THE OXFORD HANDBOOK OF

PRISONS AND IMPRISONMENT

GENERAL EDITOR: MICHAEL TONRY

THE OXFORD HANDBOOKS IN CRIMINOLOGY AND CRIMINAL JUSTICE offer authoritative, comprehensive, and critical overviews of the state of the art of criminology and criminal justice. Each volume focuses on a major area of each discipline, is edited by a distinguished group of specialists, and contains specially commissioned, original essays from leading international scholars in their respective fields. Guided by the general editorship of Michael Tonry, the series will provide an invaluable reference for scholars, students, and policy makers seeking to understand a wide range of research and policies in criminology and criminal justice.

THE OXFORD HANDBOOK OF

PRISONS AND IMPRISONMENT

Edited by

JOHN WOOLDREDGE

PAULA SMITH

OXFORD
UNIVERSITY PRESS

OXFORD

UNIVERSITY PRESS

Oxford University Press is a department of the University of Oxford. It furthers
the University's objective of excellence in research, scholarship, and education
by publishing worldwide. Oxford is a registered trade mark of Oxford University
Press in the UK and certain other countries.

Published in the United States of America by Oxford University Press
198 Madison Avenue, New York, NY 10016, United States of America.

© Oxford University Press 2018

CIP data is on file at the Library of Congress
ISBN 978-0-19-994815-4

1 3 5 7 9 8 6 4 2

Printed by Sheridan Books, Inc., United States of America

For their love and support, this book is dedicated to
Amy, Michael, Sara, and Esmiana

Contents

SECTION V: SPECIAL OFFENDER POPULATIONS AND INMATE WELL-BEING

SECTION VI: PRISON POLICY

Preface

THERE is a dearth of scholarly books on institutional corrections that encompass theoretically grounded and critical discussions of the many issues facing both prisoners and prison organizations that interfere with the goals of incarceration and ultimately inflict harms on both groups. The rarity of these types of books is understandable, however, given the need to cover these issues from multiple perspectives (from the social and behavioral sciences) while offering thorough reviews of sometimes divergent literatures and making sense of emerging themes and lessons that can subsequently contribute to "best practices."

Most of the existing books covering these issues are primarily "readers" or collected snippets of published research, each including a relatively small cross-section of extant research on only a small portion of the topics covered in this volume. On the other hand, "encyclopedias" of corrections and related areas such as sentencing cover a broad swathe of topics but without in-depth and critical discourses. The best original treatments of some of these topics have been provided in the *Crime and Justice* series, although most of the entries in related volumes include literature reviews that would now be considered outdated. The *Oxford Handbook on Prisons and Imprisonment* provides updated reviews on the more popular topics covered in these previous volumes including conditions of confinement and prisoner subcultures, and also provides reviews on topics that have taken or are destined to take greater priority in the field such as inmate victimization, special offender populations, prisoner re-entry, and privatization. Aside from being an important resource for both academics and practitioners, university students will also benefit from this collection of essays. Most criminal justice academic programs now offer junior/senior undergraduate courses as well as graduate seminars on institutional corrections, most often focusing on critical issues and future directions, and yet there is no contemporary original text that provides thorough discussions of the topics generally covered in a semester course.

The *Oxford Handbook on Prisons and Imprisonment* provides students, academics, and practitioners with a rich source of information on the current state of institutional corrections around the world, covering the most critical issues facing both inmates and prison staff and how these issues may impede the various goals of incarceration. It is the first original volume on prisons and prisoners to cover topics relevant to both the social and behavioral sciences with equal depth paid to each area. Focusing on the impact of these issues on the philosophies of incarceration (particularly with respect to retribution, incapacitation, and rehabilitation) is unique to a single volume, offering more scholarly treatments of these issues while also providing a larger picture of their implications and possible future directions for both policy and research.

The scarcity of related books is understandable after reviewing the history of penology and prison research. Extant studies began back in the 1940s, were conducted primarily in the United States and Great Britain and were focused mainly on inmate "subcultures" and sociological interpretations of inmate and prison guard adaptations to their environments, with ethnographic research methods being the norm. The academic focus on prisons was fairly narrow until the inmate rights "movement" in the United States during the 1960s and early 1970s, when prisons became more open to public view and, hence, of greater interest to academics in both the United States and abroad. Not until the prison "boom" of the 1980s and 1990s in the United States, however, did research noticeably expand beyond adaptation to issues related to crowding, psychological well-being, inmate suicide, managing special types of offenders, risk assessment, and so on. Also, despite the growth in the role of psychology in related research, there has been no single-volume coverage of these topics that address both individual and cultural perspectives in necessary depth. As a consequence, the field remains bipolar in the treatment of these issues.

This volume constitutes a single source that bridges social and behavioral science perspectives, providing students with a more comprehensive understanding of these topics while offering academics a knowledge base that will more effectively inform their own research. For practitioners, particularly those in the treatment sector, the book provides an excellent overview of best program practices that are empirically based and research-driven.

Aside from offering a comprehensive understanding of major issues in the field of institutional corrections, the contributors to this volume provide theoretically informed and critical discussions of these issues that facilitate more objective and realistic assessments of problems and their possible solutions. These assessments are also facilitated with multiple perspectives on the same or similar issues provided by different authors. Within each topic area, these discussions can be integrated to provide a set of broader themes related to the parameters of the harms or benefits associated with particular issues. Across topic areas, these discourses can also be integrated to identify themes regarding the common sources of "harmful" versus "useful" corrections policies. As such, the handbook offers new ideas, critical treatments of substantive topics with both theoretical and policy implications, and comprehensive literature reviews that reflect cumulative knowledge on best and worse practices. Although each chapter can be read alone or in a "vacuum," an appreciation for the broader themes will emerge from reading the entire volume.

The *Handbook* is divided into six sections, each corresponding to a topic area that we have identified as a focal point of discussion and research in the field of institutional corrections. All six parts have been the focus of discussions among both social and behavioral scientists, but one might consider the first three parts to be of greater interest to sociologists and social psychologists whereas the last three parts have more often occupied the interests of psychologists (but with important exceptions within each of these broader groups). Due to the overlap in these interests across disciplines, however, we refrained from collapsing these sections into broader groups reflecting different fields of study. We also did not combine these sections into larger groups because they are relatively distinct and do not easily lend themselves to broader themes when combined.

The era of mass incarceration beginning in the late 1970s and continuing through the mid-2000s in many industrialized countries, in conjunction with the "get tough" movement that spawned prison population growth, either generated or increased the magnitude of the most critical problems faced by prison officials today. For this reason, the *Handbook* begins with entries focusing on the origins of the inmate population boom, how it changed the composition of inmate populations and the conditions of their confinement, and cross-national differences in the use of imprisonment. The recent trend in declining prison populations across the United States offers hope for lessening the impact of some of the problems generated by mass incarceration, although the size of these populations will remain a concern in the foreseeable future. This is because (a) the US prison population is still over five times larger than the population at the beginning of the prison boom, (b) the annual incarceration rate of the United States remains the highest of any other country in the world even when adjusting for population size, and (c) most states continue to operate prisons with populations exceeding design capacities. Even if the US prison population manages to drop to 1970 levels within a few years (an unlikely scenario), discussions of the causes and consequences of large prison populations are critical for informing policies to prevent repeating these mistakes. From this perspective, Section I provides an important collection of essays for understanding the sources and implications of mass incarceration. More specifically, trends in inmate population growth since the early 1980s are described in addition to the most prominent hypothesized influences on these trends, including the shift in emphases on rehabilitation to "getting tougher" with offenders, the "war on . . ." movements, a possible contagion of incarceration policies across states, more structured sentencing schemes at the state and federal levels, and how the boom in prison construction and renovation might have fed a demand for confinement. Also discussed are how these trends and their influences may have impacted changes in the composition of inmate populations across the United States based on legal factors (i.e., types of offenses and offenders) and demographic variables (i.e., race, ethnicity, age, and sex). Confinement conditions for inmates also changed during this time, and the reasons for these changes in addition to their psychological impact on inmate well-being are considered. Section I also includes a series of cross-national comparisons in the use of imprisonment and discussion of possible reasons for this variation (including social, political, and economic influences). The role of public opinion is explored, including similarities and differences in cultural attitudes regarding incarceration and capital punishment.

Section I provides a context for the topics of Section II, which focus on the impact of these changes and the nature of current prison environments on inmate subcultures, the expansion of prison gangs, sex differences in adaptation to confinement, and the consequences of mass incarceration for other populations including inmates' families and the neighborhoods in which they reside as well as correctional officers. The evolution of our understanding of inmate subcultures since Clemmer's work in Illinois prisons has been dramatic in that more current research underscores much greater heterogeneity in subcultures, a greater prevalence of street gangs in maximum security prisons for men, and some dramatic differences in adaptations to confinement between women and men. Over the past 40 years, there has also been a growing appreciation for the relevance of targeting and addressing inmate needs for psychological "well-being" during confinement. Related to this idea, Section II also provides an in-depth discussion of the unique or "disproportionate" problems faced by women in prisons today that can interfere with their adaptation to confinement (e.g., pregnancies, recent births, separation from children, histories of abuse, greater reliance on drugs as a coping mechanism, etc.). A review of "gender-responsive" programs and discussion of why some programs should not be used for both men and women are also provided. Finally, the impact of changing prison environments on correctional officers cannot be ignored. Treatment of how officers, in turn, influence prison climates is also important in addition to understanding their roles in impeding or facilitating the goals of confinement and their impact on a climate supportive of offender change.

Given the priorities placed on inmate and staff safety by prison officials and state departments of correction, Section III turns to discussions of the ramifications of large inmate populations and inmate maladaptation for the safety of prisoners and staff and the effective and ineffective methods used by prison officials to deal with individual crimes in prison, drug use, and collective violence. This section covers the literature on best practices for predicting (and preventing) institutional misconduct as well as the empirical literature on a possible link between engaging in misconduct during confinement and post-release recidivism. Considering aggregate level misconduct, theories of prison riots are also presented and critiqued in terms of their applicability to the most serious riots in the past half-century. Turning to more specific types of prison crime, this section also covers drug use and both violent and property victimizations in prison. Specifically, the proliferation of drugs inside American prisons over the past 30 years and explanations for these trends are discussed, as well as changes in the incidence of sexual victimization, other violent victimizations, and property-related victimizations. The degree of overlap between "offenders" and "victims" is also discussed in addition to theories of inmate victimization. Attention is also paid to official responses to these events, including the detection and investigation of inmates' crimes and other rule infractions, their apprehension, determination of guilt, and opportunities for appeal. Special attention is given to due process considerations and how these procedures have evolved since the inmate rights movement. Specific to the in-house sanctions for inmate offenses, given the debate over the extent to which some inmates should be isolated from others within prison, this section examines the impact of isolation on psychological well-being during confinement and the implications for super-max prisons with 23-hour lockdown. The need for administrative segregation and solitary confinement is also assessed in the context of improving the safety of individual inmates as well as preventing collective violence.

Sections IV and V place heavier emphases on psychological perspectives of incarceration due to the focus on prison programming and the psychological harms of confinement to special offender groups. Section IV provides comprehensive discussions of "best practices" in institutional programming and how we arrived at this juncture by learning from past mistakes. This focus includes effective treatment programming for general population inmates as well as for special populations (sex offenders and substance abusers), skills training for more effective integration back into communities upon release from prison, and the more effective reintegration strategies following release. The importance of using actuarial approaches to predicting the risk of both institutional misconduct and post-release offending is discussed, as well as the inclusion of static and dynamic factors in composite measures of offender risk and need. The history of the rehabilitative ideal in corrections is also reviewed along with the contributions of meta-analyses that have evaluated the effectiveness of prison treatment programs. "What works" for reducing post-release recidivism is described in conjunction with how the principles of effective intervention are applied to institutional settings. Given the unique needs of incarcerated sex offenders, the challenges associated with managing these offenders in prison are also identified, including the problems posed by other inmates and the low status of sex offenders in the general prison population. This section also covers the challenges associated with post-release supervision and service delivery, including the potentially deleterious effects of long prison sentences and certain prison environments, as well as the development, implementation, and evaluation of prisoner reentry programs. Finally, the challenges of transferring the "what works" literature from research into practice are presented.

Section V logically follows the discussions in Section IV with a focus on particular groups that are growing yet pose significant challenges to the goals of effective treatment and reintegration (mentally disordered offenders and juveniles bound over to the adult system). Inmates at high risk of attempting suicide and suicide prevention strategies are also described, including the use of screening and prevention programs. The relative contributions of environmental and operational factors to suicide risk are reviewed. Correctional mental health care is also considered in an historical and international context, and the unique challenges posed by mentally disordered offenders in terms of prison management and service delivery are discussed. Approaches for housing juvenile offenders in adult correctional facilities (i.e., straight adult incarceration, graduated incarceration, and segregated incarceration) are described in addition to the special considerations that must be made for prison management and service delivery.

Finally, Section VI is devoted to future directions of prison policy (program innovations, inmate management, recognizing the limits of confinement for achieving crime control the role of prison privatization, and lessons learned from "harmful" policies). The empirical evidence regarding the (in)effectiveness of prisons for reducing crime, specifically through deterrence and incapacitation, is reviewed. An overview of the current state of practice, policy, and research related to privately operated prisons in the United States is provided, and current knowledge regarding the limits of both private and public prisons is assessed. Section VI concludes with a synthesis of useful prison policies discussed throughout this volume. The sources of useful versus harmful policies in addition to the implications of the latter are discussed.

Instructors using this text in graduate seminars or upper level undergraduate courses might consider tying these issues back to the different philosophies or justifications for confinement (retribution, incapacitation, deterrence, and rehabilitation). Useful discussions include how these issues might be manifestations of emphases on particular philosophies (e.g., mass incarceration during the 1980s from a heavier emphasis on retribution relative to rehabilitation) and how they might interfere with the pursuit of particular philosophies (e.g., inmate gangs and violence interfering with potentially effective treatment programs). The evolution and culmination of these philosophies over time have shaped many of the current issues, and so it is also important to discuss the *relative* priorities currently placed on retribution, incapacitation, deterrence, and rehabilitation and how this ranking potentially impacts these various issues (e.g., how a heavier focus on incapacitation relative to rehabilitation impacts available treatment resources). These types of discussions might help students to appreciate the disjuncture between certain philosophies and the realities of imprisonment.

John Wooldredge and Paula Smith
Cincinnati, Ohio
February 2018

List of Contributors

Kristina M. Blackwood is a clinical psychologist who is currently employed by the New Zealand Department of Corrections. She has worked for the past 14 years at a special treatment unit at Auckland Prison, delivering group therapy to men who have sexually offended against children. Her current interests include providing group therapy to men with intellectual disabilities.

Brandy Blasko, PhD, joined Sam Houston State University as Assistant Professor of Criminal Justice and Criminology after completing an interdisciplinary Postdoctoral Fellowship in the Departments of Criminology, Law & Society and Psychology at George Mason University. Dr. Blasko worked for a number of years in prisons conducting treatment, assessments, and research with offending populations. Lying at the intersection of criminal justice and psychology, Dr. Blasko's research focuses broadly on how custodial environments shape interactions and outcomes. Dr. Blasko is currently involved in research on: (1) conditions of confinement; (2) the exercise of discretion in decision making by prison staff and wardens; (3) prisoner suicide; and (4) the therapeutic alliance in the context of sexual offender treatment. As a licensed clinician, her clinical interests and expertise are in the assessment and treatment of individuals convicted of sexual crimes.

James Bonta, PhD, is a Fellow of the Canadian Psychological Association, a recipient of the Criminal Justice Section's Career Contribution Award for 2009, the Queen Elizabeth II Diamond Jubilee Medal, 2012, the Maud Booth Correctional Services Award (2015) and the 2015 Community Corrections Award, International Corrections and Prisons Association. Upon graduating from the University of Ottawa in 1979, Dr. Bonta was the Chief Psychologist at the Ottawa-Carleton Detention Centre, a maximum security remand centre for adults and young offenders. During his 14 years at the Detention Centre he established the only full-time psychology department in a jail setting in Canada. In 1990 Dr. Bonta joined Public Safety Canada where he was Director of Corrections Research until his retirement in 2015. Throughout his career, Dr. Bonta has held various academic appointments, professional posts and he was a member of the Editorial Advisory Boards for the *Canadian Journal of Criminology* and *Criminal Justice and Behavior*. He has published extensively in the areas of risk assessment and offender rehabilitation. Dr. Bonta's latest publications include a book co-authored with the late D. A. Andrews entitled *The Psychology of Criminal Conduct* now in its sixth edition (with translations in French and Chinese). He is also a co-author of the Level of Service offender risk-need classification instruments which have been translated into six languages and are used by correctional systems throughout the world.

Calli M. Cain is a doctoral candidate in the School of Criminology and Criminal Justice at the University of Nebraska, Omaha. Her primary research interests include the victim–offender overlap, gender differences, corrections, and juvenile delinquency. She has recently published in *Criminal Justice & Behavior, Violence & Victims, Criminal Justice Policy Review,* and *Trauma, Violence, & Abuse.*

Sharon Calci received a B.A. in sociology from the University of Rhode Island, working under the direction of Dr. Leo Carroll while assisting on this essay.

Scott D. Camp, PhD, joined the Office of Research and Evaluation at the Federal Bureau of Prisons in the early 1990s. He has worked on major evaluations, such as the use of private prisons by the BOP and the role of faith-based programming in federal prisons. He is currently engaged in research to develop a new risk prediction tool for post-incarceration of federal inmates and to understand the role of employment in risk of incarceration and return to crime after incarceration. The latter project is undertaken in conjunction with the U.S. Bureau of the Census. Dr. Camp publishes widely in various academic journals on topics such as affirmative action in prisons, program evaluations, indicators of prison performance derived from behavioral and attitudinal measures, prison-level influences on inmate misconduct and recidivism, and correlates of participation in prison programs.

Robert D. Canning, PhD, is a Senior Psychologist with the California Department of Corrections and Rehabilitation. Since 2005 Dr. Canning has been a suicide prevention subject matter expert for the department and has designed trainings for hundreds of clinicians working in California's prisons. He is also a member of the American Association of Suicidology for whom he trains mental health clinicians in suicide risk assessment. In the last year he has been a collaborator on a project to develop machine learning algorithms to stratify suicide risk for prison inmates and use as a clinical aid.

Leo Carroll, PhD, teaches courses in policing, punishment and corrections, and criminal justice policy at the University of Rhode Island where he also serves as the chair of the Department of Sociology and Anthropology. He has authored or co-authored two books and more than thirty articles in professional journals and collections of scholarly works. In recognition of his scholarship, Carroll has served as a Visiting Research Fellow in the Center for Criminal Justice at Harvard Law School, as a fellow at the Economic and Social Research Institute in Dublin, Ireland, and as the George Beto Professor in the College of Criminal Justice at Sam Houston State University in Texas. One of his books *Lawful Order: Correctional Crisis and Reform* was named the Outstanding Book by a member of the Academy of Criminal Justice Sciences in 2000. He is also a recipient of the URI President's Award for Excellence in Teaching.

Aaron Chalfin, PhD, is an Assistant Professor in the Department of Criminology at the University of Pennsylvania. He studies criminal justice policy and the economics of crime. His current research portfolio contains a mix of evaluation research and prediction projects that leverage insights from machine learning to guide the efficient allocation of scarce criminal justice resources. His past research has considered the effect of police manpower on crime, the relationship between crime and unauthorized immigration and the cost and deterrent effect of capital punishment. He is also interested in research that advances social science research methods and has written on topics such as measurement errors in observational data and cost-benefit analysis.

Todd R. Clear, PhD, is University Professor of Criminal Justice at Rutgers University. The author of 13 books and over 100 articles and book chapters, Clear's most recent book is *The*

Punishment Imperative (with Natasha Frost). He is currently involved in studies of mass incarceration, the criminological implications of "place," and the economics of justice reinvestment, and college programs in prisons. His work has been recognized through awards given by the American Society of Criminology, the Academy of Criminal Justice Sciences, the Rockefeller School of Public Policy, the American Probation and Parole Association, the American Correctional Association, and the International Community Corrections Association. He was the founding editor of the journal *Criminology & Public Policy*, published by the American Society of Criminology.

Joshua C. Cochran, PhD, is an Assistant Professor at the University of Cincinnati, School of Criminal Justice. His research interests include criminological theory, imprisonment, and sentencing. His work has appeared in *Criminology, Journal of Quantitative Criminology, Journal of Research in Crime and Delinquency, Justice Quarterly*, and in the book *Prisoner Reentry in the Era of Mass Incarceration* (Sage).

Ben Crewe, PhD, is Reader in Penology and Deputy Director of the Prisons Research Centre at the Institute of Criminology, University of Cambridge. He is currently leading a European Research Council funded study titled 'Penal Policymaking and the Prisoner Experience: A Comparative Analysis.' Ben is on the editorial board of the *British Journal of Criminology, Palgrave Communications*, and the *Prison Service Journal*. He is an International Associate Board member of *Punishment and Society*, and is one of the series editors of Palgrave Studies in Prisons and Penology (with Yvonne Jewkes and Thomas Ugelvik).

Scott H. Decker, PhD, is Foundation Professor in the School of Criminology and Criminal Justice at Arizona State University. His main research interests are in gangs, violence, and criminal justice policy. He is a Fellow in both the American Society of Criminology and the Academy of Criminal Justice Sciences. He is the author of seventeen books and over 120 scientific articles, including *Life in the Gang: Family, Friends and Violence* (Cambridge, 1996), *Confronting Gangs: Crime and Community* (Oxford, 2015), and *Policing Immigrants: Local Law Enforcement on the Front Lines* (University of Chicago, 2016). He served as a Member of the Missouri Sentencing Commission for ten years and as a member of the Arizona POST Board for five years.

Joel A. Dvoskin, PhD, is a clinical psychologist, licensed in the State of Arizona since 1981 and the State of New Mexico since 2005. He has authored numerous articles and chapters in professional journals and texts, including a number of articles that deal with treatment of persons with serious mental illness and co-occurring substance use disorders. Dr. Dvoskin is a member of several expert teams for the Civil Rights Division of the U.S. Department of Justice (USDOJ), focusing on the rights of inmates, detainees, and patients housed in various forms of secure confinement. He frequently provides training to clinicians in the treatment of persons with serious mental illness and/or substance abuse disorders and assessing the risk of violence to self and others.

Natasha A. Frost, PhD, is a professor in the School of Criminology and Criminal Justice at Northeastern University in Boston, Massachusetts. She also serves as associate dean for graduate studies in the College of Social Sciences and Humanities. Her primary research and teaching interests in the area of punishment and social control, with a focus on mass incarceration. Professor Frost has served as a consultant for the Massachusetts State Parole

Board, conducted correctional program assessment and recidivism studies for several Massachusetts counties, and continues to work collaboratively with the Massachusetts Department of Correction on research related to officer wellbeing. Professor Frost recently completed a study of the impact of incarceration on crime in communities funded by the National Institute of Justice (NIJ) and is currently conducting NIJ funded research on correctional officer stress. In 2016, Frost and her colleague, Carlos Monteiro, were awarded federal funding to study the many impacts of correctional officer suicide, with a specific focus on its impacts on the officer's families, friends, co-workers and supervisors and on the well-being of those who continue to work in correctional settings.

Paul Gendreau, OC, PhD, is Professor Emeritus, University of New Brunswick, New Brunswick, Canada. He has received the Order of Canada for his contributions to the correctional field. He has published over 200 articles on correctional issues primarily in the areas of effective correctional treatment, the prediction of recidivism and the effects of prison life. He was the first researcher to experimentally explore the effects of solitary confinement on offenders.

Claire Goggin, PhD, is an Assistant Professor in the Department of Criminology and Criminal Justice at St. Thomas University, Fredericton, New Brunswick where she teaches undergraduate courses in research methods and statistics, corrections, and criminal behavior. Research interests include correctional program evaluation, including the effects of imprisonment; empirical research methodologies and statistics, particularly meta-analysis; and knowledge cumulation and transfer. Recent projects include an examination of inscription practices in selected scientific disciplines; a meta-analysis of the effects of imprisonment on offender recidivism and emotional well-being; an examination of the relationship between rates of homicide and capital punishment in Canada between 1920–1949; and a prospective study of the socialization process among police officers.

Deborah Kant is a PhD student at the Institute of Criminology, Cambridge University. Her thesis, entitled 'Under threat? A social and occupational history of prison officers,' is supervised by Prof. Alison Liebling. Previously, she worked as a research assistant at the Prisons Research Centre, University of Cambridge.

Roy D. King is Emeritus Professor of Criminology and Criminal Justice in the University of Wales. From 2004 to 2011 he taught at the Univeristy of Cambridge, Institute of Criminology where he remains a Visiting Research Fellow. His comparative research has focussed on prisons in the UK, the USA, the Netherlands, Russia, Romania and Brazil. He has been an advisor to both the prison service of England and Wales and the US Federal Bureau of Prisons, and has acted as a consultant for both the Council of Europe and Amnesty International. His publications include Albany Birth of a Prison-End of an Era (1977, with Elliot), The Future of the Prison System (1981, with Morgan), Prisons in Context (1994, edited with Maguire), The State of Our Prisons (1995, with McDermott) and Doing Research on Crime and Justice (2000, 2008, edited with Wincup) as well as numerous articles and book chapters. He is currently working on a new analysis of the prison system in England and Wales.

Ryan M. Labrecque, PhD, is an Assistant Professor in the Department of Criminology and Criminal Justice at Portland State University. His research focuses on the evaluation of correctional interventions, the effects of prison life, the development of risk and needs assessments for community and institutional corrections settings, and the transfer of knowledge to practitioners and policy makers. His work has appeared in *Criminal Justice Policy Review; Journal of Crime and Justice; Psychology, Public Policy, and Law; Victims and Offenders; Violence and Victims*; and most recently in *Corrections: Policy, Practice and Research*.

Jodi Lane, PhD, is Professor of criminology in the Department of Sociology and Criminology & Law at the University of Florida. She is interested in reactions to crime from both an individual and policy perspective. Her primary research areas include the causes and consequences of fear of crime and juvenile justice and corrections policy. She and colleagues recently authored *Fear of Crime in the United States: Causes, Consequences and Contradictions* (2014) and *Encountering Correctional Populations: A Practical Guide for Researchers* (in press, 2018).

Lonn Lanza-Kaduce, JD, PhD, has been at the University of Florida for the last 37 years, and has served as a center director, department chair, and undergraduate coordinator. He teaches courses on Law & Society, Introduction to Law Enforcement, Juvenile Law, and Criminal Law and Procedure. His research interests in the areas of law, juvenile justice, policing, and substance use often have a policy and/or theory focus. His grant work and publications have dealt with the transfer of juveniles to criminal court, faith-based juvenile corrections, policing issues, and crime/deviance generally.

Ben Laws is a doctoral candidate in his third year, supervised by Dr Ben Crewe, in the Institute of Criminology at the University of Cambridge. Over the past year he has been collecting data for his ESRC funded study of prisoner emotion (titled: 'Emotions in prison: an exploration of space, emotion regulation and expression'). He has been investigating the ways in which prisoners regulate and express their emotions under conditions of confinement by using a combination of research methods (through semi-structured interviews and prisoner shadowing). He hopes that his findings will help us to learn more about the emotional 'survivability' of different prisons and to assist management and practitioners to ensure that prisons are positive, secure and safe environments for managing offenders.

Alison Liebling, PhD, is Professor of Criminology and Criminal Justice at the University of Cambridge and the Director of the Institute of Criminology's Prisons Research Centre. Her most recent research explores the moral quality of prison life, and the changing nature of staff-prisoner and prisoner-prisoner relationships in high security prisons. She was awarded an ESRC–funded 'Transforming Social Science' research contract in 2012-14 to explore the location and building of trust in high security settings and is currently writing up that work, with colleagues. Her books include *Prisons and their Moral Performance, The Effects of Imprisonment, Legitimacy and Criminal Justice*, and *The Prison Officer*. She is a co-editor of *Punishment and Society* and the Oxford *Clarendon Series on Criminology*.

Mona Lynch, PhD, is Professor and Chancellor's Fellow in Criminology, Law and Society and, by courtesy, the School of Law at the University of California, Irvine. Trained as a social psychologist, her research focuses on criminal justice and punishment processes, and on institutionalized forms of bias within legal organizations. Her scholarship has been published in a wide range of journals, law reviews, and edited volumes. She is the author of *Sunbelt Justice: Arizona and the Transformation of American Punishment* (2009, Stanford

University Press) and *Hard Bargains: The Power to Punish in Federal Court* (2016, Russell Sage Foundation). She is also co-editor of the journal *Punishment & Society*.

Sarah M. Manchak, PhD, is an assistant professor in the School of Criminal Justice at the University of Cincinnati. Her works seeks to inform risk assessment, treatment, and management of offenders and improve efforts to translate empirical research into routine correctional practice. Areas of research interest include offenders with mental disorders, substance addiction, coping with trauma, practitioner-offender/client relationships and criminal justice-treatment agency partnerships.

James Marquart, PhD, is Provost and Vice President for Academic Affairs at Lamar University. One of the nation's leading experts on prison systems, Dr. Marquart's extensive academic record includes more than $2 million in funded research activity, 50 presentations, more than 60 peer-reviewed journal articles and book chapters, and 7 books. Research and teaching interests include prison organizations, capital punishment, and criminal justice policy. Previous professional activities include service as president of the Academy of Criminal Justice Sciences and selection as an academic fellow for the Foundation for Defense of Democracies. He has received the 2005 Bruce Smith Senior Award from the Academy of Criminal Justice Sciences, the Leverhulme Visiting Professorship in 1998 from Queen Mary and Westfield College-University of London, the American Library Association's Outstanding Book Award for 1995, and the ACJS Outstanding Book Award in 1991.

Paul Mazerolle, PhD, is Professor and Pro Vice Chancellor of Arts, Education and Law and the Director of the Violence Research and Prevention program at Griffith University. His research examines processes that shape offending behavior across the life-course. His primary focus is in building knowledge in the area of violence to inform theories, advance understanding, and improve policy and practices to reduce or prevent violence, in particular related to youth violence, intimate partner violence and homicide.

James McGuire, PhD, is a clinical and forensic psychologist and Emeritus Professor of Forensic Clinical Psychology at the University of Liverpool. He has worked in intellectual disabilities services and in a high security hospital and has carried out research in prisons, probation services, youth justice, and other settings on aspects of psychosocial rehabilitation. He has conducted psycho-legal assessments for courts, parole and review hearings. He has acted in an advisory capacity for the National Institute of Health and Clinical Excellence, the Correctional Services Advisory and Accreditation Panel, and with criminal justice agencies in a number of countries.

Samara McPhedran, PhD, is a Senior Research Fellow in the Violence Research and Prevention Program at Griffith University. Her background is in psychology, and she has worked across a wide range of policy-focused research fields, with emphasis on lethal violence, firearm-related violence, domestic and family violence, and mental health. Before joining Griffith University in 2012, she worked for a number of years in the public sector in a range of research, policy, and program management roles.

Daniel P. Mears, PhD, is the Mark C. Stafford Professor of Criminology at Florida State University's College of Criminology and Criminal Justice. He conducts research on crime and policy. His work has appeared in such journals as *Criminology* and the *Journal of Research in Crime and Delinquency*, as well as several books, including *Out-of-Control*

Criminal Justice (Cambridge University Press), *American Criminal Justice Policy* (Cambridge University Press), and *Prisoner Reentry in the Era of Mass Incarceration* (Sage).

Robert D. Morgan, PhD, is currently the John G. Skelton, Jr. Regents Endowed Professor in Psychology at Texas Tech University. His research and scholarly activities include treatment and assessment of mentally disordered offenders, malingering, and professional development and training issues. His research has been funded by the National Institute of Mental Health, the National Institute of Justice, and the Center for Behavioral Health Services & Criminal Justice Research. He has authored or co-authored over 90 peer reviewed publications and book chapters, as well as three books: *Careers in psychology: Opportunities in a changing world* (3rd ed.), *Life after graduate school in psychology: Insider's advice from new psychologists*, and *Clinician's Guide to Violence Risk Assessment*. He has provided forensic mental health services at the request of courts, defense, and prosecution, and consults with state and private correctional agencies to inform practice.

Andrea E. Moser, PhD, is currently the Director General, Women Offender Sector, Correctional Service of Canada (CSC). She has published several articles and book chapters and has presented at national and international workshops and conferences on a variety of topics related to corrections including offender mental health, addictions, effective correctional programming and radicalized offenders. Recently, Dr. Moser was a member of the United Nations Office of Drugs and Crime (UNODC) expert working group that developed the Handbook on the Management of Violent Extremist Prisoners and the Prevention of Radicalization to Violence in Prison. She was also the recipient of the International Corrections and Prisons Association (ICPA) 2016 Research Award.

Lindsey M. Mueller is a doctoral student in the School of Criminal Justice at the University of Cincinnati. Her research interests include correctional rehabilitation, institutional corrections (inmate deviance), and program fidelity.

Devon L. L. Polaschek, PhD, DipClinPsyc, is a clinical psychologist and professor of psychology in the School of Psychology and the New Zealand Institute of Security and Crime Science, University of Waikato, New Zealand. Her research interests include theory, intervention, and intervention evaluation with serious violent and sexual offenders, family violence, psychopathy, desistance, reintegration, and parole. Devon is the author of more than 110 journal articles, book chapters and government reports, and a fellow of the Association for Psychological Science. Her research has been supported by a decade of funding from the Department of Corrections, in order to develop a better understanding of high-risk violent male prisoners: their characteristics, and what works to reduce their risk of future offending. In 2015, she was the recipient of a Fulbright Scholar Award, which she spent at John Jay College of Criminal Justice in New York, and is the 2016 recipient of the NZ Psychological Society's Hunter Award for lifetime excellence in research, scholarship, and professional achievement in psychology.

David Pyrooz, PhD, is Assistant Professor of Sociology and Faculty Associate of the Institute of Behavioral Science at the University of Colorado Boulder. His research interests are in the areas of gangs and criminal networks, incarceration and reentry, and developmental and life course criminology. He received the Ruth Shonle Cavan Young Scholar Award from the American Society of Criminology and New Scholar Award from the Academy of Criminal

Justice Sciences. His recent research has appeared in *Criminology, Journal of Quantitative Criminology, Journal of Research in Crime and Delinquency*, and *Justice Quarterly*.

Nancy Rodriguez, PhD, is a Professor in the Department of Criminology, Law and Society at the University of California, Irvine. Her research interests include inequality (race/ethnicity, class, crime and justice) and the collateral consequences of mass incarceration. In October 2014, Nancy Rodriguez was appointed by President Barack Obama to serve as the Director of the National Institute of Justice, the scientific research arm of the U.S. Department of Justice.

John Rynne, PhD, is Associate Professor and Director of the Griffith Youth Forensic Service. He has extensive theoretical and applied knowledge of Australian and international criminal justice systems, and in particular prison reform. Rynne's academic qualifications are in psychology and he is a member of the Australian Psychology Society. He is currently undertaking research in applied prison reform and organizational development via 'through-the-gate' approaches to prison rehabilitation and community re-entry. Prior to joining academia, John worked in the Queensland criminal justice system for approximately 15 years in management and operational roles in custodial and community corrections.

Paula Smith, PhD, is an Associate Professor in the School of Criminal Justice at the University of Cincinnati. Her research interests include offender classification and assessment, correctional rehabilitation, the psychological effects of incarceration, program implementation and evaluation, the transfer of knowledge to practitioners and policy-makers, and meta-analysis. She is co-author of *Corrections in the Community*, and has also authored more than thirty journal articles and book chapters. Dr. Smith has directed numerous federal and state funded research projects, including studies of prisons, community-based correctional programs, juvenile drug courts, probation and parole departments, and mental health services. Furthermore, she has been involved in evaluations of more than 280 correctional programs throughout the United States.

Benjamin Steiner, PhD, is a professor of criminology and criminal justice at the University of Nebraska at Omaha. Dr. Steiner's research interests focus on issues related to juvenile justice and corrections. He has published more than 80 journal articles and book entries related to these topics. Dr. Steiner's research has been funded by agencies such as the National Institute of Justice, National Science Foundation, and the American Statistical Association.

Sarah Tahamont, PhD, is an Assistant Professor in the Department of Criminology and Criminal Justice at the University of Maryland. Broadly, her research interests concentrate in three areas: 1) estimating the effects of criminal sanctions on individual outcomes with a particular focus on corrections, 2) examining the theoretical parameters of the criminal career paradigm in the context of a *criminal justice* career, and 3) research that advances criminological research methods. Her past research characterized the relationship between prison visitation and inmate outcomes and examined the patterns of criminal justice contact that precede a first prison sentence. Her current research includes projects that examine the consequences of errors introduced by matching administrative data, estimate the effect of facility security placement on institutional misconduct, and consider incarceration as a turning point in the life-course.

Faye S. Taxman, PhD, is a University Professor in the Criminology, Law and Society Department and Director of the Center for Advancing Correctional Excellence at George Mason University. She is recognized for her work in the development of systems-of-care models that link the criminal justice system with other service delivery systems, as well as her work in reengineering probation and parole supervision services and in organizational change models. She developed the RNR Simulation Tool (www.gmuace.org/tools) to assist agencies to advance practice. Dr. Taxman has published more than 195 articles, and many books including *Tools of the Trade: A Guide to Incorporating Science into Practice* and *Implementing Evidence-Based Community Corrections and Addiction Treatment* (Springer, 2012 with Steven Belenko). She is co-Editor of the *Health & Justice*. The American Society of Criminology's Division of Sentencing and Corrections has recognized her as Distinguished Scholar twice as well as the Rita Warren and Ted Palmer Differential Intervention Treatment award. She received the Joan McCord Award in 2017 from the Division of Experimental Criminology.

Kathleen Thibault, MSW, is a Registered Social Worker and Psychotherapist who has worked with incarcerated individuals in Canada. She has also worked as a Policy Analyst, Research Manager and Project Manager in corrections and the criminal justice field specializing in mental health and addictions policy, research and evidence-based program development. Kathleen holds a bachelor of arts degree in psychology from Queen's University and bachelors and masters degrees in social work from McGill University. Kathleen has completed all-but-dissertation of a doctorate in Health Policy from the University of Toronto.

Chad Trulson, PhD, is Professor of Criminal Justice in the Department of Criminal Justice at the University of North Texas. Dr. Trulson has worked in various positions in juvenile justice such as a juvenile resident counselor, juvenile detention officer, and a juvenile parole officer. He has published numerous articles in leading criminal justice journals has published four books: *Juvenile Justice: System, Process, and Law* (Cengage, 2006), *First Available Cell: Desegregation of the Texas Prison System* (University of Texas Press, 2009), *Applied Research Methods in Criminal Justice and Criminology* (McGraw-Hill, 2013), and *Lost Causes: Blended Sentencing, Second Chances, and the Texas Youth Commission* (University of Texas Press, 2016). He also serves as Editor-in-Chief of the highly ranked journal *Youth Violence and Juvenile Justice* (SAGE).

Jillian J. Turanovic, PhD, is an Assistant Professor in the College of Criminology and Criminal Justice at Florida State University. Her current research examines victimization and offending over the life course, correctional policy, and the collateral consequences of incarceration. Jillian is a Graduate Research Fellow and W.E.B. DuBois Fellow of the National Institute of Justice.

Susan Turner, PhD, is a Professor in the Department of Criminology, Law and Society at the University of California, Irvine. She also serves as Director of the Center for Evidence-Based Corrections and serves as an appointee of the President of the University of California to the California Rehabilitation Oversight Board (C-ROB). Dr. Turner's areas of expertise include the design and implementation of randomized field experiments and research collaborations with state and local justice agencies. At UCI, she has assisted the California Department of Corrections and Rehabilitation in the development and validation of a risk assessment tool as well as evaluations of targeted parole programs. She is also collaborating with the Orange County Reentry Initiative to map gaps in local services for offenders returning to the community.

Bert Useem, PhD, is Professor of Sociology at Purdue University. He is the coauthor of three books that analyze the cause, course, and consequences of prison riots. Recent articles, in the *American Journal of Sociology* and *American Sociological Review*, with Jack Goldstone, develop the idea that theories of revolution can be used to explain prison riots.

Anjuli Verma, PhD, is a Chancellor's Postdoctoral Fellow in Jurisprudence and Social Policy at the University of California, Berkeley. Her research examines punishment, law, and inequality from an interdisciplinary perspective using multiple methods. Anjuli's work appears in *Law & Society Review*, *The Annals of the American Academy of Political and Social Science*, *The British Journal of Criminology*, *The American Journal of Bioethics* and is forthcoming in *Sociological Perspectives* and *The Oxford Research Encyclopedia of Criminology and Criminal Justice*. In 2018, Anjuli will join the Politics Department at the University of California, Santa Cruz as an Assistant Professor.

John R. Weekes, PhD, has worked in the corrections, criminal justice and forensic psychology research communities in Canada and internationally for over 35 years. Currently, he is Director of Research for the Correctional Service of Canada. He is trained as both a clinical and a research psychologist, before earning his doctorate from Ohio University. He is Adjunct Research Professor of Forensic Psychology and Addictions in the Forensic Psychology Research Centre of the Department of Psychology at Carleton University where he teaches and supervises undergraduate and graduate student research. Dr. Weekes is also a research affiliate of the Centre for Forensic Behavioural Sciences and Justice Studies at the University of Saskatchewan and the Canadian Institute for Public Safety Research and Treatment at the University of Regina. He consults widely in Canada and internationally, including in England and Wales, Ireland, the US, and Scandinavia. He is a past Chair of the American Correctional Association's (ACA's) Substance Abuse Committee, and served on the ACA's Best Practices Coordinating Council. Dr. Weekes is a continuing member of the Correctional Services Accreditation and Advice Panel, Her Majesty's Prison and Probation Service, Ministry of Justice, UK. He has also served as Chair of the Volunteers of America (Delaware Valley) ad hoc Research Committee. Dr. Weekes is a scientific advisor to the Breaking Free Group – a computer-assisted therapy online service provider based in Manchester, UK. He has published and presented extensively on substance misuse, addictions, forensic psychology, clinical psychopathology, motivational interviewing, evidence-informed treatment, computer-assisted therapy, and treatment-outcome research.

Michael Wheatley, M.St., is a qualified social worker and experienced commissioner and practitioner with Her Majesty's Prison and Probation Service to lead the Health Team within the Rehabilitation Services Group on prison substance misuse provision. In this role he works with Government Ministers, other Government departments, other HMPPS directorates, prison Governors, local health commissioners and service providers to support the design, development and implementation of bespoke substance misuse services. Currently, Michael is embedded into HMP Holme House leading on the development of a Drug Recovery Prison concept. Previously, Michael was a senior manager responsible for delivering, co-ordinating and supporting the commissioning of interventions designed to reduce reoffending in high security prisons. He has also worked as a community probation officer. Michael holds a bachelor of arts degree in Applied Social Studies, a Certificate in Qualified Social Work from Sheffield Hallam University and a Master of Studies in Applied Criminology, Penology and Prison Management from Cambridge University.

Amber Wilson received a B.A. in sociology from the University of Rhode Island, working under the direction of Dr. Leo Carroll while assisting on this essay.

Nancy Wolff, PhD, an economist and distinguished professor, is the director of the Bloustein Center for Survey Research and former director of the Center for Behavioral Health Services & Criminal Justice Research (NIMH funded from 2002-2014) at Rutgers University. Since 1995, she has increasingly focused on public policies and justice practices that influence the incarceration and rehabilitation of justice-involved people. Her work has focused on the prevalence of trauma among incarcerated men and women and its effective treatment. Dr. Wolff spends two days a week at prisons in Pennsylvania and New Jersey teaching and leading reading and skill-building groups. She is the founder of Books Behind Bars, a prison-based literacy program, for which she received a Russell Berrie Award for Making a Difference in 2008.

John Wooldredge, PhD, is a professor in the School of Criminal Justice at the University of Cincinnati. His research and publications focus on institutional corrections (crowding, inmate crimes and victimizations) and criminal case processing (sentencing and recidivism, and micro- versus macro-level extralegal disparities in case processing and outcomes). He is currently involved in an NIJ funded study of the use and impacts of restrictive housing in Ohio prisons (with Josh Cochran), and in projects focusing on prison program effects on subsequent misconduct during incarceration and post-release recidivism, and extralegal disparities in prison sanctions imposed for rule violations.

J. Stephen Wormith, PhD, is a professor in the Psychology Department and Director of the Centre of Forensic Behavioral Science and Justice Studies at the University of Saskatchewan. He has worked as a psychologist, researcher, and administrator in both federal and provincial correctional jurisdictions in Canada. His research interests include offender risk and psychological assessment, offender treatment, sexual offenders and crime prevention. Dr. Wormith is on the editorial board of three criminal justice journals, is a Fellow of the Canadian Psychological Association (CPA), and represents CPA on the National Associations Active in Criminal Justice (NAACJ). In 2015, he received the Edwin I. Megargee Distinguished Contribution Award from the International Association for Correctional and Forensic Psychology.

Emily M. Wright, PhD, is a professor in the School of Criminology and Criminal Justice at the University of Nebraska at Omaha. Her research involves neighborhoods, intimate partner violence, victimization, exposure to violence, and female offenders. Her research has appeared in *Criminology, Child Abuse & Neglect, Journal of Research in Crime and Delinquency*, and *Trauma, Violence, & Abuse*.

THE OXFORD HANDBOOK OF

PRISONS AND IMPRISONMENT

SECTION I

TRENDS
IN IMPRISONMENT

CHAPTER 1

THE IMPRISONMENT BOOM OF THE LATE TWENTIETH CENTURY
Past, Present, and Future

MONA LYNCH AND ANJULI VERMA

No warning systems were in place for the tidal wave of incarceration in the late twentieth century. Even the most renowned criminologists of the era had no idea it was coming. Most famously, Alfred Blumstein and Jacqueline Cohen published "A Theory of the Stability of Punishment" in 1973, just as the ascent in incarceration rates began. Characterized by Franklin E. Zimring as "the most important and certainly the most ironically timed article" (2010, p. 1226) in the twentieth-century criminological field, Blumstein and Cohen used the relatively flat line of US incarceration rates from 1930 to 1970[1] to support their contention that societies' punishment levels are static and that definitions of punishable crime adapt to maintain that stasis. An instance of such irony is that, in noting that "the imprisonment rate since 1961 has shown a distinct downward trend," Blumstein and Cohen (1973, p. 202) identified declining—not rising—incarceration rates as a possible threat to the stability theory.

A few years later, Stanley Cohen (1979, p. 341) famously described that downward trend as no less than an historic paradigm shift, in which prisons were "becoming places of *last* resort [and the] notion of abolition, rather than reform became common talk." His essay warned of an amorphous wave of prison alternatives in the form of "community corrections" permeating all spheres of social life. Ultimately, the result would be the "punitive city" in which the traditional prison was merely the cardinal point on a continuum of control. While Cohen was clear that the place of the prison in his model remained a huge "question mark" (p. 358), he centered a rising tide of non-incarcerative sanctions, not a prison explosion, as the looming trend.

We begin with these two iconic pieces of scholarship not to draw attention to the authors' inability to see the future but rather to focus on two important concepts. First we foreground the difficulties of any "history of the present," whether that involves looking back over the previous 10 years (about the length of the decarceration period referenced by Cohen), 30 years (as we have been asked to do here), or 40 years, as Blumstein and Cohen (1973) endeavored. Thus in this essay we describe the contours of the inmate population boom since the 1980s and present some of the prevailing explanations for it. In an even riskier endeavor, we also examine what appears to be an emerging period of stability in incarceration. In doing both, we do not assert a single "correct" explanation for these phenomena, knowing that the long view of history would likely contradict us if we did and that the complex drivers of incarceration rates defy singular causation.

Second, while these scholars (among others) did not successfully predict exactly how penal practices were manifested in the following years, they offered enduring insights about the nature of contemporary punishment from which we draw in this essay. For instance, although the prediction about its effect was not borne out, Blumstein and Cohen's (1973) model highlighted the fluid and constructionist underlying nature of the category of "crime" that deserves state punishment in any given society, a lesson that sometimes gets lost in empirical criminological literature.[2] For his part, Cohen (1979, 1985) was a pioneer in conceptualizing modern penality as something that may take the form of state imprisonment but that can take many other forms, each with its own ramifications for social and political life.

This essay begins by describing what has happened since the 1970s—namely the US prison population increase beginning in that decade, which then metastasized into what became known by the 1980s and 1990s as "mass incarceration."[3] Within section I, we delineate some of the features central to mass incarceration, including the race, class, and gender dimensions; the particular role that the "war on drugs" played in the incarceration explosion; the geographical and jurisdictional variation in imprisonment; and, to a much lesser extent, the changed nature of the incarceration experience.

Section II offers a brief sketch of various theoretical explanations for the emergence of mass incarceration in the United States, as well as the evidence in support of those theories. We make a point to supplement these theories with perspectives that attend to the significant variations in how imprisonment has been used at the state and local levels in an effort to highlight more empirically nuanced, midrange theoretical understandings of mass incarceration as well. In this section, we also briefly examine the various forms of incarcerative punishment and consider the important but understudied role of local jails in the imprisonment explosion. This leads us to our examination of the present in section III, in which we argue that the stabilization trends in state imprisonment rates that emerged in the mid-2000s may be misleading indicators of a retrenchment from mass incarceration. Using the California case as one example, we suggest that the kinds of punishment dispersal strategies identified by Cohen (1979) may once again be flourishing in troubling ways. Finally, section IV discusses future directions for theory-building, research, and policy reform. The main conclusions of the essay are as follows:

- Key defining features of the late twentieth century imprisonment boom include (a) global notoriety; (b) persistent racial disparities; (c) the role of felony drug filings, convictions, and sentences in fueling both the scale and racial disparities of imprisonment; and (4) regional and jurisdictional variation on three planes: federal–state, interstate, and intrastate. This final less appreciated but no less significant feature is fundamental to adequate accounts of both the rise in imprisonment and its stabilization in the late 2000s.
- The scholarship attempting to explain the swiftness, magnitude, and persistence of the late twentieth century rise in incarceration has emerged from a variety of

disciplines and has ranged from highly functionalist structural accounts to more culturally embedded midrange ones. Local criminal courts, county-level criminal justice administration, and jails are especially promising sites of future research and theory-building, as they are the very linkage points between the broader political economy of punishment (at the macro level) and geographically-specific day-to-day punitive action (at the micro level).

- While it is tempting to look to major law changes by way of Congressional acts and US Supreme Court rulings as the most dispositive catalysts for ending mass incarceration, the highly localized, federated structure of American government in general and criminal justice administration and politics in particular strongly suggest that the most viable pathways out of the imprisonment boom will solidify at the municipal, county, and state levels. Specifically, state-level sentencing reform, as well as measures that build fiscal and political accountability into county-level criminal justice administration, such as California's 2011 Realignment law (A.B. 109 2011), have the potential to force local justice workgroups to weigh the costs, risks, and benefits of relying on incarceration in local jails as the primary crime and punishment policy.

- Overall incarceration rates at the state level began to stabilize and slightly decline by 2007. There is reason to believe this stabilization may reflect changing public attitudes about the role of imprisonment in society, in reaction to the fiscal crises, racial disparities, and community destruction wrought by over four decades of high reliance on incarceration. At the same time, these may be misleading indicators of a genuine retrenchment from mass incarceration, and we must remain cognizant of the troubling dispersal of punishment that may accompany prison downsizing developments. Indeed, the latest data evinces the precarious and possibly short-lived nature of this stabilization period: the US prison population began increasing again from 2012 to 2013 (Carson 2014). This is just one signal that we should not expect the consistency or scale of observed imprisonment declines to come anywhere close to that of its precipitous rise during the late twentieth century. Even small reductions will be hard-fought, given the massive institutional arrangements that facilitated the incarceration boom in the first place, as these institutions, like all institutions, tend to resist changes that threaten their very existence.

I. CONTOURS OF THE LATE TWENTIETH CENTURY PRISON POPULATION BOOM

United States incarceration rates in state and federal prisons remained remarkably stable throughout the better part of the twentieth century, averaging just over 108 people per 100,000 from 1925 to 1973 (Cahalan 1986).[4] The incarceration rate resisted fluctuation amidst some of the most chaotic and transformative eras in American history, including the Great Depression and the repeal of alcohol prohibition in the early 1930s, the Second World War, the internment of Japanese Americans and the race riots and labor strikes of the 1940s, the dawn of the Cold War, the nuclear age and the Red Scare in the 1950s, along with the civil rights movement, the end of de jure segregation of public schools and accommodations, and the assassination of President John F. Kennedy by the mid-1960s. Indeed, throughout the 1960s, incarceration rates seemed impervious to the major social turmoil and transformation associated with the Vietnam War; highly publicized race riots in Watts, Detroit and elsewhere; and the Summer of Love. It is no wonder that, by 1973, the prevailing view of imprisonment among criminologists was a working "Theory of the Stability of Punishment" (Blumstein and Cohen 1973).

Just one decade later, however, the rate of US imprisonment increased by over 40 percent, from 97 per 100,000 people in 1970 to 139 per 100,000 people in 1980—the first increase of this magnitude in American history (Cahalan 1986). That increase would be dwarfed, however, by what happened over the next quarter century: Between 1980 and the mid-2000s, the incarceration rate nearly quadrupled, reaching an all-time high of 506 per 100,000 people by 2007, amounting to a total of 1,596,835 state and federal prisoners (see Figure 1.1; Beck and Gilliard 1995; Beck and Harrison 2001; Carson and Sabol 2012). If one includes the estimated 780,174 people incarcerated in local jails that year, by 2007 a total of 2,377,009 people were living behind bars in the United States, or approximately 1 in 100 US adults (Pew Charitable Trusts 2008). Even before mass incarceration reached its zenith in the mid-2000s, statisticians with the US Bureau of Justice Statistics in 2001 predicted that if the trends of the 1980s and 1990s continued, nearly 1 in 15 Americans born at the turn of the twenty-first century would serve time in prison during their lifetime—this projection did not even account for the likelihood of serving time in jail (Bonzcar 2003). This prediction was borne out for adult African American males, of whom 1 of 15 was incarcerated by 2008 (Pew Charitable Trusts 2008) and partially for the US population as a whole: By 2012, 1 in 35 US adults was estimated to be living under some form of correctional supervision, which includes jail, prison, parole, or probation (Glaze and Herberman 2013).

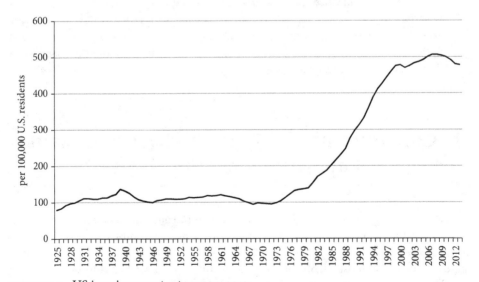

FIGURE 1.1. US imprisonment rates, 1925–2013.

Sources: 1925–1980: Cahalan (1986); 1980–2013: US Bureau of Justice Statistics (2014).

Note: Does not include those incarcerated in jails.

While the first social fact of incarceration to be explained was the remarkable stability of punishment from 1925 to the 1970s, the emergent social fact of incarceration during
the latter third of the twentieth century was the remarkable acceleration of punishment to
heights never before seen in American—or global—history. This social fact, now known
as "mass incarceration,"[5] contains several defining features: its global notoriety, persistent
racial disparities, and the role of felony drug filings, convictions, and sentences in fueling
both the scale and racial disparities of imprisonment. A less appreciated but no less significant feature of mass incarceration is its regional and jurisdictional variation, which we view
as fundamental to adequate accounts of both the rise in imprisonment and its stabilization
since 2007 (if one is measuring the rate of incarceration) or 2009 (if one is measuring the
total imprisoned population). In an effort to further specify the contours of the late twentieth century prison population boom, we examine these defining features in turn. While we
view the changing nature of the incarcerative experience as a central and crucially important aspect of mass incarceration, it is outside the scope of this essay and so is not addressed
in any systematic way here.[6]

First, we consider the prison boom's global notoriety. By the dawn of the twenty-first
century, the United States imprisoned more people in absolute numbers and per capita
than any nation in the world. Even China, which has 1 billion more people than the United
States, trailed behind, incarcerating approximately 1.6 million persons in jails and prisons
at a rate of 121 per 100,000 by 2011, compared to the incarcerated US population (in both
jails and prisons) of nearly 2.3 million people at a rate of 716 per 100,000 that same year
(Walmsley 2013). Moreover, the imprisoned populations and rates of imprisonment of the
next highest incarcerating nations, Russia, Brazil, and India, lagged well behind US figures
(International Center for Prison Studies 2013). Since 1991, the US imprisonment rate increase
has been more unidirectional and pronounced than all but one (Brazil) of the world's four
next largest jailers. As shown in Figure 1.2, however, even the case of Brazil is unique in
that its highest rates never approached the lowest rates in the United States. The scale of US

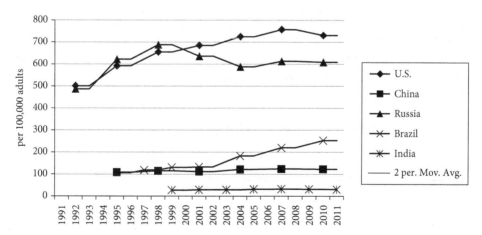

FIGURE 1.2. Imprisonment rates of countries with the world's five largest prison populations, 1991–2011.

Source: International Center for Prison Studies (2013).

Note: Includes those incarcerated in jails.

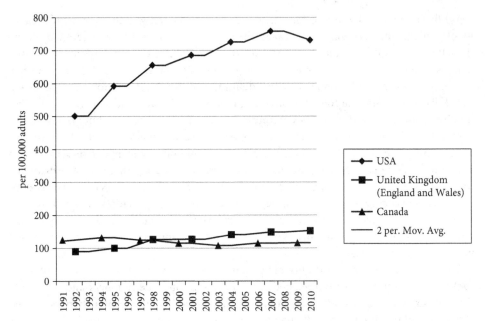

FIGURE 1.3. Imprisonment rates of United States, Canada, and United Kingdom, 1992–2010.

Source: International Center for Prison Studies (2013).

Note: Includes those incarcerated in jails.

imprisonment is even more striking when examined alongside arguably more comparable Western European counterparts, such as the United Kingdom (England and Wales) and Canada, whose incarceration rates have barely risen since 1991(see Figure 1.3). Even the incarcerated populations of some state correctional systems within the United States dwarf the imprisoned populations of entire countries. For example, as Margo Schlanger (2013) explains, if the state of California were a country, its prison and jail populations combined would be the ninth largest in the world.

The second defining feature of the late twentieth century's prison population explosion is the persistent racial disparity among those incarcerated. While an estimated 1 in 100 US adults was living behind the bars of either a prison or a jail by 2007, incarceration rates were even higher for racial and ethnic minorities. The Pew Charitable Trusts (2008) reported that while 1 in 106 white adult males was incarcerated by the mid-2000s, that figure was 1 in 36 for Hispanic adult males, 1 in 15 for adult African American males, and 1 in nine for African American males ages 20 to 34 years old. Racial disparities in the incarceration of women are similarly striking, particularly among the adult women aged 35 to 39: 1 in 355 white women was incarcerated during this same time period, and that figure rises to 1 in 297 for Hispanic women and 1 in 100 for African American women.

As Michael Tonry (2011) described in his analysis of the racial composition of America's imprisoned population, for the past two decades the total imprisonment rate in state and federal prisons and jails for African Americans has been five to seven times that of whites. The *increase* in African American incarceration rates between 1980 and 2006 alone was almost four times the total rate of incarceration for whites in 2006. By 2006, the white rate of incarceration (483 per 100,000 whites) had failed to reach the rate of African American incarceration 56 years earlier in 1950 (598 per 100,000 African Americans). To put this point into greater relief, in many of the years between 1991 and 2008, the one-year increases in the rates of African American incarceration alone exceeded the total imprisonment rates of Canada in many years and of many European countries at any time in the past 40 years.[7]

In particular, poor, undereducated African American men bore the brunt of mass incarceration. As Bruce Western (2006, p. 50) points out, while "poor and minority men were much less involved in crime in 2000 than twenty years earlier . . . their chances of going to prison rose to historically high levels." Indeed, he estimated that 60 percent of African American men born in the 1960s and who dropped out of high school had been in prison by the time they reached their 30s (see also Currie 1998).

The third defining feature of the late twentieth century imprisonment boom, related to its first and second features, is the role of felony drug filings, convictions, and sentences. As a result of punitive drug legislation passed by Congress and by some state legislatures during the 1980s and 1990s that prescribed mandatory, lengthy periods of incarceration even for first-time drug law violators with no histories of violence, a staggering number of people in the United States were arrested and incarcerated for drugs for longer periods of time than in most other countries (Horne and Farrell 1999). While the general population has grown by 50 percent since 1980 (US Census Bureau 2010), the United States saw an increase of over 1,000 percent in the number of people in state and federal prisons and jails for drug law violations—from an estimated 41,100[8] people incarcerated for drug convictions in 1980 (Beck and Gilliard 1995; Mauer and King 2007) to an estimated 464,300[9] by year-end 2012 (Dorsey and Middleton 2002; Carson 2014). Simply put, the number of people incarcerated for drug law violations at the time of this writing almost reaches the number of people incarcerated for all crimes in 1980 (Beck and Gilliard 1995).[10]

This trend is most pronounced in the federal system. The US Sentencing Commission predicted these results as the most punitive drug war legislation, including the notorious mandatory minimum statutes for crack cocaine offenses, was gaining steam in Congress in the mid-1980s. The Commission foresaw a federal prison population reaching at least 100,000 people by 2002, roughly one-half of whom would be incarcerated for drug law violations (US Sentencing Commission 1987). Drug offense incarceration has surpassed the Commission's prophecy: by fiscal year-end 2010, federal prisons housed over 210,000 people, 51.4 percent (108,057) for whom a drug law violation was their most serious conviction (Federal Bureau of Prisons 2010). In addition, by year-end 2012, over 210,000 people were incarcerated in state prisons for drug law violations, accounting for 16 percent of all state prisoners (Carson 2014) (see Figure 1.4). And, in the most recent year for which such data is available, an additional estimated 155,900 people were held in jails for drug law violations, accounting for almost 25 percent of all jail inmates (James 2004). Although a growing proportion of inmates are incarcerated in federal prisons for immigration- and weapons-related offenses, the largest portion of newly admitted inmates are incarcerated for drug offenses (James 2013).

In this respect, federal prison offender populations diverge from those of state prisons. For instance, by year-end 2012, drug offenders constituted over half of the federal prison population (50.7 percent), followed by those serving sentences for weapons offenses (15.5 percent), other public-order offenses (10.4 percent), immigration offenses (9.9 percent), and a range of economic, violent, and miscellaneous other offenses (Carson 2014).

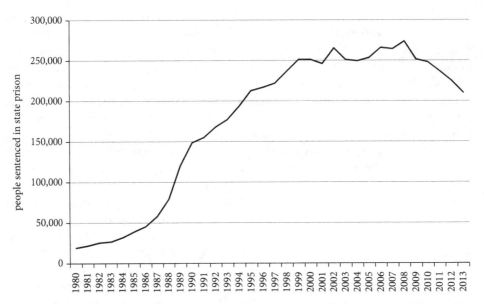

FIGURE 1.4. Number of state prisoners whose most serious offense was a drug law violation, 1980–2013.

Source: US Bureau of Justice Statistics (2014).

By contrast, the majority of offenders held in state prisons by 2013 were serving sentences for violent crimes (53.8 percent), followed by property crimes (18.8 percent), drug crimes (16 percent), and public-order offenses (10.7 percent) (Carson 2014).

The growth in the rate of women incarcerated for drug convictions outstrips that of men. The overall rate of incarceration increased at a pace nearly double for women compared to men (Frost, Greene, and Pranis 2006), and, by 2003, roughly one-third (31.5 percent) of the women in state prisons were behind bars for drug law violations, compared to roughly one-fifth (20.7 percent) of men (Frost et al. 2006). Between 1986 and 1991, the number of women incarcerated for drug law violations jumped by 433 percent (Frost et al. 2006). Women of color were especially impacted: White women's rate of incarceration for drugs rose by 241 percent, Latina women's rate rose by 328 percent, and African American women's drug incarceration rate rose by 828 percent (Frost et al. 2006).

The final defining feature of the late twentieth century's imprisonment boom—which has only recently received in-depth scholarly attention—is the notable regional and jurisdictional variation in incarceration rates. There are three planes of variation: federal–state, interstate, and intrastate. Beginning with the federal–state plane, state prisons and local jails account for the vast majority of US imprisonment. In 2007, the year distinguished by the highest rate of incarceration on record, state prisons held 1,397,217 inmates (58.8 percent of the total incarcerated population) and local jails held 780,174 inmates (32.8 percent), while federal prisons held only 199,618 inmates (8.3 percent) that same year (Carson and Sabol 2012). While the federal system accounts for a relatively small proportion of those incarcerated in the United States, federal imprisonment has been the fastest and most consistently growing incarceration sector. State and local jail imprisonment levels rose steadily throughout the 1980s and 1990s but began to flatten out by 2000, whereas growth in the federal imprisonment rate has shown few signs of subsiding. Between 1995 and 2003, the increase in federal incarceration was nearly three times that of state and local incarceration (The Sentencing Project 2004).

Imprisonment rate variation transcends the federal–state distinction, however. Virtually all 50 US states exhibited significant increases in incarceration between 1980 and 2000, and Zimring and Hawkins (1991) demonstrated that, at least in the early stages of the prison boom, the *magnitude* of growth was similar across all states, suggesting a meaningful national trend. As imprisonment continued to increase over the next two decades, however, rates of per capita incarceration and rates of growth began to show notable interstate variation (Beckett and Western 2001; Greenberg and West 2001). By 2011, while the national incarceration rate (in both federal and state prisons) was 492 people per 100,000 (Carson and Sabol 2012), one state, Louisiana, exceeded this average by nearly double (865 people per 100,000), and the next highest incarcerating states, Mississippi, Alabama, Texas, and Oklahoma, exceeded the national rate by between 28 and 40 percent (The Sentencing Project 2013).[11] Alternatively, the national incarceration rate in 2011 was nearly three and a half times that of the lowest incarcerating state, Maine (147 per 100,000) (The Sentencing Project 2013).[12] This snapshot reflects consistent regional variation in state-level incarceration trends. For example, between 1990 and 2000, northeastern states showed the lowest percentage increase in state imprisoned populations (40 percent),[13] while southern states showed the highest increase (87.2 percent), followed by western states (76.8 percent) and midwestern states (62.2 percent) (Beck and Harrison 2001).

Finally, within states, counties vary immensely in the rates at which they send people to state prisons and utilize local jails, even after controlling for crime rates. As Lynch (2011) has emphasized, this intrastate variation highlights the importance of accounting for highly localized criminal justice system dynamics in explaining national trends in US incarceration levels. Emerging scholarship in New York (Schupp and Riviera 2010) and California (Ball 2012; Verma 2013), for example, illuminate vast differences in county-level imprisonment rates. Paul Schupp and Craig Riviera (2010) found that the 61 counties of New York showed six distinct patterns of imprisonment[14] between 1990 and 2000 (and that such patterns were not associated with prospective changes in violent or property crime rates). Between 2000 and 2009, Ball (2012) demonstrated the highly disparate rates by which California's 58 counties sent people to state prison. After controlling for county population and crime levels for each year, Ball found that the same "high prison use" counties repeatedly fell into the top quartile of counties that sent the most offenders to state prison for nearly all of the 10 years during the period of his study. At the other end of the spectrum, the same "low use" counties repeatedly fell in the lowest quartile for nearly all of the years studied. Such phenomena are by no means limited to these two states; Schupp and Riviera (2012) also found significant variation in the rate of court commitments to prison among the counties of the 28 states included in the National Corrections Reporting Program, and they identified at least 11 distinct trajectories of county-level imprisonment between 1990 and 2003. These trajectories included groups of counties that demonstrated either sharply increasing, stable to low level, or decreasing imprisonment rates over time. This subnational variation suggests that there are a host of local factors—including perhaps sociolegal norms around defining crime dangerousness and the appropriate responses to criminality—that are influential beyond the formal law in prompting both inter- and intrastate differences in incarceration rates.

In summary, a suitable analysis of the late twentieth century's prison population explosion begins with an appreciation of its anomaly in the American penological history of stable imprisonment rates up until 1973. The major contours of the sharp and swift upsurge of imprisonment since then include its global status, in that the United States is now the world's largest jailer (both per capita and in absolute numbers), the racial disparities within the incarcerated population that grew wider in concert with the population explosion, the role of the "war on drugs" in fueling both the racial disparities and the scale of imprisonment, and the variations in incarcerating behavior (a) between federal and state jurisdictional levels, (b) among states, and (c) among counties within states.

II. How and Why Did It Happen?

There is no one explanation for the social fact of mass incarceration as it emerged in the United States in the late twentieth century. The lack of a universally accepted "account" can be understood on practical as well as ontological grounds. Practically, the study of punishment, and particularly the notable penal transformations of the late twentieth century, has been spread among many disciplines; this can, in turn, be understood as the natural result of the ontology of mass incarceration, which, as summarized earlier, exhibits meaningful variation on multiple planes, including across time; the race, class, and gender of those imprisoned; the changing definitions of imprisonable offenses; geography; and jurisdiction.[15] In step with the many others who have attempted to tackle this expansive domain, we therefore do not intend to settle on any one explanation—and in any case do not submit to the view that any one explanation exists—but rather attempt to draw out the important knowledge thus far produced. In doing so, we take the view that, while macro-sociological explanations have supplied crucial theoretical footing, more empirically grounded mid-range explanations have served as something of a corrective in illuminating the qualitative features of mass incarceration, as well as the multiple pathways to it.

The first generation of scholarly literature can be viewed as a reaction to what we call the *conventional crime narrative*, which positions the remarkable rise in US imprisonment as a direct response to a similarly remarkable rise in violent crime during the same time period (Dilulio 1991; Bennett, Dilulio, and Walters 1996). Violent crime began rising in the mid-1960s and did not decline appreciably until the 1990s (Zimring 2007). This narrative, which Francis Cullen and colleagues (1985) termed the "democracy-at-work" thesis, held a great amount of popular appeal for its simplicity, common-sense rationale, and strategic political value (Beckett 1997). The scholarly literature that emerged during this period, however, challenged this narrative in several important ways. First, it explicated the role of imprisonment in the mass incarceration era as shifting from a largely individualistic enterprise aiming to rehabilitate each offender through various forms of "penal welfarism" (Garland 1985) to a politically, economically, and culturally intertwined device for managing entire classes of people (Feeley and Simon 1992; see also Harcourt 2003, 2007 on the "risk managment" model). As such, this line of theorizing argued against the simple linear relationship between crime incidence and responsive use of imprisonment. Rather, penal strategies came to be used for "herding a specific population that cannot be disaggregated and transformed, but only maintained" (Feeley and Simon 1992, p. 470).

These analyses also challenged the conventional crime narrative by theorizing mass incarceration as a policy adaptation to the public's waning faith by the 1970s in the state's ability to produce sustained economic opportunity, generate upward mobility (particularly but not exclusively among racial minorities and the lower classes), and stem steeply rising violent crime rates through nonincarcerative, governmental social engineering programs (Savelsberg 1994; Caplow and Simon 1999; Garland 2001b; Gottschalk 2006; Simon 2007). While these analyses did not deny the role of rising crime rates (see especially Garland 2001b), they endeavored to link the massive transformation in penal logics and practices to structural sociopolitical changes, some of which also impacted crime incidence. Consistent with this, scholars have argued that the increased use of imprisonment is linked to the rise of neoliberalism, whereby the fundamental restructuring of the economy that was taking place in the late twentieth century, which entailed deindustrialization, globalization, and economic deregulation, rendered sizeable classes of people unemployable due to decreased demand for so-called unskilled manual labor. Prisons and jails, in this view, became tools for isolating and managing these "surplus" populations (Beckett and Western 2001; De Giorgi 2007; Gilmore 2007; Wacquant 2009; Harcourt 2010, 2011). As we discuss later, scholars have also highlighted how the decentralized political structure that characterizes the United States, including the fragmentation of power between multiple jurisdictions, has both historically (Gottschalk 2006) and in contemporary times (Miller 2008; Scheingold 1991) created the nation's unique capacity for mass incarceration.

In a related set of theoretical treatments, mass incarceration has been conceptualized as a post–civil rights tool of racial subjugation (Wacquant 2000; Alexander 2010; see also Tonry 1995, 2011). Michelle Alexander (2010) has perhaps most forcefully made this argument to broader audiences outside of academe in her book, *The New Jim Crow: Mass Incarceration in the Age of Colorblindness*, in which she explains mass incarceration as the latest manifestation of a historically patterned process of racial casting in the United States.

These social structural and functionalist accounts provide overlapping theoretical backdrops for understanding the general conditions of possibility for the rise of mass incarceration in this specific historical period, including the particular political and institutional arrangements that allowed for such rapid and sustained prison growth. Ultimately, these accounts have complicated the popularly held assumption that mass incarceration was primarily or singularly a method of crime control.

What might be considered the second generation of this literature explores more empirically grounded, midrange explanations, often for geographically specific sites of prison growth. These studies excavate and explain multiple pathways to mass incarceration among different locales and penal sites, even as they exist under the same general social organization that earlier theorists identified as characteristic of late modernity (such as a weak state, neoliberal restructuring, cynicism about the state's ability to prevent crime, etc.). Additionally, this literature has delved more deeply into the qualitative features of mass incarceration that distinguish it from previous penal eras in American history, such as the emerging prevalence of "super-maximum" isolation housing and increased overcrowding coupled with austere, depriving conditions of confinement (see, e.g., Toch 1985; Haney and Lynch 1997; Haney 2003, 2006; Terry 2004; Reiter 2012; Lynch 2013).

Just as earlier studies complicated the conventional crime narrative, this generation of scholarship confounded another prevailing narrative: the increased sentencing severity wrought by the shift from indeterminate to determinate sentencing was a major cause of mass incarceration (e.g., Langan 1991; Freeman 1996; Boggess and Bound 1997; Blumstein and Beck 1999, 2005; Garland 2001b; Whitman 2003). Unlike the conventional crime narrative, the sentencing severity narrative predominated academic as much as popular discourse. However, as empirical legal studies scholars such as John Pfaff (2008, 2011, 2013) and Kevin Reitz (2005), as well as social scientists such as Jon Sorensen and Don Stemen (2002) have shown, determinate sentencing, which prescribes mandatory sentence lengths or ranges that offer limited or no judicial discretion to hand down shorter terms of imprisonment, has exerted little causal effect on the rise and scale of US imprisonment. Thus it appears that it is not the mere form of statutory structure, but rather how criminal laws are deployed, that accounts for many of the features of mass incarceration (Lynch 2011).

Indeed, as Pfaff (2011) shows, it has been the rise in felony filings, as a rate of arrests, by prosecutors who enjoy sole discretion in the decision to file a new felony charge. Previous studies that attributed increased incarceration to an increase in prison admissions per arrest—which suggests more severe sanctioning throughout the various levels of the criminal justice system (Langan 1991; Boggess and Bound 1997; Blumstein and Beck 1999, 2005)—failed to disaggregate data to show the multiple decision points by multiple institutional actors between the event of an arrest and that of handing down a prison sentence. Pfaff's (2011, p. 19) findings "consistently identify the same institutional actor as the central engine of prison admission growth: the prosecutor."[16]

Reitz (2005), as well as Sorensen and Stemen (2002), demonstrate that neither sentencing policies nor changes in parole policies, such as the removal of discretionary parole, explain much of the variation among state imprisonment rates, while a combination of "[c]rime rates, the percentage of the population that is Black, and citizen ideology have the greatest influence on the rates of incarceration and admission across states" (Sorensen and Stemen 2002, p. 456). Such findings are replicated in the empirical literature explaining intrastate (i.e., intercounty) imprisonment variation, which identifies the causal effects of additional variables such as the proportion of nonwhite populations, poverty rate, degree of urbanization, ideological and political conservatism, and location in the southern US region on prison admission levels (McCarthy 1990; Jacobs and Helms 1996; Arvanites and Asher 1998; Jacobs and Carmichael 2001; Kane 2003; Weidner and Frase 2003; Percival 2010).

Perhaps most simply put, William J. Stuntz (2011, p. 47) states: "Today's justice system does punish crime more severely than in the past—but its defining feature is that it punishes vastly *more often*" (emphasis added). The conventional narrative about lengthier sentencing driving the imprisonment boom, then, is not entirely wrong. The shift to determinate sentencing was a major driver of this punitive turn that swelled US incarceration levels, not just because it expanded the potential for longer sentences but because it restructured and consolidated the power to punish squarely within the hands of prosecutors. Specifically, it appears to have done so through shifting discretionary power from judges to prosecutors, who are better positioned to maneuver around highly structured sentencing regimes through charging decisions and plea-bargaining negotiations that occur prior to a criminal case formally coming before a judge. As comparative studies emphasize, however, even the rise of the prosecutor would not self-evidently lead to more prolific punishment but for the federated, highly localized political system unique (though certainly not exclusive) to the United States (e.g., Zimring and Hawkins 1991; Savelsberg 1994; Gottschalk 2006; Miller 2008). The federal–state–county–municipal layering of the criminal justice system in the United States means that prosecutors, in turn, are each situated within a particular "locale"

significant pressure to shed prisoners in the state, but nonetheless the state's budget shortfalls had made it virtually impossible to devote more resources to prisons.

As Realignment is implemented, it is unclear how California counties, each facing local fiscal crises of their own, will respond. Will they use the discretion afforded to them under this new law to deploy alternative sanctions that do not require offenders to spend lengthy periods of incarceration in local jails? Or will they continue their historic reliance on incarceration by placing offenders in local jails merely as a substitute for sending them to state prisons? Initial evidence suggests that, while the total number of people incarcerated in prisons and jails does not appear to have grown since the enactment of Realignment, the overall decreases observed in the state prison population mask the underlying persistence of incarceration, which, for this class of low-level, "realigned" offenders, is now served behind the bars of county jails rather than state prisons.

In a study of this question, Magnus Lofstrom and Steven Raphael (2013) found that between June 2011 and June 2012 (a time period containing the first nine months of Realignment), California's prison population decreased by approximately 27,000 people while the average daily population of California's jails grew by about 8,600 inmates (about 12 percent). Lofstrom and Raphael also point out that 16 counties are operating jails above rated design capacity (up from 11 counties in the previous year) and that, statewide, county jails have been operating above 100 percent of rated capacity since February 2012 (four months after the enactment of Realignment). This emerging data does not demonstrate a "one-to-one transfer of felons from state prison to county jails" (Lofstrom and Raphael 2013, p. 2). Rather, they estimate that "Realignment increased the average daily jail population by roughly one inmate for every three fewer offenders going to state prison" (p. 19).

In line with wide historic intercounty imprisonment variation in California (Ball 2012), Lofstrom and Raphael (2013) also found that the effect of Realignment on jail populations varies among counties, with some counties incarcerating much higher percentages of their Realignment caseloads in local jails. In summary, the concern that Realignment "will have simply changed the inmate's address from state prison to county jail" (Petersilia and Snyder 2013, p. 41) appears to have only partially come to fruition—at least according to early data.

There is a risk, though, that the correspondence between realigned defendants and jail growth will grow closer once the current wave of jail construction underway in many California counties is completed. Indeed, the California legislature amended a separate piece of legislation in the wake of the *Brown v. Plata* (2011) order and the enactment of Realignment, which authorized $1.2 billion in lease revenue bonds for the construction of an estimated 10,000 new county jail beds in the state (Public Policy Institute of California 2013). A second potential contributor to a transcarceral (rather than decarceral) effect of Realignment is the county-specific response to recidivism. Joan Petersilia and Jessica Snyder (2013, p. 41) used historical rates of recidivism to project overall incarceration levels by 2017 and predicted that the total jail plus prison population will actually be about 5,000 people higher than it was prior to the enactment of Realignment, suggesting that Lofstrom and Raphael's (2013) findings may be premature. Beyond the question of whether recidivism rates among realigned offenders will be comparable to, lower, or higher than pre-Realignment rates, is how each of California's counties will choose to sanction recidivism. Because Realignment leaves wide discretion to counties in this respect, it remains to be seen whether the overall jail population will continue to rise due to returns to jail and, if so, how much county policies and practices will vary on this point.

This kind of localization policy also runs the risk of replicating the very problems that prompted its innovation in the first place, given the growing problem with overcrowding that is already occurring in county jails. As Schlanger (2013) makes clear, conditions of confinement, like the kind of extreme overcrowding that ultimately resulted in the *Plata* decision (and prompted the Realignment legislation), will be much harder to monitor and challenge in the state's more than 50 local jail systems. Thus she warns of "the hydra risk" whereby the courts "chopping the head off of unconstitutional prison conditions could cause many of the fifty-eight counties to, in turn, develop unconstitutional conditions of jail confinement" (p. 210). Moreover, faith in jails as an ameliorative for unconstitutional treatment appears misguided. For instance, the Los Angeles County jail system, which is larger than fully half of US states' prison systems, has been plagued by years of documented abuses against inmates, including serious and fatal beatings by guards that have resulted in federal intervention and judgments against the jailers and the county (Faturechi and Leonard 2013b). In late 2013, more than a dozen Los Angeles Sheriff's jail personnel were federally indicted on civil rights and corruption charges stemming from systemic use of violence by jail staff against inmates (Faturechi and Leonard 2013a).

Finally, Cohen's (1979) dystopic prospect of the "punitive city" urges us to look beyond incarceration—whether in state and federal prisons or county jails—as the only meaningful metric of the societal effects of correctional control (see also Beckett and Murakawa 2012). Data on the *total* population under some form of correctional supervision in California, which includes prison, jail, and community supervision programs, such as probation or parole, show a slight decline from 725,085 (2.8 percent of California adults) in 2004 (Lin and Jannetta 2006) to 632,878 adults (2.13 percent of California adults) by year-end 2012 (Petersilia and Snyder 2013). These data, however, tell us nothing about how the sentence lengths of community supervision might be increasing or about how the qualitative features of community supervision (see, e.g., Phelps 2013) and incarceration in jails versus prisons might be changing in important ways. While Cohen's trepidation that alternatives to incarceration would result in "widening the net" (whereby "the new diversion diverts—for better or worse—*into* the system" [1979, p. 349]) have not so far been clearly borne out in California, the longer term effects of these kinds of prison downsizing mandates remain to be seen, and the critical—if often difficult to answer—questions raised by Cohen remain as timely as ever.

IV. CONCLUSION

Much of the theoretical and empirical scholarship that has tried to explain the rise of mass incarceration has looked to an array of predicate causes that are, at times, quite distant from this phenomenon as effect. As John Levi Martin (2011) suggests, this is in part a product of the social scientific intellectual enterprise, where we gain the greatest rewards for the most creative and (often) least intuitive causal models. As a result, we have some brilliant and creative ideas about how many huge, complex, structural forces have transformed punishment in the United States and beyond—but ideas that often sacrifice theoretical and empirical accounts of the precise triggers and actions that moved millions of our population into carceral institutions.

We have often been loath to examine the more on-the-ground, proximate potential causes of mass incarceration, even when we recognize them, since such approaches may lack the grandeur and sense of importance that attends macro-theoretical approaches. This is a mistake, not only for the sake of theory but also for policy and practice. The rollback of mass incarceration, if it is to happen, will require a much more nuanced understanding of how day-to-day institutional power is reshaped, in multifarious ways, as levers are pulled or pathways to action are blocked. Harkening back to Cohen (1979), we must be prepared to see how the power to punish, by a much larger and highly resourced set of criminal justice systems than was in place in the 1970s, is manifested into punitive action as states and localities begin to cut off some of the direct flow to prisons. This is necessarily an on-the-ground and close-up endeavor that begins with some common principles of action but that also is quite variegated as a function of specific times, people, and places. We do not foresee a wholesale shrinkage of the myriad institutions that comprise criminal justice on the horizon; rather, we should be prepared for new, recycled, or reinvented modes of intervention that nonetheless aim to sustain the relevance of those institutions.

We end by returning to Pfaff's (2011, 2013) critical work on the role of prosecutors, which, while impressively creative, is also intuitive and commonsensical both theoretically and as a matter of empirical reality (especially to those with direct experience with the day-to-day realities of the criminal justice system). As noted already, his work shows that increased prosecutorial filings per arrests accounts for more of the prison growth than any of the other common explanations. These findings not only underscore the centrality of local criminal justice action to mass incarceration but also suggest that we must attend more closely to those operations that we cannot readily observe. Thus, while the politics of law and order, the proliferation of social surveillance, expanded police forces (especially in urban settings), and even overburdened criminal courts are visible and accessible, the prosecutor's office remains a black box, particularly in terms of the early-stage decision-making process as to whether and what to charge in any given law enforcement referral.

Thus Pfaff's (2011, 2013) findings suggest to us that we need to change the nature of our empirical questions about mass incarceration. Most fundamentally, they suggest a pivot away from the big "why" questions to more precise "how" questions, which may be especially useful to generate modes of intervention to temper the enormous power that resides with prosecutors. Specifically, they suggest that local criminal courts are the very linkage point between the political economy of punishment and punitive action, prompting the question of how just one arm of the courtroom workgroup could impose so much more business on systems that have been overtaxed long before the advent of mass incarceration (see, e.g., Zeisel, Kalven, and Buchholz 1959; Meeker and Pontell 1985). Did this new pressure catalyze new modes of adjudication that privileged efficiency over due process? Why was there no countervailing pressure on prosecutors' offices from judges and county officials against the increased caseloads? How did the prevailing politics allow prosecutors to become revered and unassailable figures in the "war on crime" (see Simon 2007)? Finally, how precisely did the punitive innovations and impulses happening at local and state levels, especially those of prosecutors (McCoy 1993; Campbell 2011), transcend jurisdictional boundaries to metastasize into mass incarceration?

If the emergent stabilization, and even decline, of imprisonment observed in the United States does in fact prove epochal in the long view of history (which we hope it does, even if we remain skeptical), it will no doubt have been because fundamental changes to the institutions that comprise the criminal justice system—and the public opinion that buttresses them—took root at the turn of the twenty-first century, a time in which economic recession forced many states and municipalities to scale back on public works, including corrections. While it is tempting to look to major law changes by way of Congressional acts and US Supreme Court rulings as the most dispositive catalysts for ending mass incarceration, the highly localized, federated structure of American government in general and criminal justice administration and politics in particular strongly suggest that the most viable pathways out of the imprisonment boom will solidify at the municipal, county, and state levels. For example, while major sentencing reform at the federal level remains unlikely, sentencing reform at the state level that decriminalizes low-level drug offenses appears viable in many states. Indeed, at the time of this writing, 13 states and the District of Columbia treat personal use drug possession offenses as misdemeanors rather than felonies (Hopper, Austin, and Foreman 2014), and two states have removed criminal penalties altogether for adult use of marijuana. Sentencing reform measures such as these, while no panacea, modify the relatively unfettered discretion of prosecutors to initiate felony drug filings by meaningfully shrinking the universe of offenses that can be classified as imprisonable felonies, thus slowing the flow of people into correctional institutions in the first place.

Beyond sentencing reform, measures that build fiscal and political accountability into county-level criminal justice administration, such as California's Realignment law, force local justice workgroups (including district attorneys) to weigh the costs, risks, and benefits of relying on incarceration in local jails as the primary crime and punishment policy. It is likely no coincidence that the stabilization of imprisonment roughly coincided with the Great Recession of the late 2000s. Eliminating (or limiting) the "free lunch" (Zimring and Hawkins 1991) that counties have historically been receiving in virtually all states by sending people to state prisons without bearing any of the costs stands to change fundamental institutional practices and how counties relate to state governments in this policy area.

Because of the changed nature of the economy, it appears as if resources to build new prisons will not be available on the scale they once were; nor does the political will to invest in prisons to the detriment of other public works, such as education and health care, appear to exist in this "new" economy. These conditions offer at least some limiting principles for even the most punitive local governments. While the institutional arrangements of the past allowed locally elected criminal justice officials to deploy "tough on crime" policies as powerful political capital, the fiscal and legal limits placed on today's institutions may in fact render them political liabilities. Indeed, we have already witnessed a pivot in the conservative rhetoric, from getting tough on crime to getting "smart on crime," as exemplified by the advocacy group, Right on Crime (2013), which makes "the conservative case for reform" on mainly fiscal grounds. Nonetheless, we cannot rely on tight economic conditions as the solution to mass incarceration, especially given the history of penal expansion under previous recessionary periods (see Gottschalk [2010] for a review; see also Aviram 2015). Indeed, economic scarcity and insecurity can have countervailing effects. As Gottschalk (2010) has warned, punitive tendencies often rise under tough economic conditions, and in the recent Great Recession, the signs of rollback are quite meager given the scale of financial woes.

Finally, and also related to the US governmental structure, is the role of special-interest groups and social movements in shaping the crime policies of the twenty-first century. One common lesson from what we have called a "second generation" of research attempting to explain the rise and entrenchment of mass incarceration is the formidable (and sometimes dispositive) role that district attorney, law enforcement, and prison guard professional associations and unions, as well as conservative victims' rights groups, have played in blocking genuine retreats from mass incarceration (Zimring et al. 2001; Gottschalk 2006; Barker 2009; Lynch 2009; Campbell 2011; Page 2011; Hopper et al. 2014). Without being overly quixotic, however, there is reason to believe that public attitudes about the role of imprisonment in society are changing in reaction to the fiscal crises, racial disparities, and community destruction wrought by an overreliance on incarceration (see Hopper et al. [2013] for a discussion of shifting public opinion specifically in California). National surveys, such as a study conducted by the Pew Charitable Trusts (2012), show that American voters believe too many people are in prison and that the nation spends too much on imprisonment, and they voice overwhelming support for a variety of policy changes that shift nonviolent offenders from prison to more effective, less expensive alternatives. The study also showed that support for sentencing and corrections reforms (including reduced prison terms) is strong across political parties, regions, and age, gender, and racial/ethnic groups. While these opinion shifts signal precisely the kind of punishment dispersal strategies Cohen (1979) augured, they also open up political space to question the singularity of conservative victims' rights groups and the primacy of the voices of prosecutors and law enforcement—to the virtual exclusion of others—in shaping American criminal justice policy.

NOTES

1. They also examined Norway's rates to support their claims.
2. All too often, measures of crime are inserted in models as unproblematic representations of an agreed-on, objectively based concept that may suffer from measurement error but not definitional differences across time and place. See also Donald Black's (1970) iconic piece, "The Production of Crime Rates" on this point.
3. The concept of "mass incarceration," or "mass imprisonment," is not fully defined in the literature, although, in general, the following elements are commonly assumed: vast numbers of imprisoned citizens and skyrocketing rates of imprisonment, overcrowded facilities, and the concentrated impact on minorities and the poor (Garland 2001a). It has additionally been defined by a qualitative shift in the prison as a living institution, as an explicitly punitive operational ethos began to supersede the logic of rehabilitation in many state penal systems (Lynch 2009).
4. Unless otherwise specified, we do not include local jail incarceration in our reported incarceration rates.
5. See note 3.
6. See Haney (2006) for a full examination of the psychological impacts of the mass incarcerative experience.
7. For instance, in some years between 1991 and 2008, the African American incarceration rate increased by more than 100 per 100,000 African Americans. The overall annual

imprisonment rates for the Scandinavian countries ranged from 65 to 74 per 100,000 population during the same time frame. The annual rates for France, Germany, and Belgium were between 88 and 96 per 100,000. The Canadian rate was just above 100 per 100,000 (Tonry 2011, pp. 35–36).

8. In 1980, there were 19,000 drug offenders in state prisons, 4,900 in federal prisons (Beck and Gilliard 1995), and 17,200 in jail (Mauer and King 2007).

9. By year-end 2012, there were an estimated 210,200 sentenced drug offenders in state prisons (Carson 2014, Table 14), and 98,200 in federal prisons (Carson 2014, Table 15).

10. There were a total of 501,886 federal and state prison and jail inmates in 1980 (Beck and Gilliard 1995).

11. Mississippi's incarceration rate was 690 per 100,000; Alabama's was 650 per 100,000; Texas's was 632 per 100,000; and Oklahoma's was 631 per 100,000 (Carson and Sabol 2012).

12. The next four lowest, Minnesota (183 per 100,000), Rhode Island (196 per 100,000), New Hampshire (198 per 100,000), and Massachusetts (206 per 100,000) were each less than half the national rate (The Sentencing Project 2013).

13. It is important, however, not to lose sight of how aggressive even a 40 percent increase is, based on the incarceration trajectories throughout most of American history.

14. Measured as the percentage of felony convictions resulting in a state prison commitment, separately for each year from 1990 to 1999.

15. We differentiate "geography" from "jurisdiction" to acknowledge that both are legal constructions that do not necessarily match one another. For example, criminal justice adjudicatory and administrative bodies may encompass multiple states, counties, and municipalities, or they may be divided into subunits. The federal court system offers one example, in that it divides the United States into federal circuits that each contains multiple states, which are, in turn, divided into districts that are, at their largest, the size of single states.

16. Pfaff documents a spiraling effect of the general late twentieth century law and order movement; that is, that system expansion has created many more people with felony records, who in turn are especially likely to have felony charges filed against them because they may come to be seen by prosecutors as prosecution-worthy by dint of their record. He posits that this is how the "war on drugs" has had its impact—by the rise discretionary arrests for drug offenses and subsequent convictions, the pool of those deemed worthy of felony filings across all offense types has increased.

17. The incarceration *rate* began slowing in 2007, however.

18. For the first time since 1980, however, federal imprisonment decreased by 0.9 percent from 2012 to 2013 (Carson 2014). Whether this indicates a prolonged stabilization at the federal level, only time will tell.

19. The states with the next greatest declines were New Hampshire (5.3 percent), Connecticut (5.2 percent), and New Jersey (4.7 percent; Carson and Sabol 2012).

References

Alexander, Michelle. 2010. *The New Jim Crow: Mass Incarceration in the Age of Colorblindness.* New York: New Free Press.

Arvanites, Thomas, and Martin A. Asher. 1998. "State and County Incarceration Rates: The Direct and Indirect Effects of Race and Inequality." *American Journal of Economics and Sociology* 572:207–221.

Aviram, Hadar. 2015. *Cheap on Crime: Recession-Era Politics and the Transformation of American Punishment*. Berkeley: University of California Press.

Ball, David. 2012. "Tough on Crime (on the State's Dime): How Violent Crime Does Not Drive California Counties' Incarceration Rates—and Why It Should." *Georgia State Law Review* 28:987–1084.

Barker, Vanessa. 2009. *The Politics of Imprisonment: How the Democratic Process Shapes the Way America Punishes Offenders*. New York: Oxford University Press.

Beck, Allen J., and Darrell K. Gilliard. 1995. *Prisoners in 1994*. Washington, DC: US Department of Justice, Bureau of Justice Statistics.

Beck, Allen J., and Paige M. Harrison. 2001. *Prisoners in 2000*. Washington, DC: US Department of Justice, Office of Justice Programs, Bureau of Justice Statistics.

Beckett, Katherine. 1997. *Making Crime Pay: Law and Order in Contemporary American Politics*. New York: Oxford University Press.

Beckett, Katherine, and Naomi Murakawa. 2012. "Mapping the Shadow Carceral State: Toward an Institutionally Capacious Approach to Punishment." *Theoretical Criminology* 162:221–244.

Beckett, Katherine, and Bruce Western. 2001. "Governing Social Marginality: Welfare, Incarceration, and the Transformation of State Policy." *Punishment & Society* 3:43–59.

Bennett, William J., John J. Dilulio, and John P. Walters. 1996. *Body Count: Moral Poverty— and How to Win America's War against Crime and Drugs*. New York: Simon & Schuster.

Black, Donald J. 1970. "Production of Crime Rates." *American Sociological Review* 35:733–748.

Blumstein, Alfred, and Allen J. Beck. 1999. "Population Growth in the U.S. Prisons, 1980– 1996." In *Prisons*, edited by Michael Tonry and Joan Petersilia. Chicago: University of Chicago Press.

Blumstein, Alfred, and Jacqueline Cohen. 1973. "Theory of Stability of Punishment." *Journal of Criminal Law and Criminology* 642:198–207.

Blumstein, Alfred, and Allen J. Beck. 2005. "Reentry as a Transient State between Liberty and Recommitment." In *Prisoner Reentry and Crime in America*, edited by Jeremy Travis and Christy Visher. Cambridge, UK: Cambridge University Press.

Boggess, Scott, and John Bound. 1997. "Did Criminal Activity Increase During the 1980s? Comparisons Across Data Sources." *Social Science Quarterly* 783:725–39.

Bonzcar, Thomas P. 2003. *Prevalence of Imprisonment in the U.S. Population, 1974–2001*. NCJ 197976. Washington, DC: Bureau of Justice Statistics.

Cahalan, Margaret Werner. 1986. *Historical Corrections in the United States, 1850–1984*. Washington, DC: Bureau of Justice Statistics.

Campbell, Michael C. 2011. "Politics, Prisons, and Law Enforcement: An Examination of the Emergence of 'Law and Order' Politics in Texas." *Law & Society Review* 453:631–665.

Campbell, Michael C., and Heather Schoenfeld. 2013. "The Transformation of America's Penal Order: A Historicized Political Sociology of Punishment." *American Journal of Sociology* 1185:1375–1423.

Caplow, Theodore, and Jonathan Simon. 1999. "Understanding Prison Policy and Population Trends." *Crime and Justice* 26:63–120.

Carson, E. Ann. 2014. *Prisoners in 2013*. NCJ 247282. Washington, DC: US Department of Justice, Office of Justice Programs, Bureau of Justice Statistics.

Carson, E. Ann, and Daniela Gollineli. 2013. *Prisoners in 2012—Advance Counts*. NCJ 242467. Washington, DC: US Department of Justice, Office of Justice Programs, Bureau of Justice Statistics.

Carson, E. Ann, and William J. Sabol. 2012. *Prisoners in 2011*. NCJ 239808. Washington, DC: US Department of Justice, Office of Justice Programs, Bureau of Justice Statistics.

Cohen, Stanley 1979. "Punitive City: Notes on the Dispersal of Social Control." *Contemporary Crises* 34:339–363.

Cohen, Stanley. 1985. *Visions of Social Control: Crime, Punishment, and Classification*. Oxford: Polity Press.

Cullen, Francis, Gregory A. Clark, and John F. Wozniak. 1985. "Explaining the Get-Tough Movement: Can the Public Be Blamed?" *Federal Probation* 452:16–24.

Currie, Elliott. 1998. *Crime and Punishment in America*. New York: Metropolitan Books.

De Giorgi, Alessandro. 2007. "Toward a Political Economy of Post-Fordist Punishment." *Critical Criminology* 153:243–265.

Dilulio, John J. 1991. *No Escape: The Future of American Corrections*. New York: Basic Books.

Dorsey, Tina L., and Priscilla Middleton. 2002. *Drugs and Crime Facts*. Washington, DC: US Department of Justice, Bureau of Justice Statistics.

The Economist. 2012. "California's Overcrowded Prisons: The Challenges of 'Realignment.'" May 19. http://www.economist.com/node/21555611.

Faturechi, Robert, and Jack Leonard. 2013a. "FBI Arrests Sheriffs Officials in L.A. County Jails." *Los Angeles Times* (December 9). http://www.latimes.com/news/local/la-me-ln-fbi-sheriff-arrests-jail-20131209,0,2818116.story.

Faturechi, Robert, and Jack Leonard. 2013b. "U.S. Launches Probe into Abuse at L.A. County Jails." *Los Angeles Times* (September 6). http://www.latimes.com/local/lanow/la-me-ln-justice-department-probe-la-jails-20130906,0,792120.story#axzz2nIhoaAWZ.

Federal Bureau of Prisons. 2010. *State of the Bureau 2010*. Washington, DC: US Department of Justice.

Feeley, Malcolm, and Jonathan Simon. 1992. "The New Penology: Notes on the Emerging Strategy of Corrections and Its Implications." *Criminology* 304:449–474.

Freeman, Alexa P. 1996. "Unscheduled Departures: The Circumvention of Just Sentencing for Police Brutality." *Hastings Law Journal* 47:677–777.

Frost, Natasha A., Judith Greene, and Kevin Pranis. 2006. *Hard Hit: The Growth in the Imprisonment of Women, 1977–2004*. New York: Women's Prison Association and Institute on Women and Criminal Justice.

Garland, David. 1985. *Punishment and Welfare: A History of Penal Strategies*. Aldershot, UK: Gower.

Garland, David. 2001a. *Mass Imprisonment: Social Causes and Consequences*. Thousand Oaks, CA: SAGE.

Garland, David. 2001b. *The Culture of Control: Crime and Social Order in Contemporary Society*. Chicago: University of Chicago Press.

Gilmore, Ruth Wilson. 2007. *Golden Gulag: Prisons, Surplus, Crisis, and Opposition in Globalizing California*. Berkeley: University of California Press.

Glaze, Lauren E., and Erinn J. Herberman. 2013. *Correctional Populations in the United States, 2012*. NCJ 243936. Washington, DC: US Department of Justice, Office of Justice Programs, Bureau of Justice Statistics.

Goodman, Phil. 2008. "'It's Just Black, White, or Hispanic': An Observational Study of Racializing Moves in California's Segregated Prison Reception Centers." *Law and Society Review* 424:735–770.

Gottschalk, Marie. 2006. *The Prison and the Gallows: The Politics of Mass Incarceration in America*. Cambridge, UK: Cambridge University Press.

Gottschalk, Marie. 2010. "Cell Blocks and Red Ink: Mass Incarceration, the Great Recession and Penal Reform." *Daedalus* 139:62–73.

Greenberg, David F., and Valerie West. 2001. "State Prison Populations and Their Growth, 1971–1991." *Criminology* 393:615–654.

Haney, Craig. 2003. "Mental Health Issues in Long-term Solitary and 'Supermax' Confinement." *Crime & Delinquency* 491:124–556.

Haney, Craig. 2006. *Reforming Punishment: Psychological Limits to the Pains of Imprisonment*. Washington, DC: American Psychological Association.

Haney, Craig, and Mona Lynch. 1997. "Regulating Prisons of the Future: A Psychological Analysis of Supermax and Solitary Confinement." *NYU Review of Law and Social Change* 23:477–570.

Harcourt, Bernard E. 2003. *Guns, Crime, And Punishment in America*. New York: New York University Press.

Harcourt, Bernard E. 2007. *Against Prediction: Profiling, Policing, And Punishing in an Actuarial Age*. Chicago: University of Chicago Press.

Harcourt, Bernard E. 2010. "Risk as a Proxy for Race." University of Chicago Law and Economics Olin Working Paper No. 535, University of Chicago Public Law Working Paper No. 323. Chicago: Law School, University of Chicago.

Harcourt, Bernard E. 2011. *The Illusion of Free Markets: Punishment and the Myth of Natural Order*. Cambridge, MA: Harvard University Press.

Hopper, Allen, James Austin, and Jolene Foreman. 2014. "Shifting the Paradigm or Shifting the Problem? The Politics of California's Criminal Justice Realignment." *Santa Clara Law Review* 54:527-621.

Horne, Sheryl Van, and Graham Farrell. 1999. *Drug Offenders in the Global Criminal Justice System*. HEUNI Paper No. 13. Helsinki: European Institute for Crime Prevention and Control.

International Center for Prison Studies. 2013. "World Prison Brief." http://www.prisonstudies.org/info/worldbrief.

Jacobs, David, and Jason T. Carmichael. 2001. "The Politics of Punishment across Time and Space: A Pooled Time-Series Analysis of Imprisonment Rates." *Social Forces* 80:61–89.

Jacobs, David, and Ronald E. Helms. 1996. "Toward a Political Model of Incarceration: A Time-Series Examination of Multiple Explanations for Prison Admission Rates." *American Journal of Sociology* 102:323–357.

James, Doris J. 2004. *Profile of Jail Inmates, 2002*. Washington, DC: US Department of Justice, Bureau of Justice Statistics.

James, Nathan. 2013. *The Federal Prison Population Buildup: Overview, Policy Changes, Issues, and Options*. Washington, DC: Congressional Research Service.

Kane, Robert J. 2003. "Social Control in the Metropolis: A Community-Level Examination of the Minority Group-Threat Hypothesis." *Justice Quarterly* 20:265–295.

Langan, Patrick A. 1991. "America's Soaring Prison Population." *Science* 251(5001):1568–1573.

Lin, Jeffrey, and Jesse Jannetta. 2006. *The Scope of Correctional Control in California*. Irvine: Center for Evidence-Based Corrections, University of California-Irvine.

Lofstrom, Magnus, and Steven Raphael. 2013. *Impact of Realignment on County Jail Populations*. San Francisco, CA: Public Policy Institute of California.

Lynch, Mona. 2009. *Sunbelt Justice: Arizona and the Transformation of American Punishment*. Palo Alto, CA: Stanford University Press.

Lynch, Mona. 2011. "Mass Incarceration, Legal Change and Locale: Understanding and Remediating American Penal Overindulgence." *Criminology and Public Policy* 10:671–698.

Lynch, Mona. 2013. "The Social Psychology of Mass Imprisonment." In *The SAGE Handbook of Punishment and Society*, edited by Jonthan Simon and Richard Sparks. London: SAGE.

Lynch, Mona, and Marisa Omori. 2014. "Legal Change and Sentencing Norms in the Wake of Booker: The Impact of Time and Place on Drug Trafficking Cases in Federal Court." *Law & Society Review* 48:411–445.

Martin, John Levi. 2011. *The Explanation of Social Action*. New York: Oxford University Press.

Mauer, Marc, and Ryan S. King. 2007. *A 25-Year Quagmire: The War on Drugs and Its Impact on American Society*. Washington, DC: The Sentencing Project.

McCarthy, Belinda R. 1990. "A Micro-Level Analysis of Social Structure and Social Control: Intrastate Use of Jail and Prison Confinement." *Justice Quarterly* 72:325–340.

McCoy, Candace. 1993. *Politics and Plea Bargaining: Victims' Rights in California*. Philadelphia: University of Pennsylvania Press.

Meeker, James W., and Henry N. Pontell. 1985. "Court Caseloads, Plea Bargains, and Criminal Sanctions: The Effects of Section 17 PC in California." *Criminology* 231:119–143.

Miller, Lisa. 2008. *The Perils of Federalism: Race, Poverty, and the Politics of Crime Control*. Oxford: Oxford University Press.

Page, Joshua. 2011. *The Toughest Beat: Politics, Punishment, and the Prison Officers' Union in California*. New York: Oxford University Press.

Percival, Garrick L. 2010. "Ideology, Diversity, and Imprisonment: Considering the Influence of Local Politics on Racial and Ethnic Minority Incarceration Rates." *Social Science Quarterly* 91:1063-1082.

Perkinson, Robert. 2010. *Texas Tough: The Rise of America's Prison Empire*. New York: Picador.

Petersilia, Joan, and Jessica Greenlick Snyder. 2013. "Looking Past the Hype: 10 Questions Everyone Should Ask about California's Prison Realignment." *California Journal of Politics and Policy* 52:266–306.

Pew Charitable Trusts. 2008. *One in 100: Behind Bars in America 2008*. Washington, DC: Pew Charitable Trusts.

Pew Charitable Trusts. 2012. *Public Opinion on Sentencing and Corrections Policy in America*. Washington, DC: Pew Charitable Trusts.

Pfaff, John F. 2008. "The Empirics of Prison Growth: A Critical Review and Path Forward." *Journal of Criminal Law and Criminology* 982:547–619.

Pfaff, John F. 2011. "The Myths and Realities of Correctional Severity: Evidence from the National Corrections Reporting Program on Sentencing Practices." *American Law and Economics Review* 132:491–531.

Pfaff, John F. 2013. "A Plague of Prisons: The Epidemiology of Mass Incarceration in America." *Michigan Law Review* 111(6): 1087–1110.

Phelps, Michelle S. 2013. "The Paradox of Probation: Community Supervision in the Age of Mass Incarceration." *Law and Policy* 35(1–2): 51–80.

Public Policy Institute of California. 2013. Just the Facts: California's County Jails. http://www.ppic.org/main/publication_show.asp?i=1061.

Reiter, Keramet A. 2012. "The Most Restrictive Alternative: A Litigation History of Solitary Confinement in US Prisons, 1960–2006." *Studies in Law, Politics, and Society* 57:71–124.

Reitz, Kevin R. 2005. "Don't Blame Determinacy: U.S. Incarceration Growth Has Been Driven by Other Forces." *Texas Law Review* 84:1787–1802.

Right on Crime. 2013. "What Conservatives Are Saying About Criminal Justice Reform and Right on Crime." http://www.rightoncrime.com/the-conservative-case-for-reform/what-conservatives-are-saying.

Savelsberg, Joachim. 1994. "Knowledge, Domination and Criminal Punishment." *American Journal of Sociology* 994:911–943.

Scheingold, Stuart A. 1991. *The Politics of Street Crime: Criminal Process and Cultural Obsession.* Philadelphia: Temple University Press.

Schlanger, Margo. 2013. "*Plata v. Brown* and Realignment: Jails, Prisons, Courts and Politics." *Harvard Civil Rights-Civil Liberties Law Review* 48:165–215.

Schoenfeld, Heather. 2010. "Mass Incarceration and the Paradox of Prison Conditions Litigation." *Law & Society Review* 443(4): 731–768.

Schupp, Paul, and Craig Riviera. 2010. "Identifying Imprisonment Patterns and Their Relation to Crime among New York Counties 1990–2000: An Exploratory Application of Trajectory Modeling." *Criminal Justice Policy Review* 211:50–75.

Schupp, Paul, and Craig Riviera. 2012. "County-Level Imprisonment Patterns and Their Macro-Level Crime Control Effects." Paper presented at the American Society of Criminology conference, Chicago, November 16.

Simon, Jonathan. 2007. *Governing through Crime: How the War on Crime Transformed American Democracy and Created a Culture of Fear.* Oxford: Oxford University Press.

Simon, Jonathan. 2013. "The Return of the Medical Model: Disease and the Meaning of Imprisonment from John Howard to *Brown v. Plata*." *Harvard Civil Rights-Civil Liberties Law Review* 48:217–235.

Simon. Jonathan. 2014. *Mass Incarceration on Trial: A Remarkable Court Decision and the Future of Prisons in America.* New York: New Press.

Sorensen, Jon, and Don Stemen. 2002. "The Effect of State Sentencing Policies on Incarceration Rates." *Crime & Delinquency* 483:456–475.

Stuntz, William J. 2011. *The Collapse of American Criminal Justice.* Cambridge, MA: Belknap Press of Harvard University Press.

Terry, Charles M. 2004. "Managing Prisoners as Problem Populations and the Evolving Nature of Imprisonment: A Convict Perspective." *Critical Criminology* 121:43–66.

The Sentencing Project. 2004. "The Federal Prison Population: A Statistical Analysis." http://www.sentencingproject.org/doc/publications/inc_federalprisonpop.pdf.

The Sentencing Project. 2013. "Trends in U.S. Corrections Factsheet." http://sentencingproject.org/doc/publications/inc_Trends_in_Corrections_Fact_sheet.pdf.

Toch, Hans. 1985. "Warehouses for People?" *Annals of the American Academy of Political and Social Science* 4781:58–72.

Tonry, Michael H. 1995. *Malign Neglect—Race, Crime, and Punishment in America.* New York: Oxford University Press.

Tonry, Michael H. 2011. *Punishing Race: A Continuing American Dilemma.* New York: Oxford University Press.

US Bureau of Justice Statistics. 2014. "Data Collection: National Prisoner Statistics Program." http://www.bjs.gov/index.cfm?ty=dcdetail&iid=269.

US Census Bureau. 2010. "2010 Census Data." http://www.census.gov/2010census/data/.

US Sentencing Commission. 1987. "Supplementary Report on the Initial Sentencing Guidelines and Policy Statements." https://www.ncjrs.gov/App/publications/abstract.aspx?ID=106173.

Verma, Anjuli. 2013. "De-Incarceration or Trans-Incarceration? An Examination of the Multiple Developmental Pathways to Present-Day Imprisonment Levels among California

Counties 2000–2010." Paper presented at the American Society of Criminology conference, Atlanta, November 20.

Wacquant, Loïc. 2000. "The New 'Peculiar Institution': On the Prison as Surrogate Ghetto." *Theoretical Criminology* 43:377–389.

Wacquant, Loïc. 2009. *Punishing The Poor: The Neoliberal Government of Social Insecurity.* Durham, NC: Duke University Press.

Walmsley, Roy. 2013. *World Prison Population List*, 10th ed. Essex, UK: University of Essex, International Center for Prison Studies.

Weidner, Robert R., and Richard S. Frase. 2003. "Legal and Extralegal Determinants of Intercounty Difference in Prison Use." *Criminal Justice Policy Review* 143:377–400.

Western, Bruce. 2006. *Punishment and Inequality in America.* New York: Russell Sage Foundation.

Whitman, James Q. 2003. *Harsh Justice: Criminal Punishment and the Widening Divide between America and Europe.* Oxford, New York: Oxford University Press.

Zeisel, Hans, Harry Kalven, and Bernard Buchholz. 1959. *Delay in the Court.* Boston: Little, Brown.

Zimring, Franklin E. 2007. *The Great American Crime Decline.* Oxford: Oxford University Press.

Zimring, Franklin E. 2010. "Scale of Imprisonment in the United States: Twentieth Century Patterns and Twenty-First Century Prospects." *Journal of Criminal Law and Criminology* 1003:1225–1246.

Zimring, Franklin E., and Gordon Hawkins. 1991. *The Scale of Imprisonment.* Chicago: University of Chicago Press.

Zimring, Franklin E., Gordon Hawkins, and Sam Kamin. 2001. *Punishment and Democracy: Three Strikes and You're Out in California.* Oxford: Oxford University Press.

Cases and Laws Cited

Brown v. Plata, 563 U.S. (2011).

California Assembly Bill No. 109, 2011-2012 Regular Session, Ch.15 (Cal. 2011); see also Cal. Penal Code section 17.5(a).

Public Safety and Offender Rehabilitation Services Act of 2007, A.B. 900, 2007-2008 Regular Session, Ch. 7 (Cal. 2007); S.B. 1022, 2011-2012 Regular Session, Ch. 42 (Cal. 2012); see also Cal. Gov't Code § 15819.40, et seq.

CHAPTER 2

....

WHO GOES TO PRISON?

....

DANIEL P. MEARS AND JOSHUA C. COCHRAN

AGAINST a backdrop of historically unprecedented and sustained growth in incarceration over the past three decades in the United States, this essay examines three questions. First, what is the composition of the inmate population in the United States with respect to legal characteristics (e.g., types of offenses and offenders) and to select demographic and social characteristics (e.g., age, race, ethnicity, sex, education, employment, drug abuse, and mental health), and what is the importance of each particular characteristic? Second, what, more generally, is the relevance of inmate composition, as well as inmate experiences, for anticipating prison bed space needs and for understanding inmate behavior and prisoner reentry? Third, what factors have influenced the composition of prison inmates?

To address these questions, this essay proceeds as follows. Section I examines the composition of inmates along the previously specified dimensions. Other dimensions that warrant consideration in scholarship and policy discussions about inmates are identified as well. Section II discusses why variation in inmate composition matters. A central reason is that some groups may be more likely to be incarcerated and may have different experiences in prison. These differences in turn may affect the behavior of individuals while incarcerated and after release. Section III turns to a focus on some of the factors that contribute to prison population characteristics. Here we explore several possibilities, such as crime, the roles of the police and courts, the implications of the shift from decision-making based on substantive rationality to more structured (formally rational) decision making, increased prosecutorial attention to community well-being and the effect of crime on it, the influence of drug wars, and trends in prosecuting juveniles as adults. Section IV then concludes with a call for research that documents patterns and trends in the composition of prison populations and the consequences of both for bed space forecasting, inmate management, and prisoner reentry.

The main conclusions discussed in this essay include the following:

- In the federal justice system, almost half (48 percent) of incarcerated individuals consist of drug offenders and 8 percent consist of violent offenders; among state prison systems, 17 percent consist of drug offenders and more than half (53 percent) consist of violent offenders. These percentages vary greatly among state prison systems and over time.

- Approximately three-fourths of state prison inmates have previously been incarcerated or on probation and almost half (47 percent) have had three or more prior sentences to prison or probation. Estimates indicate that, among released inmates, the average number of prior arrests is eight and the median is six.
- In 2009 released inmates served approximately 2.1 years in prison, on average. Time served among inmates increased by more than nine months from 1990 to 2009.
- Most inmates (62 percent) are age 39 or younger; in recent decades, the age of the inmate population has increased; that is, there has been a "graying" of the inmate population.
- Black incarceration rates are substantially greater than those of whites and Hispanics; over time, these differences have become more pronounced for black males in particular as compared to other groups.
- More than 90 percent of inmates in state and federal prisons are males. Males are more likely to be incarcerated for violent offenses whereas females are more likely to be incarcerated for drug crimes.
- More than 40 percent of inmates have not graduated from high school and approximately 21 to 38 percent of inmates were unemployed just prior to incarceration; more generally, individuals in prison have substantially worse educational and employment histories as compared to the general population.
- More than half of inmates report drug abuse in the month prior to being sent to prison, and more than half have some type of mental health problem; over time, the number and percentage of inmates with mental illness or a drug problem in prison have increased.
- Many other dimensions bear consideration when profiling the inmate population, including the availability of educational and rehabilitative programming, extent of family support, marital and parental status, proximity to home communities, visitation, the types and amounts of programming and abuse in prisons, variation in prison culture within and across prison systems, presence and influence of gangs or "security threat groups," and changes in administrative practices.
- Prison inmate characteristics are consequential for several reasons, including creation of more accurate bed space forecasting, developing more effective prison management strategies, and identifying ways to improve reentry experiences and outcomes for diverse groups of individuals released from state and federal prisons.
- Many factors may influence the composition of inmates in state and federal prison systems, as well as changes in the composition of inmates. Scholarship has identified as leading explanations such factors as levels and changes in crime, police and court practices and emphases, shifts to structured sentencing that emerged in the 1980s and continued to be widely implemented by states in ways that appear to contribute to disproportionate minority confinement, a deemphasis on rehabilitation and a corresponding emphasis on punishment and social control, the large-scale and sustained war on drugs, and the trend toward punishing juveniles as adults.

I. Composition of Prison Inmates

The main finding stemming from many descriptive accounts of inmates is that the individuals in prison come from impoverished backgrounds and therefore bring with them a considerable risk of failing to lead prosocial lives after release, irrespective of any potentially beneficial impact of incarceration (see, e.g., Petersilia 2003; Irwin 2005; Travis and Visher 2005; Gottschalk 2006, 2011; Western 2006; Useem and Piehl 2008; Mears 2010). Given the limited evidence that prison reduces recidivism (Nagin, Cullen, and Jonson 2009), there is, then, considerable basis for concern, especially since estimates indicate that over two-thirds of prisoners are rearrested within three years of release (Langan and Levin 2002).

In this section, we briefly describe some of the characteristics of prison inmates and the basis for this concern. To this end, we build on Petersilia's (2003, 2005) descriptive accounts and those of many others, including those in Bureau of Justice Statistics reports (e.g., Carson and Sabol 2012) and scholarly articles and books (e.g., Lynch and Sabol 2001; Irwin 2005; Travis 2005; Western 2006; Useem and Piehl 2008; Gottschalk 2006, 2011; Mears and Cochran 2012). A veritable flood of publications has emerged that examines inmate populations and prisoner reentry. As we emphasize further later, when all is said and done—and when we move beyond a focus on precise estimates of specific inmate characteristics—the profile that emerges is largely the same, regardless of the account. Inmates are disadvantaged in many ways, the in-prison experiences that they have vary enormously and may be criminogenic, and these individuals typically return to areas marked by high levels of social disadvantage. In addition, the factors that determine inmate composition in any given state in any given year vary and can influence greatly the need for prison bed space and the types of management and reentry approaches that may be most effective. As we also discuss, the dimensions examined here only scratch the surface of those that may be relevant to understanding inmate experiences, variations in experiences for different inmate populations, and how variation in inmate characteristics and experiences may influence inmate behavior and reentry outcomes.

A. Legal Factors and Time Served

1. *Types of Offenses and Offenders*

Offense type is an important part of understanding prison system populations. In 2011, 8 percent of the 197,050 federal prison inmates were incarcerated for violent crimes, 5 percent for property offenses, 48 percent for drug crimes, and 35 percent for public order crimes (Carson and Sabol 2012, p. 10). In 2010, 53 percent of the 1,362,028 state prison inmates were incarcerated for violent crimes, 18 percent for property offenses, 17 percent for drug crimes, and 10 percent for public order crimes (Carson and Sabol 2012, p. 10).

Such information provides insight into the broad categories, or types, of offenses or offenders targeted by state and federal law enforcement agencies and by the courts. It also is useful for anticipating the fiscal costs of imprisonment. For example, violent offenders are likely to serve lengthier sentences. Accordingly, knowing the proportion of inmates incarcerated for violent crime or other offenses that result in lengthy sentences is useful for forecasting prison capacity and, in turn, impending resource demands. Understanding the composition of offenders in prison can also provide insight into prison management challenges and needs, both current and anticipated. Research suggests, for example, that violent offenders may be more likely to engage in prison violence (Gendreau, Goggin, and Law 1997; Steiner 2009; Arbach-Lucioni, Martinez-Garcia, and Andres-Pueyo 2012; see also Cunningham, Sorensen, and Vigen 2011). Other groups, such as sex offenders, may be more at risk for victimization (Beck and Johnson 2012). Thus these types of offenders may require special attention and surveillance from prison staff over the course of incarceration.

The utility of descriptive accounts like these are useful primarily in a heuristic manner. Such accounts, however, obscure important considerations. For example, prisons are used for punishing a range of offenses, and the prevalence of any given type of offender in prison may stem from the amount of a particular type of crime in a state or such factors as law enforcement or prosecutorial priorities. Thus the prevalence of certain types of offenders in prison systems should not be taken to reflect only or even primarily rates of related crime. In addition, most offenders are generalists (Blumstein et al. 1986). Any classification system like those used in many descriptive accounts thus is only broadly useful for understanding inmate populations, given that inmates typically have committed many other types of crimes and thus are not purely or exclusively "violent" offenders, "property" offenders, or the like.

Another consideration is that prevalence estimates, using any given offender classification system, may vary greatly across states, and within any given state they may vary over time. Although estimates will not change dramatically from year to year, shifts can occur over longer periods. Examination of these trends is useful for identifying changes in crime or in the priorities of the justice system and, in turn, for anticipating potential needs for changes in prison programming, treatment, and services. For example, as a consequence of increased attention to drug crimes over the past 40 years (Blumstein and Beck 1999; Alexander 2010; Mauer 2011), the proportion of drug offenders in state prisons was three times larger in 2010 than it was in 1980 (17 percent in 2010 vs. 6 percent in 1980). The proportion in federal prisons doubled during that same period of time (52 percent in 2010 vs. 25 percent in 1980; Brown et al. 1996; Carson and Sabol 2012). In addition, today's prisons contain a substantially lower percentage of property offenders. Such changes highlight the potential need for prison systems to monitor dimensions related to the composition of the inmates. For example, as more and more drug-involved offenders enter a given prison system, there likely should be increased attention to potential drug trafficking within the system and to providing drug treatment.

2. *Prior Record*

The prior record of inmates also can be helpful for understanding the individuals who enter prison and how they may act. Inmates who have been in prison before may bring different views or attitudes about how to navigate interactions with prison officials and inmates and, more broadly, the prison system. In addition, they may pose different challenges than inmates who are in prison for the first time. A prison facility or system with a greater percentage of inmates previously arrested or incarcerated for violent crimes, for example, might want to consider management strategies that differ from those in prisons or states where inmates have less extensive records of violence. Similarly, first-time inmates may pose special risks, such as a greater likelihood of committing suicide (Adams 1992; Liebling 1999). Prior record thus can be useful for informing prison management approaches and strategies. In addition, prior record provides an indication of the criminality of the prison population, which may assist with developing management strategies and recidivism risk profiles and reentry plans.

National estimates suggest that most offenders in prison have prior experience with the correctional system. Approximately 75 percent of state inmates have been in prison or on probation prior to admission (Harlow, Snell, and Mumola 2000). Thus about 25 percent of prisoners are there for the first time. Among the previously incarcerated group, a greater proportion typically are violent recidivists (47 percent). In addition, a substantial percentage of returning prisoners have experienced multiple stints of punishment. Estimates suggest that almost half (47 percent) of soon-to-be-released state inmates have had three or more prior sentences to probation or prison (Petersilia 2005, p. 23). Prisoners typically have also had repeated contact with law enforcement. For example, in a study of inmates released in 1994 from 15 states, the average number of prior arrests was 8.8 and the median was 6.0 (Langan and Levin 2002, p. 2). It is not clear, however, whether prior experiences with the justice system have increased among the inmate population over time. The expanded use of incarceration suggests that individuals have more opportunities to be incarcerated. At the same time, and as discussed later, offenders are spending more time in prison, which could reduce the frequency of justice system contacts in the long term. In short, the inmate population varies greatly in its prior exposure to the criminal justice system, but, on average, most have had extensive justice system involvement. That in turn raises questions about the effectiveness of the prior arrests, convictions, and sanctions and the likely effectiveness of additional sanctions, including incarceration. It also raises questions about the potential need for more intensive programming or treatment, or different sanctions, for reducing offending and improving other life outcomes.

3. *Time Served*

The length of time inmates serve provides a rough indicator of the seriousness of the inmate population—lengthier sentences typically indicate that individuals committed more serious crimes. It can also provide an indication of how punitive a given state is. By extension, trends in time served provide an indicator of changes in crime or punitiveness. If inmates are serving longer sentences than in previous years, it may indicate that the courts are administering tougher sanctions. Such changes, especially in recent decades, may stem from broad-based policy efforts aimed at allowing for and encouraging longer sentences. For example, the implementation of truth-in-sentencing and mandatory minimum legislation in recent decades has led to lengthier terms of incarceration across the United States, which increased, on average, nine months from 1990 to 2009 (Pew Center on the States 2012).

Increases in average time served are relevant for many reasons. For example, longer prison terms place greater demand on existing bed space and, unchecked, require investment in more prison capacity to accommodate existing inmate populations and new admissions. Longer prison terms also have implications for prison order. On average, inmates who serve lengthier terms may have less incentive to behave. There also is the need to consider how time served may affect participation in, or the effectiveness of, treatment and vocational programs. It may be more effective, for example, to provide some types of treatment later in a prison term rather than at the beginning. From a reentry perspective, lengthier stays in prison can make planning for release more challenging. For example, incarceration can contribute to severed ties to family and friends, a possibility that becomes more likely with each additional month or year that an individual remains in prison (Uggen, Wakefield, and Western 2005; Meade et al. 2013).

How long do inmates typically stay in prison? On average, inmates in 2009 served approximately 2.1 years (Guerino, Harrison, and Sabol 2011; Pew Center on the States 2012). Notably, this figure is skewed upward by a small percentage of long-term inmates—the median amount of time served in 2008 was sixteen months (Bureau of Justice Statistics 2011). There is also substantial variation in time served across offender groups and over time. Specifically, estimates by the Pew Center on the States (2012) show that, across the three main offender groups—violent, property, and drug—average time served varied greatly and, for each group, has increased over time. Nationally, violent offenders in 2009 served 5 years compared to 3.7 years in 1990, property offenders served 2.3 years in 2009 compared to 1.8 years in 1990, and drug offenders served 2.2 years compared to 1.6 years in 1990. Similar types of variation, of course, exist at the state level. For example, according to the Pew Center on the States (2012), some states, such as Florida, increased time served from 1980 to 2009 by more than 160 percent, whereas others, such as Illinois, shortened their average time served.

B. Demographics

1. Age

Age is another factor that we can use to understand better the overall composition of the prison population and to anticipate the challenges administrators may face. Younger inmates are more aggressive and have a higher propensity to engage in serious misconduct than older inmates (e.g., Gendreau, Goggin, and Law 1997; Wooldredge, Griffin, and Pratt 2001; Sorensen and Cunningham 2010). They also require different and more diverse kinds of programs and services, which can place added strain on correctional staff and resources. We can anticipate different prison and reentry experiences for different age groups. For example, younger inmates, as compared with middle-aged and older inmates, may be more likely to maintain relationships with their social networks and families during and after incarceration (Rose and Clear 2003; Uggen and Wakefield 2005).

Increasingly, as inmates serve longer sentences than in decades past, and do so for a wider range of offense types, the US prison population has grown older over time. In 1991 more than 80 percent of inmates were under the age of 40; as of 2011, 62 percent of adult inmates were under this age (Beck and Mumola 1999; Carson and Sabol 2012). This "graying" of the inmate population has posed new challenges for correctional systems. Elderly inmates require more extensive health services and thus impose greater financial costs on prison systems (Chiu 2010; Stal 2013). Some estimates suggest that housing inmates age 55 or older incurs costs that are roughly three times greater than what arise when housing younger inmates (Petersilia 2005, p. 18). The silver lining may be that older inmates, on average, are less likely to offend and thus should be less likely to recidivate. Any such benefit, however, may be offset by the substantially greater incarceration costs and by potentially comparable or greater adverse effects on homelessness and joblessness among released older inmates. Although research on the implications of incarceration and reentry for elderly inmates is needed, the increased costs, the heightened risks of adverse effects, and the reduced risks of recidivism seem to imply that, at some point, alternative sanctions to prison might be more effective for elderly inmates; they may help, for example, to reduce the financial costs and potential harms associated with their imprisonment.

2. Race and Ethnicity

The overrepresentation of minority citizens in prison is well documented (see, e.g., Mann 1993; Tonry 1995, 2011; Alexander 2010). Western's (2006) account, in *Punishment and Inequality in America*, provides a succinct quantitative summation of the racial and ethnic disparities in punishment and in incarceration in America that date back almost a century: "Blacks have been more likely than whites to go to prison, at least since the 1920s . . . The basic brute fact of incarceration in the new era of mass imprisonment is that African Americans are eight times more likely to be incarcerated than Whites" (p. 3).

That assessment remains true in contemporary times. Among the total male population in the United States, as of 2010, 0.5 percent of whites, 3 percent of blacks, and 1.2 percent of Hispanics were in prison (Carson and Sabol 2012). Across all age and gender categories, blacks and Hispanics are incarcerated at higher rates than whites, though the disparities are largest in the younger age groups. According to Bureau of Justice Statistics data, black males aged 18 to 19 are incarcerated at a rate nine times that of white males of the same age (1,544 per 100,000 vs. 166 per 100,000, respectively) and nearly three times that of Hispanic males of the same age (574 per 100,000). Similarly, black females aged 18 to 19 are incarcerated at a rate three times that of whites (41 per 100,000 vs. 14, respectively) and nearly two times that of Hispanics (25 per 100,000; Carson and Sabol 2012). The black male incarceration rate in particular has increased dramatically over recent decades. Western's (2006, p. 17) analyses show that from 1980 to 2000, peak years in the rise of "get tough" punishment, the percentage of all black men aged 18 to 65 incarcerated in prison or jail went from 3.0 percent to 7.9 percent; by contrast, among whites during this same time period, the increase was from 0.7 percent to 2.1 percent, and for Hispanics it was from 1.6 percent to 3.3 percent.

What do these disparities mean? The disproportionate representation of minority groups is likely due to many factors (Petersilia 2005). It may stem from greater involvement in crime. It may stem from greater policing of citizens who live in poor, urban areas and who typically are more likely to be racial or ethnic minorities (Petit and Western 2004; Clear 2007; Mears et al. 2008; Tonry 2008, 2011). It may stem, too, from conscious or unconscious discrimination in the processing of minorities through the criminal justice system. Such effects, in turn, can compound one another and result in the pronounced overrepresentation of minorities in prisons. The extent to which any one factor, or a combination of them, contributes to disproportionate minority incarceration likely varies from state to state and over time. Accordingly, for any given state, the salience of any one study for understanding and assessing racial and ethnic differences in incarceration may be minimal. A central task for states, then, is to undertake studies that identify the unique factors specific to them that create overrepresentation of minorities in the prison system and ways to address them.

3. *Sex*

The federal and state prison systems house mostly male inmates. Indeed, in 2011, 93 percent of inmates in state and federal prisons were men (Carson and Sabol 2012), and males were incarcerated at a rate more than 14 times higher than that of females (932 per 100,000 vs. 65, respectively). Notably, however, the rate of female incarceration has increased dramatically over time, and, in fact, the female inmate population has actually grown at a higher rate than that of males (see, e.g., Harrison and Beck 2005). A large literature suggests that males and females both experience prison and cope with the strains of incarceration differently and, by extension, may benefit from gender-specific management and programming approaches (Blevins et al. 2010; Solinger et al. 2010; Wolff and Shi 2011; Cobbina et al. 2012). Female inmates, for example, are more likely to have dependent children and thus may require special services or accommodations so that they can maintain relationships with their children and families (Matthews and Hubbard 2008; Wright et al. 2012). They also have unique physical and mental health needs. For example, female inmates have a higher prevalence of preexisting infectious diseases and chronic illness and are likely to have reproductive issues that require screening, testing, and treatment (Guthrie 2011). Female inmates also have a higher prevalence of mental illness and are more likely than males to have been victims of physical and sexual abuse (James and Glaze 2006; Wright et al. 2012).

In addition, female inmate populations typically consist of different types of offenders. For example, females are less likely to be imprisoned for violent crimes—to illustrate, in 2010 37 percent of females were violent offenders, as compared to 54 percent of males. Females were, however, substantially more likely to be incarcerated for drug offenses—25 percent of females were drug offenders compared to 17 percent of males (Carson and Sabol 2012). Notably, the rate of incarceration of female offenders has increased substantially more than it has for male offenders, and the increases have been more pronounced for African American and Hispanic females (Chesney-Lind and Pasko 2013). Here again, the implication is that variation in the percentage of females inmates—and in the percentages of females inmates with specific physical health, mental health, or other needs—presents management and reentry challenges that may require gender-specific treatment and services.

C. Social Demographics

1. *Education*

Most prisoners are unlikely to have graduated from high school and are even less likely to have attended college. For example, in a study of state and federal prisoners in 1997, 41 percent had some high school or less, 23 percent had a GED, 23 percent had a high school diploma, and about 13 percent had at least some postsecondary education (Harlow 2003). The same study suggests that these estimates appear to be fairly stable over time. A larger body of prison and reentry scholarship reveals the same basic pattern—relatively low educational attainment among inmate populations—and identifies that inmates are substantially more likely to have learning disabilities (Hayes 2002; Herrington 2009; McKenzie et al. 2012). The overrepresentation of individuals with less education in prison results from a variety of factors. One factor, of course, is that education provides a conduit for opportunities for legitimate work. But less education itself can be a proxy for exposure to social disadvantage, which, in turn, can contribute to a greater risk of recidivism (Gottfredson, Wilson, and Najaka 2002; Harlow 2003; Petersilia 2005). That risk arises in part from the fact that finding employment, after prison, is difficult (Wang, Mears, and Bales 2010). As discussed in the next section, many inmates are unemployed prior to incarceration, and, with little education, attaining steady employment after prison poses an even greater challenge (Petersilia 2003; Uggen, Wakefield, and Western 2005). The extant literature has not systematically identified how variation in education affects prison or reentry experiences (see, however, Visher, Debus-Sherrill, and Yahner 2010), but it nonetheless constitutes a central dimension that may influence prison order and reentry outcomes.

2. *Employment*

Not only are inmates unlikely to have graduated from high school or college, but they are also likely to be have been unemployed or employed in a low-paying job at the time of arrest. Nationally, 21 to 38 percent of inmates report being unemployed in the month prior to incarceration (Harlow 2003; see also Petersilia 2005). An increasingly large body of research implicates employment as an important factor for helping offenders desist from crime (Uggen, Wakefield, and Western 2005; Bushway, Stoll, and Weiman 2007; Mears et al. 2008; Wang, Mears, and Bales 2010). However, inmates typically face considerable challenges finding gainful employment after release (Holzer 1996; Pager 2003; Uggen, Wakefield, and Western 2005). They have poor employment records, a felony record that precludes some type of work, and limited educational attainment. In addition, ex-prisoners typically return to areas where employment opportunities may be limited, a situation that worsened during the economic downturn in the late 2000's (Wang, Mears, and Bales 2010). Going forward, it can be anticipated that during periods of economic downturn, when levels of resource deprivation and unemployment are higher, ex-prisoners will face even greater challenges attaining stable work, which in turn can decrease the likelihood of successful reintegration (Bushway, Stoll, and Weiman 2007; Mears et al. 2008; Wang, Mears, and Bales 2010). Prison-based vocational programming may help offset these conditions somewhat, but their effectiveness is limited both by reduced funding for such programming (Lynch and Sabol 2001; Travis 2005) and by the difficulties inherent in matching inmates to the types of work for which they might have the greatest likelihood of being hired (see, generally, Bushway and Apel 2012).

D. Drug Abuse and Mental Health

Prisoners generally are at a higher risk of disease, mental illness, and, not least, drug abuse than are members of the general public (Mears and Cochran 2012). One national estimate indicates that over half (56 percent) of state inmates report drug use in the month prior to incarceration (Mumola and Karberg 2007). Greater numbers and percentages of inmates in state and federal prison systems over time has resulted in part from the get tough punishment trend that began in the 1980s and that included a war on drugs. Inmates' substance abuse histories have important implications for the operations of the prison. The prevalence of substance abuse and dependency among prisoners suggests that prisons have some responsibility to provide addiction treatment and drug counseling. Drug problems, of course, bring with them the risk of drug dealing and contraband in prisons, which in turn can create conflict, violence, and disorder. In addition, if substance abuse problems go unaddressed, the likelihood of recidivism, homelessness, and unemployment may increase. In short, failing to address drug problems among the inmate population may impose costs on prison systems, but, at the same time, treatment for drug problems and efforts to control trafficking also generates costs.

Nationally, an estimated 53 percent of state inmates have some type of mental health problem (James and Glaze 2006). About 43 percent of state inmates meet the criteria for a mania disorder, 23 percent meet the criteria for a major depressive disorder, and 15 percent meet the criteria for a psychotic disorder. Petersilia (2003, pp. 36–37) has reported that the number of inmates with mental illness has increased over time in part due to deinstitutionalization efforts that intensified in the 1970s. Based on these estimates, compared to the general population, prisoners are 5 to 24 times more likely to have one of these disorders. The high rate of mental illness in prisons has important implications (see, generally, Mears 2004). Mentally ill prisoners may need treatment and counseling. They also may require increased supervision— for example, inmates with mental disorders are more likely to engage in misconduct and to be victimized (Guy et al. 2005; James and Glaze 2006; Steiner and Wooldredge 2009; Felson, Silver, and Remster 2012; Houser, Belenko, and Brennan 2012). If untreated, the condition of prisoners' mental illness can worsen, increasing the probability of harm to themselves or others, and there can also be implications upon release. For example, ex-offenders with mental illness have an increased risk of recidivism, homelessness, and unemployment (Petersilia 2003; Travis 2005; James and Glaze 2006; Cloyes et al. 2010).

E. Concluding Observations

When we examine the characteristics of prisoners, we find that the typical inmate is male, black, under the age of 40, and incarcerated for a violent offense. He or she has previously been incarcerated or on probation and, based on median length of stay, will serve roughly 16 months in prison. In addition, he or she did not graduate from high school, was unemployed or working a low-wage job, and will face considerable challenges finding work after prison. Not least, the typical inmate enters prison with a prior substance abuse history and a history of mental illness. Whether such dimensions have made inmates more difficult to manage or treat remains understudied. One large-scale study undertaken by Useem and Piehl (2008) indicates that, notwithstanding the growth in incarceration and changes in inmate composition, prison violence has not greatly increased and, if anything, it has decreased. Few studies, however, have systematically and empirically linked changes in inmate composition to inmate behavior and prison order.

As emphasized earlier, these dimensions—offense type, prior record, age, race and ethnicity, sex, education, employment, drug abuse, and mental health—only touch on the broad contours of the inmate population. Other dimensions may matter as much if not more for understanding what inmates experience in prison, what contributes to these experiences, and what influences the ways that individuals act while incarcerated and after release into society. Some other dimensions that may be relevant are as follows.

- Inmate exposure to and participation in prison programs, including educational, vocational, and rehabilitative programs and, in particular, exposure to high-quality programming (Lynch and Sabol 2001).
- Inmate family support, marital status, and parental status (Travis 2005).
- Inmate proximity to home communities, including families and friends (inmates are housed, on average, 100 miles away from home; Mumola 2000).
- The amount and quality of visitation and other contact with family and friends (Cochran 2012; Cochran and Mears 2013).
- Trajectories of experiences within prison settings, such as varying patterns of visitation, inmate programming, abuse, transfer to other facilities, and more, over the "life course" of an individual while incarcerated (Mears, Cochran, and Siennick 2013).
- The culture—however defined or operationalized—among inmates, within a facility and across a prison system (Bottoms 1999).
- The administrative or management philosophies and approaches undertaken by prison officials and wardens and the implementation of these philosophies and approaches by officers (Reisig 1998).
- Changes in the composition of inmates over time, such as the infusion of gang members or leaders, or in the staffing or resources available to manage, assist, educate, train, or supervise inmates.

In the end, precision about the prevalence of these and other characteristics is only helpful as a broad guidepost for the potential need to consider how best to plan for bed space capacity and programming in the prison system and how best to manage inmates or ensure that they have successful reentry outcomes. Here again, the main theme that emerges from the literature is that the typical inmate has a broad array of disadvantages and limitations that make their prospects for prosocial behavior while in prison and after release dim. Further precision in estimates will not likely change that conclusion. Indeed, precision is ephemeral. The characteristics of inmates varies greatly among states and, over time, within states. And for many of the dimensions about which we might be concerned—such as the amount and quality of programming or the gaps in providing needed services—there remains little systematic empirical evidence (Mears 2010). Accordingly, a critical goal for the federal government and for individual states ideally is to develop the research infrastructure for carefully describing and monitoring inmate composition over time and linking patterns and trends to inmate behavior and reentry outcomes and to the factors that contribute to any observed associations.

II. WHY PRISON POPULATION CHARACTERISTICS MATTER FOR UNDERSTANDING BED SPACE NEEDS, INMATE BEHAVIOR, AND PRISONER REENTRY

The interest in prison population characteristics—that is, who goes to prison—is relevant for many reasons. One is the effect that these characteristics may have for anticipating bed space needs in prisons. A second is that they may be relevant to understanding how best to manage inmates. A third, although the list is not exhaustive, is that they can inform efforts to improve reentry experiences and outcomes. These dimensions were alluded to in the previous discussion. We discuss these in more detail because they provide some of the central reasons scholars or policymakers care about any specific inmate characteristic.

A. The Relevance of Variation in Inmate Characteristics for Bed Space Forecasting

The past three decades have witnessed historically unprecedented growth in prison populations. Many factors, discussed in the next section, contributed to these changes. Increased crime, for example, can result in more arrests, more convictions, and, in turn, more individuals sent to prison. Beyond that possibility, though, is the fact that the characteristics of the individuals sent to prison can greatly influence the need to expand prison capacity.

As a general matter, if any given characteristic is related to length of stay, then it will influence the need for bed space. For example, if blacks consistently receive lengthier terms of incarceration, and if there is an increase in their incarceration rate, then the average length of stay of inmates as a whole will increase. In turn, prison expansion must be undertaken or inmates must be released earlier into their prison term.

This example reflects precisely a central dynamic that has affected many state prison systems. Indeed, nationally and in many states, mass incarceration has involved greater increases in rates of incarceration of blacks, frequently for lengthier terms of imprisonment (see, e.g., Travis 2005; Gottschalk 2006; Western 2006). In some cases, however, there may be increases or decreases among other groups, such as drug offenders (Blumstein and Beck 1999) or sex offenders, that drive the average lengths of stay and, in turn, bed space needs. In the end, no single profile of an inmate population suffices to determine bed space needs. Instead, each state, and the federal prison system, must determine what the precise profile is of the entering inmate population, what the average lengths of stay are that can be anticipated for each group (as defined by any characteristic that may be associated with length of stay), and what the differences mean, when aggregated, for bed space needs (Mears 2010).

B. The Relevance of Variation in Inmate Characteristics for Prison Management

Inmate profiles may also be relevant for determining how best to manage inmates. Here again, though, no uniform guidance exists about how to proceed. In part that is because the characteristics of inmates varies across states, and within states, over time, and their association with adjustment and misconduct may vary as well. Mental illness, for example, is associated with inmate maladjustment in prison, especially in high-security facilities (Haney 2003). Yet this association may stem from many factors. Mentally ill inmates may act out more; they may have treatment needs that, if unaddressed, result in misconduct; or their behavior may be misunderstood by officers, resulting in more supervision and disciplinary reports. This issue is one that confronts efforts to understand, more broadly, the relationship between mental illness and offending (Mears 2004). Regardless, the different possibilities leave prison systems with a basic need—that of identifying the extent of mental illness and then of identifying how best to treat and manage such inmates. In some states, mental health treatment may be needed; in others, there may be a greater need to emphasize officer education about mental illness and ways to manage inmates who may have a mental disorder.

Under an ideal prison research and monitoring approach, states would profile their inmate populations along a range of dimensions (e.g., age, sex, race, ethnicity, education, mental health) and do so with an eye toward addressing specific needs that groups may have and toward identifying how the dimensions may be associated with adjustment and misconduct (Adams 1992; Mears 2012). Such monitoring, too, ideally would examine factors that might be related to adjustment and misconduct in general or among specific groups of inmates. In turn, states would have information that could be used to help determine what management approaches might be most effective. For example, a facility that houses primarily younger inmates likely will have higher rates of misconduct, but those rates may stem not only from age itself but also from how officers respond to younger inmates. Having both sources of information—about the higher rates of involvement in misconduct among younger inmates and the cause of it—can highlight the need for a specific strategy, such as staff training, for making prisons safer.

C. The Relevance of Variation in Inmate Characteristics for Prisoner Reentry

Inmate characteristics also may have implications for reentry experiences and outcomes (Petersilia 2003; Visher and Travis 2003, 2011; Travis 2005). Here, then, it is not only prisons but also agencies charged with supervising or assisting released inmates that have an interest in understanding better the characteristics of inmates and how these may be related to successful transitions to housing, employment, treatment for physical or mental illness, and, not least, lifestyles that encourage desistance from crime. The same challenge for bed space forecasting and inmate management surfaces again—that is, there is a need for population-specific and area-specific analyses that are coupled with assessments of available resources for supervising and assisting ex-prisoners. Black inmates, for example, may be more likely to return to areas where unemployment rates are especially high and, concomitantly, may face employer discrimination (Western 2006; Wang, Mears, and Bales 2010). To the extent that such differences exist, then efforts ideally would be targeted toward helping black ex-prisoners negotiate such contexts. The same logic applies for any other dimension, including those discussed previously (e.g., age, sex, prior record). In short, national ex-prisoner profiles take us only so far. From a policy perspective, information about the characteristics of inmates released to specific areas, and the resources and capacities of these areas, is needed to identify how best to increase the chances of successful reentry.

III. Factors that Influence Prison Population Characteristics

Inmate characteristics and experiences matter in part because they help us to understand who exactly it is we are incarcerating and how to plan for bed space needs. They also matter because they may affect how inmates behave in prison and how well they transition back into society. Such insights are especially helpful if we couple them with a greater understanding of who is sent to prison and why. For example, a state, or the country as a whole, may move in the direction of placing more drug offenders in prison. This information is useful for understanding that greater attention may be needed toward implementing strategies or approaches for managing this particular population and for assisting and supervising them during reentry.

Accordingly, in the next sections we briefly discuss several factors that can contribute to the types of offenders that states incarcerate. The extent to which any one factor influences the characteristics of the prison population may vary, of course, among states and over time. Their significance lies in illustrating the need to understand what drives prison growth, the types of individuals incarcerated, and, in turn, the need for management and reentry strategies that will be most useful in maintaining prison order and improving reentry outcomes.

A. Crime

The amount and rate of crime in general, and of specific types of crime, fuels the criminal justice system. If violent crime increases dramatically, we can expect that more arrests for violent crime will occur and that there will be more convictions and more sentences to prison, possibly for longer periods of time. Even so, the relationship between crime and incarceration is complicated. For example, violent crime was stable or declining during the 1970s and early 1980s, and yet, in the latter period, policymakers embarked on an aggressive path toward toughening sentencing laws. Then, from approximately 1986 to 1994, violent crime, murder in particular, escalated, before declining steadily over the subsequent decade (Mears 2010). Throughout this entire period of time, however, policymakers—at state and federal levels—continuously passed laws that placed more discretion in the hands of prosecutors. These laws toughened penalties for various offenses, especially those involving drugs and guns, and provided greater levels of funding for law enforcement, the courts, and corrections. The disjuncture, therefore, between levels of crime and levels of investment in punishment is considerable (Travis 2005; Blumstein and Wallman 2006; Gottschalk 2011). That does not mean that crime has no influence on punishment, only that the relationship is complicated.

B. Roles of Police and Courts

The police and the courts represent the first and second entrance points to the prison system. Expansion of police forces, greater deployment in certain areas, and increased focus by the police on certain types of crimes or offenders can directly contribute to the amount and composition of individuals who are arrested for crimes. The number and rate of arrests, in turn, affect the composition of individuals brought before the court. For example, an increased police presence in areas that are poor and that consist primarily of minority populations is likely to lead to more arrests and, in turn, more incarceration of citizens from those areas (Pettit and Western 2004; Warren et al. 2006; Clear 2007).

Such activities may fuel resentment and mistrust of law enforcement officers as well as cynicism regarding the legitimacy of formal social control mechanisms, including not only law enforcement but also the courts (Mears 2010). Ultimately, these changes may reduce the effectiveness of the police and courts. Among other things, minority groups may be less willing to seek assistance from or cooperate with these agents of social control. For example, blacks in low-income communities may be less willing to participate in community policing efforts even though crime may be substantially higher in these areas (Skogan 2003). Ultimately, then, higher rates of incarceration, less satisfaction with the police, and unchanged or increased crime may be more likely in minority communities as a result of police and court practices. The implications carry forward into prisons as well—black inmates may be less trusting of prison officials and staff and thus less likely to cooperate with or seek assistance from prison authorities. To the extent that minorities are targeted in similar ways in prisons, this dynamic may repeat itself and fuel even greater levels of mistrust and recidivism upon release from prison.

In the same way, court actors, including prosecutors and judges, may have changing priorities over time that can lead to increased or decreased likelihoods of incarceration for certain types of crimes or offenders and varying sentence lengths (Kramer and Ulmer 2009; Tonry 2011). The courts, for example, may crack down on drug- or gang-related crimes. They also may associate such crimes with minorities, per focal concerns and racial threat theories (Mears 2010). From these and related perspectives, the courts rely on shorthand assumptions that enable them to process cases more rapidly. For example, the assumption may be that young, black males are much more likely to commit violent crime. From that perspective, then, prosecutors and the courts may view arrested young, black males as almost invariably guilty and view criminal cases in that light (Steffensmeier, Ulmer, and Kramer 1998; Wang and Mears 2010).

The end result may be a direct or indirect targeting of minorities for tougher punishment. Any such stereotypes could carry substantial implications for minorities. Incarceration for drug offenses, for example, has increased dramatically. In recent decades, increasingly more drug offenders have been sent to prison and for longer periods of time (Blumstein and Beck 1999; Pew Center on the States 2012). The result is an increase in the number and percentage of inmates in prison who have committed drug or drug-related crimes. This increase reflects shifting law enforcement and court priorities, as well as the enactment of laws that place greater discretion in the hands of prosecutors. Violent offending remains a relatively constant priority of law enforcement and the courts, but priorities related to other types of crime, such as drug, sex, or gang-related offending, can vary dramatically.

In recent decades, funding for law enforcement and the courts increased dramatically—between 1982 and 2006, a period arguably capturing the peak of the get tough trend in punishment, police expenditures grew from $19 billion to almost $100 billion while court expenditures grew from $8 billion to $47 billion (Mears 2010, p. 17). Accordingly, the potential for all of this added capacity to be targeted toward certain areas and populations, even if only indirectly through prioritizing certain crimes, was great and serves here to underscore the role that the police and courts may have in affecting who is sent to prison.

C. Implications of the Shift to Structured Decision-Making

In the 1980s, the federal government enacted sentencing guidelines; many states then followed suit (Petersilia 2003; Travis 2005; Gottschalk 2006; Clear 2007). The impetus varied, but a central motivation was the concern that the courts were too lenient and too inconsistent at a time when crime seemed to be worsening. More structured decision-making in the form of sentencing guidelines was intended to reduce judicial discretion so that "like" cases would be treated in "like" ways, and sentencing disparities based on an offender's race, ethnicity, gender, and so on would be eliminated. Scholarly accounts framed the issue as one of emphasizing formally rational criteria, such as the use of prior record, offense severity, and harm to victims, to guide sentencing decisions.

Formally rational approaches, at least in theory, should lead to more consistent and appropriate sanctions across similar offenses committed by offenders with similar criminal histories. The concern, however, was that the approach would lead to substantively irrational decisions due to other unique circumstances of the offenses and the offenders no longer considered by court actors. Under informal arrangements, prosecutors, judges, and defense counsel can consider a range of factors, including the likelihood that an offender can be rehabilitated or deterred, and then arrive at a sanction that is believed to be most effective for that individual. This individualistic approach has guided the US juvenile justice system and was central to adult case processing prior to the get tough movement. Guidelines emerged, however, in part from the concern that substantively rational decision-making leads to wildly disparate sentences for cases involving similar offenses. Another concern in the 1980s and 1990s that continues to the present is that the individualistic approach to sentencing led to sentences that were too lenient relative to the offenses.

Although there is a large body of empirical scholarship on sentencing, the effects of more structured sentencing practices remain unclear. One difficulty in assessing the impact of guidelines is determining how to define "consistent" sentencing. Indeed, it remains unclear whether sentencing guidelines have reduced disparities in sentencing or whether they have merely changed the nature of the disparities. For example, a central conclusion from extant research is that reducing judicial discretion under guidelines has only displaced discretion to prosecutors (Mears 2010). In recent decades, this may have contributed to higher rates of incarceration and longer sentences for minorities (Gottschalk 2011; Tonry 2011).

Structured decision-making, such as occurred with sentencing guidelines, three-strikes laws, and other such approaches to sentencing, shifted the balance of power toward prosecutors and did so at a time when caseloads increased dramatically. This shift in turn contributed substantially to ever-greater numbers of individuals being sent to prison and a greater emphasis on retribution and incapacitation. It arguably led as well to the incarceration of ever-greater numbers of blacks and minorities (Western 2006) relative to whites. As discussed previously, such a shift could arise from prosecutors and the courts adhering to focal concerns perspectives, such as an emphasis on tougher punishment of individuals, such as young, black males, assumed to be somehow more "criminal." It also could arise from greater prosecutorial emphasis on certain types of crimes, such as drug offenses. The most prominent example involves crack cocaine—in the 1980s, states enacted ever-tougher penalties for crimes involving this drug. Indirectly, this approach targeted blacks and contributed, in a context of getting tough on crime, to higher rates of incarcerating blacks relative to whites (Mauer 2009, 2011).

What the future holds is, of course, uncertain. What we know, though, from existing scholarship is that discretion is central to court processing. How that discretion is distributed can play a fundamental role in who goes to prison or remains in the community.

D. A Focus on Community Well-Being and Less Attention to Rehabilitation

These changes occurred during a period when prosecutors—and the criminal laws in general—placed a high premium on protecting communities. The effects of public disillusionment with rehabilitation began in the 1970s and surfaced in the 1980s. Less and less attention to and support for probation, intermediate sanctions, and, more broadly, rehabilitation programs existed (Cullen and Gilbert 2013). This shift in sentiment aligned with perceptions that crime was out of control, resulting in tougher sentencing laws, increased prosecutorial discretion, and greater funding for prisons (Mears 2010). The end result was a focus on punishment and a greater emphasis on the idea that more punishment would be effective in promoting public safety. This emphasis is reflected, in part, in reductions in educational and vocational programming for prisoners during the 1990s. It is also reflected in the growing investment in incarceration across the United States during the past several decades without a comparable (proportionate) investment in alternatives to incarceration and public health approaches to reducing crime.

E. Influence of Drug Wars

As discussed previously, an increased focus on drug crimes by the criminal justice system has led to dramatic changes in the number and types of people in prison. The infamous "war on drugs," declared by President Nixon in the early 1970s and implemented, in varying forms, with increased vigor in the 1980s and 1990s has evolved over the past 40 years (Mauer 2009; Whitford and Yates 2009). It has resulted in a dramatic increase both in state and federal prison populations and in the proportions of inmates incarcerated for drug-related crimes (Blumstein and Beck 1999). As noted earlier, in 2011, 48 percent of federal inmates were incarcerated for drug crimes and, in 2010, 17 percent of state inmates were incarcerated for drug crimes (Carson and Sabol 2012, p. 10).

The war on drugs constitutes perhaps the most vivid example of how a shift in the focus of the justice system can alter the composition of prison populations. Among other things, it led to a greater police emphasis on drug-crime arrests and heightened efforts by the courts to punish drug offenders severely. Compared to what would have happened in previous decades, drug offenders since the 1980s are more likely to be sent to prison and to serve lengthier terms of incarceration. Drug offenders are also more likely to be minorities, which causes further expansion of the minority prisoner population.

Although drug offenses still garner severe punishments today, some scholars, judges, and policymakers have called for a public health response to drug-related crimes rather than a primarily or exclusively punishment-oriented response. Under President Obama, for example, the Office of National Drug Control Policy (2013), in a press release, called for just such an approach: "Today [April 24, 2013] we are releasing a science-driven plan for drug policy reform in America to build upon this progress. This 21st century drug policy outlines a series of evidence-based reforms that treat our Nation's drug problem as a public health issue, not just a criminal justice issue. This policy underscores what we all know to be true: we cannot arrest or incarcerate our way out of the drug problem." If a shift in the punishment of drug offenders was to occur—one focused more toward a public health perspective rather than a punishment perspective—this shift would also change the profile of prisoners over time.

F. Trends in Prosecuting Juveniles as Adults

In the 1990s, in step with the focus on tougher criminal justice responses to crime, states increasingly "criminalized" their juvenile justice systems. They did so through many reforms, but perhaps the most prominent shift consisted of new and expanded ways of transferring juveniles to the adult justice system. Sometimes referred to as "waiver" or "certification" to adult court, transfer is justified in part as a way to provide tougher, more "adult-like" penalties for serious, violent crimes. The effects of these laws and practices on the adult prison system remain unclear because national statistics on different types of transfer do not exist and because transfer appears to fluctuate broadly over time. Consider judicial transfer, one of several types of transfer and the only one for which national data exist: from 1985 to 1994, the peak year for transfers, the number of cases sent to adult court increased from 7,200 to 13,800, respectively, but then declined, by 2009, to 7,600 cases (Adams and Addie 2012, p. 2). National trend data for other types of transfer do not exist (Mears 2010).

Not all youth who are transferred to adult court are convicted or, if convicted, sent to prison (Mears 2003; Redding 2010). Even so, it appears plausible that juvenile transfers to adult court—including judicial, prosecutorial, and legislative—contributed to the growth in the adult prison system. Tougher punishment of young offenders in general, such as those aged 24 and younger, also may have been a central factor that contributed to the growth (Mears and Travis 2004; Loeber and Farrington 2012). This phenomenon is notable in part because some evidence suggests that juvenile transfer increases recidivism (Mears 2003; Redding 2010) and because young offenders may be more disruptive in adult prisons and the adult prison system may be criminogenic, or more criminogenic, for youthful offenders, whether placed in the system as juveniles or as young adults (Loeber and Farrington 2012).

G. Summary Observations

These factors in reality constitute but a sampling of the range of factors that can influence the profile of the inmate population nationally and among states. Economic conditions, changing political climates, shifting social and political priorities, and more may affect crime, punishment, or both. In the context of this essay, the salience of the factors lies in underscoring the complexity of prison growth. No static assessment of inmate characteristics is, on its own, especially helpful in planning for bed space capacity, prison management, or reentry preparation and assistance. Rather, what ultimately is likely to be most helpful to the federal prison system or to state prison systems is to (a) monitor changes in inmate populations; (b) identify the factors that contribute to those changes and the characteristics that are linked to lengths of stay, inmate adjustment, misconduct, and reentry experiences and outcomes; (c) determine what strategies and approaches may be most appropriate or effective in reducing the need for prisons and for managing or assisting these specific populations; (d) assess which of these strategies may be more feasible and cost-effective;

(e) implement them well; and (f) adjust policy over time to reflect changes in the prison population. Such an approach holds the potential for more efficiently and effectively anticipating necessary changes in bed space and programming and for effectively meeting those needs. This approach could also help with identifying groups, such as young or mentally ill offenders, who may need special attention, and it could potentially lead to the creation of more effective reentry plans for inmates.

IV. CONCLUSION

Prisoners constitute a challenging group for policymakers and practitioners. The individuals who land in prison have committed the types of crimes that society, or particular states, have deemed worthy of incarceration, whether to achieve a given level of retribution, deterrence, incapacitation, rehabilitation, or some combination of these. On average, they have accumulated repeated contacts with law enforcement and the correctional system. Compared to inmates in the past, the inmates of today serve lengthier periods of time behind bars and receive less programming and treatment. Compared to individuals in the general population, they typically are substantially less educated, have poor employment histories, are more drug-involved, and are more likely to have mental health and physical health problems. They are also more likely to be homeless and to have learning disabilities.

All of these factors and more make it difficult to arrive at uniform prison management or reentry strategies that will work equally well for all inmates in all settings and places. They also make it challenging for the communities to which inmates return. In essence, these individuals enter prisons with various disadvantages and sometimes return to their communities with even more, not to mention that the communities themselves are often characterized by high levels of social and economic disadvantage.

If federal, state, and local governments, as well as local communities, are to improve the effectiveness of their criminal justice and prisons systems, they will need to understand better who it is that they incarcerate. They will need, for example, to monitor inmate composition patterns over time and do so with considerable care. The resulting information in turn can be used to inform efforts to plan for bed space capacity, to understand the effects of prison, and to identify how to improve prison order and reentry outcomes.

REFERENCES

Adams, Benjamin, and Sean Addie. 2012. *Delinquency Cases Waived to Criminal Court, 2009.* Washington, DC: Office of Juvenile Justice and Delinquency Prevention.

Adams, Kenneth. 1992. "Adjusting to Prison Life." *Crime and Justice* 16:275–359.

Alexander, Michelle. 2010. *The New Jim Crow: Mass Incarceration in the Age of Colorblindness.* New York: The New Press.

Arbach-Lucioni, Karin, Marian Martinez-Garcia, and Antonio Andres-Pueyo. 2012. "Risk Factors for Violent Behavior in Prison Inmates: A Cross-Cultural Contribution." *Criminal Justice and Behavior* 39:1219–1239.

Beck, Allen J., and Candace Johnson. 2012. *Sexual Victimization Reported by Former State Prisoners, 2008*. Washington, DC: Bureau of Justice Statistics.

Beck, Allen J., and Christopher J. Mumola. 1999. *Prisoners in 1998*. Washington, DC: Bureau of Justice Statistics.

Blevins, Kristie R., Shelley Johnson Listwan, Francis T. Cullen, and Cheryl Lero Jonson. 2010. "A General Stain Theory of Prison Violence and Misconduct: An Integrated Model of Inmate Behavior." *Journal of Contemporary Criminal Justice* 26:148–166.

Blumstein, Alfred, and Allen J. Beck. 1999. "Population Growth in U.S. Prisons, 1980–1996." In *Prisons*, edited by Michael H. Tonry and Joan Petersilia. Chicago: University of Chicago Press.

Blumstein, Alfred, Jacqueline Cohen, Jeffrey A. Roth, and Christy Visher. 1986. *Criminal Careers and Career Criminals*, Vol. 1. Washington, DC: National Academy Press.

Blumstein, Alfred, and Joel Wallman. 2006. *The Crime Drop in America*, 2d ed. New York: Cambridge University Press.

Bottoms, Anthony E. 1999. "Interpersonal Violence and Social Order in Prisons." *Crime and Justice* 26:205–281.

Brown, Jodi M., Darrell K. Gilliard, Tracy L. Snell, James J. Stephan, and Doris James Wilson. 1996. *Correctional Populations in the United States, 1994*. Washington, DC: Bureau of Justice Statistics.

Bureau of Justice Statistics. 2011. *State Prison Releases, 2008: Time Served in Prison, by Offense and Release Type*. Washington, DC: Bureau of Justice Statistics.

Bushway, Shawn D., and Robert Apel. 2012. "A Signaling Perspective on Employment-Based Reentry Programming: Training Completion as a Desistance Signal." *Criminology and Public Policy* 11:21–50.

Bushway, Shawn D., Michael Stoll, and David Weiman, eds. 2007. *Barriers to Reentry? The Labor Market for Released Prisoners in Post-Industrial America*. New York: Russell Sage.

Carson, E. Ann, and William J. Sabol. 2012. *Prisoners in 2011*. Washington, DC: Bureau of Justice Statistics.

Chesney-Lind, Meda, and Lisa Pasko, eds. 2013. *The Female Offender: Girls, Women, and Crime*. Thousand Oaks, CA: Sage.

Chiu, Tina. 2010. *It's About Time: Aging Prisoners, Increasing Costs, and Geriatric Release*. New York: Vera Institute of Justice.

Clear, Todd R. 2007. *Imprisoning Communities: How Mass Incarceration Makes Disadvantaged Neighborhoods Worse*. New York: Oxford University Press.

Cloyes, Kristin G., Bob Wong, Seth Latimer, and Jose Abarca. 2010. "Time to Prison Return for Offenders with Serious Mental Illness Released from Prison: A Survival Analysis." *Criminal Justice and Behavior* 37:175–187.

Cobbina, Jennifer E. 2012. "Men, Women, and Postrelease Offending: An Examination of the Nature of the Link between Relational Ties and Recidivism." *Crime and Delinquency* 58:331–361.

Cochran, Joshua C. 2012. "The Ties that Bind or the Ties that Break: Examining the Relationships between Visitation and Prisoner Misconduct." *Journal of Criminal Justice* 40:433–440.

Cochran, Joshua C., and Daniel P. Mears. 2013. "Social Isolation and Inmate Behavior: A Conceptual Framework for Theorizing Prison Visitation and Guiding and Assessing Research." *Journal of Criminal Justice* 41:252–261.

Cullen, Francis T., and Karen E. Gilbert. 2013. *Reaffirming Rehabilitation*, 2d ed. Waltham, MA: Elsevier.

Cunningham, Mark D., Jon R. Sorensen, and Mark P. Vigen. 2011. "Correlates and Actuarial Models of Assaultive Prison Misconduct Among Violence-Predicted Capital Offenders." *Criminal Justice and Behavior* 38:5–25.

Felson, Richard B., Eric Silver, and Brianna Remster. 2012. "Mental Disorder and Offending in Prison." *Criminal Justice and Behavior* 39:125–143.

Gendreau, Paul, Claire E. Goggin, and Moira A. Law. 1997. "Predicting Prison Misconduct." *Criminal Justice and Behavior* 24:414–431.

Gottfredson, Denise, David B. Wilson, and Stacy Najaka. 2002. "The Schools." In *Crime: Public Policies for Crime Control*, edited by James Q. Wilson and Joan Petersilia. San Francisco, CA: ICS Press.

Gottschalk, Marie. 2011. "The Past, Present, and Future of Mass Incarceration in the United States." *Criminology and Public Policy* 10:483–504.

Gottschalk, Marie. 2006. *The Prison and the Gallows: The Politics of Mass Incarceration in America*. New York: Cambridge University Press.

Guerino, Paul, Paige M. Harrison, and William J. Sabol. 2011. *Prisoners in 2010*. Washington, DC: Bureau of Justice Statistics.

Guthrie, Barbara. 2011. "Toward a Gender-Responsive Restorative Correctional Health Care Model." *Journal of Obstetric, Gynecologic, and Neonatal Nursing* 40:497–505.

Guy, Laura S., John F. Edens, Christine Anthony, and Kevin S. Douglas. 2005. "Does Psychopathy Predict Institutional Misconduct Among Adults? A Meta-Analytic Investigation." *Journal of Consulting and Clinical Psychology* 73:1056–1064.

Haney, Craig. 2003. "Mental Health Issues in Long-Term Solitary and 'Supermax' Confinement." *Crime and Delinquency* 49:124–156.

Harlow, Caroline Wolf. 2003. *Education and Correctional Populations*. Washington, DC: Bureau of Justice Statistics.

Harlow, Caroline Wolf, Tracy L. Snell, and Christopher J. Mumola. 2000. *Correctional Populations in the United States, 1997*. Washington, DC: Bureau of Justice Statistics.

Harrison, Paige M., and Allen J. Beck. 2005. *Prison and Jail Inmates at Midyear 2004*. Washington, DC: Bureau of Justice Statistics.

Hayes, Susan Carol. 2002. "Early Intervention or Early Incarceration? Using a Screening Test for Intellectual Disability in the Criminal Justice System." *Journal of Applied Research in Intellectual Disabilities* 15:120–128.

Herrington, V. 2009. "Assessing the Prevalence of Intellectual Disability Among Young Male Prisoners." *Journal of Intellectual Disability Research* 53:397–410.

Holzer, Harry J. 1996. *What Employers Want: Job Prospects for Less-Educated Workers*. New York: Russell Sage Foundation.

Houser, Kimberly A., Steven Belenko, and Pauline K. Brennan. 2012. "The Effects of Mental Health and Substance Abuse Disorder on Institutional Misconduct Among Female Inmates." *Justice Quarterly* 29:799–828.

Irwin, John. 2005. *The Warehouse Prison: Disposal of the New Dangerous Class*. Los Angeles, CA: Roxbury Press.

James, Doris J., and Lauren E. Glaze. 2006. *Mental Health Problems of Prison and Jail Inmates*. Washington, DC: Bureau of Justice Statistics.

Kramer, John H., and Jeffery T. Ulmer. 2009. *Sentencing Guidelines: Lessons from Pennsylvania*. Boulder, CO: Lynne Rienner.

Langan, Patrick A., and David J. Levin. 2002. *Recidivism of Prisoners Released in 1994*. Washington, DC: Bureau of Justice Statistics.

Liebling, Alison. 1999. "Prison Suicide and Prison Coping." In *Prisons*, edited by Michael H. Tonry and Joan Petersilia. Chicago: University of Chicago Press.

Loeber, Rolf, and David P. Farrington, eds. 2012. *From Juvenile Delinquency to Adult Crime: Criminal Careers, Justice Policy, and Prevention*. New York: Oxford University Press.

Lynch, James P., and William J. Sabol. 2001. *Prisoner Reentry in Perspective*. Washington, DC: Urban Institute.

Mann, Coramae R. 1993. *Unequal Justice: A Question of Color*. Bloomington: Indiana University Press.

Matthews, Betsy, and Dana Jones Hubbard. 2008. "Moving Ahead: Five Essential Elements for Working Effectively with Girls." *Journal of Criminal Justice* 36:494–502.

Mauer, Marc. 2009. *The Changing Racial Dynamics of the War on Drugs*. Washington, DC: The Sentencing Project.

Mauer, Marc. 2011. "Addressing the Political Environment Shaping Mass Incarceration." *Criminology and Public Policy* 10:699–705.

McKenzie, Karen, Amanda Michie, Aja Murray, and Charlene Hales. 2012. "Screening for Offenders with an Intellectual Disability: The Validity of the Learning Disability Screening Questionnaire." *Research in Developmental Disabilities* 33:791–795.

Meade, Benjamin, Benjamin Steiner, Matthew Makarios, and Lawrence Travis. 2013. "Estimating a Dose–Response Relationship Between Time Served in Prison and Recidivism." *Journal of Research in Crime and Delinquency* 50:525–550.

Mears, Daniel P. 2003. "A Critique of Waiver Research: Critical Next Steps in Assessing the Impacts of Laws for Transferring Juveniles to the Criminal Justice System." *Youth Violence and Juvenile Justice* 1:156–172.

Mears, Daniel P. 2004. "Mental Health Needs and Services in the Criminal Justice System." *Houston Journal of Health, Law and Policy* 4: 255–284.

Mears, Daniel P. 2010. *American Criminal Justice Policy*. New York: Cambridge University Press.

Mears, Daniel P. 2012. "The Prison Experience: Introduction to the Special Issue." *Journal of Criminal Justice* 40:345–347.

Mears, Daniel P., and Joshua C. Cochran. 2012. "U.S. Prisoner Reentry Health Care Policy in International Perspective: Service Gaps and the Moral and Public Health Implications." *The Prison Journal* 92:175–202.

Mears, Daniel P., Joshua C. Cochran, and Sonja E. Siennick. 2013. "Life-Course Perspectives and Prisoner Reentry." In *the Handbook of Life-Course Criminology: Emerging Trends and Directions for Future Research*, edited by Marvin D. Krohn and Chris L. Gibson. New York: Springer-Verlag.

Mears, Daniel P., and Jeremy Travis. 2004. "Youth Development and Reentry." *Youth Violence and Juvenile Justice* 2:1–20.

Mears, Daniel P., Xia Wang, Carter Hay, and William D. Bales. 2008. "Social Ecology and Recidivism: Implications for Prisoner Reentry." *Criminology* 46:301–340.

Mumola, Christopher J. 2000. *Incarcerated Parents and Their Children*. Washington, DC: Bureau of Justice Statistics.

Mumola, Christopher J., and Jennifer C. Karberg. 2007. *Drug Use and Dependence, State and Federal Prisoners, 2004*. Washington, DC: Bureau of Justice Statistics.

Nagin, Daniel S., Francis T. Cullen, and Cheryl L. Jonson. 2009. "Imprisonment and Reoffending." *Crime and Justice* 38:115–200.

Office of National Drug Control Policy. 2013. "Drug Policy Reform in Action: A 21st Century Approach." Press release, April 24. Washington, DC: Office of National Drug Control Policy. http://www.whitehouse.gov/ondcp/news-releases/2013-national-drug-policy-strategy-release.

Pager, Devah. 2003. "The Mark of a Criminal Record." *American Journal of Sociology* 108:937–975.

Petersilia, Joan. 2003. *When Prisoners Come Home: Parole and Prisoner Reentry.* New York: Oxford University Press.

Petersilia, Joan. 2005. "From Cell to Society: Who Is Returning Home?" In *Prisoner Reentry and Crime in America*, edited by Jeremy Travis and Christy Visher. New York: Cambridge University Press.

Petit, Becky, and Bruce Western. 2004. "Mass Imprisonment and the Life Course: Race and Class Inequality in U.S. Incarceration." *American Sociological Review* 69:151–169.

Pew Center on the States. 2012. *Time Served: The High Cost, Low Return of Longer Prison Terms.* Washington DC: Pew Charitable Trusts.

Redding, Richard E. 2010. *Juvenile Transfer Laws: An Effective Deterrent to Delinquency?* Washington, DC: Office of Juvenile Justice and Delinquency Prevention.

Reisig, Michael D. 1998. "Rates of Disorder in Higher-Custody State Prisons: A Comparative Analysis of Managerial Practices." *Crime and Delinquency* 44:229–244.

Rose, Dina R., and Todd R. Clear. 2003. "Incarceration, Reentry, and Social Capital: Social Networks in the Balance" In *Prisoners Once Removed: The Impact of Incarceration and Reentry on Children, Families, and Communities*, edited by Jeremy Travis and Michelle Waul. Washington, DC: Urban Institute Press.

Skogan, Wesley G, ed. 2003. *Community Policing: Can It Work?* Belmont, CA: Wadsworth.

Solinger, Rickie, Paula C. Johnson, Martha L. Raimon, Tina Reynolds, and Ruby C. Tapia. 2010. *Interrupted Life: Experiences of Incarcerated Women in the United States.* Berkeley: University of California Press.

Sorensen, Jon, and Mark D. Cunningham. 2010. "Conviction Offense and Prison Violence: A Comparative Study of Murderers and Other Offenders." *Crime and Delinquency* 56:103–125.

Stal, Marina. 2013. "Treatment of Older and Elderly Inmates Within Prisons." *Journal of Correctional Health Care* 19:69–73.

Steffensmeier, Darrell, Jeffery Ulmer, and John Kramer. 1998. "The Interaction of Race, Gender, and Age in Criminal Sentencing: The Punishment Cost of Being Young, Black, and Male." *Criminology* 36:763–798.

Steiner, Benjamin. 2009. "Assessing Static and Dynamic Influences on Inmate Violence Levels." *Crime and Delinquency* 55:134–161.

Steiner, Benjamin, and John Wooldredge. 2009. "Individual and Environmental Effects on Assaults and Nonviolent Rule Breaking by Women in Prison." *Journal of Research in Crime and Delinquency* 46:437–467.

Tonry, Michael H. 1995. *Malign Neglect: Race, Crime, and Punishment in America.* New York: Oxford University Press.

Tonry, Michael H. 2008. "Crime and Human Rights—How Political Paranoia, Protestant Fundamentalism, and Constitutional Obsolescence Combined to Devastate Black America: The American Society of Criminology 2007 Presidential Address." *Criminology* 46:1–34.

Tonry, Michael H. 2011. *Punishing Race: A Continuing American Dilemma.* New York: Oxford University Press.

Travis, Jeremy. 2005. *But They All Come Back: Facing the Challenges of Prisoner Reentry.* Washington, DC: Urban Institute Press.

Travis, Jeremy, and Christy Visher, eds. 2005. *Prisoner Reentry and Crime in America.* New York: Cambridge University Press.

Uggen, Christopher, and Sara Wakefield. 2005. "Young Adults Reentering the Community from the Criminal Justice System: The Challenge." In *On Your Own Without a Net*, edited by Wayne D. Osgood, Michael E. Foster, Constance Flanagan, and Gretchen P. Ruth. Chicago: University of Chicago Press.

Uggen, Christopher, Sara Wakefield, and Bruce Western. 2005. "Work and Family Perspectives on Reentry" In *Prisoner Reentry and Crime in America*, edited by Jeremy Travis and Christy Visher. New York: Cambridge University Press.

Useem, Bert, and Anne M. Piehl. 2008. *Prison State: The Challenge of Mass Incarceration*. New York: Cambridge University Press.

Visher, Christy A., Sara A. Debus-Sherrill, and Jennifer Yahner. 2010. "Employment After Prison: A Longitudinal Study of Former Prisoners." *Justice Quarterly* 28:698–718.

Visher, Christy A., and Jeremy Travis. 2003. "Transitions from Prison to Community: Understanding Individual Pathways." *Annual Review of Sociology* 29:89–113.

Visher, Christy A., and Jeremy Travis. 2011. "Life on the Outside: Returning Home after Incarceration." *The Prison Journal* 9:102–119.

Wang, Xia, and Daniel P. Mears. 2010. "A Multilevel Test of Minority Threat Effects on Sentencing." *Journal of Quantitative Criminology* 26:191–215.

Wang, Xia, Daniel P. Mears, and William D. Bales. 2010. "Race-Specific Employment Contexts and Recidivism." *Criminology* 48:201–241.

Warren, Patricia, Donald Tomaskovic-Devey, William Smith, Matthew Zingraff, and Marcinda Mason. 2006. "Driving While Black: Bias Processes and Racial Disparity in Police Stops." *Criminology* 44:709–738.

Western, Bruce. 2006. *Punishment and Inequality in America*. New York: Russell Sage Foundation.

Whitford, Andrew B., and Jeff Yates. 2009. *Presidential Rhetoric and the Public Agenda: Constructing the War on Drugs*. Baltimore, MD: Johns Hopkins University Press.

Wolff, Nancy, and Jing Shi. 2011. "Patterns of Victimization and Feelings of Safety Inside Prison: The Experience of Male and Female Inmates." *Crime and Delinquency* 57:29–55.

Wooldredge, John, Timothy Griffin, and Travis Pratt. 2001. "Considering Hierarchical Models for Research on Inmate Behavior: Predicting Misconduct with Multilevel Data." *Justice Quarterly* 18:203–231.

Wright, Emily M., Patricia Van Voorhis, Emily J. Salisbury, and Ashley Bauman. 2012. "Gender-Responsive Lessons Learned and Policy Implications for Women in Prison: A Review." *Criminal Justice and Behavior* 39:1612–1632.

CHAPTER 3

MASS INCARCERATION AND CONDITIONS OF CONFINEMENT

LEO CARROLL, SHARON CALCI, AND AMBER WILSON

SINCE 1975 the proportion of the nation's population that is in prison or jail has grown dramatically. This mass incarceration has drawn much attention from scholars, most of which has centered on its causes and its consequences for the wider society. Despite the fears of some critics that the strain produced by vastly increased numbers would plunge the prison system into chaos, there has been comparatively little research into how the prison system has coped with the crisis of large numbers. Here we explore the impact of mass incarceration on conditions of confinement in U.S. prisons.

There are over 1,300 federal and state prisons in the United States. Some of these facilities are well managed and safe and provide adequate care and opportunities for prisoners to improve their lives. Conditions in others—because they are old or poorly managed or underfunded or overcrowded or whatever—may be so harsh as to constitute cruel and unusual punishment. Thus, no generalization will apply to the conditions in each and every prison, and our evidence must, of necessity, be qualified with terms such as "in general" or "on average." Having said this, however, our basic conclusion is that the prison system did not collapse under the weight of numbers, and that conditions in most prisons today are perhaps somewhat better, and certainly no worse, than they were in the 1970s.

In support of our conclusion, we offer the following arguments:

- Data regarding violence and disorder, health and health care, and rehabilitative treatment suggests that prisons today are certainly safer, possibly healthier, and perhaps more rehabilitative than were those in operation prior to the population boom.
- Judicial intervention eliminated some of the most onerous conditions and set standards that prison conditions must meet in order to be constitutionally permissible. Much of this litigation directly concerned overcrowding and substantially alleviated the pressures produced by overcrowding, albeit often by indirectly causing the construction of more prisons.

- Another factor, at least partially attributable to litigation, has been the professionalization of corrections. Professional associations have set detailed standards in key areas and have begun accrediting prisons; national institutes have been established to provide assistance to state and local systems and offer advanced training for correctional managers; agencies have increased support for research and the wide dissemination of evidence-based best practices; and there is more and better training for correctional officers.

I. Evolution of Prison Environments

A. Population Growth and Prison Construction

At the beginning of the twentieth century, there were less than 60,000 offenders incarcerated in state and federal prisons, a rate of about 69 per 100,000 population (Cahalan 1986, Tables 3-2 and 3-3). For most of the century, the number in prison grew only slightly faster than the increase in population with the result that the rate of incarceration was relatively stable, increasing in some decades such as the 1930s but declining in others such as the 1960s even as the crime rate rose. Some scholars theorized that the level of formal punishment in a society may be stable and as serious crime rises, minor offenses are increasingly tolerated (Blumstein, Cohen, and Nagin 1977; Berk, Rauma, Messinger, and Cooley 1981).

The "stability of punishment" thesis was called into question by events occurring even as researchers debated it. In 1970 the rate of incarceration stood at 98 per 100,000 population, only 31 percent higher than it had been 60 years before (Bureau of Justice Statistics 1986; Cahalan 1986, Table 3-3). Over the next five years the rate increased to 111 per 100,000, and then it exploded. The incarceration rate rose by more than 80 percent between 1975 and 1985, and then the inmate population more than doubled between 1985 and 1995. Growth then slowed somewhat to slightly less than 500 per 100,000 population (Carson and Sabol 2012) (Figure 3.1).

Many scholars feared that this rapid buildup in the prisoner population would overwhelm the system and result in an upsurge of violence and disorder. John Hagan (1995, p. 524) warned that "increased imprisonment will lead to more disruptions and riots in prison." Several years later, Blomberg and Lucken believed that Hagan's fears had been realized: "Prison riots, hostage taking, gang warfare, and inmate to inmate, inmate to staff, and staff to inmate violence are all increasingly routine aspects of everyday operations" (2000, p. 132).

However, the system expanded rapidly to accommodate the population increase. The *1984 Census of State Adult Correctional Facilities* (Stephen 1987, Table 1) reported that there were 694 state-operated prisons that year. In 2005, the year of the most recently available census, there were 1,190. There were also 102 federal prisons in 2005, up from 80 in 1990. In addition, there were 107 private prisons operating under contracts with either state or federal correctional agencies in 2005 (Stephen 2008, Appendix Table 2).

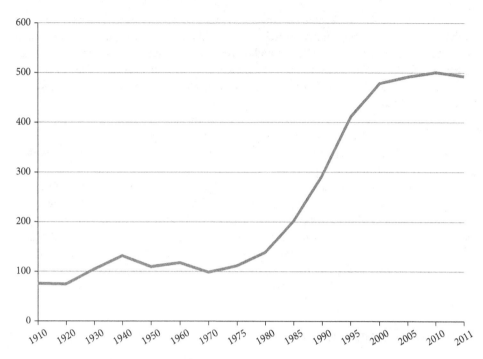

FIGURE 3.1. Incarceration rates per 100,000 population, 1910–2011.

Nearly three-quarters of correctional facilities[1] are relatively small, with capacities less than 500, and the majority are rated as minimum security (Stephen 2008, Table 1). However, a disproportionate number of the *newly* constructed facilities are large, maximum-security prisons. From 1990 to 2005, the number of correctional facilities of all kinds grew by 41.5 percent, but the number of maximum-security prisons increased by 59 percent, and the number of prisons with capacities of 2,500 or greater nearly tripled, with 50 of these "warehouse prisons" added to the 26 in existence in 1990 (Stephen 2008, Appendix Table 5). Along with the number of prisons, the number of people employed in prisons also grew rapidly, increasing by over 70 percent. This growth, however, did not keep pace with the increased number of prisoners, and the ratio of prisoners to staff grew from 2.9 in 1990 to 3.3 in 2005.

Newly constructed prisons bear little resemblance to those of the past, some of which, however, remain in use. Irwin (2005, p. 58) observed that three principles have guided their construction: security, efficiency, and economy. Massive walls and grand entrances have been replaced by double rows of steel fences, rolls of razor wire between them, and rather ordinary-looking steel doors. The buildings inside these walls are constructed of prefabricated steel-reinforced concrete slabs. Prisoners are more commonly housed in triangular or circular pods holding 100 to 200 individuals rather than in long, cavernous cell blocks. To better protect officers, cell doors are now solid steel rather than barred. Through a strategically located control center, one officer can observe all activity in a housing unit and can open and close cells by the push of a button. Movement about the institution is no longer controlled by "turnkeys" who open and close gates, but by electronic doors manned by officers secure in a control center viewing the gate remotely through a camera. The "yard" in the center of the compound is sparsely landscaped and often just plain dirt, asphalt, or concrete and frequently divided into smaller areas by high chain-link fences. Critics such as Irwin (2005) and Wacquant (2001, p. 109) view these new prisons as "race-divided and violence-ridden 'warehouse[s]' geared solely to neutralizing social rejects by sequestering them physically from society."

Many of these new facilities are exactly what the critics claim. They are "super-maximum-security" (supermax) prisons designed to house prisoners in conditions that minimize their ability to engage in serious misconduct. Contrary to popular belief, there is no precise definition of a "supermax" prison. They may be standalone facilities or special housing units within a larger complex, but they share certain characteristics: Prisoners are typically kept in solitary confinement for close to 24 hours a day, are fed in their cells, are provided little in the way of programming, take recreation by themselves in a caged-in area, and have few if any visits. In the words of Kurki and Morris, these institutions are a "new form of double incapacitation: [serving] not only to isolate prisoners from the rest of society but to isolate the worst of them from other prisoners and the staff" (2001, p. 391).

B. Judicial Intervention

Prior to the 1960s, courts had, by and large, maintained a "hands-off" policy with respect to the operation of prisons. This policy was justified by the belief that offenders had sacrificed their constitutional rights, and they were, in the words of an 1871 Virginia court, "slaves of the state" (*Ruffin v. Commonwealth*, 62 Va. 790). Judges were also reluctant to intervene because they interpreted the separation of powers to mean they lacked authority to inter-fere in the operation of executive agencies, and because they lacked sufficient penological expertise. The civil rights movement, however, drew prison conditions within the orbit of the courts and triggered the beginning of a "hands-on" era.

In the first case in which the U.S. Supreme Court took notice of prisoners' claims, *Cooper v. Pate* (378 U.S. 546, 1964), the Court recognized the standing of Black Muslim prisoners to challenge the constitutionality of prison regulations that denied them any opportunity to worship. The law under which the prisoners were found to have standing was Section 1983 of the U.S. Code, originally passed in 1871, to protect former slaves from abuses of their civil rights by persons "acting under the color of law."

Judicial recognition of prisoners' rights and access to the courts created a tidal wave of litigation. Prisoners filed 218 Section 1983 lawsuits in federal courts in 1966; that number grew to over 26,000 in 1992 (Hanson and Daley 1994, p. 2). Some of the major decisions recognizing prisoner rights by the U.S. Supreme Court are listed in Tables 3.1 and 3.2. These and numerous other decisions by lower courts affirmed that prisoners retain certain fun-damental rights such as the right to practice their religion even if it is an unconventional one, freedom of expression, meaningful access to the courts, and basic due process in hear-ings regarding serious disciplinary infractions. In other decisions, however, the Court made clear its concern with institutional security. For example, regulations banning union meet-ings, solicitation of union membership, and bulk mailings by North Carolina prisoners were found to be rationally related to reasonable objectives of prison administration. For

Table 3.1. Selected decisions of the U.S. Supreme Court concerning prisoners' rights during the "hands-on" period, 1965–1980

Case	Decision
Lee v. Washington 390 U.S. 333(1968)	Mandatory racial segregation in a state prison is unconstitutional.
Johnson v. Avery 393 U. S. 483 (1969)	Regulations prohibiting inmates from assisting each other in preparing petitions for post-conviction relief are unconstitutional unless the state provides them with a reasonable alternative.
Cruz v. Beto 405 U.S. 319 (1972)	Prisoners who hold unconventional religious beliefs must be given opportunities to practice their beliefs comparable to those who hold more conventional beliefs.
Procunier v. Martinez 416 U.S. 396 (1974)	Censorship of prisoner mail is permitted only to further governmental interests in security, order, or rehabilitation and is no greater than is necessary to protect the governmental interest involved.
Wolff v. McDonnell 418 U.S. 539(1974)	Prison disciplinary proceedings that can result in the loss of good time or transfer to punitive segregation must contain the basic elements of due process to accord with the Fourteenth Amendment.
Estelle v. Gamble 429 U.S. 97 (1976)	"Deliberate indifference" by prison personnel to a prisoner's serious illness or injury constitutes cruel and unusual punishment in violation of the Eighth Amendment.
Bounds v. Smith 430 U.S. 817 (1977)	The right of access to the courts requires prison authorities to assist prisoners in the preparation and filing of legal papers by providing them with an adequate law library or assistance from persons trained in the law.

Table 3.2. Selected decisions of the U.S. Supreme Court concerning prisoners' rights during the deference period, 1980–present

Case	Decision
Rhodes v. Chapman 452 U.S. 337 (1981)	Double-celling inmates in cells designed for one does not, in itself, constitute cruel and unusual punishment in violation of the Eighth Amendment.
O'Lone v. The Estate of Shabazz 482 U.S. 342 (1987)	Rules that prohibit inmates from attending religious services do not violate the free exercise clause of the First Amendment so long as they are reasonably related to a legitimate penological objective.
Wilson v. Seiter 501 U.S. 294 (1991)	Prisoners challenging the conditions of their confinement must show a culpable state of mind on the part of prison officials, to wit "deliberate indifference."
Rufo v. Inmates of Suffolk County Jail 502 U.S. 367 (1992)	A consent decree may be modified if the party seeking modification shows that a significant change in the facts or the law warrant the revision, and that the proposed modification is suitably tailored to the changed circumstances.
Sandin v. Conner 515 U.S. (1995)	Confinement for 30 days in punitive segregation is not the kind of atypical and significant deprivation that requires due process protections before imposition.

example, a prisoners' union may become an adversarial organization that poses a threat to order and security (*Jones v. North Carolina Prisoners' Union*, 433 U.S. 119, 1977).

The most sweeping and controversial decisions of the "hands-on" period were Eighth Amendment cases in which federal district courts found that the "totality of conditions" in a particular prison or an entire state's prison system constituted cruel and unusual punishment. In the first such case, a federal district court found that confinement in the Arkansas prison system "is characterized by conditions and practices so bad as to be shocking to the conscience of reasonably civilized people" (*Holt v. Sarver*, 309 F. Supp. 362, pp. 372–373, 1970). Similar conditions were found following litigation over the next several years in Alabama (*Pugh v. Locke*, 406 F. Supp. 318, 1976), Rhode Island (*Palmigiano v. Garrahy*, 443 F. Supp. 956, 1977), and Texas (*Ruiz v. Estelle*, 503 F. Supp. 1265, 1980). Other states with equally deplorable prison conditions entered into consent decrees rather than go to trial, including Mississippi (*Gates v. Collier*, 390 F. Supp. 492, 1975) and Georgia (*Guthrie v. Evans*, C.A. 73-3068, 1973). These cases necessitated extensive remedial action by the state, often involved the use of a special master to monitor compliance, and placed the institution or system under court supervision, sometimes for as long as 15 years, until compliance was achieved.

By 1984, 166 prisons were operating under a court order or consent decree (Stephen 1987, Table 15), and the number of petitions filed by inmates continued to grow. In an effort to stem the tide of litigation, the U.S. Supreme Court began to define prisoners' rights in ways that limited them and showed greater deference to the expertise of correctional administrators. A sample of these cases is summarized in Table 3.2. Of particular significance are the cases of *Rhodes v. Chapman* (452 U.S. 337, 1981) and *Wilson v. Seiter* (501 U.S. 294, 1991). In the former, the Court held that double-celling prisoners in cells designed for one and in which they spend most of their time each day did not violate the Eighth Amendment because the practice did not result in an increase in violence and the prisoners were not deprived of basic human needs such as food, medical care, and sanitation. In the latter, the Court ruled that a prisoner challenging the conditions of confinement must show not only that the conditions are inhumane but that they result from the "deliberate indifference" of authorities.

Under pressure from governors and state attorneys general, the U.S. Congress took steps to stem the tide of litigation in 1996, passing the Prison Litigation Reform Act (PLRA). The PLRA was also intended to prevent judges from "micromanaging" state prisons and local jails. The PLRA requires prisoners to exhaust all available administrative remedies before filing suit, requires those unable to pay the full filing fee to pay an initial fee plus installments, and prohibits those who have had three suits dismissed as frivolous from filing *in forma pauperis* (allowing a poor person to bring suit without liability for the costs) unless they face an imminent threat of serious physical injury. The PLRA also limits the amount of attorney's fees that can be awarded when prisoners prevail, and the powers of special masters, appointed by the court to oversee implementation of its orders. The relief that courts can order must relate only to constitutional violations, be no further than is required to remedy that violation, and be the least intrusive means of correcting it. Moreover, any prospective relief ordered by a court can be stayed for 30 days, and possibly up to 60 days, upon a motion for termination by the defendants (Palmer 2010, pp. 413–417).

Since passage of the PLRA, the number of Section 1983 filings by prisoners has declined to about 17,000 per year (*Sourcebook* 2010, Table 5.65). However, the PLRA has not been the death knell of prison reform as some had feared. For example, the Court recently upheld a California decision finding that overcrowding was the primary cause of constitutionally inadequate medical and mental health care in the prison system and ordered the state to reduce the prison population by some 40,000 (*Brown v. Plata*, 131 S.Ct. 1910, 2011).

C. Professionalization

Fifty years ago, prisons sat on the periphery of society. Set in remote areas, surrounded by high walls with limited communication with the outside world, they existed in geographic and cultural isolation from other institutions and their core values. Those in charge treated the prison as their personal fiefdom and ruled it autocratically, with little or no accountability. Some of these leaders were larger-than-life figures such as Joe Ragen of Stateville (Jacobs 1977) and George Beto of Texas (Crouch and Marquart 1989) who—through a combination of charisma, ability, and intimidation—operated institutions that were safe, clean, and orderly if not altogether humane. More commonly, however, the leaders were political operatives whose main task was to keep the lid on and the institution off the front page.

Events of the 1970s blew the lid off, however. Widespread acceptance of the rehabilitative ideal led to the development of a collaborative management philosophy in which correctional managers would share power with inmates in the governance of the prison. Attempts to implement the philosophy, however, often produced disastrous results. The sharp break with autocratic rule fractured the prison hierarchy, pitting coalitions of administrators and prisoners against correctional officers. The basic conditions of life—food, sanitation, medical care, and so forth—deteriorated while administrators made promises of reform and rehabilitation; violence escalated as gangs stepped into the vacuum left by the retreat of the correctional officers; and the number of riots increased as heightened expectations went unfulfilled (Carroll 1974; Jacobs 1977; Useem and Kimball 1989).

Regaining control and restoring order, while meeting the demands posed by court orders and a growing population, necessitated the development of complex bureaucracies and rational-legal forms of control. Prisons, which had been relatively autonomous, began in the 1970s to be integrated into newly established state departments of correction. In many cases, federal judges intervened and set concrete objectives and timeframes by which administrators could set priorities and order decision making; and the attainment of constitutionality replaced the more ambiguous goal of rehabilitation. Professional associations began to work in partnership with the courts. The American Correctional Association instituted an accreditation program for facilities and certification programs for personnel; the National Institute of Corrections was established to provide expertise in the form of technical assistance and training to state agencies; and the National Commission of Correctional Health Care and the American Association of Correctional Psychology, among others, were founded and continue to set standards and offer continuing education and training in key areas.

New construction required managers with requisite skills to span the boundaries of the prison and to work successfully with the private sector. Correctional administrators looked outside the field for management models and found ways to modify the traditional quasi-military bureaucracy. In the most progressive systems, decision making began to be delegated to the lowest possible level. Lower-level staff members such as officers, counselors, and teachers were consulted in decisions regarding their areas of responsibility; performance was evaluated by agreed-upon quantifiable metrics; and personnel from different departments were assigned to work groups to accomplish specific tasks such as case management and coordinating schedules more effectively.

One of the best examples of this type of decentralization is the unit-management system found in many state prisons and the entire federal system. Although unit management can be implemented in most institutions, it is particularly suited to the modular construction of most new prisons. The basic concept of unit management is to subdivide the larger population into smaller groups of between 75 and 250 inmates whose needs for supervision and programs are similar to each other. Each group is housed together in the same unit, many services are provided within the unit, and the group remains together for as many activities as possible (e.g., dining, recreation) outside the unit. Unit staff are permanently assigned and typically consist of a unit manager, one or more case managers and counselors, a unit secretary, and a part-time mental health worker. Correctional officers are assigned on a rotating basis, but optimally are posted to the unit for nine months to a year (Gerard 1991; Levinson 1999).

Sound classification of prisoners is essential to the operation of a safe and orderly prison, and is particularly important to sustain unit management. In the past, the assignment to housing, work, and programs was largely a subjective decision made by a team (usually composed of representatives from custody, counseling, and education) following a review of the prisoner's records and a brief interview. These decisions were frequently the subject of lawsuits (e.g., *Morris v. Travisono*, 310 F. Supp. 857, 1970; *Ramos v. Lamm*, 485 F. Supp. 122, 1979), as the courts required an equitable process, and administrators found it difficult to demonstrate that the criteria employed were valid and applied consistently. In response to this problem, researchers set about developing objective classification systems that use valid and reliable criteria to assess prisoners' risks and needs. There are now several such instruments that have been shown to outperform more subjective determinations in assessing both risk and needs (Austin and Hardyman 2004; Gendreau, Andrews, and Theriault 2010).[2]

In sum, faced with both external challenges from the courts and internal threats posed by a rapidly growing prisoner population, corrections has become an increasingly complex field and correctional administration, by and large, has become increasingly rational. Formerly isolated prisons have become integrated into statewide bureaucracies. Written policies and procedures now govern the conduct of all offices. Decision making is located at different levels, increasingly based on measurable criteria, and reviewed at higher levels. Correctional standards have been established by courts and professional associations, and pre-service and in-service training at all levels has been emphasized and upgraded.

II. Prison Conditions

What are conditions in prisons like today? How have they been affected by the changes just described? We now turn to these questions focusing on violence and disorder, health and medical care, mental illness, and access to treatment and meaningful activity. Again, we caution that not all prisons are alike. Some are harsh, brutal, dangerous places in which inmates may be deprived of basic necessities; others are relatively safe, orderly institutions in which prisoners are provided opportunities to improve their lives after release. Treating this wide variation in conditions is far beyond the scope of this chapter, which must, of necessity, be restricted to aggregate data and selected examples.

A. Violence and Disorder

The 1970s was a violent decade in America's prisons. It began with the Attica (New York) riot in which 39 people were killed and ended with a particularly brutal riot at the New Mexico State Penitentiary in 1980. During much of the decade the homicide rate in prisons was seven to ten times that of the nation at large (Bowker 1980, p. 27). As the numbers in prison swelled in the following years, many feared that authorities would completely lose control and life inside the walls would descend into a Hobbesian war of all against all. Available data, however, indicate that these fears were unfounded and that, if anything, there is less violence in prisons today than there was 30 or 40 years ago.

In their study of the impact of mass incarceration in the United States, Bert Useem and Anne Morrison Piehl (2008, Chapter 4) looked closely at indices of prison disorder over time. There were over 350 riots in American prisons reported by major news media from 1971 through 1975. Thirty years later, from 2001 through 2005, there were fewer than ten riots. A search we conducted found only seven American riots reported by the *New York Times* from 2006 through 2012.[3]

Much the same picture emerges from the data Useem and Piehl present on prison homicide and suicide rates. In 1980 there were 54 homicides and 34 suicides per 100,000 inmates. By 1990 those rates had fallen by 85 and 53 percent, respectively. These rates have stabilized since then; in 2010 the homicide rate was 5 per 100,000 and the suicide rate was 16 (Noonan 2012, i4). To provide some perspective, according to the National Center for Health Statistics (2012), the 2009 U.S. homicide rate for the population aged 18 to 24 was 14 and the suicide rate was 12. For those aged 25 to 44, the respective rates were 8 and 15 (Figure 3.2).

In the public mind, violence in prison is commonly associated with sexual assault. Until recently, however, there have been no reliable data by which to estimate how frequent sexual assault in prison actually is. Since 2008, the Bureau of Justice Statistics has conducted surveys of inmates concerning sexual victimization and has published the results of its third survey.[4] That report estimates that about 4 percent of the prisoner population, some 68,900 prison inmates, was victimized during 2011–2012 (Beck, Berzofsky, Caspar, and Krebs 2013). Slightly less than half of these incidents involved unwanted contact or activity with another inmate, and slightly more than half involved staff misconduct, although the inmates characterized about half of these latter incidents as "willing." Force or the threat of force was used in approximately two-thirds of the inmate-on-inmate incidents and about 35 percent of those involving staff, and injuries occurred in about one in four of the former incidents and in 10 percent of the latter.

The percentage of inmates reporting "willing" sexual involvement with staff declined slightly between 2008–2009 and 2011–2012, but the estimates of other types of sexual contact/activity remained stable. Thus, while it is not possible to estimate whether the level of sexual victimization in prison has increased or decreased with the buildup of the prisoner

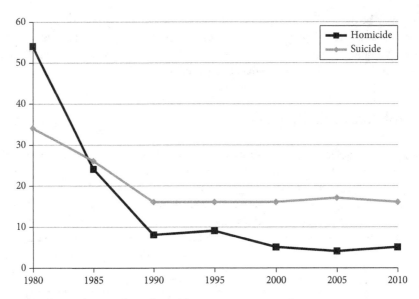

FIGURE 3.2. Prison homicide and suicide rates per 100,000 inmates.

population over the past 40 or so years, it appears not to have changed substantially over the past five years.

The data on serious disorder and violence clearly do not support the dire predictions of some scholars regarding the consequences of the growth of incarceration. Indeed, prisons today are much safer and more orderly than they were in the 1970s when the number of prisoners was less than 15 percent of what it is today. The argument we have advanced above is that strong leadership, improved management, and better-designed facilities spurred on by court orders and consent decrees has succeeded not only in containing violence but actually reducing it.

Correctional administrators attribute much of the reduction in violence and disorder to the growth of "supermax" prisons and Secure Housing Units. Thirty years ago, there was only one supermax prison in the United States—the federal penitentiary at Marion, Illinois. By 2004, however, there were at least 57 such facilities and 44 states had at least one (Mears and Watson 2006). When asked if supermax facilities have been effective, some 90 percent of the state prison wardens surveyed responded that they thought supermaxes improved systemwide order, safety, and control (Mears and Castro 2006, p. 45).

The scant research available, however, does not entirely support the beliefs of the authorities. Two of the most rigorous evaluations were conducted by Chad Briggs, Thomas Castellano, and Jody Sundt. The first study (Briggs et al. 2003) focused on four states, three of which had supermaxes and one that did not. They found little evidence that the opening of the supermaxes produced an overall reduction in violence. Inmate-on-inmate assaults were not affected, and the data on inmate–staff assaults were contradictory. In one state (Illinois), there was evidence of a reduction in inmate-on-staff assaults, but in another (Arizona) they increased. The second study (Sundt et al. 2008) examined the opening of the Illinois facility in more depth. Their findings were consistent with those of the first study regarding assaults, but they found that, following the opening of the facility, there was a sharp and permanent reduction in the number of days that prisons within the state had to be locked down in order to restore order.

Although these two studies provide some support for the argument that supermax prisons reduce violence and restore order, that evidence is only partial and somewhat contradictory. In discussing their results, Sundt et al. (2008, p. 117) cautioned that, given the paucity of research and the limitations in their own study, it is not possible "to conclude with confidence that the effect of super-max on safety or prison order observed here can be generalized to other prison systems or over time within this prison system."

Mississippi reduced the number of inmates held in long-term administrative segregation at the Parchman Penitentiary. Evidence from that experience suggests that use of long-term administrative segregation may not be essential to maintaining security and order, and the number so confined may be sharply reduced. Some 1,000 prisoners, including those on death row, had been kept isolated in Unit 32. Conditions were filthy; prisoners spent their days in almost complete idleness and had little access to exercise. Disruptive behavior and staff use of force were an everyday occurrence. Those on death row filed suit against the state in 2002, and that was followed by a suit filed on behalf of those held in administrative segregation, many of whom were housed permanently in Unit 32 (Kupers et al. 2009).

Rather than go to trial, the Mississippi Department of Corrections chose to negotiate a consent decree with the plaintiffs. The Department agreed to improve the physical conditions in Unit 32, revise its classification system, develop means by which prisoners could earn their way out of administrative segregation, and establish a secure treatment unit as an alternative for prisoners suffering from serious mental illness. Within 18 months, those with a serious mental illness were transferred to a stepdown unit where they were provided treatment by mental health professionals, and nearly 80 percent of the remaining population had been reclassified from administrative segregation to general population. Also, those individuals remaining in administrative segregation could work their way out. Misconduct rates among the mentally ill and those reclassified to the general population fell sharply, as did incidents in which the staff used force (Kupers et al. 2009).

Despite the beliefs of correctional authorities, there is little evidence to support the contention that the emergence of the supermax prison has been a major factor in the restoration of order and stability in American prisons. States have begun to realize that the operation of these facilities is very costly, and some have recently been converted to general-population use. Research on the effects of these conversions on security and order are needed before we can offer a more definitive assessment of their utility. But even if these facilities are found to have a positive influence on reducing violence, this influence must be balanced against any negative effects of such extreme deprivations. Isolation, idleness, and lack of stimulation cause both physical and mental deterioration, and the perception of being treated unfairly can also produce rage, all of which are frequently manifested in disruptive and violent behavior. Those who must respond to this behavior and work in the same tense and depressing environment tend to become callous and even vengeful, perhaps provoking incidents that require them to use force and abusing those who are almost completely dependent upon them. Such conditions likely breed what Haney (2008) has termed a "culture of harm" in which there is as much or more violence than that which is prevented.

B. Health and Medical Care

The U.S. Supreme Court concluded in *Estelle v. Gamble* (429 U.S. 97, 1976, p. 105) that "deliberate indifference to the serious medical needs of prisoners constitutes the unnecessary and wanton infliction of pain . . . proscribed by the Eighth Amendment." Despite this constitutional protection and the development of standards and guidelines for correctional health care, there continues to be a steady stream of litigation regarding medical care in prisons around the country. In perhaps the most prominent case, California in 2002 stipulated that the prison medical care system was constitutionally deficient, and several years later did not contest a finding by the court that "on average an inmate in one of California's prisons needlessly dies every six to seven days due to constitutional deficiencies in . . . the medical delivery system" (Schlanger 2013, p. 174). Growth in California's prisoner population frustrated the state's efforts to remedy the deficiencies, and in 2011 the U.S. Supreme Court in *Brown v. Plata* (131 S.Ct. 1910, 2011) upheld a district court order requiring the state to reduce the prisoner population to 137.5 percent of the system's rated capacity by the end of 2013.[5]

Unlike the situation in *Plata*, most of the litigation regarding medical care concerns the treatment of individual inmates. Palmer (2010, pp. 229–233) presents a veritable litany of such cases. In a 1994 case, a physician's treatment of a prisoner was found to constitute cruel and unusual punishment because he failed to inform his patient that he had two broken pins in his hip, and then delayed surgery for two years despite the inmate's constant complaints of pain. In another case decided in 2001, prison officials were held to be deliberately indifferent for not providing an inmate with his needed heart medication or his dentures, with the result that he experienced severe chest pain and could not chew or eat properly. In a 2008 case, correctional officers were found to be deliberately indifferent to the serious medical needs of an inmate who died from asphyxia after being repeatedly pepper-sprayed during a cell extraction.

Rates of serious medical conditions among prisoners are two to three times higher than rates in the non-institutionalized population. An analysis of the medical data collected in the 2004 *Survey of Inmates in State and Federal Correctional Facilities* (SISFCF) disclosed that 38 and 42 percent of federal and state prisoners, respectively, reported having a serious chronic medical condition (Wilper et al. 2009). Between 5 and 6 percent of the prisoners reported having persistent hepatitis, which compares to about 2 percent of the population at large. Only 1.5 percent of the prisoner population has been diagnosed with HIV/AIDS, and that percentage is declining, but that figure is still three times higher than for the general population. Further, the Centers for Disease Control and Prevention (n.d.) reports that the 1 percent of the prisoner population diagnosed with tuberculosis accounts for close to 4 percent of those diagnosed with tuberculosis each year in both institutional and non-institutional populations combined.

Data from the SISFCF on access to medical care revealed that the cases cited above are not atypical (Wilper et al. 2009, p. 670). Nearly 15 percent of the federal inmates and some 20 percent of the state inmates who reported having a persistent medical problem[6] had not received a medical examination since admission. About one in seven prisoners reported that they were a taking a prescription medication at the time of their incarceration; of these, about 20 and 24 percent of the federal and state prisoners (respectively) reported that they had stopped taking their medications since admission. On the other hand, about 96 percent of those who had a condition requiring routine blood tests[7] had been tested at least once since entering prisons, and 92 percent of the federal prisoners and 88 percent of the state prisoners who reported sustaining a serious injury also reported that they had been seen by medical personnel following the injury. The researchers stressed, however, that they were measuring what were, at best, minimal standards and that overall access in prisons, though better than in jails, was substandard (Wilper et al. 2009, pp. 669–670).

However inadequate prison medical care may be, research on mortality rates suggests that, California notwithstanding, the increase in the prisoner population has not caused a rise in the number of inmates dying today because of insufficient care compared to 1994 (when these statistics were first collected). The crude death rate for state prisoners remained relatively constant from 2001 through 2010, rising slightly until 2008 and then dropping back to its 2001 level. The same trend is evident for federal prisoners, although the actual rates are from 10 percent to 37 percent lower than the state rates. Nearly 90 percent of state prisoner deaths are from illness. The major causes of death are heart disease and cancer, which together account for over 50 percent of the deaths. Although the mortality rate from heart disease has remained constant since 1994, that for cancer increased by over 20 percent, probably because of the older population. During the same period, however, due to advances in treatment, the rate of deaths from AIDS-related causes dropped by almost 75 percent (Noonan 2012, Tables 13 and 14).

From 2001 to 2004, death rates for state prisoners were 19 percent lower than the rate for all U.S. residents, and it was 57 percent lower among black prisoners compared to blacks in the non-institutionalized population (Mumola 2007, p. 3). A study examined this "protective" function of prison in more detail by following the survival over 15 years, from 1991 to 2006, of a cohort of 23,510 persons incarcerated in Georgia prisons on June 30, 1991 (Spaulding et al. 2011). Mortality rates standardized for age, sex, race, and socioeconomic status were calculated and compared to similar rates for the Georgia population at large. Deaths during incarceration were about 15 percent lower than expected while postrelease deaths were about 54 percent higher than expected. The lower mortality rates in prison were due primarily to lower rates of homicide, transportation injuries, accidental poisoning (drug overdoses), and suicide. Slightly more than 60 percent of the postrelease excess mortality was due to deaths resulting from homicide, transportation injuries, and accidental poisoning, followed by deaths from HIV infection, cancer, and cirrhosis. However, only black men experienced significantly lower mortality rates while in prison whereas white men experienced somewhat elevated rates during incarceration. We recognize that the compassionate release of moribund prisoners may explain a large portion of the low mortality in prison, but the data suggest that prisons may offer inmates, especially black men, protection from the even more potentially fatal circumstances and situations they face on the outside.

Any protection from mortality afforded by prisons, however, appears to be short term. Patterson (2013) studied the ten-year survival of 111,509 New York prisoners released to parole from 1989 to 2003. After adjusting for a variety of offense-related factors and several demographic variables known to be related to mortality, she found that each additional year in prison produced a 15.6 percent increase in the odds of death for parolees, which translated into a two-year decline in life expectancy for each year served in prison. Thus, Patterson estimated that a 30-year-old prisoner who had served the average length of time

(21.7 months) could expect to live approximately 3.6 years less than a person of the same age who had never been incarcerated. Patterson's data did not include cause of death, nor was she able to trace the pathways to the higher mortality rates, so it not clear what conditions of confinement account for the inverse relationship between time served and life expectancy. This is certainly an area in need of further research.

C. Mental Health

Based on the belief that most people with a mental illness could be better treated in the community, psychiatric hospitals across the country began to close in the 1970s, and this process of "de-institutionalization" has continued. However, the community-based services that were supposed to replace these hospitals were never fully developed. Consequently, many of the mentally ill are unable to obtain the necessary treatment and are often unable to satisfy their basic needs. In a tragic irony, many of them end up incarcerated, making prisons and jails the largest provider of mental health services in the country.

Estimates of the number of prisoners who have significant mental health problems vary greatly. There is nonetheless general agreement that the proportion of prisoners suffering from a mental disorder of some type has increased over the past 30 to 40 years and that they now make up a significant portion of those in prison. Based on self-reports, a recent estimate by the Bureau of Justice Statistics is that 56 percent of state prisoners and 45 percent of those in federal custody in 2004 had a mental health problem as defined by a recent history of symptoms (James and Glaze 2006, p. 1). In the 12 months prior to the SISFCF interviews, nearly 40 percent of the prisoners displayed symptoms of a mania disorder, about one in five had symptoms of major depression, and some 15 percent had delusions or hallucinations symptomatic of psychoses (James and Glaze 2006, Table 1).

Prisons were not meant to be psychiatric hospitals and, despite improvements in the past several decades, they are ill equipped to be so today. To the contrary, prison can be a toxic environment for people with serious mental health issues. Their limited coping skills make it difficult for them to navigate in this regimented yet dangerous world, and extreme behaviors symptomatic of their illnesses are likely exacerbated by the tension and stress produced by overcrowding. Many of them may stubbornly refuse to follow routine orders. The behavior of some may at times become aggressive, belligerent, and even violent toward both staff and other inmates. Bizarre behavior or withdrawal and passivity may mark them for bullying, manipulation, exploitation, sexual assault, or other forms of victimization.

It is scarcely surprising, then, that the 2004 SISFCF found that prisoners with mental problems were between 33 and 50 percent (state versus federal) more likely to have been charged with a rule violation since their admission, nearly twice as likely to have assaulted someone, and twice as likely to have been injured in a fight than were those without mental problems (James and Glaze 2006, Table 16). The third National Inmate Survey conducted by the Bureau of Justice Statistics as mandated by the Prison Rape Elimination Act of 2003 revealed that, compared to inmates with no mental health problems, those in serious psychological distress were nine times more likely to have been sexually victimized by another inmate in the previous year, and five times more likely to have been victimized by a staff member (Beck et al. 2013, Table 14).

In *Bowring v. Godwin* (551 F.2d 44, 1977), the Fourth Circuit Court of Appeals found there to be no distinction between the right to medical care for physical ills and that for mental ills. In other words, the constitutional right to medical treatment established in *Estelle v. Gamble* (429 U.S. 97, 1976) also includes psychiatric treatment for inmates with serious mental illness. In recognition of a prisoner's right to mental health treatment, all federal prisons and most state prisons are required to provide mental health services to inmates, including screening inmates at intake for mental health problems, providing therapy or counseling by trained mental health professionals, and distributing psychotropic medication. Relatively few of those in need of such services actually receive them, however. Of the nearly 50 percent of state prisoners identified as having a mental problem in the 2004 SISFCF, only one-third reported having received any form of treatment since their admission. Similarly, of the federal prisoners identified as having mental health problems, only one in four had received any treatment since admission. In both state and federal prisons, the most common form of treatment received was prescribed medications (James and Glaze 2006, Table 14).

A somewhat better picture is presented by Wilper et al. (2009, Table 4). Drawing upon the same data, they looked at the treatment of those who had a previously diagnosed mental illness such as schizophrenia or bipolar disorder. Nearly 15 percent of the federal inmates and 25 percent of those in state custody reported a previous diagnosis. Of these inmates, two-thirds had taken medication since admission and about 60 percent had received counseling. So it would seem that prisoners who are seriously ill receive treatment of some kind more frequently than those who *may* have mental health problems but without a previously diagnosed condition. This means, however, that the majority of prisoners displaying symptoms of mental illness and a sizable percentage of those with diagnosed conditions do not receive treatment for their conditions while confined.[8]

Lack of mental health treatment increases the probability that a mentally ill prisoner will be disruptive, and continual disruption may lead to indefinite administrative segregation. A study by the Human Rights Watch (2003, pp. 147–148) found that the mentally ill were disproportionately represented among those in segregation. The study cited testimony in a 1997 case in Iowa, for example, that found that nearly half of the mentally ill inmates in the state penitentiary were in either disciplinary or administrative segregation. In another example, a report by the State of California indicated that nearly 32 percent of prisoners held in administrative segregation across the state during July 2002 were on the mental health caseload.[9]

Being locked in a cell for 23 hours a day with little to do and minimal interaction with others, as is the case in administrative segregation whether it is a supermax prison or a special housing unit within a prison, would be stressful for anybody. Most mental health experts, including those who work in corrections, think it is particularly destructive for those with a mental illness. Prolonged confinement in such conditions will cause them to deteriorate and regress. Those who are prone to depression are apt to become severely depressed and possibly suicidal. The mood swings of those with bipolar disorder may be accentuated. Those prone to psychosis may decompensate and lose touch with reality. For prisoners with mental health issues, segregation in isolation produces a downward spiral whereby their isolation causes them to reproduce the very behaviors that led to their placement in segregation, and those behaviors prolong their stay.

There has been considerable litigation over the years concerning a prisoner's right to treatment for mental illness, and progress has been made, but the process has been slow and frustrated by the growth in the prisoner population. A suit filed in Iowa in 1990, for example, challenging a variety of conditions including treatment of the mentally ill, was not settled until 1997 (Human Rights Watch 2003, p. 48). At that time, the court ordered the Iowa Department of Corrections to develop a plan to correct the constitutional violations. Development of the plan took another two years. The completed plan included construction of a 200-bed special-needs unit for the mentally ill at the Iowa State Penitentiary to begin operation in 2001. Opening of that facility was delayed until 2002 and initially consisted of only 40 beds, the rest to be built later.

The Iowa Department of Corrections later retained a consultant to complete a "systematic study" of the Iowa correctional system. The report was delivered in April 2007 (Durrant Group 2007, Ch.3). The consultants reported that, in 2006, some 40 percent of the prisoner population had a mental illness and the illness was persistent for two-thirds of this group. The ratio of inmates taking psychotropic medication to available psychiatrists on staff was 717:1, compared to the 150:1 ratio recommended by the American Psychiatric Association, and there was an acute shortage of other trained mental health professionals. The Special Needs Unit at the Iowa State Penitentiary had been constructed and housed about 175 inmates, and other special-needs units had been constructed at other institutions. These units, however, mainly provided intensive outpatient treatment and only short-term hospitalization. There were too few psychiatric beds for prisoners at the state psychiatric hospital, so "acute/hospital level care for male offenders is primarily provided in segregation cells. There are no psychiatric beds for female offenders; females who require single cells are mixed with males in IMCC (Iowa Medical and Classification Center) segregation unit" (Durrant Group 2007, pp. 46–47). In other words, 16 years after the suit had been filed there had been some improvements, but treatment of the mentally ill remained poor.

A somewhat better outcome seems to have occurred in Massachusetts. In 2007, following a rash of suicides by mentally ill inmates confined in administrative segregation, the Disabilities Law Center filed suit against the Massachusetts Department of Corrections concerning their policies and practices regarding those with mental health problems. With some persuasion from the judge, the two parties negotiated a private settlement agreement[10] that was approved by the federal district court in 2012. The Massachusetts Department of Corrections agreed to develop a mental health classification system, to integrate mental health professionals into the discipline process, and to establish seven Secure Treatment Units for inmates with a serious mental illness or at risk for deterioration if confined in segregation for a long period of time. Placement in one of these Treatment Units is to be determined by the risk of self-injurious behavior and/or the degree of maladaptive coping. Treatment in the unit is to be provided by mental health professionals and oriented to the individual's needs and learning style. Compliance with the agreement is to be monitored by an expert who is retained by the Disabilities Law Center and who has unrestricted access to the units. At the time the agreement was approved by the court, all seven of the Secure Treatment Units were operational (*DLC v. MDOC*, C.A. 07-10463-MLW, 2012).

Due to the closing of psychiatric hospitals, the rise in the number of prisoners with mental health problems has increased more dramatically than has the overall prisoner population. Correctional administrators have been hard pressed to meet this demand, and prison mental health services, on the whole, are inadequate. Some improvements in treatment and service have been secured through court intervention, especially in cases where the respondents have cooperated, but often this process has been drawn out over long periods of time during which the increased demand has swamped the remedies provided.

D. Programming

Because of the uncertainty of treatment and possible liability if a state does not successfully "treat" a prisoner, courts have been unwilling to recognize a constitutional right to rehabilitative treatment. However, when examining the totality of conditions within an institution, the presence or absence of rehabilitative programs may be considered as a factor in determining if conditions are in violation of the Eighth Amendment, but the lack of such programs is not, in and of itself, a constitutional violation. Thus, if other major defects are corrected, conditions in an institution may be found to be constitutionally permissible even without rehabilitative programs. However, courts have also made it clear that institutions cannot be run in a way that hinders prisoners' attempts at rehabilitation or to avoid physical or mental deterioration (Palmer 2010, p. 222). Judges, it seems, have been less concerned with effective treatment than with having prisons that are morally acceptable (Feeley and Rubin 1998, p. 265).

The dramatic increase in the number of prisoners during the 1980s and 1990s was fueled by a punitive ideology. Offenders came to be defined as incorrigible, and incapacitation displaced rehabilitation as the primary goal of the prison. As one of the leading proponents of the new ideology, James Q. Wilson, put it, "Wicked people exist. Nothing avails except to set them apart from innocent people" (1975, p. 235). Assuming that the punitive rhetoric is indicative of what is happening in practice, more critical scholars claim that prisons have become nothing more than human warehouses (Wacquant 2001; Irwin 2005); even those with more mainstream views wonder "if education and training programs are seen as futile, why should the state spend money on them?" (Rothman 2003, p. 407).

There is evidence, however, that correctional administrators are not fully in agreement with the hardline "law and order" rhetoric, and have not abandoned support for treatment programs. A survey of prison wardens by Cullen et al. (1993) revealed that although wardens view incapacitation as the primary goal of prisons, they rated rehabilitation as the second most important goal. Nor do they see a contradiction between the two. In the minds of most wardens, programming makes for good security, and the majority of them favor expanding education, vocational training, and counseling.

Michelle Phelps (2011) used both staffing data from the *Censuses of State and Adult Correctional Facilities* and inmate participation data from SIFSCF to document trends in several types of prison programs in state prisons between 1974 and 2005. She uncovered several different trends over that 30-year period. Exclusive of teachers, the ratio of inmates to professional staff, for instance, fell from 40 in 1974 to 29 in 2005. By contrast, the ratio of inmates to teachers more than doubled over the same time, rising from 53 in 1974 to 112 in 2005. She concludes that taken together these trends suggest a switch in "rehabilitative" programming over the past 30 years: from education and training to a focus on preparation for release and reentry into the community.

Trends in inmate program participation also differed over time. Programming actually expanded from 1979 through 1990, but not sufficiently to keep up with the number of prisoners, which more than doubled. From 1990 to 2004 there was a sharp decline in inmate participation in educational programs (43 to 27 percent) and a slight decline (by 1 percent) in their participation in vocational programs, consistent with the aforementioned increase in the inmate-to-teacher ratio. Participation in other types of programs did not decline, however; in fact, the percentage of prisoners who reported receiving counseling actually increased by nearly 30 percent between 1991 and 2004. However, the greatest growth was in programs oriented to reentry, such as life skills, community adjustment, job application training, financial planning, and so forth: Between 1991 and 2004, the percentage of inmates having participated in such programs increased from 15 to 25 percent.

Based on these trends, Phelps concluded that

> Despite rapid increases in imprisonment, U.S. prisons did not become "warehouses" devoid of any opportunities for rehabilitation . . . Instead, throughout the entire period under study in this article, programming rates have been quite modest and in most cases fairly consistent across time . . . Only after 1990, fully a decade and a half after the infamous Martinson report (1974), did programming rates show substantial change, and even in this instance, the data suggest that this was more of a shift from academic programs to reentry-related general counseling programs rather than a uniform decline. (2011, pp. 53, 59)

Martinson's report (1974) is indeed infamous, but more because of his sweeping declaration that "nothing works" rather any misrepresentation of the research he reviewed. Other reviews in and around the same time (e.g., Greenberg 1977), while more cautious in their conclusions, nonetheless found few correctional treatment programs that had been successful in reducing recidivism when evaluated by well-designed research. Most of the programs at the time lacked a theoretical base and often were not well implemented. There was, in fact, little rehabilitation in the "rehabilitative era."

Research on "what works" has continued, much of it in Canada, over the past three decades, and there is now an impressive body of knowledge on what treatment modalities are most successful in reducing recidivism and on the characteristics of effective programs (MacKenzie 2006). Briefly put, programs that are the most effective in reducing recidivism employ a cognitive-behavioral treatment modality, target moderate- to high-risk offenders, are directed at criminogenic needs, and are responsive to differences in target populations that may affect their ability to benefit from treatment, such as differences by gender, race, IQ, learning style, and mental illness (Latessa, Smith, and French 2006). There are now valid and reliable instruments to assess offenders' risks and needs (e.g., Gendreau et al. 2010) and to assess the extent to which particular programs have the components to be successful, such as risk/needs assessment, aftercare, and frequent process and outcome evaluations (Lowenkamp, Latessa, and Smith 2006). Hopefully, in the years ahead, more institutions will apply these principles in order to improve prison program effectiveness, and will at the same time offer incentives to increase inmate participation in these programs.

III. Conclusion

In an effort to present a balanced view of conditions in today's prisons, we have presented data drawn from court cases involving abuses of prisoners' rights as well as aggregate data on prison violence, health care, and programming. It is clear that conditions are far from optimal and are in many respects substandard. But the dire predictions of some scholars and critics that the system would be overwhelmed by the increase in numbers and that prisons would become human warehouses in which are staged wars of all against all are without foundation. Although the widespread use of long-term administrative segregation is troublesome and may be unnecessary, there is no question that prisons today are much more orderly and much less violent than they were in the 1970s. Attention to the routine medical and mental health needs of inmates is inadequate, but those with serious needs are now more likely to receive adequate care compared to the care provided in prisons in the past, and for many, the care they now receive in prison is better than what they received outside the walls. Educational programming has declined, but that decline has been balanced by a growth of programming in other areas so that, overall, the level of programs available to inmates has remained relatively stable since the 1970s, as has the level of inmate program participation, which remains modest.

We have argued that prison systems were able to cope with the dramatic rise in prisoner populations for three major reasons. First, overcrowding produced a boom in construction of new facilities that, while coldly efficient in design, increased safety through better physical control and surveillance. Much of the construction was undertaken in response to court decrees ordering reductions in overcrowding or by efforts to avoid such decrees.

Our second reason, judicial intervention, actually began before the rapid buildup of prisoner populations, so constitutional rights for inmates had already been established by the beginning of the era of mass incarceration. Through a veritable tidal wave of litigation, courts across the country in partnership with professional associations established standards in key areas that prison conditions must meet to be constitutionally permissible. While the ability of prisoners to pursue claims in the courts has been greatly weakened by the PLRA, judicial intervention remains a powerful force, as demonstrated recently in California.

The third reason that prison systems have not collapsed under the weight of rising populations is the advent of more professional management. This is, in no small measure, also due to court intervention. Meeting court demands for accountability required a new breed of correctional administrators who were pragmatic, less wed to the ideological divide of custody versus treatment, and committed to managing through the development and implementation of policies and practices rationally related to specific goals. Training in all sectors and at all levels increased and the communication of best practices improved through professional associations and institutes. Research has produced important management tools such as more valid and reliable instruments with which to classify inmates, assess risk and needs, and identify the types and characteristics of programs that are most effective in treating offenders.

Nonetheless, there remains much in our prisons that is undesirable and in need of improvement. Overcrowding may not have caused an upsurge in violence as was feared, but it has undoubtedly had a negative impact on the delivery of medical and mental health services. Although the number of prisoners has begun to decline in the past few years, the federal system and at least 50 percent of the state systems continue to operate above capacity. Steps must be taken to accelerate the decline in numbers and to reduce the large number of those released who subsequently return to prison. Increased use of earned good time is one way to relieve overcrowding, and high-quality programs to facilitate reentry are necessary to reduce recidivism.

Aside from crowded living conditions, individuals who have served prison time are, on average, in worse health than those never incarcerated. This situation presents both an opportunity and a challenge. With some 700,000 prisoners released annually, providing quality health care to those in prison could have a positive impact on public health, and our failure to do so appears to have had the opposite effect. Legislators and the public must be educated to the fact that what happens in prison does not stay in prison. Short-term measures to balance the budget such as having prisoners make co-payments for health care may be counterproductive if they deter sick prisoners from seeking medical treatment, and those released from prison should be targeted for treatment with the expansion of Medicaid under the Affordable Care Act.

Another consideration involves diverting offenders with mental health problems, especially those with serious mental illness, out of the criminal justice system when feasible. Those who must be sent to prison should be housed in secure treatment units where they are treated by mental health professionals and are less likely to be victimized. Under no circumstances should prisoners with serious mental health issues be confined to long-term or indefinite segregation.

The use of long-term administrative segregation, whether it is in a supermax prison or a secure housing unit within a prison, should be greatly reduced. There is no conclusive evidence that administrative segregation has reduced violence and disorder, and there is evidence that long-term isolation and idleness cause mental and physical deterioration. Classification to administrative segregation should involve due process protections (see *Wilkinson v. Austin*, 545 U.S. 209, 2005), periodic reviews of the classification, and stepdown units by which those so classified may have increased programming and privileges while gradually being reintegrated into the general prisoner population.

Finally, confinement conditions might improve with more program opportunities and higher levels of program participation. Good programs not only contribute to lower odds of recidivism but also help to reinforce order and security. Probably no more than half of all prisoners participate in a rehabilitative program, and even program participants are idle for much, if not most, of the day. The cost of adding programs may be reduced by contracting with agencies in surrounding communities, and participation levels may rise with more incentives such as earned good time. If these programs help to reduce recidivism, they may pay for themselves.

NOTES

1. The 1990 Census was the first to include both state and federal correctional facilities. The data are aggregated in different ways in different censuses so that it is not always possible to get data on confinement and community correctional facilities separately. When referring to prisons we use that term or confinement facility; otherwise we refer to all correctional facilities.

2. One such instrument that is widely used is the List of Service Inventory – Revised, a 54 item instrument composed of 10 sub-components that have been demonstrated to measure an offender's risk of recidivism and treatment needs. As the instrument contains both static and dynamic factors, re-assessment at periodic intervals provides a measure of change over time.

3. Useem and Kimball (1989:94) defined a riot as an incident involving 30 or more inmates, lasting 30 minutes or more that resulted in serious injury or significant property damage, and/or in which inmates took hostages or forcibly expelled prison authorities from a section of the institution.

4. The Prison Rape Elimination Act of 2003 (P.L. 108-79; PREA) requires the Bureau of Justice Statistics (BJS) to carry out a comprehensive statistical review and analysis of incidents and effects of prison rape for each calendar year.

5. Rather than release these inmates outright, California has chosen to house them in county jails and has moved some out of state. As Schlanger (2013: 196–215) points out, this may resolve the health care crisis in prisons only to create an even more serious one in the jails.

6. Persistent medical problems included pregnancy at time of admission, diabetes mellitus, persistent heart or kidney problems, persistent hypertension, cancer, stroke or brain injury, paralysis, cirrhosis, arthritis asthma, hepatitis or a sexually transmitted disease.

7. Active medical conditions requiring routine blood tests included cirrhosis, diabetes, HIV, persistent kidney problems, persistent hypertension, and prior myocardial infarction. Serious injuries included broken bones, being knocked unconscious, gunshot or knife wounds, internal injuries and sexual assault.

8. It should be noted, however, that they are more likely to receive treatment while in prison than they were in the community during the 12 months prior to their arrest (James and Glaze, 2006: Table 14; Wilper, et al., 2009: Table 4).

9. The case cited in the report is Goff v. Harper, Findings of Fact and Conclusions of Law, No. 4-90-CV-50365 (S.D. Iowa, June 5, 1997). The California report is California Department of Corrections, Health Care Placement Unit, "Mental Health Adseg/SHU/PSU," population chart created on July 25, 2002.

10. A private settlement agreement differs from a consent decree in that the court is not involved in the negotiation and does not order any relief; it merely approves the agreement. This frees the agreement from the restrictions the Prison Litigation Reform Act placed on prospective relief that is ordered by a court.

REFERENCES

Austin, James, and Patricia Hardyman. 2004. "The Risks and Needs of the Returning Prisoner Population." *Review of Policy Research* 21:13–29.

Berk, Richard A., David Rauma, Sheldon L. Messinger, and Thomas F. Cooley. 1981. "A Test of the Stability of Punishment Hypothesis: The Case of California, 1851–1970." *American Sociological Review* 46:805–829.

Beck, Allen J., Marcus Berzofsky, Rachel Caspar, and Christopher Krebs. 2013. *Sexual Victimization in Prisons and Jails Reported By Inmates, 2011–12*. Washington, DC: Bureau of Justice Statistics.

Blomberg, Thomas G., and Karol Lucken. 2000. *American Penology: A History of Control*. New York: Aldine de Gruyter.

Blumstein, Alfred, Jacqueline Cohen, and Daniel Nagin. 1977. "The Dynamics of a Homeostatic Punishment Process." *Journal of Criminal Law and Criminology* 67:317–354.

Bowker, Lee H. 1980. *Prison Victimization*. New York: Elsevier.

Briggs, Chad S., Jody L. Sundt, and Thomas C. Castellano. 2003. "The Effect of Supermaximum Security Prisons on Aggregate Levels of Institutional Violence." *Criminology* 41:1341–1378.

Bureau of Justice Statistics. 1986. *State and Federal Prisoners, 1925–1985.* Washington, DC: Bureau of Justice Statistics.

Cahalan, Margaret W. 1986. *Historical Corrections Statistics in the United States: 1850–1984.* Washington, DC: Bureau of Justice Statistics.

Carroll, Leo. 1974. *Hacks, Blacks and Cons: Race Relations in a Maximum Security Prison.* Lexington, MA: Lexington Books.

Carson, E. Ann, and William J. Sabol. 2012. *Prisoners in 2011.* Washington, DC: Bureau of Justice Statistics.

Centers for Disease Control, "Diseases and Conditions." Accessed May 17, 2013, at http://www.cdc.gov/diseasesconditions.

Crouch, Ben M., and James W. Marquart. 1989. *An Appeal to Justice: Litigated Reform of Texas Prisons.* Austin: University of Texas Press.

Cullen, Francis T., Edward J. Latessa, Velmer S. Burton, and Lucien X. Lombardo. 1993. "The Correctional Orientation of Prison Wardens: Is the Rehabilitative Ideal Supported?" *Criminology* 31:69–92.

Durrant Group. 2007. *State of Iowa Systemic Study for the State Correctional System.* Des Moines, IA: The Durrant Group.

Feeley, Malcolm M., and Edward L. Rubin. 1998. *Judicial Policy Making and the Modern State: How the Courts Reformed America's Prisons.* New York: Cambridge University Press.

Gendreau, Paul, Donald A. Andrews, and Yvette Theriault. 2010. *Correctional Program Assessment Inventory—2010.* St. John, New Brunswick: University of New Brunswick Press.

Gerard, Roy E. 1991. "The Ten Commandments of Unit Management." *Corrections Today* 53:32–36.

Greenberg, David. F. 1977. "The Correctional Effects of Corrections: A Survey of Evaluations." In *Corrections and Punishment*, edited by David F. Greenberg. Newbury Park, CA: Sage.

Hagan, John. 1995. "The Imprisoned Society: Time Turns a Classic on Its Head." *Sociological Forum* 10:519–525.

Haney, Craig. 2008. "A Culture of Harm: Taming the Dynamics of Cruelty in Supermax Prisons." *Criminal Justice and Behavior* 35:956–984.

Hanson, Roger, and Henry W. K. Daley. 1994. *Challenging Conditions of Confinement in Prisons and Jails: A Report on Section 1983 Litigation.* Washington, DC: Bureau of Justice Statistics.

Human Rights Watch. 2003. *Ill-Equipped: U.S. Prisons and Offenders with Mental Illness.* New York: Human Rights Watch.

Irwin, John. 2005. *The Warehouse Prison: Disposal of the New Dangerous Class.* Los Angeles: Roxbury Publishing Co.

Jacobs, James B. 1977. *Stateville: The Penitentiary in Mass Society.* Chicago: University of Chicago Press.

James, Doris, and Lauren Glaze. 2006. *Mental Health Problems of Prison and Jail Inmates.* Washington, DC: Bureau of Justice Statistics.

Kupers, Terry A., Theresa Dronent, Margaret Winter, James Austin, Lawrence Kelly, William Cartier, Timothy J. Morris, Stephen F. Scanlon, Emmitt L. Sparkman, Parveen Kumar, Leonard C. Vincent, Jim Norris, Kim Nagel, and Jennifer McBride. 2009. "Beyond Supermax Administrative Segregation: Mississippi's Experience Rethinking Prison

Classification and Creating Alternative Mental Health Programs." *Criminal Justice and Behavior* 36:1037–1050.

Kurki, Leena, and Norval Morris. 2001. "The Purposes, Practices, and Problems of Supermax Prisons." *Crime and Justice* 28:385–424.

Latessa, Edward J., Paula Smith, and Sheila French. 2006. "The Theory of Effective Correctional Intervention: Empirical Status and Future Direction." In *Taking Stock: The Status of Criminological Theory*, edited by Francis T. Cullen, John P. Wright, and Kristie R. Blevins. New Brunswick, NJ: Transaction.

Levinson, Robert B. 1999. *Unit Management in Prisons and Jails.* Alexandria, VA: American Correctional Association.

Lowenkamp, Christopher T., Edward J. Latessa, and Paula Smith. 2006. "Does Correctional Program Quality Really Matter? The Impact of Adhering to the Principles of Effective Intervention." *Criminology and Public Policy* 5:201–220.

Mackenzie, Doris L. 2006. *What Works in Corrections: Reducing the Criminal Activities of Offenders and Delinquents.* New York: Cambridge University Press.

Martinson, Robert. 1974. "What Works? Questions and Answers About Prison Reform." *The Public Interest* 35:22–54.

Mears, Daniel P., and Jamie Watson. 2006. "Towards a Fair and Balanced Assessment of Supermax Prisons." *Justice Quarterly* 23:232–270.

Mears, Daniel P., and Jennifer L. Castro. 2006. "Wardens' Views on the Wisdom of Supermax Prisons." *Crime and Delinquency* 52:398–431.

Mumola, Christopher J. 2007. *Medical Causes of Death in State Prisons, 2001–2004.* Washington, DC: Bureau of Justice Statistics.

National Center for Health Statistics. 2012. "QuickStats: Suicide and Homicide Rates—United States—2009." Accessed May 17, 2013, at http://www.cdc.gov/mmwr/preview/mmwrhtml/mm6128a8.htm?.

Noonan, Margaret E. 2012. *Mortality in Local Jails and State Prisons, 2000–2010—Statistical Tables.* Washington, DC: Bureau of Justice Statistics.

Palmer, John W. 2010. *Constitutional Rights of Prisoners*, 9th ed. Cincinnati: Anderson Publishing.

Patterson, Evelyn J. 2013. "The Dose–Response of Time Served in Prison on Mortality: New York State, 1989–2003." *American Journal of Public Health* 103:523–528.

Phelps, Michelle S. 2011. "Rehabilitation in the Punitive Era: The Gap Between Rhetoric and Reality in U.S. Prison Programs." *Law and Society Review* 45:33–68.

Rothman, David J. 2003. "The Crime of Punishment." In *Punishment and Social Control*, edited by Thomas Blomberg and Stanley Cohen. New York: Aldine de Gruyter.

Schlanger, Margo. 2013. "*Plata v. Brown* and Realignment: Jails, Prisons, Courts, and Politics." *Harvard Civil Rights-Civil Liberties Law Review (CR-CL)* 48:166–215.

Sourcebook of Criminal Justice Statistics. 2010. http://www.albany.edu/sourcebook.

Spaulding, Anne C., Ryan M. Seals, Victoria A. McCallum, Sebastian D. Perez, Amanda K. Brzozowski, and N. Kyle Steenland. 2011. "Prisoner Survival Inside and Outside of the Institution: Implications for Healthcare Planning." *American Journal of Epidemiology* 173:479–487.

Stephen, James J. 1987. *Census of State Adult Correctional Facilities, 1984.* Washington, DC: Bureau of Justice Statistics.

Stephen, James J. 2008. *Census of State and Federal Correctional Facilities, 2005.* Washington, DC: Bureau of Justice Statistics.

Sundt, Jody L., Thomas C. Castellano, and Chad S. Briggs. 2008. "The Sociopolitical Context of Prison Violence and its Control: A Case Study of Supermax and its Effect in Illinois." *The Prison Journal* 88:94–122.

Useem, Bert, and Peter Kimball. 1989. *States of Siege: U.S. Prison Riots, 1971–1986.* New York: Oxford University Press.

Useem, Bert, and Anne Morrison Piehl. 2008. *Prison State: The Challenge of Mass Incarceration.* New York: Cambridge University Press.

Wacquant, Loic. 2001. "Deadly Symbiosis: When Ghetto and Prison Meet and Mesh." *Punishment and Society* 3:95–133.

Wilper, Andrew P., Steffie Woolhandler, J. Wesley Boyd, Karen E. Lasser, Danny McCormick, David H. Bor, and David U. Himmelstein. 2009. "The Health and Health Care of U.S. Prisoners: Results of a Nationwide Survey." *American Journal of Public Health* 99:666–672.

Wilson, James Q. 1975. *Thinking About Crime.* New York: Random House.

Cases Cited

Bounds v. Smith, 430 U. S. 817 (1977).

Bowring v. Godwin, 551 F. 2D 44 (4th CIR. 1977).

Brown v. Plata, 131 S. CT. 1910 (2011).

Cooper v. Pate, 378 U.S. 546 (1964).

Cruz v. Beto, 405 U. S. 319 (1972).

Disability Law Center v. Massachusetts Department of Corrections, C.A. NO. 07-10463- MLW (D. C. MA 2012).

Estelle v. Gamble, 429 U.S. 97 (1976).

Gates v. Collier, 390 F. SUPP. 492 (N. D. MISS. 1975).

Guthrie v. Evans, C. A. 73-3068 (S. D. GA. 1973).

Holt v. Sarver, 309 F. SUPP. 362 (E. D. ARK. 1970).

Johnson v. Avery, 393 U. S. 483 (1969).

Jones v. North Carolina Prisoners' Labor Union Inc., 433 U. S. 119 (1977).

Lee v. Washington, 390 U. S. 333 (1968).

Morris v. Travisono, 310 F. SUPP. 857 (D.R.I. 1970).

O'Lone v. The Estate of Shabazz, 482 U. S. 342 (1987).

Palmigiano v. Garrahy, 443 F. SUPP. 956 (D.R.I. 1977).

Procunier v. Martinez, 416 U. S. 396 (1974).

Pugh v. Locke, 406 F. SUPP. 318 (M. D. ALA. 1976).

Ramos v. Lamm, 485 F. SUPP. 122 (D. COLO., 1979).

Rhodes v. Chapman, 452 U. S. 337 (1981).

Ruffin v. Commomwealth, 62 VA. (21 GRATT.) 790 (1871).

Rufo v. Inmates of Suffolk County Jail, 502 U. S. 367 (1992).

Ruiz v. Estelle, 503 F. SUPP. 1265 (S. D. TEX.1980).

Sandin v. Conner, 515 U. S. 472 (1995).

Wilkinson v. Austin, 545 U.S. 209 (2005).

Wilson v. Seiter, 501 U.S. 294 (1991).

Wolff v. McDonnell, 418 U. S. 539 (1974).

CHAPTER 4

···

EXPLORING IMPRISONMENT
ACROSS CROSS-NATIONAL
CONTEXTS

···

PAUL MAZEROLLE, JOHN RYNNE,
AND SAMARA MCPHEDRAN

SINCE the 1980s, rising rates of incarceration in many Western countries have received significant research attention and have invited an expansion of analyses on comparative contexts with respect to the use of imprisonment. Nations with similar crime rates can have dissimilar incarceration rates. Incarceration rates, to a degree, therefore signify the presence of different policy choices rather than "different behaviors" (Raphael 2009; Lynch and Pridemore 2011; Mackenzie 2012). Those policy choices cannot be viewed in isolation. Every policy setting around incarceration reflects, and is affected by, a diverse range of macro-level factors, including social and cultural context, prevailing political ideologies, and concepts of the relationship between the state and the individual, as well as the broader economic climate within a given nation at a given time (e.g., Caplow and Simon 1999; Jacobs and Kleban 2003; Mauer 2003; Lynch and Pridemore 2011).

The current essay explores cross-national contexts in the use of imprisonment as a penal policy. The essay

- provides an overview of how international comparisons of incarceration rates are typically used within discourse;
- presents incarceration figures from a selection of countries with accompanying discussions of methodological and measurement challenges; and
- explores how similar incarceration policies and practices across different countries embody similar macro-level elements of managerialism and risk assessment, using the rise of private prisons and "supermax" incarceration as examples.

A detailed description of the complex interactions between different macro-level domains, and the micro-level components within them (e.g., individual support for the use of incarceration as a function of education or political inclinations), far exceeds the scope of the current essay. Briefly, though, factors such as a nation's historical and legal traditions, demographic composition including racial and ethnic profiles (Carmichael 2005; Zhang, Maxwell, and Vaughn 2009), drug policies (Riveland 1999; Arditti and McClintock 2002; Bewley-Taylor Hallam, and Allen 2009), philosophical propensity toward criminalizing certain activities (Brownlee 1998; Brayne 2013), levels of social and economic inequality (Carmichael 2005), perceived or actual public support for the use of imprisonment (Wilkins and Pease 1987; Zimring 2001; Nagin et al. 2006; Piquero and Steinberg 2010), and perceived or actual fears about public safety (Cook and Lane 2009; Lappi-Seppala 2011; Shannon and Uggen 2012) have all been commonly implicated as playing a role in the use of incarceration across nation-states. However, this does not necessarily imply that variations in these factors suffice to explain differences in the use of incarceration within and between countries. Also, the degree of empirical support linking each of these factors with incarceration rates and practices is variable, and the oft-cited role of public support as a driver for incarceration, in particular, has been questioned (Van Kesteren 2009). Alongside these considerations, pragmatic questions such as available prison capacity, changes in prison population sizes, and fiscal ability for expansion or creation of new facilities can also contribute to the use of (or inclination away from) incarceration within and between different countries (D'Alessio and Stolzenberg 1997; Ruddell and Mays 2007).

A majority of studies into incarceration rates, and factors contributing to those rates, focus on the United States. In terms of the much smaller body of comparative research that seeks to quantify and explore differences between countries, there is a tendency to consider why the United States has higher rates of incarceration than other countries and to intensively examine US practices that may explain observed incarceration rates in that particular country as well as "set it apart" from other nations (Cavadino and Dignan 2006). While this type of approach can provide useful insights, it has also been suggested that different countries' use of incarceration may reflect the presence of fundamentally different conceptual frameworks regarding imprisonment, making it difficult to translate understandings and observations from one country to another (Sparks 2001). A complementary argument, however, is that *similar* conceptual frameworks may be found in different countries, which can contribute to explaining why similar practices and policies around incarceration have been adopted across a range of different countries. This does not negate the principle articulated by Sparks (2001); rather, it extends that principle by allowing for the presence of multiple different conceptual drivers of incarceration within and between different countries, which may or may not be consistent with one another.

The interrelated sociocultural, political, and economic domains within a society not only affect rates of incarceration (e.g., through their relationship to sentencing policies) but also have bearing on policies and practices around the actual nature of incarceration itself (i.e., how prisons are operated and how prison inmates are housed). From a global perspective, certain striking examples act as a helpful focal point for broader debate about macro-level factors and conceptual frameworks influencing the use of imprisonment and may facilitate comparisons between different nations. Two particularly illustrative examples are the privatization of prisons and the rise of super maximum security ("supermax") facilities. In these two examples, an array of different sociocultural, political, and/or economic considerations converge around the broad and often overlapping themes of *managerialism* (i.e., the ethos that a society centers around organizations, not citizens), and *risk and risk assessment*. These themes have received relatively little attention as drivers of incarceration practices, except in discourse concerning the "new penology" (Feeley and Simon 1992), a conceptual framework that emphasizes the rise of "risk-based" terminology and systems-analysis approaches to managing prison populations and that has often been cited as a correlate of practices such as mandatory sentencing (see Matthews 2005 for a critique). However, recognizing the limitations and criticisms of this paradigm (e.g., Cheliotis 2006; Cliquennois 2013), the current essay also considers these themes from a broader social theory perspective of "new public management" (e.g., Gruening 2001), which operates at a "whole of society" level that, in turn, can affect decisions around penal practice.

I. INTERNATIONAL INCARCERATION RATE COMPARISONS

Comparative rates of incarceration are commonly used as a proxy for assessing international differences in "punitiveness" (Pease 1994). Given the often contentious nature of the debate around punitiveness and what constitutes "appropriate" penalization for breaking legal rules, incarceration rates commonly illuminate politicized overtones—Is one country more "punitive" than another, and, if so, is this an indictment of its broader values? Are high incarceration rates, relative to some other country or countries, a sign that a nation should shift its policies concerning the use of incarceration? If a country has low incarceration rates, does that mean its imprisonment policies would produce the same low rates in another country, or should more general questions of social and justice policy be addressed to produce low incarceration rates? However, a realistic appraisal of comparative imprisonment rates is simply that they provide a more or less "objective" indicator that different countries do indeed have different observed uses of imprisonment. Cross-national rate comparisons do not in themselves answer these deeper questions about the nature of, or reasons for, incarceration, given they provide only a simple metric about the extent to which incarceration is used. However, they do pave the way for a far more careful examination of why certain countries may have different incarceration rates (or, indeed, similar rates) and how such differences may have arisen.

A useful element in understanding international variation in the use of incarceration is consideration of factors that do *not* provide a satisfactory explanation for intercountry differences. Arguably the most important of these factors is actual crime rates. While countries with higher rates of violent crime (and/or that treat certain crimes as extremely "serious") in particular may have higher rates of incarceration than countries with lower rates of the same type of crime, there is little evidence to support the possibility of a direct relationship between crime rates and incarceration rates (e.g., Mauer 1995; Sprott and Doob 1998; Neopolitan 2001). Incarceration rates can change (typically rise) markedly in the absence of matching changes (rises) in crime rates, and rises in incarceration rates in various countries have not been compellingly linked with corresponding rates of decline in crime (which would be expected, if there was a direct relationship between crime rates and incarceration rates; Subramanian and Shames 2013).

Nor does the efficacy of incarceration as a crime reduction (or prevention) measure appear to satisfactorily explain differences in incarceration rates between countries. There is little evidence from any country to suggest that, among a variety of available policy options, incarceration is the most effective response to criminal behavior. Rather, a wide range of incarceration rates are documented in different countries where there exists similar evidence around the efficacy or otherwise of incarceration as a crime reduction measure (whether through deterrence, incapacitation, or both).

Recent estimates suggest that there are around 10.2 million people incarcerated worldwide, with around half of those in the United States, China, and Russia. When population size is taken into account, the highest incarceration rate is found in the United States at around 716 persons per 100,000, while a number of countries report incarceration rates of less than 100 persons per 100,000 (Walmsley 2013). Regarding international comparisons of trends in the use of incarceration over time, although time-series data should be viewed with due care, there is no consistent pattern between countries.

It should be noted that population size (both general and prison) influences the observed figures. A small change in prison population numbers in a country with a small population may produce a striking increase in apparent incarceration rates over time, while the same change in numbers in a country with a much larger population will produce little appearance of change over time. Also, the use of only two time points to establish a "trend" merits interpretive caution. Nonetheless, it is apparent that there is no global consistency in incarceration trends in the 10-year period examined. Irrespective of whether the change in number or rate is considered, some countries have experienced strong increases in their prison population, others have undergone declines, and others have remained relatively stable over time. Table 4.1 provides an overview of incarceration rates per 100,000 persons in the general population, over time, across a number of different countries. Particular emphasis is given to industrialized nations, to facilitate later comparisons.

A noteworthy aspect of international incarceration rate comparisons is that, while female incarceration as a proportion of the total prison population is typically low, countries with very different overall rates of incarceration may nonetheless have similar proportions of females imprisoned (Table 4.2). For example, while Australia, Finland, and the United States have strikingly different overall incarceration rates, they have similar—and comparatively higher—proportions of females among the total prison population, relative to other nations. Where time-series data about female prison population numbers are available, they reveal—in keeping with overall incarceration figures—inconsistent trends (Walmsley 2012). Nor are trends in female imprisonment within a particular country necessarily consistent with overall trends in that country. Reasons cited for international differences in female incarceration typically include differing gender norms and gender role definitions and expectations (and differences in how the justice system responds to women), as well as different levels of "social control" exerted over women, with lower levels of control linked by some to higher incarceration levels (Heidensohn and Silvestri 2012).

Differences in the types of crimes for which females, relative to males, are incarcerated have also been noted; females are typically less likely to be incarcerated for violent crimes, for instance, and more likely to be incarcerated for drug-related crimes (which may again reflect different countries' approaches to drug criminalization; e.g., Mauer, Potler, and Wolf 1999; Chesney-Lind 2002; Johnson 2004). Collectively, these figures point to the need for gender disaggregation when trying to understand factors driving imprisonment (Pantazis and Gordon 1997; Heimer 2000; Gustafson 2009).

Table 4.1. Comparative use of incarceration between selected countries, over time

Country	Numberª	Numberᵇ	Rateª	Rateᵇ	Change in number (%)	Change in rate (%)
England and Wales	74,452	84,430	141	148	13.4	5.0
N/Ireland	1,220	1,851	70	101	51.7	44.3
Scotland	6,569	7,855	129	147	19.6	14.0
Belgium	9,253	12,126	89	108	31.0	21.3
France	55,382	62,443	93	98	12.7	5.4
Germany	81,176	64,379	98	79	−20.7	−19.4
Netherlands	16,239	13,749	100	82	−15.3	−18.0
Switzerland	4,987	6,599	68	82	32.3	20.6
Hungary	16,700	18,388	165	186	10.1	12.7
Greece	8,500	12,479	80	111	46.8	38.8
Italy	56,574	64,835	100	106	14.6	6.0
Russia	864,590	681,600	606	475	−21.2	−21.6
Poland	83,113	83,610	218	217	0.6	−0.5
Lithuania	9,217	9,729	266	329	5.6	23.7
Australia	22,492	29,383	115	130	30.6	13.0
New Zealand	5,881	8,597	155	192	46.2	23.9
United States	2,033,331	2,239,751	701	716	10.2	2.1
Canada	36,024	40,544	116	118	12.5	1.7
Brazil	284,989	54,8003	160	274	92.3	71.3
Japan	67,255	64,932	53	51	−3.5	−3.8
Denmark	3,439	4,091	64	73	19.0	14.1
Finland	3,617	3,134	70	58	−13.4	−17.1
Sweden	6,506	6,364	73	67	−2.2	−8.2

Note: Years for which data are available differ between countries, and the most recent year of data may not be the closest year to the year of publication.
ª Published in 2003.
ᵇ Published in 2013.
Adapted from Walmsley (2003) and Walmsley (2013).

II. METHODOLOGICAL LIMITATIONS TO CONDUCTING RESEARCH ON CROSS-CULTURAL DIFFERENCES IN INCARCERATION

It is unquestionable that incarceration rates vary dramatically between different countries and, indeed, within countries, especially among those countries with a "federated" system of states that may each set its own policies around incarceration. However, achieving perfectly matched comparisons across countries is subject to significant challenges. Changing data collection practices and standards, for instance, can dramatically change the way in

Table 4.2. Cross–country variation in female imprisonment, as a proportion of total prison population

Country	Number	Proportion of total prison population (%)
England and Wales	4,060	4.7
Ireland	44	2.6
Scotland	449	5.6
Belgium	419	4.0
France	2,411	3.5
Germany	3,869	5.6
Netherlands	731	6.1
Switzerland	324	5.3
Hungary	1,033	6.3
Greece	554	4.9
Italy	2,808	4.2
Russia	59,200	7.8
Poland	2,529	3.1
Lithuania	421	4.6
Australia	2,028	7.0
New Zealand	499	5.9
United States of America	201,200	8.8
Canada	1,971	5.1
Brazil	35,596	6.9
Japan	5,305	7.1
Denmark	179	4.4
Finland	228	7.1
Sweden	390	5.8

Adapted from Walmsley (2012).

which a particular nation's use of incarceration may appear "on paper," as can the availability and reliability of population estimates used for calculation of rates. However, three key concepts merit attention when quantifying incarceration; counting rules, the relative influence of remand (i.e., bail) and sentenced populations, and admissions and the length of detention (Young and Brown 1993).

Of these, the impact that counting rules can have on producing the appearance of intercountry variations in recorded incarceration use is a relatively simple concept; the way in which a particular country defines incarceration, and measures its incarcerated population, will necessarily dictate the level of incarceration recorded in that country. Examples of intercountry differences include whether all persons in detention or only adult persons are counted as "incarcerated," whether all persons incarcerated or only those who have been sentenced (relative to being held on remand pending trial/sentencing) are defined as being incarcerated, and whether all forms of incarceration (penal and psychiatric) are included. The particular metric chosen for quantifying incarceration can also influence observed rates; for example, measures of "admissions" (i.e., people entering prison during a particular time period) may give a different estimate of prison use, relative to indicators of the total "population" (the number of people in prison at a given point in time); one metric reflects the influence of custodial sentencing practices while the other is more strongly impacted by average sentence length (see Young and Brown [1993] for a more detailed discussion).

Practices around remand can also impact observed rates of incarceration. Aside from intercountry variations in the definition of "the population in remand" and "the sentenced population," changes in remand practices over time can create the appearance of variation in incarceration figures within a particular country, if the population held in custody on remand is counted in overall incarceration figures (Young and Brown 1993). Variations within a country over time may not accurately reflect any changes in the use of incarceration within sentencing practices but may nonetheless create the appearance that a particular nation has experienced substantial change in its use of incarceration as a punitive measure. Similarly, variations between countries may not reflect differences in the use of incarceration within sentencing practices but may instead demonstrate the impact of differential pretrial/pre-sentencing practices. The difficulty of obtaining incarceration data which disentangles these groups (pre-sentenced and sentenced), and the limits this can impose on analyses, have been discussed elsewhere (Hucklesby 2009; Wan et al. 2013).

III. The Role of Sentencing Practices

Sentencing practices deserve particular attention, as both a methodological consideration when considering variations in incarceration use and as an explanatory factor underlying international variations in incarceration rates. Sentencing practices—for example, mandatory custodial sentences for certain crimes and mandatory minimum sentence lengths—significantly affect both the number of admissions to prisons and the duration of an individual's stay in prison, which have the collective effect of increasing total incarceration figures (e.g., Young and Brown 1993; Lynch 1998; Freiberg and Ross 1999; Spelman 2009). From a methodological perspective, in considering intercountry variation, it is important to identify as far as possible the individual contribution each of these factors makes to observed incarceration rates; however, such data may not be routinely collected or made available at the national level and may also be affected by different counting rules.

From the perspective of *explaining* international variations, there is ample evidence demonstrating relationships between higher incarceration rates and "harsher" sentencing practices that characteristically incorporate mandatory sentencing and minimum sentence length components (e.g., Sorensen and Stemen 2002; Nicholson-Crotty 2004, but see also Zhang, Maxwell, and Vaughn 2009). In short, such practices—which in various countries (such as the United States, United Kingdom, and Australia) are increasingly set out in legislation rather than left as a matter for judicial discretion—are likely to incarcerate more people, for longer periods, leading to higher overall numbers of people incarcerated. There is a degree of evidence that when different sentencing practices, as well as crime type and conviction likelihood, are controlled for, then many intercountry differences in incarceration rates are ameliorated (Lynch and Pridemore 2011).

However, this begs the question: What drives different sentencing practices across different jurisdictions? Generally, political factors are involved, such as a prevailing ideology within a particular governing party toward "get tough" policies, or perceived public (and/ or media) support for implementing those policies (or both) (e.g., Shichor 1997; Brownlee 1998; Jerre 2014). However, political responses to crime can emerge in response to a perceived crisis or change to social order and conditions. Indeed, Garland (2001) has observed that changes in cultural conditions related to attitudes toward crime coupled with structural changes related to increases in rates of poverty and urban decline can foster changes toward punitive penal practices. Others have found that levels of welfare spending as well as institutional arrangements and structures (e.g., centralized versus diffused arrangements) can inform variations in incarceration rates within the United States and across countries (Savelsberg 1994; Sutton 2000)

The tendency to frame policies favoring incarceration in political terms frequently invokes "party-based" explanations for national differences in incarceration policies, highlighting differences in sentencing and incarceration-related policy positions between right- and left-wing political parties, for example. This approach overlooks comparable sets of policies that have been adopted in different countries under governing parties from different "sides" of the political divide. Also, it does not take into account that policy decisions can often remain in place through various changes in government. This consistency and continuity bespeaks a need to examine systemic, rather than strictly political, factors underlying incarceration policies and practices.

IV. SYSTEMIC FACTORS CONTRIBUTING TO CROSS-NATIONAL DIFFERENCES IN INCARCERATION POLICIES AND PRACTICES

This section focuses primarily on incarceration practices[1] in industrialized democracies with a common law heritage (e.g., the United Kingdom, Australia, Canada, and the United States). These countries were selected to facilitate comparisons and to reflect the concept that countries that are "more similar" tend to have "more similar" use of incarceration (although there are certainly exceptions to this). This approach also recognizes the common practice of "policy transfer" between such countries, whereby policies from one country are "picked up" and adopted in another country, often with very few adjustments (e.g., Dolowitz and Marsh 1996; Stone 2001). Two key systemic issues are considered: "managerialism" and a "culture of risk assessment." These are explored through analysis of two striking similarities in those countries' incarceration policies and practices: privatization of prisons and the rise of the supermax facility.

"Managerialism" has been given a variety of definitions, depending on the context in which it is invoked. For the purpose of this discussion, the term is used to refer to the expansion of what have traditionally been corporate (private-sector) ideals and techniques such as cost-efficiency and profitability, accountability and performance targets, and centralized decision-making bodies (at the senior management level) into other sectors (including the public sector). It is also used to capture the ideological premise that a range of social, economic, and political challenges can be resolved through application of particular management practices (Cunliffe 2009), irrespective of the exact nature and setting of those challenges.

A "culture of risk assessment" in this context denotes the widespread adoption, across many sectors, of processes of evaluating and ranking potential risks (financial, human wellbeing, or otherwise) that may be associated with a particular activity or decision. Although associated with "offender risk assessment" (i.e., assessing the level of threat posed by a particular offender on measures such as likelihood of causing harm to others), the culture of risk assessment is a far broader concept that applies risk assessment to all aspects of organizational or institutional practice. The term "culture of risk assessment" is also used in the current context to identify the spread of, and emphasis given to, "risk-based terminology" within public discourse (e.g., Furedi 2009), irrespective of whether that discourse is accompanied by or grounded in the application of any technical risk assessment processes. There are close connections between managerialism and a culture of risk assessment, which have been noted elsewhere (e.g., Phillips 2011).

A. Private Prisons

Across the globe, the delivery of services to the custodial sector by nongovernment providers occurs in various forms including financing and constructing prisons; management, staffing, and operation of prisons; and the provision of specific services such as health care, prisoner rehabilitation, and education programs (Kyle 2013; Mennicken 2013; Volokh 2014). Accordingly, a single definition of private prisons can be problematic. For this discussion, a private prison is defined as one in which the state tenders contracts for the partial or total delivery of custodial services that include the design, construction, finance, and management of the prison or parts thereof (Harding 2001).

The emergence of contemporary private adult custodial facilities commenced in earnest in 1984, when Corrections Corporation of America was awarded a contract from the US Immigration and Naturalization Service to design, construct, finance, and operate a Houston detention center (Mattera, Khan, and Nathan 2003). From this point, privatization spread throughout other American states; Australia (Borallon Queensland 1990); UK (The Wolds 1992);[2] Scotland (HMP Kilmarnock March 1999); the Netherlands Antilles (Koraal Specht prison, Curacao 1999); New Zealand (Auckland Central Remand Prison 2000);[3] Canada (Central North Correctional Centre, Ontario 2001); and South Africa (Manguang maximum security prison, Bloemfontein 2001) (Prison Privatization Report International 2000; Goyer 2001; Harding 2001; Moore, Burton, and Hannah-Moffat 2003). Currently, 12 countries have some form of private prison involvement in adult custodial corrections (see Table 4.3). The United States leads the world with the most private prisons and prisoners held in those facilities (137,220 prisoners representing 8.7 percent of the total US prison population; Carson 2014). International comparisons of rates or percentages of prisoners held in private facilities show Australia has 19 percent (Productivity Commission 2013), followed by Scotland (17 percent), England and Wales (14 percent), New Zealand (11 percent), and South Africa (4 percent) (Mason 2013).

Initially, private prisons predominantly occurred in Anglophone countries with similar systems of government, criminal justice, and custodial punishment. Despite these similarities, the reasons for introducing privatization, as well as its delivery modes and controversies,

Table 4.3. International private prisons 2014

Country	Number of Prisons	Contract Type	Features
Australia	8 (1 under tender)	Varies DCFM 15–25 years	Varies depending on contract. Private operation including all security functions in some cases.
Brazil	17	State owned	State funds construction, retains ownership and appoints warden and deputy. Private sector provides guards, in-prison and rehabilitation services renewed every five years.
Chile	10	BOO	State responsible for custodial services and prisoner finances.
	2	20-year lease back contracts. State owned and leased	Private sector operates prison including custodial functions.
England and Wales	14	Varies DCFM 15–25 year contracts	Varies depending on contract. Private operation including all security functions in some cases.
France	40 (as at 2009)	BOO Hybrid model	Warden, prison security, administration, legal assistance, and health care government controlled.
Germany	3	BOO 20- to 25-year lease back	State owns prisons and responsible for custodial services. Purchases private ancillary services.
Holland		Hybrid model	State owns prisons and responsible for custodial services. Purchases private ancillary services.
Hungary	2	BOM 15 year	State owns prisons and responsible for custodial services. Purchases private ancillary services.
Japan	7	2 x BOM; 20-year lease back to government. Five existing facilities outsourced	Public sector responsible as warden and for prisoner discipline. Private sector staff governed by same code as public sector staff.
New Zealand	2	DCFM 25-year lease back	Private operation including all security functions in some cases.

Table 4.3. Continued

Country	Number of Prisons	Contract Type	Features
Scotland	2	DCFM 25-year lease back	Varies depending on contract. Private operation including all security functions in some cases.
South Korea	1	BOO	State provides 90% of the operating costs. Private partner provides remaining 10% and runs the prison.
United States	14 FBP, 31 States have private prisons or jails	Varies DCFM	Varies depending on contract. Private operation including all security functions in some cases.

Note: DCFM = design, construct, finance and manage; BOO = build, own, operate; BOM = build, own, manage; FBP = Federal Bureau of Prisons.

vary considerably. Harding (2001) proposes that the challenges correctional agencies across the world were confronted with can be summarized in six catalysts that strongly influenced the reintroduction of private prisons (albeit with considerable variation in the extent to which each catalyst influenced individual jurisdiction's decisions). These catalysts include

> a) exponential increases in incarcerated populations, b) overcrowding in federal court intervention, c) legal and political inhibitions upon capital expenditure by governments, d) concern about recurrent costs, e) growing impatience with the perceived obstructionism of unionised labour, and f) some concern for regime improvement. (Harding 2001, p. 269)

Private prisons were promoted from the 1980s onward as a means of improving effectiveness and efficiency in comparison to that which currently existed. These developments also are a reflection of the growing managerialism ethos within the public sector at that time. In addition, this narrative of effectiveness and efficiency fits within a risk management framework, as a means to reduce perceptions of cost-inefficiency and financial risk associated with the traditional "state-run" prison model.

Despite the varying micro-level factors across different countries that have introduced private prisons, their changing political and correctional landscapes have been driven by similar pressures, which have led to the goal of managing prisons in the most cost-effective and efficient means possible (i.e., economic managerialism). By the late 1980s, prison systems across the Anglophone countries were under extraordinary pressure. Policies that emphasized being "tough on crime," waging the "war on drugs," and making changes to sentencing patterns following legislation like the "three strikes" rule drove increases in prison populations (Blumstein and Beck 1999; Caplow and Simon, 1999). Coupled with the social restructuring of prisons via deinstitutionalization of the mentally ill, governments were under considerable pressure to alleviate the problems of prisoner overcrowding and to do it quickly and efficiently (Logan 1990; Caplow and Simon 1999; Hinds 2002; Scottish Executive 2002; Shichor and Sechrest 2002).

Coinciding with expanding prison populations in the Organisation for Economic Co-operation and Development countries, including the United States, United Kingdom, and Australia, was a change in economic policy that drove public-sector reform, fed into a culture of increased financial risk management, and fueled the growth of "new public management" more generally (Raine and Willson 1997; Hancock 1998; Pollitt and Bouckaert 2000). The influence of economic rationalization, "neoliberalism" (Sinden 2003), or "free market" (Rutherford 1990; Lane 2001) models on private prisons can be seen in nations such as the United States, Australia, and the United Kingdom, where private prisons take on most or all custodial functions traditionally served by the state. Outsourcing public-sector responsibilities to the private sector was seen as a viable alternative to state management if it was able to deliver greater cost-efficiency, irrespective of what those services may entail. In contrast, the model of privatization in France, Germany, and Holland—described as "semi-privées" (Harding 2001, p. 274)—retains custodial functions under state authority and control while ancillary services like prisoner programs, health services, and (in Holland) prison kitchen services are tendered. In the French hybrid model, the private sector is tendered to build the prisons but overall responsibility for the management, security, and operational staff is maintained by the public sector (Vagg 1994; Kenter and Prior 2012; Cabral and Saussier 2013).

A managerial approach toward incarceration can also be seen in the context of a drive toward "smaller government" and greater competition. In Australia, for example, proliferation of government-owned corporations in the 1980s and the microeconomic reforms of the Hilmer and Taperell report into national competition policy (Hilmer and Taperell 1993; Davis and Wood 1998) promoted public-sector reform through reducing its role and size to improve efficiency and effectiveness. Reducing the size of government was achieved through divesting service delivery sector monopolies to the private sector or parts thereof. Various mechanisms were developed to outsource these functions including, for example, complete sale of assets to the private sector, public/private partnerships, or private finance initiatives (Osborne and Gaebler 1992; Domberger and Jensen 1997; Carter 2001; Sachdev 2001). Through introducing private-sector acumen and competition to previously sacrosanct public-sector domains, it was proposed that greater efficiency and effectiveness would be achieved (Rutherford 1990; Osborne and Gaebler 1992). The assumption was that the profit-driven efficiency and effectiveness of the private sector, which was considered superior to existing public administration processes, could be replicated in public sector service delivery (Harding 1997; Austin and Coventry 2001).

1. Inhibitions to Increased Capital Expenditure

Innovative solutions were required to fund infrastructure and prison overcrowding problems in an era of tight fiscal control (McDonald et al. 1998). With governments restrained from further borrowing to build more prisons, private prisons became an attractive and viable accounting option to control annual expenditures. In tendering prison construction and management, it was proposed that governments would reduce annual expenditures by deferring the costs of prisons across the life of the contract, for example 25 years (Logan 1990; McDonald 1990).[4] Design, construct, finance, and manage contracts provided governments with a means of defraying capital outlay costs while implementing infrastructure growth to match growing prisoner populations (Harding 1998).

The private sector also promoted more efficient procurement processes than the public sector to improve the delivery time for new prisons to meet the ever-increasing prisoner demand (Austin and Coventry 2001; Segal and Moore 2002; Mattera, Khan, and Nathan 2003). As government rules or political issues like location objections did not restrict the private sector, it was capable of building new and innovative facilities faster and more inexpensively than the public sector. Austin and Coventry (2001) provide evidence for this by indicating that, in the US experience, the public sector takes between five and six years to build a prison, whereas some private-sector agencies can take approximately half that time, with considerable savings.

2. *Reducing Recurrent Costs*

In an era that emphasized public-sector effectiveness and efficiency, private prisons were seen as a means of reducing recurrent operating costs. Proponents argued that the profit incentive of the private sector would ensure prisons were operated more effectively and efficiently than by the public sector (Austin and Coventry 2001). Through innovative staffing establishments combined with architecture innovation and new technologies like CCTV, operating costs could be substantially reduced (House of Commons Committee of Public Accounts 2003). In some jurisdictions, projected cost savings are paramount when awarding a prison contract. For example, in Florida, state legislation requires that a private prison contract can only be let after it has been established that savings of at least 7 percent in comparison to potential public-sector operating costs will be achieved (McDonald et al. 1998). In this instance, decisions on awarding the contract are based solely on efficiency or cost reduction. Improved service delivery at albeit a higher cost (i.e., value-for-money outcomes) is not considered.

3. *Service Delivery Reform*

The introduction of privatization in corrections was not solely motivated by cost efficiency. In the UK, Australia, and to a lesser extent the United States, prison privatization was initiated as an organizational development catalyst (McDonald 1999; Harding 2001; Sturgess 2003). That is, privatization was a planned process initiated as a strategy to change "risky" organizational culture, environment, and climate (Saylor 1984; Schein 1990; Harding 1997, 2001), the outcomes of which would include improvements in the quality of service delivery. A review of the numerous external and internal investigations and inquiries into the prison regimes of the UK and Australia since 1980 indicates that not only was public prison infrastructure inadequate, but organizational cultures were dysfunctional, as was service delivery (Nagle 1978; Longland 1985; Kennedy 1988; Johnston 1991; Woolf and Tumim 1991). That is, prison regimes were seen to lack quality and contain multiple failure risks.

It may also be argued that, while the numerous styles of privatization represent specific jurisdictional responses, the global rise of privatization reflects a change in long-standing concepts of the relationship between the state and the individual and how those relationships are reflected in law. Traditionally, "the state" has been seen as the only entity rightfully permitted to punish citizens for transgressing legal rules, with state-owned and -managed prisons a tangible demonstration of this principle. The global emergence of privatized prisons, however, demonstrates a shift in thinking away from the philosophical and "rights-based" principle of "who has the right" to administer punishment to individuals toward considerations of which model of administration and type of organization—private or public—will lead to the greatest cost-efficiency in service delivery. This indicates a strong managerial approach that centers around organizational influences on decision-making rather than the relationship between state and citizens.

B. "Supermax" Facilities

There is no agreed-on definition of what constitutes a supermax facility (Butler, Griffin, and Johnson 2012). For instance, facilities may be stand-alone or situated as a unit within a lower security rated facility. They may be purpose-built or a refit of existing facilities. They are variously labeled as "supermax," "special management units," "administrative segregation," or "control units." Their physical characteristics vary; while significant security measures are always present, the exact technologies used and implementation of these measures can range substantially across different facilities. Nor is there a single set of shared practices in terms of the characteristics of incarceration in these types of facilities. For example, in some facilities inmates have access to certain privileges such as television, while in others all privileges are withdrawn. However, human contact is typically kept to a bare minimum and visits from outside parties are heavily restricted or not permitted.

This section does not adopt a strict definition of supermax incarceration, but—following Dowker and Good (2002)—concentrates on the use of a model of incarceration that features three specific characteristics: prisoners are kept in solitary confinement for 22 or 23 out of every 24 hours, the conditions exist permanently (rather than as a "temporary lockdown") and as part of prison policy, and the conditions are not described as punishment but as an "administrative measure." This refers to the typical processes used in assigning prisoners to a supermax facility; generally, assignment of an individual to supermax incarceration is not a judicial decision but a decision made within the management structure of the prison system. It is not the result of a particular disciplinary process (or used for protective custody purposes) but is an institutional mechanism to control certain inmates on the basis of real or perceived likelihood of those inmates representing a threat (i.e., a risk) to the safety and/or security of the prison system (O'Keefe 2008). The administrative nature of supermax incarceration is particularly important for understanding systemic contributors to the spread of the supermax model and is discussed in greater detail later.

1. *Administrative or Punitive?*

The supermax concept is not new; solitary confinement has a long history within penal practice. However, while historical models are interpreted in contemporary discourse as favoring the use of "solitary contemplation" as a means (however unsuccessful) to encourage rehabilitation through penance (Ross 2013b), the modern use of solitary confinement—particularly in the "extreme" form found in supermax facilities—has been argued to align with a more "punishment-oriented" perception of the role of prisons in general (Feeley and Simon 1992; Roberts et al 2003; Pratt and Clark 2005). In the context of the supermax incarceration model, despite that model being characterized as an administrative rather than punitive measure, ongoing isolation indicates a management regime geared toward precluding rehabilitative strategies being implemented for individuals in those facilities (Pizarro, Stenius, and Pratt 2006). This accords with the theoretical perspective that prisons are increasingly seen as places to "manage" intractable individuals and the perceived risk they pose to others, rather than places where an attempt to "normalize" those individuals can be made (Simon 1998).

2. *Extent of Use*

Given the definitional issues associated with supermax incarceration (Reiter 2012), the number of countries using this model is somewhat challenging to determine. It is possible that many countries may use the model to some degree even if it is not overtly acknowledged. With that limitation noted, a number of authors have documented the spread of modern supermax incarceration facilities over the past two decades (see King 1999; Pizarro and Stenius 2004; Mears 2008; Ross 2013a). While the number of supermax facilities remains highest by far in the United States (estimated as having facilities in over 40 of its states [Mears 2006]), the model has also been adopted to various degrees in countries including Canada, Mexico, Brazil, South Africa, the Netherlands, England and Wales, Australia, and New Zealand (indeed, supermax facilities are found in many of the same countries that have shifted toward privatized prisons).

There is a small but growing body of literature on the use of supermax facilities globally, as well as the efficacy and legal and ethical implications of such facilities, and these issues are discussed in far greater detail elsewhere in this volume. However, the spread of the supermax incarceration model remains largely understudied relative to other aspects of imprisonment, and many studies focus on issues such as inmates' experiences and psychological well-being while in supermax facilities (e.g., Pizarro and Stenius 2004; Haney 2008; King, Steiner and Breach 2008). Little consideration has been given to the factors that underlie this global trend in prison design and use. Political explanations have been popularly invoked, such as governments implementing policies that are promoted as "getting tough on the worst of the worst offenders" (Pizarro and Narag 2008; Brown and Carlton 2013; Mears et al 2013; Newbold 2013), and using the supermax prison as symbolic of that "tough stance" (e.g., Mears 2008). This may also be set against a background of a high-profile incident, or cumulative series of incidents, such as prison riots, harm to prison staff, or escapes from maximum-security facilities by prisoners considered to pose a significant danger to the public (e.g., King and Resodihardjo 2010; West Crews 2013). While rare, the latter, in particular, has been linked at times with perceptions of public fear (based on the premise that the state is not able to control dangerous prisoners) culminating in pressure (real or perceived) on governments to take action by improving security arrangements (Pizarro, Stenius, and Pratt 2006; Shalev 2009).

However, the extent to which those circumstances, singly or cumulatively, may contribute to different countries' adoption or otherwise of the supermax incarceration model is unclear. Moreover, almost all research into the use of supermax facilities comes from the United States, making it extremely challenging to understand international similarities and variations in the uptake of this model across countries. Although political explanations are appealing, it is unrealistic to expect that any one factor can adequately explain the rise of the supermax model. Like penal practice more generally, the emergence of the supermax model cannot be reduced to a single prevailing ideology but should instead be viewed as having multiple origins that have converged around a particular type of discourse. This discourse, in turn, can be seen as one that focuses on risk and "control" or management of a particular "category" of prisoner.

3. *The Role of "Risk"*

Arguably, a shared and rising culture of risk and risk assessment has played a pivotal role in justifying the use of supermax incarceration across different countries. Discourse about supermax facilities places significant emphasis on risk as well as managerialism through the control of internal, systemic processes (Feeley and Simon 1992). The concept and language of risk is used consistently across different countries in the context of supermax facilities and applies in two specific ways. First, "risk" is the term commonly used to describe why such facilities are needed, and second, risk underlies the processes that are applied to justify incarceration of certain prisoners within those facilities. These concepts are examined separately later.

The objectives of different supermax facilities—if ever explicitly stated—vary within and between jurisdictions (Mears 2008). No compelling explanation has been provided for why this is the case, and, again, research is very heavily skewed toward US facilities. However, a shared characteristic across jurisdictions is the stated or implied use of supermax facilities as a risk management tool, for both external (public safety) and internal (prison staff and inmate safety) reasons (Shalev 2009; King and Resodighardjo 2010; Buntman and Muntingh 2013; de Jesus Filho 2013; Newbold 2013). Of course, this characteristic does not equate to an objective demonstration of certain risks existing at a level that requires a particular response, or to any empirical evidence of particular outcomes being delivered (Mears 2013). It is simply an observation about the language employed to frame the use of supermax incarceration.

4. *Risks to Public Safety*

In terms of public safety, supermax incarceration is typically framed—irrespective of jurisdiction—as an important measure to prevent escapes by the "most dangerous" prisoners, and public support for supermax incarceration appears to vary as a function of whether those prisons are perceived as benefiting public safety (Mears et al. 2013). The actual number of escapes by prisoners considered dangerous to the public, and the frequency and likelihood or probability of those events occurring, does not appear to materially influence risks to public safety being invoked as justification for supermax facilities; rather, it is the *possibility* of such events and the risk that entails that appears as the most prominent theme within discourse (see Furedi 2009, for a thought-provoking critique of probabilistic versus possibilistic risk assessment in general). This raises the question: While public safety risk has been typically invoked by those countries with supermax facilities, why have certain other countries that have also experienced prison escapes by "dangerous" inmates—and thus can reasonably be seen to have experienced the same objective "risks" to public safety as those countries who have invoked this risk as justification for creating supermax facilities—not gone down the supermax path? Although it is intuitively appealing to link this outcome with a lower uptake in those other countries of the new public management philosophy (or, in the specific context of criminology, a less prominent adoption of new penology principles outlined by Feeley and Simon 1992), available evidence is insufficient to test this premise.

A potential explanation arising from this observation is that the expansion of supermax facilities has occurred primarily in affluent countries during periods when those countries have experienced significant growth in the prison population. Rising prison populations create a range of corresponding challenges associated with managing those populations. This, in turn, raises questions about whether a rise in prison populations necessarily means an increase in the number of "high-risk" prisoners in that system, sufficient to justify higher levels of prison security for housing that population. The matter of "risk level" categorization is discussed next.

5. *Risks to Prison Order*

The second way in which risk discourse is consistently used in different countries to justify supermax incarceration is in the context of internal safety risks—that is, risks to prison staff or other inmates. Risks to staff, especially, have been cited as justifying a need for higher security housing for certain inmates (e.g., Newbold 2013; Resodihardjo 2013). This does not necessarily reflect a direct risk posed by individual inmates toward staff—although that has certainly been flagged as one form of risk—but also refers more broadly to the risk of staff losing control over inmates (e.g., a hostage or riot situation) and the risk of certain inmates inciting wider violence or organizing other disruptive activities (e.g., Pizarro and Stenius 2004; Shalev 2009). While there is no question that such incidents have occurred, the similar language of risk used across different countries on these issues does not denote that the same types of experiences with those types of incidents within prisons have occurred across all different countries with supermax facilities.

Also, there is ample evidence that internal prison security risks occur across many different countries, yet not all have responded by increasing the security settings of housing for certain inmates or by moving away from a "dispersal" theory[5] of behavioral control. This again begs the question of why only certain countries have chosen to manage perceived or actual internal risks by implementing supermax incarceration models. One possibility is that the relationships between correctional systems officials and policymakers may be similar across those countries with supermax facilities. Although this has not been well explored, perceptions of a "need" for supermax facilities by correctional administrators has been documented and (in the United States in particular) has been associated with an accompanying culture of deference by policymakers and the judiciary toward prison administrators (Weidman 2003).

6. *"Dangerous Groups"*

The focus on supermaxes as a risk management response to disruptive behavior and/or to inmates' organizing disruptive or illicit activities offers another thread of commonality between different countries in that supermax incarceration appears to be seen as one part of an institutional response to organized criminal activity (or "gang activity"). Potentially, then, a part of the spread of supermax incarceration across different countries may be explained through shared organizational perceptions of the extent and nature of gang-related activity by inmates—irrespective of how different those types of gangs may look across different countries (Tachiki 1995; Buntman and Muntigh 2013; Newbold 2013).

The premise of "gang" problems or unlawful "group" activity also relates to the way in which risk-based discourse features in managerial categorization of particular "risk" groups. While assessment of the appropriate security settings within which each individual inmate should be housed is certainly not new in the corrections system, a range of authors have explored changing practices in inmate classification since the 1980s (e.g., Gottfredson 1987; Simon 1998; Kemshall 2003). A change in how risk is conceptualized may be seen as both partially driving the use of supermax facilities (Mears 2008) and as a reason for why it is difficult to adequately document or understand the factors contributing to use of supermax facilities across different countries. That is, it is not clear whether supermax facilities are used for the same purposes or to house the same "types" of inmates across different countries, despite the shared physical and policy conditions used to conceptualize supermax incarceration.

It has been argued that, in contrast to earlier assessment practices that focused on a particular individual, supermax facilities' expansion across countries has been accompanied by growing emphasis on assigning individuals to a "risk level" based (seemingly) on the main criteria of "group membership" (Kurki and Morris 2001). While supermax facilities were originally described as a means of housing the most violent and disruptive inmates (based on their behaviour while incarcerated in other facilities), there is evidence that supermax facilities in different countries are increasingly being used to house individuals because of their membership in gangs (or terrorist organizations) or as a result of their having committed a particular "class" of offense (e.g., multiple killings). To an extent, then, the use of supermax facilities to house certain "groups" of inmates may reflect an increasingly globalized view of those types of groups that society deems as acting "most outside" the boundaries of sanctioned behavior and most "deserving" of retribution (e.g., Garland 1990; Toch 2007; von Hirsch 2012).

It appears, then, that across multiple countries the purpose of supermax facilities has slowly shifted from management of individuals considered to represent a high risk to public safety or prison security to a means of managing inmates who belong to a particular group that has been defined (potentially quite arbitrarily and/or based on punitive rather than administrative goals) as requiring the highest available level of behavioral management, irrespective of their individual propensity toward violence and/or escape (Shalev 2009). Unfortunately, policies concerning the exact way in which risk assessment is used in the context of supermax facilities are not routinely available, which means more precise comparisons between jurisdictions cannot be drawn. Nonetheless, these observations—incomplete though they are—accord with the spread of an ethos of managerialism that emphasizes interactions between defined "groups" of individuals rather than focusing on individuals themselves.

Unfortunately, however, given the difficulties of defining and identifying supermax incarceration as well as the dearth of detailed comparative international research into this question, these matters remain open questions that require further study. Also, and interestingly from a policy perspective, in various locations in the United States where there is an apparent shift away from the use of supermax facilities, evidence is emerging that the justification for that measure is framed in economic risk management terms rather than around a lessening of safety risks (see Mears [2013] for a summary). This highlights the multiple different policy and conceptual frameworks at concurrent play within the penal system in that countries that have emphasized cost-efficiency in their introduction of private prisons can simultaneously introduce supermax facilities, which are argued to be very costly to run (e.g., Mears and Bales 2009). This reinforces the malleable way in which particular "styles" of incarceration (or, indeed, the use of incarceration overall) are described within a public policy context. It remains to be seen whether the trend toward declining use of supermax incarceration will spread from the United States to other countries.

The purpose of this section was not to consider evidence for, or against, the effectiveness of private prisons and the supermax model of confinement. These matters have been debated elsewhere and—as is proper—will no doubt continue to be subject to scrutiny. However, in the interests of completeness, it is relevant to make a very brief comment on the relationships between managerialism, risk assessment, and impact evaluation (i.e., the assessment of effectiveness). A persistent concern about the managerial ethos is that while it touts accountability, the form of accountability it tends to emphasize is often based around process-focused goals (such as having a certain number of beds available in a facility or maintaining a certain level of documentation) rather than outcome-based goals (e.g., Parker and Gould 1999; Burton and van den Broek 2009). Consequently, the "targets" used to assess a measure's "effectiveness" may not have any bearing on assessing whether the original purpose of that measure has been met (if indeed those goals were ever explicitly defined—and a lack of which further impedes evaluation). Similarly, if a measure was intended to reduce the risk of a particular event, the absence of objective baseline data about the nature, prevalence, and likelihood of that event occurring— as well as an unclear understanding of how different risks are "weighted" against one another—will significantly affect the quality of any subsequent evaluations of that measure's impact.

V. Conclusion

It is impossible to capture in a brief essay the immense complexity of factors contributing to international differences and similarities in the use of incarceration and related practices and policies. However, this essay has emphasized that while cross-national differences in incarceration *rates* highlight the presence of different conceptual frameworks and policy choices, it can also be valuable to consider why different countries may have made similar sets of choices in certain aspects of their incarceration *practices*. Although there remain substantial gaps in knowledge, it seems reasonable to suggest that future efforts at understanding international trends in incarceration should not seek to understand those trends from a single conceptual framework but should instead embrace multiple conceptual understandings of how incarceration may operate by a comparable suite of drivers or influences yet at the same time be shaped by distinctly different factors owing to local contexts. It is to that challenge, understanding both the common and the distinct, the macro and the local contextual, to which future research efforts should focus that will inform a broader understanding of the cross-national contexts of incarceration as a penal response.

NOTES

1. Immigration detention and detention for military purposes is excluded.
2. In this research, the UK refers to England and Wales.
3. On March 11, 2003, the Corrections Bill No.34-1 was introduced into New Zealand parliament. In updating the Penal Institutions Act 1954, the bill removes the ability of the chief executive, Department of Corrections to enter into any new prison management contracts or extend the existing contract for the Auckland Central Remand Prison past its due date of July 12, 2005. To date, indications are that the center has run successfully as it has received all possible performance-linked fees (Barry 2003; Kerr 2003). Despite the intentions of the public provider to replicate the existing service delivery efficiency, this appears unlikely (Barry 2003).
4. Particularly in the United States, by 1986 many states had reached debt ceilings and were unwilling or unable to approach voters for approval to borrow further to fund prisons (McDonald et al. 1998). To overcome the funding problems, the private sector would issue bonds to construct the center, which would then be leased back to the state (McDonald et al. 1998).
5. This refers to the practice of dispersing (for example) "high-risk" offenders across a range of different institutions/parts of an institution, rather than "concentrating" all those offenders together in one location.

REFERENCES

Arditti, Joyce A., and Charles McClintock. 2002. "Drug Policy and Families: Casualties of the War." *Marriage and Family Review* 32(3–4): 11–32.

Austin, J., and Coventry, G. 2001. *Emerging Issues on Private Prisons*. Washington, DC: US Department of Justice, Office of Justice Programs, Bureau of Justice Assistance.

Barry, Phil. 2003. "Privately Provided Prison Services." New Zealand Business Roundtable. http://nzinitiative.org.nz/site/nzinitiative/files/releases/releases-2003/031117prisonpaper.htm

Bewley-Taylor, Dave, Chris Hallam, and Rob Allen. 2009. *The Incarceration of Drug Offenders: An Overview*. Beckley Foundation Drug Policy Programme, Report No. 16. London: International Centre for Prison Studies, King's College, University of London.

Blumstein, Alfred, and Allen J. Beck. 1999. "Population Growth in U.S. Prisons, 1980–1996." In *Prisons: Crime and Justice: A Review of Research, Vol. 26*, edited by Michael Tonry and Joan Petersilia. Chicago: University of Chicago Press.

Brayne, Sarah. 2013. "Explaining the Unites States' Penal Exceptionalism: Political, Economic, and Social Factors." *Sociology Compass* 7:75–86.

Brown, David, and Bree Carlton. 2013. "From 'Secondary Punishment' to 'Supermax': The Human Costs of High-Security Regimes in Australia." In *The Globalization of Supermax Prisons*, edited by Jeffrey I. Ross. New Brunswick, NJ: Rutgers University Press.

Brownlee, Ian. 1998. "New Labour—New Penology? Punitive Rhetoric and the Limits of Managerialism in Criminal Justice Policy." *Journal of Law and Society* 25:313–335.

Buntman, Fran, and Lukas Muntingh. 2013. "Supermaximum Prisons in South Africa." In *The Globalization of Supermax Prisons*, edited by Jeffrey I. Ross. New Brunswick, NJ: Rutgers University Press.

Burton, Judith, and Diane van den Broek. 2009. "Accountable and Countable: Information Management Systems and the Bureaucratization of Social Work." *British Journal of Social Work* 39:1326–1342.

Butler, H. Daniel, O. Hayden Griffin, and W. Wesley Johnson. 2012. "What Makes You the 'Worst of the Worst'? An Examination of State Policies Defining Supermaximum Confinement." *Criminal Justice Policy Review* 24:676–694.

Cabral, Sandro, and Stéphane Saussier. 2013. "Organizing Prisons through Public–Private Partnerships: A Cross-Country Investigation." *Brazilian Administration Review* 10(1): 100–120.

Caplow, Theodore, and Jonathan Simon. 1999. "Understanding Prison Policy and Population Trends." In *Prisons: Crime and Justice: A Review of Research, Vol. 26*, edited by Michael Tonry and Joan Petersilia. Chicago: University of Chicago Press.

Carmichael, Jason T. 2005. "The Determinants of Jail Use Across Large US Cities: An Assessment of Racial, Ethnic, and Economic Threat Explanations." *Social Science Research* 34:538–569.

Carson, E. Ann. 2014. *Prisoners in 2013*. Washington, DC: US Department of Justice, Office of Justice Programs, Bureau of Justice Statistics.

Carter, Patrick. 2001. *Review of PFI and Market Testing in the Prison Service*. London: Author.

Cavadino, Michael, and James Dignan. 2006. *Penal Systems: A Comparative Approach*. London: Sage.

Cheliotis, Leonidas K. 2006. "How Iron Is the Iron Cage of New Penology? The Role of Human Agency in the Implementation of Criminal Justice Policy." *Punishment & Society* 8:313–340.

Chesney-Lind, Meda. 2002. "The Forgotten Offender: Women in Prison." In *Exploring Corrections: A Book of Readings*, edited by Tara Gray. Boston: Allyn & Bacon.

Cliquennois, Gaëtan. 2013. "What Penology for Decision Making in French Prisons?" *Punishment & Society* 15:468–487.

Cook, Carrie L., and Jodi Lane. 2009. "The Place of Public Fear in Sentencing and Correctional Policy." *Journal of Criminal Justice* 37:586–595.

Cunliffe, Ann L. 2009. *A Very Short, Fairly Interesting, and Reasonably Cheap Book About Management*. London: Sage.

D'Alessio, Stewart J., and Lisa Stolzenberg. 1997. "The Effect of Available Capacity on Jail Incarceration: An Empirical Test of Parkinson's Law." *Journal of Criminal Justice* 25:279–288.

Davis, G., and Wood, T. 1998. "Is There a Future for Contracting in the Australian Public Sector?" *Australian Journal of Public Administration* 57(4): 85–97.

de Jesus Filho, José. 2013. "The Rise of the Supermax in Brazil." In *The Globalization of Supermax Prisons*, edited by Jeffrey I. Ross. New Brunswick, NJ: Rutgers University Press.

Dolowitz, David, and David Marsh. 1996. "Who Learns What from Whom: A Review of the Policy Transfer Literature." *Political Studies* 44:343–357.

Domberger, Simon, and Paul Jensen. 1997. "Contracting Out by the Public Sector: Theory, Evidence, Prospects." *Oxford Review of Economic Policy* 13(4): 67–78.

Dowker, Fay, and Glenn Good. 2002. "Control Units as a Control Mechanism." In *Exploring Corrections: A Book of Readings*, edited by Tara Gray. Boston: Allyn & Bacon.

Feeley, Malcolm M., and Jonathan Simon. 1992. "The New Penology: Notes on the Emerging Strategy of Corrections and its Implications." *Criminology* 30:449–774.

Freiberg, Arie, and Stuart Ross. 1999. *Sentencing Reform and Penal Change: The Victorian Experience*. Melbourne: Federation Press.

Furedi, Frank. 2009. "Precautionary Culture and the Rise of Possibilistic Risk Assessment." *Erasmus Law Review* 2:197–220.

Garland, David. 1990. *Punishment and Modern Society: A Study in Social Theory*. Chicago: University of Chicago Press.

Garland, David. 2001. *The Culture of Control: Crime and Social Control in Contemporary Society*. Chicago: Chicago University Press.

Gottfredson, Don M. 1987. "Prediction and Classification in Criminal Justice Decision Making." *Crime and Justice* 9:1–20.

Goyer, Kathryn C. 2001. *Prison Privatization in South Africa: Issues, Challenges and Opportunities*. Monograph 64. Pretoria, South Africa: Institute of Strategic Studies.

Gruening, Gernod. 2001. "Origin and Theoretical Basis of New Public Management." *International Public Management Journal* 4:1–25.

Gustafson, Kaaryn. 2009. "The Criminalization of Poverty." *Journal of Criminal Law and Criminology* 99:643–716.

Hancock, Linda. 1998. "Contractualism, Privatisation and Justice: Citizenship, the State and Managing Risk." *Australian Journal of Public Administration* 57(4): 118–127.

Haney, Craig. 2008. "A Culture of Harm: Taming the Dynamics of Cruelty in Supermax Prisons." *Criminal Justice and Behavior* 35:956–984.

Harding, Richard W. 1997. *Private Prisons and Public Accountability*. Buckingham, UK: Open University Press.

Harding, Richard W. 1998. Private Prisons in Australia: The Second Phase. Canberra: Australian Institute of Criminology. http://www.aic.gov.au/publications/current%20series/tandi/81-100/tandi084.html

Harding, Richard W. 2001. "Private Prisons." In *Crime and Justice: A Review of Research*, Vol. 28, edited by Michael Tonry. Chicago: University of Chicago Press.

Heidensohn, Frances, and Marisa Silvestri. 2012. "Gender and Crime." In *Oxford Handbook of Criminology, 5th ed.*, edited by Mike Maguire, Rod Morgan, and Robert Reiner. Oxford: Oxford University Press.

Heimer, Karen. 2000. "Changes in the Gender Gap in Crime and Women's Economic Marginalization." In *Criminal Justice 2000, Vol. 1: The Nature of Crime and Continuity and Change*, edited by G. LaFree. Washington, DC: National Institute of Justice.

Hilmer, Frederick M., and Geoffrey Taperell. 1993. *National Competition Policy: Report of the Independent Committee of Inquiry into Competition Policy in Australia*. Canberra: Australian Government Publishing Service.

Hinds, Lyn R. 2002. Law and Order: The Politics of Get Tough Crime Control. Ph.D. dissertation, Griffith University, Brisbane.

House of Commons Committee of Public Accounts. 2003. *The Operational Performance of PFI Prisons*. London: Author.

Hucklesby, Anthea. 2009. "Keeping the Lid on the Prison Remand Population: The Experience in England and Wales." *Current Issues in Criminal Justice* 21:3–23.

Jacobs, David, and Richard Kleban. 2003. "Political Institutions, Minorities, and Punishment: A Pooled Cross-National Analysis of Imprisonment Rates." *Social Forces* 80:725–755.

Jerre, Kristina. 2014. "More Sanctions—Less Prison? A Research Note on the Severity of Sanctions Proposed by Survey Participants and How It Is Affected by the Option to Combine a Prison Term with Other Sanctions." *European Journal on Criminal Policy and Research* 20:121–136.

Johnson, Holly. 2004. *Drugs and Crime: A Study of Incarcerated Female Offenders*. Research and Public Policy Series No. 63. Canberra: Australian Institute of Criminology.

Johnston, Elliot. 1991. *Report of the Royal Commission into Aboriginal Deaths in Custody*. Canberra: Australian Government Publication Service.

Kemshall, Hazel. 2003. *Understanding Risk in Criminal Justice*. Berkshire, UK: Open University Press.

Kennedy, James J. 1988. *Commission of Review into Corrective Services in Queensland, Final Report*. Queensland: Australia Government Printer.

Kenter, Robert C., and Susan V. Prior. 2012. "The Globalization of Private Prisons." In *Prison Privatization: The Many Facets of a Controversial Industry*, Vol. 1, edited by Byron E. Price II and John C. Morris. Santa Barbara, CA: Praeger.

Kerr, Roger. 2003. "Ideology Locks Away Choice" *Otago Daily Times* (November 21).

King, Kate, Benjamin Steiner, and Stephanie Ritchie Breach. 2008. "Violence in the Supermax: A Self-Fulfilling Prophecy." *The Prison Journal* 88:144–168.

King, Roy D. 1999. "The Rise and Rise of Supermax: An American Solution in Search of a Problem?" *Punishment & Society* 1:163–186.

King, Roy D., and Sandra L. Resodihardjo. 2010. "To Max or Not to Max: Dealing with High Risk Prisoners in the Netherlands and England and Wales." *Punishment & Society* 12:65–84.

Kurki, Leena, and Norval Morris. 2001. "The Purposes, Practices, and Problems of Supermax Prisons." *Crime and Justice* 28:385–424.

Kyle, Peter H. 2013. "Contracting for Performance: Restructuring the Private Prison Market." *William & Mary Law Review* 54:2087.

Lane, Jan-Erik. 2001. "From Long-Term to Short-Term Contracting." *Public Administration* 79:29–47.

Lappi-Seppälä, Tapio. 2011. "Explaining Imprisonment in Europe." *European Journal of Criminology* 8:303–328.

Logan, Charles H. 1990. *Private Prisons: Cons and Pros*. New York: Oxford University Press.

Longland, David. 1985. *Enquiry into the Management Practices Operating at H.M. Prison Brisbane*. Brisbane: Government Printer.

Lynch, James P., and William A. Pridemore. 2011. "Crime in International Perspective." In *Crime and Public Policy*, edited by James Wilson and Joan Petersilia. New York: Oxford University Press.

Lynch, Mona. 1998. "Waste Managers? The New Penology, Crime Fighting, and Parole Agent Identity." *Law & Society Review* 32:839–869.

Mackenzie, Doris L. 2012. "From Theory to Policy: Evidence-Based Corrections." In *Correctional Theory: Context and Consequences*, edited by Francis Cullen and Cheryl Johnson. Thousand Oaks, CA: Sage.

Mason, Cody. 2013. *International Growth Trends in Prison Privatization*. Washington, DC: The Sentencing Project.

Mattera, Philip, Mafruza Khan, and Stehpen Nathan. 2003. *Corrections Corporation of America: A Critical Look at Its First Twenty Years*. Charlotte, NC: Grassroots Leadership.

Matthews, Roger. 2005. "The Myth of Punitiveness." *Theoretical Criminology* 9:175–201.

Mauer, Marc. 1995. "The International Use of Incarceration." *The Prison Journal* 75:113–123.

Mauer, Marc. 2003. *Comparative International Rates of Incarceration: An Examination of Causes and Trends.* Washington, DC: The Sentencing Project.

Mauer, Marc, Cathy Potler, and Richard Wolf. 1999. *Gender and Justice: Women, Drugs, and Sentencing Policy.* Washington, DC: The Sentencing Project.

McDonald, Douglas C. 1990. *Private Prisons and the Public Interest.* New Brunswick, NJ: Rutgers University Press.

McDonald, Douglas C. 1999. Performance Issues. Paper presented at the Private Prison Workshop, Institute of Criminal Justice, University of Minnesota, Minneapolis.

McDonald, Douglas C., Elizabeth Fournier, Malcolm Russell-Einhorn, and Stephen Crawford. 1998. *Private Prisons in the United States: An Assessment of Current Practice.* Cambridge, MA: Adt Associates.

Mears, Daniel P. 2006. *Evaluating the Effectiveness of Supermax Prisons.* Washington, DC: Urban Institute.

Mears, Daniel P. 2008. "An Assessment of Supermax Prisons Using an Evaluation Research Framework." *The Prison Journal* 88:43–68.

Mears, Daniel P. 2013. "Supermax Prisons: The Policy and the Evidence." *Criminology and Public Policy* 12:681–718.

Mears, Daniel P., and William D. Bales. 2009. "Supermax Incarceration and Recidivism." *Criminology* 47:1131–1165.

Mears, Daniel P., Christina Mancini, Kevin M. Beaver, and Marc Gertz. 2013. "Housing for the 'Worst of the Worst' Inmates: Public Support for Supermax Prisons." *Crime & Delinquency* 59:587–615.

Mennicken, Andrea. 2013. "'Too Big to Fail and Too Big to Succeed': Accounting and Privatisation in the Prison Service of England and Wales." *Financial Accountability & Management* 29:206–226.

Moore, Dawn, Kellie Leclerc Burton, and Kelly Hannah-Moffat. 2003. "'Get Tough' Efficiency: Human Rights, Correctional Restructuring and Prison Privatization in Ontario, Canada." *Capitalist Punishment: Prison Privatization and Human Rights*, edited by Andrew Coyle, Allison Campbell, and Rodney Neufeld. Atlanta: Clarity Press.

Nagin, Daniel S., Alex R. Piquero, Elizabeth S. Scott, and Laurence Steinberg. 2006. "Public Preferences for Rehabilitation Versus Incarceration of Juvenile Offenders: Evidence from a Contingent Valuation Survey." *Criminology and Public Policy* 5:627–652.

Nagle, Justice F. 1978. *Report of the Royal Commission into New South Wales Prisons.* Sydney: NSW Government Printer.

Neopolitan, Jerome L. 2001. "An Examination of Cross-National Variation in Punitiveness." *International Journal of Offender Therapy and Comparative Criminology* 45:691–710.

Newbold, Greg. 2013. "The Emergence of the Supermax in New Zealand." In *The Globalization of Supermax Prisons*, edited by Jeffrey I. Ross. New Brunswick, NJ: Rutgers University Press.

Nicholson-Crotty, Sean. 2004. "The Impact of Sentencing Guidelines on State-Level Sanctions: An Analysis Over Time." *Crime & Delinquency* 50:395–411.

O'Keefe, Maureen L. 2008. "Administrative Segregation from Within: A Corrections Perspective." *The Prison Journal* 88:123–143.

Osborne, David, and Ted Gaebler. 1992. *Reinventing Government: How the Entrepreneurial Spirit Transforming the Public Sector.* New York: Plume/Penguin.

Pantazis, Christina, and David Gordon. 1997. "Television Licence Evasion and the Criminalisation of Female Poverty." *The Howard Journal* 36:170–186.

Parker, Lee, and Graeme Gould. 1999. "Changing Public Sector Accountability: Critiquing New Directions." *Accounting Forum* 23:109–135.

Pease, Ken. 1994. "Cross-National Imprisonment Rates: Limitations of Method and Possible Conclusions." *British Journal of Criminology* 34:116–130.

Phillips, Jake. 2011. "Target, Audit, and Risk Assessment Cultures in the Probation Service." *European Journal of Probation* 3(3):108–122.

Piquero, Alex, and Laurence Steinberg. 2010. "Public Preference for Rehabilitation Versus Incarceration of Juvenile Offenders." *Journal of Criminal Justice* 38:1–6.

Pizarro, Jesenia M., and Raymund E. Narag. 2008. "Supermax Prisons: What We Know, What We Do Not Know, and Where We Are Going." *The Prison Journal* 88:23–42.

Pizarro, Jesenia, and Vanja M. K. Stenius. 2004. "Supermax Prisons: Their Rise, Current Practices, and Effect on Inmates." *The Prison Journal* 84:248–264.

Pizarro, Jesenia, Vanja M. K. Stenius, and Travis C. Pratt. 2006. "Supermax Prisons: Myths, Realities, and the Politics of Punishment in American Society." *Criminal Justice Policy Review* 17:6–21.

Pollitt, Christopher, and Geert Bouckaert. 2000. *Public Management Reform: A Comparative Analysis*. Oxford: Oxford University Press.

Pratt, John, and Marie Clark. 2005. "Penal Populism in New Zealand." *Punishment & Society* 7:303–322.

Prison Privatization Report International. 2000. Prison Privatisation Report International 67 (March). Available at http://www.psiru.org/justice/

Productivity Commission. 2013. *Report on Government Services 2013*. Canberra: Steering Committee for the Review of Commonwealth/State Service Provision. http://www.pc.gov.au/research/recurring/report-on-government-services/2013/2013

Raine, John W., and Michael J. Willson. 1997. "Beyond Managerialism in Criminal Justice." *The Howard Journal* 36:80–95.

Raphael, Steven. 2009. "Explaining the Rise in U.S. Incarceration Rates." *Criminology and Public Policy* 8:87–95.

Reiter, Keramet A. 2012. "Parole, Snitch, or Die: California's Supermax Prisons and Prisoners, 1997–2007." *Punishment & Society* 14:530–563.

Resodihardjo, Sandra L. 2013. "Analyzing the Supermax Prisons in the Netherlands: The Dutch Supermax." In *The Globalization of Supermax Prisons*, edited by Jeffrey I. Ross. New Brunswick, NJ: Rutgers University Press.

Riveland, Chase. 1999. "Prison Management Trends, 1975–2025." In *Prisons. Crime and Justice: A Review of Research*, Vol. 26, edited by Michael Tonry and Joan Petersilia. Chicago: University of Chicago Press.

Roberts, Julian V., Loretta J. Stalens, David Indermaur, and Mike Hough. 2003. *Penal Populism and Public Opinion: Lessons from Five Countries*. New York: Oxford University Press.

Ross, Jeffrey I. 2013a. "The Globalization of Supermax Prisons: An Introduction." In *The Globalization of Supermax Prisons*, edited by Jeffrey I. Ross. New Brunswick, NJ: Rutgers University Press.

Ross, Jeffrey I. 2013b. "The Invention of the American Supermax Prison." In *The Globalization of Supermax Prisons*, edited by Jeffrey I. Ross. New Brunswick, NJ: Rutgers University Press.

Ruddell, Rick, and G. Larry Mays. 2007. "Rural Jails: Problematic Inmates, Overcrowded Cells, and Cash-Strapped Counties." *Journal of Criminal Justice* 35:251–260.

Rutherford, Andrew. 1990. "British Penal Policy and the Idea of Prison Privatization." In *Private Prisons and the Public Interest*, edited by Douglas McDonald. New Brunswick, NJ: Rutgers University Press.

Sachdev, Sanjiv. 2001. "Contracting Culture: From CCT to PPPs." In *The Private Provision of Public Services and Its Impact on Employment Relations*. Kingston, UK: Unison.

Savelsberg, Joachim. 1994. "Knowledge, Domination, and Criminal Punishment." *American Journal of Sociology* 99:911–943.

Saylor, William G. 1984. *Surveying Prison Environments*. Washington, DC: Federal Bureau of Prisons. https://www.bop.gov/resources/research_projects/published_reports/cond_envir/oresaylor2.pdf

Schein, Edgar H. 1990. "Organizational Culture." *American Psychologist* 45:109–119.

Scottish Executive. 2002. *Consultation Paper on the Future of the Scottish Prison Estate*. Edinburgh, UK: Scottish Executive.

Segal, Geoffrey F., and Adrian Moore. 2002. *Weighing the Watchmen: Evaluating the Costs and Benefits of Outsourcing Correctional Services Part I: Employing a Best-Value Approach to Procurement and Part II: Reviewing the Literature on Cost and Quality Comparisons*. Los-Angeles: Reason Public Policy Institute.

Shalev, Sharon. 2009. *Supermax: Controlling Risk through Solitary Confinement*. Portland, OR: Willan.

Shannon, Sarah, and Christopher Uggen. 2012. "Incarceration as a Political Institution." In *The Wiley-Blackwell Companion to Political Sociology*, edited by Edwin Amenta, Kate Nash and Alan Scott. West Sussex, UK: Blackwell.

Shichor, David. 1997. "Three Strikes as Public Policy: The Convergence of the New Penology and McDonalidization of Punishment." *Crime & Delinquency* 43:470–492.

Shichor, David, and Dale K. Sechrest. 2002. "Privatization and Flexibility: Legal and Practical Aspects of Interjurisdictional Transfer of Prisoners." *The Prison Journal* 82:386–407.

Simon, Jonathan. 1998. "Managing the Monstrous: Sex Offenders and the New Penology." *Psychology, Public Policy, and Law* 4(1–2):452–467.

Sinden, Jeff. 2003. "The Problem of Prison Privatization: The US Experience." In *Capitalist Punishment: Prison Privatization and Human Rights*, edited by Andrew Coyle, Allison Campbell, and Rodney Neufeld. London: Zed Books.

Sorensen, Jon, and Don Stemen. 2002. "The Effect of State Sentencing Policies on Incarceration Rates." *Crime & Delinquency* 48:456–475.

Sparks, Richard. 2001. "Degrees of Estrangement: The Cultural Theory of Risk and Comparative Penology." *Theoretical Criminology* 5:159–176.

Spelman, William. 2009. "Crime, Cash, and Limited Options: Explaining the Prison Boom." *Criminology and Public Policy* 8:29–77.

Sprott, Jane B., and Anthony N. Doob. 1998. "Understanding Provincial Variation in Incarceration Rates." *Canadian Journal of Criminology* 40:305–322.

Stone, Diane. 2001. Learning Lessons, Policy Transfer, and the International Diffusion of Ideas. CSGR Working Paper No. 69/01. Centre for the Study of Globalisation and Regionalisation. Coventry, UK: University of Warwick.

Sturgess, Gary. 2003. *Competition: A Catalyst for Change in the Prison Service*. London: Confederation of British Industry.

Subramanian, Ram, and Alison Shames. 2013. *Sentencing and Prison Practices in Germany and the Netherlands: Implications for the United States*. Center on Sentencing and Corrections. New York: VERA Institute of Justice.

Sutton, John. 2000. "Imprisonment and Social Classification in Five Common-Law Democracies, 1955–1985." *American Journal of Sociology* 106:350–386.

Tachiki, Scott N. 1995. "Indeterminate Sentences in Supermax Prisons Based upon Alleged Gang Affiliations: A Re-Examination of Procedural Protection and a Proposal for Greater Procedural Requirements." *California Law Review* 83:1117–1149.

Toch, Hans. 2007. "Sequestering Gang Members, Burning Witches, and Subverting Due Process." *Criminal Justice and Behavior* 32:274–288.

Van Kesteren, John. 2009. "Public Attitudes and Sentencing Policies Across the World." *European Journal on Criminal Policy and Research* 15:25–46.

Vagg, Jon. 1994. *Prison Systems: A Comparative Study of Accountability in England, France, Germany, and the Netherlands*. Oxford: Oxford University Press.

Volokh, Alexander. 2014. "Prison Accountability and Performance Measures." *Emory Law Journal* 63:339–416.

von Hirsch, Andrew. 2012. "Just Deserts: Doing Justice or Getting Tough?" In *Correctional Theory Context and Consequences*, edited by Francis Cullen and Cheryl Jonson. Thousand Oaks, CA: Sage.

Walmsley, Roy. 2003. *World Prison Population List*, 5th ed. London: Home Office.

Walmsley, Roy. 2012. *World Female Imprisonment List*, 2d ed. London: International Centre for Prison Studies.

Walmsley, Roy. 2013. *World Prison Population List, 10th ed.* London: International Centre for Prison Studies.

Wan, Wai-Yin, Steve Moffatt, Zachary Xie, Simon Corben, and Don Weatherburn. 2013. Forecasting Prison Populations Using Sentencing and Arrest Data. *Crime and Justice Bulletin No. 174*. New South Wales: New South Wales Bureau of Crime Statistics and Research.

Weidman, Mikel-Meredith. 2003. The Culture of Judicial Deference and the Problem of Supermax Prisons. *UCLA Law Review* 51:1506–1553.

West Crews, Angela. 2013. "The Growth of the Supermax Option in Britain." In *The Globalization of Supermax Prisons*, edited by Jeffrey I. Ross. New Brunswick, NJ: Rutgers University Press.

Wilkins, Leslie T., and Pease, Ken. 1987. "Public Demand for Punishment." *International Journal of Sociology and Social Policy* 7(3): 16–29.

Woolf, the Rt. Hon. Lord Harry, and the Hon. Judge Stephen Tumim. 1991. *Prison Disturbances, April 1990: Report of an Inquiry by the Rt. Hon. Lord Justice Woolf (Parts 1 and 2) and His Honour Judge Stephen Tumim (Part 2), Cm. 1456*. London: HMSO.

Young, Warren, and Mark Brown. 1993. "Cross-National Comparisons of Imprisonment." *Crime and Justice* 17:1–49.

Zhang, Yan, Christopher D. Maxwell, and Michael S. Vaughn. 2009. "The Impact of State Sentencing Policies on the U.S. Prison Population." *Journal of Criminal Justice* 37:190–199.

Zimring, Franklin E. 2001. "Imprisonment Rates and the New Politics of Criminal Punishment." In *Mass Imprisonment: Social Causes and Consequences*, edited by David Garland. London: Sage.

CHAPTER 5

....

THEORIES OF MASS
INCARCERATION

....

NATASHA A. FROST AND TODD R. CLEAR

WITH combined jail and prison populations across the country exceeding 2 million people every year since 2002, America has long led the world in its willingness to incarcerate many of its people (Harrison and Karberg 2003). With the passage of that 2 million mark, what used to be referred to as simply incarceration is now almost invariably described as mass incarceration. Literally millions of people spend time in prisons and jails across the United States, with 1 in 100 persons in the general population incarcerated on any given day (Pew Center on the States 2008). Indeed, although once only a relatively remote possibility for the average American, an imprisonment experience is increasingly common (1 in 31 persons can now claim this dubious distinction) and has become nearly ubiquitous for some segments of the population (Rose and Clear 2004; Pew Center on the States 2009; Western and Muller 2013).

In all but the most extreme circumstances (such as those that occur during times of war, for example), mass incarceration does not just occur overnight. Years—indeed decades—of subtle, and not so subtle, shifts in policy and practice lead to changes in the way that we approach crime prevention and control, and those shifts ultimately explain changing rates of incarceration (National Research Council 2014). The size of prison and jail populations, after all, depends entirely on who goes in and how long they stay there. Elsewhere we have referred to these dynamics as the "iron law" of prison populations (Clear and Austin 2009; Clear and Frost 2014). So explaining increases (or decreases) in prison populations is fairly straightforward—it is invariably a question of policies that drive prison populations up or down. Explaining what led to those policies, how they came to exist, and why they were deemed necessary is much more complicated. Indeed, there are almost as many theories of mass incarceration as there are scholars of mass incarceration—each with his or her own take on what led to the situation we now face. Each year, new articles and books offer a slightly new perspective on an old explanation, and the plethora of explanations grows, but when these explanations are grouped together in terms of common central themes, a number of dominant perspectives that seem worthy of classification as more or less distinct theories of mass incarceration emerge.

In this essay we identify five dominant theories of mass incarceration: the first casts incarceration as a rational response to increasing crime; the second describes mass incarceration as the result of the imperfect fusion of politics and public opinion; the third suggests that mass incarceration is inextricably tied to the control of marginal populations (poor, unemployed, mentally ill, etc.); the fourth, is related to the third but more prominently emphasizes the racial (and racist) aspects of criminal justice policy, casting the prison as the new urban ghetto and the policies that led to mass incarceration as the new Jim Crow; and the fifth imagines mass incarceration as a grand social experiment, not unlike other grand experiments in social policy across American history. Through this review of the major theoretical perspectives on mass incarceration, we reach the following conclusions:

- No one dominant theory of mass incarceration has yet emerged but instead there are a number of competing, and in some respects complimentary, perspectives.
- All theories of mass incarceration acknowledge the centrality of policy choices to the rapid increase of incarceration. At issue is most often what drove those policy choices.
- There is growing evidence that the overreliance on incarceration has reached a turning point and the recent (small) declines in rates of incarceration may signal the beginning of the end of the era of mass incarceration.
- Tests of theories of mass incarceration have been few, largely because crime is overdetermined and the theoretically specified constructs are difficult to operationalize and measure with any precision.

I. Is It the Beginning of the End of the Era of Mass Incarceration?

We would be seriously remiss if we did not begin this essay with a critical discussion of some fairly dramatic policy shifts occurring across the country that, if pursued unabated, will lead to a slow but steady decline in the size of prison populations over time (Clear and Frost 2014). Indeed, for the past four years, the United States has seen small but notable declines in the size of prison populations across much of the country and the emergence of a new bipartisan emphasis on making serious efforts to substantially reduce prison populations. Today it is almost impossible to find someone who argues that we need to increase prison populations further, with most claiming that the time to reduce prison populations is past due (Jacobson 2005; Lucken 2011; Simon 2011; Mauer and Ghandnoosh 2013). Part of the change in the tenor of the discussion can be attributed to two decades of declining crime rates—crime rates have fallen dramatically since 1994 when we saw the first declines in violent crime, and those declines have occurred across all states—including those that maintained relatively lower rates of incarceration (Blumstein and Wallman 2005; Zimring 2007).

But dropping crime rates is only one of the reasons the public affection for mass incarceration is waning. The cost of a large prison system is prohibitive. Beginning in 2008, when a nationwide recession left state and local governments extremely pressed for cash, policymakers began to look at correctional systems as one of the places to cut costs. After all, if crime rates were dropping, why could there not be something of a "safety dividend" reflected by lower prison populations? A policy open to reducing prison populations was created by two kinds of evidence that had gradually been accumulating. First, in the public consciousness, a developing awareness of the collateral consequences of mass incarceration grew out of a spate of stories in the popular media that documented the personal, community, and racial consequences of having large numbers of poor people cycle through the prison system. This meant that among politicians it was no longer toxic to consider prison reform as a policy option. Second, among scholars a growing awareness of the failure of prisons to affect crime rates created an evidence base that justified a new approach to punishment—a point we discuss more later. This was a policy reform triple-play: dropping crimes rates, fiscal stress, and a growing public sentiment questioning the value of prisons.

Some critics retain a sense that the drop in crime has been due to the rise in the number of prisoners. This is not surprising, since the original rationale for growing the number of prisoners drew strong social science support. It is remarkable, then, that the science in favor of more prisons has become a less prominent factor in the public debates. Part of this has to do with studies that show how weak the connection is between the size of the prison population and the amount of crime (see Western 2006 for a review). But certainly some of the reason for this change has to do with a growing recognition of the importance of the impact of the growth of prisons on noncrime outcomes.

The coming challenge for theories of mass incarceration then will be their ability to explain what several scholars are describing as early signs of the beginning of the end of mass incarceration (Goode 2013; Clear and Frost 2014). Indeed, we are increasingly seeing scholars who have for decades lamented the constantly rising prison populations expressing (perhaps cautious) optimism about the first series of decreases in rates of incarceration in almost forty years (Clear and Frost 2014; Petersilia and Cullen 2014). Each of the five theoretical perspectives are described in turn and then, in a concluding paragraph, briefly assessed for their ability to explain the recent shift away from what we have elsewhere described as a "punishment imperative" (Clear and Frost 2014).

II. MASS INCARCERATION AS A RATIONAL RESPONSE TO INCREASING CRIME

Although the precise year in which we began down the path to mass incarceration is difficult to isolate, most would agree that the beginning of the era of mass incarceration was the early 1970s and the shifts that preceded it were born in the late 1960s. The most straightforward explanations for the rise of mass incarceration begin from that observation and tie increases in crime and social unrest through the 1960s to the beginning of marked increases in incarceration that followed beginning in the early 1970s. This type of explanation is most often related to some of the early writings of political scientists such as James Q. Wilson and

Charles Murray. To these scholars, and many others who agreed with them, the impetus for the punitive turn in criminal justice policy was increasing crime. Crime, it was argued, had been increasing dramatically through the 1960s and had reached a point at which it could no longer be tolerated. In the now classic Thinking About Crime, Wilson pointed to Uniform Crime Report evidence that the levels of property and violent crime had each more than doubled over the 1960s, with violent crime rising even more rapidly than property crime. Writing about the 1960s Wilson (1975/2013, pp. 3–4) argued, "Crime soared. It rose at a faster rate and to higher levels than at any time since the 1930s and, in some categories, to higher levels than any experienced in this century . . . It all began in about 1963. That was the year, to overdramatize a bit, that a decade began to fall apart." More recently, scholars have called attention to some of the problems with those Uniform Crime Report estimates over the decade in question (Useem, Liedka, and Piehl 2003), but, at the time, all evidence suggested that crime was increasing at a fairly astounding rate.

Something had to be done, and that something involved getting notably tougher on crime and on drugs. Wilson argued cogently for the rational choice model for explaining crime. According to rational choice models, all behavior, including criminal behavior, is shaped by systems of rewards and penalties (if one is psychologically oriented) or costs and benefits (if one is more economically oriented). If behavior is shaped by rewards and penalties, then, by extension, behavior can best be modified or controlled through imposing systems of punishment that would increase the costs of engaging in criminal behavior. No one explains the appeal of this logic better than Wilson (1975/2013, p. 105) himself:

> The average citizen hardly needs to be persuaded that crimes will be committed more frequently if, other things being equal, crime becomes more profitable than other ways of spending one's time. Accordingly, the average citizen thinks it obvious that one major reason why crime has increased is that people have discovered they can get away with it. By the same token, a good way to reduce crime is to make its consequences to the would-be offender more costly (by making penalties swifter, more certain, or more severe), or to make the value of alternatives to crime more attractive (by increasing the availability and pay of legitimate jobs), or both.

Like Wilson, proponents of the theory that the rise in mass incarceration is best explained by increasing crime tend to rely on rational choice–based theories when explaining the rise in crime and criminal behavior. Here the argument is that people choose crime because crime pays—the consequences of crime were simply not outweighing the benefits. Crime paid in part because the risk of getting caught and punished was simply too low and in part because, once caught, the penalties were simply too soft (Murray 1997). In other words, the chances of getting punished were rather remote and, in the rare event that an offender was caught and punished, the potential punishments were not sufficiently painful.

Adjustments could be (and were) made to increase the likelihood that one would get caught for criminal behavior (more police were hired, more police training was funded, etc.), but those calibrations were dependent on so many factors beyond the control of policymakers that it was in many ways both simpler and more intuitive to get tough on crime by increasing the likelihood that one would go to prison once caught (often referred to as "imprisonment risk") and by increasing the length of time that one would stay there once incarcerated. Adjustments on both sides of the equation (e.g., who goes in and how long they stay) took place to varying degrees across all of the states over the period immediately preceding the steady and rapid rise in rates of incarceration (Frost 2006). Through manipulation of these dual determinants, some states saw their prison populations grow quickly and dramatically while others were able to maintain relatively low rates of incarceration, but all states experienced growth over the period (Frost 2008).

While plausible and intuitively appealing as an explanation for mass incarceration, decades of research has demonstrated that crime and incarceration, while related, are actually surprisingly loosely coupled (Young 1999; Clear and Frost 2014). Indeed, after the mid-1970s, rising incarceration rates were seemingly impervious to often fairly dramatic shifts in crime. Incarceration rates continued their upward climb regardless of what was happening in terms of crime. And although few would argue that crime and incarceration are entirely disconnected, many have demonstrated that the connection is tenuous and that the relationship between changing rates of incarceration and fluctuating rates of crime is at best imperfect (Young 1999). As a crime control strategy, incarceration is supposed to prevent crime through one of two primary mechanisms—incapacitation or deterrence—but each of these mechanisms has proven to be of relatively limited efficacy. A large body of research has shown that although incapacitation effects exist, they tend to be relatively low in magnitude and begin to lose explanatory power with each additional incarceration as a result of diminishing marginal returns that had already been reached at current levels of incarceration (Spelman 2000). The now large body of deterrence literature has also shown the limited effectiveness of deterrence-based strategies (Blumstein, Cohen, and Nagin 1978; Tonry 2008; Nagin 2013a, 2013b). Deterrence has proven so limited in part because the ability to achieve deterrence relies on the certainty, celerity, and severity of punishment, but we only really have the capacity to effect changes in severity, which is arguably the least important of the three (Nagin, Cullen, and Jonson 2009). One of the foremost experts on deterrence summarized the evidence on deterrence as follows:

> First, there is little evidence that increases in the length of already long prison sentences yield general deterrent effects that are sufficiently large to justify their social and economic costs. . . . Second . . . there is little evidence of a specific deterrent effect arising from the experience of imprisonment. . . . Instead, the evidence suggests that reoffending is either unaffected or increased. Third, there is substantial evidence that increasing the visibility of the police by hiring more officers and allocating existing officers in ways that materially heighten the perceived risk of apprehension can deter crimes. (Nagin 2013a, p. 201)

In other words, we have the greatest capacity to deter crime at the apprehension phase and very little power to deter crime through punishment. To conclude, although the theory that mass incarceration was primarily the product of increasing crime has intuitive appeal, there are few, if any, that would still argue that changes in rates of crime alone can explain changes in rates of incarceration.

On the other hand, the drop in crime is often cited as a good reason the time has come to try to reduce imprisonment. Certainly declining crime rates have reduced the pressure policymakers feel to privilege public safety over any other policy priority in the penal system. So if concern about crime gave rise to the great era of prison-based punishment, the decline has signaled the arrival of a time when a new set of ideas might emerge.

III. Public Opinion, Politics, and Mass Incarceration

A second theory of mass incarceration starts from a similar place as the first, but here the emphasis tends to be on fear of crime, rather than actual crime, and the ways in which politicians have responded to (or, depending on the perspective, generated) public opinion around crime. These theorists argue that politics, public opinion, and the punitive turn in criminal justice policy that led to mass incarceration are tightly coupled.

While there is little doubt that there has been much public support for punitive responses to crime over the past four decades, there are several competing theories of the relationship between public opinion and the growth in punitiveness that ultimately led to mass incarceration. Most theorists have argued that public opinion has pushed public policy steadily in a more punitive direction, but debate remains about the relationship between public opinion and public policy (Roberts 1992; Roberts, Hough, and Hough 2002). The idea that public opinion rather directly drives policy has been referred to as the "democracy-at-work" thesis (Beckett 1997). According to this perspective, the public has increasingly demanded harsher punishment in response to increasing crime (or fear of crime). Others have argued that political posturing shapes and then manipulates public opinion—a perspective generally referred to as "penal populism" or "populist punitiveness" (Bottoms 1995). Still more have argued that the relationship between public opinion and political maneuvering is more complex and almost certainly reciprocal (Beckett 1997; Green 2006).

The "democracy-at-work" thesis suggests that there is a direct link between public opinion about crime and punishment and the enactment of punitive policies that led to mass incarceration (Beckett 1997; Roberts et al. 2002). According to this model, the perception of rapidly increasing levels of crime in the late 1960s and through the early 1970s served as the genesis for increasingly punitive responses to crime. Put simply, during that period Americans believed we needed to get "tough on crime" because they believed crime was spiraling out of control and they were becoming increasingly fearful. According to this democracy-at-work model, the relationship between public opinion and public policy is direct and travels in just one direction. As the public becomes increasingly fearful of crime and criminal offenders, it becomes increasingly punitive toward them. Public punitiveness is related as much to fear of crime as it is to actual trends in crime, and punitive crime control policies simply reflect a responsive legislature's attempt to assuage fear and fulfill the fearful public's desire to see criminal offenders punished ever more harshly. Under this conception, the fearful public becomes increasingly punitive and demands harsher punishment, and the legislature dutifully delivers. Politicians from the left and right tend to endorse this thesis to argue that they are enacting (or supporting) increasingly punitive legislation because that is what their constituents are demanding—in other words, they are simply being responsive to the people they serve. Overly simplistic in its characterization of politics and public opinion, the democracy-at-work thesis is often criticized for failing to take into account the complexity of both the political process and the public sentiment that is thought to drive that process. Years of public opinion research, for example, has demonstrated that public opinion is both less unidimensionally punitive and more nuanced than a simple review of polling data would suggest (Roberts and Stalans 1997; Cullen, Fisher, and Applegate 2000; Cullen et al. 2002).

Other theorists have argued that over the period in which we have seen mass incarceration flourish there has been a concomitant rise in what has alternately been called either "penal populism" (Roberts et al. 2002) or "populist punitiveness" (Bottoms 1995). These scholars argue that, far from being responsive, politicians are pandering to an overly punitive public and using the crime issue to their advantage. These pandering politicians advance policies that are popular with the public with little to no regard for their effectiveness or for their impact in terms of justice or fairness. Roberts and colleagues (2002, p. 65), for example, distinguish policies that are responsive to public opinion from those that are populist, arguing that "the difference between the democracy-at-work thesis and penal populism is a subtle one, to do with the intentions underlying political initiatives." Populist policies exploit punitive public sentiment to the politician's advantage and are pursued largely for political gain—to shore up support from constituents or to win the next election.

Populist policies often fail to recognize the diversity of public opinion around issues of crime and punishment and that public opinion regarding crime and punishment is complex and often contradictory (Cullen et al. 2000). These politicians deal in absolutes with no room for nuance that is so central to a sophisticated understanding of public opinion (Green 2006). Those familiar with the research on public opinion know that it has repeatedly shown that the American public knows shockingly little about the actual nature and extent of crime, almost always believing it to be far more prevalent and serious of a problem than it actually is, and knows even less about the nature and extent of punishment, believing the system to be far more lenient than it actually is (see Roberts 1992; Roberts and Stalans 1997; Cullen et al. 2000). In other words, the public usually thinks policies are not punitive enough but lacks knowledge with regard to just how punitive criminal justice policies actually are (Hough and Roberts 1999; Mirrlees-Black 2002; Gray 2009). Crucially, even though the public is quite punitive in its orientation, Cullen and colleagues (2000, p. 66) note that "policy makers invariably overestimate rather than underestimate the punitiveness of the public" and thus when they respond in populist ways, they are almost certainly overdoing it (see also Roberts 1992; Roberts and Stalans 1997; Roberts and Hough 2002).

According to both of these perspectives regarding what drove the punitiveness that led to mass incarceration, the development of increasingly harsh policies is depicted as a bottom-up process with the overly punitive public driving public policy in a harsher direction. The politicians writing the legislation that would lead to mass incarceration are generally depicted as either being responsive to the public's demands (democracy-at-work) or exploiting the public's punitive sentiment (penal populism). Others (perhaps most notably Katherine Beckett [1997] in *Making Crime Pay*) have characterized the relationship between public opinion, politics, and mass incarceration as more insidious. Beckett offered an elite manipulation thesis that characterized the development of public opinion as a top-down process where politicians shape and then exploit public sentiment for political gain. According to this view of the relationship, representations of crime and punishment are constructed for political gain and support a broader political ideology. A number of other important and influential books describing the politics of crime and punishment during the era of mass incarceration exist (Chambliss 2001; Gest 2001; Gottschalk 2006; Hagan 2010). Most theorists trace the beginning of the punitive turn in public opinion to the late 1960s. Many have argued that it is no coincidence that this is precisely when conservative political elites were trying to win electoral support and therefore began to frame the problem of crime in ways that would resonate with politically important segments of the electorate.

The theory of "elite manipulation" rests on the premise that the public was manipulated by political elites into believing that crime is a social problem of utmost concern and that increasingly punitive criminal justice interventions were the most viable, and perhaps only, appropriate response. Just as Roberts and others have tried to distinguish responsive policies from receptive policies, Beckett (1997) goes to great lengths to distinguish *public initiative* from *public receptivity* and forcefully argues that the American public was receptive to the conservative crime control ideology from the 1960s through the 1980s precisely because it resonated with central values in American culture. A belief in individualism and in individual responsibility are widely held core American values, and politicians, knowing that the public responds to rhetoric and policies that emphasize these core American values, have exploited these beliefs for political gain. Elizabeth Brown (2009, 2011) has undertaken qualitative work to further our understanding of the processes and mechanisms by which politicians construct and then use public opinion around penal policy for political gain.

It is likely that the "public mind" about incarceration is more complex than these simple theories would suggest. Large segments of the population, especially people of color living in impoverished urban settings, experience incarceration directly themselves or through family members. This affects their beliefs about the wisdom of large prison populations. Likewise, the linkage between law enforcement policy and race in America means that we must understand public perceptions of criminal justice expansion with some nuance. What works for some politicians in some settings will not necessarily work everywhere.

We would be remiss if we concluded this section on politics, public opinion, and mass incarceration without explicitly acknowledging the increasingly important role of the media in the formation of public opinion and the development of criminal justice policy. The media are, in many ways, the crucial middlemen in the development of punitive public opinion (Beckett 1997). Because most Americans with political capital have had very little direct experience with the criminal justice system, they tend to build their knowledge about crime and punishment from secondary indirect sources—most notably, the media (Brown 2006). In reporting on crime, the media tend to rely on government sources (especially politicians) because they have the means of packaging information in ways that are useful and the stature to make them good official sources. In other words, the public tends to trust government sources. Through an overreliance on government sources, the media allows government sources, or "claims-makers" as Beckett (1997) refers to them, to shape the conversation about crime, criminals, and appropriate punishments. In an insidious self-promoting cycle, the politicians then use growing media coverage of crime, which they helped to create and shape, as evidence of growing public concern about crime.

Clearly, a shift of public opinion has been a factor in the emerging dynamic that prison populations nationally have stabilized and are starting to decline. In the days when prison populations rose annually regardless of crime rate changes, the political environment for crime policy was simply too heavily charged to allow a dispassionate assessment of what was needed. Electoral candidates for almost any kind of office felt the need to take an unremittingly tough stance on crime—and many electoral campaigns devolved into who-can-get-tougher contests (Gest 2001). That political reality, ubiquitous just a few years ago, has—almost astonishingly—basically vanished. Whether the change in public sentiment is a cause or a consequence is not easy to disentangle, but it is definitely a correlate.

IV. Mass Incarceration as the Control of Marginal Populations

The images of crime and criminals portrayed through media frames have a very distinct bent. Indeed, a number of scholars have argued that it was the pairing of images of crime and welfare through the 1970s and 1980s that helped drive some of the early increases in punitiveness and the resulting increases in rates of incarceration of largely poor, minority, inner-city Americans.

Incarceration rates have always been higher for the poor and people of color. This has led some writers to argue that prison is used to control marginal subgroups that have insignificant roles in the contemporary economy (Pettit and Western 2004). This analysis begins with the observation that incarceration is concentrated among young men who have not finished school, particularly those of color, and these are precisely the people for whom a postindustrial economy has trouble finding a place.

All societies have marginal populations—the poverty-stricken, the sick, the mentally ill, the unemployed, and so on. While representing diverse subgroups of the population, all of these groups have at least one thing in common: there is no role for them in the modern labor market economy. All societies ultimately have to devise an approach for dealing with those who cannot contribute to the labor market in a meaningful way, and a number of scholars have argued that mass incarceration has become one of the primary mechanisms by which the United States has dealt with its marginal populations, in many ways replacing the welfarist approach associated with previous generations (Garland 1985).

In *The Exclusive Society*, Jock Young (1999) argued that societies can either absorb their deviants or spit them out, and he maintained that this was an essential difference between inclusive and exclusive societies. Inclusive societies tend to emphasize the social causes of marginality and make more concerted efforts to integrate those in society who are deemed socially marginal through offering relatively expansive social welfare and integration programs. By contrast, in exclusive societies individual responsibility is emphasized, the socially marginal are depicted as undeserving, and exclusionary social policies (such as incarceration) are devised to ultimately control marginal populations. Penal and social policy then target the same group—the socially marginal—and, it has been argued, together constitute a more or less coherent policy regime (Beckett and Western 2001). Under this conception, imprisonment is characterized as an exclusionary penal policy for dealing with the socially marginal and can be contrasted with welfare, which represents a far more inclusionary approach of dealing with the very same population. These scholars and others have noted that it is perhaps no coincidence that the rise in incarceration coincided with a significant critique of, and withdrawal from, the welfarist approach to dealing with marginal populations (Garland 1985; Beckett and Western 2001; Tonry 2009).

For more critical social scientists, then, the roots of mass incarceration can be traced to a crisis in the labor market rather than to a rise in crime or fear of crime. Although Loic Wacquant (2008, 2009a, 2009b) has been one of the most consistent and persistent advocates of this perspective, many others have turned to labor market explanations for mass incarceration (Western and Beckett 1999; Beckett and Western 2001; Pettit and Western 2004; Western and Pettit 2005; Beckett and Herbert 2010; Western and Muller 2013). Here we can give only a cursory description of the central arguments made about mass incarceration from this perspective, and this summary description draws on elements of the work of many of those cited earlier.

From the labor market perspective, the rise in incarceration coincided with some fundamental shifts in the economy. Mass incarceration began at a point when labor market demand for semiskilled and unskilled labor started to decline precipitously and the competition for these low-skill jobs became increasingly fierce. Manufacturing jobs were rapidly disappearing, and service-sector jobs that had previously been dominated by lower and working-class males were increasingly sparse as women began entering the low-wage labor market in far greater numbers. In other words, a whole sector of the population was rapidly losing relevance to the shifting labor market economy. Unemployment among young, mostly black males grew quickly, and political leaders were challenged to figure out what to do with these large numbers of young males for whom there was no place in the emerging labor market. At the same time that work was disappearing (Wilson 1996), American welfare policy shifted away from broad-based, government-funded social welfare programs to work-oriented, time-limited welfare policies (Wacquant 2009b).

Fairly rapid changes in the labor market were particularly damaging to inner-city urban communities, and simultaneous declines in the availability of welfare only made the situation more urgent. The void created by a rapidly changing labor market was quickly replaced by emerging drug markets that could provide the cash and opportunities that were no longer available through legitimate means (see Johnson, Golub, and Dunlap 2000). The emergence of drug markets, and the violence sometimes associated with them, offered a new opportunity for criminalization. Media attention to drugs and the associated problems with drug markets, particularly surrounding what was described as the crack epidemic, only bolstered public concern. Debate remains over whether public concern preceded or followed increasingly punitive drug legislation, but, regardless, throughout the 1980s during both the Reagan and the Bush presidencies, the edge of drug laws became ever sharper with the introduction of mandatory lengthy terms of imprisonment for drug crimes. Perhaps more important, these images of drug markets, and the (primarily) young black men depicted as most closely associated with them, only served to stoke public fears about crime and to more firmly link young black men and black inner-city communities with criminality. Prison became the most obvious solution for this marginal group cut off from the legitimate labor market. Drug markets became the enemy and the dominant mechanism by which to move people from the unemployment lines to the prison system.

The dynamics of this kind of economy for people who live on its margin could not be better organized to produce mass incarceration. There is no access to good work, but there is an easy availability of vibrant drug markets. These markets are policed by law enforcement, providing both a steady flow of young men for imprisonment and also destabilizing the drug markets themselves enough that young men who might otherwise not become involved are able to do so (often referred to as the replacement effect). The insidious racism of drug laws is one of the points Michael Tonry (2011) made in his book, *Punishing Race*. Any reasonable person would have known that the policies that were being put into place would differentially affect young black men, placing them in prison and thereby removing them from the economy.

Ironically, while the trajectory of prison populations is changing, the rhetoric about people in trouble with the law is also shifting. Debates about criminality over the ages have often turned on conceptions of "evil" versus "troubled" and "bad" versus "sick." The tone of the public sentiment about people in prison is beginning to emphasize addiction and substance abuse, lack of education, and inequality. While the demographics of the people in prison and under state control have themselves not changed very much since the 1990s, the symbolism of their social circumstances has evolved away from conceptions of evil. Cynics can say that the rhetoric masks a continuing agenda: dealing with people who exist on the economic and social margin. The language may not emphasize control in the same blatant way that it did, but the system still engages in an ever far-reaching labyrinth of control—in the cells and on the streets, with the seamless exercise of power in each of those settings.

V. MASS INCARCERATION AS THE NEW JIM CROW

Theories that emphasize the undeniable link between race and incarceration are related to those that emphasize marginality but put race at the center of the discussion. Such theories invariably recognize the undeniable contribution that the war on drugs has made to the rise in prison populations (Donziger 1996; Mauer 1999; Bobo and Thompson 2006; Alexander 2010). Virtually all theories of mass incarceration recognize the role of the drug war in increasing prison populations and in exacerbating racial disparities throughout the criminal justice system. Some theorists, however, have argued that disparate racial impacts should be the dominant focus of any discussion of the causes or consequences of mass incarceration. Michael Tonry (2004, p. vii) perhaps made this point most evocatively when he argued that "the United States has a punishment system that no one would knowingly have built from the ground up," adding that, "it is often unjust, it is unduly severe, it is wasteful, and it does enormous damage to the lives of black Americans."

There is general agreement that the punitive turn in American penal policy can be tied to some fundamental social, political, and cultural shifts in the 1960s and that the tough-on-crime movement that ushered in unprecedented levels of incarceration was in many ways part of a political strategy. Although many have highlighted the blatantly racist undertones of the 1964 Goldwater campaign (and the more subtly racist 1968 Nixon campaign), scholars are more divided on how intentionally racist the policy choices made in the forty-plus years since have been. In one of the earliest books to focus exclusively on punishment and race in the era of mass incarceration, Tonry (1995, p. 4) argued that even if the policies themselves were not deliberately racist, "the rising levels of Black incarceration did not just happen" but instead "were the foreseeable effects of deliberate policies." Marc Mauer (1999, pp. 158–159) has similarly argued that "most police and prosecutors are not consciously racist in pursuing the drug war. Many firmly believe that they are aiding beleaguered communities caught in a vicious cycle of drug abuse and lack of opportunity." These scholars generally refrain from calling the policies or their authors deliberately racist. Others have been notably more pointed, with scholars like Michelle Alexander (2010, p. 57) arguing that covert racism still drove the political choices, pointing out that "the mass incarceration of communities of color was explained in race-neutral terms, an adaptation to the needs and demands of the current political climate."

The connection between race and penal policy has deep roots. Based on an historical analysis of southern rates of incarceration over an extended time-series, Alex Lichtenstein (2001) has demonstrated that there were actually two surges in the rates of incarceration of African Americans, and these surges followed the two most prominent emancipation movements: the emancipation of African American slaves following the Civil War in the 1860s and the emancipation of African Americans following the demise of Jim Crow segregation laws following the civil rights movement in the 1960s. Lichtenstein provides an example of the post-emancipation incarceration rates in Georgia:

> In 1871 the overall incarceration rate in Georgia was 38 per 100,000; by 1896 it was roughly 100 per 100,000, having reached the plateau that characterized national rates of incarceration throughout the first three-quarters of the 20th century. . . . It is worth noting, however, that Georgia's incarceration rate for whites in 1896 was approximately 15 per 100,000 (the corresponding figure for blacks was 150 per 100,000), suggesting either a massive racial bias in the pattern of imprisonment or else the unlikely prospect that the state's white population was the most law-abiding citizenry in human history. (p. 190)

Lichtenstein uses this example to make an important point—there is nothing new about the racialized aspects of the US system of punishment. Race, and more specifically white fear of African Americans, preceded both historical surges in rates of black incarceration.

Michelle Alexander (2010) similarly offered an historical analysis of not only the war on drugs but also the ever-growing number of collateral consequences of incarceration for those who are no longer in prison. One of the features of Jim Crow was that laws placed restrictions on the job prospects and public accommodations for African Americans. The result was that, in the South, black people could not fully participate in society as equals of whites. In a similar way, the myriad restrictions placed on people with criminal convictions—particularly after they have been incarcerated—acts to limit full participation in society. Restricting access to voting, prohibiting certain kinds of employment, limiting the availability of housing and areas to live—these are all evocative of the days of Jim Crow, when black people faced restrictions that were very much like these. Alexander links these restrictions to the war on drugs and incarceration policies that have steadily grown the number of young black men affected by imprisonment and argues that mass incarceration really is the New Jim Crow. Alexander (2010, pp. 180–181) explains "how the system works" eloquently:

> The War on Drugs is the vehicle through which extraordinary numbers of black men are forced into the cage. Vast numbers of people are swept into the criminal justice system by the police, who conduct drug operations primarily in poor communities of color. In fact,

police are allowed to rely on race as a factor in selecting whom to stop and frisk . . . effectively guaranteeing that those who are swept into the system are primarily black and brown. . . . Prosecutors are free to "load up" defendants with extra charges, and their decisions cannot be challenged for racial bias. Once convicted . . . drug offenders spend more time under the criminal justice system's formal control . . . than drug offenders anywhere else in the world. . . . The final stage . . . [is] a period of invisible punishment . . . laws [that] operate collectively to ensure that the vast majority of convicted offenders will never integrate into mainstream, white society . . . they will eventually return to prison and then be released again, caught in a closed circuit of perpetual marginality.

Although women still make up a relatively small minority of those incarcerated, representing about 10 percent of the overall prison population, the war on drugs was especially central to the increase in the number of women, and minority women in particular, serving time in US prisons (Bush-Baskette 1999; Lapidus et al. 2005). As Lapidus and colleagues have argued, it was not only targeted law enforcement practices, prosecutorial and judicial discretion, or changes in sentencing policies that led to a dramatic increase in women of color serving time for drug offenses—it was also the policing of minority communities in terms of child welfare and more extensive testing of minority women for maternal drug use. Moreover, conspiracy laws and an increasing commitment to pursuing women for accomplice liability meant that women who had a very minimal role in the drug-related crimes of their partners were sentenced to prison for exceptionally lengthy periods of time. Few can forget the story of Kemba Smith, who was just twenty-four years old when she pled guilty to conspiracy to distribute drugs and was sentenced to almost twenty-five years in prison (Lapidus et al. 2005). Her sentence was famously commuted in 2000 by President Bill Clinton as he left office, but not before Kemba had served more than six years for what many have argued were largely the crimes of her boyfriend.

The mandatory minimum sentences that have become so closely associated with the war on drugs targeted not only drug offenses but also repeat offending, violent offenses, sexual offenses, weapons offenses, and drunk driving offenses (Bureau of Justice Assistance 1998). Every state passed mandatory minimum sentencing laws for one or more of these classes of offenses during the 1980s and 1990s. Mandatory sentencing laws are often characterized as central to the build-up of mass incarceration precisely because they allow for no reasoned consideration of circumstances, roles, or consequences. Mandatory minimums represent the epitome of the notion that "you do the crime, you do the time, period," Although they were cast as ways to reduce disparities in sentencing—when written to target specific classes of crime dominated by inner-city urban youth—the disparate racial impacts of these laws should have been plain.

There can be no doubt that social realities of racial injustice are deeply entangled with penal policy. It is not possible to encounter prison and post-prison supervision without becoming immediately aware of the fact that people under correctional control are disproportionately people of color. Some of the energy for prison reform today comes from outrage about the racially disparate collateral consequences of prison policy—for people who end up in the system and for the people who live in the communities from which they come. The fact that the prison system occupies this troubling space in the heritage of American racial policy is without doubt a strong source of the energy for current efforts by reformers to reduce mass incarceration.

VI. MASS INCARCERATION AS A GRAND SOCIAL EXPERIMENT

America has a long and storied tradition of grand experimentation in social policy. Although not the first to refer to America's experience with incarceration as a grand social experiment (Gottschalk 2006; Loury 2008), we were among the first to identify some of the key characteristics of mass incarceration that could qualify it as a grand social experiment (Frost and Clear 2009)—and, more recently, have called the grand social experiment in mass incarceration the "punishment imperative" (Clear and Frost 2014). Grand social experiments have three defining features: first, they emerge around what is increasingly perceived to be "a pressing social problem requiring a transformative kind of action" (Frost and Clear 2009, p. 163). In other words, the emerging social problem is deemed to be so extraordinary that old ways of addressing social problems simply will not suffice. Although the social problem predates the public alarm about the issue, the public becomes so galvanized around the issue that an all new approach is called for—one "that turns the status quo on its head." Next, "public alarm and political will begin to coalesce around a new understanding of the social problem and a new approach" (Frost and Clear 2009, p. 163). During this phase, the problem is "defined" or, perhaps more accurately, "redefined." New understandings of underlying causes and consequences are offered, and a logical strategy for addressing that problem (given its redefinition) begins to emerge. The third defining feature is the emergence of that new idea, a new way of addressing the problem based on the shift in the way the problem is perceived, that gains momentum. Given these defining features, a grand social experiment is most accurately described as the "adoption of a new, largely unproven, strategy for a high-priority social problem based on a reformulated understanding of that problem" (Frost and Clear 2009, p. 163).

America's experiment with mass incarceration qualifies as a grand social experiment because it has each of these defining features as hallmarks. As most histories of the era explain, the impetus for the rapid increase in incarceration emerged in the 1960s when concern about crime and disorder reached a pinnacle. Most of these social histories describe the tumultuous 1960s as a time when crime seemed to be rising out of control, the level of civil unrest was palpable, and a general fear of lawlessness was gripping much of the nation. Politicians began capitalizing on growing public fear through making increasingly alarmist cries for law and order, and, in relatively short order, a new understanding of the problem of crime began to emerge. For at least the past generation (the era of Johnson's Great Society) there had been widespread agreement that criminal offending arose from a combination of poor social conditions. In such a conception, criminal offending and other problem behaviors could be ameliorated through eliminating poverty, improving living conditions and access to education, and providing adequate treatment and rehabilitation. Indeed, many of the Great Society programs had been explicitly designed to provide access to opportunities that would eliminate inequalities and begin to alleviate social problems that were borne of them, such as crime. The new wisdom that began to emerge suggested that, far from being the solution, our welfarist approach to social problems like crime *was* precisely the problem because it contributed to a culture of nonaccountability and dependence (Murray 1994).

A new way of thinking about the problem of crime began to emerge. Central to that new way of thinking was the rational choice model described earlier, which suggests that criminal offending not only made sense but was actually incentivized. According to the arguments that began to garner widespread support, the system had long been too soft on crime, and, as a result, the benefits of crime had long outweighed the threatened costs. A consensus began to coalesce around the notion that what criminals needed was not help or treatment but harsher punishment. The rhetoric that began to emerge in the late 1960s around the problem of crime and lawlessness suggested that tinkering around the edges would never be enough to quell the swelling tide of crime—what we needed was a wholesale new approach to crime control and punishment. Wilson's (1975/2013) *Thinking about Crime* in many ways epitomized the coalescing sentiment of the time.

In the foreword to the latest edition of Wilson's classic book, Charles Murray argues that "[*Thinking about Crime*] changed the criminal justice system" (Wilson 2013/1975, p. xiii). While that might be somewhat of an overstatement, there is no question that Wilson's work was influential and contributed to a fundamental change in the debate around crime prevention and control in part because of how well it resonated with public sentiment and the prevailing political will of the time. The treatment and rehabilitation orientation that had been fundamental to the US correctional system for more than 100 years became almost immediately passé, and fundamental changes to the criminal justice system emerged to fit with this new way of thinking about crime and punishment. We should be clear that there was nothing really new about this way of thinking—the so-called father of modern criminal justice, Cesare Beccaria, had argued for a remarkably similar rational choice–based system more than 200 years prior—but for the new generation of Americans hearing them, these were novel ideas that resonated with, and in many ways shaped, their own evolving way of thinking about crime. In other words, general alarm about rising crime eventually evolved into a new broad narrative about crime, its causes and its control, and that narrative led to a new approach that emphasized punishment and retribution over treatment and rehabilitation. Over the course of a decade, we witnessed the emergence of that new, unproven strategy (mass incarceration) as an approach for dealing with this reformulated problem (crime as a rational choice).

For the next three decades, policy choices were made that fit this "new" markedly more punitive approach. Clear and Frost (2014, p. 76) described this increasing harshness in punishment as "an imperative: the penal system *must* be made harsher, more unforgiving, more punitive." Sentencing policies such as mandatory minimums, three-strikes, and truth-in-sentencing all but ensured that levels of incarceration across the United States would reach previously unthinkable levels. This was the grand social experiment in mass incarceration.

If we think about the forty-year growth in incarceration as a grand social experiment, it is possible to see this experiment as coming to an end. Many social policies ebb and flow. The very idea of a social experiment suggests not only a rationale and a policy intervention but also a beginning and an end. If indeed the growth in imprisonment—the advent of mass incarceration—was the consequence of a loosely coupled but cogent social policy experiment, then it is consistent with that metaphor to say "the results are in." Perhaps the outcome of a four-decade fascination with growing prison rates is a kind of collective search for a new way to think about the response to crime.

VII. Conclusion

The five competing theories—or, perhaps more appropriately, theoretical perspectives—are in many ways overlapping and complimentary, and so it is not surprising that none has yet emerged as the dominant explanation for mass incarceration. Each is plausible and has some intuitive appeal, but theories of mass incarceration are notoriously difficult to test because crime is an overdetermined phenomenon and because many of the constructs theories point to are difficult to operationalize and measure with any precision. If we are correct that we are witnessing the beginning of the end of mass incarceration, the causes of mass incarceration might be revealed through watching its demise, and the next generation of scholars might be better positioned to explain both the rise and fall of mass incarceration.

References

Alexander, Michelle. 2010. *The New Jim Crow: Mass Incarceration in the Age of Colorblindness*. New York: New Press.

Beckett, Katherine. 1997. *Making Crime Pay: Law and Order in Contemporary American Politics*. New York: Oxford University Press.

Beckett, Katherine, and Steve Herbert. 2010. *Banished: The New Social Control in Urban America*. New York: Oxford University Press.

Beckett, Katherine, and Bruce Western. 2001. "Governing Social Marginality: Welfare, Incarceration, and the Transformation of State Policy." *Punishment & Society* 3(1): 43–59.

Blumstein, Alfred, Jacqueline Cohen, and Daniel S. Nagin. 1978. *Deterrence and Incapacitation: Estimating the Effects of Criminal Sanctions on Crime Rates*. Washington, DC: National Academy of Sciences.

Blumstein, Alfred, and Joel Wallman. 2005. *The Crime Drop in America*, 2d ed. New York: Cambridge University Press.

Bobo, Lawrence D., and Victor Thompson. 2006. "Unfair by Design: The War on Drugs, Race, and the Legitimacy of the Criminal Justice System." *Social Research* 73: 445–472.

Bottoms, Anthony. 1995. "The Philosophy and Politics of Punishment and Sentencing." In *The Politics of Sentencing Reform*, edited by Chris Clarkson and Rod Morgan. New York: Oxford University Press.

Brown, Elizabeth K. 2006. "The Dog That Did Not Bark: Punitive Social Views and the Professional Middle Classes." *Punishment & Society* 8: 287–312.

Brown, Elizabeth K. 2009. "Public Opinion and Penal Policymaking: An Examination of Constructions, Assessments, and Uses of Public Opinion by Political Actors in New York State." Unpublished doctoral dissertation, New York State University at Albany.

Brown, Elizabeth K. 2011. "Constructing the Public Will: How Political Actors in New York State Construct, Assess, and Use Public Opinion in Penal Policy Making." *Punishment & Society* 13: 424–450.

Bureau of Justice Assistance. 1998. *1996 National Survey of State Sentencing Structures*. Washington, DC: Government Printing Office.

Bush-Baskette, Stephanie R. 1999. "The 'War on Drugs': A War against Women?" In *Harsh Punishment: International Experiences of Women's Imprisonment*, edited by Sandy Cook and Susanne Daives. Boston: Northeastern University Press.

Chambliss, William J. 2001. *Power, Politics, and Crime*. Boulder, CO: Westview Press.

Clear, Todd R., and James Austin. 2009. "Reducing Mass Incarceration: Implications of the Iron Law of Prison Populations," *Harvard Law and Policy Review* 3: 307–324.

Clear, Todd R., and Natasha A. Frost. 2014. *The Punishment Imperative: The Rise and Failure of Mass Incarceration in America*. New York: New York University Press.

Cullen, Francis T., Bonnie S. Fisher, and Brandon K. Applegate. 2000. "Public Opinion about Punishment and Corrections." In *Crime and Justice: A Review of Research*, Vol. 27, edited by Michael Tonry. Chicago: University of Chicago Press.

Cullen, Francis T., Jennifer A. Pealer, Bonnie S. Fisher, Brandon K. Applegate, and Shannon A. Santana. 2002. "Public Support for Correctional Rehabilitation in America: Change or Consistency?" In *Changing Attitudes to Punishment: Public Opinion, Crime and Justice*, edited by Julian V. Roberts and Mike Hough. Portland, OR: Willan.

Donziger, Steven. 1996. *The Real War on Crime: The Report of the National Criminal Justice Commission*. New York: HarperPerennial.

Frost, Natasha A. 2006. *The Punitive State: Crime, Punishment and Imprisonment across the United States*. New York: LFB Scholarly Publications.

Frost, Natasha A. 2008. "The Mismeasure of Punishment: Alternative Measures of Punitiveness and their (Substantial) Consequences." *Punishment & Society* 10: 277–300.

Frost, Natasha A., and Todd Clear. 2009. "Understanding Mass Incarceration as a Grand Social Experiment." *Studies in Law, Politics, and Society* 47: 159–191.

Garland, David. 1985. *Punishment and Welfare: A History of Penal Strategies*. Brookfield, VT: Gower.

Gest, Ted. 2001. *Crime & Politics: Big Government's Erratic Campaign for Law and Order*. New York: Oxford University Press.

Goode, Erica. 2013. "U.S. Prison Populations Decline, Reflecting New Approach to Crime." *New York Times*, July 25. http://www.nytimes.com/2013/07/26/us/us-prison-populations-decline-reflecting-new-approach-to-crime.html

Gottschalk, Marie. 2006. *The Prison and the Gallows: The Politics of Mass Incarceration in America*. New York: Cambridge University Press.

Gray, Jacqueline M. 2009. "What Shapes Public Opinion of the Criminal Justice System?" In *Changing Attitudes to Punishment: Public Opinion, Crime and Justice*, edited by Julian V. Roberts and Mike Hough. Portland, OR: Willan.

Green, David A. 2006. "Public Opinion Versus Public Judgment about Crime: Correcting the 'Comedy of Errors.'" *British Journal of Criminology* 46: 131–154.

Hagan, John. 2010. *Who Are the Criminals? The Politics of Crime Policy from the Age of Roosevelt to the Age of Reagan*. Princeton, NJ: Princeton University Press.

Harrison, Paige M., and Jennifer C. Karberg. 2003. *Prison and Jail Inmates at Midyear 2002*. Washington, DC: Department of Justice, Bureau of Justice Statistics.

Hough, Mike, and Julian V. Roberts. 1999. "Sentencing Trends in Britain: Public Knowledge and Public Opinion." *Punishment & Society* 1: 11–26.

Jacobson, Michael. 2005. *Downsizing Prisons: How to Reduce Crime and End Mass Incarceration*. New York: New York University Press.

Johnson, Bruce D., Andrew Golub, and Eloise Dunlap. 2000. "The Rise and Decline of Hard Drugs, Drug Markets, and Violence in Inner-City New York." In *The Crime Drop in America*, edited by Alfred Blumstein and Joel Wallman. Cambridge, UK: Cambridge University Press.

Lapidus, Lenora, Namita Luthra, Anjuli Verma, Deborah Small, Patricia Allard, and Kirsten Levingston. 2005. *Caught in the Net: The Impact of Drug Policies on Women and Families*. Santa Cruz, CA: ACLU Drug Law Reform Project.

Lichtenstein, Alex. 2001. "The Private and the Public in Penal History: A Commentary on Zimring and Tonry." *Punishment & Society* 3: 189–196.

Loury, Glenn C. 2008. *Race, Incarceration and American Values*. Cambridge, MA: MIT Press.

Lucken, Karol. 2011. "Leaving Mass Incarceration." *Criminology and Public Policy* 10: 707–714.

Mauer, Marc. 1999. *Race to Incarcerate*. New York: New Press.

Mauer, Marc, and Nazgol Ghandnoosh. 2013. "Can We Wait 88 Years to End Mass Incarceration?" *Huffington Post*, December 20. http://www.huffingtonpost.com/marc-mauer/88-years-mass-incarceration_b_4474132.html

Mirrlees-Black, Catriona. 2002. "Improving Public Knowledge about Crime and Punishment." In *Changing Attitudes to Punishment: Public Opinion, Crime and Justice*, edited by Julian V. Roberts and Mike Hough. Portland, OR: Willan.

Murray, Charles A. 1994. *Losing Ground: American Social Policy, 1950–1980*, 2d ed. New York: Basic Books.

Murray, Charles A. 1997. *Does Prison Work?* London: Institute of Economic Affairs.

Nagin, Daniel S. 2013a. "Deterrence: A Review of the Evidence by a Criminologist for Economists." *Annual Review of Economics* 5: 83–105.

Nagin, Daniel S. 2013b. "Deterrence in the Twenty First Century." In *Crime and Justice in America 1975–2025*, edited by Michael Tonry. Chicago: University of Chicago Press.

Nagin, Daniel, Francis T. Cullen, and Cheryl Lero Jonson. 2009. "Imprisonment and Reoffending." In *Crime and Justice: A Review of Research, Vol. 38*, edited by Michael Tonry. Chicago: University of Chicago Press.

National Research Council. 2014. *The Growth of Incarceration in the United States: Exploring Causes and Consequences*. Washington, DC: National Academies Press.

Petersilia, Joan, and Francis T. Cullen. 2014. "Liberal But Not Stupid: Meeting the Promise of Downsizing Prisons." *Stanford Journal of Criminal Law and Policy*. http://nicic.gov/library/028481

Pettit, Becky, and Bruce Western. 2004. "Mass Imprisonment and the Life Course: Race and Class Inequality in US Incarceration." *American Sociological Review* 69: 151–169.

Pew Center on the States. 2008. *1 in 100: Behind Bars in America 2008*. Washington, DC: Pew Charitable Trusts.

Pew Center on the States. 2009. *1 in 31: The Long Reach of Corrections*. Washington, DC: Pew Charitable Trusts.

Roberts, Julian V. 1992. "Public Opinion, Crime and Criminal Justice." In *Crime and Justice: A Review of Research, Vol. 16*, edited by Michael Tonry. Chicago: University of Chicago Press.

Roberts, Julian V., Mike Hough, and J. M. Hough. 2002. *Changing Attitudes to Punishment: Public Opinion, Crime and Justice*. Portland, OR: Willan.

Roberts, Julian V., and Loretta J. Stalans. 1997. *Public Opinion, Crime, and Criminal Justice*. Boulder, CO: Westview Press.

Rose, Dina R., and Todd R. Clear. 2004. "Who Doesn't Know Someone in Jail? The Impact of Exposure to Prison on Attitudes Toward Informal and Formal Controls." *The Prison Journal* 84: 228–247.

Simon, Jonathan. 2011. "Editorial: Mass Incarceration on Trial." *Punishment & Society* 13: 251–255.

Spelman, William. 2000. "The Limited Importance of Prison Expansion." In *The Crime Drop in America*, edited by Alfred Blumstein and Joel Wallman. Cambridge, UK: Cambridge University Press.

Tonry, Michael. 1995. *Malign Neglect: Race, Crime, and Punishment in America*. New York: Oxford University Press.

Tonry, Michael. 2004. *Thinking about Crime: Sense and Sensibility in American Penal Culture*. Studies in Crime and Public Policy. New York: Oxford University Press.

Tonry, Michael. 2008. "Learning from the Limitations of Deterrence Research." In *Crime and Justice: A Review of Research, Vol. 37*, edited by Michael Tonry. Chicago: University of Chicago Press.

Tonry, Michael. 2009. "Explanations of American Punishment Policies." *Punishment & Society* 11: 377–394.

Tonry, Michael. 2011. *Punishing Race: A Continuing American Dilemma*. New York: Oxford University Press.

Useem, Bert, Raymond V. Liedka, and Anne Morrison Piehl. 2003. "Popular Support for the Prison Build-Up." *Punishment & Society* 5: 5–32.

Wacquant, Loic. 2008. *Urban Outcasts: A Comparative Sociology of Advanced Marginality*. Malden, MA: Polity Press.

Wacquant, Loic. 2009a. *Prisons of Poverty*. Minneapolis: University of Minnesota Press.

Wacquant, Loic. 2009b. *Punishing the Poor: The Neoliberal Government of Social Insecurity*. Durham, NC: Duke University Press.

Western, Bruce. 2006. *Punishment and Inequality in America*. New York: Russell Sage Foundation.

Western, Bruce, and Katherine Beckett. 1999. "How Unregulated is the U.S. Labor Market? The Penal System as a Labor Market Institution." *American Journal of Sociology* 104: 1030–1060.

Western, Bruce, and Becky Pettit. 2005. "Black–White Wage Inequality, Employment Rates, and Incarceration." *American Journal of Sociology* 111: 553–578.

Western, Bruce, and Christopher Muller. 2013. "Mass Incarceration, Macrosociology, and the Poor." *ANNALS of the American Academy of Political and Social Science* 647: 166–189.

Wilson, James Q. 2013. *Thinking About Crime*, 3d ed. New York: Random House. (Originally published 1975)

Wilson, William Julius. 1996. *When Work Disappears: The World of the New Urban Poor*. New York: Random House.

Young, Jock. 1999. *The Exclusive Society: Social Exclusion, Crime and Difference in Late Modernity*. Thousand Oaks, CA: Sage.

Zimring, Franklin E. 2007. *The Great American Crime Decline*. Studies in Crime and Public Policy. New York: Oxford University Press.

....

INMATE ADAPTATION TO THE PRISON ENVIRONMENT

....

CHAPTER 6

··

SUBCULTURAL ADAPTATIONS
TO INCARCERATION

··

BEN CREWE AND BEN LAWS

In his imperious book *The Big House*, Cox (2009, pp. 123–24) depicts Stateville penitentiary, as it was in 1935:

> The yard housed a village of eight-three wooden shacks—a Grand Bazaar of inmate clubs and stores where liquor was dispensed, gambling casinos were operated, and young men were sold as sex toys. Some of the acreage was devoted to marijuana cultivation. Inmates crammed their cells with overstuffed chairs and put curtains over the bars to ensure privacy from prying guards. Cells hosted cats, dogs, rabbits, and canaries—as many as two hundred birds per cell, bred for the pet shop market. Pigeons were raised for cooking on improvised stoves.

Describing Jackson prison in the 1940s and early 1950s, Cox (2009, p. 129) provides an equally striking image: "favored convicts followed the institutional custom of driving around southern Michigan in prison vehicles—running errands, going to ballgames, and visiting bars. Other inmates paid taxi drivers or guards to take them to houses of prostitution . . . The prison was a classic example of inmate control."

Both of these portrayals point to the distinctive social arrangements that characterized the American prison of these decades. The prison was a total institution, a "self-sufficient purposely nonnatural world" (Cox 2009, p. 97) but with an extensive informal economy and a semiofficial interior hierarchy that rendered it sprawling and socially vibrant.

Contrast this with recent descriptions of American "supermax" establishments, where prisoners are held in almost complete segregation:

> Confined to their small, densely walled cells along the periphery of the units, prisoners are both physically and psychologically distant from the officers who move briskly down the tiers or stand in the center looking out at them with the grave disengagement of the police . . . Prisoners depend on the staff to bring them everything—food, toilet paper, books, and letters from home. . . . Officers and prisoners agree on the deadening effects of an atmosphere in which is so little room for maneuver. (Rhodes 2004, pp. 30–31)

Designed "for the creation of a potentially absolute social exclusion" (Rhodes 2004, p. 7), supermax prisoners have no opportunities to mix with each other, let alone seek positions of influence that might allow them glimpses of normal social or sexual relations. As one prisoner explains, "They put you in an environment where you can't talk to anybody else, you can't have any contact . . . unless you yell or scream" (Rhodes 2004, p. 31). As suggested here, then, while supermax confinement does not completely prevent social interaction, the "forms of sociality" that it fosters are highly distorted (Rhodes 2004, p. 34).

Here, then, we begin to see the span of social arrangements that prisons engender and the futility of trying to discuss prison subcultures with any sense of generality. Meanwhile, a major impediment to any attempt to describe and contrast prisoner subcultures is the fundamental difficulty of assembling relevant empirical material. The kinds of ethnographic accounts of the prisoner community that are required for such purposes are uncommon—increasingly so, in countries such as the United States, as the gates of the prison have been closed in the face of researchers (see Simon 2000; Wacquant 2002)—leaving a knowledge base that is threadbare and dispersed. In the United States, many of the most influential accounts of prisoner culture (e.g., Sykes 1958; Jacobs 1977) have been undertaken in maximum-security contexts, or in particular state jurisdictions, such as California and Texas (Crouch and Marquart 1989; Irwin 1980, 2004). Scholarly pragmatism means that generalizations about penal culture are often drawn from single-site studies, with insufficient attention given to the particular locations, eras, and contexts in which these institutions are situated. In particular, Gresham Sykes's *The Society of Captives* has become the comparator and reference point for most studies of prisoner subculture, something that might be justified by the book's conceptual and empirical lucidity and by its emphasis on the inherent qualities of imprisonment but that risks disembedding its findings from important contextual coordinates.

With such limitations and concerns in mind, the aim of this essay is not to attempt a comprehensive overview of prisoner subculture.[1] Instead, it provides a selective description of a number of historically and geographically specific "models," both to highlight the range of social and subcultural arrangements in prisons and to help set out a framework that might help explain *why* we find such variation and what questions we should ask of any descriptive account of the prisoner social world. Section I describes the kinds of penal establishments that provided the basis for many of the classic postwar studies of prison sociology but whose conditions require historical contextualization. Sections II and III focus on the two models that superseded earlier institutional forms: the supermax prison, which represents the ultimate in coercive control, and the more typical "warehouse prison." By highlighting some of the characteristic features of prisons in England and Wales, section IV emphasizes differences between imprisonment practices and outcomes in North America and Europe, while section V seeks to summarize forms of organization and social structure in the Global South. Each section is, unavoidably, somewhat reductive, glossing over important differences within national and international jurisdictions in order to provide a rather general picture. Overall, though, the aim is to

- Emphasize the heterogeneity of institutional forms and the subcultures that exist within them.
- Explain these differences by elaborating on the broader institutional aims, conditions, and practices that determine prison social life and culture.
- Suggest the need for an alternative framework through which to think about the determinants of these aspects of prison life, whose starting point is the way that any

institution deals with the issues of power, order, and governance that are essential to all prisons, and set the conditions for prisoners' adaptations and social practices.

I. The "Big House" and The Early Postwar Prison

In *Prisons in Turmoil*, John Irwin (1980, p. 5) describes the "Big House" prison as an "asphalt monstrosity . . . a place of banishment and punishment," whose main characteristics were "isolation, routine, and monotony. Its mood was mean and grim, perforated here and there by ragged-edged vitality and humor." Despite paying lip service to ideas of reform, these 19th-century institutions had little purpose beyond incapacitation, so the main aim of staff was to ensure a basic level of control and security, but beyond this the prisoner society was relatively autonomous. Thus the daily routine was strict and tightly scheduled (prisoners often ate in silence and moved in lockstep), but the prisoner subculture was the kind of bustling social marketplace described earlier—in Cox's (2009, p. 122) terms, "Soulless regimentation on the surface, soulful turbulence underneath." Within the walled boundaries of the institution was a world that was both deeply antithetical to life outside and in many ways a parallel structure, with an extensive informal economy and a steep internal hierarchy. This subculture was not just tolerated by the official institutional structure but enabled by it. Greatly outnumbered by prisoners and lacking sophisticated tools of compliance, to ensure that the prison met all of its daily tasks, including the basic requirement of institutional stability, staff selected certain prisoners for semiofficial jobs, or informal perks and privileges; the men were expected to assist in the running of the prison. They held considerable influence over the lives of their peers, for example, in their ability to allocate cells and work assignments or in their capacity to distribute the minor goods and services that were otherwise scarce. Meanwhile, prior to the postwar era of "treatment," indeterminate sentencing, and official privileges, prisons made few efforts to assess and determine how prisoners behaved, so long as their actions were not disruptive or disobedient: what went on between prisoners beyond this was not tightly governed by institutional processes or practices.

Such were the prisons described in two of the earliest and most influential accounts of prison social life: Clemmer's (1940) *The Prison Community* and Sykes's (1958) *The Society of Captives*. Both texts depicted a rich and internally stratified prisoner culture, functioning almost autonomously from official structures, whose norms appeared at odds with those of the authorities and alien from those of the outside world. The culture was marked by distinctive forms of slang, homosexual relationships (both coercive and consensual), gambling, fraud, and violence, which Sykes (1958, p. 102) noted, ran "like a bright thread through the fabric of life" in the maximum-security prison in which he undertook his research. Meanwhile, prisoners espoused and promoted an "inmate code"—emphasizing honor, mutual aid, loyalty, masculine stoicism, and an attitude of controlled opposition toward the institution—that at the same time they frequently breached. It was this code that Sykes placed at the center of his theorization of social behavior and relations. The roots of this inmate code, he argued, were the "pains of imprisonment" that he considered to be inherent to imprisonment: the deprivations of liberty, security (or personal safety), autonomy, goods and services, and heterosexual relationships. Such deprivations created the "energy" for the entire social system, which was organized around attempts by prisoners to mitigate the daily frustrations and scarcities that they encountered. The code represented a functional response to these pains and served as a collective coping mechanism: the greater the number of prisoners who conformed to it, "the greater the likelihood that the pains of imprisonment will be rendered less severe for the inmate population as a whole" (Sykes 1958, p. 107). Most prisoners alleviated their predicament not through normative conformity but by victimizing others (e.g., stealing from or defrauding others; engaging in sexual coercion), capitalizing on their needs (e.g., through trade), or responding to their predicament in ways that were to the detriment of others (e.g. "informing" to staff; engaging in expressive violence in the face of irritation). Yet the code still shaped prisoner behavior to some extent, curbing conflicts and serving as a guide to personal conduct.

Meanwhile, Sykes (1958) posited that the prisoner leaders who embodied the inmate code were crucial in maintaining institutional order, for they kept in check prisoners who were altogether more "antisocial," disruptive and antagonistic to the authorities, and "with their commitment to loyalty among prisoners, the sharing of scarce goods, the curbing of hostility and exploitation, and so on" (Sykes 1958, p. 124) helped ease the tensions that might otherwise lead to disorder. It was these prisoners who were most likely to find themselves brokering between the authorities and their peers, because their attitude of honorable stoicism meant that they were respected by both groups and could distribute the illicit goods and privileged information that they received from staff within the prisoner community as a means of keeping the peace. These "accommodations" between guards and prisoners were inevitable, Sykes believed, given that prisoners had little internalized moral commitment to obey and official incentives and disincentives were ineffective in shaping their behavior. Without such mechanisms of compliance, order depended on trade-offs and compromises, and the greatest risk to institutional stability was the stripping away of informal power from the cohesively oriented prisoner. Counterintuitively, then, even in an institution of almost total control, Sykes believed that some power had to be transferred from official to unofficial hands and that order could not be accomplished without harnessing the internal dynamics of the prisoner subculture. Ironically, the task of the authorities was aided by a code that stated its opposition to their goals, values, and personnel. As explained next, such arrangements are still found in some jurisdictions globally, often in the more organized form of prison gangs. At the same time, in the United States, the supermax prison represents the antithesis of the power-sharing model of prison governance.

II. SUPERMAX PRISONS

The description of subculture in supermax establishments is hamstrung by two main issues. The first is that supermax prisons are "secretive institutions," which rarely allow external investigation (Rhodes 2009, p. 196). The second is that they are specifically designed to *segregate* prisoners from each other, to dissolve and preclude collective action and interaction (see Shalev 2013). Often considered to be the "end of the line" for the "worst of the worst" prisoners (Mears and Reisig 2006), supermax establishments demonstrate the essence of penal "concentration strategies" (Mears and Reisig 2006) that seek to neutralize and contain the system's most dangerous and recalcitrant prisoners. In this respect, they epitomize a wider penal ideology of managerial efficacy, risk management (Feeley and Simon 1992; Pizarro, Vanja, and Pratt 2006) and a "structured, security-orientated administration" (Shalev 2013, p. 160), which itself is a direct response to "the breakdown of the governance strategies anchored in inmate society and thus in prison sociology" (Simon 2000, p. 298). To put this another way, the supermax prison seeks to bypass the "social" in its mode of governance and to obliterate it in its everyday organization (as do other aspects of prison administration, such as the move toward smaller facilities and the more frequent transfer of prisoners between units and facilities). To quote Sharon Shalev (2013, p. 163), this "is not a side effect of supermax confinement, but one of the very central features of its rationale."

Supermax establishments—sometimes referred to in the United States as "special housing units," "control units," or "maximum security units" (Rhodes 2004)—comprise small, self-contained units where prisoners' reside for 23 hours a day under conditions of extreme sensory deprivation (Irwin 2004; Reiter 2012). By "immobilizing the convicts in concrete caverns" and employing modern technology, they attempt to "eliminate problems of order, discipline and surveillance" (Cox 2009, p. 177), creating a regime that is highly mechanical and emotionally sterile. This mechanization is evident in the "relationships" between officers and prisoners in which the latter are infantilized and deliberately subjected to "impersonal distance" (Rhodes 2009, p. 196). Further, the use of personal discretion by officers is largely proscribed, with staff instead trained to apply "pervasive and all-encompassing" rules in a manner that is "rote and routinized" (Haney 2008, p. 968). Even if this minimization is not absolute, so that officers may tolerate minor rule infractions, the opportunities for prisoners to develop relationships with staff, or to negotiate aspects of their situation, are minimal.

The impact of these practices on prisoner dynamics and social relationships is in some ways self-evident. As Simon (2000, p. 302) highlights: "The 'super-max' reduces prison social order to its lowest possible relevance by increasing the level of isolation of the inmate from both other inmates and the staff toward the theoretical limit points of total segregation." At first glance, then, what is striking about the supermax is the apparent absence of a prisoner subculture. As Sykes (1958, p. 5) noted, the development of a prisoner society requires social interaction, and when men are "locked forever in their cells," what results is "a mass of isolates rather than a society." Indeed, the majority of research within supermax prisons has documented the atomization of prisoners, a weakening of prisoner solidarity, and the replacement of a collectivist inmate code with a culture in which informing on (or falsely accusing) others for personal gain may be approved of by other prisoners (Irwin 2004). The conditions of supermax confinement, including their intentional forms of social and sensual deprivation, may also lead to a range of psychological pathologies, agitating or originating mental illness in what Haney (2006, p. 958) has termed an "ecology of cruelty" (see also Haney and Lynch 1997; Toch 2001; Elsner 2006; Mears and Reisig 2006).

Despite all of these limitations, however, evidence suggests the existence of a limited prisoner subculture even in supermax conditions. First, verbal communication is not suppressed completely, as prisoners exchange information by shouting back and forth to one another, often through ventilation or water pipes (Rhodes 2004). Meanwhile, prisoners achieve minimal but significant forms of physical contact through "finger shaking," which involves them exploiting the perforated holes in cell doors during transitions to and from cells (Shalev 2013). Second, through a range of surreptitious methods, including the inscription of messages on documents and letters (using urine as ink or "ghost writing" with pencil) and by flinging elastic threads beneath cell doors, prisoners are able to deliver messages, and sometimes other items, to their peers (Shalev 2013). Thus a *sub rosa* economy of sorts endures.

Third, while supermax confinement can inhibit the influence of gangs within the correctional system by segregating key players and personnel (Crouch and Marquart 1989), it is by no means clear that this policy is entirely successful. Supermax prisons may have high levels of "active gang and clique participation" (Irwin 2004, p. 130)—a matter that might not be of concern to administrators, if the aim is merely one of containment, but may solidify gang commitment and forms of symbolic solidarity: "The dynamics of being held in close, exclusive interaction with them [other gang members] strengthens the bonds among them. Consequently, a prisoner with a weak or no gang affiliation is often converted to full membership to that gang by the lock-up decision" (Irwin 2004, p. 142).

Indeed, although opportunities for physical interaction are sparse during supermax confinement, the experience of collective adversity may produce "an upper class of prisoners whose survival . . . affords them high status. This status allows them great influence on daily events in the prison" (Hartman 2008, p. 169). Gang culture, then, is not simply imported into the prison but is a direct response to environmental pressures that bond people in shared, extreme circumstances and create a "new standard of toughness" (Hartman 2008, p. 169).

While supermax conditions prevent prisoners from engaging in traditional forms of collective organization and resistance, this does not mean that their acts are devoid of social meaning. Rhodes (2004) reports that prisoners describe throwing urine and feces at officers as a highly meaningful, "distinctly social act" (p. 44), often undertaken for an audience, to reverse the normal "trajectory of contempt" (p. 45) and to reflect the prisoner's sense that he himself is treated as a form of human excrement. Similarly, while social interaction is profoundly curtailed, collective action remains a possibility. In summer 2013, at Pelican Bay State Prison in California, four alleged leaders of rival prison gangs coordinated a hunger strike that lasted for almost two months and involved nearly 30,000 prisoners across the Californian prison system, both within and beyond supermax facilities (Wallace-Wells 2014). The strike was profoundly "social" in its origins, aims, and organization. Its four initial protagonists were purported to be the leaders of rival, ethnic gangs who had been separated from members of their own gangs to inhibit their influence but who, after several years in the same housing corridor, began to work together on the basis of a political and class consciousness. Having declared an end to hostilities between racial groupings in the prison, their implicit message was one of inmate solidarity. They collaborated initially through conversations "yelled across the pod and through the concrete walls of the exercise room" (Wallace-Wells 2014), and the fact that the strike took hold around the state was indicative of the capillary networks, hierarchical structure, and sheer influence of the gang organizations. Meanwhile, one of the core demands was to be allowed "meaningful contact" with other people (one of the leaders, Todd Ashker, declared to a journalist that he had "not had a normal face-to-face conversation with another human being in 23 years"; Wallace-Wells 2014). Even in conditions of profound social and relational minimalism, then, social and relational energies can be inhibited but not suppressed.

III. WAREHOUSE PRISONS

> For decades, prisons were referred to as warehouses, but this label was inaccurate. It masked the existence of the complex social organizations that existed in earlier institutions. Since 1980, many prisons in states such as California and Texas that rapidly expanded their prison populations have become true human warehouses. In these warehouses, prisoners endure deeply reduced mobility, activities, and involvement in prison programs and are merely stored to serve out their sentences. (Irwin 2004, p. 57)

As suggested in John Irwin's statement, the warehouse prison represents a relatively recent model of imprisonment, marked by rigidity, overcrowding, and institutional torpor. Robertson (1997) argues that among the forces that have underpinned and fueled modern warehousing are the rapid growth in the prison population that resulted from the "war on crime" from the mid-1970s onward and a loss of faith in offender rehabilitation. Such establishments, whose primary concerns are incapacitation, efficiency, and economy, do "little more than provide secure confinement" (Birkbeck 2011, p. 308) and may be seen as the outcome of a wider penal culture whose aim is "identifying and managing unruly groups" (Feeley and Simon 1992, p. 455) without pursuing traditional aims of personal transformation. Compared to the Big House, cell blocks are considerably smaller, designed to enable staff surveillance, and control is enabled by a range of electronic and technological devices. Prisoners themselves have considerably less autonomy within the institution.

Even if, as Sykes (1958) noted, the inmate code never in fact generated a culture of loyalty and solidary cooperation, descriptions of the warehouse prison consistently portray a world in which allegiance to a collective prisoner identity has disintegrated (Irwin 2004), and whatever code endures is far looser, more contested, and more individualized than in earlier decades (Trulson 2005; Copes, Brookman, and Brown 2013). Certainly, Hassine, Bernard, and Wright's (1996, p. 42) elaboration of the contemporary prisoner code (in a maximum-security prison) is striking in advocating a form of defensive social minimalism: "Don't gamble, don't mess with drugs, don't mess with homosexuals, don't steal, don't borrow or lend, and you might survive." Winfree, Newbold, and Tubb (2002, p. 229) note that this emphasis on doing "your own time" reflects "some of the strongest elements of the inmate social system originally identified by Sykes and Messinger (1960)" and concludes that "the culture of the incarcerated remains relatively unaltered" (p. 230). But while it is helpful to question whether the prisoner world has changed as much as is often implied, particularly since every generation of older prisoners proclaims a decline in honor and respect among younger cohorts (see Hunt et al. 1993), there are good grounds for believing that the subculture of American prisons is more heterogeneous, less monolithic, and more marked by conflict and volatility than in the postwar years (Pollock 2004).

Hunt et al. (1993, p. 398) describe the warehouse prison as an "increasingly unpredictable world in which prior loyalties, allegiances, and friendships [are] disrupted" and argue that the seemingly "arbitrary and ad hoc events" of modern imprisonment contrast sharply with a time when there were clear social divisions (prisoners vs. officers, blacks vs. whites) but life was in many ways "orderly." In the contemporary environment, gangs and cliques have proliferated, creating "new clefts and competing allegiances" (p. 407), organized along racial and ethnic lines (Irwin 2004). Prison yards are "balkanized into racial groupings" (Pollock 2004, p. 106), and although these groups are not necessarily openly hostile to each other (Irwin 2004), it is to these subgroups, rather than a broader "inmate class," that prisoners express and act out their loyalties. In his description of Solano prison, Irwin suggests that, within these racial groupings, prisoners socialize in loose and unstructured friendship groups but may organize into neighborhood-based "cars," or more formally structured gangs.

The underlying reasons for these shifts in inmate culture are unclear. Faulkner and Faulkner (1997, p. 67) argue that the "dilution" of the code has resulted from restrictions on prisoner movement, which have weakened the "communication system among inmates" and the threat of long periods of supermax confinement for prisoners who participate in fights, which diminishes motivations to enforce inmate norms. It seems equally plausible, though, that, as Carroll (1974) argued, the splintering of collective commitments was an outcome of penal institutions becoming less "total," in part due to legal interventions into institutions that had previously been relatively impermeable. This development, driven by the inmate rights movement, enabled prisoners to retain and express their external identities to a greater degree than when the prison was a more psychologically isolating and depriving domain, in which prisoners were primarily defined by their shared circumstances rather than their prior identities.

It is worth noting, too, that the fracturing of the prisoner population occurred well before the supermax era. Irwin argues that the solidary nature of the inmate social system had begun to break down in the 1950s and 1960s, due to a significant increase in the proportion of ethnic minority prisoners and "lowriders"—young, criminally unskilled men, who had little sense of loyalty to those beyond their cliques and were highly volatile and aggressive. As James Jacobs (1977) documented in *Stateville* (see also Carroll 1974), by the 1970s the flow into maximum-security prisons of urban street-gangs, and their growing political and ethno-racial consciousness, had altered the dynamics between prisoners, and between prisoners and the institution, all the more profoundly. Inmate leaders were no longer the upstanding men described by Sykes but were instead gang leaders, who promoted a culture of "toughness" over "honor," such that nonaffiliated prisoners were victimized with impunity. At the same time, a defiant form of racial consciousness and the power of prison gangs to improve the lot of their members led to the breakdown of traditional accommodations between inmate leaders and the institution.

Yet the animosities of this period may have taken on new forms. Irwin contends that the threat of transfer to supermax facilities for prisoners thought to have gang affiliations, and the deliberate design of the warehouse prison to minimize disruption, has curtailed blatant forms of violence and gang activity. The result is a form of "détente" between a range of prisoner groupings. Pollock (2004, p. 107) claims that "tension between racial gangs today has as much to do with financial interests as it does racial prejudice" and that the illicit economy that has always been a defining quality of the prisoner community has become its primary determinant. Business interests are prioritized over other concerns, with ethnically homogenous groupings willing to "sell their drugs to anyone and avoid a lockdown by working together" (Trammell 2009, p. 769). Similarly, Hassine et al. (1996, p. 42) observed that "every inmate in general population was either a buyer or a seller," and that it was therefore "to everyone's benefit to abide by the Inmate Code."

Drawing on economic theories rather than the conventional frameworks of prison sociology, Skarbek (2012) takes this analysis further. Prison gangs, he argues, developed in the United States due to three primary shifts: a rapidly expanding prisoner population, increased crowding, and changes in prisoner demography. In this context, the system of social norms that had functioned in early periods became an ineffective basis for governance among prisoners. The inmate community was too large and anonymous for a reputation-based system to work, as the number of interactions and relationships between prisoners increased; there was greater competition for scarce inmate resources, resulting in higher levels of conflict and violence; and a growth in the proportion of first-time offenders meant that fewer incoming prisoners were familiar with the existing normative system. In such circumstances, Skarbek suggests, as norms failed, and in the absence of protection and oversight from the authorities, prisoners created and sought out alternative institutions of governance in the form of gangs, which mediated conflicts, enforced agreements, and functioned as protective organizations.

Skarbek's (2012) principal point is that, in the absence of other structures of governance, gangs stepped in to fill important institutional voids (in more conventional terms, gangs are a functional response to the deprivations of the environment) and "transformed the inmate subculture to a gang culture" (Trulson 2005, p. 107). Having established their power, they were then able to take over and enforce prison drug markets, contributing significantly to what Carceral (2006) describes as a "wild west" environment of predatory behavior. As others have noted, rates of violence, misconduct, and prisoner homicide increase substantially with the prevalence of gang membership (Gaes et al. 2002; Drury and De Lisi 2011). In other words, while gangs often employ violence in nonarbitrary ways, to enforce order, and may "sacrifice one of their own men if he runs up a drug debt or refuses to follow the rules about maintaining order" (Trammell 2009, p. 768), it remains an empirical question as to whether, overall, they contribute to positive forms of order—in which prisoners are held accountable to a set of codified and recognized rules—or promote an environment of fear, chaos, and violence.

IV. Prisons in Contemporary England and Wales

While ethnographic prison research in North America has dwindled, in England and Wales a steady stream of in-depth studies has endured, providing considerable insight into the daily dynamics of men's (much more than women's) imprisonment. In the medium-security men's training prison in which Crewe (2009) conducted his ethnography, among the most powerful determinants of the prisoner society was the reach of the institution (i.e., the capacity of institutional policies to shape prisoner behavior) and the relative psychological proximity of release. Most prisoners were in the later stages of their sentence and did not want to jeopardize their progression through the system. Meanwhile, a range of compliance mechanisms, including an incentives and earned privileges scheme, mandatory drug testing, and reports written by a range of wing staff and specialists, encouraged them to police not only their personal behavior but their social allegiances. As a result, the prisoner community was individualized and splintered into localized peer networks, with few prisoners willing to engage in collective protest. Code violations were often left unpunished because the potential penalties that resulted from norm enforcement outweighed the benefits. Similarly, because of concerns about being drawn into "trouble" and the long-term implications of having negative content on one's personal file, prisoners' loyalties toward each other were often limited and conditional: most differentiated between "real friends" for whom they would be willing to make personal sacrifices and whom they tended to know prior to imprisonment and "associates," with whom they socialized and shared scarce resources (such as cigarettes) but whom they scarcely trusted and were unwilling to take risks, whether physical or emotional. In the absence of organized gangs, the social world comprised a series of interlocking and often fluid groupings based primarily around local loyalties and ethnoreligious identities, with conflicts generally arising as a result of interpersonal tensions. Alongside these groups were a multitude of small "cliques," often based on little more than mutual interests, shared backgrounds, and experiences.

The primary sources of power were the limited social networks in which prisoners were embedded, as well as forms of personal reputation, often related to criminal sophistication, and the supply and distribution of drugs (heroin in particular). Yet many prisoners who had the potential to orchestrate the activity of others were reluctant to do so, recognizing the risks—in terms of sentence progression—of being visibly influential. For most prisoners, what mattered was to be "above the line" of vulnerability, that is, safe from the threat of exploitation. This could be accomplished not only through "reputation" or perceptions of violent potential but through being considered "a good lad": reliable, straightforward, and relatively loyal to others. Most prisoners differentiated between those whom they "respected"—a term that often implied fear—and those they "admired." Men who were volatile and violent were generally respected but not admired, while those who were smart and could navigate or manipulate the prison bureaucracy generated considerable kudos. In contrast, the prisoners who were most stigmatized were those who were mentally and physically vulnerable or who infringed on the norms of the prisoner community by exploiting others, denigrating the collective dignity of the prisoner community, and exhibiting various forms of weakness as a result of drug addiction (Crewe 2005, 2009).

Indeed, Crewe (2005, 2009) argues that the prisoner subculture could not be understood without an analysis of the drug economy, both inside and outside the prison. Drugs such as cannabis and heroin were among the most significant coping mechanisms available to prisoners, providing forms of sanctuary and diversion, alleviating distress, accelerating the passing of time, and "bringing down the walls" temporarily. Drug use itself brought together prisoners who in the past would not have affiliated with each other (due to differences in criminal background, for example) and diminished the reputation of men whose crimes and charisma would otherwise position them relatively high up in the prisoner hierarchy. In this respect, drugs functioned as a kind of social equalizer. At the same time, the presence of drug addicts, willing to manipulate and steal from others to feed their habits, and drug dealers, liable to use violence to enforce debts, were threats to social loyalty and solidarity, diminishing levels of interpersonal trust and humanity. Drug dealers were powerful and were admired by some of their peers due to their resourcefulness and material wealth, but their actions also generated resentment among prisoners who abhorred drugs, exploitation, and the abuse of power.

Meanwhile, drug addiction prior to imprisonment is central to two of the orientations that Crewe (2009) outlines in his typology of adaptive styles: first, among "enthusiasts," whose feelings of shame about their behavior as drug users led them to align themselves normatively with the institution, and second, among the "retreatists," who experienced the pains of imprisonment as less severe than the pains of drug addiction. Among the other adaptive positions that Crewe elaborates are the volatile and often vulnerable "pragmatists," who acted instrumentally in order to improve their daily predicament; "stoics," who were generally long-term prisoners, resigned to being enduringly compliant; and "players," often drug dealers and semi-organized criminals, who combined backstage resistance with a strategic, front-stage performance of compliance. Crewe describes considerable variation between these groups in terms of their attitudes to staff, their relationships with other prisoners, and their commitment to an inmate code that remains redolent of Sykes' description, albeit in somewhat diluted form. Thus enthusiasts identified with staff, made new friends within prison (because they felt liberated from their previous identities and were looking to develop new networks of trust and support), and did not consider it inappropriate to inform on drug dealers; stoics acted toward staff with detached courtesy, limited their social obligations, and sought to uphold a solidary version of the code; while players expressed contempt toward uniformed staff when among their peers, established instrumental relationships with others to assist them in illicit activity, and promoted a version of the code that was highly self-serving.

Compared to the American prisons literature, the relatively harmonious nature of ethnic and religious relations in England and Wales is striking. Since the 1980s, a number of studies in England and Wales have reported that while relationships between white and black or ethnic minority prisoners are often characterized by mutual suspicion and submerged hostility, these relationships are, on the whole, relatively peaceful (e.g., Genders and Player 1989; Crewe 2009), and neither ethnicity, race, nor religion are the determining features of the prisoner social world. More recently, Phillips (2012, p. 86) reports that most prisoners in her study expressed "a desire to see themselves and others simply as human beings, not defined by their race or ethnicity," with cultural identities serving as sources of pride and affiliation but not as the basis for intergroup hostility. Indeed, if anything, the public discourse of imprisonment was one of tolerance and diversity, so that being explicitly racist was taboo (as well as hazardous; Phillips 2012; see also Crewe 2009). Beneath this "fragile calm" (Crewe 2009) or "multicultural conviviality" (Phillips 2012, p. 124) was a more complex set of sentiments, in particular a perception among white prisoners of social and cultural marginalization (both in prison and in the wider society), resentment and envy about the greater solidarity of black or ethnic minority groups, and growing unease about the unity and increasing collective power of Muslim prisoners.

In England and Wales, the playing out of the dynamics and politics of race appears considerably more developed in high-security prisons. In a repeat study of HM Prison Whitemoor, Liebling and colleagues (Liebling and Arnold 2012; Liebling, Arnold, and Straub 2012) describe an establishment that, over a twelve-year period, had become a great deal more violent and lacking in trust and whose social relations were marked primarily by the increasing social and cultural power of Islam. Relationships between prisoners were "fractured," individualized, and characterized by a pervasive fear of violence—prisoners described life in the establishment as like "swimming in a shark tank" (Liebling and Arnold 2012, p. 420). A hierarchy that, twelve years earlier, had been dominated by organized, professional criminals, operating relatively cooperatively with the institution, no longer held sway. Social power instead lay in the form of Islam, which offered forms of fraternity and safety that were otherwise scarce within a harsher and more austere penal culture and a means of coping with the existential insecurities of long-term imprisonment. While in the 1980s Asian prisoners were generally considered highly compliant "model prisoners" (Genders and Player 1989), Muslim prisoners (and faith identities generally) had, in a relatively short period of time, become collectively powerful and oppositional to the institution. Many had no desire for any kind of relationship with the prison authorities—indeed, relationships between staff and prisoners in general were characterized by antipathy, suspicion, and cultural distance, shaped partly by resentment about increasingly long sentences and broader feelings of sociopolitical injustice. For some prisoners, Islam served as a screen or resource for bullying, trade, and the settling of interpersonal scores, in part because the institutional culture of risk assessment—which made prisoners very aware of the need to appear compliant—inhibited the more open expression of conflict and in part because sensitivities about respecting religious rights alongside insecurities about Islam had made faith the new "no-go" area of prison life—a place of sanctuary for prisoners, beyond the normal reach of power.

V. Prisons in the Global South

As Martin, Jefferson, and Bandyopadhyay (2014, p. 4) reflect, "prisons of the global South remain systematically ignored and, when deigned worthy of consideration, poorly understood." Typically, they are characterized by underresourcing, crowding, and a "paucity of staff" who lack "appropriate training and leadership" and are poorly paid (King and Valensia 2014, p. 510). Birkbeck (2011) cites figures that contrast the staff–prisoner ratio of 1 to 5 in the United States with those of 1 to 17 in Venezuela, while Darke (2013b), writing about prisons in Brazil, reports that for every officer on duty there are typically between 200 and 300 prisoners. Given that prisons in the Global South do not tend to have the technological features that are central to North American prisons, they operate with even lower levels of surveillance than staffing figures imply (Birkbeck 2011). In light of these factors, the most noteworthy characteristic of these low-cost, low-staff prisons is that they do not descend into total lawlessness. Instead, most develop forms of power-sharing, in which, to varying degrees, officials rely on and appeal to prisoner leadership structures to fill voids in power and control (Akoensi 2014).

One version of this is a form of "shared governance" whereby staff members allocate responsibility for the enforcement of order to groups of senior-ranking prisoners and establishments are "characterised by mutual dependencies and situational adjustments" (Garces, Martin, and Darke 2013, p. 27). In such circumstances, what Le Marcis (2014, p. 11) calls "governance from within," a subset of prisoner rules runs parallel to the official administration, and the prisoner hierarchy is harnessed in the daily operation and self-maintenance of the institution. For example, Akoensi (2014, p. 38) observes that, in Ghanaian prisons, "inmate leaders supplement the work of prison officers in the administration (control, supervision, and running) of the prisons on a daily basis." The rewards and incentives for performing these tasks include living in less crowded cells and greater freedom of movement across the establishment (Le Marcis 2014, p. 13).

The delegation of responsibilities to prisoners is typically structured around an established hierarchy of roles, ranging from low-level cell-checkers (who perform daily headcounts), middle managers who control single cells with multiple occupants, and senior-ranking prisoners who enforce order across entire buildings (Akoensi 2014). In the military argot of a Cameroonian institution (Morelle 2014), the senior prisoners are termed "Chef Cour," those beneath them are "Commandants," while at the lower end of the pyramid are "Escadrons" (squadrons). The tasks performed by such trusted prisoners range from low-level janitorial tasks (cooking, cleaning, counting) to the completion of the kinds of security and disciplinary tasks that are normally performed by prison officers (Garces et al. 2013). Indeed, Darke (2013a, p. 18) notes that, because some prisoners are involved in "handcuffing and escorting, searching cells and food parcels for contraband, eavesdropping for plans to rebel or escape," it is difficult to "distinguish trusties and inmate leaders from prison officers, not only in terms of function, but also of command" (p. 19). This kind of double administration may bring a degree of order to daily life, which may be highly valued by prisoners and staff alike (Le Marcis 2014).

In other prisons in the Global South (e.g., in Brazil), the term *self-governance* is a more accurate descriptor than *shared governance* because prison life is largely organized by gangs, and "gang affiliation is a defining feature of prison leadership" (Akoensi 2014, p. 35). Interpretations of such arrangements vary. Darke (2013a, p. 21), for example, argues that gang leadership can help to "maintain basic levels of security, discipline and welfare" and rejects the view that these relations of power represent a form of lawlessness: "The prevailing Hobbesian image of Brazilian prisons as places of abandon, conflict and extraordinary pain and violence . . . is reductionist and dystopian, over-reliant on anecdotal reports of individual incidences of violence, and premised in a lack of knowledge of the depth of inmate participation in prison regimes and prison management, and only partial understanding of the nature of inmate/inmate-staff relations that have arisen" (Darke 2013b, p. 280).

Some other scholars of prisons in the Global South concur with Darke (2013b, p. 272) that staff–prisoner relations are "characterised less by conflict and power as by accommodation and reciprocity." Shared conditions of privation and poverty may generate forms of humanity and cohesion both among prisoners and between prisoners and staff, particularly in postcolonial justice contexts, where underpaid and relatively powerless staff (themselves living away from home, in poor conditions) may feel sympathy with the circumstances of those they guard (see Bandyopadhyay 2010; Akoensi 2014).

King and Valensia (2014, p. 518) are considerably more circumspect, noting that "although there are elements of mutual benefit, the balance [of power] is more often asymmetric than reciprocal." That is, gang leaders exert total control of the internal operation of the prison, including internal discipline, while prison management attempts only to secure the perimeter walls (Jones 2014). The attitude of staff toward "the march of prison gangs" is one of "helpless resignation" (King and Valensia 2014, p. 516). Meanwhile, the prevalence of subcultural violence orchestrated by prison gangs should not be downplayed. For example, the Primeiro Comando da Capital in Brazil operates extensive drug networks, kidnappings, and robberies while also orchestrating large-scale prison riots and hostage-taking on demand (Macaulay 2013), and, as King and Valensia (2014) describe, vulnerable and affluent individuals may be systematically and brutally abused. Moreover, the fact that visitors and prisoners' families can themselves become "prey to the depredations of prison gangs" (King and Valensia, 2014, p. 526) while officers "turn a blind eye" (p. 534) is a reminder not to romanticize the forms of stability that gangs may secure when their power is almost entirely unchecked. Adorno and Salla (2007, p. 16) assert that "violence constitutes a normative code of behavior" for prisoners in Brazil, infiltrating all aspects of daily prison life:

> Everything is subject to dispute: conflicts between gangs; suspected informants; involvement in drug trafficking, the exploitation of internal activities, the trafficking of influence over the "powerful," whether those in the inmate population or the administration; possession of personal objects; obtaining sexual favors, which involve not only inmates, particularly the younger ones and first timers, who are often sold within the population, but also their wives, girlfriends and daughters; maintenance of privileges won or granted and disputes over work posts. (Adorno and Salla 2007, p. 16)

Thus while Darke (2013b) claims that violence is the exception rather than the norm in Brazilian prisons, because conflict is of benefit to neither prisoner nor staff, order may be predicated on the underlying threat of violence from gang factions "over the mass of inmates who lack the power or capacity to counter the organizations on their own" (Adorno and Salla 2007, p. 16). In some senses, this form of order, in which coercion is at the same time both largely absent and constantly present, embodies the prison as an institution.

Similarly, based on research undertaken in South African prisons, Lindegaard and Gear (2014) note that the acceptance by some prisoners of some forms of subcultural violence shields them from more undesirable attacks: by accepting subjection to particular forms of gang-related violence, or taking on protective "husbands," lower level gang members and feminized prisoners avoid more serious forms of sexual abuse and assault. Thus the absence of violence may reflect deeply hierarchical and problematic divisions between prisoners, whereby status distinctions "shape and inform inmates' relations to the informal prison economy (including access to smuggling networks, extra food, and other commodities), to physical spaces of the prison, including access to the courtyard, to participation in violence and sex, and to the risks of being abused" (Lindegaard and Gear 2014, p. 41).

VI. Conclusion

With regard to theoretical frameworks, the sociology of imprisonment has been dominated by an increasingly stale debate about whether prison life is determined by the deprivations of the environment or by social and behavioral patterns imported into the prison from the community. This debate is so often rehearsed that it needs little airing here (see Steiner, this volume). Moreover, as Irwin and Cressey (1962) made clear in their initial challenge to the "deprivation" framework, the two perspectives are not at all incompatible. To summarize rather crudely: prisoners encounter a set of problems and frustrations, such as loss of moral status, privacy, and control over many minor aspects of daily life, as well as limits on who they can trust and what they can obtain materially and emotionally. Most of these problems are inherent to their basic situation of being imprisoned but will vary according to the particular goals and culture of the institution, such as its security level; its relative emphasis on custody, retribution, or rehabilitative treatment; and the behavior of its staff. The painfulness of these issues, and the degree to which each has "bite," will vary according to prisoners' personal needs, prior identities, and expectations of life, both within the prison and on release. Prisoners "resolve" them individually and collectively (i.e., try to secure forms of respect, safety, comfort, intimacy, etc., or compensate for their loss) by drawing on preexisting psychological and social resources (e.g., family support, external reputations, personal resilience) and by using and exploiting whatever resources are available to them within the prison, whether these are official (such as educational programs) or unofficial (such as illicit drugs and the slim resources of their peers).

This framework—put simply: *deprivation, institution, importation*—remains of use to anyone seeking to understand the determinants and dynamics of the prisoner society. But rather than seek to "test" the relative explanatory power of the framework's constituent parts, a more helpful approach may be to explore qualitatively how they interact. Here the institutional level should not just be a proxy for "deprivation" factors—that is, it represents more than variations in institutional aims or staff behaviour *as they pertain to* the burdens and deprivations that prisoners encounter. Rather, it should take into consideration specific aspects of institutional culture, ethos, and practices and should account for the fact that institutional policies and practices do not only "deprive" prisoners (unless the definition of deprivation is made extremely broad) but also entail a set of incitements and requirements: to engage with the regime and self-govern in various ways (see Crewe 2009). An alternative way of thinking about prisoner social life and subculture—one that this essay has hinted at throughout—is to shift the object of analysis from prisoner to prison. That is, rather than focusing on how prisoners mitigate and negotiate their predicament, another starting point would be to assess how any institution deals with the issues of power, order, and governance that are fundamental to the environment. For, paradoxically, imprisonment is about the state-sanctioned removal and exercise of power, and yet as Sparks, Bottoms, and Hey (1996) argue in *Prisons and the Problem of Order*, one of the extraordinary things about prisons—given that prisoners are held against their will in conditions they tend not to like and generally outnumber staff—is that they are ordered at all. As we have seen, however, different "models" of imprisonment involve very different configurations of power and very different solutions to this "problem." What differs most between them is, first, how much power they seek to exercise and in what forms; second, how exactly they seek to shape the behavior of prisoners (from "discipline" to "obedience" to more intrusive forms of subjectification); and third, how much power they choose—and are required—to share with prisoners. These variables set the conditions for prisoner social life, establishing the conditions that prisoners need to address, distributing power among prisoners, encouraging and inhibiting different kinds of social relations, or enabling alternative structure of governance.

NOTE

1. Due to space limitations and the presence in this volume of a specific essay on women in prison, this essay focuses exclusively on the imprisonment of men.

REFERENCES

Adorno, Sergio, and Fernando Salla. 2007. "Organized Criminality in Prisons and the Attacks of the PCC." *Estudos Avançados* 21(61): 7–29.

Akoensi, Thomas D. 2014. "Governance through Power Sharing in Ghanaian Prisons: A Symbiotic Relationship between Officers and Inmates." *Prison Service Journal* 212: 33–38.

Bandyopadhyay, Mahuya. 2010. *Everyday Life in a Prison: Confinement, Surveillance, Resistance.* New Delhi: Orient BlackSwan.

Birkbeck, Christopher. 2011. "Imprisonment and Internment: Comparing Penal Institutions North and South." *Punishment & Society* 13: 307–332.

Carceral, K. C. 2006. *Prison, Inc.: A Convict Exposes Life Inside a Private Prison.* New York: New York University Press.

Carroll, Leo. 1974. *Hacks, Blacks and Cons: Race Relations in a Maximum-Security Prison.* London: DC Heath.

Clemmer, Donald. 1940. *The Prison Community.* New York: Rinehart & Company.

Copes, Heith, Fiona Brookman, and Anastasia Brown. 2013. "Accounting for Violations of the Convict Code." *Deviant Behavior* 34: 841–858.

Cox, Stephen D. 2009. *The Big House: Image and Reality of the American Prison.* New Haven, CT: Yale University Press.

Crewe, Ben. 2005. "Prisoner Society in the Era of Hard Drugs." *Punishment & Society* 7: 457–481.

Crewe, Ben. 2009. *The Prisoner Society: Power, Adaptation and Social Life in an English Prison.* Oxford: Oxford University Press.

Crouch, Ben. M., and James W. Marquart. 1989. *An Appeal to Justice: Litigated Reform of Texas Prisons.* Austin: University of Texas Press.

Darke, Sacha. 2013a. "Entangled Staff-Inmate Relations." *Prison Service Journal* 207: 16–22.

Darke, Sacha. 2013b. "Inmate Governance in Brazilian Prisons." *The Howard Journal of Criminal Justice* 52: 272–284.

Drury, Alan. J., and Matt DeLisi. 2011. "Gangkill: An Exploratory Empirical Assessment of Gang Membership, Homicide Offending, and Prison Misconduct." *Crime & Delinquency* 57: 130–146.

Elsner, Alan. 2006. *Gates of Injustice: The Crisis in America's Prisons.* River, NJ: Prentice Hall.

Faulkner, Paula. L., and William R. Faulkner. 1997. "Effects of Organizational Change on Inmate Status and the Inmate Code of Conduct." *Journal of Crime and Justice* 20: 55–72.

Feeley, Malcolm. M., and Jonathan Simon. 1992. "The New Penology: Notes on the Emerging Strategy of Corrections and Its Implications." *Criminology* 30: 449–474.

Gaes, Gerald. G., Susan Wallace, Evan Gilman, Jody Klein-Saffran, and Sharon Suppa. 2002. "The Influence of Prison Gang Affiliation on Violence and Other Prison Misconduct." *The Prison Journal* 82: 359–385.

Garces, Chris, Tomas Martin, and Sacha Darke. 2013. "Informal Prison Dynamics in Africa and Latin America." *Criminal Justice Matters* 91: 26–27.

Genders, Elaine, and Elaine Player. 1989. *Race Relations in Prison.* Oxford: Oxford University Press.

Haney, Craig. 2006. *Reforming Punishment: Psychological Limits to the Pains of Imprisonment.* Washington, DC: American Psychological Association.

Haney, Craig. 2008. "A Culture of Harm: Taming the Dynamics of Cruelty in Supermax Prisons." *Criminal Justice and Behavior* 35: 956–984.

Haney, Craig, and Mona Lynch. 1997. "Regulating Prisons of the Future: A Psychological Analysis of Supermax and Solitary Confinement." *New York University Review of Law and Social Change* 23: 477–570.

Hartman, Kenneth. E. 2008. "Supermax Prisons in the Consciousness of Prisoners." *The Prison Journal* 88: 169–176.

Hassine, Victor, Thomas J. Bernard, and Richard A. Wright. 1996. *Life without Parole: Living in Prison Today*, edited by Richard McCleary. Los Angeles, CA: Roxbury.

Hunt, Geoffrey, Stephanie Riegel, Tomas Morales, and Dan Waldorf. 1993. "Change in Prison Culture: Prison Gangs and the Case of the Pepsi Generation." *Social Problems* 40: 398–409.

Irwin, John. 1980. *Prisons in Turmoil*. Boston: Little, Brown and Company.

Irwin, John. 2004. *The Warehouse Prison: Disposal of the New Dangerous Class*. Los Angeles, CA: Roxbury.

Irwin, John, and Donald R. Cressey. 1962. "Thieves, Convicts and the Inmate Culture." *Social Problems* 10: 142–155.

Jacobs, James. 1977. *Stateville: The Penitentiary in Mass Society*. Chicago: University of Chicago Press.

Jones, Clarke. 2014. "Prison Gangs and Prison Governance in the Philippines." *Griffith Asia Quarterly* 2: 57–74.

King, Roy D., and Bruna Valensia. 2014. "Power, Control, and Symbiosis in Brazilian Prisons." *South Atlantic Quarterly* 113: 503–528.

Le Marcis, Frédéric. 2014. "Everyday Prison Governance in Abidjan, Ivory Coast." *Prison Service Journal* 212: 11–15.

Liebling, Alison, and Helen Arnold. 2012. "Social Relationships between Prisoners in a Maximum Security Prison: Violence, Faith, and the Declining Nature of Trust." *Journal of Criminal Justice* 40: 413–424.

Liebling, Alison, Helen Arnold, and Christina Straub. 2012. *An Exploration of Staff-Prisoner Relationships at HMP Whitemoor: Twelve Years On*. London: Ministry of Justice.

Lindegaard, Marie. R., and Sacha Gear. 2014. "Violence Makes Safe in South African Prisons: Prison Gangs, Violent Acts, and Victimization Among Inmates." *Focaal* 68: 35–54.

Macaulay, Fiona. 2013. "Modes of Prison Administration, Control and Governmentality in Latin America: Adoption, Adaptation and Hybridity." *Conflict, Security & Development* 13: 361–392.

Martin, Tomas M., Andrew M. Jefferson, and Mahuya Bandyopadhyay. 2014. "Sensing Prison Climates: Governance, Survival, and Transition." *Focaal* 2014(68): 3–17.

Mears, Daniel. P., and Michael D. Reisig. 2006. "The Theory and Practice of Supermax Prisons." *Punishment & Society* 8: 33–57.

Morelle, Marie. 2014. "Power, Control and Money in Prison: The Informal Governance of the Yaoundé Central Prison." *Prison Service Journal* 212: 21–26.

Phillips, Coretta. 2012. *The Multicultural Prison: Ethnicity, Masculinity, and Social Relations*. Oxford: Oxford University Press.

Pizarro, Jesenia, M., Vanja M. Stenius, and Travis C. Pratt. 2006. "Supermax Prisons Myths, Realities, and the Politics of Punishment in American Society." *Criminal Justice Policy Review* 17: 6–21.

Pollock, Joycelyn M. 2004. *Prisons and Prison Life: Costs and Consequences*. Los Angeles, CA: Roxbury.

Reiter, Keramet. A. 2012. "Parole, Snitch, or Die: California's Supermax Prisons and Prisoners, 1997–2007." *Punishment & Society* 14: 530–563.

Rhodes, Lorna A. 2004. *Total Confinement: Madness and Reason in the Maximum Security Prison*. Berkeley: University of California Press.

Rhodes, Lorna A. 2009. "Supermax Prisons and the Trajectory of Exception." *Studies in Law, Politics, and Society* 47: 193–218.

Robertson, James E. 1997. "Houses of the Dead: Warehouse Prisons, Paradigm Change, and the Supreme Court." *Houston Law Review* 34: 1003–1064.

Shalev, Sharon. 2013. *Supermax: Controlling Risk through Solitary Confinement*. Devon, UK: Willan.

Simon, Jonathan. 2000. "The 'Society of Captives' in the Era of Hyper-Incarceration." *Theoretical Criminology* 4: 285–308.

Skarbek, David. 2012. "Prison Gangs, Norms, and Organizations." *Journal of Economic Behavior & Organization* 82: 96–109.

Sparks, Richard, Anthony Bottoms, and Will Hey. 1996. *Prisons and the Problem of Order*. Oxford: Oxford University Press.

Sykes, Gresham. 1958. *The Society of Captives: A Study of a Maximum-Security Prison*. Princeton, NJ: Princeton University Press.

Sykes, Gresham, and Sheldon L. Messinger. 1960. "The Inmate Social System." In *Theoretical Studies in Social Organization of the Prison*, edited by Richard. A. Cloward, Donald. R. Cressey, George. H. Grosser, Richard McCleary, Lloyd. E. Ohlin, Gresham M. Sykes, and Sheldon. L. Messinger. New York: Social Science Research Council.

Toch, Hans. 2001. "The Future of Supermax Confinement." *The Prison Journal* 81: 376–388.

Trammell, Rebecca. 2009. "Values, Rules, and Keeping the Peace: How Men Describe Order and the Inmate Code in California Prisons." *Deviant Behavior* 30: 746–771.

Trulson, Chad. 2005. "The Social World of the Prisoner." In *Prisons: Today and Tomorrow*, edited by Joycelyn M. Pollock. London: Jones & Bartlett Learning.

Wacquant, Loic. 2002. "The Curious Eclipse of Prison Ethnography in the Age of Mass Incarceration." *Ethnography* 3: 371–397.

Wallace-Wells, Benjamin. 2014. "The Plot from Solitary." *New York Magazine*: Feb 24. http://nymag.com/news/features/solitary-secure-housing-units-2014-2/

Winfree, Thomas L. T., Greg Newbold, and Houston S. Tubb. 2002. "Prisoner Perspectives on Inmate Culture in New Mexico and New Zealand: A Descriptive Case Study." *The Prison Journal* 82: 213–233.

CHAPTER 7

·····

THE REAL GANGBANGING IS
IN PRISON

·····

SCOTT H. DECKER AND DAVID PYROOZ

THE title of this essay is a quote from a 30-year-old former gang member in Fresno, California. The presence of gangs and gang members in custody produces a number of challenges for correctional staff. Prison gangs and gang members also face challenges, some of which extend to the street. Prison gangs and gang members elevate the risks for involvement in violence and increase threats of interpersonal violence within the prison that can extend to the street. These challenges are not inconsequential in number or magnitude. Gang members comprise at least 13 percent of jail populations (Ruddell, Decker, and Egley 2006), 12 to 17 percent of state prison populations (Kreinert and Fleisher 2001; Griffin and Hepburn 2006), and 9 percent of the federal prison population (Gaes et al. 2002). Each of these estimates is dated and likely undercounts the overall percentage of incarcerated individuals who are affiliated with a gang of some sort given the growth of gangs and their continued involvement in crime. The threat of violence posed by these groups is significant, particularly since gang members on the street are reported to have homicide rates 100 times higher than national homicide rates (Decker and Pyrooz 2010). By the very fact that gang members in prison have undergone a "filtering process" that has eliminated the least serious individuals and targeted the most serious, the prison gang population represents a deep-end population of gang members. These figures take on added significance when considering the violence associated with gangs, inside and outside prison walls. Because involvement in crime is one of the key distinguishing features of gang membership (Klein and Maxson 2006; Decker and Pyrooz 2010), the pooling of gang members in incarcerated settings is a matter of considerable policy concern, not only for their violence and misconduct while in prison (Griffin and Hepburn 2006; Huebner, Varano, and Bynum 2007) but also for their rates of recidivism.

While we know that large numbers of gang members are in custody and that gang membership may be a risk factor for imprisonment, we know little about what life in the gang—in prison—is like. There is strong evidence that the presence of gang members increases violence in prison, which may in turn spur group formation and enhance cohesion among those groups. But the consequences of prison gangs extend well beyond threats of violence between gangs; they influence the safety of correctional officials and impede programming designed to change gang and criminal behavior. These are important challenges for a variety of reasons. Correctional work is inherently dangerous: what other job, for example, would involve employment in the company of proven offenders, many of whom have extensive involvement in violence? The disruption and violence caused by gang members may also disrupt the very programming and environments designed to reduce recidivism and offending on the street. While recidivism rates remain high among prisoners in general, estimated at nearly two-thirds by Petersilia (2009) and others (e.g., Langan and Levin 2002), there is concern that rates of failure among gang members are even higher.

The lack of information about these hypotheses may be attributed to the lack of solid research examining these issues. There are administrative challenges to examining issues of prison misconduct and gang membership. Such studies may not fit the narrow interests of correctional agencies that seek to improve operational and programmatic functions. In addition, institutional review boards are often loath to approve research that involves individuals who are incarcerated. Further, it is difficult to conduct field studies of prison gangs and gang members. As a consequence, we are often left with indirect or secondary information about prison gangs, which is filtered through the lens of prison staff or prison records, each of which carry their own biases (Gaes et al. 2002). The validity of prison record data is often difficult to establish due to variability in definitions across institutions and differences in disciplinary policies.

This essay addresses many of these issues. The first section is built primarily on the foundation of what is known about prison gangs and gang members in the current literature (despite the acknowledged shortcomings of that literature). We begin by examining the similarities and differences between street and prison gangs and what differentiates them from other types of criminal groups. We then turn to a brief review of what is known about the appearance and expansion of prison gangs and gang members. Here we pay attention to both the patterns of prison gangs as well as theories that may account for their emergence and growth. This is followed by an examination of correctional programming designed to address the unique needs of incarcerated gang members.

The second half of the essay examines original data collected as part of a larger study of gangs in four cities. Here we focus explicitly on the views of gang members while they were imprisoned, the relationship between their prison and street gang activity, and the role of the prison in the decisions of some gang members to leave their gang. We conclude this section by discussing an emerging topic of importance in understanding prison gangs: the availability and role of technology in prison.

The main conclusions discussed in this essay are

- Gang members enter prison with high levels of criminal activity in their background (particularly violence), immersion within subcultural codes that condone violence, and other psychological and social deficits in their backgrounds. These issues are exacerbated by continued gang affiliation, the filtering of street gang affiliations into prison gang "nations," ongoing gang rivalries, and criminal opportunity, which results in higher levels of misconduct among these inmates.
- Gang and racial/ethnic tensions multiply motivations and opportunities for misconduct, in turn presenting serious challenges for the control of these behaviors. As a result, such patterns of misconduct further distance gang members from programs and experiences that will help them transition to legitimate society.

- There are few programming opportunities directed specifically at gang members. Rather, gang members are more often targeted for segregation and other isolating activities that may make it easier to manage prison but are unlikely to improve their chances of early release. The dynamic nature of the landscape for conventional (e.g., the labor market) and unconventional (e.g., street gang) outlets is challenging to adapt to, as large-scale changes occur even after a few years in prison.
- As a consequence of the risks associated with gang-related behaviors and processes, gang members are at the highest risk of returning to prison. While considerable effort has been expended on prevention of gang formation, little has been done to encourage disengagement from gangs, particularly on reentry after prison.

A few words on terminology are in order. *Prison gang* is used to describe gangs in incarcerated facilities, which also includes jails and other settings. In many jurisdictions (including the Federal Bureau of Prisons) the official label for such groups is *security threat groups*, but we refer to these groups as *prison gangs* for ease of discussion of the movement from the street to the prison and back.

I. Street Gang, Prison Gang: What's the Difference?

Criminal activity is a hallmark of both prison and street gangs. This behavior does not distinguish them from other groups that engage in offending, even at high levels of serious offending. As such they share a number of characteristics with groups that smuggle drugs, traffic in humans for sex or labor purposes, engage in acts of terror, move guns illegally, or use their influence to produce financially favorable outcomes. These shared characteristics include a group of offenders, commitment to deviant norms, and a group process. Despite these similarities, gang members (both prison and street) can be distinguished from other offending groups (Decker and Pyrooz 2010) as well as from each other. A key difference between street and prison gangs and these other groups is that gangs tend to have a longer life and establish and hold on to a collective identity. The durability of prison gangs reflects their age structure, higher level of organization, and expanded role in illicit activity.

Despite the similarities between street and prison gangs, they are distinguished by a number of other characteristics. These include durability and identity. We enumerate these differences in Table 7.1. As defined by Klein and Maxson (2006, p. 4), street gangs are "durable, street-oriented youth group[s] whose involvement in illegal activity is part of its group identity." Lyman (1989, p. 48), who has proffered the accepted definition of a prison gang, argues that such a gang is "an organization which operates within the prison system as a self-perpetuating criminally oriented entity, consisting of a select group of inmates who have established an organized chain of command and are governed by an established code of conduct." This definition is now over two decades old, yet it has not been challenged empirically or conceptually in the literature. While the street gang literature is replete with tests of validity (Esbensen et al. 2001; Decker and Pyrooz 2010), definitions of gangs in prison have not been met with the same degree of scrutiny as street gangs. It is likely that the difference in attention to definitional issues stems from the lack of research on prison gangs and gang members.

Table 7.1 provides a set of comparisons between prison and street gangs as outlined in Pyrooz, Decker, and Fleisher (2011). These characteristics are drawn widely from the research literature. Prison gangs appear to be more organized versions of street gangs. Key differences, however, include the observation that prison gangs have higher levels of control and are more organized than street gangs. Prison gangs also have higher levels of organization and structure and engage in more entrepreneurial activities. Key indicators of this include the role of instrumental violence, covert behavior, drug dealing, and higher levels of loyalty. Perhaps the most significant difference is the role of race in prison gangs. While race clearly has an impact on patterns of street gang membership, it is a defining characteristic of prison gangs. On the street, gangs are usually drawn together because of neighborhood origins; in the prison system, race is an organizing attribute that is institutionalized within the system itself (see, e.g., Trulson, Marquart, and Kawucha 2006; Goodman 2008). We return to issues of race in the second half of this essay. Unlike gang-related behaviors and processes in prison settings, street gangs differ as membership tends to be fluid, leadership is situational, violence is less coordinated and more symbolic, and drug dealing tends to be individualistic rather than collective (Fleisher 2006; Klein and Maxson 2006; Curry, Decker, and Pyrooz 2013). Maxson (2012) finds that these comparisons are likely limited to adult facilities, as she observed little evidence of such sharp divergence between street and prison gangs in California youth facilities.

II. Gang Activity in Incarcerated Settings

A. Emergence and Growth of Prison Gangs

Formed in Washington state in the early 1950s, the Gypsy Jokers were the first documented American prison gang (Stastny and Tyrnauer 1983; Orlando-Morningstar 1997, pp. 1–13). *La Eme* (the Mexican Mafia) was first documented in California in the late 1950s. This is an important prison gang for several reasons. It was the first prison gang with alleged nationwide ties and the first documented Hispanic prison gang. The first attempt to document the prison gang problem nationally came with Camp and Camp's 1985 national prison survey. This study found that there were more than 110 prison gangs that had a membership of roughly 13,000 inmates. The Camp and Camp study examined prison gangs in 49 state prisons, 33 of which reported the presence of gangs. Twenty-six of these had street gang counterparts. Illinois, Pennsylvania, Texas, and California had more prison gangs and prison gang members than other states (Ralph and Marquart 1991). As gangs grew on the street, they also grew in prison; the American Correctional Association reported that prison gang membership tripled between 1985 and 1992, from 12,624 to 46,190 (Baugh 1993).

The growth in prisons and prison population has been matched by the growth of prison gang members. Useem and Piehl (2008) identified four distinct periods of prison growth from the Great Depression to the end of the 20th century: 1930–1960 was the period of a "trendless trend"; 1961–1972 was a period of "large to modest decline"; 1973–1988 was "the buildup begins" trend; and 1989–2005 was the period of "accelerated growth." It makes

Table 7.1. A Comparison of Prison and Street Gangs

Variable	Prison Gang	Street Gang
Race/ethnicity	Single race or ethnicity	Mostly single race or ethnicity
Age	Concentrated in mid-20s, with members 30s–40s	Average age in upper teens
Organizational structure[a]	Hierarchical	Situational/hierarchical
Sources of violence	Symbolic and instrumental; core activity	Symbolic; core activity
Offending style[b]	Entrepreneurial	Cafeteria style
Visibility of behavior	Covert	Overt
Drug trafficking	Major activity; organized, collective	Varies; mostly individualistic
Loyalty to gang	Absolute	Weak bonds
Key to membership	Unqualified fidelity, abide by gang rules; willingness to engage in violence	Real or perceived fidelity; hanging out; abide by street rules
Key psychological attributes[c]	Oppositional, intimidation, control, manipulation	Oppositional, intimidation, camaraderie

Note: Adopted from Pyrooz, Decker, and Fleisher (2011).
[a] *Situational* refers to structural flexibility from loose to more rigid.
[b] *Entrepreneurial activity* refers to specific types of profit-generating activity. *Cafeteria-style activity* refers to a range of profit-generating activities.
[c] *Oppositional* refers to attitudes toward correctional supervision in the case of prison gangs. For street gangs it reflects a generalized opposition to authority.

sense that the growth of prison gangs is consistent with these trends, and some argue that these trends can be linked to national crime policy (Lawrence and Travis 2004). The growth in prisoner population at the end of the 20th century is well established: between 1980 and 1989, the prisoner population grew from 315,974 to 680,907 inmates; from 1990 to 1999 it expanded from 739,980 to 1,304,074 inmates; and growth slowed between 2000 and 2007 from 1,331,278 to 1,532,800 inmates. In 2000 there were 84 federal and 1,023 state confinement facilities totaling 1,107 state and federal prisons (United States Bureau of Justice Statistics 2003). By year-end 2005 there were 1,821 state and federal correctional facilities.

It seems odd that while we document the growth in the number of prisons and the size of the inmate population, there are no longitudinal data at any geographic level that track the growth of street gang membership in state or federal prisons. It is possible to estimate the number of imprisoned gang members from the percentage of street gang members per 1,000 state residents.

Efforts to estimate the number of gang members by state have improved. The National Gang Intelligence Center (2009) provided data on gang members per capita. They found that the state of Illinois had the highest rate per capita (8 to 11 per 1,000 residents); California, Colorado, New Mexico, and Nevada had the second highest rates at 5 to 7 per 1,000; and Idaho

and Florida were third highest with 4 per 1,000. Estimating the size of prison gang populations is particularly difficult and provides only a broad sense of the magnitude of the problem.

B. Explaining Gang Emergence and Gang Violence in Prison

The emergence of gangs in prison has been guided by well-articulated theoretical perspectives. The adaptation/deprivation (Fishman 1934; Clemmer 1940) arguments are built on
Fishman's (1934) early description of deprivation of liberty and the freedoms associated
with life "outside the walls." In his landmark work, *The Prison Community*, Clemmer developed the concept further. He argued that isolation, identified as a structural constraint,
serves to strip inmates of their identity. This loss of identity creates a void in which new
identities are formed. As an adaptive response to prison conditions, prison cultures endogenous to the institution emerge. Gangs are one of the adaptive responses. Once created, new
inmates are then socialized gradually into various prison subcultures (see also Jacobs 1974).

The second perspective, importation (Irwin and Cressey 1962), also focuses on culture.
It argues that inmates bring characteristics with them into the prison and that these in turn
shape prison culture. Such characteristics reflect the backgrounds of inmates, including their
demographic characteristics, cultures, and personalities. Together these characteristics produce the "prison culture." From this perspective, prison gangs do not emerge due to indigenous conditions within the prison; instead, these gangs are imported into the prison by
individuals who participated in the gang lifestyle before coming to prison. This is referred
to by Schwartz (1971) as "cultural drift," as these preexisting factors transcend prison life. As
such, gang members bring their individual and cultural histories with them into prison.

Both the importation and deprivation models, which have been very important to prison
gang research over a fifty-year period, find support in the street gang literature. This is especially true with regard to the role of gangs in amplifying criminal behavior. Some contend
that the emergence of gangs is consistent with the principles of homophily, where similarly
situated and like-minded individuals come together because of personality deficiencies
and geographical proximity (Gottfredson and Hirschi 1990). From this view, the low self-
control that produces increased criminal propensity draws individuals together and toward
the gang. This view accounts for both the cohesion within street gangs as well as the initial
impetus to form the gang. In this sense, importation can be found both on the street and in
the prison, and these characteristics draw gang members and inmates together. The driving
forces in these processes are propensity and other individual characteristics. The counterpart
to this argument, consistent with the deprivation hypothesis, stems from the classic work on
delinquency that emphasizes the role of neighborhood subculture and socioeconomic conditions on opportunity structures. Cloward and Ohlin (1960), Cohen (1955), Miller (1958),
and Thrasher (1927) each own a piece of the argument that conditions of economic, social, or
cultural deprivation produce conditions that yield higher levels of delinquency.

Thornberry et al. (1993) advanced selection, facilitation, and enhancement models to
explain the relationship between gang membership and offending. Selection occurs when
offending is high both before and after gang membership but does not increase during
periods of gang membership. The analogue to the prison context would be the importation
model (e.g., offending levels are the same before and during incarceration). Facilitation

occurs when offending increases during periods of gang membership but is low prior to join-ing the gang. This view is analogous to the deprivation explanations of prison culture (e.g., offending escalates as a consequence of exposure to the prison environment). Thornberry and colleagues recognize that it is possible that both selection and facilitation could co-occur, and they referred to this explanation as enhancement. Tests of these hypotheses (Krohn and Thornberry 2008) concluded that there is more evidence to support the facili-tation effect than the selection effect. These explanations are consistent with explanations of behavior in the prison context, where individuals with a high level of criminal involvement are kept together in prison. Facilitation and enhancement also take place within the prison, particularly among prison gang members. Prison gang membership elevates the level of criminal activity because of the facilitation effects provided by prison gangs.

Membership in a prison gang is related to prison misconduct but not as systematically as what researchers observe in street settings. In general, studies tend to find that gang members engage in higher rates of misconduct when incarcerated, particularly for violent forms of misconduct (Kreinert and Fleisher 2001; Huebner, 2003; Trulson 2007; Tasca, Griffin, and Rodriguez 2010; Wooldredge and Steiner 2014). Griffin and Hepburn's (2006) research on inmates in Arizona state prisons is an example of a typical study in the litera-ture: Based on three years of official records from 2,158 male inmates admitted in 1996, 17 percent of whom were recorded as gang affiliated, the authors found that nearly half of gang inmates engaged in violent misconduct, whereas about one-quarter of nongang inmates engaged in violent misconduct. Once Griffin and Hepburn took into consideration demographics, incarceration history, and security level, they found that gang affiliations increased the likelihood of assault and threat misconduct but not the likelihood of fighting and weapon misconduct. The findings on gang membership and prison misconduct tend to have contingencies associated with the research. For example, some studies differenti-ate between pre-incarceration street gang activity and prison gang activity (e.g., DeLisi, Berg, and Hochstetler 2004; Berg and DeLisi 2006). Another key difference from the street gang literature is that studies are based on official rather than survey data. In other words, both the independent and dependent variables—gang affiliation and misconduct—are not determined by the individual but by prison staff. Finally, as we discuss later, corrections officials frequently use administrative segregation to move gang members out of the gen-eral population, thereby eliminating inter-inmate contact and reducing the likelihood of violence.

Worrall and Morris's (2012) study of inter-inmate violence illustrates intriguing possi-bilities for understanding gangs and gang violence. Based on a random sample of 2,000 inmates housed in facilities within a large southern state, Worrall and Morris drew from intergroup conflict theory and argued that the prevalence of gang members and the diver-sity of gang affiliations within a unit should correlate with incidents of inmate violence, even after accounting for a host of individual-level characteristics. The results of their study were generally mixed. While there were correlations between inmate violence and both gang prevalence and gang integration, only the latter remained related to the outcome after taking into consideration a host of individual-level characteristics. There is a good deal to learn about how gangs behave in incarcerated settings, with implications that likely extend to street settings. The Worrall and Morris study is but one of many ways researchers can advance knowledge of gang-related behaviors and processes.

III. Responding to Prison Gangs

Although there are a number of prison and jail gang intervention strategies, few of them have been evaluated, consistent with our general lack of research on prison gangs. It should not be surprising that correctional agencies have developed policies and programs to deal with the misbehavior of gang members in their custody. As is the case on the street, gang members in prison engage in higher levels of misconduct and crime than their nongang counterparts (even considering the qualifications noted earlier). Inmates, especially gang members, form disruptive groups in prison. This extends their behavior from the street into the institutional setting (Jacobs 1977; Hunt et al. 1990).

Gaes and his colleagues (2002, p. 30) found that "compositional and contextual effects of staff, inmate, and ecological variables impact the probability of many forms of misconduct in addition to, and separate from, individual-level characteristics of inmates." This observation is consistent with a line of both prior and subsequent research. Jacobs (1977, pp. 138–174) argued that the courts weakened the authority of correctional officers to control the influence of gangs in US prisons. The ability of prison administrators to curb the behavior of violent groups in their custody has been limited by judicial decisions, at least for the past 30 years. Increases in prison gang activity may occur in institutions with weaker controls over inmates and in facilities that have come under judicial scrutiny. This finding clearly supports the view that gangs engage in a considerable amount of "oppositional" behavior (DiIulio 1987; Ralph and Marquart 1991; Fong, Vogel, and Buentello 1995).

The impact of suppression and intervention strategies in prison affect gang and nongang inmates differently. In a comparison of sixty gang and nongang inmates, Shelden (1991) found that they shared similar socioeconomic backgrounds, education levels, marital status, and substance abuse problems. Gang members had more deficits than nongang inmates, as they were less likely to have ever held a job, much more likely to have a juvenile record, and accrued more lifetime arrests. Perhaps not surprisingly but important nonetheless, gang members were more likely to have used a weapon. While in custody, gang members had significantly more rule and drug violations, engaged in more fights, and were less likely to be involved in treatment. These individuals were not well prepared to re-enter the community after release from prison.

Prisons have employed a number of methods to control the behavior of gang members in their custody. These include both covert and overt strategies, such as inmate informants, administrative segregation for prison gang members, isolating prison gang leaders, lockdowns, prosecution of crimes committed by prison gang members, and interrupting the communications of prison gang members. Despite these efforts, there are no solid evaluations of these strategies.

Administrative segregation—colloquially known as "ad seg"—is a common inmate control procedure. This practice locks inmates in a single cell for twenty-three hours a day. In 1985 Texas put all known prison gang members into segregation in an attempt to limit their impact on the behavior of other inmates. Violence in the general population decreased. By 1991 this process included more than 1,500 gang members (Ralph and

Marquart 1991). Such policies are popular among prison officials (Knox 2000), despite the fact that a majority of them do not believe that such practices reduce misconduct. By isolating prison gang leaders, officials attempted to reduce communication among gang members to reduce the strength of gang ties. On some occasions, gang members are transferred from one institution to another. A related practice is "jacketing," where a note placed in an inmate file follows the inmate and allows authorities to transfer him to a high-security facility. In some instances, release from ad seg is contingent upon reporting information about the gang (Hunt et al. 1990). There is widespread agreement that better information-gathering and sharing between law enforcement and corrections is needed (Orlando-Morningstar 1997). Upon entry to prison, law enforcement can provide corrections officials with useful information about an individual's conflicts and prior behavior. Similarly, corrections officials can provide law enforcement with information about known associates in the institution as inmates are released back to the community. Following the lead of law enforcement, prisons now use databases to track prison gang members and gang activities. This allows for more effective communication between corrections and law enforcement. The New York City Department of Correction uses digitized photos that document gang member marks and/or tattoos. The efficiency of an online system provides for an effective tool in prison gang management.

There is very little in the way of alternative programming in prisons for gang members. There are a few exceptions, however. In Hampden County (Massachusetts), a graduated program for release from segregation was developed for prison gang members. Two years into the program, 190 inmates were enrolled and 17 were returned to segregation for gang activities (Toller and Tsagaris 1996), though no details of the program's evaluation are available.

The transfer of gang members to out-of-state facilities has become a more common control strategy. The theory is that by transferring a leader out of state, his influence is diminished. This strategy, despite its popularity, is yet to be evaluated. There is some concern that such actions may simply transport gang problems to other prisons (United States Department of Justice 1992). Other approaches include assigning members of different gangs to the same work assignment or cell block. The results of such an approach are not promising, however. In Illinois, for example, the inmate prison gang population was too large to assign to a few locations (United States Department of Justice 1992). A national survey conducted by Camp and Camp (1985) found that transfer was the most popular strategy followed by the use of informants, lockdown, and segregation.

There are some positive signs. Training for correctional officers has improved (Knox 2000), and over two-thirds of the 133 facilities surveyed by Camp and Camp (1985) provided some gang training. Despite this, only 20 percent of prison administrators surveyed by Knox (2005) indicated that they had programming for gang members who wanted to leave the gang. These experts—correctional administrators—identified six potential solutions to make their institutions safer: (a) increased sanctions against gang members, (b) special housing for gang members, (c) restricting benefits (commissary, phone calls, etc.) for prison misconduct, (d) new services for prison gang members, (e) new policies to deal with prison gang members, and (f) increased staffing and resources.

IV. FROM THE PRISON TO THE STREET

Prisoner re-entry is an important consideration when thinking about gangs in prison. The growth in imprisonment has led to an increased number of gang members behind prison walls. This has led, appropriately, to closer consideration of issues regarding the re-entry of gang members. While the number of individuals released from prison has reached record numbers, perhaps as high as 750,000 per year (Petersilia 2009), the real issue is how well they do once they are released. It is well understood that release from prison is a traumatic time. The "impact of release is dramatic. . . . The problems of the first weeks are usually staggering and sometimes insurmountable . . . and for many impossible" (Irwin 1970, p. 107). Those with a strong family support system may do better, although considerable challenges remain.

As a large number of gang members end up in prison, it is reasonable to attempt to assess how they behave upon release. It is assumed that most return to the communities in which they resided before going to prison. This makes it likely that they will reacquaint themselves with members of their former gang (Petersilia 2009; Pyrooz, Decker, and Webb 2014). However, allegiances and associations may have changed during their time in prison. It is certainly the case that the dynamics of their gang have changed. In short, gang members who leave prison go back to a community that is different and has a very different gang scene than before they went to prison. Gang members have a large number of risk factors, including little education, poor mental health, insufficient job skills, and reduced levels of social support in the community (Decker, Melde, and Pyrooz 2013). There is also the question of where these individuals will work after release from prison. They may well find that opportunities for legitimate employment are slim (see, e.g., Pager 2003; Huebner 2005), but opportunities for illegitimate money-generating activities are everywhere. Thus many gang members end up back in prison shortly after their release.

The knowledge base about why street gang members leave their gang or desist from crime is growing (Pyrooz et. al. 2014; Pyrooz and Decker 2011; Decker et al. 2013). Despite these advances in our knowledge about the desistance of street gang members, we still know very little about why prison gang members leave their gang or stop their involvement in crime. Integrating prison gang members into mainstream society should be a high priority, owing to their high levels of involvement in crime. There is a risk, though, that prisons may further alienate individuals who are already marginalized from society. Further, once released from prison, there is considerable evidence that the welfare of formerly imprisoned gang members is not a high priority for communities. This may be a "mistake" (Dupont-Morales and Harris 1994; Tonry 2004) due to the damage that such individuals can do to the community.

There is emerging evidence about the recidivism of gang members, with studies conducted in three of the United States (Olson and Dooley 2006; Huebner et al. 2007; Caudill 2010; Trulson et al. 2011, 2012), Singapore (Chu et al. 2012), and Quebec, Canada (Guay 2012). Across these studies, there is a great deal of evidence indicating that gang members fare worse when released from prison. Olson and Dooley's study is a typical example. They examined data from more than 3,300 probationers discharged from supervision and 2,500 prison releases/parolees in Illinois. Within two years, 64 percent of gang probationers (compared to 30 percent of nongang probationers) and 75 percent of gang prison releases/parolees (compared to 65 percent of nongang releases/parolees) were rearrested for a new crime.

Huebner and colleagues (2007, p. 208) concluded that gang membership was a "difficult barrier to overcome and [has] important effects on the timing of post release convictions."

V. What Do Prison Gang Members Have to Say About All of This?

Missing in prison research more generally and prison gang members more specifically are the views of gang-affiliated inmates. Such work is rare, as we noted in the introduction, as it is difficult to conduct and is generally not popular among funding sources or those who manage prisons. The second part of this essay examines original data collected as part of a larger study of gangs in four cities. Here we focus explicitly on the views of gang members while they were imprisoned, the relationship between their prison gangs and the street, and the role of the prison in the decisions of some gang members to leave their gangs. We conclude this section by discussing an emerging topic of importance in understanding prison gangs: the availability and role of technology in prison. These data were collected from individuals in street outreach programs in Los Angeles and Phoenix, inmates of the Fresno County Jail, and probationers and parolees in St. Louis. All of the individuals reported on here had been incarcerated in federal, state, or local facilities.

There has been a dearth of research on prison gangs. The work we report on here was not explicitly a study of gang members in prison. The study was designed to examine the process of desisting from gangs, with a focus on what role (if any) technology played in that process. In the course of our interviews, however, a large number of the subjects discussed their experiences in prison. We report on those perspectives here. Four categories of responses were identified in the interviews: (a) the interrelationship between prison and street gangs, (b) the role of technology in prison gangs, (c) the salience of race in prison gangs, and (d) the influence of imprisonment on the decision to leave the gang.

A. Prison to the Street

Despite being locked up, often for long stretches of time, imprisoned gang members continue to be impacted by the role of the street. For one gang member from Los Angeles (LA), the street was omnipresent and created distractions that he did not see as positive.

> Thinking about the streets is what eats a lot of people up in prison. Thinking about what is going on out there in the streets. LA, Hispanic male, 31

But other gang members found that prison gangs were different than gangs on the street, and still others told us that they joined their gang in prison and that prison gangs were more serious than street gangs.

> When I went to prison it was like here I am amongst my enemies [rival gang members] and it's like, we can get along in here. So it's like . . . I mean I have a lot of friends from different

neighborhoods. You know the prison system is different [than the street]. LA, Hispanic male, 49

I went to prison in '79. I sympathized with them [Black Guerilla Family] before I joined, but I joined in prison. Fresno, African American male, 54

Bulldogs [Fresno Bulldogs] didn't mean anything on the street, but it did in prison. The real gang banging is in prison as opposed to the street. Fresno, Hispanic male, 30

According to gang members in prison, gang activity in prison is unlike gang activity on the street; it symbolizes achieving a higher level of seriousness that simply cannot be obtained on the street. That seriousness includes both the emotional commitment to the gang as well as the actions that support that commitment—actions that are often violent.

Just as prison gangs have an impact on the street, street gangs have an influence on those in prison. A gang member told us that he expected the support and care from his street gang when he was in prison but found that was not forthcoming. Ironically, that lack of support played a role in "opening his eyes" to the fact that his gang was not as supportive as he had imagined.

They was supposed to help me and look out for me when I was in there and they [the gang] didn't. Prison opened my eyes. The gang didn't help when I went to jail. LA, African American male, 56

A St. Louis gang member struck a chord that we heard over and over again: prison gangs are different from street gangs, and gang rivalries on the street do not necessarily carry over into prison.

INTERVIEWER: So, when you're in prison, are there other 62 Brims locked up with you?

RESPONDENT: Yeah.

INTERVIEWER: And is the prison gang rivalry like it is on the street?

RESPONDENT: Yeah, yeah . . . because it's, now it's to the point where you can be a Blood and associate with a Crip.

INTERVIEWER: So when you came back after being away [in prison] for five years, and you came back on the street, did you just walk back into the gang like you had never been gone?

RESPONDENT: Like I said, I still was in it . . . it was, it was a lot of new people I didn't know about, or I knew when I had left they was not there. So you find out more information in prison than you do on the street anyways. So at the same time I was hearing who was comin' to the hood or something. St. Louis, African-American male, 25

The differences between street and prison gangs were described by one member of our sample from Phoenix in terms of their level of organization, a fact he believed was tied to the money made by prison gangs.

All my friends are in prison now. I went from being a Southside Phoenix gang member to being more Mexican Mafia in prison, which is more like organized crime: money, respect. Phoenix, Hispanic male, 19

B. Technology

We include a few insights into the use and availability of technology in prison because of the growing importance of technology in the lives of street gangs. Technology has penetrated most every aspect of contemporary society, including the prison, even when that technology is treated as contraband and expressly prohibited from being used in the prison. In particular, the availability of smartphones has created opportunities for texting, the use of social media, and advanced forms of communication. Gangs and gang members are active users of this technology (Pyrooz, Decker, and Moule 2015), apparently even in prison where the possession of such technology is expressly prohibited. Such phones were used to post pictures to Facebook by one Fresno gang member, as well as to communicate with the street. Another subject told us that he used his phone to stay in touch with family.

> The gang used the Internet to communicate from prison to the hood. Cell phones were used to take gang pictures in prison and post them on Facebook. Fresno, Hispanic male, 26

> In prison, using cell phones is a whole different thing. You have to use them to get info instead of waiting for a homie to get transferred. I had my own phone. I paid $400 because my homie was the main guy who would get them, so I got a discount. Normally they would go for $800. I just used my phone to call my wife and girls. Fresno, Hispanic male, 30

> People meet up through Facebook. They do that and they text in prison. Fresno, white male, 20

Technology presents gangs and gang members opportunities to expand and enhance their relationships with their street gang counterparts. It also allows them to quickly learn of recent events taking place on the street, as well as inform the street of events taking place in prison. Technology can also allow them to communicate to the street and "direct" activities in cases where imprisoned gang members still have sway over the gang. Indeed, technology is an important component of street and prison gang life, one that we anticipate will increase in importance as technology, as well as technological competency, advances.

C. Role/Salience of Race in Prison Gangs

Perhaps the most consistent message about the differences between life in a street gang and in a prison gang is the role of race as a means of affiliating with a prison gang. Intraracial rivalries on the street did not carry over to prison, where race was the major characteristic used to determine patterns of affiliation and grouping. While street affiliations were remembered, they did not necessarily determine who an individual aligned himself with in prison, as race was the primary mobilizing force for group membership in prison. This was true for Hispanic, black, and white members of our sample.

> Now you know, Mexicans and blacks don't like each other. They, you know, I don't know if it comes from the prison thing, come from bein' in prison, comin' out and still having that mentality, or the fact that blacks and Mexicans were, you know, Mexicans have all the marijuana and blacks want marijuana. Yeah, race, based, yeah. Mexicans have to eat with Mexicans, blacks have to eat with blacks, whites have to eat with whites. And . . . a lot of that was based

on hate, you know, I'd overhear stuff. "The fuckin' niggers," you know, whites say that and like Mexicans, "pinche miates." Blacks will be like, "So-and-so" I'm like, "Man, there's a lot of hate here, I don't hate that guy. I don't even know that guy. Why am I gonna hate this guy right here?" You know, so, I think that has to do a lot with the race relations now. Phoenix, African American male, 42

Um, gangs are not really associated in incarceration. Uh, you gonna have to get along with Bloods, you gonna have to get along with Crips. Incarcerations is, is more of a color thing. You with your color. It's all about race in jail. It's all about blacks with blacks, kinfolk with kinfolk, Chicanos with Chicanos, Pisas with Pisas, the Woods with the Woods and Chiefs with the Chiefs. It's all about your race when you're incarcerated. Phoenix, African American male, 19

Thus race is the organizing principle within the prison system, as recognized in prior research (Goodman 2008; Jacobs 1974; Maxson 2012), and especially among whites:

I put in work with the white boys in YA [California Youth Authority] before I joined. Always back up your race—Aryan Brotherhood, Nazi WW Rider, Peckerwood. Fresno, white male, 20

But the gang still matters to some extent.

INTERVIEWER: Was your gang [in prison]?
RESPONDENT: Yeah, but they were all like Southerners [southern California]. So they're just under the same umbrella.
INTERVIEWER: So were the stabbings you did in prison having to do with gang rivalry?
RESPONDENT: Yeah. It was mainly like racial.
INTERVIEWER: Was there a lot of division in there [prison] like Hispanic, black?
RESPONDENT: Yeah, that [race] is real . . . real bad. LA, Hispanic male, 27

D. Impact of Prison on Leaving the Gang

For many members of our sample, prison was a very negative experience. That, combined with maturational reform, led many of them to make a decision about leaving the gang. Prison seemed to suggest alternatives to being in the gang that perhaps they had not fully assessed prior to their time behind the walls.

INTERVIEWER: Before you went to prison, had you thought about leaving the gang?
RESPONDENT: No, absolutely not.
INTERVIEWER: When did you first think about leaving the gang?
RESPONDENT: Uh, when I was gonna go back to prison. 1990. I went back to prison. I came out and went "never mind" [to the gang]. Phoenix, African American male, 51

Prison is an experience that helped many gang members, usually older ones, reexamine their current life state and reconsider all of the negative consequences associated with gang involvement and their criminal activity.

Like I don't want to be incarcerated any longer. I'm tired of getting arrested. Then, I didn't see anything positive with my life coming above being a gang member, bein' out there. I seen death or prison. And really, that's the reality of it. So I didn't want that no more. I'm still kind like going through a transition 'cause I just got out of prison [after fourteen years]. LA, Hispanic male, 46

Today, I have to wake up and I look in the mirror and I realize, if I allow myself to think the way I used to, then I could create all kinds of chaos and the end result for me is . . . I'll spend the rest of my life in prison. I've been back to prison, thirty-two months for a two-inch knife. LA, Hispanic male, 49

Sometimes the gang leaves an individual very little choice but to exit, as illustrated in one interview with a 26-year-old Hispanic former gang member in Fresno:

There was a bogus call on me. Bulldogs made a call on me saying that I was a snitch. They sliced me, so I said I was done. I got jumped three times for the same thing, but I was fighting it, stopping it. They took it to the extreme. If they didn't make the call, I would be in it still.

When asked what he had to do to leave:

I just walked away, but they [classification officers] ad seg'd me in SNY [special needs yard] because of the incident. It took me one day from being active to being a D/O [dropout].

As Toch (2007) recognized, the gang classification system within prison involves a level of institutionalization and bureaucracy, with little recourse to inmates who are suspected of gang affiliation. As noted by another former gang member, a 54-year-old African American male:

INTERVIEWER: How did you get out?
RESPONDENT: I debriefed. I went straight to classification and debriefed. I was in Pelican Bay with an undetermined sentence. I went to an officer and debriefed.
INTERVIEWER: Did you tell the gang first?
RESPONDENT: Hell no. They would've killed me. I quit in New Folsom and went straight to the SNY.

Debriefing, or informing to correctional officials of the inner workings of the gangs, is avoided by some inmates out of fear of the consequences for "snitching," while others are extremely cautious. The last quoted inmate remains in a dropout pod (also known as special needs yard or ad seg) to this day, despite having debriefed over a decade ago.

Threats do not diminish once an inmate has debriefed. Problems continue to surface in dropout pods, as noted by several former gang members in Fresno.

There's more activity in D/O than the main pods because there's no order [no gang structure]. Fresno, white male, 20

When asked if he was worried about his former gang attacking him:

I'd be lying if I said I wasn't [worried]. I gotta watch out for sleepers, dropouts that fake leaving to get sent to the D/O pod and take care of old guys like me. Fresno, Hispanic male, 39

VI. Conclusion

This review has documented the magnitude of the problem posed by incarcerated gang members. Gang members enter prison with very high levels of crime in their background. They are more prone to be involved in violence, have weak community ties and are not well integrated into conventional society, and possess deficits that impede their employment opportunities upon re-entry. Once in prison, opportunities for involvement in crime abound. Whether by affiliating with members of their own gang or new prison gangs, members tend to engage in higher levels of institutional misconduct. This misconduct can take a variety of forms, including but not limited to violence, extortion, and the sale of drugs and other contraband.

The presence of white hate groups in prison exacerbates the tensions and conflicts in prison, multiplying the opportunities for misconduct and increasing the risk of isolation and longer prison sentences that can result from such behavior. Such patterns of deviance further distance gang members from opportunities to learn skills and gain experiences that will help them transition to legitimate society. As a consequence of prison misconduct, there are few programming opportunities directed specifically at gang members. They are more often the target of segregation, jacketing, or isolation, activities that may (or may not, as our review documents) make it easier to manage prisons but are not likely to improve the chances of gang members successfully transitioning from the prison back to the street. When gang members are released back into their communities, they find a different environment in many ways. The labor market is certainly dynamic and demands new skills that many gang members lack when entering prison and fail to acquire before release. The criminal landscape along with the power relationships among and within gangs also changes. A gang "leader" who is incarcerated for several years may return to his community only to find that his gang has been absorbed into a new gang with a new leader and new activities. Gang members returning from prison also may not be known by a new "generation" of gang members, as these generations turn over with great frequency.

We know far more about how gang members get from "the street to the prison" and far less about how they get from "the prison to the street." The evidence that does exist is only suggestive, but several tentative conclusions can be drawn. First, gang members are "hard cases"; that is, they are likely to become the targets of institutional control through misconduct, disciplinary hearings, segregation, and jacketing. Second, and as a consequence of engaging in institutional misconduct, gang members are isolated from routine programming and education/employment opportunities available to the general prison population. Third, while in prison, gang members are likely to form new alliances with gangs different from those they belonged to prior to incarceration. Fourth, when leaving prison, gang members often find that the criminal landscape has changed along with the structure and status of the gangs they once belonged to. Finally, as a consequence of these other processes, gang members are among the highest risks for returning to prison. While considerable effort is expended on prevention of gang membership, little has been done to encourage desistance by gang members upon re-entry after prison.

References

Baugh, Dennis G. 1993. *Gangs in Correctional Facilities: A National Assessment*. Laurel, MD: American Correctional Association.

Berg, Mark, and Matt DeLisi. 2006. "The Correctional Melting Pot: Race, Ethnicity, Citizenship, and Prison Violence." *Journal of Criminal Justice* 34: 631–642.

Camp, George M., and Camille G. Camp. 1985. *Prison Gangs: Their Extent, Nature, and Impact on Prisons*. Washington, DC: US Government Printing Office.

Caudill, Jonathan W. 2010. "Back on the Swagger: Institutional Release and Recidivism Timing among Gang Affiliates." *Youth Violence and Juvenile Justice* 8: 58–70.

Chu, Chi Meng, Michael Daffern, Stuart Thomas, and Jia Ying Lim. 2012. "Violence Risk and Gang Affiliation in Youth Offenders: A Recidivism Study." *Psychology, Crime, and Law* 18: 299–315.

Clemmer, Donald. 1940. *The Prison Community*. New York: Holt, Rinehart, and Winston.

Cloward, Richard, and Lloyd Ohlin. 1960. *Delinquency and Opportunity: A Theory of Delinquent Gangs*. New York: Free Press.

Cohen, Albert. 1955. *Delinquent Boys: The Culture of the Gang*. New York: Free Press.

Curry, G. David, Scott H. Decker, and David C. Pyrooz. 2013. *Confronting Gangs: Crime and Community*, 3d ed. New York: Oxford University Press.

Decker, Scott H., Chris Melde, and David C. Pyrooz. 2013. "What Do We Know about Gangs and Gang Members and Where Do We Go From Here?" *Justice Quarterly* 30: 369–402.

Decker, Scott H., and David C. Pyrooz. 2010. "Gang Violence Worldwide: Context, Culture, and Country." In *Small Arms Survey 2010: Gangs, Groups, and Guns*. Cambridge, UK: Cambridge University Press.

Decker, Scott H., David C. Pyrooz, and Richard K. Moule. 2013. "Disengagement from Gangs as Role Transitions." *Journal of Research on Adolescence* 23: 1–22.

DeLisi, Matt, Mark T. Berg, and Andy Hochstetler. 2004. "Gang Members, Career Criminals and Prison Violence: Further Specification of the Importation Model of Inmate Behavior." *Criminal Justice Studies* 17: 369–383.

DiIulio, John J. 1987. *Governing Prisons: A Comparative Study of Correctional Management*. New York: Free Press.

DuPont-Morales, M. A., and Jean E. Harris. 1994. "Strengthening Accountability: Incorporating Strategic Planning and Performance Measurement into Budgeting." *Public Productivity & Management Review* 17: 231–239.

Esbensen, Finn-Aage, L. Thomas Winfree Jr., Ni He, and Terrance J. Taylor. 2001. "Youth Gangs and Definitional Issues: When Is a Gang a Gang, and Why Does It Matter?" *Crime & Delinquency* 47: 105–130.

Fishman, Joseph. 1934. *Sex in Prison: Revealing Sex Conditions in American Prisons*. New York: National Library.

Fleisher, Mark S. 2006. "Gang Management in Corrections." In *Prison and Jail Administration: Practice and Theory*, 2d ed., edited by P. Carlson and J. S. Garrett. Gaithersburg, MD: Aspen.

Fong, Robert S., Ronald E. Vogel, and Salvador Buentello. 1995. "Blood in, Blood Out: The Rationale Behind Defecting from Prison Gangs." *Journal of Gang Research* 2: 45–51.

Gaes, Gerald G., Susan Wallace, Evan Gilman, Jody Klein-Saffron, and Sharon Suppa. 2002. "The Influence of Prison Gang Affiliation on Violence and Other Prison Misconduct." *The Prison Journal* 82: 359–385.

Goodman, Philip. 2008. "'It's Just Black, White, or Hispanic': An Observational Study of Racializing Moves in California's Segregate Prison Reception Centers." *Law & Society Review* 42: 735–770.

Gottfredson, Michael, and Travis Hirschi. 1990. *A General Theory of Crime*. Redwood City, CA: Stanford University Press.

Griffin, Marie L., and John R. Hepburn. 2006. "The Effect of Gang Affiliation on Violent Misconduct among Inmates during the Early Years of Confinement." *Criminal Justice Review* 33: 419–448.

Guay, Jean-Pierre 2012. *Predicting Recidivism with Street Gang Members*. Ottawa: Public Safety Canada. https://www.publicsafety.gc.ca/cnt/rsrcs/pblctns/2012-02-prsgm/index-eng.aspx

Huebner, Beth M. 2003. "Administrative Determinants of Inmate Violence: A Multilevel Analysis." *Journal of Criminal Justice* 31: 107–117.

Huebner, Beth M. 2005. "The Effect of Incarceration on Marriage and Work over the Life Course." *Justice Quarterly* 22: 281–303.

Huebner, B. M., S. Varano, and T. S. Bynum. 2007. "Gangs, Guns and Drugs: Recidivism among Serious, Young Offenders." *Criminology & Public Policy* 6: 183–222.

Hunt, Geoffrey, Stephanie Riegel, Tomas Morales, and Dan Waldorf. 1990. "Changes in Prison Culture: Prison Gangs and the Case of the 'Pepsi Generation.'" *Social Problems* 40: 398–409.

Irwin, John. 1970. *The Felon*. Berkeley: University of California Press.

Irwin, John, and Donald R. Cressey. 1962. "Thieves, Convicts, and the Inmate Culture." *Social Problems* 10: 142–155.

Jacobs, James B. 1974. "Street Gangs Behind Bars." *Social Problems* 21: 395–409.

Jacobs, James B. 1977. *Stateville: The Penitentiary in Mass Society*. Chicago: University of Chicago Press.

Klein, Malcolm, and Cheryl L. Maxson. 2006. *Street Gang Patterns and Policies*. New York: Oxford University Press.

Knox, George W. 2000. "National Assessment of Gangs and Security Threat Groups (STGs) in Adult Correctional Institutions: Results of the 1999 Adult Corrections Survey." *Journal of Gang Research* 7: 1–45.

Knox, George W. 2005. *The Problem of Gangs and Security Threat Groups (STGs) in American Prisons Today: Recent Research Findings from the 2004 Prison Gang Survey*. Peotone, IL: National Gang Research Center. http://www.ngcrc.com/corr2006.html

Kreinert, Jessie L., and Mark S. Fleisher. 2001. "Gang Membership as a Proxy for Social Deficiencies: A Study of Nebraska Inmates." *Corrections Management Quarterly* 3: 47–58.

Krohn, Marvin, and Terence Thornberry. 2008. "Longitudinal Perspectives on Adolescent Street Gangs." In *The Long View of Crime: A Synthesis of Longitudinal Research*, edited by Akiva Liberman. New York: Springer.

Langan, Patrick A., and David J. Levin. 2002. *Recidivism of Prisoners Released in 1994*. Bureau of Justice Statistics Special Report. Washington DC: US Department of Justice.

Lawrence, Sarah, and Jeremy Travis. 2004. *The New Landscape of Imprisonment: Mapping America's Prison Expansion*. Washington, DC: Urban Press.

Lyman, Michael D. 1989. *Gangland*. Springfield, IL: Charles C. Thomas.

Maxson, Cheryl L. 2012. "Betwixt and Between Street and Prison Gangs: Defining Gangs and Structures in Youth Correctional Facilities." In *Youth Gangs in International Perspective: Results from the Eurogang Program of Research*, edited by Finn-Aage Esbensen and Cheryl L. Maxson. New York: Springer.

Miller, Walter. 1958. "Lower Class Culture as a Generating Milieu of Gang Delinquency." *Journal of Social Issues* 14: 5–19.

National Drug Intelligence Center. 2009. "Gangs." In *2009 National Gang Threat Assessment*. Washington, DC: US Department of Justice. https://www.justice.gov/archive/ndic/pubs31/31379/gangs.htm

Olson, David E., and Brendan D. Dooley. 2006. "Gang Membership and Community Corrections Populations: Characteristics and Recidivism Rates relative to Other Offenders." In *Studying Youth Gangs*, edited by James F. Short and Lorine A. Hughes. New York: Altamira Press.

Orlando-Morningstar, Dennise. 1997. "Prison Gangs." *Special Needs Offender Bulletin* 2: 1–13.

Pager, Devah. 2003. "The Mark of a Criminal Record." *American Journal of Sociology* 108: 937–975.

Petersilia, Joan. 2009. *When Prisoners Come Home: Parole and Prisoner Reentry*. New York: Oxford University Press.

Pyrooz, David C., Scott H. Decker, and Mark Fleisher. 2011. "From the Street to the Prison, From the Prison to the Street: Understanding and Responding to Prison Gangs." *Journal of Aggression, Conflict and Peace Research* 3: 12–24.

Pyrooz, David C., Scott H. Decker, and Richard K. Moule Jr. 2015. "Criminal and Routine Activities in Online Settings: Gangs, Offenders, and the Internet." *Justice Quarterly* 32: 471–499.

Pyrooz, David C., Scott H. Decker, and Vincent J. Webb. 2014. "The Ties that Bind: Desistance from Gangs." *Crime & Delinquency* 60: 491–516.

Ralph, Paige H., and James W. Marquart. 1991. "Gang Violence in Texas Prisons." *The Prison Journal* 71: 38–49.

Ruddell, Rick, Scott H., Decker, and Arlen Egley Jr. 2006. "Gang Interventions in Jails: A National Analysis." *Criminal Justice Review* 31: 1–14.

Schwartz, Barry. 1971. "Pre-institutional vs. Situational Influence in a Correctional Community." *Journal of Criminal Law, Criminology, and Police Science* 62: 532–542.

Shelden, Randall G. 1991. "A Comparison of Gang Members and Non-Gang Members in a Prison Setting." *The Prison Journal* 71: 50–60.

Stastny Charles, and Gabrielle Tyrnauer. 1983. *Who Rules the Joint? The Changing Political Culture of Maximum-Security Prisons in America*. Lexington, MA: Lexington Books.

Tasca, Melinda, Marie L. Griffin, and Nancy Rodriguez. 2010. "The Effect of Importation and Deprivation Factors on Violent Misconduct: An Examination of Black and Latino Youth in Prison." *Youth Violence and Juvenile Justice* 8: 234–249.

Thornberry, Terence, Marvin Krohn, Alan Lizotte, and Deborah Chard-Wierschem. 1993. "The Role of Juvenile Gangs in Facilitating Delinquent Behavior." *Journal of Research in Crime and Delinquency* 30: 55–87.

Thrasher, Frederic. 1927. *The Gang: A Study of 1,313 Gangs in Chicago*. Chicago: University of Chicago Press.

Toch, Hans. 2007. "Sequestering Gang Members, Burning Witches, and Subverting Due Process." *Criminal Justice and Behavior* 34: 274–288.

Toller, William, and Basil Tsagaris. 1996. "Managing Institutional Gangs: A Practical Approach Combining Security and Human Services." *Corrections Today* 58: 100–111.

Tonry, Michael H. 2004. *Thinking about Crime: Sense and Sensibility in American Penal Culture*. New York: Oxford University Press.

Trulson, Chad R. 2007. "Determinants of Disruption: Institutional Misconduct among State-Committed Delinquents." *Youth Violence and Juvenile Justice* 5: 7–34.

Trulson, Chad R., Jonathan W. Caudill, Darin R. Haerle, and Matt DeLisi. 2012. "Cliqued Up: The Post-Incarceration Recidivism of Young Gang-Related Homicide Offenders." *Criminal Justice Review* 37: 174–190.

Trulson, Chad R., Darin R. Haerle, Matt DeLisi, and James W. Marquart. 2011. "Blended Sentencing, Early Release, and Recidivism of Violent Institutionalized Delinquents." *Prison Journal* 91: 255–278.

Truslon, Chad R., James W. Marquart, and Soraya K. Kawucha. 2006. "Gang Suppression and Institutional Control." *Corrections Today* 68: 26–31.

United States Bureau of Justice Statistics. 2003. *Sourcebook of Criminal Justice Statistics 2003.* Washington, DC: US Department of Justice. http://www.albany.edu/sourcebook/pdf/t1103.pdf

United States Department of Justice. 1992. *Management Strategies in Disturbances and with Gangs/Disruptive Groups.* Washington, DC: US Government Printing Office.

Useem, Bert, and Anne Morrison Piehl. 2008. *The Challenge of Mass Incarceration.* New York: Cambridge University Press.

Wooldredge, John, and Benjamin Steiner. 2014. "A Bi-Level Framework for Understanding Prisoner Victimization." *Journal of Quantitative Criminology* 30: 141–162.

Worrall, John L., and Robert G. Morris. 2012. "Gang Integration and Inmate Violence." *Journal of Criminal Justice* 40: 425–432.

CHAPTER 8

....

WOMEN IN PRISON

....

EMILY M. WRIGHT AND CALLI M. CAIN

WOMEN have comprised a small proportion of the prison population throughout the world, but their growth rates in some countries (i.e., United States, England, Australia, and Netherlands) have surpassed that of men's in the past two decades (Walmsley 2009). Further, the magnitude of women incarcerated in the United States is unmatched; almost one-third of females incarcerated throughout the world are in US prisons (Walmsley 2009). The number of women in the United States criminal justice system can no longer be described as trivial. More women are incarcerated now than ever before. In fact, the number of women sanctioned by the criminal justice system has given rise to questions regarding whether a "new" female offender—one that is more violent and substantially more criminogenic—has emerged (Chesney-Lind 2002; Steffensmeier et al. 2006). Such a possibility could account for why the gender gap in crime, the difference between male and female involvement in crime, may be closing (Heimer, Lauritsen, and Lynch 2009; Lauritsen, Heimer, and Lynch 2009; Schwartz et al. 2009). Alternatively, policy and societal changes (e.g., the War on Drugs and the demise of rehabilitation; Garland 2001) may better account for females' increased criminal involvement and subsequent criminal justice sanctioning (Bush-Baskette 1998; Heimer, Wittrock, and Unal 2006) given that, for the most part, females tend to engage in similar crimes as they did in the past and continue to be less violent and pose lower risk than male offenders (e.g., Bloom, Owen, and Covington 2004; Kruttschnitt and Gartner 2008). Female offenders are primarily nonviolent offenders, engaging mostly in drug and property crimes (US Department of Justice 2010). Further, they are typically the primary caretakers of young or dependent children and are characterized by social and economic marginalization, high victimization and abuse, mental illness, and substance abuse problems (Owen and Bloom 1995; Bloom, Owen, and Covington 2005; Wright et al. 2012). Female offenders bring these characteristics with them into the criminal justice system, and eventually into prisons, which in turn can affect their adjustment to confinement, their programming and service needs, and the administration and management styles used in prisons for women.

This essay details how females' unique characteristics impact their pathways into prison, their response to confinement, and the potential implications for prison management and programming services that arise when responding to females' needs. Section I presents a brief history of the rising incarceration rates among females in the United States. Section

II provides an overview of the female offenders' "gender-responsive" characteristics, such as substance use, mental illness, victimization, and childcare, while section III describes how these gender-responsive characteristics are related to females' adjustment to prison conditions. Sections IV and V describe how prison management, policies, and services can be more gender-informed in order to respond more effectively to female offenders' unique characteristics. Finally, section VI outlines what gender-responsive policies and programs within corrections might entail in the coming years. The main conclusions discussed in this essay are the following:

- Although their numbers in the criminal justice system have been rising, female offenders continue to be primarily nonviolent property and drug offenders.
- Female offenders appear to be unique from male offenders in that they more often engage in qualitatively different offenses than males (primarily nonviolent ones), do so for different reasons, pose less of a threat of violence across criminal justice settings, and come under criminal jurisdiction via different paths than men.
- Gender-responsive characteristics for women include past histories of and/or ongoing abuse from others, unhealthy relationships with others, social and economic marginalization, substance abuse, and mental or physical health problems; these factors are either not typically seen among men, are seen among male offenders but occur at a higher frequency among females, or occur in relatively equal frequency among male and female offenders but affect women in unique ways.
- Some gender-responsive characteristics influence women's adjustment to prison, and prisons should consider making changes to their policies, management styles, and programming or service provisions in order to better respond to women's unique needs.
- The future of gender-responsiveness in corrections will likely entail an expanded recognition of gender-responsive needs and, eventually, the implementation of a wide range of services across all correctional systems (e.g., pretrial, probation, prison, parole).

I. Rising Incarceration Rates among Females

The long-term trend in state and federal prison populations across the United States indicates that incarceration levels rose between 2002 and 2011, with the number of women incarcerated in the United States increasing by approximately 1.4 percent each year during that time (compared to a 1.1 percent yearly increase among males; Carson and Golinelli 2013). Females comprise a smaller proportion of violent offenders incarcerated in state institutions than males (36.8 percent and 54.3 percent, respectively), yet a higher proportion of property offenders (27.8 percent compared to 17.7 percent for males) and drug offenders (25.1 percent compared to 16.2 percent for males) (Carson and Golinelli 2013). The fact that female offenders engage in more property and drug crimes than violent, person-oriented crimes has remained largely unchanged for many years (Steffensmeier et al. 2006; Kruttschnitt and Gartner 2008; Schwartz et al. 2009).

Although the sheer numbers of women incarcerated has risen over the years, scholars warn against assuming that female offenders or females in general have become significantly "worse"—more violent or more criminogenic—during this time (Kruttschnitt and Gartner 2008). Instead, they suggest that policy changes have "widened the net" cast over female offenders, essentially bringing more women into the criminal justice system than had previously been warranted by their behavior (Chesney-Lind 2002, 2006; Steffensmeier et al. 2006; Feld 2009). The US War on Drugs imposed stiffer penalties for a range of drug crimes, expanded the types of drug offenses for which women were incarcerated, and lengthened the sentences for these crimes (Javdani, Sadeh, and Verona 2011). Other "get tough" policies include truth-in-sentencing polices, such as mandatory minimum sentences and three-strikes laws, as well as pro-arrest policies for domestic and family violence–related offenses. Because female criminal behavior is frequently linked with drug use (females often report using drugs at the time of the offense or engaging in crime to support their drug habit, see Mumola and Karberg 2006), the more rigorous enforcement of drug laws brought a large influx of female offenders—particularly African American women—into the criminal justice system (Bush-Baskette 1998; Young and Reviere 2006). In many cases, scholars contend that these policy changes disproportionately impacted women relative to their harms to society (e.g., drug abuse versus sales; Bloom, Owen, and Covington 2004).

Pro-arrest, dual-arrest, and mandatory arrest policies for domestic and family violence have also tended to bring more victimized females into the criminal justice system (Muftic et al. 2007; Javdani, Sadeh, and Verona 2011) and likely increased the numbers of status-offending girls into the juvenile justice system (Feld 2009). Many scholars contend that these policies have not only artificially increased the number of females entrenched in the criminal justice system (by bringing certain types of offenses under system jurisdiction that were not previously criminalized), but they also tend to ignore the context in which females' criminality occurs, including their roles in and motivations for crime (Chesney-Lind 2002; Bloom, Owen, and Covington 2004). For instance, mandatory dual arrest policies for domestic violence that stipulate that both parties involved in a violent incident should be arrested, regardless of the true "perpetrator" or "victim," appear to ignore the roles that women's abuse histories may play. Other policy changes related to welfare benefits, education, housing, and employment opportunities changed alongside the War on Drugs, as many services became closed off to felony-convicted women (Bloom, Owen, and Covington 2004).

Parole has also played a large role in the growing imprisonment rate of women. Caplow and Simon (1999) argued that parole is no longer an alternative to prison but a back-door route to prison, especially for female offenders. The percentage of female parolees increased from 8 percent to 12 percent between 1990 and 2007 (Petersilia 1999; Glaze and Bonczar 2008), and the percentage of female parolees returned to prison for parole violations also increased during this period (Greenfeld and Snell 1999; Glaze and Bonczar 2008). Some scholars argue that females on parole are more likely to be returned to prison than males due to the increasingly difficult conditions of parole (Carlen and Tombs 2006). Female parolees may face more challenges than males because they are more likely to have a substance abuse problem and more likely to have been unemployed or homeless prior to incarceration (Bureau of Justice Statistics 2000a, 2000b). Many scholars reiterate the importance of safe and adequate housing for women on parole, which is sometimes complicated by policies that restrict offenders with certain types of convictions from residing there (e.g., drug offenders are not eligible to live in federal low-income housing; Young and Reviere 2006). These disadvantages can make meeting parole conditions (e.g., maintaining employment and adequate housing, reporting regularly to a parole officer, notifying a parole officer of an address change, etc.) especially difficult for female offenders.

The results of these policies not only led to increased numbers of female offenders in the criminal justice system but also impacted the national profile of female offenders: The typical female offender is minority, socially and economically marginalized, the primary caretaker of dependent children, and characterized by substance use or abuse, victimization histories, and various health-related problems (Owen and Bloom 1995; Bloom, Owen, and Covington 2003, 2005). Each of these characteristics has the potential to impact women while they are under the custody and supervision of the criminal justice system. We turn next to describing women's gender-responsive characteristics and their impact on female offenders' institutional adjustment.

II. FEMALE OFFENDERS' GENDER-RESPONSIVE CHARACTERISTICS

Female offenders appear to be unique from male offenders in that they more often engage in qualitatively different offenses than males (primarily nonviolent ones), do so for different reasons, pose less of a threat of violence across criminal justice settings, and come under criminal jurisdiction via different paths than men (Bloom, Owen, and Covington 2005; Belknap 2007; Wright et al. 2012). Of particular importance to the paths that women take into criminal behavior are past histories of and/or ongoing abuse from others, unhealthy relationships with others, social and economic marginalization, substance abuse, and mental or physical health problems (Bloom, Owen, and Covington 2005; Brennan et al. 2012). These factors are said to be "gender-responsive" because they are either not typically seen among men, are seen among male offenders but occur at a higher frequency among females, or occur in relatively equal frequency among male and female offenders but affect women in unique ways (Salisbury and Van Voorhis 2009; Van Voorhis et al. 2010). For instance, although both male and female offenders report high levels of victimization, females tend to experience much more abuse during their lifetimes (Harlow 1999; Belknap and Holsinger 2006)—in fact, over 70 percent of incarcerated women report having histories of physical and/or sexual victimization (Browne, Miller, and Maguin 1999; McDaniels-Wilson and Belknap 2008; Tripodi and Pettus-Davis 2013), while about 35 percent of women in the general population experience physical and/or sexual assault in their lifetime (UN Women 2012). Further, the effect of abuse at an early age appears to impact women in different ways than males; females are more likely to run away (Kaufman and Widom 1999; Chesney-Lind and Shelden 2004), turn to drugs and alcohol as coping mechanisms (Grella, Stein, and Greenwell 2005; Widom, Marmorstein, and White 2006), develop mental health problems as a result of the trauma (Jordan et al. 2002; Tripodi and Pettus-Davis 2013), and/or engage in illegal activity to escape, survive, or cope with the victimization (Daly 1992; Gilfus 1992). The patterns of behavior after being victimized appear to be different for males and females and thus are considered "gender-responsive."

A. Victimization, Substance Use, and Mental and Physical Health

The prevalence of victimization, substance use, and mental and physical health problems appears to be higher among female offenders than male offenders, which supports their consideration in corrections as gender-responsive factors. Women in prison experience higher levels of mental illness, substance abuse, and poor health than their male counterparts or females in general population (Greenfeld and Snell 1999; James and Glaze 2006; Mumola and Karberg 2006; Maruschak 2008; Zlotnick et al. 2008). In a study of nearly 3,000 federal inmates, proportionately more female offenders suffered from a serious mental illness than male offenders (17.4 percent versus 9.6 percent) and had previously used psychotropic medications (24.3 percent versus 11.4 percent) (Magaletta et al. 2009). Among females in state prisons, an estimated 73 percent had a mental health problem and 23 percent had been diagnosed with a mental disorder in the past 12 months, compared to 55 percent and 8 percent of males, respectively (James and Glaze 2006). A high proportion of female offenders also report suffering from medical or physical problems, with approximately 52 percent of female federal inmates reporting one or more medical problems (as opposed to 37 percent of male federal inmates) (Maruschak 2008). Poor health could be a reflection of low socioeconomic status and poverty among female offenders and their inability to receive adequate health care (Bloom, Owen, and Covington 2004), or it could reflect the physical consequences of enduring years of abuse (Anderson, Rosay, and Saum 2002). Finally, substance use—although common among male offenders too—appears to be more prevalent and potentially more strongly connected to females' criminality than to males' (McClellan, Farabee, and Crouch 1997; Bush-Baskette 1998). Some scholars argue that female inmates' high level of substance abuse represents a form of self-medication used to deal with the chronic pain of mental or physical illness or to cope in the aftermath of victimization (Sacks 2004). Indeed, more female than male offenders meet the diagnostic criteria for drug dependence or abuse and more report using drugs at the time of their offense (Mumola and Karberg 2006). Much evidence indicates that women's reliance on drugs is a major facilitator to their criminal behavior (Owen 1998; Salisbury and Van Voorhis 2009).

In fact, the *co-occurrence* between victimization, substance use/abuse, and mental health problems also appears to be particularly strong and unique among female offenders (Houser, Belenko, and Brennan 2012). The comorbidity of mental illness and drug use/abuse disorders is supported in the literature (Center for Substance Abuse Treatment 2005; James and Glaze 2006; Peters et al. 2008), as is the overlap of these problems with abuse and victimization (Houser, Belenko, and Brennan 2012; Tripodi and Pettus-Davis 2013). Several studies have confirmed that women in prison have higher prevalence rates of mental illness, substance abuse, and co-occurring disorders than male inmates (Bloom, Owen, and Covington 2003; Hills 2004; James and Glaze 2006; Mumola and Karberg 2006). For instance, Messina and colleagues (2007) reported that female drug offenders had greater exposure to childhood adverse events, such as abuse and neglect, than male drug offenders and that while the impact of these adverse events significantly affected both males' and females' distress levels (e.g., anxiety, depression, sleep disturbance), women experienced higher levels of overall distress. Almost three-quarters (74 percent) of the women incarcerated in the United States meet the criteria for comorbid psychiatric and substance use disorders, as set forth in the *Diagnostic and Statistical Manual of Mental Disorders* (4th ed.; American Psychiatric Association 2000), compared with 41 percent of their male counterparts (James and Glaze 2006). The specific relationship between victimization, substance use, and mental health problems is difficult to ascertain due to temporal ordering: While victimization or abuse often occurs first among female offenders, depression, anxiety, posttraumatic stress disorder, and other mental health problems often begin very soon after the abuse and many times co-occur simultaneously with the development of substance use or dependence (Jordan et al. 2002; National Institute on Drug Abuse 2008; Asberg and Renk 2013). Additionally, drug use can be used to "treat" both mental health symptoms and trauma (physical or emotional) brought on by victimization (e.g., DeHart 2008), further complicating the interrelationship. These co-occurring disorders pose an especially complex problem for female inmates because their symptoms stem from two or more disorders, which make it difficult for accurate assessment, treatment, and clinical prognosis in correctional settings compared to inmates with singular disorders (Dennison 2005; Peters et al. 2004, 2008).

B. Relationships with Significant Others, Family, and Children

The influence of relationships with others, including family, children, and significant others, may be unique among female offenders as well. Among males, marriage may be a stabilizing and protective factor against criminality (Laub, Nagin, and Sampson 1998), yet relationships with significant others among females may actually be crime promoting (Daly 1992; Carbone-Lopez and Kruttschnitt 2010; Brennan et al. 2012). Studies suggest that, at younger ages, female offenders tend to associate with older, more criminogenic males and may be introduced to criminal behavior and/or drug use by these significant others as well as by family members (Brown 2006; Smith, Rodriguez, and Zatz 2006; Maher and Hudson 2007: Seffrin et al. 2009). Victimization at the hands of these people may increase females' subsequent maladaptive behaviors, such as drug use or other forms of criminal behavior.

Further, although children are often cited as positive influences and sources of motivation among women to change their criminal behavior (Wright et al. 2013), pregnancy and childcare responsibilities may also affect women's criminal trajectories more so than men's. More female offenders than male offenders are the primary caregivers for dependent children, both before they are entwined in the criminal justice system as well as when they are released (Mumola 2000; Glaze and Maruschak 2008). While many women may temporarily or altogether discontinue criminal behavior for the sake of their children (Wright et al. 2013), many also report that their caregiving responsibilities may actually lead to crime (Gilfus 1992) or are intricately linked to their criminal behavior in some way (Brown 2006). For instance, in an effort to provide financially for their families, females may engage in theft or fraud. Once incarcerated, mothers in prison are less likely to have their children reside with the other parent while they serve their time than are fathers (37 percent versus 88 percent, respectively), and proportionately more children of incarcerated mothers than fathers reside in foster care, which can create additional stress and anxiety for mothers (Glaze and Maruschak 2008). The gender-responsive factors discussed here are considered to embody the ways in which males and females differ, and it is not surprising that these factors are also thought to influence the ways in which women respond to criminal justice sanctioning.

III. Females' Adjustment to the Prison Environment

A. Prison Misconduct

Inmate maladjustment refers to the inability of inmates to adapt to or cope with the prison experience and includes indicators such as rule infractions, mental health problems, and disruptive behavior (Toch, Adams, and Grant 1989; Adams 1992; Kruttschnitt and Gartner 2005). Inmate characteristics such as the gender-responsive characteristics described previously can contribute to how well women adjust to prison. Prior victimization, mental health problems, substance use problems, and the co-occurrence of these factors increase women's rates of rule violations. For instance, Salisbury, Van Voorhis, and Spiropoulos (2009) found that adult victimization and childhood abuse were related to the number of serious misconducts women incurred while incarcerated, while Wright et al. (2007) noted that childhood abuse (but not adulthood abuse), depression/anxiety, and psychosis were predictive of women's misconducts in prison during the first 12 months of incarceration. Additionally, Van Voorhis and colleagues (2010) reported that childhood abuse was related to various measures of institutional misconducts among women in three separate state prisons. Results by Steiner and Wooldredge (2009) indicate that women with histories of physical or sexual abuse *and* those with prior mental health troubles (e.g., they had stayed overnight in a mental health program prior to their incarceration) were more likely to engage in violent assaults and nonviolent rule-breaking while in prison than women without histories of either problem. These researchers also found that women who were prescribed medication for mental illness while incarcerated were at increased risk for prison misconduct.

Mental illness as a risk factor for prison misconduct is further exacerbated when a substance use disorder is co-occurring (Houser, Belenko, and Brennan 2012; Houser and Welsh 2014). Additionally, female inmates with mental health problems may be more likely to engage in misconduct than their male counterparts (McCorkle 1995). Adams (1986) argued that institutional misconduct by mentally ill inmates often reflects symptoms of their psychiatric condition (e.g., self-injurious behavior, refusing to follow instructions, refusing to come out of their cell, lack of personal hygiene, destroying prison property, etc.). Indeed, James and Glaze (2006) found that inmates with mental health problems were more likely to have been charged with a rule violation than other inmates (58 percent versus 43 percent), and inmates with co-occurring disorders have also been shown to exhibit more self-harm and suicidal behavior, more frequent hospitalizations, and more difficulty with social functioning (Hills 2004; Peters et al. 2008). Houser and colleagues (2012) also found that women with co-occurring drug dependence and mental health disorders were more likely than those with no disorders to engage in both minor and serious rule violations: Women with co-occurring disorders were approximately 3.2 times more likely than those with no disorder to incur a serious misconduct, with 1.8 times the odds for minor misconduct, while women with mental illness were 2.7 times more likely to incur a serious misconduct and 1.5 times more likely to incur a minor infraction compared to women with no disorder. Furthermore, women with histories of sexual or other forms of physical victimization were approximately 1.4 times more likely to engage in serious misconduct while incarcerated (Houser, Belenko, and Brennan 2012). These patterns largely held when using a different sample of female offenders (Houser and Welsh 2014).

Although relationships have been less often examined for their impact on prison misconduct among women, there is some evidence that women who were engaged in criminal and unsupportive romantic relationships prior to incarceration are more likely to incur serious misconduct violations within one year of imprisonment than women who were not involved in such relationships (Wright et al. 2007; Van Voorhis et al. 2010). The knowledge in this area is complicated in that many studies examining the impact of prior abuse histories (especially when experienced as an adult) on prison adjustment may actually reflect the impact of poor relationship quality (i.e., abusive relationships) on prison misbehavior, even if the latter is not included in statistical models.

The impact of women's relationships with their children on prison misbehavior is also complicated. Both men and women report that separation from children while in custody is one of the most painful aspects of incarceration (Magaletta and Herbst 2001; Arditti and Few 2008; Loper et al. 2009). However, the separation experience may impact females more so because they are typically the primary caregivers of their children immediately before incarceration, yet they are less likely than men to receive visits from family members while incarcerated (Bloom 1995). This situation likely exists because there are fewer prisons for women than for men, and, as such, facilities for women are often located in more rural or inaccessible areas miles away from the cities where most resided prior to incarceration. The impact of this sort of stress can be multifaceted. Some studies have reported that having children reduces prison misconduct, such as assaults, among women (e.g., Steiner and Wooldredge 2009), while others (e.g., Houck and Loper 2002; Wright et al. 2007; Loper et al. 2009) find positive relationships for serious misconduct, and still others (e.g., Gover, Perez, and Jennings 2008; Van Voorhis et al. 2010) find no relationship with violent or nonviolent misconduct. In a series of studies on female offenders and their gender-responsive risk and need factors, Wright and colleagues (2007) reported that parental stress was associated with more misconducts among female prisoners six months after intake but was not significant by 12 months. Additional research by this group suggests that stresses associated with being a parent (e.g., providing financially for dependent children) become significant risk factors for recidivism as well as for technical violations among female offenders in community settings, either when they are on probation or once they are released back into the community on parole (e.g., Salisbury, Van Voorhis, and Spiropoulos 2009; Van Voorhis et al. 2010).

B. Self-Harm and Suicidal Behavior

Women in prison have higher rates of self-reported suicide attempts than women in the general population (Fazel and Danesh 2002). While men in the general population are more likely to commit suicide than women, female inmates are just as likely to commit suicide as male inmates (Fazel et al. 2011). Most of the research on self-injury and suicide attempts among female inmates has focused on background risk factors, such as substance abuse, physical or sexual abuse, family disruptions, and personality disorders (Kruttschnitt and Gartner 2003; Borrill et al. 2005; Thomas et al. 2006). It is possible that disproportionately high rates of trauma and victimization may contribute to the greater prevalence of suicidal behavior among women in prison (Harlow 1999; Messina and Grella 2006; Swogger et al. 2011). Some scholars have suggested that suicidal behaviors are primarily due to the psychological distress caused by abuse—for instance, that depression, anxiety, or posttraumatic stress disorder, among other negative emotions, might be the "link" between victimization and suicidal and self-harming behaviors (e.g., Dye and Aday 2013). Gunter et al. (2012) reported that exposure to trauma predicted elevated suicide risk, lifetime psychosis, antisocial personality disorders, adult attention deficit hyperactivity, and anxiety and mood disorders among both male and female inmates. Though these researchers did not assess whether problems such as anxiety, psychosis, or mood disorders mediated the relationship between trauma and suicide risk, the way in which a woman copes with trauma may in fact influence her risk of suicidal thoughts and behaviors in the future. Dye and Aday (2013) suggest that depression in particular is potentially more important to women's current thoughts about suicide and self-harm than past histories of abuse and trauma.

However, others have argued that abuse maintains a significant and direct effect on suicidal behaviors among female prisoners that is not fully mediated by psychological adjustment (e.g., Ullman 2004; Verona, Hicks, and Patrick 2005; Clements-Nolle, Wolden, and Bargmann-Losche 2009). Indeed, abuse appears to be a strong predictor of suicidal behavior and ideation among females in both general population and prison samples (Dube et al. 2001; Ullman 2004; Joiner et al. 2007; Afifi et al. 2008). A study of female prisoners who had attempted suicide in the past and prisoners who reported they may commit suicide in the future found that childhood trauma (physical and/or sexual abuse and physical and/or emotional neglect in childhood) was an independent risk factor for suicide attempts among women in prison that could not be fully explained by psychological distress, illicit drug use, or incarceration duration (Clements-Nolle, Wolden, and Bargmann-Losche 2009). Furthermore, women in prison who experienced childhood victimization, neglect, and lack of support from others were significantly more likely to have attempted suicide at least once in their lives; those who experienced higher frequencies of both childhood physical victimization and childhood sexual victimization had a higher likelihood of suicidal behavior (Tripodi, Onifade, and Pettus-Davis 2014).

Because female offenders have often been victimized numerous times or by several forms of violence, and because their victimization often co-occurs with other problems (e.g., substance use and mental health ailments), it is not surprising that women with these histories have more adjustment problems in prison. Although elements of the prison environment such as deprivation and crowding can increase adjustment problems (including suicidal behavior; see Sharkey 2010), it is perhaps more likely that women's past—and current—experiences with victimization, abuse, substance use, mental health problems, and other difficulties lead to their elevated risk of misconduct and/or self-harming behaviors because they tend to bring these gender-responsive risk factors into prisons with them. To demonstrate, Tripodi and Pettus-Davis (2013) reported that women who had experienced multiple types of childhood victimization were not only more likely to be hospitalized for psychological or emotional problems as adults, but they were also more likely to attempt suicide *prior* to their incarceration. These women could also be at increased risk of suicidal behavior while they are incarcerated. For example, Friestad and colleagues (2014) found that childhood emotional, physical, and sexual abuse and neglect significantly increased the risk of suicide attempts and drug abuse among female prisoners in Norway, and Tripodi and colleagues (2014) reported that childhood physical and sexual abuse as well as substance abuse disorders independently predicted suicide attempts among female prisoners in North Carolina, even after controlling for race and age.

In sum, studies regarding gender-responsive characteristics among women and their maladjustment to prison suggest four conclusions: First, the co-occurrence of victimization, substance use, and mental health problems among female offenders is so severe that it becomes very difficult to separate their unique effects on prison maladjustment, and some scholars (Covington 2000) suggest that all three problems should be simultaneously addressed with treatment and appropriate supervision strategies. At the very least, the unique impacts of victimization, substance use, and mental health are often difficult to tease out, and continued research in this area is gravely needed. Second, some gender-responsive factors do impact women's behavior while they are under the supervision of the criminal justice system, as they are indeed risk factors for prison maladjustment indicators (misconduct and suicidal thoughts and behaviors) among females. These findings potentially hold policy implications for prison management styles, supervision strategies, and programming needs. Third, the type and timing of gender-responsive factors is very important to consider as their effects may differ across various measurements. For instance, it may be relevant to demarcate between past histories of mental health problems versus current mental health problems, as they may impact women's behaviors differently (Steiner and Wooldredge 2009); likewise, childhood versus adulthood victimization may elicit unique effects among women and should be distinguished when possible. Last, the impact of gender-responsive factors on females' behaviors in the criminal justice system appears to be dynamic and might depend somewhat on the setting in which females are situated; that is, some gender-responsive factors may be problematic in certain environments (e.g., prisons) versus others (e.g., community settings; see Van Voorhis et al. 2010). Not surprisingly, these findings may also significantly affect the supervision and management styles needed to most effectively address the needs of female, as opposed to male, offenders. We turn next to describing the management and programming responses in prisons that arise because of women's gender-responsive characteristics and their impact on female offenders' institutional adjustment.

IV. Prison Management and Policies in Women's Prisons

Given that female offenders bring gender-responsive characteristics into prison, which can impact their behavior while under supervision, prison management styles and programming services need to be altered in order to better accommodate female offenders and address their unique characteristics. While some prison systems across the United States are making strides in providing more gender-responsive environments, many are not; this is likely due to several factors (e.g., low proportions of female prisoners, cost for services, philosophical barriers prioritizing punishment over treatment, department of corrections' and/

or administrators' unwillingness to change, etc.). Certainly, becoming a gender-responsive prison takes "buy in" from several key stakeholders including state legislators, department of corrections administrators, prison wardens, and staff. Although it may be easier to simply apply men's policies and management strategies to prisons for women, it makes little sense to do so given what we know regarding differences between male and female offenders' violence levels and needs. Overall, prisons that strive to be gender-responsive will likely promote safer and more humane adjustment among female prisoners, staff may feel more safe and satisfied, and fewer women may recycle back into the prison system.

At the facility level, administrators can move their prisons toward gender-responsiveness in a variety of ways, though all are likely interrelated (see also Wright et al. [2012] for an in-depth discussion of these recommendations). To be more gender-responsive, first, the missions of women's prisons should more closely align with a rehabilitative, rather than punitive, orientation. Many of the factors that increase women's risk of criminal behavior—both within and outside of prisons—are, in fact, changeable through treatment (e.g., substance use, mental health problems). Thus rehabilitative services should be prioritized. While accountability for women's crimes is also an important goal for women's institutions, many scholars have argued that "fair" punishment does not necessarily mean "equal" punishment between males and females (Bloom, Owen, and Covington 2004; Chesney-Lind 2006); indeed, given the many differences between male and female offenders, it makes little sense to expect that the same punishment and confinement conditions would influence both equally. We suggest that prison conditions should reflect the populations they house—in this case, female offenders who are less violent than men, are more drug dependent, suffer from unique mental and physical health needs, have been victimized by others, and have primary care-giving responsibilities to dependent children. Prisons should therefore focus on treatment and services that address these issues. As Wright and colleagues (2012) discuss, prison environments that are conducive to treatment and rehabilitation provide feelings of safety, security, and nonconfrontation so that women can focus on positive change (Covington and Bloom 2006). Prisons that reduce their emphasis on punishment and enhance their service environments in these ways will likely see benefits in terms of less institutional misconduct, healthier incarcerated women, and safer staff. Furthermore, if prisons use effective treatments, there may be fewer women returning back to these facilities.

Second, yet related, prisons would be more gender-responsive if they provided the appropriate programming and services needed to address the factors associated with women's institutional maladjustment. Substance abuse problems, victimization, mental health (especially depression and co-occurring disorders), unhealthy relationships, and family unification difficulties appear to be particularly salient for women in prison. Prisons would be more gender-responsive and possibly provide safer and more humane environments if they targeted these issues in treatment. Some of these problems (e.g., substance abuse, mental health problems, trauma, unhealthy relationships, parental stress, employment, safe housing, child care, financial assistance, and education) have also been demonstrated as risk factors to recidivism (Salisbury, Van Voorhis, and Spiropoulos 2009; Van Voorhis et al. 2010), and reducing these problems in prison may translate into higher success rates once women return to the community. We discuss specific programming needs in the next section.

Third, prison operations, including the overall environment, management practices, policies, and staff procedures, would be more gender-responsive if they were trauma-informed.

That is, policies and procedures should be implemented in ways that do not "re-victimize" women (Wright et al. 2012). Recall that the majority of women in prison have been abused or victimized at some point in their lives (McDaniels-Wilson and Belknap 2008). Staff can be trained to understand the impact of victimization on women's lives within and outside of prison, as well as on their interactions with others (including correctional officers). Additionally, appropriate rules and regulations could be created to ensure that procedures do not risk revictimizing these women (e.g., strip searches by male correctional officers, forced treatment or sharing of trauma stories; see Wright et al. [2012] for a more detailed discussion).

Trauma-informed services are being identified as some of the "best practices" to use in corrections. Other elements of evidence-based practices, such as the use of valid—and for women, gender-responsive—risk assessment tools, should also be utilized in prisons. For instance, risk factors, such as criminal history, which increase women's institutional (and community) misbehavior, should not only be assessed but so should women's criminogenic *needs*—those factors in women's lives that can be changed through treatment and thus lower the odds of criminal behavior. These should be assessed at intake (and again after an adjustment period, see Wright et al. 2012) using a valid assessment tool. Further, the information derived from these assessments should be used to make correctional decisions regarding level of supervision, programming, and case-management decisions. Although some gender-neutral risk and need assessment tools (e.g., the Level of Service Inventory) have been shown to be valid predictors of women's institutional and community criminal conduct (Smith, Cullen, and Latessa 2009), these tools were created for men and applied to women; we suggest that gender-responsive tools may be more accurate because they have been tailored to assess the aforementioned ways in which female offenders differ from male offenders (Van Voorhis et al. 2010). Few gender-responsive assessments are available, but the Women's Risk Needs Assessment (Van Voorhis et al. 2008, 2010) has demonstrated strong support for use among women in prison, probation, and prerelease settings, and it not only identifies risk levels but also assesses needs (e.g., drug use, mental health services) and suggests case management/planning decisions. Importantly, this tool does not recommend increased custody scores based on problems such as histories of abuse but instead identifies treatment targets and suggestions for treatment plans so that treatment can be best utilized to reduce women's risk and need levels (Van Voorhis et al. 2008).

A focus on treatment instead of punishment requires that prison administrators also hire and train staff members who are qualified for and amenable to case planning for female prisoners (Wright et al. 2012). Positive staff characteristics include listening and communication skills, being patient, and having a desire to work with female offenders. Further, staff can be trained to better appreciate the differences between male and female inmates and to understand how these differences translate into sex-specific behaviors within and outside of prisons. Staff members who possess this knowledge may be better able to negotiate their roles and relationships with the inmates (e.g., overlooking minor violations, doing favors, using exchange as a strategy to gain inmate compliance; see Farkas 2000) and be more prepared for the challenges of working with highly traumatized and potentially co-disordered women. For instance, a better understanding of how victimization affects women's lives may make staff more receptive to using trauma-informed policies within the prison. Additionally, staff can be trained on the need for and use of gender-responsive assessments, particularly regarding how (and why) they should talk to women about victimization, personal relationships, and mental health programs in a sensitive manner. They can also be trained regarding how to most effectively use motivational interviewing techniques—interview strategies that motivate offenders to change by helping prisoners uncover and explore their own ambivalence to change (as opposed to using alternative techniques of arguing, threatening, or coercion to motivate change; Miller and Rollnick 2002)—with female prisoners, as well as the need for gender-specific case management and planning.

Last, prison management and staff members striving to be gender-responsive would be wise to plan for the issues that women will have to negotiate upon reentering the community, such as parenting and mental health problems, and they should work with community agencies to provide wraparound services outside of the prison (Covington and Bloom 2006; Wright et al. 2012). Prison administrators who work collaboratively with community agencies to ensure that released prisoners have access to services once they are in the community are vital advocates for female offenders. Many women lack proper mental health care, medical services, safe housing, and so forth prior to incarceration; while some may receive these services while they are in prison, most return to the same communities and situations they lived in prior to their sentence (Dodge and Pogrebin 2001; Richie 2001). Thus many women are faced with a new set of challenges upon reentry: finding and keeping jobs, providing for themselves and their children, learning to cope with rejection from employers, and satisfying the conditions of their supervision (Wright et al. 2012). Many women may be unprepared to meet these challenges, and the treatment and programming they received while incarcerated may not translate to community settings where they have no ties to local agencies (e.g., mental health services, drug programs, shelters). Prison administrators who address these needs within their own institutions while also linking women to the programs they will need upon reentry would be addressing gender-responsive factors in a holistic way.

V. Programming Needs and Services in Women's Prisons

Our second point recommended that gender-responsive prisons provide the appropriate programming and services needed to address the gendered factors associated with women's misbehavior, whether in the institution or in community settings (wardens also need to determine which outcomes to focus on that best serve their institution). Wright and colleagues (2012) provide guidance regarding specific programming needs for women in prisons, and we only summarize their main points regarding substance abuse problems, victimization, mental health (especially co-occurring disorders), unhealthy relationships, and family unification difficulties here. First, in general, programs should be cognitive-behavioral in nature, utilize a relational component, and incorporate women's strengths, such as women's relationships with positive others and children (see Matthews and Hubbard 2008). Cognitive behavioral therapies restructure offender's thoughts, values, beliefs, skills, and behavior to evoke more prosocial thoughts, attitudes, and behaviors (see Van Voorhis, Braswell, and Lester 2009); incorporating a relational component into such therapies would involve utilizing women's relationships with others (e.g., counselors, children) to evoke such change (Matthews and Hubbard 2008).

Second, drug and alcohol programming should be provided in prison and should focus not only on drug-free behavior within the prison but also on teaching coping and avoidance skills for when the women return to the community. These programs should also recognize and potentially accommodate the comorbidity between substance abuse, victimization, and mental health problems (Covington 2008). Third, victimization programs that treat women in the aftermath of abuse or trauma are also needed in prison settings. These programs should not only teach women how to recognize abusive relationships and trauma (e.g., what is or is not normative and healthy behavior), but they should also strive to treat the many outcomes of victimization, such as mental health problems and substance use, and to prevent future revictimization. Fourth, prisons need to offer mental health services for women. General mental health services are helpful, but we suggest that specific treatments target the disorders seen most often among female offenders: depression, anxiety, co-occurring drug abuse and mental health problems, psychosis, posttraumatic stress disorder, anger, mood disorders, and even suicidal thoughts and behaviors. While these appear to be either the most prevalent or most detrimental mental illnesses among female inmates, additional research is needed to identify other specific areas of need. Bloom and Covington (2009) suggest such programs focus on helping women recognize symptoms (e.g., "What does posttraumatic stress disorder look like?") and understand how it might affect their lives; further, positive coping skills should be taught and reinforced so that women have these in their "tool kit" upon reentry.

Because relationships are central elements of women's lives, prison administrators should consider providing services that facilitate and enhance women's healthy relationships with others, such as their children, family, and other positive influences. Programs that teach women how to build and maintain healthy relationships that are supportive, loving, nonabusive, and free from criminal activity, inside and outside of prison, may help women deal with stress in a more positive way (e.g., through social support networks versus substance use; Wright et al. 2012). Domestic and family violence (including child physical and sexual abuse, maltreatment, and neglect) loom large in female offenders' lives—not only have many female offenders experienced these abuses prior to incarceration, but they also run the risk of recycling the violence in their own homes after incarceration (e.g., extreme poverty may contribute to child neglect). Programs are needed to help women identify and utilize healthy relationships with others, as well as to maintain these relationships using positive interaction techniques rather than resorting to anger and hostile/coercive behaviors.

Other programs devoted to pregnancy, parenting, and family reunification are also needed in women's prisons. Indeed, many facilities already provide these accommodations. Yet, because of the numbers of women giving birth while incarcerated each year and because most women are eventually released back into the community, a discussion of continued services for these needs is warranted. It is estimated that approximately 9 percent of incarcerated women give birth while in prison (Knight and Plugge 2005; Nelson 2006). These pregnancies are considered high risk because several factors can negatively impact pregnancy and birth outcomes for women in prison (e.g., homelessness prior to incarceration, inadequate health services or prenatal care prior to incarceration, histories of poor nutrition, poverty, smoking, drug and alcohol abuse, physical and sexual abuse, mental illness, HIV and sexually transmitted infections) (Sable et al. 1999; Fogel and Belyae 2001;

Knight and Plugge 2005; Hotelling 2008). Consequently, pregnant inmates often have an increased need for prenatal care, education, counseling, and substance abuse treatment programs (Knight and Plugge 2005).

Some studies have shown that babies can actually benefit from their mothers being incarcerated because it ensures they will receive food, shelter, protection from abusive partners, access to prenatal care, and more limited access to drugs and alcohol (Knight and Plugge 2005; Tanner 2010). On the other hand, the prison environment can impose additional stress and anxiety on pregnant prisoners, and some facilities may not be able to provide adequate prenatal care, exercise, education regarding childbirth and parenting, or preparation for the mother's separation from the baby after delivery (Beck 2001; Kurshan 2006; Chambers 2009). The National Commission on Correctional Health Care (2008) and the American Public Health Association (2003) created standards for pregnancy-related health care in prisons, but there is no mandatory accreditation process that facilities must go through to ensure they adhere to these standards. Additionally, many prisons do not have any written policies regarding the management of pregnant inmates (Bloom, Owen, and Covington 2003).

The issue of shackling pregnant women—placing restraints or chains around their ankles, waist, and hands—while they are transported to hospitals for prenatal care and during delivery has also been a controversial subject that warrants discussion because it pertains to the gender-responsive characteristic of childbirth. Many advocacy groups view shackling pregnant women as dangerous, inhumane, and degrading (International Human Rights Clinic, Chicago Legal Advocacy for Incarcerated Mothers and American Civil Liberties Union 2013). The Eighth Circuit Court of Appeals ruled that shackling women in late-stage labor, in the absence of a security need, constitutes cruel and unusual punishment and is in violation of the Eight Amendment of the US Constitution (*Nelson v. Correctional Medical Services*, 583 F.3d 522, 526 [2009]). Several well-known national organizations have become involved in advocating for the abolition of shackling pregnant women, arguing that physical restraints can interfere with the ability of medical personnel to practice medicine safely during childbirth, which can put women and the unborn child at risk (American Civil Liberties Union 2009; American Medical Association 2010; Williams 2011). The Bureau of Prisons (2008) banned the use of restraints for pregnant women in Federal prisons during transport, labor, delivery, and postdelivery recuperation, except in extreme circumstances where it is deemed necessary, such as when the woman presents a serious flight risk or presents a threat to herself and/or others that cannot be prevented by other means. At the end of 2013, 18 states had passed legislation prohibiting or restricting the use of shackles for pregnant prisoners, to varying degrees (International Human Rights Clinic et al. 2013).

Not surprisingly, many female inmates report feeling a profound sense of loss, pain, grief, and anxiety after being separated from their baby after birth (Wismont 2000; Schroeder and Bell 2005; Chambers 2009). Current prison policies allow little time for mothers to bond with newborns, and the majority of mothers are separated from their newborns immediately after giving birth (Schroeder and Bell 2005). Nine states have prison nursery programs in place—California, Illinois, Indiana, Ohio, Nebraska, New York, South Dakota, Washington, and West Virginia—which allow mothers who meet certain criteria (i.e., no prior convictions of serious child abuse and proximal release dates) to keep their baby with them in prison for 12 to 24 months, depending on the state (Women's Prison Association 2009). So far, these programs have demonstrated positive outcomes for participating mothers and babies, such as secure attachment, increased childcare knowledge, and decreased recidivism rates (Byrne, Goshin, and Blanchard-Lewis 2012). We commend such efforts and suggest continued progress in this area.

While prisons have begun to accommodate additional and expanded childcare and/or visitation programs, more could still be done. It is important to attempt to foster healthy bonds between the mother and her children, as many women report that separation leads to negative feelings such as depression, anxiety, and stress (Arditti and Few 2008; Loper et al. 2009); alternatively, women report increased motivation to change "for" their children. Thus we suggest that reinforcing these potentially crime-inhibiting relationships will benefit many female inmates, as well as the prison environment. Other types of programs, such as family reunification and parenting skills classes, continue to be necessary in women's prisons because of the high likelihood that women will regain childcare responsibilities upon release (Snyder 2009; Wright et al. 2012). These programs should address issues that tend to create stress and conflict in a woman's life, such as renegotiating her role within the family upon release (Brown and Bloom 2009), dealing with the guilt and shame of having left her children, and knowing how to manage potential conflicts that arise between family members (e.g., abuse, drug use). Additionally, women will need to be prepared to meet the conditions of their release while also fulfilling familial roles and responsibilities—women who are prepared for how to cope with and manage these issues may be more successful upon release and may also respond better to the prison environment.

VI. Conclusion

Academics and practitioners alike agree that female offenders are unique from male offenders in many ways. Although practice has generally lagged behind research endeavors, it is beginning to catch up: Many correctional entities across the United States now recognize the need for gender-responsive practices, such as gender-specific caseloads, trauma-informed services, and enhanced treatment and programming services. The next steps to be taken in embracing gender-responsiveness throughout corrections will likely involve an expanded recognition of these needs and, eventually, the implementation of a wide range of services across all correctional systems (e.g., pretrial, probation, prison, parole). However, research in this area is far from finished. More research is needed to determine whether some aspects of the gender-specific pathways described here apply to male offenders as well or whether these pathways are only relevant for females. Male offenders also have a high prevalence of substance abuse and mental health issues, although at lower rates than female offenders (Mumola and Karberg 2006), and it is important to understand how the associations between drug use, mental health, victimization, relationships, and so forth impact male offenders' criminal pathways and their adjustment to prison compared to females. Most might argue this has already been done since researchers and practitioners alike have traditionally focused primarily on male offending and not female offending; however, we should not disregard males' pathways to incarceration in the same way we disregarded females' for so long. Most scholars would agree there is still much we need to understand about how specific types of victimization (e.g., childhood versus adulthood, physical versus sexual, stranger versus nonstranger), mental health issues, and substance abuse affect males' and females' pathways to criminal activity and their adjustment to incarceration.

We are encouraged that there are some gender-responsive programs being used in prisons today that focus on coping with trauma, healthy relationships, self-efficacy, self-defeating thoughts, antisocial attitudes, stress management, and building social support (e.g., Moving On, Helping Women Recover, and Beyond Trauma; see Van Dieten 1998; Messina et al. 2010) and that gender-responsive risk/needs assessment tools are also available (Van Voorhis et al. 2008, 2010). Furthermore, the National Institute of Corrections continues to provide training to prison administrators regarding the need for and application of gender-responsive strategies in prisons—all of these advancements bring research into practice across the United States. However, researchers must continue to evaluate these programs, assessment tools, and policy initiatives in order to determine how much they "work," how they work, and how they can be made more effective. To do this is to truly adhere to a "best practices" philosophy.

Finally, both scholars and practitioners should continue to advance gender-responsive strategies by working collaboratively to recognize inherent differences between male and female offenders, why they end up in prison, how they behave while incarcerated, and what they do once released back into the community. They should not focus solely on the risk factors that facilitate criminal behavior but should also strive to understand the crime-reducing impacts of offenders' "strengths," or the positive aspects of their lives. A greater understanding of how to promote offenders' strengths and capitalize on their crime-inhibiting capabilities is likely a next step in curbing women's criminal behavior and helping them reintegrate back into the community. Although we believe that much has been done to improve our understanding of and effective responses to female criminality, there is more to do. In sum, the correctional system must utilize a gender-specific model that focuses on an understanding of women's involvement in criminal activities, the influence of gender-responsive characteristics on offenders, and how incarceration is experienced differently by women and men in order to most appropriately respond to female offenders in correctional systems.

REFERENCES

Adams, Kenneth. 1986. "The Disciplinary Experiences of Mentally Disordered Inmates." *Criminal Justice and Behavior* 13:297–316.

Adams, Kenneth. 1992. "Adjusting to Prison Life." In *Prisons*, edited by Michael Tonry. Vol. 16 of *Crime and Justice: A Review of Research*, edited by Michael Tonry. Chicago: University of Chicago Press.

Afifi, Tracie O., Murray W. Enns, Brian J. Cox, Gordon J. Asmundson, Murray B. Stein, and Jitender Sareen. 2008. "Population Attributable Fractions of Psychiatric Disorders and Suicide Ideation and Attempts Associated with Adverse Childhood Experiences." *American Journal of Public Health* 98:946–952.

American Civil Liberties Union. 2009. State Standards for Pregnancy-Related Health Care and Abortion for Women in Prison. https://www.aclu.org/state-standards-pregnancy-related-health-care-and-abortion-women-prison-map

American Medical Association. 2010. "Shackling of Pregnant Women During Labor." Resolution 203. In *Proceedings of the 2010 Annual House of Delegates*. Chicago: Author. www.ama-assn.org/resources/doc/hod/a10-resolutions.pdf

American Psychiatric Association. 2000. *Diagnostic and Statistical Manual of Mental Disorders*, 4th ed. Washington, DC: Author.

American Public Health Association. 2003. "Health Services for Women." In *Standards for Health Services in Correctional Institutions*, edited by American Public Health Association: Washington, DC: Author.

Anderson, Tammy L., Andre B. Rosay, and Christine Saum. (2002). "The Impact of Drug Use and Crime Involvement on Health Problems among Female Drug Offenders." *The Prison Journal* 82:50–68.

Arditti, Joyce, and April Few. 2008. "Maternal Distress and Women's Re-Entry into Family and Community Life." *Family Process* 47:303–321.

Asberg, Kia, and Kimberly Renk. 2013. "Comparing Incarcerated and College Student Women with Histories of Childhood Sexual Abuse: The Roles of Abuse Severity, Support and Substance Use." *Psychological Trauma: Theory, Research, Practice, and Policy* 5:167–175.

Beck, A. J. 2001. *Prisoners in 1999*. Bureau of Justice Statistics Special Report NCJ-183476. Washington, DC: US Department of Justice.

Belknap, Joan. 2007. *The Invisible Woman: Gender, Crime, and Justice*, 3rd ed. Belmont, CA: Thompson Wadsworth.

Belknap, Joan, and Kristi Holsinger. 2006. "The Gendered Nature of Risk Factors for Delinquency." *Feminist Criminology* 1:48–71.

Bloom, Barbara. 1995. "Imprisoned Mothers." In *Children of Incarcerated Parents*, edited by Katherine Gabel and Denise Johnston. New York: Lexington Books.

Bloom, Barbara, and Stephanie Covington. 2009. "Addressing the Mental Health Needs of Women Offenders." In *Women's Mental Health Issues across the Criminal Justice System*, edited by Rosemary L. Gido and Lanette Dalley. Upper Saddle River, NJ: Pearson Prentice Hall.

Bloom, Barbara, Barbara Owen, and Stephanie Covington. 2003. *Gender-Responsive Strategies: Research Practice and Guiding Principles for Women Offenders*. Washington, DC: US Department of Justice, National Institute of Corrections.

Bloom, Barbara, Barbara Owen, and Stephanie Covington. 2004. "Women Offenders and the Gendered Effects of Public Policy." *Review of Policy Research* 21:31–48.

Bloom, Barbara, Barbara Owen, and Stephanie Covington. 2005. *Gender-Responsive Strategies for Women Offenders: A Summary of Research, Practice, and Guiding Principles for Women Offenders*. Washington, DC: US Department of Justice, National Institute of Corrections.

Brennan, Tim, Markus Breitenbach, William Dieterich, Emily J. Salisbury, and Patricia Van Voorhis. 2012. "Women's Pathways to Serious and Habitual Crime: A Person-Centered Analysis Incorporating Gender-Responsive Factors." *Criminal Justice and Behavior* 39:1481–1508.

Brown, Marilyn. 2006. "Gender, Ethnicity, and Offending Over the Life-Course: Women's Pathways to Prison in the Aloha State." *Critical Criminology: An International Journal* 14:137–158.

Brown, Marilyn, and Barbara Bloom. 2009. "Reentry and Renegotiating Motherhood: Maternal Identity and Success on Parole." *Crime & Delinquency* 55:313–336.

Browne, Angela, B. Miller, and E. Maguin. 1999. "Prevalence and Severity of Lifetime Physical and Sexual Victimization among Incarcerated Women." *International Journal of Law and Psychiatry* 22:301–322.

Borrill, Jo, Louisa Snow, Diana Medlicott, Rebecca Teers, and Jo Paton. 2005. "Learning from 'Near Misses': Interviews with Women Who Survived an Incident of Severe Self-Harm in Prison." *The Howard Journal* 44:57–69.

Bureau of Justice Statistics. 2000a. *Correctional Populations in the U.S., 1997.* Bureau of Justice Statistics Special Report NCJ-177613. Washington, DC: US Department of Justice, Bureau of Justice Statistics.

Bureau of Justice Statistics. 2000b. *Incarcerated Parents and Their Children.* Bureau of Justice Statistics Special Report NCJ-182335. Washington, DC: US Department of Justice, Bureau of Justice Statistics.

Bureau of Prisons. 2008. Barring the Shackling of Pregnant Women Inmates in Federal Prisons in All But the Most Extreme Circumstances. www.aclu.org/files/pdfs/prison/bop_policy_escorted_trips_p5538_05.pdf

Bush-Baskette, Stephanie R. 1998. "War on Drugs as a War against Black Women." In *Crime Control and Women: Feminist Implications of Criminal Justice Policy*, edited by Susan Miller. Thousand Oaks, CA: Sage.

Byrne, Mary W., Lorie Goshin, and Barbara Blanchard-Lewis. 2012. "Maternal Separations during the Reentry Years for 100 Infants Raised in a Prison Nursery." *Family Court Review: A Interdisciplinary Journal* 50:77–90.

Caplow, Theodore, and Jonathan Simon 1999. "Understanding Prison Policy and Population Trends." In *Prisons*, edited by Michael Tonry and Joan Petersilia. Vol. 26 *of Crime and Justice: A Review of Research*, edited by Michael Tonry. Chicago: University of Chicago Press.

Carbone-Lopez, Kristen, and Candice Kruttschnitt. 2010. "Risky Relationships? Assortive Mating and Women's Experiences of Intimate Partner Violence." *Crime & Delinquency* 56:358–384.

Carlen, Pat, and Jacqueline Tombs. 2006. "Reconfigurations of Penality: The Ongoing Case of the Women's Imprisonment and Reintegration Industries." *Theoretical Criminology* 10:337–360.

Carson, E. Ann, and Daniela Golinelli. 2013. *Prisoners in 2012—Advance Counts.* Washington, DC: Bureau of Justice Statistics.

Center for Substance Abuse Treatment. 2005. Substance Abuse Treatment for Persons with Co-Occurring Disorders. Report to Treatment Improvement Protocol (TIP) Series, No. 42. Rockville, MD: Substance Abuse and Mental Health Services Administration.

Chambers, Angelina N. 2009. "Impact of Forced Separation Policy on Incarcerated Postpartum Mothers." *Policy, Politics and Nursing Practice* 10:204–211.

Chesney-Lind, Meda. 2002. "Criminalizing Victimization: The Unintended Consequences of Pro-Arrest Policies for Girls and Women." *Criminology & Public Policy* 2:81–91.

Chesney-Lind, Meda. 2006. "Patriarchy, Crime, and Justice: Feminist Criminology in an Era of Backlash." *Feminist Criminology* 1:6–26.

Chesney-Lind, Meda, and Randall G. Shelden. 2004. *Girls, Delinquency, and Juvenile Justice*, 3rd ed. Belmont, CA: Thompson Wadsworth.

Clements-Nolle, Kristen, Matthew Wolden, and Jessey Bargmann-Losche. 2009. "Childhood Trauma and Risk for Past and Future Suicide Attempts Among Women in Prison." *Women's Health Issues* 19:185–192.

Covington, Stephanie. 2000. "Helping Women to Recover: Creating Gender-Specific Treatment for Substance Abusing Women and Girls in Community Corrections." In *Assessment to Assistance: Programs for Women in Community Corrections*, edited by Meave McMahon. Lanham, MD: American Correctional Association.

Covington, Stephanie. 2008. *Helping Women Recover: A Program for Treating Substance Abuse. Special Edition for Use in the Criminal Justice System.* San Francisco: Jossey-Bass.

Covington, Stephanie, and Barbara Bloom. 2006. "Gender Responsive Treatment and Services in Correctional Settings." *Women and Therapy* 29(3–4): 9–33.

Daly, Kathleen. 1992. "Women's Pathways to Felony Court: Feminist Theories of Lawbreaking and Problems of Representation." *Southern California Review of Law and Women's Studies* 2:11–52.

DeHart, Dana D. 2008. "Pathways to Prison: Impact of Victimization in the Lives of Incarcerated Women." *Violence Against Women* 14:1362–1381.

Dennison, Sylvia J. 2005. "Substance Use Disorders in Individuals with Co-Occurring Psychiatric Disorders." In *Substance Abuse: A Comprehensive Textbook*, 4th ed., edited by Joyce H. Lowinson, Pedro Ruiz, Robert B. Millman, and John G. Langrod. Philadelphia, PA: Lippincott Williams and Wilkins.

Dodge, Mary, and Mark R. Pogrebin. 2001. "Collateral Costs of Imprisonment for Women: Complications of Reintegration." *The Prison Journal* 18:42–54.

Dube, Shanta R., Robert F. Anda, Vincent. J. Felitti, Daniel P. Chapman, David F. Williamson, and Wayne H. Giles. 2001. "Childhood Abuse, Household Dysfunction, and the Risk of Attempted Suicide throughout the Lifespan." *Journal of the American Medical Association* 286:3089–3096.

Dye, Merideth H., and Ronald H. Aday. 2013. "'I Just Wanted to Die': Preprison and Current Suicide Ideation among Women Serving Life Sentences." *Criminal Justice and Behavior* 40:832–849.

Farkas, Mary Ann. 2000. "A Typology of Correctional Officers." *International Journal of Offender Therapy and Comparative Criminology* 44:431–449.

Fazel, Seena, and John Danesh. 2002. "Serious Mental Disorder in 23000 Prisoners: A Systematic Review of 62 Surveys." *The Lancet* 359:545–550.

Fazel, Seena, Martin Grann, Boo Kling, and Keith Hawton. 2011. "Prison Suicide in 12 Countries: An Ecological Study of 861 Suicides During 2003–2007." *Social Psychiatry and Psychiatric Epidemiology* 46:191–195.

Feld, Barry C. 2009. "Violent Girls or Relabeled Status Offenders? An Alternative Interpretation of the Data." *Crime & Delinquency* 55:241–265.

Fogel, Catherine I., and Michael Belyae. 2001. "Psychosocial Risk Factors in Pregnant Inmates." *Maternal Child Health* 261:10–15.

Friestad, Christine, Rustad Ase-Bente, and Ellen Kjelsberg 2014. "Adverse Childhood Experiences among Women Prisoners: Relationships to Suicide Attempts and Drug Abuse." *International Journal of Social Psychiatry* 60:40–6.

Garland, David. 2001. *The Culture of Control: Crime and Social Order in Contemporary Society.* Chicago: University of Chicago Press.

Gilfus, Mary E. 1992. "From Victims to Survivors to Offenders: Women's Routes of Entry and Immersion into Street Crime." *Women and Criminal Justice* 4:63–90.

Glaze, Lauren E., and Thomas P. Bonczar 2008. *Probation and Parole in the United States, 2007.* Bureau of Justice Statistics Special Report NCJ-224707. Washington, DC: U.S. Department of Justice, Bureau of Justice Statistics.

Glaze, Lauren E., and Lauren M. Maruschak. 2008. *Parents in Prison and Their Minor Children*. Bureau of Justice Statistics Special Report NCJ-222984. Washington, DC: National Criminal Justice Reference Service.

Gover, Angela R., Deanna M. Perez, and Welsey G. Jennings. 2008. "Gender Differences in Factors Contributing to Institutional Misconduct." *The Prison Journal* 88:378–403.

Greenfeld, Lawrence A., and Tracy L. Snell. 1999. *Women Offenders*. Bureau of Justice Statistics Special Report NCJ-175688. Washington, DC: US Department of Justice.

Grella, Christine E., Judith A. Stein, and Lisa Greenwell. 2005. "Associations among Childhood Trauma, Adolescent Problem Behaviors, and Adverse Adult Outcomes in Substance-Abusing Women Offenders." *Psychology of Addictive Behaviors* 19:43–53.

Gunter, Tracy D., John T. Chibnall, Sandra K. Antoniak, Brett McCormick, and Donald W. Black. 2012. "Relative Contributions of Gender and Traumatic Life Experiences to the Prediction of Mental Disorders in a Sample of Incarcerated Offenders." *Behavioral Science and the Law* 30:615–630.

Harlow, Caroline W. 1999. *Prior Abuse Reported by Inmates and Probationers*. Bureau of Justice Statistics Special Report NCJ-1728797. Washington, DC: US Department of Justice.

Heimer, Karen, Janet L. Lauritsen, and James P. Lynch. 2009. "The National Crime Victimization Survey and the Gender Gap in Offending: Redux." *Criminology* 47:427–438.

Heimer, Karen, Stacy M. Wittrock, and Halime Unal. 2006. "The Crimes of Poverty: Economic Marginalization and the Gender Gap in Crime." In *Gender and Crime: Patterns in Victimization and Offending*, edited by Karen Heimer and Candice Kruttschnitt. New York: New York University Press.

Hills, Holly. 2004. *The Special Needs of Women with Co-Occurring Disorders Diverted from the Criminal Justice System*. Delmar, NY: National GAINS Center for People with Co-Occurring Disorders in Contact with the Justice System.

Hotelling, Barbara. 2008. "Perinatal Needs of Pregnant Incarcerated Women." *Journal of Perinatal Education* 17:37–44.

Houck, Katherine D., and Ann B. Loper. 2002. "The Relationship of Parenting Stress to Adjustment among Mothers in Prison." *American Journal of Orthopsychiatry* 72:548–558.

Houser, Kimberly, Steven Belenko, and Pauline Brennan. 2012. "The Effects of Mental Health and Substance Use Disorders on Institutional Misconduct among Female Inmates." *Justice Quarterly* 29:799–828.

Houser, Kimberly, and Wayne Welsh. 2014. "Examining the Association between Co-occurring Disorders and Seriousness of Misconduct by Female Prison Inmates." 41 no. 5 650-666 *Criminal Justice and Behavior* 41:650–666.

International Human Rights Clinic, Chicago Legal Advocacy for Incarcerated Mothers, and American Civil Liberties Union. 2013. "The Shackling of Incarcerated Pregnant Women: A Human Rights Violation Committed Regularly in the United States." Report to the United Nations Human Rights for the Committee's Fourth Periodic Review of the United States. https://ihrclinic.uchicago.edu/page/shackling-pregnant-prisoners-united-states

James, Doris J., and Lauren E. Glaze. 2006. *Mental Health Problems of Prison and Jail Inmates*. Bureau of Justice Statistics Special Report NCJ-213600. Washington, DC: National Criminal Justice Reference Service.

Javdani, Shabnam, Naomi Sadeh, and Edelyn Verona. 2011. "Gendered Social Forces: A Review of the Impact of Institutionalized Factors on Women and Girls' Criminal Justice Trajectories." *Psychology, Public Policy, and Law* 17:161–211.

Joiner, Thomas, Natalie Sachs-Ericsson, LaRicka Wingate, J. Brown, M. Anestis, and E. Selby. 2007. "Childhood Physical and Sexual Abuse and Lifetime Number of Suicide Attempts: A Persistent and Theoretically Important Relationship." *Behaviour Research and Therapy* 45:539–547.

Jordan, Kathleen, Elizabeth Belle Federman, Barbara J. Burns, William E. Schlenger, John A. Fairbank, and Juesta M. Caddell. 2002. "Lifetime Use of Mental Health and Substance Abuse Treatment Services by Incarcerated Women Felons." *Psychiatric Services* 53:317–325.

Kaufman, Jeanne G., and Cathy S. Widom. 1999. "Childhood Victimization, Running Away, and Delinquency." *Journal of Research in Crime and Delinquency* 36:347–370.

Knight, Marian, and Emma Plugge. 2005. "Risk Factors for Adverse Perinatal Outcomes in Imprisoned Pregnant Women: A Systematic Review." *BMC Public Health* 5:111. http://www.biomedcentral.com/1471-2458/5/111

Kruttschnitt, Candice, and Rosemary Gartner. 2003. "Women's Imprisonment." In *Crime and Justice: A Review of Research*, Vol. 30, edited by Michael Tonry. Chicago: University of Chicago Press.

Kruttschnitt, Candace, and Rosemary Gartner. 2005. *Marking Time in the Golden State: Women's Imprisonment in California.* New York: Cambridge University Press.

Kruttschnitt, Candice, and Rosemary Gartner. 2008. "Female Violent Offenders: Moral Panics or More Serious Offenders?" *Australian & New Zealand Journal of Criminology* 41:9–35.

Kurshan, Nancy. 2006. Women and Imprisonment in the U.S. History and Current Reality. www.freedomarchives.org/Documents/Finder/DOC3_scans/3.kurshan.women.imprisonment.pdf

Laub, John H., D. Nagin, and Robert J. Sampson. 1998. "Trajectories of Change in Criminal Offending: Good Marriages and the Desistance Process." *American Sociological Review* 63:225–238.

Lauritsen, Janet L., Karen Heimer, and James P. Lynch. 2009. "Trends in the Gender Gap in Violent Offending: New Evidence from the National Crime Victimization Survey." *Criminology* 47:361–400.

Loper, Ann B., Wrenn Carlson, Lacy Levitt, and Kathryn Scheffel. 2009. "Parenting Stress, Alliance, Child Contact and Adjustment of Imprisoned Mothers and Fathers." *Journal of Offender Rehabilitation* 48:483–503.

Magaletta, Philip R., Pamela M. Diamond, Erik Faust, Dawn Daggett, and Scott Camp. 2009. "Estimating the Mental Illness Component of Service Need in Corrections: Results from the Mental Health Prevalence Project." *Criminal Justice and Behavior* 36:229–244.

Magaletta, Philip R., and Dominic P. Herbst. 2001. "Fathering from Prison: Common Struggles and Successful Solutions." *Psychotherapy: Theory, Research, Practice, Training* 38:88–96.

Maher, Lisa, and Susan L. Hudson. 2007. "Women in the Drug Economy: A Metasynthesis of the Qualitative Literature." *Journal of Drug Issues* 37:805–826.

Maruschak, Lauren M. 2008. *Medical Problems of Prisoners.* Bureau of Justice Statistics Special Report NCJ-221740. Washington, DC: US Department of Justice.

Matthews, Betsy, and Dana L. Hubbard. 2008. "Moving Ahead: Five Essential Elements for Working Effectively with Girls." *Journal of Criminal Justice* 36:494-502.

McClellan, Dorothy S., David Farabee, and Ben M. Crouch. 1997. "Early Victimization, Drug Use, and Criminality: A Comparison of Male and Female Prisoners." *Criminal Justice and Behavior* 24:455–476.

McCorkle, Richard C. 1995. "Gender, Psychopathology, and Institutional Behavior: A Comparison of Male and Female Mentally Ill Prison Inmates." *Journal of Criminal Justice* 23:53–61.

McDaniels-Wilson, Cathy, and Joan Belknap. 2008. "The Extensive Sexual Violation and Sexual Abuse Histories of Incarcerated Women." *Violence Against Women* 14:1090–1127.

Messina, Nena, and Christine Grella. 2006. "Childhood Trauma and Women's Health Outcomes in a California Prison." *American Journal of Public Health* 96:1842–1848.

Messina, Nena, Christine Grella, William Burdon, and Michael Prendergast. 2007. "Childhood Adverse Events and Current Traumatic Distress: A Comparison of Men and Women Drug-Dependent Prisoners." *Criminal Justice and Behavior* 34:1385–1401.

Messina, Nena, Christine Grella, Jerry Cartier, and Stephanie Torres. 2010. "A Randomized Experimental Study of Gender-Responsive Substance Abuse Treatment for Women in Prison." *Journal of Substance Abuse Treatment* 38:97–107.

Miller, William R., and Stephen Rollnick. 2002. *Motivational Interviewing*. New York: Guilford Press.

Muftic, Lisa R., Jeff A. Bouffard, and Leana A. Bouffard. 2007. "An Exploratory Study of Women Arrested for Intimate Partner Violence: Violent Women or Violent Resistance?" *Journal of Interpersonal Violence* 22:753–774.

Mumola, Christopher J. 2000. *Incarcerated Mothers and Their Children*. Bureau of Justice Statistics Special Report NCJ-182335. Washington, DC: Department of Justice.

Mumola, Christopher J., and Jennifer C. Karberg. 2006. *Drug Use and Dependence, State and Federal Prisoners, 2004*. Bureau of Justice Statistics Special Report NCJ-213530. Washington, DC: US Department of Justice.

National Commission on Correctional Health Care. 2008. *Standards for Health Services in Prisons*. Chicago: Author.

National Institute on Drug Abuse. 2008. *Comorbidity: Addiction and Other Mental Illnesses*. National Institute of Health Report Number 10-5771. Washington, DC: US Department of Health and Human Services.

Nelson, Roxanne. 2006. "Laboring in Chains: Shackling Pregnant Inmates, Even During Childbirth, Still Happens." *American Journal of Nursing* 106:25–26.

Owen, Barbara. 1998. *In the Mix: Struggle and Survival in a Women's Prison*. New York: State University of New York Press.

Owen, Barbara, and Barbara Bloom. 1995. "Profiling Women Prisoners: Findings from National Surveys and a California Sample." *The Prison Journal* 75:165–185.

Peters, Roger H., Marla G. Bartoi, and Pattie B. Sherman. 2008. *Screening and Assessment of Co-Occurring Disorders in the Justice System*. Delmar, NY: Center for Mental Health Services National GAINS Center.

Peters, Roger. H., Michelle E. LeVasseur, and Redonna K. Chandler. 2004. "Correctional Treatment for Co-Occurring Disorders: Results of a National Survey." *Behavioral Science and the Law* 22:563–584.

Petersilia, Joan. 1999. Parole and Prisoner Re-Entry in the United States. In *Prisons*, edited by Michael Tonry and Joan Petersilia. Vol. 26 *of Crime and Justice: A Review of Research*, edited by Michael Tonry. Chicago: University of Chicago Press.

Richie, Beth. 2001. "Challenges Incarcerated Women Face as They Return to Their Communities: Findings from Life History Interviews." *Crime & Delinquency* 47:368–389.

Sable, Marjorie R., John R. Fieberg, Sandra L. Martin, and Lawrence L. Kupper. 1999. "Violence Victimization Experiences of Pregnant Prisoners." *American Journal of Orthopsychiatry* 69:392–397.

Sacks, JoAnn Y. 2004. "Women with Co-Occurring Substance Use and Mental Disorders (COD) in the Criminal Justice System: A Research Review." *Behavioral Sciences and the Law* 22:449–466.

Salisbury, Emily J., and Patricia Van Voorhis. 2009. "Gendered Pathways: A Quantitative Investigation of Women Probationers' Paths to Incarceration." *Criminal Justice and Behavior* 36:541–566.

Salisbury, Emily J., Patricia Van Voorhis, and Georgia V. Spiropoulos. 2009. "The Predictive Validity of a Gender-Responsive Needs Assessment: An Exploratory Study." *Crime & Delinquency* 55:550–585.

Schroeder, Carole, and J. Bell. 2005. "Doula Birth Support for Incarcerated Pregnant Women." *Public Health Nursing* 22:53–58.

Schwartz, Jennifer, Darrell Steffensmeier, Hua Zhong, and Jeff M. Ackerman. 2009. "Trends in the Gender Gap in Violence: Reevaluating NCVS and Other Evidence." *Criminology* 47:401–424.

Seffrin, Patrick M., Peggy C. Giordano, Wendy D. Manning, and Monica A. Longmore. 2009. "The Influence of Dating Relationships on Friendship Networks, Identity Development, and Delinquency." *Justice Quarterly* 26:238–267.

Sharkey, Lauren. 2010. "Does Overcrowding in Prisons Exacerbate the Risk of Suicide Among Women Prisoners?" *The Howard Journal* 49:111–124.

Smith, Hilary, Nancy Rodriguez, and Marjorie Zatz. 2006. "No Place for Girls to Go: How Juvenile Court Officials Respond to Substance Abuse among Girls and Boys." In *Gender and Crime: Patterns in Victimization and Offending*, edited by Karen Heimer and Candice Kruttschnitt. New York: New York University Press.

Smith, Paul, Francis T. Cullen, and Edward J. Latessa. 2009. "Can 14,737 Women Be Wrong? A Meta-Analysis of the LSI-R and Recidivism for Female Offenders." *Criminology & Public Policy* 8:183–208.

Snyder, Zoann K. 2009. "Keeping Families Together: The Importance of Maintaining Mother–Child Contact for Incarcerated Women." *Women and Criminal Justice* 19:37–59.

Steffensmeier, Darrell, Hua Zhong, Jennifer M. Ackerman, Jeff Schwartz, and Suzanne Agha. 2006. "Gender Gap Trends for Violent Crimes, 1980 to 2003: A UCR-NCVS Comparison." *Feminist Criminology* 1:72–98.

Steiner, Benjamin, and John Wooldredge. 2009. "Individual and Environmental Effects on Assaults and Nonviolent Rule Breaking by Women in Prison." *Journal of Research in Crime and Delinquency* 46:437–467.

Swogger, Marc T., Sungeun You, Sarah Cashman-Brown, and Kenneth R. Conner. 2011. "Childhood Physical Abuse, Aggression, and Suicide Attempts among Criminal Offenders." *Psychiatric Research* 185:363–367.

Tanner, Richard. 2010. "Pregnancy Outcomes at the Indiana Women's Prison." *Journal of Correctional Health Care* 16:216–219.

Thomas, Jim, Margaret Leaf, Steve Kazmierczak, and Josh Stone. 2006. "Self-Injury in Correctional Settings: 'Pathology' of Prisons or Prisoners?" *Criminology & Public Policy* 5:193–202.

Toch, Hans, Kenneth Adams, and James Douglas Grant. 1989. *Coping: Maladaptation in Prison*. New Brunswick, NJ: Transaction.

Tripodi, Steven J., Eyitayo Onifade, and Carrie Pettus-Davis. 2014. "Nonfatal Suicidal Behaviors among Women Prisoners: The Predictive Roles of Childhood Victimization, Childhood Neglect, and Childhood Positive Support." *International Journal of Offender Therapy and Comparative Criminology* 58:394–411.

Tripodi, Steven J., and Carrie Pettus-Davis. 2013. "Histories of Childhood Victimization and Subsequent Mental Health Problems, Substance Use, and Sexual Victimization for a Sample of Incarcerated Women in the US." *International Journal of Law and Psychiatry* 36:30–40.

Ullman, Sarah E. 2004. "Sexual Assault Victimization and Suicidal Behavior in Women: A Review of the Literature." *Aggression and Violent Behavior* 9:331–351.

UN Women. 2012. Violence Against Women Prevalence Data: Surveys by Country. http://www.unwomen.org/en/what-we-do/ending-violence-against-women/facts-and-figures#notes pdf.page 8

US Department of Justice. 2010. *Crime in the United States 2009: Uniform Crime Reports.* Washington, DC: Federal Bureau of Investigation, US Government Printing Office.

Van Dieten, Marilyn. 1998. *Moving On.* Toronto: Orbis Partners.

Van Voorhis, Patricia, Michael Braswell, and David Lester. 2009. *Correctional Counseling and Rehabilitation,* 7th ed. Cincinnati, OH: Anderson Publishing Co.

Van Voorhis, Patricia, Emily J. Salisbury, Emily M. Wright, and Ashley Bauman. 2008. *Achieving Accurate Pictures of Risk and Identifying Gender-Responsive Needs: Two New Assessments for Women Offenders.* Report submitted to the National Institute of Corrections, Washington, DC.

Van Voorhis, Patricia, Emily M. Wright, Emily J. Salisbury, and Ashley Bauman. 2010. "Women's Risk Factors and Their Contributions to Existing Risk/Needs Assessment: The Current Status of a Gender-Responsive Supplement." *Criminal Justice and Behavior* 37:261–288.

Verona, Edelyn, Brian M. Hicks, and Christopher H. Patrick. 2005. "Psychopathy and Suicidality in Female Offenders: Mediating Influences of Personality and Abuse." *Journal of Consulting and Clinical Psychology* 73:1065–1073.

Walmsley, Roy. 2009. *World Female Imprisonment List,* 8th ed. London: King's College London, International Centre for Prison Studies.

Widom, Cathy S., Naomi R. Marmorstein, and Helene R. White. 2006. "Childhood Victimization and Illicit Drug Use in Middle Adulthood." *Psychology of Addictive Behaviors* 20:394–403.

Williams, Tonya M. 2011. "Giving Birth Behind Bars: A Guide to Achieving Reproductive Justice for Incarcerated Women." Atlanta, GA: SPARK Reproductive Justice NOW. http://www.sparkrj.org/download/307/

Wismont, Judith M. 2000. "The Lived Pregnancy Experience of Women in Prison." *Journal of Midwifery and Women's Health* 45:292–300.

Women's Prison Association. 2009. Prison Nursery Programs a Growing Trend in Women's Prisons. http://www.corrections.com/news/article/21644

Wright, Emily M., Dana D. DeHart, Barbara A. Koons-Witt, and Courtney A. Crittenden. 2013. " 'Buffers' Against Crime? Exploring the Roles and Limitations of Positive Relationships among Women in Prison." *Punishment & Society* 15:71–95.

Wright, Emily M., Emily J. Salisbury, and Patricia Van Voorhis. 2007. "Predicting the Prison Misconducts of Women Offenders: The Importance of Gender-Responsive Needs." *Journal of Contemporary Criminal Justice* 23:310–340.

Wright, Emily M., Patricia Van Voorhis, Emily J. Salisbury, and Ashley Bauman. 2012. "Gender-Responsive Lessons Learned and Policy Implications for Women in Prison: A Review." *Criminal Justice and Behavior* 39:1612–1632.

Young, Vernetta D., and Rebecca Reviere. 2006. *Women Behind Bars: Gender and Race in U.S. Prisons.* Boulder, CO: Lynne Rienner.

Zlotnick, Caron, Jennifer G. Clarke, Peter D. Friedmann, Mary B. Roberts, Stanley Sacks, and Gerald Melnick. 2008. "Gender Differences in Comorbid Disorders among Offenders in Prison Substance Abuse Treatment Programs." *Behavioral Science and the Law* 26:403–412.

CHAPTER 9

··

IMPACT OF INCARCERATION ON FAMILIES AND COMMUNITIES

··

NANCY RODRIGUEZ AND JILLIAN J. TURANOVIC

IN light of the penal harm movement and imprisonment being "embraced as the linchpin of the nation's response to crime" (Cullen, Fisher, and Applegate 2000, p. 2), US incarceration rates rose dramatically during the last part of the twentieth century. After reaching historically unprecedented levels and peaking after a five-fold exponential increase between 1972 and 2009, there were more than 1.6 million people incarcerated in state and federal correctional facilities (Carson and Sabol 2012). While imprisonment rates have leveled off—and in some states have even declined—incarceration remains a salient aspect in the lives of many Americans.

The debate over the value, impact, and wisdom of the American brand of mass incarceration is one that has been highly polarized between most scholars and policymakers (Currie 1998; Pratt 2009; Sampson 2011). Under the assumption that offenders are bad people, deadbeat parents, and even "superpredators" with no morals or regard for rules (Bennett, DiIulio, and Walters 1996), policymakers have stated explicitly that we are better off if these individuals are removed from society (DiIulio 1994; Irwin and Austin 1994; Gest 2001; Irwin 2005). Yet these claims are at odds with an impressive body of evidence demonstrating the potentially harmful effects of incarceration on families and communities. Specified most clearly in a series of works by Todd Clear and colleagues, evidence suggests that offenders typically have complex relationships with their families and communities in which they are often the primary sources of income for their households; they also play an important role in child-rearing despite having a criminogenic lifestyle (Rose and Clear 1998; Clear 2007). The removal of these citizens from the community amounts to a form of "coercive mobility" that, in the long run, does more harm than good (Clear et al. 2003). Accordingly, a body of empirical literature has emerged demonstrating the harmful "collateral consequences" of incarceration not only for offenders but also for the communities, families, and children they leave behind (Hagan and Dinovitzer 1999; Clear 2002; Geller et al. 2009; Western and Wildeman 2009).

Accordingly, in this essay we review what is currently known about the impact of incarceration on communities and families. And while we certainly know a lot, there is much left to learn. We therefore also highlight important avenues that should arguably take center stage in the next generation of research. In particular, section I presents a broad overview of research on the collateral harms of incarceration on communities and families. Section II examines recent literature that explores variability in the effects of incarceration on families and also details particular methodological and conceptual challenges in this line of work. Section III extends the discussion of the collateral consequences of incarceration to the communities and families of Latinos. Section IV discusses the importance for future research to link immigration with criminal justice policy to best understand the next era of the collateral consequences of incarceration in the United States. The main conclusions discussed in this essay are the following:

- There is a vast literature demonstrating the many unintended consequences of incarceration on communities and families of prisoners that include coercive mobility, weakened social controls, family disruption, and stigmatization.
- Recent studies have uncovered a great deal of variability in the effects of incarceration on family systems, where family members and children may be affected positively, negatively, or not at all by the imprisonment. This variability often depends on how the person was influencing family life prior to being incarcerated.
- Research on the collateral consequences of incarceration has virtually ignored the impact on Latino families and communities, despite the fact that Latinos represent the fastest growing segment of the US correctional population.
- Although overall state and federal prison populations have plateaued and declined in recent years, it is arguably premature to conclude that this era of punitiveness is over. As crime control policies become inextricably linked to immigration discourse, the collateral consequences of incarceration will likely be felt for years to come, particularly for Latinos.

I. Collateral Consequences
of Incarceration

Soaring rates of incarceration and the cycling of people in and out of US prisons have spurred a wealth of research on the communities and families of prisoners. The ripple effects of the prison boom are concentrated among those most impoverished and disadvantaged in society, particularly those in America's inner cities (Western 2006; Sampson and Loeffler 2010). The communities most affected by incarceration therefore tend to be those in which crime is high and social controls are low, where conditions of economic deprivation are the norm, and where residential mobility and family disruption are commonplace (Pratt and Cullen 2005; Wakefield and Uggen 2010). Rather than making these communities "better" or "safer," scholars have argued that high incarceration rates tend to exacerbate these very conditions and make life even more difficult for those left behind (Rose and Clear 1998; Foster and Hagan 2007).

In particular, incarceration can introduce "coercive mobility" into communities by increasing residential turnover and disrupting the social networks that constitute the basis for informal social control (Clear, Rose, and Ryder 2001). Coercive mobility can destabilize neighborhoods by increasing levels of disorganization when offenders are removed to go to prison and also when those individuals reenter the community (Rose and Clear 1998; Clear et al. 2003). With such mobility, few residents have a vested interest in the health of the community and therefore withdraw from public and social action, including efforts of crime prevention (Coleman 1990; Putnam 2000). Essentially, such communities have very little in the way of "social capital," or a shared set of prosocial values among community residents and a commitment to solve neighborhood problems collectively (Coleman 1988; Hagan 1994).

Due to the extreme socioeconomic segregation of US housing, a small number of impoverished, predominantly minority neighborhoods bear the brunt of mass imprisonment. In such places, parent-aged adults—especially young African American men—cycle through stays in prison and jail at high rates. Although their time away may be brief, when added up across numerous years, incarceration in such neighborhoods is nearly ubiquitous (Lynch and Sabol 2001; Clear 2007). Given the racially disparate patterns of imprisonment, many scholars have pointed out that incarceration has become a normative "rite of passage" for many disadvantaged, young African American men (Maruna 2011). This "rite" is not necessarily a welcomed badge of honor but rather is considered an inevitable aspect of the maturation process for many low-income children of color (Massey 2007). Indeed, incarceration rates are about eight times higher for African Americans than whites, where young African American males under the age of thirty-five who have dropped out of high school are more likely to be incarcerated (37 percent) than to hold a job (26 percent) (Western 2006).

As many scholars have pointed out, imprisonment removes potential workers from the labor force and can deteriorate already weak employment prospects in poor urban communities. People do not often return from prison better equipped to secure employment (Sampson 1995). Instead, incarceration can stigmatize those convicted of crimes (Pager 2003) and damage the social networks that they may use to find jobs (Smith 2008). Western (2006, p. 128), for instance, estimates that going to prison reduces one's lifetime annual earnings by about one-third and that incarceration can also confine ex-prisoners to positions that are characterized by high turnover and "little chance of moving up the ladder." These problems manifest in a large concentration of residents who are less engaged in the job market and who earn diminished income (Pager 2003; Western 2006). In addition, incarceration can also reduce the marriageability of men and thereby lead to increases in the number of female-headed households in an area (Sampson 1995; Lynch and Sabol 2004). Male marriageability is reduced by their physical removal via incarceration or the stigma of their criminal record on the prospects of securing employment. Ultimately, by reducing the number of men available to guide and monitor children, it is theorized that social controls in these communities weaken, adolescents become more delinquent, and crime rises (Wilson 1987; Clear 2007).

While it may be true that some offenders are bad neighbors, absentee fathers, and a general drain on their communities' resources, such qualities do not fully characterize all those who go to prison. Instead, many offenders contribute "both positively and negatively toward family and neighborhood life" (Rose and Clear 1998, p. 442), where they often shift between legal and illegal means of securing income to support their loved ones. Even though it is possible that imprisoning offenders compensates for some of the damage they inflict on their respective communities, such incapacitation benefits are understood to be negligible relative to the consequences of imprisoning large numbers of community members (Pratt and Cullen 2005).

Not surprisingly, research has found that the incarceration of large numbers of adults, specifically parents and spouses, increases family disruption. Strong associations exist between imprisonment and divorce and separation (Western, Lopoo, and McLanahan 2004; Huebner 2005; but see Lopoo and Western 2005), where the likelihood of marital success is diminished when monetary and emotional strains are placed on remaining loved ones (Huebner 2007; Geller, Garfinkel, and Western 2011). For those who are left behind with minimal resources, the imprisonment of a spouse can worsen their situation, since these individuals must then assume additional roles and responsibilities in light of the family member's absence. These added strains can negatively affect the family system and are often compounded when children are involved. For example, research focusing on marginalized women left behind shows that mothers must typically rely on friends and family members to provide money, childcare, and companionship during their partners' absence (Clear 2007). By straining their close ties, women's support systems can become exhausted, whereby women and children become even more socially excluded than they were before the spouse's imprisonment (Schwartz-Soicher et al. 2011; Turney, Schnittker, and Wildeman 2012).

Family members of prisoners may also experience an array of emotional difficulties associated with incarceration that can hinder effective family functioning in the family member's absence. These emotional reactions can stem from the physical absence of the individual (e.g., loneliness, missing the person's presence) and can also be tied to the nature of the absence (e.g., the stigma inflicted on the family by the incarceration). Arditti (2005, p. 253) conceptualizes these responses as "disenfranchised grief," suggesting that the families of prisoners experience a type of loss that is "not openly recognized and not defined as socially significant." Family members live and work outside the prison setting and are exposed to the judgment of their neighbors, churchgoers, coworkers, supervisors, employers, and other community members. According to Braman's (2007) ethnographic findings, even those who reside in communities characterized by high rates of incarceration feel a great deal of shame and humiliation regarding the incarceration of a loved one, which in turn can contribute to lack of social support. Indifferent, hostile, or disapproving social attitudes can therefore intensify the pain of losing a family member to imprisonment (Braman 2007; Murray and Farrington 2008), especially for female romantic partners.

As Comfort (2008) has highlighted, many women provide tremendous support to their incarcerated loved ones in efforts to mitigate the deprivations of imprisonment. In shouldering a portion of the burden of "doing time," numerous facets of women's everyday lives are altered according to dictates of the prison regime. Nonincarcerated women may forfeit their own privacy, deplete their scarce resources, and jeopardize their emotional well-being in efforts to support their imprisoned partners, thus experiencing a form of "secondary prisonization" that can also extend to their children (Comfort 2008, p. 15). Women who visit loved ones in prison may assume the peculiar status of "quasi-inmate," a phenomenon Comfort (2003, p. 102) described as the "collapse of institutional differentiation between visitors and inmates." Through this experience, women are subjected to a version of the elaborate regulations, concentrated surveillance, and corporeal confinement that govern the lives of those behind bars. While some women may take refuge in the closeness they develop with their partners during the imprisonment, sustained contact with the correctional institution may worsen disenfranchised grief and secondary prisonization.

When parents of minor children are incarcerated, a host of problems can arise. Family members may be forced to change residences with children due to financial strains (Tasca, Rodriguez, and Zatz 2011) or may struggle to maintain employment, all while attempting to exert adequate controls over children's behavior (Green et al. 2006). The bulk of childcare responsibilities may be shifted to other family members during parental imprisonment, and, in many cases—particularly in urban minority communities—a large portion of this burden is assumed by grandparents. Becoming a custodial grandparent can constitute a major and unexpected role transition in the life course of older adults, especially for those who find themselves doing "double duty" by caring for their grandchildren in addition to their adult kin (Burnette 1999). Grandparents who assume this physically, emotionally, and financially demanding role tend to have limited resources and multiple needs themselves, including high rates of depression and multiple chronic health problems (Burton 1992; Poehlmann 2003). They may also feel shame or guilt regarding their effectiveness as surrogate parents, as their own children are often the ones incarcerated. Moreover, grandparents typically assume their caregiving roles without any monetary remuneration or support from public aid programs, since many choose to care for their grandchildren "informally" (Hayslip and Kaminski 2005). Obtaining legal custody of children is often an expensive and time-consuming process that can cause family tension, particularly if parents are unwilling to surrender their parental rights to grandparents.

Assuming childcare responsibilities of prisoners' children may prove most challenging for those caring for difficult or troubled children (Pruchno and McKenney 2002). Several studies have illustrated that children of incarcerated parents are more likely to engage in crime, both in the short and long term (Roettger and Swisher 2011; Murray, Farrington, and Sekol 2012). Such children are also more likely to experience mental health difficulties, aggression, troubles in school, and substance abuse problems (Murray and Farrington 2008). Because of the problems often linked to parental incarceration—particularly delinquency and school failure—imprisonment can lead to many negative long-term outcomes for children, including sustained economic deprivation, social isolation, arrest, and imprisonment (Murray and Farrington 2008; Western and Muller 2013). Moreover, parental incarceration may be an especially confusing form of separation for children, as it is often unexpected and rarely explained to them in a way that they can fully understand (Eddy and Poehlmann 2010). Accordingly, they may suffer from guilt, anger, and separation anxiety in response to their parent's absence or agonize over the well-being of their mother or father in prison (Branch and Brinson 2007).

Taken together, the majority of research on the collateral consequences of incarceration highlights the negative impact on families and communities. These findings have inspired statements such as the one made by Braman (2002, pp. 135, 122) that incarceration is among the "bluntest of social instruments" that has been "pulling apart the most vulnerable families in our society." While there is no doubt that these consequences are real, these effects are unlikely to be either exclusive (i.e., incarceration has *only* a negative impact) or universal (i.e., incarceration affects *all* families and communities similarly) (Hagan and Dinovitzer 1999; Turanovic, Rodriguez, and Pratt 2012). Instead, incarceration may be only one of many social ills plaguing disadvantaged high-crime communities and one that may not always initiate a cascade of hardships for family members left behind. As a result, Sampson (2011, p. 824) recently called for researchers of mass imprisonment to embrace a "social ledger," where the full range of collateral consequences—positive, negative, and null—are assessed.

II. Variability in the Effects of Incarceration on Families

Families, by their very nature, are dynamic social systems (Bronfenbrenner 1979; Cox and Paley 1997; Crosnoe and Cavanagh 2010). The roles of parents, caregivers, and children can be adaptable as family members respond to changing circumstances to meet each other's needs and have their needs met. Each individual connected to his or her family contributes to the system in unique ways—some may be positive, others dysfunctional. But to understand fully the impact of imprisonment on the family system, there needs to be an appreciation for *how* the prisoner was influencing family functioning prior to being incarcerated.

To that end, a body of research has begun to emerge regarding the collateral consequences of parental incarceration for certain elements of family structure (e.g., changes in child guardianship and breaks in spousal or parent–child attachments; see Geller, Garfinkel, and Western 2009; Tasca, Rodriguez, and Zatz 2011). This work is definitely a good start and is consistent with the general literature on family disruption (Amato 2000; Hetherington 2003), but focusing solely on such structural arrangements restricts our ability to understand how familial processes are affected by the imprisonment of a parent (see Giordano 2010; Kruttschnitt 2011). Taking into account broader familial processes requires researchers to look beyond dyadic parent–child or parent–spouse disruptions and instead to look at the family as a *system*, with a history (Sameroff 1994; Parke and Clarke-Stewart 2003). Family members of prisoners have likely been subjected to various highs and lows throughout the history of their relationships with these individuals, making it likely that prisoners have affected family functioning in complex ways.

If, for example, the offender was engaging in dangerous or reckless behaviors before imprisonment, his or her incarceration may allow for the remaining family system to function more positively. Substantial research has uncovered a variety of problems in the dynamics of families where antisocial conduct is prevalent, such as chaotic interaction patterns, poor communication skills, role distortion, dysfunctional boundaries, and considerable conflict (Capaldi and Patterson 1991; Ammerman et al. 1999; Carlson and Corcoran 2001). These problems may be further aggravated within families where the offender also suffers from a mental illness or substance abuse problem (Goglia et al. 1992; Mucowski and Hayden 1992; Whitaker et al. 2006). In such cases, critical family resources can be drained to finance an addiction, children may be exposed to drug or alcohol use (and the events proceeding such activities), and family life may be disrupted by the unpredictable behavior of those struggling with such issues (Cummings and Davies 2010). As a result, family members may feel burdened and place their own needs and wishes behind those of the troubled offender or feel "on guard" in the presence of someone who is volatile or unstable (Turanovic et al.

2012). Thus, for some families, the removal of a high-risk, high-need individual—even via the method of incarceration—may provide some relief, even if such relief is temporary.

Not surprisingly, issues of mental illness, substance addiction, and physical and sexual abuse are disproportionately common among prisoners and particularly among incarcerated parents. According to Bureau of Justice Statistics estimates (Glaze and Maruschak 2008), an estimated 73 percent of mothers and 55 percent of fathers incarcerated in state prisons meet *Diagnostic and Statistical Manual of Mental Disorders* diagnoses for mental illness; nearly 65 percent of mothers and 64 percent of fathers in state prisons are characterized as substance-dependent; and 60 percent of imprisoned mothers and 16 percent of imprisoned fathers have histories of sexual or other physical abuse. These problems are pervasive and may hinder parents' ability to provide a stable and nurturing home environment that ensures the healthy development of their children and the well-being of their loved ones (Mustillo et al. 2011). As Comfort argues (2008, p. 184), some family members may even come to rely on penal intervention to remove such individuals from the home and restore a "semblance of order on tumultuous and troubled existences." In situations like these, the incarceration of a high-risk parent represents an opportunity for those who may be better qualified to assume full caretaking duties of children and to begin to provide a healthier home life for all of those involved in the remaining family system.

In light of these issues, recent studies have emerged suggesting that there is substantial heterogeneity in the effects of incarceration, particularly among children of incarcerated parents. These studies reveal both negative (e.g., increased emotional and behavioral problems in children) and positive (e.g., reduced exposure to violence) outcomes, as well as the finding that parental incarceration often is unrelated to these kinds of problems net of other adversities in children's lives (Murray, Loeber, and Pardini 2012; Shlafer, Poehlmann, and Donelan-McCall 2012; Van de Rakt, Murray, and Nieuwbeerta 2012). Indeed, several studies have demonstrated the relationship between parental incarceration and child well-being to be rendered null once controlling statistically for familial adversities such as family victimization, sibling delinquency, and parental conflict (e.g., Aaron and Dallaire 2010; Besemer et al. 2011).

Looking beyond the effects on children, Turanovic, Rodriguez, and Pratt (2012) qualitatively examined the effects of incarceration on those caring for children of incarcerated parents. Their findings revealed that many of the caregivers were affected negatively by the parent's imprisonment (58 percent), yet a nontrivial number experienced either positive changes in his or her life (20 percent) or no changes at all (22 percent) as a result of the incarceration. Turanovic et al. (2012) also found that the variation in these experiences could be determined by three causal processes: (a) the nature of prior parental involvement on the part of the prisoner, (b) the quality of the interpersonal relationship between the caregiver and the prisoner, and (c) the family support system of caregivers. These three themes, although discussed separately, are very much interconnected. In particular, under conditions where prisoners had poor quality or sporadic involvement in their children's lives; where caregivers had violent, volatile, or dysfunctional relationships with prisoners; and where the caregiver received social support from other family members, caregivers experienced either *positive changes* or *no changes* in their lives as a result of incarceration. Although the majority of incarcerated parents in this study provided care to their children and emotional and financial support to their families prior to imprisonment, many incarcerated mothers and fathers were found to have no involvement in their children's lives and were reportedly cut off from family systems long before going to prison. These findings speak to the critical need for research assessing the impact of incarceration on families to take into account the extent and degree of prisoners' involvement in their family systems and their relationships with family members prior to incarceration.

It is important to note, however, that the micro-level processes typically found to influence how family members and children fare are likely *endogenous* to (i.e., the products of) larger macro-social processes. Put simply, families and children affected by imprisonment are embedded in a broader social–structural context. As such, they will be influenced by the kinds of ecological processes (e.g., chronic resource deprivation, weakened institutions of social support, and low levels of collective efficacy) that set the stage for both the causes and consequences of incarceration (see, e.g., Sampson, Raudenbush, and Earls 1997; Triplett, Gainey, and Sun 2003). We highlight the importance for future work to examine the consequences of incarceration through the lens of structured inequality and concentrated disadvantage. These concepts are well established in the criminological literature generally (Pratt and Cullen 2005), but they have been largely absent from discussions of the consequences of incarceration (for exceptions, see Rose and Clear 1998; Clear 2007).

The daunting—and yet critically important—task for future research will be to measure *directly* (as opposed to indirectly or not at all) social processes specified at the neighborhood level so that the full pathways between incarceration and social outcomes can be assessed (Sampson 2011). To do so, we must move beyond treating social processes as a "black box" where theoretically plausible (but typically unmeasured) phenomena occur (Turanovic et al. 2012). This is not something we tend to do very well in the social sciences in general or in criminology in particular (Abbott 1997; Sampson 2012). Part of the problem can be attributed to data limitations, since few of the large and publicly available data sets that are typically used to test the effects of incarceration contain rich measures of these social processes.

Although recent research has overcome many methodological limitations plaguing earlier work (e.g., problems with causality and selection; see Wildeman, Wakefield, and Turney 2013), three additional issues remain. First, there needs to be greater theoretical and empirical focus on the degree to which prisoners are embedded within the larger context of families. It is critical that inquiries of those left behind extend beyond romantic partners or a single focal child. Prisoners, like most people, have ties with other family members aside from their spouses, and many have multiple children with multiple partners (LeBlanc 2003; Comfort 2008; Arditti 2012). Indeed, the experiences of grandparents, siblings, aunts, uncles, mothers, and fathers are inevitably intertwined—each individual contributes to the functioning of the family system in unique ways that can moderate the effects of incarceration on others (Turanovic et al. 2012).

Second, greater care needs to be taken to disentangle the effects of preexisting hardships from the impact of incarceration, particularly in the case of maternal imprisonment. As has been shown consistently in prior work, incarcerated women disproportionately experience numerous life traumas (e.g., childhood victimization and sexual abuse, interpersonal violence, mental illness, and drug addiction) that can negatively affect their competence as parents and their ability to maintain stable relationships with their children. Since incarcerated mothers are also more likely to have experienced an *accumulation* of these difficulties (Arditti and Few 2006; Glaze and Maruschak 2008), problems experienced by their children or family members are likely heavily influenced by circumstances that predate the imprisonment. Maternal incarceration is a relatively rare phenomenon, and oftentimes data that capture paternal incarceration are easier to come by. Yet the few studies that have examined maternal incarceration net of preexisting problems call into question whether maternal incarceration truly diminishes child well-being (e.g., Cho 2009, 2011; Siegel 2011) or healthy family functioning (e.g., Turanovic et al. 2012).

Third, there needs to be greater appreciation for the problems associated with how incarceration is measured at the individual level. Many data sets that are commonly used in this literature (e.g., The Fragile Families and Child Wellbeing Study and the National Longitudinal Study of Adolescent Health) do not differentiate between incarceration in jail or prison. This is an important methodological distinction. Offenders serving lengthy sentences in prison are likely to have had relationships with their families, children, and communities that are qualitatively different from those offenders who may be serving a short stint in a local jail. Nevertheless, these are practical issues—certainly not intellectual ones—and such challenges should not discourage us from trying to understand more fully the complicated impact of incarceration.

III. Understanding the Impact of Incarceration on Latinos

In recent decades, soaring rates of immigration have dramatically changed the demographic landscape of the United States, due in no small part to the growth in Latino residents. The number of Latinos has increased to over 50 million, representing the largest minority group in the nation. Incarceration is typically neglected as a source of social stratification for Latinos independent of immigration laws (Massey 2007). This oversight is problematic given that incarceration carries many long-term social consequences that may manifest in family disruption and depleted social capital and that produce and exacerbate inequalities through education and employment (Pettit and Western 2004). Thus the very institutions that mitigate the criminogenic effects of disadvantage on Latino communities—such as familism and ties to the labor force (Martinez 2002)—can be undermined by disparate increases in imprisonment.

A review of the number of Latinos incarcerated in state and federal correctional facilities shows their startling rate of increase. The Latino correctional population increased by over 200 percent between 1990 and 2010—nearly doubling in size between 2000 and 2010 (Guerino, Harrison, and Sabol 2011). And while trends in rising imprisonment are certainly not at odds with American history, the recent increase in Latino imprisonment is particularly alarming since it occurred while state and federal prison populations were otherwise leveling off and declining. Indeed, in 2010, the combined US state and federal prison population declined for the first time in nearly forty years, with half of all state departments of corrections reporting decreases in their prison populations (Guerino et al. 2011).

Despite changes in demographics and the rapid increase in the incarceration of Latinos, we currently know very little about Latino imprisonment or its consequences on families and communities. Race—rather than ethnicity—has traditionally stratified US society, and thus the bulk of incarceration research has been devoted to understanding *racial* disparities (i.e., black–white differences) in the effects of imprisonment. As a result, the ethnic-specific consequences of Latino incarceration have remained grossly underexplored. To a certain extent this focus on race is not surprising given the demography of incarceration and its disproportionate impact on black communities. Black males are currently incarcerated at rates that are over seven times higher than white males and more than double that of Latino males. In 2011, for instance, more than 3.0 percent of black males in the United States were incarcerated in state and federal correctional facilities, relative to only 0.4 percent of all white males and 1.2 percent of all Latino males (Carson and Sabol 2012). Still, understanding the ethnic-specific consequences of incarceration is critical given that there were more than 350,000 Latinos incarcerated in state and federal correctional facilities in 2011 (Carson and Sabol 2012)—more than the total number of people incarcerated in US prisons in 1980 and larger than the entire population of St. Louis. Put simply, this is a problem that affects a significant and growing proportion of the American population.

In order to identify the ways in which Latinos left behind are affected by incarceration, one must consider their geographic clustering across various jurisdictions and how it differs from that of African Americans. Latinos, unlike African Americans, are less likely to live in segregated areas and instead reside in areas that border white neighborhoods or live in mixed communities (Peterson and Krivo 2010). Importantly, Latino ties to the labor force, which present a significant window of opportunity, are largely absent in African American communities. Greater economic resources naturally translate into other benefits (e.g., residential stability, educational prospects for children), which impact overall well-being. Given these larger structural forces and economic opportunities, Latino families may fare better than African American families in light of incarceration.

Aside from the larger community context of African Americans and Latinos, a distinctive feature among racial and ethnic minority families is the role of extended family and kinship networks. Specifically, kin networks (e.g., grandparents, uncles, and aunts) play a critical role in the care and supervision of children and adolescents. Among African American families, kinship support, whether formal or informal, has enabled children to remain with family members when parents have been unable to provide daily care and supervision. Although extended families are quite common among Latinos and family members may assist in providing care for children as needed, the supervision and control of children falls upon mothers and fathers. Marriage and cohabitation are highly valued among Latinos, with mothers playing an instrumental role in childrearing practices. The authoritarian parenting style among Latinos, coupled with deference toward fathers and emphasis on the traditional role of women, lead to very different roles for extended kin (Wilkinson 1987). Given these familial differences among African Americans and Latinos, Latino children may fare worse when faced with parental incarceration.

Research indicates that family disruption has a more adverse effect on whites than African Americans, with Latinos resembling whites in this effect. The less normalized nature of transitions as experienced by whites and Latinos relative to African Americans may explain these differences. In other words, African American youths' resiliency to family disruption may be due to the more frequent nature of family instability in their lives. Here the role of extended kin among racial/ethnic groups (Ruggles 1994; Dunifon and Kowaleski-Jones 2002) becomes key when families are fragmented due to incarceration and face subsequent adversities. While family disruption and parental incarceration may lead to negative outcomes (e.g., emotional difficulties, economic strain) among certain children, family systems can be instrumental in shaping the incarceration. Whether this manifests in more adversities for one group than the other remains unknown.

IV. The Immigration and Justice Nexus

Any discussion on the changing demographics in the United States must be placed in the broader context of immigration. There are more than 11 million undocumented immigrants in the United States, with 1 million of these immigrants under the age of eighteen. There are also a significant number of children in families with mixed legal status. According to the Migration Policy Institute (2012), one-fourth of US-born children have a least one parent who is undocumented. This demographic landscape is particularly important given the heightened focus on immigration law and policies and the resulting sheer number of Latinos in state and federal prisons and deportation centers. A comprehensive review of the collateral consequences of incarceration on families and communities must acknowledge the recent and ongoing attempts by government to address immigration. Such efforts have significantly altered the way of life for Latinos, especially for those who come into contact with the justice system.

Security safeguards post-9/11, the creation of the Department of Homeland Security, and failed attempts by the Bush and Obama administrations to pass comprehensive immigration legislation have all in some way contributed to anti-immigrant initiatives (Varsanyi 2010). Fueled by myths that characterize immigrants as criminally involved and a threat to public safety (Bender 2003; Portillos 2006; Chavez 2008), an array of local and state anti-immigrant initiatives have been proposed. These efforts have resulted in the enforcement of civil immigration laws by local and state police, the expansion of offenses that qualify for mandatory deportation, and the restriction of discretion of immigration judges to consider the impact on US citizen family members. Collectively, these strategies led to the confinement of an unprecedented number of immigrants (authorized and unauthorized) in state and federal correctional institutions and deportation centers.

Given the integration of immigration and criminal justice data management systems, not surprisingly, unauthorized migrants are now more likely to be detected, detained, and deported. Deportations were at an all-time high in 2012, with 409,849 deportations in fiscal year 2012 (Immigration and Customs Enforcement, Department of Homeland Security [ICE] 2012a). An important characteristic of the deportee population is how many are parents of US citizens. Children of immigrants who are born in the United States are automatically granted citizenship. Official statistics indicate that 23 percent of all deportations since mid-2010 were parents of US children (Wessler 2011; see also ICE 2012a). The deportation and absence of immigrants—many of which are parents—has significant implications for a large segment of the population in this country.

Criminal activity plays a central role in the volume of recent deportations. The basis for crime-related removals can include criminal histories, DUI offenses or other public safety offenses, or prior immigration violations. Importantly, deportees often serve time in correctional facilities before being deported. During the mid-1980s, crime-related deportations increased rapidly and now comprise the majority of all deportations (Legomsky 2007). During fiscal year 2012, 55 percent of all deportations involved crime-related removals

(ICE 2012a, 2012b). Figures indicate that more than a third of these removals involved drug or DUI offenses. A significant number of individuals deported through the Secure Communities program (38 percent) had prior records comprised of less serious crimes, including traffic violations (Wessler 2012).

Undoubtedly, the removal of these individuals has a significant impact on immigrant families and communities. This is especially the case for US children who have at least one parent who is an immigrant. To date, we know little about the effects of parental immigration detention and the subsequent deportation. We know that family members are disconnected from one another and the resulting disruption of the family unit may be short or long term. Children's care becomes a central matter for these families, who often struggle with the social and emotional stress and trauma caused by the incarceration of their loved ones (Rabin 2011; Wessler 2011, 2012; Phillips et al. 2013). The absence of a parent due to detention and deportation not only leads to adverse behavioral changes in children (e.g., change in sleeping patterns, eating habits, stress and anxiety, and poor educational outcomes) but also produces reduced economic capacity, mobility, and mistrust of the justice system (Suárez-Orozco, Todorova, and Louie 2002; Chaudry et al. 2010; Menjívar 2012). Unfortunately, for many, reunification between parents and children is very difficult. For children who have entered the child welfare system, there is currently little coordination between immigration and child welfare systems, making it difficult for children to visit parents or have access to family court proceedings. Identifying how these processes affect the well-being of immigrant families will be crucial in light of changing demographics, immigration, and the continued use of imprisonment, detention, and deportation to control and punish offenders.

V. CONCLUSION

Generally speaking, policymakers have not embraced scholarly research on the harmful collateral consequences of incarceration. Yet, faced with strapped budgets and declining revenues, many legislators have recently confronted the fact that correctional spending must be scaled back. A growing consensus now exists—between both sides of the political spectrum—that mass imprisonment is an unsustainable enterprise (Cullen and Gilbert 2013). There is a push to move as many low-risk offenders into the community as soon as possible, and there is a corresponding desire to be more judicious regarding who is sent to prison in the first place (Cullen and Jonson 2012). Nevertheless, those who interpret recent declines in overall prison populations as evidence that the "grand social experiment in mass incarceration" is over may be guilty of wishful thinking (Frost and Clear 2009, 2012). When considering the popularity of tough-on-immigration policies and the recent spike in Latino imprisonment, it seems premature to conclude that this era has drawn to a close. The large volumes of US prisoners being released to overburdened community corrections and swelling local jail populations foreshadow the consequences of America's punishment binge for decades to come.

We encourage the next era of research on the collateral consequences of incarceration to be mindful of structural inequality and concentrated disadvantage across various racial and ethnic groups. Research must also focus on Latino families and communities and examine variation in the consequences of imprisonment at the family and community levels. Last, identifying and measuring the social processes at play that lead to adverse outcomes due to incarceration must be central in this line of inquiry. Doing so may help to minimize the collateral harms inflicted on family members who are not responsible for committing the crime but are still forced to pay for it.

References

Aaron, Lauren, and Danielle H. Dallaire. 2010. "Parental Incarceration and Multiple Risk Experiences: Effects on Family Dynamics and Child Delinquency." *Journal of Youth and Adolescence* 39:471–484.

Abbott, Andrew. 1997. "Of Time and Space: The Contemporary Relevance of the Chicago School." *Social Forces* 75:1149–1182.

Amato, Paul R. 2000. "The Consequences of Divorce for Adults and Children." *Journal of Marriage and the Family* 62:1267–1287.

Ammerman, Robert T., David J. Kolko, Levent Kirisci, Timothy C. Blackson, and Michael A. Dawes. 1999. "Child Abuse Potential in Parents with Histories of Substance Use Disorder." *Child Abuse & Neglect* 23:1225–1238.

Arditti, Joyce A. 2005. "Families and Incarceration: An Ecological Approach." *Families in Society* 86:251–258.

Arditti, Joyce A. 2012. *Parental Incarceration and the Family: Psychological and Social Effects of Imprisonment on Children, Parents, and Caregivers.* New York: New York University Press.

Arditti, Joyce A., and April L. Few. 2006. "Mothers' Reentry into Family Life after Incarceration." *Criminal Justice Policy Review* 17:103–123.

Bender, Steven W. 2003. *Greasers and Gringos: Latinos, Law, and the American Imagination.* New York: New York University.

Bennett, William J., John J. DiIulio, and John P. Walters. 1996. *Body Count: Moral Poverty . . . and How to Win America's War against Crime and Drugs.* New York: Simon & Schuster.

Besemer, Sytske, Victor van der Geest, Joseph Murray, Catrien C. J. H. Bijleveld, and David P. Farrington. 2011. "The Relationship between Parental Imprisonment and Offspring Offending in England and the Netherlands." *British Journal of Criminology* 51:413–437.

Braman, Donald. 2002. "Families and Incarceration." In *Invisible Punishment: The Collateral Consequences of Mass Imprisonment,* edited by Marc Mauer and Meda Chesney-Lind. New York: New Press.

Braman, Donald. 2007. *Doing Time on the Outside: Incarceration and Family Life in Urban America.* Ann Arbor: University of Michigan Press.

Branch, Marie Louise, and Sabrina A. Brinson. 2007. "Gone But Not Forgotten: Children's Experiences with Attachment, Separation, and Loss." *Reclaiming Children and Youth* 16:42–45.

Bronfenbrenner, Urie. 1979. *The Ecology of Human Development: Experiments by Nature and Design.* Cambridge, MA: Harvard University Press.

Burnette, Denise. 1999. "Social Relationships of Latino Grandparent Caregivers: A Role Theory Perspective." *The Gerontologist* 29:49–58.

Burton, Linda M. 1992. "Black Grandmothers Rearing Children of Drug Addicted Parents: Stressors, Outcomes and Social Service Needs." *The Gerontologist* 32:744–751.

Capaldi, Deborah M., and Gerald R. Patterson. 1991. "Relation of Parental Transitions to Boys' Adjustment Problems: I. A Linear Hypothesis: II. Mothers at Risk for Transitions and Unskilled Parenting." *Developmental Psychology* 27:489–504.

Carson, E. Anne, and William J. Sabol. 2012. *Prisoners in 2011*. Washington, DC: US Department of Justice.

Chavez, Leo R. 2008. *The Latino Threat: Constructing Immigrants, Citizens, and the Nation*. Stanford, CA: Stanford University Press.

Chaudry, Ajay, Randy Capps, Juan Manuel Pedroza, Rosa Maria Castañeda, Robert Santos, and Molly M. Scott. 2010. *Facing Our Future: Children in the Aftermath of Immigration Enforcement*. Washington, DC: Urban Institute.

Cho, Rosa. 2009. "The Impact of Maternal Imprisonment on Children's Probability of Grade Retention: Results from Chicago's Public Schools." *Journal of Urban Economics* 65:11–23.

Cho, Rosa. 2011. "Understanding the Mechanism behind Maternal Imprisonment and Adolescent School Dropout." *Family Relations* 60:272–289.

Clear, Todd R. 2002. "The Problem with 'Addition by Subtraction': The Prison–Crime Relationship in Low-Income Communities." In *Invisible Punishment: The Collateral Consequences of Mass Imprisonment*, edited by Marc Mauer and Meda Chesney-Lind. New York: New Press.

Clear, Todd R. 2007. *Imprisoning Communities: How Mass Incarceration Makes Disadvantaged Neighborhoods Worse*. New York: Oxford University Press.

Clear, Todd R., Dina R. Rose, and Judith A. Ryder. 2001. "Incarceration and the Community: The Problem of Removing and Returning Offenders." *Crime & Delinquency* 47:335–351.

Clear, Todd R., Dina R. Rose, Elin Waring, and Kristen Scully. 2003. "Coercive Mobility and Crime: A Preliminary Examination of Concentrated Incarceration and Social Disorganization." *Justice Quarterly* 20:33–63.

Coleman, James. 1988. "Social Capital in the Creation of Human Capital." *American Journal of Sociology* 94:S95–S120.

Coleman, James. 1990. *Foundations of Social Theory*. Cambridge, MA: Harvard University Press.

Comfort, Megan. 2003. "In the Tube at San Quentin: The 'Secondary Prisonization' of Women Visiting Inmates." *Journal of Contemporary Ethnography* 32:77–107.

Comfort, Megan. 2008. *Doing Time Together: Love and Family in the Shadow of the Prison*. Chicago: University of Chicago Press.

Cox, Martha J., and Blair Paley. 1997. "Families as Systems." *Annual Review of Psychology* 48:243–267.

Crosnoe, Robert, and Shannon E. Cavanagh. 2010. "Families with Children and Adolescents: A Review, Critique, and Future Agenda." *Journal of Marriage and the Family* 72:594–611.

Cullen, Francis T., Bonnie S. Fisher, and Brandon Applegate. 2000. "Public Opinion about Punishment and Corrections." In *Crime and Justice: A Review of Research*, Vol. 27, edited by Michael Tonry and Joan Petersilia. Chicago: University of Chicago Press.

Cullen, Francis T., and Karen E. Gilbert. 2013. *Reaffirming Rehabilitation, 30th Anniversary Edition*. Waltham, MA: Anderson.

Cullen, Francis T., and Cheryl Lero Jonson. 2012. *Correctional Theory: Contexts and Consequences*. Thousand Oaks, CA: Sage.

Cummings, E. Mark, and Patrick T. Davies. 2010. *Marital Conflict and Children: An Emotional Security Perspective*. New York: Guilford Press.

Currie, Elliot. 1998. *Crime and Punishment in America*. New York: Henry Holt.

DiIulio, John J. 1994. "Let 'em Rot." *The Wall Street Journal*, January 26, p. A14.

Dunifon, Rachel., and Lori Kowaleski-Jones. 2002. "Who's in the House? Race Differences in Cohabitation, Single Parenthood, and Child Development." *Child Development* 73:1249–1264.

Eddy, J. Mark, and Julie Poehlmann. 2010. *Children of Incarcerated Parents: A Handbook for Researchers and Practitioners*. Washington, DC: Urban Institute Press.

Foster, Holly, and John Hagan. 2007. "Incarceration and Intergenerational Social Exclusion." *Social Problems* 54:399–433.

Frost, Natasha A., and Todd R. Clear. 2009. "Understanding Mass Incarceration as a Grand Social Experiment." *Studies in Law, Politics, and Society* 47:159–191.

Frost, Natasha A., and Todd R. Clear. 2012. "New Directions in Correctional Research." *Justice Quarterly* 29:619–649.

Geller, Amanda, Irwin Garfinkel, Carey E. Cooper, and Ronald B. Mincy. 2009. "Parental Incarceration and Child Well-Being: Implications for Urban Families." *Social Science Quarterly* 90:1186–1202.

Geller, Amanda, Irwin Garfinkel, and Bruce Western. 2011. "Paternal Incarceration and Support for Children in Fragile Families." *Demography* 48:25–47.

Gest, Ted. 2001. *Crime and Politics: Big Government's Erratic Campaign for Law and Order*. New York: Oxford University Press.

Glaze, Lauren E., and Laura M. Maruschak. 2008. *Parents in Prison and Their Minor Children*. Washington, DC: Bureau of Justice Statistics.

Giordano, Peggy C. 2010. *Legacies of Crime: A Follow-Up of the Children of Highly Delinquent Girls and Boys*. New York: Cambridge University Press.

Goglia, Linda R., Gregory J. Jurkovic, Afton M. Burt, and Katherine J. Burge-Callaway. 1992. "Generational Boundary Distortions by Adult Children of Alcoholics: Child-as-Parent and Child-as-Mate." *American Journal of Family Therapy* 20:291–299.

Green, Kerry M., Margaret E. Ensminger, Judith A. Robertson, and Hee-Soon Juon. 2006. "Impact of Adult Sons' Incarceration on African American Mothers' Psychological Distress." *Journal of Marriage and the Family* 68:430–431.

Guerino, Paul, Paige M. Harrison, and William J. Sabol. 2011. *Prisoners in 2010*. Washington, DC: Bureau of Justice Statistics.

Hagan, John. 1994. *Crime and Disrepute*. Thousand Oaks, CA: Pine Forge Press.

Hagan, John, and Ronit Dinovitzer. 1999. "Collateral Consequences of Imprisonment for Children, Communities and Prisoners." In *Crime and Justice: A Review of Research*, Vol. 26, edited by Michael Tonry and Joan Petersilia. Chicago: University of Chicago Press.

Hayslip, Bert, and Patricia L. Kaminski. 2005. "Grandparents Raising Their Grandchildren: A Review of the Literature and Suggestions for Practice." *The Gerontologist* 45:262–269.

Hetherington, E. Mavis. 2003. "Intimate Pathways: Changing Patterns in Close Personal Relationships across Time." *Family Relations* 52:318–331.

Huebner, Beth M. 2005. "The Effect of Incarceration on Marriage and Work in the Life Course." *Justice Quarterly* 22:281–301.

Huebner, Beth M. 2007. "Racial and Ethnic Differences in the Likelihood of Marriage: The Effect of Incarceration." *Justice Quarterly* 24:156–183.

Immigration and Customs Enforcement, Department of Homeland Security. 2012a. "Deportation of Parents of U.S.-Born Citizens: Fiscal Year 2011 Report to Congress, Second Semi-Annual Report." March 26. http://www.scribd.com/doc/87388663/ICE-Deport-of-Parents-of-US-Cit-FY-2011-2nd-Half

Immigration and Customs Enforcement, Department of Homeland Security. 2012b. "FY 2012: ICE Announces Year-End Removal Numbers, Highlights Focus on Key Priorities and Issues New National Detainer Guidance to Further Focus Resources." December 24. http://www.ice.gov/news/releases/1212/121221washingtondc2.htm

Irwin, John. 2005. *The Warehouse Prison: Disposal of the New Dangerous Class*. Los Angeles: Roxbury.

Irwin, John, and James Austin. 1994. *It's About Time: America's Imprisonment Binge*. Belmont, CA: Wadsworth.

Kruttschnitt, Candace. 2011. "Is the Devil in the Details? Crafting Policy to Mitigate the Collateral Consequences of Parental Incarceration." *Criminology & Public Policy* 10:829–837.

LeBlanc, Adrian Nicole. 2003. *Random Family: Love, Drugs, Trouble, and Coming of Age in the Bronx*. New York: Scribner.

Legomsky, Stephen H. 2007. "A New Path of Immigration Law: Asymmetric Incorporation of Criminal Justice Norms." *Washington and Lee Law Review* 64:469–528.

Lopoo, Leonard M., and Bruce Western. 2005. "Incarceration and the Formation and Stability of Marital Unions." *Journal of Marriage and the Family* 67:721–734.

Lynch, James P., and William J. Sabol. 2001. *Crime, Coercion, and Communities: The Effects of Arrest and Incarceration Policies on Informal Social Control in Communities*. Washington, DC: National Institute of Justice.

Lynch, James P., and William J. Sabol. 2004. "Assessing the Effects of Mass Incarceration on Informal Social Control in Communities." *Criminology & Public Policy* 3:267–294.

Martinez, Ramiro Jr. 2002. *Latino Homicide: Immigration, Violence, and Community*. New York: Routledge.

Maruna, Shadd. 2011. "Reentry as a Rite of Passage." *Punishment & Society* 13:3–28.

Massey, Douglas S. 2007. *Categorically Unequal: The American Stratification System*. New York: Russell Sage Foundation.

Menjívar, Cecilia. 2012. "Transnational Parenting and Immigration Law: Central Americans in the United States." *Journal of Ethnic and Migration Studies* 38:301–322.

Migration Policy Institute. 2012. "As Many as 1.76 Million Unauthorized Immigrant Youth Could Gain Relief from Deportation under Deferred Action for Childhood Arrivals Initiative. "August 7. http://www.migrationpolicy.org/news/2012_08_07.php

Mucowski, Richard J., and Robert Hayden. 1992. "Adult Children of Alcoholics: Verification of a Role Typology." *Alcoholism Treatment Quarterly* 9:127–140.

Murray, Joseph, and David P. Farrington. 2008. "The Effects of Parental Imprisonment on Children." In *Crime and Justice: A Review of Research*, Vol. 27, edited by Michael Tonry and Joan Petersilia. Chicago: University of Chicago Press.

Murray, Joseph, David P. Farrington, and Ivana Sekol. 2012. "Children's Antisocial Behavior, Mental Health, Drug Use, and Educational Performance After Parental Incarceration: A Systematic Review and Meta-Analysis." *Psychological Bulletin* 138:175–210.

Murray, Joseph, Rolf Loeber, and Dustin Pardini. 2012. "Parental Involvement in the Criminal Justice System and the Development of Youth Theft, Marijuana Use, Depression, and Poor Academic Performance." *Criminology* 50:225–302.

Mustillo, Sarah A., Shannon Dorsey, Kate Conover, and Barbara J. Burns. 2011. "Parental Depression and Child Outcomes: The Mediating Effects of Abuse and Neglect." *Journal of Marriage and the Family* 73:164–180.

Pager, Devah. 2003. "The Mark of a Criminal Record." *American Journal of Sociology* 108:937–975.

Parke, Ross D., and K. Allison Clarke-Stewart. 2003. "The Effects of Parental Incarceration on Children: Perspectives, Promises, and Policies." In *Prisoners Once Removed: The Impact of Incarceration and Reentry on Children, Families, and Communities*, edited by Jeremy Travis and Michelle Waul. Washington, DC: Urban Institute Press.

Peterson, Ruth, and Lauren Krivo. 2010. *Divergent Social Worlds: Neighborhood Crime and the Racial- Spatial Divide.* New York: Russell Sage Foundation.

Pettit, Becky, and Bruce Western. 2004. "Mass Imprisonment and the Life Course: Race and Class Inequality in U.S. Incarceration." *American Sociological Review* 69:151–169.

Phillips, Susan D., Wendy Cervantes, Yali Lincroft, Alan J. Dettlaff, and Lara Bruce. 2013. *Children in Harm's Way: Criminal Justice, Immigration Enforcement, and Child Welfare.* Washington, DC: The Sentencing Project and First Focus.

Poehlmann, Julie. 2003. "An Attachment Perspective on Grandparents Raising their Very Young Grandchildren: Implications for Intervention and Research." *Infant Mental Health Journal* 24:149–173.

Portillos, Edwardo L. 2006. "Latinos, Gangs, and Drugs." In *Images of Color, Images of Crime,* edited by Coramae Richey Mann, Margorie S. Zatz, and Nancy Rodriguez. Los Angeles: Roxbury.

Pratt, Travis C. 2009. *Addicted to Incarceration: Corrections Policy and the Politics of Misinformation in the United States.* Thousand Oaks, CA: Sage.

Pratt, Travis C. and Francis T. Cullen. 2005. "Assessing Macro-Level Predictors and Theories of Crime: A Meta-Analysis." In *Crime and Justice: A Review of Research,* Vol. 32, edited by Michael Tonry. Chicago: University of Chicago Press.

Pruchno, Rachel A., and Dorothy McKenney. 2002. "Psychological Well-Being of Black and White Grandmothers Raising Grandchildren: Examination of a Two-Factor Model." *Journal of Gerontology* 57:444–452.

Putnam, Robert. (2000) *Bowling Alone: The Collapse and Revival of American Community.* New York: Simon and Schuster.

Rabin, Nina. 2011. *Disappearing Parents: A Report on Immigration Enforcement and the Child Welfare System.* Tucson: University of Arizona. http://sirow.arizona.edu/sites/sirow.arizona.edu/files/disappearing_parents_report_final.pdf

Roettger, Michael E., and Raymond R. Swisher. 2011. "Associations of Fathers' History of Incarceration with Sons' Delinquency and Arrest among Black, White, and Hispanic Males in the United States." *Criminology* 49:1109–1147.

Rose, Dina R., and Todd R. Clear. 1998. "Incarceration, Social Capital, and Crime: Implications for Social Disorganization Theory." *Criminology* 36:441–480.

Ruggles, Steven. 1994. "The Transformation of American Family Structure." *American Historical Review* 99:103–128.

Sameroff, Arnold. 1994. "Developmental Systems and Family Functioning." In *Exploring Family Relationships with Other Social Contexts,* edited by Ross D. Parke and Sheppard G. Kellam. Hillsdale, NJ: Erlbaum.

Sampson, Robert J. 1995. "Unemployment and Imbalanced Sex Ratios: Race-Specific Consequences for Family Structure and Crime." In *The Decline in Marriage among African Americans: Causes, Consequences, and Policy Implications,* edited by M. Belinda Tucker and Claudia Mitchell-Kernan. New York: Russell Sage Foundation.

Sampson, Robert J. 2011. "The Incarceration Ledger: Toward a New Era in Assessing Societal Consequences." *Criminology & Public Policy* 10:819–828.

Sampson, Robert J. 2012. *Great American City: Chicago and the Enduring Neighborhood Effect.* Chicago: University of Chicago Press.

Sampson, Robert J., and Charles Loeffler. 2010. "Punishment's Place: The Local Concentration of Mass Incarceration." *Daedalus* 139:20–31.

Sampson, Robert J., Stephen W. Raudenbush, and Felton Earls. 1997. "Neighborhoods and Violent Crime: A Multilevel Study of Collective Efficacy." *Science* 227:916–924.

Schwartz-Soicher, Ofira, Amanda Geller, and Irwin Garfinkel. 2011. "The Effect of Paternal Incarceration on Material Hardship." *Social Service Review* 85:447–473.

Shlafer, Rebecca J., Julie Poehlmann, and Nancy Donelan-McCall. 2012. "Maternal Jail Time, Conviction, and Arrest as Predictors of Children's 15-year Antisocial Outcomes in the Context of a Nurse Home Visiting Program." *Journal of Clinical Child and Adolescent Psychology* 41:38–52.

Siegel, Jane A. 2011. *Disrupted Childhoods: Children of Women in Prison*. Piscataway, NJ: Rutgers University Press.

Smith, Sandra Susan. 2008. "'Don't Put My Name on It': Social Capital Activation and Job Finding among the Black Urban Poor." *American Journal of Sociology* 111:1–57.

Suárez-Orozco, Carola, Irina L.G. Todorova, and Josephine Louie. 2002. "Making Up for Lost Time: The Experience of Separation and Reunification among Immigrant Families." *Family Process* 41:625–643.

Tasca, Melinda, Nancy Rodriguez, and Marjorie Zatz. 2011. "Family and Residential Instability in the Context of Paternal and Maternal Incarceration." *Criminal Justice and Behavior* 38:231–247.

Triplett, Ruth A., Randy R. Gainey, and Ivan Y. Sun. 2003. "Institutional Strength, Social Control and Neighborhood Crime Rates." *Theoretical Criminology* 7:439–467.

Turanovic, Jillian J., Nancy Rodriguez, and Travis C. Pratt. 2012. "The Collateral Consequences of Incarceration Revisited: A Qualitative Analysis of the Effects on Caregivers of Children of Incarcerated Parents." *Criminology* 50:913–959.

Turney, Kristin, Jason Schnittker, and Christopher Wildeman. 2012. "Those They Leave Behind: Paternal Incarceration and Maternal Instrumental Support." *Journal of Marriage and Family* 74:1149–1165.

Van de Rakt, Marieke, Joseph Murray, and Paul Nieuwbeerta. 2012. "The Long-Term Effects of Parental Imprisonment on Criminal Trajectories in Children." *Journal of Research in Crime and Delinquency* 49:81–108.

Varsanyi, Monica W. 2010. *Taking Local Control: Immigration Policy Activism in U.S. Cities and States*. Stanford, CA: Stanford University Press.

Wakefield, Sara, and Christopher Uggen. 2010. "Incarceration and Stratification." *Annual Review of Sociology* 36:387–406.

Wessler, Seth Freed. 2011. "U.S. Deports 46K Parents with Citizen Kids in Just Six Months." *Colorlines*, November 3. http://colorlines.com/archives/2011/11/shocking_data_on_parents_deported_with_citizen_children.html

Wessler, Seth Freed. 2012. "Nearly 205K Deportations of Parents of U.S. Citizens in Just Over Two Years." *Colorlines*, December 17. http://colorlines.com/archives/2012/12/us_deports_more_than_200k_parents.html

Western, Bruce. 2006. *Punishment and Inequality in America*. New York: Russell Sage Foundation.

Western, Bruce, Leonard M. Lopoo, and Sarah McLanahan. 2004. "Incarceration and the Bonds between Parents in Fragile Families." In *Imprisoning America: The Social Effects of Mass Incarceration*, edited by Mary Patillo, David Weiman, and Bruce Western. New York: Russell Sage Foundation.

Western, Bruce, and Christopher Muller. 2013. "Mass Incarceration, Macrosociology, and the Poor." *Annals of the American Academy of Political and Social Science* 647:166–189.

Western, Bruce, and Christopher Wildeman. 2009. "The Black Family and Mass Incarceration." *Annals of the American Academy of Political and Social Science* 621:221–242.

Whitaker, Robert C., Sean M. Orzol, and Robert S. Kahn. 2006. "Maternal Mental Health, Substance Use, and Domestic Violence in the Year after Delivery and Subsequent Behavior Problems in Children at Age 3 Years." *Archives of General Psychiatry* 63:551–560.

Wildeman, Christopher, Sara Wakefield, and Kristin Turney. 2013. "Misidentifying the Effects of Parental Incarceration? A Comment on Johnson and Easterling (2012)." *Journal of Marriage and Family* 75:252–258.

Wilkinson, D. (1987). "Ethnicity." In *Handbook of Marriage and the Family*, edited by S. K. Steinmetz and M. B. Sussman. New York: Plenum.

Wilson, William J. 1987. *The Truly Disadvantaged: The Inner City, the Underclass, and Public Policy*. Chicago: University of Chicago Press.

CHAPTER 10

···

THE TWO CULTURES
Correctional Officers and Key Differences in Institutional Climate

···

ALISON LIEBLING AND DEBORAH KANT

At the end of the day, nothing else that we can say will be as important as the general proposition that *"staff professionalism"* and *"legitimate practices" are at the heart of the whole prison system* and that control and security flow from getting these right.

> Liebling 2011, p. 485, revising the May Committee statement,
> Home Office 1984

What makes a good officer? . . . I don't know. It must be a pretty hard balance because I mean you've got to try and develop your interpersonal relationships with others so that you can control an environment without resorting to violence every minute of the day. And you've got to be aware of security requirements as well. I think . . . you need somebody who's very comfortable with themselves so that they feel secure enough . . . I'm sure a lot of it comes with experience and time in the job and . . . you know, learning from past errors and so forth, but I think you need people with brains . . . I don't think it's just a matter of being able to turn up here . . . I think there's a lot more to it.

> Liebling, Price, and Shefer 2011, p. 1

ONE of the most striking characteristics of prisons within a single jurisdiction is the extent to which they differ. Despite the tendency in prison sociology to attempt to characterize "the prison," and the mechanical familiarity and rigidity of the typical prison day or routine, there are important and significant moral and relational differences between them. These differences in the forms and legitimacy of the power being deployed reflect distinct visions of who prisoners are (e.g., Lerman 2013) and distinct emotional and cultural climates (Liebling, assisted by Arnold 2004). Since human beings can only survive and flourish in environments containing "the virtues" (of justice, recognition, and humanity), some prison environments are literally more survivable for prisoners than others (Liebling 2014). More legitimate prison climates generate fewer suicides and less violence and may lead to better outcomes on release (Liebling 2015b). Prison climates are always more legitimate where less use is made of imprisonment in the first place.

The question addressed in this chapter is: What role do prison officers play in the institution's social climate? Does their orientation toward prisoners shape the moral climate, or levels of violence, in prison? What explains correctional officers' well-documented distrust of managers, their cynicism toward correctional reform, and their alienation from liberal humanitarian goals (Thomas 1972)? Are the explanations structural and inherent in the prison? Or do correctional staff cultures differ so greatly across prisons that other explanations must play a part?

This chapter suggests that there are two basic cultures detectable in prisons: the "professional-supportive" and the "resistant-punitive." One is more prevalent and powerful than the other, but both require explication if we are to describe and understand the prison and its variations more fully. The two cultures described are "ideal types," and the variations between even poor cultures are, like bad families, many and significant. The two ideal types are grounded in empirical research. There are common features of each correctional staff culture, including the presence of hierarchy, the dominance of idealized masculine strength, and a susceptibility to abuses of power. But partly because of this susceptibility, the most positive as well as the most negative examples of prison staff culture stand in need of theoretical explanation. The less common examples of outstanding and progressive staff cultures may be fragile, imperfect, and exceptional, but they require authentic description and reconciling with existing theories of prison staff culture. Measuring institutional climates closely, and drawing on ethnography-led measurement (see Liebling 2015a), helps in the task of understanding these complex aspects of institutional life and culture.

This chapter begins with an outline of "the two cultures." In Section I we describe the "professional-supportive" culture. In Section II we outline the "traditional-resistant" culture, before returning to the existing literature and some empirical evidence in the light of our account of these "ideal types." In Section III we draw on Muir's (1977) analysis of cynical and tragic perspectives in relation to the use of power, and the distinctive orientation toward prisoners these perspectives support. In Section IV we draw on survey data from three establishments to illustrate four different institutional climates: (a) "traditional-resistant," (b) "contested," (c) "traditional-relational," and (d) "professional-skilled." Finally, in Section V we call for a more refined research agenda on prison staff cultures, and more effective methods of measurement of institutional cultures, in the future.

We draw the following main conclusions:

- Prison staff cultures shape institutional climate and affect the survivability of the prison environment.
- Prison staff cultures fall into two broad types: the "professional-supportive" and the "traditional-resistant." The first type is overlooked in empirical research.
- At their best, "professional-supportive" officers embody the "tragic" perspective. They are future-focused moral dualists, who tend to be confident, authoritative, and prisoner oriented.

- "Traditional-resistant" officers embody the "cynical" perspective. They tend to be authoritarian, nostalgic, resistant to change, security driven, and staff oriented.
- "Tragic" or "cynical" perspectives influence officers' orientations toward safety, control, and the purpose of prison work. These orientations shape institutional climates within the prison setting.

I. Penal Climates at Their Best: Professional Authority Embodied

Eighty percent of the costs of a prison are accounted for by staff. In the same way, we argue, around 80 percent of the "moral climate" in a prison can be accounted for by staff attitudes and practices. They are gatekeepers to activities, people, goods, and services, and the best prison officers are also skilled "peacekeepers" (Toch 1976; Liebling, Elliott, and Price 1999). Counterintuitively, given the punishment function of the prison, in practice the best officers offer "containment" in the therapeutic-psychoanalytic rather than increasingly salient penal sense, offering "supportive limit setting" or combining authority and discipline with care (Liebling, assisted by Arnold 2004).[1] They embody and generate structure-as-support, as well as structure-as-order, with confidence, engaging positively with prisoners and getting to know them well. They are leaders and effective negotiators.

These kinds of officers can be described as "traditional-professional"; that is, they have professional pride, they respect the rules but use them wisely, and they operate with considerable, well-judged discretion aimed at the accomplishment of social order (Liebling, Price, and Shefer 2011; Crewe, Liebling, and Hulley 2014). They have patience, energy and physical courage. They have an open and nondefensive style and show a willingness to use force, but as a last resort (Liebling 2011). They are supportive, honest, and good humored. They recognize, but know how to manage, their own emotions and those of others (Arnold 2005). They are authentically grounded in the harsh realities of prisoners' lives but see offenders as people with futures, and themselves as equipped to help bring about a better future. They are interested in finding the way forward with troubled, difficult individuals, and in the meaning of behavior. They believe in the importance of human relationships in growth and development. They have an optimistic, but realistic, outlook and a capacity and willingness to resolve rather than exacerbate conflict. They have consistent, clearly communicated boundaries, moral strength, verbal skills, and an awareness of the effects of their own power on prisoners, as well as an understanding of the painfulness of prison. They can keep calm under pressure, are reliable, and can use their most prized skill—straight talk—with even the most challenging prisoners. They use authority appropriately, neither avoiding nor over-claiming it (Hepburn 1975; Gilbert 1977; Liebling, Price, and Shefer 2011). They are physically fit and have interests beyond the prison, often in sports, practical hobbies, family life, and the community.

These officers may have had exposure to diverse and vulnerable populations as part of their own life experience. They hold a "tragic" perspective on the use of imprisonment as inherently flawed (Muir 1977; Liebling 2011; see also Garland 1990). The best officers are "moral dualists," combining the values of authority, safety, security, predictability, and stability (the *protective* values) with those of respect, tolerance, cooperation, and the development of individual potential (*other-oriented* values). This value combination (e.g., of punctuality or cleanliness, with generosity and forgiveness) is both rare and demanding (Ohlin 1960; Braithwaite 1994; Liebling, assisted by Arnold 2004). Paradoxically, moral character is as important in successful prison officer work as technical skill.

These kinds of officers are not "typical" but can be found everywhere in prison systems, albeit in small numbers. They tend to appear disproportionately in small, special and therapeutic wings,[2] where they have cultural permission and time to work progressively with prisoners. They may not be aware of, or be able to articulate, their own skills but regard much of what they do as "common sense" (Sparks, Bottoms, and Hay 1996). As one of us has argued elsewhere (Liebling, Elliott, and Price 1999; Liebling, Price, and Shefer 2011; see also Hay and Sparks 1991) this is far from the case. Their skills represent a kind of "practical consciousness," acquired and refined over time, although they may build on strong foundations based on aspects of character, personality, and prior life or work experience. These officers work hard and often have some passion for their professional organization, establishment, and vocation. The many and varied characteristics described above are by no means exclusively masculine, but there is a kind of idealized "masculine strength"— controlled, courageous, and steeped in camaraderie—detectable in the account. This has its dangers, as we acknowledge more fully below. Where officers of this variety are present in reasonable numbers, the climate is characterized by the "professional use of authority" (see Crewe, Liebling, and Hulley 2011, 2014) and prisoners describe a less damaging prison experience (Liebling 2006, 2007).

II. The Characteristics of "Traditional-Resistant Cultures"

The above account has its opposite, in "traditional-resistant" staff cultures. Despite some important variations (Liebling, assisted by Arnold 2004), there is a "typical" ("hard end") large local public sector prison culture, often (but not exclusively) found in the largest and oldest local prisons in the United Kingdom (which serve the courts, housing prisoners awaiting trial and serving short sentences). These establishments tend to have long-serving staff who are "trapped in the past." This means they operate according to a set of attitudes and beliefs shaped by romanticized "relics of repression" (Morris and Morris 1968, p. 161). During the late 1990s and early 2000s, several reports published by Her Majesty's Chief Inspector of Prisons (HMCIP 1999a,b,c; 2000a,b,c,d)[3] attributed the state of "failing prisons" (a term used at the annual prison governors' conference by then Chief Executive Martin Narey) to the negative influence of recalcitrant, change-resistant staff cultures (HMCIP 2000d, p. 6) inhabited by officers who were "firmly stuck in days long gone" (HMCIP 2000a, p. 24). Thomas (1972) suggests that these cultures are the result of a paramilitary service designed to exert control. In these past-oriented cultures, containment of a different kind, linked to control, is prized above care and rehabilitation:[4]

> Back in them early days it was absolutely us and them. Everybody was ex-military—you played hard. We were very unprofessional, but extremely effective . . . . You hurt me and I'm going to hurt you more. That was how the whole place existed. That's how 1555 men could be kept completely subdued by 600. (Senior officer, in Kant in progress)

My secondary goal then moves to the prisoners—I'll treat them all with equal contempt, if you like. I will treat them firmly but fairly. You'll . . . if you are in genuine need I will go out of my way to help you. If you are the average prisoner, who just moans and groans for the sake of it, you will get nothing. Piss off, I'm not even interested, I'm not even going to listen. (Senior officer, in Kant in progress)

My job first and foremost is to protect the public and make sure that none of these get out. I stop you getting raped and murdered because I work here. (Senior officer, in Kant in progress)

Liebling, Price, and Shefer (2011) argued that negative traditional cultures are characterized by a preoccupation with discipline, distrust of management, resistance to change, cynicism, and a negative stance toward care for prisoners. These attitudes can coalesce into punitive or neglectful regimes, and other forms of brutality. Managers in such institutions can experience significant obstruction to the introduction of new practice as change is dismissed in favor of "the way things have always been done around here":

You get them less now, but there's the staff who've been in twenty-five years and think, "well, I've done it like this for this long and I'm alright, so I'm not going to change for you or anyone." (Officer, in Kant in progress).

The poorest staff cultures tend to be found in the public sector rather than in the newly experimental and incentives-driven private sector (e.g., Page 2011; Crewe, Liebling, and Hulley 2011, 2014), although as the private sector expands globally, examples of such cultures have been reported (e.g., Hopkins 2015). They operate according to a security or custodial model of confinement (a "no frills" model, in which prisoner rehabilitation is absent as a goal). This reflects the most limited vision of the prison officer role and is reactive. It tends to be characterized by indifferent, aggressive, and punitive attitudes, and demoralization or laziness. There is a lack of engagement with prisoners and a staff orientation (that is, overt self-interest) among officers, for example in the organization of the prison day. There is direct resistance to senior managers, often demonstrated in artificially high sickness absence, and resentment of its management. There is a preoccupation with discipline and an over-reliance on the use of segregation (over control). There are frequently reprisals for, or resistance to, prisoner complaints (prisoners describe this as bullying). Staff display a cynical orientation, which includes hostility to, and suspicion of, specialists and outsiders. They often operate a restricted regime (with a reliance on, but indifference to, cell buzzers when prisoners need attention or assistance). System processes, or the mechanics of a limited regime ("system maintenance"), are prioritized over rehabilitation, or meaningful or creative activities.

In these cultures, there is often delegation of some power to "trusted" prisoners or favorites (a form of "unofficial bargaining"; see Liebling et al. 2015). These prisoners are disproportionately white, are often long-serving, and tend to be "respectable criminals" (for example, those involved in fraud or organized crime) who are generally well disposed toward authority (see Cohen and Taylor 1972; Liebling et al., in progress). Recent research has found that prisoners with a history of military or naval service may appear disproportionately in this framework. Generalized sexism (which can be targeted at female staff, uniformed and otherwise) and racism may also characterize these cultures (see Cheliotis and Liebling 2006). Staff are often out of touch with prisoners in these climates: They may misperceive prisoners as compliant and assenting and overestimate the quality of relationships and the regime. While wings or units within the prison may vary in quality, these cultures are resilient and difficult to change. The "regime" (the daily routine of the prison in which tasks are accomplished according to a predetermined timetable—essentially a set of social practices requiring actions; see Sparks, Bottoms, and Hay 1996) is unresponsive, inactive, and restricted: there is a lack of "delivery" of essential services to prisoners. They are well oiled in the sense that routines are implemented without "drift," but staff may lock up earlier than necessary and unlock late, curbing prisoners' access to valued time carrying out domestic tasks or speaking with family members on the phone.

The local Prison Officers' Associations in these establishments are often powerful. The mode of authority is cynical (that is, heavy, casual, and sometimes overtly punitive). Security is dominant. There is much pride and peer loyalty among staff (as well as loyalty to "their prison") but little vision or "professional morality." Staff tend to be exceptionally good at, or preoccupied by, "maintaining edge" or status in these establishments (Tait 2011). There is often an absence of vision among managers as well as staff in these prisons, with a "traditional" composition of the senior management team (older men of mixed ability, about whom staff are also cynical). The buildings and infrastructure in these establishments tend to be poor, but architecture is not determinative: Some of the best staff cultures can be found in outdated and dilapidated buildings. Prisoners in these kinds of cultures describe a lack of care, stagnation, and a feeling of indifference and brutality. There may be outstanding staff in these "thoughtless" prison environments, but they are frequently isolated and burned out.

Many examples of such cultures exist in the literature (e.g., Clemmer 1940; Thomas and Pooley 1980; Kauffman 1988; Owen 1988; Fleisher 1989; Scraton, Sim, and Skidmore 1991; Jameson and Allison 1995; Farkas 1997; Cook and Davies 1999; Conover 2000; Zimbardo 2007; Page 2011). Liebling and Crewe provide an account of prison governors in England and Wales describing their own exposure to such cultures while under training, and their powerlessness to challenge or shape them (Liebling and Crewe 2012). Such studies are important but arguably dominate the field, to the exclusion of some important variations. Some of the earliest studies reflect a kind of standoff between officers and sociological researchers, whereby little empirical description is included and staff remain distant figures, as we describe below.

In the first systematic sociological study of the prison community, Clemmer briefly described officers as "the wheel-horses of the prison" (Clemmer 1940, p. 62)—their main occupation was long hours of repetitive drudgery for little pay. Conducted at the height of unemployment during the Great Depression, Clemmer described a staff body that had been somewhat reinvented after "many of the older, poorly trained, poorly disciplined, and lazy job-holders" were replaced by "younger, more interested, and efficient men" (Clemmer 1940, p. 64). Despite the national employment shortage during the period, the work of correctional officers represented little prospect of promotion, and few officers with prospects stayed past four years. Clemmer portrays the guards in his study as a largely disinterested group who had undergone a process of "acculturation" (Crawley 2004, p. xv) to the existing institutional climate, which refocused their priorities on the implementation of discipline over reform. They were at best disinterested and in search of an easy life; at worst they had "a spirit of retaliation towards inmates" (Clemmer 1940, p. 185). Guard culture, Clemmer argued, was an exaggerated version of the society they inhabited in the outside world— prison work reflected the values and preoccupations of the general public, intensified.

One of the first UK studies to include an account of prison officers is Morris and Morris's sociological study of Pentonville prison, published in 1968. HMP Pentonville is a Category B male local prison serving the courts of North London. The prison was built in 1842. It was the first Victorian prison in England and Wales to be modeled on the "Pennsylvania system" of silence and separation. The prison was built in the traditional radial design of four wings emanating from a center. The approach to and portrayal of officers in the book is harsh and unforgiving, although the culture was undeniably brutal. It was "a prison in which reformist, punitive and apathetic attitudes are quite fantastically confused" (Morris and Morris 1968, p. 106). Their chapter on "the prison staff" draws on observations and interviews with 52 staff who agreed to be interviewed as part of the Morris's study. Twenty-six staff—disproportionately long serving and "Pentonville only" staff—declined. Three were "intensely and actively hostile towards the research." The controversies of this book when published related to a depiction of the staff as very similar to prisoners in their backgrounds, values, and culture. The comparisons are graphic and include an observation (made by a prison officer) that Pentonville is a "dumping ground for the poorest officer material" (Morris and Morris 1968, p. 99–100). The authors hypothesize that the prisoner "tends to be the expression of his own worst self."

On the other hand, the authors' accounts of the split between those officers with a vocation and those trapped or hostile toward the job, of other conflicts and resentments between staff from different specialties or areas, of the monotony experienced in their work, their organizational "malaise" or confusion, and lack of enthusiasm, their fear of the forces of permissiveness and their nostalgia for discipline, and their despair of the idealism of "headquarters," are all recognizable in contemporary prisons. The Morris's accounts of the way officers use "an excess of power," decide on the worthiness of prisoners, and use formal reporting processes differently, and yet find that prisoners can make things happen that they cannot, are insightful and sensitive and anticipate some of the work carried out on prison officers since (see Sparks, Bottoms, and Hay 1996; Crawley 2004; Crewe, Liebling, and Hulley 2011; Liebling, Price, and Shefer 2011).

Cohen and Taylor's account of Durham's high-security prison, carried out in the late 1960s, is also typical of the approach to research on prisons and prison officers found in sociological studies at this time. The two young sociology lecturers, who were delivering a series of seminars to prisoners, were identified by staff with the "general forces of permissiveness." They took an explicit stance toward the officers from the outset ("we were foolish enough to visit the officers' social club"; Cohen and Taylor 1972, p. 44). Officers saw them as "in league" with prisoners. They saw themselves as engaging in a *reciprocal granting of elite status*: "We are university teachers, they are Category A prisoners. Outside on the landing sat the plebs" (Cohen and Taylor 1972, p. 33). Despite this being one of the best studies of the experience of long-term imprisonment available (see further, Liebling in press), the authors' orientation toward officers is dismissive, selective, and lacking in scholarly curiosity.

A more detailed and sympathetic account of the role of "The English Prison Officer since 1850" was published by J. E. Thomas in 1972 (the "first serious attempt at a study of the prison officer to match the scores of books on the prisoner and prison culture"; Fairn 1973, p. 100). Thomas argued that prison officers were structurally embedded in a major conflict of role, and that this confusion—between security and rehabilitation—formed the substance of much of the history of prison work and culture. He argued that, as the penal system's officials declared increasingly reformative goals, prison officers were excluded from their implementation:

> In spite of assertions that the officer has been . . . associated with these goals . . . his role has always been to control . . . his success or failure as an officer is measured against his ability to do that. In fact, his opportunities to take on work which is not solely custodial, have been narrowed in the past ninety years. (Thomas 1972, p. xiv)

Thomas argued that the paramilitary (uniformed and hierarchical) and "crisis-controlling" structure of prison staff organization inevitably resulted in a top-down occupation where training was limited, discretion was minimal, and tasks were clearly prescribed. In this kind of organization, discipline and custody were primary and were naturally embodied in the role of the chief officer—the highest uniformed rank until organizational reforms made it possible for prison officers to rise into the governor grades in 1986. Prestigious specialist work was offered to others appointed for the purpose or became the preserve of nonuniformed (direct entrant) governor grades (fast-tracked university graduates), increasingly regarded by the organization as the moral guardians of their charges but as naïve, misguided, and privileged by uniformed staff. The "golden age of prison reform" (1930s–1970s) left officers to one side, to be castigated as obstructive, antireformist opponents of "progress" (Thomas 1972, pp. 152–180). There were important exceptions, for example the "Norwich system" (Emery 1970) and Grendon Underwood therapeutic community (Genders and Player 1995), but, in general, officers' attempts to become more professionally involved in welfare were unsuccessful. Officers watched discipline decline and became caught up in an alienating position, on the one hand "protesting about the ill-effects of reformation" and on the other "demanding that they be involved in it" (Thomas 1972, p. 206). This ambivalence toward "progressive" work, the tension between this and traditional prison work (and the organization of it), and a preference for the custodial and control tasks, characterized the English prison officer:

> The English prison service from 1877 to 1965, in which most of the features of the officer's role were established, had a clear task. It was a small service, tightly knit and organized in a para-military structure. Since there was clarity of task there was clarity of role. As a result the Commissioners knew what kind of officers they were looking for . . . The Gladstone Committee[5] began that process of organisational confusion which, even at a distance of seventy years, culminated in the Mountbatten Report.[6] These years saw the increasing alienation of the prison officer from the aims of the organisation, aims which he found confusing, and in some cases, repugnant. A very important factor in this alienation was the drawing together of the Commissioners and governor grades, and the prisoners . . . The variation of the governor's role to that of a reformer, led the officers to believe that they were now second in importance to the prisoners. (Thomas 1972, p. 218)

There are other explanations for officers' ambivalence about rehabilitative work with prisoners. Like the police, prison staff culture is thought to arise as a coping mechanism in response to a dangerous occupational and ambiguous organizational environment (Terrill, Paoline, and Manning 2003). Clearly prison officers face problems in their work, including exposure to danger, a feeling of individual accountability when things go wrong, a sense of feeling invisible to and misunderstood by senior managers, and, increasingly, inroads being made into their pay and working conditions in the face of private sector competition. Prison staff carry out unpopular work, with conflicting goals, behind the scenes, in a low-visibility arena. Their failures (escapes, suicides, disturbances) receive far more attention from the public and from managers and politicians than their successes. Under these conditions, prison staff tend to adopt an insular, conservative, and somewhat defensive posture, and to focus on their own safety. In prisons with poor cultures in particular, staff tend to express these sentiments powerfully, and to feel undervalued and overly preoccupied with control. This type of culture is not universal, however.

III. Tragedy, Cynicism, Relationships, and Power

It is clear that the policing literature has much to offer those interested in studying the work of prison officers. There is a longer history of explorations of police staff culture (linked to their greater visibility), and many of the same patterns of legitimate/illegitimate uses of power and order/disorder arise (see, for example, Lord Scarman's report of the Brixton riots, 1981, in which disproportionate and indiscriminate policing of the black community led to violent protest, and the more recent account of the London 2011 riots by Newburn 2015). Interestingly, the underuse of police powers can be as significant in major disturbances as the (especially selective) overuse of police powers (Waddington 2007).

Just as in policed communities, in prisons, different "policing" styles arise in different prison locations. The nature and quality of adjudications in different areas of a prison or between prisons, for example, can indicate this. Some wings have higher rates of offenses against prison discipline, but staff on those wings also tend to bring charges against prisoners for different offense types, ranging from assaults on one wing to threatening and abusive language and disobeying a lawful order on another (see Sparks, Bottoms, and Hay 1996; Liebling and Price 2001). Staff responses to prisoner behavior are different, reflecting their "policing priorities" and their vision of what or whom represents a threat to order. It is a truism in prison management that the best prison officers use informal tactics of conflict resolution first, and that resorting to disciplinary procedures is, in some sense, a failure of authority. Relationships, and the ways in which they are built, deployed, and broken by staff (and prisoners), are fundamental in shaping the way power works in prison.

In a continuing "dialogic" cycle of approach and response, officers establish relationships of some kind with prisoners, and these relationships then influence the type of power they can use. Too much power, of the wrong sort, unmediated by relationships, can generate resistance (for a case study, see Liebling 2000). The six types of power bases staff might draw upon in a prison, as set out by Hepburn 1985, are: (i) coercive power (segregation, searches, transfer, and the disciplinary system); (ii) reward power (the distribution of privileges, prized jobs, or favorable reports); (iii) legitimate power (formal authority, or the "rule of law"); (iv) exchange power (the informal reward system, or under-enforcement); (v) expert or "professional" power (expertise—e.g., in resolving conflicts, or competence); and (vi) respect or personal authority (the manner of working with prisoners, or leadership skills). Too much use of exchange and reward power can become "collusion and laxity;" too much use of coercive power can be alienating and can become "heavy." Different power bases are emphasized or made available to staff over time and may vary according to the resources, training and professional development, and management style of the prison.

The two "ideal type" models of officer orientation—the "traditional-professional" and the "traditional-resistant"—can be understood using Muir's analysis of "tragic" and "cynical" perspectives in policing (Muir 1977). William Muir suggested in his classic study of police recruits under development that two aspects of his/her character shape conduct: attitude toward the use of coercion and attitude toward the human condition. Officers could have either a "tragic" view of the world ("one that sees individuals as essentially alike") or a "cynical" view that regards human beings as falling into two camps, the good and the bad. The tragic view sees common ground between human beings and understands the importance of context in human decision making. Muir argues that three interrelated elements of the police officer's working personality—"their intellectual outlook on the world, their emotional feelings about power and their self-imposed moral definitions of success" (p. 14–15) shape decision making in different ways. Liebling found that three key aspects of the working lives of prison officers in particular (their attitudes toward safety, their attitudes toward discipline, and their levels of confidence) vary according to this "tragic" versus "cynical" disposition (Liebling 2011). Prison staff cultures can be characterized using this framework.

Underlying each culture is a distinct criminology of the offender. The security-custody model (the cynical perspective, in Muir's typology) tends to regard offending as the result of individual choice and individual offenders as "other." An observation by a specialist staff member at Pentonville illustrates this perspective: "There are murderers and whatnot on these landings. These aren't normal people. They aren't like you and me" (Kant in progress). Offenders cannot be trusted, are dangerous and manipulative, and may condition naïve staff. The professional perspective (the tragic perspective, in Muir's typology) makes room for a more discretionary approach to offenders and to the possibilities for change (or "treatment" in a now old-fashioned language). In this model, prisoners can be trusted, for the right reasons, and more complex judgments are made about when and how such guarded forms of trust might be extended. Each culture is based upon a different vision of the prisoner, a different approach to relationships, a distinct vision of the accomplishment of order, and, linked to this, a different approach to power.

Muir's typology is useful in showing that both laxity (the underuse of power) and overbearing heaviness arise from a "cynical" position (Table 10.1). The "enforcer" and the "avoider" are both cynical, adopting a dualistic view of human nature, but they have distinct

Table 10.1. Typology of officer working personalities

	Enforcer	Reciprocator	Avoider	Professional
Perspective	Cynical	Tragic	Cynical	Tragic
Morality of Coercion	Integrated	Conflicted	Conflicted	Integrated
Passion	Yes	No	No	Yes
Perspective	No	Yes	No	Yes
Definition and standards of success	Perfectionist	Interactive	Easy life	Not exacting (realistic)

approaches to the use of coercion. The enforcer embraces it with enthusiasm (here, passion) or is overeager to use it. The avoider feels conflicted about it, and so chooses the "easy life."

The reciprocator and the professional share a tragic view of human nature, empathizing with human frailty, but the reciprocator is conflicted about coercion whereas the professional has integrated or accepted it. The professional is morally reconciled to the use of coercion, yet at the same time can reflect empathetically on the condition of mankind. He or she does not rush to use it but will do so when it is required. This is a fundamental and distinctive characteristic of the best officers and is a difficult position to maintain.

Distinct visions of safety, order, and prison work arise from these positions (Table 10.2). So, for example, "reassurance safety" is a defensive strategy based on maintaining distance and control, whereas "relational safety" resembles a more dynamic, interactive, and confident model of authority grounded in a vision of prisoners as "redeemable" and capable of good action. "Reassurance safety" (Model A) represents "discipline" and "relational safety" (Model B) represents "good authority" (Liebling 2000; Mulgan 2007; Liebling in press). The models correspond broadly with the "situational" versus "social" approaches to order

Table 10.2. Officer orientations toward safety

A. Reassurance safety (Cynical)	B. Relational safety (Tragic)	C. Disregard for safety
Suspicion: prisoners as manipulative; self-harm as a threat to authority	Approachability, accessibility; (some) trust	Avoidance or indifference
Vigilant (distant) observation	Interactive observation	Non-observation
Resort to force	Intervenes verbally in fights and disputes	Does not see incidents
Reactive	Proactive	Not active
Controlled/restricted unlock	Unlock a priority	Flexibility
Assistance limited	Practical help offered	"Sloping shoulders"
Maintaining "edge," aggression, control	Humor, banter, talk	Naïveté, unclear boundaries
Yearning for (more) discipline, swift resort to disciplinary procedures	Informal resolution of conflicts; comfortable with amount of power	Resignation
IEP[1] as punishment and control	IEP as primarily reward and progression	IEP not used
Specialists as "risk"	Specialists as "support"	
Police "access" to civilians, resources (and prisoners)	Facilitate access to civilians, resources (and prisoners)	
Resist implementation of new initiatives	Less resistance to implementation of new initiatives (conditional)	

[1] Incentives and earned privileges: a system of (mainly material) rewards and sanctions for behavior.

outlined by Sparks and Bottoms in their study of problems of order (Sparks and Bottoms 1995) and with the "security" versus "harmony" distinction outlined in *Prisons and Their Moral Performance*, with Model A representing a security orientation. The cynical, dualistic, "us/them" approach to prison work described above, in which danger becomes the "determinant of [the officer's] personal philosophy" (Muir 1977, p. 182) produces the need for reassurance safety; the tragic perspective, whereby empathy and a sense of perspective are maintained, produces a more relational (and effective, in the longer term) vision of safety. The tragic perspective "presupposes that all individuals possessed simultaneously qualities of civility and rebellion" (Muir 1977, p. 182).

Model C, a disregard for safety, found in some newly emerging under-resourced prisons, is characterized by indifference and resignation and can also be regarded as "cynical." In Model A establishments, staff often wield considerable power and yet feel a need for more, whereas staff in Model B establishments tend to use (and feel the need for) less. Professional confidence shapes officers' model of safety and their perceptions of risk and danger (see further Liebling 2007; Liebling, Arnold, and Straub 2012).

These kinds of differences in models of safety and officer orientation can be found at wing level in establishments (Liebling 2011). Prisoners identify "the best officers" as "professional" officers who do not rely on their coercive authority to achieve safety but who are comfortable in their relationships with prisoners and can command respect via an authoritative presence combined with support. Power flows more unobtrusively, and effectively, on these wings or in these kinds of establishments. These essentially qualitative distinctions can be captured using a combination of survey and interview questions asked of both prisoners and staff.

IV. Measuring Staff Culture and Institutional Climate

A team of researchers at the Institute of Criminology in Cambridge have attempted over a number of years to develop meaningful measures of these complex relational aspects of an institution's climate. One aspect of this work has been an attempt to operationalize and measure aspects of staff culture, including their orientation toward prisoners and senior managers (the SQL survey; see Liebling 2007; Liebling, Price, and Shefer 2011). Since prison staff are not always reliable evaluators of their own performance and orientation (they can feel under pressure to report "as officers should" rather than as how they work, and they are not always aware of the complexities of their approach in practice), data from prisoners about their quality of life may be a more reliable indicator of the institutional climate than staff self-report data (although we have drawn selectively on some of the staff data below).[7] Some areas within the prisoner survey are particularly instructive.

The "MQPL" (Measuring the Quality of Prison Life) survey is a "tick box questionnaire" for prisoners designed and refined over several research projects aimed at improving our understanding of prison life and its effects. Unlike many surveys used to measure prison quality, it has a highly standardized format but has been developed analytically and inductively from extensive, grounded explorations with staff and prisoners, including observations about what matters in prison, drawing on the method of Appreciative Inquiry (see

Liebling, assisted by Arnold 2004). It has an underlying conceptual framework incorporating notions of legitimacy, "right relationships," and "value balance." The concepts of "staff–prisoner relationships," "staff professionalism," and "use of authority" have emerged as key components in this framework (e.g., Crewe, Liebling, and Hulley 2011; Liebling 2011), confirming the centrality of the work of prison officers to the quality of life in prison. The survey consists of 21 of these kinds of empirical-conceptual dimensions, including "respect," "humanity," "fairness," "organization and consistency," "policing and security," "personal development," and "well-being," which reflect aspects of prison life that matter most (for a detailed account of its development and current content, see Liebling, assisted by Arnold 2004; and Liebling, Price, and Shefer 2011). Each dimension is represented via a series of statement-items with which prisoners are invited to agree or disagree on a five-point Likert scale. We refer to this methodology as *ethnography-led measurement* (Liebling 2015a). Its administration is supplemented by qualitative exploration, and the dimensions in it are grounded in qualitative work. Reading and interpreting the survey results is therefore a qualitative as well as quantitative exercise. The quantitative data help to "check," direct, and inform the overall analysis. One way of reading the data is to look at which dimensions score three or above. These scores arguably reflect the "value culture" of the establishment (see Liebling, assisted by Arnold 2004, Chapter 4, for further detail).

The MQPL Dimensions with the most significant variation between prisons are also those that tend to have the lowest overall mean scores[8] (suggesting both that it is difficult to "do well" on these dimensions and that prisons differ significantly in accomplishing them). They are "staff professionalism," "organization and consistency," "staff–prisoner relationships," "fairness," "decency," "help and assistance," and "bureaucratic legitimacy."[9] Prisons with the lowest scores on these dimensions, as experienced by prisoners, tend to be characterized by more "traditional-resistant" staff cultures. In more professional-supportive cultures, prisoners report feeling safe, receiving help and support, and feeling able to focus on and find opportunities for personal development. These results tend to hold true across the prison estate and are relatively unaffected by the age or gender of prisoners or the security category of the establishment. Table 10.3 shows the dimension results in these key areas from four distinct prison climates in three prisons: two "poor end" local prisons, an unusually relational maximum-security prison, and a special, psychologically informed planned environment within that prison. These are illustrative, and many other prison climates could have been chosen. These four climates might be described as (i) "traditional-resistant" (cynical), (ii) "contested" (a mixture of "traditional-resistant" and "traditional-professional"), (iii) "traditional-relational," and (iv) "professional-skilled." Prisoners reported entirely different experiences in these four settings. We would also expect them to have quite different outcomes. We briefly describe aspects of these climates, drawing on a number of research exercises, below.

A. "Traditional-Resistant"

The climate at Pentonville showed many of the characteristics of the negative culture described above: a culture still associated with traditional and poor- or lower-performing public sector local prisons (see Liebling 2007; Liebling 2012; and Kant in progress). Officers

Table 10.3. Dimension scores in four prison climates

MQPL Dimensions	HMP Pentonville	HMP Birmingham	HMP Frankland	HMP Frankland PIPE
	2011 $N = 111$ "Traditional-resistant" (cynical)	2011 $N = 111$ "Contested" (mixed)	2014 $N = 165$ "Traditional-relational" (tragic)	2014 $N = 5$ "Professional-skilled" (tragic)
Staff–prisoner relationships	2.88	2.91	3.06	4.10
Staff professionalism	2.99	3.14	3.14	3.87
Bureaucratic legitimacy	2.52	2.59	2.34	2.64
Fairness	2.63	2.60	2.69	3.60
Organization and consistency	2.39	2.46	2.84	3.63
Decency	2.53	2.54	2.83	3.96
Help and assistance	2.93	2.85	3.00	3.80
Personal development	2.62	2.68	2.85	4.15

at Pentonville operated to an "us versus them" paradigm that distanced or denigrated managers and prisoners. Officers were nostalgic and cynical, and while not expressing overtly hostile feelings, they excelled in a form of "passive" resistance to the implementation of change (Ministry of Justice 2011; Liebling 2012; Kant in progress). The climate was characterized by apathy, exhaustion, and indifference to prisoners' needs:

> They drag their feet here. Unless you have someone—a governor or something—behind you to exert pressure, nothing gets done, and unfortunately that is the Pentonville way. (Specialist staff member, in Kant in progress)

Officers were preoccupied with safety, yet they simultaneously neglected important control and security aspects of their work and reported "stepping back" from the landings and from prisoners: They felt "too unsafe" to enforce the rules. This preoccupation with their own safety led to further feelings of intimidation, in a vicious circle of distance from and "othering" of prisoners. The prison was short of staff, exacerbated by high rates of sickness absence and high staff turnover. In a climate of resentment, staff shortages contributed to feelings of stress and overwork; officers reported feeling disconnected from the prison and its mission and unable to do the job that others wanted them to do:

> That's the problem with Pentonville,—it's just constantly people walking around saying "well that's not my job, so I'm not doing it", instead of just getting on with something that needs doing. (Senior Officer, in Kant in progress)

As we have found in other prisons, staff were uncomfortable with a changing, more diverse population of prisoners and felt unable to deal with the unique challenges they presented (see Liebling, Arnold, and Straub 2012). As staff withdrew from the landings, they reported relying on established relationships with known, "professional" (white, mature adult) prisoners. They worked increasingly in a culture of uncertainty. One of the most important aspects of their job was relying on backup from their colleagues in the face of violence, but many officers reported they no longer felt certain that this support would come. A few officers commented that when they *had* found themselves in danger, their colleagues had not responded to alarms (see also Liebling, Arnold, and Straub 2012). These narratives of fear, risk, and disintegration of "the officer code" made their way through the establishment. Some officers admitted to nurturing closer relationships with a few trusted prisoners they felt would support them in a crisis while at the same time withdrawing from prisoners as a group. They felt that rehabilitation was not possible due to the nature of the local population, the shortage of staff, and the infrastructure of the prison. These dynamics have been seen in other "low resource" model prisons (see Symkovych 2011; Akoensi 2014; Liebling et al. 2015).

Relationships within the staff group were fractured. The prison had experienced several publicized incidents of staff corruption, and the staff group had been affected by these experiences. There was a trend, especially among long-serving, male officers, to see inexperienced staff as especially susceptible to corruption, and many officers reported that they were consciously limiting their interactions with incoming staff for fear of being affected. Differentials in pay and conditions contributed to this climate. Prisoners reported a lack of information or responsiveness to complaints and applications, inconsistencies in the regime, and an inability to "get things done." Staff were described by prisoners as lazy, disrespectful, and antagonistic (see Ministry of Justice 2011).

B. "Contested"

Somewhat similarly, in a recent study of Birmingham prison conducted by the authors and colleagues, clear signs of this "Pentonville" culture were found (Liebling et al. 2015). Birmingham prison shared many similarities with Pentonville. It was built in 1849; it is a "typical" traditional, busy, and complex public sector local prison, with poor buildings and infrastructure, occupied by long-serving but therefore highly experienced staff who had been operating a well-oiled but restricted regime to a mainly "cynical" or overly casual model of authority for many decades. For example, prisoners complained that staff did not unlock them on time—a typical characteristic of a "traditional" culture reflected in daily practice. Prisoners had to "choose between a shower or exercise." Applications and letters went missing. Staff did not mix with prisoners on the exercise yard. The prison was operating an impoverished, inconsistent, and, some would argue, brutal regime.

In a survey of prisoners' quality of life carried out in 2012, 73 percent of the prisoners agreed that they were "doing" rather than "using" time. Forty-seven percent did not feel that they were "treated as a human being." Prisoners reported that they were spoken to "like shit" by the "bad" staff, who responded to requests with, for example,

"I don't give a shit" and "fuck off." Fifty-four percent of prisoners agreed that "staff are argumentative," and 73 percent of prisoners agreed that "to get things done they had to ask and ask and ask." Prisoners felt tension and frustration in their daily lives. Sixty-one percent of prisoners indicated that their time at Birmingham felt "very much like a punishment." Fifty-eight percent felt that their "experience in this prison had been stressful," and half disagreed that "Birmingham is a decent prison." An Inspectorate Report on Birmingham prison published in December 2011 described prisoners' existence as "pitiful."

The prison staff at Birmingham were not the most cynical we have surveyed, but they were not actively assisting prisoners. Twenty-one percent of uniformed staff agreed that "most prisoners are decent people," compared to zero percent at another prison, Garth, for example (see Crewe, Liebling, and Hulley 2011). Twenty-six percent of staff believed that "most prisoners can be rehabilitated" (44 percent disagreed). Eighty-three percent of staff agreed that "officers should be involved in rehabilitation programmes."

One of the distinctive characteristics of the culture at Birmingham, however, was the way some staff challenged or complained about others. Eighty-six percent of staff agreed that "some staff get away with coasting in this prison." Complacent or unwilling colleagues had "held the prison back" and staff were on the whole (despite the emotional toll that departures and disciplinary action took on all staff) hopeful that "lazy" or "incompetent" staff (including managers of all grades) would be exposed under a privatization exercise that brought with it new working conditions. Some staff felt "liberated" by an unprecedented program of reform (which included privatizing the prison) aimed at improving its quality. Over time, we saw some aspects of the quality of life at Birmingham improve and some of the better professional uses of authority gather strength (see Liebling et al. 2015; Liebling and Ludlow under review).

C. "Traditional-Relational"

At Frankland, we observed something very different. At this maximum-security prison, we found long-term prisoners reporting somewhat more positively about their relationships with staff and significantly higher levels of "organization and consistency." This (and the still relatively low score for "bureaucratic legitimacy") was in part due to the longer-term population and the closer management oversight and procedural specifications for high-security prisons, but the scores throughout the survey also reflect a more individualized and progressive culture, in which prisoners felt "known" and somewhat helped (e.g., 55 percent of prisoners agreed or strongly agreed that "I have been helped significantly by a member of staff in this prison with a particular problem," and 42 percent agreed or strongly agreed that "I feel I have been encouraged to address my offending behaviour in this prison"). At Frankland, a friendly interpersonal style, a more professional use of authority, and a more helpful orientation toward prisoners generated a better overall climate and a significantly less negative score on "personal development." We have found considerably higher scores than these in some local prisons (e.g., see our account of Altcourse in Crewe, Liebling, and Hulley 2011, 2014), showing that prison type, or security level, is not the most important determinant of institutional climate.

D. "Professional-Skilled"

In a much more positive prison climate within the overall more "relational" prison (Frankland's Psychologically Informed Planned Environment [PIPE][10]), prisoners reported very high scores for these dimensions. There were up to 21 prisoners on the unit, and many spoke with passion and energy about their experiences on this and a related unit in Frankland (Westgate) for 55 prisoners diagnosed with severe personality disorder. The purpose of both units was to support prisoners with complex needs and personality-related difficulties. Staff had received additional training, supervision, and support from psychologists and specialists in mental health, and this greater understanding encouraged them to provide support and to attribute meaning to difficult or challenging behavior. Staff understood the importance of creating a supportive environment and had increased psychological understanding of their work. This model also operates in other settings and prison types. Prisoners rated the relationships they had with staff outstandingly positively and also rated their own personal development very highly. The only dimension not to score above three was "bureaucratic legitimacy," but it scored significantly higher than in the other three sites and was shaped to a larger degree than the other dimensions by external characteristics of the long and complex sentences being served, the security categorization process, and the length of time it took to make progress. Prisoners were so enthusiastic about the climate they experienced in this unit that they sometimes interrupted the research interviews to invite their personal officers in to provide a joint account of "the progress they had made." Staff and prisoners talked about it as "a progression environment" and extensive use was made of the creative arts and music, as well as structured activities. Staff on the unit had been through their own "transformation" process, as they moved from "being a dinosaur," or occupying a "traditional-cynical" position, to "finding individual pathways for prisoners." They seemed particularly skilled at the therapeutic (as opposed to punitive) art of "containment" whereby "the [staff member] has sufficiently understood the nature and degree of the anxiety or emotional pain, the patient feels soothed and able to think more clearly without having to resort to acting out" (Mollon 1993, p. 188). As one prisoner said:

> This unit has allowed me to be myself, and bond and make relationships with staff. I was the last person anyone could trust. They listened to me, and worked with me. I am a different person now. (Prisoner, PIPE)

Staff were enthusiastic and motivated in their work, saying: "we know it's good. You see change." Their model of prisoners was of "complex people on a journey" and they collaborated with specialist staff of all grades and varieties to "support prisoners" on this personal development trajectory (see Turley, Payne, and Webster 2013).

These are imperfect comparisons, as so many prison comparisons are, due to differences in function, population, architecture, and geographical location, but our purpose in making them here is to show that (a) prison climates can be conceptualized and evaluated in meaningful ways, (b) careful measurement can be highly informative, and (c) staff cultures differ in ways that "ethnography-led measurement" can illuminate, and that challenge and supplement some of the taken-for-granted assumptions of prison sociology. The officers in prisons 3 and 4 (and in others we have studied) are selected, and paid, in the same way as officers in prisons 1 and 2. The climates, and outcomes, are very different.

V. Conclusion

Prison staff remain remarkably understudied sociologically compared to their counterparts in the police, despite their clear significance in shaping the quality of life, the "penal field" (Page 2011), and the meaning of punishment for prisoners. Prison officers often share concerns with prisoners, or mirror their experience, so that issues of fairness, dignity, and well-being stand out in their accounts of their experience (e.g., Liebling 1994; Cox 2013), and are regarded, as they are by prisoners, as in short supply. Establishing the links between staff attitudes, values, and behavior and the treatment of prisoners should be a methodological as well as a theoretical priority.

Much of the "institutional climate" in a prison is determined by the behavior and practices of prison staff. They "embody" a prison's regime, shaping how much authority and control, and of what kind, is exerted over prisoners. Their role is symbolic and infused with meaning, but it can be occupied in quite different ways. Prisoners *feel* their imprisonment via the actions and orientations of prison staff and respond differently to these different approaches to control. Power can be used arbitrarily or consistently, heavily or lightly (Crewe, Liebling, and Hulley 2014). Prisoners prefer the boundaries to be set by officers rather than by other prisoners, so the underuse of power can be as treacherous in its outcomes as the overuse of power. Deficiencies in some power bases lead to the establishment of others, so that insufficient coercive power may lead to the establishment of reciprocity or "exchange" (accommodations). This is especially likely in low-resource model prisons. The best prison officers enforce their authority rather than "the rules." They are willing, not reluctant, nor overeager, to use force. The use of language rather than action is central to the effective use of authority, but as talk becomes more guarded, prison staff sometimes feel disabled and cautious about what can be said to whom (Liebling, Arnold, and Straub 2012). The best officers can justify each decision they make in terms of a broad set of principles that would apply to all like cases. This makes them moral actors—a role often felt to be the exclusive preserve of their senior managers. Despite some fundamental changes to their working conditions in neoliberal countries (for example, reductions in their pay, conditions, and numbers), prison officers are still "figures with power"—the *moral* power of regard and recognition, and the *instrumental* or material powers of access, distribution, and force. Prisoners have as much to say about officers' moral power to grant or withhold respect and recognition as they do about access to material goods and services in describing the quality of their lives in prison, although they might not use this terminology (see Liebling, assisted by Arnold 2004).

Prison sociologists should take the practices, attitudes, and effects of prison officer cultures more seriously and should attempt to describe them and the variations between them authentically and in more detail. Studies often explore what prison officers *think* rather than what they do, in part because access is difficult and also because prison ethnography is time-consuming and in conflict with institutional priorities (Simon 2002). Recent research (particularly in Europe) has begun to focus more ethnographically on the work and working lives of prison officers (e.g., Johnsen, Helgesen, and Granheim 2011; Nylander, Lindberg, and Bruhn 2011; Kolind et al. 2015), and there exist some helpful recent quantitative analyses of staff attitudes and their relationship to aspects of institutional life and culture (e.g., Byrne,

Taxman, and Hummer 2005, 2007; Lerman and Page 2012; Lerman 2013). Distinctions between prison staff cultures are underemphasized in research.[11] Empirical exploration shows that staff can create either safety, support, and assurance among prisoners or fear, frustration, anxiety, and distress, leading to higher rates of violence, disorder, and suicide, and a different, more oppositional form of prisoner leadership (Liebling, Durie, Stiles, and Tait 2005; Liebling 2015b). There is a "dark side" to prison culture, but that is not all there is to describe and explain.

Paradoxically, prison officers report feeling relatively powerless, in a hierarchical organization that increasingly treats them as commodities. Their power is largely downward-facing. In relation to their managers, and the organization, they are relatively subordinate, except when representing, or being represented by, their union (see Page 2011).

Toch and Klofas (1982) suggest that long-serving officers who spent their formative years working in authoritarian, rigid regimes may experience difficulty adapting to modern, more "lenient" times. Arguably, those lenient times are now barely in view, and penal systems are being reshaped in both cost-cutting and punitive ways. So this raises new questions for prison sociology and the exploration of prison climates: How do contemporary prison officers regard their work? How do they use their power, and with what ends in mind? How much of what kind do they have? What shapes the approach they take to the power they hold, and what impact does this have on their relationships with prisoners? How confident are they in making claims about which kinds of power they draw on? What do they see as the main source of their legitimacy—security, public protection, or the meeting of standards of justice (Bottoms and Tankebe 2012)? How do prison officers regard those they imprison? Are prisoners human beings with futures? Under what circumstances does this vision become possible? Finally, in the current climate of spending less money on more prison places, is there a link between resources, officer stress, and punitiveness? Page and Lerman suggest that there is.

Notes

1. The importance of "containment" to growth and development in the field of juvenile delinquency formed an important part of the standard work of early criminology (e.g., Winnicott 1984; Casement 1985; Bowlby 1988), but its practice has been associated professionally with social work rather than prison work. The recent development (and relative success) of "enabling environments" or "psychologically informed planned environments" brings it back into the penal field, albeit in a challenging (more punitive) climate. See later.
2. Like Grendon, Psychologically Informed Planned Environments (PIPEs), and historically in some small units for difficult prisoners (see Bottomley, Liebling, and Sparks 1994).
3. In particular, those for Birmingham, Brixton, Chelmsford, Feltham YOI, Preston, Rochester, and Wandsworth.
4. "Past-oriented cultures" are characterized by generalized nostalgia rather than precise historical context.
5. Gladstone Report. The Departmental Committee on Prisons was established under the chairmanship of Herbert Gladstone in 1894. It was a response to intense criticism by newspapers and periodicals such as *The Daily Chronicle* and *The Fortnightly Review* of

the existing prison system and of the Chairman of Prison Commissioners, Edmund Du Cane. Though the Committee accepted that deterrence must lie at the heart of penal policy, it also stressed the ability of prisons to reform offenders and made various recommendations to this effect. Du Cane resigned a few days after the report was published. He was succeeded by Evelyn Ruggles-Brise. The period following the Gladstone Report saw the establishment of borstal training, open prisons, greater emphasis on treatment and training, and the symbolic promotion of the purpose of helping prisoners to lead a "good and useful life" to Rule 1 (now Rule 3) of the Prison Rules. (The Prison Rules govern the management of prisons and incorporate guidelines on the treatment of prisoners, the duties of staff, and the powers of the Independent Monitoring Board. Rule 3 states: "The purpose of the training and treatment of convicted prisoners shall be to encourage and assist them to lead a good and useful life."

6. The Mountbatten Report into escapes and security (Home Office 1966) established the rank of senior officer and the system of security categorization that is still in use today.

7. Some items in the staff survey are highly instructive, so that high agreement with a single item, "prisoners who attempt suicide are usually being manipulative and attention-seeking," predict a more "traditional-resistant" and cynical culture overall. See the correspondence with "reassurance safety" and the cynical perspective in Table 10.2. See further Liebling (2007).

8. On a five-point scale, where a "3" is a neutral score; anything above it reflects positive evaluations by prisoners and anything below it reflects negative evaluations overall.

9. The dimensions are defined as follows: help and assistance: "support and encouragement given to prisoners for problems including drugs, healthcare and progression;" staff professionalism: "staff confidence and competence in the use of authority;" bureaucratic legitimacy: "the transparency and responsiveness of the prison/prison system and its moral recognition of the individual;" organization and consistency: "the clarity, predictability and reliability of the prison;" personal development: "an environment that helps prisoners with offending behaviour, preparation for release and the development of their potential" (see further Liebling, Price, and Shefer 2011; Liebling et al. in progress).

10. A PIPE is a "whole unit" rather than "treatment" approach based on the principles of the Enabling Environment, an initiative led by the Department of Health, the NHS, and the NOMS Personality Disorder Team and supported by (among other things) the Good Lives model (Ward, Mann, and Gannon 2007). It is "a place where positive relationships promote well-being for all participants; where people experience a sense of belonging; where all people involved contribute to the growth and well-being of others; where people can learn new ways of relating; a place that recognises and respects the contributions of both parties in a helping relationship and that recognises that carers also need to be cared for" (Turner and Bolger 2015). There are 10 PIPEs in prisons in England and Wales.

11. Some studies have explicitly compared prison cultures, usually by comparing two or occasionally more prisons (e.g., Vinter and Janowitz 1959; Berk 1966; Street, Vinter, and Perrow 1966; Sparks, Bottoms, and Hay 1996; Kruttschnitt and Gartner 2000). Very few explore within-security-level differences, which we find to be highly significant (Liebling et al. in progress). The account we develop here is aimed at elucidating in particular a distinction between more or less legitimate forms of staff power embodied in various cultures.

References

Akoensi, Thomas. 2014. *A Tougher Beat? The Work, Stress and Well-Being of Prison Officers in Ghana*. PhD dissertation, University of Cambridge.

Arnold, Helen. 2005. "The Effects of Prison Work." In *The Effects of Imprisonment*, edited by Alison Liebling and Shadd Maruna. Cullompton, Devon: Willan Publishing.

Berk, Bernard. 1966. "Organizational Goals and Inmate Organization." *American Journal of Sociology* 71:522–534.

Bottomley, Keith, Alison Liebling, and Richard Sparks. 1994. *Barlinnie Special Unit and Shotts Unit: An Assessment*. Scottish Prion Service Occasional Paper no. 7/1994, Edinburgh: Scottish Prison Service.

Bottoms, Anthony E., and Justice Tankebe. 2012. "Beyond Procedural Justice: A Dialogic Approach to Legitimacy in Criminal Justice." *Journal of Criminal Law and Criminology* 102:119–170.

Bowlby, John. 1988. *A Secure Base: Parent–Child Attachment and Healthy Human Development*. London: Routledge.

Braithwaite, Valerie. 1994. "Beyond Rokeach's Equality-Freedom Model: Two-Dimensional Values in a One-Dimensional World." *Journal of Social Issues* 50(4):67–94.

Byrne, James, Faye Taxman, and Donald Hummer. 2005. *An Evaluation of the Implementation and Impact of NIC"s Culture Initiative*.

Byrne, James, Faye Taxman, and Donald Hummer. 2007. *The Culture of Prison Violence*. Boston, MA: Allyn and Bacon.

Casement, Patrick. 1985. *On Learning from the Patient*. London: Tavistock Publications.

Cheliotis, Leonidas, and Alison Liebling. 2006. "Race Matters in British Prisons: Towards a Research Agenda." *British Journal of Criminology* 46:286–317.

Clemmer, Donald. 1940. *The Prison Community*, New York: Holt, Rinehart and Winston.

Cohen, Stanley, and Laurie Taylor. 1972. *Psychological Survival: Experience of Long-Term Imprisonment*. Harmondsworth: Penguin Books.

Cook, Sandy, and Susanne Davies, eds. 1999. *Harsh Punishment: International Experiences of Women's Imprisonment*. Boston, MA: Northeastern University Press.

Conover, T., ed. 2000. *Newjack: Beyond the Stereotype of the Brutal Guard*. New York: Random House.

Cox, Alexandra. 2013. "Juvenile Facility Staff Responses to Organizational Change." State University of New York, New Paltz.

Crawley, Elaine M. 2004. *Doing Prison Work. The Public and Private Lives of Prison Officers*. Portland, OR: Willan Publishing.

Crewe, Ben, Alison Liebling, and Susie Hulley. 2011. "Staff Culture, the Use of Authority, and Prisoner Outcomes in Public and Private Prisons." *Australian and New Zealand Journal of Criminology* 44:94–115.

Crewe, Ben, Alison Liebling, and Susie Hulley. 2014. "Heavy/Light, Absent/Present: Rethinking the 'Weight' of Imprisonment." *British Journal of Sociology* 65:387–410.

Emery, Fred. 1970. *Freedom and Justice Within Walls: the Bristol Prison Experiment*. London and New York: Tavistock Publications.

Fairn, Duncan. 1973. "'The English Prison Officer Since 1850: A Study in Conflict' by James E. Thomas." *British Journal of Criminology* 13(1):71–73.

Farkas, Mary Ann. 1997. "Normative Code Among Correctional Officers: An Exploration of Components and Functions." *Journal of Crime and Justice* 20:23–36.

Fleisher, Mark S. 1989. *Warehousing Violence*. London: Sage Publications.

Garland, David. 1990. *Punishment and Modern Society: A Study in Social Theory*. Oxford: Oxford University Press.

Genders, Elaine, and Elaine Player. 1995. *Grendon: A Study of a Therapeutic Prison*. Oxford: Oxford University Press.

Gilbert, Michael J. 1977. "The Illusion of Structure: A Critique of the Classical Model of Organisation and the Discretionary Power of Correctional Officers." *Criminal Justice Review* 22(1):49–64.

Hay, Will, and Richard Sparks. 1991 "What Is a Prison Officer?" *Prison Service Journal* 83:2–7.

Hepburn, John R. 1975. "The Role of the Audience in Deviant Behavior and Deviant Identity." *Sociology and Social Research* 59:387–406.

Hepburn, John R. 1985. "Exercise of Power in Coercive Organizations—A Study of Prison Guards." *Criminology* 23:145–164.

HMCIP. 1999a. *Report on an Unannounced Full Inspection of HM Prison Feltham 30 November– 4 December 1998*. London: HMCIP.

HMCIP. 1999b. *Report on a Short Unannounced Inspection of HM Prison Rochester 31 August–3 September*. London: HMCIP.

HMCIP. 1999c. *Report on an Unannounced Follow-up Inspection of HM Prison Wandsworth*. London: HMCIP.

HMCIP. 2000a. *Report on a Full Announced Inspection of HMP Birmingham 10–18 July 2000*. London: HMCIP.

HMCIP. 2000b. *Report on a Short Unannounced Inspection of HM Prison Brixton 26–29 June 2000*. London: HMCIP.

HMCIP. 2000c. *Report on an Unannounced Follow-Up Inspection of HM Prison Chelmsford 11–12 April*. London: HMCIP.

HMCIP. 2000d. *Report on a Full Announced Inspection of HM Prison Preston 14th–23rd June 1999*. London: HMCIP.

Home Office. 1966. *Report of the Inquiry into Prison Escapes and Security* (Command Paper No. 3175).

Hopkins, Ruth. 2015. "South African Prisoners Sue G4S over Torture Claims." *The Guardian* (accessed February 16, 2015).

Jameson, Nicki, and Eric Allison. 1995. *Strangeways 1990: A Serious Disturbance*. London: Larkin Publications.

Johnsen, Berit, Per K. Granheim, and Janne Helgesen. 2011. "Exceptional Prison Conditions and the Quality of Prison Life: Prison Size and Prison Culture in Norwegian Closed Prisons." *European Journal of Criminology* 8:515–529.

Kant, Deborah. In progress. *Under Threat? A Social and Occupational History of Prison Officers*. PhD dissertation, University of Cambridge.

Kauffman, Kelsey. 1988. *Prison Officers and Their World*. Cambridge, MA: Harvard University Press.

Kolind, Torsten, Vibeke A. Frank, Odd Lindberg, and Jouni Tourunen. 2015. "Officers and Drug Counsellors: New Occupational Identities in Nordic Prisons." *British Journal of Criminology* 55:303–320.

Kruttschnitt, Candace, and Rosemary Gartner. 2000. *Marking Time in the Golden State. Women's Imprisonment in California*. Cambridge: Cambridge University Press.

Lerman, Amy E. 2013. *The Modern Prison Paradox. Politics, Punishment and Social Community*. Cambridge: Cambridge University Press.

Lerman, Amy E., and Joshua Page. 2012. "The State of the Job: An Embedded Work Role Perspective on Prison Officer Attitudes." *Punishment and Society* 14:503–529.

Liebling, Alison. 1994. "Suicides Amongst Women Prisoners" *Howard Journal* 33:1–9.

Liebling, Alison. 2000. "Prison Officers, Policing and the Use of Discretion." *Theoretical Criminology* 4:333–357.

Liebling, Alison. 2006. "The Role of the Prison Environment in Prisoner Suicide and Prisoner Distress." In *Preventing Suicide and Other Self-Harm in Prison*, edited by Greg E. Dear. London: Palgrave-Macmillan.

Liebling, Alison. 2007. "Why Prison Staff Culture Matters." In *The Culture of Prison Violence*, edited by James Byrne, Faye Taxman, and Donald Hummer. Boston, MA: Allyn and Bacon.

Liebling, Alison. 2011. "Distinctions and Distinctiveness in the Work of Prison Officers: Legitimacy and Authority Revisited." *Special Issue of European Journal of Criminology* 8:484–499.

Liebling, Alison. 2012. "Pentonville Revisited: An Essay in Honour of the Morrises' Sociological Study of an English Prison, 1958–1963." *Prison Service Journal* 209:29–35.

Liebling, Alison. 2014. "Can Human Beings Flourish in Prison? Prison Phoenix Trust First Annual Lecture." London (published at http://www.theppt.org.uk/documents/Can%20Human%20Beings%20Flourish%20in%20Prison%20-%20Alison%20Liebling%20-%20May%202012.pdf).

Liebling, Alison. 2015a. "Description at the Edge? I-It / I-Thou Relations and Action in Prisons Research." *International Journal for Crime, Justice and Social Democracy* 4:18–32.

Liebling, Alison. 2015b. "Appreciative Inquiry, Generative Theory, and the 'Failed State' Prison." In *Advances in Criminological Theory: The Value of Qualitative Research for Advancing Criminological Theory*, edited by Jody Miller and Wilson Palacios. New Brunswick, NJ, and London: Transaction Publishers.

Liebling, Alison. In press. *Penal Legitimacy, Well-Being and Trust: The Role of Empirical Research*.

Liebling, Alison, Ruth Armstrong, Ryan Williams, and Richard Bramwell. In progress. *Prisons and the Problem of Trust*.

Liebling, Alison, assisted by Helen Arnold. 2004. *Prisons and Their Moral Performance: A Study of Values, Quality and Prison Life*. Oxford: Clarendon Press.

Liebling, Alison, Helen Arnold, and Christina Straub. 2012. *An Exploration of Staff–Prisoner Relationships at HMP Whitemoor: Twelve Years On*. London: National Offender Management Service.

Liebling, Alison, and Ben Crewe. 2012. "Prisons Beyond the New Penology: The Shifting Moral Foundations of Prison Management." In *Handbook on Punishment and Society*, edited by Jonathan Simon and Richard Sparks. London: Sage Publishing.

Liebling, Alison, Linda Durie, Annick Stiles, and Sarah Tait. 2005. "Revisiting Prison Suicide: The Role of Fairness and Distress." In *The Effects of Imprisonment*, edited by Alison Liebling and Shadd Maruna. Cullompton, Devon: Willan Publishing, pp. 209–231.

Liebling, Alison, Charles Elliott, and David Price. 1999. "Appreciative Inquiry and Relationships in Prison." *Punishment and Society: The International Journal of Penology* 1(1):71–98.

Liebling, Alison, and Amy Ludlow. Under review. *Privatising Public Prisons: Theory, Law and Practice*.

Liebling, Alison, and David Price. 2001. *The Prison Officer*. Cullompton, Devon: Willan Publishing.

Liebling, Alison, David Price, and Guy Shefer. 2011. *The Prison Officer*, 2nd ed. Cullompton, Devon: Willan Publishing.

Liebling, Alison, Bethany Schmidt, Ben Crewe, Katherine Auty, Ruth Armstrong, Thomas Akoensi, Deborah Kant, Amy Ludlow, and Alice Ievins. 2015. *Birmingham Prison: the Transition from Public to Private Sector and Its Impact on Staff and Prisoner Quality of Life— A Three-Year Study*. National Offender Management Service.

Ministry of Justice. 2011. *MQPL Survey Research Carried out at HMP Pentonville*. Audit and Assurance: National Offender Management Service.

Mollon, Phil. 1993. *The Fragile Self: Structure of Narcissistic Disturbance*. London: Whurr.

Morris, Terence, and Pauline Morris. 1968. *Pentonville: A Sociological Study of an English Prison*. London: Routledge.

Muir, William. 1977. *Police: Streetcorner Politicians*. Chicago and London: University of Chicago Press.

Mulgan, Geoff. 2007. *Good and Bad Power: The Ideals and Betrayals of Government*. London: Penguin.

Newburn, Tim. 2015. "The 2011 English Riots in Recent Historical Perspective." *British Journal of Criminology* 55:39–64.

Nylander, Per-Åke, Odd Lindberg, and Anders Bruhn. 2011. "Emotional Labour and Emotional Strain Among Swedish Prison Officers." *European Journal of Criminology* 8:469–483.

Ohlin, Lloyd E. 1960. "Conflicting Interests in Correctional Objectives." In *Theoretical Studies in Social Organization of the Prison* by Richard A. Cloward, Donald R. Cressey, George H. Grosser, Richard McCleery, Lloyd E. Ohlin, Gresham M. Sykes, and Sheldon L. Messinger. New York: Social Science Research Council, pp. 111–129.

Owen, Barbara. 1988. *In the Mix: Struggle and Survival in a Women's Prison*. Albany: State University of New York Press.

Page, Joshua. 2011. *The Toughest Beat: Politics, Punishment, and the Prison Officers Union in California*. New York: Oxford University Press.

Report of the Departmental Committee on Prisons. 1895. Parliamentary Papers, Cmd. 7703 (the Gladstone Report).

Scraton, Phil, Joe Sim, and Paula Skidmore. 1991. *Prisons Under Protest*. Milton Keynes: Open University Press.

Simon, Jonathan. 2002 "The Curious Eclipse of Prison Ethnography in the Age of Mass Incarceration." *Ethnography* 3:371–397.

Sparks, Richard, and Anthony E. Bottoms. 1995. "Legitimacy and Order in Prisons." *British Journal of Sociology* 46:45–62.

Sparks, Richard, Anthony E. Bottoms, and William Hay. 1996. *Prisons and the Problem of Order*. Oxford: Clarendon Press.

Street, David, Rovert D. Vinter, and Charles Perrow. 1966. *Organization for Treatment. A Comparative Study of Institutions for Delinquents*. New York: Free Press.

Symkovych, Anton. 2011. *Power Relations in a Ukrainian Prison*. PhD dissertation, University of Cambridge.

Tait, Sarah. 2011. "A Typology of Prison Officer Approaches to Care." *European Journal of Criminology* 8:440–454.

Terrill, William, Eugene A. Paoline, and Peter Manning. 2003. "Police Culture and Coercion." *Criminology* 41:1003–1034.

Thomas, John E. 1972. *The English Prison Officer Since 1850: A Study in Conflict*. London: Routledge and Kegan Paul Books.

Thomas, John E., and Richard Pooley. 1980. *The Exploding Prison*. London: Junction books.

Toch, Hans. 1976. *Peacekeeping: Police, Prisons, and Violence*. Lexington, MA: Lexington Books.

Toch, Hans, and John Klofas. 1982. "Alienation and Desire for Job Enrichment Among Correctional Officers." *Federal Probation* 46:35–44.

Turley, Caroline, Colin Payne, and Stephen Webster. 2013. *Enabling Features of Psychologically Informed Planned Environments*. National Offender Management Service.

Turner, Kirk, and Lucinda Bolger. 2015. "A Guide to Psychologically Informed Planned Environments (PIPEs)."

Vinter, Robert, and Morris Janowitz. 1959. "Effective Institutions for Juvenile Delinquents: A Research Statement." *Social Service Review* 23:118–130.

Waddington, David P. 2007. *Policing Public Disorder: Theory and Practice*. Portland, OR: Willan Publishing.

Ward, Tony, Ruth E. Mann, and Theresa A. Gannon. 2007. "The Good Lives Model of Offender Rehabilitation: Clinical Implications." *Aggression and Violent Behavior* 12:87–107.

Winnicott, Donald. 1984. *Deprivation and Delinquency*. London: Tavistock Publications.

Zimbardo, Philip. 2007. *The Lucifer Effect: Understanding How Good People Turn Evil*. New York: Random House.

SECTION III

PRISON ORDER AND DISORDER

CHAPTER 11

....

MEASURING AND EXPLAINING INMATE MISCONDUCT

....

BENJAMIN STEINER

CRIMES are behaviors that violate the criminal law (Sutherland and Cressey 1978), whereas *inmate crimes* or *misconduct* are behaviors that violate the rules of the prisons in which inmates are confined (Eichenthal and Jacobs 1991; Wooldredge 1994; Steiner and Wooldredge 2014). Institutional safety or order is often evaluated by the level of misconduct within a prison (DiIulio 1987; Bottoms 1999; Steiner and Wooldredge 2009b), and the priority that prison administrators place on these issues has generated numerous studies of the causes/ correlates to inmate misconduct.

Researchers have generally relied on three theoretical perspectives to identify potential sources of inmate misconduct. Deprivation theory suggests that inmate behaviors are manifestations of how inmates adapt and cope with the "pains" inflicted by the prison environment, whether through participation in a social system that helps to reduce these deprivations (Clemmer 1940; Sykes 1958) or through individual choices that help to facilitate need satisfaction (Goodstein, MacKenzie, and Shotland 1984; Goodstein and Wright 1989). Importation theory holds that prisons are not completely closed systems and that inmate behaviors are shaped primarily by individuals' preinstitution characteristics, beliefs, and experiences (Irwin and Cressey 1962; Irwin 1980). Management perspectives, such as administrative control theory or inmate balance theory, suggest that variation in inmate behaviors are primarily the result of differences in prison management practices (DiIulio 1987; Useem and Kimball 1989; Colvin 1992; Useem and Reisig 1999).

In this essay I review and assess these predominate theories of inmate misconduct, as well as other more general theories of criminality that have been applied to the study of misconduct. Section I describes the concept of inmate misconduct and discusses how researchers have measured the phenomenon in related studies. Section II outlines the traditional theories of inmate misconduct and evaluates each theory in terms of its empirical support and capacity to offer a comprehensive explanation of misconduct. Section III discusses the application of general theories of crime and deviance to the study of inmate misconduct. Finally, section IV offers some conclusions regarding the existing theories of inmate misconduct as well as suggestions for the study of inmate misconduct moving forward. The main conclusions discussed in this chapter are

- Inmate misconduct reflects crime and deviance within prison, and there is variation in misconduct between inmates in a prison and in misconduct rates across prisons.
- The traditional theories of inmate misconduct (deprivation theory, importation theory, and management perspectives) have each attained empirical support in the extant literature.
- None of the traditional theories of inmate misconduct offer a comprehensive explanation of inmate misconduct.
- Researchers have applied general theories of crime and delinquency to the study of inmate misconduct.
- General theories of crime and deviance offer a comprehensive explanation of misconduct and permit consideration of incarceration as a stage (or stages) in an offender's life course that may encourage desistance from offending or induce further criminality.

I. Defining and Measuring Misconduct

Accrediting agencies such as the American Correctional Association have recommended that the rules within a prison should prohibit behaviors that can have an adverse effect on the inmates (e.g., poor mental health, injury) or on institutional order and security (American Correctional Association 2003). In response to these recommendations, prison systems have typically defined inmate misconduct to include behaviors that would be considered criminal acts if they were committed within society (e.g., assaults) and behaviors that have been prohibited in an effort to maintain order and security within a prison (e.g., not remaining in designated areas, disrespecting staff). Researchers have used assorted definitions of misconduct in related studies.

Scholars have examined both self-reported and official misconduct, with the latter being used more frequently in studies published after 1990. Official measures of misconduct underestimate the volume of misconduct within a facility because many offenses go undetected. Official measures are also influenced by the discretionary decisions made by prison officials (e.g., whether a ticket is issued), and the inherent discretion in these decisions can threaten the validity of official data as an indicator of misconduct (Hewitt, Poole, and Regoli 1984; Light 1990; Steiner and Wooldredge 2014).

Self-report data can overcome the potential problems related to underestimation and recording requirements that are associated with official data. However, self-report measures can generate systematic errors resulting from poor recall and overreporting or underreporting by certain groups of respondents. Self-report data are also based on persons who agree to participate in related studies, which raises the possibility of sample selection effects (Steiner and Wooldredge 2014). These limitations aside, both self-report and official measures of misconduct are considered valid indicators of inmate behavior (Van Voorhis 1994; Steiner and Wooldredge 2014).

Researchers of misconduct have examined pooled measures of all types of rule violations combined (e.g., whether an inmate has engaged in any rule violation), while other researchers have specified their analyses by categories of misconduct such as violence, property offenses, assaults on other inmates, drug or alcohol offenses, and so forth. Consideration of specific types of rule infractions implies that some influences on misconduct may only be relevant for certain offense types, whereas focusing on a pooled measure of misconduct assumes a general explanation to inmate offending (see Gottfredson and Hirschi 1986; Blumstein, Cohen, and Farrington 1988 for related discussions concerning specialization and criminal careers in the broader criminological literature). Researchers who have examined different categories of misconduct have uncovered differences in the statistical significance of some predictor variables across models of different types of offenses (e.g., Harer and Steffensmeier 1996; Camp et al. 2003). Steiner and Wooldredge (2013) went one step further and examined the magnitude of the differences in the effects of routinely examined predictors of misconduct across nine different offense types. They found that the magnitude of the effects of the predictor variables were similar across most categories of misconduct; however, they did find significant differences in the strength of some effects derived from models of assaults on inmates or staff versus drug/alcohol violations versus all other nonviolent violations. Thus it appears that some inmates who engage in misconduct may exhibit a degree of offending specialization, although more research is needed to substantiate these observations.

Researchers have also examined both the prevalence and incidence of misconduct. The prevalence of misconduct is defined as whether the inmate committed misconduct during a study period, whereas the incidence of misconduct is the frequency of misconduct in the study period. The examination of both the prevalence and incidence of misconduct might provide a more comprehensive description of misconduct (i.e., some predictors may be more relevant for understanding whether an inmate ever engages in misconduct while others may be stronger predictors of the frequency of misconduct). Blumstein, Cohen, and Nagin (1978) made a similar argument with regard to the analysis of recidivism. However, few researchers have examined both the prevalence and incidence of misconduct within the same study (but see Steiner 2008; Steiner and Wooldredge 2008).

Finally, researchers have uncovered variation in the prevalence and incidence of misconduct between inmates and variation in misconduct *rates* between facilities and states (e.g., Wooldredge, Griffin, and Pratt 2001; Camp et al. 2003; Steiner and Wooldredge 2008; Steiner 2009). Theories that do not offer a multilevel explanation of misconduct necessarily ignore a significant portion of the variation in this phenomenon. A comprehensive theory of inmate misconduct should include concepts that can account for the variation in misconduct across inmates, prisons, and perhaps even states.

II. Traditional Theoretical Perspectives on Inmate Misconduct

As mentioned earlier, researchers of inmate misconduct have typically drawn from three theories to identify potential influences on misconduct: deprivation theory, importation theory, and management perspectives. I discuss each of these perspectives here and, in doing so, trace the development of knowledge regarding the sources of inmate misconduct.

A. Deprivation Theory

Early ethnographic studies of inmate adaptation to imprisonment highlighted the relevance of environmental "deprivations" suffered by inmates as the result of their incarceration. Researchers who conducted these studies argued that inmates formed a social system or subculture that reduced conflict among the inmates and isolated them from the harshness of the prison environment (e.g., Sykes and Messinger 1960). For instance, Clemmer (1940) offered a perspective on inmate assimilation ("prisonization") based on the Marxian view that a society's economy, and corresponding cultural attributes such as language, norms, and stratification system, are shaped by the physical environment and its available resources for human survival. Clemmer observed that even though prison environments place more restrictions on individuals' personal freedoms, individuals adapt to these restrictions by using the resources available to them. In Clemmer's prisons, inmates adopted a value system that strengthened inmate solidarity and insulated them as a group from administrators and staff. Stratification systems developed that provided materials and services denied by the administration (e.g., alcohol, sex, legal advice, protection), which were aided in part through a barter economy based on items more readily available to prison inmates (e.g., cigarettes). The inmates' value system and stratification system generated enduring routines and patterns of interaction among the inmates and correctional officers, which provided stability to the systems of living, working, and disciplining within an institution, despite changes in the inmate population (Clemmer 1940).

Sykes (1958) provided a social psychological perspective of inmate adaptation. He observed that incarceration coincided with specific environmental and psychological deprivations, such as denial of autonomy, freedom of movement, access to goods and services, heterosexual relationships, and security (safety). Sykes argued that these "pains of imprisonment" provided the energy for the inmate society or subculture as a system of action that served to mitigate the confinement experience. Sykes explained differences in behaviors between inmates by how the pains of imprisonment were felt and how inmates prioritized their needs. Inmates adapted to prison by taking on argot roles characterized by their behaviors, which were influenced by how they prioritized their needs and the degree to which particular environmental characteristics inhibited their satisfaction of each need. The other inmates and prison officials recognized these roles. For example, some inmates took on the role of the "gorilla" and sought to overcome deprivations at the expense of other inmates. "Wolves" were inmates who aggressively forced themselves on other inmates in an effort to satisfy their need to feel masculine (Sykes 1958; Sykes and Messinger 1960). Other roles included "rats," "squealers," "merchants," "punks," "fags," "hipsters," "toughs," "real men," and "ball busters." Thus deprivation theory holds that some inmates, when placed in an environment that denies them access to the means of satisfying certain needs, may seek illegitimate alternatives to need satisfaction (Clemmer 1940; Sykes 1958; Sykes and Messinger 1960).

The applicability of the deprivation perspective discussed here may have been significantly reduced over time because many of the environmental deprivations described by Clemmer (1940) and Sykes (1958) were lessened due to the inmate rights movement and the evolution of prisons from closed to more open systems (Jacobs 1977, 1980; Irwin 1980). For instance, the inmates' rights movement forced states to improve conditions of confinement and provide prisoners with a number of basic rights such as access to religion and legal materials. The inmate rights movement also disrupted the balance of power between prison staff and inmates by forcing staff to adhere to some basic procedures when handling prison rule violations (Jacobs 1980). These legally driven changes forced a greater reliance on methods of formal control and deteriorated the reciprocal exchange of power between staff and inmates that existed in many prisons. For example, Marquart and Crouch (1985) observed that *Ruiz v. Estelle* ended Texas prison officials' reliance on a "building tender" system, where inmate leaders (building tenders) were permitted certain extra privileges in exchange for informally settling many of the mundane problems of prison life (e.g., minor disputes between inmates). After *Ruiz*, prison officials were given sole responsibility for order maintenance, which decreased social distance between the inmates and staff, predictably increasing the level of officially recorded misconduct.

The inmate rights movement drew attention to the environmental conditions of prisons that potentially impact the lives of inmates, and researchers still recognize the importance of environmental influences on need satisfaction and inmate adaptation. Toch (1977), Goodstein et al. (1984), and Wright (1985, 1991) have discussed the psychological aspects of adaptation, with a more specific focus on inmate needs and the consequences of inhibiting need satisfaction. For example, Goodstein et al. underscored the relevance of inmates' need for "personal control" over their environment. Individuals have greater personal control when they have (a) outcome control (the ability to achieve desired results), (b) choice (multiple options from which to select), and (c) predictability (foreseeable consequences for actions). Prison environments that limit personal control by restricting outcome control, choice, or predictability may interfere with an individual's ability to cope with his surroundings and elicit maladaptive responses (Goodstein et al. 1984; MacKenzie, Goodstein, and Blouin 1987). Following in part from deprivation theory, empirical studies have revealed that a number of environmental characteristics of prisons (e.g., crowding, prison security level) are linked to inmate misconduct (see Steiner 2008; Meade 2012 for reviews of this literature).

B. Importation Theory

The deprivation perspective discussed here has been criticized because it places too much importance on structural deprivations resulting from incarceration (e.g., Irwin and Cressey 1962; Jacobs 1976). Irwin and Cressey argued that the inmate social system was in part a reflection of a larger criminal subculture that was not indigenous to the prison environment. They did not disagree that the total set of relationships referred to as the inmate social system was a response to imprisonment. They maintained, however, that inmates' solutions to the problems of imprisonment were not found within prison but instead were a manifestation of latent culture or preincarceration experiences. Therefore, the importation perspective holds that inmates with values and beliefs endorsing or tolerating deviant behavior may be more likely to engage in rule-breaking while they are incarcerated.

The importation perspective was initially criticized because it placed too much emphasis on preprison characteristics, experiences, and values while downplaying the relevance of environmental conditions and prison administration (e.g., Roebuck 1963). However, in the 1960s and 1970s, when the inmate rights movement reduced many of the differences in environmental conditions between prisons and introduced legal obstacles to prison administrators' abilities to exercise particular mechanisms of formal control (e.g., limits on punitive segregation, abolition of corporal punishment), scholars reemphasized the relevance of individual differences for understanding variation in inmate misconduct (e.g., Carroll 1974; Jacobs 1977; Irwin 1980). The inmate rights movement also coincided with an unprecedented increase in the incarceration of minorities (see Mauer 2006), and so these discussions often centered on potential racial and ethnic differences in inmate behavior.

Jacobs (1977), Carroll (1974), and Irwin (1980) have offered related discussions on how the increase in the incarceration of minority inmates, when coupled with the weakening of formal controls, allowed racial tension to become an important influence on levels of conflict in state prisons. Stratified subcultures (often based on race and ethnicity) that existed in urban areas emerged inside prisons and contributed to conflict between inmates. Conflict between staff and inmates was also frequent, due to growth in the number of nonwhite inmates from urban areas that were subjected to control and supervision by predominantly white guards who were typically from rural areas (Jacobs and Kraft 1978; Irwin 1980). The cultural differences between the nonwhite inmates from urban areas and white guards from rural backgrounds obstructed communication patterns and stimulated tensions between inmates and staff (Carroll 1974; Jacobs 1977; Jacobs and Kraft 1978). As a result of these processes, the 1960s and 1970s has been considered a period of heightened violence in many prisons (Irwin 1980; Colvin 1992; Irwin 2005).

In its original form, importation theory can be considered a cultural deviance model. Irwin and Cressey (1962) argued that inmates typically participated in one of three subcultures: thief, convict, or legitimate. Inmates who belonged to the thief subculture held lower class values such as toughness, smartness, and autonomy, along with reliability, trustworthiness, and level-headedness. Inmates who characterized the convict subculture valued utilitarianism and manipulation toward the goal of achieving status within the prison hierarchy. The legitimate subculture included inmates who rejected the thief and convict subculture, valued goal achievement through legitimate means, and were often social isolates within prison. Irwin and Cressey suggested that inmates' behavior patterns were explained in terms of the subculture with which they aligned.

Scholars have criticized cultural deviance models because they cannot be falsified due to their conceptual complexity and vagueness (Hirschi 1969; Kornhauser 1978). Similar problems exist for importation theory. In fact, I am not aware of any direct tests of the subcultural aspect of importation theory (see also Lahm 2008; Mears et al. 2013). To be sure, only a few researchers have examined the impact of preincarceration beliefs on offending in prison (Mears et al. 2013). Still, the ideas put forth in the importation perspective contributed to the examination of the effects of preprison characteristics on inmate misconduct. Thus, regardless of the limitations of the perspective, Irwin and Cressey (1962), and subsequently Carroll (1974) and Jacobs (1977), highlighted the importance of considering differences between individuals, even if the differences were not cultural differences per se. Researchers have identified a number of individual characteristics of inmates such as age, race, or involvement in conventional pursuits (e.g., education) that improve prediction of inmate misconduct (see Meade 2012; Schenk and Fremouw 2012 for reviews of this literature).

C. Management Perspectives

In addition to the deprivation perspective outlined here, Sykes (1958) also provided a theory of inmate collective violence (e.g., riots). Sykes concluded that the riot at the New Jersey State Prison where he was conducting his study occurred because of administrative actions (e.g., crackdowns) that affected the distribution of benefits to the leaders of the inmate social system. He observed that once the equilibrium of the social system was upset, the inmate leaders' ability to control the other inmates was undermined. More inmates adopted other roles within the social system, many of which resulted in deviant activities in order to satisfy their self-interests. Under such conditions, Sykes argued that the prison was more likely to experience collective violence. Inmate balance theory, therefore, predicts that inmate misconduct and disturbances are a reaction to a disruption of the inmate social system, which results from prison management taking abrupt actions to reestablish control (Sykes 1958; Colvin 1992). Sykes's management perspective has been used to explain not only riots but also other forms of violence and collective action (see, e.g., Useem and Reisig 1999).

DiIulio (1987) also offered a managerial perspective to explain differences in order between prisons. DiIulio observed variation in eight interrelated features that are common to models of prison management (formalness of organizational communication, formalness of personal relations, formalness of inmate/staff communication, staff discretion, regimentation of inmate lives, response to inmate rule violations, response to inmate disruptiveness, and inmate participation in decision-making). Based on variations in these features, he classified prison managerial styles into three different models: the control model, the consensual model, and the responsibility model. The control model adhered to a correctional philosophy that emphasized inmate obedience, work, and education, in that order. Each facility is run as a maximum-security facility. The responsibility model emphasized procedures that maximize inmates' responsibility for their own actions. This approach used classification to fit inmates into the least restrictive setting. Last, the consensual model was a mixture of the control and responsibility models. Consistent with the control model, the correctional staff were organized according to a paramilitary scheme, but the communication patterns between staff and between staff and inmates were informal, which is consistent with the responsibility model. The consensual model relied on informal discipline and classification but also allowed for inmate grievance procedures. The emphasis was on less restriction rather than more, although there was substantial intersystem variation. Prison governance was often shaped by the population composition of the inmates. Prisons with a large percentage of gang members, for instance, operated more similarly to the control model, whereas prisons with an older, presumably less deviant population operated more in line with the responsibility model.

DiIulio's (1987) ethnographic case study of the Texas, California, and Michigan penal systems revealed that the control model of facility management (Texas) achieved the most orderly prisons. Thus administrative control theory predicts that collective violence or higher rates of misconduct are the result of inadequate or weak facility management. As suggested by Useem and Kimball (1989) in their application of this perspective to prison riots, under periods of administrative breakdown, inmates come to believe that their conditions of confinement are unjust. Correctional officers and prison supervisors begin to neglect various day-to-day security measures, allowing for the formation of inmate groups that may mobilize collective action.

Inmate balance theory and administrative control theory are explanations of differences in violence across prisons as opposed to across inmates within the same prison. Both of these perspectives have ascertained at least some empirical support in prior studies of inmate deviance, although scholars have noted that neither of these perspectives has been able to account for the range of factors that lead to collective violence (e.g., Useem and Goldstone 2002). Even though it has been argued that these theories seemingly predict in the opposite direction (e.g., Useem and Reisig 1999), they actually share many common elements. Both theories underscore that rapid organizational change, contradictory goals, disorganized operations, and inconsistency in rule enforcement can have a negative impact on inmates' behaviors (i.e., generate more problem behaviors). Both theories suggest that these factors contribute to inmates' perceptions of injustice, which, in turn, may fuel conflict. It could be that inmates' perceptions of injustice and their belief in the legitimacy of the legal authorities and the rules they enforce are the driving forces that contribute to disturbances, conflicts, and higher rates of misconduct. Similar observations have been made by researchers of inmate deviance and collective disturbances in European prisons (e.g., Sparks et al. 1996; Liebling 2004; Carrabine 2005).

Colvin (1992) also underscored the relevance of disorganization, inconsistent rule enforcement, and administrative change for understanding collective violence in prison. Drawing from organizational theories of compliance, Colvin argued that the 1980 riot at the New Mexico State Penitentiary occurred primarily because of a managerial shift from reliance on remunerative to coercive means of controls. Inmate leaders who had assisted the administration in maintaining order were also removed from their positions of power, creating a disruption in the inmate social system. Colvin's account of the New Mexico riot could be viewed as evidence in support of inmate balance theory. However, the more important contribution of Colvin's work may have been his observations regarding the different types of strategies prison staff may use to formally control inmate behavior. Both remunerative and coercive controls are formal means used by staff to control inmates' behaviors. Remunerative controls, however, function as incentives for inmates to comply with facility rules (e.g., paid work assignments), whereas coercive controls (e.g., segregation) isolate inmates who do not comply with the rules. Even though Colvin documented the switch from primarily remunerative controls to strictly coercive controls as the primary cause of the New Mexico riot, he observed that prison officials used both types of control during a period of "good order" in the New Mexico prison. Thus both types of controls can be used in conjunction with one another to achieve order, although Colvin advocated for a greater reliance on remunerative controls. Colvin also attributed a period of reduced violence after the riot to the consistent application of specific procedures pertaining to inmate discipline, security, and staff training. It could be that the increased consistency in rule enforcement may have influenced the inmates to become less cynical regarding the legitimacy of the rules and the staff. If more inmates perceived the rules and staff as legitimate, then they may have been more likely to comply with the facility rules because their beliefs regarding the moral validity of the formal mechanisms of control may have strengthened their ties to convention. Colvin (2007) recognized the potential validity of these ideas in his application of differential coercion and social support theory to the New Mexico riot.

Bottoms (1999) developed a working model of prison order organized around the concept of legitimacy: the belief that authorities, institutions, and social arrangements are appropriate, proper, and just (Tyler 2006). Bottoms's model also includes the concepts of power and routines, normative involvement in projects, inmate population characteristics, incentives and disincentives, degree of physical constraint, specific incidents (e.g., riots), and staff deployment, approaches, and skills, the latter of which mediates the effects of all other concepts. Legitimacy is then predicted to mediate staff deployment, approaches, and skills. Bottoms noted, however, that his model is a working model requiring testing and refinement. Nonetheless, Bottoms's observations, along with Colvin's (2007) more recent perspective, underscore the potential relevance of correctional officer legitimacy. Legitimacy may be relevant to the prison environment because whether staff are viewed as legitimate may be linked to inmate compliance with the rules that the staff enforce (DiIulio 1987; Irwin 1980; Hepburn 1985; Lombardo 1989; Bottoms 1999). On the other hand, inconsistent application of rule enforcement can influence perceptions of authority as illegitimate and, in turn, provoke defiance (Sherman 1993; Colvin 2007). Whereas the perspectives of prison management discussed earlier (e.g., administrative control, administrative balance theory) are macro-level theories, inclusion of inmates' perceptions regarding correctional officer legitimacy incorporates a micro-level dimension to the management perspective, suggesting that it could be the normal everyday encounters between inmates and line-level correctional staff that have the strongest influence on inmate compliance. However, few studies have examined the impact of correctional officer legitimacy on inmate misconduct (Reisig and Mesko 2009; Steiner 2008).

D. Observations Concerning Existing Theories of Inmate Misconduct

Based on the previous discussion and related empirical evidence, a comprehensive theory of inmate misconduct should be able to explain the differences in misconduct between inmates, as well as differences in misconduct levels between facilities and perhaps even states. Following the preceding discussion, a comprehensive theory of inmate misconduct should also include concepts reflecting characteristics of inmates, facility environments, and management practices.

The three dominant theories of inmate misconduct—deprivation theory, importation theory, and management perspectives—have generated valuable insights into the sources of inmate behaviors. To be sure, these theories have provided the theoretical foundations that influenced researchers to offer empirical evidence regarding the relevance of characteristics of inmates, facility environments, and management practices. Yet scholars have recognized their limitations as standalone explanations of inmate behavior (e.g., Thomas 1970, 1977; Sparks et al. 1996; Cao, Zhao, and Van Dine 1997; Byrne, Hummer, and Taxman 2008; Hochstetler and DeLisi 2005; Lahm 2008; Mears et al. 2013), and, based on the evidence discussed earlier, none of these perspectives offers a comprehensive explanation of inmate misconduct.

Deprivation theory neglects to consider differences in the preincarceration experiences of individuals that have been determined to be relevant to an explanation of misconduct, at least to some extent. Importation theory's sole emphasis on preincarceration factors does not permit an explanation of differences in how environmental characteristics of facilities and variation in management practices may influence misconduct. Finally, management perspectives do not incorporate concepts reflecting the differences between individuals or facility environments that the extant evidence suggests are relevant to an explanation of misconduct. Each of these existing theories of inmate behavior, while straightforward, logical, and to an extent empirically supported, is limited in that none can account for the variation in misconduct at both the micro and macro levels while incorporating all relevant sources. Simply put, current perspectives are inadequate as explanations of misconduct.

Bottoms's (1999) theoretical model of prison order is a comprehensive theory of misconduct. This perspective recognizes that there are explainable differences in the level of misconduct between inmates and between facilities. His model appropriately acknowledges the relevance of inmate characteristics and features of facility environments, although he suggests that their effects are mediated by staff deployment, approaches, and skills, which are then mediated by the legitimacy of correctional staff. In Bottoms's model, staff deployment, approaches, and skills still maintain direct effects on misconduct, however. His model also differs from other management perspectives by incorporating a micro-level dimension of prison management: correctional officer legitimacy. Researchers have investigated aspects of Bottoms's model and revealed some support for a relationship between correctional officer legitimacy and misconduct (e.g., Reisig and Mesko 2009; Steiner 2008). These researchers have also found that characteristics of inmates and facility environments directly affect misconduct, suggesting that Bottoms's model may not be a sufficient explanation of inmate misconduct. By placing an emphasis on the proximate effect of prison management, Bottoms's theory succumbs to some of the same criticisms that can be applied to the more traditional theories of inmate behavior. As Carrabine (2005, p. 897) convincingly argued with regard to prison order, "the problem of order is multi-faceted and any account that relies on a singular solution to the neglect of others is unlikely to grasp the variable ways in which economic interest, political force, and moral commitment might *combine* to sustain stable and orderly patterns of life" (emphasis added).

The inadequacies of the existing theoretical perspectives described here could be due in part to researchers' focus on prisons as "special environments" that require their own theory (see, e.g., Sparks et al. 1996). Long ago, McCleary (1961, p. 184) observed that "there is little place for a special theory of penal administration as such, and a significant number of problems in prison administration grow from the failure to treat the prison as a social and political community." Although McCleary was referring to theories of prison management, his point could just as easily be applied to other theories of inmate behavior (e.g., importation, deprivation). Although there are differences between prisons and what we normally conceive of when we think of other social collectives (e.g., organizations, communities), there are also a striking number of similarities. Further, from a life-course perspective, incarceration is simply a residential change that could induce a turning point in an individual's offending trajectory, possibly inducing or contributing to an individual's desistance from offending (Sampson and Laub 1993; Laub and Sampson 2003). Thus it may be that a better understanding of inmate misconduct could be gained through consideration of more general explanations of crime and deviance.

III. General Explanations of Crime, Deviance, and Misconduct

Imprisonment has many goals, several of which are utilitarian goals designed to reduce offenders' odds of reoffending (e.g., deterrence). Inmate misconduct reflects offending in prison, and misconduct has been linked to offending after inmates have been released (e.g., Trulson, DeLisi, and Marquart 2011). Thus misconduct may be an indicator of whether imprisonment has contributed to lower odds of offending among incarcerated individuals or whether imprisonment has amplified the odds that individuals exhibit offending continuity. Theoretical perspectives that seek to explain offending across the life course may then apply to offending in prison. Following this logic, researchers have applied general strain theory and control theory to inmate behavior.

A. General Strain Theory

Strain theories assume that individuals are rule abiding under normal conditions. Experiencing strain induces pressure to engage in rule-breaking. Strain is the result of individuals' social experiences. Merton (1938) posited that strain was the result of individuals' failure to achieve their goals. Agnew (1985, 2001) identified additional sources of strain: (a) exposure to negative stimuli, and (b) removal of positively valued stimuli. Agnew also argued that some factors can decrease the risk of criminal behavior resulting from strain (e.g., social support), while other factors can increase the odds of strain induced criminality (e.g., delinquent associates). Agnew further observed that strain was most likely to stimulate criminal behavior when the strain was perceived as unjust, high in magnitude, associated with low self-control, or offered incentive to engage in criminal behavior. Researchers have applied general strain theory to understand offending among individuals and across social contexts (e.g., neighborhoods). General strain theory also recognizes that individuals cope with strain in different ways, which could account for offending specialization (e.g., drug use vs. physical assault).

Blevins et al. (2010) argued that concepts often considered under deprivation theory might also reflect categories of strain that affect many inmates. Blevins et al. also observed that antisocial values and associates, considered to be relevant based on importation theory, could make misconduct more likely, while exposure to supportive relationships or coping resources could reduce inmates' odds of offending. Thus general strain theory might provide a promising avenue for integrating measures previously considered relevant under importation or deprivation theory. Taking this one step further, management perspectives may also be relevant under a strain perspective. Prison administrators or staff could generate situations that induce strain (e.g., coercive controls such as lockdown) or promote formal mechanisms that reduce or moderate strain (e.g., remunerative controls such as rehabilitative programming or extra visitation). Considering factors previously framed under deprivation, importation, or management perspectives within a general strain framework might provide a more comprehensive explanation of misconduct and overcome some of the limitations of the traditional explanations of misconduct discussed earlier (see also Blevins et al., 2010).

Testing strain theory among a sample of inmates would require direct measures of all of the relevant concepts of the theory, and such a scenario is unlikely given the practical constraints associated with original data collection and the preference in related studies to rely on official sources of data. However, it is possible to offer partial tests of the theory or consider other routinely examined predictors of misconduct as proxies for the concepts associated with general strain theory (Morris et al. 2012). For instance, in a study of the sources of misconduct among female inmates, Steiner and Wooldredge (2009a) discussed how inmates with histories of abuse and/or mental illness might feel greater strain due to their greater difficulty in coping with imprisonment, possibly increasing their odds of misconduct. Prisons that are more crowded may also be a source of structurally induced strain if such environments interfere with prison administrators' ability to facilitate adaptation to confinement, possibly contributing to higher levels of misconduct. Thus strain theory could be a unified comprehensive framework for considering the micro- and macro-level sources of misconduct identified by the empirical literature.

B. Control Theory

Control theory may be relevant to an explanation of misconduct because control in a prison environment is necessarily linked to a common interest among inmates and staff to live or work in an orderly and safe environment (Irwin 1980; Sparks et al. 1996; Bottoms 1999). Control can reflect formal practices used by correctional staff to maintain order, but it also reflects the ability of inmates to realize common goals (e.g., reside in a safe environment) among themselves (e.g., willingness to intervene). A control perspective assumes a relatively constant innate motivation to deviate from rules across individuals. Variations in levels of deviance across individuals and across areas are explained by differences in the strength of controls (Hirschi 1969; Janowitz 1975; Kornhauser 1978).

Controls are actual or potential rewards and punishments that accrue from conformity to or deviation from the norms of society. Controls can be internal (invoked by the individual) or external (enforced by others). Controls can be direct or indirect. Direct controls are purposeful efforts to prevent or restrict deviance, whereas indirect controls are the result of role relationships established for other reasons (e.g., marriage) and are the components of role exchanges (e.g., rewards for restraint; Kornhauser 1978). A control perspective also recognizes the potential contributions of both individual- (inmate) and societal- (facility, state) level effects on deviance (Reiss 1951; Janowitz 1975; Sampson 1986; Sampson and Laub 1993; Wooldredge et al. 2001). Offending specialization can also be explained by the impact of controls on opportunity structures (Felson 1986; Steiner and Wooldredge 2013). For example, a control perspective permits consideration of individual characteristics such as personal or self-control, the ability of an individual to refrain from satisfying his or her needs in ways that violate the norms and rules of a society (Reiss 1951; Janowitz 1975; Gottfredson and Hirschi 1986), as well as ties to conventional society or stakes in conformity (e.g., family, employment) that may counteract low self-control (Toby 1957; Briar and Pilavin 1965; Hirschi 1969; Sampson and Laub

1993; Wooldredge et al. 2001). Macro-level processes related to administrative (formal) or nonadministrative (informal) controls at the aggregate level (Sampson 1986; DiIulio 1987; Useem and Kimball 1989; Colvin 1992; Useem and Reisig 1999), as well as environmental conditions that influence control structures (Kornhauser 1978; Useem 1985, Wooldredge et al. 2001), are also relevant under a control perspective. Thus concepts that have been framed within existing perspectives of inmate deviance could also reflect sources of or barriers to control.

Similar to the earlier discussion concerning general strain theory, a test of control theory among an inmate sample would require direct measures of all of the relevant concepts of the theory, and such a scenario is unlikely in a prison context. Partial tests of the theory or treating other routinely examined predictors of inmate offending as proxies or structural antecedents of the more direct measures of the concepts discussed earlier could be informative, however (Steiner 2008). For instance, the often-observed inverse relationship between age and misconduct could be considered within a control perspective. Younger inmates often have fewer stakes in conformity (Toby 1957; Wooldredge et al. 2001). Younger individuals also generally have fewer "conventional" relationships (with, e.g., partners and/or their own children) and are less likely to be involved in activities reflecting more conformist lifestyles (such as full-time jobs; Briar and Pilavin 1965; Steiner and Wooldredge 2009b).

At the macro level, a prison's security level could be relevant under a control perspective. Differences in facility security level typically coincide with differences in physical environments that may either promote or inhibit opportunities for rule violations. For example, the environment of a maximum-security prison is often more sterile and authoritative compared to less secure facilities. Although maximum-security facilities typically contain more guards, they also contain more dangerous and higher risk inmates. For all of these reasons, higher security facilities or facilities with higher proportions of inmates classified as high security might experience more misconduct.

Controls stemming from prison administrators such as remunerative and coercive controls could also be considered under a control perspective. Measures of coercive controls could include factors such as the ratio of staff to inmates, disciplinary housing use, or administrative transfers (Steiner 2009). By contrast, remunerative controls involve the manipulation of material rewards or incentives (Colvin 1992; Bottoms 1999). Remunerative controls could include the use of facility programming, paid work assignments, furloughs, visitation, and so forth.

Finally, state-level factors could also be considered under a control perspective. For example, fiscal stress could ultimately affect the level of misconduct by undermining the balance between the prison administration's resources and its responsibilities, not to mention contributing to poorer conditions of confinement (Colvin 1992; Goldstone and Useem 1999; Steiner 2009). The potential relevance of fiscal stress is consistent with macro-social theories of social control, which hypothesize an inverse relationship between neighborhood- or community-level economic disadvantage (i.e., socioeconomic status) and levels of crime (e.g., Shaw and McKay 1942; Sampson and Groves 1989; Sampson, Raudenbush, and Earls 1997). With regard to prisons, however, economic disadvantage operates at the state level, since prison resources are distributed by state departments of corrections (or other state agencies) in which they are located.

IV. Conclusion

The incarceration of criminal defendants is a selection process that generates a population of individuals at high risk to reoffend. The majority of these individuals will return to communities (Petersilia 2003); prison is merely a residential change. Inmate misconduct or rule violations reflect offending in prison, and misconduct has been associated with continuity in offending upon release (Trulson et al. 2011). Thus an understanding of offending in prison may shed light on the sources of criminality among high-risk offenders as well as on whether incarceration, types of incarceration (e.g., confinement in maximum security vs. minimum security), or processes that occur within a prison (e.g., treatment programs) are effective at initiating desistance from offending. From a more practical standpoint, institutional safety and order are reflected by the level of inmate misconduct within a facility, and identifying the sources of offending within prison could aid correctional administrators in developing strategies for reducing the problem (e.g., more structured routines, assessment tools).

The traditional theories of inmate behavior (deprivation theory, importation theory, and management perspectives) have contributed handsomely to our understanding of offending in prison. Deprivation theory has highlighted the relevance of environmental conditions of prisons for predicting misconduct. Importation theory has informed researchers' assessments of individual characteristics that are associated with misconduct. Management perspectives have underscored the influence of prison administrations and custodial staff on inmate behavior. To be sure, these theories have informed many of the empirical studies that have underscored the relevance of related concepts depicting variations in inmates, prison environments, and prison management for explaining misconduct at the micro and macro levels.

In this essay I have shown how each of the traditional theories of inmate misconduct is limited, either because it cannot explain misconduct at both the micro and macro level or because it is not inclusive of the range of factors that have been empirically determined to be relevant to an explanation of misconduct. For the most part, these theories were also developed under the notion of prisons as a unique or "special" environment. Prisons are certainly distinctive environments in some respects, but so are schools, disadvantaged neighborhoods, and corporations. Yet researchers do not rely on special theories of offending within these contexts. Instead, they assess the generality of existing theories of crime and deviance by applying these theories to different subpopulations and contexts. A better understanding of inmate behavior could be gained by applying these theories to an understanding of inmate misconduct.

A life-course perspective recognizes age-graded roles and social transitions embedded in social institutions (Sampson and Laub 1993). For many offenders, incarceration is a very real social transition that has the potential to induce change in their offending trajectory, or temporarily displace it within prisons. Inmate misconduct is deviation from the rules of a prison, and so perpetration of misconduct reflects continuity in offending behavior. If imprisonment is conceived of as a residential or situational change in an offender's life course, then offending in prison could be explained by considering the sources of offending more generally, while also taking into account variations in the relevant situational aspects of the prison context. To this end, researchers have applied general theories of crime to the study of inmate misconduct.

Scholars have used both general strain theory and theories of social control to explain offending in prison (e.g., Wooldredge et al. 2001; Steiner and Wooldredge 2009a, 2009b; Blevins et al. 2010; Morris et al 2012). On the one hand, these theories are multilevel theories; that is, they are inclusive of concepts that could explain variation in misconduct between inmates, prisons, and states. Concepts within these theories also reflect characteristics of inmates, prison environments, and prison management. Thus they are comprehensive theories of inmate misconduct. On the other hand, general strain theory and control theory also attempt to explain offending across the life course (e.g., Sampson and Laub 1993; Agnew 2006), and so the application of these theories to offending in prison permits assessment of generality of these theories during a stage (or stages) of an offender's life course (imprisonment) that is an all too frequent reality for many offenders (Western 2006).

The application of general theories of crime and deviance to inmate behavior might prove to be a fruitful avenue of research for several reasons. First, as discussed earlier, most general theories of criminality can offer a more comprehensive explanation of misconduct than the traditional theories of inmate behavior (i.e., explain misconduct at the micro and macro levels and include all of the factors that have been determined to be relevant to an explanation of misconduct). Second, application of general theories of criminality to inmate behavior permits consideration of an individual's period of incarceration as a stage in his life course. By considering incarceration as a stage (or stages) in an individual's life course, examination of prison offending might be able to shed light on the sources of offending among individuals regardless of whether they are in the community or in prison. Identifying these risk factors could be informative for developing interventions designed to encourage desistance from offending. In contrast, identifying the sources of prison offending that are unique to inmate samples might be informative for correctional administrators seeking to reduce misconduct in their own facilities (i.e., these factors might be situational and subject to administrative manipulation). Finally, application of general theories of crime and deviance to prison offending permits an assessment of the generality of these theories. Prison inmates are a high-risk population, most of which will return to communities (Petersilia 2003). If a theory cannot explain offending among this population, then the theory's applicability to explaining desistance from offending should be questioned.

Inmate misconduct reflects deviance within prison. An understanding of the sources of misconduct is important because misconduct threatens the order and safety of a prison and because misconduct is an indicator of continuity in offending after incarceration. I have argued that the traditional theories of inmate misconduct should be discarded in favor of more general explanations of offending such as general strain theory or control theory. Incarceration should also be considered a period (or periods) in an offender's life course, since it is a social transition that is typical for many offenders. An adequate life-course perspective should be able to account for offending behavior in all social transitions, including incarceration. By applying a general explanation of criminality to offending in prison, we might gain a better understanding of the sources of offending among high-risk offenders and the sources of offending that are unique to inmates within prisons. Such information is critical to public and prison safety.

REFERENCES

Agnew, Robert. 1985. "A Revised Strain Theory of Delinquency." *Social Forces* 64: 151–167.

Agnew, Robert. 2001. "Building on the Foundations of General Strain Theory: Specifying the Types of Strain Most Likely to Lead to Crime and Delinquency." *Journal of Research in Crime and Delinquency* 38: 319–361.

Agnew, Robert. 2006. *Pressured into Crime: An Overview of General Strain Theory.* New York: Oxford University Press.

American Correctional Association. 2003. *Standards for Adult Correctional Institutions*, 4th ed. Lanham, MD: American Correctional Association.

Blevins, Kristie R., Shelley Johnson Listwan, Francis T. Cullen, and Cheryl Lero Jonson. 2010. "A General Strain Theory of Prison Violence and Misconduct: An Integrated Model of Inmate Behavior." *Journal of Contemporary Criminal Justice* 26: 148–166.

Blumstein, Alfred, Jacqueline Cohen, and David Farrington. 1988. "Criminal Career Research: Its Value for Criminology." *Criminology* 26: 1–36.

Blumstein, Alfred, Jacqueline Cohen, and Daniel Nagin. 1978. *Deterrence and Incapacitation: Estimating the Effects of Criminal Sanctions on Crime.* Report of the Panel on Research on Deterrent and Incapacitative Effects. Washington, DC: National Research Council, National Academy of Sciences.

Bottoms, Anthony E. 1999. "Interpersonal Violence and Social Order in Prison." In *Crime and Justice: A Review of Research*, edited by Michael Tonry and Joan Petersilia. Chicago: University of Chicago Press.

Briar, Scott, and Irving Pilavin. 1965. "Delinquency, Situational Inducements, and Commitment to Conformity." *Social Problems* 13: 35–45.

Byrne, James, Don Hummer, and Faye S. Taxman. 2008. *The Culture of Prison Violence.* Boston: Allyn & Bacon.

Camp, Scott, Gerald G. Gaes, Neal Langan, and William Saylor. 2003. "The Influence of Prisons on Inmate Misconduct: A Multilevel Investigation." *Justice Quarterly* 20: 501–533.

Cao, Liqun, Jihong Zhao, and Steve Van Dine. 1997. "Prison Disciplinary Tickets: A Test of the Deprivation and Importation Models." *Journal of Criminal Justice* 25: 103–113.

Carrabine, Eamonn. 2005. "Prison Riots, Social Order and the Problem of Legitimacy." *The British Journal of Criminology* 45: 896–913.

Carroll, Leo. 1974. *Hacks, Blacks, and Cons: Race Relations in a Maximum Security Prison.* Lexington, MA: Lexington Books.

Clemmer, Donald. 1940. *The Prison Community.* New York: Rinehart & Company.

Colvin, Mark. 1992. *The Penitentiary in Crisis: From Accommodation to Riot in New Mexico.* Albany: State University of New York Press.

Colvin, Mark. 2007. "Applying Differential Coercion and Social Support Theory to Prison Organizations: The Case of the Penitentiary of New Mexico." *The Prison Journal* 87: 367–387.

DiIulio, John. 1987. *Governing Prisons: A Comparative Study of Correctional Management.* New York: Free Press.

Eichenthal, David, and James B. Jacobs. 1991. "Enforcing the Criminal Law in State Prisons." *Justice Quarterly* 8: 283–303.

Felson, Marcus. 1986. "Linking Criminal Choices, Routine Activities, Informal Control, and Criminal OUTCOMES." In *The Reasoning Criminal*, edited by Derek Cornish and Ronald V. Clarke. New York: Springer-Verlag.

Goldstone, Jack, and Bert Useem. 1999. "Prison Riots as Microrevolutions: An Extension of State-Centered Theories of Revolution." *The American Journal of Sociology* 104: 985–1029.

Goodstein, Lynne, Doris L. MacKenzie, and R. Lance Shotland. 1984. "Personal Control and Inmate Adjustment to Prison." *Criminology* 22: 343–369.

Goodstein, Lynn, and Kevin Wright. 1989. "Inmate Adjustment to Prison." In *The American Prison: Issues in Research and Policy*, edited by Lynn Goodstein and Doris L. MacKenzie. New York: Plenum Press.

Gottfredson, Michael, and Travis Hirschi. 1986. "The True Value of Lambda Would Appear to be Zero: An Essay on Career Criminals, Criminal Careers, Selective Incapacitation, Cohort Studies, and Related Topics." *Criminology* 24: 213–233.

Harer, Miles, and Darrell Steffensmeier. 1996. "Race and Prison Violence." *Criminology* 34: 323–355.

Hepburn, John. 1985. "The Exercise of Power in Coercive Organizations: A Study of Prison Guards." *Criminology* 23: 145–164.

Hewitt, John, Eric Poole, and Robert Regoli. 1984. "Self-Reported and Observed Rule Breaking in Prison: A Look at Disciplinary Response." *Justice Quarterly* 1: 437–447.

Hirschi, Travis. 1969. *Causes of Delinquency*. Berkeley: University of California Press.

Hochstetler, Andy, and Matt DeLisi. 2005. "Importation, Deprivation, and Varieties of Serving Time: An Integrated Lifestyle-Exposure Model of Prison Offending." *Journal of Criminal Justice* 33: 257–266.

Irwin, John. 1980. *Prisons in Turmoil*. Boston: Little, Brown.

Irwin, John. 2005. *The Warehouse Prison: Disposal of the New Dangerous Class*. Los Angeles, CA: Roxbury Press.

Irwin, John, and Donald R. Cressey. 1962. "Thieves, Convicts, and the Inmate Culture." *Social Problems* 10: 142–155.

Jacobs, James B. 1976. "Stratification and Conflict Among Prison Inmates." *Journal of Criminal Law and Criminology* 66: 476–482.

Jacobs, James B. 1977. *Stateville: The Penitentiary in Mass Society*. Chicago: University of Chicago Press.

Jacobs, James B. 1980. "The Prisoners' Rights Movement and its Impact, 1960–1980." In *Crime and Justice: A Review of the Research.*, edited by Norval Morris and Michael Tonry. Chicago: University of Chicago Press.

Jacobs, James B., and Lawrence Kraft. 1978. "Integrating the Yeepers: A Comparison of Black and White Prison Guards in Illinois." *Social Problems* 25: 304–18.

Janowitz, Morris. 1975. "Sociological Theory and Social Control." *The American Journal of Sociology* 81: 82–108.

Kornhauser, Ruth. 1978. *Social Sources of Delinquency: An Appraisal of Analytical Models*. Chicago: University of Chicago Press.

Lahm, Karen. 2008. "Inmate-on-Inmate Assault: A Multilevel Examination of Prison Violence." *Criminal Justice and Behavior* 35: 120–137.

Laub, John H., and Robert J. Sampson. 2003. *Shared Beginnings, Divergent Lives: Delinquent Boys to Age 70*. Boston: Harvard University Press.

Liebling, Allison. 2004. *Prisons and Their Moral Performance: A Study of Values, Quality, and Prison Life*. New York: Oxford University Press.

Light, Stephen. 1990. "Measurement Error in Official Statistics: Prison Rule Infraction Data." *Federal Probation* 54: 63–68.

Lombardo, Lucien. 1989. *Guards Imprisoned: Correctional Officers at Work*, 2d ed. Cincinnati, OH: Anderson Publishing.

MacKenzie, Doris L., Lynne Goodstein, and David Blouin. 1987. "Personal Control and Prisoner Adjustment: An Empirical Test of a Proposed Model." *Journal of Research in Crime and Delinquency* 24: 49–68.

Marquart, James W., and Ben Crouch. 1985. "Judicial Reform and Prisoner Control: The Impact of Ruiz v. Estelle on a Texas Penitentiary." *Law & Society Review* 19: 557–586.

Mauer, Mark. 2006. *Race to Incarcerate*, 2d ed. New York: New Press.

Meade, Benjamin. 2012. Examining the Effects of Religiosity and Religious Environments on Inmate Misconduct. Unpublished doctoral dissertation, University of South Carolina.

Mears, Daniel P., Eric A. Stewart, Sonja E. Siennick, and Ronald L. Simons. 2013. "The Code of the Street and Inmate Violence: Investigating the Salience of Imported Belief Systems." *Criminology* 51: 695–728.

Merton, Robert K. 1938. "Social Structure and Anomie." *American Sociological Review* 3: 672–682.

McCleary, Richard. 1961. "The Governmental Process and Informal Social Control." In *The Prison: Studies in Institutional Organization and Change.*, edited by Donald R. Cressey. New York: Holt, Rinehart and Winston.

Morris, Robert G., Michael Carriaga, Brie Diamond, Nicole Leeper Piquero, and Alex R. Piquero. 2012. "Does Prison Strain Lead to Prison Misbehavior? An Application of General Strain Theory to Inmate Misconduct." *Journal of Criminal Justice* 40: 194–201.

Petersilia, Joan. 2003. *When Prisoners Come Home: Parole and Prisoner Reentry*. New York: Oxford University Press.

Reisig, Michael, and Gorazd Mesko. 2009. "Procedural Justice, Legitimacy, and Prisoner Misconduct." *Psychology, Crime and Law* 15: 41–59.

Reiss, Albert. 1951. "Delinquency as the Failure of Personal and Social Controls." *American Sociological Review* 16: 196–207.

Roebuck, Julian. 1963. "A Critique of 'Thieves, Convicts and the Inmate Culture.'" *Social Problems* 11: 193–200.

Sampson, Robert J. 1986. "Crime and Cities: The Effects of Formal and Informal Social Control." In *Crime and Justice: A Review of Research*, edited by Albert Reis and Michael Tonry. Chicago: University of Chicago Press.

Sampson, Robert J., and Byron Groves. 1989. "Community Structure and Crime: Testing Social Disorganization Theory." *The American Journal of Sociology* 94: 774–802.

Sampson, Robert J., and John H. Laub. 1993. *Crime in the Making: Pathways and Turning Points Throughout Life*. Cambridge, MA: Harvard University Press.

Sampson, Robert, Stephen Raudenbush, and Felton Earls. 1997. "Neighborhoods and Violent Crime: A Multilevel Study of Collective Efficacy." *Science* 277: 918–924.

Schenk, Allison M., and William J. Fremouw. 2012. "Individual Characteristics Related to Prison Violence: A Critical Review of the Literature." *Aggression and Violent Behavior* 17: 430–442.

Shaw, Clifford, and Henry McKay. 1942. *Juvenile Delinquency and Urban Areas*. Chicago: University of Chicago Press.

Sherman, Lawrence. 1993. "Defiance, Deterrence, and Irrelevance: A Theory of the Criminal Sanction." *Journal of Research in Crime and Delinquency* 30: 445–473.

Sparks, J. Richard, Anthony E. Bottoms, and Will Hay. 1996. *Prisons and the Problem of Order*. Oxford: Oxford University Press.

Steiner, Benjamin. 2008. Maintaining Prison Order: Understanding Causes of Inmate Misconduct Within and Across Ohio Prisons. Doctoral dissertation, University of Cincinnati.

Steiner, Benjamin. 2009. "Assessing Static and Dynamic Influences on Inmate Violence Levels." *Crime & Delinquency* 55: 134–161.

Steiner, Benjamin, and John Wooldredge. 2008. "Inmate Versus Environmental Effects on Prison Rule Violations." *Criminal Justice and Behavior* 35: 438–456.

Steiner, Benjamin, and John Wooldredge. 2009a. "Individual and Environmental Effects on Assaults and Nonviolent Rule-breaking by Women in Prison." *Journal of Research in Crime and Delinquency* 46: 437–467.

Steiner, Benjamin, and John Wooldredge. 2009b. "The Relevance of Inmate Race/Ethnicity Versus Population Composition for Understanding Prison Rule Violations." *Punishment & Society* 11: 459–489.

Steiner, Benjamin, and John Wooldredge. 2013. "Implications of Different Outcome Measures for an Understanding of Inmate Misconduct." *Crime & Delinquency* 59:1234–1262.

Steiner, Benjamin, and John Wooldredge. 2014. "Comparing Self-Report to Official Measures of Inmate Misconduct." *Justice Quarterly* 31:1074–1101.

Sutherland, Edwin H., and Donald R. Cressey. 1978. *Criminology*, 10th ed. Philadelphia, PA: J. B. Lippincott.

Sykes, Gresham. 1958. *The Society of Captives*. Princeton, NJ: Princeton University Press.

Sykes, Gresham, and Sheldon Messinger. 1960. "The Inmate Social System." In *Theoretical Studies in Social Organization of the Prison*, edited by Social Science Research Council. New York: Social Science Research Council.

Thomas, Charles. 1970. "Toward a More Inclusive Model of the Inmate Contraculture." *Criminology* 8: 251–262.

Thomas, Charles. 1977. "Theoretical Perspectives on Prisonization: A Comparison of the Importation and Deprivation Models." *Journal of Criminal Law and Criminology* 68: 135–145.

Toby, Jackson. 1957. "Social Disorganization and Stake in Conformity: Complementary Factors in the Predatory Behavior of Hoodlums." *Journal of Criminal Law and Criminology* 48: 12–17.

Toch, Hans. 1977. *Living in Prison*. New York: Free Press.

Trulson, Chad R., Matt DeLisi, and James W. Marquart. 2011. "Institutional Misconduct, Delinquent Background, and Rearrest Frequency Among Serious and Violent Delinquent Offenders." *Crime & Delinquency* 57: 709–731.

Tyler, Tom R. 2006. "Psychological Perspectives on Legitimacy and Legitimation." *Annual Review of Psychology* 57: 375–400.

Useem, Bert. 1985. "Disorganization and the New Mexico Prison Riot of 1980." *American Sociological Review* 50: 677–688.

Useem, Bert, and Jack Goldstone. 2002. "Forging Social Order and its Breakdown: Riot and Reform in U.S. Prisons." *American Sociological Review* 67: 499–525.

Useem, Bert, and Peter Kimball. 1989. *States of Siege: U.S. Prison Riots, 1971–1986*. New York: Oxford University Press.

Useem, Bert, and Michael Reisig. 1999. "Collective Action in Prisons: Protests, Disturbances, and Riots." *Criminology* 37: 735–759.

Van Voorhis, Patricia. 1994. "Measuring Prison Disciplinary Problems: A Multiple Indicators Approach to Understanding Prison Adjustment." *Justice Quarterly* 11: 679–710.

Western, Bruce. 2006. *Punishment and Inequality in America*. New York: Russell Sage Foundation.

Wooldredge, John. 1994. "Inmate Crime and Victimization in a Southwestern Correctional Facility." *Journal of Criminal Justice* 22: 367–381.

Wooldredge, John, Timothy Griffin, and Travis Pratt. 2001. "Considering Hierarchical Models for Research on Inmate Behavior: Predicting Misconduct with Multilevel Data." *Justice Quarterly* 18: 203–231.

Wright, Kevin. 1985. "Developing the Prison Environment Inventory." *Journal of Research in Crime and Delinquency* 22: 257–277.

Wright, Kevin. 1991. "A Study of Individual, Environmental, and Interactive Effects in Explaining Adjustment to Prison." *Justice Quarterly* 8: 217–242.

CHAPTER 12

....

PRISON RIOTS

....

BERT USEEM

THE field of prison studies has made significant strides in its effort to understand what makes prisons orderly and why, sometimes, they fall into riots. A prison is, first and fore-most, a system of cooperation, although a hierarchical and authoritarian one.[1] The prison staff issue orders to inmates and judge their compliance with those orders and the course of interaction that follows. Inmates live where they are told to live, possess only property that prison officials allow, and have their communications monitored without warrant. Force alone, however, cannot run a modern prison. Under normal circumstances, a mod-ern prison looks like a beehive of activity. The bulk of inmates move to and from congregate meals, recreational activities, work, and rehabilitative services.

Inmate resistance may disrupt or destroy the system of cooperation needed for the normal range of activities. Resistance takes many different forms and comprises varying degrees of defiance. Low-level defiance includes inmate complaints, expressions of disrespect toward correctional staff, refusals to follow simple orders, possession of contraband, and general disorderliness. Prison authorities must respond to low-level defiance, to the extent that it (a) impedes the cooperation needed to operate a prison, and (b) portends higher levels of resistance, that is, open rebellion. The latter includes physical assaults on correctional staff, arson, and inmate "strikes." At the highest end are prison riots.

The distinctive feature of a prison riot is that authorities lose control over a significant por-tion of the prison and a significant number of prisoners for a significant amount of time. For a time, there are two centers of power—prison authorities and inmates. This essay considers the conditions that permit low-level resistance to become a prison riot. I distinguish several approaches to the causes of prison riots and then turn to their course and consequences.

The core ideas developed in this essay are the following:

- Several competing theories can help explain riot causation. No single theory has gained dominance.
- Most work on prison riots has focused on organizational aspects. Individual-level explanations are needed.
- Internal governance units (IGUs) are regulatory organizations that function to main-tain order and stability in a field. Two IGUs in corrections play this role, lowering the probability of prison riots.

- Prison riots pass through a set of stages, which can be formally stylized.
- Actual riots develop in a dynamic relationship between rioting inmates and prison authorities. As a result, pre-riot factors, such as inmate ideologies, can help explain the course of a riot, but not completely.

I. Incidence and Sources of Prion Riots

Two points can be made about the incidence of prison riots: (a) they are not very common, and (b) their incidence varies over time. For example, in the half-dozen years from 1971 to 1976, there were 81 prison riots, or 13.5 riots per year. In contrast, in the half-dozen years from 2007 to 2012, there were 21 prison riots, or 3.5 riots per year. This decrease over time is even starker when the growth in the prison population is taken into account. In the first period, on average, there were 220,043 prisoners; in the second period, on average, there were 1,544,850 prisoners. Thus while the number of inmates increased seven-fold from the first to second period, the number of riots decreased in this same period nearly four-fold. Many more prisoners were seeing many fewer riots.[2]

A. Prison Riots as Social Disintegration

An early work that attempts to explain the transition to prison riots is Gresham Sykes's (2007 [1958]) *Society of Captives*, first published a half century ago and recently re-released with a new epilogue by the author. Sykes argues that the inmates bind together in solidarity and steadfast opposition to the prison authorities (the "screws") to create their own social order. Informal inmate leaders emerge and are normally given special favors by prison authorities. In return, these inmate leaders help the administration preserve order so as not jeopardize their special privileges. They keep a lid on defiance, meaning no riots. From time to time, however, prison authorities feel compelled to tighten up prisons. Strictly enforcing the rules disrupts the inmate society. The inmate leaders oriented toward cohesion and stability lose their power. Unstable, more aggressive inmates fill the leadership vacuum, setting the stage for a riot. "The system breeds rebellions by attempting to enforce the system's rules. The custodians' efforts to secure a greater degree of control result in the destruction of that control, temporary though it may be, in those uprisings we label riots" (Sykes 2007, p. 124).

Evidence on Sykes's thesis is inconsistent. Mark Colvin (1982, 1992) found support for Sykes's argument in his study of the 1980 riot at the Penitentiary of New Mexico at Santa Fe. (I describe this riot in greater detail later.) According to Colvin, the stage for a riot was set when, in 1975, a new prison administration began to crack down on drug trafficking and eliminated previously established prison programs. These efforts to tighten up the prison dismantled the informal inmate social structure that had served to maintain order in prison. Younger, more violent inmates took over and fueled the rebellion—Sykes's riot thesis.

Another study, however, set out explicitly to test Sykes's argument but found little supportive evidence (Useem and Reisig 1999). A survey was distributed to a nationwide sample of 317 medium- and maximum-security prisons. The prison official respondents were asked whether their facility had implemented policies that tightened restrictions on (a) inmate cell assignments, (b) inmate movement, (c) inmate personal property, and (d) inmate work assignments. The responses to these four questions were combined to create a "crackdown" scale. Respondents were also asked about the occurrence of a riot in their facility, to test whether imposing restrictions on inmates increase the likelihood of riots. There was no statistically significant association between the crackdown variable and riot occurrence. Prisons that tighten up controls to regain power were no more likely than other prisons to experience riots. Arguably, however, the four "crackdown" questions are highly imperfect measures of Sykes's key independent variable. The process may be more subtle, entailing a deeper meaning of "reform," than that captured in a survey. While the book on Sykes's riot thesis is not closed, the greater challenge has come from the emergence of a competing line of analysis.

B. Prison Riots as Failed Governance

A second line of research views prison riots as products of flawed, troubled, or otherwise ineffective leadership and management (Dilulio 1987; Useem and Kimball 1989; Hamm 1995; Carroll 1998; Boin and Rattray 2004; Carrabine 2005). In one formulation, "administrative breakdown" includes poor communication among correctional officials, scandals, incoherent rules for inmates and correctional officers, and sharp conflict between correctional officers and senior administrators. Inmates then see their conditions as not merely grinding and unpleasant but illegitimately bad. In contrast, well-managed and well-led correctional systems and prisons, with adequate staff and physical structures, create a sense among inmates that the system meets reasonable standards of imprisonment. Prison officials are not merely powerful in the eyes of inmates but also the legitimate holders of criminal offenders who have forfeited their right to freedom. If inmates were in the shoes of correctional staff, they would do the same. Legitimacy is central.

Two studies illustrate the approach. First, Rynne, Harding, and Wortley (2008) examined the effort by Australia's Queensland Correctional Services to open a new prison in a liberalizing direction but without sufficient attention to the necessity of creating effective correctional leadership. To develop a new staff culture, anchored in the ethos of inmate rehabilitation and therapy rather than custody, senior and line staff were hired who had little or no correctional experience. There was, as well, a deliberate attempt to keep costs low. The progressive effort fell apart: "Insufficient staff, shift problems, and conflict between program, security, and unit staff, combined to cause considerable internal tension. These types of issues were raised repeatedly with prison management and consequently senior management but to no avail" (p. 132). Inmates rioted three weeks after the prison opened.

A second study, Goldstone and Useem (1999), emphasized the destabilizing effect of prison reform and had a surface resemblance to Sykes's position that reform yields disturbances. The authors drew on case studies of 13 major riots that occurred at medium- and high-security prisons in the United States from 1952 to 1993. Their central finding: it is not the direction of reform—toward a more liberal, inmate-accommodating regime or, alternatively, toward a more conservative, controlling prison regime, per Sykes's position—but rather whether the change is well or poorly implemented and subsequently accepted by inmates. For example, if prison officials impose stricter limitations on inmates, do they provide an acceptable rationale for the change—say, a mass escape, high rates of inter-inmate violence, or the murder of a correctional officer? Then inmates are likely to say that, while they do not like the change, they understand it as a reasonable response to circumstances. Or is the rationale perceived as an excuse to tighten the screws one more turn for no discernible purpose other than to put inmates in their place? In the latter case, inmates' sense of deprivation and anger may well fuel a riot.

This second approach implies a conscious plan by inmates as a collective to rebel. Inmates ask: Are the prisons safe, secure, healthful, humane, rehabilitative, nondiscriminatory? If answers are in the negative, a prison riot may be in the air. But it is also possible that inmates use a riot situation as little more than an opportunity for individual violence; all the talk of reform may be a pretext for individual-level aggression. If this is fundamentally true, the second perspective may be attributing political content to riots where none exist.

C. Individual Correlates of Riot Participation

Christine Graeve, Matt DeLisi, and Andy Hochestler (2007, p. 407) are correct to argue "penologists have studied prison riots for decades but virtually all of this research has employed a macrosociological or structural perspective." To fill this gap, Graeve and colleagues (2007) collected information from the dossiers of a random of sample 831 male inmates in an unidentified southwestern state. The dependent variable, an official citation for prison rioting, was defined as "inciting or participating in riot, disturbance, demonstration or work stoppage" (p. 414)—a more inclusive definition of "rioting" than used in this essay. Nevertheless, this excellent study found that individual-level characteristics explained 40 percent of the variation in rioting among the male prisoners sampled. Four blocks of independent variables were used: criminal history (9 measures), social demographics (5 measures), social "risk" (4 measures), and prison infraction history (18 measures).

Nine of these measures were significantly related to rioting. Prison rioters were more likely than nonrioters to have been cited for threating staff, in-prison theft, drug possession, and weapons possession. Prison arsonists were less likely to be involved in riots, though the authors suggest perhaps this is because they were put in segregation. Race, alien status, and age were unrelated to rioting. Criminal history was unrelated to rioting, except for the variable "arrest history," although in the opposite of the predicted direction. The authors concluded by sensibly arguing that individual-level and structural variables need to be incorporated in to "more sophisticated multilevel analyses" (Graeve et al. 2007, p. 417).

D. A Missing Independent Variable: Internal Government Units

In prior work on causes of prison riots, no attention has been given to what Neil Fligstein and Doug McAdam (2012) term "internal governance units" or IGUs. This refers to organizations that serve to ensure that an industry or other social arenas ("fields") avoid destabilizing conflict and run smoothly. Examples of IGUs include the commissioner's office in a major sport, an industry trade association, a state bar association, and an accreditation association in higher education. The responsibilities of IGUs vary widely but typically involve collecting and disseminating information, credentialing employees with skills, and identifying and formalizing best practices. As a working hypothesis, two IGUs in corrections have become central in avoiding riots. One, the Association of State Correctional Administrators (ASCA), is an association of the directors of state departments of corrections, the Federal Bureau of Prisons, the largest U.S. jails, and Canadian national and provincial correctional agencies. The ASCA provides newly appointed directors with training, as well as annually for all members; collects prison and department-level information monthly on key performance measures; and addresses specific policy issues facing corrections through the promulgation of formal resolutions as well as through study of critical issues, such as racial disparity and the use of administrative segregation. The ASCA is a voluntary organization, and its continued existence depends on delivering value to its members and the field of corrections.

Working closely with the ASCA, the American Correctional Association (ACA) is a mass-membership organization. It develops positions on correctional policy issues and advocates these positions to Congress, state and local government, and the general public. Perhaps most critically, the ACA has established an accreditation system, which verifies that correctional agencies and facilities meet national correctional standards as established by ACA policy committees. Auditors make three-day site visits to facilities. They assess the facility's strengths and weaknesses, ensure the implementation of state of the art policies and procedures, establish guidelines for day-to-day operations, and identify strategies to increase professionalism and morale.

I know of no work measuring the impact of these two IGUs on corrections. Still, it is reasonable to argue that they reduce the incidence of prison riots through several routes. First, the two IGUs provide correctional agencies and facilities with knowledge about what works in correctional management and leadership. Second, they assist correctional agencies in implementing those standards through the audit process. Variation from one facility to next is reduced, bringing into line riot-prone outliers. Third, the audit process contributes to staff morale, as staff see their efforts as having measureable and valued outcomes. More work is need to develop and verify the argument.

II. Riot Stages and Variation

Even if one accepts that prison riots are born from a common cause, they vary in how they start, how they expand, what inmates do in their period of power, and how they end. The action of each side—rioting inmates and responding prison authorities—depends on the other.[3] This makes the course and outcome of any disturbance highly uncertain, in the same way that a chess game cannot be predicted from the opening gambits, though influenced by them.

A. Pre-Riot Stage

The "pre-riot stage" is the period during which both prison authorities and inmates ready themselves for a riot situation. Inmates' readiness to act may be enhanced by "preparation," a time during which the pace of conflict escalates. The challenges may come in the form of escapes, strikes, demonstrations, or horseplay that goes unstopped. Inmates learn that prison security may be breached and, by inference, riot initiators will not be stopped dead in their tracks and promptly locked up.

Also in the pre-riot stage, prison authorities must plan and prepare for what they will do in a prison disturbance. Elements of preparation include the acquisition of resources (organization, equipment, and information) for use in a riot situation, the development of a strategy for the use of these resources, and the mental readiness to respond to an incident. These efforts may serve as well as riot avoidance, as suggested by the Latin dictum *Si vis pacem, para bellum*—if you want peace, prepare for war.

B. Initiation

The major challenge to starting a riot is to get inmates to act in concert. A few inmate "radicals" may be the first or second to throw a rock or slug a correctional officer. But most inmates will join a riot only if significant others are already participating. Their participation is contingent on "safety in numbers"—the idea of "I'll join only if others are with me" (Granovetter 1978). How is safety in numbers achieved? There are three mechanisms. One is a riot plan. Inmates collectively decide to take over the prison. While a plan is hard to stop, it is also risky to the planners. If the plan is exposed, the planners may be sent to a punishment cell or charged with a new crime. Even if the inmate rioters are not identified, rumors of riot may be leaked to authorities and the prison may go into a lockdown—a costly outcome to inmates.

A second mechanism is a set of escalating events. A fight on the yard may grow until it becomes a full-scale disturbance. The decisive moment of spillover is when correctional officers retreat. However, if sufficient numbers of prison authorities are present and are poised to act, there may be a reverse bandwagon: danger in small numbers replaces safety in large numbers, and increasingly so.

A third mechanism is a signaling event that tells inmates that if they act, others will act with them. A riot in another state facility, for example, may alert inmates that a riot is on the agenda in their facility. Another signal may be a change in policy that many inmates perceive to be unfair. In this case, not only are inmates put on edge by substance of the policy change, but they are aware that other inmates are also tense and may be ready to act in concert. While it would be useful to know whether one mechanism is more common than the others, no research has been done on this. Also, it should not be assumed that the course of a riot can be directly inferred from which of the three mechanisms started the riot. For example, the New Mexico riot (see later discussion) began as a planned takeover but quickly devolved into a chaotic conflict. Likewise, the Attica riot began as a snowballing set of events but then became organized.

Crucial to initiation is the response of state authorities. Are they quick and decisive, or sluggish and uncoordinated? Often the same factors that give rise to a rebellion impede the response.

C. Expansion

For inmates, the goal of the riot in this stage is likely to be to take control of as much territory and free as many inmates as possible. Prisoners may or may not seize hostages, depending on their priorities. For example, inmates may see taking hostages as an opportunity to exact retribution. Or, if they see the riot as a chance to negotiate with prison authorities, prisoners may take hostages for use as "chips" in the negotiations.

Expansion may last from a few minutes to several hours. As with initiation, much depends on the planning and preparation of the correctional staff. Do they have a riot plan to limit the scope of a riot? Have they rehearsed the plan? Are they ready? Are security gates locked? Also important: Does the prison architecture facilitate or impede expansion? For example, Morris and Worrall (2014) observe that a telephone style layout may impede riot control, but more work is needed to firmly establish this.

D. Inmate Sovereignty/State of Siege

Once inmates become a functioning power center, they must decide what rules, if any, will govern. Prison riots become famous, or infamous, based on the rules they choose. In some prison riots, inmates make demands for reform and seek to exchange their hostages for promises of improved living conditions. In others, inmates brutally attack one another and their hostages, and no demands are made. Other riots resemble giant racial or ethnic brawls. Some prison riots are conducted by criminal gangs, others by political radicals aligned with the broad social movements of the day, and still others by inmates with the narrowest of personal agendas.

One factor that may explain this variation is inmate ideology. Several ideologies have been identified (Goldstone and Useem 1999). *Rationalism* is the belief that that the prison is hobbled because correctional authorities do not perform their job. For example, inmates may see the correctional staff as poorly trained, lazy, or abusive and senior administrators as incompetent or corrupt. Rebellion is justified as an effort to "force" prison officials to do what they are paid to do. *Legalism* is the belief that the constitution and laws bind the government to providing decent living conditions and services. If conditions fall below those levels, then the state has violated the law. Collective action by inmates is framed as an effort to uphold legal standards. *Rehabilitationism* is the belief that the state should provide job training, educational programs, counseling, and drug rehabilitation. If the prison authorities instead leave inmates idle except for recreation, then inmates are deprived of the "right" to reenter society successfully after their prison term is up. *Revolutionism* is the ideology that offenders are imprisoned not because the state has a responsibility to uphold the law but rather because of their race or poverty or other illegitimate reasons that serve the interests of the powers that be. If prison is an instrument of repression, it is a short step to the position that a riot is rebellion against an illegitimate authority. *Hobbism* is the belief prison officials have a responsibility to maintain safety behind bars. If inmate life is instead unsafe and chaotic, prison officials are to blame. Rebellion is a demand for more authority or, at least, less chaos. The immediate enemy may be identified as staff or inmates who have offended other prisoners. Exacting vengeance may then be a "means of reassertion of human dignity or worth, after damage" (Moore 1978, p. 17).[4]

It is tempting to argue that the choices made during riots depend on the dispositions and ideologies that inmates bring into them. Some connections are easily drawn. For example, an ideology of rehabilitationism may lead to reformist demands to improve inmates' services. Similarly, if there is strong inter-inmate hostility, then the war of all against all will become fully manifest during the riot when restraints are lifted. To date, however, no research has been able to demonstrate these connections in a systematic way.

Prison officials must manage their own forces and decide on their rules of engagement. Perhaps most important, a central command must be able to exercise authority and direction over the forces and resources available. The longer a riot lasts, more agencies become involved, and the larger the area and the number of hostages held by inmates, the more complex command becomes. The challenge is met, in part, through achieving unity of command and determining the best level and location of command.

Unity of command, the principle that all forces report to a single individual with requisite authority, is important for developing a coherent response. (Napoleon reportedly said that the only thing worse than a bad general is two good ones.[5]) *Level of command* must be addressed—does the governor, the state commissioner of corrections, the warden, or the watch commander take charge? *Location of command* must also be decided. Is the command center located on site at the prison or in the state capital?

E. Termination

Prison authorities have three main options to end a riot. They may use force to retake the prison (the tactical solution), they may end the riot through talking (the negotiation solution), or they may let the riot die of its own accord (the waiting solution). Prison officials must weigh the costs and benefits of the three options. I briefly consider each.

In general, the administration can end a riot at any time if it is willing to use overwhelming force. This option, however, may be costly. Inmates may commit to injuring or killing hostages if force is used. Shots fired can kill hostages. If prison authorities are to use force, they cannot merely "apply" force but must develop strategies that are effective to minimize casualties.

Negotiations may take place between prison authorities and inmates. The dialogue may be an exercise in bargaining. Inmates use hostages as chips, seeking to trade those chips for publicity, amnesty, improved conditions, or other benefits. Staff may use promises of new programs, better food, or other organizational changes as their negotiating chips. The riot ends when the negotiating parties come to an agreement about the future. Alternatively, prison authorities may use negotiations as an element of situation management. They seek not a "deal" but to stabilize the situation, obtain information, or lower inmate vigilance against an assault.

The third strategy for riot resolution is to wait it out. The premise is that hostage takers may develop sympathy for the hostages, develop a bond with the official negotiators, or simply get tired of rioting. A strategy of waiting can be accelerated by making inmates more uncomfortable, for example, by depriving them of food, water, or heat. One problem with this is the hostages are likely to endure the same deprivations. Another is that inmate anger toward the state may increase and their position is hardened rather than softened. Examples of the three strategies are given in the following.

III. Case Studies

As noted at the outset, prison riots vary greatly in their form and course. Five case studies are selected to illustrate this variation.[6] They include protracted riots, lasting several days or longer, which are often the more famous (or notorious) riots, and contracted riots, lasting just a few hours, which are generally lesser known. A comprehensive theory of prison riots would link the causes of prison riots to the course and outcome. No one has done this in a systematic way.

A. Attica State Correctional Facility: September 9–13, 1971

This riot was set in motion by events in one of the prison's four exercise yards. In a confrontation between several correctional officers and inmates, an inmate struck an officer. The officer backed down. In the evening, the inmate accused of striking the officer was moved from his cell to a disciplinary cell-block. He resisted. As he was being carried away, inmates threw debris and screamed insults at the officers. The next morning, inmates jumped and assaulted the officer who was involved in the confrontation the previous day. The inmates quickly attacked several other officers, killing one. The inmates grabbed the officers' keys and released inmates from one of the prison's four cell blocks. They destroyed the immediate area. A security gate had a defective weld and broke, allowing the inmates to spread the riot to other blocks.

Inmates, initially disorganized, gathered in one of the four exercise yards. They milled around, chatted with friends, and looted the inmate store. After several hours, a loosely organized leadership group emerged. The group gained control over the yard.

Most of those in leadership positions had not been involved in the initial confrontation and violence. Using a bullhorn, inmate leaders urged inmates to act respectfully toward one another. The leaders drafted a set of demands addressed to President Richard Nixon and New York Governor Nelson Rockefeller. They called for amnesty for participation in the riot, transportation to a "non-imperialistic" country for those inmates who wanted it, the intervention of the federal government to help inmates, and the "reconstruction" of the prison under inmate "supervision." Inmates also demanded that several outside observers be admitted to the prison, including radical attorney William Kunstler, a liberal New York State Assemblyman, heads of the Black Panther Party and Young Lords, journalist Tom Wicker, and an Urban League activist. The leadership group established a set of rules for inmates: no harm was to be inflicted on the 43 hostages; homosexual relations, fighting, and taking drugs were forbidden. No inmate was to leave the yard without permission. A group of black Muslims took charge of the hostages and "security guards" enforced the other rules. On the second day the informally established leadership was replaced by an elected committee. Residents of each cell-block assembled in a different part of the yard to elect their representatives. Many inmates, perhaps a majority, sought no part in the riot. Some barricaded themselves in their cells; others positioned themselves on the perimeter of the yard. Inmates killed three other inmates. Inmates regarded one as an informant, another as an open white racist, and a third as mentally unstable and dangerous.

During four days of negotiations, the crisis became increasingly tense. Authorities agreed to most of the inmate demands but refused to yield on granting inmates clemency for participating in the riot and the dismissal of the prison's superintendent. Governor Rockefeller ordered state troopers to retake the prison, during which 29 inmates and 10 correctional staff were killed. This termination is an example of the force strategy but, in this case, poorly implemented.

B. Penitentiary of New Mexico: February 2–3, 1980

At about 1:30 AM on February 2, 1980, several inmates overpowered, stripped, and severely beat four correctional officers conducting a routine inspection of a dormitory in the prison's south wing. Correctional officers stationed at other south wing dormitories were quickly subdued. A number of security lapses allowed the inmates to take control over the entire institution: a security gate separating the south wing from the rest of the institution was unlocked; a recently installed window protecting the control center broke easily; and renovation crews left behind acetylene torches, which were used to open locked gates. No group of inmates attained leadership status. Control over hostages, walkie-talkies, and negotiations was fragmented, personalistic, and fleeting. Some inmates, alone and in groups, used the opportunity to beat, rape, torture, and mutilate other inmates. The assaults and killings were selective. Inmates targeted informants ("snitches") and objects of personal grudges. Thirty-three inmates were killed. Twelve correctional officers were taken as hostages; some were severely beaten and sodomized.

Not all inmates participated in the violence. The prison's 120 African American inmates organized themselves for self-protection and fled from the riot. By the second day, over two-thirds of the white and Hispanic inmates had surrendered to authorities. Some members of the initiating group attempted to negotiate with the administration, but their efforts were disorganized and had little impact on the course of the riot.

The riot ended after 36 hours primarily because inmates became exhausted and were tired of rioting. State police tactical teams entered the prison, encountering little resistance. This termination was primarily a waiting solution, highlighting its potential costs.

C. US Penitentiary, Atlanta: November 23–December 4, 1987

On November 20, 1987, the US State Department announced that Cuba had agreed to an accord that would allow the return of 2,500 Cuban nationals to Cuba. Included would be Cubans who fled to the United States in the 1980 Mariel boatlift and were released on "immigration parole" but were being held in a federal prison after having been convicted of a crime. Three days after the announcement, the detainees seized control of the US Penitentiary in Atlanta, part of the Bureau of Prisons, US Department of Justice. The central demand was not to be repatriated to Cuba.

During the few days immediately preceding the riot, there was evidence that a riot might be impending. In one unit, detainees had remained dressed overnight. Also, the volume of outgoing mail was several times heavier than normal, and detainees were removing family photographs from their lockers. The Atlanta officials were aware of the possibility of a riot. The warden met several times with his executive staff and department heads to determine whether a lockdown was warranted. Still, the evidence they obtained was not sufficient to order a lockdown.

The riot began when hundreds of detainees in three locations in the prison began seizing hostages and securing control of units. A group of inmates charged a gate in an attempt to escape but was stopped by warning shots from an officer in a tower. Over a 20-minute period, the riot expanded. The detainees gained control over much of the prison and 100 hostages.

The detainees dispersed their hostages among several buildings behind fortified barricades and pledged to kill them if an assault were launched. This precluded a quick tactical rescue. Nearly without exception, the hostages received reasonably good care.

Attorney General Edwin Meese personally directed the overall response. After 11 days of negotiations, detainees and officials reached an agreement. It provided that each detainee would receive a fair hearing to determine if he could be released and a promise to limit prosecutions for participation in the riot. The government would not agree to the primary demand to ban deportations to Cuba. This resolution illustrates a successful termination through negotiations.

D. New Castle Correctional Facility, Indiana: April 24, 2007

In March 2007, Arizona contracted with Indiana to transfer 1,300 of its medium-security inmates to facilities in Indiana. Arizona prisons were overcrowded; Indiana had more cells than inmates. Soon after the first 630 inmates arrived in Indiana, a rebellion broke out at the New Castle Correctional Facility, a privately owned prison that had accepted Arizona inmates.

The Arizona inmates felt aggrieved by the transfer and judged it to be illegitimate. Not only were inmates being moved far from their home, making visits difficult, the transfer was conducted suddenly, without providing inmates an opportunity to say good-bye to families and friends. Inmates were told at midnight that they were being moved to another state and boarded a plane at 5 AM. Even once on the plane, they were not told of their destination.

In addition, the Arizona inmates perceived Indiana prisons to have been more austere than what they had been accustomed to. For example, Indiana did not allow prisoners to smoke, and the recreation schedules were shorter. Prisoners were not told about these differences when they were being moved.

The riot began when a group of inmates refused to dress in prison-issued uniforms prior to entering the dining hall. They forced their way through staff blocking the entrance. Other inmates, then in a housing unit, heard the commotion. They broke through (defective) security windows and locked doors to join the disturbance. In total, about 500 inmates joined the riot and took control of a portion of the prison. They took no hostages. The facility's emergency response team quickly mobilized. They established a skirmish line and fired warning shots. An assault team retook the prison about two hours after the riot began. No demands were issued or negotiations conducted.

E. Apodaca, Mexico: February 19, 2012

Soon after taking office in December 2006, Mexican President Felipe Calderon declared a "war" against drug traffickers and organized crime. Many arrests were made, filling prisons beyond capacity. In 2008, the government announced that it would construct eight new maximum-security prisons; none were built.

At Apodca prison in northern Mexico, 3,000 inmates were housed in space designed for 1,500. Members of two competing drug cartels, Los Zetas and Gulf Cartel, were housed in separate cell blocks. On the streets, the two cartels had been engaged in a violent conflict over control of drug routes and markets.

The riot began when, at 2 AM, correctional staff unlocked the gates between the two units. The members of the Los Zetas surged into the Gulf Cartel block. They killed (beheaded, stabbed, hanged) 44 members of the Gulf Cartel. Mattresses were set on fire. In the overall confusion, 30 Los Zetas members escaped the prison, including a prominent leader. No demands were made. Order was restored by 6 AM. A month after the riot, the prison director and 21 staff members were arrested for their alleged role in the prison break.

IV. CONCLUSION

Do prison riots bring about change in the broader penal system? There is no simple answer to this question. Much depends on whether institutional confusion of a prison riot (prisoners in charge for a time) resonates with tensions in the broader penal system. If the penal system appears sound—in its policies and procedures, in its fiscal condition, in its rationale for confinement of those behind bars—then the post-riot reforms may go no further than improving the agency's riot-response capability. Where these conditions do not hold, when the prison system appears to be in crisis, then prison riots may signal the need for change. Effective institutional leadership will listen to the signal and act. That institutional leadership, however, may or may not be there.

Prisons are a system of cooperation, but that cooperation may be disrupted at a low level by everyday forms of resistance and at a high level through prison riots. The most general conclusion that can be drawn about prison riots is that multiple sets of factors—as identified by competing theories—may give rise to their occurrence. Administrative crackdowns may, as Sykes (2007) argues, be an underlying cause of some prison riots. But the evidence suggests that this explanation cannot account for prison riots in a more general way. A more general explanation focuses on administrative breakdown. The center cannot hold, and the chaos of a riot is summoned forth. Still, no single theory has swept away the others to gain dominance. Perhaps this is because prison riots are too disparate a phenomenon to allow for theoretical unity.

Missing from all previous theories of prison riots has been the role of IGUs—regulatory units that help safeguard stability within a broad field of action. The IGUs within corrections, the ASCA and ACA, appear to bring stability to corrections, including riot avoidance. They achieve this by devising workable solutions to substantive issues facing corrections; training senior personnel in best practices; and, through facility audits, infusing correctional staff with a commitment to professionalism and pride when certification is achieved. IGUs have little or no power to formally regulate or tax; they can be effective only to the extent they are perceived to be genuinely adding value to the field.

While prison riots may or may not arise from a common cause, they certainly take many forms. In some riots, inmates issue demands and use their hostages to bargain with the state. In others, inmates turn against each other. In still others, inmates use the occasion of a riot to attempt to escape. One reason for this variability is that prisoners bring different ideologies to the riot. For example, do they harbor grave hostility toward each other, the ideology of Hobbism, which may be expressed in inter-inmate vengeance and retaliation? Or, under an ideology of rehabilitationism, do inmates see the riot as an opportunity to bargain with the state to effect change?

A second reason for the variability is that prison riots entail a strategic, interactive element. Each side responds to the moves of the other side, followed by a further back and forth, and so on. This interactive component may produce diverse outcomes. For example, a first move, such as inmates taking hostages, may help set the course of a riot, but further moves and countermoves may take it in unexpected directions. Likewise, prison authorities may, at any time, terminate the riot by using overwhelming force. This, though, depends on administrative skill and leadership. The state's options are expanded to the extent to which it addresses its core tasks in riot resolution. They include achieving unity of command, or an appropriate level and location of command, planning, and preparation—another set of variables impacting a riot's course.

In sum, prison riots may be born from multiple causes. There develops a dynamic relationship between state actors and the inmates who challenge them.

NOTES

1. Walter (1969) develops the point that even the most brutal authoritarian systems require an element of cooperation. For an expansion of this argument, see Useem and Piehl (2008, pp. 83–85).
2. Both the absolute number of riots and the ratio of riots to inmates declined over time. Useem and Piehl (2008, p. 94) report the latter.
3. This section of the essay draws on the work of Useem and Kimball (1989) and Useem, Camp, and Camp (1996). More recent work on riot stages is needed but unavailable.
4. Along these lines, Gresham Sykes (2007, p. 79) argues that much of inmates' defiant behavior can be understood as an effort to reaffirm their dignity and vitality.
5. Pointed out by Posner (1999, p. 251).
6. There are numerous descriptive and analytic accounts of each of these riots. The reader may refer to the following: New York Special Commission on Attica (1972); Saenz (1986); US Department of Justice, Federal Bureau of Prisons (1988); Archibold (2012); de Cordoba (2012); Fox (2012); Useem and Piehl (2008).

References

Archibold, Randal C. 2012. "Gangs Blamed as Riot Kills Dozens at Prison in Mexico." *New York Times* (February 19). http://mobile.nytimes.com/2012/02/20/world/americas/in-mexico-prison-riot-kills-at-least-44-people.html

Boin, Arjen, and William A. R. Rattray. 2004. "Understanding Prison Riots: Toward a Threshold Theory." *Punishment & Society* 6:47–65.

Carrabine, Eamonn. 2005. "Prison Riots, Social Order and the Problem of Legitimacy." *British Journal of Criminology* 45:896–913.

Carroll, Leo. 1998. *Lawful Order: A Case Study of Correctional Crisis and Reform.* New York: Garland Publishing.

Colvin, Mark. 1982. "The 1980 New Mexico Riot." *Social Problems* 29:49–63.

Colvin, Mark. 1992. *The Penitentiary in Crisis: From Accommodation to Riot in New Mexico.* Albany: State University of New York Press.

de Cordoba, Jose. 2012. "Jail Riot in Mexico Was Diversion for Escape." *Wall Street Journal* (February 21). http://www.wsj.com/articles/SB10001424052970203358704577235411760082478

Dilulio, John J. Jr. 1987. *Governing Prisons: A Comparative Study of Correctional Management.* New York: Free Press.

Fligstein, Neil, and Doug McAdam. 2012. *A Theory of Fields.* New York: Oxford University Press.

Fox, Edward. 2012. "Zetas-Gulf Cartel Prison Fight Leaves 44 Dead." Insight Crime (February 20). http://www.insightcrime.org/news-briefs/zetas-gulf-cartel-prison-fight-leaves-44-dead

Goldstone, Jack A., and Bert Useem. 1999. "Prison Riots as Revolutions: An Extension of State-Centered Theories of Revolution." *American Journal of Sociology* 104:985–1029.

Granovetter, Mark. 1978. "Threshold Models of Collective Behavior." *American Journal of Sociology* 83:1420–1443.

Graeve, Christine M., Matt DeLisi, and Andy Hochstetler. 2007. "Prison Rioters: Exploring Infraction Characteristics, Risk Factors, Social Correlates, and Criminal Careers." *Psychological Reports* 100:407–419.

Hamm, Mark S. 1995. *The Abandoned Ones: The Imprisonment and Uprising of the Mariel Boat People.* Boston: Northeastern University Press.

Morris, Robert G., and John L. Worrall. 2014. "Prison Architecture and Inmate Misconduct: A Multilevel Assessment." *Crime & Delinquency* 60(7):1083–1109.

Moore, Barrington Jr. 1978. *Injustice: The Social Bases of Obedience and Revolt.* White Plains, NY: M. E. Sharpe.

New York Special Commission on Attica. 1972. *Attica: The Official Report of the New York State Special Commission on Attica.* New York: Bantam Books.

Posner, Richard A. 1999. *An Affair of State: The Investigation, Impeachment, and Trial of President Clinton.* Cambridge, MA: Harvard University Press.

Rynne, John, Richard W. Harding, and Richard Wortley. 2008. "Market Testing and Prison Riots: How Public-Sector Commercialization Contributed to a Prison Riot." *Criminology and Public Policy* 7:117–142.

Saenz, Adolph. 1986. *Politics of a Prison Riot: The 1980 New Mexico Prison Riot, Its Causes and Aftermath.* Corrales, NM: Rhombus.

Sykes, Gresham M. 2007. *The Society of Captives: A Study of a Maximum Security Prison.* Princeton, NJ: Princeton University Press. (Originally published 1958)

US Department of Justice, Federal Bureau of Prisons. 1988. *A Report to the Attorney General on the Disturbances at the Federal Detention Center, Oakdale, Louisiana and the U.S. Penitentiary, Atlanta, Georgia.* Washington, DC: US Department of Justice, Federal Bureau of Prisons.

Useem, Bert, Camille Camp, and George Camp. 1996. *Resolution of Prison Riots: Strategy and Policies.* New York: Oxford University Press.

Useem, Bert, and Peter A. Kimball. 1989. *States of Siege: US Prison Riots, 1971–1986.* New York: Oxford University Press.

Useem, Bert, and Anne Morrison Piehl. 2008. *Prison State: The Challenge of Mass Incarceration.* New York: Cambridge University Press.

Useem, Bert, and Michael D. Reisig. 1999. "Collective Action in Prisons: Protests, Disturbances, and Riots." *Criminology* 37:735–759.

Walter, Eugene V. 1969. *Terror and Resistance: A Study of Political Violence.* New York: Oxford University Press.

CHAPTER 13

DRUGS AND PRISONS

MICHAEL WHEATLEY, JOHN R. WEEKES,
ANDREA E. MOSER, AND KATHLEEN THIBAULT

How is it possible that drugs can enter a secure environment like a prison? This is a perfectly reasonable question for a layperson to ask. Correctional institutions are, by definition, the most secure and controlled physical environments in existence. How is it, then, that drugs, weapons, and other forms of prohibited items or "contraband" penetrate such a secure and monitored context? In this essay, we explore the issues of drugs in correctional institutions. In doing so, we discuss the kinds of drug contraband that have been discovered in correctional institutions, and we provide an overview of attempts by various correctional jurisdictions and agencies to eliminate their availability. Our discussion takes account of a variety of psychoactive substances, including ethyl alcohol and a broad range of illicit (illegal) and licit (legal) drugs that have been found in institutions.[1]

We first consider the extent to which drugs and drug users are found in American prisons and compare this with other jurisdictions, finding:

- The United States has a very high rate of imprisonment compared with other Western jurisdictions, and in part this is explained by the criminalization of drug use, although this is a common behavior in U.S. society.
- Many of those incarcerated in the United States are drug or alcohol abusers but convicted of other types of offenses, further increasing the number of prisoners who can be described as "drug involved."
- The criminalization of drug use in the United States is explained by a public policy position that asserts drug use can be reduced by deterrence and punishment. This is an intuitive and political rather than evidence-based position.
- Because the incarcerated population combines drug users with those involved in the drug trade, it is inevitable that drug demand and supply will become an important part of the illicit prison economy.

We then consider the problems associated with drug use inside prison walls, concluding:

- The experience of being incarcerated exacerbates people's desire to get involved with drug use—to self-medicate against the pains of imprisonment, to pass the time, to forge social networks, to promote social status, and/or for financial gain.

- If the authorities manage to reduce illicit drug supply, alternatives will be found, including prescription medication or homemade alcohol, which generates other health and control problems.
- Drugs are a principal component of the "illicit economy" found in every prison. Drug trading in prison can be extremely lucrative for the trader who is often connected to organized crime networks operating outside the prison walls.
- The use of drugs in prisons is intrinsically linked to prison violence and to serious health complications among prisoners.

Drug use in prison needs to be managed by a careful combination of control and care mechanisms:

- To disrupt drug supply, the most common interdiction methods used include searches, use of drug detection equipment and detection dogs, and mandatory drug testing of prisoners.
- More therapeutic approaches to reduce drug demand vary among jurisdictions, but some common approaches include pharmaceutical (e.g., opiate-replacement treatment) and therapeutic (e.g. therapeutic communities, cognitive behavioral programs).
- It is vital to find the correct balance between care and control strategies. If there is tight control but poor provision of therapy, the needs of drug-involved prisoners will inevitably broaden and may create more serious threats to order and control. On the other hand, even extensive provision of therapy will be undermined if drugs are plentiful and cheap.

I. Drugs and American Prisons

A. America and Imprisonment

The United States has the highest documented incarceration rate in the world (Walmsley 2013). Joseph Califano (2010), in his foreword to *Behind Bars II: Substance Abuse and America's Correctional Institution Population*, stated that the United States makes up only 5 percent of the world's population but imprisons 25 percent of the world's incarcerated offenders. Glaze and Herberman (2013) cited statistics from the U.S. Department of Justice, which stated that, in 2012, 1 of every 108 adult residents was incarcerated in a correctional institution or jail (approximately 21 percent of the correctional population or 920 per 100,000 U.S. adult residents). Also, in 2013, the Bureau of Justice Statistics reported a total of 2,228,400 offenders incarcerated in the United States—216,900 in federal correctional institutions, 1,267,000 in the state-run systems, and 744,500 in local and city jails.

The World Prison Population List (10th ed.) quotes the prison population rate (per 100,000 of national population) as 716 for the United States compared with 118 for Canada, 148 for England and Wales, 147 for Scotland, and 101 for Northern Ireland (Walmsley 2013). These figures illustrate the popularity of imprisonment by American jurisdictions.

The Justice Policy Institute (2008) reported that the growth in the correctional population continues to be driven largely by the fact that the United States incarcerates more people for drug offenses than any other country; approximately 25 percent of incarcerated offenders are convicted of a drug offense, including possession and trafficking. Further, the Sentencing Project (2016) estimated that the total number of people incarcerated for drug offenses has virtually exploded over the span of just 30 years—from approximately 41,000 in 1980 to 489,000 in 2014 (see Figure 13.1).

As well as those incarcerated for drug offenses, there was also a significant proportion of offenders with substance abuse and dependence problems who were convicted of other offenses but who also met clinical criteria for drug use disorders. These individuals are often referred to as "substance involved," and, as we will highlight later in the chapter, for a significant portion of these individuals, their abuse of alcohol and other drugs is not directly related to their offending.

In 2012, an estimated 23.9 million Americans aged twelve or older declared using illicit drugs in the month prior to a survey interview (Substance Abuse and Mental Health Services Administration 2013). Illicit drugs included marijuana, cocaine (including crack), heroin, hallucinogens, inhalants, or the nonmedical use of a range of prescription medications such as pain relievers (e.g., opioids), tranquilizers, stimulants, and sedatives. It has been estimated that almost seven million Americans struggle with symptoms of drug abuse, ranging from problematic use to full dependence (Justice Policy Institute 2008). Americans

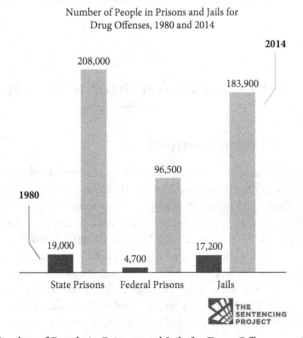

FIGURE 13.1. Number of People in Prisons and Jails for Drug Offenses, 1980 and 2014.

Sources: Carson, E. A., 2015. *Prisoners in 2014*. Washington, DC: Bureau of Justice Statistics; Mauer, M. and R. King. 2007. *A 25-Year Quagmire: The War on Drugs and Its Impact on American Society*. Washington, DC: The Sentencing Project; Glaze, L. E. and E. J. Herberman. 2014. *Correctional Populations in the United States, 2013*. Washington, DC: Bureau of Justice Statistics.

consume around two-thirds of the world's illegal drugs (Califano 2010). Thus, the linkage between drug use and the correctional system in the United States quickly emerged as a significant challenge, to say the least.

B. Substance-Involved Offenders in American Prisons

The relationship between substance abuse and America's prison population was examined by the National Center on Addiction and Substance Abuse at Columbia University (CASA) using various data sources between 1996 and 2006 (National Center on Addiction and Substance Abuse 2010). CASA researchers found that despite an unprecedented decline in violent and property crimes during this decade, the rate of incarceration that was linked in some way to alcohol and other drugs continued to grow. While the general U.S. population grew by 12.5 percent during this period, the proportion of incarcerated adults grew by almost 33 percent, and the percentage of substance-involved offenders (drugs and alcohol actively contributing to their offending behavior) behind bars rose even more rapidly, by slightly more than 43 percent. The CASA study highlighted that four out of five of America's 1.7 million incarcerated people were involved with alcohol and other drugs based on 1996 survey data. In 2006, 2.3 million adults were behind bars with 1.9 million (approximately 85 percent) being substance involved and almost two-thirds (64.5 percent) meeting established criteria for an alcohol or other drug use disorder (National Center on Addiction and Substance Abuse 2010). For example, in state correctional institutions, 63 percent of property and drug offenders were likely to be drug abusing or dependent, and 47 percent of violent offenders met the Diagnostic and Statistical Manual of Mental Disorders—4th ed. (DSM-IV) criteria for drug dependence or abuse.[2] In federal correctional institutions, 52 percent of the population was made up of drug offenders with approximately 50 percent meeting drug dependence or abuse criteria (Mumola and Karberg 2006). Clearly, there is a relationship between drugs, offending, and incarceration, and the earlier noted percentages underscore the fact that correctional institutions house the largest and most seriously substance-abusing segment of society.

While the increase in the incarcerated substance-involved population is striking, gender differences and the massive racial and ethnic disparities in the incarceration rates of drug offenders merit additional attention. In 2011, 111,387 women resided in the federal and state correctional systems and 93,300 in local jails (Carson and Sabol 2012; Minton 2012). Women represent just over 9 percent of the incarcerated population in the United States compared with 10.6 percent in Canada, 4.5 percent in England and Wales, 5.4 percent in Scotland, and 3.1 percent in Northern Ireland according to the World Prison Brief (Institute for Criminal Policy Research 2015). At the end of 2010, 25 percent of female offenders in state correctional institutions were incarcerated for drug crimes, compared with 17 percent of their male counterparts (Carson and Sabol 2012).

With regard to racial background, according to the National Association for the Advancement of Colored People (NAACP), African Americans constitute, approximately, a staggering one million of the total 2.3 million incarcerated population (NAACP 2013). This is nearly six times the incarceration rate of white Americans. Together, African Americans and Hispanic Americans represented 58 percent of all incarcerated offenders in 2008 despite making up only approximately 25 percent of the U.S. population. Yet, whites are reportedly using drugs at five times the rate of African Americans, and African Americans are sent to correctional institutions for drug offenses at ten times the rate of white Americans. This compares with approximately 9.5 percent of black offenders in federal incarceration in Canada in 2013 (black people make up roughly 3 percent of Canada's population) (Office of the Correctional Investigator 2013) and 10 percent from a black ethnic group in the British national prison population (significantly higher than the 2.8 percent of the general population they represent) (Prison Reform Trust 2015).

C. U.S. Drug Policy and Its Impact on the Prison Population

Epidemics related to heroin (late 1960s to early 1970s), powder cocaine (mid-1970s to mid-1980s), crack cocaine (mid 1980s), methamphetamine (late 1990s) and marijuana (particularly 1970s) have influenced and shaped the drug policy landscape in the United States. The resulting highly punitive regime for drug offenders is largely a response to the association of these perceived epidemics with crime waves (Pollack, Reuter, and Sevigny 2010). Despite these epidemics occurring decades ago, they still remain relevant to understanding why so many drug offenders or those who are substance involved continue to land in America's prisons and jails.

Numerous politicians and policymakers believed, and still do, that eliminating drug use will reduce crime. The use of incarceration became a popular way to achieve this goal. The policy landscape relating to drug offenses in the United States began to change, and a succession of presidents sought electoral approval via their hard line responses to drug abuse and associated crime. In short, the enactment of major drug policy legislation initiated by Ronald Reagan, promoted by George Bush, developed by Bill Clinton, and enabled by George H. W. Bush, meant more people were incarcerated in America than ever before, quadrupling to over two million. A public health approach to address drug use and abuse was replaced by law enforcement.[3] Drug use became regarded not as a health issue but was deemed immoral and illegal. Accordingly, punishing drug offenders was considered to be the priority to deter drug use rather than providing help for people to change their drug use behavior. The war on drugs became a bipartisan effort supported by Democrats and Republicans alike; it appeared that nothing was to be gained politically by protecting drug abusers from excessive punishment. Drug control legislation was proposed during every congressional election year in the 1980s. Election years often inspired bold, new drug-control schemes to the appreciation of the American voters.

Drug users and abusers form a large proportion of correctional populations in most developed countries (Dolan, Khoei, Brentari, and Stevens 2007). In the United States, it is estimated that 85 percent of incarcerated offenders have a substance abuse problem with 65 percent meeting the diagnostic criteria for a drug dependence disorder (National Center on Addiction and Substance Abuse 2010). Similar statistics are reported by other jurisdictions such as the United Kingdom (Her Majesty's Prison Service 2003), Canada (Kitchin 2006; Kunic and Grant 2006; Babooram 2008), and New Zealand (Morris 2001). In addition, a notable proportion of offenders, particularly in the United States, are incarcerated for offenses related to drug manufacturing and distribution (National Center on Addiction and Substance Abuse 2010). It is not surprising, then, that placing individuals with extensive drug use problems in a closed environment such as a correctional institution alongside those who have been principally involved in the drug trade sets up a potentially volatile and lucrative economy of supply and demand for illicit substances inside prison.

II. Problems Associated with Drug Use in Prison

A. Drug-Seeking Behavior

Many of the people in correctional institutions have been taken from a world where the use of illicit (illegal) drugs is endemic and the misuse of licit (legal) drugs is increasing markedly (Fischer, Gittins, and Rëhm 2008). Many offenders are problem drug users, and drugs may be the reason, or one of the reasons, why they are incarcerated (Blakey 2008). Given the "normality" of drug use by these individuals to relieve boredom, cope with stress, or as an established defense against feelings of social isolation, it is not surprising that they attempt to bring that normality into the prison setting (Blakey 2008; Woodall 2012). Prison can exacerbate, rather than lessen, individuals' inclinations to use illicit substances (Swann and James 1998; Stark et al. 2006). Wheatley (2007) offered a five-part explanatory model to account for this. First, he proposed that drugs are used in prison to "self-medicate" as a response to the tedium and pains of institutional life. Second, drug use can be used to pass the time and to counteract the boredom or to "slip away" from the realities of prison life (see Cope 2003; Stöver and Weilandt 2007). Third, prisoners' drug use promotes a social network forging relationships and connections through shared enterprise that can buffer feelings of social isolation and encourage solidarity (see Tompkins et al. 2007). Fourth, drug taking can inflate a prisoners' reputation within the establishment and promote social status within a constructed group hierarchy because it is a high-risk endeavor (see Courtenay and Sabo 2001). Finally, drug seeking behaviors are driven by economic incentives as prisoners influence others to use drugs so that they can exploit vulnerabilities and make financial gains (see Crewe 2005). Between those who deal the drugs and those who use, there will always be someone trying to move drugs into an institution.

As noted previously, the majority of offenders enter correctional institutions with a substance abuse problem. However, once incarcerated, the institutional environment may have an impact on offenders' drug using behavior; Shewan et al. (1994), for example, suggested that drug use in custody is reduced by prison walls, surveillance, and lack of availability. In some cases, institutional authorities' efforts to stop drugs entering a prison often leads to offenders stopping their drug use or using less frequently (Dolan et al. 2007). However, studies have also suggested that imprisonment may result in offenders switching to different drugs than they used on the street, and that this is influenced by factors such as length of incarceration, interdiction programs like mandatory drug testing (MDT), psychosocial characteristics of offenders, and the availability of substances (Boys et al. 2002; Standing Committee on Public Safety and National Security 2012).

Clearly, the use of extensive and extreme security measures limits the availability of drugs, drug paraphernalia, and other forms of contraband in a correctional institution—the setting is dramatically different from the street. When the supply and availability of illicit substances is severely decreased, offenders resort to the misuse of other types of substances, including prescription medications or homemade alcohol referred to colloquially as "brew" or "hooch" depending on the country and jurisdiction (Standing Committee on Public Safety and National Security 2012; Woodall 2012). Certain medications are available to offenders with mental health disorders, chronic pain, substance abuse, and other physical health issues. The use of medically prescribed drug replacement therapies such as methadone maintenance treatment and buprenorphrine (Suboxone) have become increasingly popular with correctional agencies around the world as effective solutions to chronic use of opioid analgesics by injection drug users. All substances, illicit and prescription, vary in the length of time that they can be identified through urinalysis, making those with shorter detection times more desirable. This can create the unintentional consequence of putting those who are taking prescribed medications at risk of being coerced, intimidated, and bullied by other inmates for their medications.

B. Drugs and the Illicit Economy in Prisons

The "illicit prison economy" refers to trade between prisoners that is forbidden by law or by prison rules. It cannot be emphasized enough that drugs are a principal driver of an illicit prison economy that also includes the misuse of licit drugs. Illicit drug distribution in prison can be a lucrative business, with substances worth three to four times their street value (Crewe 2005), which may encourage networks of organized crime both inside and outside the correctional institution, with arrangements for the trafficking of illicit items into prisons and payment of outstanding associated debts, and prison violence.

C. Other Problems Associated with Drugs in Prison

Inside, drug use and drug trafficking can lead to institutional violence (including acts of extreme violence and murder for drug debts) and create serious difficulties for correctional authorities to manage the offender population (Standing Committee on Public Safety and National Security 2012). Drugs and violence have been described as being related in three possible ways: economically, systematically, and psychopharmacologically (Goldstein 1985). The economic model suggests that some drug users engage in economically orientated violence, such as robbery, to support the costs of using drugs. The systemic model describes violence as being intrinsically involved with drug use as part of the traditionally aggressive patterns of interaction within the system of drug distribution (turf wars) and enforcing "hierarchical" codes associated with the drug or group culture. The psychopharmaceutical model suggests that some individuals, as a result of taking drugs, may become excitable, irrational, aggressive, agitated, and even violent. Some evidence does exist to suggest that taking drugs, particularly stimulants, may lead to violence by exacerbating existing psychopathological and social problems or by increasing the risk of paranoid or psychotic episodes. That said, no psychoactive substance can be said to have universal criminogenic properties, and both individual and environmental factors can influence how the use of psychoactive substances impacts behavior (European Monitoring Centre for Drugs and

Drug Addiction 2012). This serious problem is evident throughout the world as one the most challenging issues in contemporary corrections. The presence of drugs within correctional institutions puts the safety of staff, prisoners, prisoner's families, and the public in jeopardy through the health risks associated with taking illicit drugs and potential violence linked to the illicit economy.

III. MANAGEMENT OF DRUG USE IN PRISONS

A. Stifling Availability

Significantly disrupting the entry of drugs into an institution is much more complex and costly than it appears on first glance (Blakey 2008; Standing Committee on Public Safety and National Security 2012). Correctional institutions are among the most secure and controlled establishments anywhere, but they also operate as micro-communities replete with their own "subcultures" (Blakey 2008; Djemil 2008). In order to function, institutions need to admit goods, services, and people from the outside on a daily basis—perhaps with a level of frequency that far surpasses what might appear to be the case on superficial consideration. This provides a number of opportunities and entry routes for drug-related contraband (and other contraband items) despite security features like walls, fences, cameras, and patrols.

How do drugs enter a correctional institution? In fact, there are myriad entry points and routes for drugs to enter correctional institutions. Research in this area has identified five of the most common entry points for drugs and drug contraband (Feucht and Keyser 1999; Penfold, Turnbull, and Webster 2005; Blakey 2008; Djemil 2008; Standing Committee on Public Safety and National Security 2012)[4]:

1. Thrown, launched or dropped over the fence or wall to be retrieved by offenders.
2. Through visits (both personal and official).
3. Through the mail (including letters with bogus "official" labels).
4. Via those returning to the institution following temporary absences.
5. Through correctional institution staff. (This is a potential entry route into correctional institutions that is often not discussed. It is important to note that it only takes a few corrupt staff to bring a substantial amount of drugs into prison through various means.)

While the above have been identified as the "main" entry routes, these routes do not operate in isolation from each other. These (or other) entry routes and the amount of drug entry that takes place along them are affected by each other and will vary across time and place (Blakey 2008). When one supply route closes, another one opens up. Different routes also vary in the quantity or types of drugs that they can supply. For example, prison staff or contractors can bring in larger quantities of drugs than can be sent through the mail. It is a well-known adage in correctional institution culture that offenders can be exceptionally creative, and every correctional agency has examples of innovative and unique ways in which drugs, drug paraphernalia, and other types of contraband are smuggled into an institution (tucked in a baby's blanket, stamps laced with suboxone, methadone-soaked underwear, hidden in visitors' body cavities, etc.).

B. Drug Interdiction Approaches

Undoubtedly, addressing the availability of drugs in correctional institutions requires ongoing action through a comprehensive and integrated interdiction and supply reduction approach. As noted by Blakey (2008), security and increasing the detection of drugs through the use of advanced technology are essential elements of any effective correctional drug strategy.

Blakey (2008) identified five means of coordinating supply disruption to be used in an overall strategy: (1) employing good correctional practices, such as effective interdepartmental exchanges of information and communication; (2) disrupting the use of cell phones through better utilization of detection technologies leading to confiscation; (3) consistent and effective searching of inmates, visitors, and staff; (4) using trained and supported search dogs; and (5) promulgating legislation that helps enforce the consequences of inappropriate conduct and makes prosecutions possible that may help deter undesirable behavior. He added that in order for drug trafficking to be disrupted in correctional institutions on a long-term basis, three things need to take place: (1) develop and exploit available detection and interdiction technology, such as ion-mobility spectrometry drug detection machines, X-ray and metal detection portals, and cell phone detectors; (2) improve and maintain relationships with police and other law enforcement and criminal justice agencies to disrupt serious organized crime through the better exchange of information and intelligence; and (3) expand and advance the efficacy of the correctional institution intelligence system by being better linked to extended networks for help and support.

A recent international review of drug detection strategies in correctional institutions echoed some of Blakey's findings and identified four main interdiction approaches that are used: (1) canine detection units, (2) trace detection technology, (3) bulk detection technology, and (4) mandatory drug testing (Dastouri, Johnson, and Moser 2012). Each of these methods is described in detail. This review highlighted the fact that an extensive research base examining these approaches and their efficacy is lacking.

1. *Canine Detection Units*

Dogs' mobility and unique ability to detect a wide variety of substances in a short period of time are factors related to the long history of use of canine detection units worldwide in policing and correctional settings (Gravett 2000; Parmeter et al. 2000). A canine can search a large vehicle in five minutes, a small vehicle in one minute, and over 2,300 kilograms of mail in approximately thirty minutes (Parmeter et al. 2000). In addition to drugs, canines have been used for explosives and mobile phone detection (Blakey 2008).

Internationally, two types of drug detector dogs have been utilized in correctional environments. The first are "passive" drug dogs (PDDs), which are often kept on leash under the control of a trained handler and are used primarily to search offenders and visitors (Gravett 2000; Parmeter et al. 2000). These dogs indicate when a drug is present with a passive sign such as sitting down, a stare freeze, or a short bark. This makes them popular for searching prisoners, visitors, and staff. PDDs may also be used to search buildings and other areas off leash, as long as they are always under the control of the handler. It is important that PDDs have the appropriate temperament; they should not react aggressively toward those they patrol. The second are "active" drug dogs (ADDs), which are not generally used to search people but are instead often allowed off leash to search buildings, hallways, and out-side perimeters for drugs (Gravett 2000). ADDs must always be under the control of han-dlers and must have the appropriate temperament to adapt to adverse working conditions, such as night-shift work, disruptive offenders, and overall high noise levels (Gravett 2000). ADDs can behave in different ways depending on training to acknowledge an indication, such as scratching the area or barking when they detect a scent.

Although canines as a group are known to have the capability to detect any drug, an average of nine substances appears to be the maximum number of drug types that any one drug dog can accurately detect without having its detection abilities and reliability com-promised (Parmeter et al. 2000). The use of canines in correctional facilities is beneficial in that they are less likely to detect minute traces of a substance compared with trace detecting devices such as ion scanners (Parmeter et al. 2000). Overdetection of minute quantities of drugs can lead to increased "false positives,"[5] possibly leading to inappropriate reporting, responses, or sanctions. Correctional officers often question people or search items follow-ing an indication to mitigate the risk of false positives.

One of the limitations of detector dogs, however, is the short duration that they may work (approximately one hour) before needing to rest and change focus (Parmeter et al. 2000). Anecdotally, it is well recognized by correctional authorities that the accuracy and reliability of a detector dog drops dramatically when they have been overused and over-stimulated. As well, a drug-detecting canine is unable to inform its handler which drug it has discovered, only that the detection of a scent associated with an illicit item has been made (Parmeter et al. 2000). It is often believed that the possibility of being searched by a drug detection dog deters people from engaging in trafficking of illicit items.

2. Trace Detection Technology

Trace detection refers to the practice of identifying microscopic particles of different sub-stances (Dastouri et al. 2012). A person who comes in contact with a large quantity of a prohibited substance is very likely to have "particulate" or particles of that substance on their person. By collecting a sample via vacuum or swiping clothing, skin, hair, or personal items, a trace detector can identify whether a person or object has been in contact with an illicit substance provided that molecular compound has been programmed into the unit (Parmeter et al. 2000). In prisons, the substances of interest are most often illicit drugs.

The main form of trace technology currently utilized in correctional environments is ion-mobility spectrometry (IMS). IMS, better known as an "ion scanner," is a type of trace-detecting device that measures the deflection of particles after they are exposed to an elec-tric field. Those unfamiliar with correctional security procedures will recognize the use of IMS technology as a regular part of modern airport security screening procedures. The speed in which the particles move helps determine the type of larger particle from which they came (Parmeter et al. 2000). In a correctional setting, the ion scanner can be placed at the front entrances or in the mailroom of a correctional institution. Here, it is possible to scan any object—a piece of mail, a driver's license, a wallet, or a purse—and submit the sample to the IMS unit. Within seconds the IMS unit can identify whether there are drug particles or vapors present on the item in question.

While the efficiency and portability of IMS units have made them a marketable tool for combating drug supply in correctional institutions, as Dastouri and colleagues (2012) note, there are several drawbacks to the technology in correctional environments. Specifically, IMS is not able to trace a drug to its source, unlike drug-detecting canines (SCA Inc. 2001). Another drawback is that IMS technology measures drug particulate down to the nanogram, identifying "false positives" frequently (SCA Inc. 2001). As previously stated, correctional officers often question people or search items following a positive result to mitigate the risk of a false positive. Also, its oversensitivity can be buffered through the use of other detection strategies, such as manual searches or drug-detecting canine units (National Law Enforcement and Corrections Technology Center 2002), to corroborate a result.

3. *Bulk Detection*

Bulk detection techniques focus on identifying larger objects being smuggled into correctional institutions, such as weapons, cell phones, or large quantities of drugs (Wright and Butler 2001). Bulk detection techniques may be employed on a person (as seen in airport security areas) or on an object. Methods used in correctional facilities include backscatter X-rays, computed tomography scans (CT scans), X-rays, body orifice scanning systems (BOSS Chairs), and metal detectors. The primary benefit of bulk technology seems to be its ability to identify large quantities of contraband hidden in larger parcels (Paulter 2001). More frequent use of this technology is limited by size and weight, making portable deployment difficult. However, as advancements are made, the technologies become more lightweight and portable, and many prisons have seen bulk detection technology deployed in residential units, workshops, or admissions units.

4. *Mandatory Drug Testing (MDT)*

In addition to interdiction techniques aimed at restricting the flow of illicit substances into correctional facilities, mandatory drug testing aims to play a dual role of reducing drug use through deterrence (via charges and consequences for positive drug tests) and also as a mechanism to monitor the effectiveness of other interdiction measures, by tracking drug activity within an institution. Randomly choosing inmates is one method of selection for MDT. With this technique, offenders are aware that they could be asked to submit to a drug test at any time. More targeted MDT is also used in correctional environments. Specifically, those who have been previously caught using or bringing drugs into the facility are often selected to provide a sample, as are those who are returning from day parole or lengthy periods of time outside the institution (Gravett 2000). Furthermore, various correctional programs include participation in drug testing, where the inmate must submit a clean urine sample as mandated by a program in order to continue their involvement (Gravett 2000). Finally, if there are reasonable grounds to believe someone is abusing drugs within the institution, a urine sample can be requested as a requirement (Gravett 2000).

Four main biological specimens that are typically used for MDT are urine, blood, hair, and saliva. Urine is the biological specimen most commonly used to test for drug metabolites in a correctional setting (Dastouri et al. 2012). When a person consumes a drug, its decomposition within the body reduces it to its respective metabolites, and these metabolites act as fingerprints identifying the drug consumed. Since the metabolites are excreted through the body via urine, collecting urine samples provides correctional staff with a concentrated base of possible drug metabolites with which to determine the presence of drugs in their facilities (Makkai 2000). With increasing use of drugs over a long period of time, urine will become more concentrated with metabolites (Makkai 2000).

Overall, results on the effectiveness of urinalysis as a deterrent are mixed. Issues of concern include the challenges of maintaining urine specimen integrity, such as making sure it is a fresh, uncontaminated sample from the person being tested, and the variability of duration of detectability associated with the biological half-life of different compounds (some break down quicker than others). For example, cannabis can be detected in urine for much longer periods of time relative to opiates. This may result in drug-using offenders choosing to switch to more harmful drugs with a shorter biological half-life or novel psychoactive substances, which cannot be detected easily in urine. However, unequivocal evidence to support this contention is not currently available (Dastouri et al. 2012).

C. Search and Seizure Techniques and Approaches

The interventions mentioned earlier are often included as part of standard security procedures for searching staff, visitors, and prisoners as well as building structures and prison grounds. Officials also monitor prisoners' movements throughout prisons, watch them in their cells, and conduct manual operational searches of areas accessible to prisoners within and around the facility (Penfold et al. 2005). Operational search methods may use any combination of the methods outlined previously but often rely heavily on manual searching by the officers.

Search and seizure policy and procedure are developed and implemented at the institutional level under the responsibility of the facility head as is laid out in governing legislation. This varies by country and could include federal, state, and/or local laws. Three federal examples are: The Correctional and Conditional Release Act (S.C. 1992, c. 20), Government of Canada; Corrective Services Act, 2006, Queensland Parliamentary Counsel; and, Code of Laws of the United States of America, U.S. government. It is within these high-level polices that correctional staff are given the power to search for and to seize drugs and other contraband brought into prisons.

Institutions develop search plans outlining the number and location of searches that must occur within specific timeframes (e.g., monthly). These plans specify the regular search routines in specific areas of the institution, such as living units, classrooms, common areas, and work buildings, in accordance to jurisdictional authorities. Additional routine searches may be completed to those outlined in the search plans and may include searching vehicles entering and leaving the prison property, frisk searches of inmates as they enter or leave a specific location in the institution (such as visiting areas or work areas), and other manual and visual inspections of the institution and property. These types of searches are often completed regularly and at the discretion of the correctional staff during their shift.

There are a number of nonroutine searches that may also be performed under specific or exceptional circumstances. These searches may require additional authorizations or occur in an emergency situation and be based on reasonable grounds that contraband may exist in the area. These searches include strip-searching inmates or securing and searching an entire unit, wing, or institution. An example of a nonroutine or exceptional search is the intensive search that takes place after a potentially dangerous object has been reported missing from a prison work location (e.g., tool from a wood shop or a kitchen utensil). When a seizure is made, the correctional staff completes the itemization and documentation that is required by the process established in institutional policy. Outside authorities may also be contacted, possibly resulting in criminal charges.

IV. Effectiveness of Drug Interdiction Approaches

Overall, research into the effectiveness of drug detection tools shows them capable of detecting drugs. Each method has benefits and disadvantages. What remains unclear is which tool or combination of technologies yields the most accurate, cost-effective results and what works best to deter, detect, and disrupt challenging drug-related behaviors. Many of the research evaluations of drug detection technologies lack scientific rigor and are not easily comparable due to the inconsistent collection and presentation of data. Furthermore, the apparent lack of accurate baseline data in many jurisdictions renders it difficult to determine the overall effect of any single interdiction method on the amount of illicit drugs entering facilities (Dastouri et al. 2012).

In addition, all the methods described in this essay are only effective if used correctly and consistently. For example, drug dogs, ion scanners, and bulk detection technologies are only effective if they are used by trained staff who are aware of the limitations of each technique. Also, there must be consistency in the application of the drug detection strategies. For example, it was noted that corrupt staff are a potential conduit of drugs in correctional institutions. Therefore, an effective drug strategy should require staff to be subjected to consistent search procedures when they enter a correctional facility, similar to others entering the facility.

Furthermore, the drug detection techniques described in this review are not completely effective to address all possible methods of getting drugs into correctional institutions. Specifically, it was noted that one common method of contraband entry is throwing objects over the walls or fences. Obviously, the use of static detection techniques, such as ion scanners and bulk detection, are not useful in combating this mode of entry. Correctional authorities need to constantly remain vigilant and explore new ways of working supported by new technology to be proactive in the fight to stop drugs getting into prisons.

It is hard to describe treatment approaches for drug use in prison because it varies greatly between one jurisdiction and another (but see Taxman and Blasko, this volume). Despite this there are some common principles; for example, no one would dispute that interventions to reduce demand for drugs in prisons should be evidence-based. The Department of Health (2010) commissioned a systematic review of available research to assess the effectiveness of treatment modalities in prisons. High standards of scientific rigor were met, and interventions were rated on the effectiveness of reducing drug use in general, reducing drug use in prison, and reducing reoffending. Six interventions showed particular promise in delivering positive outcomes: opioid-substitution therapy, children and family support, high-intensity programs, enhancing life skills, therapeutic communities, and intensive support upon release.

Pharmaceutical interventions should be made available in all prisons to manage drug and alcohol dependency and associated health issues. This service, largely involving medicines such as methadone, has been shown to be effective in reducing drug use, in-jail drug use, and reoffending (Haig 2003; Hedrich et al. 2012). Failure to implement these interventions in prisons represents a missed opportunity to engage high-risk drug users in treatment, which can have significant consequences both in prison and following release into the community. Psychosocial interventions are recommended as a core component of any intervention. Weekes et al. (2013) list psychosocial interventions based on social learning and cognitive behavioral approaches, motivational enhancement techniques, inclusion of a maintenance and aftercare component, and demonstration of therapeutic integrity as essential elements. Aftercare or throughcare following release is particularly important as research indicates that the duration of care is often more important than the amount of care (Crits-Christoph and Siqueland 1996; Moos et al. 2000).

McSweeney et al. (2008) stated that prisons are environments where drugs are in demand and are valuable as both currency and commodity. The presence of drug markets in prisons is considered to cause violence, intimidation, and corruption. These markets are shaped by complex interactions between demand, supply, security and enforcement, and treatment strategies. Consequently, a careful balance needs to be struck between justice, care, and control. Tight security coupled with inadequate treatment may lead to wider problems and undermine broader efforts at reducing demand.

V. Conclusion

A consensus has emerged that mass incarceration, particularly for drug-related offending, is problematic. As well as potentially stifling opportunities for rehabilitation, it can destroy families and communities. Drugs and prisons is a complex issue. It requires a pragmatic approach ably supported by a complementary political response.

For those in prison with drug-related problems, demand for drugs has to be reduced. This can be addressed by trained health-care professionals who screen, assess, and effectively intervene and treat. This is in addition to providing care for co-occurring physical and mental issues. Delivering comprehensive prerelease planning and aftercare are also essential elements in promoting recovery and rehabilitation that can help reduce the number of people returning to prison. Drugs also need to be kept out of prison. Justice authorities tasked to deliver safe and secure custodial environments need to fully utilize all the interdiction tools available to them. This should be undertaken in consultation with treatment providers for a comprehensive and coordinated response.

Politicians have been promising to address drug-related problems for decades. Approaches to policing, prosecution, sentencing, and incarceration results in higher costs for taxpayers, less opportunity for affected people, and undermines any hope for both racial and sexual equality. Prison reform has to be a top political priority. Political reforms could include eliminating policies that result in disproportionate arrests and incarcerations by changing police policies, decriminalizing drug possession, promoting treatment-based alternatives to prison, and redirecting law enforcement agencies to prevent serious and violent crime. Reviewing harsh mandatory minimum sentences and reducing sentencing disparities will also make a positive contribution to prison reform.

It will take time to wean people off the excessive use of imprisonment, but it has to be done. Attending to reforming the criminal justice system, making it fairer, and being smarter in how crime is reduced are steps in the right direction.

ACKNOWLEDGMENTS

The authors would like to thank Chad Dubeau, Information Specialist with the Canadian Centre on Substance Abuse (www.ccsa.ca), for his assistance with the background research for this chapter. The views and opinions expressed in this chapter are those of the authors and do not necessarily reflect the policies and views of the Correctional Service of Canada, Public Safety Canada, or the National Offender Management Service, Ministry of Justice, United Kingdom.

NOTES

1. The term "psychoactive" refers broadly to drugs (licit and illicit) and other substances that cross the blood-brain barrier and act on the central nervous system that have the potential to affect a range of mental processes and diverse aspects of cognitive functioning and emotional regulation.
2. DSM-IV has been replaced recently by Diagnostic and Statistical Manual—Fifth Edition (DSM-V) and is published and maintained by the American Psychiatric Association.
3. The approach to medicine that is concerned with the health of the community as a whole to protect, promote, and restore peoples' health.
4. Other dangerous types of contraband such as firearms and explosives can be introduced into institutions in the same ways. Importantly, the presence of a handgun and bullets is considered by corrections officials to be more dangerous and concerning than drug-related contraband.
5. In this context, a false positive refers to the detection of truly insignificant trace amounts of a class of drug.

REFERENCES

Babooram, Avani. 2008. *The Changing Profile of Adults in Custody—2006-2007*. Statistics Canada: Juristat (December). Available at http://www.statcan.gc.ca/pub/85-002-x/2008010/article/10732-eng.htm

Blakey, David. 2008. *Disrupting the Supply of Illicit Drugs Into Correctional Institutions*. Report for the Director General of National Offender Management Service (May 30). Available at http://insidetime.org/download/research_and_reports/blakey-report_Drugs-Prisons.pdf

Boys, A., M. Farrell, P. Bebbington, T. Brugha, J. Coid, R. Jenkins, G. Lewis et al. 2002. "Drug Use and Initiation in Prison: Results from a National Prison Survey in England and Wales." *Addiction* 97:1551–1560.

Califano, Joseph. 2010. Foreword. *Behind Bars II: Substance Abuse and America's Prison Population*. New York: National Center on Addiction and Substance Abuse.

Carson, E. Ann, and William Sabol. 2012. *Prisoners in 2011*. Washington, DC: U.S. Department of Justice, Bureau of Justice Statistics.

Cope, Nina. 2003. "It's No Time or High Time: Young Offenders Experiences of Time and Drug Use in Prison." *Howard Journal* 42:158–175.

Courtenay, Will H., and Don Sabo. 2001. "Preventive Health Strategies for Men in Prison." In *Prison Masculinities*, edited by Don Sabo, Terry Kupers, and Willie London. Philadelphia, PA: Temple University Press.

Crewe, Ben. 2005. "Prisoner Society in the Era of Hard Drugs." *Punishment and Society* 7:457–481.

Crits-Christoph, Paul, and Lynne Siqueland. 1996. "Psychosocial Treatment for Drug Abuse: Selected Review and Recommendations for National Health Care." *Archives of General Psychiatry* 53:749–756.

Dastouri, Serenna, Sara Johnson, and Andrea E. Moser. 2012. *Drug Detection Strategies: International Practices within Correctional Settings*. Ottawa: Correctional Service Canada. Available at https://www.publicsafety.gc.ca/lbrr/archives/cn21488-eng.pdf

Department of Health. 2010. *Changing the Outlook: A Strategy for Developing and Modernising Mental Health Services in Prisons*. Available at http://webarchive.nation-alarchives.gov.uk/+/www.dh.gov.uk/en/Publicationsandstatistics/Publications/PublicationsPolicyAndGuidance/DH_4009699

Djemil, Huseyin. 2008. *Inside Out: How to Get Drugs Out of Correctional Institutions*. London: Centre for Policy Studies.

Dolan, Kate, Effat Merghati Khoei, Cinzia Brentari, and Alex Stevens. 2007. *Prisons and Drugs: A Global Review of Incarceration, Drug Use and Drug Services*. Oxford: Beckley Foundation Drug Policy Programme. Available at http://kar.kent.ac.uk/13324/2/Beckley_RPT12_Prisons_Drugs_EN.pdf

European Monitoring Centre for Drugs and Drug Addiction. 2012. "*Prisons and Drugs in Europe: The Problem and Responses*." Publications office of the European Unit, Luxembourg.

Feucht, Thomas E., and Andrew Keyser. 1999. "Reducing Drug Use in Prisons: Pennsylvania's Approach." *National Institute of Justice Journal* (Oct.):11–15.

Fischer, Benedikt, Jude Gittins, and Jurgen Rehm. 2008. "Characterizing the 'Awakening Elephant' of Prescription Opiod Misuse in North America: Epidemiology, Harms, Interventions." *Contemporary Drug Problems* 35:397.

Goldstein, Paul. J. 1985. "The Drugs/Violence Nexus: A Tripartite Conceptual Framework." *Journal of Drug Issues* 39:143–174.

Glaze, Lauren, and Erinn Herberman. 2013. *Correctional Populations in the United States, 2012*. Washington, DC: U.S. Department of Justice, Bureau of Justice Statistics.

Gravett, Steve. 2000. *Drugs in Prison*. London: Continuum.

Haig, T. 2003. "Randomized Controlled Trial Proves Effectiveness of Methadone Maintenance Treatment in Prison." *Canadian HIV/AIDS Policy and Law Review* 8 (3):48–48.

Hedrich, Dagmar, Paula Alves, Michael Farrell, Heino Stöver, Lars Møller, and Soraya Mayet. 2012. "The Effectiveness of Opioid Maintenance Treatment in Prison Settings: A Systematic Review." *Addiction* 107:501–517.

Her Majesty's Prison Service. 2003. *The Prison Service Drug Strategy*. London: Her Majesty's Prison Service.

Institute for Criminal Policy Research. 2015. *World Prison Brief*. London: Institute for Criminal Policy Research.

Justice Policy Institute. 2008. *Substance Abuse Treatment and Public Safety*. Washington, DC: Justice Policy Institute.

Kitchin, Heather. A. 2006. "Addictions Programming: A Perspective on Corrections in Nova Scotia." *Forum on Corrections Research* 18:9–11.

Kunic, Dan, and Brian A. Grant. 2006. *The Computerized Assessment of Substance Abuse (CASA): Results from the Demonstration Project*. Ottawa: Correctional Service Canada.

Makkai, Toni. 2000. *Drug Use Monitoring in Australia (DUMA): 1999 Annual Report on Drug Use Among Adult Detainees*. Canberra City: Australian Institute of Criminology.

McSweeney, Tim, Paul J. Turnbull, and Mike Hough. 2008. *Tackling Drug Markets and Distribution Networks in the UK*. London: Drug Policy Commission.

Minton, Todd D. 2012. *Jail Inmates at Midyear 2011-Statistical Tables*. Washington, DC: Office of Justice Programs, Bureau of Justice Statistics.

Moos, Rudolf H., John W. Finney, Elizabeth B. Federman, and Richard Suchinsky. 2000. "Specialty Mental Health Care Improves Patients' Outcomes: Findings from a Nationwide Program to Monitor the Quality of Care for Patients with Substance Use Disorders." *Journal of Studies on Alcohol* 61:704–713.

Morris, Richard. 2001. "Alcohol and Drugs: A Perspective from New Zealand." *Forum on Corrections Research* 13:18–19.

Mumola, Christopher, and Jennifer Karberg. 2006. *Drug Use and Dependence, State and Federal Prisoners, 2004*. Washington, DC: Office of Justice Programs, Bureau of Justice Statistics.

National Association for the Advancement of Colored People. 2013. "Criminal Justice Fact Sheet." Available at http://www.naacp.org/pages/criminal-justice-fact-sheet

National Center on Addiction and Substance Abuse. 2010. *Behind Bars II: Substance Abuse and America's Prison Population*. New York: National Center on Addiction and Substance Abuse.

National Law Enforcement and Corrections Technology Center. 2002. "The Check Is in the Mail." *TechBeat*, Summer.

Office of the Correctional Investigator. 2013. "The Changing Face of Canada's Prisons: Correctional Investigator Reports on Ethno-Cultural Diversity in Corrections." Available at http://www.oci-bec.gc.ca/cnt/comm/press/press20131126-eng.aspx

Parmeter, John E., Dale W. Murray, David W. Hannum, Sandia National Laboratories, and United States of America. 2000. *Guide for the Selection of Drug Detectors for Law Enforcement Applications*. Washington, DC: National Institute of Justice.

Paulter, Nicholas G. 2001. *Guide to the Technologies of Concealed Weapon and Contraband Imaging and Detection*. Washington, DC: National Institute of Justice.

Penfold, Clarissa, Paul J. Turnbull, and Russell Webster. 2005. *Tackling Prison Drug Markets: An Exploratory Qualitative Study*. London: Home Office, Home Research Development and Statistics Directorate.

Pollack, Harold, Peter Reuter, and Eric Sevigny. 2010. "If Drug Treatment Works So Well, Why Are So Many Drug Users in Prison?" In *Controlling Crime: Strategies and Tradeoffs*, edited by Philip J. Cook, Jens Ludwig, and Justin McCrary. Chicago: University of Chicago Press.

Prison Reform Trust. 2015. "Projects and Research: Race." Available at http://www.prisonre-formtrust.org.uk/projectsresearch/race

SCA Inc. (2001, October 1). *Mailroom Scenario Evaluation Final Report.* Retrieved from: http://www.ncjrs.gov/pdffiles1/nij/grants/199048.pdf

Shewan, David, Martin Gemmell, and John B. Davies. 1994. "Prison as a Modifier of Drug Using Behaviour." *Addiction Research* 2: 203–215.

Standing Committee on Public Safety and National Security. 2012. *Drugs and Alcohol in Federal Penitentiaries: An Alarming Problem.* 41st Parliament, 1st Session, 2011–2012. Ottawa: Public Works and Government Services.

Stark, Klaus, Ute Herrmann, Stephan Ehrhardt, and Ulrich Bienzle. 2006. "A Syringe Exchange Programme in Prison as Prevention Strategy against HIV Infection and Hepatitis B and C in Berlin, Germany." *Epidemiology and Infection* 134: 814–819.

Stöver, Heino, and Caren Weilandt. 2007. "Drug Use and Drug Services in Prison." In *Health in Prisons*, edited by L. Møller, H. Stöver, R. Jürgens, A. Gatherer, and H. Nikogosian. Copenhagen: WHO.

Substance Abuse and Mental Health Services Administration. 2013. "Results from the 2012 National Survey on Drug Use and Health: Summary of National Findings." Available at http://www.samhsa.gov/data.NSDUH/2012SummNatFindDetTables/NationalFindings/NSDUHresults2012.htm

Swann, Rachel, and Pam James. 1998. "The Effect of the Prison Environment upon Inmate Drug Taking Behaviour." *Howard Journal of Criminal Justice* 37: 252–265.

The Sentencing Project. 2016. "Fact Sheet: Trends in U.S. Corrections." Available at http://www.sentencingproject.org/wp-content/uploads/2016/01/Trends-in-US-Corrections.pdf

Tompkins, Charlotte NE, Joanne Neale, Laura Sheard, and Nat MJ Wright. 2007. "Experiences of Prison Among Injecting Drug Users in England: A Qualitative Study." *International Journal of Prisoner Health* 3: 189–203.

Walmsley, Roy. 2013. *World Prison Population List.* 10th ed. King's College, London: International Centre for Prison Studies.

Weekes, John R., Andrea E. Moser, Michael Wheatley, and Flora I. Matheson. 2013. "What Works in Reducing Substance-Related Offending?" In *What Works in Offender Rehabilitation: An Evidence-Based Approach to Assessment and Treatment*, edited by Leam A. Craig, Theresa A. Gannon, and Louise Dixon. London: Wiley-Blackwell.

Wheatley, Michael. 2007. "Drugs in Prison." In *Handbook on Prisons*, edited by Yvonnes Jewkes, Jamie Bennett, and Ben Crewe. New York: Routledge.

Woodall, James. 2012. "Social and Environmental Factors Influencing In-correctional Institution Drug Use." *Health Education* 112: 31–46.

Wright, Stacy, and Robert F. Butler. 2001. "Technology Takes on Drug Smugglers: Can Drug Detection Technology Stop Drugs from Entering Prisons?" *Corrections Today* 63: 66–69.

CHAPTER 14

··

A GENERAL MODEL OF HARM
IN CORRECTIONAL SETTINGS

··

NANCY WOLFF

*If men are to remain civilized or to become so, the art of associating together must
grow and improve in the same ratio in which the equality of conditions is increased.*

Alexis de Tocqueville (1956, p. 110)

THAT prisons, as social institutions, are harmful is an accepted fact by corrections experts, although the fact is rarely found acceptable. Factually, we know harm inside prison ranges from bullying (Ireland 2005) to homicide and suicide (Noonan 2012), and such manifestations of harm are often persistent, repetitive, and range in severity (Irwin 1980; Bottoms 1999; Human Rights Watch 2001). Epidemiologic evidence suggests that harm inside prison is common when displayed physically (i.e., an incarcerated person is hit, kicked, stabbed, shot, or choked). Over a six-month period, Wolff, Shi, and Siegel (2009b) found that one in five inmates (male or female) experienced some form of physical victimization by another inmate, increasing to one in three if the offender is defined to include staff. Sexual victimization is less common. Two recent studies conducted by the US Bureau of Justice Statistics estimate the prevalence of sexual victimization at 4.4 percent (based on reports from current prison inmates; Beck et al. 2010) and 9.6 percent (based on reports of former state inmates; Beck and Johnson 2012). Another way of looking at harm focuses on bullying, defined as direct or indirect aggression that creates fear of future harm. Ireland (2005) estimates that slightly more than half of incarcerated persons are bullied by others. These prevalence estimates frame the qualitative accounts of prison life documented by researchers in the 1950s, 1960s, and 1970s (Sykes 1958; Carroll 1974; Toch 1977; Irwin 1980).

In this essay harm is examined as an interdependent dyadic event involving a perpetrator and victim, where the roles of perpetrator and victim are potentially interchangeable and the forces motivating the event are both dynamic and welfare based. It is for this reason that inmate misconduct (measuring perpetrator behavior) and inmate victimization are considered together. As such, this essay integrates the theory and empirical evidence on inmate misconduct and victimization. Section I begins by defining harm conceptually and its limits constitutionally. Next, in Section II, the literature on harm within prison settings is reviewed with an emphasis on the prevalence, predictors, and consequences associated with inmate misconduct, physical victimization, and sexual victimization. In Section III, a dyadic model of harm is developed that draws on routine activities theory and rational choice theory to more clearly and systematically predict the effects of harm- and victim-propensity attributes of incarcerated people and correctional facilities on levels of harm. Section IV summarizes. The major conclusions drawn from this essay are

- Harm is endemic to incarceration and within correctional settings.
- Incarceration itself causes *welfare harm*, which activates environmental conditions and amplifies individual predispositions toward interpersonal harm.
- Harm is imprecisely and unevenly measured inside prison. Sexual victimization is measured relatively more precisely, but its prevalence is low. More common is physical violence and victimization, which are measured with imprecision.
- If harm is to be reduced, a more integrated model of harm is needed to understand the etiology and pathogenesis of harmful behavior inside prison.
- The general model of harm proposed identifies policy instruments for harm reduction and related hypotheses for empirical investigation.

I. Harm and Its Limits

A. Meaning of Harm

What is meant by "harm to people confined in correctional settings"? The answer hinges centrally on the definition of harm. According to dictionary definitions, "harm" connotes injury, wrongdoing, hurt, or damage. Taken together, the synonyms of "harm" imply that some action creates impairment. Applied to incarcerated persons, it refers generally to their being damaged or injured (impaired) by *something* (e.g., the loss of liberty from confinement, the conditions of confinement) or *someone* (e.g., other incarcerated persons, custody officers, treatment providers).

While the subject of harm is the incarcerated person,[1] the object of harm is unclear. Here the object of harm could be defined in terms of the composite self or the interests of the self. The former refers to the physical and psychological wellness of the self, which could be damaged or injured by the wrongful actions of others (Liebling 2004). Physical and sexual victimization, as well as bullying or degrading interpersonal interactions, could harm a person physically and/or psychologically (Cohen and Taylor 1972; Toch 1992; Bottoms 1999; Liebling 1999, 2004; Ireland 2005). Alternatively and more philosophically, Feinburg (1984, p. 37) defines the object of harm in terms of the "setback to interests," which from a welfare perspective "interests" include

the continuance for a foreseeable interval of one's life, and the interests in one's own physical health and vigor, the integrity and normal functioning of one's body, the absence of absorbing pain and suffering or grotesque disfigurement, minimal intellectual acuity, emotional stability, the absence of groundless anxieties and resentments, the capacity to engage normally in social intercourse and to enjoy and maintain friendships, at least minimal income and financial security, a tolerable social and physical environment, and a certain amount of freedom from interference and coercion.

Welfare interests as delineated by Feinburg provide a broader framework in which to conceptualize the harm created by confinement. According to deprivation theory, confinement creates pain through deprivation (Clemmer 1940; Sykes 1958). Confinement deprivation, an intentional punishment, however, is also a collateral setback to welfare interests and, as such, creates harm.[2] The severity and magnitude of welfare harm depends centrally on how confinement is operationalized by prison officials. Given their control of and power over confinement, the actions and inactions of prison officials and staff create conditions, processes, and practices that set the foundation for the social, economic, and psychological environment of prisons. In terms of welfare interests, these interests are inversely related to the degree of material, psychological, and social deprivation associated with confinement, the nonrandomness of its distribution, and the unpredictability of its delivery. Connecting environment conditions to welfare interests of incarcerated people provides a "something" source of harm, which might causally motivate interpersonal or intrapersonal harm to the composite self. That is, physical or psychological damage by something (e.g., conditions of confinement) can create strains and pressures on an incarcerated person who then directly harms himself or others.

For purposes of clarity, interpersonal harm and welfare harm are defined uniquely, although I acknowledge their interdependence and address it in Section III. That said, *interpersonal harm* is defined as words or actions by peers or prison staff that cause or threaten economic, physical, or psychological injury to an incarcerated person. This would include but not be limited to bullying, stolen or damaged property, and physical and sexual violence. *Welfare harm* is the loss in well-being caused by confinement conditions, processes, or practices that deprive or threaten to deprive confined people of a stable, physically and psychologically safe, and humane living environment. Examples of such confinement conditions, processes, or practices are mass punishment, punitive degradation by officers, selective enforcement of official rules, overcrowding, and reduction in programming or employment opportunities.

B. Limits to Harm

Harm within prisons, by all accounts, is endemic, yet it is far from acceptable within the United States, constitutionally or morally. Incarcerated people have the right to be protected from harm by the governmental entities confining them. Beginning in the 1980s, US federal courts imposed a safety requirement on correctional systems in response to prisoner litigation.[3] In 1980 the US District Court ruled that the Texas Department of Corrections must comprehensively remediate the conditions under which prisoners were held. The plaintiffs in the case alleged that the conditions of their incarceration, including overcrowding, insufficient health care, and abusive security practices, were a violation of their constitutional rights. In *Ruiz v. Estelle* (1980, p. 26), the Court ruled that the Texas Department of

Corrections "failed to furnish minimal safeguards for the personal safety of the inmate." A decade later the Supreme Court interpreted the Eighth Amendment's prohibition of "cruel and unusual punishment" in ways that impose a duty of protection on the government for the people it confines in correctional institutions. In *Farmer v. Brennan* (1994, p. 832), the Supreme Court ruled

> The Constitution "does not mandate comfortable prisons," *Rhodes v. Chapman*, 452 U.S. 337, 349 (1981), but neither does it permit inhumane ones, and it is now settled that "the treatment a prisoner receives in prison and the conditions under which he is confined are subject to the scrutiny under the Eighth Amendment." Helling, 509 U.S., at __ (slip op., at 5). In its prohibition of "cruel and unusual punishments," the Eighth Amendment places restraints on prison officials, who may not, for example, use excessive physical force against prisoners. See *Hudson v. McMillian*, 503 U.S. 1 (1992). The Amendment also imposes duties on these officials, who must provide humane conditions of confinement; prison officials must ensure that inmates receive adequate food, clothing, shelter and medical care, and must "take reasonable measure to guarantee the safety of the inmates." *Hudson v. Palmer*, 468 U.S. 517, 526–527 (1984). See *Helling, supra*, at__ (slip op., at 5); *Washington v. Harper*, 494 U.S. 210, 225 (1990); *Estelle*, 429 U.S., at 103. Cf. *DeShaney v. Winnebago County Dept. of Social Services*, 489 U.S.189, 198–199 (1989).

Accordingly, once a person's liberty is deprived by a governmental entity, a public duty follows that prison officials must take "reasonable measures" to preserve and protect the confined person's personal safety. This protection, however, is not unbounded. The Supreme Court in its *Farmer v. Brennan* (1994, p. 825) ruling limited the liability of prison officials to a standard of "deliberate indifference":

> A prison official may be held liable under the Eighth Amendment for acting with "deliberate indifference" to inmate health or safety only if he knows that inmates face a substantial risk of Page II serious harm and disregards that risk by failing to take reasonable measures to abate it.

Subsequent to this ruling, Human Rights Watch, an international advocacy organization, conducted two investigations into violence and victimization within correctional settings. These investigations documented sexual victimization of male prisoners (Human Rights Watch 2001) and mistreatment and victimization of incarcerated people with mental illnesses (Human Rights Watch 2003). Evidence of abject abuse inside prisons and jails fomented moral outrage and elevated inmate victimization to the policy level, culminating in federal legislation known as the Prison Rape Elimination Act (PREA) of 2003 (Bureau of Justice Statistics 2004). Never before had a consortium of policymakers, researchers, advocates, practitioners, and citizens coalesced centrally around the theme of prisoner's rights. The message was clear: rape inside prison should be prevented in accordance with basic human rights.

Judicial and legislative actions over the past 40 years have not eliminated harm within prisons. At best, judicial rulings have created standards for and placed pressures on prison officials to be "on guard" with respect to the safety needs of incarcerated persons, while legislative actions have focused security attention on particular types of harm that are socially objectionable (e.g., rape). With PREA funding, sexual victimization is now more rigorously measured, studied, monitored, and sanctioned (see Mazza 2012).[4] Mandated attention on sexual victimization, however, has overshadowed other more prevalent types of harm within prisons, such as bullying, nonviolent offending, and physical assault.

Clearly, reducing harm within prisons is socially desirable. How to achieve this goal is less straightforward. In a public health context, "harm reduction" refers to policies, programs, or practices that minimize the harmful health, social, and economic effects associated with risky human behaviors, such as prostitution and drug, alcohol, or tobacco use (Marlatt, Larimer, and Witkiewitz 2012). The philosophy of harm reduction recognizes that abstinence from high-risk behavior (e.g., sex, drugs, alcohol, tobacco) is either impractical or unfeasible, and, as such, the focus is to reduce the harms associated with risky behavior. Examples of harm-reduction interventions include substitution among drug types (e.g., noninjectable methadone for injected heroin), reduction in usage (e.g., moderate drinking for heavy drinking), and needle exchange programs. The goal of these interventions is to make risky behaviors less harmful, and research evidence suggests that such approaches effectively reduce morbidity and mortality associated with risky behaviors (see Kilmer et al. 2012; Larimer et al. 2012; Peake, Andrasik, and Lostutter 2012; Phillips et al. 2012).

In correctional settings, "aggression" is the risky behavior that generates physical and psychological harm. Given that aggression abstinence is not feasible, a harm-reduction approach inside prison might include policies, interventions, and practices that attempt to modify, adjust, or lower aggressive behavior to achieve a better outcome—that is, less harm. For example, if there was a legitimate outlet for fighting, like boxing, incarcerated persons might choose to take their disputes to the ring (which is supervised), instead of fighting in areas that are unmonitored and unregulated for safety. Similarly, a rapid-response relocation program (substituting one prison or cell block for another) that quickly moves potential victims away from harmful people would minimize harm. These are not novel practices; random prisons across the United States have implemented and sustained programs like these for years. More generally, however, minimizing harm within correctional settings would require changing the behavior of incarcerated persons and staff through well-designed intervention. Such a strategy requires understanding the manifestations of harm, the individual factors associated with aggressive behavior, the environmental conditions needed for aggression to be activated, and the social dynamic that facilitates the transmission of aggression. These issues are discussed in turn next.

II. Manifestations of Harm

There are two ways to explore harm. The first focuses on the evidence of misconduct, representing the behavior of those who do harm, while the second examines the evidence of victimization, representing the harm done. For completeness, both perspectives are explored, as they are, in fact, different sides of the same coin. In this section, the literatures on misconduct, physical victimization, and sexual victimization are summarized with emphasis on the nature and extent of harm and the adverse consequences associated with the experience of harm.

A. Inmate Misconduct

1. Definition of Inmate Misconduct

Incarcerated people are subject to rules that stipulate what actions, conduct, and possessions are allowed and disallowed. Rule infractions, when detected and formalized, can be
officially sanctioned with loss of job, privileges, cell assignment, material possessions, and
autonomy and in some cases can result in formal criminal charges. Some forms of misconduct are unique to confinement, such as failure to stand for count, failure to clean one's cell,
hygiene violations, interference with the count, tattooing, and refusal to work. By contrast,
other types of misconduct fall within Group A and B offense categories of the National
Incident Based Reporting System.[5] Misconducts analogous to Group B offenses include
littering, malingering, disorderly conduct, loitering, and violation of noise ordinances.
More serious and often violent Group A offenses include counterfeiting, theft, gambling,
property damage, arson, escape, extortion, hostage-taking, rioting, simple and aggravated
assault, drug distribution, weapons possession, threatening staff, rape, attempted murder,
and homicide.

2. Prevalence of Misconduct

The US Bureau of Justice Statistics, based on data self-reported by prisons and jails, reports
national statistics on prisoner violations. According to official statistics, since their admission to prison, 43 percent of state inmates (in 2002) without mental health problems were
charged with a rule violation (e.g., possession of a weapon, stolen property or contraband,
drug law violations, setting fires, being out of place, disobeying orders, abusive language,
horseplay, and assaults), increasing to 57.7 percent for inmates with mental health problems.
Roughly one in seven inmates without mental health problems had violations for nonlethal
physical or verbal assault on correctional staff or another inmate (James and Glaze 2006).

The research literature provides some details about misconduct among prison inmates.
DeLisi (2003) examined misconduct patterns for a random sample of 1,005 inmates supervised by a single state department of corrections. Misconduct histories were constructed for
the full period of incarceration. Based on these data, roughly one in five inmates received a
citation at some point during their incarceration for theft and one in six for simple assault.
Fewer than one in 10 inmates had *ever* received a citation for aggravated assault, rioting,
sexual behavior, extortion, arson, rape, homicide, or fraud, while a significant minority
received six or more misconducts.

Using a small random sample of inmates (n = 194), Jiang and Fisher-Giorlando (2002)
aggregated misconduct data drawn over a six-month period. Of the 428 incidents, 70 percent were nonviolent and 11 percent were against inmates. Misconducts against an inmate
were limited to three types: fighting, aggravated fighting, and theft. Cunningham and
Sorensen (2007), using a larger sample (n = 24,517), found half of the inmates had at least
one violation during a calendar year. Roughly one in 20 inmates received an assault violation, although approximately one in seven received a potentially violent violation.

While these studies shed some light on the prevalence of misconduct among inmates, it
is limited for two reasons. The first concerns measurement error. Official records incom-
pletely capture the extent and nature of misconduct among inmates in part because the

misconduct activity goes undetected by officers and in part because the misconduct that is detected is subject to the discretion of the officer (Poole and Regoli 1980; DeLisi 2003). Inmates have a vested interest in keeping their illegal activities hidden from officers and developing an informal enforcement mechanism to keep other inmates from reporting such activities to authorities (aka "snitches get stitches"; Wolff et al. 2007). In terms of officer behavior, while officers may not control the formation of rules, they do control the interpretation and application of the rules, as well as the assessment of the situation and the misconduct observed. Moreover, they are likely to consider the hassle associated with writing up the inmate and the possible hostile dynamic that might ensue in its aftermath. Relatedly, formal misconduct violations can be overturned by the hearing board, adding yet another layer of discretionary decision-making. There are, however, also rules of enforcement that can lead to false misconducts. For example, if contraband (e.g., a weapon) is found in a two-man cell, both inmates are charged and they split the sanction, unless the guilty inmate confesses, in which case he faces the full sanction. Furthermore, with intention, officers or inmates can set up an inmate for a violation in an effort to teach him a lesson, retaliate for cause, or make a personal statement. Taken together, underdetection, selective enforcement, evidentiary discretion, and fraud biases reporting of misconduct in ways that could misreport, underreport, or overreport types of misconduct, yielding unreliable and invalid misconduct data.

The second concern is analytic in nature. Misconduct data, as analyzed, was not intended to examine the connection between misconduct and interpersonal harm; rather, the three studies cited earlier and others like it (McCorkle, Miethe, and Drass 1995; Harer and Steffensmeir 1996; Cao, Zhao, and Van Dine 1997) were designed to explain and predict adaptation to prison life with an emphasis on the marginal effects of individual and institutional variables. For this reason, it is difficult to assess from the data how much of the *reported* misconduct exposes inmates to interpersonal harm. That is, while some inmates may be doing harm, it is not clear whether and to what extent their misconduct directly caused or threatened economic, physical, or psychological injury to an inmate. This ambiguity exists because misconduct is not defined in ways that reveal its impact or target.

3. *Predictors of Misconduct*

Two competing theories are most often used to explain inmate misconduct. The *deprivation model* argues that oppressive conditions (a) inside prison (e.g., overcrowding, restrictive programming and visitation policies, control and command management regimes), and (b) caused by incarceration (i.e., deprivation of liberty and humanity) stress human survival (i.e., create welfare harm) in ways that motivate violence (Sykes 1958; Goffman 1961). By contrast, the *importation model* focuses on preexisting traits and behaviors of people entering prisons, such as their personal histories and social network, that support a pattern of misconduct and violence during incarceration (Irwin and Cressey 1962). Using different samples, statistical techniques, and variables (see Schenk and Fremouw 2012), researchers have identified a variety of inmate and institutional characteristics that are associated with prison misconduct and violence (Gendreau, Goggin, and Law 1997; Schenk and Fremouw 2012).

Inmate characteristics most consistently found to increase levels of misconduct and violence are *gender* (male; Craddock 1996; Felson, Silver, and Remster 2012); *age* (young; McCorkle 1995; Craddock 1996; Bench and Allen 2003; Camp et al. 2003; DeLisi 2003; Cunningham and Sorensen 2007; Lahm 2008; Felson et al. 2012); *race and ethnicity* (particularly Hispanic and American Indian; Wooldredge 1994; Gaes et al. 2002; Camp et al. 2003; DeLisi 2003; Berg and DeLisi 2006; Griffin and Hepburn 2006); *education* (lower; DeLisi, Berg, and Hochstetler 2004; Cunningham, Sorensen, and Reidy 2005; Berg and DeLisi 2006); *extensive and/or violent criminal histories* (Wooldredge 1991, 1994; McCorkle 1995; Craddock 1996; DeLisi 2003; Gaes et al. 2002; DeLisi et al. 2004; Cunningham et al. 2005; Griffin and Hepburn 2006; Felson et al. 2012); *weak social ties* (Coa et al. 1997; McCorkle 1995; Reisig and Lee 2000; Jiang and Fisher-Giorlando 2002; DeLisi et al. 2004; Berg and DeLisi 2006); *gang affiliation* (Gaes et al. 2002; DeLisi 2003; Huebner 2003; DeLisi et al. 2004; Griffin and Hepburn 2006); and *histories of drug or alcohol use* (Felson et al. 2012).

By contrast, no consistent relationship has been found between time served and misconduct (Flanagan 1980; Wooldredge 1991; Wright 1991; Zamble 1992; Craddock 1996; Camp et al. 2003). Mixed results also have been found for mental disorder. Several studies have found no relationship between mental health problems and prison infractions (Baskin, Sommers, and Steadman 1991; McCorkle 1995; Porporino and Motiuk 1995), while a recent study by Felson et al. (2012) found a strong association between major depression and psychosis and prison offending.

Researchers have also explored the impact of prison conditions (i.e., the source of welfare harm) on levels of inmate misconduct and violence. Prison conditions have been characterized by aggregate (distributional) characteristics of the inmate population (e.g., size, demographics, criminal offense history), crowding, security level, staffing characteristics (e.g., inmate–officer ratio, officer turnover), programming, and management style. Across studies, the aggregate characteristics of the inmate population associated with levels of inmate misconduct are age, race, violent offenses, and prior incarceration (Gaes and McGuire 1985; Camp et al. 2003; Lahm 2008; Steiner and Wooldredge 2008; Lahm 2009; Steiner 2009). The effect of population density on inmate misconduct is mixed (see Steiner and Wooldredge 2009), with some studies finding a positive association between levels of misconduct and overcrowding (Gaes and McGuire 1985; Harer and Steffensmeier 1996; Wooldredge, Griffin, and Pratt 2001; Lahm 2009), while others have found no association (Ekland-Olson 1986; Camp et al. 2002; Steiner 2009). McCorkle and colleagues (1995) found rates of assault on inmates and staff increased with poor prison management and higher security level. Similarly, focusing on variation in levels of misconduct across facilities, Griffin and Hepburn (2006) found security level along with aggregate characteristics of the inmate population and the prison environment significantly affect the level of inmate misconduct. Administrative control, measuring the balance of coercive (i.e., use of threats and physical sanctions) and remunerative (i.e., positive and often material incentives) strategies applied within a prison to control inmate behavior also has been found to predict rates of misconduct, with higher levels of misconduct in prisons relying more on coercion relative to institutions with a more balanced use of coercion and remunerative control strategies (Wright 1994; Reisig 1998; Huebner 2003).

B. Physical Victimization

1. *Definition of Physical Victimization*

Definitions of physical victimization vary across studies. In some cases, "physical victimization" is defined in terms of types of harm: suicide, homicide, or assaults (James and Glaze 2006). Although such discrete incidents are easy to measure and commonly reported, they underrepresent the nature of physical harm within a correctional setting and narrowly measure its prevalence. More recently, researchers have conducted victimization surveys inside prisons, which have broadened the definition of bodily harm. Wooldredge (1994, 1998) defined "physical harm" to include bodily harm (e.g., assaults) and harm to property (e.g., theft). While more inclusive, this definition fails to probe the nature, severity, and perpetrator of bodily harm. Wolff, Shi, and Bachman (2008), using the National Violence Against Women and Men surveys (Tjaden and Thoeness 2000), expanded the definition of physical victimization to include general questions of physical victimization ("Have you been physically assaulted by an inmate or staff person" within a defined period of time?) and specific questions about the nature of victimization ("Have you been slapped, hit, kicked or bit; choked or attempted to drown; hit with object with intent to harm; beat up; threatened with harm with a knife or shank; had a loved one threatened with bodily harm; or had something of yours taken or stolen?"). Prevalence rates become more accurate when the definition is more inclusive and the probes more specific (see Wolff et al. 2006).

2. *Prevalence of Physical Victimization*

Remarkably little research attention has focused on estimating the prevalence of physical victimization inside prisons. According to official statistics, about one in 10 state prison inmates was injured in a fight since admission to prison (James and Glaze 2006). At the extreme, for 2010, there were 67 homicides (5 per 100,000 inmates) and 215 suicides (16 per 100,000 inmates) reported by state prisons (Noonan 2012).

To date, there has been no nationally representative survey of physical victimization that improves on the official reports of homicide, suicide, and assaults reported by prisons to the US Bureau of Justice Statistics. Consequently, what is known is based on inmate survey samples drawn from state prison systems using a variety of sampling and survey techniques. The first study of its kind was based on a survey of 231 inmates at a single prison. Of those responding to a survey distributed to their cells, 14 percent reported being a victim of a personal crime over a three-month period, whereas 20 percent reported being a victim of property crime (Wooldredge 1994). In a subsequent study based on a sample of 581 inmates drawn from three Ohio prisons, Wooldredge (1998) estimated that one in 10 inmates reported being physically assaulted in the previous six months, compared to one in four reporting being a victim of theft during the same time frame. When robbery, simple assault, and property damage were added to the measure of victimization, the rate of victimization increased to one out of every two responding inmates.

Wolff and colleagues (2007), drawing on data from over 8,000 inmates residing in 13 adult prisons for men and one prison for women, identified two perpetrators (inmate and staff) and seven types of physical victimization. Overall, for male inmates, property victimization (24 percent) was more prevalent than personal victimization (20.5 percent) between inmates during a six-month period. By contrast, female inmates reported higher rates of property victimization by other inmates (48.1 percent) but equal levels of personal victimization (20.6 percent; Wolff and Shi 2009c). Rates of inmate-on-inmate and staff-on-inmate personal victimization varied across facilities of different size. Inmate-on-inmate personal victimization ranged from 129 to 346 per 1,000 inmates, compared to 101 to 321 per 1,000 inmates for staff-on-inmate victimization (Wolff et al. 2007).

Synthesizing the findings across these three studies is challenging for several reasons. First, prevalence estimates are sensitive to how survey questions about victimization are posed, with rates significantly increasing with question specificity, definition of the perpetrator, and clustering of behaviors probed (Wolff et al. 2008). The definitions of physical victimization used by Wooldredge (1998) and Wolff and colleagues (2007) differed in terms of the (a) definition of victimization (Wooldredge excluded harm triggered by an aggressive act by the "victim"; Wolff et al. included any harm independent of its instigation); (b) specificity of personal victimization (Wooldredge used a two-question probe; Wolff et al. used a six-question probe); and (c) framing of the perpetrator (Wooldredge combined inmate and staff probes; Wolff et al. separated inmate and staff probes). Second, the reflection period for prevalence estimates vary, with two of the studies estimating physical victimization over a six-month period (Wolff et al. 2007; Wooldredge 1998) and one using a three-month period (Wooldredge 1994). Third, these studies used different sampling strategies, had different response rates, and attempted to represent facilities within a single department of corrections, limiting their within- and between-population generalizability.

With these limitations in mind, the research on physical victimizations suggests that inmate-on-inmate property victimization (~24 percent for males; ~48 percent for females) is more common than inmate-on-inmate personal victimization (~20 percent); staff-on-inmate personal victimization is higher for male inmates (~25 percent) than females (~8 percent); and rates of inmate-on-inmate and staff-on-inmate physical victimization vary across facilities. When combining personal (e.g., simple and aggravated assault and threats of bodily harm) and property victimization (e.g., robbery, theft, property damage) by staff and inmates, estimates of physical victimization approaches one out of every two inmates. In terms of exposure to physical harm, these findings suggest inmates experience more physical harm during confinement than what is reported officially through misconduct data in terms of theft (20 percent) and assault (5 to 14 percent).

3. Predictors of Physical Victimization

Some inmates are at greater risk of physical harm than others. Researchers have used individual- and institutional-level variables to identify risk differentials among inmates (Wooldredge 1994, 1998; Gaes et al. 2002; Griffin and Hepburn 2006; Lahm 2009; Wolff, Shi, and Siegel 2009a). Characteristics of the individual, such as race, age, mental illness, offense history, and gang affiliation, have been found to predict differential risk, although the direction and significance of the effect varies by type of victimization and sample. Wooldredge (1994, 1998) found no consistent racial or offense history pattern, although younger age consistently predicted personal and property victimization. Wolff and colleagues, controlling for variation among prison facilities and inmate characteristics, found the risk of personal victimization increased if an inmate had any of the following characteristics: young, white, had a nonserious mental disorder (e.g., depression, anxiety, posttraumatic stress disorder), committed a sex crime, experienced some form of physical victimization prior to age 18, and thought gang activity was high at the facility. Some of these same characteristics predicted risk of property victimization: nonserious mental disorder, prior physical victimization, and thought gang activity was high. They also found that facilities with poorer inmate relations (measured as dissatisfaction with the way an inmate was treated by correctional officers or other inmates) had higher personal victimization rates compared to prisons with better inmate relations. This finding is consistent with Wooldredge (1994), who found inmates with more unfavorable attitudes toward the facility were more likely to be victims of personal crime.

Overall, younger inmates, compared to older inmates, are more likely to experience personal and property victimization inside prison (Porporino, Doherty, and Sawatsky 1987; Cooley 1993; Maitland and Sluder 1998; Wooldredge 1998; Wolff et al. 2009a). The effect of race on victimization is mixed; whites have been found to be less at risk for victimization than Hispanics (Wooldredge 1994), but more at risk than blacks for inmate-on-inmate physical victimization (Wolff et al. 2008; Lahm 2009; Wolff et al. 2009a), although blacks and Hispanics were found at greater risk of staff-on-inmate physical victimization compared to whites (Wolff et al. 2009a). Other studies have found that race did not significantly predict physical victimization (Cooley 1993; Wooldredge 1998). Numerous studies have found a positive relationship between education level and physical victimization (Wooldredge 1998; Lahm 2009; Wolff et al. 2009a).

Levels of physical and property victimization vary across prisons (Wolff et al. 2009a). Characteristics of the prison found to increase victimization rates include poorer inmate relations (Wolff et al. 2009a), security level (Gaes and McGuire 1985; Cooley 1993; Lahm 2009), and lower officer-to-inmate ratios (Fuller and Orsagh 1977).

C. Sexual Victimization

1. *Definition of Sexual Victimization*

Sexual victimization is defined as *nonconsensual sexual acts*, which consists of forced sex acts, including oral, vaginal, and anal sex (referred to as sexual assault or rape), and *abusive sexual contacts*, inclusive of intentional or threatening touching of specific areas of the body (e.g., breasts, buttocks, penis; Basile and Saltzman 2002). Prior to the passage of the PREA of 2003, estimates of sexual victimization in prison ranged from as high as 41 percent to as low as 1 percent, with an average prevalence rate of prison sexual assault estimated at 1.9 percent (Gaes and Goldberg 2004).

2. *Prevalence of Sexual Victimization*

Wide variation in the prevalence of sexual victimization reflects methodological disparities (see Wolff et al. 2006; Wolff et al. 2008). Studies conducted prior to 2003 used a variety of study designs and definitions for sexual victimization. Some studies elicited information using questions that asked about "being coerced to engage in a sex act or have sexual contact," while others framed questions in terms of "being raped or sexually assaulted."

Contemporary sexual victimization research indicates that questions focusing on specific behavior produce more valid responses (Lynch 1996; Bachman 2000; Williams, Siegel, and Pomeroy 2000; Wolff et al. 2008). These studies also focused primarily on a single or small number of prisons and on small numbers of inmates (less than 15 percent) within a facility (Lockwood 1980; Nacci and Kane 1982; Wooden and Parker 1982; Tewksbury 1989; Struckman-Johnson et al. 1996; Maitland and Sluder 1998; Struckman-Johnson and Struckman-Johnson 2000; Hensley, Tewksbury, and Castle 2003). Estimates of sexual victimization at a single facility are unlikely to be representative because prison environments are heterogeneous in their management, operations, and inmate populations (Camp et al. 2003). Researchers conducting these studies elicited information about sexual victimization using either mail surveys or face-to-face interviews. Because sexual victimization often invokes feelings of shame and stigma, computer-assisted self-administered interviewing with audio assistance (A-CASI) is the most reliable method for eliciting information about stigmatizing behavior (Tourangeau and Smith 1996, 1998; Newman et al. 2002).

The goal of PREA was to rigorously estimate the prevalence of sexual victimization in prisons and to develop interventions to treat victims and prevent future victimization (Bureau of Justice Statistics 2004). In 2007 the US Bureau of Justice (BJS) conducted the first National Inmate Survey designed to measure sexual victimization in prisons. The survey included 130 state adult prisons, which held 250,873 inmates (20 percent of all inmates held in state prisons nationwide). Also included were 20 facilities operated under the auspices of the (federal) Bureau of Prisons. The survey was administered by A-CASI and completed anonymously. The questions probed specific acts ranging from inappropriate touching to sexual acts, explored the extent to which the activity was coerced, and distinguished between actions by inmates and staff over a 12-month period (Beck and Harrison 2007).

Based on this methodology, the BJS estimated that 4.5 percent of all state and federal prison inmates ($n = 60,500$) experienced some form of sexual victimization[6] over a 12-month period. Nationwide, the estimated rate for nonconsensual sexual conduct (i.e., rape) involving an inmate or staff person was 3.3 percent. An incident of sexual victimization involving another inmate was reported by 2.1 percent of inmates, compared to 2.9 percent for incidents involving staff. Nationally, of the estimated 27,500 inmates experiencing inmate-on-inmate sexual victimization, 61 percent ($n = 16,800$) experienced a nonconsensual sexual act (i.e., rape). Rates, however, were not uniform across facilities. Of the prison facilities surveyed, six had no incidents of sexual victimization reported by the sampled inmates, while 10 had sexual victimization rates ranging from 9.3 percent to 15.7 percent (Beck and Harrison 2007). A follow-up study conducted by the BJS in 2008–2009 estimated similar aggregate rates for sexual victimization but reported higher inmate-on-inmate sexual victimization among female inmates than males (Beck et al. 2010).

In 2008 the BJS commissioned the first National Former Prison Survey, which surveyed former state inmates about sexual victimization while incarcerated. From 40 states, 317 parole offices were randomly included in the survey sample. An estimated 9.6 percent of former state prisoners reported some form of sexual victimization during the most recent period of incarceration. Among the three confinement sites—jail, prison, or community-treatment facility—sexual victimization rates were highest in state prison and lowest in the community-treatment facility. Of the 27,300 former state inmates estimated to have experienced an inmate-on-inmate sexual incident during their most recent confinement, 68 percent reported being forced or pressured to have nonconsensual sex (Beck and Johnson 2012).

3. *Predictors of Sexual Victimization*

Researchers have drawn on the victimology literature to explain sexual victimization inside prison. This literature offers a variety of victim typologies (Schafer 1968; Sparks 1982) and theories of victimization (Fattah 2000). Sparks (1982), using the most integrative typology, identified six explanatory factors for victimization: facilitation, precipitation, vulnerability, impunity, attractiveness, and opportunity.[7] The advantage of Sparks's framework is it focuses on characteristics of the victim, which can be used to identify inmates at greatest risk. Characteristics frequently identified as making an inmate vulnerable to sexual victimization are sexual orientation, race, and physical appearance (Carroll 1974; Bowker 1980; Lockwood 1980). Wolff and colleagues (2006) asked more than 6,000 inmates to identify attributes that made inmates vulnerable to sexual assault. The most common responses were being homosexual, weak, small, or a pretty boy and having an offense against a child or one that involved domestic violence. Prior sexual victimization also has been found to increase the risk for future sexual victimization (Messman and Long 1996; Neumann et al. 1996; Arata 2002; Siegel and Williams 2003).

Wolff and colleagues (2007) found risk factors for sexual victimization varied by type of facility, perpetrator, and victimization type. Significant predictors for inmate-on-inmate sexual victimization in male general-population prisons were mental disorder, prior sexual victimization before the age of 18, higher levels of education, and elevated impressions of gang activity. Similar characteristics predicted staff-on-inmate sexual victimization but also included younger age, race (African American), and violent conviction. Females were at greater risk of sexual victimization if they had been sexually victimized prior to age 18 and thought gang activity was high. Younger age and higher education predicted staff-on-inmate sexual victimization for females. Using national data collected by the BJS, Beck, Harrison, Berzofsky et al. (2010) found inmate-on-inmate sexual victimization to be significantly higher for inmates with any of the following characteristics: female, white, multiracial, college education, never married, sexual orientation other than heterosexual, and prior sexual victimization.

D. Consequences of Harm

The physical and psychological consequences of inmate victimization were first reported by Carroll (1974) and Toch (1977). In the extreme, violence, manifested as victimization, culminates in death, either directly (murder) or indirectly (suicide); disfigurement; and chronic physical and psychological disability. Incarcerated people who experience violence also endure psychological trauma, pain, suffering, fear, rage, and the loss of quality of life, sometimes for years following the attack (Lockwood 1980). They also, depending on the nature of the violence, may be at increased risk of HIV and other sexually transmitted diseases (Knowles 1999). Rape, in particular, may challenge the person's self-identity and ability to resume a normal life (Lockwood 1980; Knowles 1999).

More is known about the consequences of rape inside prison than other types of victimization. Over the past 40 years, a variety of studies have explored the consequences of prison rape. The multidimensional impact of prison-based sexual assault on physical, emotional, and psychological well-being were documented by Lockwood (1980), Knowles (1999), Struckman-Johnson and colleagues (1996, 2006), and Wolff and Shi (2009b, 2009c, 2011).

In recent years, researchers have expanded the purview of analysis to examine the relative consequences of physical and sexual victimization on the well-being of inmate victims. While similarities in consequences were found between types of victimization, there were also important differences. Wolff and Shi (2009b) found that physical injuries (inclusive of internal injuries and head trauma) were more likely to result from inmate-on-inmate sexual assaults compared to inmate-on-inmate physical assaults. Virtually all victims of sexual and physical assaults reported emotional reactions as a consequence. For those physically assaulted, anger was the most common emotional reaction. By contrast, nearly half of victims of sexual assault reported feelings of depression and anger, difficulty sleeping, nightmares, and fear—consequences symptomatic of posttraumatic stress disorder. Similar patterns were reported by victims of staff-on-inmate assaults.

Not surprisingly, victims of physical and sexual violence feel less safe inside prison. Inmates who had experienced physical assault in the past six months reported feeling most unsafe from future physical or property victimization. They also were more likely to feel least safe from use of force by staff, especially if they had experienced some form of staff victimization in the past six months. Inmates reporting sexual victimization felt most unsafe relative to inmates without any victimization and those experiencing physical assault. They felt more at risk for sexual pressure, HIV, physical and property victimization, and staff abuse, especially if they were victims of staff sexual victimization (Wolff and Shi 2009c).

Victims of sexual and physical assault frequently change their behavior in the aftermath of the attack (McCorkle 1992). To protect themselves from harm, victims respond in one of three ways: fight, flight, or freeze (Cannon 1929). Those who opt for flight become more reclusive and keep to themselves, either with or without protective custody or administrative segregation, thereby avoiding people and places perceived as risky. Those who feel more powerless and helpless tend to "freeze" and give in to the demands of aggressors in their efforts to minimize harm (Greenfield 1980; Lockwood 1980). At the other extreme are the fighters. They engage in countervailing aggression, which may include securing a weapon, associating with a gang, bulking up—they fight more or become more effective fighters to deter future victimization (Irwin 1980; Lockwood 1980). Studies of the precautionary behaviors of victims post-attack have found that inmates engage in all three forms of protective behaviors: fight, flight, and freeze (McCorkle 1992; Wolff and Shi 2009b).

Most prevalent among the protective behaviors is flight (McCorkle 1992; Wolff and Shi 2009b). Wolff and Shi (2009b), studying approximately 1,400 inmate victims, found that victims of physical and sexual assault were most likely to adopt a flight response to violence: staying more to themselves and avoiding risky persons and places. However, a significant minority, particularly those who were victims of sexual or physical assault that resulted in injury, were most likely to carry a weapon, bulk up, fight more, or join a gang. In this case, violence begets more violence, with those more severely harmed opting to defensively arm themselves to return violence for violence if deemed necessary to protect or avenge.

III. General Model of Harm

Violence and victimization occur jointly; one person's act of violence is another person's incident of harm.[8] For this reason, harm via criminal conduct is modeled as a dyadic event (Toch 1977; Cohen and Felson 1979; Cook 1986; Wener 2012). The most robust analytic of this dyadic event is routine activities theory, which models the event of crime as the confluence of three elements: potential offenders, suitable targets or victims, and the absence of capable guardians (Cohen and Felson 1979). Routine activities theory, focusing on the environment of place, predicts that crime will be higher in places where guardians (e.g., police, correctional officers) are ineffective either because they are absent, incompetent, or corrupt.

Rational choice theory, focusing on the behavior of the person, can be used to explain the choices of potential offenders and victims (Cook 1986). Microeconomic theory of choice assumes that people rationally choose their behavior and are motivated to avoid pain and pursue pleasure (i.e., maximize utility). As such, people, in choosing among options (or behaviors), use a decisional balance that compares the (marginal) benefits and costs associated with each course of action and select the option that yields the most valued outcomes (i.e., greatest net benefits). The costs and benefits associated with crime can be manipulated by environmental conditions (e.g., presence of effective guardians, surveillance cameras), incentive and disincentive strategies (e.g., criminal sentencing, weapon recycling), and welfare conditions (e.g., level of deprivation). Everything else equal, when the benefits (i.e., material, emotional, or justice gains) are high and the costs are low (i.e., low effort and minimal likelihood of detection), offenders will be motivated to search for high-yield victims. Victims, also motivated by self-interest, have an incentive to engage in precautionary behaviors (e.g., avoiding high-risk areas and people, changing their demeanor, evincing less wealth). Victims attempt to change the perceptions of potential offenders about the benefits they would derive from preying on them while increasing the effort offenders would have to expend to successfully overwhelm them.

Here rational choice, combined with routine activities theory, is used to explain the prevalence of interpersonal harm (i.e., victimization) within correctional settings, as well as the variation in the prevalence of interpersonal harm across facilities. The model is developed in ways that incorporate the importation and deprivation models used to explain misconduct and violence inside prison, with the goal of presenting an integrated micro-macro model of the dyadic event: interpersonal harm, which is caused by offenders and results in victims. The utility of this model is its ability to identify strategies and practices for reducing levels of violence and victimization inside correctional facilities.

A. Assumptions

Economic models of individual behavior begin with an assumption of rational choice in which individuals engage in behavior that maximizes their self-interest. My model assumes rational choice but advances different assumptions about human behavior under conditions of confinement. I assume that (a) people who are confined seek to survive physically and psychologically, (b) their actions are motivated by "survival" instincts as it relates to their welfare interests, and (c) they act rationally in pursuit of survival. With incarceration, the goal is survival, simply because the hallmark of prisons is their deprivation, as articulated by Sykes (1958). Conditions of deprivation inside prisons are multifaceted and include the dispossession of material, social, sexual, security, and existential benefits, creating welfare harm. Focusing first on physical survival, the living conditions inside prison may fluctuate but are bounded by constitutional protections that place a ceiling on welfare harm—the level of material, social, and security deprivation allowed by law. To physically survive confinement, incarcerated persons draw on their learned abilities and social networks to minimize the setback to welfare interests caused by confinement while managing the dangers that threaten life and safety (i.e., interpersonal harm). Here the focus is on defending the body and its needs. Rationally, to survive, incarcerated people act purposefully to secure resources to nourish the body in preferred ways and protect it from harm.

Surviving psychologically requires protecting the self-concept (i.e., self-image or self-perception; Sykes 1958; Cohen and Taylor 1972; Tonry 2004). Incarceration begins with the moral rejection of the person by the community (Sykes 1958), whereby he is labeled a "threat to society" and relegated to the status of a social outcast. The attack on the self continues with confinement through the loss of privacy, civility, and agency within the prison's power structure (Irwin and Owen 2005) and is furthered by the loss in personal identity as the person becomes an inmate number (aka "prisonized"; Sykes 1958; Goffman 1961). By internalizing the social disapproval for their crime and adopting the dehumanized status of "inmate" (i.e., welfare harm), the self withers away as the incarcerated conform to and become the stigmatizing labels imposed on them by society (Tannenbaum 1938; Gove 1980; Braithwaite 1989). To psychologically survive, incarcerated people draw on and adapt their learned abilities, coping strategies, and social networks to create and sustain opportunities to maintain beliefs, values, and aspirations that connect them with their cultural heritage and perceptions of humanity.

Next I assume that harm is an instrument of survival. It is used strategically to obtain possessions and positions of value, including material goods and services, power, and status, and to defensively prevail over threats to physical and psychological survival (i.e., minimize setbacks to welfare interests and interpersonal harm). Material deprivation often motivates people to steal in order to survive. Similarly, life-threatening dangers trigger the fight response where a person rationally chooses lethal means to prevail. Threats to self-worth also elicit an instinct to survive psychologically. For example, censoriousness of prison staff, where staff compromise their professionalism to gratuitously flaunt and abuse their power over incarcerated persons (Mathiesen 1965), can trigger violence if those who are treated inhumanly or unfairly retaliate aggressively to assert their right to be treated fairly and respectfully. Indeed, Gilligan (2003) argues that violence arises from anger caused by actions intended to shame. Being talked to or treated with contempt, disdain, or disrespect threatens the person's worthiness and triggers a survival response. Wilson, Drozdek, and Turkovic (2006, p. 139), in describing the effects of shame, state that "shame damages the soul of the person, his or her most cherished and inner sense of identity and humanity." Protecting their concept of self (including manhood, adulthood, racism, religious convictions, or gang identity) can be expected to invoke strong fight–flight responses among incarcerated persons, especially if it triggers wounds of trauma.

As noted earlier, most people come to prison with a legacy of victimization, which also puts them at greater risk for victimization inside prison (Wolff and Shi 2009a). Trauma exposure among incarcerated people, in general, is positively associated with psychopathology, including self-regulation problems and aggressive behavior (Wolff and Shi 2012).

Hypersensitivity to shame is also symptomatic of trauma exposure (Budden 2009). Budden (p. 1037) argues that "psychological traumas are, in a very profound way, about threat to the social self. Overwhelming social threats tear away the fibers of one's very being." As such, confrontational and aggressive styles of engagement, emanating from power asymmetries, threaten the incarcerated persons' welfare interests, triggering fight–flight coping strategies that foment inter- and intrapersonal violence.

In summary, the use of acts of harm to survive is influenced but not strictly determined by environmental and organizational characteristics of the prison (deprivation model: setback to welfare interests), the characteristics of the people who are incarcerated (importation model, including trauma exposure), and the interactions among these characteristics.

Further, I assume violence and victimization are interdependent.[9] Violence, like an infectious disease, can spread through victimization, creating more violence. More specifically, an act of violence creates a victim, who may, in retaliation, harm someone else, creating a contagion of violence. A contagion can be instigated by direct acts of aggression by inmates against inmates or staff against inmates or by styles of engagement that engender sentiments of injustice. I do not, however, assume that violence and victimization are uniquely dependent. For example, acts of injustice or aggression by staff against inmates may create tensions and strains among inmates that manifest as violence directed at inmates, not staff, simply because the penalty of harm against staff is greater than those same acts directed at inmates (i.e., net benefits are higher if harm is directed at inmates than staff).

B. The Market for Harm

The level of interpersonal harm within a correctional setting is determined by the demand to harm and the supply of victims. Here I model harm directly done to and by incarcerated people, not staff. Staff can influence harm indirectly through their words and actions that threaten the welfare interests of incarcerated people. For clarification, I begin with a diagram (Figure 14.1) that shows graphically the "markets" for physical and sexual victimization,

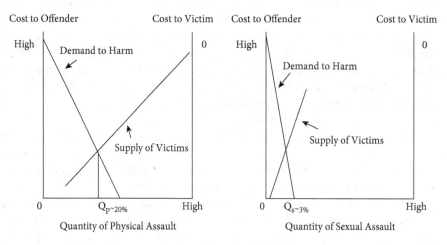

FIGURE 14.1. Graphical representation of "markets" for harm in correctional settings.

reflecting the average prevalence rates for each type of victimization found in the literature. On the vertical axis of each graph is the personal cost of interpersonal harm and, on the horizontal axis, the quantity of interpersonal harm. The demand for interpersonal harm slopes downward to the right,[10] showing that as the personal cost associated with harming others increases, the quantity of harm decreases, while the supply of victims slopes upward to the right, indicating that the number of suitable victims decreases as the personal cost of harm increases (note the reversal of the cost scale on the right side of each graph). The equilibrating outcome of interest is the quantity of interpersonal harm (i.e., its prevalence), not its cost. The (entire) demand or supply curve can shift right or left when harm-promoting or -preventing (individual or institutional) factors change, causing a change in the equilibrium level of interpersonal harm.[11]

1. *Demand to Harm*

At the individual level, the demand to harm someone depends on motivation and ability. People are motivated to harm to protect their welfare interests, which includes defending themselves against physical and psychological harm. For example, conditions of material deprivation motivate stealing, while interference with agency and the integrity of self motivates interpersonal harm. Violence is often the consequence of efforts to control or coerce people against their will or of words or actions of others that are interpreted as disrespectful, disloyal, or shaming of self, family, culture, or gang. Violence, as a learned behavior, may be more reflexive for some (i.e., habit persistence), as well as fueled by revenge against contemporary or historical enemies. As such, not all individuals have equal predispositions to harm. Conditions and conditioning create nonrandom variation in the motivation to harm across individuals. Likewise, people vary in their ability to mobilize the intent to harm. To act on the intent to harm, a person must have the skills, resources, and opportunity to do harm. Harm cannot be operationalized if people lack the skill set or resources to mobilize the intent or the opportunity to engage the intended target. Some people who are incapacitated (e.g., locked in, isolated within a facility) may contract with surrogates to activate their intent to harm, while the lack of skills and resources creates the incentive for others to build that capacity.

A demand to harm exists when people are both willing *and* able to do harm. But the amount of harm exhibited will depend on the price people are willing to pay to harm another person. The "price" of harm is its personal costs, which equals what is potentially lost if the person is caught and punished. In prison terms, the personal cost of harm equals the probable loss of privileges (e.g., job, visits, education, yard time), gains in deprivation (e.g., time in administrative segregation, reclassification, new street charges), and pain and suffering (e.g., beat downs). Rational people are willing to pay a price to harm that is equal to the value of what is gained. The personal benefit from harming equals the satisfaction from knowing justice has been rendered, revenge exacted, values or beliefs defended, or status through reputation gained. More harm will be conducted when the personal cost is lower, yielding levels of harm that are inversely related to the personal cost of harm, everything else equal.

The aggregate demand to harm within a correctional facility is the sum of all demand to harm curves across inmates at a particular facility. Assuming equal welfare conditions across facilities, the aggregate demand to harm will vary across facilities by the distribution of harm-propensity characteristics of individuals within the facility (importation theory). Harm-propensity characteristics are those that predispose people to disproportionately react protectively to efforts to control or coerce them against their will (e.g., trauma exposure) or to interpret words, actions, or situations as threatening (e.g., gang affiliation, racist orientation), combined with the reflexive and socialized tendency and ability to act on the motivation (e.g., gang affiliation, young age, history of violence, male). Nonrandom variation in individual attributes associated with the willingness and ability to do harm shifts the aggregate demand to harm. Everything else equal, above-average levels of inmates within a facility who are male, young, gang affiliated, traumatized, habituated toward violence, or have racist orientations shift the (entire) aggregate demand to harm to the right, increasing the level of harm at every personal cost measured in terms of consequences.

Assuming equal distributions of harm-propensity characteristics within inmate populations across facilities, the aggregate demand curve would vary by deprivation conditions across facilities (i.e., relative deprivation). Any condition within a facility that systematically sets back the welfare interests of incarcerated persons has the potential to shift the (entire) aggregate demand to harm to the right. Physical conditions of deprivation that cause intolerable pain and suffering through inadequate nutrition, social or sensory stimulation (e.g., overcrowding), or social isolation (e.g., routine lockdowns) will trigger survival instincts that motivate harm. People are more inclined to steal, fight, and abuse others when the integrity of body and self are at greater risk due to extreme poverty of privacy, quiet, and nourishment. Similarly, the lack of opportunities for self-development through education, treatment programs, extracurricular activities, as well as the lack of opportunities for self-preservation through social engagement with the outside world, puts the psychological self at risk, motivating the survival instinct. Facilities that deprive incarcerated people of opportunities for self-development and self-preservation lower the personal cost of harm at all levels while also motivating the instinct to protect psychological integrity. Restricting healthy socialization stimulates instincts (i.e., protective aggression) that subvert the very qualities that the individual is trying to protect. That is, making incarcerated people feel powerless over their exposure to life-sustaining comfort and support from the outside community causes them to act out abusively toward others inside to regain a sense of power and respect.

Exploitation of power asymmetries by staff also increase the demand to harm. Leadership or management styles that are unfair, capricious, cruel, or illegitimate attack the psychological welfare of people, who in reaction respond strategically to preserve their psychological survival. In addition, while illegitimate acts of power dominance by officers (i.e., censoriousness) over incarcerated persons may bolster the egos of officers, these acts also initiate a contagion of harm among incarcerated persons if, in an effort to restore their weakened egos, incarcerated people mimic officer behavior by exacting their power advantage over weaker peers. Systematic abuse of incarcerated persons by their peers may, in turn, instigate the need to invest in the ability to do harm (e.g., bulk up, acquire weapons, join a gang). Taken together, institutional characteristics associated with environmental conditions of oppression and privation will shift the aggregate demand to harm to the right, everything else equal.

In other ways, institutional characteristics can constrain the demand to harm through physical design, movement policies, and punishment strategies. The ability to harm another

person presumes freedom to move and congregate. By limiting movement and controlling association, facilities limit the opportunity to mobilize the intent to harm. Likewise,
through design, facilities can increase surveillance and detection efforts, limiting areas for
harm to be conducted. By increasing the predictability and penalties associated with harm,
facilities increase the price of harm at all levels, lowering the demand to harm. All things
equal, facilities that limit movement, congregation, and unsupervised areas, or increase the
harshness and predictability of penalties associated with harm, will have aggregate demand-
to-harm curves that are lower vis-à-vis facilities without such practices.

2. *Supply of Victims*

The supply of potential victims is bounded by the size of the inmate population. But
not all incarcerated persons are equally likely to be a victim (i.e., equally "suitable targets"). Like the demand to harm, the supply of victims depends on the willingness of
an individual to be in harm's way and his ability to be harmed (Cohen and Felson 1979).
The willingness to associate creates opportunities for victimization. Socializing through
attending programs, church, work, educational classes, yard, mess, or clinic appointments reduces social distance between people, satisfying the need to be connected to
others while also creating opportunities to be victimized either in a congregate setting or
along the way to that setting. People put themselves at risk of harm because they derive
benefits from socializing, movement, and scheduled activities (e.g., eating, work, exercise, medical treatment, worship, education, group treatment). Some people invite the
risk of harm by socializing in ways that are illegal or illegitimate. For example, they may
participate in activities such as gambling, drug distribution, running "stores" or scams,
and snitching, which create debts and hostilities often remedied with violence. However,
willingly exposing oneself to harm does not, in and of itself, result in victimization. The
ability to be harmed, once exposed, depends in part on the person's abilities to defend
himself through reputation, associations, resources, and related proficiencies.[12] Being
willing and able to fight, having associates ready to retaliate and/or a reputation of ruth-
lessness, and having resources and communication proficiencies to negotiate a nonviolent settlement serve as protective assets against harm. Countervailing these assets are
the person's vulnerability liabilities (i.e., target suitability), which might include cognitive
disabilities (e.g., developmental or mental disorders), offense stigmas (e.g., sex crimes,
crimes against family or gang members), and sexual orientation (e.g., homosexuality). At
the individual level, the potential supply of victims, therefore, depends on the willingness
of people to expose themselves to harm and their relative stocks of protective assets and
vulnerability liabilities.

To be included in the supply of victims, individuals must be willing and/or able to be
harmed. Again, assuming rationality, people would be expected to lower their exposure
to victimization as the cost of victimization increases, where the cost of victimization is
the expected pain and suffering associated with being harmed. Incarcerated people would
expose themselves to violence to the point where the personal gains (i.e., satisfaction from
association, movement, returns from legitimate/illegitimate activities) equal the personal
costs (i.e., pain and suffering associated with harm). This yields a supply of victims where
the number of potential victims decreases as the personal cost of victimization increases,
everything else constant.

The aggregate supply of victims is influenced by the size of the inmate population and the distribution of inmate and institutional characteristics within and across facilities. First, assuming homogenous welfare conditions across facilities, the potential supply of victims within a facility will depend on the distribution of victim-propensity characteristics of the incarcerated population (importation theory). Victim-propensity characteristics include the affinity for risk-taking (e.g., history of gambling, running scams, drug dealing, snitching), addiction problems (e.g., drug, alcohol, gambling addictions), or vulnerability risks (e.g., sexual orientation, sex offender, developmental or mental disability, small stature, trauma exposure). Nonrandom variation in victim-propensity attributes within an inmate population shifts the aggregate supply of victims. Everything else equal, above-average levels of inmates within a facility who are risk-loving, active in their addictions, or have vulnerability risks shift the aggregate supply of victims to the right, increasing the level of potential victimization at every personal cost.

If the distribution of victim-propensity characteristics among inmate populations is assumed equal across facilities, the aggregate supply of victims would vary by the distribution of welfare conditions (i.e., relative deprivation) across facilities. Conditions within facilities that set back the welfare interests of inmates (i.e., low-quality food, low levels of state-issued supplies, higher commissary prices, lower wage rates, higher unemployment rates, limited number of higher paying jobs) motivate welfare-enhancing risk-taking, such as gambling, running stores, scamming, and selling information to staff, which increases the number of potential victims at all costs, everything else equal. Contrariwise, facilities with controlled movement that economize on educational, social, and treatment programming deprive incarcerated people of the opportunity to move and congregate, which shifts the aggregate supply of potential victims to the left.

The relative coverage, competence, and vigilance of security staff also affect the potential supply of victims. As posited by routine activities theory (Cohen and Felson 1979), the absence of effective guardians increases the likelihood of victimization. Incarcerated persons are at greater risk of victimization when officer supervision is spatially uneven (opening up spatial opportunities for harm), which may be imperfectly captured by inmate-to-staff ratios. Prison design and use of surveillance cameras, in combination with the spatial distribution of officers, determine the extent to which incarcerated persons are protected from harm. Facilities that are designed and staffed to increase surveillance, everything else equal, will have aggregate supply of victim curves that are lower than those facilities without such surveillance/security protections. Surveillance effectiveness, however, is weakened by officers who are inattentive, corruptible, or negligent in the execution of their responsibilities to protect incarcerated persons. By overtly or covertly turning a blind eye to the environment, officers increase the likelihood of victimization. Indirect measures of officer ineffectiveness include poor work ethic, low morale, high turnover, or absenteeism of staff, while more direct measures include high rates of staff suspensions or firing for misconduct and negative attitudes about inmates and their jobs. The aggregate supply of victims shifts to the right for facilities with above-average levels of security ineffectiveness. Alternatively, to protect at-risk inmates from predators, facilities may use classification systems that separate people inclined to victimize from those easily victimized. Such policies, if effective, would shift the aggregate supply of victims to the left, everything else constant.

3. *Predicting and Preventing Harm*

The demand to harm and the supply of potential victims as described here provide a framework for predicting and preventing harm in correctional settings. Harm can be delineated into four "markets": for physical victimization, property victimization, sexual victimization, and personal harm (e.g., attempted suicides, suicide, self-cutting). Each market has unique "demand to harm" and "supply of potential victims" curves. The level of harm, distinct to each facility, reflects the mix, distribution, and interactions among harm- and victim-propensity characteristics of the inmate population and institution. Table 14.1 summarizes the variables associated with the shape and movement of the demand and supply curves.

Lowering levels of victimization through harm-reduction interventions is not straightforward because of the interdependencies among individual and institutional harm-propensity characteristics, as well as among harm- and victim-propensity characteristics at the individual and institutional levels. It is further complicated by interactions among property harm, physical interpersonal harm, sexual interpersonal harm, and intrapersonal harm. The scope and multitude of interdependencies explain in part why different studies exploring inmate misconduct and victimization yield disparate findings regarding the independent effects of individual and institutional characteristics on harm. Another reason concerns the samples used to test for these effects. Measuring the effects of harm- and victim-propensity characteristics is sensitive to sample design, particularly whether the sample is drawn from one facility (minimizing interfacility variation but drawing into question the facility's representativeness) or many facilities (better representing interfacility variation, which is then imperfectly specified with hierarchical modeling). Similar imprecision problems occur when dependent and independent variables are measured with nonrandom error and relevant variables are omitted from the model. Using theory, however, we can anticipate the direction of the effects, which then can be tested empirically with sample designs suited for specific hypothesis testing.

As an illustration, assume that the goal is to reduce physical victimization. According to Table 14.1, policy instruments available to lower harm are decreasing deprivation (physical, social, financial), decreasing movement, increasing surveillance, decreasing ineffective security, increasing the severity and predictability of punishment, and improving the classification of inmates by risk. Faced with these options, Facility A elects a strong social control approach and adopts three instruments: decreasing movement, increasing surveillance of inmate areas, and increasing the severity and predictability of punishment. Together, these policies decrease opportunities for harm and increase the detection and punishment cost of harm, lowering the willingness to harm. These changes, however, also unleash countermanding effects. Increasing levels of physical and social deprivation intensively and extensively threaten physical and psychological survival. Urges to survive by force or flight, as a consequence, build up during isolation. If movement is sharply limited, rage will be externalized using all available instruments (e.g., food, excrement, insults, taunting) or internalized through self-injury (e.g., suicide, cutting, malicious destruction). When movement is allowed, the demand to harm explodes against inmates and staff. If there is nothing to lose, the demand to harm is costly to contain. Not only are these strategies likely to increase harm, but they also can be expected to drive up mental health and facility maintenance costs.

Alternatively, Facility B opts for a balanced social control–remunerative approach by implementing more educational and vocational programming, raising the wage rate of

Table 14.1 Summary of Individual and Institutional Characteristics Influencing the Demand to Harm and Supply of Victims

Market	Type	Variable	Definition/Motivation	Effect	Interaction	Interaction
Demand	**Harm**	**Price**	**Increases with deprivation and suffering**	**Negative**		
Harm-propensity Variables	Individual	Trauma exposure	Increases sensitivity to psychological and physical harm through abuses of power	Shift Right	Institution—abuses of power; Contagion effect; Shift Right	Institution—restricted movement; Shift Left
		Gang affiliation	Increases sensitivity to physical harm through abuses of power	Shift Right		
		Racist orientation	Increases sensitivity to physical and psychological harm triggered by perceived racism	Shift Right		
		Violence history	Increases predisposition to react to physical or psychological harm with violence due to habit persistence	Shift Right		
		Young/Inexperience	Increases predisposition to react to physical or psychological harm with violence due to developmental stage	Shift Right		
		Male	Increases predisposition to react to physical or psychological harm with violence due to social conditioning	Shift Right		
	Institution	Deprivation—physical conditions	Increases threat to physical and psychological survival	Shift Right		
		Deprivation—social	Decreases prices of harm and increases threat to psychological survival	Shift Right		
		Deprivation—movement	Decreases opportunity for harm	Shift Left		

Category	Variable	Description	Effect	Contagion	
Supply	Ineffective security	Increases perceived threat	Shift Right	Contagion Shift Right	Contagion Effect: Demand to Harm shifts Right
	Censoriousness	Increases perceived threat	Shift Right	Contagion Shift Right	
	Surveillance	Decreases opportunity to harm	Shift Left		
	Punishment	Increases prices of harm	Shift Left		
	Security Level	Decreases opportunity to harm	Shift Left		
Victims	Price	Increases with pain and suffering	Negative		
Victim-propensity Variables	Individual				
	Affinity for or expansion of risk taking	Increases willingness to engage in activities associated with being harmed	Shift Right	Ineffective security Shift Right and Left	
	Addiction problems				
	Vulnerability risks—development or mental disorder, sex offender, sexual orientation	Decreases ability to protect self from being harmed	Shift Right	Ineffective security Shift Right	
	Institution				
	Deprivation—lower quality of life	Increases need to engage in welfare-enhancing activities	Shift Right		
	Deprivation—decrease association	Decrease opportunities to associate	Shift Left		
	Ineffective security	Increase opportunities for harm	Shift Right		
	Segregated classification	Decrease opportunities for harm	Shift Left		
	Surveillance	Decrease opportunities for harm	Shift Left		

inmates by 10 percent, increasing surveillance on officers and inmates, and increasing the severity and predictability of punishment for misconduct by inmates and staff. This approach increases movement and group association, which amplifies the risk of victimization. However, because these new programming opportunities enhance psychological well-being and increase the personal cost of harm across the board, the demand to harm those now in the position to be victimized is lowered. Similarly, increasing the wage rate increases the personal cost associated with harm, lowering the aggregate demand to harm further while decreasing the need to engage in welfare-enhancing risk-taking, thus decreasing the supply of potential victims. Increasing surveillance on inmates and staff improves information about misconduct, while increasing the penalties when detected raises the cost of violating inmate and professional rules of conduct, reducing the demand to harm (by both inmates and staff). Any instruments that curb abuses of power by staff within a facility are expected to significantly reduce levels of harm, given their contagion effects on violence and victimization.

IV. Conclusion

Harm reduction (i.e., safety) is a preeminent goal of correctional agencies. This can be achieved in a myriad of ways, some of which are more likely to be successful than others. My general model of harm identifies a mix of policy instruments, some more punitive than others, and explains how they are likely to influence the willingness and ability of incarcerated persons to harm and be harmed. The advantage of this model is it integrates importation and deprivation variables, through routine activities theory and rational choice theory, into a dyadic and dynamic framework of physical and psychological survival where security staff activates, directs, and energizes the dynamic through how they interact with the principal actors (incarcerated persons). The logic of this model suggests that direct effects of policy interventions can be swamped by offsetting secondary reactions, which may in part explain why our empirical evidence is so mixed and the rates of harm are so difficult to change.

Reducing harm in correctional settings is all about managing people effectively. Effective management of people, whether confined or not, requires a blend of "carrot and stick" approaches. When managing incarcerated persons, it is vital to remember that their goal is physical and psychological survival in a jungle where scarcity is king. More scarcity will not invite more civilized behavior. Likewise, more potent or pervasive cruelty will not quell these primal instincts. Counter to conventional wisdom, prison leadership and staff must make prisons more civilized if they are to host civil behavior. Indeed, spending money on civility and civilized conditions might actually save money through lower medical, disability, and maintenance costs. Equality of conditions, in the words of Alex de Tocqueville (1956), improves the art of association. The challenge, therefore, is to engage and work with the survival instincts of incarcerated persons by finding a balance in the "setback to interests" caused by confinement that will support and encourage more civility and safety and, in turn, less harm.

NOTES

1. It is beyond the scope of this essay to explore harm to staff, although the extension is easily accommodated within the definition of harm to be developed herein.

2. The argument here is not normative; rather, it is a statement of fact: confinement deprivation causes a setback to welfare interests—welfare harm. Although it may be considered socially appropriate to impose welfare harm on incarcerated people, incarcerated people experience the deprivation, even if morally or socially deserved, as harmful to their welfare interest.

3. A duty of protection is imposed on correctional institutions under Article 10 of the International Covenant on Civil Rights and Political Rights (ICCRPR), which states that "[a]ll persons deprived of their liberty shall be treated with humanity and with respect for the inherent dignity of the human person" (Rodley 1999, p. 286). Although the United States ratified the ICCRPR, it has not been incorporated into domestic law. Hence this international standard of protection is rarely invoked by incarcerated persons; rather, they look to the US Constitution for relief.

4. For a comprehensive review of PREA and related literature, visit http://nicic.gov/prea.

5. See http://www.icpsr.umich.edu/icpsrweb/NACJD/NIBRS/ for more details.

6. Sexual victimization includes *nonconsensual sexual acts* (i.e., forced sex acts, including oral, vaginal, and anal sex) and *abusive sexual contacts* (i.e., intentional or threatening touching of specific areas of the body (e.g., breasts, buttocks, penis) (Basile and Saltzman 2002).

7. A related but more macro-environmental theory of victimization is routine activities theory, which focuses on how the normal routine activities of daily living create opportunities for crime as they bring together suitable targets and motivated offenders, where capable guardians may be absent or ineffective (Cohen and Felson 1979).

8. The person initiating the harm may ultimately be the victim if the intended victim subdues the instigator of harm. Likewise today's victim may be tomorrow's perpetrator. In modeling harm, the emphasis is on the inextricable and interdependent connection between violence and victimization, not on uniquely labeling who is blameworthy for initiating the violence.

9. Again, it is important to keep in mind that "victim" and "offender" labels are dynamic and organic; a person could be an offender at the outset but a victim at the conclusion of the event, a victim in a previous event but the offender in a later event, or simultaneously the offender and victim, in the case of self-abuse.

10. The linearity or non-linearity of the demand and supply curves are not relevant; what is relevant is directionality; people do less harm when the cost of harm increases (negative association between cost and quantity), and fewer people are available to be harmed when the cost of harming increases (positive association between lower cost and quantity).

11. For example, in traditional markets, an increase in personal income will increase the demand (shift the demand curve to the right) for goods like cars, computers, books, and so forth. That is, people will buy more of these goods at all prevailing prices because they have more money to spend.

12. Issues of "guardianship" (Cohen and Felson 1979) will be addressed later in terms of local facility conditions.

REFERENCES

Arata, Catalina. M. 2002. "Child Sexual Abuse and Sexual Victimization." *Clinical Psychology* 9: 135–164.

Bachman, Ronet. 2000. "A Comparison of Annual Incidence Rates and Contextual Characteristics of Intimate-Partner Violence Against Women from the National Crime Victimization Survey (NVAWS)." *Violence Against Women* 6: 839–867.

Basile, Kathleen C., and Linda E. Saltzman. 2002. *Sexual Violence Surveillance: Uniform Definitions and Recommended Data Elements*. Atlanta, GA: National Center for Injury Prevention and Control, Centers for Disease Control and Prevention.

Baskin, Deborah R., Ira Sommers, and Henry J. Steadman. 1991. "Assessing the Impact of Psychiatric Impairment on Prison Violence." *Journal of Criminal Justice* 19: 271–280.

Beck, Allen J., and Paige M. Harrison. 2007. *Sexual Victimization in State and Federal Prisons Reported by Inmates, 2007*. Special Report of the Bureau of Justice Statistics. (No. NCJ 219414). Washington, DC: Bureau of Justice Statistics, US Department of Justice.

Beck, Allen J., Paige M. Harrison, Marcus Berzofsky, Rachel Caspar, and Christopher Krebs. 2010. *Sexual Victimization in Prisons and Jails Reported by Inmates, 2008–2009*. Special Report of the Bureau of Justice Statistics. (No. NCJ 231169). Washington, DC: Bureau of Justice Statistics, US Department of Justice.

Beck, Allen J., and Candace Johnson. 2012. *Sexual Victimization Reported by Former State Prisoners, 2008*. Special Report of the Bureau of Justice Statistics. (No NCJ 237363). Washington, DC: Bureau of Justice Statistics, US Department of Justice.

Bench, Lawrence L., and Terry D. Allen. 2003. "Investigating the Stigma of Prison Classification: An Experiential Design." *The Prison Journal* 83: 367–382.

Berg, Mark T., and Matt DeLisi. 2006. "The Correctional Melting Pot: Race, Ethnicity, Citizenship, and Prison Violence." *Journal of Criminal Justice* 34: 631–642.

Bottoms, Anthony. 1999. "Interpersonal Violence and Social Order in Prisons." In *Prisons*, edited by Michael Tonry and Joan Petersilia. Chicago: University of Chicago Press.

Bowker, Lee. 1980. *Prison Victimization*. New York: Elsevier North Holland.

Braithwaite, John. 1989. *Crime, Shame, and Reintegration*. Cambridge, UK: Cambridge University Press.

Budden, Ashwin. 2009. "The Role of Shame in Posttraumatic Stress Disorder: A Proposal for a Socio-Emotional Model for DSM–V." *Social Science and Medicine* 69: 1032–1039.

Bureau of Justice Statistics. 2003. *Census of State and Federal Correctional Facilities 2000* (No. NCJ 198272). Washington, DC: Bureau of Justice Statistics, US Department of Justice.

Bureau of Justice Statistics. 2004. *Data Collections for the Prison Rape Elimination Act of 2003*. Washington, DC: US Department of Justice.

Camp, Scott D., Gerald G. Gaes, Neal P. Langan, and William G. Saylor. 2003. "The Influence of Prisons on Inmate Misconduct: A Multilevel Investigation." *Justice Quarterly* 20: 501–533.

Cannon, Walter B. 1929. *Bodily Changes in Pain, Hunger, Fear, and Rage*. New York: Appleton-Century-Crofts.

Cao, Liqun, Jihon Zhao, and Steve Van Dine. 1997. "Prison Disciplinary Tickets: A Test of the Deprivation and Importation Models." *Journal of Criminal Justice* 25: 103–111.

Carroll, Leo. 1974. *Hacks, Blacks, and Cons: Race Relations in a Maximum Security Prison*. Prospect Heights, IL: Waveland Press.

Clemmer, Donald. 1940. *The Prison Community*. New York: Holt, Rinehart and Winston.

Cohen, Lawrence, and Marcus Felson. 1979. "Social Change and Crime Rate Trends: A Routine Activities Approach." *American Sociological Review* 44: 588–608.

Cohen, Stanley, and Laurie Taylor. 1972. *Psychological Survival: The Experience of Long-Term Imprisonment*. Harmondsworth, UK: Penguin.

Cook, Phillip J. 1986. "The Demand and Supply of Criminal Opportunities." *Crime & Justice* 7: 1–27.

Cooley, Dennis. 1993. "Criminal Victimization in Male Federal Prisons." *Canadian Journal of Criminology* 4: 479–495.

Craddock, Amy. 1996. "A Comparative Study of Male and Female Prison Misconduct Careers." *The Prison Journal*, 76: 60–80.

Cunningham, Mark D., and Jon Sorensen. 2007. "Predictive Factors for Violent Misconduct in Close Custody." *The Prison Journal* 87: 241–253.

Cunningham, Mark D., Jon Sorensen, and Thomas Reidy. 2005. "An Actuarial Model of Assessment of Prison Violence Risk among Maximum Security Inmates." *Assessment* 12: 40–49.

de Tocqueville, Alexis. 1956. *Democracy in America*. New York: Knopf.

DeLisi, Matt. 2003. "Criminal Careers Behind Bars." *Behavior Sciences and the Law* 21: 653–669.

DeLisi, Matt., Mark T. Berg, and Andy Hochstetler. 2004. "Gang Members, Career Criminals, and Prison Violence: Further Specification of the Importation Model of Inmate Behavior." *Criminal Justice Studies* 17: 369–383.

DeShaney v. Winnebago Cty. DSS 489 U.S. 189 (1989).

Ekland-Olson, Sheldon. 1986. "Crowding, Social Control, and Prison Violence: Evidence from the Post-Ruiz years in Texas." *Law & Society Review* 20: 389–421.

Estelle v. Gamble, 429 U.S. 97 (1976)

Farmer v. Brennan, 511 U.S. 825 (1994).

Fattah, Ezzat A. 2000. "The Vital Role of Victimology in the Rehabilitation of Offenders and Their Reintegration into Society." *Resource Material Series* 56: 71–86.

Feinburg, Joel. 1984. *Harm to Others. Moral Limits of Criminal Law 1*. New York: Oxford University Press.

Felson, Richard B., Eric Silver, Brianna Remster. 2012. "Mental Disorder and Offending in Prison." *Criminal Justice and Behavior* 39: 125–143.

Flanagan, Timothy J. 1980. "Time-Served and Institutional Misconduct Patterns of Involvement in Disciplinary Infractions Among Long-Term and Short-Term Inmates." *Journal of Criminal Justice* 8: 357–367.

Fuller, Dan A., and Thomas Orsagh. 1977. "Violence and Victimization within a State Prison System." *Criminal Justice Review* 2: 35–55.

Gaes, Gerald G., and Andrew L. Goldberg. 2004. *Prison Rape: A Critical Review of the Literature*. Washington, DC: National Institute of Justice.

Gaes, Gerald G., and William McGuire. 1985. "Prison Violence: The Contribution of Crowding Versus Other Determinants of Prison Assault Rates." *Journal of Research in Crime and Delinquency* 22: 41–65.

Gaes, Gerald G., Susan Wallace, Evan Gilman, Jody Klein-Saffan, and Sharon Suppa. 2002. "The Influence of Prison Gang Affiliation on Violence and Other Prison Misconduct." *The Prison Journal* 82: 359–385.

Gendreau, Paul, Claire E. Goggin, and Moira A. Law. 1997. "Predicting Prison Misconducts." *Criminal Justice and Behavior* 24: 414–431.

Gilligan, James. 2003. "Shame, Guilt, and Violence." *Social Research* 70: 1149–1180.

Goffman, Erving. 1961. *Asylums: Essays on the Social Situation of Mental Patients and Other Inmates.* Garden City, NY: Anchor Books.

Gove, Walter R. 1980. *The Labeling of Deviance: Evaluating a Perspective,* 2d ed. Beverly Hills, CA: Sage.

Greenfield, Lawrence A. 1980. *Assessing Prison Environments: A Comparative Approach.* Hackensack, NJ: National Council on Crime and Delinquency.

Griffin, Marie L., and John R. Hepburn. 2006. "The Effect of Gang Affiliation on Violent Misconduct Among Inmates During the Early Years of Confinement." *Criminal Justice and Behavior* 33: 419–448.

Harer, Miles, and Darrell Steffensmeier. 1996. "Race and Prison Violence." *Criminology* 34: 323–355.

Helling v. McKinney, 509 U.S. 25 (1993).

Hensley, Christopher, Richard Tewksbury, and Tammy Castle. 2003. "Characteristics of Prison Sexual Assault Targets in Male Oklahoma Correctional Facilities." *Journal of Interpersonal Violence* 18: 595–607.

Hudson v. Palmer, 468 U.S. 517 (1984).

Huebner, Beth M. 2003. "Administrative Determinants of Inmate Violence." *Journal of Criminal Justice* 31: 107–117.

Human Rights Watch. 2001. *No Escape: Male Rape in US Prisons.* New York: Human Rights Watch.

Human Rights Watch. 2003. *Ill-Equipped: U.S. Prisons and Offenders with Mental Illness.* Washington, DC: Human Rights Watch.

Ireland, Jane L. 2005. *Bullying Among Prisoners: Innovations in Theory and Research.* Portland, OR: Willan.

Irwin, John. 1980. *Prisons in Turmoil.* Boston: Little, Brown.

Irwin, John, and Donald R. Cressey. 1962. "Thieves, Convicts, and the Inmate Culture." *Social Problems* 10: 142–155.

James, Doris J. and Lauren E. Glaze. 2006. *Mental Health Problems of Prison and Jail Inmates.* Bureau of Justice Statistics (No. NCJ 213600). Washington, DC: Department of Justice, Office of Justice Programs.

Jiang, Shanhe, and Marianne Fisher-Giorlando. 2002. "Inmate Misconduct: A Test of the Deprivation, Importation, and Situational Models." *The Prison Journal* 83: 335–358.

Kilmer, Jason R., Jessica M. Cronce, Scott B. Hunt, and Christine M. Lee. 2012. "Reducing Harm Associated with Illicit Drug Use." In *Harm Reduction: Programmatic Strategies for Managing High-Risk Behaviors,* edited by G. Alan Marlatt, Mary E. Larimer, and Katie Witkiewitz. New York: Guilford Press.

Knowles, Gordon. 1999. "Male Prison Rape: A Search for Causation and Prevention." *The Howard Journal* 38: 267–282.

Lahm, Karen F. 2008. "Inmate-on-Inmate Assault: A Multilevel Examination of Prison Violence." *Criminal Justice and Behavior* 35: 120–137.

Lahm, Karen F. 2009. "Physical and Property Victimization Behind Bars: A Multilevel Examination." *International Journal of Offender Therapy and Comparative Criminology* 53: 348–365.

Larimer, Mary E., Tiara M. Dillworth, Clayton Neighbors, Melissa A. Lewis, Heidi Montoya, and Diane E. Logan. 2012. "Harm Reduction for Alcohol Problems." In *Harm Reduction: Programmatic Strategies for Managing High-Risk Behaviors,* edited by G. Alan Marlatt, Mary E. Larimer, and Katie Witkiewitz. New York: Guilford Press.

Liebling, Alison. 1999. "Doing Research in Prison: Breaking the Silence." *Theoretical Criminology* 4: 333–357.

Liebling, Alison. 2004. *Prisons and Their Moral Performance: A Study of Values, Quality, and Prison Life*. Oxford: Clarendon.

Lockwood, Daniel. 1980. *Prison Sexual Violence*. New York: Elsevier.

Lynch, James L. 1996. "Clarifying Divergent Estimates of Rape from Two National Surveys." *Public Opinion Quarterly* 60: 410–430.

Maitland, Angela S., and Richard D. Sluder. 1998. "Victimization and Youthful Prison Inmates: An Empirical Analysis." *The Prison Journal* 78: 55–73.

Marlatt, G. Alan, Mary E. Larimer, and Katie Witkiewitz. 2012. *Harm Reduction: Pragmatic Strategies for Managing High-Risk Behaviors*. New York: Guilford Press.

Mathiesen, Thomas. 1965. *The Defences of the Weak*. London: Tavistock.

Mazza, George. 2012. "What Might PREA Mean to Female Correctional Staff?" *Corrections Today* 74: 28–32.

McCorkle, Richard C. 1992. "Personal Precautions to Violence Inside Prison." *Criminal Justice and Behavior* 19: 160–173.

McCorkle, Richard C. 1995. "Gender, Psychopathology, and Institutional Behavior: A Comparison of Male and Female Mentally Ill Inmates." *Journal of Criminal Justice* 23: 53–61.

McCorkle, Richard C., Terance D. Miethe, and Kriss A. Drass. 1995. "The Roots of Prison Violence: A Test of Deprivation, Management, and 'Not-So-Total' Institution Models." *Crime & Delinquency* 41: 317–331.

Messman, Terri, and Patricia Long. 1996. "Child Sexual Abuse and Its Relationship to Revictimization in Adult Women: A Review." *Clinical Psychology Review* 16: 397–420.

Nacci, Peter L., and Thomas R. Kane. 1982. *Sex and Sexual Aggression in Federal Prisons*. Washington, DC: Federal Bureau of Prisons.

Neumann, Debra, Beth Houskamp, Vicki Pollock, and John Briere. 1996. "The Long-Term Sequelae of Childhood Sexual Abuse in Women: A Meta-Analytic Review." *Child Maltreatment* 1: 6–16.

Newman, Jessica, Don Des Jarlais, Charles Turner, Jay Gribble, Phillip Cooley, and Denise Paone. 2002. "The Differential Effects of Face-to-Face and Computer Interview Modes." *American Journal of Public Health* 92: 294–297.

Noonan, Margaret E. 2012. *Mortality in Local Jails and State Prisons, 2000–2010: Statistical Tables*. Washington, DC: Office of Justice Programs.

Peake Andrasik, Michele, and Ty W. Lostutter. 2012. "Harm Reduction for High-Risk Sexual Behavior and HIV." In *Harm Reduction: Programmatic Strategies for Managing High-Risk Behaviors*, edited by G. Alan Marlatt, Mary E. Larimer, and Katie Witkiewitz. New York: Guilford Press.

Phillips, Carl V., Karyn K. Heavner, Paul L. Bergen, and Catherine M. Nissen. 2012. "Tobacco: Untapped Potential for Harm Reduction." In *Harm Reduction: Programmatic Strategies for Managing High-Risk Behaviors*, edited by G. Alan Marlatt, Mary E. Larimer, and Katie Witkiewitz. New York: Guilford Press.

Poole, Eric D., and Robert M. Regoli. 1980. "Role Stress, Custody Orientation, and Disciplinary Actions—A Study of Prison Guards." *Criminology* 18: 303–314.

Porporino, Frank J., Phyllis D. Doherty, and Terence Sawatsky. 1987. "Characteristics of Homicide Victims and Victimization in Prisons. A Canadian Historical Perspective." *International Journal of Offender Therapy and Comparative Criminology* 31: 125–136.

Porporino, Frank, and Laurence L. Motiuk. 1995. "The Prison Careers of Mentally Disordered Offenders." *International Journal of Law and Psychiatry* 18: 29–44.

Reisig, Michael D. 1998. "Rates of Disorder in Higher-Custody State Prisons: A Comparative Analysis of Managerial Practices." *Crime & Delinquency* 44: 229–244.

Reisig, Michael D., and Yoon Ho Lee. 2000. "Prisonization in the Republic of Korea." *Journal of Criminal Justice* 28: 23–31.

Ruiz v. Estelle, 503 F. Supp. 1265 (S.D. Tex. 1980).

Schafer, Stephen. 1968. *Restitution to Victims of Crime*. London: Stevens and Sons.

Schenk, Allison M., and William Fremouw. 2012. "Individual Characteristics Related to Prison Violence: A Critical Review of the Literature." *Aggression and Violent Behavior* 17: 432–442.

Siegel, Jane, and Linda Williams. 2003. "Risk Factors for Sexual Victimization of Women: Results from a Prospective Study." *Violence Against Women* 9: 902–930.

Sparks, Richard. 1982. *Research on Victims of Crime: Accomplishments, Issues, and New Directions. Crime and Delinquency Issues*. Washington, DC: US Department of Health and Human Services.

Steiner, Benjamin. 2009. "Assessing Static and Dynamic Influences on Inmate Violence Levels." *Crime & Delinquency* 55: 134–161.

Steiner, Benjamin, and John Wooldredge. 2008. "Inmate Versus Environmental Effects on Prison Rule Violations." *Criminal Justice and Behavior* 35: 438–456.

Steiner, Benjamin, and John Wooldredge. 2009. "Rethinking the Link Between Institutional Overcrowding and Inmate Misconduct." *The Prison Journal* 89: 205–233.

Struckman-Johnson, Cindy, and David Struckman-Johnson. 2006. "A Comparison of Sexual Coercion Experiences Reported by Men and Women in Prison." *Journal of Interpersonal Violence* 21: 1591–1615.

Struckman-Johnson, Cindy, and David Struckman-Johnson. 2000. "Sexual Coercion Rates in Seven Mid-Western Prison Facilities." *The Prison Journal*, 80: 379–390.

Struckman-Johnson, Cindy, David Struckman-Johnson, Lila Rucker, Kurt Bumby, and Stephen Donaldson. 1996. "Sexual Coercion Reported by Men and Women in Prison." *Journal of Sex Research* 33: 67–76.

Sykes, Gresham M. 1958. *The Society of Captives: A Study of a Maximum Security Prison*. Princeton, NJ: Princeton University Press.

Tannenbaum, Frank. 1938. *Crime and the Community*. New York: Columbia University Press.

Tewksbury Richard. 1989. "Fear of Sexual Assault in Prison Inmates." *The Prison Journal* 69: 62–71.

Tjaden, Patricia, and Nancy Thoennes. 2000. *Full Report of the Prevalence, Incidence, and Consequences of Violence Against Women*. Washington, DC: Office of Justice Programs.

Toch, Hans. 1992. *Mosaic of Despair: Human Breakdown in Prison*. Washington, DC: American Psychological Association.

Toch, Hans. 1977. *Living in Prison: The Ecology of Survival*. New York: Free Press.

Tonry, Michael. 2004. *The Future of Imprisonment*. Oxford: Oxford University Press.

Tourangeau, Roger, and Tom W. Smith. 1996. "Asking Sensitive Questions: The Impact of Data Collection Mode, Question Format, and Question Context." *Public Opinion Quarterly* 60: 275–304.

Tourangeau, Roger, and Tom W. Smith. 1998. "Collecting Sensitive Information with Different Mode of Data Collection." In *Computer Assisted Survey Information Collection*, edited by Mick P. Cooper. Baker, NY: Wiley.

Washington v. Harper, 494 U.S. 210 (1990).

Wener, Richard E. 2012. *The Environmental Psychology of Prisons and Jails*. Cambridge, UK: Cambridge University Press.

Williams, Linda, Jane Siegel, and Judith Jackson Pomeroy. 2000. "Validity of Women's Self Reports of Documented Child Sexual Abuse." In *The Science of Self-Report: Implications for Research and Practice*, edited by Arthur Stone, Christine Bachrach, Jared Jobe, Howard Kurtzman, and Virginia Cain. Mahwah, NJ: Erlbaum.

Wilson, John P., Boris Drozdek, and Silvana Turkovic. 2006. "Posttraumatic Shame and Guilt." *Trauma, Violence & Abuse* 7: 122–141.

Wolff, Nancy, Cynthia Blitz, Jing Shi, Ronet Bachman, and Jane Siegel. 2006. "Sexual Violence Inside Prison: Rates of Victimization." *Journal of Urban Health* 83: 835–848.

Wolff, Nancy, Cynthia Blitz, Jing Shi, Jane Siegel, and Ronet Bachman. 2007. "Physical Violence Inside Prison: Rates of Victimization." *Criminal Justice and Behavior* 34: 588–599.

Wolff, Nancy, and Jing Shi. 2009a. "Contextualization of Physical and Sexual Assault in Male Prisons: Incidents and Their Aftermath." *Journal of Correctional Health Care* 15: 58–77.

Wolff, Nancy, and Jing Shi. 2009b. "Feelings of Safety Inside Prison Among Male Inmates with Different Victimization Experiences." *Violence and Victims* 24: 800–816.

Wolff, Nancy, and Jing Shi. 2009c. "Type, Source, and Patterns of Physical Victimization: A Comparison of Male and Female Inmates." *The Prison Journal* 89: 172–191.

Wolff, Nancy, and Jing Shi. 2011. "Patterns of Victimization and Feelings of Safety Inside Prison: The Experience of Male and Female Inmates." *Crime & Delinquency* 57: 29–55.

Wolff, Nancy, Jing Shi, and Ronet Bachman. 2008. "Measuring Victimization Inside Prison: Questioning the Questions." *Journal of Interpersonal Violence* 23: 1343–1362.

Wolff, Nancy, Jing Shi, Cynthia Blitz, and Jane Siegel. 2007. "Understanding Sexual Victimization Inside Prisons: Factors that Predict Risk." *Criminology and Public Policy* 6: 201–231.

Wolff, Nancy, Jing Shi, and Jane Siegel. 2009a. "Patterns of Victimization Among Male and Female Inmates: Evidence of an Enduring Legacy." *Violence and Victimization* 24: 469–484.

Wolff, Nancy, Jing Shi, and Jane Siegel. 2009b. "Understanding Physical Victimization Inside Prisons: Factors that Predict Risk." *Justice Quarterly* 26: 445–475.

Wooden, Wayne S., and Jay Parker. 1982. *Men Behind Bars: Sexual Exploitation in Prison*. New York: Plenum Press.

Wooldredge, John D. 1991. "Correlates of Deviant Behavior among Inmates in U.S. Correctional Facilities." *Journal of Crime and Justice* 14: 1–25.

Wooldredge, John D. 1994. "Inmate Crime and Victimization in a Southwestern Correctional Facility." *Journal of Criminal Justice* 22: 367–381.

Wooldredge, John D. 1998. "Inmate Lifestyles and Opportunities for Victimization." *Journal of Research in Crime and Delinquency* 35: 480–502.

Wooldredge, John D., Timothy Griffin, and Travis Pratt. 2001. "Considering Hierarchical Models for Research on Inmate Behavior: Predicting Misconduct with Multilevel Data." *Justice Quarterly* 18: 203–232.

Wright, Kevin N. 1991. "A Study of Individual, Environmental, and Interactive Effects in Explaining Adjustment to Prison." *Justice Quarterly* 8: 217–242.

Wright, Kevin N. 1994. *Effective Prison Leadership*. Binghamton, NY: William Neil.

Zamble, Edward. 1992. "Behavior and Adaptation in Long-Term Prison Inmates: Descriptive Longitudinal Results." *Criminal Justice and Behavior* 19: 409–425.

CHAPTER 15

....

UNDERSTANDING THE CONTOURS OF PRISON DISCIPLINARY PROCEDURES

....

JAMES MARQUART AND CHAD TRULSON

WHAT to do about prisoner deviance and rule violations has been a complex issue since institutions were first constructed in the United States in the early 1800s. To an outsider, regardless of the time period, it would seem that obtaining compliance from an already subjugated inmate population would be an easy, relatively simple task—"just make them obey and be done with it." But maintaining control and order in prisons has been anything but easy or simple. The regime of prison discipline has transformed numerous times, evolving from near complete informality, whim, and the "creativity" of staff to a highly rigid, legally complex, and overwhelmingly bureaucratic system of "cans and cant's" backed up by the courts' evolving standards of constitutional interpretation.

In this essay, we seek to broadly examine the changes over time to the prisoner disciplinary process in the United States, both informal and formal, and end with a discussion of the lot of prisoners today when it comes to formal responses to inmate deviance behind bars. We also examine recent changes and fads in the control and discipline of problem prisoners broadly, but we also specifically study the contours of prison discipline experienced by one state—Texas. We have long been students of organizational change within the Texas prison system, and the story of prisoner discipline in this state mirrors roughly what has transpired throughout the US state prison systems. The Texas experience is to a large degree a microcosm of this nation's experience with the changing nature of dealing with prisoners.

Section I examines the shift in institutional disciplinary tactics between 1875 and 2012. Section II examines the efforts of external agents, such as state political groups, interest groups, and the courts, to control the custodial regime's discretion in obtaining prisoner compliance. Section III analyzes the due process revolution concerning the disciplinary process within prison organizations. Section IV examines official responses to prisoner deviance and "crime" in the contemporary prison. Finally, section V discusses, from our vantage point, future directions and issues concerning institutional disciplinary procedures and the formal responses to inmate deviance behind bars. The main conclusions discussed in this essay are the following:

- Disciplinary processes in prisons will continue to follow bureaucratic and legalized guidelines. The days of informal approaches to inmate deviance and rule violations are over.
- Disciplinary procedures in correctional institutions will continue to evolve and parallel "free world" criminal procedures. Prison inmates will more and more be held criminally accountable for their in-prison behavior.
- The prisoner population will be sorted and split into various risk groupings coupled with the demand for new and different institutions to handle the growth in risk groups. Efforts to further incapacitate problem prisoners "within" the prison facility, such as supermax, will continue to accommodate risk groupings.
- The social distance between keeper and kept will continue to grow.

I. Historical Context

In April 1875, the Texas prison system in the United States was rocked with scandal due to the horrific treatment of its prisoners. The ill treatment of prisoners became publicized when investigators from the Attorney General's office descended upon the prison facilities and convict camps to interview and take statements from the prisoners. Convict Fred Stone described the tenor of the guards' regime of discipline and order:

> I am a convict and will tell you all I know, relying on your assurance that I shall not be punished for it. I am in for ten years and shall die here. The character of punishment is just what the guards like to inflict. I was an inmate of the penitentiary for two months before conviction; was sent here for safe keeping. I had been here but three weeks when I was taken out of my bed and put in the "stocks" and left there for thirty or forty minutes. He also whipped me. They said I was in a plot to get out all the prisoners. I lay in the "blind cell" for about a week. There are some here who will tell you everything, but they are afraid. That man there has his back so injured by punishment that he cannot work at all. I have known persons die in the stocks. I did not see it but I know it. (Texas State Library and Archives Commission 2013c)

Roughly 137 years or 50,000 days later, in April 2012, the Texas Department of Criminal Justice "went live" with the newest version of its "Disciplinary Rules and Procedures for Offenders" on its official website. The following is the foreword to the now 46-page manual:

> It is the policy of the Texas Department of Criminal Justice (TDCJ) to operate a swift and fair disciplinary process that embodies constitutional and statutory standards. The goals of the offender disciplinary process are to 1) Maintain order and control of institutional safety; 2) Ensure offenders are not disciplined unfairly; 3) Ensure the constitutional rights are protected; 4) Modify offender behavior in a positive manner; and 5) Maintain an official record of an offender's disciplinary history. This plan is in compliance with Texas Government Code §§ 493.001, 494.002, 499.102(a) (9), 493.005, 493.0051, 497.051, 499.004. Reference: American

Correctional Association (ACA) Standards 4-4097 and 4-4347. Supersedes: GR-106, *Disciplinary Rules and Procedures for Offenders January 2005*. (Texas Department of Criminal Justice 2013)

How and why did these changes occur in a mere century and a half—changes from a largely informal-based system of convict control and punishment to a system mired in formalities and bureaucracy and constitutional concerns for the now known "offenders?" How and why did the status of prisoners transform from "slaves of the state" with little in the way of rights or redress when it came to discipline in the prison setting to a group perhaps more protected and fawned over than any other group in American society, institutionalized or not, criminal or not? The role reversal witnessed in American prisons concerning the treatment of prison inmates is interesting on many levels, but perhaps most interest surrounds the issue of what to do about prisoner rule violations and deviance.

A. Near Complete Discretion

For the most part, the dawn of legally prescribed and mandated institutional disciplinary procedures began in the 1960s, as a key element within the prisoners' rights movement. Bureaucratization of order maintenance in the prison setting was both a mechanism of enhancing fairness and predictability for the inmates and a device to control the behavior of the custodial regime (see section C: "Change Agents and the Legal Landscape" for a discussion of why these issues emerged). Interestingly, the changes experienced in the prison environment and shifting focus away from the kept toward the keepers originated outside of the prison and outside of the system of state government—the federal court system.

This is not say that state oversight over the internal workings of prison discipline and order was nonexistent prior to the 1960s. It must be remembered that Fred Stone's tales of harsh treatment in 1875 was communicated to Texas state officials. Whether or not his tales led to relevant or lasting change is another matter. We simply do not know, but we must assume that few changes were ever operationalized, as the Texas prison system was embroiled in a cycle of reform and neglect from the period of Reconstruction (1865–1877) through the closing days of World War I. While little was done in these years to afford inmates with procedural due process protections in disciplinary affairs, some efforts were made to eliminate or control the more extreme modes of corporal punishment to keep convicts in line. Indeed, on November 30, 1909, the members of the Texas Prison Board met to discuss, among other things, the use of the "bat"—a three-foot-long, three-inch-wide leather strap attached to a short wooden handle—an instrument that harkened back to the days of slavery and was considered by far the most effective form of prisoner discipline in the South. Prison staff used the bat to whip the backs and buttocks of disobedient convicts—the inmate was made to lie face down on the ground while the whip handler administered the strokes. As expected, abuses surfaced in the media and forced prison board members to review and revise prison policy on the use of the bat.

> The question of changing the rules as to corporal punishment was considered and discussed, the following resolution being adopted by the Board: "No punishment shall be administered except upon a written order from an Inspector," and the rule as to the number of licks to be

administered for any offense was amended so as to hereafter and "not more than twenty licks shall be administered for any one offense."

Each application and order for punishment shall be filed with the Board of Penitentiary Commissioners by the Superintendent at its next Regular meeting each month. No whipping shall be applied by any officer except in the presence of the Prison Physician and a private citizen, whenever practicable, and each report shall be endorsed by the Physician and citizen, if present, and shall show the nature of the offense, the time of punishment, and number of licks administered.

The inspector shall be required to spend one full day in each month at each Camp in his District and shall personally inspect the exposed bodies of the convicts and ascertain what character of punishment has been administered, reporting immediately to the Superintendent of Penitentiaries, and the Penitentiary Board, whether or not the punishment was excessive or in any manner inhuman, and whenever it shall appear that in administering punishment the law has been violated, or cruelly practiced, it shall be the duty of the Inspector, and he is hereby commanded, to report such violations to the nearest Magistrate and to furnish the name of the official who has been guilty of said violation and such proof as is available, to the end that said official shall be properly prosecuted. (Texas State Library and Archives Commission 2013b)

Not surprisingly, however, abuses continued, and even though inspectors were to scrutinize whippings, they used their ingenuity and signed their names on stacks of blank whipping orders and left them for the camp managers to use as they saw fit—business continued as it always had. The bat as a mechanism of discipline and punishment, though praised by some prison administrators for its curative properties (Simmons 1957), was forever banned in 1926 in Texas.

The onset of the Great Depression in 1929 and intervening war years through 1945 kept any public interest in upgrading the daily experience of Texas prisoners or reforming the prison system to a minimum. In these years, the prison system slid into darkness, accelerated by public apathy as attention was turned toward the European and Pacific war fronts, and prisoner discipline remained highly unregulated and dependent upon the "ingenuity" of the security staff. The light was about to shine on the Texas prison system due to the efforts of the Texas Council of Methodist Women, who took up the cause of prison reform following the war. In 1947, the famed criminologist Austin McCormick was commissioned to examine prison conditions in Texas, and his report, titled "Committee Report on Investigation of Penitentiaries," in April 1947 contains many descriptions of the disciplinary tactics used by the guards in this time period.

Tear gas is used extensively and often on the tanks [large open dormitories]. Especially in the ward where the men are in Solitary Confinement (locked in separate cells.) If any one man causes trouble, tear gas in large quantities is shot in the cells and all the men suffer for the wrongs of one man. This was the most consistent gripe of all the men.

The Solitary confinement cells were inspected and there the Committee found two men locked up with their hands handcuffed at their backs. One man was 17 years old, namely, Kenneth Clem of Dallas who had been there in Solitary Confinement so handcuffed for the period of two days with no blanket to sleep on, and with his hands behind his back in such a way that sleep must have been might near impossible in the first place. He said he was given water and one piece of bread every eight hours and a square meal every 36 hours. It was this man who had attempted to hang himself, but was foiled in the attempt. The young man looked tired, and cringed from fear of the Committee. He was a pitiful sight; a boy who almost cried when being talked to by the Committee.

In the next cell, in darkness and handcuffed the same way, the Committee found a man named Cecil Bear from Houston who had been found by the guards in the act of mutilating himself. He was put here further because of his refusal to work. This man had been in this same cell for 48 hours and was unable to sleep on the concrete floor with his hands handcuffed to his back. He said he was being fed once every 36 hours. He had no milk, only water to drink while in this place. He had been beaten with a rubber hose by guards, earlier, he related, in front of the tanks on the second floor of the building. He further said that he had been informed by Captain Easton that he would stay in that cell for 30 days handcuffed until he was released. He told the Committee that the guards cursed the men continuously and beat them in the fields with rubber hoses for talking to each other and for other minor reasons. He had no complaints on the fare of food offered in regular meals.

Men put in Solitary Confinement on little or no cause. Left there for days handcuffed. As many as 6 men are put in at a time handcuffed together so they can't sleep. Not enough room to lie down—its [sic] too crowded.

The food given to the men in Solitary Confinement is found to be: 4 spoonfuls of water gravy, 1 spoonful of beans, small piece of dry salt bacon, 3 biscuits and water. No milk or coffee. This they have every 36 hours as a square meal.

Men are handcuffed to the bars in the "schoolroom" and made to stand there for hours. One man was handcuffed and made to sit from 3:00 [P.M.] one day until 8:00 P.M. the next day on his hands on the stool in the cell.

One man who had cut his fingers (3) off, was taken directly to the dispensary and bandaged, but was then beaten for 30 minutes with hose for mutilating himself. (Texas State Library and Archives Commission, 2013a)

These inmate narratives of punishment provide us today with a unique window into prisoner discipline in the 1940s. Two systems were operating simultaneously. One, a formal one, was seen through the use of solitary cells for those engaged in misconduct. We cannot, however, locate empirical data to substantiate usage patterns or the processes that led to this form of punishment. Control and order were also maintained through a second, more elaborate system of informal mechanisms, including fear, extreme physical coercion, and near complete staff discretion in the treatment and control of the convict population.

It should be noted that, originally, scrutiny of the prison system in the 1940s came from within the state's governmental institutions and various state-organized prison reform groups. The impetus for reform came from state government, and the prison situation was so dire that the governor of Texas brought in noted prison manager O. B. Ellis, from Memphis, Tennessee, to institute wholesale changes in anticipation of coming reforms.

B. A Tale of Two Prison Worlds: The Emerging Formal Disciplinary Mechanism of Prisoner Control

Noted criminologist and prison scholar Gresham Sykes (1958) made the observation nearly 60 years ago that prison walls are permeable and that changes in the broader society eventually filter or meander their way into the cellblocks, halls, turn rows, dining halls, and administrative bureaucracy of prisons. The 1960s was a period of major social and legal change in the wider society. The relationship between the accused and the state was changing, and these changes were ushered into the fabric of US society by such major Supreme Court cases as *Mapp v. Ohio* (1961), *Gideon v. Wainwright* (1963), *Escobedo v. Illinois* (1964), and *Miranda v. Arizona* (1966). However, prescient Texas prison administrators implemented important procedures within their own institutional disciplinary proceedings. In some instances, they did not wait for changes in the wider society to filter inside and force change.

As evidence, we examined disciplinary reports of the Texas prison system, the earliest dated September 20, 1963, as part of a book project on racial desegregation in the Texas prison system (Trulson and Marquart 2009). The report date is important, as it predates many important landmark US Supreme Court rulings pertaining to procedural due process protections in the free world. It should also be noted that the accused inmate, Allen Lamar, was a well-known inmate writ writer within the Texas prison system, who in the next decade acquired "fame" in a major lawsuit (*Lamar v. Coffield* 1977) challenging successfully the practice of racial segregation within the prison system. Lamar was no stranger to the security staff, or to the disciplinary system of the day.

We cite this factual record with the intent to show that some aspects of the Texas prisoner disciplinary system in the 1960s were formal and bureaucratically complex. We make no judgment as to Lamar's rule violations (impudence and laziness were the violations he was charged with and categories that later came under intense scrutiny in another major landmark Texas prisoner lawsuit *Ruiz v. Estelle* [1980]); rather, in this disciplinary report one can find

1. A detailed description of the infraction
2. An investigation into the situation
3. An assessed punishment decided by several employees
4. A review of the case and punishment by a unit disciplinary committee
5. A final review and approval by the director of the state prison system

One can argue that the aforementioned procedures were merely "for show" or a front-stage activity designed to demonstrate an appearance of formality, process, and oversight. While this assertion may be true, the fact remains that a codified disciplinary system was in place in Texas prisons long before any Miranda rights were established for arrested citizens in the free world. Our point is that, between 1945 and 1960, rapid change befell the prison system on many fronts, along with advances in the system of discipline and punishment. Bureaucratic formalities, paperwork, and layers of review were beginning to become customary.

We are also not claiming that order and control prevailed in Texas prisons as a result of the detailed paperwork described here. Nor was there a custodial regime hell-bent on rule enforcement and record-keeping. In fact, an elaborate informal system of discipline and order existed at the same time based on fear and physical coercion from guards and co-opted inmate enforcers, much like the guards had relied on in the decades prior to the Second World War. This informal system of control in Texas has been well described elsewhere (Crouch and Marquart 1989), and was characteristic of other prison systems across the United States, particularly in the South. What we are suggesting is that two systems of discipline and order were evident—a key feature in most total institutions (Goffman 1961). The first system was in keeping with the emerging legal standards of the day, or the front-stage disciplinary apparatus. The second was the "deeper," more traditional control system—a system nearly devoid of outside review and one that relied on informal exchanges between keepers and the kept—and a system that utilized co-opted inmate enforcers, extensive snitch networks, and extreme intimidation, fear, and physical punishments. It was the traditional control system that slowly eroded under pressure from outside entities. And most of this pressure from outside entities came from the federal courts.

C. Change Agents and the Legal Landscape

Fast-forward in time, and the extensive snitch networks, co-opted inmates, and extreme physical punishments—informal and largely institution specific methods used to deal with prisoner deviance, rule violations, and general intransigence—were on the brink of change. Instead of "no limits" afforded to the keepers in the discipline of the kept, formerly out-of-sight/out-of-mind prison institutions (and their administrators and officers) were facing full scrutiny in their overall treatment of prisoners.

Interestingly, this scrutiny came primarily from the lower federal courts in the 1960s, and they were backed by the final decisions of the U.S. Supreme Court ("Court") (Trulson and Marquart 2009). This shift in judicial temperament and involvement was somewhat surprising considering the federal courts' historical stance on prison-related matters and their belief that wardens, not the courts, should superintend prisons. But all this changed, and by the 1960s, the Arkansas prison system was already embroiled in a massive surge of institutional litigation challenging the totality of all conditions in that prison system, including complaints of severe institutional brutality and torture (Harris and Spiller 1977; Feeley and Rubin 1999). In short order, significant legal pressure was being applied to dozens of prison systems across the nation. Not surprisingly, most of this pressure was applied to southern prison systems in states like Mississippi, Texas, Louisiana, Alabama, and Georgia with their distinctly southern mix of chain gangs, hoe squads, inmate enforcers and/or armed trusties, field camps and turn rows, and penal farms (Feeley and Rubin 1999; Trulson and Marquart 2010). While court pressure was uneven and occurred on different timetables throughout the South, and then into other states, the fact remained that prison institutions would never be the same again.

By most accounts, attention by the federal courts was the change agent that held most sway in the transformation of American prisons from paternalistic and repressive places to legalistic and bureaucratic and constitutional organizations (Dilulio 1987; Crouch and Marquart 1989; see also, for a more thorough discussion of change agents involved in the prisoners' rights movement, Jacobs 1983). The judicial attention spanned the spectrum of prison-relevant areas including but not limited to court access, equal protection, religious freedom, conditions of confinement (e.g., crowding, sanitation, health care, mental health programs, classification), and, eventually, prisoner discipline and due process (Jacobs, 1983; Feeley and Rubin, 1999; Smith, 2000). But why the courts took such a keen interest in prisons and prisoners was peculiar, especially since prisoners in America had always been considered more or less "slaves of the state"—members of an excluded class not eligible for the rights and privileges enjoyed by free citizens (Trulson and Marquart 2009). And, prior to the 1960s, no one seemed to really care about prisoners anyway, as long as they were contained within the high stone walls of urban prisons or kept at bay by the natural boundaries, trusty shooters, and ferocious dog packs of the southern prison farms. Nonetheless, change was coming, and on that horse came the death of the backstage disciplinary control systems.

Instead of change coming from the inside out, the sea change laid at the doorstep of prison institutions originated largely outside of the prison walls. As noted by Jacobs (1983), court intervention focused on changing the status of prisoners was heavily influenced by the broader civil rights movement that rose during the turbulent 1950s and 1960s. It was because of this movement outside of prison walls that marginalized groups such as women, minorities, and juveniles were given standing in the societal mainstream. This movement was also influenced by the rapid expansion of minorities who were being sent to prisons at a more rapid pace, most of whom were poor and black, and who also became considered "victimized minorities" like their peers outside of prison walls (Jacobs 1983, p. 35). With the marginalized groups finding ground to stand on outside of prison walls, it was a natural progression then that prisoners, perhaps American society's most marginalized group, would eventually press for a more equalized status in mainstream society, despite their incarceration status. The vehicle prisoners used to tap into this mainstream was the courts and a cadre of well-trained civil rights lawyers, fresh off major victories involving voting rights and equal access to education. The court's receptivity to prisoner complaints, just as it had occurred outside of prison walls for other marginalized groups, was the key.

Fast forward again—some two decades into the late 1980s—and prisoners had carved a place for themselves in the so-called societal mainstream as a result of judicial intervention. But these changes did not happen overnight. This was especially the case concerning prisoner discipline. That the issue of prisoner discipline took longer to be addressed than many other prison issues should cause no surprise. Indeed, issues such as improved sanitation, better health care, improved infrastructure, and reducing overcrowding were never really met with strong resistance, even from the strictest prison administrators (Crouch and Marquart 1989; Trulson and Marquart 2009). But autonomy in maintaining control of the prisoner population has always been a staunchly defended feature of prison administrations. Beyond the general disdain prison administrators had for judges dictating any prison operation, administrators held tight to the traditional inmate disciplinary structure, both informal and whatever formal and bureaucratic means existed, out of fear that judicial tinkering with established inmate discipline and control systems would undermine their authority, increase expectations among inmates, politicize prisoners, demoralize staff ranks, and, at the end of the day, disrupt the delicate control balance in institutions (Carroll 1974; Jacobs 1983). In short, major change to the inmate control and discipline structure would take time and momentum. In the meantime, several important court cases were decided that had major impacts on the lot of prisoners and served to build the momentum to eventually address the issue of prisoner discipline and control.

II. Due Process in Prisons and Formal Responses to Inmate Deviance

A. Building Momentum

No case was perhaps as important to the building of change momentum as the Supreme Court's 1964 ruling in *Cooper v. Pate. Cooper* involved an appeal from a black Muslim inmate incarcerated in the Illinois State Penitentiary (Stateville). He claimed prison administrators who denied him access to his Koran and an opportunity to worship his religion were violating his rights to religious freedom. Receiving the case from the Seventh Circuit Court of Appeals, which originally denied Cooper relief and maintained that prison administrators and not federal courts should dictate prison operations, the US Supreme Court reversed the Seventh Circuit and broadly held that prisoners had a right to sue state government officials in federal court for violating their constitutional rights and those rights given by federal law. In short, this decision and related others significantly transformed the place of prisoners in American society, for they gave prisoners standing in the federal court system instead of the politically charged judiciary at state levels (Smith 2000). The result, as noted by Trulson and Marquart (2009, pp. 67–68), was that the "once marginalized, invisible, and excluded class of prisoners was now highly visible and charged . . . hundreds of prisoners' rights lawsuits followed in the late 1960s and 1970s."

As cases poured into the federal courts, there was little doubt that the issue of prisoner control and discipline and, more broadly, the subject of inmate due process would eventually work its way to the forefront of prison legal issues. And in 1974 it did. In that year, the Court dealt with one of the most significant cases of prison officials' responses to inmate deviance and general disciplinary issues. In *Wolff v. McDonnell* (1974), the Court addressed the question of whether inmates enjoy due process rights and protections when facing internal prison disciplinary proceedings. McDonnell was a prisoner in Nebraska who filed a lawsuit after he was found guilty of a prison infraction and then lost a significant portion of his good time credits toward prison release. In line with most other decisions of this newly labeled "hands-on era," the Court ruled that prisoners do not shed all due process protections as a result of being confined, and when faced with disciplinary sanctions, prisoners must be afforded such protections.

Beyond the general ruling that prisoners enjoy due process rights in prison disciplinary proceedings, the Court went further than most other legal holdings of this era and fashioned a set of minimum and specific due process protections for prisoners facing disciplinary sanctions. Although the Court stopped short of affording inmates the whole panoply of due process rights afforded to free citizens facing a criminal trial, for example, it significantly expanded protections. According to the Court's ruling in *Wolff*, minimum due process rights for prisoners facing disciplinary proceedings included

1. Advance written notice of the claimed violation
2. A period of time after the notice, no less than 24 hours, to allow the inmate to prepare a defense before the disciplinary committee
3. The ability to call witnesses and present evidence to aid in the inmate's defense, as long as allowing such does not threaten institutional security, safety, or correctional goals
4. There is no right to counsel, but when an illiterate inmate is facing disciplinary sanction and/or when the case is so complex that it would make it unlikely for the inmate to collect and present evidence, the inmate should be free to speak to a fellow inmate, or if that is forbidden, to have aid in the form of help from staff or another competent inmate as designated by staff

5. Written statement of the fact-findings, the evidence used to reach the fact-findings, and reasons for the disciplinary action taken
6. An impartial committee must decide the decision on disciplinary action (Belbot and Hemmens 2010)

Legally, the *Wolff* decision was a juggernaut in that in one fell swoop it addressed most of the pressing due process questions relative to formal inmate discipline for prison deviance and general rule violations. Following *Wolff*, other cases provided further clarification to the rules governing inmate discipline and due process, some that extended inmate due process rights and others that did not. For example, in *Baxter v. Palmigiano* (1976), the Court reaffirmed that prisoners do not enjoy a due process right to legal counsel in disciplinary hearings and that prison officials could treat a prisoner's silence in a disciplinary hearing as evidence of guilt. Whereas *Baxter* failed to extend inmate due process rights, *Hutto v. Finney* (1978) indirectly extended them. In this case, the Court decided that presiding lower courts could place limits on the amount of time a prisoner should spend in punitive segregation. This decision was made in context of the Arkansas prison system, which was declared wholly unconstitutional by the presiding federal district court and a case in which the Court wanted to affirm the power of courts to remedy unconstitutional conditions in Eighth Amendment cases. Those collateral issues aside, the Court in *Hutto* affirmed the power of courts to limit punitive segregation for inmates in disciplinary cases. Further, in 1983, the Court in *Hewitt v. Helms* declared that placing an inmate in administrative segregation (as opposed to punitive segregation) also must be supported by due process considerations, including at minimum an informal review of evidence, a notice of the charges to the prisoner, and an opportunity for the inmate to submit a statement to officials—unless the prisoner's segregation placement was required in the face of emergency conditions (*Hughes v. Rowe* 1980).

In other cases related to inmate discipline and due process, the Court has ruled that removing an inmate's good time must be supported by a modicum of evidence to meet due process requirements (*Superintendent v. Hill* 1985), that due process does not require prison administrators to note their reasoning for certain decisions involved in a due process disciplinary hearing, such as refusing to allow an inmate witness (*Ponte v. Real* 1985), or that a due process hearing is not required for certain aspects necessary for prison administration, such as the transfer of an inmate to a facility within the same state (*Meachum v. Fano* 1976), the transfer of an inmate within the same state even if it is for disciplinary reasons (*Montanye v. Haymes* 1976), or the involuntary transfer of an inmate to a mental hospital (*Vitek v. Jones* 1980).

Taken together, the legal evolution in formal responses to inmate discipline suggests a significant expansion of inmate rights, but at the same time, clear limits as to how far the notion of due process or fundamental fairness must extend in the prison environment. These major cases also, slowly but surely, laid waste to the old, informal mechanisms of control and order. By the year 2000, inmate trusty systems and other informal measures of control reliant on physical coercion and fear were gone from the American prison landscape. The custodial regime's response to inmate deviance and disorder became "rationalized" with a main feature being the tight control of discretion—everyone was to be treated the same. Equality and formality transplanted individuality and informality.

B. The Time-Bound Nature of the Due Process Movement and Concerns in the Contemporary Prison

Unlike the protracted prisoner cases centering on the totality of conditions of confinement, the issue of due process relative to inmate discipline and formal responses to inmate deviance was all but legally decided by the Court in *Wolff*. However, *Wolff* and its progeny was limited in a sense, because, in context, such decisions were based in a particular time period—a time period before the massive expansion of prison systems, before the changing nature of correctional populations (e.g., younger), before the officer shortages, before the unintended consequences of prison reform could be realized, and, more recently, before the increased attention and relevance given to criminal behavior and victimization behind prison walls. Related to the last issue, the legal decisions and their evolution previously examined focused solely on administrative rule violations and related sanctions to gain inmate rule compliance such as the taking of good time, privilege reduction, and time in solitary or punitive confinement. To be sure, these are still relevant considerations in the contemporary prison, but these issues are, for all intents and purposes, routine and old news.

A discussion of formal responses to inmate deviance in the contemporary prison must be broadened to include a focus on criminal behavior behind prison walls and, specifically, how correctional institutions and their administrators and officers are responding to this growing concern in today's prisons. Indeed, until relatively recently, correctional scholars largely viewed a prison stint as more or less an interruption in a criminal career (DeLisi 2003). Today, however, there is increasing recognition that incarceration, instead of a period marked by desistance in criminal offending, is for many a period of continued involvement not only in institutional misconduct and rule infractions but also a time of continuity in criminal offending (Trulson et al. 2010). Indeed, a burgeoning body of research has revealed that a prison sentence for many has simply become an extension of an already problematic criminal career (see, e.g., Eichenthal and Blatchford 1997; DeLisi 2003; Steiner and Wooldredge 2008; Drury and DeLisi 2010; Trulson et al. 2010; Drury and DeLisi 2011; Sorensen et al. 2011).

Although the extent of actual crime in prison is unknown on any systematic national level (see, generally, Allard, Wortley, and Stewart 2008), some insight is provided by examining recent statistics on the incidence of prison rape victimization (see, e.g., Beck and Johnson 2012). In their study of sexual victimizations reported by former state prisoners, Beck and Johnson revealed that nearly 10 percent of former state prisoners were the victims of at least one incident of sexual victimization while confined. While it is not known how these victimizations would fit relative to penal code categorization outside of prison walls, certainly nonconsensual and abusive sexual victimizations perpetrated by other inmates would be considered criminal violations on some level. Absent systematic nationwide data on the incidence of criminal violations in prisons, these findings tacitly suggest that there is a significant dark figure of prison crime.

This is not to suggest that criminal behavior behind prison walls has never occurred or has just been discovered. Criminal offenses among the incarcerated have probably always been a feature of prison institutions since their inception, even in the most controlled settings. The point is, however, that along with "regular" and expected forms of inmate misconduct or disciplinary rule violations, today there is increasing emphasis on attending to actual crimes that occur behind prison walls. This emphasis started in earnest for sexual victimizations but, more frequently, is expanding to other forms of criminal violations inside prisons.

Central to the issue of formal responses to inmate deviance, the issue of criminal behavior behind bars has hastened the need for correctional organizations to develop elaborate processes for detecting and investigating such behaviors, apprehending and processing prison "suspects," and, ultimately, punishing such offenders. Inasmuch as the history of responding to inmate deviance in the prison setting has gone from complete informality to more formal and bureaucratic procedures, the attention to "prison crime" will slowly but surely lead to significant changes in the contemporary prison relative to formal responses to inmate deviance. At the most basic level, the notion of inmate "deviance" has expanded considerably in the contemporary prison.

III. Prisoner Crime and Formal Legal Control in the Contemporary Prison

In many respects, early prison scholars such as Gresham Sykes and Donald Clemmer or, for that matter, old-time prison administrators such as George Beto and Joseph Ragan, would not recognize the contemporary prison institution—at least in terms of the processes related to the control and discipline of the inmate population (Dilulio 1987). Unlike the autonomous, self-contained, and largely invisible prison systems these individuals studied and operated in, contemporary prison institutions are no longer "places apart." In fact, take away the prison façade and the uniforms and the processes and operations in the contemporary prison involving prison inmates are hardly distinguishable from other institutions and processes in criminal justice (e.g., law enforcement, court processing).

These changes are perhaps no more evident than in official reactions to deviance and crime in prisons today. For an example of this transformation, one needs only to examine a rules and regulations manual in a contemporary prison. A cursory review would leave no doubt that the informal and haphazard responses to prisoner deviance of old have given way to constitutionalized, bulky, and legally sterile manuals and processes outlining in precision the rules, what constitutes a violation of rules, the procedures for "offenders" facing a rule violation, and the potential punishment assessed. The Texas Department of Criminal Justice manual for Disciplinary Rules and Procedures for Offenders cited at the outset of this essay, for example, is now 46 pages long and reads like a code of criminal procedure, chockfull with "legalese" verbiage. Interestingly, the Texas prison system Disciplinary Rules and Procedures manual says nothing about criminal behavior behind prison walls—how it is dealt with or punishments that could be faced by offenders.

More than 20 years ago, Eichenthal and Jacobs (1991) published their study on criminal law enforcement in state prisons. In this survey of 40 state prison directors, the authors revealed that only half of surveyed departments possessed data on the number of prison crime cases referred to free-world authorities, and only California, Illinois, Texas, and New York maintained data on the disposition of prosecuted cases. At the time, the Eichenthal and

Jacobs' study was one of the first to systematically delve into the issue of prisoner crime and responses to such behavior in prison settings. A few years later, Eichenthal and Blatchford (1997) studied prison crime in New York State and uncovered thousands of prison incidents that would have been considered crimes if committed outside of prison walls. Beyond the incidence of crime behind bars, however, Eichenthal and Blatchford noted that few of the criminal incidents they uncovered behind bars were ever referred for prosecution or prosecuted at all. On the research front since then, the evidence is still quite lean.

There is no doubt a dark figure of in-prison crime. In fact, the study of crime behind prison walls is perhaps one of the most elusive statistics in criminal justice. And despite major efforts in the past decade to understand one form of prison crime (prisoner rape), simply little is known relative to how much additional crime occurs behind prison walls. What is less elusive, however, is information on the responses to this elevated form of prisoner behavior behind bars.

A. Detecting and Investigating Crime and Deviance Behind Bars

Among all efforts related to investigating, processing, and punishing criminal behavior behind bars, it is the processes of detecting and investigating that have witnessed the most development. Relative to detection, the list of usual technological suspects is being utilized or at least considered in a number of capacities in prison organizations: closed-circuit televisions, IP cameras with remote Internet access for off-site monitoring, microphones, monitors of varying sorts with motion-detection functions and the ability to email or text staff members in cases of tampering, and so on. The claims of such equipment run the gamut from preventing violent crime and incidents in prison to lowering general disorder to uncovering contraband networks. Legally, the major benefit of these technological innovations is having visual and/or audio evidence of incidents occurring within prisons for disciplinary procedures or criminal indictments.

Beyond the technical gadgetry and tinkering, one of the most compelling changes in the formal response to prisoner deviance has come to the investigation of crime behind bars. Investigation activities have evolved over the past several decades from having a convict snitch or two to utilizing precise undercover operations; cultivating cadres of confidential informants; utilizing social networking sites for intelligence gathering using extensive phone, mail, and visitation surveillance; code cracking; information sharing with free-world law enforcement and other investigative agencies; multiagency collaboration, including the development of fusion centers; and the mobilization of special intelligence departments or extended task forces across correctional organizations (Bell 2002; see generally Winterdyk and Ruddell 2010).

Among all operations, the move toward specialized intelligence departments within prison organizations appears to be one of the most prevalent investigation strategies, especially as related to gang intelligence and monitoring (Winterdyk and Ruddell 2010; National Gang Intelligence Center 2011). Although no national-level data exist on the prevalence of such departments in correctional agencies, one need not look far for evidence that these types of specialized units exist in some way, shape, or form. Take, for example, Operation

Black Widow in 1998. Black Widow was a three-year multimillion-dollar collaboration between the FBI and local authorities in California to gain intelligence and prosecute the most violent and problematic members of the Nuestra Familia operating within California prisons (Trulson, Marquart, and Kawucha 2006). This multiagency cooperation led to dozens of indictments and convictions for both in-and out-of-prison crimes committed or facilitated by Nuestra Familia members. The City of New York Department of Corrections has also established an intelligence unit, which was formed to assess the nature and extent of gang activity within correctional facilities. Today, the now-evolved Gang Intelligence Task Force monitors and tracks members of security risk groups (i.e., gangs) not only for internal management but also for such activities as information sharing and database construction with other law enforcement and correctional agencies. Even the Correctional Corporation of America, the leading private correctional industry in America, utilizes an inmate management system to monitor and track gang members.

A survey conducted by Bell (2002) sheds more light on the investigation function in the contemporary prison. In a survey sent to 50 state departments of correction (overall response rate of 66 percent, or 33 of 50 states), roughly 67 percent of responding correctional agencies reported using prison-specific investigators. Roughly 52 percent of prison investigators were reported to have "full police powers." Furthermore, almost all respondents noted that prison investigators share their intelligence information with outside law enforcement agencies, prepare criminal cases for local district attorneys, testify as advisory witnesses, and prepare affidavits and warrants. Interestingly, when asked whether prison investigators process crime scenes, all but one respondent agency indicated that prison investigators did process crimes scenes partially or fully in the prison setting. Even crime-scene investigation has evolved from the outside world to the inside world on a more regular basis.

Again, while systematic evidence on the extent of these initiatives in prisons is incomplete, the point here is that the boundary between the "inside" and "outside" world continues to erode when it comes to detecting and investigating criminal behavior. Where prisons were once places apart from the wider society—they are virtually indistinguishable now from other institutional contexts, free world or not. Whereas prisoners were once slaves of the state who received little attention, both in-prison criminals and their victims have grabbed a more prominent place in public discourse. Indeed, crime on the inside is treated—investigated, processed, punished—much like it would be for any free citizen involved in the criminal justice process. This is much different than just 40 or 50 years ago, when the informal ways of prison discipline still held sway and what happened behind prison walls, stayed there.

B. Processing Crime and Deviance Behind Bars

Unlike the internal and largely decided due process procedures in place to deal with non-criminal prisoner misconduct, processing crime behind bars is still in its infancy. Among all efforts, the development of Prison Prosecution Units, Special Prosecution Units, or other similarly named entities is perhaps the most unique development as a formal response to inmate crime and deviance on the processing front. Generally, a Special Prosecution Unit functions as an independent department that works with and supports local district attorneys in prosecuting criminal offenses that occur within correctional institutions. In short, they are the entities that spearhead "free-world prosecutions" on criminally involved prisoners. Like most other developments in the formal response to prisoner deviance, especially those in response to prisoner crime, such specialized units are more of the exception than the rule—at least for now.

To our knowledge, Texas is the only state in the nation that utilizes a special prosecution entity on any larger scale specifically focused on prison crimes. Procedurally in Texas, the Office of the Inspector General investigates in-prison crimes and, when deemed appropriate, refers them to the Special Prison Prosecution Unit. Originally, the Texas prosecution unit was developed in the 1980s in response to a massive increase in murders generally and gang-related murders specifically in the aftermath of the *Ruiz v. Estelle* (1980) remedies (e.g., removal of the building tender system, mobilization of a new prisoner classification system) (Baird 1986; Trulson and Marquart 2009). In the thick of the *Ruiz* implementations in 1984 and 1985, the Texas prison system witnessed 53 killings, 74 percent of which were gang-related (Trulson and Marquart 2009, p. 132). The violence and ferocity of the killings in the formerly calm and controlled Texas prison system was simply too much for the prisoner disciplinary system to handle; therefore additional means were utilized to effectively punish offending prisoners. While the main thrust behind the Special Prison Prosecution Unit in Texas today centers on prisoner rape and prosecuting these offenses, the Special Prison Prosecution Unit remains the statewide entity that can potentially process any in-prison crime from contraband offenses to murder.

Despite the absence of academic and professional literature on the prevalence of such programs, not to mention the absence of evaluations of such programs, those who have studied the issue more generally advocate for these initiatives (Eichenthal and Jacobs 1991; Eichenthal and Blatchford 1997). In addition to providing a prosecution vehicle for in-prison crime, Eichenthal and Blatchford have noted that such units help to enhance investigations in prisons by allowing investigators to develop experience and expertise in the unique prison environment such as cultivating witnesses and gaining the cooperation of victims (see, e.g., Bell 2002 on the unique nature of practical criminal investigation in correctional facilities including but not limited to evidence collection, understanding the "convict," and preparing usable information, intelligence, and reports for prosecutors).

Beyond the issue of crime incidence or prevalence of specialized prosecution units, however, there are collateral issues involved in a discussion of prosecuting in-prison crime. One issue surrounds the goal of prosecuting in-prison crimes: Are such activities meant for vindicating public justice as they are in free-world prosecutions (Eichenthal and Blatchford 1997), or are they meant to enhance prison order and control by somehow further incapacitating the in-prison "criminals" so to protect other inmates in prison, or are both of these goals relevant? Another issue surrounds the fact that it appears most prison crimes are not prosecuted at all by outside authorities (Eichenthal and Blatchford 1997). This perspective brings up the issue of victim worth as noted by Trulson (2005) almost a decade ago (in the context of victim rights and services for criminals who become victimized, or victims in the prison context). On the prosecution front, these and related issues will continue to influence efforts to deal with criminal behavior behind the walls of the contemporary prison. Despite not having answers to these and other issues, the fact remains that in the evolution of formal responses to inmate discipline, prosecuting in-prison crimes is at the forefront.

C. Punishing Crime and Deviance Behind Bars

Managing inmate deviance, especially through formal and legal processes, has always been a challenge to administrators. While the keepers of past decades utilized informal and sometimes violent means to curtail and/or respond to inmate deviance, those days are long gone. Without the ability to beat or otherwise physically coerce inmates into submission, the development of formal and legalized punishment systems in prisons evolved to rely on a now-familiar set of punishments (or incentives) to maintain prisoner control—removal of good time, restriction of visitation privileges, reduction in autonomy, reduced or suspended employment, removal of program participation privileges, suspending of commissary privileges, and so on. While these types of punishments were also used decades ago, today they are nearly the only means to elicit inmate obedience—with one major exception.

Beyond these standard punishments, there is perhaps no other change more dramatic relative to formal responses to both inmate deviance and inmate crime than the move to supermaximum incarceration facilities. Known by many names (e.g., supermax, administrative separation, administrative segregation, Secure Housing Unit), super-secure and super-austere housing has garnered increased attention over the past several years as the go-to method to deal with the most violent and intransigent inmates in any particular prison system. Inasmuch as prisons were once considered "places apart" from the wider society, supermax prison institutions are now the new places apart within contemporary prison systems.

To be sure, prison systems have always had places to house the most problematic and incorrigible prisoners. The D-Blocks (Alcatraz) or Unit 32s (Mississippi), the Shamrock's (Texas) or Siberias (Idaho), and the "holes," "boxes," and "cages" served to contain those who were the most extreme disciplinary problems in the prison environment. But, for the most part, these places were meant for punishment and, following court decisions, were used for shortened periods of time. Supermax confinement, on the other hand, was not developed as a punishment per se but rather as an administrative housing alternative to be used either pre-emptively for imminent threats or postincident to isolate and contain prison-system incorrigibles.

To be sure, the use of supermax confinement is far from uniform across the United States. This variability in use notwithstanding, since supermax imprisonment emerged as the new trend on the correctional scene, it has been subject to much research and commentary. This research has explored the historical development of the supermax (King 1999); how supermax confinement may achieve prison order and control (Mears and Reisig 2006); the placement, duration, and timing of supermax practices and issues surrounding offender entrance back into general prison populations or mainstream society following supermax placements (Mears and Bales, 2010); the impact of supermax confinement on postrelease recidivism (Mears and Bales 2009; public support for supermax (Mears et al. 2013); and more generalized information on supermax practices such as entry and exit criteria and evolving legal challenges (Pizarro and Stenius 2004; Pizarro and Narag 2008). This list is by no means exhaustive and does not even begin to address the substantial literature examining the impacts of supermax confinement on mental health and related issues (see, e.g., Arrigo and Bullock 2008; Haney 2008).

Overall, supermax confinement functions as the end-of-the-line response to prison crime and deviance in the contemporary prison. While the prosecution and punishment of in-prison criminal behavior may result in the assessment of an additional prison sentence, a possible death sentence in rare cases, and/or more routine prison disciplinary sanctions (e.g., reduction in good time, restricted visitation), in the contemporary prison, supermaximum confinement is, for the majority of serious prison-based rule violators and criminals, their final destination.

IV. Conclusion

Maintaining control and order in the contemporary prison is as much a problem and issue for today's custodial regime as it was for our forbearers. Whim, personal ingenuity and discretion, and physical coercion were key elements driving offender compliance with the rules. Fear was the order of the day, and this system prevailed for much of the twentieth century. Major social, political, and criminal justice reforms paved the way for change behind the walls. By the last decade of the twentieth century the transition from informality to formality, highlighted by intense bureaucratization, had taken place. The old ways of maintaining order were gone, replaced by rigid adherence to processes and procedures much like the legal processing system in the free community. Fear of violating the rules was replaced with a regimen of control with roots deep in the world of the actuary—risk assessment.

Today the inmate community has been sorted and split into subdivisions to ease control and order. Categorization is now the order of the day: gang/nongang, dangerous/nondangerous, youthful offender/nonyouthful offender, work capable/not capable, upper bunk/bottom bunk, medically fit/unfit, geriatric/nongeriatric, and so forth. Special facilities and institution types have been constructed to house a continuum of offender types paralleling biological evolution. Solitary confinement has morphed into administrative segregation, and administrative segregation has evolved into so-called supermax facilities. While Alcatraz may be uninhabited, Pelican Bay and the United States Penitentiary, Administrative Maximum Facility, to name a few, currently house hundreds of prisoners determined by staff to be disruptive and/or too dangerous to be confined in a general prisoner population setting. Such facilities are also replete with the newest technological devices to aid in the surveillance and control of the offenders—many of who will spend the remainder of their lives in these sterile settings with little contact from anyone. It would be interesting to know what Jeremy Bentham would say about these "modern" facilities, which seem to embrace the notion of the panopticon—inmates in supermax today are to be seen, but not see.

The regime of disciplinary control in prisons will no doubt follow the leads and trends in social control evolving in the wider society. This suggests the continued movement away from physicality to technologically driven modes of control and restraint. The social distance between keeper and kept will increase as an intended ploy to reduce the risk of responsibility, and hence, litigation. At the same time our ability to assess risk and dangerousness will sharpen and foster further the evolution of specific institutional types to house specific offender types. All the while prisons will continue to be microcosms of the larger society, as they have always been, and what happens out there will eventually filter into the prison walls. Relative to formal responses to prisoner deviance, one needs only to look at current practices focused on prosecuting and otherwise attending to criminal behavior behind prison walls for evidence of this reality.

REFERENCES

Allard, Troy, Richard Wortley, and Anna Stewart. 2008. "The Effect of CCTV on Prisoner Misbehavior." *The Prison Journal* 88:404–422.

Arrigo, Bruce, and Jennifer Bullock. 2008. "The Psychological Effects of Solitary Confinement on Prisoners in Supermax Units." *International Journal of Offender Therapy and Comparative Criminology* 52:622–640.

Baird, L. H. 1986. "Prison Gangs: Texas." *Corrections Today* 48(5):12–22.

Beck, Allen, and Candace Johnson. 2012. *Sexual Victimization Reported by Former State Prisoners, 2008*. Washington, DC: Bureau of Justice Statistics.

Belbot, Barbara, and Craig Hemmens. 2010. *The Legal Rights of the Convicted*. El Paso, TX: LFB Scholarly Publishing.

Bell, William. 2002. *Practical Criminal Investigations in Correctional Facilities*. New York: CRC Press.

Carroll, Leo. 1974. *Hacks, Blacks, and Cons: Race Relations in a Maximum Security Prison*. Prospect Heights, IL: Waveland Press.

Crouch, Ben, and James Marquart 1989. *An Appeal to Justice: Litigated Reform of Texas Prisons*. Austin: University of Texas Press.

Delisi, Matt. 2003. "Criminal Careers Behind Bars." *Behavioral Sciences and the Law* 21:653–669.

Dilulio, John. 1987. "Prison Discipline and Prison Reform." *The Public Interest* 89:71–90.

Drury, Alan, and Matt DeLisi. 2010. "The Past Is Prologue: Prior Adjustment to Prison and Institutional Misconduct." *The Prison Journal* 90:331–352.

Drury, Alan, and Matt DeLisi. 2011. "Gangkill: An Exploratory Empirical Assessment of Gang Membership, Homicide Offending, and Prison Misconduct." *Crime & Delinquency* 57:130–146.

Eichenthal, David, and Laurel Blatchford. 1997. "Prison Crime in New York State." *The Prison Journal* 77:456–466.

Eichenthal, David, and James Jacobs. 1991. "Enforcing the Criminal Law in State Prisons." *Justice Quarterly* 8:283–303.

Feeley, Malcolm, and Edward Rubin. 1999. *Judicial Policymaking and the Modern State*. Cambridge, UK: Cambridge University Press.

Goffman, Erving. 1961. *Asylums*. New York: Anchor Books.

Haney, Craig. 2008. "A Culture of Harm: Taming the Dynamics of Cruelty in Supermax Prisons." *Criminal Justice and Behavior* 35(8):956–984.

Harris, Kay, and Dudley Spiller. 1977. After Decision: Implementation of Judicial Decrees in Correctional Settings. Report to the National Institute of Law Enforcement and Criminal Justice. Washington, DC: US Department of Justice.

Jacobs, James. 1983. *New Perspectives on Prisons and Imprisonment*. New York: Cornell University Press.

King, Roy. 1999. "The Rise and Rise of Supermax." *Punishment & Society* 1:163–186.

Mears, Daniel, and William Bales. 2009. "Supermax Incarceration and Recidivism." *Criminology* 47:1131–1165.

Mears, Daniel, and William Bales. 2010. "Supermax Housing: Placement, Duration, and Time to Reentry." *Journal of Criminal Justice* 38:545–554.

Mears, Daniel, Christina Mancini, Kevin Beaver, and Marc Gertz. 2013. "Housing for the 'Worst of the Worst' Inmates: Public Support for Supermax Prisons." *Crime & Delinquency* 59(4):587–615.

Mears, Daniel, and Michael Reisig. 2006. "The Theory and Practice of Supermax Prisons." *Punishment and Society* 8:33–57.

National Gang Intelligence Center. 2011. *National Gang Threat Assessment: Emerging Trends.* Washington, DC: US Department of Justice.

Pizarro, Jesenia, and Raymund Narag. 2008. "Supermax Prisons: What We Know, What We Do Not Know, and Where We Are Going." *The Prison Journal* 88:23–42.

Pizarro, Jesenia, and Vanja Stenius. 2004. "Supermax Prisons: Their Rise, Current Practices, and Effect on Inmates." *The Prison Journal* 84:248–264.

Simmons, Lee. 1957. *Assignment Huntsville: Memoirs of a Texas Prison Official.* Austin: University of Texas Press.

Smith, Christopher. 2000. "The Governance of Corrections: Implications of the Changing Interface of Courts and Corrections." In *Boundary Changes in Criminal Justice Organizations*, edited by Charles M. Friel. Washington, DC: US Department of Justice.

Sorensen, Jon, Mark Cunningham, Mark Vigen, and S. O. Woods. 2011. "Serious Assaults on Prison Staff: A Descriptive Analysis." *Journal of Criminal Justice* 39:143–150.

Steiner, Benjamin, and John Wooldredge. 2008. "Inmate Versus Environmental Effects on Prison Rule Violations." *Criminal Justice and Behavior* 35:438–456.

Sykes, Gresham. 1958. *The Society of Captives: A Study of a Maximum Security Prison.* Princeton, NJ: Princeton University Press.

Trulson, Chad. 2005. "Victims' Rights and Services: Eligibility, Exclusion, and Victim Worth." *Journal of Criminology and Public Policy* 4:399–414.

Trulson, Chad, Matt DeLisi, Jonathan Caudill, Scott Belshaw, and James Marquart. 2010. "Delinquent Careers Behind Bars." *Criminal Justice Review* 35:200–219.

Trulson, Chad, and James Marquart. 2009. *First Available Cell: Desegregation of the Texas Prison System.* Austin: University of Texas Press.

Trulson, Chad, and James Marquart. 2010. "Who Rules the Joint Revisited: Organizational Chance and the Importance of Prison Leadership." *International Journal of Punishment and Sentencing* 6:71–83.

Trulson, Chad, James Marquart, and Soraya Kawucha. 2006. "Gang Suppression and Institutional Control." *Corrections Today* 68(2):26–31.

Winterdyk, John, and Rick Ruddell. 2010. "Managing Prison Gangs: Results from a Survey of U.S. Prison Systems." *Journal of Criminal Justice* 38:730–736.

Cases and Laws Cited

Baxter v. Palmigiano, 425 U.S. 308 (1976).

Cooper v. Pate, 378 U.S. 546 (1964).

Escobedo v. Illinois, 378 U.S. 478 (1964).

Gideon v. Wainwright, 372 U.S. 335 (1963).

Hewitt v. Helms, 459 U.S. 460 (1983).

Hughes v. Rowe, 449 U.S. 5 (1980).

Hutto v. Finney, 437 U.S. 638 (1978).

Lamar v. Coffield, Consent Decree, Civil Action No. 72-H-1393 (S.D. Tex. 1977).

Mapp v. Ohio, 367 U.S. 643 (1961).

Miranda v. Arizona, 384 U.S. 436 (1966).

Meachum v. Fano, 427 U.S. 215 (1976).

Montanye v. Haymes, 427 U.S. 236 (1976).

Ponte v. Real, 471 U.S. 491 (1985).

Ruiz v. Estelle, 503 F. Supp. 1265 (1980).

Vitek v. Jones, 445 U.S. 480 (1980).

Superintendent v. Hill, 472 U.S. 445 (1985).

Texas Department of Criminal Justice. 2013. Disciplinary Rules and Procedures for Offenders. http://www.tdcj.state.tx.us/documents/cid/Disciplinary_Rules_and_Procedures_for_Offenders_English.pdf.

Texas State Library and Archives Commission. 2013a. Committee Report on the Investigation of the Penitentiary. Accessed May 31, 2013. https://www.tsl.state.tx.us/exhibits/prisons/reform/investigationreport_1947_1.html.

Texas State Library and Archives Commission. 2013b. Reform and Reaction. https://www.tsl.state.tx.us/exhibits/prisons/reform/page2.html.

Texas State Library and Archives Commission. 2013c. Testimony of Fred Stone. https://www.tsl.state.tx.us/exhibits/prisons/lease/fred_stone_apr15_1875_1.html.

Wolff v. McDonnell, 418 U.S. 539 (1974).

....

CHAPTER 16

THE EFFECTS OF
ADMINISTRATIVE
SEGREGATION
A Lesson in Knowledge Cumulation

....

PAUL GENDREAU AND RYAN M. LABRECQUE

THE effective management of prisons has been a magnet for polarizing views among penologists. Recall the "nothing works" debate (Martinson 1974), which focused on the failure of prison treatment programs (Cullen and Gendreau 1989). Those who opposed Martinson's position swiftly became the targets of ad hominem attacks (see Gendreau and Ross 1979; Palmer et al. 2012). More recently, the professional competency and ethics of researchers (see O'Keefe et al. 2010) examining the effects of administrative segregation (AS) have similarly come under fire from those (e.g., Mohr 1985; Grassian 2010) who have disputed the findings that AS does not uniformly result in debilitating psychological effects for all inmates.

Before addressing the crux of this issue—namely, the magnitude of the effects of AS—we provide some background information on the history of AS. The informative reviews by Haney (1997) and Scharff-Smith (2006) on the evolution of the use of AS in corrections would prove helpful in this respect. Nowadays, AS is typically defined as 23 hours a day of lockup in an environment with severe restrictions placed on auditory, visual, and kinesthetic stimulation. By comparison, regular living conditions within prisons or jails provide inmates with access to various activities (i.e., programming, recreation), which affords them a degree of meaningful social interaction. Inmates in AS are not representative of the general population as typically they have posed a threat to the good order of the prison or they have been placed in AS at their own request for various reasons (Pizarro and Narag 2008). There is also considerable variation in the administration of AS across jurisdictions, particularly in the United States (Metcalf et al. 2013) as compared with that of other countries (e.g., Canada, the UK) where federal authorities are responsible for the great majority of inmates.

In assessing the effects of AS, this essay proceeds in the following manner. Section I discusses the three dominate schools of thought on the topic. In order to assess the validity of these competing perspectives, the essay examines three relevant and distinct literatures: the general prison life literature (Section II), the sensory deprivation (SD) literature (Section III), and solitary confinement (SC) studies involving prisoners (Section IV). Section V offers a rationale for why some offenders may report greater distress while in AS. Section VI outlines what needs to be done in terms of additional research and suggests several clinical practice guidelines that will ensure inmates are treated more humanely while in AS. The main conclusions discussed here include the following:

- Examination of the general prison incarceration literature, the studies on SD for both nonoffender and offender samples, and a meta-analysis of the studies on inmates exposed to AS does not support the view that AS produces dramatic negative psychological effects unless extreme conditions apply.
- These findings are consistent with predictions from two of the theories of prison life and the perceptual sensory adaptation literature. It is likely that the failure to recognize the confounding effects of response bias factors has led to previous overestimations of the negative effects of AS.
- When negative effects from AS occur, it is primarily due to how offenders are managed by prison authorities.
- We recommend that to better understand the effects of AS researchers must rely on a meta-analytic perspective and work directly in prisons to gain the necessary data. Researchers must gather information on how correctional officers supervise inmates, search for individual differences among inmates that predict a negative response to AS, and study the effects of AS in those prisons whose substandard physical conditions, lack of treatment programming, and extreme length of stay may produce iatrogenic consequences.
- In order to reduce the use of AS in prisons, recommendations are made regarding the clinical management of mentally disordered offenders, the monitoring of the psychological health of inmates in AS, and development of incentive programs to encourage inmates to return to the general population.

I. The Effects of AS

There are two schools of thought regarding the effects of AS. The first characterizes AS as a form of torture, resulting in an environment that is psychologically crippling and sufficiently destructive to promote self-harm among inmates (Jackson 1983). Proponents of this view have been unwavering in their belief that AS is capable of producing ubiquitous pathological effects that quickly lead to lasting emotional damage, functional disability, and psychosis (Grassian 1983; Scharff-Smith 2006; Kupers 2008; Haney 2012).

The second position is that AS produces much less intense effects and only for some inmates in prisons that meet basic standards of humane care (Suedfeld et al. 1982; Gendreau and Bonta 1984; Wormith 1984; Clements et al. 2007; O'Keefe et al. 2010; Gendreau and Thériault 2011; Gendreau and Goggin 2013; O'Keefe et al. 2013; Valera and Kates-Benman 2015: O'Donnell 2016), rather, other factors in the prison environment put offenders at greater risk of psychological harm.

In attempting to establish the validity of these two schools, we take as our starting point Toch's (1984, p. 514) call for a "science of imprisonment as well as a science of inmate reactions to imprisonment." In so doing, we adhered to the investigative process adopted by the Canadian school of rehabilitation in their development of a viable theory of effective offender treatment (Gendreau, Smith, and French 2006; Andrews and Bonta 2010; Cullen and Jonson 2011). Their approach involved the search for convergent validity from diverse empirical and theoretical literatures in order to demonstrate that certain types of treatment programs produce robust, replicable effects that will both protect the public and benefit inmates. As part of this process, a meta-analysis was used to quantitatively synthesize the results. In contrast to narrative reviews, which often reach inaccurate conclusions, meta-analysis provides a point estimate of the effect size (ES) and an estimate of its precision (Beaman 1991; Schmidt 1992; Cooper and Hedges 1994).

In this essay we follow a similar investigative route in the hopes of improving our understanding of the issue by examining three distinct literatures as a means of assessing the relative consistency of findings regarding the effects of AS. We start with a review of the effects of general conditions of prison life, followed by a summary of experimental studies on SD in the field of sensation and perception, and finally, a meta-analysis of SC studies involving offenders.

II. The Effects of Prison Life: The General Case

If AS represents the most powerful prison "dosage" that results in the most psychological pain among inmates, it would be reasonable to assume that being exposed to a lesser dosage of prison should produce psychological distress, although to a lesser extent. Three theories of the effects of prison life offer some predictions in this matter (Gendreau and Smith 2012). One of them directly contradicts the point of view that AS necessarily has vivid negative effects on inmates' psychological health, while the other two focus on other outcomes (i.e., misconducts, recidivism) that have been ignored in the AS literature.

In the first case, a theory originally known as the importation model (Thomas and Foster 1973), that goes under the colorful title of "behavioral deep freeze" (Zamble and Porporino 1988, 1990), submits that prisons are relatively neutral environments. Framed in the language of coping theory, Zamble and Porporino (1988, 1990) asserted that inmates who cope badly with prison have typically demonstrated inadequate coping skills throughout much of their lifespan.[1] In fact, inmates may cope better with prison life than in the outside world because, there, behaviors are restricted by the prison regime. This theory also accounts for how extra-prison factors (e.g., family, friends) may affect coping behaviors in prison. The evidence in support of this theory comes from a number of studies with large sample sizes using cross-sectional and longitudinal designs ranging from brief periods of several months to more than 10 years that assessed inmate adjustment to prison life (see Wormith 1984; Bonta and Gendreau 1990). On the basis of this literature, as well as his work with Porporino, Zamble (1992, p. 420) concluded that "the most striking result was in the total absence of any evidence for *general* or *widespread* deteriorative effects" of incarceration (emphasis added). The deep freeze theory also applies to mentally disordered offenders. Hodgins and Côté (1991) reported that 86 percent of mentally disordered offenders exhibited similar pathology prior to being admitted to prison and being placed in AS.

Subsequently, two reports have appeared that are in agreement with Zamble's (1992) conclusion. Walker et al.'s (2014) narrative review of 10 prison studies found that offenders reported mental health problems upon first entering prison, but in 7 of the 10 studies an improvement in mental state over time was reported. Two studies reported little change in mental health status, and one study showed a decline. Second, the Bauer (2012a) cross-sectional study found mixed results: some inmates responded poorly to incarceration, while others adjusted quite well (see Morgan et al. 2014).

In the absence of a meta-analysis of this literature, there are no estimates of the precise magnitude of the effects of prison life, although we expect it is likely close to zero given the previous summary of results. Until one is conducted, we are left with two meta-analyses on crowded living conditions, which should, ostensibly, result in greater levels of inmate distress than living in prisons that have adequate housing space. The interpretation of the magnitude of the effects from crowding studies, however, depends on what one considers a large effect. We took the data from Table 1 of Bonta and Gendreau's (1990, p. 352) meta-analysis on prison crowding and converted their ESs into r values, with accompanying 95 percent confidence intervals (CI). This offers a plausible range of ES values. The correlation between *density of living conditions* and *physiological indices* (e.g., elevated heart rate, blood pressure) and *feelings of personal discomfort* were $r = .20$ (CI = .14, .26) and $r = .22$ (CI = .15, .29), respectively. We regard estimates of this width as being too imprecise to form more definitive conclusions for policy purposes (i.e., CI width > .10; Gendreau and Smith 2007). When it comes to expressions of behavioral outcomes such as assaults and misconducts, the point estimate for crowding was quite a bit less and the estimate was more precise (.06–.08). The CI predicts that there is an 83 percent chance that this CI result will include the mean of a future replication experiment (Cumming 2012). Subsequently, a meta-analysis by Franklin, Franklin, and Pratt (2006) on the effects of crowding replicated these results. These authors found an ES of $r = .07$ (CI = .02–.11).

None of these findings dismiss prison overcrowding as inconsequential to the goal of providing humane care of inmates. Future research in the area must explore how factors such as management style, staff case management practices, abrupt changes in prison population involving younger inmates, and inmates' perceptions of control and "feelings" of being crowded moderate the ESs reported here (Bonta and Gendreau 1990; Franklin, Franklin, and Pratt 2006; Steiner and Wooldredge 2008, 2009).

The other two theories of prison life have primarily focused on criminogenic outcomes. Deterrence theory rests on the assumption that the stigmatizing and humiliating experience of prison life should be an antidote for pursuing a criminal lifestyle (see Gendreau and Smith 2012). It has been proposed that prison life should be made much harsher (e.g., physical punishment) to achieve the desired effect (see Stubblefield 2002; Gendreau and Goggin 2013, p. 764). The other theory, known as the "schools of crime," predicts the reverse outcome. Through a process of prisonization and social learning, inmates adopt the antisocial culture of the setting, which in turn reinforces criminogenic values (Clemmer 1940; Buckstel and Kilmann 1980). The longer the time spent in prison, the worse the result, which should be reflected in higher rates of recidivism (Jaman, Dickover, and Bennett 1972).

The support for the deterrence school prediction is almost entirely based on anecdotal evidence (Pizarro and Narag 2008) or the weakest of quasi-experimental research designs (Ward and Werlich 2003). On the other hand, the research results support the schools of crime hypothesis. Large sample primary studies and meta-analytic summaries (the total sample sizes are several hundred thousand) that have compared offender outcomes after serving time in prison versus being placed on community sanctions as well as outcomes after serving varying lengths of sentence all indicate that time in prison increases recidivism and makes prison adjustment worse (e.g., increases misconducts), usually in the range of 5 percent to 30 percent (see Smith, Goggin, and Gendreau 2002; Gendreau and Goggin 2013). There is one major caveat to this conclusion: these negative effects appear to be moderated to a large extent by lower inmate risk levels and to a lesser degree by "harsher" prison life conditions (i.e., maximum security environments; Gaes and Camp 2009; Jonson 2010; Gendreau and Smith 2012).

In conclusion, we recognize that previously cited literature is a distal representation of the living conditions found in AS. Studies must take into account the psychological histories of inmates; otherwise there may be a misattribution of negative symptoms to the physical structure of prison environments. Finally, this literature identifies criminogenic outcomes as the most adverse outcome of incarceration.

III. SENSORY DEPRIVATION

One of the puzzling aspects of the AS debate has been the lack of recognition of the SD literature (see Zubek 1969). To use a musical analogy, in order to understand the entire "scale" of the effects of confinement, would not the first step be to learn the "root notes," which, in this case, can be found in the psychological sensation and perception literature? This field of study seems, at first glance, to be a historical oddity, far removed from the interests of penologists. To be charitable, some AS researchers may have encountered this literature but had their interest soon extinguished because SD studies are a complex mix of subtle definitions, different methods, and different procedures. This research may also have been ignored because of the intellectual egocentrism and ethnocentrism that exists within and between the disciplines that work in corrections, resulting in a silo model of knowledge generation (Gendreau 1996; Gendreau and Goggin 2013). Whatever the case, a failure to respect this body of knowledge has been most unfortunate.

The rush to judgment on the effects of SD began with the legendary McGill experiments in the 1950s (see Gendreau and Thériault 2011). In these studies, college students were subjected to conditions[2] that were more severe than those found in any AS units of which we are aware. The McGill findings produced cognitive deterioration and visual and auditory hallucinations within a relatively short time (e.g., two to three days). In later years, however, such symptoms were not replicated in studies of up to 14 days using either SD modality (Zubek 1969). The consensus among experts in the area was that the studies were influenced by the powerful demand characteristics of settings within which they were conducted. In other words, the results were contaminated by participant response bias (Orne 1962). We discuss two studies that epitomize this point.

The first, by Jackson and Kelly (1962), was a telling example of the formidable influence of instructional set. Fourteen students were subjected to just one hour of perceptual monotony conditions. They were warned to anticipate unusual effects and were administered a placebo hallucinogen they were told might facilitate these experiences. All subjects reported marked visual, auditory, somesthetic, emotional, and cognitive distortions of reality. Some thought their hallucinations were real. In the second study, by Orne and Scheibe (1964), similar findings were reported *without* employing perceptual monotony or restricted environmental stimulation. All the experimenters had to do to produce results comparable to those found at McGill was to manipulate non-SD features of the environment, such as the dress and demeanor of the experimenter, material in the room, and a medical tray full of various items, and provide a panic button in case participants felt they might be vulnerable to becoming distressed. The control group, meanwhile, was not subjected to any of these procedures while placed under the McGill-like perceptual monotony conditions. Reported symptoms among controls were three times less than that of the experimental group! Orne and Scheibe, it should be noted, did not deny that SD did produce some negative psychological effects.

By the early 1970s, several hundred SD experiments had been conducted (Zubek 1969). Suedfeld (1975) described a survey he undertook of prominent research programs in the field involving 3,300 subjects of widely varying backgrounds, both volunteers and nonvolunteers. He reported that some participants reacted negatively but "one rarely finds, particularly in more recent studies, extreme emotionality, anger, and anxiety" (p. 62). Decrements in performance were usually found in the appearance of colors, spatial orientation, or arousal to visual stimuli. The effects usually dissipated shortly after leaving the SD venue. Negligible results have been found in a number of tactual, visual, and kinesthetic tasks while improvements have been reported on auditory tests and some intellectual tasks.[3] Tolerance of SD was as high as 90 percent, and the incidence of hallucinations that lasted for a significant period of time after SD was about 1 percent.[4]

As with the general incarceration literature, theory contributes to understanding why some of these results occurred. Beginning in the 1890s, perceptual researchers revealed how the sensory system successfully adapted to acute distortions in their sensory modalities (e.g., alterations in the visual field; Stratton 1896). Subsequently, a perceptual adaptation theory was developed by Helson (1964), which laid the foundation for understanding how organisms integrate stimuli and adapt to changing patterns and magnitudes of sensory input. Thus it comes as no surprise that many SD research participants were able to cope with the lack of stimulation, recognizing that the experimental condition was generally limited (up to 14 days) and that the researchers involved took care to monitor the health of experimental subjects.

In summary, while no meta-analysis has been carried out on the perceptual literature SD studies, our estimate from Suedfeld's (1975) narrative review suggests that overall there is likely a small negative effect of SD. Admittedly, the duration of SD exposure in these studies was much less than that seen in prisons. At the same time, experimental SD subjects were totally unfamiliar with the process. This stands in contrast to the experience of offenders who may find themselves in prison SD conditions that are typically far less forgiving than those presented to college students (Zubek et al. 1969). Moreover, this literature is very strong methodologically (e.g., true experiments and quasi-experimental designs) with careful attention paid to measurement. There is also a valid theory in support of the findings.

Last—and this is a crucial point regarding the generalizability of results from SD non-prison settings to SC in prisons—it has been found that the SC situation within prison is a reasonable facsimile for the SD literature. The replicable findings found in SD experiments (e.g., EEG and plasma cortical stress levels, arousal to sensory input, perceptual adaptation, and health outcomes) have also been corroborated in prison SC settings (e.g., Ecclestone, Gendreau, and Knox 1974; Gendreau et al. 1972). Next we explore the prison AS studies, the ultimate test of the two schools of thought on the effects of AS.

IV. PRISON AS STUDIES

The debate over the reputed harmful effects of AS gained momentum 30 years ago with the publication of a study by Grassian (1983). His assessment of 14 inmates in AS alleged that they suffered from massive free-floating anxiety, aggressive fantasies, and paranoia, among other responses. This study was an instant classic in the field and became a mantra in the media (Gawande 2009; Keim 2013). Fast-forward to 2010 and the publication of O'Keefe et al.'s (2010) Colorado AS study, later published in the *Journal of the American Academy of Psychiatry and the Law* (O'Keefe et al. 2013).[5] This study has quickly become infamous, especially among its detractors.

In our view, the Colorado study was an outstanding example of applied correctional research. It was planned with great care, the choice of dependent variables for measuring mental health symptoms were state of the art, and the design was rigorous with repeated measures encompassing a variety of constructs within a one-year follow-up. The sample size ($n = 247$) was impressive for a study of this type. The results are about as conclusive as possible that the experience of AS within the Colorado penitentiary studied did not result in an escalation of psychological problems. The data for this study are presented in two composite figures (see Figures 16.1 and 16.2), which we adapted from O'Keefe et al. (2010). As can be seen in Figure 16.1, with the exception of one outcome, inmates with no mental illness demonstrated an initial *decline* in symptomology with a subsequent rise to approximately initial levels.

Figure 16.2 depicts that mentally ill inmates reported, as expected, more symptomology at the first assessment period, but, with one exception, there was a slight decline in six of the seven symptom domains. Overall, 20 percent of the inmates showed improvement over time while 7 percent continued to get worse (Metzner and O'Keefe 2011).

Not surprisingly, some of the reactions to O'Keefe et al.'s (2010) findings were histrionic. Grassian (2010, p. 4) and Grassian and Kupers (2011) accused O'Keefe et al. of gross incompetency for producing "garbage in and out" results. What is more, they claimed that the findings were biased because of the "attractiveness" of one of the investigators, which apparently intimidated inmates in AS from revealing their "real" feelings so as to protect their self-worth. Some of the other criticisms of O'Keefe et al. (see Gendreau and Thériault 2011; Grassian and Kupers 2011; Metzner and Maureen 2011) were characteristic of standard knowledge destruction techniques commonly used in corrections where information is accepted and/or rejected according to moral and/or personal values, raising suspicions about errors in measurement and claiming a phenomenological inquiry is superior because human experience cannot be captured by checklist measures (e.g., Beck Depression

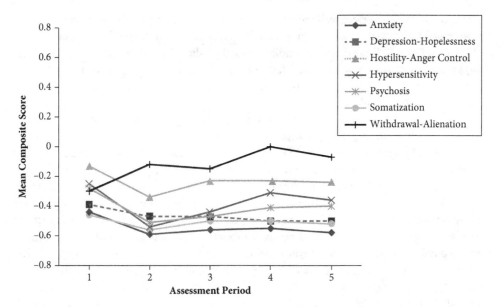

FIGURE 16.1. Mean scores on the seven composite measures over time for segregated group of inmates with no mental illness.

Source: Figures based on data reported in O'Keefe et al. (2010)

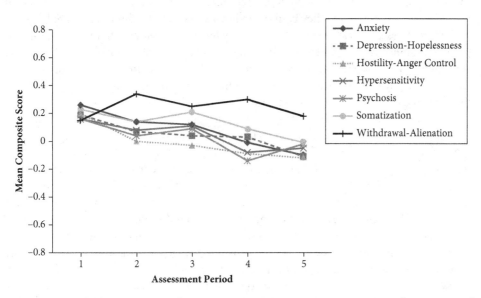

FIGURE 16.2. Mean scores on the seven composite measures over time for segregated group of inmates with mental illness.

Source: Figures based on data reported in O'Keefe et al. (2010)

Inventory) even if they are well validated. Interestingly, the only researchers to use a phenomenological measure that interprets people's experience from their own perspective (i.e.,
Repertory Grid Technique) in AS studies was led by the first author (see Ecclestone et al.
1974). This study found no adverse effects of AS on inmates' personal constructs. For the
record, O'Keefe et al. provided a cogent defense of their methodology and discussed the
limitations of their research.

In contrast to the Colorado study, what is the quality of the evidence touted by critics as
being the "truth" about AS? And what is their theory? Regarding the evidence, there are
two issues. One concerns response bias and the second study quality. We have already provided two persuasive examples for one type of response bias (e.g., Jackson and Kelly 1962;
Orne 1962). A second form comes from the field of cognitive psychology, where memory
researchers have demonstrated that it is easy to influence how people respond to questions
(Gudjonsson 1986; Fisher and Geiselman 1992; Gudjonsson 1992; Loftus 2003). Participants
are often eager to take the path of least resistance and provide the answer that they believe
is acceptable to the experimenter, whose position of authority has a powerful influence. The
interviewee does this to protect his or her self-esteem and/or because it serves some instrumental gain. Moreover, subtle wording of questions and instructions, even the altering of
one subtle word, can change recollections of past events (Loftus 2003). Ultimately, research
has shown that poor questioning practices can produce unreliable information. Could any
of these processes been in effect in the Grassian (1983) and Haney (2003) studies? How
reliable were the responses that they obtained? No mention was made of accounting for
the influence of response bias factors. In fact, interrogators in these two studies appeared
to encourage response bias. They commented that some inmates did not seem to be aware
of the dire stress they were experiencing so they had to be prompted to divulge the appropriate symptoms. A third variation of response bias found in the Grassian study, and one
frequently cited in support of his results (see Brodsky and Scogin 1988), was that inmates
were involved in a lawsuit against the state at the time of the interviews. It is plausible that
they had much to gain by responding negatively to the interviewers' questions.

Next we turn to a frequently cited review of the AS literature. This review relied on 11
studies that used quantitative data that included a comparison group and 17 that were qualitative (Scharff-Smith's 2006).[6] The author used a vote-counting method to summarize studies, a procedure that has historically led to substantial inaccuracies in summarizing the
magnitude of ES (Hunter and Schmidt 2004). The qualitative studies were treated at face
value despite the fact they were based on simple common-sense heuristics (see Gendreau
et al. 2002).[7] No criteria were reported for what constituted a minor versus serious effect.

Regarding theory, Scharff-Smith (2006) seem to maintain that inmates are blameless
victims of the situation; in other words, AS is the primary driving force that creates the
psychological malaise of inmates who, prior to the experience of AS, had no such problem
(O'Keefe et al. 2013). In essence, this reasoning is textbook radical behaviorism, a theory
that once dominated the field of learning (Bowers 1973). We are not denying the potential for situations to significantly shape behavior, but psychologists now acknowledge that
both situations and traits meaningfully contribute to behavior (Bowers 1973; Fleeson and
Noftle 2009).

In an effort to test this theory, we submitted the quantitative studies cited by Scharff-
Smith (2006), plus others located from an ongoing analysis of the effects of AS, to the meta-
analytic test (Labrecque, Smith, and Gendreau 2013).[8] The inclusion criteria required that

the study take place in a correctional setting with prisoners, had a comparison group, and contained sufficient data to calculate an ES. Of the 150 studies located, 15 met the criteria and were suitable for analysis. Two hundred and forty-six ESs from the 15 studies were collected and categorized by type of outcome: behavioral ($k = 9$), physiological ($k = 24$), or psychological ($k = 213$). The majority of ESs for length of stay in AS were 60 days or more. The mean ESs for each category are presented in Table 16.1, where a positive valence indicates an iatrogenic effect (i.e., AS correlates with an increase in the outcome of interest).

The overall mean effect of AS was $r = .04$ (CI = .03, .05), with the largest negative effects coming from studies with the weakest research designs[9] ($r = .06$ as compared to $r = .02$ for studies of stronger design). The largest negative effects were reported for medical/physiological outcomes, although this magnitude is deceiving as increases in visual-evoked potentials and a decline in EEG were coded as negative outcomes. From a psychophysiological perspective the direction of these results represents an appropriate response by the organism to SD (Helson 1964; Myers 1969; Zubek 1969).[10]

The second highest magnitude of AS effects was for behavioral outcomes, as measured by institutional misconduct and postrelease recidivism ($r = .04$, CI = .02, .07). Recall that deterrence theory predicts a suppression effect, while the schools of crime view is the opposite. Despite the relatively weak effect of AS on behavioral indicators, this domain deserves some additional comment. There were five studies in this category that correlated AS experience with recidivism. The ES for recidivism was an r of .07 with a CI of .04 to .10. Is this convincing evidence in support of the school of crime view? It would be tempting to think so, but the lack of information about the comparison groups in AS studies raises some doubts. This is not a criticism of the investigators involved, as they had to rely on the limited evidence provided by prison authorities. It is likely that the offenders in AS were already assessed as higher risk to reoffend unless these samples were comprised of largely low-risk inmates, which would be most unlikely. Risk to recidivate in the five studies was generally based on one or two static variables, notably criminal history and age. Dynamic risk factors (e.g., antisocial attitudes, antisocial values), which are useful predictors of risk (Gendreau, Little, and Goggin 1996; Andrews and Bonta 2010), were not available to the researchers involved. Inmates are also sent to AS based on situational factors involving prison management (e.g., sudden transfers of inmates) and the quality of life (i.e., prison climate; e.g.,

Table 16.1. Mean effect sizes by outcome category type

Outcome	K	n	r	95% CI
Behavioral	9	6,267	.04	[.02, .07]
Medical/ Physiological	24	1,046	.15	[.09, .21]
Psychological	213	11,608	.03	[.01, .05]
Total	246	18,921	.04	[.03, .05]

Note: CI = confidence interval.

Gendreau, Goggin, and Law 1997; Goggin 2009), but this information also was not available to the researchers. Finally, theory states that for a school of crime effect to occur, many opportunities for social learning and modeling must be present, which would necessarily be limited due to the social isolation conditions inherent to AS. Last, the weakest data in support of adverse outcomes for AS were found in the psychological domain ($r = .03$; CI = .01, .05) with the majority of the outcomes emanating from the Colorado study.

In keeping with our objective at the outset, we have confirmed the convergent validity of the effects of AS from the available literature on confinement. Two sources of data on confinement are consistent with the results of the AS studies in establishing that the effects of confinement are negative but do not produce "lasting emotional damage, if not full-blown psychosis and functional disability" (Kupers 2008, p. 1006). But that is not the end of the story. To cite an old cliché, there remains an elephant in the phone booth regarding the AS issue. In the next section we identify the culprit and then outline the type of research that will be required to determine the conditions under which AS may have differential effects. Last, we present several clinical practice and management guidelines to limit the use of AS.

V. Identifying the Elephant and Deciding What To Do About It

In our opinion, the driving force behind most of the irrational behavior that clinicians and correctional staff witness on the part of AS inmates is the result of how they are treated (Gendreau and Thériault 2011; Valera and Kates-Benman 2015). Observers representing both schools of thought (e.g., Jackson 1983; Brodsky and Scogin 1988; Wormith, Tellier, and Gendreau 1988; Haney 2009; Gendreau and Thériault 2011; Grassian and Kupers 2011), as well as those who were ostensibly "neutral" before being asked to conduct special investigations on prison life (e.g., Vantour 1975; Arbour 1996), agree on one key point. When inmates are treated mean spiritedly and capriciously, kept in a fog of uncertainty about their circumstances, and generally feel that they have been treated unjustly, then negative effects are much more likely to manifest themselves (Gendreau and Bonta 1984; Jackson 2001). In effect, we are faced with a human relations and programming problem much more so than a prison architectural design issue (Gendreau and Thériault 2011). As Haney (2008, p. 982) admitted, it is folly to think that "mere tinkering with its [AS] design can produce a beneficial or palliative response." As testimony to this observation, Jackson (1983) documented that when physical living conditions where improved considerably (e.g., access to TV, recreation, more programming), inmates still complained of cruel and unusual punishment for the reasons noted previously.

So what is to be done? Some advocate that AS should be banished entirely (Andersen et al. 2000). This sentiment is well intended but is it politically realistic, especially in the United States, where supermax facilities have become a standard way of doing business that traps correctional administrators into short-term thinking and primitive solutions to handling inmates (Gendreau 2012a; F. Porporino, personal communication, June 30, 2014)? Nevertheless, we cannot cavalierly dismiss the reality that there are a meaningful proportion of inmates who are truly dangerous and psychopathic or minimize the difficult job that prison managers encounter in settings where gang culture dominates the lives of inmates and staff alike. All the same, AS will always be part of prison operations; it can be relied upon to a much lesser extent in the future using strategies that are described in the forthcoming section on clinical practice.

VI. Being Proactive About AS: Research and Clinical Practice

Despite all that has been written about AS, recommendations regarding what research to pursue in order to better understand its effects and the clinical practices that need to be in place to reduce potential harm have been lacking (see Gendreau and Bonta 1984; Haney and Lynch 1997; Gendreau and Thériault 2011). We begin this section by outlining the research questions that need to be addressed.

A. Research

Gendreau and Thériault (2011) affirmed that for any progress to be made, a meta-analytic perspective is necessary. Otherwise, policy decisions about AS will be of little utility as they will be based on the law of small numbers and hampered by sampling error and bad common-sense reasoning. The meta-analysis reported here must be replicated, hopefully with additional studies.[11] While the estimates of the effects of AS from our database are precise and unlikely to change to any marked degree, the Colorado study, which contributed a substantial amount of data to our meta-analysis, has provided a limited number of point estimates. It is imperative researchers assess other AS settings whose standards of care are much less than that witnessed at the Colorado site.[12] We understand that some of the research we recommend will likely meet with resistance from many correctional authorities and may not be undertaken for quite some time. Nevertheless, asking the following questions might prevent a rush to judgment and help us to rethink the putative effects of AS. The clinical implications of this research, where they are relevant, are discussed later.

1. Is AS Really an SD Condition?

Clearly, that was the conclusion from the Ontario evaluations (Gendreau et al. 1972) and no doubt applies to many AS cells in use today. Figure 16.3 shows an AS cell in a maximum-security penitentiary, which was almost identical to the 1960s' versions used by Gendreau et al. (1972) and Ecclestone et al. (1974).

Some AS settings, however, do not meet the definition of SD because inmates may have access to radio, TV, books, other inmates, and activities, which better approximates the sensory input level found for non-AS inmates. Meanwhile, we are aware that prison administrators use euphemisms (e.g., intensive support units, secure living environments) to hide the fact that they have cell accommodations that have unnecessarily low levels of sensory input (Zinger 2013). Future studies on the effects of AS must first make an objective

FIGURE 16.3. A maximum-security cell.

determination as to whether the conditions of restricted environmental stimulation are present. If the conditions do not apply, researchers are likely addressing a research question relevant to the effects of prison life in general rather than AS per se.

2. Individual Differences

As noted at the outset, AS inmates are a heterogeneous group. Based on our experience and the Canadian data (Public Safety Canada 2013), it is possible that about 20 to 30 percent of inmates are in AS for reasons of personal preference. We predict that future studies will find that the reactions to AS of such "volunteers" are different from those who are sent there against their will. Second, whatever the case, some percentage will cope badly under AS conditions; whether it is less than 10 percent as Metzner and O'Keefe (2011) discovered remains to be seen.

As of yet, we are unable to predict with any certitude which inmates will react poorly to AS. Gendreau and Thériault (2011) have listed just a few of the characteristics (e.g., biochemical, stimulation seeking, conceptual level, risk level) of offenders that may enhance their vulnerability to the negative effects of AS. To that list we would add measures of coping style (e.g., task oriented, avoidance, and reactive coping styles) that predict prison adjustment and might well apply to AS (Gullone, Jones, and Cummings 2000; Zamble and Porporino 1988). In addition, there is recent work that demonstrates the coping styles that inmates may use to adjust to AS (O'Donnell 2014; Valera and Kates-Benman 2015). Research that examines the interrelationships among reasons for being in AS and individual differences will make a truly significant contribution to the literature. Any correctional system that is at all concerned about its inmates should be able to generate individual predictive validities fairly readily, assuming they are using intake assessment protocols that collect such information.

3. Assessing the Contribution of "the Real Culprit" to ES Estimates

The quality of interaction between correctional officers and inmates should be evaluated via videotape and, where possible, factored into the designs of future AS studies. To prove our point made previously, we predict that when relations markedly deteriorate between the keepers and the kept, negative behaviors will increase substantially over the results reported in our meta-analysis. Similar assessments of the inmate–staff interactions should be taken of non-AS prison settings. For example, experts working as prison ombudsmen, whose role is to investigate the quality of prison life, have commented that, in some instances, living conditions in "regular" prison accommodations are actually more uncomfortable and stressful than those in AS (I. Zinger, personal communication, October 10, 2013). In this regard, more research on the "climate" of prisons, whatever their designation, particularly when there appears to be a culture of harm (see Haney 2008) is urgently needed (see Wright 1991; Goggin 2008).[13] If more prisons followed the guidelines suggested by Toch (1992) for managing prisons in a safe and humane fashion, the reliance on AS to control behavior might diminish.

4. AS as a Punisher

Some anecdotes suggest that AS serves as an effective punisher for suppressing antisocial behavior within prison (Pizarro and Narag 2008). One study, conducted by Briggs, Sundt, and Castellano (2003), found that US states with supermax prisons did not have lower levels of inmate-on-inmate violence, but did find mixed support for its ability to increase staff safety. We can see no possible reason for results that produced a reduction of inmate-on-staff assaults in view of how the laws of punishment function.[14] Such a finding is probably a result of sampling error, the nature of the comparison group, and the use of aggregate-level data, which can inflate ES (Gendreau and Smith 2007). Moreover, for a percentage of inmates, living in AS might be seen as a reinforcer given some of the negative aspects that occur in routine prison life. More recently, the second author examined the impact of disciplinary segregation on institutional behavior in a sample of inmates ($n = 14,311$) in the Ohio prison system and found that neither the experience of segregation, nor the number of days spent in the setting, had any significant effect on the subsequent occurrence of violent, nonviolent, or drug misconduct (see Labrecque 2015).

5. Researcher Accountability

It is one thing to recommend these research agendas, but what of the responsibilities of the research communities? Who is going to conduct the studies? Very few prisons have the staff with the inclination or skill set to do so. Haney and Zimbardo (1998) recognized this point and called out criminologists and psychologists for abandoning the study of prisons, the reasons for which were summarized by Gendreau and Smith (2012). On the other hand, we recognize that there are serious barriers to conducting research in prisons. Some correctional jurisdictions have been antagonistic to external parties "meddling" in their affairs (Ward and Werlich 2003; Bauer 2012b). Given the inherent problems of relying on prison officials for secondary data, researchers must gather the necessary data on-site themselves, or at least work in collaboration with prison officials to establish better record-keeping and clinical documentation. Otherwise, AS research will continue to be plagued by the limitations of the available data in regard to the myriad of personal and situational variables that determine critical outcomes.

B. Clinical Practice

Clinical practice refers to ethically defensible and humane plans of action that can be taken by those staff (e.g., psychologists, social workers, correctional officers) whose duties focus on encouraging inmates to adjust to prison life in a prosocial manner.

1. *Mentally Disordered Offenders*

Much of the focus on the effects of AS has focused on mentally disordered offenders (MDOs). The assumption that time spent in AS will exacerbate their illness is naïve and one that is not predicted from theory (Bentler 1990). Mentally disordered offenders function best in quiet environments, which reduce confusing perceptual and cognitive stimuli, a point made by Grassian and Friedman (1986) and one reinforced in the Colorado study (see data for depression-hopelessness and psychosis in Figure 16.2).

Is AS the appropriate placement for MDOs? Obviously not, as MDOs require clinical supervision to ensure that they take their medications, a major predictor of relapse along with that of expressed emotion (Smith, Gendreau, and Goggin 2007). Mental health care should take place in a psychiatric hospital wing of the prison run by mental health professionals who are bound by the mental health acts of their state or province. It is vitally important that these professionals are also responsible for security decisions. Otherwise, the mental health unit will become just another prison. Typically, when MDOs misbehave because of their illness, prison officers react as one would expect they would, which is to use AS as a punisher (Office of the Correctional Investigator 2013). A worthwhile example of a mental health model for MDOs can be found in the Mississippi State penitentiary treatment program (Kupers et al. 2009).[15]

Once MDOs' symptoms are under control, clinicians then face two crucial decisions. If MDOs are assessed as low risk to reoffend, they should remain in the psychiatric unit to prevent the schools of crime effect from occurring by mixing them with high-risk inmates. If they are low risk, treatment for criminogenic needs is a low priority. High-risk MDOs should be returned to regular cell accommodations once their symptoms abate and also be enrolled in programs designed to reduce their antisocial behaviors (Gendreau 2012b).

A final point concerns the identification of MDOs. In our view, the difficulties in this area have been glossed over. First, it seems that almost any malaise ranging from antisocial, comorbidity, dysthymic, oppositional, and posttraumatic stress disorder makes one eligible for an MDO classification. Throw in alienation, attention deficient hyperactivity disorder, low self-esteem, mental retardation, self-injurious and suicidal behaviors, and substance abuse into the diagnostic pot, as some are wont to do, and one would not be surprised to find that almost all offenders would qualify for the MDO designation (Smith et al. 2007; Andrews and Bonta 2010). We are traditionalists in this matter and adhere to the *Diagnostic and Statistical Manual of Mental Disorders* (fifth edition) criteria for MDOs (i.e., schizophrenia, debilitating depression, and bipolar disorder; American Psychiatric Association 2013). Second, there is another problem when it comes to identifying MDOs: just because a measure purports to assess the *Diagnostic and Statistical Manual of Mental Disorders* symptoms does not mean that it necessarily has predictive validity. As of several years ago, there were 419 measures used to assess mental disorders (Smith et al. 2007). Sadly, Smith et al. found only 17 percent reported any predictive validities and just 1 percent had more than 10 ESs with relapse and/or rehospitalization. Of the latter 1 percent, a measure of expressed emotion (the Camberwell Family Interview) far surpassed the others in predictive accuracy.

2. *Inmate Monitoring*

For whatever reason, some observers have argued for AS stays of up to 90 days with a maximum of monthly on-site clinical reviews (Jackson 1983; Haney and Lynch 1997). Those who have worked in prisons and monitored inmates in SC as part of their clinical duties have adopted even stricter guidelines, such as limiting the length of stay to 14 days and performing daily clinical check-ups (Gendreau and Bonta 1984; M. Bettman, personal communication, October 10, 2013). Interestingly, a quarter of a century later some authorities are proposing the same recommendation (Kates 2014). The reason is that small effects of AS should not go unheeded as they could have serious consequences later on.[16] An additional issue that affects the humane care of inmates in AS has been the lack of communication and consistency in decision-making by staff regarding inmates' needs, due to brief duty rotations. This factor alone causes inmates distress, as they are unsure of where they stand and their requests get lost in the shuffle because good case management practices are not in effect. For case management to work effectively, it is therefore recommended that correctional staff have the training needed to deal with the presenting problems that are typical of AS inmates (e.g., acting-out behavior, social withdrawal) before being assigned to an AS inmate caseload.

3. *Prevention*

Administrative segregation was initially used to house a prison's most disruptive inmates. Treatment programs modeled on Andrews and Bonta's (2010) risk-need-responsivity model of rehabilitation has been shown to be highly effective in reducing prison misconducts (French and Gendreau 2006). In addition, reducing misconducts has substantial cost-saving benefits (Lovell and Jemelka 1996). There are also risk measures available for clinicians to identify inmates who are at risk for misconduct behaviors and who can then be placed in programs (Gendreau et al. 1997; Campbell, French, and Gendreau 2009; Gendreau and Goggin 2013).

Two other policies can help limit the use of AS. One is to design prison environments in such a way as to discourage the assaults that lead to AS (see Wortley 2002). No doubt cynics will ridicule the following suggestion as being unrealistic—maybe so, but why not limit the number of AS cells and length of time in AS? In one prison in which the senior author has worked as a clinician/administrator, five AS cells were available and inmates had to leave within a week. With these policies in place, staff and inmates learned to cope with this reality. Waiting lists all but disappeared and inmates returned to their normal living accommodations. When the AS accommodations were increased later on by another administration, AS cells were quickly filled to capacity despite there being no changes in the inmate composition or the prison climate. The cliché "build it and they will come" was proven once again.[17]

4. Incentives to Leave AS

Once inmates find life in AS to be tolerable, it can be extremely difficult to encourage them to return to the general population. One form of programming that, unfortunately, has been relegated to the dustbin of offender treatment methods is what is known as contingency management. By far the most common strategy of this type of programming is the token economy, where receipt of tangible and social rewards is made contingent on inmates' behavior. Forty years ago in corrections, token economies were in great favor, but they were attacked as being unduly coercive and later were supplanted by the cognitive behavioral revolution (Gendreau et al. 2014). These authors revisited this literature to determine the magnitude of the effect of token economies on a variety of inmate behaviors. The results were truly impressive, with a 64 percent improvement recorded for a variety of within-prison prosocial behaviors. Having said that, token economies, in particular, are vulnerable to being easily sabotaged unless there is wholehearted support from all stakeholders in the prison and the contingencies are followed to the letter (see also Liebling 2008). For the interested reader, Gendreau et al. (2014) provides a detailed list of the "dos and don'ts" of successful token economy management. We have also been made aware of a recent attempt to establish a token economy-like program at Alger Correctional Facility in Michigan that has had marked success in returning inmates to the regular population (C. Bauman, personal communication, August 9, 2013).

VII. CONCLUSION

This essay examined the two opposing schools of thought on the effects of AS. We searched for convergent validity from diverse empirical and theoretical literatures as a means of assessing the relative consistency of the findings to establish the validity of these two perspectives. First, we examined the general prison life literature, which revealed support for the schools of crime hypothesis. Prisons, in general, are criminogenic primarily for low-risk offenders (i.e., increased antisocial behavior in prison and postrelease recidivism) but do not produce much in the way of adverse mental health outcomes.

Next we reviewed the SD literature in the field of sensation and perception. Although the McGill experiments in the 1950s reported cognitive deterioration and visual and auditory hallucinations within a relatively short time (see Gendreau and Thériault 2011), the vast majority of studies in this area found only weak negative effects and that only in the areas of textual, visual, and kinesthetic sensation (Suedfeld 1975). One of the potential causes for extreme results in this area is participant response bias (see Orne 1962). It is rather unfortunate that this SD literature has largely been ignored in the AS debate despite its obvious relevance. For example, the replicable findings found in SD experiments (e.g., EEG and plasma cortical stress levels, arousal to sensory input, perceptual adaptation, and health outcomes) have also been corroborated in prison SC settings (e.g., Gendreau et al. 1972; Ecclestone et al. 1974).

Finally, we explored the SC studies involving offenders in custodial settings. In the 30 years since the publication of the Grassian (1983) study, there has been a contentious debate regarding the harmful effects of AS on inmates. Although some of this literature has been limited in terms of the methodological quality, the recent O'Keefe et al. (2010) Colorado study was of particularly high quality (e.g., quasi-experimental, repeated measures, variety of mental health constructs, one-year follow-up). The results of this study indicated that the majority of inmates in the Colorado prison did not experience any escalation of psychological symptoms (Metzner and O'Keefe 2011). In our meta-analysis of this literature, we discovered relatively weak effects of AS on inmate outcomes ($r = .04$; Labrecque et al. 2013). In addition, more extreme effects were noted for studies employing weaker designs ($r = .06$) compared to those with stronger designs ($r = .02$). Our contention is that when negative effects occur in AS, it is primarily due to how inmates are treated by correctional staff and managed in general by prison administrators.

We caution policymakers, however, to be leery of basing decisions about AS exclusively on the results of any one particular study and most certainly on those that are qualitative. Instead, we maintain that a meta-analytic perspective is necessary in order to understand the effects of AS on subsequent inmate outcomes. Future investigations on the effects of AS should be conducted with greater methodological quality and with the careful attention to clinical outcomes typified by the Colorado evaluation. It is also imperative that forthcoming evaluations investigate moderators (e.g., inmate and prison characteristics, the relationship between keepers and kept); we expect that these factors combined with excessively long periods (i.e., >30 days to several years in U.S. prisons) in AS will produce iatrogenic consequences that will violate reasonable standards of humane care. In the meantime, several clinical practice and programming policies should be initiated to ensure that inmates are treated humanely and to discourage prison authorities to rely on the use of AS.

NOTES

1. The life-span psychology literature has generated considerable evidence that personality traits are consistent over the lifetime and relatively impervious to environmental influences (Costa and McCrae 1997).
2. These studies were of a form of SD called perceptual deprivation whereby the sensory environment is made as monotonous as possible. Student volunteers in the McGill studies were instructed to lie on a bed wearing translucent goggles and body cuffs

to reduce tactile stimulation. There was a constant buzzing noise. For an example of even more extreme restrictions see Zubek, Bayer, and Shephard (1969). The other type of SD, typical of prison environments, is that of restricted environmental stimulation where sensory stimulation is much lower than "normal" (Gendreau et al. 1972; Suedfeld 1980). Perceptual deprivation seems to produce more cognitive impairment (Zuckerman 1969).

3. Based on supporting evidence from his own work with offenders and research results from developmental psychology and the psychiatric literature, Suedfeld (1980) has proposed that restricted environmental conditions can have beneficial effects. Oddly enough, Grassian and Friedman (1986) are in agreement with Suedfeld on this point for some mentally disordered offenders.

4. Even under the most extreme SD conditions (e.g., up to 14 days of perceptual deprivation) tolerance levels were high (i.e., 67 percent) and hallucinatory reactions were almost totally absent (Zubek 1964). One condition of SD that does seem to affect tolerance rates is the addition of kinesthetic immobilization (i.e., students placed in coffin-like boxes) to visual and auditory deprivation (Zubek et al. 1969). In that study, tolerance rates were 40 percent.

5. While this study has drawn almost all of the attention, we also recommend the reports by Suedfeld et al. (1982) and Zinger, Wichmann, and Andrews (2001), which reported results similar to the Colorado group.

6. The Grassian (1983) and Haney (2003) studies were included in his review. The former did not include a comparison group, and the latter compared his results to a nonprison nonoffender sample; neither study empirically assessed previous mental health histories of their inmates.

7. Examples of common-sense arguments include relying on testimonials from authority, "what everybody knows" claims, resorting to explanation by naming, and accepting ideographic laws of behavior. Scharff-Smith (2006) also accepted the validity of the McGill studies.

8. Interested readers can access the final report from the second author. Data presented in this document may slightly deviate from Table 16.1.

9. Labrecque et al. (2013) defined weak designs as those that did not use a comparison group that was similar to the treatment group on at least five empirically relevant characteristics.

10. Coding the studies in this way reversed the ES to r of –.25 with a CI of –.42 to .07.

11. Robert Morgan and colleagues are conducting a separate meta-analysis, and the results analyzed to date are similar to ours (see note 8).

12. Consider the deplorable third-world physical conditions in AS at Mississippi State Penitentiary (Kupers et al. 2009, p. 1039). In another southern state, the first author of this chapter was asked to bring basic toiletries (e.g., soap, toothbrush, etc.) for inmates. These kinds of conditions should produce psychological problems greater than our meta-analysis indicates.

13. Mention must be made of the Goggin (2008) analysis of a correctional climate survey in the Canadian correctional system. Its scope was extraordinary. Forty-three prisons contributed data; the sample sizes were 4,283 inmates and 2,717 staff.

14. There are 14 steps that must be fulfilled to ensure the maximal effect of punishment (e.g., escape from the punishing stimuli is not possible, punishment is administered immediately with maximum intensity at every occurrence of the target behavior; see Matson and DiLorenzo 1984).

15. While we obviously have our points of contention with Dr. Kupers, all credit is due to him and his colleagues for their innovative program (which must have had any number of serious barriers to overcome) that has resulted in robust effects for reducing rule violations besides improving inmates' mental health. Their description is also noteworthy for detailing how many inmates were misclassified for AS in the first place (see also Ward and Werlich 2003).

16. Determining what would qualify as a significant clinical effect is very difficult. From a research perspective, just because a large sample of inmates shows an increase of a few points on a clinical scale may demonstrate only statistical conclusion validity.

17. As a point of emphasis regarding the overuse of AS in the United States, Canada, a country with a population about the size of California's, has only one maximum security supermax housing unit (SHU). This facility houses 72 inmates at any given time. The country also has other units designated as AS, which house about 5 percent of the prison population. Two-thirds of these inmates spend less than 60 days in AS (Public Safety Canada 2013). In the past year, Public Safety Canada reduced their admissions to AS by 50 percent (I. Zinger, personal communication, February 25, 2016). In comparison, California's Pelican Bay state prison alone has approximately 1,300 inmates in SHU (King, Steiner, and Ritchie-Breach 2008). Across the entire Canadian federal system, 6 percent (of approximately 15,000 inmates) are in an AS cell at any one time, 48 percent have been in AS for less than 30 days, and 17 percent less than 120 days. Naday, Freilich, and Mellow (2008) reported that there were 23,252 SHU inmates in the US state prisons alone (which does not include the number of federal inmates in SHU). Bauer (2012b) reported that 563 inmates were in the Pelican Bay SHU for at least five years. For other indices of overuse of AS in other states, see Mears and Bales (2010).

REFERENCES

American Psychiatric Association. 2013. *Diagnostic and Statistical Manual of Mental Disorders*, 5th ed. Arlington, VA: American Psychiatric Publishing.

Andersen, Henrik S., Dorte Sestoft, Tommy Lillebaek, Gorm Gabrielsen, Ralf Hemmingsen, and Peter Kramp. 2000. "A Longitudinal Study of Prisoners on Remand: Psychiatric Prevalence, Incidence and Psychopathology in Solitary vs. Non-Solitary Confinement." *Acta Psychiatrica Scandinavica* 102:19–25.

Andrews, Don A., and James Bonta. 2010. *The Psychology of Criminal Conduct*, 5th ed. Cincinnati, OH: Anderson Publishing.

Arbour, Louise. 1996. *Commission of Inquiry into Certain Events at the Prison for Women in Kingston*. Ottawa, ON: Public Works and Government Services of Canada.

Bauer, Rebecca L. 2012a. "Implications of Long-Term Incarceration for Persons with Mental Illness." PhD dissertation. Texas Tech University, Lubbock, TX.

Bauer, Shane. 2012b. "Solitary in Iran Nearly Broke Me. Then I Went Inside America's Prisons." *Mother Jones* (November/December). http://www.motherjones.com/politics/2012/10/solitary-confinement-shane-bauer.

Beaman, Arthur L. 1991. "An Empirical Comparison of Meta-Analytic and Traditional Reviews." *Personality and Social Psychology Bulletin* 17:252–257.

Bentler, Peter M. 1990. "Comparative Fit Indexes in Structural Models." *Psychological Bulletin* 107:238–246.

Bonta, James, and Paul Gendreau. 1990. "Reexamining the Cruel and Unusual Punishment of Prison Life." *Law and Human Behavior* 14:347–366.

Bowers, Kenneth S. 1973. "Situationism in Psychology: An Analysis and a Critique." *Psychological Review* 80:307–336.

Briggs, Chad S., Jody L. Sundt, and Thomas C. Castellano. 2003. "The Effect of Supermaximum Security Prisons on Aggregate Levels of Institutional Violence." *Criminology* 41:1341–1376.

Brodsky, Stanley L., and Forrest R. Scogin. 1988. "Inmates in Protective Custody: First Data on Emotional Effects." *Forensic Reports* 1:267–280.

Buckstel, Lee H., and Peter R. Kilmann. 1980. "Psychological Effects of Imprisonment on Confined Individuals." *Psychological Bulletin* 88:469–493.

Campbell, Mary A., Sheila French, and Paul Gendreau. 2009. "The Prediction of Violence in Adult Offenders: A Meta-Analytic Comparison." *Criminal Justice and Behavior* 36:567–590.

Clements, Carl B., Richard Althouse, Robert K. Ax, Phillip R. Magaletta, Thomas J. Fagan, and J. Stephen Wormith. 2007. "Systematic Issues and Correctional Outcomes: Expanding the Scope of Correctional Psychology." *Criminal Justice and Behavior* 34:919–932.

Clemmer, Donald. 1940. *The Prison Community*. New York: Rinehart.

Cooper, Harris, and Larry V. Hedges. 1994. *The Handbook of Research Synthesis*. New York: Russell Sage Foundation.

Costa, Paul T., and Robert R. McCrae. 1997. "Longitudinal Stability of Adult Personality." In *Handbook of Personality Psychology*, edited by Robert Hogan, John Johnson, and Stephen Briggs. San Diego: Academic Press.

Cullen, Francis T., and Paul Gendreau. 1989. "The Effectiveness of Correctional Rehabilitation." In *The American Prison: Issues in Research Policy*, edited by Lynne Goodstein and Doris L. MacKenzie. New York: Plenum.

Cullen, Francis T., and Cheryl L. Jonson. 2011. "Rehabilitation and Treatment Programs." In *Crime and Public Policy*, edited by James Q. Wilson and Joan Petersilia. New York: Oxford University Press.

Cumming, Geoff. 2012. *Understanding the New Statistics: Effect Sizes, Confidence Intervals, and Meta-Analysis*. New York: Routledge.

Ecclestone, C. E. J., Paul Gendreau, and Clifford Knox. 1974. "Solitary Confinement of Prisoners: An Assessment of Its Effects on Inmates' Personal Constructs and Adrenalcortical Activity." *Canadian Journal of Behavioural Science* 6:178–191.

Fisher, Ronald P., and R. Edward Geiselman. 1992. *Memory-Enhancing Techniques for Investigative Interviewing: The Cognitive Interview*. Springfield, IL: Charles C. Thomas.

Fleeson, William, and Erik Noftle. 2009. "The End of the Person–Situation Debate: An Emerging Synthesis in the Answer to the Consistency Question." *Social and Personality Psychology Compass* 2:1667–1684.

Franklin, Travis C., Cortney A. Franklin, and Travis C. Pratt. 2006. "Examining the Empirical Relationship between Prison Crowding and Inmate Misconduct: A Meta-Analysis of Conflicting Research Results." *Journal of Criminal Justice* 34:401–412.

French, Sheila A., and Paul Gendreau. 2006. "Reducing Prison Misconducts: What Works!" *Criminal Justice and Behavior* 33:185–218.

Gaes, Gerald G., and Scott D. Camp. 2009. "Unintended Consequences: Experimental Evidence for the Criminogenic Effect of Security Level Placement on Post-Release Recidivism." *Journal of Experimental Criminology* 5:185–218.

Gawande, Atul. 2009. "Hellhole." *The New Yorker* (March 30). http://www.newyorker.com/magazine/2009/03/30/hellhole.

Gendreau, Paul. 1996. "Offender Rehabilitation: What We Know and What Needs To Be Done." *Criminal Justice and Behavior* 23:144–161.

Gendreau, Paul. 2012a. *Everything You Wanted to Know About Prisons.* Keynote address at the October conference for the Association for the Treatment of Sexual Abuse, Denver, CO.

Gendreau, Paul. 2012b. *The Principles of Effective Intervention with MDOs.* Paper presented at the St. Lawrence Valley Correctional and Treatment Centre, Ontario Ministry of Community Safety and Correctional Services, Brockville, Ontario, Canada (May).

Gendreau, Paul, and James Bonta. 1984. "Solitary Confinement Is Not Cruel and Unusual Punishment: Sometimes People Are!" *Canadian Journal of Criminology* 26:467–478.

Gendreau, Paul, N. Freedman, G. J. S. Wilde, and G. D. Scott. 1972. "Changes in EEG Alpha Frequency and Evoked Response Latency During Solitary Confinement." *Journal of Abnormal Psychology* 79:54–59.

Gendreau, Paul, and Claire Goggin. 2013. "Practicing Psychology in Correctional Settings." In *The Handbook of Forensic Psychology*, 4th ed., edited by Irving B. Weiner and Randy K. Otto. Hoboken, NJ: John Wiley.

Gendreau, Paul, Claire Goggin, Francis T. Cullen, and Mario Paparozzi. 2002. "The Common-Sense Revolution and Correctional Policy." In *Offender Rehabilitation and Treatment: Effective Programmes and Policies to Reduce Reoffending*, edited by James McGuire. West Chichester, UK: Wiley.

Gendreau, Paul, Claire Goggin, and Moira A. Law. 1997. "Predicting Prison Misconducts." *Criminal Justice and Behavior* 24:414–431.

Gendreau, Paul, Shelley J. Listwan, Joseph B. Kuhns, and Lynn Exum. (2014). "Making Prisoners Accountable: Are Contingency Management Programs the Answer?" *Criminal Justice and Behavior*, 41:1079–1102.

Gendreau, Paul, Tracy Little, and Claire Goggin. 1996. "A Meta-Analysis of the Predictors of Adult Recidivism: What Works?" *Criminology* 34:575–607.

Gendreau, Paul, and Robert R. Ross. 1979. "Effective Correctional Treatment: Bibliotherapy for Cynics." *Crime & Delinquency* 25:463–489.

Gendreau, Paul, and Paula Smith. 2007. "Influencing the 'People Who Count': Some Perspectives on the Reporting of Meta-Analytic Results for Prediction and Treatment Outcomes with Offenders." *Criminal Justice and Behavior* 34:1536–1559.

Gendreau, Paul, and Paula Smith. 2012. "Assessment and Treatment Strategies for Correctional Institutions." In *Using Social Science to Reduce Violent Offending*, edited by Joel A. Dvoskin, Jennifer L. Skeem, Raymond W. Novaco, and Kevin S. Douglas. New York: Oxford University Press.

Gendreau, Paul, Paula Smith, and Sheila French. 2006. "The Theory of Effective Correctional Intervention: Empirical Status and Future Directions." In *Taking Stock: The Status of Criminological Theory*, Vol. 15, edited by Francis T. Cullen, John P. Wright, and Kristie R. Blevins. New Brunswick, NJ: Transaction.

Gendreau, Paul, and Yvette Thériault. 2011. "Bibliotherapy for Cynics Revisited: Commentary on One Year Longitudinal Study of the Psychological Effects of Administrative Segregation." Corrections and Mental Health Update. Washington, DC: National Institute of Corrections.

Goggin, Claire. 2009. "Is Prison 'Personality' Associated with Offender Recidivism?" PhD dissertation, University of New Brunswick, Fredericton, New Brunswick, Canada.

Grassian, Stuart. 1983. "Psychopathological Effects of Solitary Confinement." *American Journal of Psychiatry* 140:1450–1454.

Grassian, Stuart. 2010. " 'Fatal flaws' in the Colorado Solitary Confinement Study." Solitary Watch, November 15. http://solitarywatch.com/2010/11/15/fatal-flaws-in-the-colorado-solitary-confinement-study/.

Grassian, Stuart, and Nancy Friedman. 1986. *International Journal of Law and Psychiatry* 8:49–65.

Grassian, Stuart, and Terry Kupers. 2011. "The Colorado Study vs. the Reality of Supermax Confinement." *Correctional Mental Health Report* 13:1–16.

Gudjonsson, Gisli H. 1986. "The Relationship Between Interrogative Suggestibility and Acquiescence: Empirical Findings and Theoretical Implications." *Personality and Individual Differences* 7:195–99.

Gudjonsson, Gisli H. 1992. *The Psychology of Interrogations, Confessions and Testimony.* New York: John Wiley.

Gullone, Elenora, Tessa Jones, and Robert Cummings. 2000. "Coping Styles and Prison Experience as Predictors of Psychological Well-Being in Male Prisoners." *Psychiatry, Psychology, and Law* 7:170–181.

Haney, Craig. 1997. "Psychology and the Limits of Prison Pain: Confronting the Coming Crisis of the Eighth Amendment Law." *Psychology, Public Policy and Law* 3:499–588.

Haney, Craig. 2003. "Mental Health Issues in Long-Term Solitary and 'Supermax' Confinement." *Crime & Delinquency* 49:124–156.

Haney, Craig. 2008. "A Culture of Harm: Taming the Dynamics of Cruelty in Supermax Prisons." *Criminal Justice and Behavior* 35:956–984.

Haney, Craig. 2009. "The Social Psychology of Isolation: Why Solitary Confinement Is Psychologically Harmful." *Prison Service Journal* 181:12–20.

Haney, Craig. 2012. "Testimony of Professor Craig Haney to the Senate Judiciary Subcommittee on the Constitution, Civil Rights, and Human Rights Hearing on Solitary Confinement (June 19, 2012)." http://www.judiciary.senate.gov.

Haney, Craig, and Mona Lynch. 1997. "Regulating Prisons of the Future: A Psychological Analysis of Supermax and Solitary Confinement." *N.Y.U. Review of Law & Social Change* 23:477–570.

Haney, Craig, and Philip Zimbardo. 1998. "The Past and Future of U.S. Prison Policy: Twenty-Five Years After the Stanford Prison Experiment." *American Psychologist* 53:709–727.

Helson, Harry. 1964. *Adaptation-Level Theory.* New York: Harper & Row.

Hodgins, Sheilagh, and Gilles Côté. 1991. "The Mental Health of Penitentiary Inmates in Isolation." *Canadian Journal of Criminology* 33:175–182.

Hunter, John E., and Frank L. Schmidt. 2004. *Methods of Meta-Analysis: Correcting Error and Bias in Research Findings,* 2d ed. Newbury Park, CA: Sage.

Jackson, C. Wesley Jr., and E. Lowell Kelly. 1962. "Influence of Suggestion and Subjects' Prior Knowledge on Sensory Deprivation." *Science* 135:211–212.

Jackson, Michael. 1983. *Prisoners of Isolation: Solitary Confinement in Canada.* Toronto: University of Toronto Press.

Jackson, Michael. 2001. "The Psychological Effects of Administrative Segregation." *Canadian Journal of Criminology* 43:109–116.

Jaman, Dorothy R., Robert M. Dickover, and Lawrence A. Bennett. 1972. "Parole Outcome as a Function of Time Served." *British Journal of Criminology* 12:5–34.

Jonson, Cheryl L. 2010. "The Impact of Imprisonment on Reoffending: A Meta-Analysis." PhD dissertation, University of Cincinnati.

Kates, Graham. 2014. "Limiting Solitary." *The Crime Report* (January 31). http://www.thecri-mereport.org/news/inside-criminal-justice/2014-01-limiting-solitary.

Keim, Brandon. 2013. "The Horrible Psychology of Solitary Confinement." *Wired* (July 10). http://www.wired.com/2013/07/solitary-confinement-2/.

King, Kate, Benjamin Steiner, and Stephanie Ritchie-Breach. 2008. "Violence in the Supermax: A Self-Fulfilling Prophecy." *The Prison Journal* 88:144–168.

Kupers, Terry A. 2008. "What To Do with the Survivors? Coping with the Long-Term Effects of Isolated Confinement." *Criminal Justice and Behavior* 35:1005–1016.

Kupers, Terry A., Theresa Dronet, Margaret Winter, James Austin, Lawrence Kelly, William Cartier, Timothy J. Morris, Stephen F. Hanion, Emmitt L. Sparkman, Parveen Kumar, Leonard C. Vincent, Jim Norris, J. Kim Nagel, and Jennifer Mcbride. 2009. "Beyond Supermax Administrative Segregation: Mississippi's Experience Rethinking Prison Classification and Creating Alternative Mental Health Programs." *Criminal Justice and Behavior* 36:1037–1050.

Labrecque, Ryan M. (2015). *The Effect of Solitary Confinement on Institutional Misconduct: A Longitudinal Evaluation.* Washington, D.C.: U.S. Department of Justice.

Labrecque, Ryan M., Paula Smith, and Paul Gendreau. 2013. "The Effects of Solitary Confinement on Prisoners in Custodial Settings: A Meta-Analysis." Paper presented at the annual meeting of the Academy of Criminal Justice Sciences, Dallas, TX (March).

Liebling, A. 2008. "Incentives and Earned Privileges Revisited: Fairness, Discretion, and the Quality of Prison Life." *Journal of Scandinavian Studies in Criminology and Crime Prevention* 9:25–41.

Loftus, Elizabeth F. 2003. "Make-Believe Memories." *American Psychologist* 58:864–873.

Lovell, David, and Ron Jemelka. 1996. "When Inmates Misbehave: The Costs of Discipline." *The Prison Journal* 76:165–179.

Martinson, Robert. 1974. "What Works? Questions and Answers About Prison Reform." *Public Interest* 25:22–25.

Matson, Johnny L., and Thomas M. DiLorenzo. 1984. *Punishment and Its Alternatives: A New Perspective for Behavior Modification.* New York: Springer.

Mears, Daniel P., and William D. Bales. 2010. "Supermax Housing: Placement, Duration, and Time to Re-Entry." *Journal of Criminal Justice* 38:545–554.

Metcalf, Hope, Jamelia Morgan, Samuel Oliker-Friedland, Judith Resnik, Julia Spiegel, Haran Tae, Alyssa R. Work, and Brian Holbrook. 2013. *Administrative Segregation, Degrees of Isolation, and Incarceration: A National Overview of State and Federal Correctional Policies.* New Haven, CT: Liman Public Interest Program.

Metzner, Jeffrey L., and Maureen L. O'Keefe. 2011. "Psychological Effects of Administrative Segregation: The Colorado Study." *Correctional Mental Health Report* 13:1–2, 12–15.

Mohr, J. W. 1985. "The Long-Term Incarceration Issue: The Banality of Evil and the Pornography of Power." *Canadian Journal of Criminology* 27:103–112.

Morgan, Robert D., Stephanie A. Van Horn, Nina MacLean, Angelea Bolanos, Andrew L. Gray, Ashley Batastini, and Jeremy F. Mills. 2014. "Administrative Segregation: Is It a Harmful Correctional Practice?" Paper presented at the annual meeting of the American Psychology-Law Society, New Orleans, LA (March).

Myers, Thomas I. 1969. "Tolerance for Sensory and Perceptual Deprivation." In *Sensory Deprivation: Fifteen Years of Research,* edited by John P. Zubek. New York: Appleton-Century-Crofts.

Naday, Alexandra, Joshua D. Freilich, and Jeff Mellow. 2008. "The Elusive Data on Supermax Confinement." *The Prison Journal* 88:69–93.

Office of the Correctional Investigator. 2013. *Risky Business: An Investigation of the Treatment and Management of Chronic Self-Injury Among Federally Sentenced Women*. http://www.oci-bec.gc.ca/cnt/rpt/pdf/oth-aut/oth-aut20130930-eng.pdf.

O'Donnell, Ian. (2014). *Prisoners, Solitude, and Time*. Oxford, UK: Oxford University Press.

O'Keefe, Maureen L., Kelli J. Klebe, Jeffrey Metzner, Joel Dvoskin, Jamie Fellner, and Alysha Stucker. 2013. "A Longitudinal Study of Administrative Segregation." *Journal of the American Academy of Psychiatry and the Law* 41:49–60.

O'Keefe, Maureen L., Kelli J. Klebe, Alysha Stucker, Kristin Sturm, and William Leggett. 2010. *One Year Longitudinal Study of the Psychological Effects of Administrative Segregation*. Colorado Springs: Colorado Department of Corrections.

Orne, Martin T. 1962. "On the Social Psychology of the Psychological Experiment: With Particular Reference to Demand Characteristics and their Implications." *American Psychologist* 17:776–783.

Orne, Martin T., and Karl E. Scheibe. 1964. "The Contribution of Non-Deprivation Factors in the Production of Sensory Deprivation Effects: The Psychology of the 'Panic Button.'" *Journal of Abnormal Psychology* 68:3–12.

Palmer, Ted, Patricia Van Voorhis, Faye Taxman, and Doris McKenzie. 2012. "Insights from Ted Palmer: Experimental Criminology in a Different Era." *Journal of Experimental Criminology* 8:103–115.

Pizarro, Jesenia M., and Raymond M. Narag. 2008. "Supermax Prisons: What We Know, What We Do Not Know, and Where We Are Going." *The Prison Journal* 88:23–42.

Public Safety Canada. 2013. *Corrections and Conditional Release Statistical Overview*. https://www.publicsafety.gc.ca/cnt/rsrcs/pblctns/ccrso-2013/index-en.aspx.

Scharff-Smith, Peter. 2006. "The Effects of Solitary Confinement on Prison Inmates: A Brief History and Review of the Literature." In *Crime and Justice: A Review of Research*, Vol. 34, edited by Michael Tonry and Joan Petersilia. Chicago: University of Chicago Press.

Schmidt, Frank L. 1992. "What Do Data Really Mean? Research Findings, Meta-Analysis, and Cumulative Knowledge in Psychology." *American Psychologist* 47:1173–1181.

Smith, Paula, Paul Gendreau, and Claire Goggin. 2007. "'What Works' in Predicting Psychiatric Hospitalization and Relapse: The Specific Responsivity Dimension of Effective Correctional Treatment for Mentally Disordered Offenders." In *Corrections, Mental, and Social Policy: International Perspectives*, edited by Robert K. Ax and Thomas J. Fagan. Springfield, IL: Charles C. Thomas.

Smith, Paula, Claire Goggin, and Paul Gendreau. 2002. *The Effects of Prison Sentences and Intermediate Sanctions on Recidivism: General Effects and Individual Differences*. Ottawa, ON: Solicitor General Canada.

Steiner, Benjamin, and John Wooldredge. 2008. "Inmate Versus Facility Effects on Prison Rule Violations." *Criminal Justice and Behavior* 35:438–456.

Steiner, Benjamin, and John Wooldredge. 2009. "Re-Thinking the Link Between Institutional Crowding and Inmate Misconduct." *The Prison Journal* 89:205–233.

Stratton, George M. 1896. "Some Preliminary Experiments on Vision Without Inversion of the Retinal Image." *Psychological Review* 3:611–617.

Stubblefield, Roger. 2002. "Prisons Should Not Coddle Inmates." In *America's Prisons: Opposing Viewpoints*, edited by Roman Espejo. San Diego, CA: Greenhaven Press.

Suedfeld, Peter. 1975. "The Benefits of Boredom: Sensory Deprivation Reconsidered: The Effects of Monotonous Environments Are Not Always Negative; Sometimes Sensory Deprivation has High Utility." *American Scientist* 63:60–69.

Suedfeld, Peter. 1980. *Restricted Environmental Stimulation: Research and Clinical Applications.* New York: John Wiley.

Suedfeld, Peter, Carmenza Ramirez, John Deaton, and Gloria Baker-Brown. 1982. "Reactions and Attributes of Prisoners in Solitary Confinement." *Criminal Justice and Behavior* 9:303–340.

Thomas, Charles W., and Samuel C. Foster. 1973. "The Importation Model Perspective on Inmate Social Roles: An Empirical Test." *The Sociological Quarterly* 14:226–234.

Toch, Hans. 1984. "Quo Vadis?" *Canadian Journal of Criminology* 26:511–516.

Toch, Hans. 1992. *Living in Prison: The Ecology of Survival.* Washington, DC: American Psychological Association.

Valera, Pamela, & Kates-Benman, Cheryl L. (2015). Exploring the Use of Special Housing Units by Men Released from New York Correctional Facilities: A Small Mixed-Methods Study. *American Journal of Men's Health.* Advance on-line publication.

Vantour, James A. 1975. *Report of the Study Group on Dissociation.* Ottawa, ON: Solicitor General Canada.

Walker, J., C. Illingworth, A. Canning, E. Garner, J. Woolley, P. Taylor, and T. Amos. 2014. "Changes in Mental State Associated with Prison Environments: A Systematic Review." *Acta Psychiatrica Scandinavica* 129:427–436.

Ward, David A., and Thomas G. Werlich. 2003. "Alcatraz and Marion: Evaluating Supermaximum Custody." *Punishment & Society* 5:53–75.

Wright, Kevin N. 1991. "A Study of Individual, Environmental, and Interactive Effects in Explaining Adjustment to Prison." *Justice Quarterly* 8:217–242.

Wormith, J. Stephen. (1984). The controversy over the effects of long-term incarceration. *Canadian Journal of Criminology* 26:423-437.

Wormith, J. Stephen, Marie-Claude Tellier, and Paul Gendreau. 1988. "Characteristics of Protective Custody Offenders in a Provincial Correctional Center." *Canadian Journal of Criminology* 30:39–58.

Wortley, Richard. 2002. *Situational Prison Control: Crime Prevention in Correctional Institutions.* Cambridge, UK: Cambridge University Press.

Zamble, Edward. 1992. "Behavior and Adaptation in Long-Term Prison Inmates: Descriptive Longitudinal Results." *Criminal Justice and Behavior* 19:409–425.

Zamble, Edward, and Frank J. Porporino. 1988. *Coping, Behavior, and Adaptation in Prison Inmates.* New York: Springer-Verlag.

Zamble, Edward, and Frank J. Porporino. 1990. "Coping, Imprisonment, and Rehabilitation." *Criminal Justice and Behavior* 17:53–70.

Zinger, Ivan. 2013. "Segregation in Canadian Federal Corrections: A Prison Ombudsman's Perspective." Paper presented at the International Conference on Human Rights and Solitary Confinement, Winnipeg, Manitoba, Canada (March).

Zinger, Ivan, Cherami Wichmann, and Don A. Andrews. (2001). The Psychological Effects of 60 Days in Administrative Segregation. *Canadian Journal of Criminology* 43(1): 47-83.

Zubek, John P. 1964. "Behavioral and EEG Changes after 14 Days of Perceptual Deprivation." *Psychonomic Science* 1:57–58.

Zubek, John P. 1969. *Sensory Deprivation: Fifteen Years of Research.* New York: Appleton-Century-Crofts.

Zubek, John P., L. Bayer, S. Milstein, and Jean M. Shephard. 1969. "Behavioral and Physiological Changes During Prolonged Immobilization Plus Perceptual Deprivation." *Journal of Abnormal Psychology* 74:230–236.

Zubek, John P., L. Bayer, and Jean M. Shephard. 1969. "Relative Effects of Prolonged Social Isolation and Confinement: Behavioral and EEG Changes." *Journal of Abnormal Psychology* 74:625–631.

Zuckerman, Marvin. 1969. "Variables Affecting Deprivation Results." In *Sensory Deprivation: Fifteen Years of Research*, edited by John P. Zubek. New York: Meredith.

CHAPTER 17

....

A COMPARISON OF BRITISH AND AMERICAN POLICIES FOR MANAGING DANGEROUS PRISONERS

A Question of Legitimacy

....

ROY D. KING

THERE has been a long history of cross-fertilization of penological ideas between Britain and the United States, but the traffic has been mostly from west to east. Nevertheless, Britain[1] and the United States have followed different paths in their attempts at dealing with difficult and dangerous prisoners, and those exchanging the ideas have not always understood the context within which the other's contributions were made. In the United States, high-security prison policies have tended to be driven by the pursuit of *order and control within the walls* while coincidentally also dealing with the containment of escape-prone prisoners. In Britain, policies have been driven primarily by fears about prisoners *getting over the walls*, in a search for security procedures that would prevent escapes, and only secondarily by behaviors inside prison, which latterly at least have been dealt with separately. Escape fears have loomed less large in America, in part because of the presence in most states of armed perimeter guards: in Britain, prison officers were required to give up their firearms in 1953. Issues of security have often been conflated conceptually with questions of order and control—not surprisingly because some prisoners, probably a rather small minority, will be both escape risks and control risks. However, the degree of overlap is an empirical question that needs to be established, not simply assumed, and basing policies on wrong assumptions can call their legitimacy into question. The notion of *legitimacy* used here broadly rests on the three criteria required by Beetham (1991), namely conformity to rules, the justifiability of those rules in terms of shared beliefs, and the expression of consent. It is useful to maintain the distinction between escape risks and control risks because the policy solutions to them seem to be different. In a word, the solution to issues of escapes lies in expensive technology, and parsimony would dictate a policy of concentration in as few facilities as possible. The solution to issues of order and control, on the other hand, lies in better management throughout the system, and for small numbers of the most difficult to manage prisoners, this is best provided in small, differentiated units. Failure to distinguish between security and control issues clearly has bedeviled policies in both countries and led to misunderstandings on both sides of the Atlantic.

Rather than listing policy developments in these areas in the two countries separately, this essay is organized in three chronological periods—from 1960 to 1979, from 1980 to the mid-1990s, and from the mid-1990s to the present day—in the hope that moving the discussion between the two countries will better bring out the similarities and differences.

I. The Period from 1960 to 1979

Until the 1960s, Britain had no exceptionally high-security prisons: there were closed prisons, with walls around them, and open prisons, surrounded at best by fences beyond which prisoners were trusted not to go. There was no security categorization and no attempt to identify prisoners in terms of the control problems they presented. Instead, different classes of prisoner were identified in part by the sentence of the court—with or without hard labor, or preventive detention, for example—and by whether they were in prison for the first time ("stars") or had been so sentenced previously ("ordinaries"). Whether a prisoner could be transferred to an open prison depended on local judgments on whether he or she could be trusted, the stage of sentence reached, and various restrictions agreed with the local community.

All of this began to change on August 12, 1964, when Charles Wilson, one of the "great train robbers," escaped from Winson Green prison assisted by underworld colleagues who broke into the prison and unlocked his cell. The mail train robbery netted £2.6 million (£45 million, or $70 million in today's money), but the 30-year sentences handed down by the courts were unprecedented, and the fact that big money was available on the outside to fund organized escape attempts caught the Prison Service unprepared. Then-Assistant Under-Secretary of State at the Home Duncan Fairn phoned Myrl Alexander, the mild-mannered professorial director of the Federal Bureau of Prisons (BoP) seeking friendly advice. "Come on Duncan," said Alexander. "You know the answer to that one. All you gotta do is put some damn guns up on your towers!" (Author interview with Alexander 13th July 1984). This is a minor example of not knowing where the other is coming from, but British prisons do not have towers.

The following year Ronnie Biggs, another of the train robbers, escaped from Wandsworth prison by scrambling up rope ladders thrown over the wall and on to the roof of a furniture removal van parked outside by accomplices.[2] Fairn dispatched Hugh Kenyon, a member of the Prisons Board, to the States to see what could be gleaned from American experience, though it is not entirely clear with what result. According to Alexander, however, the incident caused some amusement, not to say disbelief, among his security colleagues.

Three temporary special wings were hastily created, with an overbearing staff presence and exceedingly restrictive regimes. But worse was to come. In 1966 the spy George Blake, sentenced to an exceptional forty-two years, escaped from Wormwood Scrubs prison and made his way to the Soviet Union.[3] Two days later, Earl Mountbatten of Burma was appointed to conduct an inquiry into prison escapes and security. His report (Home Office 1966) essentially comprised two sets of recommendations: first, that prisoners should be classified into four categories—A to D—according to their likelihood of making escape bids and the threat they would pose to the public, the police, and the state should they be successful (paras. 212, 217), and second, that prisons should be graded according to their level of security and that the highest security risk prisoners in Category A (of whom he estimated there would be no more than 120 for the whole of England and Wales) should be concentrated in a new fortress prison (paras. 212, 215), to which a second could be added, if needed (para. 214). As Price (2000) has noted, Mountbatten is chiefly remembered for the second of these proposals, even though it was never acted upon, whereas the first, which was implemented and remains in force, has attracted less attention.

Mountbatten's analysis of security risks and how to house them appropriately was a task he accomplished better than anyone before or since. However, the recommendation for a fortress prison was ridiculed by the liberal press and criminologists (Fowler 1967; Klare 1968; Taylor 1968; Morris 1968; Cohen and Taylor 1972; Taylor et al. 1975) but, as I have argued elsewhere, most of the criticisms were ill founded (King and Elliot 1977; King and Morgan 1980), not least because there is an important distinction to be made between the particulars of Mountbatten's *prison design*, on the one hand, and the *policy of concentrating escape risks* in one prison, or more as needed, on the other. Unfairly, Mountbatten— a second cousin of the queen, Admiral of the Fleet, and the last viceroy of India—was regarded by his critics as having no qualifications to speak on prison matters. It is thus worth remembering that he castigated the conditions in the special wings, and the plan for a new high-security prison was already part of the Prison Department's policy in the wake of the escapes. Moreover, he not only eschewed arming guards (para. 294) but insisted that his proposals not affect the rest of the system and its policies on employment, education, and rehabilitation (para. 14). Indeed, Mountbatten argued in his report that many prisoners currently housed in closed prisons could be safely transferred to open prisons (para. 208). Finally, he was the first to advocate for a professional head of the Prison Service (as distinct from a career civil servant; para. 251) and for the inspection of prisons (para. 238) although, confusingly, he rather conflated those roles. It was another fifteen years before a system of independent inspection was established and more than a quarter of a century before the idea of a professional prisons person as head of the service became the norm. It is important to note that Mountbatten made no mention of control problems, for the good reason that there was no serious problem of order and control in British prisons at that time.

Home Secretary Jenkins, aware of the concerns expressed by many about Mountbatten's proposed fortress prison, referred the matter of the regime for prisoners in long-term imprisonment to the Advisory Council on the Penal System. They delegated the matter to a subcommittee under the chairmanship of Leon Radzinowicz, then director of the Institute of Criminology in Cambridge,[4] and the subcommittee visited many prisons in the United States, specifically for our purposes here, the Federal penitentiaries at Lewisburg, Terre Haute, and Marion. In my 1984 interview, Myrl Alexander recalled that the group was particularly interested in the closure of Alcatraz and what had happened to the prisoners who had been housed there. When informed that the subcommittee was told that most had been transferred to other penitentiaries without causing serious problems and that this had been interpreted as evidence in favor of dispersal over concentration, Alexander suggested that it was an oversimplification and only partly reflected the bureau's position at that time. Alcatraz closed because the structure was crumbling away and the cost of shipping fresh water and supplies across San Francisco Bay had become prohibitive. Moreover, Alexander continued, Alcatraz had served mostly as a *symbolic* way of dealing with notorious gangsters like Machine Gun Kelly and Al Capone, who were not necessarily difficult prisoners (see also Ward and Kassebaum 2009), and its soulless regime was intended as a deterrent to others.

The original plans for replacing Alcatraz involved building a single penitentiary at Marion, Illinois, but in the event, Marion opened "without the intended surrounding wall" in what Norman Johnston (1973, p. 62) called "a determined attempt to break away from the more traditional architectural treatment of very high security facilities." Not surprisingly, in the words of Ward and Breed (1984, p. 2), Alcatraz prisoners "were seen as posing too severe a test for a new facility" and instead were transferred back to the Federal penitentiaries at Leavenworth and Atlanta from which most had come. Bureau of Prisons Research Analyst Larry Karacki, in an unpublished internal report (Karacki 1984b, p. 65), noted that the general operating philosophy of the bureau at that time was that "as long as appropriate security at the perimeter is established and maintained, a fairly open and relaxed atmosphere can be provided within the institution" and that "institutional control" could be "based upon interpersonal relationships with inmates." Alexander conceded that the bureau had difficulties in reconciling the dead-end image of Alcatraz with more high-minded concerns of the rehabilitative ideal and so the Radzinwicz sub-committee could have felt that this supported their conclusion that it was better to disperse such prisoners rather than to concentrate them. But he pointed out that the bureau was already experiencing problems that were leading to a rethink, and, as Ward and Breed noted, "by the late 60s" (i.e., around the time of the Radzinowicz visit), some of the ex-Alcatraz prisoners began to be transferred to Marion.

Ultimately, however, it is less important whether Radzinowicz tapped into the end of a fairly brief experiment than that there was a lack of clarity—on both sides of the Atlantic—about the presenting problems. On the American side, the position was neatly characterized by Karacki (1984a, p. 9): "In the Federal Prison System, while one can draw a distinction between [security level (escape risks) and custody level (disciplinary problems)], they ultimately tend to mesh together at the top and consequently are more or less treated as one and the same—penitentiary-type inmates." The Radzinowicz subcommittee, like Mountbatten before it, was dealing with the regime for escape-risk prisoners, but its recommendations were predicated on the anticipatory fear that putting them all together in a single prison would be unmanageable for staff (Advisory Council on the Penal System 1968, paras. 34–38)—in other words, it simply assumed that escape risks either already had control problems or else would develop them if lumped together. In both countries, this failure to think through the implications of the distinction led to serious problems in the management of difficult and dangerous prisoners.

By the late 1960s and early 1970s, growing racial tensions had led to an increase of violent incidents in Federal penitentiaries with a number of inmate deaths (see Mears and Cochran in this volume). In July 1972 a de facto return to a policy of concentration was affected when H Unit at Marion was reconfigured as a control unit, to which the most difficult prisoners were transferred. In the early days, according to Karacki (1984b, p. 70), it was said "that white inmates at Marion try to escape, Mexicans run drugs and rackets, and blacks look to do easy time." But that did not last long, and the next decade saw a significant increase in activities by gangs, usually organized along racial lines, such as the Aryan Brotherhood, the Mexican Mafia, the Black Guerilla Family, and myriad offshoots and local chapters, whose rivalries have caused major difficulties both in state and Federal institutions. In 1979, in an attempt to preserve order in the rest of the system, a new classification of prisons and prisoners was introduced by the bureau that placed Marion as the only Level VI establishment, in which there was a buildup of the most difficult prisoners, including many whom state systems were unable to control. There are few research studies that have analyzed the effect of these changes on the experience of imprisonment, although some sense of this can be found in Irwin (1970, 1980) and Jacobs (1974, 1977, 1983).

In Britain, surprising though it may seem, the loss of order happened even more quickly, but it was a loss of order of a different kind. Whereas in the United States the problems involved random, apparently noninstrumental though often drug-related violence and intergang rivalries and killings, in Britain the disorder largely took the form of organized protests, initially inspired by a fledgling prisoners' rights movement but that sometimes descended into riots and the destruction of whole sections of prisons (see also Adams 1992). Radzinowicz (Advisory Council on the Penal System 1968) had proposed that the 138 prisoners who had been identified as Category A—the highest security risk—should be dispersed among (para. 62) and occasionally transferred between (para. 154) three or four prisons with strengthened perimeter security. There they would experience a liberal regime within a secure perimeter (para. 48), which would include observation towers (para. 53) manned by armed officers (para. 61)[5]. It was assumed that any threat posed by Category A prisoners would be diluted by the presence of a majority of lower security risk prisoners, but any who became recalcitrant would be moved as necessary into segregation units within each dispersal prison (para. 164). The first prisoners were transferred from the special wings to Parkhurst, Wakefield, and Wormwood Scrubs with newly strengthened perimeters. Gartree and Hull were added in 1969 and Albany in 1970, doubling the minimum size of the system that Radzinowicz had envisaged from three to six. At first there was a genuine attempt to make the system work in accordance with the Radzinowicz proposals, and the dispersal prisons held Category B and C prisoners and even some Category D prisoners who would normally have been eligible for open conditions. A standard Category A regime was introduced with prisoners able to spend a great deal of time outside their cells and relative freedom of movement to and from a wide variety of program activities, as well as to central dining halls.

During these years no prisoner escaped from the dispersal prisons, but these prisons soon became the locations of the most serious disturbances and riots: at Parkhurst in October 1969, Albany in August 1972, Gartree in November 1972, Hull in August and September 1976, Gartree again in 1978, Parkhurst again in March 1979, Hull again in April 1979, and Wormwood Scrubs in August 1979 (see Home Office 1984, Annex D). The response of the Prison Service started from the assumption that the mayhem was caused by a few troublemakers, and the ringleaders, once identified, were transferred from one dispersal segregation unit to another at three monthly intervals—what eventually became known officially as the Continuous Assessment Scheme and to prisoners as the Magic Roundabout. The liberal regime, however, was whittled away and the security of the perimeter moved ever closer to the interior of the prisons. Movement was restricted, activities and programs were curtailed, and prisoners spent more time in their cells, including during meals. The lower security risk prisoners in Category D and Category C were gradually removed from the system. Briefly, in 1974, two control units were announced, although one was never used and the other was abandoned after a storm of protest. It is perhaps easy to see from this distance that these measures mirrored some of the American experience, though remarkably the

Prison Service did not question the dispersal policy itself, instead arguing that *more* dispersal prisons were required, especially ones that were built specifically for that purpose: Long Lartin had been added in 1973, and two new prisons—Frankland and Full Sutton soon followed. At its height, with only modest increases in the number of Category A prisoners, the planned dispersal system had grown to nine prisons—three times the minimum envisaged by Radzinowicz. It housed, as a matter of policy, large numbers of prisoners in conditions of security that, by definition, they did not need. The logic of Mountbatten, which linked the security risk of prisoners to the security of prisons in which they were housed, had been turned on its head. The fears about disorder that had been entertained for a policy of concentration had turned out to be the defining attribute of a policy of dispersal.

One of the few accounts that attempted a conceptual analysis of riots in the dispersal system is King and Elliot's (1977) study of Albany. They located the problem in the operation of the dispersal policy itself. They hypothesized that prisoners who caused trouble in prisons were not necessarily the same as those who were most at risk of escape, and they advocated that the Prison Service classify prisoners in terms of their prison behavior as well as likelihood of escape. But they also hypothesized that a prisoner might be "difficult" in one setting but not in another, so that any classification by behavior needed to be context specific and allow for an individual to change. The point of such a classification would be to keep incompatible individuals or groups separate from one another, they suggested, but carried no necessary implication for more restrictive regimes. They also argued that riots and disturbances are best understood in terms of the relations between staff and prisoners in situations not wholly within their own control. In 1979 this analysis was presented to the May Committee of Inquiry, which had been created in the wake of industrial disputes amounting to a struggle between the Prison Officers' Association and prison governors (wardens) over who managed the prisons. In spite of a vigorous defense of dispersal by the Home Office (1979b), it was fairly clear that the two main principles underlining the policy—that of absorbing difficult prisoners among lower security prisoners and that of a liberal regime within a secure perimeter—were incompatible. The committee, however, recommended that "in present operational conditions" the dispersal policy should be retained not so much because of "the strength of the arguments in favour of dispersal but of those against concentration" (Home Office 1979a, para. 6.72). The most important of those arguments against concentration was undoubtedly the possibility of an armed attack by the Irish Republican Army (IRA) on a single maximum-security prison, which at that time would have included a significant number of Irish "terrorists." In truth there was some merit to that position—the loss of such a prison to terrorist action would have been hugely embarrassing as well as a danger to the police and the public—although, as the committee conceded, Mountbatten had acknowledged the potential need for a second such prison.

II. The Period from 1980 to the Mid-1990s

By 1980 the BoP in the United States had returned to a policy of concentration for prisoners who were deemed to be uncontrollable in ordinary penitentiaries—but life in the Marion Control Unit was far from stable. In Britain, the dispersal policy for escape-risk prisoners continued--at least in name—but problems of order remained endemic. One of the more curious developments in Britain was that the Prison Service had begun to allocate some non-Category A prisoners to the dispersal prisons not because they would "dilute" the control problem in line with Radzinowicz thinking but because they "needed" dispersal level security due to their difficult behaviors (King and Morgan 1980; see also Price 2000). Indeed, it is hard at this point to distinguish between the British policy and the characterization by Karacki (1984a, p. 9) of bureau policy whereby escape risks and control risks were "treated more or less the same—as penitentiary type inmates"—except, of course, that the British dispersal policy still kept large numbers of prisoners in conditions of security higher than they needed.

The dispersal prisons continued to simmer, and in May 1983 a major incident in Albany was followed by another in Wormwood Scrubs. In September of that year the Prison Service established the Control Review Committee (CRC) to consider "the maintenance of control in the prison system . . . with particular reference to the dispersal system." In October Home Secretary Leon Brittan, reflecting the emergence of a tougher stance on law and order, announced restrictions on the parole eligibility for long-term prisoners, and this added urgency to the committee's task. The Report of the CRC (Home Office 1984) was a masterpiece of diplomacy. The authors deftly suggested that a solution to the concentration versus dispersal debate had to wait on the development of a prison design that avoided the criticisms of Mountbatten's fortress yet could meet the criteria of Radzinowicz's aspiration for a liberal regime. That design they found in a particular example of a so-called "new generation" prison at Oak Park Heights in Minnesota.

Oak Park Heights opened as a state-of-the-art new-generation maximum-security prison in 1982, after the neighboring old-style penitentiary at Stillwater had suffered a sea of troubles including homicides, suicides, and gang activities (see Ward and Schoen 1981). Only the low-level administration building of Oak Park Heights can be seen from the road; behind and below that is the main prison. A chain of seven self-contained living "complexes," plus a mental health unit and an infirmary, linked by "racetrack" corridors, actually constitute the perimeter. A single armed guard can patrol the entire prison from the flat roofs. Because it was built into the contours of the hillside, the prison is "earth sheltered" on three sides, and a high wall completes the perimeter defense on the fourth side. The corridors are on two levels: one at ground floor for prisoners and above that one for staff only; these give access to all of the prison's facilities. Prisoners enter their complex via an electronically controlled sally port next to a security bubble, which has sightlines along the corridor as well as virtually complete observation of the interior of the living unit. The seven living units each have 52 single cells arranged in small groups on two tiers along one wall, and each cell has a window looking out over the central area of the prison. Immediately outside each group of cells is a small recreation–cum–dining area with fixed tables and chairs, which is only for the use of those occupants. Between these "defendables," as they are known in the local argot, and the security bubble lies a larger communal area, shared by both staff and prisoners. Each complex has a servery with cooking facilities, a television room, a fitness room, and a laundry.

From the security point of view there is no possibility of escaping by digging tunnels through the hillside from the closely observed corridor to which prisoners have only limited controlled access. On the other hand, the prisoners do have relatively free access to an enclosed recreation area immediately outside each complex, and on a more limited basis to the large central area with a running track and baseball diamond, but this only takes them further away from the perimeter. From a regime point of view, Oak Park Heights offers secure access to facilities that can be operated flexibly. Immediately above each complex there is an area for daytime activity—initially three complexes were given over to industries, one to education, and another to sex offender and drug dependency programs. Complex 6 was for segregation and Complex 7 for prisoners engaged in services, such as cleaners (known locally as "swampers") and kitchen workers. Apart from those in "services," prisoners do not have to leave their complex for these activities but simply ascend a staircase: similarly, staff, including those in the security bubbles, can use their own staircases to observe the workshops or classrooms.

The prison was born amid controversy. Why did Minnesota, with one of the lowest incarceration rates, need such a secure prison? The decision to build was regretted by some because, during the long planning and building process, Frank Wood, who was to become the charismatic first warden of Oak Park Heights, had succeeded in returning Stillwater to a state of good order. However, anyone visiting Oak Park Heights and Stillwater in 1983 would have no doubt as to which offered the better security or safer and more rewarding regimes. Wood enjoyed the luxury of interviewing all the staff for the new prison, whom he eyeballed and declared that he wanted them to treat prisoners as they would want their fathers, brothers, or sons to be treated if they were in prison. He also insisted that staff must not retreat behind physical or electronic barriers but instead seek close working relationships with prisoners. To that end, the staffing of each living unit comprised one officer in the bubble and two on the floor sharing space with prisoners. Members of the CRC were informed of the preliminary findings from King's study of Oak Park Heights and looked forward to the results from his proposed comparative study of Gartree dispersal prison. In what is still the only direct comparison of a British and American maximum security prison, King (1991) was able to show that Oak Park Heights in 1984 was more secure, safer for both staff and prisoners, and provided a much fuller and more varied regime than Gartree in 1986.

Oak Park Heights not only attracted the attention of the British but became a prison of great interest to the Federal BoP, because of growing tension in Marion, including rising levels of assaults on staff, hostage takings, and killings of prisoners. Things came to a head at Marion on October 22, 1983, when Officers Clutts and Hoffman were stabbed to death in separate but near-identical incidents. Marion Control Unit went into complete long-term lock down. Norman Carlson, then director of the BoP, was considering whether Oak Park Heights could be transferred to the Federal jurisdiction.[6] Although the living units of some Federal facilities—for example, Butner, Otisville, and Pleasanton—shared some of the new-generation features of Oak Park Heights, none was suitable as a maximum-security prison. The bureau then decided to build its own new administrative segregation (ADX) facility at Florence in Colorado to replace Marion. But by the time that was built, the notion of "new-generation" architecture had morphed into the idea of "supermax" prisons, and there was a headlong charge into the proliferation of last-resort prisons (King 1999). According to Riveland (National Institute of Corrections 1997), nineteen states had established supermax facilities before the Federal Bureau built their ADX in Florence, and this was followed by more than a dozen others in short order. The claim that such facilities were for the "worst of the worst," based on the notion that "bad behavior gets you in and good behavior gets you out," and offered little or nothing in the way of privileges or programs provided politicians and administrators alike with a self-validating demonstration of the "new penology" in action.

Insofar as the driving forces of supermax custody have any intellectual underpinnings, they probably come from John DiIulio's (1987) comparative study of prison governance in California, Texas, and Michigan. DiIulio famously claimed that American prisons had failed (and thereby allowed gang culture to flourish) "because they have been ill-managed, under managed or not managed at all" (DiIulio 1987, p. 7). There was much to be said for his diagnosis. My own impressions, at that time, were that few Departments of Correction exerted much control over individual prisons with the result that wardens often had, for good or ill, considerable freedom. Wardens in turn often exerted little supervision over what went on in living units, which might be managed by sergeants with occasional, but often predictable, visits by a lieutenant. DiIulio was highly critical of both rehabilitative rhetoric and sociological attempts at understanding the prisoner community. He was particularly scathing about the work of Clemmer (1940) and Sykes (1968), for example, which, in his view, had led to a laissez faire style of management that accommodated inmate culture. But his conclusions that prisons should be run by highly disciplined authorities who are strong enough to control prisoners but obliged to control themselves, and that the aims of imprisonment should be limited to the delivery of order, amenity, and services, have had unfortunate consequences. As Sparks, Bottoms, and Hay (1996, p. 84) have pointed out, the prime legitimating principle underlying his control model is "efficient service delivery and consistent application of known rules, anything more is unrealistic." In many supermax prisons, amenity in DiIulio's terms often amounts to no more than "three hots and a cot" (though by the time the meals arrive they are often cold and the cot is made of poured concrete), and services are at best negligible and often nonexistent. Order is maintained by extreme situational control backed up by the reiteration of the company line that "bad behavior gets you in and good behavior gets you out" and a constant assertion that prisoners simply need to obey the rules. Given that it is often not true that "bad behavior gets you in" and getting out is often at the arbitrary discretion of staff, and that the rules are often irrational and disproportionate, it is not hard to see how there is a significant legitimacy gap. Such an approach also shows the same kind of error about the mainsprings of human motivation and behavior that economists so frequently make about the rational nature of markets.

It could be said that management in supermax facilities have fulfilled DiIulio's hope that they are mostly strong enough to control prisoners, but they have frequently failed in their obligation for staff to control themselves. Some of the worst examples of abuse have been found in California at Pelican Bay, although many others could be cited from elsewhere. In 1995, in *Madrid v. Gomez*,[7] Federal District Court Judge Thelton Henderson, in an extensive judgment that took in not just deliberate acts of brutality and excessive use of force but also the general regime in the Special Housing Unit (SHU) found the latter to "hover on the edge of what is humanly tolerable for those with normal resilience" (*Madrid v. Gomez* 1995, p. 1280). However, with a reluctant nod toward the rights of individual states to determine their own policies within the federal union, Judge Henderson ruled that those conditions did not breach Eighth Amendment protections against cruel and unusual punishment because it had not been demonstrated that they created "a sufficiently high risk to *all* inmates of incurring a serious mental illness" (p. 1267, emphasis added). I have argued elsewhere both that the judgment sets a legal standard for Eighth Amendment rights that would be extremely difficult to meet (King 2005) and that what went on in Pelican Bay in relation to suspected gang members (see also Reiter 2012) may have subliminally prepared the public for—if not quite legitimated—the abuses of suspects at Abu Graib and detainees in Guantanamo Bay in the post 9/11 "war on terror" (King 2008). However, it is important to note that the Madrid Court did set an important precedent, since upheld by other decisions, concerning prisoners with mental illness in supermax, although the problem has not gone away because of poor mental health screening and lack of other facilities.

Back in Britain, the CRC marked a watershed in the development of policy. It assumed that the actual need for very high security accommodation was "unlikely to be more than 300–400" prisoners and recommended that the possibility of accommodating them in two small new-generation prisons be "urgently examined" (Home Office 1984, para. 20). It acknowledged that the dispersal system had grown because of a mistaken assumption that each dispersal prison should have "no more than a small pre-determined percentage [about 10 percent] of Category A prisoners" (para. 129). In the same paragraph, the committee recognized that it was now "a truism that many prisoners requiring high security do not present a control threat" and that it was the proportion of high control-risk prisoners rather than high security-risk prisoners that was at issue. While it was important to separate control-risk prisoners from the rest of the population, this did not require "entire new prisons" but could instead be managed in "smaller specialized plant[s]" (para. 129).

The CRC recommended the immediate reduction of the dispersal system to seven prisons (para. 135) and proposed several measures for dealing with the control problem. These included better central assessment and allocation policies (para. 134), clearer incentives for good behavior (para. 133), and the creation of a small number of specialized units offering different programs for those disruptive prisoners who did not respond to these other initiatives (para. 135). The committee rejected the notion of developing a control classification, preferring a more flexible analysis of, and response to, problems as they arose (para. 88); it also rejected the idea that any of the new units should be either punitive in intent or last-resort control units (paras. 66–67). Instead, the proposed new units would be developed with advisory input from academics, in an attempt to evolve a range of complementary regimes from which prisoners could be returned to normal locations with the general population, and they would be subject to evaluation as part of a wider program of independent research (paras. 69 and 119).

The CRC had visited many establishments in the United States other than Oak Park Heights and had high-level discussions with senior academics as well as prison administrators.[8] Its report was certainly read in Washington, DC. But it seems to have had a slightly odd reception. In a thoughtful unpublished internal paper comparing the Federal experience of controlling dangerous prisoners with that of the British Prison Department, Karacki (1984a, p. 9) mistakenly attributed the problems of the dispersal system to the British distinction between "security cases (escape risks) and control cases (disciplinary problems)." "It would be fine" he wrote, "if one could see some demonstrated value in this approach, but it appears instead to be a source of confusion and continuing problems." In fact, the analysis of the CRC (and of this essay) is the very opposite: the initial *failure* to distinguish between security and control risks was a major cause of the problems of the dispersal system; making the distinction clear offered a possible solution. Ironically, Karacki (1984a, p. 10) found that Marion (to which both control risks and escape risks had been allocated) suffered much the same problems as the dispersal prisons and "moved from an open regime to semi-lockdown to total lockdown operation with a corresponding decrease in programs." Nevertheless, Karacki concluded that the CRC's proposal that instead of a control unit it should create "a number of fairly experimental specialized units providing different programs and levels of custody within a prison setting" went "beyond what we have attempted at the federal level, except at Butner and Springfield. If actually implemented, these experimental units could be a valuable source of information and program ideas about disciplinary cases and for this reason should be carefully monitored" (Karacki 1984a, p. 11).

It would be a mistake to pretend that the CRC report solved all of Britain's problems. There was resistance within the Prison Service by the defenders of the dispersal system—if only on the basis of "the devil you know" and the costs of change. However, a working party set up to study new generation design (Home Office 1985) agreed that "Oak Park Heights . . . offers a valuable model of the application of new generation concepts to a maximum security establishment" (Home Office 1985, p. 93). But although new-generation concepts influenced the design of lower security establishments, Britain has never built a new-generation maximum-security prison.[9] If the CRC's hope that the dispersal system would be replaced by two new-generation prisons never came to fruition, the report marked the end of expansion and the beginning of consolidation into a much more compact high-security estate. Nor could it be said that the CRC units provided an immediate answer to control problems. The full range of units was never established. It was hard to resist staff and union pressures to create something like an American-style control unit, and various euphemisms were sought to provide one small unit with a deliberately "structured" and "austere" regime. Another unit was for prisoners with mental health problems, which in effect was a reinvention of an earlier experiment. A third involved a regime based on psychological counseling and social learning. A planned fourth unit with more specialized psychological interventions never got off the ground, and a fifth that might have resembled the famous Barlinnie unit in Scotland (see Cooke 1989) was from the start politically unacceptable because it involved prisoners in some decision-making. The units were duly evaluated (Bottomley 1995). For the most part, they seemed to do a reasonably good job with the small number of prisoners they dealt with, but they were seen as remote by dispersal prison governors who continued to rely on transfers under the continuous assessment scheme, which the CRC had hoped to avoid. There was also a danger that the units could seem to be rewarding bad behavior with better regimes, which would be hard to justify. However, the operation and evaluation of the units did provide an experience from which the Prison Service learned a great deal.

The other recommendations of the CRC, including better assessment and allocation procedures and sending the right signals through rationalizing incentives to good behavior, seemed to quiet things down in the high-security prisons, but there were serious problems elsewhere in the system. A quarter of a century of underinvestment had led to overcrowding and poor sanitation, especially in the local remand prisons, and the impoverishment of regimes in prisons of all types (see King and McDermott 1989). Things came to a head in Strangeways prison in Manchester in April 1990 when rooftop protests developed into a 25-day siege that sparked sympathy riots in several other establishments. An important public inquiry was conducted by Lord Justice Woolf. Prominent in the evidence to the inquiry were the preliminary findings from the work by Bottoms and colleagues (Bottoms 1992; Sparks, Bottoms, and Hay 1996) arising from their comparison of two dispersal prisons, the riot-prone Albany and Long Lartin, one of only two dispersals that had escaped serious disturbances. It was expected that close study would reveal a list of things to avoid from the experience of Albany and a replicable formula for success from Long Lartin. However, their research, which had been sponsored by the CRC, produced surprising results. Albany was unpopular with prisoners, but its restrictive, "situational" approach to restoring and maintaining order was effective. Long Lartin's more "social" approach based on more relaxed interpersonal relationships was popular with prisoners, but a number of problems lurked beneath the surface. Neither regime was fully successful in establishing its legitimacy, they argued, and they suggested (unlike DiIulio in the United States) that elements of *both* approaches were essential to good governance.

The concept of *legitimacy* loomed large in the thinking enshrined in Lord Justice Woolf's report (Home Office 1991), and for the first time there was an overwhelming consensus in the evidence from academic research, nongovernmental organizations concerned with human rights and prison reform, and senior figures in the administration of prisons about the way forward. Underlying the concept of legitimacy were the notions of rationality, proportionality of the regime to the nature of the risks, and the sense of fairness and consistency in what, after all, was a key part of the criminal *justice* system—in a word, its *justifiability*. This was essentially summed up by Woolf as the need to hold security, control, and justice in proper balance.[10] The Woolf report was, somewhat surprisingly, embraced by the Conservative Home Secretary Kenneth Baker in a new White Paper, and the Criminal Justice Act of 1991 sought, in part, to bring down the prison population through what came to be called proportionate or "principled" sentencing. But the consensus was short-lived. Baker's successor, Kenneth Clarke, reviewed, and in part reversed, the Criminal Justice Act, and by the time he was replaced by Michael Howard the prison population had begun to rise. Howard, more than any previous home secretary, used the Home Office as a stage for a theatrically populist approach to law and order in which developments in the United States, including "three strikes" and other features of the "new penology" (Feeley and Simon 1992), became the touchstone for evaluating British policy. His speech to the Conservative Party conference in 1993 proclaiming that "prison works" dramatically changed the debate, despite the evidence to the contrary. It also marked the beginning of the erosion of the Woolf agenda.

From the 1990s onward, political populism has provided the ever-present backdrop to the work of the Prison Service. The main political parties competed to see who could be the toughest on crime. Prison administrators did their best to mitigate the attempts of politicians to micromanage the system and to preserve what had been learned through the experience of the CRC and Woolf, but their resolve was sorely tested with a renewed moral panic over escapes. In 1987 Gartree had become the first dispersal prison from which a successful escape was made by a Category A prisoner, and this led to a refinement of categorization that subdivided Category A into *exceptional, high,* and *standard risks.* But in 1994 there was a huge political outcry over what was a serious, but ultimately unsuccessful, escape attempt from the Special Security Unit at Whitemoor by five IRA prisoners.[11] Woodcock, an inspector of Constabulary appointed to conduct the inquiry, argued that, had the existing security procedures actually been implemented, there would have been no escape, yet nevertheless made 64 far-reaching new recommendations for expensive changes to security hardware and procedures (Home Office 1994, Section 10)—all of which were immediately accepted by Michael Howard. Howard had also asked for a wider review of security by a retired quartermaster General Learmont. The latter did not visit Oak Park Heights but returned from the United States enamored of the BoP's replacement for Marion at Florence and of the simplistic mantra that "bad behavior gets you in, good behaviour gets you out." Learmont endorsed Woodcock's recommendations and added a host of others, including the proposed building of an American-style supermax prison to house all exceptional and high-risk Category A prisoners (Home Office 1995; paras 5.14–5.16). He also proposed a second supermax facility as a control prison to house disruptive prisoners who were mentally disturbed, those currently held in the small CRC units and on the continuous assessment scheme, as well as young volatile offenders who disrupted Category C prisons (paras. 5.48–5.54). These prisons would sit on top of the existing dispersal prisons, which would continue to hold standard-risk Category A and Category B prisoners. While the first proposal had some merit in that it revisited Mountbatten's recommendation, the proposal for a control prison was surprising in the extreme. There had been no serious control problem since the Woolf Report; a concentration policy for disruptive prisoners had never been contemplated in Britain; and to include young Category C prisoners in a supermax facility would be seen by all informed observers as unacceptable overkill.

The director general of the Prison Service, Derek Lewis, was sacked by Michael Howard, and his successor, Richard Tilt, the first director who had actually governed prisons, appointed a working party to consider the feasibility of developing supermax prisons.[12] The working party quickly rejected the idea of a supermax prison for control purposes but hesitantly acknowledged that a supermax was feasible but only if it replaced one or preferably two dispersal prisons rather than being an additional facility.[13] In fact, after implementing all the expensive Woodcock proposals, there was no money for such a project, and by the time the working party reported, there had been a general election and the director was able to tell the incoming New Labour government that there was no longer any need for such a prison.

III. THE PERIOD FROM THE MID-1990S TO THE PRESENT

A second working party had been tasked by Director Tilt with reviewing the operation of the relatively discrete CRC small units; as a result, they were reorganized into a more closely related system and renamed Close Supervision Centers (CSCs; Prison Service 1996), which came into being in February 1998. Fundamental to the operation of the CSCs, like the CRC units before them, was that they were kept as a scarce resource with allocation to them made only after careful analysis by a Selection Committee, which also regularly reviewed inmate progress and eventual transfer out. In an attempt to reassure the press and public that the units did not become "control units," a number of independent observers, including academics and others with a knowledge of prisons and an interest in human rights, were appointed as an advisory group and given complete access to the centers, the selection process, and periodic statistics on their use. The revamped CSCs were more closely integrated with the rest of the system in that they all had a lower level of privileges than was available in the dispersal system, and they were more related to each other in that they were able to offer the possibility of progressing from one unit to another en route back to one's normal location. This involved a move away somewhat from the CRC approach of discrete, specialized regimes toward something based more on a philosophy of the "carrot and stick" in parallel with the Incentives and Earned Privileges Scheme that was being rolled out throughout the system. The CSCs were not an overnight success. They were criticized both by the Prisons Inspectorate (Home Office 2000) and by researchers (Clare and Bottomley 2001). Much of the criticism focused on the operation of the most restrictive of the units (D Wing at Woodhill), which for a time was characterized by confrontation and a prolonged stand-off, staff opened a cell only when five staff "suited up" in riot gear were present, and prisoners engaged in dirty protests by smearing cells with excrement. Liebling (2001, p. 143) noted in an appendix to the evaluation report that there was a sharp distinction "between approaches which focus on carrots, in the context of a high threshold quality of life [as in the CRC Report, the Woolf Report, and so on] and an approach emphasizing the stick with a very low or austere threshold." Liebling's comments here, though, would apply with far more force to the regimes in the American supermax. Some of the criticisms by the inspectorate involved confusion, for example, as to whether the Advisory Group had, or should have, a monitoring role. But in a system that was feeling its way, not surprisingly, there were a number of detailed criticisms and recommendations that needed to be addressed.

As the CSC system developed, it was possible to move away from separate regimes for each unit toward more individualized programming within them. Over time, staff learned to undertake more careful individual risk assessments so that they could respond proportionately to those risks, with the result that, for much of the time and with most prisoners, they felt confident in opening up in shirtsleeves. Prisoners were allowed to associate with others, on a risk-assessed basis, and were not normally hand-cuffed or otherwise restrained while outside their cells and within the unit. Staff, who always outnumbered prisoners, were encouraged to have higher levels of interaction with prisoners, and it was not uncommon to see them together playing pool, cards, or board games. In a prison population with high levels of morbidity in relation to mental health issues (Singleton, Lader, and Meltzer 1998), it was not surprising that these were also found among the most difficult and dangerous offenders, and, following some prompting from the inspectorate, renewed efforts were made to provide better mental health screening. For generations it had been something of a lottery as to whether offenders with mental health problems ended up in the special hospitals run by the Health Service or in the prison system. Among the most difficult were those with severe personality disorders whom the special hospitals regarded as untreatable. An experimental unit for prisoners with dangerous severe personality disorders (DSPD) was developed at Whitemoor alongside the CSC system with built-in research evaluation. With heavy inputs from prison psychologists, work began on a Violence Reduction Programme, adapted from a Canadian model, and the first unit to deliver this was in Woodhill in 2004. This formed part of a wider violence reduction strategy for the system as a whole. With the gaining of confidence in dealing with the most difficult prisoners, the Advisory Group hoped that the experience gained could be fed through to the rest of the prison system. A later report by the inspectorate (HM Inspectorate of Prisons 2006) found many improvements in the operation of the centers, including the closure of Woodhill D wing.

For many years the Prison Service had gradually learned to live with the findings from independent research and, where possible, to act on it insofar as political and economic constraints would allow. A new generation of researchers, led by Alison Liebling, developed assessments of the "moral performance" of prisons through an exploration of the legitimacy-conferring dimensions identified around the time of the Woolf report (Liebling and Arnold 2004). Together with her colleague Ben Crewe's work on prison ethnography (Crewe 2009), they have widened and deepened the work of their predecessors. Liebling and her colleagues have utilized methods derived from "appreciative inquiry" (Elliott 1999) to provide a better understanding of the ways in which staff and prisoners experience life in prison and the values that underpin their relationships. In a remarkable rapprochement between officialdom and the research community, their Measuring the Quality of Prison Life scales have been adopted by the Prison Service for the routine monitoring of prison performance in an attempt to focus on those institutions where remedial action may be required.

Liebling's work has ranged widely over the prison system, but two important studies bear directly on the changing quality of life in Whitemoor. In 1999 Liebling and Price reported very positive relationships in the prison, but by 2008 an Inspectorate Report (HM Inspectorate of Prisons 2008) revealed a marked deterioration in these relationships. Invited by the Prison Service to return to Whitemoor, Liebling, Arnold, and Straub (2011) found many examples of good practice, especially in, but not confined to, education and the DSPD unit, but elsewhere levels of trust between staff and prisoners were low and there were high levels of suspicion and concerns about risks. These were particularly associated with a changing population with many more younger prisoners serving indeterminate sentences with fifteen- to twenty-five-year tariffs, a growing number of prisoners bringing confrontational street culture into the prison, and an influx of Muslim prisoners. Staff found it difficult to relate to Muslim prisoners, who now made up about a third of the population in Whitemoor (many having been converted in prison), and they felt that they had little support or guidance on this from managers. There was an understandable concern about "radicalization" of young Muslims. But staff tended to overestimate levels of extremism, and in an echo of King and Elliott's (1977) analysis of Albany, Liebling and colleagues reported that extremist prisoners kept their distance from staff and adopted a facade of compliance, although behind the scenes they were suspected of orchestrating acts of violence and intimidation. As of December 2013, the Prison Service held 116 prisoners suspected or convicted of offences under the various Terror Acts (so-called TACT prisoners) of whom 86 were detained in the high-security estate. The majority of TACT prisoners were regarded as Al-Qaida inspired.[14] How well the Prison Service copes with these new challenges, which seem likely to dominate concerns for at least a generation and may well generate new and poorly considered initiatives from politicians, remains to be seen.

Among the most recent developments, following the relative success of the DSPD program and consequent upon the transfer of ear-marked funding from the Health Service to the Prison Service, has been the diffusion of this psychological expertise more widely in the Prison Service into a number of what are called Psychologically Informed Planned Environments. At the same time, the Management of Challenging Behaviour Strategy (MCBS) has been launched, which seeks to identify and monitor prisoners who appear to be on the threshold of eligibility for the CSC system with the hope of diverting them from, or preparing them for, entry. In January 2013 there were 54 prisoners being observed and managed under the MCBS scheme, six of them in a central unit in Woodhill. These developments seem to be in keeping with the original hopes of the CRC and designed to encourage all prisons to manage their own difficult prisoners, rather than relying on prolonged segregation or prison transfers under the Continuous Assessment Scheme. No system will ever be perfect, and, apart from the myriad things that can go wrong on a daily basis, there are at least two actual or potential problems. The first has been evident for some time, namely that movement of prisoners out of the CSCs can be problematic, and there are undoubtedly a few who require management within the CSCs if not permanently then for a very long time. It is hoped that the creation of a progression or step-down unit at Whitemoor will facilitate transfer back into the mainstream population. The second is the possibility that individual dispersal prisons will resort to the greater use of their own segregation units, either for those needing protection or administratively for the good order of the prison, as well as for punishment for disciplinary offenses, the more serious of which are nowadays dealt with by magistrates. Segregation units were recently renamed care and reintegration units, or care and separation units, and although this might seem to be another use of euphemistic nomenclature that is so common in prison systems around the world, it is intended to mark a move away from the traditionally punitive and uncaring life in segregation toward a greater emphasis on respect and preparing prisoners for return to the general population. The jury is out on how successful this has been. Reports of the local independent monitoring boards[15] at the dispersal prisons, as well as those of the Chief Inspector of Prisons, so far suggest that the humanizing of segregation still has some way to go, and it is clear from prison officer blogs that changes have been met with resistance. Although from time to time it is reported that larger numbers of prisoners are segregated, mostly for their own protection, in the light of a growing problem of gang culture from the streets, the use of segregation does not seem to have reached the levels that were common in the dispersal prisons in the 1970s and early 1980s.

In the latest phase of its development (January 2013), the high-security estate comprises five dispersal prisons (Frankland, Full Sutton, Long Lartin, Wakefield, and Whitemoor) and three core local prisons (Belmarsh, Manchester, and Woodhill) capable of keeping small numbers of Category A prisoners on remand and containing some cells that could give temporary relief to the CSCs. All told, the dispersal prisons held about 3,200 prisoners (1,032 in Category A) or about 3.7 percent of the total prison population of about 86,000. In 1984, the year of the CRC Report, the eight dispersal prisons contained, on average, about 2,800 prisoners (273 in Category A) or about 6.8 percent of a total population of nearly 42,000. Over that period the prison population had more than doubled, and the numbers in Category A quadrupled, but there was only a modest increase of about 15 percent in the size of the dispersal prison population, and they were held in three fewer prisons. Although it is difficult to make exact comparisons, one might speculate as to what the situation would have been like today had Mountbatten's proposal been adopted or had the CRCs hope for reorganization around two new-generation prisons come to fruition, but there can be no doubt that there has effectively been a substantial move from a dispersal policy toward a policy of greater concentration.

Since the CSCs probably represent the closest comparator to American supermax facilities—at least in terms of the problematic prisoners they contain though not in terms of either regime or philosophy—it is instructive to see the very small numbers contained therein. In January 2013, there were 38 prisoners in total (less than 0.04 percent of the prison population). Of these, the two CSC units in Woodhill had 10 and 8 prisoners, respectively; Whitemoor had 12 and a further 8 prisoners were in Wakefield. It is actually quite difficult to establish just how many states operate supermax facilities and how many prisoners are held in them. I reported (King 1999) some 34 states plus the Federal BoP operated at least one supermax facility and that around 20,000 prisoners were contained in them. O'Donnell (forthcoming), as well as others in personal communications, have suggested this is an underestimate. At about the same time, the Monitoring Project (1997) claimed that 42 states had supermax prisons, and a few years later Mears (2005) suggested that about 25,000 prisoners were held in these facilities. In recent years there seems to have been at least a slowing down in the rate of growth, and some states have had second thoughts, for example Illinois, where Tamms (which inspired the wrath of Kurki and Morris [2001]) has been closed. These difficulties arise in part because of problems over definition, which I discuss later. But in the absence of exact numbers, which would require a major research project to determine, the differences in scale of use are quite extraordinary: the ratio of prisoners in US supermax prisons to all other prisoners is probably 35 to 45 times greater than the ratio of prisoners in CSC and associated units in the prison population in the UK—and the differences in philosophy, conditions, and regime in these two types of custody are very large.

In most states supermax facilities are thought of as dealing with prisoners who are described as the "worst of the worst," though this is a description that scarcely stands up under scrutiny. The worst prisoners in, say, California are likely to be rather different (worse?) from those in, say, Maine, though the latter appears to have proportionately three times as many prisoners in supermax units as the former. The two states are clearly not comparable, and neither may be their prisoners, although it could be argued that is of no matter—each state can define its problems in its own way. More important, since allocation to a supermax is by an administrative process, it is up to individual wardens within each state to put forward their own worst prisoners as candidates—but it is likely that the worst prisoners from one prison will be much less "bad" than those from another. This would not be such a problem if there were tight criteria of eligibility, but the states that I studied all included a catch-all category at the end of their lists of qualifying misbehaviors, which could sweep up nuisance prisoners rather than dangerous ones. It is perhaps understandable that administrators would not wish to lose the flexibility that such a criterion allows. The British CSC system also has a similar criterion, but because final allocation is strictly governed by the Close Supervision Selection Committee (now renamed the Management Committee) at headquarters that considers every proposal, and because the accommodation is deliberately kept as a scarce resource, it has hardly ever been used, if at all. By contrast, few American Departments of Correction appear to exercise central control of allocation, and once large numbers of supermax beds have been provided, there is a pressure not to leave them unfilled. California and Texas both have large departments devoted to the identification of security threat groups, but it should be noted that many prisoners there are held in supermax facilities on the basis of suspected gang *affiliation* or *associates* and not on gang or other *misbehaviors* in prison. I know of no systematic independent research on the allocation procedures to a supermax, but it is clear that the phrase "worst of the worst" is more a political slogan and less a serious description of the population contained in supermax facilities.

Just as it is not necessarily the case that bad behavior gets one into a supermax, it is also not necessarily the case that good behavior gets one out. In some circumstances, the period spent in a supermax may be determinate provided there have been no further misbehaviors, but the definition of "further misbehaviors" is effectively in the hands of frontline staff, and there are many reports that prisoners claim to be knocked back by staff toward the end of their term for trivial reasons or no reason at all. They then return to an earlier stage, sometimes to the beginning of their term. In other circumstances, most notably with suspected gang members in California, the period is indeterminate and getting out depends on "debriefing" (i.e., snitching on other gang members, which may simply mean exchanging a prison sentence for a death sentence or one isolation cell for another, this time under protective custody). Some states also have long memories: prisoners whose sentences expired while still serving a SHU term may be released to the streets and then, if they reoffend, find themselves returned to the SHU on a new sentence years later, before they have had any opportunity to misbehave.

Chase Riveland's survey on behalf of the National Institute of Corrections (1997) used a definition of "supermax" containing three essential elements: (a) a physically separate accommodation, in which (b) a controlled environment emphasizing safety and security, via separation from staff and other prisoners and restricted movement, is provided for, and (c) used for prisoners identified under an administrative process as needing such control on grounds of their violent or seriously disruptive behavior in other high-security units.

Not all self-reported supermax facilities are alike, however. Riveland included both newly built and retrofitted facilities, as well as facilities that had some programming and those that had none. While architecture may be expected to have some impact on the quality of life—for good or ill—the presence or absence of programs and the way in which they are delivered will almost certainly mitigate or exacerbate the conditions of confinement. But the interpretation of the separation of prisoners from staff and other prisoners can be even more crucial to the quality of life. Let us take Oak Park Heights in Minnesota by way of illustration. During my 1984 study of that prison (King 1991), there was no mention of the word "supermax." All of the complexes except one had employment or educational programs as well as indoor and outdoor recreation in the company of other prisoners. The exception was the segregation complex, then referred to as Due Process, because prisoners were mostly housed there awaiting or following a disciplinary hearing. When I did a follow-up study in 1999 (King 2005), the Department of Corrections had responded to Riveland's survey by self-defining Oak Park Heights as a supermax. But the warden ran the prison very much in the style that Frank Wood had laid down, although there had been cuts in the budget that reduced some programs. The prison had rebranded two of the complexes as SHU units, but they were still staffed with one man in the bubble and two on the floor when prisoners were out of cells for periods of association. At that time there were plans afoot to add a new complex specifically designed as a supermax facility, although most staff did not believe there was a serious justification for this. In 2009 I returned to see the new unit in operation and to interview some staff and prisoners. Significantly, prisoners in the new unit did not associate with each other and any programming was conducted in their cells. Since prisoners were never at large in a communal space, there was no need for staff on the floor. In a close-out session the warden and I reminisced about the history of the prison. She had been a junior member of staff when I first visited and was now almost certainly the last in a line of wardens all of whom had worked with, or trained under Wood. With a rueful smile, she said "That was then—this is now."

It would seem that in any operational definition of what constitutes supermax we would need to take into account both Liebling and colleagues' work on staff – prisoner relationships and the profound difference between the original complexes at Oak Park Heights where staff and prisoners shared communal areas and the new unit where they did not. If we are to speak of "supermax" in a scientifically meaningful way, we need to reserve the term for those prisons that make a complete separation between the staff and inmate world—where staff enter the living units only to make cell extractions, to serve food periodically through the "cuff port" or "bean hole" depending on the local argot, or to accompany one prisoner at a time, under physical restraints and outnumbered three to one to the shower, telephone, or dog-run exercise yards. Those restraints often involve handcuffs, leg irons, belly chains, and spit masks, and sometimes even the need to escort can be reduced or eliminated through electronic aids.

It seems likely that most of the states that declare that they have supermax facilities probably strive for, or are pressured by staff into, making the separation as complete as possible in the "interests of safety." While superficially this degree of situational control may seem to protect staff, it is not foolproof, and it sets up a never-ending struggle as prisoners look to find new areas of vulnerability and staff seek to close them off. Denied actual contact, prisoners engage in "door wars" from the safety of their cells with both staff and other prisoners knowing they will most likely never have to deliver on their threats. While solid or perforated steel doors with plexiglass covering make it harder for prisoners to pass weapons, it does not stop them from using "rat lines" to pass messages or from refining the art of "gassing"—filling plastic bottles with body waste and squirting it at staff under the door or through the bean hole. In at least one supermax, the doors were replaced with bean holes close to the floor in an attempt to maintain situational control. I have interviewed prisoners in supermax who fantasize about rolling up paper so thinly and tightly that it could be an easily concealed weapon: "One day the guard will not be paying full attention when he uncuffs one hand and chains the other to the wall [so that I can make a telephone call]. He only has to make one mistake, I have all the time in the world."

In marked contrast to the situation in Britain, comparatively little research attention has been given to ethnographic accounts of the internal operation of prisons in the United States in the past thirty years or so—and only one, by Rhodes (2004), has been conducted in a supermax. Rather, more attention has been given to the effects of supermax custody. I have reviewed these elsewhere in terms of the effects on prisoners, staff, prison systems, and society (King 2005). Grassian (1983), Haney and Lynch (1997), and others have argued that the effects of solitary confinement and supermax custody (which are not always the same but frequently conflated as though they were) are overwhelmingly negative, producing insomnia, anxiety, panic, cognitive dysfunction, and a host of other clinically observable conditions—sometimes referred to collectively as SHU syndrome. Ward and Werlich (2003), on the other hand, purport that there have been few long-term consequences in terms of mental health for prisoners who passed through Alcatraz and Marion and who resettled satisfactorily either in other prisons to which they were eventually transferred or in the community. Bonta and Gendreau (1990) have argued that until research on the effects of solitary confinement employ genuinely experimental methods, definitive conclusions cannot be reached. The controversy over the effects on prisoners reached new heights in the recent Colorado study (O'Keefe et al. 2010) that attempted to overcome methodological deficiencies in earlier studies and found that inmates housed in administrative segregation in Colorado State Penitentiary (CSP) exhibited high levels of psychological impairment, but so also did comparison groups who remained in general population in other prisons. The publication of the Colorado study was greeted by a storm of criticism, partly methodological and partly out of dismay that the research could be used to justify the extension of supermax custody, including for the mentally ill (see, e.g., Shalev and Lloyd 2011).

There is a sense, however, that most of the research so far has failed to capture the real experiences of prisoners in supermax custody. The self-reported effects that prisoners express do not neatly correspond to those measured in the psychometric tests of psychological researchers. Indeed, they often report that they—like concentration camp victims reported by Jorge Semprun (1997)—could only really talk about their experiences to those who had experienced the same thing themselves. The measures used by Ward and Werlich (2003), including later referral to mental health facilities in prison or self-referral to such facilities in the community, probably tells us as much about the screening and referral procedures as it does about the effects of supermax custody, and their results may equally call into question whether those prisoners "needed" supermax custody in the first place. And the holy grail of experimental method—randomized control trials—is unlikely ever to pass ethics committees in this context. In regard to the results in the Colorado study, it should be noted that CSP is almost certainly among the better supermax facilities, and the authors noted that the results might not be generalizable. In my own interviews with 37 prisoners in CSP and 42 prisoners in Oak Park Heights (King 2005), I asked inmates about the costs and benefits to them of being in supermax custody. Over half of the prisoners reported some positive feedback: for example, it had given them time to think and reflect, they had learned patience and control, or it had given them an opportunity to get away from the often malign influence of their peers. But for the majority of these prisoners, these positives were embedded within a wider and deeper framework of perceived negative effects. Moreover, most of these prisoners felt that the positive effects could have been achieved more quickly, in other ways, and without the levels of deprivation involved. At the other extreme, about a fifth of the prisoners were adamant that the whole experience had made them so much worse and more alienated that, if and when they came out, they would be all the more bitter and vengeful. It should come as no surprise that a supermax, or solitary confinement, will not impact all prisoners in the same way and to the same extent. There is inevitably a complex interaction between the biography of prisoners, their respective ego strengths, the levels of support they may have, and a host of other variables that might be expected to influence the effects of prolonged custody in supermax or solitary confinement—Nelson Mandela, for example. But there is a sense in which some of this research is simply beside the point. Even if it were unequivocally shown that prolonged incarceration in supermax or solitary confinement had no negative impacts on mental health, this would not alone be sufficient to justify the use of supermax custody without considering the effects on staff, the rest of the prison system, and society.

It should be clear that placing physical barriers between staff and prisoners, and limiting staff roles to escorting prisoners under restraint and providing a meal delivery service, involves deskilling relative to what Karacki (1984b) described as maintaining control through interpersonal relationships. It is ironic that these changes to the staff role came in part through pressure from staff out of concerns about safety, but they were obviously also encouraged by management. This contrasts markedly with the situation in British CSCs, where initially staff retreated behind riot gear but came to welcome a style of more personal relationships as more rewarding after this had been encouraged by management.

My first attempt at conducting research in Pelican Bay was during the early days of the Madrid Compliance Unit operating within the prison. I was allowed to review video evidence of the use-of-force incidents alongside members of that unit to assess whether the rules were followed. They mostly were. What could not be examined was whether the rules, and the circumstances of their use, were reasonable or proportionate to events. Thus staff had no problems in allowing me to stand and watch them dealing with a prisoner from the SHU unit who was refusing to re-enter his cell after returning to the pod from his dog-run exercise. He was duly warned by staff in the control room that he was "holding the pod to hostage" and that if he refused to go to his cell they would call the lieutenant. There were no other prisoners out of their cells, there was nowhere else for him to go, he had no weapons, and he was visibly upset (I learned subsequently from staff that this was because of domestic problems that emerged on a visit the previous day). The lieutenant came to the pod and repeated the order to return to his cell and warn that force would be used if he refused. Five officers were duly "suited up" and videoed giving name and function in the extraction team and declaring that they would behave properly and without undue force. A sixth officer who controlled the video camera would film the proceedings. Before they entered, however, three volleys from a 37mm gas gun were fired at the prisoner (I was given some of the rubber pellets as a souvenir), the third of which brought him to his knees. The extraction team went in, pepper-sprayed the prisoner, removed him from the pod, placed him on a gurney, took him to the showers where they bathed his eyes, and then physically returned him to his cell. All of this was done according to the rules enshrined in policy documents. No one questioned whether this was an appropriate response or whether it had adverse desensitizing effects on the staff who were carrying it out.

One of the most frequently used justifications for the use of supermax prisons, or the use of the British CSCs for that matter, is that their existence allows the rest of the system to operate more peacefully. This is notoriously difficult to assess given the methodological problems involved, including, for example, the somewhat arbitrary definitions of "unacceptable behavior" in different prisons. The most sophisticated attempt to study this was carried out by Briggs, Sundt, and Castellano (2003) who used a quasi-experimental, multiple interrupted time series design to examine system effects following the establishment of Special Management Units I and II in Arizona, Tamms in Illinois, and Oak Park Heights in Minnesota. They found a net worsening of institutional violence in Arizona, a very small reduction in assaults on staff (from 62 to 60 a month) in Illinois, and a small increase in staff assaults in Minnesota. In Britain, Clare and Bottomley (2001), on the basis of post hoc staff interviews, found that staff in the dispersal prisons believed there to have been fewer serious incidents, and the analysis of routinely recorded data showed that fewer prisoners were held in long-term segregation or transferred under the Continuous Assessment Scheme. More research is needed, but on the evidence thus far the CSCs may have produced more system benefits at much less cost.

Considering the effects on society takes us further away from the scientific arena and into the moral-political sphere, although, as we have seen, Liebling and colleagues have not shied away from the application of science to the moral performance of prisons. But there can be no doubt that the legitimacy of what goes on in prisons has a moral as well as a utilitarian dimension. I last visited Pelican Bay in 2011 shortly after the ending of one hunger strike and at the beginning of a second, called in response to what was seen by prisoners to be delays in implementing promised reforms. Some of the prisoners I had interviewed fifteen years earlier were still in the SHU, at least one of whom was still refusing to debrief concerning his suspected gang activities. He was angry because officials had not yet fulfilled their promise that, among other things, they would move away from identifying gang members through suspicion of affiliation or through association and more toward clear evidence of gang behaviors. By that time, a three-judge court had ordered California to reduce its prison population to 137.5 percent of design capacity within two years. The Supreme Court narrowly upheld the decision on appeal in *Brown v. Plata*,[16] and in a landmark majority opinion, Justice Kennedy held the state's mental health facilities in prison to be "incompatible with human dignity" and having "no place in civilized society." In a telephone conversation with Judge Henderson, he told me he regretted that he had not ruled the whole of the SHU as in breach of the Eighth Amendment all those years ago, although he was now mildly hopeful about the effectiveness of the current court orders. Not long afterward, as the hunger strikes resumed in Pelican Bay, he had the uncomfortable task of ruling that the Department of Corrections could force-feed prisoners (in marked contrast to Margaret Thatcher's decision to allow the IRA hunger strikers in Britain to starve themselves to death).

Legitimacy is, in part, a question of audience, and there may be many audiences—prisoners and their families, prison administrators and staff, politicians, the public, and the courts and various bodies, both national and international—with an acknowledged interest or jurisdiction in relevant matters. In 1995 Keohane, in a Commission on Accreditation for Corrections report responding to Amnesty International's critique of conditions on death row in Oklahoma, dismissed "reference to international standards" in favor of "court decisions, ACA standards, state legislative laws" and, ultimately, "the will and expectation of the citizens of Oklahoma." Although the United States ratified both the International Covenant on Civil and Political Rights and the Convention Against Torture and Other Cruel, Inhuman or Degrading Treatment or Punishment, it did so only insofar as "cruel, inhuman, or degrading" meant what was prohibited by the American Constitution. Haney and Lynch (1997) have reviewed the evolving jurisprudence on Eighth Amendment protections against cruel and unusual punishment and noted how Chief Justice Warren's expectation that, as society matured, so court judgments would reflect more civilized standards had been set back by recent experience. In that light, Simon (2011) has argued that Justice Kennedy's use of the word "torture" in his majority opinion in *Brown v. Plata* and his insistence that medical and mental health care had to be consistent with human dignity in a civilized society may prove to be the beginning of an emerging new consensus about the requirements for legitimacy.

IV. Conclusion

In this essay I have tried to trace the development of policies in relation to difficult and dangerous prisoners in Britain and the United States from the 1960s to the present day. I have suggested that British policy was driven more by escape than control problems and initially followed a policy of dispersing escape risks in several prisons. However, as these dispersal prisons suffered a series of control problems, the Prison Service moved toward a policy of greater concentration of prisoners considered high escape risks. That history was punctuated at several points by the temptation to emulate the model developed at Oak Park Heights in Minnesota, and later a recommendation to build two supermax prisons, although the first never came to fruition and the second was firmly rejected. Over a thirty-year period, a separate policy of dealing with the most difficult to manage prisoners in small units evolved from the recommendations of the CRC into the present-day CSCs. It is a small parsimonious system, deliberately maintained as a scarce resource, which has achieved a relatively high level of legitimacy. By contrast, in the United States, policy has been driven more by the need to control behaviors in prison, and escape-risk prisoners and control-risk prisoners have been treated more or less alike—as penitentiary types. Since the closure of Alcatraz, there has been a move via the control unit at Marion toward an ever-expanding development of supermax prisons—which now contain between 35 and 45 times as many prisoners, proportionate to the prison population, as do the British CSCs. Moreover, the gap between the penal rhetoric ostensibly justifying them and the reality of the conditions within them, the circumstances of getting in and getting out, and the effects on prisoners, staff, the rest of the system, and the public leave them with a significant legitimacy deficit.

In part, the differences in legitimacy between the two systems can be accounted for by the well-established tradition in Britain of links between prison administrators and the research community to the extent that the former now use research instruments designed to measure the moral performance of prisons as part of in-house monitoring. In part it may also be attributed to systems of scrutiny by local independent monitoring boards and the announced and unannounced inspections by Her Majesty's Inspectorate of Prisons. By contrast, the United States has relied on intervention by the Federal courts, often only after problems have become endemic. Finally, prison officials in Britain and their masters in government periodically find their feet held to the fire by the Committee for the Prevention of Torture and judgments by the European Courts regarding breaches of international covenants and conventions—pressures that have been largely resisted in the United States.

I began by asserting that the exchange of penological ideas had been largely from west to east. Perhaps it is now time to reverse the flow. Karacki (1984a) recommended that the Federal Bureau monitor the CRC's policy of small units for difficult and dangerous prisoners. As far as I am aware, that has not happened. Perhaps now it would be appropriate to examine the operation of their successors, the CSCs, as an alternative to supermax prisons and SHUs.

Notes

1. With apologies to Scotland and Northern Ireland who have their own separate prison services from the one in England and Wales, I use *Britain* and *British* here as shorthand for *England and Wales* and *English and Welsh*, respectively.

   This essay is based on my own research in the United States high-security prisons: 3 months in Oak Park Heights and several weeks in Marion, plus orientation visits to Stillwater, Leavenworth, Lewisburg, and Terre Haute in 1983–1984; several weeks each in Pelican Bay, Colorado State Penitentiary, and Oak Park Heights during the late 1990s; and orientation visits to Southport and Marcy Correctional Facilities in New York; Camp Hill and Greene County in Pennsylvania; Tamms in Illinois; Wynne, Estelle, and Terrel Units in Texas; Red Onion and Wallens Ridge in Virginia; SM Units I and II in Arizona; and Corcoran and Valley State in California. I also reported on conditions in Pelican Bay (2011), Boscobel (2001) in Wisconsin, and McAlester H Unit (1994–1995) in Oklahoma for Amnesty International. In Britain I have conducted research in many prisons, but most important for the purposes of this essay are Albany (1967–1972) and Gartree (1985–1986) when they were part of the high-security estate of "dispersal prisons." I was a member of the Research and Advisory Group for the Control Review Committee in the 1980s, academic advisor to the Feasibility of Supermax Working Group in 1996, and a member of the Advisory Group on the Close Supervision Centres.

2. Biggs eventually settled in Brazil where he remarried and fathered a son. He returned to Britain, voluntarily, in 2001 to recommence his sentence and was released on compassionate grounds in 2009 after a series of strokes.

3. As a callow postgraduate student on a placement from the Institute of Criminology, I interviewed Blake in the Scrubs in 1963, from which stemmed my lifelong interest in prison security issues.

4. Other members of the subcommittee were Leo Abse (MP), R. C. Mortimer (Bishop of Exeter), and Dr. Peter Scott (psychiatrist).

5. Peter Scott dissociated himself from the proposal for armed guards in a note of reservation, which was supported by seven of the seventeen members of the Advisory Council, and it was never implemented.

6. I was conducting research in Oak Park Heights at that time and had been granted permission to extend my research to Marion and the other Federal penitentiaries. I arrived in Marion at the end of October, and although I interviewed several prisoners and staff, it was clear that the prison was in too great a state of shock to undertake much research. The following month, at the request of Warden Keohane, I gave a short speech at a memorial service for the two murdered officers while visiting Terre Haute.

7. *Madrid v. Gomez* (1995) No.C90-3094-THE, Class Action: Findings of Fact, Conclusions of Law, and Order, US District Court for the Northern District of California, January.

8. Including Profs. Norval Morris, David Ward, and Lloyd Ohlin; Norman Carlson of the Bureau of Prisons; and representatives of the American Correctional Association and the National Institute of Corrections.

9. Oak Park Heights is probably a contender for being the most visited and least copied prison in the world.

10. *En passant*, we may note that Woolf added his voice to the desirability of "earmarking at least one new generation prison for dispersal prisoners" (paras. 12.297–12.305).

11. The prisoners were quickly caught by the last line of defense—the police outside the prison.

12. I acted as academic advisor to the working party.

13. Members of the working party had a preference for a facility along the model of Oak Park Heights but were aware that Howard preferred the Florence ADX.

14. Figures on TACT prisoners in this paragraph and current use of CSC and DSPD units in the following paragraphs were kindly supplied by HM Prison Service.

15. Every prison has an independent monitoring board whose members have the right of access to interview prisoners out of the hearing of prison officers and to report on prison conditions. This is the first level of independent scrutiny of happenings in a prison. A second is provided by the Prisons and Probation Ombudsman, who can examine complaints and is required to look at all deaths in custody. The third is the Inspectorate of Prisons, whose reports on announced and unannounced inspections and thematic reviews of particular issues are all published.

16. *Brown v. Plata* (2011) No.09-1233, US Supreme Court, May 23, 2011.

REFERENCES

Adams, Robert. 1992. *Prison Riots in Britain and the USA*. Basingstoke, UK: Macmillan.

Advisory Council on the Penal System. 1968. *The Regime for Long-Term Prisoners in Conditions of Maximum Security Custody*. Radzinowicz Report. London: HMSO.

Beetham, David. 1991. *The Legitimation of Power*. London: Macmillan.

Bonta, James, and Paul Gendreau. 1990. "Reexamining the Cruel and Unusual Punishment of Prison Life." *Law and Human Behavior* 14:347–372.

Bottomley, A. Keith. 1995. *CRC Special Units: A General Assessment.* London: Home Office Research and Planning Unit.

Bottoms, Anthony. 1992. "Violence and Disorder in Long-Term Prisons: The Influence of Institutional Environments." *Criminal Behaviour and Mental Health* 2:126–136.

Briggs, Chad S., Jody L. Sundt, and Thomas C. Castellano. 2003. "The Effect of Supermaximum Security Prisons on Aggregate Levels of Institutional Violence." *Criminology* 41:1341–1376.

Clare, E., and A. Keith Bottomley. 2001. *Evaluation of Close Supervision Centres,* Home Office Research Study 219. London: Home Office Research and Statistics Directorate.

Clemmer, Donald. 1940. *The Prison Community.* New York: Holt, Rinehart and Winston.

Cohen, Stanley, and Laurie Taylor. 1972. *Psychological Survival: The Experience of Long-Term Imprisonment.* Harmondsworth, UK: Penguin Books.

Cooke, David. 1989. "Containing Violent Prisoners: An Analysis of the Barlinnie Special Unit." *British Journal of Criminology* 29:129–143.

Crewe, Ben. 2009. *The Prisoner Society: Power, Adaptation and Social Life in an English Prison.* Oxford: Oxford University Press.

DiIulio, John J. 1987. *Governing Prisons.* New York: Simon & Schuster.

Elliott, Charles. 1999. *Locating the Energy for Change: An Introduction to Appreciative Inquiry.* Winnipeg, Manitoba: International Institute for Sustainable Development.

Feeley, Malcolm, and Jonathan Simon. 1992. "The New Penology: Notes on the Emerging Strategy of Corrections and its Implications." *Criminology* 30:449–475.

Fowler, Norman. 1967. "Hard Times for the Home Secretary." *The Times,* August 17.

Grassian, Stuart. 1983. "Psychological Effects of Solitary Confinement." *American Journal of Psychiatry* 140:1450–1454.

Haney, Craig, and Mona Lynch. 1997. "Regulating Prisons of the Future: A Psychological Analysis of Supermax and Solitary Confinement." *New York University Review of Law and Social Change* 23:477–570.

HM Inspectorate of Prisons. 2006. *Extreme Custody: A Thematic Inspection of Close Supervision Centres and High Security Segregation.* London: HM Inspectorate of Prisons.

HM Inspectorate of Prisons. 2008. *Report on an Unannounced Full Follow-up Inspection of HMP Whitemoor.* London: HM Inspectorate of Prisons.

Home Office. 1966. *Report of the Inquiry into Prison Escapes and Security.* The Mountbatten Report, Cmnd. 3175. London: HMSO.

Home Office. 1979a. *Report of the Committee of Inquiry into the United Kingdom Prison Services.* May Committee Report, Cmnd 7673. London: HMSO.

Home Office. 1979b. *Inquiry into the United Kingdom Prison Services.* Vol. II, Paper 9: The Dispersal System: England and Wales. Response to King's Evidence to the May Committee. London: HMSO.

Home Office. 1984. *Managing the Long-Term Prison System.* Report of the Control Review Committee. London: HMSO.

Home Office. 1985. *New Directions in Prison Design.* Report of a Home Office Study of New Generation Prisons in the USA. London: HMSO.

Home Office. 1991. *Prison Disturbances April 1990.* Report of an Inquiry by the Rt. Hon. Lord Justice Woolf (Parts I and II) and His Honour Judge Stephen Tumim (Part II), Cmnd. 1456. London: HMSO.

Home Office. 1994. *The Escape from Whitemoor Prison on Friday 9th September 1994.* Woodcock Report, Cmnd. 2741, London: HMSO.

Home Office. 1995. *Review of Prison Service Security in England and Wales and the Escape from Parkhurst Prison on Tuesday 3rd January 1995.* Learmont Report, Cmnd.3020. London: HMSO.

Home Office. 2000. *Inspection of Close Supervision Centres, August–September 1999.* London: HMSO.

Irwin, John. 1970. *The Felon.* Englewood Cliffs, NJ: Prentice-Hall.

Irwin, John. 1980. *Prison in Turmoil.* Boston: Little, Brown.

Jacobs, James. 1974. "Street Gangs Behind Bars." *Social Problems* 21(3): 395–409.

Jacobs, James. 1977. *Stateville: The Penitentiary in Mass Society.* Chicago: University of Chicago Press.

Jacobs, James. 1983. *New Perspectives on Prisons and Imprisonment.* Ithaca, NY: Cornell University Press.

Johnston, Norman. 1973. *The Human Cage: A Brief History of Prison Architecture.* New York: Walker and Company.

Karacki, Larry. 1984a. "Controlling Dangerous Prisoners: The Experience of the Federal Prison System and the British Prison Department." Unpublished paper for the Bureau of Prisons.

Karacki, Larry. 1984b. "The Marion Lockdown: History of Events Preceding and Following the October, 1983 Lockdown of USP Marion and Culminating in the Present High Security Operation, November 1984." Unpublished paper for the Bureau of Prisons.

King, Roy D. 1991. "Maximum Security Custody in Britain and the USA: A Study of Gartree and Oak Park Heights." *British Journal of Criminology* 31:126–152.

King, Roy D. 1999. "The Rise and Rise of Supermax: An American Solution in Search of a Problem." *Punishment & Society* 1(2): 163–186.

King, Roy D. 2005. "The Effects of Supermax Custody." In *The Effects of Imprisonment, edited by* A. Liebling and S. Maruna. Cullompton, UK: Willan.

King, Roy D. 2008. "Terror, Torture and Legitimacy." Paper presented at the Conference on Torture, Centre for the Study of Violence, São Paulo, February.

King, Roy D., and Kenneth W. Elliott. 1977. *Albany: Birth of a Prison—End of an Era.* London: Routledge and Kegan Paul.

King, Roy D., and Kathleen McDermott. 1989. "British Prisons, 1970–87: The Ever-Deepening Crisis." *The British Journal of Criminology* 29:107–128.

King, Roy D., and Rodney Morgan. 1980. *The Future of the Prison System.* Farnborough, UK: Gower.

Klare, Hugh J. 1968. "Prisoners in Maximum Security." *New Society* 11:494–495.

Kurki, Leena, and Norval Morris. 2001. "The Purposes, Practices and Problems of Supermax Prisons." In *Crime and Justice: A Review of Research,* Vol. 28, edited by Michael Tonry. Chicago: University of Chicago Press.

Liebling, Alison. 2001. "Policy and Practice in the Management of Disruptive Prisoners: Incentives and Earned Privileges, The Spurr Report and Close Supervision Centres." In *Evaluation of Close Supervision Centres,* edited by Clare and Bottomley. Home Office Research Study 219. London: Home Office Research.

Liebling, Alison, and Helen Arnold. 2004. *Prisons and Their Moral Performance: A Study of Values, Quality and Prison Life.* Clarendon Studies in Criminology. Oxford: Oxford University Press.

Liebling, Alison, Helen Arnold, and Christina Straub. 2011. *An Exploration of Staff–Prisoner Relationships at HMP Whitemoor: 12 Years On.* Revised Final Report. Cambridge, UK: Institute of Criminology, Prisons Research Centre.

Liebling, Alison, and David Price. 1999. "An Exploration of Staff-Relationships at HMP Whitemoor." Prison Service Research Report 6. London: HMPS.

Mears, Daniel P. 2005. *Evaluating the Effectiveness of Supermax Prisons.* Washington, DC: Urban Institute Justice Policy Center.

Monitoring Project. 1997. *The Use of Control Units in the United States*. Boulder. CO: Rocky Mountain Peace Project.

Morris, Terence P. 1968. "Notes on the Regime for Long-Term Prisoners in Conditions of Maximum Security." *British Journal of Criminology* 8(3): 312–314.

National Institute of Corrections. 1997. *Supermax Housing: A Survey of Current Practice, Special Issues in Corrections*. Longmont, CO. US Department of Justice, National Institute of Corrections.

O'Keefe, Maureen L., Kelli J. Klebe, Alysha Stucker, Kristin Sturm, and William Leggett. 2010. *One Year Longitudinal Study of the Psychological Effects of Administrative Segregation*. Colorado Springs: Colorado Department of Corrections.

Price, David. 2000. Security Categorisation in the English Penal System. PhD thesis, University of Cambridge.

Prison Service. 1996. "Management of Disruptive Prisoners: CRC Review Project, Final Report. "Unpublished paper.

Reiter, Keramet A. 2012. "Parole, Snitch or Die: California's Supermax Prisons and Prisoners 1997–2007." *Punishment & Society* 14:540–563.

Rhodes, Loma A. 2004. *Total Confinement: Madness and Reason in the Maximum Security Prison*. Berkeley: University of California Press.

Semprun, Jorge. 1997. *Literature or Life*. New York: Viking.

Shalev, Sharon, and Monica Lloyd. 2011. Though This Be Method, Yet There Is Madness In't: Commentary on One Year Longitudinal Study of the Psychological Effects of Administrative Segregation. Washington, DC: National Institute of Corrections.

Simon, Jonathan. 2011. "Mass Incarceration on Trial." *Punishment & Society* 13(3): 251–255.

Singleton, Nicola, Deborah Lader, and Howard Meltzer. 1998. *Psychiatric Morbidity among Prisoners in England and Wales*. London: Office for National Statistics.

Sparks, Richard, Anthony E. Bottoms, and Will Hay. 1996. *Prisons and the Problem of Order*. Oxford: Clarendon Press.

Sykes, Gresham M. 1968. *The Society of Captives: A Study of a Maximum Security Prison*. Princeton, NJ: Princeton University Press.

Taylor, Ian. 1968. "Letter." *New Society* 11:576.

Taylor, Ian, Paul Walton, and Jock Young. 1975. "Critical Criminology in Britain: Review and Prospects." In *Critical Criminology*, edited by Ian Taylor, Paul Walton, and Jock Young. London: Routledge and Kegan Paul.

Ward, David A., and A. F. Breed. 1984. *The United States Penitentiary, Marion, Illinois*. A Report to the Judiciary Committee, United States House of Representatives. Washington, DC: US Government Printing Office.

Ward, David A., and Gene Kassebaum. 2009. *Alcatraz: The Gangster Years*. Berkeley: University of California Press.

Ward, David A., and Kenneth Schoen. 1981. *Confinement in Maximum Custody*. Lexington, MA: Lexington Books.

Ward, David A., and Thomas G. Werlich. 2003. "Alcatraz and Marion: Evaluating Supermax Custody." *Punishment & Society* 5:53–75.

Court Cases

Madrid v. Gomez 889 F.Supp. 1146 - Dist. Court, ND California (1995).

SECTION IV

PRISONER REHABILITATION

CHAPTER 18

ADULT OFFENDER ASSESSMENT AND CLASSIFICATION IN CUSTODIAL SETTINGS

JAMES BONTA AND J. STEPHEN WORMITH

OFFENDER assessment and classification are two important activities that usually occur in the early stage of processing offenders as they are admitted to correctional facilities throughout the United States, Canada, the United Kingdom, and many other westernized countries. These are interrelated concepts in the sense that an effective inmate classification system is based on an assessment of the offender's risk and needs, although the nature of the assessment can vary from cursory to extremely detailed. However, offender assessment becomes effective, or of value to the correctional agency, only when it is applied to a group of offenders in some fashion that is helpful to the correctional agency. Typically, this comes in the form of housing, supervision, management, and service delivery. The critical point is that the grouping of prisoners must be meaningful to the correctional agency. Consequently, offender assessment and classification are or should be inextricably linked in correctional policy and practice.

The assessment-classification concept is not in any way original or unique to corrections; it is found in numerous disciplines and has heralded progress in sciences ranging from physics and chemistry to biology and psychiatry. Classification systems in all fields are derived from theory and research in their respective science, and offender classification is no exception. There is one important variation that is found across scientific classification systems: Some classification systems consist of unique and exhaustive groups such as women and men, while others consist of groupings along some measured continuum such as offender risk. One should be mindful of these differences when reviewing the assessment and classification of prison inmates.

In this chapter, we begin by describing the evolution of offender classification, primarily in North America. These practices consist of two major themes: brief security-oriented assessment-classification models and the assessment and classification of offenders for programming and treatment. In this latter context, particular attention is paid to the application of the principles of Risk, Need, and Responsivity (RNR) (Andrews, Bonta, and Hoge 1990) to offender assessment, classification, and subsequent work with the offender, often described as "offender case management." The assessment and classification of special groups of offenders, such as women and offenders with mental health issues, is considered. A number of particular issues pertaining to the process of offender classification are found throughout correctional agencies and warrant consideration. These include the use of the override or administrative judgment, the importance of reassessment and reclassification of offenders, and the preparation of prisoners for release.

With an understanding of how offender assessment and classification is conducted, we then turn to four reasons why offender classification is so vital to correctional agencies: (1) The safety of the institution for both staff and prisoners; (2) the human costs to the prisoner and their repercussions to the public by means of increasing subsequent reoffending; (3) the delivery of appropriate offender treatment programs and services, which may reduce further offending; and (4) the financial costs of operating prisons, which has been exacerbated by the prison population explosion after the 1970s, particularly in the United States. Although few in number, efforts to evaluate offender classification are considered with reference to two experimental field trials and correctional agencies' efforts to conduct reliable and valid offender classifications. We end with a view to the future and the pressing demands for institutional and community safety, humanitarian services, and cost-effective operations that continue to fall on these important correctional practices.

I. From Historical to Recent Developments in Offender Classification

Historically, prisons were used primarily to confine the person until a punishment could be decided upon (e.g., execution, corporal punishment). It was not until the late eighteenth century that imprisonment not only became a punishment for wrongdoing but also assumed a correctional function. Offenders were sent to prison for punishment (Jeremy Bentham's calculus that pain should outweigh the pleasure brought by crime) and for corrections (John Howard's reformation). In the beginning, young and old, male and female, with little regard to the type of offense committed, were all housed together. However, under the leadership of John Howard in England and William Penn in the United States, this warehousing of offenders was seen as inhumane and needed to change. The intermingling of offenders in unsanitary conditions made for a dangerous mix for not only the spread of disease but also for the safety of the confined.

Early efforts at inmate classification, such as separating men from women and housing youth in separate facilities, may have served a humane purpose but also contributed to the safer management of prisons. Although the assessment and classification of inmates for security reasons remains at the forefront of prison management, "reformation" or rehabilitation in today's language also plays a critical role.

A. Matching Security to Offender Risk

Upon entry into a custodial facility, offenders are assessed and security placements are determined. Is the person a threat to the security of staff and other inmates? What is the likelihood of an escape? Could the person fall prey to other inmates? These questions speak to matters of security surrounding inmates, staff, and potentially the general community. How these assessments that underlie placement decisions are conducted is the topic of this section. The question of threat to oneself will be discussed later.

Security classification decisions may be made according to (a) policy directives, (b) professional judgment, (c) objective, actuarial-based assessments, or (d) a combination thereof. Offender placement decisions based upon policy directives are the simplest, involving the most rudimentary assessment of the offender. Typically, such decisions require only knowledge of the offense or the notoriety of the offender. In these situations, policy often overrides any evidence as to the offender's true risk to security.

Security placements are limited by the availability of different levels of custody. Some prison systems may have very few levels of security and others many more. For example, the U.S. Federal Bureau of Prisons (BOP) has four levels of security along with specialized facilities such as pretrial detention centers that house all security levels (Federal Bureau of Prisons 2006). The Correctional Service of Canada (CSC) has three security levels (minimum, medium, maximum) but also includes specialized facilities such as a special handling unit for extremely violent offenders and healing lodges for Aboriginal offenders (Correctional Service of Canada 2006). Although policy considerations play a role in prison placement decisions (e.g., offenders convicted of first-degree murder or a terrorist act may automatically be placed in maximum security), many jurisdictions have come to depend upon either professional judgment or actuarial-based classification instruments. We will focus only on the actuarial measures, as the research shows that these measures are more accurate than professional judgment (Andrews, Bonta, and Wormith 2006; Hilton, Harris, and Rice 2006).

Offender risk instruments are intended to assist placement decisions that enhance the safety and security of institutions while applying the "least restrictive alternative." This principle, applied in U.S., Canadian, and European legal contexts, states that the penalty should be the least restrictive while being consistent with the goals of punishment (Rubin 1975; Hogg and Bushell 1997; Harbo 2010). In the correctional context, an offender who poses no escape risk or threat to others would not be placed in a maximum-security facility save for the policy circumstances noted above. Thus, the main goal is to match the level of security to the level of risk. To adhere to the least restrictive alternative and make placements that enhance safety, there are two general requirements: (1) One must use a reliable and valid measure that predicts threats to security (i.e., escape, prison misconducts); and (2) the application of such an assessment instrument should demonstrate that it actually "works" or achieves these goals. We begin with the assessment of risk that an offender poses to the security of the prison, staff, and other inmates.

B. Traditional Prison Classification

In the United States, the BOP has the sole responsibility for the classification or "designation" of all offenders who are sentenced in Federal District Court. Prisoner classification is based on the following general principles: (1) the level of security and staff supervision the inmate requires; (2) the level of security and staff supervision the institution provides; (3) the medical classification care level of the inmate and the care level of the institution; (4) the inmate's program needs (e.g., substance abuse treatment, educational/vocational training, individual and/or group counseling, medical/mental health treatment); and (5) various administrative factors (e.g., institution bed space capacity, judicial recommendations, security measures needed to ensure protection of victims and witnesses).

Offenders are classified based on an objective scoring system, discussed in more detail below, that includes such factors as voluntary surrender, severity of current offense, extent of criminal history, and alcohol and drug abuse. Various management issues may also be considered such as any security, location, or program recommendations made by the sentencing court, work assignment, and psychiatric status (Federal Bureau of Prisons 2006). Thus, the system allows staff an opportunity to exercise their professional judgment. Most state departments of corrections (DOCs) and county jails operate in a similar fashion, although smaller jurisdictions may have fewer options in terms of the range of placement facilities.

In Canada, responsibility for inmates can be either a federal responsibility (a sentence of two years or more) or a provincial responsibility (a sentence of less than two years). The classification of federal inmates begins with a "penitentiary placement" exercise. A standardized Custody Rating Scale, discussed in more detail below, is used to assess the offender's security needs. Not surprisingly, it is similar in content, although different in form, to the American federal classification system. Its items include, for example, involvement in previous institutional incidents, escape history, and alcohol and drug use (Correctional Service of Canada [CSC] 2012). Security level cutoff scores are then used to assign inmates to minimum-, medium-, or maximum-security institutions.

In response to what appears to have been public displeasure of the classification of homicide offenders to medium-security institutions, CSC modified its policy in 2001 requiring life sentence offenders for first- or second-degree murder to spend at least the first two years of their sentence in a maximum-security facility. Elsewhere, we have referred to this kind of mechanism as an "administrative override" (Andrews, Bonta, and Wormith 2004). The policy allows for exceptions with approval from the local warden (CSC 2006). We interpret this modification to decentralized authority as an appropriate effort to reduce the rigidity of this kind of override.

We completed a survey of classification principles, procedures, and instruments in Canadian provincial and territorial DOCs (Wormith, Ferguson, and Bonta 2013). Twelve out of 13 institutional arms of the respective agencies responded. Some jurisdictions employ a mechanism for inmate classification similar to that of the CSC described above (e.g., Alberta). Others tend to focus more on mental health issues and suicide assessment and classification (Quebec). Regardless of jurisdiction, however, we were impressed by the attention paid to criminogenic needs and the RNR principles (Andrews et al. 1990), which we will discuss later (see also Chapter 19 of this volume). We also noted that many jurisdictions were using similar assessment procedures, indeed often the same instrument, in both the institution and community arms of their organization, hence facilitating the flow of information and terminology when an offender moved from institution to community or vice versa.

C. Brief Risk Assessment for Institutional Security

Ideally, it would be informative to review all the prison risk instruments used in the United States, Canada, and other Western countries. However, this would be a daunting task for the United States, where there are federal, state, and county correctional systems, with many having developed their own security classification instruments (American Correctional Association 1982; Brennan, Wells, and Alexander 2004). Therefore, our comments will be limited and focus on two general types of inmate classification instruments: brief risk scales and the more comprehensive risk-need instruments. The latter will be discussed under the section *Classification for Treatment*.

Two widely used and representative instruments of the brief risk measures are the BOP's Security Designation (SD) scale (Federal Bureau of Prisons 2006) and CSC's Custody Rating Scale (CRS; Porporino et al. 1989). They have relatively few items, 10 items in the case of the SD scale and 12 items in the case of the CRS. Most of the items are easily accessible criminal history items (e.g., history of violence, escape history). The motivation for their development is based, in part, on the principle of the least restrictive intervention, although managing overcrowding also plays a role (Levinson and Williams 1979).

The development and evaluation of the SD and CRS followed two different lines. The SD was a product of the professional consensus of 329 staff from the BOP on the significant factors involving security and custody decisions (Levinson and Williams 1979). Through simulation exercises, it was found that the SD recommendation corresponded to the actual security designation in as much as 64 percent of the cases. Although this is not a high degree of correspondence, more inmates were placed in *lower*-security institutions (the percentage of inmates overclassified was not provided). Apparently, this type of evidence was sufficient to implement the SD systemwide in 1979. There are no published studies of the predictive validity of the SD for escapes, misconducts, or criminal recidivism.

The CRS's development arose from a systematic program of research on its predictive validity with respect to misconducts and offender recidivism. Research on the CRS began in 1987, with the instrument becoming fully operational in 1995 (Motiuk 2004). The early research reported promising results (Luciani, Motiuk, and Nafekh 1996; Grant and Luciani 1998; Luciani 2001). However, criticisms of the CRS arose due to the fact that most of the research was on males and, therefore, the instrument was not applicable to women and Aboriginal offenders (Auditor General of Canada 2003; Canadian Human Rights Commission 2003; Webster and Doob 2004a,b). The criticisms of the CRS were met with vigorous opposition by the prison service (Blanchette and Motiuk 2004). However, the exposure of the difficulties with the CRS did stimulate research to address some of the concerns for male offenders (Gobeil 2011).

The stories of the SD and CRS reflect a number of themes found in the various actuarial custody classification instruments. First, the instruments tend to be short and consist of mainly static, unchangeable, criminal history items (Brennan et al. 2004). Second, and as already noted, evidence for their predictive validity for the outcomes that matter to security (e.g., institutional misconduct) has been weak or nonexistent. Third, their usefulness is limited in a time when correctional agencies are returning to rehabilitation and "reentry" is the new buzzword in corrections. The brief custody classification instruments provide very little information about what is needed to rehabilitate and successfully reintegrate inmates into their communities. Thus, offender treatment-oriented classification systems that have been used in community corrections for many years are being introduced into prison classification systems. We will first trace the development of classification instruments that not only inform risk to security but also assess the treatment needs of inmates.

D. Classification for Treatment

We do not wish to suggest that the assessment of inmates for treatment purposes is a recent development; in fact, there is a long history of assessing inmates based upon personality type for the purpose of matching them to the appropriate treatment service. As we shall soon see, the focus on personality for offender rehabilitation yielded minimal benefits, leading to an abandonment of personality-based measures in favor of assessments based upon the more general psychology of criminal conduct.

1. *Personality-Based Classification*

One of the early assessment instruments used in prison settings was the Minnesota Multiphasic Personality Inventory (MMPI; Hathaway and McKinley 1951). The clinical scales of the MMPI cover a variety of personality maladjustments, and only one scale, the psychopathic deviate scale on the older MMPI and the Antisocial Practices scale on the MMPI-2 (Butcher et al. 1989), really is specific to criminal offenders. Although the research has shown that these scales discriminate offenders from nonoffenders (concurrent validity), the prediction of criminal behavior has been modest (Bayer, Bonta, and Motiuk 1985; Duncan, Kennedy, and Patrick 1995).

The most significant attempt to make the MMPI relevant to offender populations was the creation of typologies based upon profiles of the scales. Megargee and Bohn (1979) administered the MMPI to more than 1,200 inmates in a Florida prison and, by applying various statistical techniques, found 10 distinctive profiles. Although the research mostly suggests that the 10 profiles are replicable when based on the original MMPI, classifications based on the more recent and now more widely used MMPI-2 have been largely unreliable (Megargee 1994). More problematic has been the mixed results on the predictive validity of the typologies with respect to both institutional misconducts (Edinger and Auerbach 1978; Hanson et al. 1983; Wright 1988; Bohn et al. 1995) and recidivism (Megargee and Bohn 1979; Moss et al. 1984; Motiuk, Bonta, and Andrews 1986). Only one study reported the benefits of using the typology. Bohn (1980) found a 46 percent reduction in assaults in a Florida federal prison. Nevertheless, the Megargee MMPI system is rarely used today.

Another personality-based classification system for offenders is Quay's (1984) Adult Internal Management System (AIMS). AIMS describes five offender types using two behavioral assessment instruments, the Life History Checklist and the Correctional Adjustment Checklist, to assign offenders into one of the types. Scores on the checklists are converted into a group classification that is used to assign the inmate to specific living quarters. The five offender types are Aggressive-Psychopathic (AP), Manipulative (M), Situational (S), Inadequate-Dependent (ID), and Neurotic-Anxious (NA). Briefly, AP types constantly violate rules and search for excitement, Ms use manipulation to get their way, Ss are relatively trustworthy with a short criminal history, IDs are passive individuals who are frequently victimized by AP and M offenders, and NAs are tense and depressed and tend to lose control when under stress. The main goals of AIMS were to separate the predators from their more likely victims and to assign higher levels of supervision to those most likely to engage in institutional violence.

Research on the validity of AIMS has emphasized the impact of AIMS classification on the reduction of prison violence, despite some evidence that AIMS classification does not predict institutional misconduct (Van Voorhis 1994). Quay (1984) reported that the use of AIMS in a U.S. federal prison system reduced the inmate–staff and inmate–inmate assault rate by approximately 50 percent. Similar results have been reported by Levinson (1988) after implementation of AIMS in a state prison in South Carolina. Concerning the prediction of postrelease recidivism, Levinson (1988) collapsed the five types into three groups and reported a two-year follow-up of 220 inmates. As expected, his Heavy group (AP and M) had the highest rearrest rate. Like the Megargee MMPI, AIMS has not endured, perhaps due to the inconsistent predictive validity data and the complexity of the assessment process.

2. Some Concluding Comments on Personality-Based Assessments

Beginning with Lombroso and Freud, there has long been an interest in identifying offender types, driven by psychologists and a medical model of offenders (MacKenzie 1989). The personality-based classification systems discussed here, the Megargee MMPI and AIMS, have been influential in promoting treatment efforts with offenders because of the emphasis placed on matching the intervention to the personality type of the offender. What we conclude from this literature is that individuals differ along some important dimensions and treatment effectiveness varies with personality factors.

If researchers want to incorporate personality factors into classification systems, then they must identify relevant personality factors that are predictive of outcomes that matter to correctional staff. Such studies have been few and not very promising. What is sorely lacking is evidence on the ability of the personality-based systems to predict recidivism; the few data that exist have not been impressive (e.g., Motiuk et al. 1986; Gendreau, Little, and Goggin 1996).

One final but important comment concerns the general search for typologies. A "type" implies that there are key characteristics associated with the particular type and that one type can be clearly differentiated from another type. Taking Quay's system as an example, an AP offender has some specific characteristics that differentiate him or her from an NA offender. A typological system demands that individuals be classified as one specific type, and forcing individuals who may vary on a dimension such as risk into a particular category is likely to be problematic.

3. A More General and Useful Psychological Approach to Offender Assessment

For many years, correctional psychologists focused on indicators of psychological distress (e.g., anxiety, poor self-esteem, depression) in treatment. However, Andrews, Bonta, and Hoge (1990) turned the traditional targets of treatment on its head. Their paper laid the foundation for the RNR model of offender classification and rehabilitation. Noting that not all treatments are equally effective, Andrews and colleagues proposed three major principles hypothesized to be associated with treatment effectiveness.

The Risk principle has the following two ideas: (1) Criminal behavior can be predicted, and (2) the intensity of treatment should match the offender's level of risk. Regarding the first point, today there is no debate that criminal behavior can be predicted beyond chance levels. Regarding the second point, the research clearly indicates that providing treatment to low-risk offenders produces only very small reductions in recidivism, and larger reductions in recidivism are found when intensive services are provided to higher-risk offenders (Bourgon and Armstrong 2005; Andrews and Bonta 2010; Sperber, Latessa, and Makarios 2013).

The Need principle described the important treatment targets for correctional interventions. These treatment targets were *not* vague personal distress factors; instead, the authors argued, interventions that reduced recidivism were interventions that targeted criminogenic needs such as pro-criminal attitudes, criminal associates, and substance abuse. Evidence for the importance of criminogenic needs as treatment targets has now been widely confirmed (Andrews et al. 1990; Andrews and Bonta 2010) and today is a key feature in many correctional treatment programs.

The Responsivity principle speaks to the modality of treatment and states, in part, that cognitive-behavioral interventions are the most effective mode of treatment with offenders. A key feature of cognitive-behavioral programs is that thoughts lead to behavior, and only by changing one's thoughts will behavior change (Rugge and Bonta 2014). The Risk and Need principles play important roles in the assessment and classification of offenders; in particular, the Need principle views criminogenic needs as *dynamic* risk factors that, when changed, are associated with changes in the probability of recidivism. Thus, instruments that measure criminogenic needs are directly relevant to the treatment of offenders.

There are a number of classification instruments that measure risk and criminogenic needs. The most widely used risk-need instruments belong to the family of the Level of Service (LS) instruments. This includes the Level of Service Inventory-Revised (LSI-R; Andrews and Bonta 1995), the Level of Service/Case Management Inventory (LS/CMI; Andrews, Bonta, and Wormith 2004), the Level of Service/Risk, Need, Responsivity (LS/RNR; Andrews, Bonta, and Wormith 2008), and a brief instrument, the Level of Service-Revised: Screening Version (LSI-R: SV; Andrews and Bonta 1998). Although the LS instruments were first developed on community offender populations, they are currently being used within prison settings around the world. In Canada, eight of 13 jurisdictions use an LS instrument (Wormith, Ferguson, and Bonta 2013). In the United States, there are at least 17 state DOCs that use an LS instrument (Multi-Health Systems, personal communication, July 30, 2013). Further afield, versions of LS have been administered in prisons in Singapore (Andrews et al. 2004), Australia (Hsu, Caputi, and Byrne 2011), Germany (Dahle 2006), and the United Kingdom (Hollin and Palmer 2006).

The LSI-R consists of 54 risk/need items that are scored 0 (absent) or 1 (present), and a simple summation provides a total risk score. The LS/RNR includes much of the same items as the LSI-R but reduced and reconfigured into 42 items (the same is the case with the LS/CMI). However, both the LS/RNR and LS/CMI have additional sections that measure specific risk factors with criminogenic potential, responsivity, and other client considerations. The LS/CMI includes a case management plan embedded in the instrument.

Much of the predictive validity of the LS instruments is with respect to the prediction of offender general and violent recidivism (Gendreau, Goggin, and Smith 2002; Campbell, French, and Gendreau 2009; Andrews, Bonta, and Wormith 2010; Olver, Stockdale, and

Wormith 2014). However, there has also been a significant body of research on the prediction of prison misconduct. Noteworthy is a meta-analysis of the predictors of prison misconduct by Gendreau, Goggin, and Law (1997), in which 39 studies produced 695 effect sizes for a variety of predictors (e.g., race, educational level) including actuarial (risk scale) measures. The actuarial measures were grouped into the following four categories: LSI-R, MMPI, non-MMPI, and other, which consisted of instruments. The LSI-R displayed a significantly higher mean effect size (r = .22; 95 percent CI = .18, .27) than the other risk measures (r = .14; 95 percent CI = .11, .17). The MMPI and the other personality measures performed the worst. Although sufficient research on the LS/CMI and the LS/RNR has yet to be reported, we expect the newer instruments to perform similarly to the LSI-R given their similarity in item content (Olver, Stockdale, and Wormith 2014).

II. Special Cases and Contexts

Two groups of inmates pose special challenges to classification (women and mentally disordered offenders) and, therefore, deserve discussion. In addition, there are certain situations where classification requires a reassessment of the offender and perhaps an overriding of the actuarial-based assessment. In this section, we will also comment on the role of reclassification and the use of professional override.

A. The Classification of Women Prisoners

The classification of women offenders in custody presents a number of special issues, most of which are derived from the fact that most state and federal DOCs use a single classification instrument to assign both male and female prisoners to security level (Farr 2000). Most classification instruments are developed and validated with male offender data, and this has left many correctional workers and offender advocates dissatisfied with the manner by which women are being classified in prison. For some jurisdictions it is a moot point, as there may only be a single facility in the jurisdiction to which female offenders are sentenced. In other jurisdictions, some DOCs, such as the BOP, use the same indicators as they do for men but use different cutoff scores to assign women to security level (Federal Bureau of Prisons 2006). Moreover, the BOP has only four levels of security in its prisons for women (this adjustment is basically made by collapsing minimum and medium security into low security). Hence, this is another means of attempting to accommodate women offenders and to follow the correctional wisdom that women, generally, do not require as high a level of security as their male counterparts with similar scores on a standardized security classification instrument.

Following a scathing review of the manner in which women offenders are classified and generally treated in Canadian federal institutions (Arbour 1996), CSC embarked on an effort to revamp its classification of women offenders and the prisons in which they were placed. This included the development and implementation of a Security Reclassification Scale for Women, which was implemented in 2005 and deemed to be valid also for Aboriginal women offenders (CSC 2006). It was then revalidated in 2012, with some interesting results (Thompson, McConnell, and Paquin-Marseille 2011). The scale remained valid for Aboriginal women and was better for women than men. Most women were classified to medium security, which is very different from how the U.S. BOP classifies women offenders. The override feature was used frequently (27 percent), and two out of every three of these cases used the override to increase women's security level, typically because of their attitude or behavior since their previous classification.

It is widely held that many of the indicators that work (predict accurately) for male prisoners do not do so for female prisoners (e.g., employment, criminal associates, procriminal attitudes). Consequently, it is held that many women prisoners are classified to a security setting that is more restrictive than is necessary. Correctional administrators are then forced to exercise a professional override to adjust the security classification of many women (Farr 2000). Excessive use of an override mechanism is not good correctional practice and tends to exacerbate the problem of prediction error in efforts to improve the process (Harris and Rice 2003; Bonta and Wormith 2013).

B. Prisoners with Mental Health Problems

Forensic professionals and researchers have written extensively about the incidence of prisoners with mental health problems. In a review of correctional research, Arboleda-Florez (2009) found that estimates were highly dependent on the measure and definition of a mental health problem and varied from 5 percent to 90 percent. In a thorough interview-based survey of offenders in jails, state prisons, and federal prisons, James and Glaze (2006) estimated that about half of all incarcerated offenders have some kind of mental health problem (broadly defined). Rates varied by type of facility (jails, 64 percent; state prisons, 56 percent; federal prisons, 45 percent) and by gender, with women routinely reporting higher rates (8 percent to 18 percent greater) than men.

These figures are of interest for a couple of reasons. One, the reported gender differences are consistent with other reports that mental health issues are particularly relevant and prevalent among female offenders and may speak to a different etiology, or pathway, for their offending (Chesney-Lind 1997; Bloom, Owen, and Covington 2003), which in turn speaks to gender-specific treatment that addresses both mental health status as a responsivity factor in the delivery of intervention services and mental health issues as a criminogenic factor. Two, the substantial differences between officially diagnosed cases and all identified cases through various means suggest a failure of correctional assessment procedures to identify the majority of offenders with mental health problems in their facilities. Assessment and classification of offenders must address conditions such as depression and likelihood of suicide, which is the third most prevalent cause of death in U.S. federal and state prisons (preceded by natural causes and AIDS) (Daniel 2007). Given the sheer volume of offenders who are admitted to prisons and jails, the most common approach to identify offenders with mental health issues is to include a screening tool as part of the admissions and assessment process (Teplin and Swartz 1989). Clearly, better and more routinely administered mental health screening procedures are required in corrections.

There are two other important reasons that the offender assessment and classification process must be mindful of mental health issues. First is for the safety and security of prisoners with mental health issues; as we have noted, these offenders are vulnerable in the general population of most prisons. Second, specialized medical and psychiatric units or facilities are better designed to meet their complex clinical needs. The classification of prisoners because of their mental health problems occurs on a different level than classification for traditional security reasons. Although some mental health prisoners do pose a risk to other offenders, most are vulnerable as victims (Blitz, Wolff, and Shi 2008) and are less likely to perpetrate prison violence (DiCataldo, Greer, and Profit 1995).

C. Reclassifications and Preparation for Reintegration

In anticipation of subsequent release back to the community, many custodial agencies provide opportunities for changes in the inmate's custodial placement. Reclassification assessments contain elements of the initial classification instruments but are also related to the behavior of the prisoner in his or her current level of security and frequently take into consideration the remaining time of an offender's sentence. The goal is to reduce the security classification and placement over time and to prepare the offender for release, sometimes referred to as "cascading" down through progressively lower levels of prison security into community corrections facilities or halfway houses. Hopefully, the criminogenic needs of the offender are also taken into consideration in this process, as are factors such as proximity to family and opportunities for work and other programs outside of the institution. An accurate and thorough knowledge of an offender's criminogenic needs is vital for his or her successful reentry into the community (Bonta and Wormith 2013). A good classification system is dynamic and helps in the preparation of an offender's reentry and reintegration to the community.

Reclassification can go in the other direction as well: If an offender's behavior begins to deteriorate, his or her classification may be increased, upon a periodic review (e.g., every six months is common in many DOCs across the United States). In fact, it is not uncommon for offenders serving lengthy sentences to move back and forth between security levels during their incarceration. For these reasons, it is important that offenders be considered for reclassification on a regular basis and that the instrument used for reclassification be dynamic and sensitive to changes in the offender's risk status over time.

D. The Role of the Professional and the Integrity of Assessment

Professionals are often expected to exercise discretion in making decisions and to administer, score, and apply the results from the instrument properly. With respect to the first expectation, predictions of criminal activity are often at the heart of discretionary action. The RNR principles do not provide the final word on offender assessment. Although they provide an empirical basis to offender assessment, sooner or later there will be a case that does not fit the formula. There may be room for professional judgment, but, given its poor track record, care must be taken so that professional overrides are used judiciously and defensibly. This can be done by agencies systematically monitoring the use of overrides and, if patterns emerge, incorporating (or perhaps discovering) a new principle of assessment. Simply put, we should use science in a constructive manner.

In regard to the second expectation, administering, scoring, and applying the results from the instrument properly, much rests on the training of the assessor. Even under the best of conditions, risk-needs instruments make errors; measurement error is inherent in any assessment tool. However, another source of error, the assessor, can be better managed.

Bonta, Bogue, Crowley, and Motiuk (2001) described the importance of ensuring the integrity of offender assessment with the implementation of the LSI-R in community corrections in Colorado. Even after highly structured training in the use of the LSI-R, there remained high rates of errors (e.g., 13 percent of 336 LSI-R files reviewed had addition mistakes and misunderstandings of how some of the items were to be scored). This problem was addressed by not only continually monitoring the administration of the LSI-R but also introducing booster training sessions. Many jurisdictions fail to monitor and correct such an important process (Flores et al. 2006).

There is also some indirect evidence suggesting that staff may not fully utilize the new instruments. A number of studies have reported that staff are often reluctant to change what they have done for years and adopt a new and better assessment procedure (Bonta et al. 2001). In a study by Schneider et al. (1996), staff members were surveyed about their views of a newly introduced classification system (Wisconsin Risk and Need). Less than half of the probation officers thought it was a helpful instrument. Only 27 percent thought that the instrument was more accurate than their professional judgment. The major reason given for completing the instrument was expectations from their supervisors (78 to 83 percent range). Similar results have been reported elsewhere—for example, Prendergast (2012) asked probation staff in England about their views of the LSI-R and another risk instrument that was being pilot tested.

We cannot help but suspect that the failure by staff to recognize the benefits of empirically based classification instruments would lead to errors and a resistance to use the results in case management. The problems encountered point to a need for a high degree of training, personal professionalism, and managerial supervision. Staff members who administer offender assessment instruments must conduct the assessments conscientiously and managers must actively assist and supervise. As we have noted previously, we are encouraged by reports that many DOCs have begun to consider this task seriously and to monitor staff assessments closely.

III. WHY ARE PRISONER ASSESSMENT AND CLASSIFICATION IMPORTANT?

The classification of prisoners can vary from very straightforward to more complex and multidimensional assessments and related decisions. Regardless, the fundamental goal of offender classification in prison is to improve the operation of the correctional agency by grouping prisoners in some systematic fashion and then dealing with the respective groups in a consistent manner. An effective offender classification system can generate a number of favorable outcomes. First, it can make the facilities safer for both prisoner and staff. Second, it can minimize the potentially deleterious effects that are inherent to routine incarceration (e.g., the restrictions around freedom of movement, personal distress, access to leisure activities). Third, it can increase the prospects of treatment and rehabilitation programs for offenders. Finally, it can reduce the financial, humanitarian, and public safety costs of incarceration to the public.

A. Prison Safety

A core responsibility of correctional facilities is to maintain the safety of their prisoners and staff. This is often an onerous task. Correctional administrators are required to accommodate a diverse range of offenders from petty property offenders to seriously violent individuals. Gangs, drugs (which penetrate the prison walls despite constant surveillance), overcrowding, aging infrastructure, and limited human and financial budgets all converge on what can seem like an impossible task. Indeed, the record of prison violence, which ranges from bullying to assault, sexual assault, prison riots, and murder, is discouraging. A few sobering facts are noteworthy.

In California, the problem of overcrowding was so severe that, in 2011, a U.S. Supreme Court ruling required the early release of 37,000 California prison inmates; the Court declared that California's overcrowded prison system was a violation of the Eighth Amendment's ban on cruel and unusual punishment (*Brown v. Plata* 2011). At the time of the ruling, California's correctional facilities held some 156,000 offenders, nearly double the number they were designed to hold. Moreover, this overcrowding imposed demands well beyond the capacity of medical and mental health facilities and created unsanitary and unsafe conditions that made progress in the provision of care difficult or impossible to achieve (*Brown v. Plata* 2011).

Inmate-on-inmate assaults have increased in a number of jurisdictions. For example, in Ohio, they jumped nearly 21 percent from 2007 to 2012 (Bischoff 2011). In Arizona, they increased from 425 in 2005 to 1,758 in 2013 (Arizona Department of Corrections 2013). In Canada, the total number of assaults reported by CSC rose from 1,415 in 2009-10 to 1,669 in 2011-12 (Metro News 2013). A U.S. Department of Justice report stated that, in 2011/12, "an estimated 4.0 percent of state and federal prison inmates and 3.2 percent of jail inmates reported experiencing incidents of sexual victimization by another inmate or facility staff in the past 12 months" (Beck et al. 2013, p. 6).

Prison gangs have evolved from a group that provides protection to its members into criminal entities involved in prostitution, assaults, drugs, and murder. According to the Federal Bureau of Investigation, although gang members make up less than 0.1 percent of the prison population, they account for 20 percent of murders in the federal prison system (Holthouse 2005). In both the United States and Canada, the same basic pattern is followed: Prison gangs control the drug trade inside most facilities, which leads to violent rivalries between gangs trying to enlarge or maintain their customer base (CBC News 2012). Like their American counterparts, prison gangs in Canada are numerous and diverse. Corrections Canada has seen a 44 percent jump in gang members in federal prisons, from 1,421 in 2007 to 2,040 in 2012 (CBC News 2012).

Prison riots cost taxpayers millions of dollars. A pair of prison riots at Peco, Texas in 2009 cost more than $1 million in repairs (Associated Press 2013). In 1993, a prison riot at a maximum-security prison in Ohio cost taxpayers nearly $69 million (Associated Press 1997). At the California Institution for men in Chino, a prison riot in 2009 cost taxpayers about $6 million to make repairs and clean up debris (Associated Press 2009).

Suicide is one of the leading causes of death for inmates. In the United States, in 2011, 185 inmates took their lives in state and federal prisons; in that year, suicides made up 5.5 percent of deaths in state and federal prisons, which was more than drugs, alcohol intoxication, homicide, and accidents combined (NBC News 2013). In Canada, between 2003 and 2008, there were 46 suicides among inmates in federal custody (Power and Riley 2010). The suicide rate among offenders is four times higher than the rate in the general population.

While inmates are at risk, so are correctional staff. The Arizona Department of Corrections (2013) reported 191 assaults on staff in 2013. In California's Sacramento County Jail, assaults on staff increased more than 160 percent from 2011 to 2012; in the San Diego County Jail, assaults on staff increased more than 50 percent from 2011 to 2012 (Anderson 2013). In Canada, there were nearly 1,000 assaults on federal corrections works between 2007 and 2010, with 22 percent of those in Canada's largest province, Ontario, where 30 percent of Canada's federal prisoners are incarcerated (Tripp 2010). Offender classification is one vital tool that correctional administrators have at their disposal in their struggle to reduce these statistics.

B. Minimizing Harm

With much of the focus of inmate classification on physical safety and effective operation of correctional facilities, it is easy to overlook a related function of the classification process: the identification of low-risk offenders for the purpose of minimizing the negative effects of association with serious, high-risk offenders. Theories and perspectives ranging from differential association (Sutherland and Cressey 1978), social learning (Bandura 1977), and a general personality and social psychological perspective (Andrews and Bonta 2010) all warn about the potential harm of intense, persistent exposure to seriously criminalized peers' and associates' criminalizing impact. This is something that prison, by its very nature, accomplishes with ease through the process of "prisonization" (Clemmer 1958). A good inmate classification system will identify those most at risk of prisonization and make recommendations accordingly.

The impact of prisonization is best seen empirically through a cumulative series of meta-analyses of variations in the severity of punishments handed out by justice systems around the world and the severity of circumstances to which prisoners are assigned. Gendreau, Goggin, and Cullen (1999) conducted a meta-analysis of 50 studies involving 336,052 offenders and 325 correlations addressing the length of incarceration in relation to recidivism, and comparisons between prison and community-based sanctions (also in terms of recidivism). They found that prison corresponded with a slight increase in recidivism (about 7 percent) and that lower-risk offenders were more severely affected. Their interpretation was that "lower-risk offenders may be more adversely affected by greater lengths of incarceration through exposure to an environment typically dominated by their higher-risk, more hardcore peers" (p. 1). In a follow-up study, when only well-controlled studies were considered, the negative effect actually increased to 14 percent (Smith, Goggin, and Gendreau 2002).

Most recently, Jonson (2010) conducted a similar meta-analysis with 85 studies comparing prison to community sanctions and degrees of severity in prison settings. She found a 14 percent increase in recidivism among those sentenced to prison and a 15 percent increase in recidivism among those sentenced to a harsher condition, typically increased security. For the 35 percent of studies where risk information was available, risk level did not moderate the general findings. Consequently, we encourage clinicians and correctional administrators to keep in mind that as much attention should be devoted to the assessment and classification of low-risk, well-behaved offenders as to high-risk, problematic offenders.

Looking at the harshness of prison conditions, there is some evidence for the deleterious effects of harsher conditions on recidivism. Using individual-level data, Chen and Shapiro (2007) found that, if anything, higher security classifications and harsher prison sentences were related to increased, not decreased, recidivism rates among BOP inmates. Projecting their findings, Chen and Shapiro predicted that if all minimum-security BOP inmates were placed in higher-security institutions, their rearrest rate would increase by 41 percent. By considering this hypothetical projection in reverse, one can appreciate the value that is gained by classifying low-risk inmates to minimum-security facilities.

Elsewhere, examining a wide range of prison conditions, including overcrowding and lack of volunteers, on the postrelease behaviors of about 20,000 Italian inmates, Drago, Galbiati, and Vertova (2011) found a consistent relationship between harshness of the conditions and prisoner recidivism. However, these studies and the vast majority of studies in the aforementioned meta-analyses were correlational. Most did not control for risk level as offenders entered prison (only 35 percent in the Jonson [2010] review) or did not randomly assign offenders to prison or prison type.

In sum, prison and the severity of prison conditions does not appear to deter offenders from reoffending; indeed, it may actually be criminogenic, exacerbating one's likelihood of returning to prison.

C. Fostering Rehabilitation and Reintegration in the Community

Another important aspect of offender classification is to foster effective intervention with prisoners. Because the LS instruments are the most popular RNR-based classification instruments, our discussion on the relationship between offender assessment and treatment is focused on these instruments. The growing use of LS assessments is due to its capacity to bring information on the treatment needs of offenders to the classification process, something the brief security instruments cannot do.

The LS instruments measure the major criminogenic needs of offenders. These dynamic risk factors make up what Andrews and Bonta (2010) refer to as the Central Eight risk/need factors (Table 18.1). For example, one can make pro-criminal friends or replace pro-criminal friends with prosocial friends, or one can replace pro-criminal attitudes with prosocial attitudes. Such changes can occur through natural life events, as when an offender becomes involved in a romantic relationship with a prosocial partner. The other way that criminogenic needs can change is by planned treatment intervention. It is here that prisons

Table 18.1. The "Central Eight" risk/need factors of the Level of Service Instruments

Risk/Need Factor	Description
Criminal History	Early onset of antisocial behavior, frequent and varied antisocial acts
Pro-criminal Attitudes	Thoughts, values, and sentiments supportive of criminal conduct
Antisocial Personality Pattern	Low self-control, hostile, pleasure/thrill seeking, disregard for others, callous
Pro-criminal Associates	Friends who model, encourage, and support criminal behavior and thoughts
Education/Employment	Difficulties in school and work settings with peers and authority, poor performance
Family/Marital	Marital instability, poor parenting skills, criminality within the family and marital relationship
Substance Abuse	Alcohol and/or drug abuse, substance abuse interfering with prosocial behaviors and relationships within the context of school, work, and family
Leisure/Recreation	Lack of prosocial pursuits

Source: Andrews and Bonta (2010).

see a value for the use of risk/need assessment instruments because they identify the criminogenic needs that should be addressed by treatment programs and, because they are dynamic, correctional staff can monitor offender change through reassessment.

Why should prison officials care about identifying criminogenic needs and providing treatment programs? Would it not be cheaper for prisons to simply segregate inmates for security reasons and carry out the court-ordered sentence? There are three reasons why prisons should care. First, the evidence suggests that incapacitation has little effect on offender recidivism—in some cases, it even increases recidivism. Thus, imprisonment does little to enhance community safety in the long term. Second, helping inmates to behave in a more prosocial manner can make prison environments less disruptive and easier to manage (Gendreau, Listwan, Kuhns, and Exum 2014). Finally, treatment that follows the RNR principles within a custodial setting is associated with reduced recidivism (Andrews and Bonta 2010). This has become especially important in the United States, where financial pressure to reduce prison populations has required consideration of treatment to ensure safe reentry of prisoners into their communities. For the first time since 1972 there was a drop in the state prison population, with more inmates being released on parole (Pew Center on the States 2010). An offender assessment and classification system that can prevent harm *and* foster rehabilitation and increase public safety is a welcome change from schemes based only on security.

D. Financial Costs of High Security

An easily overlooked reason to have a good classification system pertains to the cost of building and operating higher-security prisons. This function may seem rather mercenary and out of place with the aforementioned "principled" functions of offender classification, but it is a very real issue for DOCs, where the fiscal backdrop must be weighed against efforts to achieve other goals. Recent estimates suggest that the cost of constructing a maximum-security facility is at least $100,000 per bed. Doing the math is simple: If a state requires 1,000 new beds to accommodate new maximum-security inmates or to ease overcrowding, the cost would total $100 million (Mulligan 2007).

One must also consider differences in the annual costs of operating prisons with different security levels. For a number of reasons, the annual operating costs of prisons increase with security level. One reason is the inmate-to-staff ratio. Lower-security facilities require fewer officers to patrol the facility, to operate technology, and to occupy security posts throughout the institution. Lower-security facilities can also be constructed to house more offenders and thus capitalize on economies of scale both in terms of construction and operating costs. We take the United States as a case study of the financial costs of imprisonment.

1. Incarceration Costs in the United States

State spending on corrections has skyrocketed, from $12 billion in 1988 to more than $52 billion in 2011 (Justice Center 2013). The Vera Institute of Justice (2013) estimated that among the 40 states that participated in their survey, the cost of prisons was $39 billion in 2010. Table 18.2 reports the costs of incarceration for the 40 state DOCs that participated in the survey. As seen in Figure 18.1, the lion's share of the costs of prisons is borne by state and local governments (Schmitt, Warner, and Gupta 2010). Nearly 2 percent of the prison population in the United States is housed in what are called supermax facilities. By 2006, the United States had 57 supermax facilities in 40 states. However, supermax imprisonment remains one of the most controversial developments in corrections largely due to the costs of such facilities. A typical supermax facility may represent a $1 billion investment over 30 to 40 years, the typical lifespan of a prison (Mears and Watson 2006). The per-cell "operating" cost of a supermax is about $75,000 annually, compared to $25,000 for each cell in an ordinary state prison (Ross 2007). Such high costs to taxpayers are one of the most controversial aspects of supermax prisons.

Maximum-security institutions provide the next highest level of security. In the United States, the annual cost per inmate for maximum security in the BOP was $33,930 in 2012 (LaVigne and Samuels 2012). Currently, about 30 percent of the federal inmate population is housed in medium-security facilities, where the average cost per inmate is $26,247. The cost for minimum security is $21,006 per inmate (LaVigne and Samuels 2012). However, these average annual costs vary considerably by state.

2. Does Offender Classification Work?

The answer to the question "does it work?" has two important elements. First, the classification instrument should be able to reliably predict behaviors that threaten the security of the prison (i.e., institutional misconduct and escapes). Published evidence for the predictive validity of the various instruments ranges from nonexistent (e.g., SD) to conflicting (e.g., CRS) to reasonably strong (e.g., LS instruments). The second element is that implementation of a security classification instrument should lead to a more appropriate distribution of inmates across security levels, with fewer misconducts and escapes.

Table 18.2. The price of prison for 40 states (in millions or billions)

State	Prison cost[*]
Alabama	445.5 m
Arizona	998.5 m
Arkansas	288.6 m
California	7.0 b
Colorado	584.7 m
Connecticut	613.3 m
Delaware	190.4 m
Florida	2.05 b
Georgia	1.0 b
Idaho	143 m
Illinois	1.2 b
Indiana	562.2 m
Iowa	265.4 m
Kansas	156.1 m
Kentucky	272.5 m
Louisiana	608 m
Maine	94.0 m
Maryland	731.3 m
Michigan	1.2 b
Minnesota	365.5 m
Missouri	503.9 m
Montana	74.6 m
Nebraska	158.2 m
Nevada	267.9 m
New Hampshire	80.3 m
New Jersey	1.2 b
New York	2.7 b
North Carolina	1.1 b
North Dakota	56.2 m
Ohio	1.27 b
Oklahoma	441.8 m
Pennsylvania	1.6 b
Rhode Island	159.8 m
Texas	2.5 b
Utah	178.1 m
Vermont	102 m
Virginia	712.4 m
Washington	684.6 m
West Virginia	152.1 m
Wisconsin	800.3 m

[*] In fiscal year 2010.
Source: Vera Institute of Justice (2013).

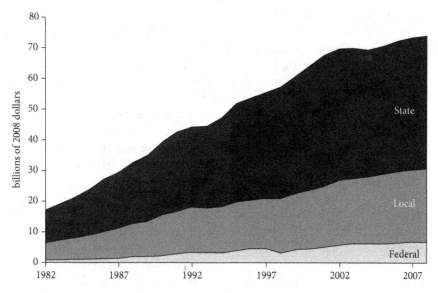

FIGURE 18.1. United States: total inflation-adjusted corrections expenditures by type of government, 1982–2008.

Although there is no predictive validity evidence on the SD, its implementation in the BOP was evaluated with respect to its impact on the appropriateness of the security classifications. Levinson (1980) found that after implementation of the SD, there was a small decrease in the escape rate but no difference in the assault rate compared to a period prior to implementation. However, the introduction of the SD did lead to placing more inmates in lower-security institutions.

Some evaluations of classification systems have relied on statistical modeling, where the question is "what if . . . ?" Bonta and Motiuk (1992) provided an estimate of the impact of using LSI-R cutoff scores on the distribution of inmates along three custody levels for the entire Ontario provincial prison system. They found that if the LSI-R was used to make placement decisions, there would be a reduction in overclassification by 38 percent. Others have also reported that the introduction of objective offender classification can lead to better use of minimum- and medium-security facilities (Baird 1993).

More rigorous evaluations of inmate classification systems have been few and far between. To our knowledge, there have only been two randomized experimental evaluations of adult classification systems. The first was conducted in Washington State, but the results for the effectiveness of the new classification system were confounded by the fact that all of the inmates were also placed in a new prison facility (Austin, Baird, and Neuenfeldt 1993).

Berk and his colleagues (2003) conducted an experimental test of the introduction of a new inmate classification system. Over 19,000 male inmates in the California DOC were participants in the experiment. California was assigning inmates to different security institutions based on scores from a risk assessment form (CDC Form 839). With the assistance of the California Center for Population Research, modifications were made to the risk form, with items added or removed and with changes to scoring weights (Berk and de Leeuw 1999). Inmates were randomly assigned to one of two conditions. Both the original and revised CDC Form 839 were completed on all inmates; custody assignment for inmates in the control condition was based on the original risk form, but custody placement for inmates in the experimental condition was based on the revised risk form. With the revised risk classification instrument, significantly more inmates were placed in minimum-security (Level I) prisons. However, more were also placed into Level III security prisons. The increase in placements in higher security was partially traced to the presence of one item—gang involvement. Finally, misconduct rates for the control and experimental inmates were similar overall, but the revised CDC Form 839 was associated with higher rates of misconduct for the experimental inmates in Level III facilities. The latter finding was unexpected given that one would expect higher security to suppress disruptive behavior.

Another fascinating double-blind experiment was conducted by Bench and Allen (2003) in the Utah State Prison. Prisoners who had been classified as maximum security were randomly assigned to either maximum- or medium-security facilities. All correctional personnel and the inmates themselves were unaware of the study. Offenders classified to medium security were not randomly assigned to maximum security, although their behavior in medium security was recorded for the purposes of this study. All offenders were monitored for disciplinary incidents and, in addition to simply counting the number of misconducts, a 4-point weighted severity system was used (1 = engaging in unauthorized communication or violation of housing unit rules; 2 = conduct threatening to the facility or any individual or possession of stolen property; 3 = deliberate destruction of state property or attempting escape; and 4 = fire setting or assault with or without weapon or taking a hostage). The hypothesis that maximum-security inmates housed in medium security would not have more (weighted) disciplinary actions than the medium-security inmates housed in medium security was supported. However, the hypothesis that maximum-security inmates housed in the medium-security setting would have fewer (weighted) incidents than maximum-security inmates housed in maximum security was not supported.

These are sobering findings and, at first blush, one may conclude that the classification system and its security rating of offenders were not working. However, Bench and Allen (2003) speculated about possible reasons for these findings. First, it is possible that the classification system is excessively cautious and generates many "false positives," or prisoners who are rated as more likely to commit serious disciplinary infractions but do not. Obviously, a high false-positive rate has financial implications (i.e., higher security is more costly) and may be iatrogenic in that overclassification may generate more disciplinary infractions—that is, maximum-security inmates are expected to act out and then do so (Shermer, Bierie, and Stock 2012).

Second, these results may be unique to the Utah DOC and its classification system. It appears that maximum-security prisoners were identified, as they are in many jurisdictions, based on the length of their sentence, the severity of their offense, their number of prior incarcerations, and their propensity for violence. From the standpoint of correctional administrators who are looking for maximum-security cells to place their prisoners, Bench and Allen (2003) pointed out that it may be heartening to learn that maximum-security offenders, at least those who were so identified by the aforementioned scheme, pose no greater risk when placed in a medium-security institution, or at least a medium-security setting as designed in the Utah DOC.

Third, on the one hand, some might suggest that the fact that there was no difference in the number of disciplinary incidents for offenders classified and housed in their "correct" and respective settings (maximum or medium) is a testament to the value of maximum security in that it "suppressed" the anticipated high number of disciplinary incidents by means of monitoring, supervision, and limited movement. On the other hand, housing maximum-security prisoners in medium-security settings appeared to have done the same thing, perhaps by another mechanism (e.g., programing and greater human contact).

Finally, the authors pointed out that they do not believe that maximum-security prisons should be abolished, as one might conclude from this study. Rather, they are convinced, as are we, that maximum-security facilities are clearly required for some prisoners for the safety of the institution and to protect other prisoners and staff. The question is, who are those prisoners and how do we identify them?

IV. Conclusion

Traditional, one-dimensional offender assessment and classifications schemes are not adequately designed to address the multidimensionality of the task when dealing with the prison population. One instrument, the LS/CMI (Andrews et al. 2004), has incorporated what are referred to as noncriminogenic needs into its offender risk/need assessment protocol. While the added component directs the assessor to also consider mental health issues that may have an impact on decisions to house and provide an array of clinical treatment services to the offender, the general risk/need portion still correlates with offender recidivism almost as well for offenders with mental disorders as with inmates without mental disorders (i.e. .39 vs. .41; Girard and Wormith 2004). We believe this is because the Central Eight risk/need domains are as applicable to offenders who have mental health problems as to those who do not (Bonta, Blais, and Wilson 2014).

We also point out that what we have called "fourth generation" risk assessment tools (Andrews et al. 2006) are important for conducting a thorough offender assessment and classification that looks beyond offender risk and criminogenic need. They consider other social health and mental health issues, as well as key responsivity considerations, that are important not only for the delivery of service and treatment for offenders but also for their ongoing case management and supervision. There was a time when mental health issues were perceived as the critical and, in some cases, the only dimension for the psychological assessment of offenders, and it is important that we do not lose sight of it in our emerging concentration on the Central Eight. Consideration of offender mental health is important for the following reasons: security and protection of vulnerable offenders; responsivity considerations in the delivery of programs and services; and a combination of humanitarian, medical, and legal reasons (Ball 2007; Gunter et al. 2008). Finally, there is a related criminogenic issue, with some mental health issues being either directly (e.g., paranoid ideation; Bettencourt et al. 2006; Carroll 2009) or indirectly (e.g., through homelessness and substance abuse) related to further criminal behavior (Parhar and Wormith 2013).

The task of correctional administrators to house prisoners is complex and at times must seem overwhelming. Competing agendas, conflicting goals, financial constraints, legal obligations, popular sentiment, political pressures, and limited space for a burgeoning population all weigh heavily on those who are responsible for correctional policy, procedures, and daily operations. Offender assessment and classification are important tools and processes that are designed to assist DOCs to meet their legal and ethical obligations to accommodate offenders in the best and most efficacious manner possible. Regardless, the onus rests with clinicians and correctional administrators to maximize the utility of offender assessment and classification for the mutual benefit of their agency and clientele.

REFERENCES

American Correctional Association. 1982. *Classification as a Management Tool: Theories and Models for Decision-Makers.* College Park, MD: American Correctional Association.

Anderson, Kristopher. 2013. *Violence on the Rise in California County Jails.* http://www.correctionsone.com/corrections/articles/6308205-Violence-on-the-rise-in-Calif-county-jails/

Andrews, Donald A., and James Bonta. 1995. *The Level of Service Inventory—Revised.* Toronto, Canada: Multi-Health Systems.

Andrews, Donald A., and James Bonta. 1998. *The Level of Service Inventory-Revised: Screening Version. User's Manual:* Toronto, Canada: Multi-Health Systems.

Andrews, Donald A., and James Bonta. 2010. *The Psychology of Criminal Conduct,* 5th ed. New Providence, NJ: LexisNexis.

Andrews, Donald A., James Bonta, and Robert D. Hoge. 1990. "Classification for Effective Rehabilitation: Rediscovering Psychology." *Criminal Justice and Behavior* 17:19–52.

Andrews, Donald A., James Bonta, and J. Stephen Wormith. 2004. *Level of Service/Case Management Inventory (LS/CMI): User's Manual.* Toronto, Canada: Multi-Health Systems.

Andrews, Donald A., James Bonta, and J. Stephen Wormith. 2006. "The Recent Past and Near Future of Risk and/or Need Assessment." *Crime and Delinquency* 52:7–27.

Andrews, Donald A., James Bonta, and J. Stephen Wormith. 2008. *The Level of Service/Risk, Need, Responsivity. User's Manual:* Toronto, Canada: Multi-Health Systems.

Andrews, Donald A., James Bonta, and Stephen J. Wormith. 2010. "The Level of Service (LS) Assessment of Adults and Older Adolescents." In *Handbook of Violence Risk Assessment,* edited by Randy K. Otto and Kevin S. Douglas. New York: Routledge.

Andrews, Donald A., Ivan Zinger, Robert D. Hoge, James Bonta, Paul Gendreau, and Francis T. Cullen. 1990. "Does Correctional Treatment Work? A Psychologically Informed Meta-analysis." *Criminology* 28:369–404.

Arboleda-Florez, Julio. 2009. "Mental Patients in Prisons." *World Psychiatry* 8(3):187–189.

Arbour, Louise. 1996. *Commission of Inquiry into Certain Events at the Prison for Women in Kingston.* Ottawa, Canada: Solicitor General of Canada.

Arizona Department of Corrections. 2013. *Inmate Assault Data.* http://www.azcorrections.gov/adc/pdf/021113_inmate_assault_data.pdf

Associated Press. 1997. *Prison Riot Cost Taxpayers $68.8M.* http://www.highbeam.com/doc/1G1-67899404.html

Associated Press. 2009. *Prison Riot to Cost California $5-$6 M.* http://www.correctionsone.com/finance-and-budgets/articles/1873744-Prison-riot-to-cost-California-5M-6M/

Associated Press. 2013. *West Texas Prison Riots Cost County $1.1 Million.* http://www.brownsvilleherald.com/news/valley/article_edcfb028-16fd-511f-a7b5-ae071a130171.html

Auditor General of Canada. 2003. *Report of the Auditor General of Canada to the House of Commons.* Ottawa, Canada: Office of the Auditor General of Canada.

Austin, James, Christopher Baird, and Deborah Neuenfeldt. 1993. "Classification for Internal Management Purposes: The Washington Experience." In *Classification: A Tool for Managing Today's Offenders*. Laurel, MD: American Correctional Association.

Baird, Christopher. 1993. "Objective Classification in Tennessee: Management, Effectiveness, and Planning Issues." In *Classification: A Tool for Managing Today's Offenders*. Laurel, MD: American Correctional Association.

Ball, W. David. 2007. "Mentally Ill Prisoners in the California Department of Corrections and Rehabilitation: Strategies for Improving Treatment and Reducing Recidivism." *Journal of Contemporary Law and Health Policy* 24:1–42.

Bandura, Albert. 1977. *Social Learning Theory*. New York: Prentice Hall.

Bayer, Betty, M., James Bonta, and Laurence L. Motiuk. 1985. "The Pd Subscales: An Empirical Evaluation." *Journal of Clinical Psychology* 41:780–788.

Beck, Allen, J., Marcus Berzofsky, Rachel Casper, and Christopher Krebs. 2013. *Sexual Victimization in Prisons and Jails Reported by Inmates, 2011-12*. Washington, DC: Bureau of Justice Statistics. http://www.bjs.gov/content/pub/pdf/svpjri1112.pdf

Bench, Lawrence, L., and Terry D. Allen. 2003. "Investigating the Stigma of Prison Classification: An Experimental Design." *The Prison Journal* 43:367–382.

Berk, Richard A., and Jan de Leeuw. 1999. *An Evaluation of California's Inmate Classification System Using a Generalized Regression Discontinuity Design*. Department of Statistics, University of California at Los Angeles.

Berk, Richard A., Heather Ladd, Heidi Graziano, and Jong-Ho Baek. 2003. "A Randomized Experiment Testing Inmate Classification Systems." *Criminology and Public Policy* 2:215–242.

Bettencourt, B. Ann, Amelia E. Talley, Arlin J. Benjamin, and Jeffrey Valentine. 2006. "Personality and Aggressive Behavior Under Provoking and Neutral Conditions. A Meta-analytic Review." *Psychological Bulletin* 132:751–777.

Bischoff, Laura A. 2011. *Assaults in Ohio Prisons up 20.6%*. http://www.springfieldnewssun.com/news/news/local/assaults-in-ohio-prisons-up-206-1/nMwmy/

Blanchette, Kelley, and Laurence L. Motiuk. 2004. "Taking Down the Straw Man: A Reply to Webster and Doob." *Canadian Journal of Criminology and Criminal Justice* 46:621–630.

Blitz, Cynthia L., Nancy Wolff, and Jing Shi. 2008. "Physical Victimization in Prison: The Role of Mental Illness." *International Journal of Law and Psychiatry* 31(5):385–393.

Bloom, Barbara, Barbara Owen, and Stephanie Covington. 2003. *Gender-Responsive Strategies: Research, Practice, and Guiding Principles for Women Offenders*. Washington, DC: National Institute of Corrections, US Department of Justice.

Bohn, Martin J. 1980. "Inmate Classification and the Reduction of Institution Violence." In *Proceedings of the One Hundred and Ninth Annual Congress of Correction*. American Correctional Association. Alexandria, VA.

Bohn, Martin J., Joyce L. Carbonell, and Edwin I. Megargee, E. 1995. "The Applicability and Utility of the MMPI-based Offender Classification System in a Correctional Mental Health Unit." *Criminal Behaviour and Mental Health* 5:14–33.

Bonta, James, Julie Blais, and Holly A. Wilson. 2014. "A Theoretically Informed Meta-Analysis of the Risk for General and Violent Recidivism for Mentally Disordered Offenders Aggression and Violent Behavior." *Aggression and Violent Behavior* 19:278–287.

Bonta, James, Brad Bogue, Michael Crowley, and Laurence Motiuk. 2001. "Implementing Offender Classification Systems: Lessons Learned." In *Offender Rehabilitation in Practice: Implementing and Evaluating Effective Programs*, edited by Gary A. Bernfeld, David P. Farrington, and Alan W. Leschied. Chichester, England: Wiley.

Bonta, James, and Laurence L. Motiuk. 1992. "Inmate Classification." *Journal of Criminal Justice* 20:343–353.

Bonta, James, and J. Stephen Wormith. 2013. "Applying the Risk-Needs-Responsivity Principles to Offender Assessment." In *What Works in Offender Rehabilitation: An Evidence-Based Approach to Assessment and Treatment*, edited by Leam A. Craig, Louise Dixon, and Theresa A. Gannon. Chichester, West Sussex, United Kingdom: Wiley-Blackwell.

Bourgon, G., and Barbara Armstrong. 2005. "Transferring the Principles of Effective Treatment into a 'Real World' Prison Setting." *Criminal Justice and Behavior* 32:3–25.

Brennan, Tim, David Wells, and Jack Alexander. 2004. *Enhancing Prison Classification Systems: The Emerging Role of Management Information Systems*. Washington, DC: U.S. Department of Justice.

Brown v. Plata. 2011. Supreme Court of the United States. 563 U.S. http://www.supremecourt.gov/opinions/10pdf/09-1233.pdf

Butcher, James N., W. Grant Dahlstrom, John R. Graham, Auke Tellegen, and B. Kaemmer. 1989. *The Minnesota Multiphasic Personality Inventory-2: Manual for Administration and Scoring*. Minneapolis: University of Minnesota Press.

Campbell, Mary Ann, Sheila French, and Paul Gendreau. 2009. "The Prediction of Violence in Adult Offenders: A Meta-analytic Comparison of Instruments and Methods of Assessment." *Criminal Justice and Behavior* 36:567–590.

Canadian Human Rights Commission 2003. *Protecting their Rights: A Systemic Review of Human Rights in Correctional Services for Federally Sentenced Women*. Ottawa, Canada: Canadian Human Rights Commission.

Carroll, Andrew. 2009. "Are You Looking at Me? Understanding and Managing Paranoid Personality Disorder." *Advances in Psychiatric Treatment* 15:40–48.

CBC News. 2012. *Rise in Prison Gangs Fuelling Violence, Drug Trade*. http://ca.news.yahoo.com/rise-prison-gangs-fuelling-violence-drug-trade-212628669.html

Chen, M. Keith, and Jesse M. Shapiro. 2007. "Do Harsher Prison Conditions Reduce Recidivism? A Discontinuity-based Approach." *American Law and Economics Review* 9:1–29.

Chesney-Lind, Meda. 1997. *The Female Offender: Girls, Women and Crime*. Thousand Oaks, CA: Sage Publications.

Clemmer, Donald. 1958. *The Prison Community*. New York: Rinehart.

Correctional Service of Canada. 2006. *Ten-Year Status Report of Women's Corrections: 1996–2006*. http://www.csc-scc.gc.ca/text/prgrm/fsw/wos24/tenyearstatusreport_e.pdf

Correctional Service of Canada. 2012. *Security Classification and Penitentiary Placement*. http://www.csc-scc.gc.ca/text/plcy/cdshtm/705-7-cd-eng.shtml#s8

Dahle, Klaus-Peter. 2006. "Strengths and Limitations of Actuarial Prediction of Criminal Reoffence in a German Prison Sample: A Comparative Study of LSI-R, HCR-20 and PCL-R." *International Journal of Law and Psychiatry* 29:431–442.

Daniel, Anasseril E. 2007. "Care of the Mentally Ill in Prisons: Challenges and Solutions." *Journal of the American Academy of Psychiatry and Law* 35(4):406–410.

DiCataldo, Frank, Alexander Greer, and Wesley E. Profit. 1995. "Screening Prison Inmates for Mental Disorder: An Examination of the Relationship Between Mental Disorder and Prison Adjustment." *Bulletin of the American Academy of Psychiatry and Law* 23:573–585.

Drago, Francesco, Roberto Galbiati, and Pietro Vertova. 2011. "Prison Conditions and Recidivism." *American Law and Economics Review* 13:103–130.

Duncan, Renae D., Wallace A. Kennedy, and Christopher J. Patrick.1995. "Four-factor Model of Recidivism in Male Juvenile Offenders." *Journal of Clinical Child Psychology* 24:250–257.

Edinger, Jack D., and Stephen M. Auerbach. 1978. "Development and Validation of a Multidimensional Multivariate Model for Accounting for Infractionary Behavior in a Correctional Setting." *Journal of Personality and Social Psychology* 36:1472–1489.

Farr, Kathryn A. 2000. "Classification for Female Inmates: Moving Forward." *Crime and Delinquency* 46:3–17.

Federal Bureau of Prisons. 2006. *Program Statement: Inmate Security Designation and Custody Classification.* P5100.08. http://www.bop.gov/policy/progstat/5100_008.pdf

Flores, Anthony W., Christopher T. Lowenkamp, Alexander M. Holsinger, and Edward J. Latessa. 2006. "Predicting Outcome with the Level of Service Inventory-Revised: The Importance of Implementation Integrity." *Journal of Criminal Justice* 34:523–529.

Gendreau, Paul, Claire Goggin, and Francis T. Cullen. 1999. *The Effect of Prison Sentences on Recidivism* (Corrections User Report 1999-3). Ottawa, Canada: Solicitor General of Canada.

Gendreau, Paul, Claire E. Goggin, and Moira A. Law. 1997. "Predicting Prison Misconducts." *Criminal Justice and Behavior* 24:414–431.

Gendreau, Paul, Claire Goggin, and Paula Smith. 2002. "Is the PCL-R Really the 'Unparalleled' Measure of Offender Risk? A Lesson in Knowledge Cumulation." *Criminal Justice and Behavior* 29:397–426.

Gendreau, Paul, Shelley J. Listwan, Joseph B. Kuhns, and M. Lyn Exum. 2014. "Making Prisoners Accountable: Are Contingency Management Programs the Answer?" *Criminal Justice and Behavior* 41(9):1079–1102.

Gendreau, Paul, Tracy Little, and Claire Goggin. 1996. "A Meta-analysis of the Predictors of Adult Offender Recidivism: What Works!" *Criminology* 34:575–607.

Girard, Lina, and J. Stephen Wormith. 2004. "The Predictive Validity of the Level of Service Inventory-Ontario Revision on General and Violent Recidivism among Various Offender Groups." *Criminal Justice and Behavior* 31:150–181.

Gobeil, Renée. 2011. *The Custody Rating Scale as Applied to Male Offenders.* R-257. Ottawa, Canada: Correctional Service of Canada.

Grant, Brian A., and Fred Luciani. 1998. *Security Classification Using the Custody Rating Scale.* Research Report R-67. Ottawa, Canada: Correctional Service of Canada.

Gunter, Tracy D., Stephan Arndt, S., Gloria Wenman, Jeff Allen, Peggy Loveless, Bruce Sieleni, B., and Donald Black. 2008. "The Frequency of Mental and Addictive Disorders Among 320 Men and Women Entering the Iowa Prison System: Use of the MINI-Plus." *Journal of the American Academy of Psychiatry and Law* 36:27–34.

Hanson, Richard W., C. Scott Moss, Ray E. Hosford, and Mark E. Johnson 1983. "Predicting Inmate Penitentiary Adjustment: An Assessment of Four Classificatory Methods." *Criminal Justice and Behavior* 10:293–309.

Harbo, Tor-Ing. 2010. "The Function of the Proportionality Principle in EU Law." *European Law Journal* 16(2):158–185.

Hathaway, Starke R., and J. Charnley McKinley. 1951. *Minnesota Multiphasic Personality Inventory.* New York: Psychological Corporation.

Harris, Grant T., and Marnie E. Rice. 2003. "Actuarial Assessment of Risk among Sex Offenders." In *Understanding and Managing Sexually Coercive Behavior,* edited by Robert Prentky, Eric Janus, and Michael Seto. New York: Annals of the New York Academy of Sciences.

Hilton, Zoe N., Grant T. Harris, and Marnie E. Rice. 2006. "Sixty-Six Years of Research on the Clinical versus Actuarial Prediction of Violence." *The Counseling Psychologist* 34:400–409.

Hogg, Peter W., and Allison A. Bushell. 1997. "The *Charter* Dialogue between Courts and Legislatures." *Osgood Hall Law Journal* 35:75–124.

Hollin, Clive R., and Emma J. Palmer. 2006. "The Level of Service Inventory-Revised Profile of English Prisoners: Risk and Reconviction Analysis." *Criminal Justice and Behavior* 33:347–366.

Holthouse, David. 2005. *Smashing the Shamrock: Intelligence Report.* http://legacysplc.wwwsplcenter.org/intel/intelreport/article.jsp?aid=569

Hsu, Ching-I., Peter Caputi, and Mitchell K. Byrne. 2011. "The Level of Service Inventory-Revised (LSI-R) and Australian Offenders: Factor Structure, Sensitivity, and Specificity." *Criminal Justice and Behavior* 38:600–618.

James, Doris J., and Lauren E. Glaze. 2006. *Mental Health Problems of Prison and Jail Inmates.* Statistics Special Report no. NCJ 213600 (September). Washington, DC: Department of Justice, Bureau of Justice Statistics.

Jonson, Cheryl L. 2010. *The Impact of Imprisonment on Reoffending: A Meta-analysis.* Unpublished dissertation, University of Cincinnati.

Justice Center. 2013. *Lessons from the States: Reducing Recidivism and Curbing Corrections Costs Through Justice Reinvestment.* http://csgjusticecenter.org/jr/publications/lessons-from-the-states/

LaVigne, Nancy, and Julie Samuels. 2012. *The Growth and Increasing Cost of the Federal Prison System: Drivers and Potential Solutions.* http://www.urban.org/publications/412693.html

Levinson, Robert B. 1980. "Security Designation System: Preliminary Results." *Federal Probation* 44(September):26–30.

Levinson, Robert B. 1988. "Developments in the Classification Process: Quay's AIMS Approach." *Criminal Justice and Behavior* 15:24–38.

Levinson, Robert, and J. D. Williams. 1979. "Inmate Classification: Security/Custody Considerations." *Federal Probation* (March):37–42.

Luciani, Fred. 2001. "Initiating Safe Reintegration: A Decade of Custodial Rating Scale Results." *Forum on Corrections Research* 13:8–10.

Luciani, Fred, Laurence Motiuk, and Mark Nafekh. 1996. An Operational Review of the Custody Rating Scale: Reliability, Validity and Practical Utility (Research Report R-47). Ottawa, ON: Correctional Service Canada.

MacKenzie, Doris L. 1989. "Prison Classification: The Management and Psychological Perspectives." In *American Prison: Issues in Research and Policy,* edited by Lynne Goodstein and Doris L. Mackenzie. New York: Plenum Press.

Mears, Daniel P., and Jamie Watson. 2006. "Towards a Fair and Balanced Assessment of Supermax Prisons." *Justice Quarterly* 23:232–270.

Megargee, Edwin I. 1994. "Using the Megargee MMPI-based Classification System with MMPI-2s of Male Inmates." *Psychological Assessment* 6:337–344.

Megargee, Edwin I., and Martin J. Bohn Jr. 1979. *Classifying Criminal Offenders: A New System Based on the MMPI.* Beverly Hills, CA: Sage.

Metro News. (2013). *Violent Assaults in Federal Prisons on the Rise.* http://metronews.ca/news/canada/289654/violent-assaults-in-federal-prisons-on-the-rise/

Moss, C. Scott, Mark E. Johnson, and Ray E. Hosford. 1984. "An Assessment of the Megargee Typology in Lifelong Criminal Violence." *Criminal Justice and Behavior* 11:225–234.

Motiuk, Laurence L. 2004. *Review of the Custody Rating Scale: A Commentary.* October 20, written communication.

Motiuk, Laurence L., James Bonta, and D. A. Andrews. 1986. "Classification in Correctional Halfway Houses: The Relative and Incremental Predictive Criterion Validities of the Megargee-MMPI and LSI systems." *Criminal Justice and Behavior* 13:33–46.

Mulligan, R. A. 2007. *Presentation at the Symposium on Incarceration and Inequality.* http://www.hks.harvard.edu/rappaport/downloads/b101/rappaport%2020071017.ppt

NBC News. 2013. *Suicides Kill More Inmates than Homicide, Overdoses, Accidents Combined.* http://www.nbcnews.com/news/other/suicides-kill-more-inmates-homicide-overdoses-accidents-combined-f8C11072563

Olver, Mark E., Keira C. Stockdale, and J. Stephen Wormith. 2014. "Thirty Years of Research on the Level of Service Scales: A Meta-analytic Examination of Predictive Accuracy and Sources of Variability." *Psychological Assessment* 26:156–176.

Parhar, Karen, and J. Stephen Wormith. 2013. "Risk Factors for Homelessness Among Recently Released Offenders." *Journal of Forensic Social Work* 3:16–33.

Pew Center on the States. 2010. *Prison Count 2010: State Population Declines for the First Time in 38 Years.* http://www.pewstates.org/uploadedFiles/PCS_Assets/2010/Pew_Prison_Count_2010.pdf

Porporino, Frank J., Fred Luciani, Laurence Motiuk, Michael Johnston, and Brian Mainwaring. 1989. *Pilot Implementation of a Custody Rating Scale: Interim Report (R-02).* Ottawa, Canada: Research Branch, Correctional Service of Canada.

Power, Jennel, and Dana L. Riley. 2010. *A Comparative Review of Suicide and Self-injury Investigative Reports in a Canadian Federal Correctional Population (R-221).* Ottawa, Canada: Correctional Services Canada.

Prendergast, Margaret. 2012. "Practitioner Perceptions on the Merits, Challenges and Ethical Dilemmas of LSI-R in Practice." *Irish Probation Journal* 9(October):111–131.

Quay, Herbert C. 1984. *Managing Adult Inmates: Classification for Housing and Program Assignments.* College Park, MD: American Correctional Association.

Ross, Jeffrey I. 2007. "Supermax Prisons." *Society* 44(3):60–64.

Rubin, Sol. 1975. "Probation or Prison: Applying the Principle of the Least Restrictive Alternative." *Crime and Delinquency* 21:331–336.

Rugge, Tanya, and James Bonta. 2014. "Training Community Corrections Officers." In *Forensic CBT: A Handbook for Clinical Practice*, edited by Raymond C. Tafrate and Damon Mitchell. West Sussex, England: John Wiley & Sons.

Schmitt, John, Kris Warner, and Sarika Gupta. 2010. *The High Budgetary Cost of Incarceration.* http://www.cepr.net/documents/publications/incarceration-2010-06.pdf

Schneider, Anne L., Laurie Ervin, and Zoann Snyder-Joy. 1996. "Further Explorations of the Flight from Discretion: The Role of Risk/Need Instruments in Probation Supervision Decisions." *Journal of Criminal Justice* 24:109–121.

Shermer, Lauren O., David M. Bierie, and Amber Stock. 2012. "Endogeneity in Prison Risk Classification." *International Journal of Offender Therapy and Comparative Criminology* 57:1248–1274.

Smith, Paula, Claire Goggin, and Paul Gendreau. 2002. *The Effects of Prison Sentences and Intermediate Sanctions on Recidivism: General Effects and Individual Differences (Corrections User Report 2002-01).* Ottawa, Canada: Ministry of the Solicitor General.

Sperber, Kimberly G., Edward J. Latessa, and Mathew D. Makarios. 2013. "Examining the Interaction Between Level of Risk and Dosage of Treatment." *Criminal Justice and Behavior* 40:338–348.

Sutherland, Edwin H., and Donald R. Cressey. 1978. *Criminology*, 10th ed. Philadelphia, PA: Lippincott.

Teplin, Linda A., and James Swartz. 1989. "Screening for Severe Mental Disorder in Jails: The Development of the Referral Decision Scale." *Law and Human Behavior* 13:1–18.

Thompson, Jennie, Ashley McConnell, and Lysiane Paquin-Marseille. 2011. *The Security Reclassification Scale (SRSW) for Shorter Review Periods Among Federal Women Offenders.* Ottawa, Canada: Correctional Service Canada.

Tripp, Rob. 2010. *Prison Staff Assaults on Rise.* http://www.thewhig.com/2010/07/19/prison-staff-assaults-on-rise-report

Van Voorhis, Patricia. 1994. *Psychological Classification of the Adult Male Prison Inmate.* Albany: State University of New York Press.

Vera Institute of Justice. 2013. *The Price of Prisons. What Incarceration Costs Taxpayers.* http://www.vera.org/sites/default/files/resources/downloads/the-price-of-prisons-40-fact-sheets-updated-072012.pdf

Webster, Cheryl M., and Anthony N. Doob. 2004a. "Classification Without Validity or Equity: An Empirical Examination of the Custody Rating Scale for Federally Sentenced Women Offenders in Canada." *Canadian Journal of Criminology and Criminal Justice* 46:395–421.

Webster, Cheryl M., and Anthony N. Doob. 2004b. "Taking Down the Straw Man or Building a House of Straw: Validity, Equity and the Custody Rating Scale." *Canadian Journal of Criminology and Criminal Justice* 46:631–638.

Wormith, J. Stephen, Myles Ferguson, and James Bonta. 2013. "Offender Classification and Case Management and Their Application in Canadian Corrections." In *Adult Corrections in Canada: A Comprehensive Overview*, edited by John Winterdyk and Michael Weinrath. Whitby, Canada: DeSitter Publications.

Wright, Kevin. 1988. "The Relationship of Risk, Needs, and Personality Classification Systems and Prison Adjustment." *Criminal Justice and Behavior* 15:454–471.

CHAPTER 19

....

PRINCIPLES OF EFFECTIVE INTERVENTION WITH INCARCERATED OFFENDERS

....

CLAIRE GOGGIN

CORRECTIONAL treatment may be defined in a number of ways (i.e., Sechrest, White, and Brown 1979, pp. 20–21). Generally, it entails structured interventions that target characteristics of offenders or their circumstances that, if ameliorated, reduce the risk of future criminal behavior. Typically, this is achieved using counseling and cognitive behavioral treatments (CBT) to shape prosocial attitudes (i.e., cognitions) and behaviors and enhance skill-building (i.e., educational/vocational aptitude, etc.). Relevant to the present discussion is the effect of such interventions in reducing inmates' antisocial behaviors (i.e., misconducts, postrelease recidivism).

This essay summarizes the literature regarding the principles of effective correctional programming—offender risk, needs, and responsivity (RNR)—and the contribution of these principles to establishing "what works" in correctional rehabilitation (Smith, Gendreau, and Schwartz 2009; Andrews and Bonta 2010). Section I lays the groundwork by providing a brief history of prisons and the origins of the rehabilitative ideal. Section II summarizes its progress through the turbulent 1960s and 1970s, including the near-fatal blow dealt by Martinson (1974). Section III describes the research response to Martinson, while Sections IV and V highlight the role of meta-analysis in resuscitating the rehabilitative ideal and developing the RNR principles. Sections VI and VII focus on issues surrounding prison treatment and describe several exemplary institutional treatment programs. Finally, Section VIII proposes next steps for research and practice in the area. The principle conclusions from this discussion include the following:

- In order to fully evaluate the effectiveness of correctional treatments, it is essential that rates of offender treatment engagement and retention be maximized. Research suggests that treatment dropouts are more likely to be assessed at highest risk and in greatest need of intervention (Olver, Stockdale, and Wormith 2011).

- Risk assessment indices should incorporate case management planning as it provides both front-line staff and researchers with a mechanism for continuous and comprehensive monitoring of offender treatment progress and program outcome.
- Evaluations of program quality should be standard practice in all correctional agencies. By evaluating the degree to which correctional treatments adhere to the RNR principles, therapeutic effectiveness can be optimized, ensuring that those in need receive appropriate levels of intervention.
- In order to enhance evidence-based practice, the field should avail itself of recent technological advances such as data registries (Turner et al. 2003; Petrosino 2013).

I. PRISON AS CONTEXT

As of 2010, 10 million people were imprisoned worldwide (Walmsley 2011). Almost 1.6 million people, approximately 743 per 100,000, were imprisoned in the United States alone during 2012 (Carson and Golinelli 2013), making the United States the world leader in incarceration rates. Accordingly, the effectiveness of inmate treatments in reducing rates of misconduct and postrelease recidivism is of primary concern to both correctional administrators and front-line workers.

To begin, it is useful to revisit the purpose of prison. Historically, it had three objectives: detention (i.e., incapacitation), specific deterrence (i.e., fear-inducing sanction), and rehabilitation (i.e., treatment). The construction of purpose-built facilities came into vogue at the end of the 18th century, in part in response to John Howard's seminal report of the dreadful conditions in jails in Britain, Europe, and the Near East (Howard 1991).

The first American penitentiaries, constructed in the early 1800s at Auburn in New York and Eastern State in Pennsylvania, were intended to promote behavior change by providing the requisite conditions for offender introspection and penitence: sanitary facilities where inmates, separated by age and gender, would work in silence by day and be housed in solitary by night. In reality, throughout most of the 19th century, conditions in North American prisons were wretched (American Correctional Association 1972; Rotman 1998) due to excessive use of corporal punishments, deplorable living conditions, limited budgets, few educational/vocational training opportunities, and generally poor management practices. At the same time, the late 19th century was a "golden age" for prison reformers, philanthropists, scholars, and bureaucrats interested in maximizing prison's potential to reform criminals (Scalia 1871; Ives 1914/1970; Wines and Dwight 1867/1973; Johnston 2000). Notably, at a pivotal conference in Cincinnati in 1879 sponsored by the National Congress on Penitentiary and Reformatory Discipline, attendees endorsed prison management principles that were prescient in their understanding of behavioral change mechanisms. They spoke of hope, promoted reform over punishment, and recognized the negative effects of physical punishments and the importance of offender participation and cooperation (Wines 1871; Guilford 1946), concepts that would later resonate in 20th-century learning theory (Mowrer 1960; Spiegler and Guevremont 2010).

In truth, this commitment to prison reform did not immediately translate into improved prison conditions as governments were ever sensitive to the guiding principle of "less eligibility": conditions of confinement for inmates should not exceed those of the working poor (Singer 1971; Sieh 1989; Carrigan 1991). Nevertheless, it did lay the groundwork for the development of a prison reform agenda (Allen 1981) that, eventually, became the prevailing ethos in North America (Cullen and Gendreau 2000). The resulting treatment paradigm, later elaborated on during the Progressive Era (Allen 1981), had important implications for modern rehabilitative practices. Specifically, it presumed that criminal behavior was rooted in a number of psychological and social factors, which, once identified, could be targeted for therapy, with the treatment agency maintaining discretion as to the timing and intensity of interventions.

During the mid-1900s, the rehabilitative ideal underwent further refinements. In 1954 the American Correctional Association was founded. Prisons were thereafter known as "correctional institutions." For rehabilitation advocates, the following decades witnessed several positive developments. Sophisticated classification systems were introduced (i.e., Warren 1969). Prison-based treatment programs were implemented, including individual and group counseling, therapeutic *milieu*, behavioral modification, and vocational and educational programming. With the advent of community corrections in the 1960s, parole decisions were often tied to inmates' progress in treatment while incarcerated. By 1975, with the establishment of the American Probation and Parole Association, many probation/ parole settings were reporting meaningful reductions in recidivism in response to correctional treatments (see Ross and Gendreau 1980).

Despite this general acceptance of rehabilitation as the preeminent correctional philosophy, it did have its critics. Beginning in the 1950s, some criminologists (i.e., Kirby 1954; Wootton 1959; Cressey 1958; Bailey 1966; Robison and Smith 1971; Logan 1972) began to suggest that the existing evidence did not support rehabilitation's effectiveness as approximately half of controlled-treatment studies reported only limited reductions in recidivism. For the moment, these criticisms were not widely adopted as rehabilitation continued to be endorsed by academics (Toby 1964; Menninger 1968), government (i.e., President's Commission on Law Enforcement and Administration of Justice 1967), and the majority of practitioners (American Friends Service Committee Working Party 1971).

II. REHABILITATION'S "CLAY FEET"

The climate began to change, however, when Martinson (1974) published a summary of Lipton, Martinson, and Wilks's (1975) comprehensive review of offender treatment studies ($k = 231$) published between 1945 and 1967. It was the catalyst for an abrupt about-face in correctional policy. Martinson's observation "that with few exceptions the rehabilitative efforts that have been reported so far have had no appreciable effect on recidivism" (p. 25) shook the foundations of the rehabilitative ideal. And his conclusion that "we haven't the faintest clue about how to rehabilitate offenders and reduce recidivism" (Martinson 1974, p. 48) posed a serious challenge to its continued viability. As Walker (1985) noted, the impact of Martinson's findings was immediate and far-reaching, attracting the attention of both the public and academics. Consequently, the merits of continuing to invest in a seemingly failed correctional policy prompted a turn to a more retributive response. If treatment did not work in reducing recidivism, perhaps punishment would (Adams 1976).

It is worth noting that, although Martinson's (1974) conclusions did not differ substantively from those of earlier critics (i.e., Kirby 1954; Cressey 1958), they had considerably more impact (Cullen 2005) and were the harbingers of what Cullen and Gilbert (2013) have called the "mean season in corrections" (p. 216). Some scholars (i.e., Cullen and Gendreau 1989; Cullen and Gilbert 2013) have suggested that this had as much to do with the period's prevailing social context as it did Martinson's message. In the turbulent social climate in the United States during the 1960s and 1970s (i.e., Kent State, Watergate, Vietnam War, etc.), the consensus was that governments, in general, were neither ethically suited to nor capable of being competent and trustworthy civil administrators (Lipset and Schneider 1983; Cullen and Gendreau 1989). This attitude was also prevalent in corrections, which witnessed increasing unrest inside prisons (i.e., riots at Attica, McAlester) and growing public controversy over judicial and parole-based decision-making (Useem and Kimball 1991; Cullen and Gendreau 2000).

As a result, both ends of the political spectrum were dissatisfied with the status of correctional policy, and each was quick to pinpoint the rehabilitative ideal as the problem. On the right, early-release policies and the perceived increase in prison unrest were taken as evidence of a weakened and ineffectual system. In the context of increasing crime rates during the 1970s, the response to Martinson's (1974) review among conservative policymakers was a "hardening" of correctional policy. Specifically, they recommended the abolition of parole; the implementation of mandatory minimum sentences, including sentencing grids such as "three strikes" laws (i.e., life sentence at the third conviction regardless of offense type); tougher prison conditions (see Shichor and Sechrest 1996; Gendreau, Goggin, and Cullen 1999); and greater restrictions on early release.

Among the political left, there was a sense that the rehabilitative ideal placed too much discretion in the hands of correctional administrators and, consequently, led to potentially unjust and coercive offender processing decisions. Treatment programs were characterized as degradation ceremonies that simply widened the net and did more harm than good (see Morris 1974; Fogel 1979; Binder and Geis 1984). Prison staff were seen as social control agents who discriminated against the oppressed. As a result, the left supported the "justice model," which emphasized the goal of fairness in criminal justice processing while downplaying crime control objectives (Cullen and Gilbert 1982). Fixed-length sentences, abolition of parole, and voluntary treatment would reduce undue discretion and ensure that offenders were protected from the vagaries of a capricious criminal justice system (Conrad 1981).

Those who attempted to rebut the new "nothing works" orthodoxy were swiftly and, often, scornfully rebuked. For example, Palmer's (1975) review of Martinson's (1974) data set revealed that, in fact, for 48 percent of treatments, recidivism was actually reduced, particularly for community-based programs and those involving juveniles or moderate-risk offenders. Palmer concluded that some programs clearly worked and suggested that recidivism could be further reduced with an improved understanding of "which methods work best for which type of offenders, and under what conditions or in what types of settings" (p. 150). Martinson's (1976) response to Palmer was both vicious and personal (see Gendreau and Ross 1979, p. 483; Palmer et al. 2012). He dismissed Palmer's analysis, particularly the idea that attending to *offender* × *treatment* × *setting* interactions would result in meaningful reductions in recidivism. Thus, at the conclusion of the 1970s, support for the rehabilitative ideal was at its nadir.

III. Rehabilitation's Rebirth: Mid-1970s to Mid-1980s

Ironically, Martinson's (1974) essay was the spark that revitalized scholars to empirically evaluate the role of rehabilitation in reducing recidivism. A first step in its revivification came with Ross and McKay's (1978) review of the behavioral modification literature. Martinson (1979) updated his earlier review of the offender treatment literature, including studies published since 1972, and stated "I have often said that treatment added to the networks of criminal justice is impotent . . . the conclusion is not correct . . . treatments will be found to be 'impotent' under certain conditions, beneficial under others, and detrimental under still others" (p. 254).

Renewed interest in rehabilitation also came from beyond the discipline of criminology, many of whose members had not been troubled by the "nothing works" credo as it was relatively consistent with their ideological ethos (Binder and Geis 1984; Cullen 2005; Cullen and Gendreau 2000). Instead, psychologists, most of whom were associated with the so-called "Canadian School" of rehabilitation (Logan et al. 1991; Cullen 2005) spearheaded the next series of studies.

Canadian School affiliates were generally scientists/practitioners and most worked within correctional settings and governmental sectors whose policies were supportive of rehabilitation. The implementation, administration, and monitoring of offender treatment programs were among their key responsibilities. As professional psychologists, they were trained in learning theory and CBT. They worked under the assumption that antisocial behavior was learned and could, therefore, be reduced through the delivery of structured, ethically appropriate treatments. The new "nothing works" doctrine that held that criminals were unable to relearn or acquire new behavioral repertoires was antithetical to them (i.e., Gendreau and Ross, 1979, p. 466).

In response to Martinson (1974), this group conducted a number of treatment demonstration projects and completed several reviews of the offender treatment literature (i.e., Ross and McKay 1978; Andrews 1979; Gendreau and Andrews 1979; Gendreau and Ross 1979, 1980, 1981a, 1981b, 1983–1984, 1987; Andrews and Kiessling 1980; Gendreau, Burke, and Grant 1980; Ross and Fabiano 1985; Andrews et al. 1986) in the hopes that the results would identify the constituents of effective, and ineffective, correctional practices. One of the more important aspects of this enterprise was an examination of the "black box" of correctional programs. In Gendreau's (1996b, p. 118) words:

> Unlike Martinson and his followers, we believe it is not sufficient just to sum across studies or file them into general categories. The salient question is what are the principles that distinguish between effective and ineffective programs?—what exactly was accomplished under the name of "employment"? As a result of endorsing the perspective of opening the "black box," we have been able to generate a number of principles of effective and ineffective intervention.

As a first step, Gendreau and Ross (1979) provided "bibliotherapy for cynics" by reviewing dozens of studies that examined treatment effects on recidivism. Some were quite robust (i.e., a 20 percent to 50 percent difference in the recidivism rates of treatment vs.

nontreatment groups). The results of these reviews (see also Andrews 1979) laid the groundwork for the development of the RNR principles.

For example, Gendreau and Ross (1979) found that the majority of the most effective programs were behavioral. Consistent with Palmer's (1975) hypothesis regarding the impact of individual differences on treatment effects, research in the post-Martinson period was dominated by studies of such effects (see Gendreau and Ross 1987, pp. 370–374, for a complete summary). *Offender risk* was identified as a potentially important individual difference variable as it was proposed that offenders rated as higher on risk (i.e., more extensive antisocial attitudes, substance abuse problems, criminal histories) might benefit most from intensive behavioral treatments (i.e., Andrews et al. 1986). In addition to identifying effective program components, the Canadian group also shed light on aspects of programs that increased recidivism. Of particular interest was the concept of therapeutic integrity, or

> To what extent do treatment personnel actually adhere to the principles and employ the techniques of the therapy they purport to provide? To what extent are the treatment staff competent? How hard do they work? How much is treatment diluted in the correctional environment so that it becomes treatment in name only? (Gendreau and Ross 1979, p. 467)

Gendreau and Ross proposed that lack of therapeutic integrity was, in fact, quite prevalent and found support in Quay's (1977) reanalysis of Kassebaum, Ward, and Wilner's (1971) renowned prison counseling program. At the time, the Kassebaum et al. study was lauded as a methodologically sound study that illustrated that correctional treatment did not work. On closer inspection, however, Quay found that the program lacked therapeutic integrity. Specifically, it was conceptually weak, included unstable counseling groups, and was staffed by unqualified, poorly trained counselors who themselves had little confidence in the program. Emery and Marholin (1977) reached a similar conclusion in their reexamination of 27 empirical investigations of applied behavioral programs for delinquency prevention. They reported that in only 9 percent of cases were the behaviors targeted for change uniquely selected per youth. Further, in only 30 percent of studies was there a match between the behaviors for which the youth were referred and the behaviors targeted for treatment (i.e., one client was referred for stealing cars but was treated for tardiness).

Other aspects of unsuccessful programs appeared to be related to individual difference factors and types of treatment. For example, the evidence indicated that even high-quality treatment services had little impact on the recidivism of low-risk offenders and that psychodynamic-oriented treatments (i.e., nondirective, insight-oriented "talk" therapies) were notably ineffective modalities (see Andrews 1979; Andrews and Bonta 2010; Gendreau and Ross 1983–1984).

IV. The Tide Shifts: The Advent of Meta-Analysis

The gradual revival of the rehabilitative ideal was the result of both an intensive research effort whose results have broadened our knowledge of what makes correctional programs effective and concurrent developments in how that knowledge is cumulated. Historically, offender treatment literature reviews were narrative in design. This technique typically assesses the merits of an issue by sampling a literature's more influential theoretical papers, examining some of the available data, and then selecting the results that tend to support the hypothesis. Critics of narrative reviews (i.e., Glass, McGaw, and Smith 1981; Beaman 1991; Rosenthal 1991) have noted that they often omit crucial data and their conclusions can be unduly effected by prejudice and ideology. Their most problematic limitation is, perhaps, the inability to measure the precise magnitude of an effect (Cooper and Rosenthal 1980). In addition, most contemporary literatures consist of, at minimum, dozens of studies (i.e., Gendreau and Ross 1987). Given the limits of cognitive processing when dealing with diverse outcomes, methodologies, and study characteristics (i.e., types of offenders, quality of research design, etc.), it is not surprising that conclusions from narrative reviews can be quite variable, making such studies difficult to replicate. With respect to narrative reviews of correctional program effectiveness, policymakers might reasonably conclude that some programs reduce recidivism but are unable to determine which are more effective and by what magnitude.

By comparison, quantitative review techniques such as meta-analysis produce more nuanced results, especially when examining complex research questions. Popularized by Glass (1976) in the late 1970s, meta-analysis is now commonplace in virtually all scientific disciplines (Hunt 1997; Hunter and Schmidt 2004; Chan and Arvey 2012). Such reviews calculate an effect size (ES), usually Pearson r with associated confidence interval (CI; i.e., Rosenthal 1991; Schmidt 1996) between predictor and outcome. Effect sizes may be limited to one or multiples per study depending on the nature of the sample (i.e., males vs. females) and/or research question (i.e., types of outcome). A second advantage of meta-analysis is the capacity to code the review sample along a number of dimensions (Wells 2009). With respect to correctional treatment studies, this may include type of sample, offender risk level, type and dosage of treatment, therapist qualifications, study setting, and quality of research design. These variables can then be correlated with outcome to evaluate their impact as moderators of treatment effect.

Of course meta-analysis is not a panacea (Gendreau, Goggin, and Smith 2000; Smith et al. 2009). Its utility is directly dependent on the quality of the studies reviewed and the fidelity with which study details are coded. Nonetheless, the consensus is that, for the purposes of summarizing extensive research literatures in order to contribute to rational policy formulation, meta-analytic strategies are definitely superior to narrative techniques (Gendreau and Smith 2007). This was confirmed by Beaman (1991) who compared the two techniques ($n = 20$ each) regarding the coding of 31 study elements (i.e., type of literature search, magnitude and direction of ES, moderator–criterion relationships) and reported that, on average, the meta-analyses provided 50 percent more information about study elements than did the narrative reviews. Perhaps the most useful aspect of any meta-analysis is its replication potential, as it provides the opportunity for independent reexamination, thereby contributing over time to knowledge synthesis within a discipline (i.e., which treatments work, which do not) and, ultimately, paradigm development (Chan and Arvey 2012). The first meta-analyses of rehabilitation program effectiveness appeared in the mid-1980s (Davidson et al. 1984; also reported in more detail in Garrett 1985; Apter and Goldstein 1986; for a review see Ross and Fabiano 1985; Gendreau and Ross 1987, pp. 391–394; Izzo and Ross 1990) and articulated themes that would be validated in subsequent reviews. They sampled largely juveniles, and the studies surveyed did not overlap greatly. On average, a modest majority of the effect sizes ($n \approx 55$ percent) indicated positive effects (i.e., reductions in recidivism).

Subsequently, Lipsey (1992) summarized a large database of juvenile interventions ($n = 443$ effect sizes), 64 percent of which were positive, representing a considerable improvement over the 50 percent baseline reported previously by Martinson (1974) and Palmer (1975). In Lipsey, the average reduction in recidivism varied from 5 percent to 9 percent depending on the statistical adjustments made to the effect sizes (i.e., weighting by n and number of ES).

Lösel (1995) later completed a comprehensive review of 13 meta-analyses of the offender treatment literature published between 1985 and 1995. Both juvenile and adult samples were represented, and he reported mean effect sizes ranging from 0.05 to 0.18, with an overall mean $r \approx 0.10$, or an approximate 10 percent reduction in recidivism. Using Rosenthal's (1991) binomial effect size display statistic, which assumes relatively equivalent base rates in outcome per group, this equates to recidivism rates of approximately 45 percent and 55 percent for the treatment and control groups, respectively. The results of later meta-analyses (Andrews, Dowden, and Gendreau 1999; Redondo, Sanchez-Meca, and Garrido 1999; Smith et al. 2009; Andrews and Bonta 2010) concurred with Lösel. Of note, these positive results were not moderated by methodological factors such as subject attrition, quality of research design, length of follow-up, or inclusion of published versus unpublished studies (Lipsey 1992, 1999).

These replications are noteworthy given the inherent variability among study samples, coding schemes, and researchers. Even criminologists who had been inimical to rehabilitation reported positive results using meta-analysis (Whitehead and Lab 1989). In addition, Lösel (1995) and Lipsey (1992) have suggested that the overall effect of treatment is likely attenuated as rehabilitation studies do not typically include treatment versus no-treatment comparisons (i.e., comparison groups typically receive "routine" programming). Equally, they usually employ dichotomous independent (i.e., treatment condition) and dependent (i.e., recidivism vs. no recidivism) measures, which tend to compromise statistical power (Cohen 1988; Lösel 1995).

Some may argue that a 10 percent reduction in recidivism is rather meager and of little applied value. Lipsey and Wilson (1993) and Rosnow and Rosenthal (1993) have noted that similar effects have translated into meaningful cost savings in other fields (i.e., incidence of serious medical illness). In that vein, Cohen (1998) gauged the cost-effectiveness of interventions for high-risk juvenile offenders. Of note, cost-benefit analyses of criminal activity can be somewhat inexact given their reliance on aggregate rates of criminal performance and the inclusion of conditions such as *prison* and *suffering* along with *property loss* and *lost wages*. Nevertheless, Cohen's analysis indicated that, over the course of a criminal career, the costs associated with a high-risk juvenile offender are in the order of $1.7 million to $2.3 million.

From this one can conclude that, depending on the timing and cost of a particular intervention, offender programming can be cost-effective even when reductions in recidivism are relatively "small" in magnitude. A comprehensive cost-benefit analysis of correctional interventions in Washington state by Drake, Aos, and Miller (2009) provides further evidence for the utility of rehabilitation. They found a 17.9 percent reduction in recidivism among juveniles enrolled in multidimensional treatment foster care (vs. regular group care) and reported a net savings of $88,953 per youth (see also Greenwood et al. 1996; Aos et al. 1999).

V. Effective Correctional Programming: Uncovering the Principles

The aforementioned meta-analyses provided a first glimpse of the key elements of effective correctional programming, and, despite somewhat dissimilar samples and methodologies, their conclusions were broadly consistent. The largest reductions in recidivism were associated with behavioral treatments or, at minimum, with treatments that included considerable structure (i.e., educational, occupational, family therapies). Mean effect sizes for behavioral programs were not large (i.e., ≈10 percent) but were decidedly greater than those for nonbehavioral interventions such as group therapy and psychodynamic or *milieu* therapies that occasionally produced slight increases in recidivism.

A box-score review by Ross and Fabiano (1985) provided additional insight in that they found that CBT strategies tended to maximize treatment effectiveness. Davidson et al.'s (1984) analysis focused on the effects of moderators on outcome and reported that variables such as *professional training* (i.e., psychology, education) and *evaluator involvement* (i.e., control of program design, implementation, and delivery) were also associated with reductions in recidivism. The results of two subsequent meta-analyses by Andrews and colleagues (1990; Andrews et al. 1999) provided further elaboration of the RNR principles that subsequent research has confirmed are essential to the delivery of effective correctional programming (for a detailed discussion see Gendreau, Cullen, and Bonta 1994; Andrews 1995; Gendreau 1996a, 1996b; Andrews and Bonta 1998).

A. Risk

According to the risk principle, treatment should be reserved for high-risk offenders as they pose the greatest potential harm to the public (see Bonta 1996). By contrast, low-risk offenders should be diverted from treatment as they have fewer needs that merit intervention and exposing them to unnecessary treatments is both costly and, potentially, iatrogenic (Andrews and Bonta 1998, p. 243). The most efficient means of determining risk is through the use of comprehensive assessment tools designed to evaluate the nature and extent of offenders' relevant risk factors.

B. Need

The need principle holds that treatments most successful in reducing recidivism are those that target offender characteristics (i.e., needs) that are robust predictors of recidivism. Typically, these are categorized as either "static" (i.e., historical factors) or "dynamic" (i.e., current factors), with the latter being distinguished as *criminogenic* (i.e., antisocial attitudes) or *noncriminogenic* (i.e., self-esteem, anxiety, depression) needs based on their predictive validity with recidivism. The importance of focusing on criminogenic needs is that they can be remediated through correctional treatment whereas historical factors (i.e., prior incarcerations) cannot. Their utility as predictors of recidivism among adult offenders was confirmed by Gendreau, Little, and Goggin (1996), who reported respective validities of $r \approx 0.18$ and $r \approx 0.05$ for criminogenic versus noncriminogenic needs, respectively.

C. Responsivity

There are two aspects to consider regarding responsivity. The first, general responsivity, addresses the nature of the treatment being delivered. The evidence indicates that the most effective treatment modalities are CBT (Lipsey, Landenberger, and Wilson 2007), and the key to their success is operant conditioning. Specifically, behaviors that are positively reinforced (i.e., receive a greater frequency and density of rewards) tend to be those that are more reliably expressed. Positive reinforcers may include both tangible (i.e., material goods, recreation, etc.) and intangible (i.e., interpersonal interaction, self-thoughts/evaluations) rewards. Conversely, behaviors that are not positively reinforced are more likely to be extinguished over time. In the offender context, effective treatments target offenders' antisocial values and beliefs, helping them to learn more adaptive prosocial behaviors that, with practice, can eventually supplant their antisocial repertoire.

A second, and equally important, aspect of responsivity attends to the specific capabilities of offenders. That is, treatment strategies and delivery styles are tailored to match their learning styles (i.e., cognitive/emotional maturity, emotional intelligence, intellectual ability) in order to maximize learning potential and, ultimately, behavioral change (Gendreau 1996b, pp. 122-123; Andrews and Bonta 1998, p. 245).

VI. Putting the Principles to Work

A. Effect of Therapeutic Integrity on Outcome

The original Andrews et al. (1990) database now includes 374 effect sizes (Andrews and Bonta 2010). Of particular interest in this data is the differential relationship with outcome based on degree of "appropriateness" of treatment (i.e., degree of adherence to RNR principles) wherein programs that use appropriate treatments tend to show the greatest reductions in recidivism (i.e., $\approx$ 30 percent). This contrasts with a 13 percent reduction in recidivism in response to unspecified interventions and a 7 percent increase in recidivism in response to inappropriate treatments.

More precisely, levels of recidivism differ based on the number of RNR principles embodied in treatment. That is, effect sizes range from $r = -0.02$ ($k = 124$), where negative correlations indicate higher recidivism, for no adherence, through $r = 0.02$ ($k = 106$) for adherence to only one principle, $r = 0.18$ ($k = 84$) for any two principles, and $r = 0.26$ ($k = 60$) for all three (Andrews and Bonta 2010). These results have also been reported among diverse correctional populations where correlations between adherence to RNR principles and recidivism range from $r = 0.46$ ($k = 193$) for juveniles, to $r = 0.56$ ($k = 45$) for females, and $r = 0.46$ ($k = 106$) for minority samples (Andrews and Bonta 2010). Similar results have also been reported for sexual offenders (odds ratio = 0.21; $k = 3$) (Hanson et al. 2009) and violent offenders ($r = 0.20$; $k = 13$; Dowden and Andrews 2000).

Regarding the effect of type of intervention, Smith et al.'s (2009) summary of the results of meta-analyses of the correctional treatment literature indicated that the vast majority ($\approx$75 percent) of effect sizes for CBTs were in the order of $r \geq 0.15$. This is consistent with the results of Andrews and Bonta (2010), where CBTs were associated with a 19 percent reduction in recidivism as compared with nonbehavioral treatments, and the meta-analysis by Lipsey et al. (2007), who reported a 25 percent reduction in recidivism in response to treatment (i.e., mean odds ratio = 1.53, $p < .001$).

B. What Does Not Work: Custody as Treatment

The same research agenda that has contributed to our understanding of the key elements of effective correctional treatment has also provided empirical confirmation of what does *not* work in attempting to reduce criminal behaviour. This includes specific deterrence-type sanctions such as incarceration, boot camp, and electronic monitoring. The premise underlying such "common-sense" notions is that offender behavior can be changed through psychological harm, humiliation, or increased surveillance (see Gendreau et al. 2002).

The literature is unequivocal, however, that incarceration, long regarded as a useful criminal sanction due to its putative aversive and stigmatizing nature (cf. Erickson and Gibbs 1979; Wood and Grasmick 1999; Applegate 2001), is neither an effective deterrent nor a prudent use of public monies (see Van Voorhis et al. 1997; Smith, Goggin, and Gendreau 2002; Goggin 2009; Listwan et al. 2013). Similarly, reviews of the literature do not support the use of either boot camps (Wilson, MacKenzie, and Mitchell 2003) or electronic monitoring (Renzema and Mayo-Wilson 2005) in attempting to reduce recidivism. That said, prison is nonetheless the context within which many offenders receive correctional programming. Is prison, then, a suitable environment in which to deliver treatment? And how might its effectiveness best be evaluated?

C. Treatment in Custody

For prison administrators, correctional staff, and inmates alike, the preeminent concern with respect to prisons is their safe and humane management. For example, it has been suggested that well-managed facilities—those that have higher ratios of correctional officers to inmates, employ professional staff, and offer programming routines for inmates—tend to have lower rates of institutional infractions (i.e., Bonta and Gendreau, 1990; Steiner, 2009; Wooldredge and Steiner, 2013). Misconducts can range from minor incidents (i.e., disobeying orders) to grave injuries (i.e., staff or inmate assaults) and may result in reduced privileges or transfer to more secure custody (i.e., administrative segregation). At minimum, they represent a potentially serious impediment to environmental stability, and high rates of infractions can have a deleterious impact on operational budgets due to the economic consequences of personal injury and property damage (Lovell and Jemelka 1996).

D. Misconducts as a Proxy for Recidivism

Of course in much of the offender treatment literature, the outcome of interest has not been misconducts. There is a long history of research, however, establishing the link between the misconducts and recidivism that supports the transfer of knowledge gained from the recidivism prediction literature to the prediction of institutional outcomes.

Schnur (1949) first documented an empirical association between the two criteria when he reported that inmates with more extensive criminal histories had higher levels of misconducts (r_{range} = 0.17–0.50; n = 1,762) and that levels of misconducts were related to postrelease recidivism. Further, inmates whose frequency of infractions increased while in custody tended to experience higher rates of postrelease recidivism. The importance of this relationship to the management of prisons lies in the fact that, if misconducts are a proxy for postrelease recidivism and recidivism can be reduced through treatment, then one would expect that the delivery of treatment within the prison context would result in lower misconduct levels. Such a result would also have an impact on reentry policies for probationers and parolees (Glaser and Stratton 1972).

There has been ample replication of Schnur's (1949) findings (see the review by Motiuk 1991; Gendreau, Goggin, and Law 1997; Cochran et al. 2012). For example, the meta-analysis by Gendreau et al. (1997) reported that both violent and nonviolent misconducts could reliably be predicted with *misconduct history* being the most robust (r = 0.21; weighted ES = 0.32) factor. These results were in keeping with those from Gendreau et al.'s (1996) meta-analysis of adult predictors of recidivism, which found criminal history, antisocial attitudes, and level of social achievement to be among the most reliable predictors.

As noted previously, the key to reliable prediction of outcome is a valid measure of offender risk. In the Gendreau et al. (1996) review, the Level of Service Inventory–Revised™ (LSI-R™; Andrews and Bonta 1995), a comprehensive measure of both dynamic and static offender attributes, produced the strongest validities with recidivism (r = 0.22, n = 2,252, k = 10). A later review by Campbell, French, and Gendreau (2009) evaluated the validity of several commonly used risk measures in predicting violent misconducts. The authors reported that the Historical-Clinical-Risk Management–20 scale (Webster et al. 1997; n = 758, k = 11) produced the highest predictive validities (r = 0.31; CI = 0.21, 0.40). Of note, the CIs about the mean effect sizes of three other instruments—the LSI-R™ (Andrews and Bonta 1995), the Psychopathy Checklist–Revised™ (Hare 2003), and the Psychopathy Checklist: Screening Version ™ (Hart, Cox, and Hare 1995)—overlapped (Cumming 2009) those of the Historical-Clinical-Risk Management–20 scale (Webster et al. 1997). Caution is advised, however, in interpreting the results from Campbell et al. (2009), as many of the study samples were relatively small in size and little descriptive information about offenders was provided (i.e., history of violence, etc.), with most being assessed as low risk. More important, the width of many of the CIs about the mean effect sizes suggested a degree of imprecision in their magnitude estimates (for CIs whose width is > .10, see Gendreau and Smith 2007).

Two additional studies have added to our understanding of the predictive relationship between misconducts and recidivism. Smith and Gendreau (2012) reported that, among a large sample of federal Canadian inmates (n = 5,038), both minor (incident reports) and major (e.g., assault) misconducts were predictive of parole revocation and reincarceration

(r_{range} = 0.16–0.22). They also noted that scores on a 7-point prison adjustment scale designed to assess misconducts, escapes, and criminal histories was also a useful predictor of postrelease recidivism (r_{range} = 0.28–0.31). In addition, Cochran et al. (2012) examined the misconduct histories (i.e., yes vs. no) of a large group of risk-matched inmates and reported that those with a history of misconducts had a 12 percent higher violent recidivism rate compared to those with no such history.

At the same time, new research cautions against the wholesale application of purpose-built indices in predicting diverse criteria. In a prospective study of mainly low-risk inmates (n = 414), Makarios and Latessa (2013) found that the magnitude of validities for two classes of instruments, risk classification and case management, were differentially sensitive to type of outcome. Specifically, validities for the risk classification tool were in the order of r = 0.37 in predicting misconducts but only r = 0.13 when predicting postrelease arrest. The reverse was true of the case management measure, where validities of r = 0.17 and r = 0.38 were reported in predicting misconducts and rearrests, respectively. The authors suggested that instruments used to predict misconducts may benefit from the inclusion of dynamic items that reflect the nature of the prison context. Additional replications of these findings should prove useful in the design and refinement of inmate assessment and classification measures.

E. RNR and Misconducts

Existing research, therefore, generally supports the use of misconducts as a proxy for recidivism. By extension, does the research record also support the effectiveness of correctional treatment as a means to reduce misconducts? There have been a variety of interventions proffered as effective strategies to control inmate behavior (see review by French and Gendreau 2006, pp. 187–188), both environmental (i.e., architectural design, climate control) and inmate-specific (i.e., diet). To date, none except correctional programming has received more than weak empirical support.

Two early meta-analyses (Keyes 1996; Morgan and Flora 2002) documented the effectiveness of custodial treatments in reducing misconducts. A third review by French and Gendreau (2006) confirmed that effective prison-based programs were those that most closely adhered to the RNR model. That is, behavioral treatments that addressed more versus fewer dynamic criminogenic needs and, importantly, scored higher on therapeutic integrity, as assessed by the Correctional Program Assessment Inventory-2010© (CPAI-2010©; Gendreau, Andrews, and Thériault 2010), reported greater reductions in recidivism than comparators. For example, effect sizes for behavioral programs were in the order of r = 0.26 as compared with r = 0.10 for nonbehavioral programs. Moreover, those programs that were most effective in reducing misconducts were equally effective in reducing recidivism (r = 0.13, CI = 0.04, 0.29, k = 12). By comparison, inmates in programs that did not reduce misconduct rates tended to have higher recidivism rates (r = −0.05, CI = −0.16, 0.07, k = 11). Caution is advised, however, in interpreting these results as these comparisons involved very few studies and the CIs about the respective mean effect sizes overlapped.

When evaluating treatment effectiveness, it is important to consider the impact of moderators such as offender risk on outcome. While French and Gendreau (2006) did not report such data, Smith and Gendreau (2012) found that interventions most consistent with the

RNR principles resulted in decreases in segregation rates among moderate-risk (i.e., 1 percent) and high-risk (i.e., 8 percent) inmates but increased segregation rates among low-risk inmates (i.e., 8 percent). Among programs that did not adhere to the RNR principles, the results were considerably worse: a 16 percent to 20 percent increase in inmate segregation rates, regardless of risk level.

VII. Inside the "Black Box": Empirical Validation of Treatment's Constituents

There is ample evidence, then, that misconducts can be reliably predicted based on an assessment of the same criminogenic need domains that predict recidivism (Gendreau et al. 1996, 1997). Similarly, the research literature indicates that prison misconducts can be reduced through the application of programs that embody the RNR principles. Further, Andrews and Bonta (2010, p. 362) note that the effects of *non*-RNR programs in custody contexts are "particularly negative." The corollary is: Can effective prison-based programming also reduce postrelease recidivism rates? Of course the basic answer to this question has been known since Andrews et al.'s (1990) classic review documented such an effect. As Gendreau (1996a) has noted, however, studies from that era did not fully describe the specifics regarding which aspects of treatment were fundamental to their success. This section showcases four programs that have contributed greatly to our understanding of treatment's essential constituents.

The first program, which dates from the Martinson era, was located at the Rideau Correctional and Treatment Centre (Bourgon and Anderson 2005), a Canadian medium-security provincial facility. It was noteworthy for its comprehensive embodiment of the RNR principles in that criminogenic needs and aspects of offender responsivity were assessed using the LSI-R™ (Andrews and Bonta 1995) and other validated psychological indices (i.e., Criminal Sentiments Scale, Beck Depression Inventory©, etc.). Based on assessed risk/need, inmates were assigned to one of three structured CBT programs lasting 5, 10, or 15 weeks. The treatment group, including nonprogram completers, was comprised of 482 inmates versus 138 in the risk-controlled comparison group. The program targeted offenders' antisocial thinking, substance abuse, and anger management issues while providing them with relapse-prevention training. Key learning tactics such as role play (i.e., step-by-step modeling of skill-building behaviors) and behavioral rehearsal (i.e., modeling target behaviors) were also emphasized.

Regarding outcome, postrelease recidivism was 13 percent lower for the treatment group during a two-year follow-up period. As inmates were assigned to varying lengths of treatment, Bourgon and Anderson (2005) were able to examine the differential effects of treatment "dosages," something that has long been of interest to researchers (see Lipsey 1995). As such, they evaluated recidivism rates by level of risk for each group of inmates and found additional reductions of 1 percent to 7 percent, depending on the risk-dosage comparison. Further, the authors noted that 300 hours was the optimum treatment exposure and estimated that recidivism rates could be lowered by 1 percent to 2 percent for each additional week in treatment.

The second program was that developed by Jack Bush in Vermont during the late 1980s. Its roots lay in Bush's (1995) conceptualization of offenders and their behavior and drew on both the offender treatment and relapse-prevention literatures (Bandura 1973; Yochelson and Samenow 1976; Andrews 1980; Marlatt and Gordon 1985; Goldstein 1999). For example, Bush did not support the notion that offenders are necessarily mentally disordered or offense specialists. Rather, the Vermont regimen engaged offenders at the level of their antisocial cognitions, focusing on the use of thinking reports (i.e., observing/recording one's thoughts/feelings in response to one's criminal activities) through which inmates could learn to recognize, and by applying newly acquired skills, correct their thinking distortions and control their impulsivity (Bush 1995). Among the keys to the program's success were relapse prevention, including postrelease community programming, role play, and behavioral rehearsal.

Henning and Frueh's (1996) evaluation of the Vermont program used a matched-comparison groups design, including treatment dropouts. They reported a 21 percent reduction in recidivism during a two-year follow-up for treatment ($n = 28$) versus nontreatment inmates ($n = 141$). While details of treatment dosage were not reported, Sadler and Powell (2008) later estimated that the minimum dosage for the Vermont program was approximately 150 hours. Such estimates are consistent with those reported by Sperber, Latessa, and Makarios (2013), who reported optimal treatment dosage for meaningful reductions in recidivism to be in the range of 200 hours, especially among high-risk offenders.

The third study is a review of treatment effectiveness in 80 state-run halfway houses and community-based correctional centers in Ohio conducted by researchers from the University of Cincinnati (Lowenkamp, Latessa, and Smith 2006; Latessa, Lovins, and Smith 2010; Latessa, Lovins, Smith, et al. 2010). Of note, there was considerable variability in terms of the treatments offered by the facilities, few of whom were *au courant* with the RNR research literature. Not surprisingly, the programs were not particularly effective in reducing recidivism (Latessa, Lovins, and Smith 2010).

When outcome was examined by risk level, however, Latessa, Lovins, and Smith (2010) found an effect consistent with the risk principle but only among community-based correctional center inmates. Specifically, high-risk inmates tended to have a lower reincarceration rate (i.e., treatment 59.7 percent vs. comparison group 60.5 percent) while those assessed as low risk experienced the opposite effect (i.e., treatment 26.6 percent vs. comparison group 16.9 percent). Risk level did not moderate treatment effect among halfway-house inmates where recidivism rates were higher among treatment participants (i.e., 38.8 percent) versus comparison group counterparts (i.e., 30.0 percent) at all risk levels.

The Latessa group was also able to examine the constituents of treatment programs in order to determine exactly what was being delivered. They used Lowenkamp et al. (2006) as a basis for comparison as that study had reported that several indices of therapeutic integrity, as measured by the CPAI-2010© (Gendreau et al. 2010), were associated with reductions in recidivism ($r_{range} = 0.25$–0.54). Latessa, Lovins, Smith et al.'s (2010) results were consistent with those of Lowenkamp et al. (2006) in that they reported reductions in recidivism in the 10 percent range for program elements such as *high-quality program leadership, well-qualified/experienced staff, use of risk assessment measures, appropriate use of punishment*, and *appropriate targeting of criminogenic needs*.

Finally, Smith and Gendreau (2012) highlighted the importance of the risk principle to program effectiveness as they reported that, among programs that were consistent with the need principle, recidivism decreased among moderate-risk and high-risk inmates by 7 percent and 11 percent, respectively, but increased by 4 percent among low-risk inmates, an effect that has been consistently replicated in the literature (Andrews and Bonta 2010). For programs that did not follow the need principle, recidivism rates were higher for inmates at each level of assessed risk but especially so for low-risk inmates (i.e., low: 14 percent, moderate: 7 percent, high: 6 percent).

As noted previously, there is mounting evidence that correctional treatments can also be cost-effective (Cohen 1998). Depending on operational definitions of effectiveness versus benefit, estimates of cost-savings range from $2,600,000 per youth whose criminal career is preempted before adulthood to $15,000 in life-cycle benefits for even small reductions (i.e., 7 percent) in recidivism (Drake et al. 2009; Farrington, Petrosino, and Welsh 2001). A recent study by Romani and colleagues (2012) provides the most nuanced examination of the cost-benefit issue as they were able to compare the cost of programs that successfully reduced recidivism by at least 1 percent relative to their adherence to the RNR principles. Specifically, they found that the average cost per 1 percent reduction was 20 times less for RNR-based versus punishment-based programs and 7 times less for RNR versus non-RNR treatments. Moreover, the effect sizes associated with the RNR programs were, on average, greater in magnitude than those of either of the other two treatment conditions.

VIII. Next Steps

While much has been learned regarding "what works" in rehabilitative programming, a number of issues merit further research. These include improving treatment engagement and retention rates, incorporating case management planning within risk assessment indices, making program evaluations standard practice, and taking advantage of available technologies (i.e., data registries) to advance the research agenda.

A. Treatment Engagement and Retention

Treatment drop-out rates continue to be a problem when evaluating program effectiveness. For example, in a recent meta-analysis ($k = 114$) of predictors of attrition, Olver et al. (2011) reported that just over 25 percent of offenders dropped out of treatment and were typically those assessed as highest risk. Dropouts were more likely to be unemployed, have lower levels of education, exhibit antisocial personality tendencies, and have prior incarceration histories, all factors predictive of both recidivism (Gendreau et al. 1996) and misconducts (Gendreau et al. 1997). Further, aspects of offender responsivity such as *denial of need for treatment, negative attitudes toward treatment, disruptive behavior during treatment*, and *lack of engagement in treatment* were among the strongest predictors of attrition.

Olver et al. (2011) were unable to determine why offenders failed to complete treatment (i.e., self-selection or dismissal), although at least one meta-analysis has reported that quality of program implementation and attrition rates are inversely related (Lipsey et al. 2007). This highlights the importance of attending to implementation issues in evaluating program effectiveness (Gendreau, Goggin, and Smith 1999) and emphasizes the need for replications of well-controlled primary studies designed to evaluate the interaction of offender, facilitator, and setting characteristics on attrition (Wormith et al. 2007; Andrews, Bonta, and Wormith 2011).

Results from neuropsychological research have also proposed a potential link between offender attrition and cognitive functioning deficits. For example, Vaske, Galyean, and Cullen (2011) reviewed the effect of CBT at the neural level and found that such programs resulted in activation in offenders' frontal, parietal, and temporal lobes (see Vaske et al. 2011 for a detailed map of relevant brain structures), areas known to govern "executive" functions such as introspection, emotional regulation, moral reasoning, self-control, motivation, appraisal of rewards/punishers, risk evaluation, and perception of social cues. Several studies (i.e., Raine, Buchsbaum, and LaCasse 1997; Raine et al. 2000; Blair 2004; Pridmore, Chambers, and McArthur 2005) have documented deficits in these brain areas among offenders. The question remains as to whether CBT might result in positive neural changes in this group, as has been documented using functional magnetic resonance imaging in patients being treated for depression (i.e., Goldapple et al. 2004; Fu et al. 2008) and panic disorder (i.e., Praško et al. 2004).

As Vaske et al. (2011) have noted, the ability to track changes in neural status through imaging techniques, or their psychometric proxies (i.e., the Stroop task), has particular import for documenting the effects of programming among difficult to treat offenders and, perhaps most important, speaks directly to offender responsivity (i.e., potential to respond to treatment). Primary studies by Fishbein and Sheppard (2006) and Fishbein et al. (2009) have shown that inmates who were more prone to impulsivity and had learning retention difficulties were also more likely to drop out of treatment or fail to make progress in treatment. Fishbein et al. suggest that, as such responsivity deficits predicted poorer outcome in their sample ($n = 224$), it would be useful to address such issues prior to beginning CBT programming in order to augment treatment readiness and improve the potential for inmates to stay engaged in treatment once enrolled (see also MacKenzie 2013).

B. Integrating Risk Assessment, Case Management, and Outcome Evaluation

The empirical validation of the RNR principles highlights the importance of sound risk assessment practices to effective correctional treatment. Andrews and Bonta (2010) have characterized risk assessment scales in "generational" terms based on theoretical grounding, the ratio of dynamic–static items, and how data are summarized and integrated in practice. For example, the Level of Service/Case Management Inventory™ (Andrews, Bonta, and Wormith 2004) is a fourth-generation scale that samples broadly from among the most robust empirically documented risk factors and incorporates measures of offender responsivity. It then combines this information with offender case management planning and outcome evaluation on an ongoing basis (Andrews and Bonta 2010; Luong and Wormith 2011).

In terms of predicting criterion, the Level of Service/Case Management Inventory™ reports validities of $r = 0.41$ and $r = 0.29$ for general and violent recidivism, respectively, where offenders assessed as high risk were more likely to recidivate (Andrews, Bonta, and Wormith 2006; see also Campbell et al. 2009). The integration of risk assessment, case management planning, and outcome evaluation components within a single scale offers a significant advantage for both front-line workers and researchers interested in tracking offender change over time in response to correctional treatment.

C. Evaluating Program Effectiveness

With the development of the CPAI-2010© (Gendreau et al. 2010), it is now possible to measure program effectiveness by evaluating the degree to which correctional treatments adhere to what the literature says about offender RNR. This inventory evaluates eight program components during on-site review including *organizational culture, program implementation/maintenance, management/staff characteristics, offender risk/need practices, program characteristics*, plus dimensions of *core correctional practice, interagency communication*, and *outcome evaluation*. Among institutional and community-based correctional programs that score well on the inventory, the CPAI-2010© has reported substantial predictive validities (r_{range} = 0.41–0.50; Andrews and Bonta 2010).

Unfortunately, the majority of programs reviewed to date have scored in the "unsatisfactory" range (i.e., less than 50 percent of ratable elements present; Matthews, Hubbard, and Latessa 2001; Andrews 2006). They were also least likely to be associated with meaningful reductions in recidivism. For example, in a matched-control study, Lowenkamp et al. (2006) reported that program quality had differential effects on recidivism rates among 3,237 offenders enrolled in 38 community-based treatments. Specifically, for programs that scored 60 percent or above on the CPAI-2010©, there was a 22-point difference in the recidivism rates of the treatment and control groups. By comparison, for programs that scored in the 50 percent to 59 percent range (k = 8), there was an 8-point difference in recidivism rates. And for programs that scored less than 50 percent, there was virtually no difference in the recidivism rates of the two groups (i.e., < 2 points; Lowenkamp et al. 2006).

These kinds of results reinforce the position taken by the field's leading scholars (e.g., Andrews, Bonta, Gendreau, Cullen) with respect to correctional treatment: ensure optimal effectiveness by using empirically validated assessment tools to identify those in greatest need of service and do so using empirically validated treatment modalities delivered by experienced and credentialed facilitators. As Cullen, Myer, and Latessa (2009, p. 210) have stated, the existing "knowledge base creates the ability to ask correctional officials and agencies a powerful question: Why aren't you doing what works?" Given what is currently known about core correctional practice, and in the face of constrained budgets, publicly financed correctional services can ill afford to leave themselves open to such a question.

D. Embracing Technology

Recent advancements in the area of data digitization and storage offer the potential to significantly affect both the volume of knowledge within a literature and the speed with which it is cumulated and disseminated. Initiatives such as the Sociological, Psychological, Educational, and Criminological Trials Register (C2-SPECTR) sponsored by the Campbell

Collaboration (C2) are positioned to dramatically influence both applied and research practice (Turner et al. 2003).

C2 is an international research network whose mandate is to provide comprehensive summaries of treatment research literatures in public policy (i.e., education, crime and justice, social welfare; Turner et al. 2003). Since 2000, C2 has sponsored 100 systematic reviews of relevant research literatures, 35 percent of which fall within the crime and justice domain (Petrosino 2013). A vital characteristic of these syntheses, and one that is crucial to furthering the knowledge base, is that virtually all of the studies included in C2 reviews are of the highest methodological quality; that is, they use randomized or quasi-experimental designs. As such, the results they produce regarding program effectiveness are considered definitive.

With the C2-SPECTR initiative, the research network has expanded its role to include web-based consolidation of key details from high-quality studies examining crime and justice issues. Currently, the majority of the 11,600 entries in the registry consist of study abstracts. The ultimate goal is to have "uniform synopses" (Turner et al. 2003, p. 219) completed for all studies in the registry. These will provide details of study elements such as purpose, research design, sample, and independent and dependent variables. Once fully operational, the C2-SPECTR registry will provide the basis for comprehensive reviews of rigorously designed studies of applied criminal justice issues.

Similar projects have also been established in the United States under the auspices of the Office of Justice Programs. For example, CrimeSolutions.gov is a website that uses program evaluation data to categorize correctional treatments by relative effectiveness: "effective," "promising," or "no effect." In keeping with C2 and equivalent initiatives (see also Perrino et al. 2013), such data registries are examples of current trends in developing models of evidence-based practice that will enable the reliable transfer of empirical results to practical reality.

IX. Conclusion

When considering future developments in the design and implementation of effective correctional programming, taking the long view provides much-needed perspective. In terms of the rehabilitative ideal, the 19th century can rightfully lay claim to generating many of the ideas about correcting offender behavior that later found empirical support in the early 20th century. And during the latter half of that century, the elements of "what works for whom" in correctional programming were empirically validated. What strides, then, will characterize the first part of the 21st century in this area?

At a minimum, the coming generation of researchers is advised to carefully nurture the knowledge of program design, elements, and implementation gained to date and to faithfully attend to its consolidation and distribution in order to benefit all constituents: the public, policymakers, and offenders alike. Cullen et al. (2009, p. 210) have identified three key objectives in this regard: *knowledge construction, knowledge dissemination*, and *knowledge fidelity*. If we are to sustain the rehabilitative ideal and safeguard its future growth, evidence-based practice rooted in the three "knowledges" must be the norm.

References

Adams, Stuart. 1976. "Evaluation: A Way Out of Rhetoric." In *Rehabilitation, Recidivism, and Research*, edited by Robert Martinson, Ted Palmer, and Stuart Adams. Hackensack, NJ: National Council on Crime and Delinquency.

Allen, Francis A. 1981. *The Decline of the Rehabilitative Ideal: Penal Policy and Social Purpose*. New Haven, CT: Yale University Press.

American Correctional Association. 1972. "Developments of Modern Correctional Concepts and Standards." In *Correctional Institutions*, edited by Robert M. Carter, Daniel Glaser, and Leslie T. Wilkins. New York: J. P. Lippincott.

American Friends Service Committee Working Party. 1971. *Struggle for Justice: A Report on Crime and Punishment in America*. New York: Hill & Wang.

Andrews, Donald A. 1979. *The Dimensions of Correctional Counseling and Supervision Process in Probation and Parole*. Toronto: Ontario Ministry of Correctional Services.

Andrews, Donald A. 1980. "Some Experimental Investigations of the Principles of Differential Association Through Deliberate Manipulations of the Structure of Service Systems." *American Sociological Review* 45: 448–462.

Andrews, Donald A. 1995. "The Psychology of Criminal Conduct and Effective Treatment." In *What Works: Reducing Reoffending*, edited by James McGuire. West Sussex, UK: John Wiley.

Andrews, Donald A. 2006. "Enhancing Adherence to Risk-Need-Responsivity: Making Quality a Matter of Policy." *Criminology & Public Policy* 5: 595–602.

Andrews, Donald A., and James Bonta. 1995. *The Level of Service Inventory-Revised*. Toronto: Multi-Health Systems.

Andrews, Donald A., and James Bonta. 1998. *The Psychology of Criminal Conduct*, 2d ed. Cincinnati, OH: Anderson.

Andrews, Donald A., and James Bonta. 2010. *The Psychology of Criminal Conduct*, 5th ed. Cincinnati, OH: Anderson.

Andrews, Donald A., James Bonta, and J. Stephen Wormith. 2004. *The Level of Service/Case Management Inventory (LS/CMI): User's Manual*. Toronto: Multi-Health Systems.

Andrews, Donald A., James Bonta, and J. Stephen Wormith. 2006. "The Recent Past and Near Future of Risk Assessment." *Crime & Delinquency* 52: 7–27.

Andrews, Donald A., James Bonta, and J. Stephen Wormith. 2011. "The Risk-Need-Responsivity Model: Does Adding the Good Lives Model Contribute to Effective Crime Prevention?" *Criminal Justice and Behavior* 38: 735–755.

Andrews, Donald A., Craig Dowden, and Paul Gendreau. 1999. *Clinically Relevant and Psychologically Informed Approaches to Reduced Re-Offending: A Meta-Analytic Study of Human Service, Risk, Need, Responsivity, and Other Concerns in Justice Contexts*. Unpublished manuscript, Carleton University.

Andrews, Donald A., and Jerry J. Kiessling. 1980. "Program Structure and Effective Correctional Practices: A Summary of the CaVIC Research." In *Effective Correctional Treatment* edited by Robert R. Ross and Paul Gendreau. Toronto: Butterworth.

Andrews, Donald A., Jerry J. Kiessling, David Robinson, and Susan Mickus. 1986. "The Risk Principle of Case Classification: An Outcome Evaluation with Young Adult Probationers." *Canadian Journal of Criminology* 28: 377–384.

Andrews, Donald A., Ivan Zinger, Robert D. Hoge, James L. Bonta, Paul Gendreau, and Francis T. Cullen. 1990. "Does Correctional Treatment Work? A Clinically Relevant and Psychologically Informed Meta-Analysis." *Criminology* 28: 369–404.

Aos, Steve, Polly Phipps, Robert Barnoski, and Roxanne Lieb. 1999. *The Comparative Costs and Benefits of Programs to Reduce Crime: A Review of National Research Findings with Implications for Washington State*. Olympia: Washington State Institute for Public Safety.

Applegate, Brandon K. 2001. "Penal Austerity: Perceived Utility, Desert, and Public Attitudes Toward Prison Amenities." *American Journal of Criminal Justice* 25: 253–268.

Apter, Steven J., and Arnold P. Goldstein. 1986. *Youth Violence: Program and Prospects*. New York: Pergamon Press.

Bailey, Walter C. 1966. "Correctional Outcome: An Evaluation of 100 Reports." *Journal of Criminal Law, Criminology and Police Science* 57: 153–160.

Bandura, Albert. 1973. *Aggression: A Social Learning Analysis*. Oxford: Prentice-Hall.

Beaman, Arthur L. 1991. "An Empirical Comparison of Meta-Analytic and Traditional Reviews." *Personality and Social Psychology Bulletin* 17: 252–257.

Binder, Albert, and Gilbert Geis. 1984. "Ad Populum Argumentation in Criminology: Juvenile Diversion as Rhetoric." *Crime & Delinquency* 30: 624–647.

Blair, R. James. 2004. "The Roles of Orbital Frontal Cortex in the Modulation of Antisocial Behavior." *Brain and Cognition* 55: 198–208.

Bonta, James. 1996. "Risk Needs Assessment and Treatment." In *Choosing Correctional Options that Work*, edited by A. T. Harland. Thousand Oaks, CA: Sage.

Bonta, James, and Paul Gendreau. 1990. "Reexamining the Cruel and Unusual Punishment of Prison Life." *Law and Human Behavior* 14: 347–372.

Bourgon, Guy, and Barbara Anderson. 2005. "Transferring the Principles of Effective Treatment into a 'Real World' Prison Setting." *Criminal Justice and Behavior* 32: 3–25.

Bush, Jack. 1995. "Teaching Self-Risk Management to Violent Offenders." In *What Works: Reducing Reoffending—Guidelines from Research and Practice*, edited by James McGuire. Hoboken, NJ: Wiley.

Campbell, Mary Ann, Sheila French, and Paul Gendreau. 2009. "The Prediction of Violence in Adult Offenders: A Meta-Analytic Comparison of Instruments and Methods of Assessment." *Criminal Justice and Behavior* 36: 567–590.

Carrigan, D. Owen. 1991. *Crime and Punishment in Canada: A History*. Toronto: McLelland and Stewart.

Carson, E. Ann, and Daniela Golinelli. 2013. *Prisoners in 2012: Advance Counts*. NCJ 242467. Washington, DC: US Department of Justice, Bureau of Justice Statistics.

Chan, MeowLan E., and Richard D. Arvey. 2012. "Meta-Analysis and the Development of Knowledge." *Perspectives on Psychological Science* 7: 79–92.

Cochran, Joshua C., Daniel P. Mears, William D. Bales, and Eric A. Stewart. 2012. "Does Inmate Behavior Affect Post-Release Offending? Investigating the Misconduct-Recidivism Relationship among Youth and Adults." *Justice Quarterly*, 1–30.

Cohen, Jacob. 1988. *Statistical Power Analysis for the Behavioral Sciences*, 2d ed. New York: Academic Press.

Cohen, Mark A. 1998. "The Monetary Value of Saving a High-Risk Youth." *Journal of Quantitative Criminology* 14: 5–32.

Conrad, John P. 1981. "Where There's Hope There's Life." In *Justice as Fairness: Perspectives of the Justice Model*, edited by David Fogel and Joe Hudson Cincinnati, OH: Anderson.

Cooper, Harris M., and Robert Rosenthal. 1980. "Statistical Versus Traditional Procedures for Summarizing Research Findings." *Psychological Bulletin* 87: 442–449.

Cressey, Donald R. 1958. "The Nature and Effectiveness of Correctional Techniques." *Law and Contemporary Problems* 23: 754–771.

Cullen, Francis T. 2005. "The Twelve People Who Saved Rehabilitation: How the Science of Criminology Made a Difference." *Criminology* 43: 1–42.

Cullen, Francis T., and Paul Gendreau. 1989. "The Effectiveness of Correctional Treatment: Reconsidering the 'Nothing Works' Debate." In *The American Prison: Issues in Research and Policy*, edited by Lynn Goodstein and Doris L. MacKenzie. New York: Plenum Press.

Cullen, Francis T., and Paul Gendreau. 2000. "Assessing Correctional Rehabilitation: Policy, Practice, Prospects." In *National Institute of Justice Criminal Justice 2000: Changes in Decision Making and Discretion in the Criminal Justice System*, edited by Julie Horney. Washington, DC: US Department of Justice, National Institute of Justice.

Cullen, Francis T., and Karen E. Gilbert. 1982. *Reaffirming Rehabilitation.* Cincinnati, OH: Anderson.

Cullen, Francis T., and Karen E. Gilbert. 2013. *Reaffirming Rehabilitation*, 2d ed. Cincinnati, OH: Anderson.

Cullen, Francis T., Andrew J. Myer, and Latessa, E. J. 2009. "Eight Lessons from *Moneyball*: The High Cost of Ignoring Evidence-Based Corrections." *Victims & Offenders* 4: 197–213.

Cumming, Geoff. 2009. "Inference by Eye: Reading the Overlap of Independent Confidence Intervals." *Statistics in Medicine* 28: 205–220.

Davidson, William S. II, Rand Gottschalk, Leah K. Gensheimer, and Jeffrey P. Mayer. 1984. *Interventions with Juvenile Delinquents: A Meta-Analysis of Treatment Efficacy.* Washington, DC: National Institute of Juvenile Justice and Delinquency Prevention.

Dowden, Craig, and Donald A. Andrews. 2000. "Effective Correctional Treatment and Violent Reoffending: A Meta-Analysis." *Canadian Journal of Criminology* 42: 449–468.

Drake, Elizabeth K., Steve Aos, and Marna G. Miller. 2009. "Evidence-Based Public Policy Options to Reduce Crime and Criminal Justice Costs: Implications in Washington State." *Victims and Offenders* 4: 170–196.

Emery, Robert E., and David Marholin. 1977. "An Applied Behavior Analysis of Delinquency: The Irrelevancy of Relevant Behavior." *American Psychologist* 32: 860–873.

Erickson, Maynard L., and Jack P. Gibbs. 1979. "On the Perceived Severity of Legal Penalties." *Journal of Criminal Law and Criminology* 70: 102–116.

Farrington, David P., Anthony Petrosino, and Brandon C. Welsh. 2001. "Systematic Reviews and Cost-Benefit Analysis of Correctional Interventions." *The Prison Journal* 81: 339–359.

Fishbein, Diana, and Monica Sheppard. 2006. *Assessing the Role of Neuropsychological Functioning in Inmates' Treatment Response.* Washington, DC: National Institute of Justice.

Fishbein, Diana, Monica Sheppard, Christopher Hyde, Robert Hubai, David Newlin, Ralph Serin, George Chrousos, and Salvatore Alesci. 2009. "Deficits in Behavioral Inhibition Predict Treatment Engagement in Prison Inmates." *Law and Human Behavior* 33: 419–435.

Fogel, David. 1979. *We Are the Living Proof: The Justice Model for Corrections*, 2d ed. Cincinnati, OH: Anderson.

French, Sheila A., and Paul Gendreau. 2006. "Reducing Prison Misconducts: What Works!" *Criminal Justice and Behavior* 33: 185–218.

Fu, Cynthia H., Steven C. Williams, Anthony J. Cleare, Jan Scott, Martina T. Mitterschiffthaler, Nicholas D. Walsh, Catherine Donaldson, John Suckling, Chris Andrew, Herbert Steiner, and Robin M. Murray. 2008. "Neural Responses to Sad Facial Expressions in Major Depression Following Cognitive-Behavioral Therapy." *Biological Psychiatry* 64: 505–512.

Garrett, Carol J. 1985. "Effects of Residential Treatment of Adjudicated Delinquents: A Meta-Analysis." *Journal of Research in Crime and Delinquency* 22: 287–308.

Gendreau, Paul. 1996a. "Offender Rehabilitation: What We Know and What Needs to Be Done." *Criminal Justice and Behavior* 23: 144–161.

Gendreau, Paul. 1996b. "The Principles of Effective Intervention with Offenders." In *Choosing Correctional Interventions that Work: Defining the Demand and Evaluating the Supply*, edited by Alan T. Harland. Newbury Park, CA: Sage.

Gendreau, Paul., and Donald A. Andrews. 1979. "Psychological Consultation in Correctional Agencies: Case Studies and General Issues." In *The Psychological Consultant*, edited by Jerome J. Platt and Robert J. Wicks. New York: Grune and Stratton.

Gendreau, Paul., Donald A. Andrews, and Yvette Thériault. 2010. *Correctional Program Assessment Inventory-2010© (CPAI-2010©)*. Beresford, NB: Author.

Gendreau, Paul, Doretta Burke, and Brian A. Grant. 1980. "A Second Evaluation of the Rideau Inmate Volunteer Program." *Canadian Journal of Criminology* 22: 66–67.

Gendreau, Paul, Francis T. Cullen, and James Bonta. 1994. "Intensive Rehabilitation Supervision: The Next Generation in Community Corrections." *Federal Probation* 58: 72–78.

Gendreau, Paul, Claire Goggin, and Francis T. Cullen. 1999. *The Effects of Prison Sentences on Recidivism*. Ottawa: Solicitor General Canada.

Gendreau, Paul, Claire Goggin, Francis T. Cullen, and Mario Paparozzi. 2002. "The Common Sense Revolution and Correctional Policy." In *Offender Rehabilitation and Treatment: Effective Programs and Policies to Reduce Re-Offending*, edited by James McGuire. Chichester, UK: John Wiley.

Gendreau, Paul, Claire Goggin, and Moira Law. 1997. "Predicting Prison Misconducts." *Criminal Justice and Behavior* 24: 414–431.

Gendreau, Paul, Claire Goggin, and Paula Smith. 1999. "The Forgotten Issue in Effective Correctional Treatment: Program Implementation." *International Journal of Offender Therapy and Comparative Criminology* 43: 180–187.

Gendreau, Paul, Claire Goggin, and Paula Smith. 2000. "Generating Rational Correctional Policies: An Introduction to Advances in Cumulating Knowledge." *Corrections Management Quarterly* 4: 52–60.

Gendreau, Paul, Tracey Little, and Claire Goggin. 1996. "A Meta-Analysis of the Predictors of Adult Offender Recidivism: What Works!" *Criminology* 34: 575–607.

Gendreau, Paul, and Robert R. Ross. 1979. "Effective Correctional Treatment: Bibliotherapy for Cynics." *Crime & Delinquency* 25: 463–489.

Gendreau, Paul, and Robert Ross. 1980. *Effective Correctional Treatment*. Toronto: Butterworth.

Gendreau, Paul, and Robert R. Ross. 1981a. "Correctional Potency: Treatment and Deterrence on Trial." In *Evaluation and Criminal Justice Policy*, edited by Ronald Roesch and Raymond R. Corrado. Beverly Hills, CA: Sage.

Gendreau, Paul, and Robert R. Ross. 1981b. "Offender Rehabilitation: The Appeal of Success. *Federal Probation* 45: 45–48.

Gendreau, Paul, and Robert R. Ross. 1983–1984. "Correctional Treatment: Some Recommendations for Successful Intervention." *Juvenile and Family Court* 34: 31–40.

Gendreau, Paul, and Robert R. Ross. 1987. "Revivification of Rehabilitation: Evidence from the 1980s." *Justice Quarterly* 4: 349–407.

Gendreau, Paul, and Paula Smith. 2007. "Influencing the 'People Who Count': Some Perspectives on the Reporting of Meta-Analytic Results for Prediction and Treatment Outcomes with Offenders." *Criminal Justice and Behavior* 34: 1536–1559.

Glaser, Daniel, and John Stratton. 1972. "Measuring Inmate Change in Prison." In *Prison Studies in Institutional Organization and Change*, edited by Donald R. Cressey. New York: Holt, Rinehart and Winston.

Glass, Gene V. 1976. "Primary, Secondary, and Meta-Analysis of Research." *Educational Researcher* 5: 3–8.

Glass, Gene V., Barry McGaw, and Mary Lee Smith. 1981. *Meta-Analysis in Social Research.* Beverly Hills, CA: Sage.

Goggin, Claire. 2009. *Is Prison "Personality" Associated with Offender Recidivism?* PhD dissertation. University of New Brunswick, Fredericton.

Goldapple, Kimberley, Zindel Segal, Carol Garson, Mark Lau, Peter Bieling, Sidney Kennedy, and Helen Mayberg. 2004. "Modulation of Cortical-Limbic Pathways in Major Depression." *Archives of General Psychiatry* 61: 34–41.

Goldstein, Arnold P. 1999. *The Prepare Curriculum: Teaching Prosocial Competencies.* Champaign, IL: Research Press.

Greenwood, P. W., K. E. Model, C. P. Rydell, and J. Chiesa. 1996. *Diverting Children from a Life of Crime: Measuring Costs and Benefits.* Santa Monica, CA: RAND.

Guilford, Joy Paul. 1946. *General Psychology*, 6th ed. New York: D. Van Nostrand.

Hanson, R. Karl, Guy Bourgon, Leslie Helmus, and Shannon Hodgson. 2009. "The Principles of Effective Correctional Treatment Also Apply to Sexual Offenders: A Meta-Analysis." *Criminal Justice and Behavior* 36: 865–891.

Hare, Robert D. 2003. *The Hare Psychopathy Checklist: Revised*, 2d ed. Toronto: Multi-Health Systems.

Hart, Stephen D., David N. Cox, and Robert D. Hare. 1995. *The Hare Psychopathy Checklist: Screening Version.* Toronto: Multi-Health Systems.

Henning, Kris R., and Christopher Frueh. 1996. "Cognitive-Behavioral Treatment of Incarcerated Offenders: An Evaluation of the Vermont Department of Corrections' Cognitive Self-Change Program." *Criminal Justice and Behavior* 23: 523–541.

Howard, John. 1991. "The State of the Prisons." In *Imprisonment: European perspectives*, edited by John Muncie and Richard Sparks. New York: St. Martin's Press.

Hunt, Morton. 1997. *How Science Takes Stock: The Story of Meta-Analysis.* New York: Russell Sage Foundation.

Hunter, John E., and Frank L. Schmidt. 2004. *Methods of Meta-Analysis: Correcting Error and Bias in Research Findings.* Thousand Oaks, CA: Sage.

Ives, George. 1970. *A History of Penal Methods: Criminals, Witches, Lunatics.* Montclair, NJ: Patterson Smith. (Original work published 1914).

Izzo, Rhena L., and Robert R. Ross. 1990. "Meta-Analysis of Rehabilitation Programs for Juvenile Delinquents." *Criminal Justice and Behavior* 17: 134–142.

Johnston, Norval. 2000. *Forms of Constraint: A History of Prison Architecture.* Chicago: University of Illinois Press.

Kassebaum, Gene, David A. Ward, and Daniel M. Wilner. 1971. *Prison Treatment and Parole Survival: An Empirical Assessment.* New York: John Wiley.

Keyes, David. 1996. *"Preventing Prison Misconduct Behaviour: A Quantitative Review of the Literature."* Unpublished master's thesis. University of New Brunswick, Saint John.

Kirby, Bernard C. 1954. "Measuring Effects of Treatment of Criminals and Delinquents." *Sociology and Social Research* 38: 368–374.

Latessa, Edward J., Lori B. Lovins, and Paula Smith. 2010. *Final Report: Follow-Up Evaluation of Ohio's Community Based Correctional Facility and Halfway House Programs-Outcome Study.* Cincinnati, OH: University of Cincinnati, Division of Criminal Justice.

Latessa, Edward J., Lori B. Lovins, Paula Smith, and Matthew Makarios. 2010. *Follow-Up Evaluation of Ohio's Community Based Correctional Facility and Halfway House Programs: Program Characteristics Supplemental Report.* Cincinnati, OH: University of Cincinnati, Division of Criminal Justice.

Lipset, Seymour M., and William Schneider. 1983. *The Confidence Gap: Business, Labor, and Government in the Public Mind.* New York: Free Press.

Lipsey, Mark W. 1992. "Juvenile Delinquency Treatment: A Meta-Analytic Inquiry into the Variability of Effects." In *Meta-Analysis for Explanation: A Casebook*, edited by Thomas D. Cook, Harris Cooper, David S. Cordray, Heidi Hartmann, Larry V. Hedges, Richard J. Light, Thomas A. Lewis, and Frederick Mosteller. New York: Russell Sage Foundation.

Lipsey, Mark W. 1995. "What Do We Learn from 400 Research Studies on the Effectiveness of Treatment with Juvenile Delinquents?" In *What Works: Reducing Reoffending—Guidelines for Research and Practice*, edited by James McGuire. Oxford: John Wiley.

Lipsey, Mark W. 1999. "Can Rehabilitative Programs Reduce the Recidivism of Juvenile Offenders? An Inquiry into the Effectiveness of Practical Programs." *Virginia Journal of Social Policy and Law* 6: 611–641.

Lipsey, Mark W., Nana A. Landenberger, and Sandra J. Wilson. 2007. *Effects of Cognitive-Behavioral Programs for Criminal Offenders.* Campbell Systematic Reviews 6. Oslo: Campbell Collaboration.

Lipsey, Mark W., and David B. Wilson. 1993. "The Efficacy of Psychological, Educational and Behavioral Treatment." *American Psychologist* 48: 1181–1209.

Lipton, Douglas, Robert Martinson, and Judith Wilks. 1975. *The Effectiveness of Correctional Treatment: A Survey of Treatment Evaluation Studies.* New York: Praeger.

Listwan, Shelley J., Christopher J. Sullivan, Robert Agnew, Francis T. Cullen, and Mark Colvin. 2013. "The Pains of Imprisonment Revisited: The Impact of Strain on Inmate Recidivism." *Justice Quarterly* 30: 144–168.

Logan, Charles H. 1972. "Evaluation Research in Crime and Delinquency: A Reappraisal." *Journal of Criminal Law, Criminology and Police Science* 63: 378–387.

Logan, Charles H., Gerald G. Gaes, Miles Harer, Christopher A. Innes, Loren Karacki, and William G. Saylor. 1991. *Can Meta-Analysis Save Correctional Rehabilitation?* Washington, DC: Federal Bureau of Prisons, US Department of Justice.

Lösel, Friedrich. 1995. "The Efficacy of Correctional Treatment: A Review and Synthesis of Meta-Evaluations." In *What Works: Reducing Reoffending*, edited by James McGuire West Sussex, UK: John Wiley.

Lovell, David, and Ron Jemelka. 1996. "When Inmates Misbehave: The Costs of Discipline." *The Prison Journal* 76: 165–179.

Lowenkamp, Christopher, Edward J. Latessa, and Paula Smith. 2006. "Does Correctional Program Quality Really Matter? The Impact of Adhering to the Principles of Effective Intervention." *Criminology and Public Policy* 5: 575–594.

Luong, Duyen, and J. Stephen Wormith. 2011. "Applying Risk/Need Assessment to Probation Practice and Its Impact on the Recidivism of Young Offenders." *Criminal Justice and Behavior* 38: 1177–1199.

MacKenzie, Doris L. 2013. "First Do No Harm: A Look at Correctional Policies and Programs Today." *Journal of Experimental Criminology* 9: 1–17.

Makarios, Matthew, and Edward J. Latessa. 2013. "Developing a Risk and Needs Assessment Instrument for Prison Inmates: The Issue of Outcome." *Criminal Justice and Behavior* 20: 1–23.

Marlatt, G. Alan, and Judith R. Gordon. 1985. "Relapse Prevention: Theoretical Rationale and Overview of the Model." In *Relapse Prevention: Maintenance Strategies in the Treatment of Addictive Behaviors*, edited by G. Alan Marlatt and Judith R. Gordon New York: Guilford Press.

Martinson, Robert. 1974. "What Works? Questions and Answers about Prison Reform." *The Public Interest*, 35: 22–54.

Martinson, Robert. 1976. "California and the Crossroads." In *Rehabilitation, Recidivism and Research*, edited by Robert Martinson, Ted Palmer, and Stuart Adams. Hackensack, NJ: National Council on Crime and Delinquency.

Martinson, Robert. 1979. "New Findings, New Views: A Note of Caution Regarding Sentencing Reform." *Hofstra Law Review* 7: 243–258.

Matthews, Betsy, Dana J. Hubbard, and Edward Latessa. 2001. "Making the Next Step: Using Evaluability Assessment to Improve Correctional Programming." *The Prison Journal*, 81: 454–472.

Menninger, Karl A. 1968. *The Crime of Punishment*. New York: Penguin.

Morgan, Robert D., and David B. Flora. 2002. "Group Psychotherapy with Incarcerated Offenders: A Research Synthesis." *Group Dynamics: Theory, Research, and Practice* 6: 203–218.

Morris, Norval. 1974. *The Future of Imprisonment*. Chicago: University of Chicago Press.

Motiuk, Lawrence L. 1991. *"Antecedents and Consequences of Prison Adjustment: A Systematic Assessment and Reassessment Approach."* Unpublished PhD dissertation, Carleton University, Ottawa.

Mowrer, O. Hobart. 1960. *Learning Theory and Behavior*. New York: John Wiley.

Olver, Mark E., Keira C. Stockdale, and J. Stephen Wormith. 2011. "A Meta-Analysis of Predictors of Offender Treatment Attrition and its Relationship to Recidivism." *Journal of Consulting and Clinical Psychology* 79: 6–21.

Palmer, Ted. 1975. "Martinson revisited." *Journal of Research in Crime and Delinquency* 12: 133–152.

Palmer, Ted, Patricia Van Voorhis, Faye Taxman, and Doris L. MacKenzie. 2012. "Insights from Ted Palmer: Experimental Criminology in a Different Era—The Academy of Experimental Criminology 2011 Joan McCord Prize Lecture." *Journal of Experimental Criminology* 8: 103–115.

Perrino, Tatiana, George Howe, Anne Sperling, William Beardslee, Irwin Sandler, David Shern, Hilda Pantin, Sheila Kaupert, Nicole Cano, Gracelyn Cruden, Frank Bandiera, and C. Hendricks Brown. 2013. "Advancing Science Through Collaborative Data Sharing and Synthesis." *Perspectives on Psychological Science* 8: 433–444.

Petrosino, Anthony. 2013. "Reflections on the Genesis of the Campbell Collaboration." *The Experimental Criminologist* 8: 9–12.

Praško, Ján, Jirí Horácek, Richard Záleský, Miloslav Kopecek, Tomáš Novák, Beata Pašková, Lucie Škrdlantová, Otakar Belohlávek, and Cyril Höschl. 2004. "The Change of Regional Brain Metabolism (18FDG PET) in Panic Disorder During the Treatment with Cognitive-Behavioral Therapy or Antidepressants." *Neuroendocrinology Letters* 25: 340–348.

President's Commission on Law Enforcement and Administration of Justice. 1967. *Task Force Report—Corrections*. Washington, DC: Task Force on Corrections.

Pridmore, Saxby, Amber Chambers, and Milford McArthur. 2005. "Neuroimaging in Psychopathy." *Australia & New Zealand Journal of Psychiatry* 39: 856–865.

Quay, Herbert C. 1977. "The Three Faces of Evaluation: What Can Be Expected to Work." *Criminal Justice and Behavior* 4: 21–25.

Raine, Adrian, Monte Buchsbaum, and Lori LaCasse, 1997. "Brain Abnormalities in Murderers Indicated by Positron Emission Tomography." *Biological Psychiatry* 42: 495–508.

Raine, Adrian, Todd Lencz, Susan Bihrle, Lori LaCasse, and Patrick Colletti. 2000. "Reduced Prefrontal Gray Matter Volume and Reduced Autonomic Activity in Antisocial Personality Disorder." *Archives of General Psychiatry* 57: 119–127.

Redondo, Santiago, Julio Sanchez-Meca, and Vincente Garrido. 1999. "The Influence of Treatment Programmes on the Recidivism of Juvenile and Adult Offenders: A European Meta-Analytic Review." *Psychology, Crime and Law* 5: 251–278.

Renzema, Marc, and Evan Mayo-Wilson. 2005. "Can Electronic Monitoring Reduce Crime for Moderate to High-Risk Offenders?" *Journal of Experimental Criminology* 1: 215–237.

Robison, James, and Gerald Smith. 1971. "The Effectiveness of Correctional Programs." *Crime & Delinquency* 17: 67–80.

Romani, Christopher J., Robert D. Morgan, Nicole R. Gross, and Brendan R. McDonald. 2012. "Treating Criminal Behavior: Is the Bang Worth the Buck?" *Psychology, Public Policy, and Law* 18: 144–165.

Rosenthal, Robert. 1991. *Meta-Analytic Procedures for Social Research*. Beverly Hills, CA: Sage.

Rosnow, Ralph L., and Robert Rosenthal. 1993. *Beginning Behavioral Research*. New York: Macmillan.

Ross, Robert, and Elizabeth A. Fabiano. 1985. *Time to Think: A Cognitive Model of Delinquency Prevention and Offender Rehabilitation*. Johnson City, TN: Institute of Social Science and Arts.

Ross, Robert R., and Paul Gendreau. 1980. *Effective Correctional Treatment*. Toronto: Butterworths.

Ross, Robert, and H. Bryan McKay. 1978. "Treatment in Corrections: Requiem for a Panacea. *Canadian Journal of Criminology* 20: 279–295.

Rotman, Edgardo. 1998. "The Failure of Reform: United States, 1865-1965. In *The Oxford History of the Prison*, edited by Norval Morris and David J. Rothman. Oxford, UK: Oxford University Press.

Sadler, Christine M., and Thomas A. Powell. 2008. *The Vermont Cognitive Self-Change Program: The Case for Risk-Adjusted Classification*. Proceedings of the North American Correctional and Criminal Justice Psychology Conference, Toronto.

Scalia, Martino B. 1871. "Historical Sketch of National and International Penitentiary Conferences in Europe and America." In *Transactions of the National Congress on Penitentiary and Reformatory Discipline*, edited by Enoch C. Wines. Albany, NY: Weed, Parsons and Company.

Schmidt, Frank. 1996. "Statistical Significance Testing and Cumulative Knowledge in Psychology: Implications for Training of Researchers." *Psychological Methods* 1: 115–129.

Schnur, Alfred C. 1949. "Prison Conduct and Recidivism." *Journal of Criminal Law and Criminology* 40: 36–42.

Sechrest, Lee, Susan O. White, and Elizabeth D. Brown. 1979. *The Rehabilitation of Criminal Offenders: Problems and Prospects*. Washington, DC: National Academy of Sciences.

Shichor, David, and Dale K. Sechrest. 1996. *Three Strikes and You're Out: Vengeance as Public Policy*. Thousand Oaks, CA: Sage.

Sieh, Edward W. 1989. "Less Eligibility: The Upper Limits of Penal Policy." *Criminal Justice Policy Review* 3: 159–183.

Singer, Richard G. 1971. "Prison Conditions: An Unconstitutional Roadblock to Rehabilitation." *Catholic University Law Review* 20: 365–393.

Smith, Paula, and Paul Gendreau. 2012. "*Treatment Programs in Prisons: Prison Adjustment, Recidivism and the Risk Hypothesis.*" Unpublished manuscript.

Smith, Paula, Paul Gendreau, and Kristin Swartz. 2009. "Validating the Principles of Effective Intervention: A Systematic Review of the Contributions of Meta-Analysis in the Field of Corrections." *Victims & Offenders* 4: 148–169.

Smith, Paula, Claire Goggin, and Paul Gendreau. 2002. *The Effects of Prison Sentences and Intermediate Sanctions on Recidivism: General Effects and Individual Differences. JS42–103/ 2002.* Ottawa: Corrections Research and Development, Solicitor General of Canada.

Sperber, Kimberly G., Edward J. Latessa, and Matthew D. Makarios. 2013. "Examining the Interaction Between Level of Risk and Dosage of Treatment." *Criminal Justice and Behavior* 40: 338–348.

Spiegler, Michael D., and David C. Guevremont. 2010. *Contemporary Behavior Therapy*, 5th ed. Belmont, CA: Walworth.

Steiner, Benjamin. 2009. "Assessing Static and Dynamic Influences on Inmate Violence Levels." *Crime & Delinquency* 55: 134–161.

Toby, Jackson. 1964. "Is Punishment Necessary?" *Journal of Criminal Law, Criminology, and Police Science* 55: 332–337.

Turner, Herbert, Robert Boruch, Anthony Petrosino, Julia Lavenberg, Dorothy de Moya, and Hannah Rothstein. 2003. "Populating an International Web-Based Randomized Trials Register in the Social, Behavioral, Criminological, and Education Science." *The ANNALS of the American Academy of Political and Social Science* 589: 203–223.

Useem, Bert, and Peter Kimball. 1991. *States of Siege: US Prison Riots, 1971–1986.* New York: Oxford University Press.

Van Voorhis, Patricia, Sandra L. Browning, Marilyn Simon, and Jill Gordon. 1997. "The Meaning of Punishment: Inmate's Orientation to the Prison Experience." *The Prison Journal* 77: 135–167.

Vaske, Jamie, Kevan Galyean, and Francis T. Cullen. 2011. "Toward a Biosocial Theory of Offender Rehabilitation: Why Does Cognitive-Behavioral Therapy Work?" *Journal of Criminal Justice* 39: 90–102.

Walker, Samuel. 1985. *Sense and Nonsense About Crime: A Policy Guide.* Monterey, CA: Brooks/ Cole.

Walmsley, Roy. 2011. *World Prison Population List*, 9th ed. London: International Centre for Prison Studies.

Warren, Marguerite Q. 1969. "The Case for Differential Treatment of Delinquents." *The ANNALS of the American Academy of Political and Social Science* 62: 239–258.

Webster, Christopher D., Kevin S. Douglas, S. Derek Eaves, and Stephen D. Hart. 1997. "Assessing Risk of Violence to Others." In *Impulsivity: Theory, Assessment, and Treatment*, edited by Christopher D. Webster and Margaret A. Jackson. New York: Guilford Press.

Wells, Edward. 2009. "Uses of Meta-Analysis in Criminal Justice Research: A Quantitative Review." *Justice Quarterly* 26: 268–294.

Whitehead, John T., and Steven P. Lab. 1989. "A Meta-Analysis of Juvenile Correctional Treatment." *Journal of Research in Crime and Delinquency* 26: 276–295.

Wilson, David B., Doris L. MacKenzie, and Fawn N. Mitchell. 2003. *Effects of Correctional Boot Camps on Offending.* Campbell Systematic Reviews 1. Oslo: Campbell Collaboration.

Wines, Enoch C. 1871. "Declaration of Principles Adopted and Promulgated by the Congress." In *Transactions of the National Congress on Penitentiary and Reformatory Discipline*, edited by Enoch C. Wines. Albany, NY: Weed, Parsons and Company.

Wines, Enoch. C., and Theodore W. Dwight. 1973. *Report on the Prisons and Reformatories of the United States and Canada, Made to the Legislature of New York, January, 1867.* New York: AMS Press. (Original work published 1867)

Wood, Peter B., and Harold G. Grasmick. 1999. "Toward the Development of Punishment Equivalencies: Male and Female Inmates Rate the Severity of Alternative Sanctions Compared to Prison." *Justice Quarterly* 16: 19–50.

Wooldredge, John, and Benjamin Steiner. 2013. "Violent Victimization among State Prison Inmates." *Violence and Victims* 28: 531–551.

Wootton, Barbara. 1959. *Social Science and Social Pathology.* London: Allen & Unwin.

Wormith, J. Stephen, Richard Althouse, Mark Simpson, Lorraine R. Reitzel, Thomas J. Fagan, and Robert D. Morgan. 2007. "The Rehabilitation and Reintegration of Offenders: The Current Landscape and Some Future Directions for Correctional Psychology." *Criminal Justice and Behavior* 34: 879–892.

Yochelson, Samuel, and Stanton E. Samenow. 1976. *The Criminal Personality: Vol. 1, A Profile for Change.* New York: Aronson.

CHAPTER 20

EMPLOYMENT AND
VOCATION PROGRAMS
IN PRISON

PAULA SMITH, LINDSEY M. MUELLER,
AND RYAN M. LABRECQUE

THERE is a well-established link between employment status and criminal behavior (Sampson and Laub 1993; Andrews and Bonta 2010; Tripodi, Kim, and Bender 2010). Specifically, the empirical literature finds that employment is an important criminogenic need (i.e., dynamic risk factor) that relates to the risk to reoffend (Andrews and Bonta 2010). On average, offender populations generally lack adequate marketable job skills when compared to the general population (for reviews, see Wilson, Gallagher, and MacKenzie 2000; Andrews and Bonta 2010). However, when former prisoners are successful in gaining meaningful, legitimate employment, it significantly reduces their risk to reoffend (Sampson and Laub 1993; Uggen 2000). Programs aimed at reducing problems related to this risk factor have been suggested as a cost-effective method to increase employability and reduce recidivism upon release from prison (Aos, Miller, and Drake 2006; Drake, Aos, and Miller 2009; Sedgley, Scott, Williams, and Derrick 2010; Bohmert and Duwe 2012). Given this context, there is a need to identify the effective characteristics of prison-based employment programs that seek to develop inmates' work-related skills as a form of rehabilitation. These programs can help alleviate some of the barriers related to reentry, reduce postrelease offending, increase the chances for a successful reintegration into communities, and make the public safer.

This chapter provides an overview of the interventions, strategies, and approaches that are most effective in targeting the employability of former prisoners upon release. In order to assess the effects of prison-based employment programs, this chapter is organized in the following manner: Section I discusses the historical context for integrating work into correctional systems. In order to assess the success of prison-based employment programs, the following sections of the chapter examine the relevant literature bases: the rationale for integrating prison-based employment programs within correctional systems (Section II), a review of the literature on the effectiveness of these programs on postrelease outcomes

(Section III), and the characteristics of effective programming (Section IV). The main conclusions of this chapter include the following:

- Prison employment was initially utilized to provide institutional structure and reduce prisoner idleness but, over time, has adopted a rehabilitative approach in an attempt to reduce future criminality and enhance reintegration outcomes.
- These goals provide reason to implement prison-based employment programs that aim to reduce the barriers faced among former offenders when seeking employment and target criminogenic need areas to reduce offender's risk level.
- Effective employment and vocational programs offered in prison demonstrate short- and long-term effects on postrelease outcomes by increasing employment, reducing recidivism rates, and providing monetary benefits to taxpayers and crime victims.
- Characteristics of the effective programs include components such as incorporating multiple program components, community follow-up services, and teaching skills relevant to the current job market.

I. Historical Context

There has been a long-standing emphasis in corrections on employment training, with productive labor being an important element of correctional institutions since their inception (Piehl 1998; Gaes, Flanagan, Motiiuk, and Stewart 1999). Prison labor was introduced in American prisons during the latter part of the seventeenth century when Pennsylvania declared, "All prisons shall be work-houses" (Garvey 1998). The earliest purpose of inmate labor was economic, where it would help reduce some of the costs associated with maintaining prisoners (Miller and Grieser 1986). However, prison labor has served several functions and purposes since the earlier prison system. The creators of the early American prisons believed that prison labor confronted the main cause of crime—idleness. By incorporating labor, the inmates could (a) follow a structured daily regimen, (b) learn new habits, and (c) ultimately reform themselves (Garvey 1998).

The idea that hard, productive labor can initiate the reformation process of inmates did not come to full fruition until the expansion of prisons in the early nineteenth century (Cullen and Travis 1984; Dwyer and McNally 1993; Garvey 1998). The significance of the expansion was profound as it utilized inmate labor as a cheap source to sell to private industries and then place the products on the open market for sale (Miller and Grieser 1986; Roberts 1996; Travis 2005). However, a widespread opposition to prison industries quickly developed due to the abuse of inmate labor, economic issues concerning competition between organized labor and competing manufacturers, and the critically high national unemployment rates during the Great Depression (Miller and Grieser 1986). As a result, Congress prohibited the federal government from purchasing prison-made goods and made it illegal for states to import these products in the early parts of the twentieth century (Miller and Grieser 1986; Sexton 1995; Roberts 1996). In conjunction with the laws passed by Congress, a reform movement advocated that prison programming should take more of a rehabilitative approach rather than use it for an economic objective (Miller and Grieser 1986). These early reformers were setting the stage for the use of reformatories and treatment programs that emphasized employment training and vocational programs. By the mid-twentieth century, the rehabilitative ideal was reinforced with the reemergence of prison industries and the development of employment/vocational training services (Roberts 1996; Solomon, Johnson, Travis, and McBride 2004).

A. Prison Industry Programs

The restoration of prison industries (e.g., Affordable Homes Program [AHP], Post-Release Employment Project [PREP], and Prison Enterprises Network) was made possible in 1979 when Congress created the Prison Industry Enhancement Certification Program (PIECP). In an effort to alleviate restrictions previously imposed on state prison-made goods, the PIECP permits certified state and local corrections departments to sell inmate-made products through interstate commerce and to the federal government in amounts exceeding the limit typically placed on such trades (Bureau of Justice Assistance 2004). Specifically, the program was implemented to encourage state and local agencies to collaborate with private companies and generate products from inmate labor in a way that approximates private-sector work opportunities (Solomon et al. 2004). The program not only offers inmates vocational training but provides a realistic working environment that can translate to specific marketable skills to enhance job opportunities upon release (Richmond 2014). The underlying rationale for implementing a prison industry program is that the structured work routine and associated wages may reduce prison misconduct while increasing inmates' chance for successful rehabilitation and meaningful employment opportunities upon release (Cullen and Travis 1984; Garvey 1998).

Contemporary prison industry programs encompass a broad range of employment related activities, which produce products and services for the government and private-sector consumers (Bouffard, MacKenzie, and Hickman 2000). Prison industries typically include activities that range from "traditional work," such as laundry, food services, and license plate manufacturing to more "innovative" programs including computer refurbishing, farming, and textiles (Lawrence, Mears, Dubin, and Travis 2002). Some states create prison industries that train offenders for a specific type of job or profession; however, this is a less common approach for these types of programs. For example, the Minnesota Department of Corrections manages the AHP. The AHP provides hands-on training to inmates in the community, specifically the construction trade (Bohmert and Duwe 2012). In contrast, other states employ prison industry programs that are more diversified. To illustrate, Lawrence and colleagues (2002) found that Indiana offers over 50 different types of industries for inmates across only 14 facilities. Regardless of the specificity of the industry program, it is expected that those individuals who have at least some exposure to a wide range of work activities will have more job prospects compared to those inmates without such program exposure (Lawrence et al. 2002).

The primary goals of prison industry programs are to generate revenues that help offset the costs of incarceration, compensate crime victims, and provide financial support to the families of those incarcerated while reducing idle time in prison and increasing job-related skills (Bureau of Justice Assistance 2004; Solomon et al. 2004). According to Maguire,

Flanagan, and Thornberry (1988), Sexton (1995), and Lawrence et al. (2002), prison industries have been successful in lowering facility operating costs and reducing prisoner idleness. Maguire et al. (1988) and Sexton (1995) further note that such programming generates an income for correctional facilities through the sale of prison-made products and provides the necessary skills and training for later use by released offenders. Moreover, it is suggested that prison industry work can help inmates develop time management skills, learn self-discipline, and acquire proper work ethic (Maguire et al. 1988). Awareness of the benefits that prison industries provide has resulted in the establishment of several policies and practices aimed to prepare inmates for a successful reintegration upon release.

However, there are reasons to suspect that prison industry programs may not be effective in increasing the chance of employment opportunities upon release. Some scholars caution that many of the specific trade or industry skills learned in prison are not applicable or may not appeal to the job market once released (Maguire et al. 1988; Solomon et al. 2004). For example, Solomon and colleagues (2004) note that among the 1.1 million state and federal inmates in 2000 eligible for work, nearly half were assigned to institutional maintenance jobs (e.g., laundry and janitorial labor). This implies that the "job-related skills" offenders learn while in prison may provide a limited foundation for obtaining a high-quality position postincarceration (Lawrence et al. 2002). Maguire et al. (1988) also raised concerns that prison industry programs often train inmates in jobs that have an excess of employees or require professional licenses that are difficult for former prisoners to obtain. Job prospects may be especially limited for released inmates given that helping offenders achieve certification of a specific trade or profession is not a highly emphasized component of prison industry programs (Bohmert and Duwe 2012). For these reasons, prison programs have shifted their focus to offering vocational training and services aimed to address the limitations of prison industry programs.

B. Vocational Training and Services

Vocational training and employment service programs have a much shorter history than prison industry programs. These types of programs were established in the late 1960s and early 1970s, when rehabilitation was still at the forefront of the criminal justice system's efforts (Pollock 2013). They are predicated on the assumption that individualized vocational instruction will provide prisoners with an opportunity to learn specific skills to increase job prospects once released back into society (Austin and Irwin 2001; LoBuglio 2001). Thus employment programs seek to address certain skill deficiencies (e.g., poor educational attainment and reduced employability) in order to help offenders successfully compete in the job market (Bouffard et al. 2000; Lawrence et al. 2002).

Given the goals of vocational training and employment service programs, they integrate several different approaches to distinguish themselves from prison industry programs. In particular, vocational training and services provide apprenticeship training, where the focus is on helping offenders earn a certificate for a specific profession such as carpentry, auto mechanics, or electronic servicing (Lawrence et al. 2002; Bohmert and Duwe 2012). Additionally, courses in employment services are often offered to teach inmates basic work knowledge (e.g., life skills, time management, and work ethics) and address educational needs (Bouffard et al. 2000; Wilson et al. 2000). Further, employment programs emphasize placement assistance and intensive job preparation (Bouffard et al. 2000). Several programs (Project Re-Integration for Offenders, Project Community, Restitution, and Apprenticeship-Focused Training, and Center for Employment Opportunities [CEO]) exist that assist offenders in setting up interviews and establishing connections with outside agencies to secure a job upon release. In addition to assistance with job referrals, some employment programs offer workshops, preemployment classes, and onsite training to prepare offenders for a variety of professional careers (Finn 1998).

The establishment of vocational training and employment service programs shifted the focus to not only increase productive work while incarcerated but also to provide services aimed at enhancing specific job-related skills to help increase marketability upon release. However, some express concerns that vocational programs still attempt to train offenders in more general rather than specific fields (Lawrence et al. 2002). It is suggested that offenders will have greater job prospects and higher paying jobs if they can demonstrate mastery of a specific skill or market demand. In addition, though these programs share several similarities, the intended outcomes (e.g., reduced recidivism, job placement, and maintaining employment) may vary (Bouffard et al. 2000). Thus it is critically important to identify the types of work programs that are capable of reaching their intended outcomes to inform future policies and practices.

II. The Rationale for Prison-Based Employment Programs

There are a few reasons to justify the incorporation of work in prisons. First, research has consistently found an association between unemployment and crime (Wolfgang, Figlio, and Sellin 1972; Farrington 1986; Sampson and Laub 1993). Second, when we compare offenders to those who do not engage in crime, we can find several factors that distinguish the two. Employment, in particular, is recognized as one of the important risk factors that distinguish offenders from nonoffenders (Andrews and Bonta 2010). Third, the absence of work experience and jobs skills coupled with the barriers of finding employment upon release may contribute to former prisoners remaining unemployed and reverting to subsequent criminal behavior (Austin and Irwin 2001). Therefore, it is clear that any efforts made to enhance employment outcomes for offenders will need to provide services that address these barriers.

A. Employment as a Risk Factor for Recidivism

There is a large body of research examining conditions attributable to recidivism, which consistently documents that employment status correlates with recidivism. Specifically, Gendreau, Little, and Goggin (1996) conducted a meta-analytic review examining the literature on recidivism for adults and found that criminal background, lack of education, and inadequate employment skills were among the strongest predictors for reoffending. In addition, Simourd (1993) found that those who lack personal education and vocational achievement have a 28 percent higher chance of engaging in crime. Obtaining and maintaining employment is one factor thought to influence desistance from criminal behavior (Sampson and Laub 1993).

In addition to the findings on the relationship between employment status and recidivism, Andrews and colleagues (2010) identified a set of eight risk factors associated with an offender's risk to reoffend. Employment status is included as one of the central eight risk factors. Additionally, researchers classify employment status as a "dynamic" risk factor. Dynamic risk factors are those factors that relate to an offender's risk to reoffend but can change over time. Advocates of correctional rehabilitation argue that these crime-producing factors should be the target for treatment programs as they most strongly and consistently relate to future criminal involvement, and, when targeted for change, the chance of an offender recidivating significantly decreases (Andrews and Bonta 2010). The corrections literature categorizes dynamic risk factors into two types: (a) acute needs, which indicate that the need areas change relatively quickly, and (b) stable needs, meaning that it requires more time and effort to change the need areas (Andrews and Bonta 2010). Previous research suggests that employment is an acute need, but it is a multifaceted concept that relates to other risk factors (Latessa 2012). For instance, an individual's risk level can change quickly if one is unemployed one day and finds employment the next. However, other dynamic risk factors relate to an individual's employment success (e.g., attitudes toward work, poor problem-solving or coping skills, criminal attitudes/beliefs) and require additional time and effort to address. Thus, in order for employment programs to be effective, they will need to address acute dynamic needs as well as other related risk factors that can interfere with the ability to obtain and maintain employment.

Given this information, research has suggested that employment is not one of the "Big Four" or top-tier risk factors of criminal behavior (see Andrews and Bonta [2010] for more information). The corrections literature finds that other risk factors (i.e., peer associations, antisocial personality and cognitions) correlate more strongly with the criminal behavior of individuals compared to the second-tier or "moderate" risk factors (i.e., school/work, family/marital status, substance abuse, and leisure/recreation). For example, Bucklen and Zajac (2009) found that offender attitudes and expectations associated with employment strongly relate to success and failure and may be more critical than employment itself. This would suggest that employment programs targeting employment deficiencies should not be offered as a replacement for interventions that target top-tier risk factors but rather in conjunction with these services to address other risk factors that could hinder one's success in maintaining employment.

B. The Need for Employment Programs

While it may be a requirement for a released offender to find employment (e.g., as a condition of parole/probation), obtaining and maintaining employment may be a difficult challenge for this population. Individuals with a criminal record are already at a disadvantage when searching for employment, yet the barriers become exacerbated the longer an individual remains incarcerated. While incarcerated, commitment to conventional norms may weaken, leaving few legitimate opportunities upon release (Hagan and Dinovitzer 1999; Western et al. 2001). Having a criminal record can also hinder subsequent job wages and stability (Sampson and Laub 1997; Bushway 1998; Western et al. 2001). Previous research suggests that offenders are more likely to obtain employment in secondary labor market positions (i.e., jobs that are highly unstable, have low expectations for promotional opportunities, and provide lower pay) when compared to the general labor force, both prior to incarceration and following release (Saylor and Gaes 1997).

Other barriers faced by former offenders trying to obtain and maintain employment include poor employment history (due to incarceration), erosion of past job-related skills, and transportation difficulties (Visher, Winterfield, and Coggeshall 2005). Moreover, employers are typically reluctant to hire individuals with a criminal record (Holzer, Raphael, and Stoll 2003). In conjunction with the identified barriers, the potential threat to public safety among former offenders who remain unemployed in the community give purpose to identifying effective programming that seeks to enhance employability and lower recidivism rates for this population.

Due to the challenges faced by many former prisoners, most experts agree that deficiencies in adequate job training and employment opportunities are a critical area of concern (Turner and Petersilia 1996). In addition to the presumed benefit of employment reducing an offender's risk for future offending, employment programs can reasonably be expected to provide offenders with several advantages. First, a good job allows for adaptation to a productive lifestyle, the development of prosocial relationships and a sense of self-efficacy, and the fostering of a sense of conformity to a conventional lifestyle (Visher et al. 2005; Latessa 2012). Second, participation in employment programs may also contribute to a reduction in prison misconduct, violence, and disturbances within institutions (Saylor and Gaes 1997; Wilson et al. 2000), perhaps because inmates are utilizing their time constructively and receiving reinforcement for their prosocial behaviors (Wilson et al. 2000). It has been found that employment structures daily patterns of behavior for ex-offenders and signifies a source of informal social control (Sampson and Laub 1997; Uggen 1999; Uggen and Staff 2001; Visher et al. 2005). Finally, working while incarcerated provides inmates with an opportunity to address poor employment histories by enhancing job-related skills and learning good workplace habits (Solomon et al. 2004).

III. Current Knowledge of Employment Effects

Criminological research has previously shown an inverse relationship between employment and crime (Sampson and Laub 1993; Laub and Sampson 2003). This would suggest that former offenders who obtain employment are less likely to recidivate. As a result, there are several different types of prison-based employment programs implemented that aim to provide employment assistance to help alleviate some of the challenges faced by this population when re-entering the community (Uggen and Staff 2001). Given this information, several researchers have examined the effectiveness of these types of programs and their ability to enhance employability, decrease recidivism rates among former prisoners, and act as a cost-effective method of transitioning former offenders back into society.

A. Evaluations of Prison-Based Employment Programs

Extant studies of prison-based employment programs have looked at two primary outcomes: employment and recidivism. Among the existing studies, however, most of the research examines recidivism as the primary outcome. Some evaluations take their analysis a step further by calculating the cost of such programming (Aos et al. 2006; Drake et al. 2009; Sedgley et al. 2010; Bohmert and Duwe 2012). In general, the literature supports the use of employment programs for prisoners. The majority of the research suggests vocational and industry programs increase offender employability, reduce postrelease criminal behavior, and are a cost-effective method of repaying crime victims and taxpayers. These are important themes given that these evaluations have examined different groups of offenders and different programs and have used different methodological approaches. However, it is important to note that many of the evaluations examine the effectiveness of vocational training and employment services whereas few have focused on prison industry programs. Additionally, this area of the literature largely generalizes to male inmate populations, as many evaluations have not included females in the samples due to insufficient numbers of females available for analysis. Despite these potential shortcomings, this section reviews the effects of prison-based employment programs on employment and recidivism outcomes and examines the cost-effectiveness of such programs.

1. *Employment Outcomes*

The purpose of examining employment outcomes is to determine whether employment services offered in prison can increase the chance of former offenders obtaining and maintaining employment upon release. Following a review of the literature, there is sufficient evidence to suggest that prison-based employment programs produce positive outcomes for participants (Saylor and Gaes 1997; Smith et al. 2006; Wilson et al. 2000; Bohmert and Duwe 2012). However, there is evidence to suggest that this effect diminishes over time (Saylor and Gaes 1997; Zweig et al. 2011). Despite this limitation, two conclusions can be drawn from the literature as they relate to employment outcomes. First, employment programs are capable of increasing the employability of offenders both in the short and long run. Second, such programs assist offenders with developing specific employment-related skills and may have a marginal impact on helping former inmates obtain higher quality positions.

The literature suggests that employment programs are effective for enhancing job readiness skills and employability among former offenders (Saylor and Gaes 1997; Wilson et al. 2000; Seiter and Kadela 2003; Smith et al. 2006; Bohmert and Duwe 2012). In a meta-analysis examining the effectiveness of educational, vocational training, and work programs, Wilson and colleagues (2000) found that program participants are employed at a higher rate than comparison groups. Among the eight studies that included employment as an outcome measure, the findings revealed that program participants were twice as likely to find postrelease employment. Similarly, Bohmert and Duwe (2012) found that program completers of the AHP—a program that trains offenders in the construction trade while incarcerated—had a 14.7 percent higher employment rate upon release than nonparticipants. Further, PREP was specifically designed to evaluate the effects of employment experience, vocational training, and apprenticeship on postrelease outcomes (Saylor and Gaes 1997). Analyzing data on more than 7,000 offenders from the Federal Bureau of Prisons, the findings revealed that program participants were 24.4 percent more likely to obtain full-time employment compared to nonparticipants.

Prison-based employment programs are also associated with helping offenders obtain employment more quickly and maintain employment for longer periods (Saylor & Gaes, 1997; Smith et al., 2006; Bohmert and Duwe 2012). In a national review of the PIECP, Smith et al. (2006) found that the participants were 15 percent more likely to obtain employment faster and nearly 10 percent more likely to maintain their employment for more than one year than the comparison group. Saylor and Gaes (1997) report a similar finding in regards to long-term effects on postrelease employment outcomes, where program participants were significantly more likely to be employed at the 12-month follow-up than those who did not participate in any prison industry, vocational training, or apprenticeship program (71.7 percent vs. 63.1 percent). Though this finding is significant, it is important to note that the difference in employment rates between the two groups narrowed over time. A similar finding was produced by Zweig and colleagues (2011) evaluating the impact of the CEO program in New York State. Finally, Bohmert and Duwe (2012) found that those participants who completed the AHP program averaged 228.63 more hours worked than the comparison group.

The literature also provides some support for the notion that employment programs are effective with enhancing specific employment-related skills, and by extension, helping offenders obtain employment in a specific field (Bohmert and Duwe 2012). For example, Bohmert and Duwe (2012) found that training exclusively in the construction field (e.g., plumbing; electrical work; and highway, bridge, or street construction) increased the chances that program participants were placed in a construction-related job. Specifically, 32.1 percent of the AHP participants (including those who completed the program as well as those who did not complete the program) had a job in the construction field compared to only 16.9 percent of members in the comparison group. It is important to note that 39.7 percent of the program completers actually obtained employment in a construction-related field compared to 17.9 percent of the program terminators (those who participated in but did not complete the program).

The findings related to employment program effects on increasing the possibility of higher wages among participants are mixed. Smith et al.'s (2006) findings reveal that program participants had significantly higher wages than the comparison group. Specifically, individuals who participated in the PIECP program earned, on average, $44,263 compared to the average $27,136 earned by nonparticipants (Smith et al. 2006). Similarly, Bohmert and Duwe (2012) found that AHP program completers were significantly more likely to earn higher-paying jobs than those in the comparison group, where they earned an average of $3,351.15 more than their comparison counterparts. In contrast, Saylor and Gaes (1997) failed to find any significant differences in wages earned between the PREP participants and comparison group members.

2. Recidivism Outcomes

The purpose of examining recidivism outcomes is to determine whether employment services offered in prisons are capable of reducing reoffending among former offenders. Of the programs evaluated, two main conclusions can be drawn as they relate to recidivism. First, employment programs reduce postrelease recidivism, both in the short and the long term. Second, the findings are mixed in terms of whether employment programs can reduce institutional misconduct, but few studies have examined this concept as an outcome.

The literature demonstrates that prison work programs are effective in reducing the recidivism rates of former prisoners. In a meta-analytic review, Wilson et al. (1999) examined the effectiveness of corrections-based education, vocation, and work programs on reducing recidivism. The findings indicate that program participants were less likely to recidivate than the comparison groups. Aos et al. (2006) found a 9 percent reduction in recidivism among participants of the four prison-based vocational programs included in their meta-analysis. In addition, Aos and colleagues (2006) reported that the four correctional industry program evaluations reduced recidivism by 6 percent. Similarly, in their reviews of existing program evaluations, both MacKenzie (2000) and Seiter and Kadela (2003) concluded that vocational programs reduce recidivism. Last, Bohmert and Duwe (2012) found that AHP program completers had significantly lower recidivism rates than their counterparts. For example, the program completers had a reconviction rate that was 10.9 percent lower than the comparison group while the program terminations (those who participated in but did not complete the program) had a reconviction rate that was 10.1 percent higher than the comparison group (Bohmert and Duwe 2012).

The findings on recidivism outcomes also indicate that prison-based employment programs have long-term effects. Evaluations of the PIECP, in particular, show significant reductions in postrelease recidivism among participants (Smith et al. 2006; Hopper 2013). Using data from the Indiana and Tennessee Departments of Corrections, Hopper (2013) concluded that over one-year, two-year, and three-year postrelease periods, there were consistently significant reductions in the odds of recidivism for program participants. Similarly, Smith et al. (2006) found that PIECP participants were more likely to display lower recidivism rates and less likely to experience a subsequent arrest (59 percent vs. 53 percent), conviction (77.9 percent vs. 73.6 percent), and incarceration (93 percent vs. 89 percent) compared to their counterparts. Using a follow up period ranging from 8 to 12 years, Saylor and Gaes (1997) examined the recidivism rates of participants in vocational and apprenticeship training. The findings revealed that program participants had a 33 percent lower likelihood of reincarceration than individuals in the matched control group. Further, Sedgley et al. (2010) conducted a study that examined the recidivism rates of 4,515 male prisoners released in Ohio during the time between 1992 and 2002. They found that participation in education and employment programming is an important component to help reduce recidivism rates. The participants of the programs were able to stay out of prison at higher rates when compared to the nonparticipants (Sedgley et al. 2010). However, the effects diminished over time, so Sedgley and colleagues suggested that the programs had a marginal effect on recidivism rates.

The empirical literature has demonstrated a link between participation in prison-based programs in general and lower odds of rule violations during incarceration, but findings are mixed in terms of whether employment programs can reduce institutional misconduct. For example, Saylor and Gaes (1997) found that prison employment significantly reduced prison misconduct, where the study group members were 15 percent less likely than the comparison group to receive an incident report. In addition, members of the comparison group were more likely to be convicted of serious types of infractions and received harsher punishments for rule infractions. In contrast, a meta-analysis examining the impact of correctional programming on prison misconduct rates produced a null finding for educational and vocational programs (French and Gendreau 2006). On average, educational and vocational programs performed significantly worse than prison programs based on behavioral approaches. However, they found that educational and vocational programs had significant heterogeneity in effect sizes, which suggests that some of these programs could still play an important role in altering offenders' behaviors while incarcerated.

3. Cost-Effectiveness of Prison-Based Employment Programs

Another way to assess the effectiveness of prison-based employment programs is to determine whether the benefits of the programs outweigh the costs. For example, if programs are successful in reaching their intended outcomes (e.g., recidivism), some of the state and government costs can be avoided. Few studies have reviewed the cost-effectiveness of prison-based employment programs, but the four that exist have yielded evidence to support the notion that these programs save a substantial amount of money in incarceration costs (Aos et al. 2006; Drake et al. 2009) and help to reduce costs to the state (Sedgley et al. 2010; Bohmert and Duwe 2012). This section reviews the literature that has examined the cost-effectiveness of prison-based employment programs.

There is evidence to suggest that the costs per participant for employment-related programs offered in prison vary depending on the type of program. For example, Aos et al. (2006) found that vocational education programs cost, on average, $1,182 per participant while the marginal costs of prison industries per participant is $417. Similarly, Drake and colleagues (2009) found that the average costs per participant for vocational education programs, prison industries, and work release were $1,210, $427, and $615, respectively. Given that some of the costs to participate in these programs seem rather large, it is important to identify whether employment programs are capable of producing monetary benefits that would reduce costs paid by taxpayers and, by extension, the states.

Two studies (Aos et al. 2006; Drake et al. 2009) found substantial cost savings to taxpayers from postponing return to prison due to participation in employment services while in custody. For example, in their review of vocational education and prison industry programs in the state of Washington, Aos et al. (2006) found that a 9 percent reduction in recidivism for vocational education programs generates an estimated $14,920 benefit to taxpayers. Similarly, Drake and colleagues' (2009) findings of a 6.4 percent reduction in reoffending for prison industry programs is associated with an estimated $14,387 per participant total costs avoided by taxpayers. They also found a substantially higher estimate of costs avoided for taxpayers ($21,932) with a similar reduction in recidivism (9.8 percent) for vocational education programs (Drake et al. 2009). These examples suggest that programs capable of achieving significant reductions in recidivism rates can reduce the amount of money taxpayers spend on the criminal justice system (Aos et al. 2006; Drake et al. 2009).

In addition to these findings, evaluations of prison-based employment programs suggest large monetary benefits to state and federal government agencies. To illustrate, Bohmert and Duwe (2012) examined the relative costs avoided to the state as a result of implementing the AHP program. Specifically, they assessed the costs saved by (a) housing AHP participants in local correctional facilities (rather than prisons), (b) using inmate labor in nonprofit agencies, (c) providing no-interest loans to nonprofit agencies, (d) producing tax contributions from post-release jobs, and (e) reducing recidivism. Their findings revealed that the program produced an estimated $13.1 million in costs avoided to the state, which translates to $58,491 reduced costs to the state per participant (n = 224). The program produced a gain of $61.86 for every dollar spent. Similarly, Sedgley et al. (2010) estimated the expected savings based on the recidivism rates of individuals who participated in prison industry, educational, and general institutional work programs. Using a statistical method to control for self-selection into a program, they found an estimated savings of $3,619 in incarceration costs per individual due to a reduction in recidivism rates associated with a standard prison job. When participants participated in a prison industry program as well as a general institutional job, the results showed an additional cost savings of approximately $2,763 per person.

B. Limitations of Employment Program Evaluations

In recent decades, the research has demonstrated that prison programming can contribute to a wide range of positive outcomes. Unfortunately, tempering these encouraging findings is the fact that evaluations of prison-based employment programs to date have been limited in several ways. These caveats make it difficult to identify specific programs that are effective with their intended post-release outcomes. This section highlights the methodological limitations of extant research on the effectiveness of prison-based employment programs.

First, the most important issue to consider is that the methodological strategies for evaluating the effectiveness of prison-based employment programs have limited our ability to conclude definitively that these interventions are successful with improving outcomes among offenders (Finn 1998; Bouffard et al. 2000; Wilson et al. 2000). For example, a meta-analysis conducted by Bouffard et al. (2000) examining all of the available employment programs between the years of 1985 and 2000 revealed that only 25 evaluations (13 vocational education, 5 correctional industry, and 7 community employment) met the minimum standards of scientific rigor.

In addition, following a review of the literature, it appears that there is a direct correlation between the magnitude of the findings and quality of the study design. Specifically, studies that researchers rate as lower quality reported larger effects in comparison to studies of higher quality. Thus the effectiveness of employment programs is less conclusive when studies limit their research to high-quality studies. To illustrate, Visher et al. (2005) examined eight random assignment experimental design studies and found that job training and employment programs among ex-offenders produced modest to no effects on subsequent criminal activity. Visher and colleagues (2005) found that the mean effect size was 0.03, which was not a significant finding. This leads to the suggestion that such programs did not reduce arrest among the treatment participants by more than the amount expected by chance.

Second, a characteristic of weak research designs is that offenders often self-select into a treatment condition or volunteer for the study. This is especially true given that few prison programs are mandated (Lawrence et al. 2002) and, consequently, program participants are often more motivated. As a result, the potential for selection bias becomes a concern since there is a greater tendency for program participants to have certain characteristics that would keep them out of prison after release even in the absence of employment services

(Uggen and Staff 2001). That is, the "positive" effects of programming may be a result of the differential characteristics between the program participants and the general population of inmates instead of the actual intervention (Gaes et al. 1999). Thus comparisons between the two populations should be approached with caution.

Few studies have been able to employ designs that control for biases produced by self-selection into employment programs. To overcome the problem of selection bias, some researchers have used a statistical matching procedure—propensity score matching (see Saylor and Gaes [1997] and Sedgley et al. [2010] for examples). This two-step approach first generates a propensity score of the study group and comparison group members based on personal attributes to determine the likelihood an offender would be selected for participation in a program (Saylor and Gaes 1997). The second step involves matching program participants to comparison subjects using the propensity score in addition to other variables (Saylor and Gaes 1997). This method increases similarities between the two groups on factors that would contribute to participation in a correctional program. It is important to note that this method does not fully rule out the possibility of bias as the propensity score is estimated based only on observable attributes and the covariates included in the analysis (Sedgley et al. 2010).

Finally, some of the programs combine several components, such as vocational education, prison industry work, and job searching, to target offenders' multiple need areas (Bouffard et al. 2000). Some researchers suggest that combining several approaches may increase program effectiveness (Andrews et al. 1990; Lipsey 1992; Gendreau 1993; Bushway and Reuter 1997). While targeting multiple need areas may produce more benefits than single component programs, however, they often present challenges for evaluations of program effectiveness. As a result, it is difficult to conclude with certainty that a single program element attributes to the effectiveness of an intervention (Lawrence et al. 2002).

IV. Characteristics of Effective Programming

As previously described, a review of the literature demonstrates that prison-based employment programs are generally effective for increasing employment upon release from prison and for reducing recidivism. However, some programs are more successful than others in meeting these goals. Some evaluations have identified specific factors or characteristics that appear to relate to the most promising correctional program outcomes. It seems that programs are most successful if they teach skills relevant to the job market, include multiple program components, and integrate community follow-up services (Bushway and Reuter 1997; Wilson et al. 1999; Harrison and Schehr 2004).

Some evaluations suggest that vocational services and training may influence postrelease outcomes more positively than prison industry programs. For example, Saylor and Gaes (1997) found that inmates who participated in either vocational or apprenticeship training were 33 percent less likely to recidivate while inmates who worked in prison industries were 24 percent less likely to recidivate throughout the observation period. However, differential program type effects were not evident in all of the studies reviewed. One study in particular, Sedgley et al. (2010), found that regardless of the type of program in which the prisoner participated, the pattern of returning to prison was similar. Even so, their findings demonstrate that recidivism rates differ between those inmates who participated in prison industries, educational programs, or standard work assignments and those that chose not to participate in any programs. These findings provide further evidence that the influence of prison activities is an important component for reducing recidivism.

There are also several variables that may impact the relationship between offender employability and recidivism. For example, Uggen (2001) suggests that older subjects—defined as 27 years of age and older—benefit more from employment services than younger inmates. In addition, Lichtenberger and Weygandt (2011) found that employment programs had greater success among moderate- and high-risk offenders relative to those in the low-risk group. Similarly, Zweig et al. (2011) found that the CEO was more effective in reducing postrelease recidivism among high-risk parolees compared to low-risk parolees. Although this impact of CEO on high-risk parolees did not emerge until after the second year of starting the program, there were few program impacts on recidivism for the low-risk and medium-risk parolees. This finding is consistent with the corrections literature, which argues that correctional treatment programs should target higher risk offenders to achieve the largest reductions in recidivism (Andrews and Bonta 2010). Higher risk offenders generally have more need areas to address (i.e., more room for change) and require intensive intervention to reduce their risk to reoffend. From a theoretical standpoint, exposing lower risk offenders to such treatment can adversely affect them as it potentially increases contact with higher risk offenders, disrupts protective factors, and may increase subsequent criminal involvement (Andrews and Bonta 2010).

Perhaps more important is the aftercare component of prison-based employment programs. The concept of transitioning prisoners from institutions to communities is not a new phenomenon. However, the scale of prisoner reentry is changing. For instance, the United States releases more than 630,000 prisoners annually (Carson and Golinelli 2013). The overwhelming number of prisoners released per year presents challenges to provide enough resources to prepare individuals for a successful reintegration. As a result, it is important to identify effective employment programs that not only provide services inside of the prison but also directly link into community employment upon release.

A problem is that the majority of the implemented programs in correctional facilities in the United States do not provide services beyond incarceration. In a study that examined the amount of "prison-to-community" work programs, Krienert (2005) found that most states had available programs to enhance job-related skills and training while incarcerated, but few of those programs (37.1 percent) allowed for a smooth transition into job placement upon release. Employment readiness classes and work readiness training were among some of the most limited programs with only 5.7 percent of states reporting available employment readiness classes and 2.9 percent of states offering work readiness training. Krienert (2005) emphasizes that there is not much support within our criminal justice system to successfully reintegrate offenders back into society.

Despite the fact that many institutions do not have work re-entry programs, empirical evaluations have supported the idea of implementing prison-to-community work programs. Specifically, several programs that help offenders transition back into the community have been successful in providing former prisoners immediate employment opportunities, enhancing job-related skills, and increasing work experience for more permanent positions. This literature also highlights the importance of aftercare in the community in meeting these goals. For example, Safer Foundation is a nonprofit organization in Chicago that prepares offenders for completing job applications and teaches them appropriate job interview skills. In 1996, the program helped place 1,102 offenders in jobs in which 59 percent of the participants remained at their first position at the 30-day follow-up (Finn 1998). Similarly, Project Re-Integration for Offenders was designed to provide life skills classes, individual job readiness counseling, and help prepare offenders for job placement upon release (Finn 1998). In a 1992 evaluation of the project, 69 percent of the program participants obtained employment within one year compared to 36 percent of nonparticipants.

In addition to these findings, research has supported the idea that the length of participation in employment programs decreases the likelihood of former offender's recidivating. In their evaluation of the Preventing Parolee Crime Program (PPCP), Zhang and colleagues (2006) found that participants had an overall 8 percent lower recidivism rate than nonparticipants. Additionally, nonparticipants were 2.46 times more likely to be re-incarcerated in comparison to the PPCP participants. The likelihood of parolees recidivating decreased the longer they remained in the program. To illustrate, early dropouts (i.e., participants who had minimum participation in the program) represented the group that had the highest return to prison, followed by those who partially achieved the treatment goal (i.e., participants who received services but did not complete the treatment goal). Those participants who achieved the treatment goal were the least likely to be reincarcerated.

Collectively, the literature highlights the benefits of incorporating work programs into prison systems. The findings seem to suggest that employment programs offer prisoners opportunities to enhance job-related skills, learn how to manage employment, and sustain long-term employment. Relatedly, programs that help offenders successfully transition back into society by finding legitimate employment upon release have greater success in terms of less employment turnover and lower odds of recidivism. Based on the research, programs that integrate multiple components and target other dynamic needs related to an offender's ability to obtain and maintain employment appear to provide the most effective types of intervention.

V. Conclusion

The purpose of this chapter was to examine the effectiveness of prison-based employment programs in increasing employability and reducing recidivism among former prisoners. Based on the literature, it is clear that the notion of incorporating work in prisons is not a new phenomenon. Hard labor in prison was predicated on the assumption that individualized vocational instruction would provide prisoners with the opportunity to change for the better and to be reformed while incarcerated (Austin and Irwin 2001; LoBuglio 2001). This justification for work programs remains a fundamental component of prison operations today. Specifically, there are two main types of employment programs available to prisoners today: (a) prison industry programs, and (b) vocational training and services.

The rationale for providing employment programs to prisoners is to address their lack of sufficient job skills and related behaviors that interfere with job success. It is clear that prisoners face insurmountable barriers to obtaining and maintaining employment, and when not provided an opportunity to enhance job-related skills in prison, those individuals may revert to criminal behaviors upon release. One method of reducing the problems faced by former prisoners upon release is to direct services to the most appropriate offenders using effective strategies that will enhance employability. However, it should be recognized that employment is considered a second-tier risk factor (Andrews and Bonta 2010). This suggests that employment programs should not be offered in lieu of interventions for the top-tier risk factors (i.e., criminal attitudes/values/beliefs, antisocial peers, antisocial personality traits) but rather in conjunction with these services.

Based on the current evaluations of prison-based employment programs, it seems that they are an effective method of increasing employability and reducing recidivism among prisoners. The results indicate that employment programs can enhance specific job-related skills, increase the chances of employability, reduce recidivism, and demonstrate short- and long-term effects on postrelease employment and recidivism outcomes. Furthermore, such programming proves to be a cost-effective method by saving taxpayers' money and keeping the public safe. However, it should be noted that some programs are more successful in meeting these goals. In particular, those programs that teach prisoners specific job-related skills (e.g., apprenticeship, vocational services), incorporate community follow-up components, and integrate multiple components may be better suited for achieving the implementation goals of such programming.

Given the conclusions drawn from this evaluation, the following recommendations are offered. First, employment programs should be incorporated into the available services for offenders both inside and outside of the prison system. Second, such programming should include intensive follow-up services to monitor offender job placement and address any issues that may interfere with a successful reintegration. Third, several key components of employment programs have been identified that will lead to greater reductions in recidivism: (a) institutional job readiness training, (b) job referral assistance, and (c) transition funds to assist with expenses during job search. Finally, employment programs should combine skill acquisition with activities designed to target offender's attitudes about work.

REFERENCES

Andrews, Don A., and James Bonta. 2010. *The Psychology of Criminal Conduct*, 5th ed. Cincinnati, OH: Anderson.

Andrews, Don A., Ivan Zinger, Robert D. Hoge, James Bonta, Paul Gendreau, and Francis T. Cullen. 1990. "Does Correctional Treatment Work? A Clinically-Relevant and Psychologically-Informed Meta-Analysis." *Criminology* 28: 369–404.

Aos, Steve, Marna Miller, and Elizabeth Drake. 2006. "Evidence-Based Public Policy Options to Reduce Future Prison Construction, Criminal Justice Costs, and Crime Rates." *Federal Sentencing Reporter* 19: 275–290.

Austin, James, and John Irwin. 2001. *It's About Time: America's Imprisonment Binge*. Belmont, CA: Wadsworth.

Bohmert, Miriam Northcutt, and Grant Duwe. 2012. "Minnesota's Affordable Homes Program: Evaluating the Effects of a Prison Work Program on Recidivism, Employment, and Cost Avoidance." *Criminal Justice Policy Review* 23: 327–351.

Bouffard, Jeffrey A., Doris Layton MacKenzie, and Laura J. Hickman. 2000. "Effectiveness of Vocational Education and Employment Programs for Adult Offenders." *Journal of Offender Rehabilitation* 31: 1–41.

Bucklen, Kristofer Bret, and Gary Zajac. 2009. "But Some of Them Don't Come Back (to Prison!): Resource Deprivation and Thinking Errors as Determinants of Parole Success and Failure." *Prison Journal* 89: 239–264.

Bushway, Shawn D. 1998. "The Impact of an Arrest on the Job Stability of Young White American Men." *Journal of Research in Crime and Delinquency* 35: 454–479.

Bushway, Shawn, and Peter Reuter. 1997. "Labor Markets and Crime Risk Factors." In *Preventing Crime: What Works, What Doesn't, What's Promising*, edited by Lawrence W. Sherman, Denise C. Gottfredson, Doris L. MacKenzie, John Eck, Peter Reuter, and Shawn D. Bushway (pp. 6-1–6-59). Washington, DC: US Department of Justice, Office of Justice Programs.

Bureau of Justice Assistance. 2004. *Prison Industry Enhancement Certification Program.* Washington, DC: US Department of Justice, Office of Justice Programs.

Carson, E. Ann., and Daniela Golinelli. 2013. *Prisoners in 2012-Advance Counts.* Washington, DC: US Department of Justice, Office of Justice Programs, Bureau of Justice Statistics.

Cullen, Francis T., and Lawrence F. Travis. 1984. "Work as an Avenue of Prison Reform." *New England Journal on Civil and Criminal Confinement* 10: 45–64.

Drake, Elizabeth K., Steve Aos, and Marna G. Miller. 2009. "Evidence-Based Public Policy Options to Reduce Crime and Criminal Justice Costs: Implications in Washington State." *Victims and Offenders* 4: 170–196.

Dwyer, Diane C., and Roger B. McNally. 1993. "Public Policy, Prison Industries, and Business: An Equitable Balance for the 1990s." *Federal Probation* 57(2): 30–36.

Farrington, David P. 1986. "Age and Crime." *Crime and Justice* 7: 189–250.

Finn, Peter. 1998. "Job Placement for Offenders in Relation to Recidivism." *Journal of Offender Rehabilitation* 28: 89–106.

French, Sheila A., and Paul Gendreau. 2006. "Reducing Prison Misconduct: What Works!" *Criminal Justice and Behavior* 33: 185–218.

Gaes, Gerald, Timothy Flanagan, Laurence Motiiuk, and Lynn Stewart. 1999. "Adult Correctional Treatment." *Crime and Justice* 26: 361–426.

Garvey, Stephen P. 1998. "Freeing Prisoner's Labor." *Stanford Law Review* 50: 339–398.

Gendreau, Paul. 1993. *Principles of Effective Intervention with Offenders.* Fredericton: University of New Brunswick.

Gendreau, Paul, Tracy Little, and Claire Goggin. 1996. "A Meta-Analysis of the Predictors of Adult Offender Recidivism: What Works!" *Criminology* 34: 575–608.

Hagan, John, and Romit Dinovitzer. 1999. "Collateral Consequences of Imprisonment for Children, Communities, and Prisoners." In *Prisons*, edited by Michael Tonry and Joan Petersilia. Chicago: University of Chicago Press.

Harrison, Byron, and Robert Carl Schehr. 2004. "Offenders and Post-Release Jobs." *Journal of Offender Rehabilitation* 39: 35–68.

Holzer, Harry, Steven Raphael, and Michael A. Stoll. 2003. "Employment Barriers Facing Ex-Offenders." Urban Institute Reentry Roundtable, Employment Dimensions of Reentry: Understanding the Nexus between Prisoner Reentry and Work. Washington, DC: Urban Institute.

Hopper, Jeffrey D. 2013. "Benefits of Inmate Employment Programs: Evidence from the Prison Industry Enhancement Certification Program." *Journal of Business & Economics Research* 11: 213–222.

Krienert, Jessie L. 2005. "Bridging the Gap between Prison and Community Employment: An Initial Assessment of Current Information." *Criminal Justice Institute* 18: 293–303.

Latessa, Edward. 2012. "Why Work Is Important, and How to Improve the Effectiveness of Correctional Reentry Programs that Target Employment." *Criminology and Public Policy* 11: 87–91.

Laub, John H., and Robert J. Sampson. 2003. *Shared Beginnings, Divergent Lives: Delinquent Boys to Age 70*. Cambridge, MA: Harvard University Press.

Lawrence, Sarah, Daniel P. Mears, Glenn Dubin, and Jeremy Travis. 2002. *The Practice and Promise of Prison Programming*. Washington, DC: Urban Institute.

Lichtenberger, Eric, and Scott Weygandt. 2011. "Offender Workforce Development Services Makes an Impact." *Corrections Today* 73: 66–67.

Lipsey, Mark W. 1992. "Juvenile Delinquency Treatment: Meta-Analytic Inquiry into the Variability of Effects." In *Meta-Analysis for Explanation: A Casebook*, edited by Thomas D. Cook, Harris Cooper, David S. Cordray, Heidi Hartmann, Larry V. Hedges, Richard J. Light, Thomas A. Louis, and Frederick Mosteller. New York: Russell Sage.

LoBuglio, Stefan. 2001. "Time to Reframe Politics and Practices in Correctional Education." In *The Annual Review of Adult Learning and Literacy*, Vol. 2, edited by John Comings, Barbara Garner, and Cristine Smith. San Francisco, CA: Jossey-Bass.

MacKenzie, Doris Layton. 2000. "Evidence-Based Corrections: Identifying What Works." *Crime & Delinquency* 46: 457–471.

Maguire, Kathleen E., Timothy J. Flanagan, and Terence P. Thornberry. 1988. "Prison Labor and Recidivism." *Journal of Quantitative Criminology* 4: 3–18.

Miller, Neal, and Robert C. Grieser. 1986. "The Evolution of Prison Industries." In *A Study of Prison Industry: History, Components, and Goals*, edited by the National Institute of Corrections and the American Correctional Association. College Park, MD: American Correctional Association.

Piehl, Ann. 1998. "Economic Conditions, Work, and Crime." In *The Handbook of Crime and Punishment*, edited by Michael Tonry. New York: Oxford University Press.

Pollock, Joycelyn M. 2013. *Prisons and Prison Life: Costs and Consequences*, 2nd ed. New York: Oxford University Press.

Richmond, Kerry M. 2014. "Why Work While Incarcerated? Inmate Perceptions on Prison Industries Employment." *Journal of Offender Rehabilitation* 53: 231–252.

Roberts, John W. 1996. *Factories with Fences: The History of Federal Prison Industries*. Washington, DC: Federal Prison Industries.

Sampson, Robert, and John Laub. 1993. *Crime in the Making: Pathways and Turning Points through Life*. Cambridge, MA: Harvard University Press.

Sampson, Robert, and John Laub. 1997. "A Life-Course Theory of Cumulative Disadvantage and the Stability of Delinquency." *Advances in Criminological Theory* 7: 133–161.

Saylor, William G., and Gerald G. Gaes. 1997. "Training Inmates through Industrial Work Participation and Vocational and Apprenticeship Instruction." *Corrections Management Quarterly* 1: 32–43.

Sedgley, Norman, H., Charles E. Scott, Nancy A. Williams, and Frederick W. Derrick. 2010. "Prison's Dilemma: Do Education and Jobs Programmes Affect Recidivism?" *Economica* 77: 497–517.

Seiter, Richard P., and Karen R. Kadela. 2003. "Prisoner Reentry: What Works, What Does Not, and What Is Promising." *Crime & Delinquency* 49: 360–388.

Sexton, George E. (1995). *Work in American Prisons: Joint Ventures with the Private Sector*. Washinton, DC: US Department of Justice, Office of Justice Programs, National Institute of Justice.

Simourd, Linda. 1993. "Correlates of Delinquency: A Look at Gender Differences." *Forum on Correctional Research* 6: 26–31.

Smith, Cindy J., Jennifer Bechtel, Angie Patrick, Richard R. Smith, and Laura Wilson-Gentry. 2006. *Correctional Industries Preparing Inmates for Re-Entry: Recidivism & Post-Release Employment.* Washington, DC: US Department of Justice, Office of Justice Programs, National Institute of Justice.

Solomon, Amy L., Kelly Dedel Johnson, Jeremy Travis, and Elizabeth C. McBride. 2004. *From Prison to Work: The Employment Dimensions of Prisoner Reentry.* Washington, DC: Urban Institute.

Travis, Jeremy. 2005. *But They All Come Back: Facing the Challenges of Prisoner Reentry.* Washington, DC: Urban Institute.

Tripodi, Stephen J., Johnny S. Kim, and Kimberly Bender. 2010. "Is Employment Associated With Reduced Recidivism? The Complex Relationship Between Employment and Crime." *International Journal of Offender Therapy and Comparative Criminology* 54: 706–720.

Turner, Susan, and Joan Petersilia. 1996. "Work Release in Washington: Effects on Recidivism and Corrections Costs." *The Prison Journal* 76: 138–164.

Uggen, Christopher. 1999. "Ex-Offenders and the Conformist Alternative: A Job Quality Model of Work and Crime." *Social Problems* 46: 127–151.

Uggen, Christopher. 2000. "Work as a Turning Point in the Life Course of Criminals: A Duration Model of Age, Employment, and Recidivism." *American Sociological Review* 65: 529–546.

Uggen, Christopher, and Jeremy Staff. 2001. "Work as a Turning Point for Criminal Offenders." *Corrections Management Quarterly* 5: 1–16.

Visher, Christy A., Laura Winterfield, and Mark B. Coggeshall. 2005. "Ex-Offender Employment Programs and Recidivism: A Meta-Analysis." *Journal of Experimental Criminology* 1: 295–315.

Western, Bruce, Jeffrey R. Kling, and David F. Weiman. 2001. "The Labor Market Consequences of Incarceration." *Crime & Delinquency* 47: 410–427.

Wilson, David B., Catherine A. Gallagher, Mark B. Coggeshall, and Doris L. MacKenzie. 1999. "A Quantitative Review and Description of Corrections-Based Education, Vocation, and Work Programs." *Corrections Management Quarterly* 3: 8–18.

Wilson, David B., Catherine A. Gallagher, and Doris L. MacKenzie. 2000. "A Meta-Analysis of Corrections-Based Education, Vocation, and Work Programs for Adult Offenders." *Journal of Research in Crime and Delinquency* 37: 347–368.

Wolfgang, Marvin, Robert Figlio, and Thorstin Sellin. 1972. *Delinquency in a Birth Cohort.* Chicago: University of Chicago Press.

Zhang, Sheldon X., Robert E. L. Roberts, and Valerie J. Callanan. 2006. "Preventing Parolees from Returning to Prison through Community-Based Reintegration." *Crime & Delinquency* 52: 551–571.

Zweig, Janine, Jennifer Yahner, and Cindy Redcross. 2011. "For Who Does a Transitional Job Program Work? Examining the Recidivism Effects of the Center for Employment Opportunities Program on Former Prisoners at High, Medium, and Low Risk of Offending." *Criminology & Public Policy* 10: 945–972.

....

CHAPTER 21

TREATING SEX OFFENDERS IN PRISON

....

DEVON L. L. POLASCHEK
AND KRISTINA M. BLACKWOOD

THEORY and research on the treatment of sex offenders is one of the most well-developed domains in offender treatment, although many important and interesting questions remain. Much of this development has occurred with some degree of separation from the more general body of knowledge on the rehabilitation of offenders, for at least two reasons. First, more than other types of serious offending, there has been a tradition of viewing sex offending as the result of a mental disorder or psychopathology (e.g., pedophilia), drawing attention to the problem from a mental health perspective and leading to the development of civil legislation for indefinite hospital-based detention.[1] Second, and relatedly, sex offenders have been treated as specialist offenders with their own unique treatment needs. But many are not specialists, and more narrowly focused interventions may overlook treatment needs that are shared with other offenders. A sex offender's next offense may not be sexual in nature, and there is therefore an obligation to provide services in order to reduce the risk of other types of offending.

Sex offenders' psychological characteristics are diverse, as are the offenses they commit and the motivations for their offenses (Beech, Craig, and Browne 2009). Most perpetrators are male, and although a significant proportion is adolescent, most offenders in prison are likely to be adults. The focus here is primarily on adult men who have committed serious contact offenses such as penetrative and nonpenetrative offenses toward children and other adults (e.g., sexual assault, sexual violation, rape).

Sex offender treatment approaches are relatively well-developed, both in the community and in prison. This essay begins, in section I, by reviewing what is known from scientific research about the most effective approaches to treatment, before moving on, in section II, to major rehabilitation theories. Section III outlines purposes, methods, and areas of offender assessment. Section IV structures programs into three phases (preparation, addressing criminogenic needs, planning for the future) and considers each phase in turn. Section V discusses a variety of issues pertinent to treatment design and process, particularly in prison environments.

The essay's main conclusions are

- Sex offender treatment can reduce recidivism. However, most offenders, whether treated or not, are not reconvicted for new sexual offenses, so on average, only about 6 men in every 100 treated desist as a result of the treatment.
- Treatment of sex offenders has been undergoing significant transformation, with the influence of strength-based and positive approaches and the increasing adoption of the Good Lives Model. However, the Risk, Need, and Responsivity principles from the Psychology of Criminal Conduct also are as empirically relevant to sex offenders as they are to other types.
- Prison environments pose a number of challenges for treatment, including the development of therapeutic relationships, group processes and communities in an institutional environment, responsivity to diverse client cultures and to offenders with low cognitive functioning, what to do with those who deny offending and with low-risk offenders, how to detect treatment change, and how to prepare offenders for release.

I. Effective Treatment with Sex Offenders: What the Research Tells Us

Research from several sources informs understanding of what is effective with sex offenders: recidivism outcome evaluations, studies of the degree to which current programs meet general principles of effectiveness, research on the predictors of sexual recidivism, and, finally, research linking treatment change to recidivism.

A. Recidivism Outcome Evaluations

Ideally, recidivism outcome evaluations compare large samples that are equivalent in all respects, except for treatment status, on an outcome with a moderate base rate (i.e., around 50 percent). Studies of sex offender programs do not generally achieve these standards. For example, there are few randomized controlled trials, and those that do exist have not always achieved group equivalence (e.g., Marques et al. 2005). Also, the methodology of randomized control trials (e.g., rigid application of identical interventions for all members of a treatment sample) itself mitigates against effective treatment (Marshall 2006; Hollin 2008).

Overall, the quality of the research remains poor; a small number of studies meet minimum quality criteria (Hanson et al. 2009). Therefore, although most researchers and practitioners likely believe that sex offender treatment *can* effectively reduce recidivism, the empirical support is limited and clearly weaker than in the general offender rehabilitation area (Lösel and Schmucker 2005). Conclusions are thus more contentious. For example, concluding that there is no evidence that treatment is effective ignores a number of outcome studies with similar effect sizes to non-sex offender rehabilitation programs (Marshall 2006).

The largest meta-analysis to date (Schmucker and Lösel 2008) found six randomized controlled trials. At best, most studies employed clearly nonequivalent control groups. Nevertheless, there was no difference in effect size for higher and lower quality designs, and the overall effect was not related to design quality. The low recidivism base-rate problem is illustrated in the overall results of this analysis. Although the mean relative reduction in later sexual recidivism achieved by the treatment groups was 37 percent, in absolute terms, the recidivism figures for both groups were quite low: 17.5 percent in comparison groups and 11.1 percent in treatment groups.[2]

Meta-analyses generally find that hormonal medications, cognitive behavioral treatment and behavioral interventions are the most effective. Cognitive behavioral treatment programs—interventions that target cognition and behavior that is thought to cause sexual offending—are the most commonly evaluated. However, all things being equal, there are arguments favoring psychological programs. The need for hormonal therapy—typically oral or injectable preparations that significantly reduce testosterone levels, often making it difficult for the man to achieve an erection—is likely to be rare in prison; it is not discussed further here (see Marshall et al. 2011). Few cost-benefit analyses are available. But those that do exist suggest that cognitive behavioral treatment programs for sex offenders are cost effective, with ratios as high as $4.13 of benefits for every dollar invested (Bakker et al. 1998; Aos et al. 2001).

B. General Characteristics of Effective Treatment

Correlations with later recidivism are used to determine empirically the characteristics of programs that may be effective or ineffective. This research suggests, first, that effectiveness is higher for programs in the community compared to those in institutions, and some meta-analyses reveal that only community modalities showed an overall effect (Schmucker and Lösel 2008).[3]

Second, treatment format may be important. Individual treatments may not be as effective as mixed formats (individual and group) and predominantly group treatments (Schmucker and Lösel 2008; Ware, Mann, and Wakeling 2009). Finally, programs that adhere broadly to the principles of risk, need, and responsivity (RNR model; Andrews, Bonta, and Hoge 1990) are also associated with larger reductions in recidivism. These programs target intensive service to higher-than-average-risk sex offenders (reflecting the risk principle). At least half of their primary treatment targets are factors previously established to predict recidivism (based on the need principle; see the next section for research on what these factors are). And they demonstrate adherence to responsivity principles by being cognitive behavioral, by making efforts to engage with offenders in ways that maximize their ability to learn, and by using skilled prosocial therapists to develop strong therapeutic attachments with offenders (Harkins and Beech 2007; Hanson et al. 2009).

Interestingly, when Hanson et al. (2009) rated how many of the three principles these programs complied with, they found that, as with the general offender rehabilitation domain, adherence to more principles corresponded with greater treatment effect. They noted that most did not give greater service to higher risk offenders but still met the criteria used for responsivity. However, to meet the study criteria for the need principle, the authors required that at least 51 percent of the program's treatment goals have an empirically established connection to sexual recidivism, and, surprisingly, the majority of programs did not meet that criterion, although all but one of the studies was published since 1990 and therefore should reflect relatively up-to-date information on effective program approaches.

C. Treatment Targets

What criminogenic needs should be addressed in sex offender treatment programs? In their most recent analysis of 82 studies and almost 30,000 offenders, Hanson and Morton-Bourgon (2005) produced a list of the most "promising dynamic risk factors" and "potentially misleading risk factors" (p. 1158). Promising factors included sexual deviancy (though not in rapists), sexual preoccupation, antisocial personality disorder, psychopathy (based on Psychopathy Checklist scores), general self-regulation problems (e.g., impulsivity, lifestyle instability), employment stability, and hostility. Two aspects of this list are interesting. First, despite the large sample, common factors addressed in sex offender treatment such as intimacy deficits and cognitions supportive of sex offending did not make the list because their relationships to sexual recidivism were small. Second, non-sex offenders share most of the factors that made the list (Andrews and Bonta 2010). In fact, the relationships between these same factors and violent and general recidivism in sex offenders suggests that, apart from sexual deviancy and preoccupation, "promising" targets are generic risk factors for offending.

More controversially, the list of "misleading" factors included those that could derail effective treatment and those that could result in negative evaluations of offenders' treatability. These include childhood history factors (sexual and physical abuse and neglect), loneliness, low self-esteem, lack of victim empathy, minimization and denial of criminal responsibility, low pretreatment motivation, and poor progress in treatment (Hanson and Morton-Bourgon 2005).

Of course, this is correlational research and the results cannot be taken to mean that these factors cause or do not cause sex offending. Nor does it address whether factors are changeable or whether they should be addressed in treatment in particular ways. However, it has served to stimulate energetic and valuable discussions among treatment providers, leading to some theoretical development and research that will ultimately improve treatment (Mann, Hanson, and Thornton 2010; Mann and Barnett 2013).

D. Is Treatment Change Related to Outcome?

Recidivism evaluations provide no meaningful information about how programs affect their outcomes. An important way of assessing the impact of programs, especially in prison contexts where release may not be imminent, is in the effects on intermediate change variables. If treatment focuses on changing variables that are related to recidivism, and we have reliable and valid ways of measuring those changes, then those who change the most should have better outcomes (and should therefore make better release prospects) than those who do not, assuming equivalent pretreatment risk level (Olver et al. 2014).

Several recent studies have been able to make these links. The Violence Risk Scale—Sexual Offender Version (VRS–SO; Wong et al. 2003) is a structured therapist-rated actuarial tool that also documents treatment change using a modification of Prochaska, DiClemente, and Norcross' (1992) stage of change model to measure the effects of change on pretreatment risk level. Using the VRS–SO, Olver and colleagues have shown that change scores predict recidivism after controlling for initial risk levels and, further, that among men who were initially equally high risk, those who made more than average changes had lower sexual recidivism than those who changed less (Olver et al. 2007; Olver and Wong 2011).

Using offender-completed psychometric scales, others have similarly linked change to recidivism, but the picture here has been mixed. Some studies have found some pretreatment scores to be better predictors than posttreatment scores (Wakeling, Beech, and Freemantle 2013), but others have confidence that the amount of change on these scales that offenders themselves report in prison-based programs can have predictive validity (see Olver et al. [2014] for a review). One advantage of using instruments with normative data available from nonoffender populations is that it is possible to identify scores representing "normal" or "healthy" functioning. Wakeling et al. (2013) found that fewer of those offenders whose scores were in the normal range before and after treatment recidivated compared to others. Again, such findings indicate that self-report information may have value in establishing treatment needs and in monitoring change.

E. Conclusions

Based on empirical research, we can conclude that sex offender treatment program attendance can lead to lower recidivism, although the absolute reduction is often small. Even so, it may be cost-effective, but more investigations are needed. Programs that adhere to the RNR principles, including targeting for change those factors with empirical links to recidivism, will be associated with greater reductions in recidivism. Finally, there is some evidence that when we look to see if there have been any changes on those targeted factors, the changes are themselves predictive of recidivism outcomes.

II. Theoretical Approaches to Treatment of Sex Offenders in Prison

A number of major etiological theories have contributed to the development of sex offender treatment programs. A detailed discussion of these theories is outside the scope of this essay (see Ward, Polaschek, and Beech [2006] for a more detailed review). Instead, we focus here on rehabilitation and treatment theories that have guided the design and delivery of treatment programs as well as the selection of treatment participants and staff.

Psychologically based sex offender treatment currently is informed by two frameworks. The RNR model (Andrews and Bonta 1994) grew in mainstream offender rehabilitation throughout the last two decades of the twentieth century, leading some to recognize its relevance to sex offender treatment and bringing this field into closer alignment with other forms of offender rehabilitation (Andrews, Bonta, and Wormith 2011). In addition to the core principles of risk, need, and responsivity, other newer principles include (a) basing the program on empirically validated psychological theory, (b) the importance of targeting a broad range of criminogenic needs, (c) the importance of assessing strengths, (d) using structured assessments of risk, and (e) using both relationship and structuring principles in staff practices with offenders (Polaschek 2012).

The RNR model has presented useful challenges for sex offender treatment in several important ways. First, it has encouraged program designers to reflect on and articulate rationales for treating noncriminogenic needs. Second, it has reminded the field that sex offenders are first and foremost offenders, leading to a broader view of the criminogenic needs they should target (e.g., criminal attitudes). Third, it has challenged the view that low-risk sex offenders need intensive treatment. However, there are a number of problems with the RNR model, particularly in how it has been implemented (Polaschek 2012). The model is not suited as a blueprint for the design and delivery of a sex offender (or any offender) treatment program; too much is left unspecified. Sex offender–specific models (e.g., the Self-Regulation Model; Ward et al. 2006) are needed to fill in the details (Polaschek 2012).

The early 2000s witnessed a punitive environment across much of Western corrections. This punitiveness arguably intruded further into therapy, especially in custodial environments, where therapy staff cannot fully shield themselves from the influence of a "get tough" milieu. New civil and criminal legislation resulted in more indefinite detention of sex offenders, increased community surveillance, and sex offender registries and residential restrictions that made it very difficult for offenders to reform and rebuild their lives. The lines between treatment and punishment became blurred (e.g., the use of polygraphs in treatment to establish self-report veracity; Kokish 2003). In this deteriorating systemic climate, a number of programs began to reclaim therapeutic values by adopting various elements of positive psychology, ranging from the very practical (e.g., couching goals in positive approach terms when working with offenders) to the complex and abstract (e.g., the Good Lives Model [GLM]; Ward and Stewart 2003).

The GLM is intended to provide all of the resources needed in a complete rehabilitation theory, including its own etiological theory of sex offending that posits that sex offenders victimize others in the thwarted and misguided pursuit of human needs that are common to all of us. This aspect harks back to anomie and strain theories in sociology and to Maslow's self-actualization hierarchy (Marshall et al. 2013). And, similarly to the Greek philosophers, the GLM proposes that we all strive to lead a flourishing life by maximizing our potential across a combination of up to nine basic human needs (health, knowledge, mastery in work and play, autonomy, inner peace, creativity, relatedness, spirituality, happiness). Treatments based completely on the GLM would therefore identify the strengths and weaknesses of each offender's current Good Life plan and then intervene to improve it. Processes and content in treatment would be directed toward achieving improvements on the plan and its implementation.

The GLM has captured the enthusiasm of a generation of therapists and program designers, and with good reason. Its humanistic approach is naturally appealing to people who genuinely want to help sex offenders live better lives. It puts sex offenders as people at the heart of the therapeutic endeavor, offers hope, and, most important, instead of casting their futures as a bleak and unrelenting quest to stamp out tendrils of risk, gives clients a reason to *want* to undertake treatment.

More recently, Ward and colleagues' Self-Regulation Model (Ward, Hudson, and Keenan 1998; Ward and Hudson 2000) has been integrated with the GLM to provide a detailed treatment strategy for sex offenders (Ward et al. 2004, 2006; Yates, Ward, and Kingston 2009). Initially set up in opposition to the RNR model (Ward and Stewart 2003), the GLM is now viewed as complementary. In reality, it is difficult to find GLM programs that do not blend the two; in fact, blending is desirable (Willis and Ward 2013).

Although the GLM is a complete rehabilitation theory (Fortune, Ward, and Willis 2012), many programs appear to have adopted only parts of it (Willis, Ward, and Levenson 2014). Its most common contribution has been to the enhancement of responsivity, leading to careful consideration of what will motivate offenders to undertake the challenges of personal change (Willis et al. 2014). Another likely benefit is in stimulating therapists to think more completely about indirect routes to changing key criminogenic needs (e.g., whether, rather than working directly to reduce alcohol use, the offender pursues the attainment of satisfying employment with people who drink little alcohol). Its key assumptions and approaches also are valuable in posttreatment prison contexts for their contributions to reintegration foci, a point we return to later.

III. ASSESSMENT FOR TREATMENT

The approach to assessing potential treatment participants should fit the purpose for which it is undertaken. For a low-intensity program, that purpose might simply be to ascertain whether the prisoner meets program eligibility requirements (e.g., level of risk, and language and intellectual capabilities). Similarly, if the main tasks of assessment are actually better achieved in the early phases of group treatment, pregroup assessment may be brief (Marshall et al. 2011).

The pretreatment assessment phase serves a variety of functions, including the initial development of the therapeutic relationship and motivation for treatment. For courses of treatment with a more idiographic approach, the main aim of assessment becomes the development of an individual formulation based on risks, strengths, and protective factors; identification of immediate responsivity issues; and the preliminary establishment of treatment goals. Gathering detailed individual information goes some way to addressing the evident heterogeneity of offenders' needs, and detailed information comes into its own when the treatment can be wholly or partly individualized (Ward and Siegert 2002). In a program that includes an RNR orientation, the most important pretreatment areas of assessment fall into several core domains of dynamic risk (Craissati and Beech 2003; Craig and Beech 2009), including cognitions supportive of sex offending (e.g., attitudes, beliefs, schemas), social and emotional functioning (e.g., hostility, emotional congruence with children, strong prosocial support), general self-regulation issues (e.g., problem-solving, management of impulses and strong emotional states, other self-monitoring helpful for supporting change plans), and sexual issues (e.g., excessive preoccupation, deviant sexual interests).

The use of diverse methods of assessment is good clinical practice. Relevant information can be gathered from interviews with offenders and others who know them and from reviews of relevant file information including descriptions of offending, previous criminal history, social history, behavior in prison, previous interventions, and so on.

A wide variety of questionnaires have been developed for use with sex offender populations (e.g., Beech, Beckett, and Fisher 2003; see also Craig and Beech 2009; Marshall et al.

2011), but few have been adequately validated for use with sex offenders (Craig and Beech 2009). Beech and colleagues have undertaken much of the existing validation work, using data from UK prison and community-based sex offenders. Beech (1998) demonstrated that offenders could be classified into high and low deviancy groups based on scale scores and that high deviancy offenders needed a higher dose of treatment to make changes (Beech, Fisher, and Beckett 1999).

Clinicians routinely call into question the value of such offender self-report measures, because they appear easy to fake and there is concern that offenders may feel pressure to respond in a socially desirable way. Response bias in this domain is a very complex and interesting issue that remains poorly understood (Tan and Grace 2008). However, as the foregoing research suggests, there are no compelling reasons to discard such measures as part of a broader range of information sources, including observational information and other informants. As with all treatment information, questionnaires are most useful when they can both identify the level of current problems—making them risk markers—as well as identify changes in response to treatment. And some psychometric scales used with sex offenders can do both. Although few studies have linked changes on psychometric self-report scale data to outcomes (see Beech and Ford 2006), this picture is no worse than it is for most types of therapist-based ratings (e.g., Looman et al. 2005). The problem may lie more with unreliable tools or with what is being measured than with the self-report method per se.

The assessment of sexual interests has attracted the most technically sophisticated methodologies. Penile plethysmography (PPG)—the measurement of penile tumescence in response to stimulus presentation—has dominated the domain since the 1970s. For child-sex offenders—but not consistently rapists of adults—PPG-based sexual interest is an established predictor of sexual recidivism (Hanson and Morton-Bourgon 2005). But its utility is limited: "it is expensive, invasive, labour intensive, limited to males, and ideally . . . requires a motivated and responsive subject" (Gress and Laws 2009, p. 109). Moreover, there have been concerns about the ethical issues associated with the collation of stimulus sets (e.g., pictures of naked children), and it can be faked readily. Also, from a scientific validity perspective, there is no standardized methodology (Fernandez 2009; Laws 2009); in other words, variation is found in the device, the stimuli, the instructions used with offenders, and the methods of data analysis (O'Donohue and Letourneau 1992). Finally, a significant proportion of offenders who undertake the assessment show little or no response to the entire procedure, and there is a lack of consensus on how to interpret these results (Fernandez 2009). Nevertheless, it remains the most widely used of the available methods of assessing arousal, although it may be most popular in North America (Marshall et al. 2011). Internationally, the proportion of assessments for legal or treatment purposes in which the PPG has actually been used has not been reported.

More recently, in contrast to this physiological method, measures of response times have been used to tap information-processing with regard to sexual interest. These measures include, among others, the Implicit Association Test (Babchishin, Nunes, and Hermann 2013), which can measure the relative strength of associations between sexual and other relevant concepts (e.g., children); viewing time methods that covertly document the amount of time spent viewing diverse stimuli (e.g., Abel et al. 2004); and cognitive load methods such as emotional Stroop tasks where people demonstrate their preferences by taking longer to name the ink color for words that they link with emotions or with sexual interest (e.g., "child") than neutral words; thus revealing their preferences through these small delays (Gress and Laws 2009; Bourke and Gormley 2012; Price et al. 2013). Of these measures, most evaluations have focused on the viewing time and Implicit Association Test methods (Gress and Laws 2009; Babchishin et al. 2013). Gress and Laws's review suggests that although some of these methods have good potential in regard to practical utility (e.g., they are portable, inexpensive, and relatively brief), none is ready for routine clinical use at this point. Some do not reliably distinguish sex offenders from others, while others are promising but simply need more research (see also Thornton and Laws 2009).

Several therapist-rated measures are useful in treatment settings. As with self-report scales, they can assist in identifying treatment priorities. They include a number of dynamic risk assessment tools such as (a) the treatment-oriented, therapist-rated VRS–SO (Wong et al. 2003); (b) the Stable and Acute (2000/2007; Harris, Scott, and Helmus 2007; Harris and Hanson 2010), which are designed for use by supervising probation officers; and (c) the Structured Assessment of Risk and Need (Webster et al. 2006), the Sexual-Violence-Risk Management-20 (Boer et al. 1997), both structured clinical rating scales, and the Sex Offender Treatment Intervention and Progress Scale (McGrath, Lasher, and Cumming 2012), a widely used US measure suitable for repeated administration by treatment providers and probation officers.

Hanson and Harris (2000) made the theoretically important distinction between stable and acute risk factors, noting that stable factors were useful treatment targets and acute factors indicated targets for immediate risk management, particularly in the community. So existing tools recognize static, stable, and acute risk factors as distinct types. Most recently, "protective" factors—both dynamic and static—have begun to be included in both risk and treatment assessments, although the definition of protective remains unclear (de Vries Robbé and de Vogel 2013). For example, some protective factors may act to buffer the effects of risk factors when the latter are high but have no effect if risk factors are low. However, others may simply be positively worded versions of factors previously labeled as risks. For example, a risk factor such as "lack of community support" (Wong et al. 2003), for which a low score indicates that the offender has strong prosocial community support, may instead be described as a protective factor (e.g., "constructive social and professional support network"; de Vries Robbé and de Vogel 2011). More work needs to be done to place these distinctions on a strong conceptual and empirical foundation (Mann et al. 2010).

To conclude, the most important purpose for gathering assessment information is to enable the development of a treatment regimen based on factors that render the offender vulnerable to offending and, in GLM terms, "what is important to the client in his life and what his strengths are" (Yates, Prescott, and Ward 2010, p. 126). The formulation, coupled with an understanding of responsivity issues, informs the treatment plan.

IV. Program Structure and Content

A practical approach to program structure and content is to break it into three phases: (a) an introductory or preparation phase in which participants are socialized to the process of group therapy, they learn some introductory skills for managing what lies ahead, and therapeutic relationships begin to build between members and therapists; (b) a phase in which primary criminogenic needs are addressed; and (c) a preparation for the transition from treatment to the next placement or setting.

A. Preparation/Engagement

Although the preparatory phase can be included in the program as a whole, a number of jurisdictions now start with a preparatory program distinct from the main intervention(s) as a means to ensure treatment readiness (Marshall et al. 2006, 2011, 2013; Carich, Vasileff, and Glenn 2012). These programs could typically include an outline of treatment, discussion on issues of confidentiality, and skills for regulating and tolerating emotional distress. Marshall and colleagues (2006, 2011, 2013) also include exercises to assist clients in gaining empathy and to enhance self-esteem and reduce shame. The latter two factors are potential responsivity barriers that affect the men's belief in their ability to change. In their preparatory program, the men also present an offense disclosure and autobiography. These exercises are used to elicit not only deficits in their functioning but also the strengths they have exhibited in the past. In some programs there may be practice with skills such as communication and giving/receiving feedback. All these issues may be raised initially in the first phase of treatment, but it is expected that they will continue to be addressed as needed throughout subsequent treatment phases.

B. Addressing Criminogenic Needs

The second phase of treatment typically addresses criminogenic needs (Marshall et al. 2006, 2011, 2013; Carich et al. 2010). As we noted earlier, these needs can be grouped into four main areas: beliefs and other types of cognition, self-regulation, social and emotional problems, and sexual issues. Although cognitive distortions have traditionally been challenged vigorously (Salter 1988), Marshall et al. (2011) suggest that many of these forms of cognition, such as making excuses and justifying behavior, have not been shown to be predictive of recidivism (Hanson and Morton-Bourgon 2005) and are, in fact, common human responses that likely reflect an understanding that the behavior was wrong. Consequently, some programs are now less dedicated than previously to getting the offender to acknowledge full responsibility for every aspect of each offense. However, it is still considered vital to target cognitions that are predictive of reoffending, (Gannon and Polaschek 2006; Cortoni 2009; Mann and Marshall 2009; Marshall et al. 2011), including adversarial sexual beliefs such as hostile or distorted views of women, beliefs supportive of child abuse such as children enjoy sexual contact with adults, emotional identification with children, generally antisocial attitudes, viewing oneself as low risk, and a sense of entitlement (Marshall et al. 2011). Methods used to address these distorted beliefs include assisting the client to recognize the distorted thinking, gain an understanding of how this arose, and appreciate the impact of this thinking on past behavior (offending) via cognitive restructuring, challenging of beliefs, and schema therapy techniques (Mann and Beech 2003).

Difficulties with self-regulation and social and emotional problems can be seen in poor decision-making and problem-solving, urge- or distress-driven behavior, and difficulties in relationships. Relationship problems in sex offenders include difficulty achieving intimacy with adults, poor generic relationship skills, dysfunctional attachment styles, and emotional loneliness (Marshall 1989; Ward, Hudson, and Marshall 1996; Cortoni 2009; Mann et al. 2010; Marshall et al. 2011). Clients are assisted to develop prosocial skills and the changes in beliefs necessary to self-regulate their emotions and behavior and to enable them to form interpersonal relationships that meet their need for intimacy and closeness with others without impinging on the rights of others (Marshall et al. 2013).

Finally, sexual issues such as deviant sexual preferences and difficulties with sexual regulation also require attention (Ward et al. 2006; Mann et al. 2010; Marshall et al. 2011). Sexual regulation difficulties include sexual preoccupation and the use of sex as a coping strategy for dealing with negative emotion. These problems are typically addressed through discussion about healthy sexuality aimed at assessing and challenging maladaptive beliefs about sexual activity and through the acquisition of skills for managing emotions more constructively.

A number of methods have developed for treating sexual deviance. For intrusive sexual fantasies, two techniques may be used: (a) olfactory aversion therapy, which involves pairing an unpleasant smell such as ammonia with sexually deviant fantasy, and (b) covert sensitization, where an imagined situation of approaching a child or adult sexually is paired with imagined aversive consequences (e.g., getting caught). A third technique, masturbatory reconditioning, is used both to enhance preferences for acceptable sexual stimuli by pairing them with arousal and to extinguish interest in deviant fantasies due to the absence of pleasure previously associated with them. Typically, the offender practices masturbating to orgasm (satiation) with suitable adult fantasy content and then rehearses deviant fantasies while in a refractory state, unable to achieve orgasm (Ward et al. 2006; Marshall et al. 2006; Camilleri and Quinsey 2008; Marshall, O'Brien, and Marshall 2009; Marhsall et al., 2011, 2013).

C. Self-Management Plans and Safety Planning

The final phase in most treatment programs is preparation for leaving the program. Although in some prison sex offender programs this phase includes preparation for community reentry, here we separate out preparation for community release from the more general orientation to life after the program: maintaining changes, pursuing posttreatment goals, and managing threats to desistance.

Although little research has examined whether treatment gains are maintained posttreatment, both generalizing treatment change to posttreatment environments and planning for life after treatment are likely to be essential for higher risk offenders. For many years the focus of posttreatment planning was on risk management via the Relapse Prevention Model. In this model, treatment is oriented around a template of how offenses unfold over time, and treatment strategies are chosen to prevent or derail progress toward offending at each point in the chain (see Laws, Hudson, and Ward 2000). With the developing emphasis on desistance in correctional psychology, a number of more recent programs have integrated positively oriented life planning into treatment (Cumming and McGrath 2000; Willis and Grace 2009; Marshall et al. 2011).

The GLM is again useful at this stage of the process because it readily provides conceptual resources for engaging offenders in planning for a more meaningful and constructive posttreatment lifestyle. Marshall et al. (2011) provide one example of how it can be adapted to this purpose, if not used as the primary treatment approach. They have simplified the original list into six primary goods (i.e., basic human needs), expressed in straightforward language: health, mastery, autonomy, relatedness, inner peace, and knowledge and creativity. Treatment clients use this list as a basis for identifying a small number of goals and, most important, to make plans for achieving them and to carry out the first steps in those plans (prior to treatment completion).

The construction of a life plan based on the GLM should strengthen one's motivation to desist through a greater sense of purpose. The life plan complements two other pressing needs, particularly for higher risk prisoners who are approaching parole. These include strategies for managing imminent risks or threats to desistance and concrete plans for meeting the most basic of human needs (food, shelter, safety) during the first few months in the community. All three of these approaches (GLM plans, avoidance strategies, and release planning) overlap with each other in practice, but each has a slightly different focus.

Although the practice literature on sex offender treatment advocates reducing reliance on avoidance goals and plans (e.g., "I will avoid any contact with children") because of their likely detrimental effects on progress (Mann et al. 2004), they can still be useful at this phase of treatment. It is not uncommon to hear of offenders in the community who are making excellent progress but are suddenly tripped up by an unforeseen acute event, leading to new offending. For offenders whose previous offending has unfolded rapidly from some specific triggering events, the development of simple strategies for derailing acute threats to desistance may be a very helpful stopgap (e.g., staying home if drunk, practicing how to politely refuse invitations from criminal peers, self-soothing strategies for when social supports are temporarily unavailable in emotional crises, solutions to avoiding being left alone with a child) and can be developed and rehearsed in treatment. Although it is not possible to predict every scenario, developing some basic strategies for common situations may be helpful in modeling strategies for novel situations once in the community.

V. Additional Issues in the Provision of Sex Offender Treatment in Prison

A. Rolling Versus Closed-Cohort Groups

Group treatments are commonly delivered in a closed-group format, meaning that a group of participants start together as a cohort—typically 8 to 12 members with one to two therapists—and work together through a fixed sequence of program components. This format is simple and is suited to highly manualized approaches when facilitators have a limited mandate to tailor treatment to individual group members. A strong sense of "in-group" status, trust, and cohesion can develop as the cohort progresses together. On the downside, progressing together means consecutive sessions on the same topic as each group member completes it, which can lead to boredom and less ability for members to learn from each other because there are no senior role models. Perhaps the most difficult features are managing the needs of group members who learn at different paces and the effects of attrition where precious spaces are lost when participants leave early and cannot be replaced (Ware and Bright 2008).

A number of programs now use rolling group approaches. The strongest advocates for rolling group formats are Marshall and colleagues (2011). Rolling groups run continuously, and a new group member joins when a place becomes available, either through premature treatment termination or because a participant has completed his treatment goals and graduated. They require a more nuanced and sophisticated understanding of the relationship between individual clients' formulations and etiological and treatment theory, and they require therapists to use group sessions to manage the progress of multiple individuals with different needs and at different stages (Fernandez and Marshall 2000). Treatment goals and the means to achieve them can be tailored to each person who can work on his goals at the most suitable pace. Treatment length can vary widely across clients depending on their individual needs and pace of progress (Ware, Frost, and Hoy 2009). Although more challenging for emerging therapists, rolling groups are likely more satisfying and interesting for experienced staff who may even perceive them as less stressful (Ware and Bright 2008). They may also improve the experience for clients. More senior members can act as role models, consolidating their own learning (Fiorella and Mayer 2013) as they assist therapists with newer members. And, because the group always exists, some of the more difficult closed-group phases (e.g., "storming," during which members debate fundamental values and individual differences in order to settle on a modus operandi for the group; Tuckman 1965) are largely ameliorated; new members can integrate into the group quite quickly, which also makes the process less challenging for therapists (Marshall et al. 2011). A potential disadvantage is that they may lend themselves to overtreatment. Although overtreatment can occur in any format, a therapist's caution may lead to retention of participants longer than would be possible in a closed format, and sometimes that may be longer than necessary. Little is yet known about whether different formats vary in their effectiveness or efficiency.

B. Therapist Factors and the Therapy Alliance

The importance of therapist characteristics and behaviors, as well as the quality of the bond between therapists, has sometimes been overlooked in sex offender treatment (Marshall and Serran 2004). The therapeutic alliance itself has received little attention in empirical research. However, more recent positive and strength-based treatment philosophies have rejuvenated interest in therapist features and their relationships to treatment change (Marshall et al. 2003; Marshall 2005). For example, treatment change has been shown to correlate positively with therapist characteristics of interpersonal warmth, empathy, rewardingness, and directiveness and negatively with aggressive confrontations (Marshall and Serran 2004), highlighting the importance of training therapists in process skills and not simply in content delivery.

C. Creating Group Cohesion

Related to effective therapist behaviors are various other process issues for sex offender treatment. For group treatment, these issues include the effective functioning of the group and understanding and exploiting group processes in creating change. The few studies examining group cohesion have all been conducted using the Moos (1994) Group Environment Scale, which includes one scale that measures cohesion. This research has found that good or very good group functioning can be achieved (Beech and Hamilton-Giachritsis 2005). Although these scores have not been correlated with recidivism (Harkins and Beech 2008), they may have an important indirect role. For example, they may facilitate increases in treatment change on key variables (e.g., offending–supportive attitudes; Beech and Hamilton-Giachritsis 2005), such as by influencing the quality of prosocial interactions between group members outside of group sessions (Frost and Connolly 2004).

D. Therapeutic Communities

The development of a program setting into a community that promotes psychological change has a long tradition in forensic settings (De Leon 2000). Therapeutic communities have been viewed as stand-alone treatments for decades in some jurisdictions (Shuker 2013). There are formidable challenges to generating well-functioning facilities in many of today's prisons, but any movement toward creating a more prosocial resocializing milieu in prison should enhance rehabilitation (Antonowicz and Ross 1994). The extant research evidence on the effectiveness of therapeutic communities (TCs) as a stand-alone correctional intervention is not supportive (Lösel and Schmucker 2005). However, a number of programs, particularly for high-risk sex offenders, incorporate some form of TC into the residential environment of structured, group-based cognitive-behavioral treatment programs (e.g., Bakker et al. 1998; Olver and Wong 2013; Wilson, Kilgour, and Polaschek 2013). When combined this way, TCs can extend the structured treatment process to outside of the group sessions (Ware, Mann, and Wakeling 2009). TCs can provide (a) authentic opportunities for practicing basic interpersonal skills that often contribute to sex offending (e.g., one-to-one conflict resolution; seeking help from others with problem-solving) with other staff (e.g., custodial staff) and other prisoners; (b) adjunct experiences that address other change goals (e.g., employment); (c) extending lessons of the session itself (e.g., group "homework" exercises or behavioral experiments); and (d) normalizing community experiences (e.g., celebrating important community events; making collective decisions). However, this is certainly an area that requires further qualitative and quantitative research, particularly with regard to how prisoners themselves experience these environments (Day et al. 2012). In higher risk programs, it is likely that if the therapy regime does not have control of the climate of the unit, it is at risk of being predominantly criminogenic, since it will be dictated by the entrenched antisociality of the most socially dominant residents.

E. Cultural Responsivity

In many jurisdictions, prisoner populations comprise a wide variety of ethnic identities and cultural backgrounds. Many of our sex offender treatment approaches originate from developed nations and have a markedly Western orientation. Attending to the degree of fit between program and offender is an important part of the responsivity principle; poor fit is theorized to reduce treatment effectiveness (Andrews and Bonta 2010).

Along with cultural diversity can come a variety of other responsivity issues that may need attention, depending on both history and the current context (e.g., refugees recovering from experiences in a war-torn homeland, oppression and deculturation of indigenous people, and institutional racism). Therefore, treatment efforts inevitably will run up against the impact—often multigenerational—of destructive political and societal issues on the treatment participants. Programs for indigenous people must be particularly cognizant of these effects, resulting as they do in myriad negative health and social effects, including very high rates of family poverty and ill health, substance abuse, violence, and trauma (Ertz 1998; Queensland Corrective Services 2010), along with cognitive impairments, illiteracy, mental disorders, and shame (Cull and Wehner 1998).

The term *culture* has many definitions, including "a system of shared attitudes, values, goals, and practices that characterises an institution, organization or group" (Tamatea and Brown 2011, p. 171). As yet there is little written and even less research on therapeutic approaches that have been shaped explicitly with reference to culture. Documented program approaches to date vary from those specialized for a single, often indigenous culture to mixed-culture models. Single-culture programs allow that culture to develop more fully indigenous responses to sex offender treatment, while mixed culture programs provide the opportunity to create a culturally inclusive model, which is a particularly challenging task when Western and non-Western approaches do not readily align (Ellerby and Stonechild 1998).

In some offender populations in Western nations, people of European origins may be in the minority. Such a circumstance necessitates the development and provision of services that better fit the "cultural space(s)" of offenders (Tamatea and Brown 2011). New Zealand is one such example; indigenous Maori represent 50 percent of the prison population but just 15 percent of the country's population (Statistics New Zealand 2012) and, together with the descendants of people from the smaller neighboring nations of the Pacific (e.g., Samoa, Cook Islands, Tonga), comprise the majority in custody. An example of a prison-based model that has sought to integrate indigenous Maori and Western approaches in the treatment of child-sex offenders is New Zealand's Te Piriti Special Treatment Unit (Nathan, Wilson, and Hillman 2003; see also Larsen et al. 1998). Opened in 1994, Te Piriti offers a cognitive-behavioral group therapy program embedded in a therapeutic community that is imbued with significant traditional Maori processes and practices that serve to provide a positive and prosocial framework for the implementation of treatment for Maori and non-Maori alike. Tikanga Maori (Maori cultural knowledge, processes, and practices) is also woven into the treatment itself, wherever possible, but in abstract terms the strategies for treatment change remain cognitive-behavioral.

An evaluation of graduates in May 2001 found that Te Piriti's approach was beneficial for Maori and non-Maori alike. Two-thirds of graduates were non-Maori; most were European New Zealanders. Compared to a 21 percent recidivism rate for a similar untreated sample, Maori and non-Maori program completers' sexual recidivism was 4 percent and 6 percent, respectively. Maori cultural variables measured at both pre- and postprogram (e.g., cultural identity, knowledge of ancestry, traditional protocols, language and culture-specific skills, degree of family support) showed positive changes. However, as is often found with pre- and postprogram measures, changes were not related to reconviction (Nathan et al. 2003). Although the model thus appears to be successful, research like this generates many new questions. For example, would it be still more effective if Maori were treated alone?

Is it more effective for non-Maori than similar non-Maori–influenced programs? Besides improved desistance, what other benefits does this treatment have for Maori?

F. Treatment of Rapists and Child Molesters: Separate or Together?

Prison programs commonly mix sex offenders whose victims were adults together with child molesters (Lösel and Schmucker 2005). It has been argued that the mix is advantageous for group process and offender progress (Ware, Mann, and Wakeling 2009) and that it facilitates efficient allocation of treatment places. However, comparisons of the effectiveness across mixed and separated groups have been few. Studies of group climate have revealed mainly similarities (Harkins and Beech 2008), with the possible exception that mixed groups may be less expressive, possibly because child-victim offenders feel more uncomfortable with disclosure in these groups. To date, the extant evidence finds no difference in treatment effectiveness between mixed and more homogeneous groups (Harkins and Beech 2008), leaving the decision about whether to mix or separate to be determined according to the culture and facilities of different prisons.

In much of the Western world, sex offenders require protective segregation from other prisoners if they are to be contained humanely and safely, and prison treatment is made available in segregated facilities to ensure safety (Ward, Gannon, and Birgden 2007). However, in New Zealand, adult-victim offenders do not experience the same disdain, hostility, and threats to their lives as do child-victim offenders, and they sometimes contribute to the persecution of child-sex offenders in prison. Hence the two groups are treated separately, and rapists are currently treated in their own specialist program in units with high-risk violent offenders (Wilson et al. 2013). Problems with rapists colluding with each other in mixed groups and intimidating child abusers have also been reported in UK research (Harkins and Beech 2008) and, if severe, may not be overcome by therapist skill, rendering the treatment climate antitherapeutic and potentially unsafe.

G. Treatment of Sex Offenders with Low Cognitive Functioning

Consistent with the responsivity principle, it is sometimes necessary to tailor programs to meet the needs of men with low cognitive function (Wilcox 2004; Keeling and Rose 2006; Keeling, Rose, and Beech 2007; Murphy and Sinclair 2009; Williams and Mann 2010). The term "low cognitive functioning" rather than "intellectual disability" is used here because some programs include not only men who meet the criteria for Intellectual Disability (IQ of less than 70 and deficits in social and adaptive functioning) but also those who function in the borderline intellectual functioning range (IQ 70–80; Keeling and Rose 2006). These offenders are even more likely than other prisoners to experience serious difficulties with literacy, learning new information, abstract reasoning, communication and general social skills, insight, self-esteem, impulsivity, and emotional management (Wilcox 2004; Keeling and Rose 2006; Keeling et al 2007; Craig and Lindsay 2009), all of which may affect receptiveness to, and thus ability to learn from, treatment. Modified treatment for these offenders still covers similar core issues as mainstream groups (e.g., identifying their offending patterns, cognitive distortions, social skills, sexual regulation, and safety planning), but treatment delivery also emphasizes the use of a range of techniques and communication mediums, including pictures and symbols, frequent repetition and rehearsal, simplified presentation of concepts, visual imagery, and assistance with generalizing skills across settings. In addition, therapists need to be even more willing to adapt their style to meet the needs of clients, and it is recommended that treatment groups have a lower number of participants and shorter sessions than mainstream groups (Haaven and Coleman 2000; Wilcox 2004; Williams and Mann 2010; Sakdalan and Collier 2012).

"Old Me/New Me" is a concept that has been found to be effective for scaffolding change in men with low cognitive functioning. "Old Me" represents the thoughts, feelings and behaviors present when the individual offended, while "New Me" stands for the offense-free life the offender would like to lead (Haaven and Coleman 2000; Keeling and Rose 2006; Williams and Mann 2010). In the UK, the Sex Offender Treatment Services Collaborative in Intellectual Disabilities (SOTSIC–ID) has developed a model and treatment manual that form the basis of a comprehensive approach to working with men with cognitive disabilities (Murphy and Sinclair 2009).[4] Few studies of treatment outcome have yet been reported for this group. One using a waiting-list control design reported progress on treatment goals and low rates of reoffending (SOTSEC–ID 2010).

H. Treatment Provision for Low-Risk Offenders

Another thorny issue in prisons is what services to provide for those assessed as being at low risk of further sex offenses. On the one hand, it can be argued that all offenders should be treated regardless of risk, that any level of risk is unacceptable, that risk assessment has error rates, that it depends on how "low risk" is defined, and that treatment should aim to do more than reduce risk. Furthermore, there are wider political, social, and ethical concerns. That is, denial of services may appear to trivialize victim impact, may send a message to offenders that they are not expected to take responsibility for change, may deprive offenders who request them access to important services (Wakeling, Mann, and Carter 2012), and may prevent offenders from being released early on parole.

On the other hand, correctional resources are always limited, and, in general, there is evidence that sufficiently intensive treatment of higher risk offenders results in the prevention of a greater number of new convictions (Lowenkamp et al. 2006). Low-risk offenders, by definition, will have fewer and less serious treatment needs, suggesting that the impact of treatment on these cases will be significantly lower than on higher risk offenders (see Wakeling et al. [2012] for a review) and may be negligible.

If resources are limited, and if we can justify it on empirical grounds, should we simply decline to offer treatment to low-risk sex offenders? Hypothetically "yes," but at least two other possibilities should be considered. First, while risk of sexual reconviction may be low, some offenders may have a moderate or high risk of committing new offenses of a nonsexual nature. Some form of treatment may be desirable to prevent that next offense (Polaschek and King 2002). Second, for many sex offenders, their postrelease lifestyle—separation from family, community notification, curfews, residential restrictions, and the like—may be far harder than life prior to release. To the extent that such stressors play a part in the build-up to that person's reoffending, it may be argued that his proneness to reoffend may have increased since imprisonment, thus rendering static factor assessments based on preprison variables uninformative. For some, especially those serving very long sentences, prison itself may have had a detrimental effect on a variety of dynamic risk and protective factors (e.g., adaptive emotional regulation and access to prosocial support; Bonta and Gendreau 1990; Jamieson and Grounds 2005). Low-intensity rolling treatment groups that concentrate on reentry issues could be an efficient, humane, and defensible option.

I. Monitoring and Measuring Treatment Change in Prison

Identifying who has progressed in treatment, by how much, and on which targets is essential information for establishing posttreatment placement, support needs, and parole suitability. A number of instruments in various stages of validation as clinical assessment tools can assess pretreatment programs as well as progress in treatment. Programs have commonly readministered self-report psychometric scales and plethysmography for this purpose. A third approach has been clinical ratings of learning objectives or goal attainment at the end of each treatment component (e.g., increases in understanding one's pattern of offending). Among all three approaches there have been very few demonstrations of links between change and recidivism outcome (Beggs 2010).

When using psychometric scales, although *any* improvement in scores may be desirable, normative data can serve to establish cut-offs for "recovery" (a return to scores in the nondisordered range) and "improvement" (scores improve but remain below cut-offs for complete recovery: Mandeville-Norden, Beech, and Hayes 2008; Nunes, Babchishin, and Cortoni 2011; Beech, Mandeville-Norden, and Goodwill 2012), and for identifying treatment "responders" and "nonresponders," which, in turn, may be linked to recidivism (Beech et al. 2012).

Sometimes overlooked in the evaluation of progress in treatment is the observation of actual behavior in the treatment setting. Prisons can provide good opportunities for the observation of treatment-relevant behavior outside the sessions. The downside is that the prison context constrains behavior, and these setting effects may be particularly significant for sexual behavior. That is, offending-related behavior (e.g., hostility toward women partners, alcohol intoxication) may simply not occur at all in the custodial environment, regardless of risk. Furthermore, it may be much harder to have confidence in links between offending behavior and contemporary functioning in offenders who have spent long periods in custody or who were charged decades after the offenses occurred.

J. Treatment of Deniers

The denial of responsibility for sex offenses poses another challenge for offenders in prison who seek early or contingent release. Denial takes a number of forms (e.g., minimizing the extent and seriousness of behavior, justifying behavior, externalizing blame; Vanhoeck and Van Daele 2011) that are common in those who take part in sex offender treatment. However, categorical denial ("it wasn't me," "I didn't do anything to him," "I never even met her") has frequently resulted in denial of treatment access because of the common treatment requirement of accepting responsibility for offending and because of the focus on offending itself in the preliminary engagement phases of treatment (e.g., Marshall et al. 2011). Particularly if they are assessed as high risk, such untreated offenders may then be denied release. It is likely that a proportion of such prisoners—hopefully very small—is comprised of wrongfully convicted innocent people who should certainly be released. Also, the remainder may have criminogenic needs that could benefit from treatment despite their refusals to admit the offense.

For categorical deniers, some success has been anecdotally reported with motivational interviewing approaches and placing deniers into programs with those who admit their offenses. However, sex offender denial in those who were rightfully convicted can be maintained by strong external factors such as family and peer pressure to maintain innocence, open legal appeals against conviction, and stigma and safety concerns (Lord and Willmot 2004), making it likely that more often these approaches have failed.

A number of approaches have been suggested for working more effectively with deniers (Vanhoeck and Van Daele 2011). One approach showing tentative signs of utility is based on providing treatment without targeting the intervention at the denial itself. For example, around 1998, Marshall and colleagues (2001) piloted a treatment offered to deniers on the grounds of its potential benefit for avoiding future accusation. The program resembles conventional treatment but omits only those components that require offense disclosure or admissions of guilt. Even safety planning (to avoid further accusations) and an understanding of victim harm (generic) can be included. Participants in the program agree to undertake it to enhance parole chances or to improve their life functioning in previously problematic areas. As yet, relatively small numbers of offenders have completed this type of program, but preliminary results are reported to be promising (Ware and Marshall 2008; Marshall et al. 2011).

K. Reintegration or Reentry into the Community

Sex offender treatment has been influenced by the growing recognition of the importance of reentry preparation for prisoners (e.g., Duwe 2012). A good release plan, if implemented, may significantly stabilize a newly released prisoner, reducing the frequency of crises and encounters with destabilizing influences. Some offenders are able to draw on good community resources without assistance and are positively disposed toward making use of professional assistance and oversight. Others, particularly after long terms of imprisonment, need assistance in constructing a strong prerelease plan and may have negative attitudes toward parole compliance that also pose a threat to release success. Research on release planning has shown that the quality of plans (e.g., accommodation, social support, employment) predict sexual recidivism years later (Willis and Grace 2008, 2009), with an incremental increase in predictive power over dynamic and static risk measures (Scoones, Willis, and Grace 2012).

Another important component of the reintegration process itself is meetings between the offender in treatment and his release support network. Such meetings may need to begin quite early in treatment if one of the goals is to rebuild support by restoring relationships with estranged but willing family members. For offenders with few or no prosocial support networks—common if their offending occurred inside their family—more formal methods of developing support will need to be invoked. Some community organizations provide this type of specialist support. The best-known example is Circles of Support and Accountability (CoSA), which originated in Canada in the mid-1990s and has spread gradually to a number of Western countries. CoSA organizes a handful of community volunteers to provide a "circle of support" for high-risk sex offenders, with a second, outer circle of professionals providing more conventional external supervision (McWhinnie, Wilson, and Brown 2013).

Volunteers in CoSA are prepared for the offender's release, know something of his risk factors, and provide a variety of practical and emotional supports and positive role modeling (van Rensburg 2012). Research to date suggests they are effective. Wilson, Cortoni, and McWhinnie (2009) reported 2.3 percent sex offense reconvictions over three years postrelease—an 83 percent reduction—with similar reductions in violent and general offending for matched CoSA participants compared to non-CoSA controls. None had postrelease parole supervision. Well-managed regular support group meetings with other graduates in the community can also assist with isolation and change maintenance and are available in some locations.

In many jurisdictions, a variety of procedures that reflect the "trail 'em, nail 'em, jail 'em" philosophy (Wilson, Cortoni, and McWhinnie 2009) will also be a significant part of parolees' postrelease life (e.g., Cumming and Mcgrath 2000; Kemshall and Wood 2009). Positively managing potential public persecution, intrusive supervision and monitoring procedures, and restrictions on location and movement is an ever-increasing challenge for sex offenders. Such measures work against the establishment of a healthy lifestyle after release (Zevitz and Farkas 2004; Levenson and Cotter 2005) and exacerbate the likelihood of recidivism with no commensurate increase in public safety (Nobles, Levenson, and Youstin 2012). Although interventions like CoSA can provide a balance to these more difficult aspects of release, preparation for the likely emotional and practical impacts of postrelease conditions is also important, especially if they are complex and difficult to remember or will leave the offender isolated and with few meaningful daily activities for some time.

VI. Conclusion

The treatment of sex offenders in prison has steadily evolved in sophistication and diversity over the past 20 years. Although helpful research has continued to grow, many of the nuances of effective treatment remain untested. Much sex offender treatment occurs in prisons, which pose some distinctive challenges for the safe provision of services, the opportunities to generalize behavior, and the monitoring of treatment change. New developments in the past decade or so include the GLM, rolling group formats, preparatory programs, programs for categorical deniers, therapeutic communities for cognitive behavioral treatment, and an increase in reentry planning. Substantial inroads remain to be made in the provision of treatments proven to be effective with indigenous and non-European offenders.

NOTES

1. For example, California's Sexual Violent Predator statute and indefinite detention in UK Special Hospitals under Sections 37 and 41 of the Mental Health Act (1983).
2. The absolute difference is therefore 17.5–11.1 percent = 6.4 percent. However, the relative difference represents the proportion of reduction from 17.5 percent: 6.4 represents 37 percent of 17.5.
3. But two more rigorously selective recent analyses were favorable for prison treatments (Hanson et al. 2009; *Treatment for Adult Sex Offenders: Technical Report 2012*).
4. See www.kent.ac.uk/tizard/sotsec/index.html.

REFERENCES

Abel, Gene G., Alan Jordan, Joanne L. Rouleau, Robert Emerick, Sharen Barboza-Whitehead, and Candice Osborn. 2004. "Use of Visual Reaction Time to Assess Male Adolescents Who Molest Children." *Sexual Abuse: A Journal of Research and Treatment* 16:255–265.

Andrews, Donald Arthur, and James Bonta. 1994. *The Psychology of Criminal Conduct*. Cincinnati, OH: Anderson.

Andrews, Donald Arthur, and James Bonta. 2010. *The Psychology of Criminal Conduct*, 5th ed. New York: Routledge.

Andrews, Donald A., James Bonta, and Robert D. Hoge. 1990. "Classification for Effective Rehabilitation: Rediscovering Psychology." *Criminal Justice and Behavior* 17:19–52.

Andrews, Donald A., James Bonta, and J. Stephen Wormith. 2011. "The Risk-Need Responsivity Model: Does the Good Lives Model Contribute to Effective Crime Prevention?" *Criminal Justice and Behavior* 38:735–755.

Antonowicz, Daniel H., and Robert R. Ross. 1994. "Essential Components of Successful Rehabilitation Programs for Offenders." *International Journal of Offender Therapy and Comparative Criminology* 38:97–104.

Aos, Steve, Polly Phipps, Robert Barnoski, and Roxanne Lieb. 2001. *The Comparative Costs and Benefits of Programs to Reduce Crime*. Olympia: Washington State Institute for Public Policy.

Babchishin, Kelly M., Kevin L. Nunes, and Chantal A. Hermann. 2013. "The Validity of Implicit Association Test (IAT) Measures of Sexual Attraction to Children: A Meta-Analysis." *Archives of Sexual Behavior* 42:487–499.

Bakker, L., Stephen Hudson, David Wales, and David Riley. 1998. *And There Was Light: Evaluating the Kia Marama Treatment Programme for New Zealand Sex Offenders Against Children*. Christchurch, NZ: Department of Corrections Psychological Service.

Beech, Anthony R. 1998. "A Psychometric Typology of Child Abusers." *International Journal of Offender Therapy and Comparative Criminology* 42:319–339.

Beech, Anthony, Richard C. Beckett, and Dawn Fisher. 2003. "Risk Assessment of Sex Offenders." *Professional Psychology: Research and Practice* 34:339–352.

Beech, Anthony, Leam A. Craig, and Kevin D. Browne. 2009. Introduction. In *Assessment and Treatment of Sex Offenders: A Handbook*, edited by Anthony Beech, Leam A. Craig, and Kevin D. Browne. Chichester, UK: Wiley.

Beech, Anthony, Dawn Fisher, and Richard C. Beckett. 1999. *Step 3: An Evaluation of the Prison Sex Offender Treatment Programme*. London: UK Home Office. http://www.homeoffice.gov.uk/rds/adhocpubs1.html.

Beech, Anthony, and Hannah Ford. 2006. "The Relationship Between Risk, Deviance, Treatment Outcome and Sexual Reconviction in a Sample of Child Sexual Abusers Completing Residential Treatment for Their Offending." *Psychology, Crime & Law* 12:685–701.

Beech, Anthony, and Catherine E. Hamilton-Giachritsis. 2005. "Relationship Between Therapeutic Climate and Treatment Outcome in Group-Based Sexual Offender Treatment Programs." *Sexual Abuse: A Journal of Research and Treatment* 17:127–140.

Beech, Anthony, Rebecca Mandeville-Norden, and Alasdair Goodwill. 2012. "Comparing Recidivism Rates of Treatment Responders/Nonresponders in a Sample of 413 Child Molesters Who Had Completed Community-Based Sex Offender Treatment in the United Kingdom." *International Journal of Offender Therapy and Comparative Criminology* 56:29–49.

Beggs, Sarah. 2010. "Within-Treatment Outcome among Sexual Offenders: A Review." *Aggression and Violent Behavior* 15:369–379.

Boer, Douglas P., Stephen D. Hart, P. Randall Kropp, and Christopher D. Webster. 1997. *Manual for the Sexual Violence Risk–20: Professional Guidelines for Assessing Risk of Sexual Violence*. Vancouver: British Columbia Institute Against Family Violence.

Bonta, James, and Paul Gendreau. 1990. "Reexamining the Cruel and Unusual Punishment of Prison Life." *Law and Human Behavior* 14:347–372.

Bourke, Ashling B., and Michael J. Gormley. 2012. "Comparing a Pictoral Stroop Task to Viewing Time Measures of Sexual Interest." *Sexual Abuse: A Journal of Research and Treatment* 24:479–500.

Camilleri, Joseph A., and Vernon L. Quinsey. 2008. "Pedophilia: Assessment and Treatment." In *Sexual Deviance: Theory, Assessment, and Treatment*, edited by D. Richard Laws and William T. O'Donohue. New York: Guilford Press.

Carich, Mark S., J. D. Vasileff, and T. L. Glenn. 2012. *Treatment Readiness Programs for Sexual Abusers: Key Elements*. Beaverton, OR: Association for the Treatment of Sexual Offenders.

Carich, Mark S., Chris Wilson, Peter A. Carich, and Martin C. Calder. 2010. "Contemporary Sex Offender Treatment: Incorporating Circles of Support and the Good Lives Model." In *What Else Works? Creative Work with Offenders*, edited by Jo Brayford, Francis Cowe, and John Deering. Devon, UK: Willan.

Cortoni, Franca. 2009. "Factors Associated with Sexual Offending." In *Assessment and Treatment of Sex Offenders: A Handbook*, edited by Anthony Beech, Leam A. Craig, and Kevin D. Browne. Chichester, UK: Wiley.

Craig, Leam A., and Anthony R. Beech. 2009. "Psychometric Assessment of Sexual Deviance." In *Assessment and Treatment of Sex Offenders: A Handbook*, edited by Anthony Beech, Leam A. Craig, and Kevin D. Browne. Chichester, UK: Wiley.

Craig, Leam A., and William R. Lindsay. 2009. "Sexual Offenders with Intellectual Disabilities: Characteristics and Prevalence." In *Assessment and Treatment of Sex Offenders: A Handbook*, edited by Anthony Beech, Leam A. Craig, and Kevin D. Browne. Chichester, UK: Wiley.

Craissati, Jackie, and Anthony Beech. 2003. "A Review of the Dynamic Variables and Their Relationship to Risk Prediction in Sex Offenders." *Journal of Sexual Aggression* 9:41–55.

Cull, Denise M., and David M. Wehner. 1998. "Australian Aborigines: Cultural Factors Pertaining to the Assessment and Treatment of Australian Aboriginal Sexual Offenders." In *Sourcebook of Treatment Programs for Sexual Offenders*, edited by William L. Marshall, Yolanda M. Fernandez, Stephen M. Hudson, and Tony Ward. New York: Plenum.

Cumming, Georgia, and Robert J. McGrath. 2000. "External Supervision: How Can It Increase the Effectiveness of Relapse Prevention?" In *Remaking Relapse Prevention with Sex Offenders: A Sourcebook*, edited by D. Richard Laws, Stephen M. Hudson, and Tony Ward. Newbury Park, CA: Sage.

Day, Andrew, Sharon Casey, Jim Vess, and Gina Huisy. 2012. "Assessing the Therapeutic Climate of Prisons." *Criminal Justice and Behavior* 39:156–168.

De Leon, George. 2000. *The Therapeutic Community: Theory, Model and Method.* New York: Springer.

de Vries Robbé, Michiel, and Vivienne de Vogel. 2011. "Protective Factors for (Sexual) Offenders. Results with the SAPROF." Paper presented at the annual meeting of the American Psychology—Law Society/4th International Congress of Psychology and Law, Miami, FL. http://citation.allacademic.com/meta/p483330_index.html

de Vries Robbé, Michiel, and Vivienne de Vogel. 2013. "Protective Factors for Violence Risk: Bringing Balance to Risk Assessment." In *Managing Clinical Risk: A Guide to Effective Practice*, edited by Caroline Logan and Lorraine Johnstone. London: Routledge.

Duwe, Grant. 2012. "Evaluating the Minnesota Comprehensive Offender Reentry Plan (MCORP): Results from a Randomized Experiment." *Justice Quarterly* 29:347–383.

Ellerby, Lawrence, and John Stonechild. 1998. "Blending the Traditional with the Contemporary in the Treatment of Aboriginal Sexual Offenders: A Canadian Experience." In *Sourcebook of Treatment Programs for Sexual Offenders*, edited by William L. Marshall, Yolanda M. Fernandez, Stephen M. Hudson, and Tony Ward. New York: Plenum.

Ertz, Dewey J. 1998. "Treatment of United States American Indians." In *Sourcebook of Treatment Programs for Sexual Offenders*, edited by William L. Marshall, Yolanda M. Fernandez, Stephen M. Hudson, and Tony Ward. New York: Plenum.

Fernandez, Yolanda. 2009. "The Standardisation of Phallometry." In *Assessment and Treatment of Sex Offenders: A Handbook*, edited by Anthony Beech, Leam A. Craig, and Kevin D. Browne. Chichester, UK: Wiley.

Fernandez, Yolanda M., and W. L. Marshall. 2000. "Contextual Issues in Relapse Prevention Treatment." In *Remaking Relapse Prevention with Sex Offenders: A Sourcebook*, edited by D. Richard Laws, Stephen M. Hudson, and Tony Ward. Newbury Park, CA: Sage.

Fiorella, Logan, and Richard E. Mayer. 2013. "The Relative Benefits of Learning by Teaching and Teaching Expectancy." *Contemporary Educational Psychology* 38:281–288.

Fortune, Clare-Ann, Tony Ward, and Gwenda M. Willis. 2012. "The Rehabilitation of Offenders: Reducing Risk and Promoting Better Lives." *Psychiatry, Psychology and Law* 19:646–661.

Frost, Andrew, and Marie Connolly. 2004. "Reflexivity, Reflection, and the Change Process in Offender Work." *Sexual Abuse: A Journal of Research and Treatment* 16:365–380.

Gannon, Theresa A., and Devon L. L. Polaschek. 2006. "Cognitive Distortions in Child Molesters: A Re-Examination of Key Theories and Research." *Clinical Psychology Review* 26:1000–1019.

Gress, Carmen L., and D. Richard Laws. 2009. "Measuring Sexual Deviance: Attention-Based Measures." In *Assessment and Treatment of Sex Offenders: A Handbook*, edited by Anthony Beech, Leam A. Craig, and Kevin D. Browne. Chichester, UK: Wiley.

Haaven, James L., and Emily M. Coleman. 2000. "Treatment of the Developmentally Disabled Sex Offender." In *Remaking Relapse Prevention with Sex Offenders: A Sourcebook*, edited by D. Richard Laws, Stephen M. Hudson, and Tony Ward. Newbury Park, CA: Sage.

Hanson, R. Karl, Guy Bourgon, Leslie Helmus, and Shannon Hodgson. 2009. *Treatment for Adult Sex Offenders: Technical Report 2012*. Ottawa: Public Safety Canada.

Hanson, R. Karl, Guy Bourgon, Leslie Helmus, and Shannon Hodgson. 2009. "The Principles of Effective Correctional Treatment Also Apply to Sexual Offenders: A Meta-Analysis." *Criminal Justice and Behavior* 36:865–891.

Hanson, R. Karl, and Andrew J. R. Harris. 2000. "Where Should We Intervene? Dynamic Predictors of Sexual Offence Recidivism." *Criminal Justice and Behavior* 27:6–35.

Hanson, R. Karl, and Kelly E. Morton-Bourgon. 2005. "The Characteristics of Persistent Sexual Offenders: A Meta-Analysis of Recidivism Studies." *Journal of Consulting and Clinical Psychology* 73:1154–1163.

Harkins, Leigh, and Anthony R. Beech. 2007. "A Review of the Factors that Can Influence the Effectiveness of Sexual Offender Treatment: Risk, Need, Responsivity, and Process Issues." *Aggression and Violent Behavior* 12:615–627.

Harkins, Leigh, and Anthony R. Beech. 2008. "Examining the Impact of Mixing Child Molesters and Rapists in Group-Based Cognitive-Behavioral Treatment for Sexual Offenders." *International Journal of Offender Therapy and Comparative Criminology* 52:31–45.

Harris, Andrew J. R., and R. Karl Hanson. 2010. "Clinical, Actuarial and Dynamic Risk Assessment of Sexual Offenders: Why Do Things Keep Changing?" *Journal of Sexual Aggression* 16:296–310.

Harris, Andrew J. R., Terri-Lynne Scott, and Leslie Helmus. 2007. *Assessing the Risk of Sexual Offenders on Community Supervision: The Dynamic Supervision Project*. Ottawa, ON: Public Safety Canada.

Hollin, Clive R. 2008. "Evaluating Offending Behaviour Programmes: Does Only Randomization Glister?" *Criminology and Criminal Justice* 8:89–106.

Jamieson, Ruth, and Adrian Grounds. 2005. "Release and Adjustment: Perspectives from Studies of Wrongly Convicted and Politically Motivated Prisoners." In *The Effects of Imprisonment*, edited by Alison Liebling and Shad Maruna. Devon, UK: Willan.

Keeling, Jenny A., and John L. Rose. 2006. "The Adaptation of a Cognitive-Behavioural Treatment Programme for Special Needs Sexual Offenders." *British Journal of Learning Disabilities* 34:110–116.

Keeling, Jenny A., John L. Rose, and Anthony R. Beech. 2007. "Comparing Sexual Offender Treatment Efficacy: Mainstream Sexual Offenders and Sexual Offenders with Special Needs." *Journal of Intellectual and Developmental Disability* 32:117–124.

Kemshall, Hazel, and Jason Wood. 2009. "Community Strategies for Managing High-Risk Offenders: The Contribution of Multi-Agency Public Protection Arrangements." In *Assessment and Treatment of Sex Offenders: A Handbook*, edited by Anthony Beech, Leam A. Craig, and Kevin D. Browne. Chichester, UK: Wiley.

Kokish, Ron. 2003. "The Current Role of Post-Conviction Sex Offender Polygraph Testing in Sex Offender Treatment." *Journal of Child Sexual Abuse* 12:175–194.

Larsen, Jillian, Paul Robertson, David Hillman, and Stephen M. Hudson. 1998. "Te Piriti: A Bicultural Model for Treating Child Molesters in Aotearoa/New Zealand." In *Sourcebook of Treatment Programs for Sexual Offenders*, edited by William L. Marshall, Yolanda M. Fernandez, Stephen M. Hudson, and Tony Ward. New York: Plenum.

Laws, D. Richard. 2009. "Penile Plethysmography: Strengths, Limitations, Innovations." In *Cognitive Approaches to the Assessment of Sexual Interest in Sexual Offenders*, edited by David Thornton and D. Richard Laws. Chichester, UK: Wiley.

Laws, D. Richard, Stephen M. Hudson, and Tony Ward. 2000. *Remaking Relapse Prevention with Sex Offenders: A Sourcebook.* Newbury Park, CA: Sage.

Levenson, Jill S., and Leo P. Cotter. 2005. "The Impact of Sex Offender Residence Restrictions: 1000 Feet from Danger or One Step from Absurd?" *International Journal of Offender and Comparative Criminology* 49:168–178.

Looman, Jan, Jeffrey Abracen, Ralph Serin, and Peter Marquis. 2005. "Psychopathy, Treatment Change and Recidivism in High Risk and High Need Sexual Offenders." *Journal of Interpersonal Violence* 20:549–568.

Lord, Alex, and Phil Willmot. 2004. "The Process of Overcoming Denial in Sexual Offenders." *Journal of Sexual Aggression* 10:51–61.

Lösel, Friedrich, and Martin Schmucker. 2005. "The Effectiveness of Treatment for Sexual Offenders: A Comprehensive Meta-Analysis." *Journal of Experimental Criminology* 1:117–146.

Lowenkamp, Christopher T., Edward J. Latessa, and Alexander M. Holsinger. 2006. "The Risk Principle in Action: What Have We Learned from 13,676 Offenders and 97 Correctional Programs?" *Crime & Delinquency* 52:77–93.

Mandeville-Norden, Rebecca, Anthony Beech, and Elizabeth Hayes. 2008. "Examining the Effectiveness of a UK Community-Based Sexual Offender Treatment Programme for Child Abusers." *Psychology, Crime & Law* 14:493–512.

Mann, Ruth E., and Georgia D. Barnett. 2013. "Victim Empathy Intervention with Sexual Offenders: Rehabilitation, Punishment, or Correctional Quackery?" *Sexual Abuse: A Journal of Research and Treatment* 25:282–301.

Mann, Ruth E., and Anthony R. Beech. 2003. "Cognitive Distortions, Schemas and Implicit Theories." In *Sexual Deviance: Issues and Controversies*, edited by Tony Ward, D. Richard Laws, and Stephen M. Hudson. Thousand Oaks, CA: Sage.

Mann, Ruth E., R. Karl Hanson, and David Thornton. 2010. "Assessing Risk for Sexual Recidivism: Some Proposals on the Nature of Psychologically Meaningful Risk Factors." *Sexual Abuse: A Journal of Research and Treatment* 22:191–217.

Mann, Ruth E., and William L. Marshall. 2009. "Advances in the Treatment of Adult Incarcerated Sex Offenders." In *Assessment and Treatment of Sex Offenders: A Handbook*, edited by Anthony Beech, Leam A. Craig, and Kevin D. Browne. Chichester, UK: Wiley.

Mann, Ruth E., Stephen D. Webster, Caroline Schofield, and William L. Marshall. 2004. "Approach Versus Avoidance Goals in Relapse Prevention with Sexual Offenders." *Sexual Abuse: A Journal of Research and Treatment* 16:65–75.

Marques, Janice K., Mark Wiederanders, David M. Day, Craig Nelson, and Alice Van Ommeren. 2005. "Effects of a Relapse Prevention Program on Sexual Recidivism: Final Results from California's Sex Offender Treatment and Evaluation Project (SOTEP)." *Sexual Abuse: A Journal of Research and Treatment* 17:79–107.

Marshall, William L. 1989. "Invited Essay: Intimacy, Loneliness and Sexual Offending." *Behaviour Research Therapy* 27(5): 491–503.

Marshall, William L. 2005. "Therapist Style in Sexual Offender Treatment: Influences on Indices of Change." *Sexual Abuse: A Journal of Research and Treatment* 17:109–116.

Marshall, William L. 2006. "Appraising Treatment Outcome with Sexual Offenders." In *Sexual Offender Treatment: Controversial Issues*, edited by William L. Marshall, Yolanda M. Fernandez, Liam E. Marshall, and Geris E. Serran. Chichester, UK: Wiley.

Marshall, William L., Liam E. Marshall, Gerris A. Serran, and Yolanda M. Fernandez. 2006. *Treating Sexual Offenders: An Integrated Approach.* New York: Routledge.

Marshall, William L., Liam E. Marshall, Gerris A. Serran, and Matt D. O'Brien. 2011. *Rehabilitating Sexual Offenders: A Strength-Based Approach*. Washington, DC: American Psychological Association.

Marshall, William L., Liam E. Marshall, Gerris A. Serran, and Matt D. O'Brien. 2013. "What Works to Reduce Sexual Offending." In *What Works in Offender Rehabilitation*, edited by Leam A. Craig, Louise Dixon, and Theresa A. Gannon. Chichester, UK: Wiley-Blackwell.

Marshall, William L., Matt D. O'Brien, and Liam E. Marshall. 2009. "Modifying Sexual Preferences." In *Assessment and Treatment of Sex Offenders: A Handbook*, edited by Anthony Beech, Leam A. Craig, and Kevin D. Browne. Chichester, UK: Wiley.

Marshall, William L., and Gerris A. Serran. 2004. "The Role of the Therapist in Offender Treatment." *Psychology, Crime & Law* 10:309–320.

Marshall, William L., Gerris A. Serran, Yolanda M. Fernandez, R. Mulloy, R. E. Mann, and D. Thornton. 2003. "Therapist Characteristics in the Treatment of Sexual Offenders: Tentative Data on Their Relationship with Indices of Behaviour Change." *Journal of Sexual Aggression* 9:25–30.

Marshall, William L., David Thornton, Liam E. Marshall, Yolanda M. Fernandez, and Ruth Mann. 2001. "Treatment of Sexual Offenders Who Are in Categorical Denial: A Pilot Project." *Sexual Abuse: A Journal of Research and Treatment* 13:205–215.

McGrath, Robert J., Michael P. Lasher, and Georgia F. Cumming. 2012. "The Sex Offender Treatment Intervention and Progress Scale (SOTIPS): Psychometric Properties and Incremental Predictive Validity with the Static-99R." *Sexual Abuse: A Journal of Research and Treatment* 24:431–458.

McWhinnie, Andrew J., Robin J. Wilson, and Robert E. Brown. 2013. "Circles of Support and Accountability: Dimensions of Practice, Research and Inter-Agency Collaboration in Prisoner Re-Entry." *Criminal Justice Research Review* 14(5): 98–106.

Moos, Rudolf H. 1994. *Group Environment Scale Manual*, 3rd ed. Palo Alto, CA: Consulting Psychologists Press.

Murphy, Glynis, and Neil Sinclair. 2009. "Treatment for Men with Intellectual Disabilities and Sexually Abusive Behaviour." In *Assessment and Treatment of Sex Offenders: A Handbook*, edited by Anthony Beech, Leam A. Craig, and Kevin D. Browne. Chichester, UK: Wiley.

Nathan, Lavinia, Nick J. Wilson, and David Hillman. 2003. *Te Whakakotahitanga: An Evaluation of the Te Piriti Special Treatment Programme for Child Sex Offenders in New Zealand*. Wellington, NZ: Department of Corrections Psychological Services.

New Zealand Government Statistician. 2012. Maori Population Grows and More Live Longer. www.stats.govt.nz/tools_and_services/media-centre/additional-releases/maori-population-estimates-15-nov-2012.aspx

Nobles, Matt R., Jill S. Levenson, and Tasha J. Youstin. 2012. "Effectiveness of Residence Restrictions in Preventing Sex Offense Recidivism." *Crime & Delinquency* 58:491–513.

Nunes, Kevin L., Kelly M. Babchishin, and Franca Cortoni. 2011. "Measuring Treatment Change in Sex Offenders: Clinical and Statistical Significance." *Criminal Justice and Behavior* 38:157–173.

O'Donohue, William, and Elizabeth Letourneau. 1992. "The Psychometric Properties of the Penile Tumescence Assessment of Child Molesters." *Journal of Psychopathology and Behavioral Assessment* 14:123–174.

Olver, Mark E., Sarah M. Beggs Christofferson, Randolph C. Grace, and Stephen C. P. Wong. 2014. "Incorporating Change Information into Sexual Offender Risk Assessments Using the Violence Risk Scale–Sexual Offender Version." *Sexual Abuse: A Journal of Research and Treatment* 26:472–499.

Olver, Mark E., and Stephen C. P. Wong. 2011. "A Comparison of Static and Dynamic Assessment of Sex Offender Risk and Need in a Treatment Context." *Criminal Justice and Behavior* 38:113–126.

Olver, Mark E., and Stephen C. P. Wong. 2013. "A Description and Research Review of the Clearwater Sex Offender Treatment Programme." *Psychology, Crime & Law* 19:477–492.

Olver, Mark E., Stephen C. P. Wong, Terry Nicholaichuk, and Audrey Gordon. 2007. "The Validity and Reliability of the Violence Risk Scale–Sexual Offender Version: Assessing Sex Offender Risk and Evaluating Therapeutic Change." *Psychological Assessment* 19:318–329.

Polaschek, Devon L. L. 2012. "An Appraisal of the Risk-Need-Responsivity Model of Offender Rehabilitation and Its Application in Correctional Treatment." *Legal and Criminological Psychology* 17:1–17.

Polaschek, Devon L. L., and Lucy L. King. 2002. "Rehabilitating Rapists: Reconsidering the Issues." *Australian Psychologist* 37:215–221.

Price, Shelley A., Anthony R. Beech, Ian Mitchell, and Glyn W. Humphreys. 2013. "Measuring Deviant Sexual Interests Using the Emotional Stroop Task." *Criminal Justice and Behavior* 40:970–987.

Prochaska, James O., Carlo C. DiClemente, and John C. Norcross. 1992. "In Search of How People Change: Applications to Addictive Behaviors." *American Psychologist* 47:1102–1114.

Queensland Corrective Services. 2010. Rehabilitative Needs and Treatment of Indigenous Offenders in Queensland. Operational Strategy and Research, Queensland Corrective Services. http://www.premiers.qld.gov.au/publications.aspx

Sakdalan, Joseph Allan, and Vicki Collier. 2012. "Piloting an Evidence-Based Group Treatment Programme for High Risk Sex Offenders with Intellectual Disability in the New Zealand Setting." *New Zealand Journal of Psychology* 41(3): 6–12.

Salter, Anna. 1988. *Treating Child Sex Offenders and Victims: A Practical Guide.* Newbury Park, CA: Sage.

Schmucker, Martin, and Friedrich Lösel. 2008. "Does Sexual Offender Treatment Work? A Systematic Review of Outcome Evaluations." *Psicotherma* 20:10–19.

Scoones, Carwyn D., Gwenda M. Willis, and Randolph C. Grace. 2012. "Beyond Static and Dynamic Risk Factors: The Incremental Validity of Release Planning for Predicting Sex Offender Recidivism." *Journal of Interpersonal Violence* 27:222–238.

Shuker, Richard. 2013. "Treating Offenders in a Therapeutic Community." In *What Works in Offender Rehabilitation*, edited by Leam A. Craig, Louise Dixon, and Theresa A. Gannon. Chichester, UK: Wiley-Blackwell.

Sex Offender Treatment Services Collaborative—Intellectual Disabilities (SOTSEC-ID) 2010. "Effectiveness of Group Cognitive-Behavioural Treatment for Men with Intellectual Disabilities at Risk of Sexual Offending." *Journal of Applied Research in Intellectual Disability* 23:537–551.

Statistics New Zealand. 2012. New Zealand Official Yearbook: 2012 Yearbook Tables by Topic. http://www.stats.govt.nz/browse_for_stats/snapshots-of-nz/yearbook/yearbook-tables. aspx

Tamatea, Armon J., and Tansy Brown. 2011. "Culture and Offender Rehabilitation in New Zealand: Implications for Programme Delivery and Development." In *Effective Interventions with Offenders: Lessons Learned*, edited by Ken McMaster and David Riley. Christchurch, NZ: Hall, McMaster and Associates.

Tan, Lavinia, and Randolph C. Grace. 2008. "Social Desirability and Sexual Offenders: A Review." *Sexual Abuse: A Journal of Research and Treatment* 20:61–87.

Thornton, David, and D. Richard Laws (eds.). 2009. Cognitive Approaches to the Assessment of Sexual Interest in Sexual Offenders. New York: John Wiley and Sons.

Tuckman, Bruce W. 1965. "Developmental Sequence in Small Groups." Psychological Bulletin 63:384–399.

van Rensburg, Jim. 2012. "The Dawn of Circles of Support and Accountability in New Zealand." Sexual Abuse in Australia and New Zealand 4(2): 53–58.

Vanhoeck, Kris, and Els Van Daele. 2011. "Denial of Sexual Crimes: A Therapeutic Exploration." In International Perspectives on the Assessment and Treatment of Sexual Offenders: Theory, Practice, and Research, edited by Douglas P. Boer, Reinhard Eher, Leam A. Craig, Michael H. Miner, and Friedemann Pfäfflin. Chichester, UK: Wiley.

Wakeling, Helen, Anthony R. Beech, and Nick Freemantle. 2013. "Investigating Treatment Change and Its Relationship to Recidivism in a Sample of 3,773 Sex Offenders in the UK." Psychology, Crime & Law 19:233–252.

Wakeling, Helen C., Ruth E. Mann, and Adam J. Carter. 2012. "Do Low-Risk Sexual Offenders Need Treatment?" The Howard Journal of Crime and Justice 51:286–299.

Ward, T., Bickley, J., Stephen D. Webster, Dawn D. Fisher, Beech, Anthony R., and Hilary Eldridge. 2004. The Self-Regulation Model of the Offense and Relapse Process: Vol. 1, Assessment. Victoria, BC: Pacific Psychological Assessment Corporation/Trafford.

Ward, Tony, Theresa A. Gannon, and Astrid Birgden. 2007. "Human Rights and the Treatment of Sex Offenders." Sexual Abuse: A Journal of Research and Treatment 19:195–216.

Ward, Tony, and Stephen M. Hudson. 2000. "A Self-Regulation Model of Relapse Prevention." In Remaking Relapse Prevention with Sex Offenders: A Sourcebook, edited by D. Richard Laws, Stephen M. Hudson, and Tony Ward. Newbury Park, CA: Sage.

Ward, Tony, Stephen M. Hudson, and Thomas Keenan. 1998. "A Self-Regulation Model of the Sexual Offense Process." Sexual Abuse: A Journal of Research and Treatment 10:141–157.

Ward, Tony, Stephen M. Hudson, and William L. Marshall. 1996. "Attachment Style in Sex Offenders: A Preliminary Study." The Journal of Sex Research 33:17–26.

Ward, Tony, Devon Polaschek, and Anthony R. Beech. 2006. Theories of Sexual Offending. Chichester, UK: Wiley.

Ward, Tony, and Richard J. Siegert. 2002. "Toward a Comprehensive Theory of Child Sexual Abuse: A Theory Knitting Perspective." Psychology, Crime & Law 8:319–351.

Ward, Tony, and Claire Stewart. 2003. "The Treatment of Sex Offenders: Risk Management and Good Lives." Professional Psychology: Research and Practice 34:353–360.

Ward, Tony, Pamela M. Yates, and Carole A. Long. 2006. The Self-Regulation Model of the Offense and Relapse Process: Vol. 2, Treatment. Victoria, BC: Pacific Psychological Assessments Corporation.

Ware, Jayson, and David A. Bright. 2008. "Evolution of a Treatment Programme for Sex Offenders: Changes to the NSW Custody-Based Intensive Treatment (CUBIT)." Psychiatry, Psychology and Law 15:340–349.

Ware, Jayson, Andrew Frost, and Anna Hoy. 2009. "A Review of the Use of Therapeutic Communities with Sexual Offenders." International Journal of Offender Therapy and Comparative Criminology 54:721–742.

Ware, Jayson, Ruth E. Mann, and Helen C. Wakeling. 2009. "Group Versus Individual Treatment: What Is the Best Modality for Treating Sexual Offenders?" Sexual Abuse in Australia and New Zealand 2:2–13.

Ware, Jayson, and William L. Marshall. 2008. "Treatment Engagement with a Sexual Offender Who Denies Committing the Offense." Clinical Case Studies 7:592–603.

Webster, Stephen D., Ruth E. Mann, Adam J. Carter, Julia Long, Rebecca J. Milner, Matt D. O'Brien, Helen C. Wakeling, and Nicola L. Ray. 2006. "Inter-Rater Reliability of Dynamic Risk Assessment with Sexual Offenders." *Psychology, Crime & Law* 12:439–452.

Wilcox, Daniel T. 2004. "Treatment of Intellectually Disabled Individuals Who Have Committed Sexual Offences: A Review of the Literature." *Journal of Sexual Aggression* 10(1): 85–110.

Williams, Fiona, and Ruth E. Mann. 2010. "The Treatment of Intellectually Disabled Sexual Offenders in the National Offender Management Service: The Adapted Sex Offender Treatment Programmes." In *Assessment and Treatment of Sexual Offenders with Intellectual Disabilities*, edited by Leam A. Craig, William R. Lindsay, and Kevin D. Browne. Chichester, UK: Wiley.

Willis, Gwenda M., and Randolph C. Grace. 2008. "The Quality of Community Reintegration Planning for Child Molesters: Effects on Sexual Recidivism." *Sexual Abuse: A Journal of Research and Treatment* 20:218–240.

Willis, Gwenda M., and Randolph C. Grace. 2009. "Assessment of Community Reintegration Planning for Sex Offenders: Poor Planning Predicts Recidivism." *Criminal Justice and Behavior* 36:494–512.

Willis, Gwenda M., and Tony Ward. 2013. "What Works to Reduce Sexual Offending." In *What Works in Offender Rehabilitation*, edited by Leam A. Craig, Louise Dixon, and Theresa A. Gannon. Chichester, UK: Wiley-Blackwell.

Willis, Gwenda M., Tony Ward, and Jill S. Levenson. 2014. "The Good Lives Model (GLM): An Evaluation of GLM Operationalisation in North American Treatment Programs." *Sexual Abuse: A Journal of Research and Treatment* 26:58–81.

Wilson, Nick J., T. Glen Kilgour, and Devon Polaschek. 2013. "Treating High Risk Rapists in a New Zealand Intensive Prison Programme." *Psychology, Crime & Law*. 19:527–547

Wilson, Robin J., Franca Cortoni, and Andrew J. McWhinnie. 2009. "Circles of Support and Accountability: A Canadian National Replication of Outcome Findings." *Sexual Abuse: A Journal of Research and Treatment* 21:412–430.

Wong, Stephen, Mark E. Olver, Terry P. Nicholaichuk, and Audrey Gordon. 2003. *The Violence Risk Scale—Sexual Offender Version (VRS-SO)*. Saskatoon, SK: Regional Psychiatric Centre, Department of Psychology and Research.

Yates, Pamela M., David Prescott, and Tony Ward. 2010. *Applying the Good Lives and Self-Regulation Models to Sex Offender Treatment: A Practical Guide for Clinicians*. Brandon, VT: Safer Society Press.

Yates, Pamela M., Tony Ward, and Drew A. Kingston. 2009. *The Self-Regulation Model of the Offense and Relapse Process: Vol. 3, A Guide to Assessment and Treatment Planning Using the Integrated Good Lives/Self-Regulation Model of Sexual Offending*. Victoria, BC: Pacific Psychological Assessments Corporation.

Zevitz, Richard G., and Mary Ann Farkas. 2004. "Sex Offender Community Notification: Managing High Risk Criminals or Exacting Further Vengeance?" In *About Criminals: A View of the Offender's World*, edited by M. Pogrebin. Thousand Oaks, CA: Sage.

CHAPTER 22

....

THE MULTIPLE FACES
OF REENTRY

....

SUSAN TURNER

IN March 2014, the US president's budget included $115 million in continued support for
Second Chance Act (SCA) programs, extending for an additional five years programs and
services aimed at reintegrating prisoners into their communities. The reauthorization highlights the national focus on prisoner reentry in recent years. Each year, hundreds of thousands of inmates are released from prison back into their communities, and many fail, only
to return to prison. In 2012, releases from US prisons numbered 637,400. Nearly a third of
admissions that year were for parole violations (Carson and Golinelli 2013), representing
failures during supervision in the community after release.

Much has been written on the needs of offenders as they return home (Petersilia 2003,
2007; Visher et al. 2004), what offenders experience as they transition from prison to the
community (Maruna 2001), and the impact of incarceration on communities (Clear, Rose,
and Ryder 2001; Lynch and Sabol 2001; Sabol and Lynch 2003; Clear, Waring, and Scully
2005). This essay does not summarize these bodies of work. Rather, it focuses on programs
and approaches that are part of the reentry process. For purposes of discussion, *reentry* is
conceptualized broadly as a three-phase process beginning at prison admission, to preparation for release, and finally to release and supervision in the community. I use a broad
approach to paint a picture of programming in the prisons, supervision and programs in
the community, and the rise of newer models of collaboration across agencies. The essay
begins with a discussion of in-prison programming, followed by postprison reentry programming. I then discuss collaborative models of reentry and the federal government's role
in funding reentry efforts.

The main conclusions of the essay are as follows:

- Across the United States, prisons provide a variety of programs, including academic
  and career education, prison work activities, and, more recently prerelease skills.
  However, many offenders do not take part in these programs before release. Tight
  economic times have frequently resulted in cuts to rehabilitation programs in prisons.
- The majority of offenders released from prison are placed under some kind of supervision in the community. A wide variety of services are provided, including drug, sex

offender, and mental health treatment; help finding housing; and employment assistance. Based on surveys, small percentages are receiving services; most likely many more are in need of them. Although the effectiveness of postrelease supervision has not been sufficiently validated, guidelines for successful supervision have been developed.
- Collaborative models that involve multiple agencies in the community (including corrections, health, and social services) have been developed by a number of organizations; these models share key approaches and components.
- The federal government has supported a number of reentry efforts over the past 15 years; however, there is currently no central coordinating agency, and small percentages of released offenders participate in the various programs.

I. In-Prison Programming

As noted earlier, this essay envisions prison reentry as starting when offenders enter the prison system, rather than focusing only on the end of an inmate's prison term. This allows an examination of programs and services provided during an inmate's entire length of stay and highlights reentry as a continuum, with each phase integrated with a previous phase (Taxman, Young, and Byrne 2003). Each year hundreds of thousands of inmates enter state and federal facilities in the United States. In 2012, there were over 600,000 state and federal admissions to prison (Carson and Golinelli 2013). Prisons balance two missions—trying to keep institutions safe and secure for inmates and staff while protecting the public from escapes, as well as providing programming to inmates (Seiter 2014). Prisoners participate in a number of programs designed to provide rehabilitative services (e.g., academic and vocational programs, substance abuse programs), whereas other programs provide operational assistance to the prison in performing basic functions related to maintenance, food preparation, and clerical activities.

Our best national picture of program offerings and inmate participation comes from periodic surveys of state and federal prison inmates conducted by the Bureau of Justice Statistics (BJS). The surveys began in the late 1970s in an effort to collect data to assist policymakers in addressing what was then viewed as overcrowded prisons and deteriorating living conditions. They have documented (among other variables) the extent to which prisons offer programming of different types as well the participation levels of inmates. Although individual items contained on the survey as well as response options have changed over the years, the surveys provide a nationwide view of changes over time. The most recently available inmate survey at the time of this publication was fielded in 2004.

The BJS surveys show that between the early 1990s and mid-2000s, the types of programming offered reflect changes in educational and work related activities (see Table 22.1). The vast majority of prisons offer basic and secondary academic education. Since 1990, however, the percentage offering college courses has decreased, due to elimination of Pell Grants as part of the 1994 Crime Act (as amended). Vocational training, often referred to as career technical education, has been offered by about half of all state prisons; work release, however, has declined during the time period. Study release offerings have also dropped dramatically, from slightly over a third to fewer than 5 percent, a reflection of negative media

Table 22.1. Percentage of US state and federal prisons with program offerings

Variable	1974 state (N = 592)	1979 state (N = 791)	1984 state (N = 903)	1990 state (N = 1129)	1995 state (N = 1262)	2000 state (N = 1295)	2005 state (N = 1294)	1990 federal (N=80)	1995 federal (N=112)	2000 federal (N = 84)	2005 federal (N = 102)
Basic education	—	64.2	63.7	79.3	76.2	80.2	78.3	93.8	91.7	89.3	98.0
Secondary education	86.8*	37.9	68.3	80.3	80.3	83.2	85.5	93.8	100.0	90.5	98.0
College	59.0	46.5	47.4	59.3	31.5	26.6	35.6	85.0	68.8	73.8	98.0
Special education	—	19.3	27.6	49.7	33.6	39.7	39.1	65.0	34.8	54.8	98.0
Vocational training	77.2	49.6	46.5	50.9	54.8	55.8	57.4	62.5	73.2	85.7	98.0
Work release	61.7	51.2	41.3	31.4	28.8	24.9	22.0	3.8	0.0	20.2	2.0
Study release	41.0	35.0	—	35.6	9.2	7.2	4.7	3.8	5.4	5.6	0.0
Facility support	—	—	74.6	88.3	91.0	88.6	85.4	97.5	96.4	91.7	98.0
Prison industries	27.5	—	56.6	34.8	36.8	37.1	35.7	77.5	80.4	80.9	86.3
Farm	—	—	22.7	28.3	27.5	26.6	21.7	15.0	15.2	7.1	2.0
Public work	—	—	—	51.8	55.9	63.6	56.5	20.0	33.0	39.3	0.0
Life skills	—	—	—	46.5	64.1	68.7	79.8	50.0	82.1	89.3	98.0
Parenting	—	—	—	15.9	34.4	42.2	44.2	25.0	88.4	88.1	97.1
Other job	—	—	—	42.6	57.7	62.0	74.8	36.2	72.3	88.1	98.0
Other	—	—	—	1.1	18.8	26.9	16.2	0.0	7.1	13.1	0.0

Note:
* Combination of basic and secondary education for 1974 survey; analyses conducted by author on Bureau of Justice Statistics surveys.

around crimes committed by offenders released from incarceration who commit violent acts, such as Willie Horton. Over the past 20 years, almost all states have provided facility support—or activities directly related to the operations of prisons (e.g., clerical, grounds keeping)—although those offering prison industries services, in which offenders may have the opportunity to learn trades and skills relevant to the outside job market, have been consistently low at less than 40 percent. Despite the fact that the more traditional program offerings have remained fairly steady or have decreased, the surveys suggest that "reentry" programs—life skills, parenting, and employment programs—have been on the rise (see also Phelps 2011, 2012).

How do these play out in terms of offender participation? Table 22.2 shows that, despite fairly high percentages of state prison systems offering programs, the reality is that relatively few inmates participate in them. The past 20 years has seen a downward trend in participation in academic and vocational education but not in work assignments. And, over this same time period, the median hours worked by those inmates with jobs has dropped from 33 to 20 hours per week. Rates of pay are low, often cents per hour (see Table 22.3). Participation in drug and alcohol programs is also low. In 1997, of those inmates who had used drugs the month before committing their offense, 34.3 percent of state inmates and 38.8 percent of federal inmates reported having been in treatment since their admission to prison. In 2004, the percentages had risen to 39.2 percent for state and 45.3 percent for federal inmates. Self-help group/peer counseling and drug education programs were the most frequently attended. Fewer than 10 percent of inmates who had used drugs the month before committing their offense participated in a residential facility or unit (Mumola and Karberg 2006).

Program participation *is* low. To make matters worse, when we examine participation by offender program need, we also see a mismatch of need and services provisions. Petersilia (2003, 2007) selected soon-to-be-released inmates and classified them according to need for receiving relevant programs, as defined by their histories before prison entry. Her analysis showed that only 36.5 percent of state inmates with a high need for alcohol treatment participated in a treatment program; 39.6 of those with a high drug need participated in a drug program; 63.1 percent of those with high mental health needs received treatment; and 52.4 percent of those with high education/employment needs participated in a relevant program (Petersilia 2003, 2005). In California, fewer than 15 percent of moderate- to high-risk inmates released in fiscal year 2012–2013 had all of their treatment/programming needs met by the time they were released from prison, despite a concerted effort since 2007 to increase rehabilitation services (California Department of Corrections and Rehabilitation 2007; California Rehabilitation Oversight Board 2013).

In 2003, the federal government funded nearly 70 agencies to develop programs to improve criminal justice, employment, education, health, and housing outcomes for released prisoners under the Serious and Violent Offender Reentry Initiative (SVORI). In their evaluation of the effort, Lattimore, Steffey, and Visher (2010) found that even high-risk prisoners targeted for facilitated reentry programming did not reach levels one might expect. Although SVORI participants received more services and programming than a control group of offenders, they were not as high as anticipated. As an example, 30 days prior to release, 57 percent of SVORI participants reported having a reentry plan, compared to 24 percent of the control group (Lattimore, Steffey, and Visher 2010).

Why is there so much concern about program participation? In addition to program participation as a good management technique to maintain control and safety in the prison,

Table 22.2. Percentage of prisoners in US state and federal prisons who participated in program offerings

Program	1974	1979	1986	1991 state	1997 state	2004 state	1991 federal	1997 federal	2004 federal
Basic education	–	–	–	5.3	3.1	2.0	10.4	1.8	1.5
Secondary education	–	–	–	27.4	23.3	19.3	27.3	22.7	23.3
College	–	–	–	14.0	9.6	7.2	18.9	12.7	10.5
Any academic	22.2	27.1	45.3	43.6	33.5	27.1	56.3	34.5	33.1
Vocational training	27.3	31.1	19.8	31.4	31.7	27.3	29.5	28.8	31.6
Work release	5.4	8.9	10.6	9.7	10.5	7.4	.4	4.3	1.7
Work assignment	74.4	72.7	65.8	69.9	68.5	65.6	91.3	89.4	90.4
General janitorial	7.6	10.2	11.5	13.4	16.2	18.4	11.7	18.3	21.9
Grounds or road	3.3	7.3	4.8	8.2	7.5	7.9	6.5	6.9	7.5
Food preparation	11.5	11.6	12.5	12.6	12.4	11.9	13.0	15.0	14.3
Laundry	3.5	3.3	2.8	3.0	3.2	3.2	2.3	1.9	2.0
Hospital/medical	1.8	1.2	0.8	0.5	0.7	0.6	1.7	0.9	1.1
Farming/forestry	6.8	8.0	3.5	3.9	3.8	2.2	0.4	0.7	0.4
Goods production	9.7	4.9	4.2	4.3	4.0	3.3	2.9	17.3	11.7
Other prison service	6.2	17.6	7.7	8.0	6.3	6.6	14.9	10.2	12.5
Maintenance or repair	8.0	8.1	7.0	8.8	6.4	5.0	14.6	11.0	10.6
Other	15.4	0.4	11.1	12.0	11.6	10.3	24.9	9.6	9.8

Note: Analyses conducted by author on Bureau of Justice Statistics surveys.

Table 22.3. Inmate hours assigned and pay scales

Variable	1974 state	1979 state	1986 state	1991 state	1997 state	2004 state	1991 federal	1997 federal	2004 federal
Median hours worked per week	40.0	40.0	36.0	33.0	30.0	20.0	38.0	35.0	35.0
Median rate per hour	.13	.17	.25	.38	.32	.31	.14	.17	.21
Median rate per day	.55	.90	1.00	1.05	1.10	1.05	4.40	4.00	5.18
Median rate per week	3.75	4.75	6.13	6.96	5.25	5.50	11.60	20.00	10.00
Median rate per month	10.50	15.00	18.50	26.00	20.00	20.00	19.00	20.00	21.00
% paid for work (of those who work)	64.90	64.30	71.80	67.40	58.60	57.80	97.60	98.50	97.00

Note: Analyses conducted by author on Bureau of Justice Statistics surveys.

program participation can be effective in reducing individual offender recidivism after release from custody. Although the field's embrace of rehabilitative programming as crime control has fluctuated dramatically since Martinson's (1974) negative conclusions on the effectiveness of correctional programming over 40 years ago (see also Lipton, Martinson, and Wilks 1975), more recent analyses have demonstrated the effectiveness of a number of correctional programs and interventions. Reviews by MacKenzie (2006, 2012) and meta-analyses conducted by the Washington State Institute of Public Policy (Aos, Miller, and Drake 2006) show reductions in recidivism for a number of programs, including drug treatment, education, vocational programs, and cognitive behavioral interventions. A meta-analysis of correctional and vocational education completed by the RAND Corporation showed a 13 percentage-point reduction in recidivism and a 13 percent higher odds of obtaining employment (Davis 2013). Unfortunately, funding for recidivism reduction programs is not always assured. As the economy tightened in the Great Recession, many states faced a number of trade-offs in funding services for their citizens. Forty-four states responding to a Vera Institute (2010) survey reported an overall 1 percent decrease in total 2011 appropriations for corrections (although 19 states reported increases in budgets). States have been responding to recent fiscal pressures in corrections in a number of ways, such as reducing staffing, closing prisons, reducing food service charges, and introducing new technology and energy efficiency. Twenty-two of the states indicated reducing or eliminating programs as a way to reduce costs. Many states in the survey reported using American Recovery and Reinvestment Act funds to pay for corrections expenses; however, these funds were mostly expended by fiscal year 2012 (Vera Institute 2010).

As an example of cost-cutting to correctional programming, in 2009 the California Department of Corrections and Rehabilitation proposed cuts to adult offender rehabilitation programs, reducing headquarters staff, and creating new efficiencies to save over $280 million in response to the department's plan to achieve a $1.2 billion budget reduction. The department cut $250 million in rehabilitation programs for adult offenders, including layoffs of more than 700 teachers. These reductions impacted education, vocational, substance abuse, and other programs for inmates and parolees and represented over a third of the adult programs budget (California Department of Corrections and Rehabilitation 2009). Although programming dollars have increased since the cut, program capacity remains less than what it was before the budget cuts (California Rehabilitation Oversight Board 2013).

Given the mixed findings described here, most would agree that preparation for return to the community while in prison is not optimal. We turn next to services and programs offenders receive as they transition into the community.

II. Post-Prison Reentry

Although the vast majority of offenders are released into the community after serving their prison terms, many are no longer released onto parole via a traditional parole board (see Rhine [2012] for a comprehensive description). Most are still managed, however, under some form of mandatory supervision. The most recent statistics from BJS for 2012 show that 408,186 inmates were released conditionally (e.g., supervised release, probation). An additional 213,204 were released unconditionally through expiration of sentence, commutations, and so on (Carson and Golinelli 2013). Thus for more than a third of inmates leaving prisons annually, no supervision is provided and the potential formal link in a phased reentry model from prison to the community is not available. These are national rates; states vary greatly in their use of release strategies. For example, California releases virtually all its prisoners (over 97 percent) to conditional release, but virtually none of the releases is discretionary (i.e., made by a parole board). In contrast, over 70 percent of Virginia prisoners are released unconditionally.

A. Release Decisions and Reentry Challenges

Although the majority of offenders receive postrelease supervision, do the supervision and services in the community after release really help offenders? We know, for example, that the most vulnerable time for returning offenders is right after release. From a reentry or public safety view, this would argue for supervised release and provision of services in an effort not only to help the offender reintegrate into society but also to increase public safety, with the swift detection of violations of release conditions or new criminal behaviors. However, others argue from a just-desserts viewpoint that once an offender has "done the time," his or her debt to society has been paid. Why should an offender serve more time under supervision in the community? Perhaps offenders would be well served by supervision programs, such as earned discharge, that allow them to reduce the time under supervision for good behavior (Travis and Petersilia 2001; Petersilia 2007; Smith, Omori, Turner, and Jannetta 2012). Of course the choice is not that simple. States currently use a variety of sentencing and release structures that complicate the hand-off into the community and impact reentry. Traditionally, most offenders are released by a parole board after serving indeterminate sentences. The hope is that, upon release, the offender is ready for a successful return to the community. With the surge of determinate sentencing structures in the 1970s, many states are now required to release inmates based on time served calculations who may not be "ready" for parole/postrelease supervision; thus many offenders may now be at higher risk of recidivism than in the past.

B. What Do They Get Under Supervision?

As many observers note, parole has moved from a focus on social services to one largely of surveillance over the past several decades (Petersilia 2003), although the surveillance model has softened somewhat as the field has embraced the risk-needs-responsivity approach advanced by Andrews, Ivan Zinger, and colleagues (1990; Andrews and Bonta 2010; see also Goggin this volume). What do people receive in terms of services while on parole? I address this question next.

The BJS conducted a census of state parole supervising agencies in 2006 (Bonczar 2008), collecting information from 52 state agencies. Nearly all parole agencies surveyed reported requiring parolees to abide by one or more conditions of supervision when released into the community. Conditions can include drug testing, payment of supervision fees, finding employment, and fulfilling treatment requirements (Bonczar 2008).

As in prison, persons placed under community supervision or parole participate in programs after their release. Many of these programs are required as a part of their terms and conditions of release. Parole supervising agencies also provide a number of services to parolees, such as drug, sex offender, and mental health treatment; help finding housing; and employment assistance. Drug, sex offender, and mental health treatment programs are provided by nearly all agencies. For those agencies supplying enrollment information, just under 11 percent of parolees were enrolled in drug treatment programs run by formally trained professionals; 17 percent were enrolled in self-help programs or drug awareness such as Narcotics Anonymous or Cocaine Anonymous. Fewer than 4 percent of parolees were enrolled in sex offender programs, and just under 1 percent (.9 percent) were enrolled in a mental health program operated by a trained professional (Bonzcar 2008). Two in five agencies operated or contracted with a housing service, and half of parole supervision agencies offered employment assistance, usually as part of a formal employment assistance program with a state or county employment agency, a contract with a private agency, or in-house employment service (Bonzcar 2008). Given high rates of mental illness (Glaze and James 2006; Steadman et al. 2009) and substance abuse that have been reported for prison and jail populations (Fazel, Bains, and Doll 2006), these percentages suggest only a fraction of those offenders who need services are receiving them after release from prison.

C. Does Supervision Itself Make a Difference?

As noted earlier, most offenders leaving prison are placed under supervision in the community when they leave the prison gates. Community supervision is used as both a surveillance tool and a social service mechanism and ideally prevents new crimes from occurring. The hope is that supervision will make a difference in offenders' lives. But does it? The answer to this question has been approached in a number of ways.

Ideally, one would conduct a study on the effectiveness of postrelease supervision using random assignment. Unfortunately, no such studies have been done. Several studies have examined the global question of whether supervision matters using nonexperimental designs. These studies are limited in that they are essentially taking supervision as a "black box"—not knowing the extent of either surveillance or rehabilitative programming to which offenders have been exposed. Rosenfeld, Wallman, and Fornango (2005) estimated the effects of supervision on rearrests over a three-year period from release from prison in 1994 in 13 states. Controlling for prisoner demographics, imprisonment offense, prior criminal history, and state from which the offender was released, the authors found that being released on discretionary parole was associated with 36 percent fewer arrests for violent crime, 30 percent fewer property crimes, and 17 percent fewer drug crimes relative to those released unconditionally. Mandatory supervised release was associated with fewer arrests for property crime, suggesting that parole release was more effective than supervision after mandatory release (Rosenfeld, Wallman, and Fornango 2005).

The Urban Institute examined this question using prison releases from the 1994 BJS surveys, comparing those who were released to parole supervision to those released without supervision in 15 states (representing two-thirds of all prisoners released nationwide in 1994). Analyses revealed that, two years after release, 54 percent of discretionary parolees were arrested compared to 61 percent of mandatory parolees (those released under determinate sentencing policies) and 62 percent of unconditional releasees (those who maxed out and were not under any supervision after release from prison). However, when offender-level characteristics (such as criminal history and age), characteristics of the community to which the prisoner was released, and state-level characteristics were taken into account, unconditional and mandatory release predicted probabilities of rearrest after two years were 61 percent, contrasted with 57 percent for discretionary parolees, suggesting minimal differences due to supervision status. Data were not available on the nature of supervision, however, so it is not clear whether any particular parole practices were associated with better outcomes. Even so, the results suggest that parole—at least as measured as basically a "black box"—may not provide much of an effect on recidivism (Solomon 2005).

Piehl and LuBuglio (2005, p. 136) in their answer to the question "Does supervision matter?" are not sanguine about the state of community supervision:

> The logic of community supervision and its long-standing and widespread practice suggests that it has the potential to be effective, but it is quite possible that policies or practices have evolved such that we have exceeded the optimal level of interference and are 'oversupervising.' As always, how much supervision matters and how much supervision can matter depend on the way the details are implemented. Unfortunately, the research literature does not provide clear lessons about how much and in what ways supervision matters directly to crime control. One reason that it is hard to know how supervision relates to crime control is the tremendous variation across states in supervision and other policies. This variation suggests two puzzles: why have we not learned more from these "50 experiments" in supervising those released from prison and why have we not observed convergence across states to a handful of models?
>
> Although one might think that the enormous variation in sentencing laws, discretionary release policies, and supervision practices across and within states would provide natural experiments from which to learn much about the effectiveness of supervision, the inability to cleanly delineate differences in supervision practices from system differences itself makes inference from cross-jurisdictional comparisons difficult.

How little we really know about parole supervision is also echoed in a recent review of parole by Taxman (2011). According to her analysis, "Studies with similar findings are not yet sufficient in number to conclusively establish a particular framework for supervising offenders in the field that would be most beneficial" (pp. 212–213). Certain strategies of parole supervision have been shown to be ineffective, including varying caseload size and increasing the intensity of supervision (see Petersilia and Turner 1993). However, other practices may be promising, including behavioral management. As yet, Taxman (2011, p. 219) states

> research that considers different theoretical models of parole is sorely lacking. It does appear that cognitive-behavioral therapy, motivational interviewing, a working alliance between parole officer and parolee, therapeutic communities, and heroin substitution are useful means of improving outcomes, but the lack of studies on parolees limits the strength of that statement. Further, we cannot be sure about the size of the effect and the sustainability of the effect. A need exists to understand how different roles of parole officers affect outcomes and whether one theoretical approach yields stronger outcomes.

Given the consensus of a lack of empirical evidence on the effectiveness of parole, it is somewhat ironic that the field has forged ahead with recommendations for reentry on a number of fronts. Drawing from two meetings on parole supervision with national experts, the Urban Institute outlined 13 parole strategies at the organizational and individual offender levels that are designed to enhance reentry outcomes by improving public safety and using taxpayer dollars wisely (Solomon et al. 2008). With an explicit acknowledgement that the field does not have enough adequate evaluations of specific parole strategies, the report utilized a broader knowledge base as well as expert and practitioner experience to develop recommendations.

At the organizational level, strategies recommended in their report include

- define success as recidivism reduction and measure agency performance against goals set for recidivism reduction;
- tailor conditions of supervision to the individual;
- focus resources on moderate- to high-risk parolees;
- provide resources to the offender shortly after release from prison as this time period represents the highest risk for failure in the community;
- implement earned discharge as an incentive in which offenders can reduce the length of supervision provided they abide by guidelines and meet goals;
- implement place-based supervision, in which officers supervise and collaborate with agencies in the communities where the offenders live; and
- engage partners in governmental and private agencies—such as treatment, education, employment—to expand intervention capacities.

Individual level supervision strategies that are believed to produce better outcomes include:

- assess criminogenic risk and needs factors;
- develop and implement supervision case plans that balance surveillance and treatment;
- involve parolees to enhance their engagement in assessment, case planning, and supervision;
- engage informal social controls to facilitate community reintegration;
- incorporate incentives and rewards into the supervision process; and
- employ graduated, problem-solving responses to violations of parole conditions in a swift and certain manner (Solomon et al. 2008, pp. 4–5).

In many of these recommendations, one can see the influence of the concepts central to the risk-needs-responsivity literature, which employs psychological constructs to help effect offender change and the use of cognitive-behavioral strategies (Andrews, Bonta, and Hoge 1990; Andrews, Ivan Zinger, et al. 1990; Goggin this volume). However, what is also apparent is the call for more than just a single agency approach (e.g., parole) to help change the postrelease behaviors of offenders. Among the 13 strategies are clear signals that the community and other players are regarded as essential in the reentry transition.

III. Collaborative Models for More Effective Reentry

More than a decade ago, Travis and Petersilia (2001) argued that we should abolish the system of parole as we know it and replace it with a seamless prison-to-community collaborative system that considers reentry as its primary goal. Such a system would encourage a model of transition to independence. By far the greatest interest lately in rentry has been in collaborative models to provide treatment and supervision to offenders while integrating the offender into the community, although seeds of this approach existed in the 1990s (Burke 1997). What are these collaborative models, and what have been their experiences? In this final section of the essay, integrated community reentry models are discussed.

A. Reentry Policy Council

Several national initiatives over the past 10 years have focused on reentry. The 2005 report of the Reentry Policy Council—an effort spearheaded by the Council of State Governments, in collaboration with 10 project partners and 100 key leaders at the state, local, and national levels—is perhaps the most comprehensive plan for reentry initiatives.

A multiagency focus is apparent in the press release for the report: "Nearly all of the 1.6 million people incarcerated in the United States will eventually be released. Implementing evidence-based plans that provide seamless services through state and local collaboratives can improve both individual and community outcomes" (Reentry Policy Council 2005). The report presents a set of 35 policy statements covering three major areas: planning a reentry initiative, the reentry process (from an institution to the community), and the elements of effective health and social service systems. According to the Reentry Policy Council (2005, p. xx), a successful reentry effort

> requires the development of policies and programs that promote the following: smart release and community supervision decisions; support for victims; and services support for re-entering individuals, including safe places to live, substance abuse treatment, education and employment, physical and mental health treatment, and meaningful relationships (with family, peers, partners, and the faith-community). Effective implementation of each of these policy statements requires collaboration between staff inside correctional facilities and people outside the walls, including community-based health care and social services providers, relatives, victims, and community members, such as representatives of faith-based institutions.

Table 22.4 shows the important steps at various points in the inmate's journey from arrest through release into the community. What is most apparent from this approach is the multiple action points as well as the vast number of items that must be addressed for successful reentry.

B. Transition from Prison to the Community Reentry

Before the work of the Reentry Policy Council, the National Institute on Corrections had adopted a comprehensive community framework for the transition from prison. In late 2000, the institute brought together practitioners and researchers to design a model that considered effective strategies in the context of operations with the overarching goal of enhancing public safety. Success included not only recidivism reduction but also increased

Table 22.4. Reentry Policy Council stages of reentry: From admission to the institution to return to the community

Admission to the Facility	Development of intake procedure
	Development of programming plan
Prison and Jail-Based Programming	Physical health care
	Mental health care
	Substance abuse treatment
	Make available services and support for children and families of inmates
	Provide programs aimed at behaviors and attitudes
	Education and vocational training
	Work experience
Making the Release Decision	Advising the release authority
	Release decision
Managing the Key Transition Period	Housing
	Planning continuity of care
	Creation of employment opportunities
	Workforce development and the transition plan
	Prepare victims, families, and communities for offender's return to the community
	Obtain identification and apply/receive public benefits
	Design of supervision strategy
Community Supervision	Implementation of supervision strategy
	Maintaining continuity of care
	Job development and supportive employment
	Graduated responses

Source: Re-Entry Policy Council (2005, pp. xxi–xxiv).

ability of offenders to become law-abiding, contributing members of their communities. Basic premises of the model included the following:

- Stakeholders include corrections, law enforcement, and human services agencies that articulate and promote common interests, integrate and coordinate policies, and develop mutual ownership of an improved transition process.
- Information should be shared among and within organizations involved in reentry efforts.
- Proven reforms and best practices should be used.
- Reforms should be affordable, transferable to other jurisdictions, and adaptable to local situations.
- Basic transition services should be targeted to all offenders—for those with and without community supervision after release.
- The principle of risk should guide allocation of programming, supervision, and services (Burke 2008, p. 8).

According to the authors, the distinctive elements of the Transition from Prison to the Community (TPC) model that set it apart (at that time) from other models of reentry included the following:

- Reentry should be viewed broadly as a seamless process with key decision points.
- Community safety is achieved through offender success, not just surveillance and risk management.
- Involvement of noncorrectional stakeholders is needed, such as community organization and informal networks that can provide services to meet offender needs.
- System and organizational change is needed—basically changing the way correctional agencies and their partners do business (e.g., incorporating risk-needs into correctional and supervision policies).
- Collaboration between agencies as a way of doing business is needed, where agencies share common goals and share their strengths with sustained and committed partnerships.
- Collaborative teams are used to help bring the model to life, to help align current practices in a jurisdiction with the TPC model ideals.
- Evidence-based practices, shown to be effective by sound research in reducing recidivism, should be used.
- Define and measure outcome clearly and track system changes used to achieve change in an effort to improve performance (Burke 2008, p. 12).

The TPC model was pilot tested in eight states starting in 2004: Georgia; Indiana, Michigan, Missouri, North Dakota, New York, Oregon, and Rhode Island. The National Institute of Corrections provided technical assistance to the states to implement the model. Some of the lessons learned from the implementation of the TPC model included the difficulties of changing correctional culture from risk management to risk reduction; the necessity of strong leadership that is able to engage with nontraditional stakeholders in the process; challenges in sharing information about an individual between correctional and noncorrectional agencies; and the importance of noncorrectional stakeholders, including legislators, service providers, benefit agencies, and social support networks (family and faith-based groups). The use of evidence-based practices—key to the TPC model—can be challenging. For example, jurisdictions must have the capacity to provide services to address offender needs, assuring that programs are evidence-based and effective, including expectations for evaluation of program outcomes. According to Burke (2008, pp. 22–26), targeting intervention by risk of reoffense is one of the most difficult evidence-based principles to implement. Housing locations, which are often not based on risk of recidivism, often determine access to programs.

C. National Governor's Association Reentry Policy Academy

A similar effort was conducted by the National Governor's Association through its Reentry Policy Academy, reflecting interest in addressing correctional costs and high recidivism rates by focusing on pre- and postrelease services. In two rounds of funding (2003 and 2007), 12 states were selected to be involved in technical assistance and education activities.

States assembled interdisciplinary reentry policy teams from departments of corrections, public safety, welfare, human services, workforce, and housing. The project assessed the reentry process within states, identified major service gaps and other barriers, and examined relevant state data on prisoner reentry trends. Two main categories of early "lessons learned" emerged: governance and management issues and service system issues. Within the former, the importance of gubernatorial leadership was highlighted as well as interdisciplinary partnerships in the development and implementation of effective reentry strategies, the importance of data necessary to decision-making and planning, and identification of local law enforcement as a vital part of the reentry process. Within service system issues, the effort noted that planning for reentry needs to begin at prison intake, and case management should integrate institutional and community resources and provide specific plans for offenders after release. Case management should also consider, when appropriate, social support (family and other relationships) for successful reintegration. A final service system issue noted the importance of using risk assessment tools in preparing aftercare plans (National Governor's Association 2002). Among the steps that governors and other policymakers can take in rentry efforts is to raise the profile of "prisoner" as not just a corrections issue but as a public safety issue (National Governor's Association 2005).

The efforts described here reveal consistencies in many recommendations for approaches to successful reentry. In fact, according to Burke and Tonry (2006, p. 23), "the growing interest in reentry and the weight of the research evidence demonstrate that we possess the knowledge, tools and ambition to reduce re-offending rates and increase successful reentry." I turn now to how the federal government has helped in moving these agreed-on concepts into the field.

IV. Federal Support for Offender Reentry Programs

Between 2001 and 2010, the federal government authorized over \$234 million in direct appropriations for the US Department of Justice Reentry Grant Programs (James 2011). Here I discuss several of the large initiatives that incorporated the multiagency and multifaceted approaches described earlier.

The SVORI mentioned previously was a four-year, \$300 million initiative that pooled the federal offender reentry resources at the Departments of Justice, Labor, Education, and Housing and Urban Development in order to reduce recidivism. In 2003, the Office of Justice Programs distributed \$110 million to 69 grantees to provide a continuum of services to serious and violent offenders that began during incarceration and continued for several years postrelease (James 2011, 2014; Lattimore and Visher 2009). SVORI also provided states assistance in navigating the wide variety of funding mechanisms while creating their reentry programs (James 2011). An evaluation of the program conducted by Research Triangle Institute and the Urban Institute revealed that participants in these multiphased efforts often received more services than nonparticipating offenders, yielding moderately better outcomes in self-reported criminal behavior, housing, employment, and substance abuse outcomes. However, these improvements were not associated with reductions in incarceration, at least as measured by officially recorded recidivism. Cost analyses did not reveal significant differences between program participants and others in terms of net criminal justice costs (Lattimore and Visher 2009). Following SVORI, the Prisoner Reentry Initiative (PRI) was an interagency effort that also focused on providing services and assistance to formerly incarcerated persons. The program targeted offender reentry during incarceration, the transition time right before and after release, as well as long-term community transition (James 2011, 2014)—similar to SVORI. During its three-year existence, the PRI grant program focused on reducing recidivism by helping former inmates find work and providing them access to other critical services in their communities (General Accountability Office [GAO] 2012b). Funding was discontinued by Congress in fiscal year 2008.

An evaluation of 30 projects funded by PRI revealed that two-thirds of all participants found unsubsidized work and average wages just over $9/hour in the short term, although about half were employed in the quarter after leaving the program. Nearly all received workforce preparation activities, although most were placed in low-skilled positions due to limited prior work experience. The program reported low recidivism of less than 10 percent for arrests, incarceration, or revocation of parole or probation. No comparison group was included, so it is difficult to conclude whether the program was effective in reducing recidivism over routine reentry efforts in the participating sites. Sites worked on building collaborations across agencies, although substance-abuse and mental health service partnerships were difficult to forge given scare resources available (Holl, Kolovich, Belotti, and Paxton 2009).

Following after the PRI, the Second Chance Act (P.L. 110-199; SCA) authorized federal funding for a wide range of state and local governmental agencies, which provided substance abuse treatment, housing, employment assistance, mentoring, and other services to help reduce recidivism (General Accountability Office 2012b). The act sought to build on the innovative and successful program developed under SVORI. More specifically, the SCA expanded areas eligible for funding with seven broad purpose areas:

- educational, literacy, vocational, and job placement services;
- substance abuse treatment and services, including programs that start in placement and continue with the community programs that also provide housing assistance and mental and physical health services;
- programs that focus on family integration during and after placement for both offenders and their families;
- mentoring programs that start in placement and continue into the community;
- programs that provide victim-appropriate services, including those that promote the timely payment of restitution by offenders and those that offer services (such as security or counseling) to victims when offenders are released; and
- programs that protect communities from dangerous offenders, including developing and implementing the use of risk assessment tools to determine when offenders should be released from prison. (James 2014, p. 23)

A National Institute of Justice–funded evaluation recently reported on the implementation of 10 demonstration sites funded under the SCA (D'Amico et al. 2013). The researchers found significant system changes in state and local government agencies that received SCA funds. New partnerships were being developed. These included collaborations between governmental agencies (such as probation and parole) and service providers to increase the types of programming and services available to offenders returning to the community. Services were becoming more "holistic," often with the assistance of formal case managers who assessed, brokered services, and served as enforcers of supervision conditions. The authors reported on their observations of a cultural shift emerging in thinking about how services are delivered. Agencies are rethinking their surveillance focus and moving toward evidence-based practices and a rehabilitative approach. Research on the effectiveness of these changes has not yet been completed. A second part of the evaluation will examine specific outcomes of the SCA funding in demonstration sites, particularly the impact of the new reentry programs on recidivism and the program's cost-effectiveness. Those findings were due in 2015 (D'Amico et al. 2013).

Other federal agencies have implemented grant programs that support reentry services at the state and local levels. The Department of Labor implemented the Reintegration of Ex-Offenders (RExO) program in 2005 designed to strengthen communities to which the majority of former inmates return through an employment-centered program that incorporates mentoring, job training, and other comprehensive transitional services. This program seeks to reduce recidivism by helping former inmates find work when they return to their communities. An implementation and outcome study of 24 RExO grantees utilizing random assignment is currently underway. Somewhat similar to the findings from SCA, the implementation evaluation found that RExO offenders had additional services at many sites, enhanced case management, and a diverse range of partnerships. However, in the vast majority of sites, programs were either eliminated or scaled back when federal funds ended (Leshnick et al. 2012). Results from the outcome study that will measure the impacts of the program on recidivism, employment, and services received are forthcoming.

The Department of Health and Human Services (HHS) developed the Offender Reentry Program (ORP) to expand or enhance substance abuse treatment and related recovery and reentry services for former inmates returning to the community. Grantees are required to report recidivism outcomes for the program in terms of the numbers of arrests, arrests for drug-related offenses, and number of nights spent in jail or prison. In 2011 HHS reported that 4.8 percent of ORP offenders reported involvement with the justice system 30 days prior to the reporting period (General Accountability Office 2012b).

Currently there is no federal agency in charge of coordinating reentry programs. It may come as no surprise, then, that recent GAO investigations found that grant programs were fragmented, overlapping in substantive areas, and at risk of duplication of efforts across the Departments of Justice, Labor, and HHS (General Accountability Office 2012a, 2012b, 2012c). Reentry can be enhanced by coinvestment, which can then provide a variety of services. But it also points out that agencies need to be more aware of each other's projects. Recently, the Department of Justice and HHS developed intraagency working groups to internally coordinate their reentry funding efforts. A Federal Interagency Reentry Council was established in 2011 and has helped agencies to "define and articulate a common outcome, establish mutually reinforcing or joint strategies, identify and address needs by leveraging resources, and agree on roles and responsibilities" (General Accountability Office 2012b, p. 23). The National Reentry Resource Center established by SCA and managed by the Council of State Governments Justice Center promotes knowledge transfer and dissemination and evidence-based best practices. The "What Works in Reentry Clearinghouse," launched in 2012, is part of this. According to its website, "The *What Works in Reentry Clearinghouse* offers easy access to important research on the effectiveness of a wide variety of reentry programs and practices. It provides a user-friendly, one-stop shop for practitioners and service providers seeking guidance on evidence-based reentry interventions, as well as a useful resource for researchers and others interested in reentry" (http://whatworks. csgjusticecenter.org/). Coordination efforts have paid off. The most recent GAO report on inmate reentry programs analyzed primary services funded across federal agencies in 2011 and found minimal overlap. Put into perspective, however, the vast amount of funding for programs—over $75 million in 2011—does not reach a large percentage of offenders reentering their communities from prison. The GAO estimates that of the more than 700,000 releases from prison, the RExO program provided services to about 7,500 released inmates, the SCA to approximately 6,600 inmates, and the ORP program to about 3,300 inmates (General Accountability Office 2012*b*, p. 20).

V. Conclusion

This essay highlights the complex nature of reentry programs, reentry models, and federal funding without a detailed review of evidence on the implementation of these models. However, key to any intervention's success is implementation, and research often shows that programs are not delivered as planned. One of the most high-profile failures of a contemporary prisoner reentry program was Project Greenlight (Wilson and Davis 2006). The program, purportedly developed based on effective principles of offender change, did not reduce offender recidivism. Whether the poor findings reflected major challenges in the implementation of evidence-based principles in a large scale, real-world setting (Rhine, Mawhorr, and Parks 2006) or from misguided understanding of evidence-based principles (Marlowe 2006), this large-scale failure clearly highlights the great difficulty of making complicated reentry models work.

Although this may be the latest bruise to our ability to implement effective models, it is not the only large-scale effort to note less-than-intended program intensity. As Lattimore and colleagues (2010, p. 259) noted, despite participants in SVORI programs receiving more services than "business as usual," treatment was diluted, with discrepancies between what programs were designed to deliver and what they delivered and what individuals needed versus what they received. Poor implementation has plagued the field for decades. More than 20 years ago, Petersilia and Turner (1993) pointed out discrepancies between designed and delivered program components for intensive supervision probation and parole.

Since the days of Martinson (1974), concern has been voiced over the often poor quality of correctional evaluations. This concern has been echoed in the nearly 40 years since the "nothing works" pronouncement (Petersilia and Rosenfeld 2008; Taxman 2011; MacKenzie 2006, 2012). Poor-quality research designs, in which treatment and comparison groups are not comparable; different outcome measures and definitions of recidivism; infrequent use of outcome measures designed to understand moderators and mediators of recidivism— such as job attainment, reduced drug use, educational and career attainment—hinder our ability to document and understand when and how interventions are either successful or unsuccessful. Understanding the "black box" of many interventions still eludes us.

Finally, our ability to reap large changes in offender behavior may be unrealistic. Reentry programs and services are provided to offenders using an implicit model that assumes that improvement in intermediate outcomes (e.g., drug use, employment, education) will lead to reductions in recidivism. Lattimore, Steffey, and Visher (2010) performed a thought experiment on how this may translate into actual reductions in recidivism. Using different scenarios of the impact of a job training program on employment and employment on recidivism, the authors found modest potential impacts for reentry programming. Under an optimistic case scenario in which (a) job training would increase employment by 50 percent, and (b) employment would, in turn, reduce recidivism by 50 percent, we might expect to see reductions in recidivism on the order of 25 percent (Lattimore, Steffey, and Visher 2010). Systematic analyses of program effectiveness often show changes of around 10 to 30 percent in recidivism rates.

Our understanding of effective reentry strategies and their effectiveness is still very much a work in progress. This essay has focused on service provision, models for change, and funding efforts for increasing the chances of successful reentry for the hundreds of thousands of offenders returning to their communities each year. Despite the optimistic models that have been outlined, many proposed changes to our prison and community programs suggested over the past 15 years are not commonplace for all reentering offenders as of 2016. We have proposed models that promise success, but we do not yet know how well they will work.

REFERENCES

Andrews, Don A., and James Bonta. 2010. *The Psychology of Criminal Conduct.* New York: Elsevier.

Andrews, Don A., James Bonta, and Robert D. Hoge. 1990. "Classification for Effective Rehabilitation: Rediscovering Psychology." *Criminal Justice and Behavior* 17:19–52.

Andrews, Don A., Ivan Zinger, Robert D. Hoge, James Bonta, Paul Gendreau, and Francis T. Cullen. 1990. "Does Correctional Treatment Work? A Clinically Relevant and Psychologically Informed Meta-analysis." *Criminology* 28:369–404.

Aos, Steve, Marna Miller, and Elizabeth Drake. 2006. "Evidence-Based Public Policy Options to Reduce Future Prison Construction, Criminal Justice Costs, and Crime Rates." *Federal Sentencing Reporter* 19:275-290.

Bonczar, Thomas P. 2008. *Characteristics of State Parole Supervising Agencies, 2006.* Washington, DC: Bureau of Justice Statistics.

Burke, Peggy B. 1997. *Policy-Driven Responses to Probation and Parole Violations.* Silver Spring, MD: Center for Effective Public Policy.

Burke, Peggy B. 2008. *TPC Reentry Handbook: Implementing the NIC Transition from Prison to Community Model.* Washington, DC: National Institute of Corrections.

Burke, Peggy B., and Michael H. Tonry. 2006. *Successful Transition and Reentry for Safer Communities: A Call to Action for Parole.* Silver Spring, MD: Center for Effective Public Policy.

California Department of Corrections and Rehabilitation. 2007. *Expert Panel on Adult Offender and Recidivism Reduction Programming: Report to the California State Legislature.* Sacramento, CA: California Department of Corrections and Rehabilitation.

California Department of Corrections and Rehabilitation. 2009. *CDCR Reduces Offender Rehabilitation Programs: Headquarters Staff Reduced to Contain Costs and Increase Efficiencies*. Sacramento, CA: California Department of Corrections and Rehabilitation.

California Rehabilitation Oversight Board. 2013. *March 15, 2013 Biannual Report*. Sacramento, CA: Office of the Inspector General.

Carson, E. Ann, and Daniela Golinelli. 2013. *"Prisoners in 2012."* Washington, DC: Bureau of Justice Statistics.

Clear, Todd R., Dina R. Rose, and Judith A. Ryder. 2001. "Incarceration and the Community: The Problem of Removing and Returning Offenders." *Crime & Delinquency* 47:335–51.

Clear, Todd R., Elin Waring, and Kristen Scully. 2005. "Communities and Reentry: Concentrated Reentry Cycling." In *Prisoner Reentry and Crime in America*, edited by Jeremy Travis and Christy Visher. Cambridge, UK: Cambridge University Press.

D'Amico, Ron, Christian Geckeler, Jennifer Henderson-Frakes, Deborah Kogan, and Tyler Moazed. 2013. *Evaluation of the Second Chance Act (SCA) Adult Demonstration 2009 Grantees*. Oakland, CA: Social Policy Research Associates.

Davis, Lois M. 2013. *Evaluating the Effectiveness of Correctional Education: A Meta-Analysis of Programs that Provide Education to Incarcerated Adults*. Santa Monica, CA: RAND Corporation.

Fazel, Seena, Parveen Bains, and Helen Doll. 2006. "Substance Abuse and Dependence in Prisoners: A Systematic Review." *Addiction* 101:181–191.

General Accountability Office. 2012a. *2012 Annual Report: Opportunities to Reduce Duplication, Overlap and Fragmentation, Achieve Savings, and Enhance Revenue*. Washington, DC: US General Accountability Office.

General Accountability Office. 2012b. *Inmate Reentry Programs: Enhanced Information Sharing Could Further Strengthen Coordination and Grant Management*. Washington, DC: US General Accountability Office.

General Accountability Office. 2012c. *Justice Grant Programs: DOJ should do More to Reduce Risk of Unncessary Duplication and Enhance Program Assessment*. Washington, DC: US General Accountability Office.

Glaze, Lauren E., and Doris J. James. 2006. *Mental Health Problems of Prison and Jail Inmates*. Washington, DC: Bureau of Justice Statistics.

Holl, Douglas B., Lisa Kolovich, Jeanne Bellotti, and Nora Paxton. 2009. *Evaluation of the Prisoner Re-Entry Initiative*. Bethesda, MD: Coffey Consulting.

James, Nathan. 2011. *Offender Reentry: Correctional Statistics, Reintegration into the Community, and Recidivism*. Washington, DC: Congressional Research Service.

James, Nathan. 2014. *Offender Reentry: Correctional Statistics, Reintegration into the Community, and Recidivism*. Washington, DC: Congressional Research Service.

Lattimore, Pamela K., Danielle M. Steffey, and Christy A. Visher. 2010. "Prisoner Reentry in the First Decade of the Twenty-First Century." *Victims & Offenders* 5:253–267.

Lattimore, Pamela K., and Christy Ann Visher. 2009. *The Multi-Site Evaluation of SVORI: Summary and Synthesis*. Washington, DC: Urban Institute.

Leshnick, Sengsouvanh Sukey, Christian Geckeler, Andrew Wiegand, Brandon Nicholson, and Kimberly Foley. 2012. *Evaluation of the Re-Integration of Ex-Offenders (RExO) Program: Interim Report*. Oakland, CA: Social Policy Research Associates.

Lipton, Douglas, Robert Martinson, and Judith Wilks. 1975. *The Effectiveness of Correctional Treatment: A Survey of Treatment Evaluation Studies*. New York: Praeger.

Lynch, James P., and William J. Sabol. 2001. *Crime Policy Report: Prisoner Reentry in Perspective.* Washington, DC: Urban Institute.

MacKenzie, Doris L. 2006. *What Works in Corrections: Reducing the Recidivism of Offenders and Delinquents.* Cambridge, UK: Cambridge University Press.

MacKenzie, Doris L. 2012. "The Effectiveness of Corrections-Based Work and Academic and Vocational Education Programs." In *The Oxford Handbook of Sentencing and Corrections,* edited by Joan Petersilia and Kevin R. Reitz. New York: Oxford University Press.

Marlowe, Douglas B. 2006. "When 'What Works' Never Did: Dodging the 'Scarlet M' in Correctional Rehabilitation." *Criminology & Public Policy* 5:339–346.

Martinson, Robert. 1974. "What Works? Questions and Answers about Prison Reform." *The Public Interest* 35:22–54.

Maruna, Shadd. 2001. *Making Good.* Washington, DC: American Psychological Association.

Mumola, Christopher J., and Jennifer C. Karberg. 2006. *Drug Use and Dependence, State and Federal Prisoners, 2004.* Washington, DC: Bureau of Justice Statistics.

National Governors Association. 2002. *Early Lessons from the NGA Prisoner Reentry Policy Academy.* Washington, DC: National Governors Association.

National Governors Association. 2005. *Improving Prisoner Reentry through Strategic Policy Innovations.* Washington, DC: National Governors Association.

Petersilia, Joan. 2003. *When Prisoners Come Home: Parole and Prisoner Reentry.* New York: Oxford University Press.

Petersilia, Joan. 2005. "Hard Time: Ex-Offenders Returning Home After Prison." *Corrections Today* 67(2):66-71.

Petersilia, Joan. 2007. "Employ Behavioral Contracting for 'Earned Discharge' Parole." *Criminology & Public Policy* 6:807–814.

Petersilia, Joan, and Richard Rosenfeld. 2008. *Parole, Desistance from Crime, and Community Integration* Washington, DC: National Academies Press.

Petersilia, Joan, and Susan Turner. 1993. "Intensive Probation and Parole." In *Crime and Justice: A Review of Research,* edited by Michael Tonry. Chicago: University of Chicago Press.

Phelps, Michelle S. 2011. "Rehabilitation in the Punitive Era: The Gap between Rhetoric and Reality in US Prison Programs." *Law & Society Review* 45:33–68.

Phelps, Michelle S. 2012. "The Place of Punishment: Variation in the Provision of Inmate Services Staff Across the Punitive Turn." *Journal of Criminal Justice* 40:348–357.

Piehl, Anne Morrison, and Stefan F. LoBuglio. 2005. "Does Supervision Matter?" In *Prisoner Reentry and Crime in America,* edited by Jeremy Travis and Christy Visher. Cambridge, UK: Cambridge University Press.

Reentry Policy Council. 2005. *Report of the Reentry Policy Council: Charting the Safe and Successful Return of Prisoners to the Community.* New York: Council of State Governments.

Rhine, Edward. 2012. "The Present Status and Future Prospects of Parole Boards and Parole Supervision." In *The Oxford Handbook of Sentencing and Corrections,* edited by Joan Petersilia and Kevin R. Reitz. New York: Oxford University Press.

Rhine, Edward E., Tina L. Mawhorr, and Evalyn C. Parks. 2006. "Implementation: The Bane of Effective Correctional Programs." *Criminology & Public Policy* 5(2):347–358.

Rosenfeld, Richard, Joel Wallman, and Robert Fornango. 2005. "The Contribution of Ex-Prisoners to Crime Rates." In *Prisoner Reentry and Crime in America,* edited by Jeremy Travis and Christy Visher. Cambridge, UK: Cambridge University Press.

Sabol, William J., and James P. Lynch. 2003. "Assessing the Longer-Run Consequences of Incarceration: Effects on Families and Employment." *Contributions in Criminology and Penology* 55:3–26.

Seiter, Richard. 2014. *Probation, Parole and Comunity Corrections*. New York: Prentice Hall.

Smith, Sarah M., Marisa K. Omori, Susan F. Turner, and Jesse Jannetta. 2012. "Assessing the Earned Discharge Pilot Project." *Criminology & Public Policy* 11:385–410.

Solomon, Amy L. 2005. *Does Parole Work? Analyzing the Impact of Postprison Supervision on Rearrest Outcomes*. Washington, DC: Urban Institute.

Solomon, Amy L., Jenny Osborne, Laura Winterfield, Brian Elderbroom, Peggy Burke, Richard P. Stroker, Edward E. Rhine, and William D. Burrell. 2008. *"Putting Public Safety First: 13 Parole Supervision Strategies to Enhance Reentry Outcomes."* Washinton, DC: Urban Institute.

Steadman, Henry, Fred Osher, Pamela Clark Robbins, Brian Case, and Steven Samuels. 2009. "Prevalence of Serious Mental Illness among Jail Inmates." *Psychiatric Services* 60:761–765.

Taxman, Faye S. 2011. "Parole: 'What Works' Is Still Under Construction." In *Handbook of Evidence-Based Substance Abuse Treatment in Criminal Justice Settings*, edited by Carl Leukefeld, Thomas P. Gullotta, and John Gregrich. New York: Springer.

Taxman, Faye S, Douglas Young, and J. M. Byrne. 2003. *From Prison Safety to Public Safety: Best Practices in Offender Reentry*. Washington, DC: National Institute of Justice.

Travis, Jeremy, and Joan Petersilia. 2001. "Reentry Reconsidered: A New Look at an Old Question." *Crime & Delinquency* 47:291–313.

Vera Institute of Justice. 2010. *The Continuing Fiscal Crisis in Corrections: Setting a New Course*. New York: Vera Institute of Justice.

Visher, Christy Ann, Vera Kachnowski, Nancy Gladys La Vigne, Jeremy Travis, and Justice Policy Center. 2004. *Baltimore Prisoners' Experiences Returning Home*. Washington, DC: Urban Institute.

Wilson, James A., and Robert C. Davis. 2006. "Good Intentions Meet Hard Realities: An Evaluation of the Project Greenlight Reentry Program." *Criminology & Public Policy* 5:303–338.

....

CHAPTER 23

IMPLEMENTING PRISON-BASED TREATMENT PROGRAMS

....

JAMES MCGUIRE

THE objective of this chapter is to examine the issues involved in transferring what has become known as the "what works" literature from research into practice in adult prisons. There are several aspects of this that are important to consider, all of them interconnected. They range from the purposes of imprisonment itself, and the nature of prisons as organizations, to the kinds of obstacles that often make change difficult in any setting accustomed to working in a given way. Portions of what follows will focus on the development and implementation of rehabilitative programs, the provision of guidelines for applying them in practice, and the importance of monitoring and evaluating what we do while remaining responsive to changing demands. The task is analogous to one that in health care is called *translational* (Woolf 2008). But in the context of a penal institution, it presents additional hurdles and some potential traps.

A sentence of imprisonment is designed to serve multiple purposes at one and the same time. Other than where capital sentences are retained, imprisonment is classed as the most severe penalty available to the courts in most jurisdictions (Nagin, Cullen, and Jonson 2009). Its traditional objectives include the functions of *retribution, incapacitation, deterrence,* and *rehabilitation* (Pollock 2014; Ashworth 2015). The first two of those objectives are in a sense achieved through the structure of the prison itself. By depriving a citizen of liberty, society signals its denunciation of criminal activity and its determination to rectify the imbalance that was created when the offender took advantage over others, by inflicting pain on him or her in return (retribution). Through being incarcerated, the individual is removed from opportunities to cause further harm in the community (incapacitation); although, it is known that many crimes occur in prison, so arguably this may more often be a form of displacement.

Whether prison achieves the third objective, deterrence, is harder to discern. Loss of liberty is intended to precipitate change by inducing fear of consequences both in the individual made subject to it (specific deterrence) and in the public at large who are made aware that the same could happen to them (general deterrence). This expectation is grounded in the assumption of rational crime theory, that a would-be offender will weigh the imagined benefits of crime against its costs and conclude that it is not worthwhile. Such advance calculation may not, however, typify very many offenses. Moreover, the question of whether deterrence is genuinely achieved has been and continues to be a matter of debate among practitioners and policymakers in many criminal justice systems, and also among scholars across the fields of penology, criminology, law, economics, psychology and psychiatry. At least one philosopher has argued that contrary to what many see as the "common sense" approach to justice, the breaking of laws does not give the community an automatic right to punish the offender because "punishment" itself can precipitate other problems for society (Boonin 2008). That discussion is, however, beyond the scope of the present chapter.

The fourth objective, rehabilitation, is different from the others in not being inherently contained in the process of penal confinement in itself, although in the past it was often assumed to be. In many ways it sits uneasily alongside the others. Putting it bluntly, officially proclaimed investment of importance in it is often rhetorical rather than real, and it is all too frequently marginalized, even excluded, as a meaningful feature of prison agendas. But consider this scenario: Imagine you ask a child, what did you do in school today? The child describes entering a building, spending several hours there, then returning home. Despite further questioning, you cannot elicit any information suggesting that an activity took place likely to stimulate learning. You ask if a teacher was present, as there is no mention of such a person. Or perhaps a teacher was there but sat in the corner passively and did not interact with the children. If this scenario was repeated, you would surely begin to doubt whether the process we call education, usually believed to be the point of attending school, had been happening, and wonder how the children were expected to learn.

It seems odd then to expect that some desired change will take place in another setting, a prison, when there is no activity going on likely to promote it. For many decades, there appeared to be a general assumption that individuals sent to prison would somehow change, simply through the raw experience of being there. Perhaps rehabilitation was seen as a second-level by-product of confinement. Through long hours of self-reflection and contemplation, or possibly from having become religious or gained a sense of redemption (Maruna, Wilson, and Curran 2006), prisoners were thought to learn the errors of their ways and would thereby resolve to live better lives. Yes, there are occasional anecdotes and narratives illustrating such a transformation, as the autobiographies of some former prisoners describe (Morgan 1999). But a broader reckoning suggests they are the exception, and wise mentors dispensing messages about how to live a more law-abiding life are not reliably available. In most places where data have been collected, there is little to support the idea that this occurs in more than a small fraction of cases. That it can be the foundation of a general policy for using prison as a means of rehabilitation is very much at odds with what is known about most ex-prisoner careers.

For some years, therefore, the major challenge in this area has been how to instill a firmer rehabilitative ethos into systems that are not designed principally for that purpose. It is helpful that in the last few decades, since approximately the late 1970s, we have learned a great deal about the possibility of accomplishing rehabilitative goals. The widely expressed, almost dogmatic dismissiveness that was then dominant has been replaced with a recognition that, while not guaranteed, effective community reintegration and reductions in criminal recidivism can be secured after release from prison. That change has been brought about largely through the accumulation of a sizeable corpus of research findings, portions of which are reviewed elsewhere in this handbook. While inevitably there are still gaps, we have now more than 100 meta-analyses to draw upon that can inform practice and policy in this area (McGuire 2013). While there is not a total consensus on this, the preponderance of informed opinion endorses a well-tested conceptual approach, the risk-needs-responsivity (RNR) model (Andrews and Bonta 2010), as a framework for such efforts. This is based on a general theory of the development of delinquency and crime informed by research on personality and social learning. The RNR model has had a steadily growing influence on correctional professionals and systems in many countries.

Paradoxically, across the same period in which this knowledge base was developing, prison populations in some of the same countries where much of the associated work was done grew at a very rapid pace (Berman 2010; Cook and Ludwig 2011; Walmsley 2014). Although occurring in parallel, these trends were not, however, causally related. Many other factors contributed to the rise in prominence of a punitive stance and of what has been called the "penal harm" movement (Clear 1994). Yet as a result, the challenges of turning prisons into places with a rehabilitative emphasis are if anything greater today than they were three or four decades ago.

The upshot of this rather extensive preamble is to establish the point that if imprisonment is to have a positive impact in reducing subsequent recidivism, achieving that goal is likely to require providing specific activities in prison that have rehabilitation as their focus. Containment in itself, compliance with prison routines, even regular involvement in work, may not be sufficient to engender the kinds of change that are seen as desirable.

In what follows, we will consider several aspects of this in turn. First, it is important to review the effectiveness of imprisonment in itself: Does it have rehabilitative capacity through the processes of retribution, incapacitation, or deterrence that are its core features? Second, can activities in prisons with a distinct rehabilitative focus have positive effects following release? Third, when trying to install such activities in a prison regime, what obstacles are we likely to encounter? Fourth, can they be surmounted, counteracted, or neutralized, and if so, how?

I. The Effect of Imprisonment

Major questions can be raised over the effectiveness of prison for its appointed purposes. It is reasonable to claim that it succeeds as a form of retribution, since in a sense that does not appeal to measurable consequences (although crime victims sometimes express discontentment when they believe sentences are too lenient). Societal denunciation and the rebalancing of disadvantage that are the core of this penal philosophy do not rely on the evaluation of impact. The process of delivering "just deserts" is in a sense cyclical, a kind of closed loop, complete in itself. It is also valued for its symbolic significance, in reinforcing community cohesion and society's delineation of its boundaries. From that perspective, it is a fallacy to think of judicial punishment predominantly in terms of crime control (Garland 1990).

However, from other standpoints, prison is considered to serve a primary crime-preventive function (Nagin, Cullen, and Jonson 2009). We could say that imprisonment has a direct incapacitating effect on those detained, who are prevented from committing crimes in the community, and although technically intricate, that effect can be measured.

For example, analyzing crime statistics in New South Wales, Australia, Weatherburn, Hua, and Moffatt (2006) estimated that imprisonment prevented 45,000 burglaries per annum. Marvell and Moody (1994, p. 36) estimated that during the 1970s and 1980s in the United States "each additional state prisoner averted at least 17 index crimes on average, mostly larcenies." According to Levitt (2004), the steeply rising U.S. prison population was one of four factors that combined to produce the crime drop in the 1990s. (The other factors were increased police numbers, a reduction in crack cocaine use, and the legalization of abortion in the 1970s).

However, the potentially broader and longer lasting impact of incapacitation on crime rates may be weaker than these analyses suggest. Through the vagaries of crime reporting, detection, arrest, charging, prosecution, conviction, and sentencing, only a very small proportion of most types of offenses results in an offender being imprisoned. Thus an analysis by Tarling (1993) of "incapacitation models" for England and Wales found that to decrease the crime rate by just 1 percent, the prison population would need to be increased by 25 percent. In New South Wales, Weatherburn, Hua, and Moffatt (2006) estimated that to achieve a 10 percent reduction in burglary rates, imprisonment would need to be increased by 34 percent. Marvell and Moody (1994) produced a more optimistic estimate, where each 10 percent rise in prisoner numbers led to 2.5 percent fewer crimes; but the impact on assault and rape was negligible. Clearly to have any noticeable impact on crime through such a policy, the level of expenditure required is substantial and in many jurisdictions would be fiscally unsustainable.

Furthermore, while in prison some individuals maintain connections through gangs or other criminal networks with illegal activities outside. There are instances of serious crimes including homicides being ordered by cell phones from inside prison. This highlights the sizeable problem of prison indiscipline which takes numerous forms, including many that would constitute crimes in the community, such as violent assault (e.g., Wolff, Blitz, Shi, Siegel, and Bachman 2007). In the United States, it has been suggested that official statistics on prison violence considerably underestimate its actual prevalence (Byrne and Hummer 2007).

A search for firm evidence of beneficial outcomes from the use of imprisonment often turns, therefore, to its presumed deterrent or "suppressant" effects. This has been examined in many studies. Lloyd, Mair, and Hough (1994) compared the two-year recidivism rates of offenders in England and Wales subject to four different types of sentences: imprisonment, community service, probation supervision, and probation with additional requirements (e.g., to attend a day center). They employed a newly developed prediction instrument, the Offender Group Reconviction Scale (OGRS). As the most punishing sentence, prison should be the most effective deterrent and should suppress the two-year reconviction rate of those sent there below that observed for the other sentences. However, across all four categories, the rate at which individuals were reconvicted was very close to the rate at which they were predicted to be based on their criminal histories. In no case was the difference between predicted and actual rates greater than 3 percent.

This has been investigated in several other ways. Although few studies are randomized experiments, researchers can employ statistical controls to take account of differences between samples. In a study in the Netherlands, being imprisoned for the first time when aged between 18 and 38 was associated with an increased likelihood of a further prison sentence over the next three years (Nieuwbeerta, Nagin, and Blokland 2009). In the largest study of this kind, covering prisons from 46 American states over the period 1974-2002, Vieraitis, Kovandzic, and Marvell (2007) found clear evidence that released prisoners committed more crimes than they would have been expected to do. This study took account of a number of external community economic variables, such as the unemployment rate and levels of per-capita income, in arriving at this conclusion. Analysis indicated the observed effect was not a product of "reverse incapacitation" (i.e., the lowering of prison populations) but of "prisonization." The authors concluded that "imprisonment causes harm to prisoners" (2007, p. 614).

Other researchers have reported comparisons between the relative effects of prison and other types of sentences on subsequent recidivism rates. Wermink et al. (2010) compared short-term imprisonment with community service in the Netherlands. Drawing on a very large sample in Florida sentenced during the period 1994-2002, Bales and Piquero (2012) compared prison with an intensive supervision program (Community Control). This study used three different approaches to data analysis, all of which yielded the same results. Comparisons have also been made between prison and suspended sentences in Spain (Cid 2009); and in Australia (Lulham, Weatherburn, and Bartels 2009); and in the United States between imprisonment and probation (Spohn and Holleran 2002). These studies uniformly find that, rather than having a deterrent effect, sentences of imprisonment either make no difference or have a net criminogenic effect. Even when other factors associated with recidivism are controlled, those sent to prison often have a higher subsequent recidivism rate than their respective comparators. In another U.S. study, Spohn (2007) found that prison increased recidivism even amongst those with strong bonds to conventional society—with "high stakes in conformity" as measured by employment, educational, and marital status. A further aspect of this, obtained from a randomized experiment, is evidence that security level while in prison had a criminogenic effect independently of background factors (Gaes and Camp 2009).

Systematic reviews of this research have been undertaken. Nagin, Cullen, and Jonson (2009), and Durlauf and Nagin (2011a, 2011b) have reviewed studies of the relationship between imprisonment and crime rates. For the Campbell Collaboration, Villetaz, Killias, and Zoder (2006; revised and updated by Villetaz, Gillieron, and Killias 2015), reviewed studies comparing custodial with noncustodial sentences. In the modest number of studies where experimental designs were used (either randomized controlled trials or quasi-experiments), meta-analysis was conducted. In the studies that employed formal randomized designs, no differences emerged between custodial and noncustodial sentences. In the quasi-experimental studies, results favored noncustodial sentences (that is, they showed significantly lower rates of recidivism). A consensus emerges from these two sets of reviews to the effect that "an overwhelming majority of studies summarized here as well as in other reviews . . . point in the direction of criminogenic effects of imprisonment" (Villetaz et al. 2015, p. 46).

There is, of course, a frequently voiced argument that the deterrent effects of prison are weaker than they could be and should be, because prison is not sufficiently punishing. If discussion of crime and justice in the news media is an indicator, it would seem that the public often perceives sentences as too short and prison environments as too comfortable and easygoing: In the United Kingdom, they are sometimes characterized by the phrase "holiday camps." Conversely, therefore, many people expect there to be more leverage toward reducing recidivism by increasing the level of penalty and making conditions harsher.

Investigation of this, however, shows that the reverse is more likely to occur, based on studies conducted both in the United States (Chen and Shapiro 2007; Listwan et al. 2013) and among a large sample of discharged prisoners in Italy (Drago, Galbiati, and Vertova 2011). The "pains of imprisonment," to use Sykes's (1958) much-quoted phrase, are more often associated with increases in rates of postrelease recidivism and greater likelihood of later re-incarceration than with more effective deterrence. We might expect that prisoners who experience marked fear of other inmates would be more likely deterred, but a study of young offenders in Germany found the opposite (Windzio 2006). Where prison conditions are deliberately made "tougher" by adding further restrictions or deprivations, prisoners' behavior while detained usually deteriorates (Bierie 2012). When the effects of punitive sanctions have been examined more widely, severity of penalty has not been found to have any particular impact (von Hirsch, Bottoms, Burney, and Wikström 1999). There is far more purchase to be gained by increasing the likelihood of being apprehended than by increasing sentence length or making prisoners' lives more difficult (Braga and Weisburd 2012).

When penalties are toughened by increasing sentence length, they still do not reliably achieve the desired results. A notable illustration of this is the inception of habitual offender or "three strikes" legislation in a number of American states. Under these laws, following commission of a third serious felony, an offender is liable for a life sentence. Between 1994 and 2008 in California, approximately 41,500 offenders were sentenced under these laws; until 2012 the third offense could be a misdemeanor. Some positive outcomes were reported by Helland and Tabarrok (2007), who described an apparent suppressant effect among those who had acquired two prior convictions for serious crimes and who following a third would have been eligible for a very long sentence. However, other evaluations examining the broader results of this policy have found no evidence of an impact on crime rates. In California, for example, there were large variations between counties in the amount of usage of three-strikes laws: some used it up to six times more often than others. Follow-up analysis of crime data in the counties that applied the legislation *least* showed that they experienced a *greater* decline in violent crime than those counties which used it most (Center on Juvenile and Criminal Justice 2008). Similarly, Parker (2012) found that decreases in violent crime that did occur had begun before the habitual offender statutes were introduced. Trends in serious crime were unrelated to the three-strikes policy and showed a far closer relationship over time to changes in the level of alcohol consumption.

Following a further-reaching change in policy in California Public Safety Realignment, between September 2011 and May 2013, the state prison population fell by 27,846. Such an abrupt change would raise sharp fears of a spike in crime, given the numbers involved, perhaps on an unprecedented scale. Scrutinizing the data, however, Lofstrom and Raphael (2016) found no evidence of any effect on violent crime rates, the sole significant change observed being a small increase in vehicle thefts (equivalent to 1.2 car thefts per prison year not served).

Why is prison not a successful, even powerful, deterrent? One possibility is that it lacks certain archetypal features of a consistent "punisher" in behavioral terms. To be effective, painful consequences of an action should be inevitable or difficult to escape, and immediate or temporally close to the problem behavior they are intended to eradicate. But the likelihood of being imprisoned following most criminal offenses is very low, and even when it occurs, it is usually after a gap of several weeks or even months. Another possibility is that the prospect of it is not cognitively accessible to individuals in the period prior to committing a crime. They are not in what have been called "deterrable states of mind" (Walker 1991, p. 15), just as, for example, most people who drive a car know in theory they could be involved in an accident but do not think it will happen to them. A third is that many of those sent to prison find that, despite the hardships, it is not as difficult to endure as they expected (though they do not perceive it as easy). They accept it as part of the price to be paid for adopting a criminal lifestyle, to which they believe there is no real alternative (Crank and Brezina 2013).

Collectively, therefore, these individual studies and literature reviews yield very little to confirm that imprisonment accomplishes its desired effects through deterrence, with some finding that it makes no difference and many that it makes matters worse. In a sense this is a remarkable situation. If farming generally failed to produce food, or if hospitals mostly made people ill rather than better, or if evidence of their usefulness was so tenuous that only elaborate statistical analysis could isolate it, there would be widespread puzzlement, if not alarm. Despite apparently failing to achieve major parts of their appointed purpose, prisons seem to be in a unique position, in being virtually immune from criticism of their value. If their use cannot be justified in terms of denunciation, retribution, and public protection—and the last of those may be marginal at best—then in the words of a British government policy document from some years ago (Home Office 1990, p. 6) they become simply "an expensive way of making bad people worse." A similar view has been expressed by a life sentence prisoner in the United States (Soering 2004). But that discovery is far from new. "For the prison, in its reality and visible effects, was denounced at once as the great failure of penal justice." The words are not from a recent anticarceral polemic but from Foucault (1979, p. 264), summarizing numerous official reports written in the period 1820-1845, following the arrival of the penitentiary in France.

II. Rehabilitative Potential

In contrast to the previous findings mentioned, when rehabilitation programs are provided in prisons, they can have a significant impact on postrelease offending. In a meta-analysis of the effects of cognitive behavioral programs, Lipsey, Landenberger, and Wilson (2007) found equivalent reductions in recidivism for offenders in correctional institutions and community services. Of 58 studies they located, 27 were based in prisons. The mean effect size on subsequent recidivism across programs was a reduction of 25 percent. Lipsey et al. (2007, p. 23) concluded that "offenders treated in prison (generally close to the end of their sentences) showed recidivism decreases comparable to those of offenders treated in the community (e.g., while on probation, parole, or in transitional aftercare)." In some other reviews, however, average effect sizes for interventions in custodial settings have been lower than for community-based equivalents (Parhar, Wormith, Derkzen, and Beauregard 2008; Andrews and Bonta 2010). Given the often adverse effects of imprisonment reviewed here, such a disparity is perhaps not unexpected.

An offender rehabilitation program is essentially a structured, prearranged sequence of learning opportunities that can be reproduced on successive occasions (McGuire 2001). Prisoners, often (though not always) working in small groups, are taken through a series of activities designed to develop their thinking, influence their attitudes, and help them acquire skills for avoiding or managing future situations in which they would be at risk of committing another crime. Programs vary in their degree of structure and prescriptiveness. Most are supported by a specially prepared manual, but others have a more open and flexible format. All, however, require training to be provided for staff who will facilitate the sessions. Many such programs have now been devised, for addressing offending behavior in general or for focusing more closely on specific types of offenses such as violent, sex, substance-related, or property crimes. Thus in several respects this aspect of services is well developed. That is not to say it cannot evolve further, and there are still many unanswered questions in relation to it.

The majority of programs of this type are informed by the RNR model, briefly described earlier (see also Goggin in this volume). Apart from its general application with offenders who would be regarded as "versatile," having been convicted of a variety of offenses in their criminal careers, supporting evidence has also been obtained from work with those who exhibit more "specialized" forms of criminality, including sex offending (Hanson, Bourgon, Helmus, and Hodgson 2009), intimate partner violence (Stewart, Flight, and Slavin-Stewart 2013), and substance-related offending—although here it has been found to be related to crime outcomes, but less so with drug use outcomes (Prendergast et al. 2013). Attempting to have an impact on prisoners with multiple problems, rather than rely exclusively on free-standing programs, larger scale changes can be made in how a regime operates, as for example in socio-therapeutic prisons in Germany (Lösel and Koferl 1989) or in therapeutic communities (Lipton, Pearson, Cleland, and Yee 2002). Of particular interest are studies that have linked therapeutic work or prerelease preparation in prison with multiagency re-entry services, where a small number of studies with robust designs have shown positive outcomes (Braga, Piehl, and Hureau 2009; Sacks et al. 2004, 2012).

Arguably, beneficial outcomes could be secured on a larger scale, and prison systems could become more effective vehicles for crime prevention if they were to pursue a direction in which these initiatives were given higher priority and became more widely disseminated. Doing so would depend on increasing the level of investment in the time and resources needed to ensure their proper delivery. Admittedly, if prisons are endemically criminogenic environments (as the research mentioned implies), the task of converting them to a different balance of purposes is a daunting one. Most rehabilitation programs last only a few hours per day for a few weeks, though there are longer ones that take many months to complete. But on average they typically represent less than a hundred hours of structured activity. That period can be effective (e.g., Bourgon and Armstrong 2005), but the experience has to be set against many hundreds of hours of exposure to influences that may work in the opposite direction. For significant findings to have been obtained despite such counter-currents is an impressive result.

Extending the process to enable prisons to become more firmly rehabilitation-focused agencies requires not only introducing suitable programs, but it also means adapting the organizational culture to a point where participation in them is seen as a central reason for being there. As suggested earlier, the prison milieu is not one that has traditionally been formulated as a carrier of an educational or personal-change culture, to any other than a minimal extent. Indeed, depending on the unit to which they are allocated, individual prisoners may spend a large portion of their time engaged in fairly unrewarding work, feeling bored, or concerned for their personal safety; and many may be further criminalized by attitudes and values absorbed from other prisoners. A portion will be in the retrogressive and ethically indefensible state of solitary confinement (Smith 2006), a measure that does not in any case achieve its supposed main purpose of reducing violent misconduct (Morris 2016). Daily prison routines, requiring large numbers of carefully managed movements between cells, washrooms, workshops, kitchen, servery, sports hall, and journeys to the prison library or health-care center, can be tedious and time-consuming. Prisoners have to be inducted, assessed, allocated; their behavior observed; incidents recorded. While clearly there are exceptions to this, for the most part the majority of correctional staff usually has little opportunity to participate in discussion with individual prisoners or small groups. In any case, their job training does not prepare them for engaging in this in any depth.

Other professionals based in prisons, such as teachers, social workers, psychologists, or specialized therapists, are usually thinly spread. Often they have specific tasks allotted that leave little time for direct work on prisoner rehabilitation. But given the overriding concern with security, many of those tasks are seen by custody staff as distracting, inconsequential, or both. Collectively, despite hard work on the part of many people, the prospect of rehabilitation being meaningfully achieved can easily be lost in the everyday proceedings of institutional life. Several authors have attested to the pitfalls that can arise, for example, when providing drug treatment services in prisons, from negotiating the numerous "interfaces" between different stakeholder groups (Lurigio and Swartz 1994) to preoccupation with events of other kinds, such as a smoking ban or a change of treatment providers (Linhorst, Knight, Johnston, and Trickey 2001). Lehman, Greener, Rowan-Szal, and Flynn (2012) advise conducting preliminary assessment of a prison's "readiness for change," as this may uncover several impediments with respect to both the availability of resources and the organizational climate.

Researchers in this area have acknowledged that, until fairly recently, not enough attention was paid to the process of program implementation in prison settings. By comparison with the focus on the materials that constituted the programs themselves, issues of delivery and management were not only neglected but also often totally overlooked (Gendreau, Goggin, and Smith 1999). Palmer (1995) distinguished between two aspects of rehabilitation in justice services, *programatic* and *nonprogramatic*. The former refers to the nature, design, structure, content, and other ingredients of programs themselves. The latter refers to contextual and organizational factors that affect their installation and delivery. By comparison with the former, these aspects of criminal justice rehabilitation remain less developed and less well understood.

Nevertheless there have been some advances in exploring this. Gendreau, Goggin, and Smith (2001) identified a list of factors that should be considered in developing guidelines for better quality implementation procedures. Acting on them means focusing on key issues when deciding and planning to introduce interventions in penal settings. While they did not find well-designed experimental trials demonstrating this, they cite other evidence that more attention paid to the implementation process corresponds with better outcomes. They grouped the issues to be addressed into four categories. First, it is vital to consider *organizational factors*, such as whether a host agency has a track record of making innovations, and whether there is evidence of workforce stability (e.g., a low level of staff turnover). Second, *program factors* include an agreement by staff that the program is needed, that stakeholders have realistic expectations of what it can achieve, that the additional work is financially supported, and there are no major problems or other changes occurring simultaneously. Third, there should be involvement of a *change agent*, who has professional credibility and brings a sound knowledge of the nature of the change being introduced and of the agency itself. Finally, several *staff factors* are also crucial: Those involved should understand and accept the rationale for adopting the program, have the skills (or be provided the training) needed to manage and deliver it, and be provided with the resources for doing so.

Bernfeld, Farrington, and Leschied (2001) perceived the question of implementation as sufficiently important to suggest that in order to foster its development, it should be regarded as a field in its own right. Long-standing advice from those with experience of program implementation suggests that it is vital to address it on four levels: *client, program, organization*, and *community* (Bernfeld, Blasé, and Fixsen 1990). Self-evidently, a program should be designed to address the recognized needs of a client group, but to maximize the likelihood of making this happen both the organizational context and the wider community context in which it occurs also need to be taken into account. Overlooking any one of those levels is likely to mean problems will arise. McCarthy (1989, cited in Leschied, Bernfeld, and Farrington 2001) suggested a number of conditions need to be met in implementation if it is to generate larger scale and more enduring change across a service delivery system. There should be a decision at a senior level to instigate and sustain the change process. Senior staff need to foster "multilevel ownership" of the innovation. Ideally, there would be pilot projects to demonstrate the value of planned changes, and where "centers of excellence" are established they should be assured long-term monetary support. There should be active leadership to "neutralize the forces of counter-control" that are likely to develop. Leaders build wider investment in and regard for the innovation and there should be "top to bottom" training of staff to enable them to play allotted parts in the departure and to elicit and maintain their support for it. Based on their work introducing a substance abuse treatment program into prisons over a seven-year period, Linhorst, Dirks-Linhorst, Bernsen, and Childrey (2009) offered a similar set of guidance.

In a meta-analysis focused on one aspect of these specifications, Dowden and Andrews (2004) found significant relationships between staff-related factors and the outcomes of programs in terms of recidivism. They defined these factors as elements of "core correctional practice" and analyzed their effects across 273 tests from 225 separate studies. Several variables were significantly correlated with the effect sizes of interventions. This showed that skills of staff in structuring learning, modeling, and problem-solving; in showing warmth, confidence, genuineness, empathy, and other relationship-enhancement skills; and in effective use of reinforcement and of authority (a "firm but fair" approach) contributed significantly to larger effects sizes in terms of lower rates of recidivism. Using the same dataset, Andrews and Dowden (2005) probed the relationship between the effects of interventions and the integrity of program delivery. The latter was assessed with reference to a series of indicators such as fidelity to the assigned treatment model; appropriate selection, training, and supervision of staff; availability of program and training manuals; monitoring of program delivery and level of attendance at sessions, and involvement of an evaluator. Unfortunately, in many services, some (and sometimes most) of these features were absent. Across all studies, out of ten indicators of integrity the average number present was only 3.46. But "mean effect size was significantly greater with programs that incorporated elements of program integrity" (2005, p. 181). Other reviews of this issue are consolidated by Smith, Gendreau, and Swartz (2009). Similarly, in another meta-analytic review, Lowenkamp, Latessa, and Smith (2006) found that program quality, gauged in terms of the

Correctional Program Assessment Inventory (CPAI, discussed later), which records these indicators in a more formalized way, was also closely associated with outcome effectiveness.

Subsequently, Andrews (2011) analyzed the evidence pertaining to nonprogrammatic factors and their role in effective service delivery. He reviewed a set of seven program "failures" that on close examination revealed a mixture of effects. For example, when study groups were broken down, differential outcomes were observed according to whether programs had been delivered well or badly, by higher functioning versus lower functioning staff, by reliable delivery of the intended model, and by the extent of application of RNR principles. However, we should note that among the reviews just discussed, some of the interventions evaluated were for younger offenders and the majority were provided in community rather than custodial settings. Therefore caution needs to be exercised in extrapolating the reasons for failure to prison-based work.

III. Prison Environment and Organization

What steps can be taken to advance the possibility of prisons becoming places of rehabilitative work rather than expecting that they will have their effects through deterrence? A probably necessary, though almost certainly not sufficient condition, is that prisons should be well run. There should be reasonably good internal order, meaning a level of discontent and disturbance kept as low as possible, not beset by high levels of prisoner misconduct or unrest.

Many factors influence the occurrence of prison violence. The most frequently studied explanations focus on the concepts of *importation* (individuals with histories of rule breaking and, in some cases a readiness to fight, bring a propensity toward violence with them), and *deprivation* (prison hardships induce stress and conflict). There are also studies of micro-level interactions, situational flashpoints, and staff-prisoner exchanges. Various permutations of those factors have been investigated in integrative models. It is beyond the scope of this chapter to review that area in depth (see Steiner in this volume). However, there have been reviews of interventions designed to reduce rates of violent infractions. French and Gendreau (2006) reported a meta-analysis of sixty-eight studies, all employing either a randomized or comparison control group design, with an aggregate sample of 21,467 offenders, generating a total of 104 effect-size tests. The main focus of this was on the effects of prison-based treatment programs on misconduct and on recidivism after release, as well as to test whether interventions that adhered to the RNR model achieved better effects than those that did not. The overall mean effect size (r) across all studies was fairly modest at 0.14, but was 0.26 among 40 evaluations of behaviorally based programs, rising to 0.39 when weighted by sample sizes. Some other types of intervention also had positive (favorable) effects but they were weaker than for this group of studies.

Byrne and Hummer (2008) reviewed findings of 57 empirical studies, published in the period 1984-2006, concerned with several aspects of prison culture and their relationship to violent misconduct. The variables they extracted included levels of prison crowding, classification and management practices, situational controls, and prisoner profiles. They summarized the findings in relation to the relative strength of support for the two main competing models used to explain violation of prison rules. From the importation model, given that disciplinary problems are thought to arise from known troublesome prisoners, it follows they are best reduced by improved prediction, classification, and control. In the deprivation model, where such problems are seen as a function of prison environments, the best solution is thought to be more extensive provision of paid work, change programs, and ability to maintain external contacts. Although the evidence concerning this remains fairly limited, the latter policy was more strongly supported by research (Byrne and Hummer 2008; Huebner 2003).

It is difficult to envisage effective correctional rehabilitation taking place in an atmosphere of tension and disruption. If prison inmates are preoccupied with fears over personal safety or with gang rivalries, it may be difficult to focus their attention on longer term concerns. A third approach to the factors that contribute to prison indiscipline, the *administrative control* model, accords considerable importance to prison management procedures as a major factor in reducing the frequency of infractions including violence. Comparisons between different prison systems have suggested that violent indiscipline is likely to be lower where prisons are well managed. The latter is likely to be observable in rule structures, in a clear division of labor, explicit routines, communication with prisoners, well supported staff, and confident leadership. Prisoners are more likely to assent to staff authority and conform to rules when they perceive them as possessing *legitimacy* (Bottoms 1999); that is, when they see them as reasonable, justifiable, and applied fairly. While this variable is notoriously difficult to capture in research, studies by Wooldredge and Steiner (2012, 2014) have provided evidence on an association between it and lower levels of violent infractions.

It is frequently remarked in debates on penal sanctions that it is important for those who have broken the law to become more aware of the consequences of their actions. That is often interpreted, however, as vindicating the use of punitive methods to "teach them a lesson." However, methods deploying some form of *contingency management* (e.g., token economies), produce better results. This behavioral-based method has an established track record as an effective component of the treatment of substance use problems, as shown in a meta-analysis by Prendergast et al. (2006). It can be successfully used in prison-based drug treatment (Burdon, De Lore, and Prendergast 2011), and Gendreau, Listwan, Kuhns, and Exum (2014) have reported a separate meta-analysis of its use in a wider range of settings, including as an approach to increasing prisoners' accountability. This showed that contingency management can be instrumental in increasing a large variety of "target behaviors" including prosocial, cooperative action and attendance at education and work programs. However, most prison-based studies of this were done in the 1970s, and it does not currently appear to be an active area of research. Also, the inclusion of contingency management in the form of an "incentives and privileges" scheme in an atmosphere that is inimical to the approach, in being fundamentally punitive and where coercion is the modal form of power, can detract from and undermine its usefulness (Liebling 2008; Liebling and Crewe 2012).

IV. INTRODUCING AND ESTABLISHING PROGRAMS

As some of these examples imply, if prisons were to expand their levels of rehabilitative activity, including the inception of intervention programs, it is unfortunately not the case that everyone would be in favor of the development. The process through which an organization can subvert, even undermine, an attempt to change its ways of working is by no means unique to prisons. Until an initiative gains the support of a critical mass of the staff, or if there are powerful factions opposed to it, whether overtly or covertly, however much it is valued by others it may stand little chance of survival. For example, given the paramount importance of security, movement of prisoners between locations (from cell blocks to a rehabilitation unit) might be stopped or delayed on the grounds of a suspected risk or threat. Or, rooms that were reserved for a group program may somehow have been allocated for other uses, with no one apparently knowing how that occurred. Procedures for monitoring integrity and quality of delivery should be able to identify when rehabilitation programs are falling victim to problems such as these.

The everyday operation of programs can be assessed in a number of ways, and while their central aim is to help inform and guide that process, they may also expose organizational blockages of the kind just mentioned. There are ready-made instruments for carrying out this task. The most widely used is the Correctional Program Assessment Inventory (CPAI: Gendreau and Andrews 2001). It is used to map the extent to which an intervention program or service applies the principles of the RNR correctional model. It involves staff interviews and ratings across several domains of a service's work, including characteristics of offenders, staff selection and training, program features, and implementation processes. The inventory has demonstrated its usefulness in appraising programs for evaluative purposes and in delineating relationships between features of them and reductions in recidivism (e.g. Lowenkamp et al. 2010). Another instrument, the Correctional Program Checklist, is partly based on the CPAI but has additional items (University of Cincinnati Corrections Institute 2008). Adopting a different approach, Bouffard, Taxman, and Silverman (2003) considered that the CPAI relied too heavily on information provided by program staff and resorted instead to direct observation of program activity using a specially devised Structured Social Observation schedule.

There is one respect in which institution-based programs can be said to outperform their counterparts in the community: On average they have lower rates of attrition. That applies both to noncompletion of programs once begun ("dropout") and also to precommencement attrition (nonappearance or "nonstarters"). Olver, Stockdale, and Wormith (2011) reported a meta-analysis of 114 studies of attrition from treatment and analyzed moderators associated with it. There was a significant difference between custody and community-based services. For example, the average noncompletion rate for prison programs was 19.9 percent as compared with an average of 31.2 percent for community programs, and 36.9 percent for parole/probation offices. The corresponding figures with nonstarters included were 31 percent, 37.2 percent, and 44.3 percent. The reasons for this are not clear and may be varied, but we might speculate that it is a function of the closer monitoring of everyday routines in prison, and that the range of options for nonattendance is considerably narrower than in the community where there may be many other distractions.

Even so, a noncompletion rate of one in five is puzzling in what is supposedly a highly controlled environment, and worrying given the repeated finding that program attrition is associated (via other mediating variables) with a higher risk of reoffending. Given the limited alternative choices in a custodial setting, absence from programs could be an indirect sign of weak institutional support for rehabilitative activities. That, in turn, may reflect insufficient provision of staff time for escorting or other support duties. Some of this could be due to lack of resources or to administrative error. But a proportion may be a result of sabotage by staff who either do not prioritize allocation of resources to sustain programs or who deliberately sideline systems put in place for that purpose. For these reasons it is important to record attendance levels and, if possible, note reasons for nonattendance. All of this affirms the importance of tending to the context in which any adjustment is being made to "business as usual."

Possibly one of the largest scale departures of this type was begun in the 1990s when the prison service of England and Wales formulated plans for the introduction of treatment programs on a significant scale across a large number of prison units. Government policy was announced making additional resources available for this change, which would include extensive staff training, supervision, organizational change, and evaluation of both short- and long-term outcomes.

The inception of program use in the prison service of England and Wales from the mid-1990s onward was accompanied and underpinned by the introduction of a number of mechanisms intended to ensure the dissemination of programs across multiple sites, and to preserve treatment integrity, given the possibility of divergent interpretations of program materials. The process was overseen through a newly established working group within the prison service's headquarters, the Offending Behavior Programs Unit, acting in consultation with a specially convened and independent panel of experts, which has continued to the present and is currently known as the Correctional Services Advisory and Accreditation Panel. The importance of accreditation to the development of criminal justice rehabilitation has been emphasized by Lipton et al. (2000). Accounts of the process of introducing and safeguarding the accreditation framework are given by Clark (2010) and an "inside story" of the Panel's work is given by Maguire, Grubin, Lösel, and Raynor (2010).

A key task in seeking to ensure the quality of intervention services was to devise a set of criteria for the accreditation of programs. Essentially such a process is akin to one that might be found in education, health, or other locations where services are being provided, with the task of setting and then monitoring standards of delivery of those services despite variations in context. The original criteria were intermittently modified to incorporate new knowledge and also in response to the need to accommodate the changing nature of programs designed to focus on complex and challenging problems (e.g., to accommodate the design of therapeutic community regimes as compared with structured cognitive behavioral programs). The criteria as they stand at present are the following:

- *A clear model of change*: The program is based on a clear, explicit model of change with a well-articulated basis in a broader theoretical framework.
- *Selection of offenders*: There are clear and appropriate criteria for the selection and allocation of those who should take part.
- *Targeting a range of dynamic risk factors*: The program's materials and methods must target a range of dynamic risk factors (i.e., it is multimodal in format and content).
- *Effective methods*: The program entails use of demonstrably effective methods of intervention, derived from relevant research literature.
- *Skills orientated*: Methods used in the program focus on the acquisition and development of relevant skills to enable individuals to avoid reoffending.
- *Sequencing, intensity, and duration*: There are clear, explicit links between the sequencing, intensity, and duration of the program's separate components.

- *Engagement and motivation*: The methods used take account of the need to engage and motivate participants and specify how this will be done.
- *Continuity of programs and services*: The program is integrated with other aspects of service provision (e.g., sentence planning or community supervision).
- *Process evaluation and maintaining integrity*: Provision is made for monitoring integrity of delivery (i.e., to check sessions are being delivered in accordance with the planned model).
- *Ongoing evaluation*: Arrangements are in place for data collection and analysis used in ongoing outcome evaluations.

For a program to be accredited, its designers needed to prepare and submit a sizeable quantity of supporting documentation. Each program requires five manuals: A *theory manual*, presenting the intervention model and research evidence supporting it; the *program manual* itself, describing the content, exercises, and materials to be used; an *assessment and evaluation manual*, setting out procedures for prisoner selection and monitoring; a *management and operational manual*, containing guidance on program delivery within the institutional setting; and a *staff training manual*, containing materials for preparing staff to run the program.

It is important not to confuse the setting of standards with the imposition of a bland uniformity in terms of how the work was done. Prison staff members were allowed some discretion in how to adapt program materials, but it was important to distinguish which adaptations of a method were permissible and which were not. The former complied with the model underlying a program and did not threaten or compromise treatment integrity but fulfilled the principle of responsivity by addressing features of diversity among participant groups. This could have an impact on how the program was received and thereby its chances of having beneficial effects. In retrospect, it may be that this aspect of program delivery should have been given more attention than it was, as it appeared to be helpful in maintaining staff motivation so that they did not feel all aspects of the work were imposed on them and were not given credit for their adaptability and their innovation skills.

Based on the submitted documents, the panel then allots scores on each of the accreditation criteria on a 3-point scale (2 = fully met; 1 = partially met; 0 = not met). To be awarded accredited status, a program must score 18 to 20 points. At the time of this writing, a total of 33 programs have achieved this and are in current use in prisons. They include general offending-behavior programs, attended by prisoners who have been convicted of a variety of offense types, plus programs focused specifically on acquisitive crime, alcohol-related crime, substance-related offending, sex offenses, and other violent offenses. The list also includes some therapeutic community regimes, programs focused on healthy living, and a program for prisoners classified as "highly psychopathic." A separate 13 programs are accredited for use in probation services in the community, and 10 programs exist in variant forms for use in both locations (Correctional Services Accreditation Panel 2011).

To encourage the uptake of program use, the governor of each participating prison was asked to appoint a program staff team. These had a tripartite management structure, involving a program manager, usually a senior member of the prison custody staff, such as an assistant prison governor; a treatment manager, usually a forensic psychologist; and a through-care manager, usually the senior prison officer based on the prison site, who maintained contacts with outside agencies for continuity purposes before and after release.

The other members of the team were program tutors, who undertook prisoner selection, program delivery, and monitoring of prisoners' progress. Tutors were given specialized training in the program, and their work was supervised by senior staff. The delivery of offending behavior programs was made a Key Performance Indicator (KPI) of the prison service's role, and some elements of resource allocation were made dependent on achieving satisfactory scores on this indicator. This created an organizational motive for driving the associated work.

For quality assurance and integrity-monitoring purposes, a series of procedures was developed and put in place. Pivotal amongst them was an Annual Site Audit that required collating an extensive portfolio of information on program delivery. The audit covered four areas of program provision encompassing a total of 48 indicators. The first, *institutional support* comprised items requiring, for example, formal statements showing senior managers' commitment to support the program and to provide resources accordingly. There needed to be evidence of suitable management structures and of procedures to ensure continuity of personnel, attendance at designated training events, and recording of data—which included prisoner-intake assessment and progress reports, levels of inmate attendance, and postcompletion and short-term follow-up test results. As part of the objective of changing the prison culture, program teams were also required to provide quarterly awareness sessions for their colleagues elsewhere in the prison and to ensure that a certain proportion of staff attended on each occasion.

Other aspects of the audit included recording information on *treatment management*, such as procedures for staff selection and training, mentoring (working initially alongside a more experienced colleague), and regular supervision; and *through-care*, concerned with maintaining links between prison and community. This entailed effective liaison between the program team and other prison departments, conduct of review meetings at the point of program completion, and contact with probation supervisors of ex-prisoners on parole.

The final area dealt with *quality of delivery* and preservation of program integrity. To inform this, all sessions were videotaped, with the camera focusing on the program tutors. Since prisoners might, on occasion, inadvertently be seen in the recordings, they were required to sign a written agreement regarding confidentiality. An independent auditor familiar with the nature of the program viewed and rated a randomly selected sample of the recordings in terms of three main features: The tutor's adherence to the manual, appropriateness of interaction style, and group facilitation skills. Each of these headings subsumed a set of items rated on 5-point scales. Items included (for example) effective achievement of session objectives, the clarity of explanations given for exercises, making connections between different program elements, challenging offense-supportive attitudes, and managing groups such that all members had an opportunity to contribute. Scores were summed and averaged to produce an overall quality-of-delivery score. If this fell below a specified level, the issues that arose were discussed in supervision. If there was a recurrent problem of poor delivery, the tutor could be withdrawn from the role and might be asked to retrain or be reassigned to other duties. All of these quality control tasks were carried out by central (prison headquarters) staff, sometimes by staff from the prison service's regional offices, and sometimes on a peer review basis with unit teams from separate prisons evaluating each other's work.

This is an elaborate and exacting set of procedures, and some may question whether the scale of bureaucracy involved is really necessary. In contrast, there are occasions when an exceptional individual can give leadership and induce large-scale changes in single prisons or penal services, as happened for example in the now legendary Massachusetts experiment of the 1970s. There, over a period of only two years, then Commissioner of Youth Services Dr. Jerome Miller made dramatic and lasting changes by virtually emptying the state's secure training schools, without any resultant escalation in crime (Coates, Miller, and Ohlin 1978). But instances of that kind are rare, and each has unique features that may not be replicable on a larger scale or in a way that can be applied systematically as an approach to policy formation. Quality control on any sizeable scale is unfortunately hard to ensure without some reliance on recording processes that will inevitably seem somewhat bureaucratic. But in any case, Byrne and Hummer (2008) dismissed as a myth the idea that a charismatic leader is as likely to guarantee success in prison management. They noted that senior staff of correctional agencies in the United States do not usually remain in their posts for very long (usually four years or less), and the same likely applies in many other penal systems.

That will carry cost implications, and some might query the value and cost of intensive input for a group that has, after all, broken society's rules and caused harm to other people. But even if we set aside the welfare-centered aspects of this (bearing in mind that many prisoners have come from deprived and/or dysfunctional backgrounds), in terms of subsequent savings if crime is reduced, rehabilitative efforts can yield positive and highly significant benefit-cost ratios. This is amply demonstrated in the series of reports produced by the Washington State Institute for Public Policy (Lee et al. 2012), which have shown that there are healthy returns on the outlays required for properly funded offender rehabilitation programs.

While initial outcomes from the dissemination of programs across prison services in England and Wales were mixed (Friendship, Blud, Erikson, and Travers 2002; Cann, Falshaw, Nugent, and Friendship 2003), recent studies have reported clearer results. Travers, Mann, and Hollin (2014) analyzed the differences between two-year predicted and actual rates of reconviction for 21,373 male offenders. The group overall showed a 15 percent reduction in reconviction compared with predictions, which, broken down by principal offense type, showed corresponding reductions of 48 percent, 29 percent, and 22 percent for those who had committed sex, violent, and drug crimes, respectively. However, there was no difference for acquisitive offenders and a small increase (6 percent) for those whose index offense had been robbery. This type of comparison strategy is often viewed as unconvincing, and randomized controlled trials would be considered more persuasive. However, it is worth comparing these results with those of Lloyd, Mair, and Hough (1994), who found that, following different court disposals, expected and actual reconviction rates were practically identical.

V. Conclusion

If criminal justice authorities seek to make penal systems more effective, to achieve the goals of sentencing in a more judicious yet still serviceable way, it seems crucial that some form of realignment of objectives is needed in the direction outlined here. Doing so could be allied to the broader concept of *justice reinvestment* (Brown et al. 2016), in which there is a net transfer of resources from maintaining high prison volumes into community-based services. Prison places are then reserved for those who need to be incapacitated, thereby also providing them with more opportunities for genuine rehabilitation. In England and Wales this has been recommended by the House of Commons Justice Committee (2010). In the United States there are examples of what some aspects of such a departure could look like, for example in Hawaii's Opportunity Probation with Enforcement (HOPE) program (Kleiman 2011) and in policy changes in North Carolina (Justice Center 2014). A process whereby prison populations were reduced in a stepwise fashion with commensurate increases in community provision, linked to a parallel process of transferring resources from the one to the other, is feasible in principle and could be done in practice without compromising public safety (McGuire 2012). It is surely possible to conceive of a progressive justice system that affords sound protection to the public while also dealing with adjudicated offenders in a way that is both effective and humane. It is likely to be one which draws on the now substantial findings of social science research concerning each of these issues. Such things have of course been said many times before; they bear repetition nonetheless.

REFERENCES

Andrews, Donald A. 2011. "The Impact of Nonprogrammatic Factors on Criminal-Justice Interventions." *Legal and Criminological Psychology* 16:1–23.

Andrews, Donald A., and James L. Bonta. 2010. "Rehabilitating Criminal Justice Policy and Practice." *Psychology, Public Policy, and Law* 16:39–55.

Andrews, Donald A., and Craig Dowden. 2005. "Managing Correctional Treatment for Reduced Recidivism: A Meta-Analytic Review of Program Integrity." *Legal and Criminological Psychology* 10:173–187.

Ashworth, Andrew. 2015. *Sentencing and Criminal Justice*, 6th ed. Oxford: Oxford University Press.

Bales, William D., and Alex R. Piquero. 2012. "Assessing the Impact of Imprisonment on Recidivism." *Journal of Experimental Criminology* 8:71–101.

Berman, Gavin. 2010. *Prison Population Statistics*. London: House of Commons Library.

Bernfeld, Gary A., Karen A. Blase, and Dean L. Fixsen. 1990. "Towards a Unified Perspective on Service Delivery Systems: Application of the Teaching-Family Model." In *Behavioral Disorders of Adolescence*, edited by Robert J. McMahon and Ray DeV Peters. New York: Plenum Press.

Bernfeld, Gary A., David P. Farrington, and Alan W. Leschied. 2001. *Offender Rehabilitation in Practice: Implementing and Evaluating Effective Programs*. Chichester: John Wiley and Sons.

Bierie, David M. 2012. "Is Tougher Better? The Impact of Physical Prison Conditions on Inmate Violence." *International Journal of Offender Therapy and Comparative Criminology* 56:338–355.

Boonin, David. 2008. *The Problem of Punishment*. New York: Cambridge University Press.

Bottoms, Anthony E. 1999. "Interpersonal Violence and Social Order in Prisons." *Crime and Justice* 26:205–281.

Bouffard, Jeffrey A., Faye S. Taxman, and Rebecca Silverman. 2003. "Improving Process Evaluations of Correctional Programs by Using a Comprehensive Evaluation Methodology." *Evaluation and Program Planning* 26:149–161.

Bourgon, Guy, and Barbara Armstrong. 2005. "Transferring the Principles of Effective Treatment into a 'Real World' Prison Setting." *Criminal Justice and Behavior* 32:3–25.

Braga, Anthony A., Anne M. Piehl, and David Hureau. 2009. "Controlling Violent Offenders Released to the Community: Evaluation of the Boston Reentry Initiative." *Journal of Research in Crime and Delinquency* 46:411–436.

Braga, Anthony A., David L. Weisburd. 2012. "The Effects of Focused Deterrence Strategies on Crime: A Systematic Review and Meta-Analysis of the Empirical Evidence." *Journal of Research in Crime and Delinquency* 49:323–358.

Brown, David, Chris Cunneen, Melanie Schwartz, Julie Stubbs, and Courtney Young. 2016. *Justice Reinvestment: Winding Back Imprisonment*. London: Palgrave MacMillan.

Burdon, William M., Jef St. De Lore, and Michael L. Prendergast. 2011. "Intervention in Prison-Based Drug Treatment: Project BRITE." *Journal of Psychoactive Drugs* 43:40–50.

Byrne, James M., and Don Hummer. 2007. "Myths and Realities of Prison Violence: A Review of the Evidence." *Victims and Offenders* 2:77–90.

Byrne, James M., and Don Hummer. 2008. "Examining the Impact of Institutional Culture on Prison Violence and Disorder: An Evidence-Based Review." In *The Culture of Prison Violence*, edited by James M. Byrne, Don Hummer, and Faye S. Taxman. Boston: Pearson.

Cann, Jenny, Louise Falshaw, Francis Nugent, and Caroline Friendship. 2003. *Understanding What Works: Accredited Cognitive Skills Programs for Adult Men and Young Offenders*. Available at http://webarchive.nationalarchives.gov.uk/20110218135832/rds.homeoffice.gov.uk/rds/pdfs2/r226.pdf

Center on Juvenile and Criminal Justice. 2008. *Research Update: Does More Imprisonment Lead to Less Crime?* Available at www.cjcj.org

Chen, M. Keith, and Jesse M. Shapiro. 2007. "Do Harsher Prison Conditions Reduce Recidivism? A Discontinuity-Based Approach." *American Law and Economics Review* 9:1–29.

Cid, Jose. 2009. "Is Imprisonment Criminogenic? A Comparative Study of Recidivism Rates Between Prison and Suspended Prison Sanctions." *European Journal of Criminology* 6:459–480.

Clark, Danny. 2010. "Therapy and Offending Behaviour Programmes." In *Psychological Therapy in Prisons and Other Secure Settings*, edited by Joel Harvey and Kristy Smedley. Abingdon: Willan.

Clear, Todd R. 1994. *Harm in American Penology*. Albany: State University of New York Press.

Coates, Robert B., Alden D. Miller, and Lloyd Ohlin. 1978. *Diversity in a Youth Correctional System: Handling Delinquents in Massachusetts*. Cambridge: Ballinger.

Cook, Philip J., and Jens Ludwig. 2011. "Economical Crime Control." In *Controlling Crime: Strategies and Tradeoffs*, edited by Philip J. Cook, Jens Ludwig, and Justin McCrary. Chicago: University of Chicago Press.

Correctional Services Accreditation Panel. 2011. *The Correctional Services Accreditation Panel Report 2010–2011*. Available at www.justice.gov.uk

Crank, Beverly R., and Timothy Brezina. 2013. "Prison Will Either Make Ya or Break Ya: Punishment, Deterrence, and the Criminal Lifestyle." *Deviant Behavior* 34:782–802.

Dowden, Craig, and Donald A. Andrews. 2004. "The Importance of Staff Practice in Delivering Effective Correctional Treatment: A Meta-Analytic Review of Core Correctional Practice." *International Journal of Offender Therapy and Comparative Criminology* 48:203–214.

Drago, Francesco, Roberto Galbiati, and Pietro Vertova. 2011. "Prison Conditions and Recidivism." *American Law and Economics Review* 13:103–130.

Durlauf, Steven N., Daniel S. Nagin. 2011a. "The Deterrent Effect of Imprisonment." In *Controlling Crime: Strategies and Tradeoffs*, Philip J. Cook, Jens Ludwig, and Justin McCrary. Chicago: University of Chicago Press.

Durlauf, Steven N., and Daniel S. Nagin. 2011b. "Imprisonment and Crime: Can Both Be Reduced?" *Criminology and Public Policy* 10:13–54.

Foucault, Michel. 1979. *Discipline and Punish: The Birth of the Prison*. Harmondsworth: Peregrine Books.

French, Sheila A., and Paul Gendreau. 2006. "Reducing Prison Misconducts: What Works!" *Criminal Justice and Behavior* 33:185–218.

Friendship, Caroline, Linda Blud, Matthew Erikson, and Rosie Travers. 2002. *An Evaluation of Cognitive-Behavioural Treatment for Prisoners*. Available at http://webarchive.nationalarchives.gov.uk/20110218135832/http:/rds.homeoffice.gov.uk/rds/pdfs2/r161.pdf

Gaes, Gerald G., Scott D. Camp. 2009. "Unintended Consequences: Experimental Evidence for the Criminogenic Effect of Prison Security Level Placement on Post-Release Recidivism." *Journal of Experimental Criminology* 5:139–162.

Garland, David. 1990. *Punishment and Modern Society: A Study in Social Theory*. Oxford: Clarendon Press.

Gendreau, Paul, and Don A. Andrews. 2001. *The Correctional Program Assessment Inventory—2000*.

Gendreau, Paul, Claire Goggin, and Paula Smith. 1999. "The Forgotten Issue in Effective Correctional Treatment: Program Implementation." *International Journal of Offender Therapy and Comparative Criminology* 43:180–187.

Gendreau, Paul, Claire Goggin, and Paula Smith. 2001. "Implementation Guidelines for Correctional Programs in the 'Real World.'" In *Offender Rehabilitation in Practice: Implementing and Evaluating Effective Programs*, edited by Gary A. Bernfeld, David P. Farrington, and Alan W. Leschied. Chichester: John Wiley and Sons.

Gendreau, Paul, Shelley J. Listwan, Joseph B. Kuhns, and M. Lyn Exum. 2014. "Making Prisoners Accountable: Are Contingency Management Programs the Answer?" *Criminal Justice and Behavior* 41:1079–1102.

Hanson, R. Karl, Guy Bourgon, Leslie Helmus, and Shannon Hodgson. 2009. "The Principles of Effective Correctional Treatment Also Apply to Sex Offenders: A Meta-Analysis." *Criminal Justice and Behavior* 36:865–891.

Helland, Eric, and Alexander Tabarrok. 2007. "Does Three Strikes Deter? A Nonparametric Estimation." *Journal of Human Resources* 42:309–330.

Home Office. 1990. *Crime, Justice and Protecting the Public*. Cm 965. London: HMSO.

House of Commons Justice Committee. 2010. *Cutting Crime: The Case for Justice Reinvestment*. First Report of Session 2009–2010. London: The Stationery Office Limited.

Huebner, Beth M. 2003. "Administrative Determinants of Inmate Violence: A Multilevel Analysis." *Journal of Criminal Justice* 31:107–117.

Justice Center/Council of State Governments. 2014. *Justice Reinvestment in North Carolina: Three Years Later*. Available at https://csgjusticecenter.org/wp-content/uploads/2014/11/JRinNCThreeYearsLater.pdf

Kleiman, Mark A. R. 2011. "Justice Reinvestment in Community Supervision." *Criminology and Public Policy* 10:651–659.

Lee, Stephanie, Steve Aos, Elizabeth Drake, Annie Pennucci, Marna Miller, and Laurie Anderson. 2012. *Return on Investment: Evidence-based Options to Improve Statewide Outcomes, April 2012* (Document No. 12-04-1201). Olympia: Washington State Institute for Public Policy.

Lehman, Wayne E. K., Jack M. Greener, Grace, Rowan-Szal, and Patrick M. Flynn. 2012. "Organizational Readiness for Change in Correctional and Community Substance Abuse Programs." *Journal of Offender Rehabilitation* 51:96–114.

Leschied, Alan W., Gary A. Bernfeld, and David P. Farrington. 2001. "Implementation Issues." In *Offender Rehabilitation in Practice: Implementing and Evaluating Effective Programs*, edited by Gary A. Bernfeld, David P. Farrington, and Alan W. Leschied. Chichester: John Wiley and Sons.

Levitt, Steven D. 2004. "Understanding Why Crime Fell in the 1990s: Four Factors That Explain the Decline and Six That Do Not." *Journal of Economic Perspectives* 18:163–190.

Liebling, Alison. 2008. "Incentives and Earned Privileges Revisited: Fairness, Discretion and the Quality of Prison Life." *Journal of Scandinavian Studies in Criminology and Crime Prevention* 9:25–41.

Liebling, Alison, and Ben Crewe. 2012. "Prison Life, Penal Power, and Prison Effects." In *The Oxford Handbook of Criminology*, 5th ed., edited by Mike Maguire, Rod Morgan, and Robert Reiner. Oxford: Oxford University Press.

Linhorst, Donald M., P. Ann Dirks-Linhorst, Herbert L. Bernsen, and Julia Childrey. 2009. "The Development and Implementation of a Jail-Based Substance Abuse Treatment Program." *Journal of Social Work Practice in the Addictions* 9:91–112.

Linhorst, Donald M., Kevin Knight, J. Scott Johnston, and Myrna Trickey. 2001. "Situational Influences on the Implementation of a Prison-Based Therapeutic Community." *The Prison Journal* 81:436–453.

Lipsey, Mark W., Nana A. Landenberger, and Sandra J. Wilson. 2007. *Effects of Cognitive-Behavioral Programs for Criminal Offenders*. Campbell Systematic Reviews 2007:6. doi: 10.4073/csr.2007.6

Lipton, Douglas S., Frank S. Pearson, Charles M. Cleland, and Dorline Yee. 2002. "The Effects of Therapeutic Communities and Milieu Therapy on Recidivism." In *Offender Rehabilitation and Treatment: Effective Programs and Policies to Reduce Re-Offending*, edited by James McGuire. Chichester: John Wiley and Sons.

Lipton, Douglas, David Thornton, James McGuire, Frank J. Porporino, and Clive R. Hollin. 2000. "Program Accreditation and Correctional Treatment." *Substance Use & Misuse* 35:1705–1734.

Listwan, Shelley J., Christopher J. Sullivan, Robert Agnew, Francis T. Cullen, and Mark Colvin. 2013. "The Pains of Imprisonment Revisited: Impact of Strain on Inmate Recidivism." *Justice Quarterly* 30:144–168.

Lloyd, Charles, George Mair, Mike Hough. 1994. *Explaining Reconviction Rates: A Critical Analysis*. Home Office Research Study 136. London: HMSO.

Lofstrom, Magnus, and Steven Raphael. 2016. "Incarceration and Crime: Evidence from California's Public Safety Realignment Reform." *Annals of the American Academic of Political and Social Sciences* 664:196–220.

Lösel, Friedrich, and Peter Koferl. 1989. "Evaluation Research on Correctional Treatment in West Germany: A Meta-Analysis." In *Criminal Behavior and the Justice System: Psychological Perspectives*, edited by Hermann Wegener, Friedrich Lösel, and Jochen Haisch. New York: Springer-Verlag.

Lowenkamp, Christopher T., Anthony W. Flores, Alexander M. Holsinger, Matthew D. Makarios, and Edward Latessa. 2010. "Intensive Supervision Programs: Does Program Philosophy and the Principles of Effective Intervention Matter?" *Journal of Criminal Justice* 38:368–375.

Lowenkamp, Christopher T., Edward J. Latessa, and Paula Smith. 2006. "Does Correctional Program Quality Really Matter? The Impact of Adhering to the Principles of Effective Intervention." *Criminology and Public Policy* 5:575–594.

Lulham, Rohan, Don Weatherburn, and Lorana Bartels. 2009. "The Recidivism of Offenders Given Suspended Sentences: A Comparison with Full-Time Imprisonment." *Crime and Justice Bulletin: Contemporary Issues in Crime and Justice* 136. Sydney: NSW Bureau of Crime Statistics and Research.

Lurigio, Aurthur, and James Swartz. 1994. "Life at the Interface: Issues in the Implementation and Evaluation of a Multi-phased, Multi-agency, Jail-based Treatment Program." *Evaluation and Program Planning* 17:205–216.

Maguire, Mike, Don Grubin, Friedrich Lösel, and Peter Raynor. 2010. "'What Works' and the Correctional Services Accreditation Panel: Taking Stock from an Inside Perspective." *Criminology and Criminal Justice* 10:37–58.

Maruna, Shadd, Louise, Wilson, and Kathryn, Curran. 2006. "Why God Is Often Found Behind Bars: Prison Conversions and the Crisis of Self-Narrative." *Research in Human Development* 3:161–184.

Marvell, Thomas B., and Carlisle E. Moody. 1994. "Prison Population Growth and Crime Reduction." *Journal of Quantitative Criminology* 10:109–140.

McGuire, James. 2001. "Defining Correctional Programs." In *Compendium 2000 on Effective Correctional Programming*, edited by Laurence L. Motiuk and Ralph C. Serin. Ottawa: Correctional Service Canada.

McGuire, James. 2012. "Addressing System Inertia to Effect Change." In *Applying Social Science to Reduce Violent Offending*, edited by Joel A. Dvoskin, Jennifer L. Skeem, Raymond W. Novaco, and Kevin S. Douglas. New York: Oxford University Press.

McGuire, James. 2013. "'What Works' to Reduce Reoffending: 18 Years On." In *What Works in Offender Rehabilitation: An Evidence Based Approach to Assessment and Treatment*, Leam A. Craig, Loise Dixon, and Theresa A. Gannon. Chichester: Wiley-Blackwell.

Morgan, Steve. 1999. "Prison Lives: Critical Issues in Reading Prisoner Autobiography." *Howard Journal of Criminal Justice* 38:328–340.

Morris, Robert G. 2016. "Exploring the Effect of Exposure to Short-Term Solitary Confinement Among Violent Prison Inmates." *Journal of Quantitative Criminology* 32:1–22.

Nagin, Daniel S., Francis T. Cullen, and Cheryl Lero Jonson. 2009. "Imprisonment and Reoffending." In *Crime and Justice: A Review of Research*, edited by Michael H. Tonry. Chicago: University of Chicago Press.

Nieuwbeerta, Paul, Daniel S. Nagin, and Arjan A. J. Blokland. 2009. "Assessing the Impact of First-Time Imprisonment on Offenders' Subsequent Criminal Career Development: A Matched Samples Comparison." *Journal of Quantitative Criminology* 25:227–257.

Olver, Mark E., Keira C. Stockdale, and J. Stephen Wormith. 2011. "A Meta-Analysis of Predictors of Offender Treatment Attrition and its Relationship to Recidivism." *Journal of Consulting and Clinical Psychology* 79:6–21.

Palmer, Ted. 1995. "Programmatic and Nonprogrammatic Aspects of Successful Intervention: New Directions for Research." *Crime & Delinquency* 41:100–131.

Parhar, Karen K., J. Stephen Wormith, Dena M. Derkzen, and Adele M. Beauregard. 2008. "Offender Coercion in Treatment: A Meta-Analysis of Effectiveness." *Criminal Justice and Behavior* 35:1109–1135.

Parker, Robert Nash. 2012. "Why California's 'Three Strikes' Fails as Crime and Economic Policy, and What to Do." *California Journal of Politics and Policy* 5:206–231.

Pollock, Joycelyn M. 2014. "The Rationale of Imprisonment." In *Prisons Today and Tomorrow*, 3rd ed., edited by Ashley G. Blackburn, Shannon K. Fowler, and Joycelyn M. Pollock. Burlington: Jones and Bartlett Learning.

Prendergast, Michael L., Frank S. Pearson, Deborah Podus, Zachary K. Hamilton, and Lisa Greenwell. 2013. "The Andrews' Principles of Risk, Needs and Responsivity as Applied in Drug Treatment Programs: Meta-Analysis of Crime and Drug Use Outcomes." *Journal of Experimental Criminology* 9:275–300.

Prendergast, Michael L., Deborah Podus, John Finney, Lisa Greenwell, and John Roll. 2006. "Contingency Management for Treatment of Substance Use Disorders: A Meta-Analysis." *Addiction* 101:1546–1560.

Sacks, Stanley, Michael Chaple, JoAnn Y. Sacks, Karen McKendrick, and Charles M. Cleland. 2012. "Randomized Trial of a Re-Entry Modified Therapeutic Community for Offenders with Co-Occurring Disorders: Crime Outcomes." *Journal of Substance Abuse Treatment* 42:247–259.

Sacks, Stanley, JoAnn Y. Sacks, Karen McKendrick, Steven Banks, and Joe Stommel. 2004. "Modified TC for MICA Offenders: Crime Outcomes." *Behavioral Sciences and the Law* 22:477–501.

Smith, Paula, Paul Gendreau, Kristin Swartz. 2009. "Validating the Principles of Effective Intervention: A Systematic Review of the Contributions of Meta-Analysis in the Field of Corrections." *Victims and Offenders* 4:148–169.

Smith, Peter Scharff. 2006. "The Effects of Solitary Confinement on Prison Inmates: A Brief History and Review of the Literature." *Crime and Justice* 34:441–528.

Soering, Jens. 2004. *An Expensive Way to Make Bad People Worse: An Essay on Prison Reform from an Insider's Perspective.* New York: Lantern Books.

Spohn, Cassia. 2007. "The Deterrent Effect of Imprisonment and Offenders' Stakes in Conformity." *Criminal Justice Policy Review* 18:31–50.

Spohn, Cassia, and David Holleran. 2002. "The Effect of Imprisonment on Recidivism Rates of Felony Offenders: A Focus on Drug Offenders." *Criminology* 40:329–357.

Stewart, Lynn A., Jillian Flight, and Claire Slavin-Stewart. 2013. "Applying Effective Corrections Principles (RNR) to Partner Abuse Interventions." *Partner Abuse* 4:494–534.

Sykes, Gresham M. 1958. *The Society of Captives: A Study of a Maximum Security Prison.* Princeton: Princeton University Press.

Tarling, Roger. 1993. *Analysing Crime: Data, Models and Interpretations.* London: HMSO.

Travers, Rosie, Ruth E. Mann, and Clive R. Hollin. 2014. "Who Benefits from Cognitive Skills Programs? Differential Impact by Risk and Offense Type." *Criminal Justice and Behavior* 41:1103–1129.

University of Cincinnati Corrections Institute. 2008. *Evidence-Based Correctional Program Checklist.* Cincinnati: UCCI. Available at http://www.uc.edu/content/dam/uc/corrections/docs/Training%20Overviews/CPC%20ASSESSMENT%20DESCRIPTION.pdf

Vieraitis, Lynne M., Tomislav V. Kovandzic, and Thomas B. Marvell. 2007. "The Criminogenic Effects of Imprisonment: Evidence from State Panel Data." *Criminology and Public Policy* 6:589–622.

Villetaz, Patrice, Gwladys Gillieron, and Martin Killias. 2015. *The Effects on Re-Offending of Custodial vs. Non-Custodial Sanctions: An Updated Systematic Review of the State of Knowledge.* Campbell Systematic Reviews 2015:1. doi: 10.4073/csr.2015.1

Villetaz, Patrice, Martin Killias, and Isabel Zoder. 2006. *The Effects of Custodial Vs. Non-Custodial Sentences on Re-Offending: A Systematic Review of the State of Knowledge.* Campbell Systematic Reviews 2006:13. doi: 10.4073/csr.2006.13

von Hirsch, Andrew, Anthony E. Bottoms, Elizabeth Burney, and Per-Olof H. Wikström. 1999. *Criminal Deterrence and Sentencing Severity: An Analysis of Recent Research.* Oxford: Hart.

Walker, Nigel. 1991. *Why Punish? Theories of Punishment Reassessed*. Oxford: Oxford University Press.

Walmsley, Roy. 2014. *World Prison Population List*, 10th ed. University of Essex: International Center for Prison Studies.

Weatherburn, Don, Jiuzhao Hua, and Steve Moffatt. 2006. "How Much Crime Does Prison Stop? The Incapacitation Effect of Prison on Burglary." *Crime and Justice Bulletin: Contemporary Issues in Crime and Justice* 93. Sydney: NSW Bureau of Crime Statistics and Research.

Wermink, Hilde, Arjan Blokland, Paul Nieuwbeerta, Daniel Nagin, and Nikolaj Tollenaar. 2010. "Comparing the Effects of Community Service and Short-Term Imprisonment on Recidivism: A Matched Samples Approach." *Journal of Experimental Criminology* 6:325–349.

Windzio, Michael. 2006. "Is There a Deterrent Effect of Pains of Imprisonment? The Impact of 'Social Costs' of First Incarceration on the Hazard Rate of Recidivism." *Punishment and Society* 8:341–364.

Wolff, Nancy, Cuynthia L. Blitz, Jing Shi, Jane Siegel, and Ronet Bachman. 2007. "Physical Violence Inside Prisons: Rates of Victimization." *Criminal Justice and Behavior* 34:588–599.

Wooldredge, John, and Benjamin Steiner. 2012. "Race Group Differences in Prison Victimization Experiences." *Journal of Criminal Justice* 40:358–369.

Wooldredge, John, and Benjamin Steiner. 2014. "A Bi-Level Framework for Understanding Prisoner Victimization." *Journal of Quantitative Criminology* 30:141–162.

Woolf, Steven H. 2008. "The Meaning of Translational Research and Why It Matters." *Journal of the American Medical Association* 299:211–213.

SPECIAL OFFENDER POPULATIONS AND INMATE WELL-BEING

CHAPTER 24

....

PREVENTING SUICIDE IN DETENTION AND CORRECTIONAL FACILITIES

....

ROBERT D. CANNING AND JOEL A. DVOSKIN

SUICIDE is a significant and tragic public health problem. The World Health Organization estimates that 800,000 individuals die by suicide annually (see http://www.who.int/mental_health/prevention/suicide/suicideprevent/en/), making it the 15th leading cause of death worldwide. In the United States, in 2013 more than 41,000 individuals (mostly men) died by suicide (see http://webappa.cdc.gov/sasweb/ncipc/mortrate10_us.html), making it the 10th leading cause of death in the country.

Until almost 40 years ago, suicide in jails and prisons was not the subject of significant and systematic study by government agencies or academia. Hayes (1983) published the first national study of jail suicide in 1981 and later the first national study of prison suicide (Hayes 1995). Since then, due in part to the sheer increase in prison populations in the United States and the intense scrutiny this has brought, academic and governmental interest in suicide and suicide prevention in correctional settings has grown.[1] Responding to the apparent need, professional medical and mental health groups have promulgated guidelines for suicide-prevention strategies in their position statements about the treatment of correctional populations (see, e.g., American Psychiatric Association 2016).

This interest has heightened since 2000, when the US Congress passed the Death in Custody Reporting Act, which requires jurisdictions to report information on all deaths in custody (see http://www.bjs.gov/index.cfm?ty=dcdetail&iid=243). In 2001 the release of the Surgeon General's National Strategy for Suicide Prevention acknowledged the need for improved suicide prevention in the correctional environment (US Surgeon General 2001).

I. EPIDEMIOLOGY OF SUICIDE AND SUICIDE ATTEMPTS IN JAILS AND PRISONS

....

Suicide has been a leading cause of death in US correctional populations for many years. Between 2000 and 2012, suicide was the number-one cause of death among American jail prisoners (Bureau of Justice Statistics 2015). However, the frequency of suicide in jails dropped from 479 in 1979 to 327 in 2013, despite an increase in the US jail population from fewer than 200,000 prisoners in 1979 to more than 700,000 at mid-year 2013 (Hayes and Rowan 1988; Bureau of Justice Statistics 2015). Overall, the rate of suicide in American jails dropped from 129 per 100,000 prisoners in 1983 to 54 per 100,000 in 1999 (Hanson 2010) and 46 per 100,000 in 2013 (Bureau of Justice Statistics 2015).

Between 2001 and 2013, the overall rate of suicide in US state prisons was 16 per 100,000 prisoners (Bureau of Justice Statistics 2015).[2] In terms of raw numbers, the 2,577 prison inmates who died by suicide during this period were only exceeded by deaths due to cancer (11,223), heart disease (10,795), and liver disease (4,063). By comparison, during the same time period, only 762 homicides occurred in US prisons (Bureau of Justice Statistics 2015).

A. Demographic Factors

Both in the community and in correctional settings, suicide rates vary as a function of demographic characteristics. The overwhelming majority of suicide deaths in both jails and state prisons are among male prisoners. The Bureau of Justice Statistics (2015) through its Death in Custody Reporting Program reported that between 2000 and 2013, male jail prisoners committed 92 percent of suicides, while in state prison systems over 95 percent of suicides were committed by males. This large disparity is due, but only in part, to the high percentage of males held in US jails and prisons and also to the higher suicide rates for males generally.

Suicide rates in jails and prisons vary by racial group and mirror the different rates found in the community. In US jails, between 2000 and 2013, for instance, 70 percent of suicides were by white prisoners and, in state prisons, 59 percent were white prisoners, despite only 46 percent of jail prisoners and 36 percent of state and federal prisoners being white (Bureau of Justice Statistics 2015). Hispanic and African American prisoners have comparatively lower rates of suicide in both jails and prisons. In the first decade of the 21st century, Hispanic prisoners accounted for 12 percent and 16 percent of suicide deaths in jails and prisons, respectively, while African American prisoners accounted for 14 percent and 20 percent, respectively (Bureau of Justice Statistics 2015).

B. Individual Risk Factors

Risk factors for completed suicide in prison and jails are similar to those found in the community. In addition, correctional settings present a unique set of "correctional" factors that have been found to contribute to the risk for suicide.

As in the community, previous suicide attempts and psychiatric disorders are the most important risk factors for suicide among prisoners. Given the number of seriously mentally ill individuals incarcerated in the past 30 years, it is not surprising that the prevalence rate for serious mental illnesses such as schizophrenia, bipolar disorders, depressive disorders, and psychotic disorders is higher than in the community (Teplin 1994; Prins 2014). This, combined with the stressful correctional environment, increases the risk for suicide among mentally ill prisoners (Fazel et al. 2008).

A systematic review of studies of jail and prison suicides found that suicidal ideation, previous suicide attempts, a current psychiatric diagnosis, and being prescribed psychotropic medication were significant risk factors for suicide (Fazel et al. 2008). These authors point out that the combination of a psychiatric diagnosis and a history of self-harm is a particularly important risk factor for prisoners.

Although there has been substantial research on completed suicides among prisoners in the past three decades, less well understood are the numbers and rates of suicide attempts and other forms of self-injurious behavior in American prisons and jails. The one national survey that attempted to quantify the level of self-injury in prison systems nationally found that self-injury causes significant disruption, yet most states do not even keep a tally of such events. (Note, however, that many incidents of self-injurious behavior are not believed to be suicide attempts.) The authors estimate that approximately 2 percent of state prisoners engage in some form of self-injurious behavior annually (Appelbaum et al. 2011). A study of South Carolina prisoners found that those who self-harm were likely to be younger, Caucasian, unmarried, have more disciplinary infractions, and have a psychiatric diagnosis than prisoners who did not self-harm (Smith and Kaminski 2010).

Drug and alcohol use disorders are significant risk factors for suicide (Moscicki 2001; Nock et al. 2008). The high prevalence of substance use disorders in US correctional populations (Teplin 1994; National Center on Addiction and Substance Abuse 2010) likely contributes to the prevalence of suicide in jails and prisons. In jails, the likelihood of intoxication or withdrawal from drugs or alcohol may also contribute to the prevalence of suicide during the first few days of detention.

Evidence that prison populations have higher overall mortality than community populations (Patterson 2010) and that illness (Nock et al. 2008) and chronic pain (Tang and Crane 2006) are potent risk factors for suicide in the community suggest that medically ill prisoners are at increased risk of suicide (Way et al. 2005). Receiving a terminal diagnosis in prison or jail is a distressing and depressing event. Palliative care and hospice services may be limited, and the demands of treatment may be onerous and only exacerbate the poor conditions of some prisoners. Further, separation from loved ones may be especially painful when one is facing death. Prisoners faced with this situation may choose to end their own life. In addition, studies of released prisoners have found that the higher suicide risk associated with medical illness follows prisoners back into the community, resulting in high rates of suicide (and other causes of death) in a relatively short time period after leaving prison (Binswanger et al. 2007; Rosen, Schoenbach, and Wohl 2008; Zlodre, Jakov, and Fazel 2012).

Most prisoners in jails and prisons have suffered some form of childhood victimization (Maxfield and Widom 1996). In the 1980s, the intimate connection between childhood adversity and later criminal activity and psychopathology (particularly posttraumatic stress disorder) became clear (Widom 1989). Childhood maltreatment has been found to be a significant risk factor for suicide attempts (Johnson et al. 2002). Given these findings, all prisoners should be asked about a history of child maltreatment, which can be regarded as a chronic risk factor for suicide (Nock et al. 2008). Of course, because of the high prevalence of trauma in the lives of prisoners, trauma alone is a nonspecific risk factor that would yield many false positives. However, inquiry about the nature of a prisoner's trauma history can provide important insight into the nature of suicide risk.

A number of studies have found that there are unique "correctional" risk factors, related both to the individual prisoner and the context in which he or she is living. For instance, Fazel and colleagues (2008) noted that lengthy prison terms were associated with increased risk of suicide. They also found that being housed alone, preadjudication status, having a conviction for murder or a life sentence, or a violent offense were significant correlates of death by suicide.

The threat or fact of physical or sexual assault significantly increases the risk of self-harm or suicide for the victim. The Bureau of Justice Statistics (2013) reported that 4.0 percent of state prisoners and 3.2 percent of jail prisoners reported some form of sexual assault in 2011–2012. Physically small or frail, mentally disordered, intellectually disabled, homosexual, and transgendered prisoners may all be at higher risk of being assaulted by other prisoners.

The stress of life in correctional settings can take a toll on individual prisoners. Consistent with a diathesis-stress model of suicidal behavior (Mann et al. 1999), vulnerable prisoners, like vulnerable nonprisoners, may attempt suicide after exposure to a variety of life stressors. Medical illness, as mentioned, is one such stressor, but jail and prison inmates are exposed to other stressors that can increase their risk for self-harm, including suicide. For example, overcrowding has been found to increase the probability of suicide in prison populations (Huey and McNulty 2005). In addition, in a study of New York state prisoners, Way and colleagues (2005) found that receipt of "bad news" such as death of a family member increased the risk of suicide.

C. Contextual Factors

In correctional settings, the type of housing can increase the risk of suicide (Hughes and Metzner 2015). There has been much discussion in recent years (see, e.g., Berger, Chaplin, and Trestman 2013) of the deleterious effects of "segregated" housing. This type of housing can be either short term or long term and is designated in a variety of ways, such as disciplinary segregation, administrative segregation, security housing units, or supermax. In these settings, a prisoner is confined to a cell for many hours per day, and his or her interaction with other prisoners or staff can be very limited. In the most common and severe forms of segregation, a prisoner may be alone in a cell for up to 23 hours per day. Some prisons have assigned segregation prisoners to two-man cells, which remains a far cry from normal social interaction.

Bonner (2006) and Way et al. (2007) found that when prisoners are moved to higher security segregated settings, suicide risk may increase (see also Hughes and Metzner 2015.) This is particularly true if the rehousing is sudden and unexpected. The ability of staff to identify those prisoners who will suffer the most (and need more help) in segregated settings is difficult. In order to identify prisoners who are responding poorly to segregation as early as possible, many prisons now include regular rounds by mental health clinicians, typically consisting of brief cell-front conversations with every segregation prisoner. It is important to allow either the prisoner or the clinician to request a private clinical contact when requested or deemed appropriate.

One of the most pervasive and difficult problems is the predatory and violent nature of the correctional setting (see Toch 1997, as quoted in Cohen et al. 2011, pp. 13-14). Prisoners seek safe environments in which to live, and when they perceive the situation as hopeless and feel trapped, with few or no alternatives for relief, they can become suicidal. Large prison and jail systems that struggle with gang and drug problems often have gang "drop-outs" who can quickly become suicidal—even when separated and segregated for safety reasons. The anxiety and agitation these prisoners experience can rise to psychotic proportions and quickly precipitate a suicidal crisis.

The physical design of prisons and jails should always take into account the possibility of suicide. Older, many-tiered prison buildings are particularly challenging from a suicide-prevention perspective, largely due to the difficulty in observing prisoners frequently. Even modern, two-tiered prison buildings, however, are not immune to suicide risk and require the measures described here.

Designing and equipping cells with furnishings that are suicide-resistant should be part of every new facility. Among other things, the cells should be free of protrusions from which a prisoner could easily suspend a ligature. Ventilation grates should have a small enough mesh that it would be extremely difficult to suspend a ligature. Cells should also be free of sharp, protruding edges that would facilitate self-harm. Finally, cell doors should have large enough vision panels to allow observation of the entire cell from a safe distance. Obviously, all of these considerations are especially important in single-person cells and mandatory in any cell that is to be used for prisoners on suicide-precaution status.

D. Protective Factors

Protective factors or buffers are characteristics of the individual or his or her surroundings that decrease the likelihood of suicidal behavior. In the community, an important protective factor is social connectedness (Joiner, Brown, and Wingate 2005). For prisoners—already isolated from family and social networks—the presence of connections to family (correspondence and phone calls) and access to social networks in the prison environment are considered protective against suicidal behavior. In addition, studies have found that being housed with other prisoners (Fazel et al. 2008), contact with family members, and being married (although see Fazel et al. 2008 for a contrary finding) are negatively correlated with suicide.

II. Legal Basis for Suicide Prevention

There is little dispute about the constitutional and tort law necessity of a suicide-prevention system in every correctional institution. While the original jurisprudence regarding deliberate indifference emerged from Eighth Amendment claims against prisons, it is now clear that similar requirements emerge from the Fourth, Fifth, Sixth, and Fourteenth Amendments (*Bell v. Wolfish 1979*) and apply to all forms of detention and incarceration, for youth and adults alike. (For a more complete explanation of the legal basis for suicide prevention, see Cohen et al. 2011.)

Because federal courts have recognized that it is impossible to prevent all suicides, the legal requirements are that every detention correctional facility or system make reasonable efforts to prevent suicides. Even in cases where there has been no deliberate indifference, civil courts may find negligence, malpractice, or other forms of tort resulting in death. Again, the results of these cases should not be based solely on the outcome but whether the facility took the reasonable steps, such as those outlined here, to prevent suicides (see Cohen et al. 2011 for details of these cases).

1. *Ruiz v. Estelle* was the first of several landmark cases that found correctional systems in violation of the Eighth Amendment of the Constitution. In *Ruiz*, Judge Justice found that Texas had inflicted cruel and unusual punishment on prisoners by not providing adequate screening, appropriate treatment, sufficient mental health staff to support treatment, a medical records system, an up-to-date medication management system, and a program to identify and treat prisoners with elevated suicide risk.
2. *Langley v. Coughlin* extended the requirements of *Ruiz* and delineated in more detail exactly what a constitutional mental health system should look like.
3. *Farmer v. Brennan* described "deliberate indifference" as a failure to act when there is prior knowledge (either explicit or implicit) of risk. In suicide cases, this principle extends to knowledge of prior attempts and the potential for suicide.
4. *Coleman v. Wilson* applied the standard of deliberate indifference and found California's massive correctional system at fault in most of the same ways as Texas in *Ruiz*. Although the state's suicide-prevention program was not initially found deficient, overcrowding and issues of suicide among prisoners in segregated settings quickly came to the fore. The court pushed the state to expand suicide-prevention programs beyond the class of seriously mentally ill prisoners, targeting the general prisoner population, instituting suicide-prevention training for all staff (not just custodial and mental health staff), and extending screening procedures throughout the system. This case also points out the difficulty of reducing suicide rates in the context of overcrowding and poor conditions of confinement.

In addition to class actions regarding conditions of confinement, custodial suicides can also result in individual actions alleging civil tort liability for wrongful death. Depending on the circumstances, and whether the state has a cap on tort liability for government agencies, these cases can result in extremely large payouts to the estates or surviving relatives of prisoners who have committed suicide. Six- and seven-figure awards are not unheard of both in state (e.g., *Estate of Price v. Black Hawk County*, No. 00-CV-2008 [N.D. Iowa March 21, 2003], which awarded the family of a jail prisoner $300,000 after his suicide) and federal courts (e.g., *Belbachir v. County of McHenry*, No. 06-C-1392, U.S. Dist. Court [N.D. Ill.], in which the court awarded $1 million to the estate of an immigration detainee who hanged herself in custody).

The impact of 40 years of litigation on correctional health-care practices cannot be overstated. There has been a steady improvement in the conditions of confinement and better guidance for prison administrators about the boundaries of adequate and constitutionally appropriate health care, including suicide prevention.

III. National Standards and Best Practice Guidelines for Suicide Prevention in Correctional Settings

In addition to improvements in prison suicide prevention driven by litigation, other changes have come from the increased involvement of professional organizations that have written standards for care based in part on community standards of care and best practices. The National Commission on Correctional Health Care (2008), the American Psychiatric Association (2016), and the American Correctional Association (2003) have all promulgated standards for medical and mental health care that include specific recommendations for suicide-prevention programs. These standards guide correctional administrators and medical and mental health administrators and are often looked to by the courts as the minimum standards for suicide-prevention programs in correctional systems.

Until the Surgeon General's Report in 1999, implementation of systematic public health suicide-prevention programs in the community were marginally successful and thus had little influence on the organization and implementation of suicide-prevention programs in correctional settings. Recently, a number of highly successful suicide-prevention programs have been implemented in large, integrated health-care systems (Hampton 2010; Knox et al. 2010), and the lessons learned from these programs must be disseminated and implemented in correctional settings.

As part of the US Surgeon General's National Action Alliance for Suicide Prevention (2012), the Clinical Care and Intervention Task Force (2014) examined several of these integrated health-care systems. Based on their analysis, the task force recommended that suicide-prevention programs in large-scale health systems be organized around three critical principles: core values, systems management, and evidence-based clinical care practice. Many correctional systems have implemented one or even two of these principles, but few have adopted and fully implemented all three. In the next sections of this essay we discuss important components of suicide-prevention programs with these three basic principles in mind.

The evidence is clear: implementing a comprehensive public health approach to suicide prevention in jails has proven successful. According to Hayes and Rowan (1988) and Hayes (2012), the suicide rate in detention facilities throughout United States has been substantially reduced during the past 20 years, dropping from 107 jail suicides per 100,000 prisoners in 1986 to 38 jail suicide deaths per 100,000 prisoners in 2006. Hayes (2013, p. 193) writes, "Recent research has suggested that many jail suicides occur in facilities lacking comprehensive suicide prevention programs, with only 20 percent having written policies encompassing all the essential components." In other words, we know how to prevent jail suicides, even though not every jail does it.

IV. Essential Components of Correctional Suicide Prevention

A. Core Values

Based on a review of the health-care systems noted previously, the Clinical Care and Intervention Task Force recommended that all behavioral health organizations adopt a set of core values in order to implement suicide prevention effectively. The four organizations evaluated (US Air Force, Henry Ford Health System, National Suicide Prevention Lifeline, and the Central Arizona Programmatic Suicide Deterrent System Project) had strong leadership that set the organizational tone and articulated that any suicide attempt was an unacceptable event. The attitudes and beliefs of the organization emanated from the entire leadership corps. This principle was best exemplified by the US Air Force program, the epitome of a "top-down" organization, in which the cultural changes necessary to make suicide prevention a top priority were established by the chief of staff, the highest-ranking uniformed officer (Knox et al. 2010).

In correctional systems, too often suicide prevention is considered the domain of mental health programs alone. Correctional leaders must resist this bias and make suicide prevention a system-wide priority that is part of everyone's job. This is important because, due to the nature of suicide in correctional settings, many prisoners—not just those in mental health care—are at elevated risk for suicide over long periods of time; thus prevention programs need to reach all prisoners. To be fair, there are many examples where wardens, sheriffs, and jail directors have made a strong, personal investment in suicide prevention.

The Task Force recommended that suicidal behavior needs to be treated without regard to underlying pathology and requires multiple levels of service in a team environment. Linkages must be established between all levels of care, between providers of all disciplines, and over time. Especially important is the communication that allows all parts of the institution to be aware of information related to suicide risks for individual prisoners and detainees, as well as information gleaned from investigations of serious and fatal suicide attempts. For instance, implementing universal screening in primary care cannot be successful in the correctional setting without systems in place to support primary care providers and manage suicidal prisoners no matter the time of day or custodial status.

Around-the-clock management and care is required if acutely suicidal patients are to be adequately cared for. Creating trusting and productive therapeutic alliances is an important aspect of any successful treatment for suicidal patients. Fostering a culture of shared responsibility and team care can allay clinicians' anxiety, which in turn will increase the effectiveness of their interventions.

Finally, for any program to succeed, systematic evaluation of the program is an absolute necessity. This last point is particularly important. The Task Force and others (see Suicide Prevention Resource Center 2015) recommend that any suicide prevention program be accompanied at the outset by an evaluation program that delineates the important elements of the program, tracks progress, and produces feedback for the plan sponsors and participants. Without a systematic evaluation plan, programs cannot gain insights into what is or is not working. The nature of evaluation and quality improvement systems for suicide prevention must include self-critical and multidisciplinary investigations of suicide deaths and serious suicide attempts, as well as frequent audits of the suicide risk screening program and the quality of comprehensive suicide risk assessments by clinicians. Among custody staff, there must be audits of the frequency of observation of prisoners on various suicide prevention statuses.

It is especially important to resist the practice of separate investigations for custody, mental health, and health care after a completed suicide. The goal of these investigations is not to assign blame but to identify steps that can and must be taken to reduce the chances of another death under similar circumstances. These "lessons learned" seldom fall neatly into the bailiwick of one part of the organization to the exclusion of others. Communication between custody and health care is a shared responsibility whose failures can result in tragedy; separate investigations are unlikely to identify these cross-discipline areas of potential improvement and are thus presumptively inadequate.

B. Systems Management

1. *Policy and Procedures*

Specific written policies and procedures guide an institution's actions to detect and treat suicidal prisoners. An adequate suicide-prevention policy will guide the actions of all staff, including medical, mental health, and custody staff. The policy will account for all of the essential elements of suicide prevention included in this essay. Ideally, all three parts of the institutional staff will operate under the same policy. However, in many institutions, the medical and mental health providers may work under contract or through an intergovernmental agreement. If all of the groups cannot utilize the same policy, the policies in place must be compatible and explicitly reference each other. Once the policies and procedures are in place, staff at all levels must be trained in them so that they are aware of their roles and the expectations of the system for their care of suicidal prisoners. Generally, the policies and procedures of each institution should comport with the standards of the National Commission on Correctional Health Care, the American Correctional Association, or similar organizations, to assure that the national standards are met.

2. *Suicide Prevention Committees*

One of the most important innovations in suicide prevention is the creation of a suicide-prevention committee. The committee, whether system-wide or for a single institution, should be truly multidisciplinary, including representatives from various levels of security, medical, and mental health staff. The chair of the committee can be from any discipline but should be someone with a vested interest and meaningful authority in preventing suicides and able to provide leadership for the system or institution. These committees are typically responsible for development and implementation of the program's policies and procedures and for ensuring that the facility's quality improvement systems pay adequate attention to suicide prevention. If a local committee, the responsibility is to translate the larger system's policies into local procedures that fit with the mission of their institution.

For example, a high-security institution's suicide-prevention committee may want to implement a program of suicide screening of prisoners housed in segregated settings for more than a certain period of time on the theory that extended stays in segregation raise the risk of self-harm or suicide. To accomplish this, they must work with multiple stakeholders—mental health providers, nursing staff, and of course custodial employees at all levels. The program must be able to identify who should be screened (e.g., mental health patients or all segregation prisoners), who will do the screening (e.g., nursing or mental health staff), what instrument will be used, and how the screenings will be documented, in addition to ensuring the screening can be accomplished safely (e.g., the screening staff may need to be accompanied by a correctional officer). The results of the screenings must be tracked and a process put into place to ensure prisoners who "screen positive" are evaluated in a timely manner and the information from the screening is available to those who need it. Finally, the system must be evaluated over time for its effectiveness. New programs like this may be the result of court initiatives, quality management data, evaluations of recent suicide deaths, or simply informal observations by staff.

When suicide-prevention committees create procedures they must create lines of communication across all disciplines and professional boundaries in the facility. This is particularly important whether medical or mental health care is provided by a contract provider, by a separate department within the facility's jurisdiction, or through an intergovernmental agreement.

Sufficient professional and analytic staff should be devoted to the suicide-prevention program to allow it to function effectively. Leadership of suicide-prevention programs must have the support of the top-level leaders of the correctional system, whether that be a local sheriff running a 50-prisoner jail or a state-level secretary of corrections who must manage a system of thousands of prisoners in numerous institutions.

Other responsibilities of a suicide-prevention committee include review of self-harm incidents and suicide deaths. Suicide deaths are extreme and uncommon occurrences, but every system should have a set of policies and procedures to review, evaluate, and learn from these tragic events. Whatever review process a system establishes (e.g., root cause analysis, morbidity and mortality review, or psychological autopsy), the review must be integrated into the quality improvement program so the system can improve practices and move forward (Hayes 2010).

The committee's responsibilities can be quite broad, encompassing risk-reduction policies that target individual groups of prisoners (e.g., those returning from parole or court proceedings who may be at increased risk), custodial practices (e.g., regarding how often custodial officers check on prisoners in different kinds of housing units), or even architectural features of new construction to reduce the risk of hanging from furnishings and fixtures.

One of the most important tasks for any suicide-prevention committee is oversight of training. The coordination and monitoring of training for custodial, medical, and mental health staff is an essential piece of suicide prevention. Emergency response training, drills, and tracking of training are necessary to maintain readiness. It is also important to ensure that new employees are trained adequately and continuing staff have ongoing training. Particularly important are those who screen prisoners on intake and in other settings (see later discussion) and mental health staff whose duty is to make judgments of suicide risk and implement safety plans for prisoners who may have become suicidal.

3. *Managing Quality in Suicide Prevention*

Suicide-prevention committees should be embedded in the larger system's quality improvement program. Policies that delineate the nature and kind of data collected and the frequency of collection need to be in place. Ideally, a computerized tracking system affords the committee the ability to analyze trends and outcomes of the programs. In large systems with a number of jails or prisons, a central office suicide-prevention committee should be responsible for aggregation and analysis of system-wide data and devising procedures for ensuring that the information from those analyses is cycled back into the care setting and that lessons learned are shared between facilities.

Quality improvement programs should track a number of general indicators, such as staffing and training, the frequency and numbers of suicide risk assessments, referrals for suicide risk assessments and their source, and emergency responses. Exactly what is tracked depends on the type of correctional system, its size, and the resources available.

When a suicide death occurs, a suicide-prevention program should have an evaluation process ready to respond (Hayes 2010). Suicide evaluations should include a systematic inquiry into the events, both proximal and distal, that preceded the death as well as the circumstances of the event, including emergency response, and, if necessary, it should recommend corrective actions and/or investigations of the conduct of staff or the identification of policies and procedures that may need changing. Investigations may be completed by a section of the correctional department or by an independent agency; but the goal of any evaluation of these sentinel events is always prevention. As noted later, some aspects of suicide investigations may be carried out exclusively by physicians and nurses. However investigations are completed, it is imperative that the final investigation include all significant parts of the organization, including (at least) custody, mental health, and health care.

Both directed and regular peer review should be part of correctional quality improvement programs. These may range from formal procedures as part of licensed medical or professional staff organizations (often called mortality and morbidity reviews) to less formal but regular processes among a small number of mental health workers in a county jail (Ruiz 2010).

Adequate quality improvement requires that all correctional systems have processes to change and improve. This may involve giving information to decision-makers in easily understandable ways, to show compliance with quality standards and targets, or policies that require review of incidents and quality improvement plans when processes have broken down. Once a final set of recommendations emerges from these reviews and investigations, it is important to document each recommendation and track its successful implementation.

4. *Collaboration and Communication*

The principals of collaborative care must be adhered to. This is particularly important in correctional settings where multiple health care–related processes *plus* custodial processes must be followed to assure not only adequate health care but also safety and security.

Staff must both understand and believe that they are part of a larger team dedicated to reducing suicides. Just as connectedness acts as a protective buffer for those who have thoughts of suicide, team cohesiveness fosters connectedness and good communication.

5. *Trained and Skilled Work Force*

No adequate health-care system can function without a critical mass of providers who possess the appropriate skills and training to work with suicidal individuals. Staff training is an essential component of every suicide-prevention program (see American Correctional Association, American Psychiatric Association, and National Commission on Correctional Health Care standards; Hayes 2010). Systems must have in place ways to recruit and retain well-trained staff at all levels; this includes adequate salaries and benefits.

As noted, litigation following suicide deaths and class actions regarding suicide-prevention programs can have devastating effects on correctional and detention systems. These effects include not only money damages; they can also result in consent decrees, settlement agreements, and other forms of outside oversight than can negatively affect institutional morale. Prison suicide litigation has focused on a number of factors, including the need to assure the availability of an adequate number of qualified—and trained—mental health professionals. Qualified mental health professionals (QMHPs) are typically defined as professionals with at least a master's degree who are licensed in a mental health profession, such as psychiatry, clinical or counseling psychology, social work, nursing, counseling, or other related fields. QMHPs are needed to oversee the screening process, perform comprehensive suicide risk assessments, and provide the treatment that is needed for a serious mental illness or to alleviate the despair that led to the prisoner's suicidality. Whether they are provided by employees, contractors, or interagency agreement, every correctional facility must have an adequate number of trained mental health clinicians.

Specific training in suicide risk assessment is necessary given the evidence that even highly educated providers have often not been adequately trained in the details of how to talk to a suicidal individual, elicit the information necessary to make an accurate judgment of risk, and develop a safety plan to reduce the short-term risk of self-harm (Schmitz et al. 2012). But training mental health providers is not enough in today's correctional environment. Training medical, nursing, custodial, chaplaincy, and other non–health-care employees about the identification and referral of a prisoner for evaluation is necessary. Ideally, every staff member with prisoner contact should receive training that includes the identification of prisoners in need of mental health assessment, especially those for whom suicide is a current or historical issue. This includes a working knowledge of the signs and symptoms of acute and chronic suicidality, general and specific risk factors, and warning signs of short-term risk that indicate the need for emergency treatment.

All detention and correctional officers, as well as anyone else likely to perform a suicide watch, must be trained in the policies, practices, and post orders regarding the proper conducting of a suicide watch. This includes timeliness, observing signs of life, and allowing prisoners an opportunity to communicate a worsening of their condition or an intensifying of their suicidal ideations or intentions. It also includes the required documentation of watches and emergency procedures.

For staff assigned to intake screening (e.g., correctional or detention officers or nurses), special training is mandatory. This training includes when and how to inquire about ambiguous responses, how to document responses, and how and when to refer acute cases for immediate mental health assessment and treatment, as well as implementation of suicide-preventive watches until a clinician is available. Training must also include emergency preparedness, supported by ongoing drills to ensure that emergency medical and mental health responses to suicide attempts are timely and competent. The schedule of drills must be part of the system's policies and a local facility's procedures.

All correctional, mental health, and medical staff must also be well trained in how to document observations about suicide risk, and especially their documentation of serious suicide attempts, whether or not they were completed. In our experience, mistakes (or even intentional falsification) in documentation in the immediate aftermath of a suicide attempt can have pernicious effects. For example, without an accurate account, it is difficult or impossible to identify corrective actions that could prevent future tragedies. Further, staff should be clearly trained to understand that cover-ups are often far more deleterious to careers than the errors that were covered up, and, in our opinion, falsification of documentation of suicide-related events should be treated as an extremely serious and potentially lethal violation of policy.

C. Evidenced-Based Clinical Care

The National Action Alliance for Suicide Prevention (2012) made strong recommendations about the need for organizations to adopt methods of assessment and treatment that are evidence-based even while recognizing that the research base is thin (Clinical Care and Intervention Task Force 2014). This is particularly so in research in correctional mental health practice, where treatment research is difficult and complex. It also stressed that stigma can negatively affect treatment and that organizations will sometimes avoid suicidal patients because of what they call "fatalistic misperceptions" that there is nothing to do for individuals determined to take their lives. Correctional systems of care must avoid these biases and, through training and education, resist perpetuating them or creating a culture of avoidance.

Detection, assessment, and treatment of suicidal individuals are difficult tasks for both individual clinicians and systems of care. As noted earlier, collaboration and communication are essential elements of any systemic approach to the proper care of suicidal individuals. Suicide prevention is a process over time that includes screening, assessment of risk, and management of suicidal prisoners. We next discuss the important elements of suicide prevention and note evidence-based interventions that have shown efficacy in preventing suicide attempts and even suicide deaths and should be considered for implementation in correctional settings.

1. *Screening*

Although universal screening for suicide risk in the general population has shown limited utility (O'Connor et al. 2013), screening among prisoners, a population with elevated risk for suicide, is an important suicide-prevention tool in correctional settings (Hayes 1995, 2012). Screening instruments should be short, valid, and target those psychological domains and risk factors that are most appropriate for the setting in which they are used. The screening process should ideally employ a screening instrument designed for correctional settings (Maloney et al. 2015; Mills and Kroner 2005; Steadman et al. 2005; Ford et al. 2009). Every screening should include questions about suicide risk. While many of the questions seem obvious (e.g., current suicidal thoughts, recent history of attempted suicide, etc.), they provide newly admitted prisoners with an opportunity to reveal their thoughts of suicide and to get help. (For a summary of suicide prevention screening instruments, see Maloney et al. 2015.)

In addition to the choice of screening instrument, those who administer screenings must be trained on their use and the procedures when a prisoner gives positive answers to questions. Personnel who administer screenings can range from law enforcement officers in jail booking sections to nursing staff and even mental health professionals in large correctional reception centers. When a non–mental health staff member administers a screening, the measure should have built-in scoring rules to reduce the need for clinical judgment. In this situation, the measure itself makes the decision about referral rather than the person administering the measure.

The screening process should maximize false positive results and minimize false negatives. The cost of a false positive error is merely an additional assessment, while the cost of a false negative error could result in a preventable death. In other words, staff must be taught to err on the side of caution in deciding whether to refer a prisoner for further assessment. Once a screening is completed, the results must be documented and, if necessary, conveyed to other clinical staff for follow-up. Additionally, the data should be included in the quality improvement system for analysis and evaluation purposes.

Screening of prisoners should be routine at certain times and places. Transfers and entry into new facilities should occasion screening for mental health concerns and suicide risk. Because a transfer to segregation may increase the risk of suicide, screening either before rehousing or soon after may identify vulnerable prisoners in need of increased mental health attention. As noted, many jurisdictions conduct mental health rounds for all segregation prisoners at least weekly. For prisoners who endure lengthy stays in segregated housing, face-to-face, confidential assessments are typically required at regular (e.g., monthly) intervals.

Screening is important when prisoners return from hospital stays, court proceedings, parole hearings, or even after visiting. As part of an integrated health-care system, screening should (and can) be performed in medical clinics as part of routine practice. All prisoners attend medical clinics periodically and are interviewed by nurses or physicians, but typically less than 20 percent regularly receive mental health services. Research in the community has shown that it is much more likely that an individual who dies by suicide has seen a medical provider in the year before his or her death than a mental health provider (Luoma, Martin, and Pearson 2002). Thus every medical visit should include some inquiry into suicidal ideation.

2. *Assessment*

Suicide risk assessment and the judgment of suicide risk is a complex and difficult clinical task. It may be the most difficult task a clinician can perform—no matter the setting. The standard of care in suicide risk assessment is not the prediction of suicide but rather the evaluation and documentation of a systematic review of risk and protective factors (along with warning signs of very short-term risk), formulation and justification of a risk level, and construction of a plan of care based on the data gathered and the judgment of risk (Silverman 2014).

Clinicians are often asked, "If the person is really suicidal, why would they tell you?" It is important to understand that suicidal prisoners are presumptively ambivalent, as evidenced by the fact that they are (so far) still alive. Clinical experience suggests that prisoners are often frightened of their own suicidal wishes. They sincerely want to die, but something is keeping them alive, at least for the time being. The goal of suicide is often to escape the extreme psychological distress they are experiencing, and the provision of competent help can often aid the individual to get past their suicidal crisis. In other words, even if a suicidal threat or attempt is literally a "cry for help," the individual's suicidal intentions and fears are real, resulting in tragic outcomes if the help is not provided.

The use of risk factors to gauge someone's risk for suicide has a long history but is fraught with problems. It is not enough for a clinician to simply add up the risk factors, balance them with protective factors, and compute a risk "score." The process is not additive and is plagued by the lack of general consensus about how to weigh each risk and protective factor and how to designate the levels of risk. High risk for one prisoner may be only low to moderate risk for another. Additionally, suicidal states wax and wane over time, suggesting that suicide risk assessment is a process rather than a one-time event (Berman and Silverman 2014; Silverman and Berman 2014).

Experts are quick to point out that most risk factors clinicians are taught to assess give little hint about the short-term risk of suicide (Silverman and Berman 2014). For instance, a history of suicide attempts gives little information about what the person will do in the next few hours or days, and even the presence of suicidal ideation has a low correlation with eventual suicide. In addition to the assessment of risk and protective factors, it is important, particularly in crisis evaluations, to use what are called "warning signs"—signs and symptoms of near-term (hours, days, weeks) risk. The risk of suicide is analogous to the risk of heart attack. When evaluating for the short-term risk of heart attack, it is less important to evaluate the history of smoking or a family history of heart disease than to ask about shortness of breath or radiating pain in the upper left quadrant of the chest. In the same way, accurately assessing the short-term risk of suicide may depend more on warning signs than on stable risk and protective factors.

There are a number of warning sign "schemes" in the literature on suicide risk assessment, but recently the American Association of Suicidology has publicized a set of 10 warning signs that go by the acronym IS PATH WARM. These 10 warning signs (ideation, substances, purposelessness, anxiety, feeling trapped, hopelessness, withdrawal, agitation/anger, recklessness, and mood instability) were created by a consensus panel of experts and are currently being tested in a variety of settings. They can be taught to both laypersons and professionals and thus, in the correctional setting, can be taught, disseminated, and "advertised" to all staff (Rudd et al. 2006).

Recent advances in the assessment of suicide risk have pointed out the importance of stratifying risk over time (Silverman 2014). It is important to differentiate between chronic and acute risk (also called "static" and "dynamic" risk; Rudd 2006). Chronic risk factors such as historical and demographic factors are long-term risks that "prime the pump" and raise individuals' susceptibility to the effects of acute or short-term risk factors. Acute risk factors, if powerful and having significant meaning for the individual, can precipitate suicidal crises even in the absence of chronic risk.

Acute risk factors (and warning signs) are important elements for treatment planning with suicidal prisoners. Safety plans should target acute risk factors and warning signs (i.e., modifiable risk factors). For instance, in a correctional setting, placement in segregation removes a prisoner from his or her personal belongings, social group, or, possibly, school or job assignment—in short, the person experiences losses in all areas of social functioning. The provision of daily exercise (psychomotor activation), daily structured contact with staff (rounding by health care), individual in-cell activities (entertainment devices and activity booklets), and possibly group activities (relatedness) can counter the effects of isolation and provide buffers against suicidal urges.

Perhaps surprisingly, one of the most useful and important questions to ask a suicidal prisoner is: "How is it that you are still alive (i.e., in the face of all of your psychological pain and despair)?" Asked respectfully, this question can elicit protective factors that are preventing the person from acting on his or her suicidal impulses and cognitions. Examples include family connections (e.g., "I couldn't do that to my kids") or religious values (e.g., "I don't want to burn in hell"). Learning about protective factors can inform treatment interventions. Further, acknowledging the person's ability to withstand suicidal ideation allows clinicians to reinforce attributes such as resilience and courage, thereby improving a dangerously impaired self-image.

Learning about a prisoner's protective factors or "buffers" can help clinicians to reduce risk by reinforcing interpersonal relationships, maintaining contact with families, and emphasizing future orientation. Safety plans for suicidal prisoners should always focus on enhancing protective factors, if possible. However, it is important for clinicians to remember that high levels of acute risk can overwhelm the positive benefits of protective factors.

Many systems create a specific form for evaluators to fill out when a suicide risk assessment is performed. No form can substitute for clinical judgment, but a well-constructed form can provide documentation that the clinician "covered all the bases" of a reasonable and adequate risk assessment (Simon 2009). A form should contain all elements of a risk assessment: sections for chronic and acute risk and protective factors, room for a mental status examination and suicide inquiry, a section to note the risk level (commonly low, moderate, or high) and its justification, and space for a detailed safety plan that addresses the modifiable risk factors and protective factors that should be enhanced.

3. Clinical Interventions and Treatments

Treatment planning and management of suicidal prisoners begins as the assessment phase ends. Each assessment (especially those conducted in response to a crisis evaluation) should include a short-term "safety plan" that emphasizes enhancement of protective factors, reduction of acute risk factors (possibly housing issues or issues involving recent transfers), and treatment of current distress and agitation. These safety plans can be modeled after brief interventions used in emergency departments in the community (Stanley and Brown 2012) but specifically tailored to correctional settings.

Once a suicidal prisoner has been stabilized and short-term risk has subsided, the prisoner should be thoroughly assessed to determine the necessity of an individualized and targeted treatment plan that includes measurable outcomes. (Even if the suicidal episode is determined to be reactive to a recent event and of very short duration, it is important to follow up with the prisoner several days after removal from suicide observation to make sure that the assessment was accurate.) These plans are typically a product of a treatment team including psychiatry, nursing, therapists (psychologist, social worker, or counselor), and custodial staff. It is important to include custodial staff in treatment planning since one of the goals of correctional mental health treatment is to allow prisoners to function successfully in the correctional environment. Custodial staff have specialized knowledge that may be important for the team to take into account such as case factors (long sentence, adjustment in other institutions, etc.). Further, correctional officers are often in contact with inmates 24 hours per day, allowing for important observations about the prisoner's functioning when no clinical staff are present.

Treatment plans should describe in sufficient detail the problems associated with the symptoms of the prisoner's mental illness. Problems are best expressed in behavioral terms and should include ways to measure progress (or the lack thereof). Cognitive-behavior treatment protocols often focus on engaging the prisoner in a collaborative process that makes him or her an active participant in treatment. Given some prisoners' security levels and the safety of staff, special treatment arrangements sometimes must be made.

Suicide-specific treatment planning should target those specific problems that may have led to the crisis (e.g., hopelessness, social withdrawal, or psychiatric syndromes such as bipolar disorder or depression). Group treatment can be especially helpful for the interpersonal isolation and feelings of burdensomeness that can lead to suicidal thinking (Chaiken and Brizendine 2015).

As noted earlier, the evidence base for the efficacy of treatments for suicidal behavior is poor. The situation for prison and jail programs is even worse, since few psychosocial treatments have shown success in the correctional environment. Nonetheless, treatments for suicidal prisoners should adhere to what evidence does exist. The National Action Alliance for Suicide Prevention (2012) identified two carefully studied approaches to treatment for suicidal behavior: dialectical behavior therapy (Linehan 1993), and cognitive therapy for suicidal behavior (Wenzel, Brown, and Beck 2009). Of the two proposed models, dialectical behavior therapy has actually been implemented in a number of youth correctional settings and its principles have informed forensic and correctional treatment protocols (McCann, Ball, and Ivanoff 2000; McCann et al. 2007; Schmidt and Ivanoff 2014).

4. Suicide Observation

Prisoners who attempt suicide while incarcerated are often subject to increased monitoring, either in housing units or inpatient psychiatric settings. Although not technically a "treatment" of suicidal behavior, close observation can be crucial in the early stages of treatment to assure the safety of suicidal prisoners.

If a prisoner is observed harming him- or herself or makes suicidal statements, any staff member should be able to place that person on suicide observation status until he or she is evaluated by a QMHP. In general, suicide observation statuses (either constant one-to-one watch or periodic checks) occurs under conditions that make suicide extremely difficult to accomplish, such as suicide-resistant holding cells or inpatient hospital units. On the other hand, the conditions of suicide watch must never be unnecessarily punitive.

The standard of care for suicide watches is a matter of some debate. Some experts believe that a suicide watch must include constant observation by a staff member within arm's length of the prisoner at all times. Of course this is the safest method of suicide watch;

however, depending on the number of people deemed to be at high risk of suicide, it can be extremely expensive to have one staff person assigned to each prisoner on suicide precautions. In addition, security considerations can dictate that the prisoner be placed in celled housing, either in a housing unit or a dedicated psychiatric facility.

In our opinion, if a prisoner is not actively harming him- or herself and is housed in a suicide-resistant environment, it is often reasonable to observe the prisoner at variable intervals. The maximum amount of time that can elapse between observations, however, is also a matter of some debate. Some facilities continue to use 15 minutes as the presumptive interval between observations, which we believe to be unsafe. In our opinion, the emerging standard of care for observation of prisoners deemed to be at high risk of suicide is much shorter (e.g., variable observations that are never more than 5 or at most 10 minutes apart) for prisoners on suicide watch. However, a QMHP must have the latitude to order constant observation when appropriate.

After a prisoner is released from the highest level of suicide observation, it is best to have an intermediate status, often called "step-down" or safety watch status. Any change from a more stringent level of observation to a less frequent schedule of observation implies the prisoner no longer poses an immediate risk of self-harm. When such a change occurs, a QMHP must complete a risk assessment that documents the factors that have changed during the interval and justify the change in observation. The intermediate level of precaution is there to allow the staff to err on the side of caution.

Step-down or safety watch status is typically a variable observation interval not exceeding 15 minutes between observations, and again, the prisoner should be housed in an environment that is reasonably suicide resistant. Periodic welfare checks, no matter the interval, should be completed at uneven intervals ("staggering") to avoid allowing prisoners the opportunity to "time" staff and harm themselves in the interval between checks. For example, if the maximum interval between welfare checks is 15 minutes, the prisoner should be checked five times per hour at unequal intervals not to exceed 15 minutes.

Prisoners are aware of most jail and prison procedures, including the often austere conditions that prevail in correctional psychiatric units. These units may require "strip out" conditions in which the prisoner is deprived of clothes, a bed, even eyeglasses and is required to eat from paper plates. Patients in these settings are commonly provided heavy tear-resistant blankets and smocks, must sleep on tear-proof mattresses, and are often housed alone. Housing prisoners under these conditions, although believed necessary for safety reasons, can discourage prisoners from being forthcoming about their suicidal intentions. These units can thus be the antithesis of therapeutic conditions, and, despite a prisoner's dire circumstances and extreme distress, they will often deny suicidal ideation to avoid being moved to one of these settings.

Wherever a prisoner is housed on suicide observation status, the conditions must never be unnecessarily harsh or unpleasant. Treatment conditions should include adequate and supervised out-of-cell activities, whether for routine exercise or mental health treatment, and a continuation of the usual privileges afforded in regular housing units: telephone calls, mail, some personal belongings, reading materials, and visitation. Any exceptions must be based on individualized assessment and documented.

Recognizing that isolation can increase suicide risk and, conversely, that the presence of others in the living space can be protective, some facilities use multiperson dormitories as a "safe zone" to house suicidal prisoners who are not deemed to pose an immediate risk toward others. These settings also allow for one staff member to closely watch several suicidal prisoners.

One of the most common complaints of correctional mental health clinicians (and custodial staff) is that prisoners often dishonestly claim to be suicidal in order to gain some advantage. It is common to read or hear accusations of feigning, malingering, and manipulating when an inmate reports suicidal thoughts, intentions, or plans. Some clinicians claim that the best way to reduce false claims of suicidality is to make the conditions of suicide watch especially harsh. Sadly, however, harsh conditions of suicide watch will also dissuade truly suicidal inmates from asking for help, when they perceive the "help" as punitive.

Because there is no way for clinicians to "read minds," and given that suicidal prisoners are presumptively ambivalent about death, it is dangerous to jump to the conclusion that an inmate is feigning a wish to die without clear evidence that this is true. Further, even if a prisoner is malingering, it is important to try to understand his or her motive. For example, in many correctional facilities, there is a shortage of clinical staff, which means that a prisoner who is perceived to have a moderate depression will not receive much help. In such cases, prisoners might "gild the lily" and exaggerate their symptoms of depression or anxiety, simply to get some help. It is very important to avoid creating the belief that only a serious attempt will be taken seriously.

A reasonable middle ground is to avoid rewarding or punishing prisoners for expressing suicidal feelings. If the only secondary gain is treatment, it will reduce the likelihood that prisoners will see suicidal claims as a way to dramatically improve their living circumstances. Finally, it is important to compare the relative risks of respecting or rejecting a prisoner's report of suicidality. If clinicians respond to a dishonest claim of suicidality, the risk is some extra psychiatric treatment. On the other hand, cynical rejection of honest claims of suicidal intent are likely to result in preventable death. The choice is clear.

5. *Treatment Concerns and Conditions of Confinement*

Experts in correctional mental health practices have recently suggested that prisoners in treatment for serious psychiatric problems, including those who are suicidal, receive as much time out of their cells as is practically and safely possible (see recent filings in *Coleman v. Wilson*, 912 F.Supp. 1282, 1995), even when security concerns require extremely secure housing. Depending on the circumstances, staff availability, and design features, experts recommend at least 20 hours of out-of-cell activities each week. Generally, at least 10 hours per week should be devoted to some form of formal therapeutic program (e.g., individual or group psychotherapy, educational programs, etc.) with the remainder of the time devoted to informal activities such as recreation. Again, any exceptions must be carefully documented, along with interventions designed (and documented) to overcome any reasonable barriers to out-of-cell activity.

Although a very few high-security or behaviorally disordered prisoners may need restrictions on free access to reading materials, these are important tools for prisoners in treatment. Bibliotherapy (an expressive therapy technique that uses a client's relationship to the content of books) is a valuable technique that should not be restricted. Some systems have produced their own activity books or brought in treatment manuals for patients.

Some prisoners with serious mental illnesses present such a serious danger to staff and other prisoners that there is no reasonable alternative to separating them. Historically, such prisoners have often been housed in administrative segregation units, where they have received little or no meaningful treatment. While the use of long-term segregation is hotly debated, several points of consensus are clear. First, segregating prisoners with or without mental illness should only be used when absolutely necessary and when no less restrictive alternative will safely address the risk. Second, prisoners with serious mental illness who are housed in highly secure placements cannot be denied clinically appropriate mental health services. While these services must be delivered safely, they cannot be denied for nonclinical reasons. Third, when prisoners refuse such treatment, their refusals must be addressed by clinicians and documented in the prisoner's treatment plan. Interventions may include "motivational interviewing" (Hettema, Steele, and Miller 2005), more frequent cell-front visits to build trust, and, in extreme circumstances, the use of involuntary medication.

A far better way to safely serve the needs of prisoners with serious mental illness who pose a serious and imminent risk to others is to create secure therapeutic units. In recent years a number of correctional systems (e.g., Massachusetts, New York, Pennsylvania, and Colorado) have instituted special therapeutic housing units with dedicated staff and self-contained programs for prisoners with serious mental illnesses who exhibit severe behavior problems, personality disorders, or chronically elevated suicide risk. Programs vary in length of stay but are typically at least 6 months in duration and can extend to 24 or 36 months. They may be targeted at a particular treatment population (borderline personality disorder, sex offenders, or those with chronic severe psychosis) and often involve behavioral incentive programs with a step-wise progression of levels of privileges.

If secure treatment settings are created, the necessity to house a prisoner with serious mental illness in administrative segregation should be eliminated. Further, smaller correctional facilities and systems may have too few such prisoners to warrant creation of secure mental health treatment units. In the extremely rare instance when it is deemed necessary to house a prisoner with serious mental illness in a segregated setting due to violence, serious infractions, or even for personal safety concerns, additional mental health services should be provided. In some settings it may be possible to hold treatment groups and include recreation therapy for prisoners held in high-security housing. They should be afforded at least 20 hours of out-of-cell activities each week (10 hours of structured therapeutic activities and 10 hours of other recreational, vocational, or educational programs). This may include exercise yard, law library visits, recreation therapy, or, for some, group therapy sessions (Andrade and Metzner 2014). In California, for instance, prisoners with mental health problems housed in segregation units are seen at least weekly by a QMHP; they also have an assigned psychiatrist if prescribed psychotropic medications, and a QMHP attends each classification committee meeting to advise custodial staff of the needs of the prisoner and the general terms of his or her treatment.

6. Discharge Planning

Planning for discharge, whether from jail to prison, prison or jail to the community, or from a specialized treatment program to mainline prison or jail housing, can be a risky proposition for suicidal prisoners.

For those returning to the community from prison, the imminent return to the locale of a heinous crime or where social supports have disappeared after many years in prison can precipitate intense distress and possibly suicidal crises. Research has found that recently released prisoners are at high risk of mortality and morbidity from a number of causes (Pratt et al. 2006; Binswanger et al. 2007). Care planning must occur with enough lead time to arrange not only continuity of care but also the basic social infrastructure of life outside prison—identification cards, housing, and possibly employment opportunities. Prisoners, particularly "lifers" who have spent a decade or more in prison, must be prepared for "life outside."

Ideally, a parole or discharge date is known with enough leeway that planning can start 12 to 18 months prior to release. Planning may include classes on navigating social services, parole requirements, and dealing with day-to-day interactions that may trigger anger, anxiety, or frustration for someone used to the relatively regimented life inside prisons.

Discharge planning to the community from jail has a host of challenges. Jail stays are often extremely and unpredictably short, which limits the time that clinicians have to create comprehensive discharge plans. Commonly, pretrial detainees may be unexpectedly released directly from court. In such cases, treatment plans must be simple, focusing on housing, continuity of psychiatric care, and basic entitlements such as food stamps. Because many defendants were homeless when they were arrested, finding safe housing for prisoners with serious mental illness upon their release from jail is often difficult or impossible. On the other hand, because jail stays are typically of shorter duration than prison terms, reestablishing social networks may be less a worry for those prisoners who had stable housing or employment prior to their arrest. Finally, many prisoners will leave jail and move directly to state prisons. In such cases, it is imperative that the jail system transmit a discharge summary, with special attention to prisoners who are deemed to pose a chronic or acute risk of suicide.

Many prisoners, especially those with serious mental illnesses, will enter jail or prison with entitlements such as Social Security Disability Insurance or Medicaid. In the past, the benefits were terminated upon admission to a correctional institution and difficult to reinstate in a timely manner upon release. Increasingly, states are arranging for these benefits to be suspended instead of terminated, which allows for virtually immediate reinstatement upon release and continuity of mental health treatment.

Release from segregated housing or specialized treatment programs to the general population, particularly after lengthy stays, may pose increased risks for prisoners still recovering from a suicidal crisis. Some systems have created transitional housing for such prisoners who can be closely observed during the period after discharge. California's state prison system has taken an in vivo approach and houses prisoners from inpatient psychiatric programs in their original housing, providing daily mental health encounters for five days after release plus 24 hours of periodic custodial welfare checks (which can be extended). Release planning may also take into account the need for enhanced treatment services. Special care should be taken at these junctures to assure continuity of care between settings through person-to-person contacts and procedures that ensure important information is communicated.

Some prisoners will move from jail or prison to psychiatric inpatient status, typically because they are deemed to meet civil or forensic commitment standards upon their release from a correctional facility. Similarly, in some states, certain sex offenders are civilly committed as sexually dangerous persons immediately upon release from prison. In such cases, it is imperative that the sending institution provide a complete discharge summary, paying special attention to treatment received and risk factors related to suicide.

V. Special Considerations for Types of Confinement Settings

While all forms of detention and incarceration bear a responsibility to make reasonable efforts to reduce the risk of suicide, and some risks overlap across institution type, many of the specific risks vary significantly according to the type of institution and housing. For example, a high percentage of newly admitted jail and juvenile detainees are under the influence of alcohol or stimulants, which can impair impulse control and judgment, exacerbating the extreme stressor of being arrested and locked up. These substances are especially dangerous in the context of individuals whose impulse control is already weak, due to youth, head injuries, or various forms of mental illness (e.g., hyperactivity, fetal alcohol syndrome). A related problem concerns prisoners who arrive in detention facilities actively addicted to narcotics, alcohol, or other drugs, as the distress of withdrawal can lead to desperate measures, including attempted suicide (Hayes and Rowan 1988).

The presence of diverse ethnic groups is a special challenge in all forms of incarceration but especially in immigration facilities where the number of languages spoken can be quite high, making it difficult or impossible to have staff that speak every relevant language. There are no easy answers to this dilemma, but some facilities allow detainees to designate a trusted fellow detainee or officer who speaks their language to serve as a translator. While this may be a necessity in moments of crisis, it is important to understand that even well-intentioned friends are not trained interpreters and may inadvertently communicate inaccurately. Thus, as soon as possible, the most reliable arrangements should be made.

Suicide rates in prison are significantly lower than those in jail (Bureau of Justice Statistics 2014). However, reducing the number of suicides in prisons has proven to be a more difficult challenge for several reasons. First, because the incidence of suicide is lower in prisons than in jails, reductions are harder to achieve. Second, the window of risk is less clear. For example, prison suicides can occur at any time during an incarceration, often because of some form of bad news that the prisoner has received (e.g., death of a loved one, divorce, or parole rejection), unbeknownst to staff. In contrast, the majority of jail suicides have historically occurred during the first hours and days of detention, making them easier to prevent when proper suicide prevention systems are in place. Jail suicide-prevention programs have succeeded in reducing the incidence of jail suicide, mainly those that were occurring early in the person's detention. The suicides that have proven more difficult to prevent are those that are similar to prison suicides, such as those that result from bad news from home or unexpected bad results in court.

Hayes (2012) considers the jail environment to be conducive to suicide because of the environment (e.g., prisoners' lack of control, the authoritarian environment, the isolation from social networks, and the dehumanizing aspects of confinement) and the vulnerability of jail prisoners, who are often in psychological crisis. Other writers (e.g., Haycock 1991) have hypothesized that the deprivations suffered in jails (rather than the prisoners' vulnerabilities) increase suicide rates.

The notion that jail conditions may play a primary role in their high rates of suicide may have some merit given that many jail prisoners make the transition to prison and appear to function quite well in the new environment. Prisons, by their very nature, are built for long-term confinement and, although chronically stressful places, have much more to offer prisoners in the way of educational, vocational, and rehabilitative programs that can relieve the day-to-day stress and monotony of confinement and offer meaningful experiences for prisoners, thus lowering the risk of suicide.

It is now a matter of broad consensus that prisoners with current psychotic symptoms and those deemed to present an imminent risk of suicide should not be housed in segregation settings. The degree to which segregation causes psychological harm, and the characteristics of prisoners at greatest risk, remain in need of further study (Berger et al. 2013). But because segregated housing is a stressful setting, precautions should be taken to prevent the onset of new psychiatric problems and to identify prisoners whose mental health problems may have gone undetected previously.

Every segregation unit should have "rounding" on a regular basis. Rounding by nursing or mental health staff supplement security checks by custodial staff and is a recognition that these settings can increase the risk of the development of mental health symptoms. Typically all prisoners in a unit, whether or not they receive mental health treatment, are contacted at least several times per week by staff for a brief encounter in which an assessment of their mental state and well-being is made and documented. The goal is to identify problems and treat them as early as possible.

Prisoners housed in short-term segregation often do not have many of their personal belongings (television, books, letters, etc.). In-cell activities may be provided to increase stimulation and decrease boredom. Overall, increasing the opportunities for social interaction and prosocial forms of distraction (e.g., music, television) and providing ways to "cut through" the boredom and isolation of segregated settings can prevent the onset or worsening of mental health symptoms among prisoners in segregated housing.

VI. Conclusion

Some suicides are easier to prevent than others. Because suicides of both adults and juveniles in jails are often impulsive and situationally determined, the "prevention windows" of time, place, and people are narrower; thus it is easier to focus preventive attention on them. As a result, jails that have implemented relatively simple and cost-effective measures have been able to reduce the prevalence of suicide significantly during the past three decades.

Preventing suicide in prison is more challenging, though not impossible. Unlike jail, where stress is especially predictable at the front door, prison stressors (e.g., "Dear John letters," negative parole decisions, death of a loved one, etc.) can occur at any time during a prisoner's incarceration, and staff members often have no way of knowing about it. Nonimpulsive, planned suicides seem most difficult, unless one considers that many of the prisoners who engage in such behaviors have been depressed for a long time before deciding that suicide is the only way to end their psychological or physical pain. Thus the presence of user-friendly and competent mental health care, including therapeutic treatment of severe depression, is likely to prevent suicides, even if the prisoners and treatment staff are unaware of what might have happened in the absence of effective treatment.

The most vexing aspect of suicide prevention, of course, is that one often has no way of knowing what one has prevented. Further, because suicides, as rare events, are inherently unpredictable, correctional programs must be diligent in their efforts to lower the risks of suicide for all of the prisoners in their care. Correctional suicide-prevention programs, as integrated health-care systems, should adhere to the highest standards of care and adopt goals similar to those of systems that have committed to and succeeded in reducing suicide (National Action Alliance for Suicide Prevention 2012; Clinical Care and Intervention Task Force 2014). Bringing the core values, standards, and methods of correctional suicide-prevention programs into alignment with these community programs will move them toward the goal of further reductions in correctional suicide.

Finally, it is important to remember that suicide is typically borne of despair. To the extent that correctional institutions forget their correctional mission and become instruments of punishment alone, the likelihood of despair will increase. In a very real sense, all of the very useful and important tools outlined in this essay pale in comparison to instilling hope, which is the only remedy for despair that has ever worked. Helping people feel some sense of dignity and meaning in the worst of circumstances has always been the most impressive accomplishment of well-run institutions, and for those correctional leaders and advocates who have managed to create hope amid despair, we offer our profound respect. Sadly, these people will never know what they have prevented, but that does nothing to lessen the importance of their work.

NOTES

1. In general, this essay is intended to apply to all forms of correctional incarceration and detention. Except where we intend to refer to a specific type of institution, we use the words "prisoner" and "inmate" to refer to prisoners, detainees, and residents of jails, prisons, and juvenile correctional and detention facilities.
2. For comparison, the rate of suicide deaths in the United States between 2000 and 2013 was 11.7 deaths per 100,000 (Web-Based Injury Statistics Query and Reporting System, US Centers for Disease Control and Prevention, November 22, 2015).

REFERENCES

American Correctional Association. 2003. *Standards for Adult Correctional Institutions,* 4th ed. Washington, DC: American Correctional Association.

American Psychiatric Association. 2016. *Psychiatric Services in Correctional Facilities,* 3rd ed. Washington, DC: American Psychiatric Publishing.

Andrade, Joel T., and Jeffrey L. Metzner. 2014. "*Serious Mental Illness and Segregation: Recommendations for Implementing a System that Works.*" Paper presented at the Mental Health Conference of the National Commission on Correctional Health Care, Boulder, CO, July 13–14.

Appelbaum, Kenneth L., Judith A. Savageau, Robert L. Trestman, Jeffrey L. Metzner, and Jacques Baillargeon. 2011. "A National Survey of Self-Injurious Behavior in American Prisons." *Psychiatric Services* 62(2):285–290.

Berger, Robert H., M. Paul Chaplin, and Robert L. Trestman. 2013. "Commentary: Toward an Improved Understanding of Administrative Segregation." *Journal of the American Academy of Psychiatry and the Law* 41:61–64.

Berman, Alan L., and Morton M. Silverman. 2014. "Suicide Risk Assessment and Risk Formulation, Part II: Suicide Risk Formulation and Determination of Levels of Risk." *Suicide and Life Threatening Behavior* 44(4):432–443.

Binswanger, Ingrid A., Mark F. Stern, Richard A. Deyo, Patrick J. Heagerty, Allen Cheadle, Joann G. Elmore, and Thomas D. Koepsell. 2007. "Release from Prison—A High Risk of Death for Former Inmates." *New England Journal of Medicine* 356(2):157–165.

Bonner, Ronald L. 2006. "Stressful Segregation Housing and Psychosocial Vulnerability in Prison Suicide Ideators." *Suicide and Life-Threatening Behavior* 36(2):250–254.

Bureau of Justice Statistics. 2013. *Sexual Victimization in Prisons and Jails Reported by Prisoners, 2011–12* Washington, DC: US Government Printing Office.

Bureau of Justice Statistics. 2014. *"Data Collection: Deaths In Custody Reporting Program."* Washington DC: Office of Justice Programs. http://www.bjs.gov/index.cfm?ty=dcdetail&iid=243

Bureau of Justice Statistics. 2015. *Mortality in Local Jails and State Prisons, 2000–2013—Statistical Tables.* Washington, DC: US Government Printing Office.

Chaiken, Shama, and Brittany Brizendine. 2015. "Group Psychotherapy" In *Oxford Textbook of Correctional Psychiatry*, edited by Robert L. Trestman, Kenneth L. Appelbaum, and Jeffrey L. Metzner. New York: Oxford University Press.

Clinical Care and Intervention Task Force. 2014. *Suicide Care in Systems Framework.* Washington, DC: Department of Health and Human Services.

Center for Disease Control and Prevention. 2015. "Fatal Injury Reports, National and Regional, 1999–2014." Web-based Injury Statistics Query and Reporting System. http://webappa.cdc.gov/sasweb/ncipc/mortrate10_us.html

Cohen, Fred, James L. Knoll IV, Terry A. Kupers, and Jeffrey L. Metzner. 2011. *Practical Guide to Correctional Mental Health Care and the Law.* Kingston, NJ: Civic Research Institute.

Fazel, Seena, Julia Cartwright, Arabella Norman-Nott, and Keith Hawton. 2008. "Suicide in Prisons: A Systematic Review of Risk Factors." *Journal of Clinical Psychiatry* 69(11):1721–1731.

Ford, Julian D., Robert L. Trestman, Valerie H. Wiesbrock, and Wanli Zhang. 2009. "Validation of a Brief Screening Instrument for Identifying Psychiatric Disorders Among Newly Incarcerated Adults." *Psychiatric Services* 60:842–846.

Hampton, Tracy. 2010. "Depression Care Effort Brings Dramatic Drop in Large HMO Population's Suicide Rate." *Journal of the American Medical Association* 303(19):1903–1905.

Hanson, Annette. 2010. "Correctional Suicide: Has Progress Ended?" *Journal of the American Academy of Psychiatry and the Law* 38:6–10.

Haycock, Joel. 1991. "Capital Crimes: Suicides in Jail." *Death Studies* 15:417–433.

Hayes, Lindsay M. 1983. "And Darkness Closes In: A National Study of Jail Suicides." *Criminal Justice and Behavior* 10(4):461–484.

Hayes, Lindsay M. 1995. "Prison Suicide: An Overview and Guide to Prevention." *The Prison Journal* 75(4):431–456.

Hayes, Lindsay M. 2010. "Toward a Better Understanding of Suicide Prevention in Correctional Facilities." In *Handbook of Correctional Mental Health*, 2d ed., edited by Charles L. Scott. Arlington, VA: American Psychiatric Publishing.

Hayes, Lindsay M. 2012. "National Study of Jail Suicide: 20 Years Later." *Journal of Correctional Health Care* 18(3):233–245.

Hayes, Lindsay M. 2013. "Suicide Prevention in Correctional Facilities: Reflections and Next Steps." *International Journal of Law and Psychiatry* 36:188–194.

Hayes, Lindsay M., and Joseph R. Rowan. 1988. *National Study of Jail Suicide: Seven Years Later*. Alexandria, VA: National Center on Institutions and Alternatives.

Hettema, Jennifer, Julie Steele, and William R. Miller. 2005. "Motivational Interviewing." *Annual Review of Clinical Psychology* 1:91–111.

Huey, Meredith P., and Thomas L. McNulty. 2005. "Institutional Conditions and Prison Suicide: Conditional Effects of Deprivation and Overcrowding." *The Prison Journal* 85(4):490–514.

Hughes, Kerry C., and Jeffrey L. Metzner. 2015. "Suicide Risk Management." In *Oxford Textbook of Correctional Psychiatry*, edited by Robert L. Trestman, Kenneth L. Appelbaum, and Jeffrey L. Metzner. New York: Oxford University Press.

Johnson, Jeffrey G., Patricia Cohen, Madelyn S. Gould, Stephanie Kasen, Joselyn Brown, and Judith S. Brook. 2002. "Childhood Adversities, Interpersonal Difficulties and Risk for Suicide Attempts During Late Adolescence and Early Adulthood." *Archives of General Psychiatry* 59(8):741–749.

Joiner, Thomas E., Jessica S. Brown, and LaRicka R. Wingate. 2005. "The Psychology and Neurobiology of Suicidal Behavior." *Annual Review of Psychology* 56:287–314.

Knox, Kerry L., Steven Pflanz, Gerald W. Talcott, Rick L. Campise, Jill E. Lavigne, Alina Bajorska, Xin Tu, and Eric Caine. 2010. "The US Air Force Suicide Prevention Program: Implications for Public Health Policy." *American Journal of Public Health* 100(12):2457–2463.

Linehan, Marsha M. 1993. *Cognitive Behavioral Treatment of Borderline Personality Disorder*. New York: Guildford Press.

Luoma, Jason B., Catherine E. Martin, and Jane L. Pearson. 2002. "Contact with Mental Health and Primary Care Providers Before Suicide: A Review of the Evidence." *American Journal of Psychiatry* 159:909–916.

Maloney, Michael P., Joel A. Dvoskin, and Jeffrey L. Metzner. 2015. "Mental Health Screening and Brief Assessment." In *Oxford Textbook of Correctional Psychiatry*, edited by Robert L. Trestman, Kenneth L. Appelbaum, and Jeffrey L. Metzner. New York: Oxford University Press.

Mann, J. John, Christine Waternaux, Gretchen L. Haas, and Kevin M. Malone. 1999. "Toward a Clinical Model of Suicidal Behavior in Psychiatric Patients." *American Journal of Psychiatry* 156:181–189.

Maxfield, Michael G., and Cathy Spatz Widom. 1996. "The Cycle of Violence: Revisited 6 Years Later." *Archives of Pediatric and Adolescent Medicine* 150(4):390–395.

McCann, Robin A., Elissa M. Ball, and Andre Ivanoff. 2000. "DBT with an Inpatient Forensic Population: The CMHIP Forensic Model." *Cognitive and Behavioral Practice* 7:447–456.

McCann, Robin A., Andre Ivanoff, Henry Schmidt, and Bradley Beach. 2007 "Implementing Dialectical Behavior Therapy in a Residential Forensic Settings with Adults and Juveniles." In *DBT in Clinical Practice: Applications Across Disorders and Settings*, edited by Linda A. Dimeff and Kelly Koerner. New York: Guilford Press.

Mills, Jeremy F., and Daryl G. Kroner. 2005. "Screening for Suicide Risk Factors in Prison Inmates: Evaluating the Efficiency of the Depression, Hopelessness and Suicide Screening Form (DHS)." *Legal and Criminological Psychology* 10:1–12.

Moscicki, Eve K. 2001. "Epidemiology of Completed and Attempted Suicide: Toward a Framework for Prevention." *Clinical Neuroscience Research* 1:310–323.

National Action Alliance for Suicide Prevention. 2012. *2012 National Strategy for Suicide Prevention: Goals and Objectives.* Washington, DC: Department of Health and Human Services.

National Center on Addiction and Substance Abuse. 2010. *Behind Bars II: Substance Abuse and America's Prison Population.* New York: National Center on Addiction and Substance Abuse, Columbia University.

National Commission on Correctional Health Care. 2008. *Standards for Mental Health Services in Correctional Facilities.* Chicago: National Commission on Correctional Health Care.

Nock, Matthew K., Guilherme Borges, Evelyn J. Bromet, Christine B. Cha, Ronald C. Kessler, and Sing Lee. 2008. "Suicide and Suicidal Behavior." *Epidemiologic Reviews* 30:133–154.

O'Connor, Elizabeth, Bradley N. Gaynes, Brittany U. Burda, Clara Soh, and Evelyn P. Whitlock. 2013. "Screening for and Treatment of Suicide Risk Relevant to Primary Care: A Systematic Review for the U.S. Preventive Services Task Force." *Annals of Internal Medicine* 158:741–754.

Patterson, Evelyn J. 2010. "Incarcerating Death: Mortality in U.S. State Correctional Facilities, 1985–1998." *Demography* 47(3):587–607.

Pratt, Daniel, Mary Piper, Louis Appleby, Roger Webb, and Jenny Shaw. 2006. "Suicide in Recently Released Prisoners: A Population-Based Cohort Study." *The Lancet* 368:119–123.

Prins, Seth J. 2014. "Prevalence of Mental Illnesses in U.S. State Prisons: A Systematic Review." *Psychiatric Services* 65:862–872.

Rosen, David L., Victor J. Schoenbach, and David A. Wohl. 2008. "All-Cause and Cause-Specific Mortality Among Men Released from State Prison, 1980–2005." *American Journal of Public Health* 98(12):2278–2284.

Rudd, M. David. 2006. *The Assessment and Management of Suicidality.* Sarasota, FL: Professional Resources Press.

Rudd, M. David, Alan L. Berman, Thomas E. Joiner Jr., Matthew K. Nock, Morton M. Silverman, Michael Mandrusiak, Kimberly Van Orden, and Tracy Witte. 2006. "Warning Signs for Suicide: Theory, Research and Clinical Applications." *Suicide and Life-Threatening Behavior* 36(3):255–262.

Ruiz, Amanda. 2010. "Continuous Quality Improvement and Documentation." In *Handbook of Correctional Mental Health*, 2d ed., edited by Charles L. Scott. Arlington, VA: American Psychiatric Publishing.

Schmidt, Henry III, and Andre Ivanoff. 2014. "Treating Self-Injurious Behaviors in Residential Settings." *Best Practices in Mental Health* 10(1):16–28.

Schmitz, William M. Jr., Michael H. Allen, Barry N. Feldman, Nina J. Gutin, Danielle R. Jahn, Phillip M. Kleepsies, and Skip Simpson. 2012. "Preventing Suicide Through Improved Training in Suicide Risk Assessment and Care: An American Association of Suicidology Task Force." *Suicide and Life-Threatening Behavior* 42(3):292–304.

Silverman, Morton M. 2014. "Suicide Risk Assessment and Suicide Risk Formulation: Essential Components of the Therapeutic Risk Management Model." *Journal of Psychiatric Practice* 20:373–378.

Silverman, Morton M., and Alan L. Berman. 2014. "Suicide Risk Assessment and Risk Formulation, Part I: A Focus on Suicide Ideation in Assessing Suicide Risk." *Suicide and Life Threatening Behavior* 44(4):420–431.

Simon, Robert I. 2009. "Suicide Risk Assessment Forms: Form Over Substance?" *Journal of the American Academy of Psychiatry and the Law* 37:290–293.

Smith, Hayden P., and Robert J. Kaminski. 2010. "Inmate Self-Injurious Behaviors: Distinguishing Characteristics Within a Retrospective Study." *Criminal Justice and Behavior* 37(1):81–96.

Stanley, Barbara, and Gregory K. Brown. 2012. "Safety Planning Intervention: A Brief Intervention to Mitigate Suicide Risk." *Cognitive and Behavioral Practice* 19: 256–264.

Steadman, Henry J., Jack E. Scott, Fred C. Osher, Tara K. Agnese, and Pamela Clark Robbins. 2005. "Validation of the Brief Jail Mental Health Screen." *Psychiatric Services* 56:816–822.

Suicide Prevention Resource Center. 2015. The Strategic Planning Approach to Suicide Prevention. http://www.sprc.org/basics%20/about-suicide-prevention/planning

Tang, Nicole K. Y., and Catherine Crane. 2006. "Suicidality in Chronic Pain: A Review of Prevalence, Risk Factors and Psychological Links." *Psychological Medicine* 36(5):575–586.

Teplin, Linda A. 1994. "Psychiatric and Substance Abuse Disorders Among Male Urban Jail Detainees." *American Journal of Public Health* 84:290–293.

US Surgeon General. 2001. *National Strategy for Suicide Prevention: Goals and Objectives for Action*. Rockville, MD: Department of Health and Human Services.

Way, Bruce B., Richard Miraglia, Donald A. Sawyer, Richard Beer, and John Eddy. 2005. "Factors Related to Suicide in New York State Prisons." *International Journal of Law and Psychiatry* 28(3):207–221.

Way, Bruce B., D. A. Sawyer, S. Barboza, and R. Nash 2007. "Prisoner Suicide and Time Spent in Special Disciplinary Housing in New York State Prison." *Psychiatric Services* 58:558–560.

Wenzel, Amy, Gregory K. Brown, and Aaron T. Beck. 2009. Cognitive Therapy for Suicidal Patients: Scientific and Clinical Applications. Washington, DC: American Psychological Association.

Widom, Cathy Spatz. 1989. "The Cycle of Violence." *Science* 244(4901):160–166.

World Health Organization. 2016. "Mental Health." http://www.who.int/mental_health/prevention/suicide/suicideprevent/en/

Zlodre, Jakov, and Seena Fazel. 2012. "All-Cause and External Mortality in Released Prisoners: Systematic Review and Meta-Analysis." *American Journal of Public Health* 102(12):e67–e75.

CHAPTER 25

OFFENDERS WITH MENTAL ILLNESS IN PRISON

SARAH M. MANCHAK AND ROBERT D. MORGAN

OFFENDERS with mental illness represent a significant proportion of US prison populations. More than 700,000 state prisoners (56 percent) and 70,000 (45 percent) federal prisoners have either had a recent diagnosis, been recently treated, or currently have symptoms of a mental illness (James and Glaze 2006). Rates of such serious and often debilitating mental illnesses as schizophrenia, bipolar disorder, and major depression are nearly 20 percent in US prison populations (National Commission on Correctional Health Care 2002). In both the United States and a number of other industrialized Western countries, the prevalence of mental illness among prisoners is higher than that of the general population (for a review, see Watson, Stimpson, and Hostick 2004).

In this essay, we first explore why persons with mental illnesses are overrepresented in the criminal justice system. In the second section, we present the argument that the efforts to rehabilitate this population should not take place within the prison environment, but if they do, significant changes in current practices are necessary. We discuss in detail the many ways in which prisoners with mental illness pose challenges to prison officials, consider how these challenges are managed, and offer a critical discussion of these strategies. In the final section, we present an analysis of the changes that are needed to improve conditions for inmates with mental illness in prisons. This section includes a description of one promising program for treating offenders with mental illness in prison. Throughout the essay we offer some suggestions for future research with this population that will help inform and improve prison conditions for offenders with mental illness.

In this essay, we argue in support of three main points:

- Offenders with mental illness are not overrepresented in the criminal justice system *because of* their mental illness. Rather, offenders with mental illness have criminogenic risk factors similar to offenders without mental illness. As such, it is necessary to target their criminogenic needs to reduce recidivism risk and target their mental health needs to improve symptoms, functioning, and responsivity to correctional interventions.

- Offenders with mental illness present a number of complex management problems for prison officials, and prisons—as they currently operate—do not seem equipped to effectively manage and treat this population of offenders.
- Because, like general offenders, offenders with mental illness will most likely be released back into the community at some point, it is necessary that prison-based management and treatment practices for this population be improved so as to reduce recidivism and facilitate successful reintegration into the community.

I. Understanding Why Offenders with Mental Illness Are Overrepresented in the Criminal Justice System

Several theories have been posited to explain the overrepresentation of people with mental illness in the criminal justice system. One popular theory places blame on the deinstitutionalization movement in the United States during the 1950s and 1960s, arguing that the closure of state hospitals created a scenario where people with mental illness were no longer able to receive the psychiatric care they required. Therefore, the untreated mental health symptoms resulted in an increase in behaviors warranting an arrest, and many people with mental illness were displaced into the criminal justice system (see Abramson 1972; Teplin 1983). There is very little empirical evidence to support this theory, however. Instead, the research points to other viable explanations for the overrepresentation of offenders with mental illness in the criminal justice system. What is this evidence that refutes the criminalization thesis?

First, the increase in the rate of individuals with mental illness in prisons and jails does not correspond to the rate of hospital bed closures. Instead, economic and systems-based studies reveal that the increase in numbers of mentally ill persons entering jails and prisons parallel the surges in jail and prison populations that occurred throughout the United States at the time. This hike in correctional populations between the 1970s and the early 2000s is largely attributable to changes in sentencing and crime policy (e.g., "get tough" policies, the war on drugs, and mandated sentencing guidelines; see Steadman et al. 1984; Frank and Glied 2006). Still, the proportion of people with serious mental illness who have been incarcerated has been steady (~7 percent) since the 1950s (see Frank and Gleid 2006).

Second, a fairly large body of empirical evidence has robustly demonstrated that, at best, there is a tenuous relationship between mental illness and criminal behavior. To most directly address this issue, several researchers have examined detailed accounts of the crimes committed by people with mental illness to determine whether their crimes could be attributable to psychiatric symptoms. These studies uniformly indicate that symptoms influence criminal behavior for only a small subsample of offenders—and only some of the time. For example, in one study of 109 parolees with mental illness (Peterson et al. 2010) and a separate study of 113 offenders with mental illness in a jail diversion program (Junginger et al. 2006), the symptoms of psychosis (e.g., delusions and/or hallucinations) accounted for the criminal behaviors in 4 to 5 percent of cases. Only an additional 4 percent of cases were accounted for when the definition of symptoms was expanded to include depression, confusion, irritability, and thought disorder (Junginger et al. 2006).

Using a slightly different strategy, Peterson and colleagues (2014) coded the accounts of 429 prior crimes across 143 prisoners with mental illness from detailed, life calendar–approach interviews with offenders and reviews of their institutional files. Rather than using a binary index of whether symptoms influenced the criminal behavior, the researchers rated on a continuum the *extent to which* the crime was either completely independent of—or completely and directly attributable to—the symptoms of mental illness. Only 7.5 percent of crimes were deemed "direct," 10.7 percent were mostly direct, and approximately 82 percent were viewed as mostly or completely "independent." Taking these results one step further, the researchers examined whether those offenders who had committed crimes that were moderately or completely influenced by psychiatric symptoms were always influenced by their symptoms throughout their criminal histories. In this sample, there was no evidence to support the idea that any particular offender with mental illness consistently committed crime *because* of his or her mental health symptoms; approximately 67 percent of those offenders who had committed a crime strongly influenced by their symptoms had also committed a crime that was mostly or completely independent from the influence of symptoms (Peterson et al. 2014).

In addition to the three studies highlighted here that directly examine whether and how much symptoms can account for criminal involvement, several meta-analyses have revealed two important findings. First, clinical factors do not increase the risk for criminal recidivism and instead demonstrate no relationship or a negative relationship with recidivism (Bonta, Law, and Hanson 1998; Bonta, Blais, and Wilson 2013). Second, providing psychiatric treatment does not reduce recidivism risk (Martin et al. 2012).

A third body of evidence against the criminalization hypothesis suggests that something *other* than serious mental illness—which can but may not necessarily co-occur with it—can better explain the overrepresentation of people with mental illness in the criminal justice system. The violence risk assessment literature, for example, has determined that although psychosis is a risk factor for violence (Douglas, Guy, and Hart 2009), its effects on violence are not as strong as those produced by externalizing disorders (e.g., early-onset criminality, antisocial personality disorder) or by borderline and psychopathic personality traits (Douglas et al. 2009).

Similarly, in one of the most methodologically sophisticated single studies examining the link between mental illness and violence ("The MacArthur Violence Risk Study"; see Steadman et al. 1998), it was determined that substance use may be the driving factor behind psychiatric patients' involvement in violence. In this study, researchers compared 951 people with serious mental illness (e.g., schizophrenia, depression, bipolar disorder, and other psychotic disorders) recently discharged from emergency psychiatric facilities to 519 people without mental illnesses living in the same neighborhoods. Participants were interviewed five times over the course of one year to determine their involvement in violence. Holding all else constant, mental illness alone did not increase the risk for involvement in violence. Psychiatric patients were just as likely to be involved in any aggressive acts and serious violence as their relatively healthy neighbors (Steadman et al. 1998). The presence of substance use increased the prevalence of violence in both groups, but *only* when substance use was present were those with mental disorders more likely to be violent than those without mental disorders. These findings are consistent with those of a recent meta-analysis that demonstrated greater effect sizes for psychosis on violence when substance use was present (see Douglas et al. 2009).

Several other factors may also explain why there are such high rates of people with serious mental illness in the correctional system. These factors are arguably factors to which people with mental illness may be disproportionately exposed, but these factors are not necessarily *unique* to people with mental illness. For example, people with mental illness may be more likely to be exposed to homelessness, which in turn can expose individuals to a number of risk factors (see Ditton 1999; Draine et al. 2002) that are more strongly and proximately related to both crime and violence (e.g., residential and familial instability, exposure to antisocial peers, substance use; see Andrews and Bonta 1998, 2010). Not surprisingly, recent research suggests that offenders with mental illness possess many of the same risk factors for crime as people without mental illness.

To demonstrate this, one study compared the Level of Service/Case Management Inventory (Andrews, Bonta, and Wormith 2006; see also Bonta and Wormith this volume) risk assessment scores of 112 parolees with mental illness to 109 parolees without mental illness. Offenders with mental illness scored just as high or higher than those without mental illness across several dynamic (i.e., changeable) risk factors (Skeem et al. 2013). Similarly, Morgan and colleagues (2010) examined prevalence of criminal thinking, one of the primary criminal risk factors (see Andrews and Bonta 1998, 2010) and found that offenders with mental illness in multiple prison (Morgan et al. 2010; Wolff et al. 2011) and jail populations (Blank-Wilson et al. 2014) present with antisocial attitudes comparable to their non–mentally ill counterparts. Notably, this also appears true for persons with mental illness who are justice involved and in an acute psychiatric inpatient setting or outpatient community mental health setting (Gross and Morgan 2013).

Given this body of evidence, we submit that most people with mental illness are not in prisons and jails because they are mentally ill. They are incarcerated, rather, because they have committed a crime. And the same factors that increase the risk for criminal behavior among general offenders are just as likely to be risk factors for those with mental illnesses. Thus a lack of available community treatment is unlikely to directly influence the offending of people with mental illnesses, and it is unlikely to explain their involvement in the criminal justice system. Extant research suggests instead that the system should respond to offenders with mental illness in a similar manner as it does to their nondisordered counterparts. However, despite widespread agreement that offenders with mental illness must also be held responsible for their criminal behavior, and in light of a growing awareness that we must target the criminogenic needs of this population if we are to meaningfully reduce their risk for recidivism, another body of evidence seems to suggest that these goals are perhaps not best met within the confines of the prison environment.

II. The Mismatch of Offenders with Mental Illness and the Prison Context

For a number of reasons, prison may not be the most appropriate correctional environment in which to manage and rehabilitate offenders with mental illness. As discussed in this essay, prisons, as they currently operate, are not achieving the necessary psycholog-ical *and* correctional rehabilitative goals with this population. In part, this is because the confinement conditions and retributive goals of prisons create environments that do little to foster inmates' well-being and change in behavior. Indeed, there is a fundamental mis-match between the prison context and the mentally ill offender. Consider the following observations:

> In congested settings such as prisons self-insulation or privacy may become difficult to achieve. In settings that oscillate between chaos and routine (as most prisons do) stimulation levels may defy accommodation or exceed thresholds. Safety—both actual and subjective—may be impossible to come by. (Toch and Adams 1986, p. 15)

> U.S. prisons are not designed or equipped for mentally ill prisoners . . . There is an inherent tension between the security mission of prisons and mental health considerations. The for-mal and informal rules and codes of conduct in prison reflect staff concerns about security, safety, power, and control. Coordinating the needs of the mentally ill with those rules and goals is nearly impossible. (Fellner 2006, p. 391)

Prisons are undesirable environments for most psychologically healthy people. For those who are struggling with serious symptoms of mental illness, however, the prison environment could be experienced as even more aversive. This appears particularly true when looking at extended periods of confinement, as time spent in prison is associated with increased symptoms of depression and personality traits (e.g., schizoid, depressive, antisocial, aggressive, and negativistic personality traits) for those inmates suffering from mental illness (Bauer 2012). The mismatch of the person (mentally ill offender) and envi-ronment (prison) is perhaps most apparent when one considers (a) the profound needs of mentally ill offenders, the strain they place on prison resources, and the inability of the prison to adequately and effectively address these needs, and (b) the failure of prison offi-cials to alter their response to prison noncompliance in a manner that is more appropriate and responsive to the unique psychological and emotional experiences of the mentally ill offender.

Perhaps more than any other type of prisoner, those with mental illness have significant and persistent needs that can strain prison resources. First and foremost, they require basic mental health services such as psychiatric stabilization (i.e., medication, crisis intervention services), care, and monitoring (Morgan 2003). This can take the form of requiring regular administration of psychotropic medication and/or counseling services. It may also require monitoring for self-harm. Indeed, inmates with mental illness are six times more likely to commit suicide than those without (Fazel et al. 2008), and 72 percent of inmates who com-mit suicide had a psychiatric diagnosis at the time of the act (Shaw et al. 2004).

Regardless of what specific mental health services may be needed, the costs of treating offenders with mental illness is staggering. Although, on average, the annual taxpayer costs for housing an inmate is more than $30,000 (Henrichson and Delaney 2012), it can cost up to $50,000 to incarcerate one person with mental illness (Torrey et al. 2010). Psychiatric medications are costly, but much of this expense can also be attributed to increases in per-sonnel, allocating specialized housing, and treatment delivery. In total, more than $15 bil-lion per year is spent on incarcerating people with mental illnesses in jails and prisons (Maguire and Pastore 1997).

In addition to requiring psychiatric care, inmates with mental illness are also likely to have more serious and persistent general health-care needs. Individuals who have such serious mental illnesses as schizophrenia, bipolar disorder, and major depressive disorder are also likely to have co-occurring chronic physical health conditions. Diseases and illnesses such as HIV, hepatitis, and hypertension, for example, are not uncommon among people with mental illness (for a review, see De Hert et al. 2011)—and therefore not uncommon among prisoners with mental illness too. Moreover, nearly three-quarters of offenders with mental illnesses are likely to have co-occurring substance use disorders (Kessler et al. 1996; Karberg and James 2005), which can present significant physical health impairments in other areas as well (e.g., lung disorders, periodontal disease). Many individuals with mental illness who also have a history of incarceration are likely to face several of these health problems at once (Cuddeback et al. 2010).

A third area in which offenders present with significant need is in regard to their safety. Victimization is especially high among inmates with mental illness. For example, in a study of more than 7,000 adult male and female inmates randomly sampled from 13 prisons, Blitz, Wolff, and Shi (2008) found that men with a mental illness were 1.6 times more likely to be physically assaulted by another inmate and 1.2 times more likely to be assaulted by staff, relative to men without mental illness. Correspondingly, women with mental illness were 1.7 times more likely to be physically assaulted by other inmates than women without mental illness. Sexual victimization, too, is problematic. Using the same sample just mentioned, Wolff, Blitz, and Shi (2007) found that males (but not females) with mental illness were significantly more likely to be sexually victimized by another inmate (i.e., any nonconsensual sexual act) than males without a mental disorder.

It is not entirely clear why inmates with mental illness are more likely to be victimized. It may be that they are viewed as easier targets for other predatory inmates because they may appear weaker, confused, and frightened—some of which may be due to their psychiatric symptomatology. Indeed, "all inmates in jails or prisons are at risk for such attacks, but inmates who are confused by their illness and less able to defend themselves are more vulnerable" (Treatment Advocacy Center 2007, p. 4). It could also be that offenders with mental illness may not be as adept in establishing or maintaining social relationships or "connections" with other prisoners that could otherwise help protect them from victimization. A third possibility could be that the sometimes odd and erratic, and often disruptive, symptoms of serious mental illness could irk or irritate other inmates, leading them to lash out in response. Regardless, research suggests that offenders with mental illnesses are also likely to have been victimized prior to entering prison (Ditton 1999; Teplin et al. 2005). As such, prison per se may not be placing these individuals at greater risk for victimization. How prison officials respond to this victimization, however, is quite important. In the next section, we discuss how prison officials attempt to address the many needs of offenders with mental illness.

A final but important way by which offenders with mental illness pose a significant challenge to prison officials is through their institutional misconduct. Indeed, inmates with mental illness are notoriously difficult to manage in a general prison population. For example, in a systematic file review of more than 10,000 inmate cases, Toch and Adams (1986) found that inmates who had psychiatric treatment histories were significantly more likely to have committed disciplinary infractions in prison. More recent studies support the finding that inmates with mental illness commit more disciplinary infractions (Feder 1991; Ditton

1999; James and Glaze 2006; O'Keefe and Schnell 2007), which subsequently lead them to serve more time in prison because they are less likely to receive good time (Lurigio 2001) or early parole (Feder 1994). The nature of their infractions is also disconcerting.

Although violations can be for petty noncompliance or disruptive behavior, research indicates that inmates with mental illness are also more likely to engage in more serious misconduct. For example, in a nationally representative sample of more than 16,000 state and federal inmates, Felson, Silver, and Remster (2012) found that those who self-reported having previously been given a psychiatric diagnosis from a doctor were more likely to engage in nonviolent noncompliance, verbal and physical attacks on inmates and staff, drug and/or alcohol use, and weapon possession relative to those without a self-reported mental disorder. These findings held even after controlling for a number of relevant variables (e.g., gender, race, age, length of time in prison, education, and alcohol and drug problems). Fighting, in particular, seems to be a major problem for this population. Approximately 36 percent of prison inmates with mental illness have been repeatedly involved in physical fights during incarceration, as compared to 25 percent of inmates without mental illness (Ditton 1999).

In summary, offenders with mental illness not only present with significant mental and physical health needs, but they also pose a number of management challenges to correctional officials. These challenges center around not only protecting the safety of this unique prison population but also in ensuring the safety of other inmates and corrections staff and the stability of routine prison functioning. Effectively tackling all of these challenges is no easy feat, particularly when prison officials must also worry about many other administrative concerns and the much larger population of non–mentally ill offenders in the same prison. We next discuss how prisons have generally attempted to manage this unique prison population.

III. How Prisons Respond to and Manage Mentally Ill Prisoners

To what extent are prisons equipped to handle the myriad of psychological, health-care, and safety needs of inmates with mental illness? Although prisons are required by the Eighth Amendment to provide medical care and psychiatric care and protect inmate safety, the quality of this care and protection is highly variable across prisons. Some empirical data are available on service utilization, the nature of services rendered, and, to a lesser extent, the quality of services delivered. Correspondingly, information is also available about how prisons protect mentally ill inmates from victimization.

A. Correctional Psychiatric Treatment

In contrast to some of the other services prisons may provide, there is quite a bit of information available about correctional psychiatric treatment, and some (but not all) of it is promising. First, data from 1,558 state private and public correctional institutions for adults compiled by researchers from the US Department of Justice (Bureau of Justice Statistics; Beck and Maruschak 2001) indicated that most prisons offer *some* psychiatric care. Specifically, approximately 78 percent of "confinement facilities" (prisons) screen all offenders for mental illness upon intake into the facility, and about the same amount (79 percent) conduct full psychiatric assessments. Slightly more facilities provide psychotropic medications (83 percent) or psychiatric counseling (84 percent). Findings also indicate that, as of the year 2000, about 13 percent of inmates were receiving mental health counseling and 10 percent were receiving psychotropic medications. Notably, service usage is higher among women than men, consistent with prevalence rates in other correctional samples (see Teplin 1990; Teplin, Abram, and McClelland 1996).

Second, offenders with mental illness are *more* likely to receive psychiatric care while incarcerated than when in the community. For instance, one study found a substantially greater proportion of offenders with mental illness received psychiatric medication while in prison, as compared to the time of arrest (~70 percent vs. 30 percent, respectively; Wilper et al. 2009). Similarly, a Bureau of Justice Statistics study reported that whereas only one-fifth of state prison inmates with mental illness had received any psychiatric care (medication or counseling) in the year preceding incarceration, nearly two-thirds received it postadmission (James and Glaze 2006). Of course many factors could account for these trends; some may be attributable to individual factors (e.g., greater need for or adherence to treatment when incarcerated) and some to prison factors (e.g., use of medication to help keep inmates calm and maintain order, better coordination of psychiatric service delivery). Regardless, there is at least some evidence to suggest that prisons *are*, in fact, providing mental health care to inmates. Indeed, it is now well-known that several of the nation's jails and prisons (e.g., Riker's Island in New York, Cook County Detention Center in Chicago, and Twin Towers in Los Angeles) have become the largest de facto mental health care providers.

Two national surveys provide a bit more insight into what, specifically, correctional mental health treatment "looks like" in routine prison settings. In the first, Boothby and Clements (2000) surveyed 830 prison psychologists across 48 prisons. In the second, Bewley and Morgan (2011) surveyed 230 mental health professionals in 165 correctional facilities across 47 states. Across these two studies, several key findings emerged:

1. Psychiatric care is being delivered by people qualified to do so; most prisons employ a psychologist or psychiatrist, and many also have other mental health professionals on staff (e.g., drug and alcohol counselors, social workers; Bewley and Morgan 2011).
2. Prison psychologists spend much of their time administering assessments, delivering individualized services, and completing administrative paperwork (Boothby and Clements 2000; Bewley and Morgan 2011). The former two seems promising, whereas the latter suggests that psychologists' time is often directed to work that takes away from being able to provide therapy to inmates.
3. When treatment is delivered, it is more often done so in an individual (vs. group) format (Boothby and Clements 2000; Bewley and Morgan 2011). On one hand, this suggests that some inmates are receiving the important individualized attention that they may need; on the other hand, it suggests that prison psychologists could make better use of group-based treatment when it is appropriate to do so.

4. Practitioners follow an eclectic treatment approach (i.e., they utilize a variety of techniques and draw from a range of theoretical frameworks to guide treatment); most commonly, cognitive (i.e., targeting thoughts; 88 percent) and/or behavioral models (i.e., targeting behaviors; 69 percent) are emphasized (Boothby and Clements 2000). These general approaches to therapy are, indeed, supported by empirical evidence (Butler et al., 2006).

5. A variety of mental health specific services (e.g., mental illness awareness, symptom management) and nonspecific services (e.g., stress management, anger management, and problem-solving) are provided by prison-based mental health professionals (Bewley and Morgan 2011). Although a wide array of services may be available, it is unclear whether they are appropriately matched to the offender's specific treatment needs.

6. Many of the inmates who receive psychiatric services in prison do so voluntarily (50 percent). Approximately one-quarter of those who receive treatment are referred, and the remaining 25 percent are mandated to treatment by a judge or required to do so by prison officials (Bewley and Morgan 2011).

Very few studies have examined the effectiveness, or perceived effectiveness, of correctional mental health treatment. In one study, qualitative interviews with a small sample of inmates in the UK (n = 44) indicated that inmates with mental illness recognize the utility of psychotropic medications in helping to improve psychiatric symptoms (Mills et al. 2011). Furthermore, Morgan and colleagues (2012) found that correctional mental health treatment successfully reduced psychiatric symptomatology, improved inmate coping with symptoms of mental illness, and, although not conclusive, showed positive evidence for the effectiveness of correctional mental health treatment to reduce both criminal and psychiatric (i.e., rehospitalization) recidivism.

Together these two studies certainly signal the need for more research on the potential effects of treatment on the outcomes for offenders with mental illness. At present, little research has been done to determine whether inmates who are in need of counseling are able to receive it routinely and if this care is appropriate, sufficient, and consistently delivered. Furthermore, the studies that have been done are limited in their methodological rigor, doing little to advance our understanding of the prison psychiatric treatment and its potential effects. In fact, of more than 12,000 documents reviewed, Morgan and colleagues (2012) found that only 26 studies met the scientific rigor necessary to be included in a meta-analysis. Also, very little is known about whether appropriate psychotropic medications are being administered, whether this is being done in a timely manner, and whether side effects are effectively managed. In future studies, it will be crucial for researchers to more rigorously test potential changes in psychiatric symptomatology (rather than relying on self-reports) and to investigate in more detail how mental health treatment may or may not improve institutional behavior.

What is known about correctional mental health treatment is that, consistent with *Estelle v. Gamble* (1976, 429 U.S. 97), offenders with mental illness do not generally seem deprived of the *opportunity* for correctional mental health care; most prisons offer treatment and employ mental health professionals. More research is clearly needed in this area, however, to arrive at any conclusions about access to, quality of, and effectiveness of correctional mental health care. Correctional staff acknowledge that *appropriate* resources are generally unavailable to mentally ill prisoners (Lavoie, Connolly, and Roesch 2006), but much is yet to be learned from the offender's perspective. Although there are some areas of promise in correctional mental health care, there are still others that are concerning.

> The sheer number of mentally ill inmates has transformed prisons into facilities for the mentally ill. Yet prisons cannot provide the range of services mentally ill prisoners need in the necessary quantity and quality. Seriously ill prisoners confront a paucity of qualified staff to evaluate their illness, develop and implement treatment plans, and monitor their condition. They confront treatment that often consists of little more than medication—and even that may be poorly administered and supervised . . . They live without the diversity of mental health interventions they need, much less the long-term supportive and therapeutic environment that would best help many of them manage their illnesses. Without necessary care, mentally ill inmates suffer painful symptoms and their conditions can deteriorate. (Fellner 2006, p. 394)

B. Correctional Medical Treatment

With respect to medical care specifically for mentally ill inmates, less is known. No currently available research focuses specifically on medical care for inmates with mental illness. As such, what might be known about this population can only be inferred from research on offenders in general. In a secondary data analysis of surveys of nearly 7,000 jail and prison inmates initially conducted by the US Census Bureau, Wilper and colleagues (2009) found that approximately 39 percent of federal and 43 percent of state inmates had at least one chronic medical condition (e.g., diabetes, hypertension); however, 14 percent of federal and 20 percent of state inmates with these chronic health concerns did not receive a medical examination since their incarceration, suggesting that perhaps they also were not receiving treatment for their chronic illnesses (Wilper et al. 2009). Of course it may not be the case that prisons are necessarily being negligent in providing these services. Inmates must communicate their medical needs and comply with prescribed treatment regimens. Nevertheless, there is ample room for improvement in the area of correctional medical care.

C. Inmate Safety

Because inmates are at high risk for harm to themselves, for victimization from other inmates, and for engaging in institutional misconduct, prisons officials must take steps to protect inmate safety. One approach to achieve this goal, in many cases, is to place mentally ill inmates in segregation, which is sometimes referred to as administrative segregation ("ad seg"; often used to keep those with mental illness safe from victimization by other inmates or from self-harm) or disciplinary segregation (used in response to prison misconduct). In segregation units, inmates are often housed in individual cells in a special pod or section of the prison and are typically confined to the cell for 23 of 24 hours each day. If not sentenced to a supermax prison, where all inmates are in ad seg conditions for the full term of their sentence, most inmates are placed in segregation for a specified period of time (e.g., one to three months in disciplinary segregation).

Whether used as a punitive measure (to punish noncompliance and aggression) or as a safety precaution (to reduce risk for victimization, self-harm, or violence), offenders with mental illness are disproportionately assigned to solitary confinement as a correctional management strategy (Lovell et al. 2000; Fellner 2006; James and Glaze 2006; Metzer and Fellner 2010). In some states, as many as half of the ad seg inmates have mental illness (see Fellner 2006; Lovell 2008). Additionally, perhaps because of (a) the profound safety and administrative concerns posed by offenders with mental illness, (b) the persistence of behavior that may lead to repeated or continued placement in segregation (e.g., self-harm, aggression, noncompliance), or (c) correctional staffs' perceptions that "mentally ill inmates are inherently dangerous, unpredictable, and explosive" (Cloyes et al. 2006, p. 762), mentally ill prisoners may be placed in segregation for longer, more indefinite periods of time relative to other inmates.

If solitary confinement is disproportionately applied to individuals with mental illness, it is important to discuss whether this administrative response is appropriate for them. Because the psychological effects of segregation for inmates with and without mental illness is reviewed in detail elsewhere in this volume (Gendreau and Labreque), we present only a brief summary of the literature here. In short, most of the empirical evidence is quite mixed. Notably, the research on both sides of the argument (i.e., segregation is psychologically harmful vs. not harmful) has been critiqued on a number of methodological grounds such as use of small sample sizes; research duration that does not adequately reflect the use of segregation practices in the United States; selection bias; lack of an appropriate comparison group and/or randomization; issues with sample attrition and measurement of symptomatology; length of follow-up; and failure to account for baseline personality and psychiatric problems as well as the normal progression of symptoms over time (see Grassian and Friedman 1986; Bonta and Gendreau 1990; Smith 2006).

Nevertheless, at least two nonrandomized repeated measures studies comparing non-disordered inmates in segregation, inmates with mental illness in segregation, and inmates with and without mental illness in the general population seem to suggest that segregation—by itself—does not make mentally ill inmates *worse* psychologically (a finding that is consistent with two recent meta-analytic reviews on the effects of segregation; see Gendreau and Labrecque this volume; Morgan et al. 2014). In fact, symptoms generally decrease over time whether or not one is in segregation (see Andersen et al. 2003; O'Keefe 2010; O'Keefe et al. 2013). Such findings may lead some to conclude that the use of solitary confinement for prisoners with mental illness is neither harmful nor inappropriate; however, the body of research to date does suggest that the use of segregation is harmful to some inmates. Furthermore, in spite of the Andersen et al. and O'Keefe et al. studies, inmates with mental illness remain a vulnerable population when considering the use of segregation.

There are several points to consider when weighing the appropriateness of solitary confinement for mentally ill prisoners. First, it may be an ineffective strategy for preventing inmate self-injurious behavior. For example, a study of more than 150,000 prisoners in California spanning over a five-year period found that nearly half of completed suicides were done when an inmate was in an ad seg cell (Patterson and Hughes 2008; see also White, Schimmel, and Frickey 2002).

A second mitigating issue against the use of segregation for inmates with mental illness is that it may delay the natural progression (and improvement) of psychiatric symptoms over time. In one study, remand prisoners in Denmark placed in segregation (n = 133) and nonsegregation units ($n = 95$) were repeatedly assessed for changes in psychopathology and general functioning over the course of several months. Although both groups eventually saw improvement in functioning and decreased depression and anxiety symptoms over time, the changes did not occur with the segregation participants until *after* they were transferred out of the segregation units (Andersen et al. 2003).

Finally, and perhaps most important, segregation often deprives inmates of the opportunity to benefit from psychiatric treatment and correctional rehabilitation efforts. Several researchers have noted that segregation units are not only typically understaffed in general, but the nature of segregation makes it so inmates cannot leave their cells to receive needed treatment services (see Fellner 2006; Arrigio and Bullock 2008; Metzer and Fellner 2010). Thus it would follow that there is a potential for symptoms to go un- or under-treated. Moreover, inmates in solitary confinement have less access to prison programming that might otherwise help to shape and improve inmate behavior in a manner that would have significant and lasting implications for the prison milieu and public safety (Metzer and Fellner 2010). Although segregation may not make mentally ill offenders worse, it does very little to actually make them better, psychologically or behaviorally.

IV. Moving Forward: Recommendations for Improving Conditions for Mentally Ill Offenders in Prison

Thus far we have presented the theories and research to help explain why people with mental illness are overrepresented in criminal justice populations. We argued that although mental illness is unlikely to be the root cause of criminal behavior for the majority of these offenders, those with mental illness may be disproportionately exposed to other risk factors (e.g., poverty, homelessness, substance use) that more strongly influence their risk for involvement in crime. Offenders with mental illness require not only psychiatric stabilization but also interventions to help reduce those risk factors for criminality. The prison environment is one among many contexts in which these efforts can take place. However, as currently operated, the prison context may fall short in achieving this goal. We have proposed that prisons are not well-equipped to offer the kind of extensive care, services, and monitoring that this population requires and that current administrative practices for both protecting and punishing mentally ill inmates may be inappropriate.

For these reasons, both scholars and practitioners have argued that many offenders with mental illness do not belong in prison. As such, a variety of alternative programs have been developed to keep mentally ill offenders in the community (e.g., diversion, mental health courts, specialized mental health probation). Nevertheless, it is unlikely that any policy will ever prohibit any one group of offenders from being sentenced to prison. If criminal justice officials wish to impact the behavior of mentally ill prisoners within the prison context and after release, modifications to traditional practices are warranted. In this section, we offer several suggestions for improving the conditions for inmates with mental illness.

A. Stop Harmful Practices

Up to this point, we have discussed the "typical" or "average" practices for managing and treating offenders with mental illness in prisons. However, there are a number of other practices that may not be representative of prisons in general but that do occur and must be unequivocally "exnovated" (Frank and Glied 2006)—namely, any instances of abuse or neglect. Unfortunately, there are many accounts of harmful prison practices with mentally ill inmates that have been documented by the media.

For example, a recent article in *The Atlantic* featured a story about the treatment of mentally ill offenders in South Carolina's prisons. South Carolina's prisons were found by a judge to be woefully inadequate in providing psychiatric care to inmates, negligent in their attempts to prevent inmate suicide, disproportionately and inappropriately using solitary confinement to manage mentally ill offenders, and outright neglectful and abusive toward some mentally ill inmates, which resulted in their death (Cohen 2014). In New York's Rikers Island, one inmate recently succumbed to intense heat caused by a faulty thermostat that was blamed, in part, on a lack of required monitoring of the prison's mental health unit (Schwirtz 2014). In California, the prison system has been under significant scrutiny from a three-judge panel for nearly a decade, in part because overcrowded conditions have compromised mentally ill prisoners' access to psychiatric and medical care, violating offenders' Eighth Amendment rights.

It is quite understandable that many prison officials would be overwhelmed by the substantial burden and challenge that mentally ill offenders place on prison resources, but negligence and abuse are never acceptable. Prison administrators must work to implement policies and procedures to punish and eradicate harmful practices. At the same time, they must also problem-solve potential alternative solutions for managing this challenging population. Such solutions may come in the form of improvements on existing practices or introducing new promising and evidence-based practices.

B. Improve Existing Practices

Even minor changes in routine prison policy and practice can go a long way toward improving conditions for mentally ill inmates. With respect to psychiatric care, the first area in which prisons can improve is with assessment. In their survey of correctional mental health practitioners, Boothby and Clements (2000) found that the majority of psychological assessments being done actually had very little to do with psychiatric symptoms and risk and more often focused on personality and intellectual functioning. Prisons would benefit from implementing brief screening tools for mental illness such as the K-6 (Kessler et al. 2002) or Brief Jail Mental Health Screen (Steadman et al. 2005). Those who "screen in" for potential mental illness can go on for more thorough and rigorous mental health assessments that can identify the nature and severity of symptoms and aid in prison-based psychiatric case planning. Additionally, it is quite clear that prisons also need to identify ways by which correctional mental health practitioners can increase their time spent actually delivering psychiatric treatment (see Boothby and Clements 2000; Bewley and Morgan

2011). The use of technology (i.e., electronic medical records, telemedicine) and increasing staff size may help in this regard.

Improvements can also be made in existing practices designed to protect inmate safety. Namely, offenders who are a risk to themselves should not be placed in solitary confinement but should be treated in a secure setting where they are routinely monitored and given appropriate psycho-social interventions. For prison officials seeking to prevent inmates with mental illness from engaging in self-injurious behavior, segregation from the general population may be appropriate; however, long periods of isolation and inaccessibility to needed services while in segregation should be remedied. People with mental illness benefit from social support and social contact (Jacoby and Kozie-Peak 1997), and thus efforts should be made to increase social supports both within the facility as well as with family members outside the prison. Further, allowing prisoners to receive needed psychological treatment and linking mentally ill prisoners with prison programming is likely to help reduce their symptoms, functioning, and behavior (Martin et al. 2012). Finally, when using solitary confinement as a corrective tool to address inmate misconduct, officers should minimize their use of force and coercion in these settings and seclusion should be coupled with interventions to target and reduce noncompliant behavior. Prisons may also benefit from developing intermediate step-down units to help facilitate more successful transitions from solitary confinement or ad seg into the general prison population and/or into the community upon release (see Kupers et al. 2009).

A number of improvements in the general prison milieu can also be made primarily through education. Correctional administrators and practitioners (officers and treatment providers) would benefit from a better understanding of how and why offenders with mental illness come to be involved in the criminal justice system. Such education efforts may, on one hand, help reduce officers' stigmatizing attitudes about mentally ill offenders as inherently violent and unpredictable (Lavoie et al. 2006). On the other hand, this knowledge can shape correctional intervention efforts. Equipped with the knowledge that behavior change will best be effected by targeting known risk factors for institutional misconduct and crime (e.g., impulsivity, aggressiveness, and antisocial thinking) while also attending to mental illness to increase offenders' receptiveness to such interventions, correctional practitioners may better reduce mentally ill inmates' risk for recidivism and ultimately improve public safety.

Prison personnel should also be educated about symptoms of mental illness and the typical life courses of those with mental illnesses. Indeed, "officers typically do not understand the nature of mental illness and its behavioral impact. They cannot distinguish—and may not even know a distinction exists—between a frustrated or disgruntled inmate who 'acts out' and one whose 'acting out' reflects mental illness" (Fellner 2006, p. 397). Education about mental illness can improve officers' response to mentally ill inmates, allowing them to link inmates with timely and appropriate psychiatric treatment and effectively respond to behavior that may be influenced by these symptoms.

C. Implement Promising and Evidence-Based Practices

An abundance of research in both the mental health care and corrections arenas has helped to identify programs and practices that are effective for achieving particular goals. The onus is on prison administrators to ensure that their correctional practitioners deliver these evidence-based treatments. A comprehensive list of such programs is beyond the scope of this essay; however, we highlight four key principles that are supported by the empirical research.

First, to reduce criminal behavior, interventions must attend to the "principles of effective correctional intervention" (see Goggin this volume). Specifically, correctional personnel must routinely administer a valid risk assessment tool at intake and match the intensity of services to the offender's risk level, where higher risk offenders are in more programming and for longer periods of time (i.e., "risk principle"). They must also use this risk assessment tool to identify dynamic (i.e., changeable) risk factors that should be targeted in correctional interventions—and then target them (i.e., "need principle"). For most offenders with mental illness, this means working to change such factors as antisocial thinking and associates, substance use, and problems with family and employment. Finally, practitioners must deliver services in a manner that best suits offenders' learning styles (i.e., use cognitive-behavioral strategies and social learning principles; "General Responsivity Principle") and account for each offender's individual circumstances (e.g., motivation, religious or cultural beliefs, gender; "Specific Responsivity Principle"). To capitalize on correctional intervention efforts even further, personnel must use "core correctional practices" (Andrews and Kiessling 1980; Dowden and Andrews 2004) that include appropriate use of reinforcement, punishment, and authority, and the development of strong inmate-practitioner relationships characterized by caring, trust, and a firm-but-fair manner (Skeem et al. 2007).

Second, mental illness cannot be ignored. Even though addressing mental health symptoms is unlikely to reduce the risk for criminality (Martin et al. 2012), from a public health and human rights perspective, we must continue to provide efficacious treatments to incarcerated persons with mental illness. Within the principles of effective correctional intervention (Andrews and Bonta 1998, 2010), mental illness is conceptualized as a specific responsivity factor. That is, symptoms can impede an offender's responsiveness to correctional interventions. However, mental illness remains a primary risk factor for successful reentry (Feder 1991) and reintegration into the community and for psychiatric recidivism (Lovell, Gagliardi, and Peterson 2002).

Third, when offenders have mental illness and substance use problems (which applies to most offenders with mental illness; Kessler et al. 1996; Karberg and James 2005), it is better to treat the issues in tandem than in a parallel or sequential manner (see Mueser et al. 2003). Since psychiatric and substance use disorders typically require longer term care and may share similar etiological risks, and since addressing only one issue at the expense of another can complicate treatment efforts and hinder treatment progress, it has been assumed that treating mental illness and addiction in an integrated manner (i.e., by the same provider) may be more effective. As noted by Drake and colleagues (1998, p. 590), this approach can "ensure that the patient receives a consistent explanation of illness and a coherent prescription for treatment rather than a contradictory set of messages from different providers." In a systematic review of 36 studies, there was evidence that integrated dual diagnosis was a more promising approach for reducing substance use and psychiatric hospitalizations, particularly when the treatment was longer (~18 months), involved outreach components, and targeted issues with motivation (Drake et al. 1998).

Issues of mental illness, substance use, and criminality must be treated in tandem, much akin to the manner in which co-occurring mental illness and substance abuse is treated

(Draine et al. 2002; Moran and Hodgins 2004; Hodgins et al. 2007; Morgan et al. 2012, 2013). One promising program to accomplish this goal is "Changing Lives and Changing Outcomes: A Treatment Program for Offenders with Mental Illness" (Morgan et al. 2013). Preliminary results of this comprehensive psychotherapeutic program are promising, with reductions in psychiatric symptomatology as high as 48 percent; 50 percent reductions in general distress; and reductions in reactive (e.g., spontaneous, unplanned, impetuous criminal behavior, 30 percent) and current (thoughts, values, and beliefs consistent with current criminal behavior, 20 percent) criminal thinking. Further study to assess criminal and psychiatric recidivism is underway, but these preliminary findings are promising for a comprehensive and integrated treatment program targeting co-occurring issues of mental illness and criminality.

Last, reentry services need to be more widely and better implemented. Offenders with mental illness deal with complex medical, social, and personal issues upon release from prison. When they return to the communities, it is essential that they are linked with the care and services necessary for successful reintegration. It is simply not sufficient to release an inmate with mental illness from prison with a list of referral sources on a piece of paper. Successful reentry of prisoners with mental illness into the community requires close collaboration primarily between criminal justice, substance use, and mental health agencies (and other medical and social service agencies), so that released offenders can have continuity of services from prison to the community. Further, these services need to be not only adequate (e.g., evidence-based, address basic needs across domains), but they also need to be sustained over time (see Lovell et al. 2002). Two programs—the Assess, Plan, Identify, and Coordinate program (Osher, Steadman, and Barr 2003) and the Critical Time Intervention (Draine and Herman 2007)—are promising in that they incorporate continuity of care and coordination of services from before offenders are discharged from prison through their reintegration with the community.

V. CONCLUSION

We began this essay with a review of the prevalence of persons with mental illness in the justice system, arguing that their overrepresentation is not the result of a deficit in community mental health services, nor is it because mental illness increases risk for crime. Rather, offenders with mental illness present with many of the same risk factors for crime as other, nondisordered offenders *alongside* mental health and substance use problems, oftentimes complicating treatment and management efforts. As a result of this realization, prison services must adequately address both criminal and psychiatric/substance use issues. Thus treatment of offenders with mental illness should be considered within a risk–need–responsivity framework if correctional interventions are to have an appreciable effect on crime.

Correspondingly, it is important not to lose sight of mental health needs, and correctional interventions need to be modified to address the psychiatric concerns of this unique offender population. At present, prisons have a long way to go toward achieving this balance, both in terms of the treatment programming they provide and the successful management of this population. For example, segregation policies may need to be revised, and inmates may benefit from increased access to quality health and mental health care during periods of confinement. Given the continued overrepresentation of mental illness in the prison population, researchers and practitioners must work together to identify the best strategies to achieve inmate and public safety goals and public (mental) health goals. They must do so in a manner that is both cost effective and helps facilitate successful reintegration of this population upon release from prison. Going forward, it will be important to identify ways to improve the continuity of services from inside the prison walls to the outside community. Examination of the direct linkages to services and barriers to effective linkages may be particularly enlightening.

References

Abramson Marc F. 1972. "The Criminalization of Mentally Disordered Behavior." *Hospital and Community Psychiatry* 23: 101–105.

Andersen, Henrik Steen, Dorte Sestoft, Tommy Lillebaek, Gorm Gabrielsen, and Ralf Hemmingsen. 2003. "A Longitudinal Study of Prisoners on Remand: Repeated Measures of Psychopathology in the Initial Phase of Solitary Versus Nonsolitary Confinement." *International Journal of Law and Psychiatry* 26: 165–177.

Andrews, Don A., and James Bonta. 1998. *Psychology of Criminal Conduct*, 2d ed. Cincinnati, OH: Anderson.

Andrews, Don A., and James Bonta. 2010. *Psychology of Criminal Conduct*, 5th ed. Cincinnati, OH: Anderson.

Andrews, Don A., James Bonta, and J. Stephen Wormith. 2006. "The Recent Past and Near Future of Risk and/or Need Assessment." *Crime & Delinquency* 52: 7–27.

Andrews, Don A., and Jerry J. Kiessling. 1980. "Program Structure and Effective Correctional Practices: A Summary of the CaVIC Research." In *Effective Correctional Treatment*, edited by Robert R. Ross and Paul Gendreau. Toronto: Butterworths.

Arrigo, Bruce A., and Jennifer L. Bullock. 2008. "The Psychological Effects of Solitary Confinement on Prisoners in Supermax Units: Reviewing What We Know and Recommending What Should Change." *International Journal of Offender Therapy and Comparative Criminology* 52: 622–640.

Bauer, Rebecca. 2012. *"Implications of Long-Term Incarceration for Persons with Mental Illness."* Unpublished doctoral dissertation, Texas Tech University, Lubbock.

Beck, Allen J., and Laura M. Maruschak. 2001. "Mental Health Treatment in State Prisons, 2000." Washington, DC: US Department of Justice, Bureau of Justice Statistics.

Bewley, Marshall T., and Robert D. Morgan. 2011. "A National Survey of Mental Health Services Available to Offenders with Mental Illness: Who Is Doing What?" *Law and Human Behavior* 35: 351–363.

Blank-Wilson, Amy, Kathleen Farkas, Karen J. Ishler, Michael Gearhart, Robert Morgan, and Melinda Ashe. 2014. "Criminal Thinking Styles among People with Serious Mental Illness in Jail." *Law and Human Behavior* 38(6): 592–601.

Blitz, Cynthia L., Nancy Wolff, and Jing Shi. 2008. "Physical Victimization in Prison: The Role of Mental Illness." *International Journal of Law and Psychiatry* 31: 385–393.

Bonta, James, Julie Blais, and Holly Wilson. 2013. "The Prediction of Risk for Mentally Disordered Offenders: A Quantitative Synthesis." Ottawa: Public Safety Canada. http://www.publicsafety.gc.ca/cnt/rsrcs/pblctns/prdctn-rsk-mntlly-dsrdrd/index-eng.aspx

Bonta, James, and Paul Gendreau. 1990. "Reexamining the Cruel and Unusual Punishment of Prison Life." *Law and Human Behavior* 14: 347–372.

Bonta, James, Moira Law, and Karl Hanson. 1998. "The Prediction of Criminal and Violent Recidivism among Mentally Disordered Offenders: A Meta-Analysis." *Psychological Bulletin* 123: 123–142.

Boothby, Jennifer L., and Carl B. Clements. 2000. "A National Survey of Correctional Psychologists." *Criminal Justice and Behavior* 27: 716–732.

Butler, A. C., J. E. Chapman, E. M. Forman, and A. T. Beck. 2006. The Empirical Status of Cognitive–Behavioral Therapy: A Review of Meta-Analyses. *Clinical Psychology Review* 26: 17–31.

Cloyes, Kristin G., David Lovell, David G. Allen, and Lorna A. Rhodes. 2006. "Assessment of Psychosocial Impairment in a Supermaximum Security Unit Sample." *Criminal Justice and Behavior* 33: 760–781.

Cohen, Andrew. 2014. *"When Good People Do Nothing: The Appalling Story of South Carolina's Prisons."* *The Atlantic*, January 10 http://www.theatlantic.com/national/archive/2014/01/when-good-people-do-nothing-the-appalling-story-of-south-carolinas-prisons/282938/

Cuddeback, Gary, Anna Scheyett, Carrie Pettus-Davis, and Joseph Morrissey. 2010. "General Medical Problems of Incarcerated Persons with Severe and Persistent Mental Illness: A Population-Based Study." *Psychiatric Services* 61: 45–49.

De Hert, Marc, Christoph U. Correll, Julio Bobes, Marcelo Cetkovich-Bakmas, Dan Cohen, Itsuo Asai, Johan Detraux, Shiv Guatam, Hans-Jurgan Möeller, David M. Ndetei, John W. Newcomer, Richard Uwakwe, and Stefan Leucht. 2011. "Physical Illness in Patients with Severe Mental Disorders: I. Prevalence, Impact of Medications and Disparities in Health Care." *World Psychiatry* 10: 52–77.

Ditton, Paula M. 1999. Mental Health and Treatment of Inmates and Probationers. Washington, DC: US Department of Justice, Bureau of Justice Statistics.

Douglas, Kevin S., Laura S. Guy, and Stephen D. Hart. 2009. "Psychosis as a Risk Factor for Violence to Others: A Meta-Analysis." *Psychological Bulletin* 135: 679–706.

Dowden, Craig, and Don A. Andrews. 2004. "The Importance of Staff Practice in Delivering Effective Correctional Treatment: A Meta-Analytic Review of Core Correctional Practice." *International Journal of Offender Therapy and Comparative Criminology* 48: 203–214.

Draine, Jeffrey, and Daniel Herman. 2007. "Critical Time Intervention for Reentry from Prison for Persons with Mental Illness". *Psychiatric Services* 58: 1577–1581.

Draine, Jeffrey, Mark S. Salzer, Dennis P. Culhane, and Trevor R. Hadley. 2002. "Role of Social Disadvantage in Crime, Joblessness, and Homelessness among Persons with Serious Mental Illness." *Psychiatric Services* 53: 565–573.

Drake, Robert E., Carolyn Mercer-McFadden, Kim T. Mueser, Gregory J. McHugo, and Gary R. Bond. 1998. "Review of Integrated Mental Health and Substance Abuse Treatment for Patients with Dual Disorders." *Schizophrenia Bulletin* 24: 589–608.

Fazel, Seena, Julia Cartwright, Arabella Norman-Nott, and Keith Hawton. 2008. "Suicide in Prisoners: A Systematic Review of Risk Factors." *Journal of Clinical Psychiatry* 69: 1721–1731.

Feder, Lynette. 1991. "A Comparison of the Community Adjustment of Mentally Ill Offenders with Those from the General Prison Population: An 18-Month Follow-up." *Law and Human Behavior* 15: 477–493.

Feder, Lynette. 1994. "Psychiatric Hospitalization History and Parole Decisions." *Law and Human Behavior* 18: 395–410.

Fellner, Jamie. 2006. "A Corrections Quandary: Mental Illness and Prison Rules." *Harvard Civil Rights-Civil Liberties Law Review* 41: 391–412.

Felson, Richard B., Eric Silver, and Brianna Remster. 2012. "Mental Disorder and Offending in Prison." *Criminal Justice and Behavior* 39: 125–143.

Frank, Richard G., and Sherry A. Glied. 2006. Better But Not Well: Mental Health Policy in the United States Since 1950. Baltimore, MD: Johns Hopkins University Press.

Grassian, Stuart, and Nancy Friedman. 1986. "Effects of Sensory Deprivation in Psychiatric Seclusion and Solitary Confinement." *International Journal of Law and Psychiatry* 8: 49–65.

Gross, Nicole R., and Robert D. Morgan. 2013. "Understanding Persons with Mental Illness Who Are and Are Not Criminal Justice Involved: A Comparison of Criminal Thinking and Psychiatric Symptoms." *Law and Human Behavior* 37: 175–186.

Henrichson, Christian, and Ruth Delaney. 2012. "The Price of Prisons: What Incarceration Costs Taxpayers." *Federal Sentencing Reporter* 25(1): 68–80.

Hodgins, Sheilagh, Jane Alderton, Adrian Cree, Andrew Aboud, and Timothy Mak. 2007. "Aggressive Behaviour, Victimization, and Crime among Severely Mentally Ill Patients Requiring Hospitalisation." *The British Journal of Psychiatry* 191: 343–350.

Jacoby, Joseph E., and Brenda Kozie-Peak. 1997. "The Benefits of Social Support for Mentally Ill Offenders: Prison-to-Community Transitions." *Behavioral Sciences and the Law* 15: 483–502.

James, Doris J., and Lauren E. Glaze. 2006. Mental Health Problems of Prison and Jail Inmates. Washington, DC: US Department of Justice, Bureau of Justice Statistics.

Junginger, John, Keith Claypoole, Ranilo Laygo, and Annette Crisanti. 2006. "Effects of Serious Mental Illness and Substance Abuse on Criminal Offenses." *Psychiatric Services* 57: 879–882.

Karberg, Jennifer C., and Doris J. James. 2005. Substance Dependence, Abuse, and Treatment of Jail Inmates, 2002. Washington, DC: US Department of Justice, Bureau of Justice Statistics.

Kessler, Ronald C., Gavin Andrews, Lisa J. Colpe, Eva Hiripi, Daniel K. Mroczek, Sharon-Lise T. Normand, Ellen E. Walters, and Alan M. Zaslavsky. 2002. "Short Screening Scales to Monitor Population Prevalences and Trends in Non-Specific Psychological Distress." *Psychological Medicine* 32: 959–976.

Kessler, Ronald C., Christopher B. Nelson, Katherine A. McGonagle, Mark J. Edlund, Richard G. Frank, and Philip J. Leaf. 1996. "The Epidemiology of Co-Occurring Addictive and Mental Disorders: Implications for Prevention and Service Utilization." *American Journal of Orthopsychiatry* 66: 17–31.

Kupers, Terry, Theresa Dronet, Margaret Winter, James Austin, Lawrence Kelly, William Cartier, Timothy Morris, Stephen Hanlon, Emmit Sparkman, Parveen Kumar, Leonard Vincent, Jim Norris, Kim Nagel, and Jennifer McBride. 2009. "Beyond Supermax Administrative Segregation: Mississippi's Experience Rethinking Prison Classification and Creating Alternative Mental Health Programs." *Criminal Justice and Behavior* 36: 1037–1050.

Lavoie, Jennifer A., Deborah A. Connolly, and Ronald Roesch. 2006. "Correctional Officers' Perceptions of Inmates with Mental Illness: The Role of Training and Burnout Syndrome." *International Journal of Forensic Mental Health* 5: 151–166.

Lovell, David. 2008. "Patterns of Disturbed Behavior in a Supermax Population." *Criminal Justice and Behavior* 35: 985–1004.

Lovell, David, Kristin Cloyes, David Allen, and Lorna Rhodes. 2000. "Who Lives in Super-Maximum Custody? A Washington State Study." *Federal Probation* 64(2): 33–39.

Lovell, David, Gregg Gagliardi, and Paul Peterson. 2002. "Recidivism and the Use of Services among Persons with Mental Illness after Release from Prison." *Psychiatric Services* 53: 1290–1296.

Lurigio, Arthur J. 2001. "Effective Services for Parolees with Mental Illnesses." *Crime & Delinquency* 47: 446–461.

Maguire, Kathleen, and Anne L. Pastore. 1997. Bureau of Justice Statistics Sourcebook of Criminal Justice Statistics, 1996. Washington, DC: US Department of Justice, Bureau of Justice Statistics.

Martin, Michael, Shannon Dorken, Ashley Wamboldt, and Sarah Wooten. 2012. "Stopping the Revolving Door: A Meta-Analysis on the Effectiveness of Interventions for Criminally Involved Individuals with Major Mental Disorders". *Law and Human Behavior* 36: 1–12.

Metzner, Jeffrey L., and Jamie Fellner. 2010. "Solitary Confinement and Mental Illness in U.S. Prisons: A Challenge for Medical Ethics." *Journal of the American Academy of Psychiatry and the Law* 38: 104–108.

Mills, Alice, Judith Lathlean, Dan Bressington, Andrew Forrester, Wilhelm Van Veenhuyzen, and Richard Gray. 2011. "Prisoners' Experiences of Antipsychotic Medication: Influences on Adherence." *Journal of Forensic Psychiatry and Psychology* 22(1): 110–125.

Moran, Paul, and Sheilagh Hodgins. 2004. "The Correlates of Comorbid Antisocial Personality Disorder in Schizophrenia." *Schizophrenia Bulletin* 30: 791–802.

Morgan, Robert D. 2003. "Basic Mental Health Services: Services and Issues." In *Correctional Mental Health Handbook*, edited by Thomas Fagan and Robert K. Ax. Thousand Oaks, CA: Sage.

Morgan, Robert D., William H. Fisher, Naihua Duan, Jon T. Mandracchia, and Danielle Murray. 2010. "Prevalence of Criminal Thinking among State Prison Inmates with Serious Mental Illness." *Law and Human Behavior* 34: 324–336.

Morgan, Robert D., David B. Flora, Daryl G. Kroner, Jeremy F. Mills, Femina Varghese, and Jarrod S. Steffan. 2012. "Treating Offenders with Mental Illness: A Research Synthesis." *Law and Human Behavior* 36: 37–50.

Morgan, Robert D., Daryl G. Kroner, Jeremy F. Mills, Rebecca L. Bauer, and Catherine Serna. 2013. "Treating Justice Involved Persons with Mental Illness: Preliminary Evaluation of a Comprehensive Treatment Program." *Criminal Justice and Behavior* 41(7): 902–916.

Morgan, Robert D., Stephanie A. Van Horn, Nina Maclean, Angela Bolanos, Ashley Batastini, Andrew Gray, and Jeremy Mills. 2014. *"Administrative Segregation: Is It a Harmful Correctional Practice?"* Poster presented at the annual meeting of the American Psychology-Law Society, New Orleans, LA.

Mueser, Kim T., Douglas L. Noordsy, Robert E. Drake, and Lindy Fox. 2003. *Integrated Treatment for Dual Disorders: A Guide to Effective Practice.* New York: Guilford Press.

National Commission on Correctional Health Care. 2002. *Health Status of Soon-to-Be-Released Inmates.* Chicago: National Commission on Correctional Health Care.

O'Keefe, Maureen L. 2010. *"One Year Longitudinal Study of the Psychological Effects of Administrative Segregation."* Unpublished paper. https://www.ncjrs.gov/pdffiles1/nij/grants/232973.pdf

O'Keefe, Maureen L, Kelli Klebe, Jeffrey Metzner, Joel Dvoskin, Jamie Fellner, and Alysha Stucker. 2013. "A Longitudinal Study of Administrative Segregation." *Journal of the American Academy of Psychiatry and the Law* 41: 49–60.

O'Keefe, Maureen L., and Marissa J. Schnell. 2007. "Offenders with Mental Illness in the Correctional System." *Journal of Offender Rehabilitation* 45: 81–104.

Osher, Fred, Henry Steadman, and Heather Barr. 2003. "A Best Practice Approach to Community Reentry from Jail for Inmates with Co-occurring Disorders: The APIC Model." *Crime & Delinquency* 49: 79–96.

Patterson, Raymond, and Kerry Hughes. 2008. "Review of Completed Suicides in the California Department of Corrections and Rehabilitation, 1999 to 2004." *Psychiatric Services* 59: 676–682.

Peterson, Jillian, Jennifer Skeem, Eliza Hart, Sarah Vidal, and Felicia Keith. 2010. "Analyzing Offense Patterns as a Function of Mental Illness to Test the Criminalization Hypothesis." *Psychiatric Services* 61: 1217–1222.

Peterson, Jillian, Jennifer L. Skeem, Patrick J. Kennealy, Beth Bray, and Andrea Zvonkovic. 2014. "How Often and How Consistently Do Symptoms Directly Precede Criminal Behavior among Offenders with Mental Illness?" *Law and Human Behavior* 38(5): 439–449.

Schwirtz, Michael. 2014. "Warden at Riker's Island Demoted after Inmate Dies in Overheated Cell." *The New York Times*, April 3, p. A20.

Shaw, Jenny, Denise Baker, Isabelle M. Hunt, Anne Moloney, and Louis Appleby. 2004. "Suicide by Prisoners: National Clinical Survey." *The British Journal of Psychiatry* 184: 263–267.

Skeem, Jennifer, Jennifer Eno Louden, Devon Polaschek, and Jacqueline Camp. 2007. "Assessing Relationship Quality in Mandated Community Treatment: Blending Care with Control." *Psychological Assessment* 19: 397–410.

Skeem, Jennifer L., Eliza Winter, Patrick J. Kennealy, Jennifer Eno Louden, and Joseph R. Tatar II. 2013. "Offenders with Mental Illness Have Criminogenic Needs Too: Toward Recidivism Reduction." *Law and Human Behavior* 38(3): 212–224.

Smith, Peter Scharff. 2006. "The Effects of Solitary Confinement on Prison Inmates: A Brief History and Review of the Literature." *Journal of Crime and Justice* 34: 441–528.

Steadman, Henry J., John Monahan, Barbara Duffee, and Eliot Hartstone. 1984. "The Impact of State Mental Hospital Deinstitutionalization on United States Prison Populations, 1968–1978." *Journal of Criminal Law and Criminology* 75: 474–490.

Steadman, Henry J., Edward P. Mulvey, John Monahan, Pamela Clark-Robbins, Paul S. Appelbaum, Thomas Grisso, Loren H. Roth, and Eric Silver. 1998. "Violence by People Discharged from Acute Psychiatric Inpatient Facilities and by Others in the Same Neighborhoods." *Archives of General Psychiatry* 55: 393–401.

Steadman, Henry J., Jack E. Scott, Fred Osher, Tara K. Agnese, and Pamela Clark-Robbins. 2005. "Validation of the Brief Jail Mental Health Screen." *Psychiatric Services* 56: 816–822.

Teplin, Linda. 1983. "The Criminalization of the Mentally Ill: Speculation in Search of Data". *Psychological Bulletin* 94: 54–67.

Teplin, Linda. 1990. "The Prevalence of Severe Mental Disorder among Male Urban Jail Detainees: Comparison with the Epidemiologic Catchment Area Program." *American Journal of Public Health* 80: 663–669.

Teplin, Linda A., Karen M. Abram, and Gary M. McClelland. 1996. "Prevalence of Psychiatric Disorders among Incarcerated Women: Pretrial Jail Detainees." *Archives of General Psychiatry* 53: 505–512.

Teplin, Linda A., Gary M. McClelland, Karen M. Abram, and Dana A. Weiner. 2005. "Crime Victimization in Adults with Severe Mental Illness: Comparison with the National Crime Victimization Survey." *Archives of General Psychiatry* 62: 911–921.

Toch, Hans, and Kenneth Adams. 1986. "Pathology and Disruptiveness among Prison Inmates." *Journal of Research in Crime and Delinquency* 23: 7–21.

Torrey, E. Fuller, Aaron Kennard, Don Eslinger, Rochard Lamb, and James Pavle. 2010. "*More Mentally Ill Persons Are in Jails and Prisons than Hospitals: A Survey of the States.*" Arlington, VA: Treatment Advocacy Center. Retrieved from http://www.treatmentadvocacycenter.org/storage/documents/final_jails_v_hospitals_study.pdf

Treatment Advocacy Center. 2007. "Criminalization of Individuals with Severe Psychiatric Disorders." Arlington, VA: Treatment Advocacy Center. http://www.treatmentadvocacy-center.org/storage/documents/criminalization_of_ individuals_with_severe_psychiatric_disorders.pdf

Watson, Roger, Anne Stimpson, and Tony Hostick. 2004. "Prison Health Care: A Review of the Literature." *International Journal of Nursing Studies* 41: 119–128.

White, Thomas W., Dennis J. Schimmel, and Robert Frickey. 2002. "A Comprehensive Analysis of Suicide in Federal Prisons: A Fifteen-Year Review." *Journal of Correctional Health Care* 9: 321–343.

Wilper, Andrew P., Steffie Woolhandler, J. Wesley Boyd, Karen E. Lasser, Danny McCormick, D. H. Bor, and David U. Himmelstein. 2009. "The Health and Health Care of U.S. Prisoners: Results of a Nationwide Survey." *American Journal of Public Health* 99: 666–672.

Wolff, Nancy, Cynthia Blitz, and Jing Shi. 2007. "Rates of Sexual Victimization in Prison for Inmates with and without Mental Disorders." *Psychiatric Services* 58: 1087–1094.

Wolff, Nancy, Robert D. Morgan, Jing Shi, William Fisher, and Jessica Huening. 2011. "Comparative Analysis of Thinking Styles and Emotional States of Male and Female Inmates with and without Mental Disorders." *Psychiatric Services* 62: 1485–1493.

....

CHAPTER 26

THE PROBLEM OF INCARCERATING JUVENILES WITH ADULTS

....

JODI LANE AND LONN LANZA-KADUCE

THE transfer of children to adult court and hence subsequent "adult" punishment is not a new idea. There has been a longstanding historical debate about what childhood means in terms of maturity and culpability for misbehavior, and questions continue to arise in public and policy circles about how children should be controlled and socialized (Tanenhaus 2000). The development of the first separate juvenile court system in Cook County, Illinois, in 1899 signaled the beginning of almost a century of treating most children as though they were fundamentally different from adults. This trend was interrupted when serious juvenile crime increased in the 1980s and juvenile violence peaked in the mid-1990s, prompting renewed questions about the qualities that distinguished children from adults. Some scholars even characterized some young offenders as "superpredators" and undeserving as being treated as children (e.g., Bennet, DiIulio, and Walters 1996).

Prior to the development of the juvenile justice system, children were routinely incarcerated with adults and treated as if they were as culpable. But, as Tanenhaus (2000) noted, the existence of a separate juvenile court did not completely split children from adults, as some were considered too serious or not sufficiently amenable to treatment to warrant being housed with younger, less mature children. As a result, there have always been mechanisms to transfer some troubled children to the adult criminal justice system with its emphasis on culpability and punishment (Feld and Bishop 2012).

Yet, depending on the political philosophy and events of the time, the use of transfer provisions and the number of juveniles in adult prisons and jails has fluctuated. In the 1990s, as the public and policymakers were startled by a sharp increase in juvenile violence and the focus on transferring youths to adult court revitalized, policies were rewritten and more children were sent to the adult court and subsequently to adult institutions (Griffin, Torbet, and Szymanski 1998). Yet as crime declined in the past decade or so, the focus on transferring youths to adult court has eased, and fewer now are sent to adult lockups and prisons.

Since the 1990s, several other trends have emerged. Brain research accumulated to indicate that children are fundamentally different from adults in decision-making abilities and maturity. In addition, the US Supreme Court signaled a trend back toward recognizing the basic differences in culpability between children and adults in three key case decisions. *Roper v. Simmons* (2005) banned capital punishment for minors; *Graham v. Florida* (2010) blocked the use of sentences to life without parole for juveniles who had not committed murder (see Feld and Bishop 2012); and *Miller v. Alabama* (2012) extended this reasoning, finding mandatory life sentences for murders committed by youths under 18 to be unconstitutional. These recent decisions only limit the severest of sentences for juveniles convicted of crimes as adults. Many young offenders are still managing life in adult institutions and must deal with the long-term aftereffects.

This essay first briefly summarizes the history of juvenile justice, focusing primarily on the transfer to adult court and subsequent adult incarceration. Next we discuss the current situation in terms of juvenile crime and the numbers of youths facing adult punishment. The following sections discuss the experiences of youths inside adult incarceration facilities and the effects of transfer to adult court on postrelease recidivism. Finally, we summarize states' approaches to housing youths in adult incarceration facilities. The primary conclusions of this essay are

- Juvenile transfer to adult court and subsequent adult punishment is not a new idea, but it was implemented with new vigor during the 1990s when juvenile violence peaked.
- Many of the 1990s "get tough" laws focused on juveniles remain and continue to have lasting impacts on the number of youths transferred to adult court and facing incarceration in adult facilities; yet, some state legislatures have revised these laws, showing a trend back to protecting children.
- While research is inconsistent on whether juveniles transferred to adult court serve longer sentences than those who remain in the juvenile justice system, it is clear that being incarcerated in adult facilities hurts youths. Transfer to adult court and subsequent incarceration in adult facilities interferes with adolescent development; reduces youths' access to helping staff, treatment, and life-skills programming; increases their risk of victimization; and increases their risk for recidivism.
- States vary in the way they house juveniles sent to adult facilities. Juveniles held for pre-adult trial can be held in juvenile detention or adult jail. Juveniles sentenced to adult prison can be housed in separate "youthful offender" facilities, separate wings of a general population facility, in protective custody, or mixed into the general adult population.
- Psychological, criminal justice, and brain research all lead to the conclusion that transferring youths to adult court and subsequently sentencing them to adult prison should be a rarity and a last resort. The experience harms youths and by increasing recidivism decreases public safety. Moreover, teenagers have not developed the mental maturity expected of adults until they reach their 20s, indicating that it is generally bad policy to hold them to the same level of responsibility.

I. A Brief History of Juvenile Incarceration with Adults

Over the centuries in western Europe, housing juveniles in lockups with adults was normative under long-standing legal standards. Historically, the important status distinction was not "juvenile" but "infancy." Beginning in Roman law, children under the age of seven were considered to be infants and deemed not responsible for their behaviors (Champion 2001). "Infants" were different from everyone else; other children were not considered so different from adults. The English Common Law system would also adopt this concept of infancy and add to it a rebuttable presumption about 7- to 13-year-olds: youths in this age group were presumed not to be responsible for their behaviors, but that presumption could be rebutted if evidence was persuasive that they were mature enough and showed the mental capacity to be treated in the same way as adults (Reid 2013). Thus for many of those who we now define as juveniles, there was no legal bar to their being housed with adults in lockups.

In medieval Europe, children were often "abandoned, ignored, and exploited" (Thornton, James, and Doerner 1982, p. 5). They were not given a special social status beyond that recognized by the infancy defense. The norms about children began to shift in the 17th century when religious authorities stressed that education and guidance were important (Thornton et al. 1982), which would extend beyond the age of six. This helped to develop a separate notion of children, one that seems to have been reflected in the presumption of infancy adopted in the English Common Law.

The import of religion can be seen in the role of the early Court of Chancery (court of equity) in England. This court pursued remedies in equity separate from those in Common Law, and it was led by the Lord Chancellor, who almost always came from the Church. Part of the jurisdiction of the Chancery Court was over the welfare of children. Equity demanded different legal solutions for "deserving cases" (Caldwell 1972, cited in Thornton et al. 1982, p. 7), and cases involving children often called for individualized justice. The Chancery Court played an important role in the institutionalization of *parens patriae*, where the state had authority to serve as the parent of last resort to protect children (see Siegel and Senna 1991, p. 378). But the ideals of *parens patriae* were not fully developed and not strong enough to offset problems of poverty and economic shifts. Women and children were often sent to debtors' prisons and workhouses where they were housed with adults, including criminals. Lockups did not segregate criminals from "status" offenders. In fact, special legal authority was granted to place truant, incorrigible, neglected, or vagrant youth in workhouses. Indentured servitude was used for youth until age 21 (see generally Champion 2001).

The control and incarceration of children was exported with the colonists to the New World, where different local practices emerged as the Eurocentric societies took root and developed. Although much of what happened to children in rural Colonial America was left to parental control, one of the important innovations occurred at the Quaker's Walnut Street Jail in Philadelphia. It introduced a system that segregated populations by offense and kept women and children separated from hardened criminals (Champion 2001). The postcolonial American experience introduced other practices that would affect the incarceration of youth. Separate public "houses of refuge" opened for vagrant or neglected children in New York and Boston in the 1820s and spread to other areas (Siegal and Senna 1991), and reform schools were opened in many states to deal with problem juveniles (Thornton et al. 1982). John Augustus introduced probation for both adults and children in the mid-1800s in Massachusetts (Thornton et al. 1982). Massachusetts began to hold separate court trials for juveniles in 1874 without a separate court jurisdiction or separate body of law (Champion 2001).

The rapid growth, industrialization, immigration, and urbanization of the United States gave rise to various social upheavals, many of which affected or involved youth. America's

"Child Savers" movement was an effort to both control children caught up in the rapid social change and expose the poor living conditions of children (Platt 1972; see also Myers 2005). The *parens patriae* philosophy of the Child Savers also began to be reflected in legal decisions about incarceration and children. But there was tension between the near-complete authority of the state for the welfare of children (see *Ex Parte Crouse* 1838, where a parent lost his challenge in a Pennsylvania court to the commitment of his daughter to a house of refuge without a trial) versus the acknowledgment of some due process checks (see *People ex re. O'Connell v. Turner* 1870, where an Illinois court ordered a boy to be released from a Chicago reform school because he had committed no crime and had been convicted without due process).

The culmination of the Child Savers movement was the Illinois Juvenile Act of 1899, creating the first separate juvenile justice system. The Illinois law premised the new juvenile system on *parens patriae* and, unlike the adult system, required probation officers to obtain information in the best interest of the child, gave the new system civil rather than criminal court jurisdiction, and distinguished among delinquent acts, status offenses, and neglect or abuse. It prohibited children under 12 from being committed to jails and established that any child who was sentenced to confinement in places with adult inmates had the right to be separated from those adults. As to disposition, the Illinois act expressly authorized commitment of juveniles to reform schools. The 1907 amendments to the Illinois enactment extended the age of jurisdiction for delinquent acts to 17 for males and 18 for females, extended the maximum age of jurisdiction to 21 for intervention, protected juvenile records from use in other courts, and allowed for concurrent jurisdiction so that juveniles could be transferred into adult criminal court (Mack 1909). The Illinois innovation of a separate juvenile justice system spread rapidly and was adopted by all but two of the other states by 1923 as well as many other countries (Thornton et al. 1982; see also Myers 2005).

These separate juvenile justice systems almost always provided a way to transfer youth to the adult criminal justice system (Flicker 1983). For the youth, transfer meant that he or she had been determined to be sufficiently adult-like to be removed from the separate juvenile justice system and exposed to adult court processes and punishments, including incarceration in jails and prisons. Transfer could and can be done in one of three basic ways: (a) judicial waiver (where judges have primary decision-making authority after a due process hearing, which is probably the most restrictive means of transferring juveniles to the adult court),[1] (b) prosecutorial waiver or direct file (where prosecutors have broad discretion, without judicial oversight, over whether to file the case in adult rather than juvenile court; direct file has the potential to bring many more youth into the adult system), or (c) legislative waiver (where legislatures lower the traditional age of juvenile court jurisdiction for some or all offenses and thereby push large numbers of juveniles into the adult system).

Of course the more youth who are transferred to the adult system, the more youth are exposed to adult lockups. In addition, there is no separation in systems for the policing function. In other words, separate juvenile justice systems may steer many juveniles from adult lockups, but they do not erect a complete wall of separation. At the pick-up and arrest stages, juveniles may be exposed to adult facilities. Adult lockups may also be used for post-adjudication dispositions.

The ideals of *parens patriae* with its treatment orientation and civil (rather than criminal) jurisdiction were often unrealized in practice. The treatment goals were often displaced by custodial and control concerns (Street, Vinter, and Perrow 1966). This reality influenced the

US Supreme Court as it imposed a "due process" revolution in procedural law for juveniles (see *Kent v. United States* 1966; *In Re Gault* 1967; *In Re Winship* 1970; and *Breed v. Jones* 1975):

> While there can be no doubt of the original laudable purpose of juvenile courts, studies and critiques in recent years raise serious questions as to whether actual performance measures well enough against the theoretical purpose to make tolerable the immunity of the process from the reach of constitutional guaranties applicable to adults . . . . There is evidence, in fact, that there may be grounds for concern that the child receives the worst of both worlds; that he gets neither the protections accorded to adults nor the solicitous care and regenerative treatment postulated for children. (*Kent v. United States* 1966, 555)

The gap between the ideal and the real meant that, for much of the 20th century, juveniles were exposed to adult jails and prisons. This was true at arrest or intake, during pretrial detention, and at sentencing. The exposure extended to neglected and dependent children, status offenders, certain traffic offenders, and delinquents. The kinds of problems and issues attendant with juveniles exposed to adult facilities (reviewed later) helped to drive the federal government to take action. Specifically, Congress passed the Juvenile Justice and Delinquency Prevention Act of 1974 (Pub. L. No. 93-415, 42 U.S.C. § 5601 *et seq.*). Because the power to deal with the welfare and control of children was relegated to the states, the federal government's impact was through recommending standard practices and providing funding to states willing to implement them.

The federal Office of Juvenile Justice and Delinquency Prevention coordinated this enactment, which initially called for the separation of juveniles from adults and the deinstitutionalization of status offenders and eventually moved to a jail removal initiative in 1980 that took years to implement. The initiative mandated that juveniles could be held in jails or adult facilities only under very narrow conditions. Juvenile status offenders were not to be held in secure custody in a jail or adult lockup at all, and there were strict criteria for nonsecure custody of status offenders in adult facilities (e.g., only some areas in these facilities were suitable; the nonsecure custody area could not be used for residential purposes; the juvenile status offender had to be under continuous visual supervision by a law enforcement officer or facility staff member; the juvenile status offender could not be physically secured or cuffed to a rail or other stationary object). Juveniles taken into custody (on delinquency, neglect/abuse, or status offense grounds) could only be held temporarily, usually only six hours. Two exceptions to the temporary custody standard included youths placed in jail pursuant to a court order and juveniles who had been transferred to the adult criminal justice system. Juveniles in custody at an adult pretrial facility had to be separated by sight and sound from adult detainees (including trustees) and could have no regular contact with adult inmates. This requirement of no regular contact (including sight and sound) extended to youth who had been transferred to the adult system for trial and had not yet been convicted and had not been previously convicted as an adult. Sight and sound separation also extended to juveniles sent to the adult facility via a court order.

The Juvenile Justice and Delinquency Prevention Act and the jail removal initiative represented an advance in the separation of children from exposure to adult criminals. In one important way, however, the pendulum swung back sharply in the 1990s based on what may have been a "moral panic" about "superpredators" (Springer and Roberts 2011, pp. 9–11). Given the perception of a sharp uptick in violent acts committed by juveniles, almost every state expanded its transfer provisions to enable more juveniles to be transferred into the adult criminal court (Sickmund, Snyder, and Poe-Yamagata 1997; for a recent review of the laws on transfer, see Feld and Bishop 2012). These revisions, premised on what Feld (1988) terms the "principle of the offense" rather than the needs of the juvenile, made it more likely to subject those under 18 to adult punishments. The legal changes expanded legislative waiver (by increasing the number of offenses for which younger teens could be transferred to adult court and/or by lowering the maximum age of juvenile court jurisdiction) and increased the authority of prosecutors to file charges against those under 18 years of age directly in the adult criminal court. Even for judicial waiver, innovations like "presumptive" and "mandatory" waiver were instituted to reduce the discretion of judges and make it more likely for some youths to be transferred into the adult system. The mechanisms to bring juveniles into the adult system and expose them to adult punishments have been in place since shortly after the inception of a separate juvenile system (Flicker 1983). How many youth are caught up in that machinery depends on trends in delinquency and the discretion of decision-makers in both the juvenile and adult systems.[2]

II. Juvenile Crime and Imprisonment

Recent numbers show that almost 2 million juveniles are arrested each year but only about 5 percent for violent index crimes. In fact, juvenile violence declined for 10 straight years after it reached its peak in 1994, increased for a couple of years after, and then began dropping again. By 2009, juvenile violence had reached its lowest level in more than two decades (Puzzanchera and Adams 2011).

Because there are three basic ways to move teens into the adult criminal justice system, it is hard to obtain exact estimates of the numbers of youths transferred. Although youths can be sent to adult court for many types of offenses, the number of youths judicially waived to criminal court is about half of what it was in 1994, when juvenile violence peaked and policymakers and practitioners were frenzied about how to stop youths from terrorizing their communities. Currently, official statistics indicate about 9 of every 1,000 juveniles sent to court (or about 7,600 in 2009) go to the adult system through judicial waiver (Adams and Addie 2012). The Campaign for Youth Justice (2012), an advocacy organization that hopes to end transfer to adult court, estimates that 250,000 youths are "tried, sentenced, or incarcerated as adults" across the country each year if all mechanisms of transfer to adult court are considered.

Counting youths transferred is complicated for several reasons. Not all states track juvenile transfers. The mechanism used to move juveniles into the adult system also confuses matters. Some states do not generally set the lower age limit of the adult court at 18. That is, all 16- and/or 17-year-olds are sent to adult court via statutory exclusion in 13 states, and some official estimates are that there may be about 175,000 sent to adult court in this manner (Griffin et al. 2011). The number of juveniles subject to prosecutorial waiver is also hard to track. The trend in prosecutorial waivers has probably declined, as evidenced by Florida's numbers. Florida was the largest state to rely most heavily on direct file transfers for the longest period of time, and transfers there declined 44 percent between fiscal year 2007–2008 and fiscal year 2011–2012 (Florida Department of Juvenile Justice 2013b). But a decline may not be uniform across all jurisdictions. In California, for example, which introduced direct file after passing Proposition 21 in 2000, some counties have increased their use of direct file over the past decade while others have rarely used it (Males and Teji 2012).

Although transfers to adult court have decreased since the 1990s, many of the harsh policies passed in the mid-1990s in response to political and public worries about juvenile crime remain. Many of the youths who were transferred since then may still be incarcerated or under the control of the adult justice system. During the late 1980s and 1990s, state legislatures across the country rewrote their laws to make it easier to transfer youths to adult court, to allow prosecutors more power to make transfer decisions, and to include provisions for some youths to be automatically transferred rather than face a judicial decision regarding which court was most appropriate for them. Now, 38 states have automatic transfer laws, and 15 states allow prosecutors to make decisions, at least in certain cases. Many states use multiple approaches for transferring youth to the adult criminal justice system. Although juvenile crime is decreasing, states generally have not removed these harsher laws from the books (Griffin et al. 2011).

There are some exceptions. A recent report by the Campaign for Youth Justice (Arya 2011) identifies important statutory changes that have occurred across the country in the past few years that limit the number of juveniles in the adult system. Ten states changed important provisions in their transfer laws; some made it easier to obtain reverse waiver hearings,[3] some raised the age at which youths can be tried as adults, some changed provisions to the laws that required those charged as adults always be treated as adults, and others reduced the number of offenses that automatically were sent to adult court (Arya 2011). For example, three states increased the upper age limit of the juvenile justice system to 18—Connecticut for all juveniles, Illinois for misdemeanants, and Mississippi for many felons who were once automatically transferred. Illinois also stopped the automatic transfer of drug offenders to adult court. Delaware restricted automatic transfer of robbers to those who had a deadly weapon or caused serious injury (Arya 2011).

Specifically relevant to this essay are changes that directly affect jailing and imprisoning juveniles in adult facilities, and a few states have made changes in this regard (Arya 2011). Colorado specified criteria for prosecutors to use in order to determine if youths should be held pretrial in adult jails and also required educational services for those held in adult jails. Virginia went one step further, keeping all youths in juvenile facilities pretrial unless they are deemed a security threat by a judge (Arya 2011). In 2011, Texas law changed to provide local jurisdictions the option to hold transferred juveniles in either adult jail or juvenile detention while they await trial (Deitch, Galbraith, and Pollock 2012). Ohio allows for all "bindover" youth (or transfers to adult court) to be held in juvenile facilities while they wait to finish their cases in adult court, although they can also be held in adult jail (Children's Law Center 2012). According to the Campaign for Youth Justice (Arya 2011), nationally about two-thirds of transferred youths are detained pretrial in adult jails and about one-third are detained in juvenile facilities.

Other recent changes relate to handling youths postconviction. For example, as of 2008, in Maine, youth under 16 at sentencing must be housed in juvenile facilities until they turn 18. In Pennsylvania, since 2010, youths can be "decertified" after trial and sent back to the juvenile system to receive treatment based on the judge's discretion, although adult charges remain. In 2006, Colorado abolished life without parole for all youthful offenders, including murderers, and Texas followed suit in 2009, both before the Supreme Court rulings mentioned earlier. Washington eliminated mandatory sentencing in 2005 for those transferred to adult courts (Arya 2011).

Even with these changes in some states, adult jails and prisons continue to house juveniles who are younger than 18. In 2012 government statistics indicated there were about 4,600 youths being held in adult jails (Minton 2013), and, in 2010, there were 2,295 youths under 18 in prison (Guerino, Harrison, and Sabol 2012). Advocacy groups, such as the Campaign for Youth Justice (2012), however, estimate that the numbers in adult prisons and jails are much higher (roughly 10,000).[4]

Two issues complicate our understanding of what happens to juveniles who have been transferred. The first issue concerns the difficulties with projecting the course of their sentences, since many are adults when released. There are no readily available national numbers indicating how many people who were sentenced to prison as juveniles remain there after turning 18, how long they stay, or how their lives were affected by incarceration in prisons for adults (see Singer 2003). The second issue centers on comparisons between juveniles transferred to the adult system and those retained in the juvenile system. Some research finds that juveniles sent to adult prisons receive longer sentences than they would have had in juvenile facilities, especially if they committed violent offenses (e.g., Rudman et al. 1986; Houghtalin and Mays 1991; Podkapacz and Feld 1996; Singer 1996; Myers 2003; Kurlychek and Johnson 2004; Schubert et al. 2010; Jordan and Myers 2011). Sometimes transfers do not receive more time, however, such as when they commit property offenses (Gillespie and Norman 1984; Bortner 1986; Kinder et al. 1995; Podkapacz and Feld 1996). Many transfers are also sentenced to probation and are not incarcerated at all. Still others are given jail rather than prison sentences. Howell (1996) argued that the average stay for juveniles sent to prison was slightly more than two years, which was three times longer than serious offenders held in juvenile facilities.

A few studies have examined time served among specific groups, many focusing on sentences prior to the "get tough on juveniles" hype of the 1990s. Heide and colleagues (2001), for example, followed 59 juveniles who were incarcerated as adults for murder or attempted murder during the 1980s in Florida. They found that if the juvenile murderers were not sentenced to life, their average time served was slightly more than five years, despite longer initial sentences. Fritsch, Caeti, and Hemmens (1996) likewise found that youths who were waived to adult court in Texas were sentenced to much longer time than those in the juvenile system but actually served a similar amount of time to those not waived (see also Myers 2003). Yet another study revealed that transferred murderers were sentenced to an average of almost 20 years and rapists to about 12 years, while those with lesser crimes were sentenced to much less time (Clement 1997), but the study did not examine actual time served. The actual timed served was not necessarily long. Steiner (2005) found that juveniles who were sent to adult prison in Idaho served, on average, slightly more than six months.

III. WHAT WE KNOW ABOUT HOW IMPRISONMENT IN ADULT FACILITIES AFFECTS JUVENILES

No matter how much time juveniles serve in adult prison, research has shown that the experience is qualitatively different and more negative than what occurs in even deep-end juvenile institutions. There are relatively few studies on incarceration experiences for juveniles who were transferred to adult court (see Redding 2003), but research generally shows that adult incarceration is an unpleasant and harmful experience for teens (Mulvey and Schubert 2012a, 2012b). Studies have examined mental health and social development, behavior, and risk of harm, sometimes comparing the juveniles' experiences to those of juveniles housed in facilities for juveniles.

A. Mental Health and Development

Youths in adult facilities face threats to their mental, psychological, and developmental health, which might be expected given that teenage years are an especially important period of personal development. A recent study by Ng and colleagues (2011), for example, found that youths in adult prisons were significantly more likely to be depressed than those in juvenile facilities or halfway houses. Beyer (1997) found that suicide rates for youth in adult facilities were eight times the rate for juvenile facilities. He also argued that "The adult criminal justice system fails the basic test of balancing nurturance and opportunities for independence which are both needed during adolescence" (Beyer 1997, p. 18).

Others also have focused on the particularly negative impact of adult incarceration on adolescent development. Woolard et al. (2005) summarized many of the ways that youths are different from adults, discussing developmental milestones. For example, they noted that the physical maturation (e.g., hormonal changes and physical maturity), cognitive growth (e.g., thinking abilities), and social changes (e.g., peers, relationships) that occur during this time distinguish youths from adults. They argued that identity, autonomy, intimacy, sexuality, and focus on achievement all develop during the teenage years, which makes this group qualitatively different from adult inmates and calls for treating them differently.

Mulvey and Schubert (2012b, p. 845) noted that adolescents "are undergoing marked change in capacities regarding the assessment of risk, impulse control, future orientation, and susceptibility to peer influence" and argued that incarceration in adult facilities causes disruptions and difficulties for adolescent development in these areas (see also Mulvey and Schubert 2012a). For example, they argued that identity development, which generally occurs in adolescence, is more difficult because these youths face this important developmental milestone without helpful adults or positive peer relationships and in a dangerous environment. These scholars also noted that kids in adult facilities lose key opportunities to learn about how to be an adult and to learn important skills (such as how to get a job, how to manage household duties, and how to develop long-term love relationships), which creates more problems for these youths down the road. They also live in an environment where typical adolescent behaviors, such as expressing individual ideas and developing one's own path, can result in dire consequences, such as more isolation and fewer privileges in an already austere environment. Consequently, their ability to navigate the teenage years in a typical way is severely stunted (Mulvey and Schubert 2012a, 2012b).

Studies specifically on institutional behavior indicate that teens also have trouble adjusting to daily life and that sometimes they struggle more than those who are placed in juvenile facilities. McShane and Williams (1989) found that inmates in adult prison who committed their crimes before they were 17 were much more likely to be difficult inmates and to be managed under higher custody levels than were those who committed their crimes just a little later (between 17 and 21). One report showed that, in some states, youths were more likely than older inmates to get in trouble (e.g., Arkansas, Georgia, Oklahoma, Oregon; National Institute of Corrections 1995). Still, a survey of correctional administrators revealed that administrators gave different responses on this issue—some saying imprisoned teens caused more trouble and some saying they caused less (Reddington and Sapp 1997). Yet about half of the respondents said that juveniles were harder to deal with than adults. A later study by Tasca, Griffin, and Rodriguez (2010) reported that about half of juvenile prison inmates indicated they had assaulted someone in the past year, and they were more likely to have done so if they were in a gang prior to entry or if they had been threatened with a weapon themselves.

B. Harm and Help

Early research on the conditions of confinement for juveniles housed in adult facilities showed that their risk of harm was much greater and their opportunity to receive help was much less than was true of those housed in juvenile facilities (Austin, Johnson, and Gregoriou 2000). Forst, Fagan, and Vivona (1989) reported that juveniles in adult facilities were more likely to be victimized.

Similarly, Bishop and colleagues (1998) found that transferred youth were much more likely to describe their surroundings as dangerous and to report being victimized or seeing someone else hurt, either by another inmate or by a staff member, than were youths in juvenile institutions. Beyer (1997) also noted that youngsters in adult facilities were much more likely to be sexually assaulted, beaten, and attacked with a weapon than those in juvenile facilities. As Mulvey and Schubert (2012b) noted, there is not much doubt about the physical risks that youths face in prison.

When the US Congress passed the Prison Rape Elimination Act of 2003 (§15601), it reported that "Juveniles are 5 times more likely to be sexually assaulted in adult rather than juvenile facilities—often within the first 48 hours of incarceration." Reports on sexual victimization in adult facilities in 2008 indicate that youths who are admitted before they are 18 years old are more likely than people of other ages to report being victimized by other inmates (about 5 percent compared to 3 percent of 18- to 19-year-olds, 4 percent in their early 20s, and fewer than 3 percent for everyone else). Sexual assaults by staff are even more common for juveniles in adult facilities; they are almost double that of older inmates (11 percent compared to about 6 percent for 18- to 24-year-olds; Beck and Johnson 2012). Numbers from 2011–2012 raise the prospect of some improvement in that they show a lower percentage of 16- and 17-year-olds reporting sexual victimization in adult facilities (about 2 percent by inmates and about 3 percent by staff; Beck et al. 2013).

In terms of help from prison staff, Forst et al. (1989) found that youths in adult facilities felt staff were less likely to help them with peer relationships, to provide important skills to use upon release, to help them feel good about themselves, or to achieve personal goals. Youths in juvenile facilities felt much better about their case management (e.g., having a caseworker help them with their daily routines, teaching them rules, and providing counseling), their treatment programs (e.g., helping with personal issues and family relationships), and their experiences with others inside. Bishop et al. (1998) found that youths in juvenile institutions were much more likely than youths in adult institutions to describe the staff in a positive way (e.g., as helping and positive versus indifferent, hostile, or belittling). Their findings were similar with regard to institutional atmosphere. In juvenile institutions, youths described the programs as trying to make them and their lives better, while youths in adult institutions felt that the focus was on their past mistakes and lack of hope for change.

Lane and colleagues (2002) reported on the same Florida interviews with youths in juvenile and adult facilities, but they focused on the impact of experiences during confinement on youths' attitudes and behaviors. They found that when teens rated juvenile programs as effective, it was because they "gained" things (such as life skills, hope, or counseling), and they found this in the deep-end juvenile institutions rather than less intensive programs. In contrast, when the adult system made a difference, it was because youths "lost things— hope, safety, amenities, family, and people in their environments who treated them with respect" (Lane et al. 2002, p. 450). In other words, it was the pain of imprisonment rather than treatment gains that were perceived to matter. Ng et al. (2012) found similar results when they compared youths in the juvenile and adult systems in Michigan. Specifically, those in juvenile institutions had more work opportunities, more time in counseling, and better quality education opportunities (i.e., high school and college programs rather than the general education degree [GED] and vocational programs).

In contrast, Kupchik (2007) found that youths in adult facilities designed specifically for "youthful" offenders in one northeastern state were more likely to indicate that counseling services were available to them. Those in juvenile facilities, however, were more likely to indicate positive interactions with staff (e.g., fairness and mentoring). Yet, a recent report on 17-year-olds in the Massachusetts adult system found that youths are supervised by people who have little training in how to work with adolescents and rarely have access to programs that are designed for their needs. Available services also vary depending on the facility. For example, local houses of correction (adult jails) often have no educational programming available, and state prisons offer few educational opportunities except for GED classes via closed-circuit television in some of these facilities. There are often no services at all for youths with disabilities (Citizens for Juvenile Justice 2011).

Several recent reports identify limitations of the federal government's Jail Removal Initiative from the 1970s to improve conditions of juveniles in adult lockups. Recall that jail removal does not apply to transferred youths once they are convicted. Deitch et al. (2012) examined conditions for juveniles in adult jails in Texas and found that juveniles are at risk of victimization. For example, they found that of 41 jail administrators surveyed, 11 jails sometimes housed juveniles with adults and 12 jails did not prevent juveniles from coming into contact with adults when they were not in their cells. Fewer than half (18 jails) kept juveniles separate from adults at all times. They also found that most jailed youths spent considerable amounts of time isolated in their cells and had very little access to the services they needed (e.g., education, substance abuse treatment, or other programming). A recent study in Ohio suggests a management strategy to reduce that risk. In Ohio, youths are often isolated for up to 23 hours per day to keep them away from adults (Children's Law Center 2012). Such isolation may be an unintended consequence of the jail removal emphasis developed decades ago.

Educational services are rarely available for youths put in jail in Wisconsin (Wisconsin Council on Children and Families 2008). A recent Human Rights Watch (2012) report on youths serving life without parole in the United States found that almost all the youthful offenders they talked to had experienced some type of sexual advances (harassment, requests for sexual favors, rape, and/or other sexual abuse). Many also witnessed or experienced other serious types of violence (e.g., stabbings, rapes, beatings, or murders). And, like other studies have revealed, many juveniles spent a lot of time in isolation, either as a way to protect them from other inmates or as punishment. Because the youth had no prospect of getting out, they were also often denied access to educational and rehabilitative services. Moreover, they reported being afraid and depressed, and some had contemplated or attempted suicide (Human Rights Watch 2012).

IV. Recidivism Postrelease

Research on outcomes, primarily recidivism, also indicates that transferring juveniles to adult court and housing them in adult facilities is counterproductive. In the past two decades, studies have examined the impact of transfer (adult vs. juvenile processing) on recidivism and have found that juveniles in the adult system do worse. That is, transfer may actually increase offending postsentence (see Bishop 2000; McGowan et al. 2007; Redding 2010; Griffin et al. 2011).

Podkopacz and Feld (1996) examined judicial waivers in Minneapolis, where the judge reviews the case and makes the final decision about the most appropriate court to hear the case. They found that transferred youths were more likely to be convicted within two years' postrelease than were those retained in the juvenile system. Bishop and colleagues (1996) compared a matched group of juveniles transferred to adult court with juveniles retained in the juvenile justice system in Florida, finding that transfers were more likely to recidivate on all measures (rearrest, time to failure, and severity of rearrest). The same researchers examined this group over the long term and found that transfers were more likely to be rearrested for all crime categories (except property felonies) and that they were rearrested sooner and more often (Winner et al. 1997). The same Florida research group later refined their approach, using additional data and adding 12 more matching variables (e.g., priors, number charges, gang involvement, victim injury, weapons). They again found that transfers, especially violent juveniles, were more likely to reoffend compared with those retained in the juvenile system (Lanza-Kaduce et al. 2005).

Fagan (1995, 1996) examined differences in outcomes for older adolescents charged with burglary and robbery in a juvenile court in New Jersey compared to similar offenders in New York, where these youths were handled in adult court. He, too, found that transferred youths who committed robbery fared worse on rearrest, time to rearrest, and reincarceration, although differences between burglars were not significant. Myers (2001) compared youths transferred to adult court by judges with those retained in the juvenile system in Pennsylvania. He found that, once released back into the community, transfers were more likely to be rearrested more quickly. A study in Dade County, Florida, found similar results in that youths who received any adult sanction (including probation, boot camp, jail, or prison) were 1.5 times more likely to recidivate than those who were given juvenile sanctions. When technical violations were included and juvenile sanctions were compared with adult probation and boot camp, the results were even more striking. Those sent to the adult system were 2.3 times more likely to recidivate (Mason et al. 2003).

More recent research has attempted to tease out the characteristics that are relevant to recidivism among juveniles who are transferred to adult court, and much of it has resulted from the Pathways to Desistance Study using a Maricopa County subsample because this Arizona County has a high rate of transfers. Schubert et al. (2010) used an array of predictors to examine outcomes for transferred youth only, including antisocial behavior, rearrests, reincarceration, and participation in work or school. Using survival analysis, they compared youths with priors versus no priors and youths who received probation (19 percent of all transfers) versus incarceration (74 percent). In general, however, they found that most of the transfers were rearrested (62 percent), and most of those were reincarcerated (88 percent of those rearrested), typically more than once. About half of the transfers also self-reported being involved in antisocial activity (e.g., crime) postrelease. Those with priors were more likely to be rearrested, those with more priors and more antisocial friends were more likely to be rearrested more quickly, and those who were incarcerated and younger at first petition were more likely to be reincarcerated postrelease (see Mulvey and Schubert 2012a for a summary).

The same research group (Loughran et al. 2010) classified youths within similar groups based on propensity scores and also examined the effect of transfer on different types of offenders, comparing them with juvenile retainees. Overall, they found no statistically significant differences in rearrest between youths who were transferred versus those who were retained. However, they argued that the effects of transfer were negative on property offenders (more likely to recidivate) but positive for person offenders (less likely to recidivate). They did not find differential effects between those in the two systems based on number of priors but overall found that those with fewer priors did better after being sent to either court (see Mulvey and Schubert 2012a for a summary).

Interestingly, Matsuda (2009) found that it was not the court process that mattered the most but rather where youthful offenders were housed postconviction. She found that those who were housed in juvenile facilities did better in resisting recidivism over time, while those who went to adult facilities did worse. Interestingly, those who went to adult court but were housed in juvenile facilities postincarceration had better outcomes postrelease than those who were sent there by juvenile courts or who went to adult incarceration facilities. She speculated this result may have been more due to offender age differences across the two groups rather than carceral experiences specifically.

Findings from recent research conducted by a policy organization also reveal that adult correctional facilities make young offenders worse. In Wisconsin, 17-year-olds sent to adult courts had a high recidivism rate: those sent to jail fared the worst (80 percent recidivated), while 65 percent of those who went to prison or who received an adult fine or adult probation were re-arrested, but only 37 percent of those who were deferred prosecution recommitted crimes (Wisconsin Council on Children and Families 2008).

One other line of research has examined the effect of leap-frogging over more graduated sanctions. Often the youth who are transferred have not been given the full range of treatment interventions in the juvenile justice system. Using Florida data, Johnson, Lanza-Kaduce, and Woolard (2011) found that the positive relationship between transfer and recidivism disappeared when a measure of graduated sanctions was introduced into the statistical analysis. The more important variable in predicting recidivism was whether youth (transfers and juvenile justice retainees) leap-frogged over graduated sanctions. Because so many transferred youths had skipped over many sanctions in the continuum, they were more likely to be affected. A report from Texas (Deitch 2011) showed similar findings. In Texas, most of the youth who were transferred (certified) to the adult court were not different from those who were retained for juvenile treatment programming, and the transfers had not been given the opportunity to receive rehabilitative programs in the juvenile system that were shown to be effective in reducing recidivism. The implication is that the recidivism for the transferred youth might have been similarly reduced with their exposure to those programs.

V. Approaches to Housing Juveniles in Adult Facilities

Adult correctional facilities that house troubled juveniles have an added burden of providing extra protections to them compared to adults, simply because their relative mental and physical immaturity and smaller statures put them at greater risk of victimization and self-harm (Austin et al. 2000; Woolard et al. 2005; Kupchik 2007). In addition, incarcerated youths have the legal right to humane treatment, adequate mental health and medical care, educational services, and access to the courts and their families (Austin et al. 2000).

Because youths are developmentally different, scholars have argued for improving classification tools, especially those that have not yet been validated or designed specifically for adolescents. They argue for designing assessment tools to take into account the specific developmental needs of youths (Austin et al. 2000; Woolard et al. 2005). They also argue for improving assessments focused on service provision, such as those for evaluating mental health and personality characteristics at different points in time as youth mature and change, and for developing treatment programs specifically for juveniles. Finally, researchers have noted the importance of training staff to deal specifically with teenagers and their unique characteristics (e.g., higher energy and greater impulsivity compared to adults) and using discipline techniques that are developmentally appropriate for teens (e.g., avoiding solitary confinement; using alternative methods to deescalate situations; Austin et al. 2000; Woolard et al. 2005).

Despite the developmental differences between juveniles and adults, often there are no established standards for how to treat juveniles confined to adult facilities (Deitch et al. 2012). States are taking different approaches to addressing the special issues that arise when housing juveniles with adults, and there is no standard practice or list of best practices for how to deal with teens in the adult system (Austin et al. 2000). Also, there are no recent national data on state approaches to handling youths in adult facilities. Teens in the adult system are often called "youthful offenders," but the term is less than precise in that it has no standard age brackets and can refer to persons over 18 years old. Consequently, this essay refers to juveniles based on the typical 18 years of age cutoff. Again, practices vary between states and even within a state, especially in regard to different offense categories. Data from the 1990s indicated the following regarding juveniles under 18 years of age who were sentenced as adults: 6 states housed these juveniles in separate facilities or units from the adult population, 12 states housed them with other younger offenders over 18 years old, 4 states allowed them to be kept in juvenile facilities, 12 states placed them with an agency other than adult corrections, and 27 states housed them in the general adult population (or in protective custody, if required). In some states, the housing choice depended on the type of crime (National Institute of Corrections 1995).

The remainder of this section provides examples of how states currently approach the management of youthful offenders. In Massachusetts, all 17-year-olds go to adult court; they can be sent to the juvenile system until they turn 21, they can be sent to an adult prison once they turn 18, or they can serve a combined sentence involving time in a juvenile facility until age 21 followed by a suspended adult sentence at age 21 (Citizens for Juvenile Justice 2011).

Austin et al. (2000) discussed the approach of three states—Arizona, Virginia, and Florida, as well as two cities—New York and Philadelphia. According to this report, Arizona holds juveniles in different facilities or units, separate from adults. Those placed in the Special Management Unit for minors, which is in a supermaximum security prison, are housed separately from adults and must participate in and complete two of three programs (substance abuse treatment, anger management, and/or literacy) depending on their particular assessed needs.

At the time of the Austin et al. (2000) report, Virginia had one designated facility to house "youthful offenders" (St. Brides Correctional Center), and this facility was responsible for both presentence assessments and postsentence incarceration. St. Brides provided academic programs, treatment (e.g., substance abuse counseling, sex offender treatment, anger management, life skills), and vocational training (e.g., electronics, auto mechanics, and carpentry; Austin et al. 2000). In the mid-2000s, inmates at St. Brides caused a major behavioral disturbance, which led to many being sent back to court and others transferred to Indian Creek Correctional Center to be "mainstreamed with a more settled and mature prison population" (Johnson 2005, p. 2). Problems like this led to the recommendation that the youthful offenders program be disbanded (Johnson 2005). In early 2005, the youthful offender program was integrated with the therapeutic community at the Indian Creek institution (Community Education Centers 2013).

Florida has two types of prisons for young males sentenced to less than 10 years—those that house youths 14 to 18 years old and those that house 19- to 24-year-olds, although women aged 14 to 24 are housed in the same facility due to their small numbers (see Austin et al. 2000). There are also specific types of facilities (e.g., reception centers and drug treatment centers) that are designated to hold only people younger than age 25 (Florida Department of Corrections 2012). Florida's adult court judges also have the power to sentence youths to juvenile dispositions, after considering the seriousness of the offense, prior record, juvenile maturity, and so on (The 2012 Florida Statutes §985.565).

When adult sanctions are applied, those sentenced to less than 10 years become part of the Florida Department of Corrections' Extended Day Program for Youthful Offenders. This program is designed to provide at least 12 hours of daytime activities, including work assignments, education (educational and academic) programs, counseling, behavior modification, military style drills, systematic discipline, and other activities (Austin et al. 2000). Some of the programs they offer include GED, special education, autotronics, automotive technology, building maintenance, carpentry, and cosmetology (Florida Department of Corrections 2013a). Staff who work in these institutions must undergo specific training on how to interact with these youthful offenders (Austin et al. 2000).

In Ohio, young males are sent to a Youthful Offender Program until age 18, and then they are placed in the general adult prison population. By contrast, girls are sent to a women's prison immediately (Children's Law Center 2012). North Carolina designates five facilities to house youths separate from inmates ages 25 and older. Like in Florida, some facilities house youths up to age 19 and others house youths from 19 to 25 years old. These prisons typically offer the same educational and social skills programming as prisons for adults, but sometimes they also offer additional education, chemical dependency, and job skills programs (North Carolina Sentencing and Policy Advisory Commission 2007). Texas also has a Youthful Offender Program for youth under 18, but not all youth in the prison system are in this program, and programming has been cut back in recent years so that fewer than half are receiving educational programming (Deitch 2011). This Texas program, called COURAGE (Challenge, Opportunity, Understanding, Respect, Acceptance, Growth, and Education), includes many services such as anger management, goal-setting, values, life skills, and aggression replacement training. The program is available at one prison for men (Clemens Unit) and one prison for women (Hilltop Unit; Texas Department of Criminal Justice 2013).

VI. Conclusion

The research to date clearly suggests that trying youths under 18 in adult court, housing them in adult jails, and sending them to adult prisons can do more harm than good. These experiences can hurt them emotionally, developmentally, and physically and generally can make them more likely to have troubled lives upon release. Youths placed in adult institutions are more depressed, are more prone to suicide, and face greater difficulties when transitioning into functional, well-adjusted adults. They are often unsafe in adult facilities, facing victimization from other inmates and staff. Moreover, such punishment and living conditions do not appear to be useful in reducing youths' problematic behaviors upon release. Transferred youths are more likely than those who stay in the juvenile justice system to recommit crime, including more serious crimes, and to do so more quickly.

States vary in how they attempt to work with juveniles once they are convicted and sentenced to incarceration. Some states send them back to juvenile institutions until they reach legal adulthood (age 18); others designate particular facilities to house these youthful offenders separately from older inmates; and still others mix them with the general population. When transferred youths are housed in their own institutions, they sometimes have access to additional life skills programs (e.g., educational and technical) and treatment options (e.g., substance abuse and anger management) that are not available to inmates in facilities for adults. Administrators sometimes find that this group is especially difficult to manage when compared to older inmates. Still, research shows that when youths say adult institutions changed their criminal attitudes (i.e., made a difference), it is because hurtful things happened, not because they learned important skills while in prison.

Given the evidence that adult institutions allow for painful experiences and decrease life chances of conformity, scholars almost uniformly question its widespread use (e.g., Bishop et al. 1996; Winner et al. 1997; Bishop 2000; Myers 2005; McGowan et al. 2007; Feld and Bishop 2012). We wholeheartedly concur with these reservations and, like others, recommend that the use of transfer, and especially incarceration in adult prisons, be severely limited (e.g., Fagan 1995, 1996; Bishop 2000; Mulvey and Schubert 2012b). Bishop (2000, p. 86) asserted that "the goals of doing justice and controlling crime may both be advanced by retaining the vast majority of transferred offenders in a juvenile system with extended jurisdiction and an expanded portfolio of carefully selected treatment options." Fagan (1995) similarly argued that policymakers should continue to keep teens in juvenile court but should refine both juvenile court and transfer procedures if they are used (see also Fagan 1996). Mulvey and Schubert (2012a) basically suggested that transfer policies focus on serious violent offenders only because the policy backfires for others (see also Schubert et al. 2010), and Mulvey and Schubert (2012b) suggested that transfer may be warranted for certain chronic offenders. Holtzman (2004) also argued specifically that Pennsylvania should repeal 1996 statutes that increased the use of transfer because they are counterproductive.

The use of transfer and incarceration in adult jails and prisons is questionable for many reasons. As noted in this essay, the research consistently shows that these youths fare worse than those in the juvenile system, both while locked up and once they return to their communities. For policymakers, this evidence should be enough to question the practice of treating kids like adults. In addition, the public does not necessarily support sending youths to adult court and to adult prisons. According to a recent survey by the advocacy group Campaign for Youth Justice (2011), slightly more than half of respondents thought that adult prisons were inappropriate sanctions for young offenders and thought adult imprisonment would increase youths' chances of recommitting crimes. Academic research generally confirms that the public would prefer to help teens in trouble. As Piquero and colleagues (2010, p. 190) noted, "In short, studies using diverse methodologies arrive at the same conclusion: on a general level, the American public endorses efforts to save children and teens from a life of crime." They also reported that respondents in their study wanted children to be treated differently from adults, believing that youths could change. A different study found that community respondents saw an offender as more responsible as he or she aged and wanted younger juveniles to be treated differently from adults, although they were more likely to say teens should be tried as adults when crimes were more serious (Scott et al. 2006). In contrast, Jan, Ball, and Walsh (2008) found that most respondents supported waiver for serious property and violent crimes as well as for drug offenses, but their respondents were split on whether the juvenile justice system itself should focus on punishment or rehabilitation.

Especially relevant, both theoretically and philosophically, brain research continues to show that teenagers do not think like adults and they do not have the mental capacity to do so. According to Blakemore and Choudhury (2006, p. 300), "recent MRI studies indicate that the time at which the brain reaches maturity may be much later than the end of adolescence." Teenagers' reasoning develops as they progress throughout adolescence and into young adulthood. For example, one study showed that it is not until older adolescence that teenagers begin to understand the perspectives of others in social interactions (van den Bos et al. 2011). Consider the implication of these findings for how juveniles view or treat their victims.

Another study revealed that teenagers become better at controlling their behavior as they age, results that have implications for understanding impulsive criminal behaviors among youth and possibly for why we are often at a loss to explain why they do some of the things they do (Luna et al. 2001). In their summary of brain research and cognitive development, Casey and colleagues (2005) noted that cognitive abilities to filter information and to refrain from inappropriate behavior develop during the first 20 or so years of life, but they also noted that we need more studies on how learning affects maturation and neural processes. If learning affects brain development, as they suspect, it is possible that the type of learning youth do in prison may hinder their progress and therefore their ability to conform upon release. A recent study showed that the public understands that teen brains are not fully developed (Bradley et al. 2012). The majority of respondents thought that the brain is completely developed by 20 years of age (although science has demonstrated that it takes longer), but most thought that juveniles were not mature enough to appreciate the complexities of the adult court. Yet another study found that those who thought that adolescents were mature were more likely to want them to face harsher punishments, including adult prison, leading researchers to argue for public education on youth development (Allen, Trzcinski, and Kubiak 2012).

These findings and similar studies should be critically important in informing our policies toward the punishment of teenagers who commit crimes. If teens cannot fully control their behaviors and cannot understand their impact on others, and if prison experiences have the potential to permanently hinder their ability to succeed, then we should seriously question the practice of holding them fully culpable in adult criminal court and of incarcerating them in adult institutions.

NOTES

1. Various conventions structure the discretion of the judges. The most foundational are the so-called Kent criteria laid out in *Kent v. United States* (1966). Subsequently, state legislatures have structured the discretion even more completely through guidelines that judges are to follow or show reason for rejecting (presumptive waiver) or are actually mandatory, removing judicial discretion completely (Griffin et al. 1998; see Lanza-Kaduce et al. 1996 for a discussion of Florida's scheme).
2. A few studies have examined the impact of changes in transfer laws on crime generally (rather than recidivism particularly) but have yielded inconsistent results. One study found that crime went up after the law was implemented (Jensen and Metsger 1994). Three others found the legal change had no effect (Singer and McDowall 1988; Singer 1996; Steiner and Wright 2006). Yet another found the legal change was followed by decreases in both violent and property crime (Levitt 1998).
3. In reverse waiver, cases that started in the criminal court can be moved back to juvenile jurisdiction (Dawson 2000).
4. Although this essay does not specifically focus on issues of gender, race, and age, it is important to note that most research reports that older youths, males, and youths of color are disproportionately transferred to adult court and sentenced to adult punishments (Bortner, Zatz, and Hawkins 2000; Adams and Addie 2012).

REFERENCES

Adams, Benjamin, and Sean Addie. 2012. *Delinquency Cases Waived to Criminal Court, 2009.* Washington, DC: Office of Juvenile Justice and Delinquency Prevention.
Allen, Terrence T., Eileen Trzcinski, and Sheryl Pimlott Kubiak. 2012. "Public Attitudes toward Juveniles Who Commit Crimes: The Relationship Between Assessments of Adolescent

Development and Attitudes toward Severity of Punishment." *Crime & Delinquency* 58: 78–102.

Arya, Neelum. 2011. *State Trends: Legislative Changes from 2005 to 2010: Removing Youth from the Adult Criminal Justice System*, Washington, DC: Campaign for Youth Justice.

Austin, James, Kelly Dedel Johnson, and Maria Gregoriou. 2000. *Juveniles in Adult Prisons and Jails: A National Assessment.* Washington, DC: Bureau of Justice Assistance.

Beck, Allen J., Marcus Berzofsky, Rachel Casper, and Christopher Krebs. 2013. *Sexual Victimization in Prisons and Jails Reported by Inmates, 2011–2012.* Washington, DC: Bureau of Justice Statistics.

Beck, Allen J., and Candace Johnson. 2012. *Sexual Victimization Reported by Former State Prisoners, 2008.* Washington, DC: Bureau of Justice Statistics.

Bennet, William J., John J. DiIulio, and John P. Walters. 1996. *Body Count: Moral Poverty . . . and How to Win America's War Against Crime and Drugs.* New York: Simon & Schuster.

Beyer, Marty. 1997. "Experts for Juveniles at Risk of Adult Sentences." In *More than Meets the Eye: Rethinking Assessment, Competency, and Sentencing for a Harsher Era of Juvenile Justice*, edited by Marty Beyer, Thomas Grisso, and Malcolm C. Young. Washington, DC: American Bar Association.

Bishop, Donna M. 2000. "Juvenile Offenders in the Adult Criminal Justice System." *Crime & Justice* 27: 81–167.

Bishop, Donna M., Charles E. Frazier, Lonn Lanza-Kaduce, and Henry George White. 1998. "Juvenile Transfers to Criminal Court Study: Phase 1 Final Report." https://www.ncjrs.gov/pdffiles1/Digitization/179568NCJRS.pdf

Bishop, Donna M., Charles E. Frazier, Lonn Lanza-Kaduce, and Lawrence Winner. 1996. "The Transfer of Juveniles to Criminal Court: Does it Make a Difference?" *Crime & Delinquency* 42: 171–191.

Blakemore, Sarah-Jayne, and Suparna Choudhury 2006. "Development of the Adolescent Brain: Implications for Executive Function and Social Cognition." *Journal of Child Psychology and Psychiatry* 47: 296–312.

Bortner, M. A. 1986. "Traditional Rhetoric, Organizational Realities: Remand of Juveniles to Adult Court." *Crime & Delinquency* 32: 53–73.

Bortner, M. A., Marjorie S. Zatz, and Darnell F. Hawkins. 2000. "Race and Transfer: Empirical Research and Social Context." In *The Changing Borders of Juvenile Justice*, edited by Jeffrey Fagan and Franklin E. Zimring. Chicago: University of Chicago Press.

Bradley, April R., Roni Mayzer, Mallory Schefter, Erin Olufs, Joseph Miller, and Mariah Laver. 2012. "Juvenile Competency and Responsibility: Public Perceptions." *Journal of Applied Social Psychology* 42: 2411–2432.

Campaign for Youth Justice. 2011. "Youth Justice System Survey." http://www.campaignforyouthjustice.org/documents/FR_GBA_Poll_1011.pdf

Campaign for Youth Justice. 2012. "Key Facts: Youth in the Justice System." http://www.campaignforyouthjustice.org/documents/KeyYouthCrimeFacts.pdf

Casey, B. J., Nim Tottenham, Conor Liston, and Sarah Durston. 2005. "Imaging the Developing Brain: What Have We Learned about Cognitive Development." *Trends in Cognitive Sciences* 9: 104–110.

Champion, Dean J. 2001. *The Juvenile Justice System: Delinquency, Processing, and the Law*, 3d ed. Upper Saddle River, NJ: Prentice-Hall.

Children's Law Center. 2012. *Falling Through the Cracks: A New Look at Ohio Youth in the Adult Criminal Justice System.* Covington, KY: Children's Law Center. http://www.childrenslawky.

org/wp-content/uploads/2012/07/Falling-Through-The-Cracks-A-New-Look-at-Ohio-Youth-in-the-Adult-Criminal-Justice-System-May-2012.pdf

Citizens for Juvenile Justice. 2011. *Minor Transgressions, Major Consequences: A Picture of 17-Year-Olds in the Massachusetts Criminal Justice System.* Boston: Citizens for Juvenile Justice. http://www.cfjj.org/minortransgressions.php

Clement, Mary J. 1997. "A Five-Year Study of Juvenile Waiver and Adult Sentences: Implications for Policy." *Criminal Justice Policy Review* 8: 201–219.

Community Education Centers. 2013. "*Indian Creek Correctional Center.*" http://www.cecintl.com/facilities_ip_va_001.html

Dawson, Robert O. 2000. "Judicial Wavier in Theory and Practice." In *The Changing Borders of Juvenile Justice*, edited by Jeffrey Fagan and Franklin E. Zimring. Chicago: University of Chicago Press.

Deitch, Michele. 2011. *Juveniles in the Adult Criminal Justice System in Texas.* Austin: University of Texas, Lyndon B. Johnson School of Public Affairs.

Deitch, Michele, Anna Lipton Galbraith, and Jordan Pollock. 2012. *Conditions for Certified Juveniles in Texas County Jails.* Austin: University of Texas, Lyndon B. Johnson School of Public Affairs.

Fagan, Jeffrey. 1995. "Separating the Men from the Boys: The Comparative Advantage of Juvenile Versus Criminal Court Sanctions on Recidivism among Adolescent Felony Offenders." In *Serious, Violent & Chronic Juvenile Offenders: A Sourcebook*, edited by James C. Howell, Barry Krisberg, J. David Hawkins, and John J. Wilson. Thousand Oaks, CA: Sage.

Fagan, Jeffrey. 1996. "The Comparative Advantage of Juvenile versus Criminal Court Sanctions on Recidivism among Adolescent Felony Offenders." *Law & Policy* 18: 77–114.

Feld, Barry C. 1988. "The Juvenile Court Meets the Principle of Offense: Punishment, Treatment and the Difference It Makes." *Boston University Law Review* 68: 821–915.

Feld, Barry C., and Donna M. Bishop 2012. "Transfer of Juveniles to Criminal Court." In *The Oxford Handbook of Juvenile Crime and Juvenile Justice*, edited by Barry C. Feld and Donna M. Bishop. New York: Oxford University Press.

Flicker, Barbara. 1983. *Current Policy Issues: Transferring Juveniles to Adult Court for Trial.* Washington, DC: Institute of Judicial Administration.

Florida Department of Corrections. 2012. "*2012 Annual Report: Fiscal Year 2011–2012.*" http://www.dc.state.fl.us/pub/annual/1112/AnnualReport-1112.pdf

Florida Department of Corrections. 2013a. "*Department of Corrections Youthful Offenders Program.*" http://www.dc.state.fl.us/pub/youthful-deleted/index.html

Florida Department of Corrections. 2013b. "*Five Year Trends and Conditions.*" http://www.djj.state.fl.us/research/fast-facts/five-year-trends

Forst, Martin, Jeffrey Fagan, and T. Scott Vivona. 1989. "Youth in Prisons and Training Schools: Perceptions and Consequences of the Treatment-Custody Dichotomy." *Juvenile and Family Court Journal* 40: 1–14.

Fritsch, Eric J., Tory J. Caeti, and Craig Hemmens. 1996. "Spare the Needle But Not the Punishment: The Interaction of Waived Youth in Texas Prisons." *Crime & Delinquency* 42: 593–609.

Gillespie, L. Kay, and Michael D. Norman. 1984. "Does Certification Mean Prison? Some Preliminary Findings from Utah." *Juvenile and Family Court Journal* 35(3): 23–34.

Griffin, Patrick, Sean Addie, Benjamin Adams, and Kathy Firestine. 2011. *Trying Juveniles as Adults: An Analysis of State Transfer Laws and Reporting.* Washington, DC: Office of Juvenile Justice and Delinquency Prevention.

Griffin, Patrick, Patricia Torbet, and Linda Szymanski. 1998. *Trying Juveniles as Adults in Criminal Court: An Analysis of State Transfer Provisions.* Washington, DC: Office of Juvenile Justice and Delinquency Provision.

Guerino, Paul, Paige M. Harrison, and William J. Sabol. 2012. *Prisoners in 2011.* Washington, DC: Bureau of Justice Statistics.

Heide, Kathleen M., Erin Spencer, Andrea Thompson, and Eldra P. Solomon. 2001. "Who's In, Who's Out, and Who's Back: Follow-Up Data on 59 Juveniles Incarcerated in Adult Prison for Murder or Attempted Murder in the Early 1980s." *Behavioral Sciences & the Law* 19: 97–108.

Holtzman, Anthony. 2004. "Juvenile Justice? The Increased Propensity of Juvenile Transfer to the Criminal Court System in Pennsylvania and the Need for a Revised Approach to Juvenile Offenders." *Penn State Law Review* 109: 657–682.

Houghtalin, Marilyn, and G. Larry Mays. 1991. "Criminal Dispositions of New Mexico Juveniles Transferred to Adult Court." *Crime & Delinquency* 37: 393–407.

Howell, James C. 1996. "Juvenile Transfers to the Criminal Justice System: State of the Art." *Law & Policy* 18: 17–60.

Human Rights Watch. 2012. *Against All Odds: Prison Conditions for Youth Offenders Serving Life without Parole Sentences in the United States.* New York: Human Rights Watch. https://www.hrw.org/sites/default/files/reports/us0112ForUpload_1.pdf

Jan, I-Fang, Jeremy D. Ball, and Anthony Walsh. 2008. "Predicting Public Opinion about Juvenile Waivers." *Criminal Justice Policy Review* 19: 285–300.

Jensen, Eric L., and Linda K. Metsger. 1994. "A Test of the Deterrent Effect of Legislative Waiver on Violent Juvenile Crime." *Crime & Delinquency* 40: 96–104.

Johnson, Gene M. 2005. "Progress Report on the Youthful Offender Program." http://leg2.state.va.us/dls/h&sdocs.nsf/fc86c2b17a1cf388852570f9006f1299/eca10531d35675a085256e-e8006fc139/$FILE/RD257.pdf

Johnson, Kristin, Lonn Lanza-Kaduce, and Jennifer Woolard. 2011. "Disregarding Graduated Treatment: Why Transfer Aggravates Recidivism." *Crime & Delinquency* 57: 756–777.

Jordan, Kareem L., and David L. Myers. 2011. "Juvenile Transfer and Deterrence: Reexamining the Effectiveness of a 'Get Tough' Policy." *Crime & Delinquency* 57: 247–270.

Kinder, Kristine, Carol Veneziano, Michael Fichter, and Henry Azuma. 1995. "A Comparison of the Dispositions of Juvenile Offenders Certified as Adults with Juvenile Offenders Not Certified." *Juvenile and Family Court Journal* 46: 37–42.

Kupchik, Aaron. 2007. "The Correctional Experiences of Youth in Adult and Juvenile Prisons." *Justice Quarterly* 24: 247–270.

Kurlychek, Megan C., and Brian D. Johnson. 2004. "The Juvenile Penalty: A Comparison of Juvenile and Young Adult Sentencing Outcomes in Criminal Court." *Criminology* 42: 485–517.

Lane, Jodi, Lonn Lanza-Kaduce, Charles E. Frazier, and Donna M. Bishop. 2002. "Adult Versus Juvenile Sanctions: Voices of Incarcerated Youths." *Crime & Delinquency* 48: 431–455.

Lanza-Kaduce, Lonn, Donna M. Bishop, Charles E. Frazier, and Lawrence Winner 1996. "Changes in Juvenile Waiver and Transfer Provisions: Projecting the Impact in Florida" *Law & Policy* 18: 137–150.

Lanza-Kaduce, Lonn, Jodi Lane, Donna M. Bishop, and Charles E. Frazier. 2005. "Juvenile Offenders and Adult Felony Recidivism: The Impact of Transfer." *Journal of Crime and Justice* 28: 59–77.

Levitt, Steven D. 1998. "Juvenile Crime and Punishment." *Journal of Political Economy* 106: 1156–1185.

Loughran, Thomas A., Edward P. Mulvey, Carol A. Schubert, Laurie A. Chassin, Laurence Steinberg, Alex R. Piquero, Jeffrey Fagan, Sonia Cota-Robles, Elizabeth Cauffman, and Sandy Losoya. 2010. "Differential Effects of Adult Court Transfer on Juvenile Offender Recidivism." *Law and Human Behavior* 34: 476–488.

Luna, Beatriz, Keith R. Thulborn, Douglas P. Munoz, Elisha P. Mirriam, Krista E. Garver, Nancy J. Minshew, Matcheri S. Keshavan, Christopher R. Genovese, William F. Eddy, and John A. Sweeney. 2001. "Maturation of Widely Distributed Brain Function Subserves Cognitive Development." *NeuroImage* 13: 786–793.

Mack, Julian W. 1909. "The Juvenile Court." *Harvard Law Review* 23: 104–122.

Males, Mike and Selena Teji. 2012. *Charging Youths as Adults in California: A county by County Analysis of Prosecutorial Direct File Practices.* San Francisco: Center on Juvenile and Criminal Justice. http://www.cjcj.org/uploads/cjcj/documents/Charging_youths_as_ adults_in_California_Aug_2012.pdf

Mason, Craig A., Derek A. Chapman, Shau Chang, and Julie Simons. 2003. "Impacting Re-Arrest Rates among Youth Sentenced in Adult Court: An Epidemiological Examination of the Juvenile Sentencing Advocacy Project." *Journal of Clinical Child and Adolescent Psychology* 32: 205–214.

Matsuda, Kristy Nana. 2009. "*The Impact of Incarceration on Young Offenders.*" Doctoral dissertation, University of California, Irvine.

McGowan, Angela, Robert Hahn, Akiva Liberman, Alex Crosby, Mindy Fullilove, Robert Johnson, Eve Moscicki, LeShawndra Price, Susan Snyder, Farris Tuma, Jessica Lowy, Peter Briss, Stella Cory, and Glenda Stone. 2007. "Effects on Violence of Laws and Policies Facilitating the Transfer of Juveniles from the Juvenile Justice System to the Adult System: A Systematic Review." *American Journal of Preventive Medicine* 32: S7–S28.

McShane, Marilyn D., and Frank P. Williams III. 1989. "The Prison Adjustment of Juvenile Offenders." *Crime & Delinquency* 35: 254–269.

Minton, Todd D. 2013. *Jail Inmates at Midyear 2012—Statistical Tables.* Washington, DC: Bureau of Justice Statistics.

Mulvey, Edward P. and Carol A. Schubert. 2012a. *Transfer of Juveniles to Adult Court: Effects of a Broad Policy in One Court.* Washington, DC: Office of Juvenile Justice and Delinquency Prevention.

Mulvey, Edward P. and Carol A. Schubert. 2012b. "Youth in Prison and Beyond." In *The Oxford Handbook of Juvenile Crime and Juvenile Justice*, edited by Barry C. Feld and Donna M. Bishop. New York: Oxford University Press.

Myers, David L. 2001. *Excluding Violent Youths from Juvenile Court: The Effectiveness of Legislative Waiver.* New York: LFB Scholarly Publishing.

Myers, David L. 2003. "Adult Crime, Adult Time: Punishing Violent Youth in the Adult Criminal Justice System." *Youth Violence and Juvenile Justice* 1: 173–197.

Myers, David L. 2005. *Boys among Men: Trying and Sentencing Juveniles as Adults.* Westport, CT: Praeger.

National Institute of Corrections. 1995. *Offenders under Age 18 in State Adult Correctional Systems: A National Picture.* Longmont, CO: National Institute of Corrections.

Ng, Irene Y. H., Rosemary C. Sarri, Jeffrey J. Shook, and Elizabeth Stoffregen. 2012. "Comparison of Correctional Services for Youth Incarcerated in Adult and Juvenile Facilities in Michigan." *The Prison Journal* 92: 460–483.

Ng, Irene Y. H., Xiaoyi Shen, Helen Sim, Rosemary C. Sarri, Elizabeth Stoffregen, and Jeffrey J. Shook. 2011. "Incarcerating Juvenile in Adult Prisons as a Factor in Depression." *Criminal Behaviour and Mental Health* 21: 21–34.

North Carolina Sentencing and Policy Advisory Commission. 2007. "Report on Study of Youthful Offenders Pursuant to Session Law 2006-248, Sections 34.1 and 34.2". http://www.njjn.org/uploads/digital-library/resource_1094.pdf

Piquero, Alex R., Francis T. Cullen, James D. Unnever, Nicole L. Piquero, and Jill A. Gordon. 2010. "Never Too Late: Public Optimism about Juvenile Rehabilitation." *Punishment & Society* 12: 187–207.

Platt, Anthony M. 1972. *The Child Savers: The Invention of Delinquency.* Chicago: University of Chicago Press.

Podkopacz, Marcy Rasmussen, and Barry C. Feld. 1996. "The End of the Line: An Empirical Study of Judicial Waiver." *Journal of Criminal Law and Criminology* 86: 449–492.

Puzzanchera, Charles, and Benjamin Adams. 2011. *Juvenile Arrests 2009.* Washington, DC: Office of Juvenile Justice and Delinquency Prevention.

Redding, Richard E. 2003. "The Effects of Adjudicating and Sentencing Juveniles as Adults: Research and Policy Implications." *Youth Violence and Juvenile Justice* 1: 128–155.

Redding, Richard E. 2010. *Juvenile Transfer Laws: An Effective Deterrent to Delinquency?* Washington, DC: Office of Juvenile Justice and Delinquency Prevention.

Reddington, Frances P., and Allen D. Sapp. 1997. "Juveniles in Adult Prisons: Problems and Prospects." *Journal of Crime and Justice* 20: 139–152.

Reid, Sue Titus. 2013. *Criminal Law*, 9th ed. New York: Oxford University Press.

Rudman, Cary, Eliot Hartstone, Jeffrey Fagan, and Melinda Moore. 1986. "Violent Youth in Adult Court: Process and Punishment." *Crime & Delinquency* 32: 75–96.

Schubert, Carol A., Edward P. Mulvey, Thomas A. Loughran, Jeffrey Fagan, Laurie A. Chassin, Alex R. Piquero, Sandra H. Losoya, Laurence Steinberg, and Elizabeth Cauffman. 2010. "Predicting Outcomes for Youth Transferred to Adult Court." *Law and Human Behavior* 34: 460–475.

Scott, Elizabeth S., N. Dickon Reppuci, Jill Antonishak, and Jennifer T. DeGennaro. 2006. "Public Attitudes about the Culpability and Punishment of Young Offenders." *Behavioral Sciences & the Law* 24: 815–832.

Siegel, Larry L., and Joseph J. Senna 1991. *Juvenile Delinquency: Theory, Practice & Law*, 4th ed. St. Paul, MN: West.

Sickmund, Melissa, Howard N. Snyder, and Eileen Poe-Yamagata 1997. *Juvenile Offenders and Victims: 1997 Update on Violence.* Washington, DC: Office of Juvenile Justice and Delinquency Prevention.

Singer, Simon I. 1996. *Recriminalizing Delinquency: Violent Juvenile Crime and Juvenile Justice Reform.* New York: Cambridge University Press.

Singer, Simon I. 2003. "Incarcerating Juveniles into Adulthood: Organizational Fields of Knowledge and the Back End of Waiver." *Youth Violence and Juvenile Justice* 1: 115–127.

Singer, Simon I., and David McDowall. 1988. "Criminalizing Delinquency: The Deterrent Effects of the New York Juvenile Offender Law." *Law & Society Review* 22: 521–535.

Springer, David W., and Albert R. Roberts. *Juvenile Justice and Delinquency 2011.* Boston: Jones & Bartlett.

Steiner, Benjamin. 2005. "Predicting Sentencing Outcomes and Time Served for Juveniles Transferred to Criminal Court in a Rural Northwestern State." *Journal of Criminal Justice* 33: 601–610.

Steiner, Benjamin, and Emily Wright. 2006. "Assessing the Relative Effects of State Direct File Waiver Laws on Violent Juvenile Crime: Deterrence or Irrelevance?" *Journal of Criminal Law and Criminology* 96: 1451–1477.

Street, David, Robert D. Vinter, and Charles Perrow. 1966. *Organization for Treatment: A Comparative Study of Institutions for Delinquents.* New York: Free Press.

Tanenhaus, David S. 2000. "The Evolution of Transfer out of the Juvenile Court." In *The Changing Borders of Juvenile Justice: Transfer of Adolescents to the Criminal Court*, edited by Jeffrey Fagan and Franklin E. Zimring. Chicago: University of Chicago Press.

Tasca, Melinda, Marie L. Griffin, and Nancy Rodriguez. 2010. "The Effect of Importation and Deprivation Factors on Violent Misconduct: An Examination of Black and Latino Youth in Prison." *Youth Violence and Juvenile Justice* 8: 234–249.

Texas Department of Criminal Justice. 2013. "COURAGE Program for Youthful Offenders." http://www.tdcj.state.tx.us/divisions/rpd/rpd_courage.html

Thornton, Willem E. Jr., Jennifer A. James, and William G. Doerner. 1982. *Delinquency and Justice.* Glenview, IL: Scott, Foresman.

van den Bos, Wouter, Eric van Dijk, Michiel Westenberg, Serge A. R. B. Rombouts, and Eveline A. Crone. 2011. "Changing Brains, Changing Perspectives: The Neurocognitive Development of Reciprocity." *Psychological Science* 32: 60–70.

Winner, Lawrence, Lonn Lanza-Kaduce, Donna M. Bishop, and Charles E. Frazier. 1997. "The Transfer of Juveniles to Criminal Court: Reexamining Recidivism over the Long Term." *Crime & Delinquency* 43: 548–563.

Wisconsin Council on Children and Families. 2008. *Risking their Futures: Why Trying Nonviolent 17-Year-Olds as Adults Is Bad Policy for Wisconsin.* Madison: Wisconsin Council on Children and Families. http://www.ceanational.org/phorum/read.php?9,614,614

Woolard, Jennifer L., Candice Odgers, Lonn Lanza-Kaduce, and Hayley Daglis. 2005. "Juveniles within Adult Correctional Settings: Legal Pathways and Developmental Considerations." *International Journal of Forensic Mental Health* 4: 1–18.

Court Cases

Breed v. Jones (73-1995). 421 U.S. 519 (1975).
Graham v. Florida (08-7412). 560 U.S. ___ (2010).
Kent v. United States (104). 383 U.S. 541 (1966).
In Re Gault (116). 387 U.S. 1 (1967).
In Re Winship (778). 397 U.S. 358 (1970).
Ex Parte Crouse. 4 Wharton (Pa) 9 (1838).
Miller v. Alabama (10-9646). 567 U.S. ___ (2012).
People ex re. O-Connell v. Turner. 55 Ill. 280 (1870).
Roper v. Simmons. (03-633). 543 U.S. 551 (2005).

Statutes

Illinois Juvenile Court Act of 1899, 41st General Assembly Laws, Regular Session (Illinois 1899).

Illinois Juvenile Court Act of 1899, As Amended, 45th General Assembly Laws, Regular Session (Illinois 1907).

Juvenile Justice and Delinquency Prevention Act of 1974. Public Law No. 93-415, 42 U.S.C. §5601 *et seq.*

Prison Rape Elimination Act of 2003. Public Law 108-79, 108th Cong. 42 U.S.C § 15601.

Sentencing Powers; Procedures; Alternatives for Juveniles Prosecuted as Adults. The 2012 Florida Statutes. §985.565. http://www.leg.state.fl.us/Statutes/index.cfm?App_mode=Display_Statute&Search_String=&URL=0900-0999/0985/Sections/0985.565.html

SECTION VI

PRISON POLICY

....

CHAPTER 27

THE EFFECT OF PRISONS ON CRIME

....

SARAH TAHAMONT AND AARON CHALFIN

THE scale of incarceration in the United States is overwhelming and has been described as a new form of "American exceptionalism" (Raphael and Stoll 2013). The United States has, by far, the highest incarceration rate in the world—716 inmates per 100,000 residents—and well over half (65 percent) of the incarcerated population in the United States is housed in state or federal prisons as opposed to local jails (Carson and Golinelli 2013). Crime prevention is a principal motivation for mass incarceration and, accordingly, the extent to which prison prevents crime is a topic that has received considerable scholarly attention.

In general, there are two ways in which prisons might affect crime: (1) deterrence and/or criminogenesis, and (2) incapacitation.[1] Deterrence occurs when an individual chooses to abstain from criminal activity because the marginal costs of doing so outweigh the marginal benefits. As the marginal cost of crime depends critically on public crime-control inputs, we can think of prison as deterring crime when by virtue of either the experience or the threat of incarceration, an individual does not engage in criminal behavior that he or she otherwise would have. Criminogenesis is, in principle, the same mechanism as deterrence except that it captures the scenario in which public policy intervenes in a way that lowers the perceived marginal cost of crime. Prominent examples of criminogenesis include housing inmates in conditions that acculturate them to violence and a criminal lifestyle. Incapacitation, on the other hand, is largely a mechanical effect and reduces crime by removing an individual's opportunities to engage in illegal activity. In other words, an individual who is unwilling to engage in criminal behavior when he or she otherwise would have is considered deterred, whereas an individual who is willing but unable to engage in crime is considered incapacitated.

The distinction between deterrence and criminogenesis on the one hand,[2] and incapacitation on the other hand, is key to understanding the relationship between prison and crime. Prisons might deter crime through specific deterrence by altering the behavior of those who were once incarcerated but have now been released, or the threat of prison might generally deter crime by altering the behavior of those who have never been previously incarcerated. Prisons might also prevent crime by limiting the movements and interactions of incarcerated individuals. The net effect of prison depends on the empirical salience of each of these mechanisms and has profound implications for understanding the usefulness of incarceration as a tool for the promotion of public safety. However, unpacking the mechanisms is equally important, as the cost-effectiveness of incarceration depends, in large part, on whether prisons merely incapacitate or whether they also deter.

Disaggregating between the deterrence and incapacitation effects of prison is conceptually and empirically challenging. For example, research that considers the effect of a given sanction will, generally speaking, identify a combination of deterrence and incapacitation effects. By contrast, research that identifies a deterrence effect that is distinct from incapacitation must rely on a natural experiment that induces quasi-random variation in the severity of sanctions but does not induce corresponding variation in the length of time that an individual is removed from circulation.

In this chapter, we begin with a brief discussion of the mechanisms through which incarceration affects crime. We then review research that presents empirical evidence on the relationship between prisons and crime; we begin with papers that estimate the total effect of prison on crime and next turn to papers that attempt to isolate the deterrence or incapacitation effects of prison. We conclude with a brief discussion of the policy implications that follow from the empirical research.

I. The Relationship Between Prisons and Crime

In thinking about the relationship between prison and crime, it is important to note that prisons serve several different functions, each of which is weighted differently by different actors within the criminal justice system. One function of prisons is to lock inmates away to limit their contact with those outside prison, with the intention of preventing future crimes against those outside prison (i.e., incapacitation). Another function of prisons is to punish inmates for their crimes in order to create a salient negative incentive against committing future crimes (i.e., specific deterrence), or, according to some, simply to exact retribution. Others would argue that a purpose of prison is to rehabilitate inmates so that they can function as productive members of society upon release. With the exception of pure punishment, each of the functions of prison is intended to reduce crime.

All of the functions of prisons are related to the crime rate through two mechanisms: deterrence and incapacitation. Deterrence might be generated in response to any policy that changes the cost or benefits of criminal behavior, whereas incapacitation occurs only when the probability of capture or the expected length of incarceration increases. Research that identifies changes in the opportunity cost of crime is more likely to isolate deterrence. Although the incapacitation effect can be thought of as the mechanical response of crime to public policy, isolating a pure incapacitation effect can be difficult because criminal justice policies that affect incapacitation typically generate treatment effects that are a function of both incapacitation and deterrence. Later in this chapter we will discuss empirical attempts to disentangle incapacitation and deterrence, but first we will discuss the theoretical relationship between prison and crime as it operates through the mechanisms of deterrence, criminogenesis, and incapacitation.

A. Deterrence and Criminogenesis

Deterrence is an old idea that has been discussed in academic writing at least as far back as the seminal eighteenth-century treatises of Jeremy Bentham (1798) and Cesare Beccaria (1764). There are three core concepts embedded in theories of deterrence—that individuals respond to changes in the certainty, severity, and swiftness of punishment (Nagin and Pogarsky 2001; Nagin 2013). The theory of deterrence is predicated on the idea that sufficiently severe penalties, imposed sufficiently swiftly, with a sufficiently high degree of certainty will discourage criminal activity. Hence, the deterrent effect of criminal justice policies depends heavily on the probability of arrest and the probability of punishment given arrest, and, to a certain extent, the temporal proximity of the punishment to the crime as well as the severity of the punishments imposed relative to the crimes committed. As a part of our discussion of the relationship between prisons and crime we focus on deterrence because, as one of the most severe sanctions the criminal justice system metes out, prisons play a key role with respect to the severity of criminal sanctions. Recent reviews by Durlauf and Nagin (2011), Chalfin and McCrary (2017), and Chalfin and Tahamont (2016) discussed the theory of crime as it relates to deterrence in great detail; we do not discuss the details of the theoretical models and their extensions here, but we do provide a brief discussion of the formal models in order to illustrate the extent to which the deterrent effect of prisons on crime might be theoretically limited.

The standard neoclassical economic model of criminal behavior is built upon a simple expected utility model introduced in a seminal contribution by Gary Becker, winner of the 1992 Nobel Prize in Economics. The central idea of Becker's (1968) model of criminal offending is that a rational individual who is considering committing a crime faces three potential outcomes, each of which delivers a different level of utility: (1) the utility associated with the choice not to commit a crime, thereby forgoing the criminal benefit (U_{NC}); (2) the utility associated with choosing to commit a crime and not being apprehended (U_{C_1}); and (3) the utility associated with choosing to commit a crime and being apprehended and subsequently punished (U_{C_2}). Letting P denote the probability that an individual is captured conditional on having committed a crime, in this formulation, the individual chooses to commit a crime if the following condition holds:

$$\left(1 - P\right)U_{C1} + PU_{C2} > U_{NC} \tag{1}$$

That is, crime is worthwhile so long as its expected utility exceeds the utility from abstention. While Becker was the first to express crime as the outcome of a decision process by any rational individual in formal economic terms, the notion that utility guides conduct dates back to Bentham.[3]

The above formulation suggests the presence of, in addition to P, a factor that reflects the disutility associated with capture, which Becker operationalized using a single exogenous variable f, which he referred to as the severity of the criminal sanction upon capture. Typically, f is assumed to refer to something like the length of sentence.[4] However, in principle, f can be a function of many different characteristics of the sanction, including the length of the sentence, the conditions under which the sentence will be served, and the degree of social stigma that is attached to a term of incarceration, all of which are likely heterogeneous among the population. Becker used the ideas about rational utility contained in (1) to generate a function denoting the supply of offenses for a given individual and a given type of crime, which yields the following decision rule:

$$\frac{U(Y)-U_{NC}}{\left|U(Y-f)-U_{NC}\right|} > \frac{P}{1-P} \tag{2}$$

In other words, the crime is worth committing so long as the ratio of the marginal benefit of "getting away" with the crime to the marginal benefit received if captured exceeds the odds of capture. It is worth considering the properties of the expected utility function with respect to the exogenous inputs. Regardless of the individual's preference toward risk, it is easy to see that if the probability of apprehension, P, increases without a corresponding change in either the expected benefits of committing the crime, Y, or the severity of the sanction, f, the level of offending falls as fewer criminal opportunities will be worth the risk. Likewise, if the severity of sanction, f, rises, the ratio of the utility associated with the outcome when not apprehended $U(Y)$ to the utility associated with the outcome if apprehended $U(Y-f)$ decreases yielding a similar prediction. Finally, an increase in the benefits of crime, Y, leads to an unambiguous increase in crime since it leads to an expected increase in the benefit of criminal activity.

More recent additions to the neoclassical model provide some guidance as to the *relative* contribution of severity of punishment, f, and, by extension, the role of imprisonment with respect to deterrence. In particular, if individuals suffer both legal sanction costs associated with punishment and informal sanction costs associated with arrest, under all but the most extreme conceptions of criminal utility, the deterrence elasticity, or the changes in offending with respect to changes in the probability of apprehension or the severity of sanction, will be greater in certainty (P) than in severity (f). This is a formal articulation of Beccaria's (1764, p. 58) claim that "the certainty of punishment, even if it be moderate, will always make a stronger impression than the fear of another which is more terrible but combined with the hope of impunity."

It is important to note that Becker's model and its extensions are not models of deterrence per se, but rather models of criminal decision making. As a consequence, while the models demonstrate how changes to the inputs might lead to deterrence, they also demonstrate how changes to the inputs can lead to more crime. Indeed, scholars have identified some conditions under which the "deterrence elasticity" with respect to the severity of sanction, f, might be, in fact, positive. In that case prisons would not be considered deterrent but, rather, criminogenic. In particular, this can be the case when there is a shift in the distribution of sanctions that affects the variance as well as the mean.

In contrast to economic models of offending, classic literature on prison incarceration depicts prisons as institutions where inmates are socialized into a criminogenic subculture (Sykes 1958). Through this process of socialization, inmates may learn from their inmate peers to improve their skills or strengthen their attachment to criminal values. In the framework of the neoclassical model, prison experience may change perceptions of both probability of apprehension, P, and sanction severity, f. Therefore, the utility of crime increases even if no change takes place to the potential gains, and the deterrent effect of prison diminishes. The decline of perceived sanction severity has been empirically revealed as studies have found that offenders with prior prison sentences are more likely to prefer a shorter term of incarceration over a longer term of probation (Crouch 1993; May and Wood 2010). Moreover, prior prison experience considerably reduces the informal sanction costs, as Nagin (2013) proposed. As Crouch (1993, p. 84) notes, "for persons deeply involved 'in the life', prison carried only the inconvenience of the sentence, not the added loss of reputation."

Another possible criminogenic factor stems from the collateral consequences of imprisonment. A history of imprisonment subjects the inmate to a variety of legal provisions that may restrict him or her from future employment and welfare benefits (Holzer, Raphael, and Stoll 2007; Raphael and Weiman 2007). In general, these consequences, which result from a prison sentence but are not necessarily intended consequences, are barriers to the process of reintegrating formerly incarcerated individuals into society. Under the neo-classical model, one important component of the cost of engaging in criminal behavior is the opportunity cost—the loss of wages in the legal labor market. The strains on future employment introduced by a prison sentence, such as large gaps in employment history, reduce the legal wage and, therefore, reduce the cost of engaging in criminal behavior. The net benefit of crimes, Y, increases even if the loot from crimes and the punishment parameters (P and f) do not change. Thus, under the rational choice model of criminal behavior, the barriers to employment brought on by a prison sentence can make crime more desirable.

Thus far, we have discussed the theoretical parameters of the deterrent effect of prisons on crime, as specified by theory going back to Beccaria and Bentham; such theories could apply to *any* individual.[5] However, it is obvious that perceptions of the severity of sanctions vary across individuals, particularly among those who have experienced that sanction or some related punishment in the past. As a consequence, a distinction is often made between general deterrence and specific deterrence. Any deterrent effect of prisons on crime for those who have never been to prison is considered a general deterrent effect of prisons on crime. By contrast, any deterrent effect of prisons on crime for those who have previously been to prison is called specific deterrence. Throughout the remainder of the chapter, we will attempt to differentiate between general and specific deterrent effects of prison on crime.

B. Perceptual Deterrence

An important consideration with respect to describing the theoretical deterrent effect of prison on crime is the relationship between the objective parameter of sanction severity, f, and the *perceived* parameter of sanction severity. "At its core, deterrence theory is a social psychological theory of threat communication in which the causal chain runs from the objective properties of punishment through the perceptual properties of punishment to crime" (Paternoster 2010, p. 785). In other words, it is not a sufficient condition for the sanction to be severe; it must also be the case that individuals *perceive* the sanction to be severe. Though much of the perceptual deterrence literature is dedicated to understanding perceptions of the likelihood of apprehension, some studies also attend to the perceptions of punishment (e.g., Anderson 2002; Kleck et al. 2005).

With regard to general deterrence, surveys consistently find that the general public has little knowledge of specific criminal penalties or awareness of changes in the sanctions regime. In a survey of Californians conducted in the late 1960s, the general public had very little knowledge of the criminal penalties associated with different behaviors (Assembly Committee on Criminal Procedure 1968). Likewise, a more recent survey by Kleck et al. (2005) did not find a statistically significant relationship between perceptions of punishment severity and actual levels of punishment severity among a random sample of the general population in large urban counties. Cook (1980) has noted that while public perceptions of the sanctions regime are not accurate, they "tend to be systematically related to criminal justice activities" (p. 222). In other words, although individuals cannot accurately describe the sanctions regime, the perceptions differ by whether the individuals are involved in criminal activity. For example, those who commit crimes might have different perceptions of the sanctions regime than those who are not involved in criminal activity, even if the perceptions are not accurate.

The California survey, which included responses from college students, "low delinquency" high school students, "high delinquency" high school students, and inmates incarcerated by the California Youth Authority as well as the adult correctional population, also found that though there was evidence of fear of arrest, conviction, and imprisonment, generally there was no evidence that fear of lengthy sentences affected a significant number of criminal decisions (Assembly Committee on Criminal Procedure 1968). This raises an important point with respect to deterrence.

The parameter, f, is taken to represent sanction severity ranging from $f = 0$ at no punishment through the most severe punishment imaginable. Often, empirical efforts to understand the effect of sanction severity on criminal behavior exploit exogenous changes in sanction severity f, such as a change in sentence length imposed for a given crime (e.g., an increase in maximum sentence from 10 to 20 years). As is evident from survey respondents, while there is little knowledge of the specifics of the severity parameter, f, there is an understanding that $f \neq 0$, meaning that the presence of the punishment regime generates some general deterrent effect. It is important to acknowledge that even when *marginal* changes in severity do not seem to translate to perceived deterrence, the existence of the sanctions regime ($f \neq 0$), meaning prison relative to no prison, generates some unknown quantity of deterrence.

With respect to specific deterrence, it is likely that there are differences in the perceptions of the severity of sanctions between individuals in the general public and individuals who are, or who have previously been, involved in criminal behavior. As Zimring and Hawkins (1973) noted in their book *Deterrence: The Legal Threat to Crime Control*, it is possible for knowledge of the sanctions regime to be low among the general public yet high among the subpopulation involved in criminal activity. There is some early evidence that individuals involved in criminal activity are more aware than the general public of the sanctions regime. Among the adult prisoners surveyed in the 1960s in California, 76 percent were aware of the increased penalties for robbery compared to 20 percent of the general public (Assembly Committee on Criminal Procedure 1968). Compared to the general public, a more accurate perception of the sanctions regime is more valuable to individuals who are actually involved in criminal behavior because they might actually face one of the sanctions. Interestingly, a more recent survey by Anderson (2002) found a very different result; among 278 inmates in two medium-security prisons and a county jail, 26 percent of those convicted of robbery said they knew exactly what the likely punishment would be if apprehended.[6] Kleck et al. (2005) also failed to detect a relationship between perceptions of punishment severity and actual punishment severity among the portion of their sample that had been previously arrested. However, as Kleck et al. noted, this could be at least partially driven by small sample size ($N = 182$) and substantial missing data among those respondents. Both Anderson (2002) and Kleck et al. (2005) suggested that the lack of awareness or attention to the punishments translates to general ineffectiveness of *marginal increases* in the sanctions regime designed to deter future crime. Indeed, in our view, there is little evidence that a general increase in sanctions will deter crime. Later in the chapter, we will discuss empirical estimates of the effect of prison conditions, sentencing enhancements, and capital punishment statutes on crime; on the whole, these offer precious little evidence of crime reductions, let alone deterrence.

C. Incapacitation

While the hope is that the threat of prison, through general information or personal experience, deters individuals from engaging in criminal behavior, prisons are also designed to physically prevent crime through incapacitation. Models of criminal behavior necessarily assume that there is an opportunity to engage in criminal behavior. A core function of prisons is to limit the opportunities for inmates to engage in crime by eliminating, or severely limiting, their freedom of movement as well as their contact with those outside the prison environment. This is perhaps the most obvious rationale for incarceration—to physically remove an individual from free society, thereby preventing crime through incapacitation. Indeed, the only way for an individual who is incarcerated in a prison to commit a crime against someone outside prison is remotely. In removing, for the most part, the opportunity to commit crimes, the incapacitation effect can be thought of as the mechanical response of crime to correctional policy.

The best-known formal model of incapacitation was developed by Avi-Itzhak and Shinnar (1973; see also Shinnar and Shinnar 1975; Piquero and Blumstein 2007). The model assumes that the amount of crime prevented by incapacitation depends on five factors: the rate at which offenders commit crime when they are not incarcerated, the probability of apprehension and conviction, the likelihood of receiving a prison sentence given a conviction, the average time spent incarcerated, and the average duration of the criminal career (i.e., amount of time an individual would engage in crime over his or her lifetime). The fraction of crimes prevented as a result of incapacitation, I, is expressed as:

$$I = \frac{\lambda q J S\left(\dfrac{T_r}{T_r + S}\right)}{1 + \lambda q J S\left(\dfrac{T_r}{T_r + S}\right)}$$

where λ is the rate at which individuals commit crimes, q is the probability of apprehension and conviction, J is the probability of receiving a prison sentence given conviction, S is the average time in prison, and T_r is the average criminal career.

This model can also be used to derive an elasticity of crime, E, with respect to incapacitation. In other words, the model can be used to estimate the amount of crime avoided as a result of a 1 percent change in the prison population, given by:

$$E = \frac{\dfrac{1 + \lambda q J S^2 T_r}{(T_r + S)^2}}{\dfrac{-\lambda q J S T_r^2}{(T_r + S)^2}}$$

As Piquero and Blumstein (2007, p. 270) noted, the incapacitation model relies on a number of assumptions, "many of which have not been confirmed by empirical research or have not been carefully studied." Piquero and Blumstein provide a thorough analysis of the assumptions underlying the incapacitation model; we highlight several of the more problematic assumptions here. One assumption of the incapacitation model is that there is a fixed number of potential offenders in the population, so that when one individual is incarcerated there are fewer potential offenders in the population. This assumption is particularly problematic for the drug trade, because drug markets tend to recruit replacements for imprisoned participants (Blumstein 1993). However, the problem of replacement seems to be less relevant for predatory crimes (Piquero and Blumstein 2007). Another assumption of the incapacitation model is that the experience of incarceration does not change the length of the criminal career (T_r) nor the individual crime rate (λ), though the original model was updated by Canela-Cacho, Blumstein, and Cohen (1997) to include a distribution of offense rates. A final assumption of the incapacitation model that is worth highlighting is the assumption that the individual crime rate (λ) does not change over time and is homogeneous across all individuals. This is, of course, an empirical question, and estimating the value of λ for different populations has been one of the central foci of criminological research into "criminal careers."

Empirical attempts by criminologists to estimate the role of incapacitation in the relationship between prisons and crime have focused on the consequences of "taking a slice out" of an individual's criminal career (Blumstein 1983, p. 874), estimating the crimes avoided by incarcerating that individual or group of individuals. Some econometric studies have been able to disentangle the deterrent effect of prisons from the incapacitation effect; the effort has been to estimate the deterrence and not the incapacitation. Having discussed the theoretical relationship between prisons and crime, we now turn to a review of the literature that attempts to generate empirical estimates of the effect of prison on crime.

II. Estimates of the Total Effect of Imprisonment on Crime

A natural starting point in unraveling the empirical prison–crime relationship is to consider the elasticity of crime with respect to the size of the prison population. This elasticity measures the percentage change in a jurisdiction's crime rate in response to a 1 percent increase in its incarceration rate. This elasticity does not distinguish between incapacitation and deterrence, so it is best thought of as the net or "total" effect of the scale of incarceration on crime. A large crime–prison population elasticity implies that mass incarceration has been effective in reducing crime, while a small elasticity implies that the marginal offender who is either incapacitated or deterred by the experience or threat of prison is not a prolific offender. The key challenge for this literature is to identify a causal relationship between the incarceration rate and the crime rate that is not confounded by simultaneity bias, which is a first-order threat to identification, since just as the prison population may affect crime, crime has a corresponding effect on the size of the prison population.

In the modern literature, Marvell and Moody (1994) provided the first credible empirical study of the elasticity of crime with respect to prison populations, estimating an elasticity of –0.16 using a state panel. To address the possibility of simultaneity bias, the authors explicitly model the simultaneity bias using the concept of Granger causality. As the relationship between the size of the lagged prison population and contemporaneous crime was greater than the relationship between lagged crime and the size of contemporaneous prison populations, the authors concluded that larger prison populations do tend to reduce crime. While Granger causality is a useful innovation with respect to identifying causal effects, it is not robust to a more nuanced conception of how simultaneity between these two variables comes about. In particular, to the extent that a third factor drives both incarceration rates and crime, the exercise will result in a biased estimate of the effect of the scale of incarceration.

The focus of the recent literature has been on identifying more credible ways to isolate the causal effect of the imprisonment rate on the crime rate. Levitt (1996) exploited exogenous variation in state incarceration rates induced by court orders related to prison overcrowding to reduce prison populations. The intuition behind the approach is that while prison crowding might be correlated with higher crime rates, the precise *timing* of the court orders that result in discrete reductions in a state's prison population as a result of a court order should be as good as random. Using a panel of annual, state-level observations from 1971 to 1993, Levitt's estimated elasticities, –0.40 for violent crimes and –0.30 for property crimes, were considerably larger than previous estimates that did not account for the confounded relationship between incarceration rates and crime rates. The estimate was large for robbery (–0.70). Hence, a 10 percent increase in the incarceration rate would result in a 4 percent reduction in violent crime rates, a 3 percent reduction in property crime rates, and a 7 percent reduction in robberies. Spelman (2000) replicated Levitt's analysis on a slightly longer time series and reported qualitatively similar results.

Using more recent data, Johnson and Raphael (2012) developed an instrumental variable to predict future changes in incarceration rates, using variation in the scope of incarceration that is not due to contemporaneous criminal behavior. Using state-level panel data from 1978 to 2004, Johnson and Raphael estimated the elasticity of crime over the whole time period with respect to prison populations of approximately –0.10 for violent crimes and –0.20 for property crimes. Like Levitt (1996), their instrumental variables coefficients were larger in magnitude than the OLS estimates. They also generated separate estimates for an earlier time period, 1978 to 1990, and a later time period, 1991 to 2004. Though the U.S. total incarceration rate increased considerably over the entire period of the data, there were stark differences in the incarceration rate between the earlier period (196 per 100,000) and later period (428 per 100,000). It is worth noting that the estimated elasticities for the earlier time period were larger in magnitude than that of the total time series and were closer in magnitude to those estimated by Levitt. Johnson and Raphael concluded that the criminality of the marginal criminal had changed considerably over time as incarceration rates have risen, and that increases in incarceration had generated "much less bang-per-buck" in terms of crime reduction, a conclusion that was echoed by Liedka, Piehl, and Useem (2006).

The responsiveness of crime with respect to juvenile incarceration seems to be some-what larger. Using Levitt's (1998) estimates of the responsiveness of juvenile crime to the number of juveniles in custody per capita at the state level during the 1970s and 1980s, Lee and McCrary (2009) computed an implied elasticity for violent crimes of –0.40, meaning that for a 10 percent increase in the juvenile incarceration rate, the violent crime rate would decrease by 4 percent.

In sum, estimates of the elasticity of crime with respect to prison are generally modest and fall between –0.1 and –0.7. Estimates for violent and property crimes are of approximately equal magnitude, and there is evidence that the elasticity has diminished considerably over time as prison populations have grown. Our best guess is that the current elasticity of crime with respect to prison populations is approximately –0.2, as reported by Johnson and Raphael. This finding is further bolstered by a recent evaluation of "realignment," a policy implemented in California to reduce prison overcrowding by sending additional inmates to county jails, where they tend to serve shorter sentences. Lofstrom and Raphael (2013) reported that, with the exception of motor vehicle theft, there is no evidence of an increase in crime despite the fact that 18,000 offenders who would have been incarcerated are on the street due to the realignment policy. The magnitude of this elasticity leaves open the possibility for non-trivial deterrence effects of prison, but, given that prison generates sizeable incapacitation effects, the magnitude of deterrence is likely small. Finally, it is worth noting that while these studies give an overall sense of the responsiveness of the crime rate to incarceration, prison population is not a policy variable; rather, it is an outcome of sanction policies that determine who goes to prison and for how long. As a consequence, any estimate of the effect of the imprisonment rate on the crime rate overall is the net effect of many interacting "policy treatments."

III. Estimates of Deterrence and Criminogenesis

We now turn to a review of the empirical attempts to estimate the deterrent or criminogenic effects of prison on crime. We begin with a discussion of the literature examining the effect of the prison experience on future crime of released inmates, and then we turn to a discussion of sentencing enhancements and the death penalty.

The empirical literature on the effect of the prison experience focuses on two areas. The bulk of the literature examines the overall effect of incarceration on the probability that an offender reoffends, while a smaller subset of the literature examines the relationship between specific aspects of the prison experience and recidivism (also at the individual level).

The first literature examines the overall effect of incarceration on recidivism. Unlike studies that examine the effect of incarceration on overall crime rates, this literature focuses solely on the rearrests or reconvictions of formerly incarcerated individuals. The main focus of this literature is to compare the postrelease outcomes of defendants sentenced to prison and those who were sentenced to noncustodial sanctions. In doing so, these studies consider the effect of incarceration holistically, as opposed to examining the effect of any particular aspect of the incarceration experience.

Nagin, Cullen, and Jonson (2009) provide an excellent review of literature on the relationship between prison sentences and reoffending and highlight the fact that while the findings of individual studies are mixed, the literature generally finds the prison experience to have a null or mildly criminogenic effect, compared with noncustodial sanctions. The review, in particular, includes an excellent discussion on the methodological challenges inherent in studying this topic. Notably, much of the literature estimates the effect of imprisonment on recidivism using regression-based approaches that do not provide strong reasons for believing that individuals who experience prison and those who do not are equally disposed toward reoffending. Given that "in many studies important variables like prior record or age are not adequately accounted for" (p. 178), it is not clear that the majority of this literature has credibly accounted for the possibility of confounding.

A. The Experience of Prison

We begin with a discussion of research that examines the effect of specific elements of the prison experience. The primary research question in this literature is whether substantively harsher prison conditions deter or potentially increase reoffending. Prisons are typically classified into a security hierarchy ranging in level from minimum to maximum security, and each inmate is assigned to one of the security levels based on an evaluation of risk factors. There is considerable heterogeneity in prison conditions across security classifications. As a consequence, security classification assignment is the primary determinant of the set of prison conditions a given inmate will experience.

Direct estimation of the effect of prison security level on recidivism is likely to be confounded by this process since riskier inmates, who might be more likely to recidivate regardless of the prison conditions they experience, would, by default, concentrate in higher-security facilities. Chen and Shapiro (2007) addressed this problem by using a regression discontinuity design and identified the causal relationship between facility security level and recidivism for a sample of inmates from the federal prison system. In the federal prison system, inmates are assigned to a facility security level based on a custody score that is calculated for each inmate based on the characteristics of the current offense, demographic characteristics, and criminal history. The rationale for the regression discontinuity design is that inmates who have scores adjacent to the cutoff line between security levels are sufficiently similar in all aspects except for their assigned security level. Therefore, any observed differences in recidivism can, without making heroic assumptions, be causally attributed to the security levels. Chen and Shapiro found that inmates who were housed in an above-minimum-security facility increased their probability of recidivism by 14 to 21 percentage points compared to those inmates housed in minimum-security facilities.

There has been particular attention to the effect of incarceration under "supermax" conditions. Supermax conditions are characterized by solitary confinement with minimal human interaction (see Chapter 16 in this volume). Although various evidence has pointed to the detrimental influence of supermax prisons on inmates' mental health conditions (Haney 2003; Grassian 2006), evaluation of these inmates' postrelease outcomes is scarce. Lovell, Johnson, and Cain (2007) conducted a study in Washington State and found that incarceration under supermax conditions had no impact on the overall recidivism rate of their sample. However, they did find that those who were released directly from a supermax prison to the community had a higher recidivism rate and recidivated faster than those who left supermax incarceration and were incarcerated in the general prison population at least three months prior to their release. By contrast, Mears and Bales (2009) found that Florida's postrelease supermax inmates had higher recidivism rates for violent felonies, but that duration and recentness of the supermax incarceration did not appear to have an impact.

Katz, Levitt, and Shustorovich (2003) examined living conditions in prison more generally. While the majority of the studies that examined the relationship between the prison experience and recidivism used individual-level data on former inmates after release, Katz et al. used aggregate data. They examined the relationship between prison conditions, operationalized as prisoner death rates, using state-level panel data. They found a sizeable deterrent effect of prison conditions on *state crime rates*—that the elasticity of violent and property crimes with prisoner death was –0.05, or each death in prison decreases 30 to 100 violent crimes and a similar number of property crimes. Using a similar approach, but with individual-level outcome data, Drago, Galbiati, and Vertova (2011) found that harsher prison conditions did not reduce the recidivism rate for their sample of former inmates in Italy. Instead, they found a positive 0.025 elasticity of recidivism rate to prisoner death rate, meaning that inmates are more likely to recidivate as they experience harsher prison conditions as proxied by higher prisoner death rates.

A final group of studies examined the relationship between receipt of visits from loved ones and recidivism. The separation of inmates from their families and communities may be detrimental to social bonds essential for successful reentry and desistance (Maruna and Toch 2005; Harding et al. 2014), and visitation during incarceration might serve as a counterweight to the isolation and negative peer influences in prison and might serve as a way to maintain social bonds with family and friends in the community. Bales and Mears (2008), Mears, Cochran, Siennick, and Bales (2012), and Duwe and Clark (2013) conducted multivariate analyses of the impact of visits from different kinds of visitors on recidivism using administrative data from Florida and Minnesota. These studies found that visits, especially more recent visits from at least some kinds of visitors, were associated with reduced recidivism.

B. Sentence Length

The literature that considers the effect of the prison experience on future criminal behavior is limited to consideration of specific deterrence or criminogenesis. By contrast, the literature on sentence lengths includes general as well as specific deterrent effects. In our discussion of the empirical literature on the effect of sentence lengths, we consider the general deterrent effects of prison on crime and then turn to those studies that estimated the effect of prison on the future crime of those who have already experienced incarceration.

The major innovation in the literature on sentence lengths is to study the effect on crime of legislation that enhances sentences for certain crimes while leaving sentence lengths for other crimes untouched. By systematically increasing the length of a prison sentence arising from a criminal conviction, sentencing enhancements increase sentence severity and provide a means to understanding how marginal increases in prison sentence length affect both contemporaneous and subsequent crime. Early studies on sentencing enhancements generally found no deterrence effect, whereas more recent studies, employing more rigorous methodology, tend to find that longer sentences do deter criminal behavior. These findings are in contrast with those of the studies on prison conditions, which generally found harsher prison conditions to be criminogenic.

The early studies on sentencing enhancements date back to the early 1980s, when Loftin and McDowall first examined the effect of firearm laws on the violent crime rate (Loftin and McDowall 1981, 1984; Loftin, Heumann, and McDowall 1983). These papers consider specific sentencing enhancements in Michigan and Florida. The Michigan Felony Firearm Law of 1977 mandated a two-year sentencing enhancement for defendants who possessed a firearm while committing a felony. The Florida Felony Firearm Law mandated a "flat" three-year minimum sentence for those who possessed a firearm when committing certain violent felonies, and prohibited such a sentence from being suspended, deferred, or withheld. These studies generally found no significant crime-reduction effect.[7]

More recent work considers the effect of a more expansive set of sentence enhancements. Raphael and Ludwig (2003) examined the effect of Project Exile in Richmond, VA. Project Exile authorized the transfer of firearm felony offenders from state to federal courts, which typically resulted in harsher penalties.[8] They compared the city-level crime rates and concluded that Project Exile did not have a detectable deterrent effect on crime rates. They noted that although there was a decline in the murder rate after the law's enactment, it was attributable to the unusual increase in gun homicide in the decade prior to the law's enactment.

Sentencing enhancements may also target only particular groups of offenders. The most notable sentencing scheme of this type is "three strikes" laws. Under these laws, typically an individual with one strike (a conviction for a listed serious or violent felony) faces automatic doubling of sentence length upon any subsequent felony conviction (which does not have to be a "strikeable" felony), whereas an offender with two strikes faces a prison sentence of 25 years to life upon conviction for a serious or violent felony.[9] Findings from empirical studies of the effect of three-strikes laws are mixed. A number of studies failed to detect a crime-reduction effect of these laws, either in California (Stolzenberg and D'Alessio 1997; Zimring, Hawkins, and Kamin 2001; Greenwood and Hawken 2002) or among all the three-strikes states (Marvell and Moody 2001; Kovandzic, Sloan, and Vieraitis 2004; Chen 2008). In contrast, Shepherd (2002a) analyzed county-level data in California from 1984 to 1996 and found that three-strikes laws deterred strikeable offenses but not non-strikeable offenses. Shepherd attributed this finding to the notion of "full deterrence"—that is, the laws deterred not only the offenders with strikes from the second and third strike, but also offenders without any strikes from obtaining the first strike via those particular offenses. She estimated that during the first two years of the legislation, approximately 8 murders, 3,952 aggravated assaults, 10,672 robberies, and 384,488 burglaries were deterred. However, she also found a substitution effect, as the number of larcenies, a non-strikeable offense, increased by 17,700, which is explained by the shift of offenders' behaviors from strikeable offenses to non-strikeable ones like larceny. Iyengar (2008) also found a significant crime-reduction effect: She estimated that the laws reduced participation in any criminal activity by 20 percent for second-strike-eligible offenders and by 28 percent for third-strike-eligible offenders.[10]

While much of the literature on sentence enhancements focuses on changes in sentence severity induced by changes in the law, there are a few examples where sentence severity increased without a change in the law. An example of this type is a recent study by Bell, Jaitman, and Machin (2014) that examined the aftermath of the 2011 riots in London. Within the prescribed sentence range, individuals who were involved in the riots were sanctioned substantially more harshly than those who committed similar crimes but did not participate in the riots. Bell et al. found a sizeable decline in riot crimes relative to non-riot crimes in the six-month period after the riots. They also found a decline in crime rates in areas not affected by the riots. They interpreted the findings as stemming mainly from a global deterrent effect of the enhanced sanction severity, but they also admitted that they were not able to differentiate the deterrent effect from the incapacitation effect using available data.

Many studies, including those by Bell and colleagues (2014) and Iyengar (2008), acknowledged that one major difficulty in estimating the effect of prison on crime is that the deterrence and incapacitation mechanisms tend to work simultaneously. On the one hand, the fear of incarceration works as a disincentive to committing crimes. On the other hand, the physical insulation of the prison environment prevents offenses against those outside prison. Yet, in practice, the distinction between deterrence and incapacitation is important for policymakers "because the same reduction in crime is cheaper if produced by deterrence than if produced by incapacitation" (Helland and Tabarrok 2007, pp. 310–311). In the literature, two methods have been employed to differentiate between deterrence and incapacitation effects. The first is examining the reoffending behavior of certain types of released inmates (e.g., Helland and Tabarrok 2007; Drago, Galbiati, and Vertova 2009). The second method is to examine the trend of relatively serious crimes over a short period of time after a change in the law governing sentencing practices (e.g., Kessler and Levitt 1999; Shepherd 2002b; Abrams 2012).

With respect to individual incentives to commit crime, Drago et al. (2009) examined the effect of a natural experiment in Italy. In July 2006, the Italian Parliament passed the Collective Clemency Bill, which reduced the prison term of all inmates by three years. The bill resulted in immediate release of about 40 percent of Italy's prison population on August 1, 2006. A key provision of the bill mandated that if an inmate released under this bill received a sentence of two years or longer for any subsequent conviction within five years, the remainder of his or her original sentence would be appended to the sentence for the new offense. Hence, two otherwise identical cohorts of prisoners faced considerably different sanctions regimes arising from the commission of the same crime. The authors found a reduction of 0.16 of a percentage point in the probability of recidivism for every additional month expected to be served. On average, the amount of time that remained on an inmate's sentence when the cohorts were released was 14.5 months, which resulted in a reduction of 2.3 percentage points in the probability of recidivism. In a similar contribution, Helland and Tabarrok (2007) compared the subsequent arrest patterns between individuals with two convictions for strikeable offenses and those who had been tried twice for strikeable offenses but had been convicted of only one of the two offenses. Their estimates suggested that three-strikes laws reduced felony arrest rates among defendants who had two strikes by 17 to 20 percent compared with those who had only one strike.

The second group of studies examined the instantaneous effect of a sentence enhancement on crimes that would result in a lengthy prison sentence regardless of the sentence enhancement. The logic is that any observed decline in crimes immediately following a sentence enhancement cannot be due to incapacitation, since the offenders would have been incarcerated even without the enhancement, only for a shorter term. For instance, if the minimum sentence for violent crimes is three years before the enactment of a sentence enhancement, then any reduction in violent crimes in the three years immediately following the new law's enactment cannot be attributed to the sentence enhancement, because those offenders would be imprisoned under the old law as well. Studies of this type begin with Kessler and Levitt (1999), who studied the effect of California's Proposition 8 in 1982, which prescribed for those "serious" felony offenders a five-year sentence enhancement for each prior "serious" felony conviction. They estimated that Proposition 8 reduced the eligible crimes by 4 percent in the following year and by 8 percent in each of the three following years.[11]

Several other recent studies followed the same logic and examined a variety of sentencing enhancement laws. Shepherd (2002b) examined the effect of truth-in-sentencing (TIS) laws. First enacted in 1984, TIS laws required offenders to serve a substantial portion of their prison sentence and restricted parole eligibility and good-time credits. Shepherd used county-level data in all 3,054 U.S. counties between 1984 and 1996. She found that TIS laws predicted a decrease in violent crimes ranging from 12 to 24 percent but an increase in burglary by 20 percent and auto theft by 15 percent (both acquisitive crimes). Following the same logic, Abrams (2012) examined the effect of the state "add-on" gun laws. As of 1996, 30 states had enacted some type of sentence enhancement for possessing a gun while committing a crime. He found that these laws reduced gun robberies by 5 percent in a three-year follow-up period, even after state crime trends had been taken into account.

IV. Capital Punishment

Variation in the presence or intensity of capital punishment potentially generates an excellent source of variation with which to test for the magnitude of general deterrence. In particular, to the extent that variation in a state's death penalty regime is unrelated to changes in the intensity of policing, the effect of the death penalty represents a pure measure of deterrence because any response of murder rates to the presence or intensity of capital punishment is not plausibly attributable to incapacitation.

There have been two primary approaches to identifying deterrent effects of capital punishment. One approach uses granular time series data or "event studies" to identify the effect of the timing of executions on murder. The evidence from these studies is, at best, mixed and yields little evidence of deterrence. Overall, evidence of deterrence is reported by Land, Teske, and Zheng (2009), while little to no evidence of deterrence is reported by Grogger (1990), Cochran, Chamlin, and Seth (1994), Stolzenberg and D'Alessio (2004), Hjalmarsson (2009), and Zimring, Fagan, and Johnson (2010).

Broadly speaking, the time series and event studies literatures offer little support in favor of deterrence—though, as noted by Charles and Durlauf (2013), the literature is plagued by several conceptual problems that compromise the interpretability of estimated treatment effects in the context of the neoclassical model. First, the focus of the time series literature on executions as opposed to the sanctions regime more generally marks a divergence from the Becker model insofar as the occurrence of an execution does not per se change the expected severity of a criminal sanction for murder. Second, Charles and Durlauf noted that the underlying logic of time series analyses of executions and murder operationalize the dynamic correlations between a shock to one time series and the levels of another as deterrence.[12] As the authors noted, "there is no good reason to think that these dynamic correlations capture what is meant by deterrence." Notably with a limited time horizon, it is not possible to distinguish between deterrence and temporal displacement.

A second literature studies the deterrent effect of capital punishment using panel data on U.S. states to identify the effect of a capital punishment statute or the frequency of executions on murder among the public at large. In particular, these studies have exploited the fact that in addition to cross-state differences in sentencing policy, there is also variation over time for individual states in the official sentencing regime, in the propensity to seek the death penalty in practice, and in the application of the ultimate punishment (Chalfin, Haviland, and Raphael 2013). This literature has generated mixed findings, with several prominent papers (e.g., Dezhbakhsh, Rubin, and Shepherd 2003; Mocan and Gittings 2003; Zimmerman 2004, 2006; Dezhbakhsh and Shepherd 2006) finding large and significant deterrence effects versus several equally prominent papers finding little evidence in favor of deterrence (Katz, Levitt, and Shustorovich 2003; Berk 2005; Donohue and Wolfers 2005, 2009; Kovandzic, Vieraitis, and Boots 2009).

While evidence in favor of a deterrent effect of the death penalty is mixed, recent reviews by Donohue and Wolfers (2005, 2009) and Chalfin et al. (2013), as well as a 2012 report commissioned by the National Academies of Science (Nagin and Pepper 2012), point to substantial problems in a number of papers that purport to find deterrence effects of capital punishment. These problems include the use of weak and/or inappropriate instruments (Dezhbakhsh et al. 2003; Zimmerman 2004), failure to report standard errors that are robust to within-state dependence (Dezhbakhsh and Shepherd 2006; Zimmerman 2009), and sensitivity of estimates to different conceptions of perceived execution risk (Mocan and Gittings 2003). More generally, the panel data literature suffers from the threat of policy endogeneity, failure to include accurate controls, and a lack of knowledge regarding how potential offenders perceive execution risk. Perhaps the most careful paper to date is that of Kovandzic et al. (2009), who used a particularly long panel of data, employed an expanded set of control variables, and explored a wide variety of operationalizations of the effect of capital punishment and execution risk. The authors found no evidence of a deterrent effect of capital punishment.

V. Estimates of Incapacitation

We now turn to the estimates of the extent to which prisons affect crime through incapacitation. Most of the extant literature has found a significant reduction in crime due to incapacitation, though the estimates vary in magnitude. An early review by Cohen (1978) estimated elasticities ranging from –0.05 to –0.70. The interval presented by Spelman (1994) was substantially narrower, with elasticities ranging from –0.12 to –0.20. A pair of studies by DiIulio and Piehl (DiIulio and Piehl 1991; Piehl and DiIulio 1995) estimated elasticities of –0.22 for a sample of Wisconsin prisoners and –0.26 for a sample of prisoners from New Jersey. Later, Weatherburn, Hua, and Moffatt (2006) estimated an elasticity of burglary with respect to imprisonment of –0.30. These estimates are concentrated around an elasticity of approximately –0.20, which translates to an increase of 5 percent in the prison population leading to a 1 percent reduction in crime.

As we described in our theoretical discussion of incapacitation, empirical estimation of the incapacitation effect of prisons is challenging because it is difficult to estimate the counterfactual number of crimes a given individual would commit if he or she were not incarcerated. In recognition of the fact that the incapacitation effect of imprisonment is heterogeneous depending on the individual crime rate λ of the incarcerated individual, there have been some attempts to identify high-λ individuals in order to "selectively incapacitate" (Greenwood and Abrahamse 1982). Auerhahn (1999) replicated the prediction tool originally developed by Greenwood and Abrahamse using a representative sample of California state prison inmates and found that the prediction tool had only a 60 percent accuracy rate at predicting levels of criminal behavior (High, Medium, Low). In addition, the tool generated false-positive predictions for more than one-third of the predicted "High Rate" group. Piquero and Blumstein (2007, p. 272) noted that "any classification of an individual as a high- or low-λ person [would be] fraught with error. And any such attempt at identifying would introduce an inequity that was widely seen as unacceptable." However, the analysis by Canela-Cacho et al. (1997) showed that the individuals with higher levels of criminal behavior would necessarily be more likely to be sentenced to prison because they engaged in higher levels of criminal behavior and thus had more opportunities to be apprehended and then sentenced to prison, a process they called "stochastic selection." Stochastic selection showed that it was possible, indeed inevitable, to imprison higher-λ individuals without needing to make any individual estimates of λ.

VI. Conclusion

In this chapter we described the theoretical relationships between prisons and crime and assessed the empirical literature that has arisen to better understand the relationship. With respect to theory, we demonstrated that the deterrent and criminogenic effects of prison on crime operate through the severity of the sanction and that, relatively speaking, the severity of sanction as a whole and the role of prison within the severity of sanction can be shown to be theoretically limited.

The deterrent effects of prison on crime can be separated into two categories: specific and general deterrence. Prisons can deter crime through specific deterrence by altering the behavior of those who were once incarcerated but have now been released; however, the empirical literature suggests that harsher prison conditions tend to result in increasing the recidivism rates for the formerly incarcerated as opposed to deterring them.

With respect to the general deterrence of those who have never been incarcerated, we showed that aggregate crime rates are not very sensitive to marginal changes in the severity of a prison sentence. That said, there is some evidence that individuals facing different prison sentences for the same crime tend to behave differently (Drago et al. 2009), a finding that is echoed by Helland and Tabarrok (2007), who studied the behavior of individuals with two strikeable offenses in California.

Incapacitation can be thought of as the mechanical response of prison with respect to crime. Empirical attempts to estimate the role of incapacitation in the relationship between prisons and crime have focused on the consequences of "taking a slice out" of an individual's criminal career (Blumstein 1983, p. 874), estimating the crimes avoided by incarcerating that individual or group of individuals.

With respect to public policy, in particular, the distinction between deterrence and criminogenesis on the one hand and incapacitation on the other is key. Consider, for example, a utilitarian social planner who must decide how to allocate scarce crime-control resources among police and prisons. Holding all other things equal, it is more efficient to invest in the resource that generates crime reductions that accrue via deterrence as opposed to incapacitation. The costs of arrest, adjudication, and incarceration mean that incapacitation is expensive and, by contrast, deterrence is relatively cheap. In other words, efficiency concerns dictate that social planners give priority to criminal justice policies that seem likely to reduce both crime and incarceration rates (Durlauf and Nagin 2011).

NOTES

1. Although it might seem that "rehabilitation" is missing from this discussion, it is present as a factor mediating deterrence. One of the reasons individuals might be deterred from future crime after serving time in prison is that they have been "rehabilitated." It is true that while incarcerated some individuals seek out or receive treatments that they would not otherwise receive. If the effect of those treatments is to prevent the individual from future criminal behavior, then the person is deterred through rehabilitation. While it is probably true for some that treatments in prison have rehabilitative effects that are independent of their propensity to commit future crime, the general consensus is that prison has negative as opposed to positive outcomes. As a result, we are not going to address the potential general rehabilitation effects of prison.

2. Throughout the chapter we discuss deterrence and criminogenesis together because they are the inverse of one another in terms of outcomes of the rational choice model of criminal decision making. As discussed, if the marginal cost exceeds the marginal benefit of crime, then the crime is deterred, whereas when the opposite circumstance is true (MB > MC), then the conditions are criminogenic.

3. For an excellent intellectual history of deterrence theory see Paternoster (2010).

4. See Durlauf and Nagin (2011) for a discussion of the neoclassical model under this simplifying assumption.

5. Among the myriad contributions of Becker's 1968 paper was to bring deterrence theory back around to Beccaria and Bentham by suggesting that *any* individual could be at the decision margin for criminal behavior.

6. It is worth noting that unlike some of the other surveys that attempted to corroborate respondent answers with actual rates, Anderson (2002) took the self-reported answers at face value. The respondents were asked whether they knew what the likely punishment would be if apprehended and they were given a range of possible responses, from "I knew exactly what the punishment would be" to "I had no idea, or I thought I knew but I was wrong" to "I didn't think about it."

7. McDowall, Loftin, and Wiersema (1992) later combined data from the sites previously studied and found a significant deterrent effect. However, due to methodological issues these findings are considered questionable (see Durlauf and Nagin [2011] for a detailed explanation of the challenges).

8. The penalty for felony possession of a firearm under federal jurisdiction was five years without the possibility of early release; processing in the federal system also leads to a higher bail amount and a high probability of serving the prison term at an out-of-state facility.

9. In California, any felony conviction could trigger a 25-years-to-life sentence under "three strikes" until Proposition 36 changed the provision in 2012 to render only serious or violent felonies eligible for the third strike.

10. On the other hand, she found that the probability of committing violent crimes increased by 9 percentage points for third-strike-eligible offenders, which she attributed to the flattened penalty gradient (a smaller increase in the severity of sanction).

11. The findings of the Kessler and Levitt study were challenged by Webster, Doob, and Zimring (2006), which sparked a debate on this empirical approach, with a response by Levitt (2006). In an attempt to resolve the debate, Raphael (2006) commends the clever approach by Kessler and Levitt (1999) to exploit the exogenous variation induced by the change in policy, but notes that perhaps the comparisons included in that paper were not ideal because of the pre-period differences in both the crime trend and in the level of eligible and ineligible crimes in California and the rest of the United States. The trend differences were obscured by the omission of the alternate years of data in the original paper; when those alternate years were added back to the graph, the time trends looked very different.

12. What this means is that if we are analyzing the time series for both executions and murder simultaneously, we are effectively attributing the dynamic correlations between a shock, or external force, that disrupts the one time series and the levels of another time series as deterrence.

References

Abrams, David S. 2012. "Estimating the Deterrent Effect of Incarceration Using Sentencing Enhancements." *American Economic Journal: Applied Economics* 4(4):32–56.

Anderson, David A. 2002. "The Deterrence Hypothesis and Picking Pockets at the Pickpocket's Hanging." *American Law and Economics Review* 4:295–313.

Assembly Committee on Criminal Procedure. 1968. *Deterrent Effects of Criminal Sanctions*. Sacramento, CA: Assembly of the State of California.

Auerhahn, Kathleen. 1999. "Selective Incapacitation and the Problem of Prediction." *Criminology* 37:703–734.

Avi-Itzhak, Benjamin, and Reuel Shinnar. 1973. "Quantitative Models in Crime Control." *Journal of Criminal Justice* 1:185–217.

Bales, William D., and Daniel P. Mears. 2008. "Inmate Social Ties and the Transition to Society: Does Visitation Reduce Recidivism?" *Journal of Research in Crime and Delinquency* 45:287–321.

Beccaria, Cesare. 1764. *On Crimes and Punishments*. Oxford: Clarendon Press.

Becker, Gary S. 1968. "Crime and Punishment: An Economic Approach." *Journal of Political Economy* 76:169–217.

Bell, Brian, Laura Jaitman, and Stephen Machin. 2014. "Crime Deterrence: Evidence from the London 2011 Riots." *Economic Journal* 124(576):480–506.

Bentham, Jeremy. 1798. *An Introduction to the Principles of Morals and Legislation*. Oxford: Clarendon Press.

Berk, Richard. 2005. "New Claims Bbout Executions and General Deterrence: Déjà Vu All Over Again?" *Journal of Empirical Legal Studies* 2:303–330.

Blumstein, Alfred. 1983. "Incapacitation." In *Encyclopedia of Crime and Justice*, vol. 3, edited by Sanford H. Kadish, pp. 873–880. New York: The Free Press.

Blumstein, Alfred. 1993. "Making Rationality Relevant: The American Society of Criminology 1992 Presidential Address." *Criminology* 31:1–16.

Canela-Cacho, José A., Alfred Blumstein, and Jacqueline Cohen. 1997. "Relationship Between the Offending Frequency (λ) Of Imprisoned and Free Offenders." *Criminology* 35: 133–176.

Carson, E. Ann, and Golinelli, Daniela. 2013. *Prisoners in 2012*. Washington, DC: Bureau of Justice Statistics.

Chalfin, Aaron, Amelia M. Haviland, and Steven Raphael. 2013. "What Do Panel Studies Tell Us About a Deterrent Effect of Capital Punishment? A Critique of the Literature." *Journal of Quantitative Criminology* 29:5–43.

Chalfin, Aaron, and Justin McCrary. 2017. "Criminal Deterrence: A Review of the Literature." *Journal of Economic Literature* 55:5–48.

Chalfin, Aaron, and Sarah Tahamont. 2016. "The Economics of Deterrence: A Review of the Theory and Evidence." In *Deterrence, Choice, and Crime: Contemporary Perspectives*, edited by Daniel S. Nagin, Francis T. Cullen, and Cheryl Jonson. New Brunswick, NJ: Transaction.

Charles, Kerwin Kofi, and Steven N. Durlauf. 2013. "Pitfalls in the Use of Time Series Methods to Study Deterrence and Capital Punishment." *Journal of Quantitative Criminology* 29:45–66.

Chen, Elsa Y. 2008. "Impacts of 'Three Strikes and You're Out' on Crime Trends on California and throughout the United States." *Journal of Contemporary Criminal Justice* 24:345–370.

Chen, M. Keith, and Jesse M. Shapiro. 2007. "Do Harsher Prison Conditions Reduce Recidivism? A Discontinuity-Based Approach." *American Law and Economics Review* 9:1–29.

Cochran, John K., Mitchell B. Chamlin, and Mark Seth. 1994. "Deterrence or Brutalization? An Impact Assessment of Oklahoma's Return to Capital Punishment." *Criminology* 32:107–134.

Cohen, Jacqueline. 1978. "The Incapacitative Effect of Imprisonment: A Critical Review of the Literature." In *Deterrence and Incapacitation: Estimating the Effects of Criminal Sanctions on Crime Rates*, edited by Alfred Blumstein, Jacqueline Cohen, and Daniel S. Nagin. Washington, DC: National Academy Press.

Cook, Philip J. 1980. "Research in Criminal Deterrence: Laying the Groundwork for the Second Decade." *Crime and Justice* 2:211–268.

Crouch, Ben M. 1993. "Is Incarceration Really Worse? Analysis of Offenders' Preferences for Prison over Probation." *Justice Quarterly* 10:67–88.

Dezhbakhsh, Hashem, Paul H. Rubin, and Joanna M. Shepherd. 2003. "Does Capital Punishment Have a Deterrent Effect? New Evidence from Postmoratorium Panel Data." *American Law and Economics Review* 5:344–376.

Dezhbakhsh, Hashem, and Joanna M. Shepherd. 2006. "The Deterrent Effect of Capital Punishment: Evidence from a Judicial Experiment." *Economic Inquiry* 44:512–535.

DiIulio, John J., and Anne Morrison Piehl. 1991. "Does Prison Pay? The Stormy National Debate over the Cost-effectiveness of Imprisonment." *Brookings Review* 9(4):28–35.

Donohue, John J., and Justin Wolfers. 2005. "Uses and Abuses of Empirical Evidence in the Death Penalty Debate." *Stanford Law Review* 58:791–846.

Donohue, John J., and Justin Wolfers. 2009. "Estimating the Impact of the Death Penalty on Murder." *American Law and Economics Review* 11:249–309.

Drago, Francesco, Roberto Galbiati, and Pietro Vertova. 2009. "The Deterrent Effects of Prison: Evidence from a Natural Experiment." *Journal of Political Economy* 117:257–280.

Drago, Francesco, Roberto Galbiati, and Pietro Vertova. 2011. "Prison Conditions and Recidivism." *American Law and Economics Review* 13:103–130.

Durlauf, Steven N., and Daniel S. Nagin. 2011. "The Deterrent Effect of Imprisonment." In *Controlling Crime: Strategies and Tradeoffs*, edited by Philip J. Cook, Jens Ludwig, and Justin McCrary. Chicago: University of Chicago Press.

Duwe, Grant, and Valerie Clark. 2013. "Blessed Be the Social Tie That Binds: The Effects of Prison Visitation on Offender Recidivism." *Criminal Justice Policy Review* 24:271–296.

Grassian, Stuart. 2006. "Psychiatric Effects of Solitary Confinement." *Washington University Journal of Law and Policy* 22:325–383.

Greenwood, Peter W., and Allan F. Abrahamse. 1982. *Selective Incapacitation*. Santa Monica, CA: RAND.

Greenwood, Peter W., and Angela Hawken. 2002. *An Assessment of the Effect of California's Three Strikes Law*. Greenwood Associates Working Paper.

Grogger, Jeffrey. 1990. "The Deterrent Effect of Capital Punishment: An Analysis of Daily Homicide Counts." *Journal of the American Statistical Association* 85(410):295–303.

Haney, Craig. 2003. "Mental Health Issues in Long-Term Solitary and 'Supermax' Confinement." *Crime & Delinquency* 49:124–156.

Harding, David J., Jessica J. B. Wyse, Cheyney Dobson, and Jeffrey D. Morenoff. 2014. "Making Ends Meet after Prison." *Journal of Policy Analysis and Management* 33:440–470.

Helland, Eric, and Alexander Tabarrok. 2007. "Does Three Strikes Deter? A Nonparametric Estimation." *Journal of Human Resources* 42:309–330.

Hjalmarsson, Randi. 2009. "Does Capital Punishment Have a 'Local' Deterrent Effect on Homicides?" *American Law and Economics Review* 11:310–334.

Holzer, Harry J., Steven Raphael, and Michael A. Stoll. 2007. "The Effect of an Applicant's Criminal History on Employer Hiring Decisions and Screening Practices: Evidence from Los Angeles." In *Barriers to Reentry? The Labor Market for Released Prisoners in Post-Industrial America*, edited by Shawn D. Bushway, Michael A. Stoll, and David Weiman. New York: Russell Sage Foundation.

Iyengar, Radha. 2008. "I'd Rather Be Hanged for a Sheep than a Lamb: The Unintended Consequences of 'Three-Strikes' Laws." National Bureau of Economic Research working paper (No. 13784).

Johnson, Rucker, and Steven Raphael. 2012. "How Much Crime Reduction Does the Marginal Prisoner Buy?" *Journal of Law and Economics* 55:275–310.

Katz, Lawrence, Steven D. Levitt, and Ellen Shustorovich. 2003. "Prison Conditions, Capital Punishment, and Deterrence." *American Law and Economics Review* 5:318–343.

Kessler, Daniel, and Steven D. Levitt. 1999. "Using Sentence Enhancements to Distinguish between Deterrence and Incapacitation." *Journal of Law and Economics* 42:343–363.

Kleck, Gary, Brion Sever, Spencer Li, and Marc Gertz. 2005. "The Missing Link in General Deterrence Research." *Criminology* 43:623–660.

Kovandzic, Tomislav V., John J. Sloan III, and Lynne M. Vieraitis. 2004. "'Striking Out' as Crime Reduction Policy: The Impact of 'Three Strikes' Laws on Crime Rates in US Cities." *Justice Quarterly* 21:207–239.

Kovandzic, Tomislav V., Lynne M. Vieraitis, and Denise Paquette Boots. 2009. "Does the Death Penalty Save Lives?" *Criminology and Public Policy* 8:803–843.

Land, Kenneth C., Raymond H. C. Teske, and Hui Zheng. 2009. "The Short-Term Effects of Executions on Homicides: Deterrence, Displacement, or Both?" *Criminology* 47:1009–1043.

Lee, David S., and Justin McCrary. 2009. "The Deterrence Effect of Prison: Dynamic Theory and Evidence." Working paper.

Levitt, Steven D. 1996. "The Effect of Prison Population Size on Crime Rates: Evidence from Prison Overcrowding Legislation." *Quarterly Journal of Economics* 111:319–351.

Levitt, Steven D. 1998. "Juvenile Crime and Punishment." *Journal of Political Economy* 106:1156–1185.

Levitt, Stephen D. 2006. "The Case of the Critics Who Missed the Point: A Reply to Webster et al" *Criminology and Public Policy* 5:449–460.

Liedka, Raymond V., Anne Morrison Piehl, and Bert Useem. 2006. "The Crime-Control Effect of Incarceration: Does Scale Matter?" *Criminology & Public Policy* 5:245–276.

Lofstrom, Magnus, and Steven Raphael. 2013. *Public Safety Realignment and Crime Rates in California*. San Francisco: Public Policy Institute of California.

Loftin, Colin, Milton Heumann, and David McDowall. 1983. "Mandatory Sentencing and Firearms Violence: Evaluating an Alternative to Gun Control." *Law and Society Review* 17:287–318.

Loftin, Colin, and David McDowall. 1981. "'One with a Gun Gets You Two': Mandatory Sentencing and Firearms Violence in Detroit." *Annals of the American Academy of Political and Social Science* 455:150–167.

Loftin, Colin, and David McDowall. 1984. "The Deterrent Effects of the Florida Felony Firearm Law." *Journal of Criminal Law and Criminology* 75:250–259.

Lovell, David, L. Clark Johnson, and Kevin C. Cain. 2007. "Recidivism of Supermax Prisoners in Washington State." *Crime and Delinquency* 53:633–656.

Maruna, Shadd, and Hans Toch. 2005. "The Impact of Imprisonment on the Desistance Process." In *Prisoner Reentry and Crime in America*, edited by Jeremy Travis. New York: Cambridge University Press.

Marvell, Thomas B., and Carlisle E. Moody Jr. 1994. "Prison Population Growth and Crime Reduction." *Journal of Quantitative Criminology* 10:109–140.

Marvell, Thomas B., and Carlisle E. Moody. 2001. "The Lethal Effects of Three-Strikes Laws." *Journal of Legal Studies* 30:89–106.

May, David C., and Peter B. Wood. 2010. *Ranking Correctional Punishments: Views from Offenders, Practitioners, and the Public*. Durham, NC: Carolina Academic Press.

McDowall, David, Colin Loftin, and Brian Wiersema. 1992. "A Comparative Study of the Preventive Effects of Mandatory Sentencing Laws for Gun Crimes." *Journal of Criminal Law and Criminology* 83:378–394.

Mears, Daniel P., and William D. Bales. 2009. "Supermax Incarceration and Recidivism." *Criminology* 47:1131–1166.

Mears, Daniel P., Joshua C. Cochran, Sonja E. Siennick, and William D. Bales. 2012. "Prison Visitation and Recidivism." *Justice Quarterly* 29:888–918.

Mocan, H. Naci, and R. Kaj Gittings. 2003. "Getting Off Death Row: Commuted Sentences and the Deterrent Effect of Capital Punishment." *Journal of Law and Economics* 46:453–478.

Nagin, Daniel S. 2013. "Deterrence in the Twenty-First Century." *Crime and Justice* 42:199–263.

Nagin, Daniel. S., Francis T. Cullen, and Cheryl L. Jonson. 2009. "Imprisonment and Reoffending." *Crime and Justice* 38:115–200.

Nagin, Daniel S., and John V. Pepper, eds. 2012. *Deterrence and the Death Penalty*. Washington, DC: National Academies Press.

Nagin, Daniel S., and Greg Pogarsky. 2001. "Integrating Celerity, Impulsivity, and Extralegal Sanction Threats into a Model of General Deterrence: Theory and Evidence." *Criminology* 39:865–892.

Paternoster, Raymond. 2010. "How Much Do We Really Know About Criminal Deterrence?" *Journal of Criminal Law and Criminology* 100: 765–824.

Piehl, Anne. M., and John J. DiIulio Jr. 1995. "'Does Prison Pay?' Revisited: Returning to the Crime Scene." *Brookings Review* 13:20–25.

Piquero, Alex R., and Alfred Blumstein. 2007. "Does Incapacitation Reduce Crime?" *Journal of Quantitative Criminology* 23:267–285.

Raphael, Steven. 2006. "The Deterrent Effects of California's Proposition 8: Weighing the Evidence." *Criminology and Public Policy* 5:471–478.

Raphael, Steven, and Jens Ludwig. 2003. "Prison Sentence Enhancements: The Case of Project Exile." In *Evaluating Gun Policy: Effects on Crime and Violence*, edited by Jens Ludwig and Philip J. Cook. Washington, DC: Brookings Institute Press.

Raphael, Steven, and Michael A. Stoll. 2013. *Why Are So Many Americans in Prison?* New York: Russell Sage Foundation.

Raphael, Steven, and David Weiman. 2007. "The Impact of Local Labor Market Conditions on the Likelihood That Parolees Are Returned to Custody." In *Barriers to Reentry? The Labor Market for Released Prisoners in Post-Industrial America*, edited by Shawn D. Bushway, Michael A. Stoll, and David Weiman. New York: Russell Sage Foundation.

Shepherd, Joanne. M. 2002a. "Fear of the First Strike: The Full Deterrent Effect of California's Two- and Three-Strikes Legislation." *Journal of Legal Studies* 31:159–201.

Shepherd, Joanne. M. 2002b. "Police, Prosecutors, Criminals, and Determinate Sentencing: The Truth About Truth-In-Sentencing Laws." *Journal of Law and Economics* 45:509–533.

Shinnar, Shlomo, and Reuel Shinnar. 1975. "The Effects of the Criminal Justice System on the Control of Crime: A Quantitative Approach." *Law and Society Review* 9:581–611.

Spelman, William. 1994. *Criminal Incapacitation*. New York: Plenum.

Spelman, William. 2000. "The Limited Importance of Prison Expansion." In *The Crime Drop in America*, edited by Alfred Blumstein and Joel Wallman. New York: Cambridge University Press.

Stolzenberg, Lisa, and Stewart J. D'Alessio. 1997. "'Three Strikes and You're Out': The Impact of California's New Mandatory Sentencing Law on Serious Crime Rates." *Crime and Delinquency* 43:457–469.

Stolzenberg, Lisa, and Stewart J. D'Alessio. 2004. "Capital Punishment, Execution Publicity and Murder in Houston, Texas." *Journal of Criminal Law and Criminology* 94:351–380.

Sykes, Gresham M. 1958. *The Society of Captives: A Study of a Maximum Security Prison.* Princeton, NJ: Princeton University Press.

Weatherburn, Don, Jiuzhao Hua, and Steve Moffatt. 2006. "How Much Crime Does Prison Stop? The Incapacitation Effect of Prison on Burglary." *International Journal of Police Science* 2:8.

Webster, Cheryl, Anthony N. Doob, and Franklin E. Zimring. 2006. "Proposition 8 and Crime Rates in California: The Case of the Disappearing Deterrent." *Criminology and Public Policy* 5:417–448.

Zimmerman, Paul R. 2004. "State Executions, Deterrence, and the Incidence of Murder." *Journal of Applied Economics* 7:163 193.

Zimmerman, Paul R. 2006. "Estimates of the Deterrent Effect of Alternative Execution Methods in the United States: 1978–2000." *American Journal of Economics and Sociology* 65: 909–941.

Zimmerman, Paul R. 2009. "Statistical Variability and the Deterrent Effect of the Death Penalty." *American Law and Economics Review* 11:370–398.

Zimring, Franklin E., Jeffrey Fagan, and David T. Johnson. 2010. "Executions, Deterrence, and Homicide: A Tale of Two Cities." *Journal of Empirical Legal Studies* 7:1–29.

Zimring, Franklin E., and Gordon J. Hawkins. 1973. *Deterrence: The Legal Threat in Crime Control.* Chicago: University of Chicago Press.

Zimring, Franklin E., Gordon Hawkins, and Sam Kamin. 2001. *Punishment and Democracy: Three Strikes and You're Out in California.* New York: Oxford University Press.

CHAPTER 28

PRIVATE PRISONS IN A NEW ENVIRONMENT

SCOTT D. CAMP

THE reemergence of private prisons for adults in the United States occurred during the 1980s, when state prison systems were facing serious budget shortfalls at the same time that the war on drugs and determinate sentencing were placing unprecedented numbers of individuals in state and federal prisons (Blumstein and Beck 1999; Mauer 1999). Additional growth pressures emerged later as undocumented immigrants started showing up in larger numbers in prison populations, especially in the federal system with the solicitation for Criminal Alien Requirement prisons. The growth of prison populations in the 1980s coincided with the Reagan presidency and the philosophical emphasis that the private sector was superior to the public sector in efficiency and cost. Costs were primarily the focus of such discussions, as the logic of competition in capitalist markets was used to argue for private-sector superiority. There were additional arguments that the private sector provided prison programs of equal or superior quality. Ironically, the first private prison in the federal sector was proposed and implemented by the Clinton administration. The Taft Correctional Institution in California started receiving inmates in 1998 (Camp and Daggett 2005). Also, private companies, primarily nonprofit organizations, were already operating in the juvenile sector during this period. Private, nonprofit interests also kept inmates in small facilities that helped inmates make the transition from prison settings to the free community for several months prior to formal release. The facilities have been called halfway houses or reentry centers at different times.

This chapter reviews the experiences in the United States with private prisons and discusses some of the issues facing the private sector. Section I provides a brief overview of the history of the rapid growth in the private sector in the United States. Section II takes a look at the thorny issue of the costs of public and private prisons. While costs are easily quantified, assigning the proper costs to the public and private sectors has presented much controversy in previous studies. There is no general agreement about which sector operates comparable prisons at the lowest cost. Section III examines the issue of the quality of correctional services provided by public and private prisons. There is little agreement on the type of measures that allow for fair comparisons of public and private prisons. A unique factor of sections II and III is the emphasis upon the larger market in which the private-prison sector operates. Until around 2000, the prison populations of most systems in the United States rapidly expanded, creating a need for additional prison capacity. Since 2000, the pace of growth declined, and by 2009, growth had stopped or reversed in most states and even the federal sector starting in fiscal year 2014. Sections II and III discuss how this recent change affects the issues associated with cost and quality comparisons. The chapter ends with thoughts on the issues facing public and private prisons in an era marked by stability or decline as opposed to rapid growth in prison populations. The main conclusions reached in this chapter relate to:

- The new economic imperative that underlies the expansion of the private sector in providing correctional services. In the past, public-sector decisions to buy or make were predicated on whether the public or private sectors could expand capacity the most efficiently. In the near future, the decisions are more likely to be based on whether to retain public or private prisons in decisions about reducing prison capacity.
- Quality issues that are as important as cost issues in making decisions about using public or private prisons. Private prisons are not immune to operating problems, and it is important that quality issues enter equally into decisions about which prisons to shutter if/when state and federal governments reduce the overall number of prison beds.
- The private sector is better positioned in terms of physical plant to run cost-efficient prisons. During a period when few new public prisons were built, the private sector built a number of prison beds. All of these beds were built after 1984 as compared to public prisons, which can be 100 years old or more.

I. Brief History of Prison Privatization

There were no for-profit companies holding adult inmates in traditional prison settings at the beginning of the 1980s. Placing inmates in private prisons, though, was not a new idea in the 1980s, as private "prisons" for adult felons existed in the nineteenth century, especially in southern states following the Civil War. Private entrepreneurs had used inmates to produce goods on a piece-rate basis since the late colonial period. Under the piece-rate system, inmates produced finished goods from materials and tools provided by the entrepreneur, sometimes even under the supervision of the entrepreneur, but the work was done within the confines of the prison. Reconstruction in the Old South added a new twist as inmates were leased out to live and work under private interests. The convict-lease system not only aided agricultural interests in dealing with labor shortages, but leased convicts were used as strikebreakers in early industrial disputes (Weiss 2005).

The early privatization attempts ended poorly with the exposure of abuses and scandals involving the inhumane treatment of inmates and high mortality rates. There was little economic incentive to provide adequate housing, food, and medical care for leased inmates, as replacements for incapacitated inmate-workers waited in state prisons. Public exposure and the lobbying by prison reformers and religious groups led to the end of convict labor by the 1920s in the United States (Kunkel and Capps 2005). Passage of the Hawes-Cooper Act in 1929 formally outlawed the defunct practice of convict leasing by outlawing the interstate commerce of prison-manufactured goods. A key difference between the earlier use of private "prisons" and the revival of private prisons in 1984 was that early private prisons were basically arrangements to provide cheap labor to private enterprises. For the private prison operators from 1984 to the present, housing and programming the inmates was the primary focus of the economic transaction (Culp 2005; Hallett 2006). The private operators specifically focused upon three aspects. First, they noted that they could build new prisons more quickly and for lower costs given the reduction in red tape in the private sector. Second, they claimed they could utilize high levels of technology in the operations of prisons to lower operating costs. These technologies included innovations such as "just-in-time" food delivery as opposed to buying bulk, which required warehouses for storage. Finally, they noted that they could provide flexible and state-of-the-art prison programs if specified contractually. The operators claimed that contracting with the private sector for all three aspects provided the best deal for the public sector.

The dynamics that fueled the explosion of the private prison sector in the United States changed beginning around the year 2000. The 1980s and 1990s were decades of unprecedented growth in prison populations in practically every state and the federal government, but the growth in the national prison population slowed after 2000. States and the federal government scrambled to find beds for the overcrowded prisons. By 2009, in contrast, the prison population actually declined in many states, and the total number of incarcerated individuals in the United States declined for the first time in decades (Carson and Golinelli 2013). The decrease continued through 2012 although the percentage drop in 2012 was not as great as experienced in previous years (Glaze and Herberman 2013). While the overall growth was negative in 2009 through 2012, the decline was not uniform across the board; increases continued in some state systems and most notably the federal system. In the federal system, the single largest user of private prisons, the decline in prison population lagged until 2014, when the population in the Federal Bureau of Prisons declined by about 5,000 from the peak population attained in 2014.[1] Of course, in a prison system with a population of over 200,000 inmates and 31 percent overcrowding, a 2 percent decline is not as significant as could be hoped, but the change in the direction of the growth of the federal prison population is the important point to take away from this discussion. If not for the overcrowding of the Bureau of Prisons, 5,000 inmates would represent the population of two typical federal prisons.

This brief history examines the evolution of the private-sector prison from the perspective of how it was used by prison administrators to address issues in corrections. As such, the chapter is an attempt to neither discredit private prisons nor cheerlead for their continued growth. Instead, I provide an overview of the issues facing the public sector in the use of private prisons to manage correctional populations. Early on, a tenuous legal issue faced private contractors over the use of force in reacting to inmate violence and misconduct, and many private contractors operated with unresolved authority. At this point, most states have legislatively addressed the use of force by private contractors, so this issue is off the table for the most part and not discussed here.

The first private "prison" in the United States opened in Houston but was actually a detention center for illegal aliens. In 1984, the then Immigration and Naturalization Services, now Immigration and Customs Enforcement, contracted with a new corporation based in Tennessee, the Corrections Corporation of America (CCA), to operate a processing center. CCA soon obtained contracts to incarcerate adult felons in traditional prison settings, starting with a prison in nearby Kentucky, and a new industry was born. The marketing claims offered by CCA included providing prison beds at or below public costs, delivering inmate services that were on par with or better than those provided by the public sector, building prisons faster and thus providing prison beds in a more timely fashion, and giving government correctional agencies the "agility" to deal with both ups and downs in the prison population. Prison systems could reduce their capacity by canceling contracts instead of mothballing public prisons. These claims were made by all private operators and advocacy groups, such as the Reason Foundation, and even academics, most notably Charles Thomas, who was then at the University of Florida. The management of CCA was ambitious and boldly offered to operate prisons for the entire Tennessee prison system. A modified offer was tendered almost 30 years later by CCA to the 48 continental states in the United States, although there was a very important modification to the offer that is discussed in more detail below.

The major competitor of CCA initially operated as a division of the Wackenhut Corporation, a private security firm. The firm, initially known as Wackenhut Corrections Corporation, began operations in 1984 as well. By 1988, it had incorporated as a wholly owned subsidiary of the Wackenhut Corporation and changed its name to Geo Group, Inc. (GEO) in 2003. The two firms, CCA and GEO, dominated the early industry, and the domination continues to this day. While CCA, GEO, and other private-sector providers have continued to operate in an international market, discussion here focuses primarily upon the U.S. market.

By 1999, 15 years following the opening of the Houston Processing Center, private-sector prisons housed 69,188 convicted adults. CCA and GEO controlled 81 percent of the total number of these beds in the United States. CCA was the larger of the two, housing 37,244 inmates versus 19,001 in GEO facilities (Camp and Gaes 2002a, p. 431). By the end of 2000, another 16,000 inmates had been added to this population, bringing the total number of inmates in private prisons operated for states and the federal government to 85,500. Growth slowed somewhat between 2000 and 2012 in states, but the number of inmates held in private-prison beds increased to 128,300 (or 50 percent growth). The slower growth in private-prison beds under state contract during this 13-year period, from 76,100 to 96,800 (27 percent), was offset by more rapid growth in the private-prison beds contracted by the federal system, which increased from 9,400 to 31,500 (235 percent; percentages calculated from data reported in Glaze and Herberman 2013). By 2012, federal contracts accounted for 25 percent of the beds in privately operated prisons.

The growth of 50 percent in the number of private-sector prison beds over the 13 years ending in 2012 was outstanding. The rapid growth in prison populations through 2009 in most states allowed the private-sector to maintain the focus of their original marketing slogans of lower cost, improved quality, faster acquisition of beds, and flexibility in dealing with changing prison populations. Of course, the change in the prison population prior to 2006 was almost consistently positive growth.

The slowing of prison populations and eventual decline starting in 2009 in most states and the federal government probably raised concerns in both the public and private sectors about the future of specific correctional facilities. CCA, as the largest private operators, seemed confident about the future of their prisons. As noted in their 2013 10K Securities and Exchange Commission filing, 290,000 beds in U.S. prisons were in facilities 50 to 100 years old; another 100,000 beds were in prisons that were over 100 years old. CCA announced a marketing strategy to match the times. CCA executives clearly felt that they were in a superior position in competing with older prisons if contraction of correctional facilities was necessary. With all CCA-owned prisons built after 1984, even the only public prison purchased by a private operator, the Lake Erie Correctional Institution in Ohio, the capital infrastructure of CCA is much newer on average than the state or federal systems.[2]

CCA announced an aggressive strategy in 2012 as noted above. CCA sent a letter to correctional leaders in 48 states offering to purchase and run their adult prisons for the next 20 years if the prisons held 1,000 inmates or more. The offer was not extended to New Hampshire and Ohio. As part of the deal, the states would agree to guarantee payments for 90 percent occupancy in the prisons even if the actual occupancy was below 90 percent. That meant that if the rated capacity of the composition of prisons in a state was designed to hold 20,000 inmates, the state would pay a minimum fee for 90 percent of the 20,000 beds in the system—18,000 inmates—even if the state population of inmates fell below 18,000. Conversely, the state would be obligated to pay an additional per diem for any inmates over the 18,000 minimum. While some took the view that the offer by CCA was an attempt to delay or derail states' efforts at sentencing reform (Associated Press 2012), others saw the move as an attempt by CCA to exert more control over its future market by exercising more control over state prison systems (Kirkham 2012).

The conservative *Forbes* magazine noted that there were negative consequences associated with the quick infusion of cash into ailing state budgets of selling prisons to CCA:

> Once a state has sold its facility, it leaves little opportunity to contract with another prison management company in the event of a dispute or to save money. CCA, in the case of buying a prison, could be in the driver's seat to dictate prison policy to the state. And what happens when an inmate escapes? Well the state will be the one going on the hunt for the escapee, not the private prison. So the taxpayer is still on the hook. (Pavlo 2012)

None of the states took the CCA offer. The only partial exception was Ohio, which did not receive the formal proposal from CCA. In the first and only purchase of a public prison by a private vendor, and prior to the CCA offer in 2012, CCA purchased the Lake Erie Correctional Institution. CCA has a 20-year contract to operate the prison with unlimited renewals with a guaranteed capacity of 90 percent. The offer to the 48 states by CCA did contain a broadened use of an existing tool in how CCA structures contracts to protect corporate interests. When the Federal Bureau of Prisons contracted with GEO for its first private prison, a low-security prison at Taft, California, with an attached minimum-security camp, the Bureau structured the contract and subsequent contracts differently than most state contracts at the time. In particular, the Bureau wanted to avoid situations that provided an incentive for the private prison company to hold on to inmates who needed to be moved to other facilities. The Bureau accomplished this by agreeing to pay a flat fee for the management of Taft up to a certain number of inmates, and if the Bureau placed more inmates in the facility than the agreed-upon number, then the Bureau would agree to pay an additional per-diem rate based upon marginal costs. If the number of inmates remained below the agreed-upon number, then the Bureau faced the obligation to pay the flat rate for operating the prison. This model seems to have provided the template for the 2012 offer by CCA to operate entire state prison systems.

While the impetus for structuring the contract in this fashion originated in the federal sector, it obviously has clear benefits for the private provider. CCA won several contracts in the federal sector that had the guaranteed payment clause as part of the contract. Not only did CCA incorporate this guaranteed payment strategy in its offer to the 48 states, but it had already implemented this contract strategy in contracts outside of the federal government. As noted above, Ohio agreed to provide 90 percent of the capacity for CCA operations of the Lake Erie Correctional Institution. Since 2011, CCA has made similar contracts with Arizona and Georgia. The contract between CCA and the Arizona Department of Corrections calls for CCA to operate the Red Rock Correctional Center at 90 percent capacity for the next ten years, and the contract with the Georgia Department of Corrections calls for ten years of operations by CCA at the Jenkins Correctional Center. Other companies followed the lead of guaranteed capacity. A 2013 study by In the Public Interest (ITPI) examined 63 contracts, 41 of which contained provisions requiring occupancy between 80 and 100 percent (In the Public Interest 2013). ITPI identified 77 private prisons operating at the county or state level in the United States and was able to review contracts for 62 of these facilities. According to ITPI, all major private providers have incorporated what ITPI calls quotas into at least some of their contracts.

The new long-term contracts and the newer physical plant of CCA operations provide strong impetus for state agencies to continue operating private facilities even in a period of correctional downsizing. I am just describing the situation facing modern corrections as prison populations contract and not judging it to be good nor bad, although others have made judgments about this practice (In the Public Interest 2013). The structure of contracts to guarantee payments and the existence of a greater proportion of new facilities are tangible factors that must be addressed when decisions are made about correctional capacity. Certainly these factors are more tangible than the clouded knowledge about prison costs and quality I discuss next.

II. Cost Issues

The industry promise of providing correctional beds at lower costs has been hotly contested since 1984, and I will not review all the relevant studies. There have been controversies about the motives of the researchers involved. Charles Thomas was the first culprit. While a tenured faculty member at the University of Florida, Dr. Thomas was a leading proponent of private prisons in academic outlets and political forums. He was a respected scholar with prolific publications, and he testified at hearings in many state legislatures. However, Dr. Thomas's close association with and unacknowledged compensation from CCA produced suspicion about the impartiality of his scientific writings and led to accusations and a finding of ethics violations. The most recent subjects are Professors Hakim and Blackstone at Temple University. They released a working paper in 2013, "Cost Analysis of Public and Contractor-Operated Prisons," without acknowledging that the research was funded by the three largest private-prison providers. Of course, the reactions to the work of these three scholars speak as much about the passions roused by the topic of prison privatization as to the issues of transparency in scientific research.

After 30 years of experience with private prisons, the only safe conclusion is that private prisons and public prisons are competitive in terms of costs. Nobody has produced tangible examples of earth-shaking opportunities for cost savings for either public or private prisons.

Despite early claims of superior technology and efficiencies in private prisons (Logan 1990, 1992; Archambeault and Deis 1996; Thomas 1997), most of the technological edge was found in the newer designs of the prisons the private sector operated. Newer prisons are built from the ground up with lines of sight factored in, along with other design efficiencies that allowed for the use of fewer correctional staff. Generally speaking, labor costs are the area of greatest potential cost difference in prisons, as labor costs typically account for 70 percent or more of prison costs. Of course, public prisons had access to the same designs but no budgets to build new prisons to expand capacity or replace older prisons.

Gaes (2010) reviewed a couple of meta-analyses on private prison costs and quality. As he and the original authors of the meta-analyses noted, the prisons compared were rarely comparable. For example, in an early comparison of costs and quality, Perrone and Pratt (2003) noted that only two of the nine studies they examined matched public and private prisons on the basic characteristics of size, custody level, and age. In part this is a methodological shortcoming of the studies reviewed by Perrone and Pratt, but it also reflects the reality that conditions rarely allow for the comparison of similar facilities. Two exceptions presented themselves early in the push to use private prisons, one in the Louisiana Department of Corrections and the other in the Federal Bureau of Prisons. In both instances, prisons built with almost identical architectural design, including the number of beds in the main facility, were opened at the same time by the public and the private sectors. In Louisiana, three low-security prisons were built, two operated by the private sector, CCA and GEO, and the third by the state. In the Federal Bureau of Prisons, four low-security prisons were built, with only one operated by the private sector: GEO operated the Taft Correctional Institution in California. While both exceptions were intensely studied, by Archambeault and Deis in Louisiana (1996) and, in the case of the Bureau of Prisons, by an independent economist hired by the Bureau (Nelson 2005), and a study funded by the National Institute of Justice (McDonald and Carlson 2005), definitive findings accepted by all parties were not produced.

Even in these two situations of matched prisons, the methods for comparing costs were highly controversial. The biggest issue was how to account for overhead costs such as the costs of administrative staff. For example, the director of a prison system is responsible for both public and private prisons. In particular, the issue was one of assigning an appropriate portion of the overhead costs of the public system to the private operations, as these costs were not avoided by contracting for the operation of the prison. Even if all prisons were privately operated, public-sector staff would still write contracts, oversee contract compliance, and provide liaison with legislators. The true costs of operating private prisons need to reflect the fact that the public systems cannot abdicate the oversight of private prisons. Costs associated with public oversight and awarding of contracts need to be charged against the direct contractual costs of private operations. Various methods were proposed for handling these overhead costs in the case of the federal prisons, and the solutions showed that the private-sector operations produced either negligible or modest cost savings for the federal government (McDonald and Carlson 2005; Nelson 2005).

The question of whether the private sector can operate comparable prisons more cheaply than the public sector is not likely to be answered in the near future. The Louisiana and Bureau of Prisons natural experiments provided the best opportunities, and nobody seems confident in the cost assessment coming out of those two instances. All other cost studies seem to raise the question of whether the private sector, with newer facilities, can operate more cheaply than the public sector, in older prisons. It seems that is a bit of a loaded question, but nonetheless Hakim and Blackstone (2013) and others (Blumstein, Cohen, and Seth 2007) used state-level data to convince us of that very fact. Blumstein et al. (2007) went on to point out that privatization creates an incentive within public prisons to reduce costs in the face of competition, a point also made by Nelson (2005).

It seems that the real issue in the growth of privatization until the contraction of prison populations was the need for correctional agencies to quickly add prison capacity in times of restricted budgets. The Federal Bureau of Prisons, for example, last had a budget approved for building a new prison in 2009. But now the logic has changed to where decisions center on reducing prison capacity, not increasing it. The fact that the private-sector companies have all of their beds in new facilities provides them with a significant competitive edge if the declining population of inmates reaches the point where decisions must be made about how to reduce prison capacity. This is not to say that all of the advantages lie with the private sector. The Texas Department of Criminal Justice closed two private prisons in 2013 in response to declining population, thereby reducing prison capacity by 4,300 beds. One of the facilities was owned by the state and operated by the private vendor, but the other facility was both owned and managed by the private vendor. The closure of these two facilities followed the closing of an older public facility (Ward 2013). A private prison was closed in Mississippi; the closure was announced by CCA as based on declining need for the capacity of the facility (Corrections Corporation of America 2011).

Other states face the conundrum of deciding which prisons to close as they are facing smaller prison populations. In addition to Texas and Mississippi, states that closed prisons in 2013 were North Carolina, Georgia, Kentucky, New York, and Pennsylvania (Porter 2014). In some cases, private operators lost contracts as states were not satisfied with the performance of the private-sector prisons. North Carolina early on decided that the private sector provided insufficient staff and mismanaged two North Carolina prisons. By 2003, North Carolina bought the prisons from Correctional Properties Trust, the company that owned them (Chesser 2003). More recently, the scandal with CCA billing for unfilled staff hours at the Idaho Correctional Center led CCA to announce that it would not submit a bid for renewing the contract. After GEO also announced that it would not bid on the contract, the self-avowed pro-privatization Governor C. L. Otter announced that the prison would revert to state operations (Associated Press 2012; Boone 2013).

The real cost issue for states and the federal government is not who can do it cheaper but how can the government ensure that privatization arrangements are a good use of tax revenues. Nobody is interested in a repeat of the scandals listed above in either the public or private sectors. New prisons of appropriate size and design, whether operated by the public sector or the private sector, produce economies that provide for cheaper operations. Whether one sector does it with slightly different costs is not the only important issue, although introduction of competition into the system is a more compelling argument for the continued use or the introduction of private prisons in a prison system. Other issues indirectly related to cost are also compelling. What are the indirect issues involved in having tax dollars directed toward the private prisons as opposed to public prisons in terms of economic development (Genter, Hooks, and Mosher 2013)? Do communities benefit equally in community relations and charitable activities from each sector? Do private corporations, prison administrators, and public unions representing correctional workers affect the political process in similar ways? The private sector and public unions spend millions of dollars for lobbying activities. How do these activities influence criminal justice policy? These types of arguments are tertiary issues about the costs of public and private prisons and are too involved to address here, yet they are important to decisions about when to privatize and are often raised by stakeholders. The issues are broader than those typically raised but merit some attention (Hartney and Glesmann 2012; Price and Morris 2012).

III. Quality Issues

We must understand the mission of corrections to fully understand the issue of quality of services. Corrections is first and foremost part of the service sector, which is largely why many aspects of corrections resist the use of technology and other rationalization to reduce costs. The clientele is unique, but corrections policies are about housing and attending to the dietary, medical, educational, recreational, and custody needs of inmates. Corrections is about people interacting with other people to obtain major goals such as the protection of society, the protection of inmates, and the protection of staff working in corrections. The other major goal of corrections, preparing inmates for successful reentry into society, has assumed greater or lesser importance depending upon the politics and consequent funding of the time.

Correctional institutions, in both the public and private sectors, have a spotty history of providing professional services without scandal and sometimes violence. Correctional services are provided out of the public view for the most part, and care must be given to designing policies and practices that ensure proper practices. At one time, inmates served as prison tenders, or quasi-correctional officers, to control the behavior of other inmates, at least in some southern states. Even today, correctional systems place inmates in work positions where they can come into contact with prisoner files and other confidential information. The prison tender system and other uses of inmate labor provided and still provide cost savings, and oddly the prison tender system seemed to produce orderly prisons (Crouch and Marquart 1989). Of course, many alleged abuses and violence by the prison tenders helped bring these practices to an end. Breakdowns in communication and security practices have led to numerous riots in the public sector, including the notorious Attica prison riot of 1971 over conditions and political rights of inmates in New York state, the riots by Mariel Cubans in federal prisons in 1987 at Atlanta and Oakdale, Louisiana, and the extremely violent events in the New Mexico riot of 1981 (Useem and Kimball 1991).

The private sector is not without scandal either. In one of the earliest incidents, in 1999, low-security inmates at the Taft Correctional Institution, operated by GEO for the Federal Bureau of Prisons, staged a work and food strike over changes in prison policy, and the strikes ultimately escalated into a refusal of around 1,000 inmates to lock up for the 10 p.m. count. Although damage was minimal, quelling the riot included the use of tear gas, flash bangs, and sting-ball grenades. Less than lethal weapons other than those mentioned were brought into the compound (Camp and Daggett 2005, pp. 79–80). A riot occurred in 2011 at the North Fork Correctional Center in Sayre, Oklahoma, operated by CCA. A fight in the dining hall spread throughout the institution, with fighting primarily between blacks and Hispanics, especially members of Sureños. Another riot occurred at the Lake Erie Correctional Institution in Ohio after it was sold to CCA. The riot occurred in January 2013, and Ohio public personnel were activated to remove 39 inmates to a public Ohio prison (Stroud 2013). A 2013 riot at the Adams County Correctional Facility, operated by CCA for the Federal Bureau of Prisons, resulted in the death of a guard (Brooks 2012; Stroud 2014). According to the FBI, the cause of the Adams County riot was dissatisfaction with food and health care.

These cases are selective but typical of the problems faced in both the private and public correctional sectors. There have been other notable events, such as the well-publicized and initially undetected daytime escape of six violent inmates from the District of Columbia who were housed at the Northeast Ohio Correctional Center in 1998. The prison was operated by CCA. Researchers have explored whether problems of violence, riots, and escapes are more prevalent in one sector than the other (Archambeault and Deis 1996; Camp and Daggett 2005). The point of this discussion is not to belabor this debate but to acknowledge that quality issues exist in both sectors, and greater transparency in monitoring both private- and public-sector prisons is paramount (Kim and Price 2014). The million-dollar question is this: How is this monitoring accomplished? What are the components to track? The issue of monitoring has greater significance if prison populations continue to decrease in states and the federal government where the private sector has a strong presence. Monitoring is essential to ensure that correctional services are provided as decisions are made about capacity reduction.

Almost all U.S. prison systems, both public and private, try to meet the standards set by the American Correctional Association (ACA). Wardens and correctional staff take great pride in the accreditation of their facilities. In states and the federal government, if accreditation is expected of public prisons, then the same standards should apply to private prisons holding inmates from the respective jurisdictions. Less common is regulatory supervision by a state over a prison housing inmates from another state. This was the problem facing Ohio officials when District of Columbia inmates escaped from a prison in Ohio in 1998. Nonetheless, ACA standards are a requirement in all private-sector contracts of which I am aware. As does the public sector, the private sector proudly proclaims that the majority of their prisons are ACA accredited; see for example the CCA media page (CCA 2011).

Meeting ACA standards, though, does not ensure quality of operations—although it is hard to imagine quality operations in facilities not meeting ACA standards. Bad things still happen in facilities meeting ACA standards: Shortly after the 2013 riot at the Lake Erie prison, CCA announced that the facility had received an A+ accreditation rating (Stroud 2013). In early contracts for private prisons, comparability between the quality of operations in public and private prisons often was written into contracts. More recently, attention has focused upon meeting the standards written into the contract. At least one researcher took the position that satisfying the contract, basically reviewing the reports from public-sector staff who monitored the contract, was the proper method for ensuring quality (McDonald and Carlson 2005). While this is certainly a prerequisite, it seems that meeting ACA or contract standards is only the first hurdle: Prison systems should and often do go further in monitoring the quality of operations at their prisons.

One of the most common outcome measures against which prisons are assessed is inmate misconduct. Comparing misconduct is a useful exercise, but comparisons are often marred by differences between the inmate populations at the prisons being compared. For example, contracts for private prisons often include a contract provision that only healthy inmates are sent to the private facilities. While this makes sense from a management perspective and helps hold down costs at private facilities, a health-population provision has an unfortunate consequence for quality comparisons: Healthy inmates tend to be younger, and age has a well-known inverse relationship with antisocial behavior, including prison misconduct (Loeber and Farrington 2014). While the age–crime curve is bell-shaped, with an increase in the propensity to commit crime among youth and teens, by the time they become adults the propensity has peaked and declined. To ensure fair comparisons of misconduct at different prisons, statistical controls must be used to the extent possible, given the usual limitations of available data.

Research at the Federal Bureau of Prisons has demonstrated that both individual- and organizational-level variables influence the likelihood of misconduct (Harer and Steffensmeier 1996; Harer and Langan 2001; Camp et al. 2003; Camp and Daggett 2005). Excluding controls for these factors and comparing prisons on unadjusted means can provide misleading understandings of the relative performance of prisons (Camp, Saylor, and Wright 1999). Many prison systems cannot statistically model the effects of organizational factors because of the small number of prisons, but all statistical analyses of prison systems can control for individual-level effects when comparing prisons. While presenting the results of some form of regression analysis may seem complex, it is readily done. Adjusted values for each prison are readily calculated for statistical models of misconduct, whether the outcome is a rate, average, or probability. While policymakers and other consumers of prison research may not understand regression coefficients, they certainly understand results presented in such a way that prison X has twice as many instances of misconduct per month than prison Y after controlling for size and other differences in the prison population.

A path less taken in quality evaluations is using survey data to investigate prison conditions and compare prisons (for an exception, see work done at the Federal Bureau of Prison: Camp, Saylor, and Harer 1997; Camp 1999; Camp, Saylor, and Wright 1999; Camp and Gaes 2002b; Camp and Daggett 2005). Survey responses from inmates could provide information on satisfaction with the services provided to inmates. Service providers are keen to solicit feedback from their clients when the relationship between the service provider and the client is voluntary. In voluntary relationships, clients vote with their feet and use the services of other service providers when dissatisfied, whether with a hotel or restaurant. In nonvoluntary relationships such as prisons or welfare agencies, however, there seems to be trepidation about what the clients have to say about the system serving them. In nonsystematic discussions with prison administrators, prison officials have stated that inmate surveys are simply an opportunity for inmates to complain about everything under the sun. Interestingly, though, inmates do not uniformly respond with negative comments. In early research, the Federal Bureau of Prisons discovered that inmates at federal prisons, including the privately operated Taft Correctional Institution, provided more consistent results *within* prisons about local conditions than did staff when asked about similar conditions. However, there was significant variation across prisons in evaluations provided by inmates. Staff responses, on the other hand, were more consistent *across* prisons (Camp et al. 2002). In short, staff were more likely to provide similar responses to questions about the prison environment, whereas inmates provided responses that varied significantly across the different prisons.

In nonvoluntary relationships, the satisfaction of clients with services may be an interesting avenue to pursue. Especially with the wider acceptance of email and other intranet applications at prisons, data can be collected more easily than ever before. Instead of yearly data collections, data can be collected at shorter intervals at low cost, providing timelier feedback on safety, sanitation, dining, medical care, and any of the other services provided by prisons.

No one source of information adequately addresses issues of the quality of correctional services. There is little ongoing research on incorporating quality information about corrections. Compare this to the adaptation of a management tool from manufacturing industries that has produced a proliferation of hospital "scorecards" (for a recent application see Fieldston et al. 2014). Blumstein et al. (2007) note that the states that introduced private prisons into their systems saw cost savings in the public prisons. It is important to guarantee that these cost savings generated in the competition between public and private prisons do not come at the expense of the quality of services provided to inmates and the programs designed to reintroduce them into society. Prison programs are an important opportunity to provide remedial services and new training opportunities to a captive audience. This opportunity to provide programming services within a humane system of incarceration could easily fall prey to cost pressures caused by competition between the private and public sectors. Unless regulated, cost pressures can generate undesirable outcomes. My maternal grandfather told me the story of how as an adolescent he went to work in the coal mines. When he "graduated" to the job of leading the mules pulling the coal cars, he was instructed to keep the mules under the best roof possible. Even if *he* had to walk under a dangerous section of roof, he was to protect the mules because it cost money to replace the mules. The point is that actions without costs or penalties are often ignored.

Gaes et al. have discussed the unintended consequences of cost competition in correctional services (Gaes et al. 2004; Gaes 2010). In a bit of hyperbole borrowed from Ritzer (Ritzer 1993, 1998), Gaes discussed the rationalization of the work process in corrections. Ray Kroc realized that reducing tasks to their simplest elements could be accomplished in food services in the same manner that Adam Smith (1776) described for pin production. Kroc radically transformed the food service industry to where low-wage, fungible labor could be used to great profit. Ritzer picked up on this well-known example to discuss the over-rationalization of society. Apparently a similar exercise in rationalization is under way in corrections, as labor costs represent the bulk of all costs in all service industries, including corrections. The question, though, is whether there are negative consequences of these pressures. As Gaes (2010, p. 21) noted:

> Think of MacDonalds [*sic*] restaurants with cash registers that use symbols of the Big Mac and french fries, hamburgers that are already cut to specifications, pre-defined bins for each type of sandwich, and sundry other simplifications that make the routine simple and efficient. . . . Compare the correctional officer's routine of checking cells for contraband, monitoring inmate movement, and insuring doors are locked against the more subtle and perhaps more important skills of handling inmate grievances, disciplining inmates, as well as helping them through family and other personal crises. It is easy to see how the former can be re-engineered for low skilled, lower paid workers. It is more difficult to see how the latter skills can be simplified using a cookbook approach.

Private contractors have experienced problems in the past with staffing their prisons. In a preliminary examination of the effects of using lower-paid labor in the private sector, private prisons in the United States had much higher rates of turnover than the public-sector Federal Bureau of Prison prisons (Camp and Gaes 2000, 2002a). While part of this difference was the result of new prisons undergoing activation, where turnover is higher, the relationship held even for prisons that had been operating for a number of years. In at least one more recent case, CCA had difficulties maintaining an adequate workforce at the Idaho Correctional Center. CCA filed reports stating that the contractually mandated number of correctional positions had been filled but later admitted that for several months in 2012 the reports were false and the prison had been understaffed (Boone 2013).

Given pressures generated by competition between the public and private sectors, an emphasis on the quality of correctional services remains important. Ensuring that the pressures to lower costs do not have an adverse impact on correctional services may become more important if the prison industry as a whole begins to contract. The pressures actually may become more intense in the public prisons, where the prison infrastructure is older on average and cutting programs may be attractive to lower costs, although this is purely speculative. The important point is that better research and better monitoring methods are needed to provide transparency and improve the provision of correctional services.

IV. Conclusion

It is hard to imagine that the 50 percent growth in private-sector prisons, such as that experienced in the 13 years between 2000 and 2012, will continue. As prison populations contract, it is much easier to imagine that private beds will account for a greater proportion of the remaining beds in the U.S. prison population, but actual growth in the number of private beds will be much more modest. Private prisons are well positioned, at least with respect to infrastructure, to outcompete older public prisons for inmates. During the period of rapid growth in private prisons, the private sector competed with the hypothetical costs of new public prisons. Few legislatures had the funds, willingness, or even capacity requirements to construct multiple prisons for the purposes of conducting research to compare public and private operations. Plus, it was politically expedient to hide the costs of building prisons within the contracts for services to private operators. No bond referenda were needed to raise these funds. There were a few exceptions to this general pattern, such as those discussed in Louisiana and the Federal Bureau of Prisons, but no conclusive evidence was produced from the resulting studies that all parties accepted (Archambeault and Deis 1996; McDonald and Carlson 2005; Nelson 2005). With a decline in the prison population, a new economic imperative will prompt competition among the prisons currently in operation. It is here that the private sector has a significant advantage.

Corrections is an important part of modern society, even if correctional services are provided out of the public view. Correctional agencies are responsible for the lives and safety of the inmates and staff within the confines of prison and for the safety of the public beyond the confines. Given the potential for things to go wrong in modern corrections and the importance of preparing individuals for a successful return to society, the public sector must use all tools available when holding our fellow humans in custody. Most parties have recognized that private prisons are part of the arsenal of tools that address the needs of the prison system. This is not a naïve assertion that private prisons are the answer to all correctional needs; the extreme privatization argument that market forces somehow ensure success overlooks the behavior of corporations operating as oligopolies, the many scandals of private-sector cost overruns in government procurements, and the documented failures of private prisons in providing correctional services. Both private and public providers have failed, currently experience problems, and will probably continue to have at least some issues in the future. Despite mixed messages about the coddling of inmates, most Americans expect inmates to leave prison better off than when they entered (Jonson, Cullen, and Lux 2013). That is, Americans expect prisons to play some role in preventing crime. At the very least, a step toward realizing this expectation of the correctional enterprise can be taken by providing correctional services in a transparent manner.

The point implied throughout this discussion is that cost is a very important factor in the continued use of corrections, but the shift from growth to stable or declining prison populations changed the dynamic to where cost is now secondary to the issue of quality in the use of private prisons. Previously, the argument about whether to privatize was predicated on the respective abilities of the public and private sectors to operate *new* prisons. It seems clear that the private sector had a competitive advantage in adding new prison capacity, namely its ability to construct prisons quickly at lower cost. However, the advantage of the private sector in running prisons more cheaply was less clear based on the empirical evidence (Kish and Lipton 2013). What is more important in an era of stable or declining prison populations is whether to shutter public or private prisons. In that competition, the private sector will be favored when it comes to cost issues, and if they provide comparable services, then there is a clear logic to retain private prisons. To be sure, aging prisons, which are primarily held by the public sector, need to be replaced. CCA clearly believes that the number of inmates housed in aging prisons provides business opportunities for them, as noted in their 2013 10K filing with the Securities and Exchange Commission. However, it is difficult to foresee when the political will and funds for new construction will return to state and federal legislatures, which are still reeling under the impact of the massive buildup of correctional populations. It will be interesting to see if there is further consolidation in an industry already dominated by two competitors in the search for corporate growth during a period when other avenues of expansion seem to be cut off, at least in the short run.

Most of the discussion presented here was from the viewpoint of the public sector working with the private sector to secure correctional services. A perspective not usually entertained is that of the private sector itself. Until recently, the private-prison industry experienced a growth market since its inception in 1984. Demand for the product, additional beds for correctional services, expanded wildly during the period prior to 2009. It was the expanding need for additional correctional beds that led Doc Crants, Tom Beasley, and Don Hutto to join together in 1983 and form CCA. George Zoley was not far behind at Wackenhut, now GEO. The market has now entered a mature phase in which no growth or decline in the need for prison beds is the norm. In the case of corrections, the equilibrium may exist for years, at least in terms of the need for prison beds. The new competition for the private sector as it pursues growth is for existing beds in the public sector. There are a number of strategies hinted at previously that the private sector can take in response to a maturing market. One response is to consolidate the industry even further into the two largest companies, CCA and GEO, to provide growth for these two companies. There are limits to this strategy, however, as the two companies already dominate the market. The other strategy that CCA noted is to target the abundance of prison beds in older prisons as an area of private-sector growth. While CCA noted that there were almost 400,000 inmates in beds in prisons that had been in operation for at least 50 years, no information was provided on when those prisons were last renovated. Nonetheless, changing or supplementing the emphasis of political lobbying to include modernization of correctional facilities is another possible avenue for the private sector. Finally, an area where the private sector is already having some success is the holding of illegal aliens prior to hearings to determine whether the United States will proceed with deportation or whether the individuals will face incarceration for felonies committed. This is a much more volatile market, as the stays are very short, not as predictable as for sentenced inmates, and largely dependent on short-term policy shifts and budgets.

DISCLAIMER

The views expressed here are those of the author and do not represent the views of either the Federal Bureau of Prisons or the U.S. Department of Justice.

NOTES

1. In August of 2014, the Federal Bureau of Prison had 28,217 inmates in privately-operated prisons. Compare this to the total number of all federal inmates in Canada which is about 15,000 after a decade of growth (http://www.cbc.ca/news/canada-s-prison-population-at-all-time-high-1.2440039).
2. The Lake Erie Correctional facility was built in 1999 by the state of Ohio and sold to CCA in 2011.

REFERENCES

Archambeault, W. G., and D. R. Deis. 1996. *Cost Effectiveness Comparisons of Private Versus Public Prisons in Louisiana: A Comprehensive Analysis of Allen, Avoyelles, and Winn Correctional Centers*. Baton Rouge: Louisiana State University.

Associated Press. 2012. "Corrections Firm Offers States Cash for Prisons." *USA Today*, https://www.yahoo.com/news/corrections-firm-offers-states-cash-170846144.html.

Blumstein, Alfred, and Allen F. Beck. 1999. "Population Growth in U.S. Prisons, 1980–1996." In *Prisons*, edited by Michael Tonry and Joan Petersilia. Chicago: University of Chicago Press.

Blumstein, James F., Mark A. Cohen, and Suman Seth. 2007. "Do Government Agencies Respond to Market Pressures? Evidence from Private Prisons." *Vanderbilt Law and Economics Research Paper No. 03-16; Vanderbilt Public Law Research Paper No. 03-05*. Nashville, TN.

Boone, Rebecca. 2013. *AP Newsbreak: Prison Company Leaving Idaho*. AP News, http://bigstory.ap.org/article/ap-newsbreak-prison-company-leaving-idaho.

Brooks, Karen. 2012. "Inmates Riot in Mississippi Prisons, One Guard Killed." *Chicago Tribune*, http://articles.chicagotribune.com/2012-05-21/news/sns-rt-us-prison-riot-mississippibre84ko4l-20120520_1_inmates-riot-prison-yard-low-security-facility.

Camp, Scott D. 1999. "Do Inmate Survey Data Reflect Prison Conditions? Using Surveys to Assess Prison Conditions of Confinement." *Prison Journal* 79:250–268.

Camp, Scott D., and D. M. Daggett. 2005. *Evaluation of the Taft Demonstration Project: Performance of a Private-Sector Prison and the BOP*. Washington, DC: Federal Bureau of Prisons.

Camp, Scott D., and Gerald G. Gaes. 2000. *Private Prisons in the United States, 1999: An Assessment of Growth, Performance, Custody Standards, and Training Requirements*. Washington, DC: Federal Bureau of Prisons.

Camp, Scott D., and Gerald G. Gaes. 2002a. "Growth and Quality of U.S. Private Prisons: Evidence from a National Survey." *Criminology and Public Policy* 1:427–450.

Camp, Scott D., and Gerald G. Gaes. 2002b. "Quality of Prison Operations in the US Federal Sector: A Comparison with a Private Prison." *Punishment and Society* 4:27–54.

Camp, Scott D., Gerald G. Gaes, Jody Klein-Saffran, Dawn M. Daggett, and William G. Saylor. 2002. "Using Inmate Survey Data in Assessing Prison Performance: A Case Study Comparing Private and Public Prisons." *Criminal Justice Review* 27:26–51.

Camp, Scott D., Gerald G. Gaes, Neal P. Langan, and William G. Saylor. 2003. "The Influence of Prisons on Inmate Misconduct: A Multilevel Investigation." *Justice Quarterly* 20:501–533.

Camp, Scott D., William G. Saylor, and Miles D. Harer. 1997. "Aggregating Individual-Level Evaluations of the Organizational Social Climate: A Multilevel Investigation of the Work Environment at the Federal Bureau of Prisons." *Justice Quarterly* 14:739–761.

Camp, Scott D., William G. Saylor, and Kevin N. Wright. 1999. "Creating Performance Measures from Survey Data: A Practical Discussion." *Corrections Management Quarterly* 3:71–80.

Carson, E. Ann, and Daniela Golinelli. 2013. *Correctional Populations in the United States*. Washington, DC: Bureau of Justice Statistics.

Chesser, Paul. 2003. "State Sours on Private Prisons." *Carolina Journal News Reports*, http://www.carolinajournal.com/articles/display_story.html?id=957.

Corrections Corporation of America. 2011. "News Release: CCA and the State of Mississippi Announce Closure of the Delta Correctional Facility." http://ir.correctionscorp.com/phoenix.zhtml?c=117983&p=irol-newsArticle&ID=1629142&highlight=

Crouch, Ben M., and James W. Marquart. 1989. *An Appeal to Justice: Litigated Reform of Texas Prisons*. Austin: University of Texas Press.

Culp, Richard F. 2005. "The Rise and Stall of Prison Privatization: An Integration of Policy Analysis Perspectives." *Criminal Justice Policy Review* 16:412–442.

Fieldston, Evan S., Lisa B. Zaoutis, Paula M. Agosto, Annie Guo, Jennifer A. Jonas, and Nicholas Tsarouhas. 2014. "Measuring Patient Flow in a Children's Hospital Using a Scorecard with Composite Measurement." *Journal of Hospital Medicine* 9:463–468. doi: 10.1002/jhm.2202.

Gaes, Gerald G. 2010. *The Current Status of Prison Privatization Research on American Prisons*. Working Paper. Tallahassee: Florida State University.

Gaes, Gerald G., Scott D. Camp, Julianne B. Nelson, and William G. Saylor. 2004. "Measuring Prison Performance." In *Violence Prevention and Policy Series*, edited by Mark S. Fleisher. Lanham, MD: Alta Mira Press.

Genter, Shaun, Gregory Hooks, and Clayton Mosher. 2013. "Prisons, Jobs and Privatization: The Impact of Prisons on Employment Growth in Rural US Counties, 1997–2004." *Social Science Research* 42:596–610.

Glaze, Lauren E., and Erinn J. Herberman. 2013. *Correctional Populations in the United States, 2012*. Washington, DC: Bureau of Justice Statistics.

Hakim, Simon, and Erwin A. Blackstone. 2013. *Cost Analysis of Public and Contractor-Operated Prisons*. Philadelphia: Center for Competitive Government.

Hallett, Michael A. 2006. *Private Prisons in America*. Chicago: University of Illinois Press.

Harer, Miles D., and Neal P. Langan. 2001. "Gender Differences in Predictors of Prison Violence: Assessing the Predictive Validity of a Risk Classification System." *Crime and Delinquency* 47:513–536.

Harer, Miles D., and Darrell Steffensmeier. 1996. "Race and Prison Violence." *Criminology* 34:323–355.

Hartney, Christopher, and Caroline Glesmann. 2012. *Prison Bed Profiteers: How Corporations Are Reshaping Criminal Justice in the US*. National Council on Crime and Delinquency.

In the Public Interest. 2013. *How Lockup Quotas and "Low-Crime Taxes" Guarantee Profits for Private Prison Corporation*. http://www.inthepublicinterest.org/sites/default/files/Criminal-Lockup%20Quota-Report.pdf

Jonson, Cheryl Lero, Francis T. Cullen, and Jennifer L. Lux. 2013. "Creating Ideological Space: Why Public Support for Rehabilitation Matters." In *What Works in Offender Rehabilitation: An Evidence-Based Approach to Assessment and Treatment*, edited by Leam A. Craig, Theresa A. Gannon, and Louise Dixon. New York: John Wiley & Sons.

Kim, Younhee, and Byron E. Price. 2014. "Revisiting Prison Privatization: An Examination of the Magnitude of Prison Privatization." *Administration and Society* 46:255–275.

Kirkham, Chris. 2012. "Private Prison Corporation Offers Case in Exchange for State Prisons." *Huffington Post*, http://www.huffingtonpost.com/2012/02/14/private-prisons-buying-state-prisons_n_1272143.html.

Kish, Richard J., and Amy F. Lipton. 2013. "Do Private Prisons Really Offer Savings Compared with their Public Counterparts?" *Economic Affairs* 33:93–107.

Kunkel, Karl R., and Jason S. Capps. 2005. "Privatization." In *Encyclopedia of Prisons & Correctional Facilities*, edited by Mary Bosworth. Thousand Oaks, CA: Sage.

Loeber, Rolf, and David P. Farrington. 2014. "Age-Crime Curve." In *Encyclopedia of Criminology and Criminal Justice*, edited by Gerben Burinsma and David Weisburd. New York: Springer.

Logan, Charles H. 1990. *Private Prisons: Cons and Pros*. New York: Oxford University Press.

Logan, Charles H. 1992. "Well Kept: Comparing Quality of Confinement in Private and Public Prisons." *Journal of Criminal Law and Criminology* 83:577–613.

Mauer, Marc. 1999. *Race to Incarcerate*. New York: New York Press.

McDonald, Douglas C., and Kenneth Carlson. 2005. *Cost and Performance of the Privately Operated Taft Correctional Institution*. Cambridge, MA: Abt. Associates.

Nelson, Julianne. 2005. *Competition in Corrections: Comparing Public and Private Sector Operations*. Boston: CNA Corporation.

Pavlo, Walter. 2012. "Corrections Corp. of America on Buying Spree—State Prisons for Sale?" *Forbes*, http://www.forbes.com/sites/walterpavlo/2012/02/14/corrections-corp-of-america-on-buying-spree-state-prisons-for-sale.

Perrone, Dina, and Travis C. Pratt. 2003. "Comparing the Quality of Confinement and Cost-Effectiveness of Public Versus Private Prisons: What We Know, Why We Do Not Know More, and Where to Go From Here." *Prison Journal* 83:301–322.

Porter, Nicole D. 2014. *On the Chopping Block 2013: State Prison Closures*. Washington, DC: The Sentencing Project.

Price, Byron Eugene, and John Charles Morris. 2012. *Prison Privatization: The Many Facets of a Controversial Industry*, volume 1. ABC-CLIO.

Ritzer, George. 1993. *The McDonaldization of Society*. Newbury Park, CA: Pine Forge Press.

Ritzer, George. 1998. *The McDonaldization Thesis: Explorations and Extensions*. Thousand Oaks, CA: *Sage*.

Smith, Adam. 1776. *An Inquiry into the Nature and Causes of the Wealth of Nations*. London: W. Strahan and T. Cadell.

Stroud, Matt. 2013. "Ohio Prison Reboots After Weekend Riot." *Forbes*, www.forbes.com/sites/mattstroud/2013/01/13/ohio-private-prison-reboots-after-weekend-riot.

Stroud, Matt. 2014. "The Private Prison Racket." *Politico*, http://www.politico.com/magazine/story/2014/02/private-prison-racket-103893.html.

Thomas, Charles W. 1997. *Comparing the Cost and Performance of Public and Private Prisons in Arizona*. Arizona Department of Corrections.

Useem, Bert, and Peter Kimball. 1991. *States of Siege: U.S. Prison Riots, 1971–1986*. New York: Oxford University Press.

Ward, Mike. 2013. "Officials: Two Private Prisons to Close." http://www.statesman.com/news/news/officials-two-private-prisons-to-close/nYH3w/.

Weiss, Robert P. 2005. "Privatization of Labor." In *Encyclopedia of Prisons and Correctional Facilities*, edited by Mary Bosworth. Thousand Oaks, CA: Sage.

....

CHAPTER 29

POLICY AND PROGRAM
INNOVATIONS IN PRISONS

....

FAYE S. TAXMAN AND BRANDY BLASKO

U.S. PRISONS, as total institutions, are unique environments. During earlier periods, prisoners were isolated in their cells and required to remain silent. This was considered important to the reformation process because it allowed prisoners to simultaneously suffer and renounce their lives of criminal activity. Reformatories of the early 1900s allowed prisoners to interact; reduced risk for criminal activity was judged by observing the prisoner's behavior. Today, the modern U.S. prison differs significantly from prior periods. The policies that guide prison operations and the programming offered to prisoners reflect many, often conflicting, goals, such as deterrence, retribution, rehabilitation, and incapacitation, and prison managers must decide how best to administer and run their facility to meet their goals.

Section I presents advances in policies that emphasize the Risk-Need-Responsivity (RNR) framework, reentry, and good-time credits in order to emphasize how these policies provide a foundation for the expansion of prison programming. Section II outlines recent attention to novel programming approaches, including efforts to build self-efficacy through strength-based approaches, build attachments and empathy to advance interpersonal skills, and address obstacles to reentry to the community. Section III moves beyond attention to novel and innovative approaches to prison programming and considers the role of legitimacy in the prison regime and culture. A research agenda is offered to advance policy and program innovations in prison settings. The main conclusions discussed in this chapter are:

- Three main philosophies guide prison policies: RNR (Andrews and Bonta 2010), reentry policies, and earned release. Prison policies have a major impact on prison programming in defining what is acceptable to provide to inmates.
- The policy focus of a jurisdiction will influence the type of prison programs offered and the goals achieved by the institutions.
- Legitimacy in prisons is the missing component and is needed to ensure that prison policies and programs achieve their goals. Innovation in policies and programs is contingent on the prison regime's ability to maintain integrity in their operations.

I. Prison Policies

Prison policies are often developed with the input of three bodies: (a) judicial, sentencing commissions, and legislatures; (b) executive agencies; and (c) prison wardens. The perspectives of each group could differentially influence how the prison operates and which goals and objectives are emphasized. To a large extent, prison policies have a major impact on prison programming in defining what is acceptable to provide to inmates. During the 1990s and early 2000s, their focus returned to the enhancement of prison programming that would advance the offender's education and well-being. Emphasis also returned to policies of segregation and deprivation of the offender, which limited such efforts to provide personal growth and advancement. The renewed emphasis on release processes in the early 2000s, "reentry," underlined a concern for the after-prison experience, which in turn altered the focus of prison programming to focus on life skills (e.g., education, employment) (Phelps 2012). In this section we will review three main philosophies guiding prison policies: RNR (Andrews and Bonta 2010), reentry policies, and earned release.

A. RNR Framework

A focus on rehabilitation in the context of punishment and incapacitation is embedded in Andrew and Bonta's (2010) RNR model. According to the RNR framework, those at higher risk for recidivism should receive the most intensive services; services should target dynamic, criminogenic needs; and services should be tailored to meet the individual needs of prisoners (see Chapter 19 of this volume for a detailed discussion). This framework provides a way in which the information collected from a prisoner at classification and throughout incarceration can be used to inform security and treatment recommendations. For example, prisoners with more criminogenic risk factors, or dynamic risk factors that drive and contribute to criminal behavior, may be placed at a higher-risk facility and may participate in a higher dosage of treatment compared to their lower-risk counterparts (Andrews, Bonta, and Wormith 2006; Andrews and Bonta 2010). The RNR framework offers a conceptual model that can inform classification and treatment programming policies in prisons.

1. *Risk and Needs Assessment as Part of Prison Classification Policy*

The broad purpose of the initial diagnostic and classification in prisons is "to assign the inmate to the appropriate security and custody level consistent with the risk that is presented to the institution, staff, and other inmates, as well as to respond to the needs of the inmate" (Walsh 2001, p. 140). While the diagnostic and classification process can vary by jurisdiction, many prison systems use it to determine the appropriate prison and housing placement of prisoners. Questions may be asked about prior institutional violence, severity of index offense(s), assault history, and escape history. Potential security issues, such as need for separation from other prisoners or gang affiliations, are often determined and assessment tools may be used to rule out health and mental health needs.

Similar to advancements in general offender risk assessment tools, arguably more advanced assessment tools have been developed in recent years for use in prisons. Modern prison classification systems go beyond concern for institutional security and address a prisoner's program needs at the time of reception and classification. At classification, programs are recommended based upon the prisoner's needs. The intent is to consider not only the offender's behavior while in prison but also how participation in in-prison services and programs can affect transition to the community and criminal justice outcomes (e.g., arrest, substance use). As shown in Figure 29.1, the National Institute of Corrections Transition from Prison to Community (TPC; National Institute of Corrections 2002) recommends the use of standardized risk and need assessments both during the institutional phase and during the transition to the community.

Improvements in the technology of risk and need assessments and advances in research have resulted in moving away from clinical judgment and toward the use of standardized classification instruments. Using solely clinical judgment would involve staff using their discretion to determine the importance and utility of different pieces of information, such as the staff's attitudes and values regarding treatment of offenders. Relying solely on clinical judgment often results in staff failing to use policy to guide classification decisions. For example, staff may allow extralegal factors (e.g., race, geographical location) to guide decisions about service recommendations.

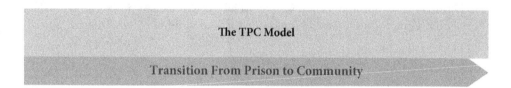

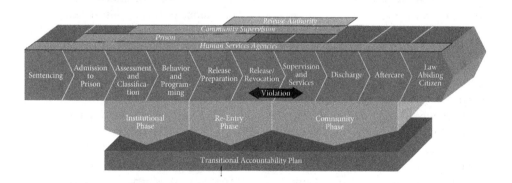

OR, MO, MI, IN, ND, RI, NY, GA

Transition from Prison to Community Initiative

FIGURE 29.1. National Institute of Corrections Transition from Prison to Community (TPC) model.

The RNR model provides a useful framework to guide risk and need assessment policy for the classification of prisoners. Pertaining to prison management, risk assessment information can inform prison behavior and recidivism after release from prison. Many actuarial risk assessment instruments are limited in that they assess only static factors related to criminal justice outcomes (e.g., history of violence). However, the assessment of both static and dynamic risk provides information that is useful when determining the service and program needs in prison to better prepare the prisoner for the transition to the community. These dynamic risk factors, which include antisocial cognitions and values, antisocial personality, antisocial peers and family networks, substance abuse, employment and education deficits, and low self-control, are believed to augment the risk assessment process to include factors amenable to change. Services and programs can then be recommended at the time of classification to address the changeable risk factors. Finally, some assessments incorporate a case planning approach to ensure that prisoners receive not only indicated and appropriate levels of care to increase the chances of change, but also ongoing assessment of dynamic risk factors throughout treatment to assess whether change is indeed evident.

Recent empirical findings question the ability of some risk assessment tools to simultaneously capture factors associated with prison misconduct and recidivism upon release from prison. Weinrath and Coles (2003) found that static risk factors were the best predictors of institutional misconduct, whereas dynamic factors predicted later criminal recidivism. Similarly, Latessa et al. (2010) found different predictors of prison behavior and release behavior. Thus far, research findings suggest dynamic, criminogenic needs predictive of recidivism upon release from prison are not useful in predicting institutional misconduct. Prison policies framed using the RNR model need to be mindful of these differences.

2. RNR in Prison Programming Policy

With regard to prisoner programming specifically, the RNR framework posits that to reduce recidivism, a prisoner's individual criminogenic needs must be targeted when recommending programs and reassessed over the course of treatment. Programs should also be flexible and allow for person-specific changes (e.g., modifications due to cognitive deficits). The use of effective treatment intervention strategies is also important. Cognitive-behavioral therapy (CBT) techniques (see Chapter 19 of this volume) are the most effective approach for the prisoner population. Prisoners who participate in CBT show a reduction in future offending by 20 to 30 percent upon release (Landenberger and Lipsey 2005) and can demonstrate a reduction in prison misconduct (French and Gendreau 2006).

While modest empirical support for rehabilitation programs that follow all three principles of the RNR model has emerged (Marques, Day, Nelson, and Miner 1989; Hanson and Morton-Bourgon 2004; Kirsch and Becker 2006), it has been argued that the treatment programs following the RNR model create necessary but insufficient conditions for effective treatment (Ward and Gannon 2006; Lindsay, Ward, Morgan, and Wilson 2007). The RNR model has been criticized for its focus on criminogenic risk factors, or deficits, to the exclusion of other variables that may help offenders lead more productive, prosocial, and fulfilling lives: strength-based approaches (e.g., motivational interviewing [Miller and Rollnick 2013], Good Lives Model [Ward and Stewart 2003; Ward and Brown 2004; Ward and Marshall 2004]). Historically, our approach to managing and treating prisoners embraced the medical model; the main emphasis was on managing and treating pathology and deficits. Strengths-based approaches represent a new paradigm in offender management and treatment. Rather than viewing the prisoner through a deficit lens, this new approach considers and focuses on both risks and strengths. The core concepts of strengths-based approaches are:

- Individuals have an innate need to recognize their strengths.
- Criminal justice practitioners should assist offenders in identifying and increasing awareness of their strengths.
- Criminal justice practitioners use the offender's existing strengths and the current situation as a starting point of treatment.
- Offenders develop an outlook that positive things can happen and that they can direct good things happening in their lives.
- The focus is on identifying risk factors and building on existing strengths identified in collaboration with the therapist or practitioner (Guterman 2006; Smith 2006).

3. *Using the Risk and Needs Assessment as Part of Prison Policy*

Using risk and need assessment frameworks to inform prison policy is important. Taxman et al. (2013) report that only 164,000 to 196,000 prisoners of the 1.2 million in need of substance abuse treatment (13 to 16 percent of all prisoners) receive services. Further, most of the available services are meant for substance abusers rather than individuals with substance dependence concerns. Placing prisoners with substance dependence in a treatment program for substance abuse means they will not receive the appropriate dosage of treatment or the appropriate clinical care to meet their needs and subsequently reduce their risk. Taxman et al. (2013) have demonstrated, using their RNR Simulation Model, that when program guidelines are modeled after risk and need components, the number of individuals returning to prison can be reduced by 3.4 percent. Finally, larger reductions of 6.7 percent can be achieved by improving policies surrounding the quality of programming (Pattavina and Taxman 2013; Taxman, Caudy, and Pattavina 2013). The application of the RNR model can produce significant improvement in incarceration rates.

B. Reentry as a Prison Policy

The concept of reentry emerged from the growing realization that nearly 650,000 individuals are released from prison each year, and that long periods of incarceration have negative impacts on resumption of civil responsibilities. While reentry ideas were welcomed, it was initially unclear whether the prison or the paroling authority was responsible for the transition period. Thus, reentry as a policy became the responsibility of prison systems in that their case management, discharge planning, treatment programming, and working relationships with the parole and/or probation systems had to be defined and operationalized.

The concept of reentry challenged the system to consider the transition point as a process that deserved separate attention. Subsequently, several models of reentry emerged. The first one in the early 2000s, the Reentry Partnership Initiative (RPI), viewed reentry as a process with multiple actors. RPI emphasized that the reentry process was not only under the ownership of the prison and parole systems, but that local police, service providers, families, religious organizations, and/or churches were also important collaborators. The notion was that the partnership should facilitate the use of formal social controls (e.g., prison, parole supervision, law enforcement) to supervise prisoners as they begin to learn to use informal social controls (e.g., family, social peers, community organizations) as a means of support. RPI provided a forum for a wide variety of organizations to become involved in the reentry process, as well as a role for the partners in facilitating successful transition of prisoners to the community. Several models resulted:

1. The police-prison-parole (or probation supervision) model: This partnership was meant to assure the returning offender that the group was there to assist with the transition process, including offering reentry sessions before release to the community.
2. The restorative justice model: This involved prison, parole, and victims, including offender–victim mediation sessions to repair harm and facilitate return to the community.
3. The family model: This focused on better linkages to support systems in the community.

These models can build partnerships, clarify roles within different components of the process, and facilitate discharge planning, to include partnering on new boundary-less systems of policies and procedures (Taxman, Young, and Byrne 2003).

The National Institute of Corrections (NIC) also developed two conceptual models of the transition process: Transition from Prison to Community and Transition from Jail to Community. The NIC models integrate the RNR framework with many of the RPI ideas into a three-stage model (see Figure 29.1) with an institutional prison phase, a reentry phase, and a community phase. The NIC models emphasize several key principles:

1. Development and use of interdisciplinary, collaborative leadership teams that are created by the leaders in corrections to address reentry efforts at state and local levels
2. Development of a strategic plan that gives attention to the unmet needs of offenders and the factors that influence recidivism, and to develop policies, procedures, and resources for reentry
3. Use of improved transitioning, including the various stages from commitment to prison and continuing through assessment, prison programming, preparation for release, release, and supervision in the community, and to develop a planned process whereby all agencies collaborate
4. Involvement of non-correctional stakeholders, such as public, private, and community agencies that can provide services and support as reentry efforts are planned and implemented
5. Assurance that offenders are provided with basic resources (e.g., food, clothing, housing, employment) and have identification documents, appropriate medications, linkages to community services and informal networks of support after they are released from prison

6. Implementation of valid risk and needs assessments at various stages of the offender's movement through the system
7. Use of effective interventions (evidence-based) that address assessment-identified risks and criminogenic needs
8. Expansion of the traditional roles of correctional staff beyond custody and security to include an integrated approach to offender management that engages offenders in the process of change
9. Means of monitoring the system through solid outcome data and information that can be used for planning.

The Transition from Prison to Community model was implemented initially in eight states as part of a demonstration project led by the NIC and collaborators. The eight states pursued different components as they advanced their reentry policies and practices. Missouri focused on developing transition housing units in their prison system to facilitate more discharge planning and to emphasize reentry programming. Georgia emphasized a fatherhood initiative program to help prisoners improve social ties and strengthen their connection with support systems and informal social controls. In Michigan, the Michigan Prisoner Reentry Initiative targeted four phases: (1) in prison, to help prisoners prepare for release; (2) during release, to assess the terms and conditions of release tied to the risk and needs assessment; (3) in the community, to use the period of supervision to provide services to improve community supervision; and (4) the case management plan, which emphasizes goals and criteria for discharge from parole. As shown in these examples, states selected different areas in which to improve reentry policies and practices, and targeted their efforts to achieve gains in developing reentry processes where none existed. A major emphasis was on using risk and need assessment and evidence-based programming in all phases of the prison-to-community efforts.

C. Good-Time Credits, Earned Credit

Good-time credits, or the awarding of credits for successful participation in prison programs, good behavior, and compliance with prison rules, was a common policy in prisons prior to the 1990s. Good-time credits could be used as incentives for prisoners to comply with the prison rules, and the policy was effective for prison managers in that it helped reduce prison overcrowding by reducing the overall length of sentences (DiIulio 1990). However, eventually mandatory-minimum policies (implemented in 1995) and truth-in-sentencing policies (with the emphasis on prisoners serving 85 percent or more of their sentence in prison) altered the degree to which good-time credits could serve as an incentive for better conduct in prison.

Earned release, another form of good-time credits, has been renewed and creatively instituted in prison policy as a way to encourage prisoners to participate in work, educational, and treatment programs. A recent survey of the National Conference of State Legislatures found that 31 states had some policies supporting earned-release credits or good-time credits. This includes 21 states that provide earned-release time credits for completing educational programs in prison and 18 states that provide credits for work-related programs. These earned credits are authorized by state legislatures and are used to recognize the importance of program participation. Most states do not allow offenders with mandatory-minimum sentences to be eligible for earned credit unless their minimum time has been served. The reinstatement of earned-credit policies is part of changing prison policy that recognizes the value of offenders participating in educational, work, or rehabilitative programs in terms of preparing them for return to the community.

II. Prison Programs

The renewed interest in changing offender outcomes after release and the expansion of policies that promote the RNR framework and reentry have contributed to a wide range of innovative programs offered in prisons today. Many prison programs are concerned with effecting offender change. This section describes some innovative programs currently offered in prisons, outlining how they are implemented based upon varying beliefs about how people can improve their quality of life both within prison and upon release.

A. Good Lives Model

Recently, in part due to the emphasis on offender-level deficits (i.e., risk and need factors) in the RNR model, the Good Lives Model and the Self-Regulation Model (SRM-R) have been developed as an alternative to existing models of offender treatment and supervision. The alternative nature is borrowed from the positive psychology movement, where the emphasis is on building on a person's strengths to counter deficits or factors that may contribute to offending. A strength-based approach recognizes that individuals have both positive and negative attributes, but the goal is to strengthen the positive factors to counter the negative ones. The Good Lives Model emerged as a therapeutic approach to focus on the individual. It has primarily been used for sex offenders (Lindsay et al. 2007; Whitehead et al. 2007), though recently it has been used with juvenile offenders, offenders with mental health concerns, and individuals under probation and parole supervision (Purvis, Ward, and Shaw 2013).

Treatment directed by the RNR framework aims primarily to reduce offenders' risk of reoffending by motivating them to address their criminogenic needs and dynamic risk factors for reoffending. Under the Good Lives Model framework, clinicians and providers are directed not only to consider the criminogenic or deficit-based dynamic factors that contribute to offending, but also to understand each prisoner's unique values, life position, and goals when conceptualizing management strategies and treatment planning. To use the Good Lives Model and the SRM-R in treatment, a distinct individualized approach is required. This framework is based on the understanding that each individual has basic or primary needs that drive human behavior, and criminal behavior represents a maladaptive way to achieve these needs (Yates, Prescott, and Ward 2010). From this conceptualization, it follows that offending may be curbed if an offender's unique needs are understood and if more adaptive means of achieving these primary needs are developed (Ward and Stewart 2003).

The Good Lives Model framework considers an offender's personal goals as important and valued and encourages offenders to recognize that the problem is not in the goal but rather in the means they are using to achieve the goal (Yates, Prescott, and Ward 2010). By examining their pathways to offending and offense-related goals and strategies (SRM-R), offenders can identify which of the primary goals outlined in the Good Lives Model are important to them: life, knowledge, being good at work and play, personal choice and independence, peace of mind, relationships and friends, community, spirituality, happiness, and creativity. For example, if an offender identifies personal choice and independence as important, one way he may have met this goal in the past was by controlling, dominating, or abusing others, viewing the world as a dangerous place, or feeling that he had to "get" others before they got him. In treatment using a CBT approach, an offender would work to realize that personal choice and independence were important to him and would continue working to achieve personal choice and independence, but by building prosocial ways to do so (e.g., by being assertive or learning to identify goals and to work toward those goals rather than to simply demand needs using control or abuse). The ultimate goal of treatment is to develop an integrated Good Lives plan. When used with sex offenders, research on the Good Lives Model and SRM-R frameworks has shown positive preliminary results (Willis and Ward 2013; Willis, Ward, and Levenson 2013). For example, sex offenders enrolled in treatment groups that use Good Lives plans versus relapse-prevention plans report improved satisfaction with programming.

It is challenging for clinicians to implement the Good Lives Model in a prison setting because it requires a great deal of individualized attention and time. Therefore, creative mechanisms, such as an entire group assisting each prisoner in identifying his or her pathway to offending rather than multiple one-on-one sessions, are likely to be necessary. It is expected that clinicians using this approach are already well versed and experienced in the assessment and treatment of offenders, and understanding and learning the Good Lives Model and SRM-R are in itself challenging for clinicians. More recently, additional treatment manuals and guides have become available to help clinicians implement the model (e.g., Yates, Prescott, and Ward 2010) and to help offenders understand the approach (Yates and Prescott 2011).

B. Restorative Justice Programs

Restorative justice approaches to rehabilitation in the prison system include prisoners *and* victims of crime as participants in the rehabilitation process. Two examples are victim–offender mediation and victim impact groups. Theoretical rationales for victim-involved interventions can be found among restorative justice principles (Braithwaite 1989, 2000, 2002). Restorative justice programs expand beyond the offender to emphasize the ways in which crime harms the victims and the community in order to promote accountability and repair among all parties (Ellsworth and Gross 1994; Garland 2001). Crime is viewed as a violation of the victim and of the community rather than of the state, and offenders are encouraged to take responsibility for their actions and repair harm by participating in mediation, restitution, competency development, and community service (Cohen 1985; Braithwaite 1989, 2002). When participating in restorative justice interventions, offenders are encouraged to take responsibility for their behavior and to feel guilt for having done wrong. Consequently, the primary goal of restorative justice programs is to reduce reoffending by helping offenders to see the negative effects of their actions on others, to empathize with the distress of their victims, and to act on the resulting inclination to repair the harm.

One example of prison programming that follows a restorative justice framework is victim impact interventions, which represent a creative application of restorative justice principles. In recent years, various victim impact interventions have been developed for use in prisons (e.g., Victim Offender Institutional Correctional Education System [VOICES], Connecticut Department of Correction 1997; Impact of Crime; Listen and Learn, National Institute of Corrections 2009). A 2004 NIC survey found that 73 percent of state correctional departments in the United States were using "victim impact education/empathy" programming (National Institute of Corrections 2004, p. 10). Such groups aim to reduce recidivism among prisoners by enhancing a sense of belongingness to the community and awareness of the impact of crime on victims and communities via direct interaction with crime victims (Monahan et al. 2004). The intervention culminates with a group community service project (e.g., creating and selling a product and donating proceeds to a local domestic violence shelter). Little research is available on the impact of these programs, but the conceptual model reinforces the importance of offenders becoming sensitive to the impact of their criminal behavior on others, with the goal of motivating offenders to change.

C. Faith-Based Prison Programs

Faith-based approaches to rehabilitation focus on a range of religious services. The Department of Justice estimates that approximately one-third of all prisoners attend religious services and are otherwise involved in religious activities while incarcerated. A vast majority of prisons offer prayer groups and personal development and parenting classes; some operate separate housing units for faith groups. For example, Florida prisons operate "faith and character-based units" dedicated to providing religious programming aimed at rehabilitation. Many faith-based programs are offered to prisoners with help from volunteers and are coordinated by faith-based groups or contractors.

Perhaps with the development of the White House Office of Faith-Based and Neighborhood Partnerships—established to encourage faith-based and other nonprofit organizations to provide social services to Americans in need—increased attention has been given to the role of faith-based programs. As a result, faith-based programs and policies have been criticized due to the lack of empirical studies showing their efficacy at reducing criminal justice outcomes. For example, of the five empirical studies investigating the link between faith-based programming and recidivism (Young et al. 1995; Johnson, Larson, and Pitts 1997; Benda, Toombs, and Peacock 2003; Johnson 2004; Duwe and King 2013), only one shows reductions in criminal justice outcomes.

In one recent study, Duwe and King (2013) evaluated the effects of religious programming on recidivism with a sample of individuals released from prison who participated in the Inner-Change Freedom Initiative program run by Prison Fellowship Ministries while they were incarcerated. This same program was evaluated previously by Johnson and Larson (2003), who found no significant difference between Inner-Change participants and nonparticipants in terms of recidivism rates.

The Inner-Change program was initiated in Texas by Prison Fellowship Ministries in 1997 and originally was designed as a values-based voluntary, prisoner reentry program (Johnson and Larson 2003; Johnson 2004; Duwe and King 2013). The program attempts to help prisoners prepare for employment, family and social relationships, and religious and community service. Specifically, participants engage in substance abuse education, victim impact awareness, life-skills development, cognitive skills development, educational attainment, community reentry, religious instruction, and moral development (Duwe and King 2013). The Inner-Change program currently operates in Arkansas, Minnesota, Texas, and Missouri and has been reorganized based on recommendations made by Johnson and Larson (2003). The most substantial change occurred in 2004 with the replacement of biblical-based instruction with values-based programming specifically addressing the criminogenic needs of participants (Johnson and Larson 2003). This change was meant to reflect the suggestions made by Cullen and Gendreau (2000) regarding the characteristics of effective correctional programs in the "what works" movement.

A study of the revised Inner-Change program examined the recidivism outcomes of participants from one adult male prison in Minnesota. The programming is reportedly similar across Inner-Change sites and consists of participants living together in a single housing unit during two structured phases initiated 18 to 24 months prior to release (Duwe and King 2013). Phase 1, which lasts approximately 12 months, consists of morning instructions followed by compulsory education and vocational programming in the evening. The morning instructions, delivered by Inner-Change counselors, are designed to introduce the core values described above, including teaching cognitive skills. In phase 2, which lasts for at least six months, prisoners work within the prison during the day and attend evening classes. These evening classes are taught by volunteers and can range from Bible study to other topical discussions. Also in this phase prisoners are introduced to individual mentors, with whom they will meet before and after release. Phase 2 consists of close interaction between mentors and offenders while in the community. It is this last component that is thought to be particularly helpful in preventing recidivism, as offenders receive a "continuum of care" before and after release.

The evaluation of the Inner-Change program was a retrospective quasi-experimental design that compared recidivism outcomes among program participants with a matched comparison group of nonparticipants who were released from Minnesota state prison between August 2003 and December 2009. Prisoners released during this period were matched (via propensity scores) to the 366 who had completed the Inner-Change program. Results showed that program participants had fewer rearrests and reconvictions but no reductions in technical violations. Duwe and King (2013) suggested that these results were likely due to program modifications designed to align with evidence-based practices and to target criminogenic needs.

It is not entirely clear that reducing criminal justice outcomes is the goal of faith-based programs and policies. Some faith-based programs state their goal as increasing positive social networks or increasing personal and emotional well-being to improve a prisoner's ability to handle stress associated with incarceration. Regardless, further research is needed, as the current literature suggests little evidence for a link between faith-based programs and policies and positive criminal justice outcomes for prisoners.

D. Prison Dog Programs

The implementation of dog programs in prisons capitalizes on findings about animals as ways to facilitate rehabilitation by helping prisoners develop attachments and learn what it means to care for someone or something outside of themselves. Dog programs in prisons take a variety of forms. In one, prisoners train service dogs for people with various disabilities who use the dogs to augment their quality of life. In another, prisoners train dogs from local shelters that would have otherwise been euthanized, later making the dogs available for adoption by the general public. The decision to implement a dog program at a given prison is more often than not the result of positive word of mouth among correctional administrators. The type of program offered at a given prison is typically determined by the dog programs operating within the local community and the warden's own experience. From the perspectives of the prison administrators, the dog program keeps inmates busy. Since these programs are primarily the responsibility of volunteers, the cost of running the program is often low and the program offers the potential for improving relations between prisons and the community.

Often the stated goal of prison dog programs is not to reduce recidivism but rather to improve the well-being of inmates while incarcerated (e.g., reduce fear and mistrust between staff and prisoners), reduce prison rule infractions, foster a sense of responsibility, and/or improve mental health. For example, Harkrader, Burke, and Owen (2004) argue that dog programs break down barriers of fear and mistrust between staff and inmates. Others argue that the programs reduce recidivism (Strimple 2003). Although there are no comprehensive data on the prevalence of dog programs in prisons, they appear popular and have been implemented in several forms in U.S. prisons. To date, there remains a paucity of empirical evidence about such programs; anecdotal accounts are often used to assess their efficacy.

E. Prosocial Networks: Programs to Maintain and Build Positive Social Networks

Prisoners have a significant amount of time to reflect upon their life circumstances, often reporting guilt or anxiety about lost relationships or fear about what will happen to their relationships with children, family, significant others, or friends while they are incarcerated. On the one hand, loss of antisocial peers or family members might be beneficial, as research suggests that association with antisocial peers or family members increases the odds of reoffending (Andrews and Bonta 2010). On the other hand, loss of positive support systems, such as family members who are frustrated with the consistent "failures" of their loved ones or a friend who cannot afford to travel the distance required to visit, could prove detrimental to a prisoner's "success." In both instances, the prisoner's adjustment to incarceration is of concern, though typically prison administration is more concerned about the mental health and well-being of prisoners rather than about on ensuring that prisoners maintain ties with family and friends. Approaches to assisting prisoners in maintaining or building positive relationships fall into two areas: structured programming and contact through letters, telephone calls, and visits.

Structured programming provided by prisons can include programs to develop parenting skills or to improve intimate relationships. Many times these programs are offered by trained counselors or psychologists. Other programs for prisoners, often facilitated by volunteer groups, are activities such as family days and audio book readings. Family days are designed to enhance the relationships between children and incarcerated parents where events are organized for both parents and their children. Audio book readings involve audiotaping incarcerated parents reading books, which are subsequently sent to their children. Prisoners may hesitate to participate in some of these programs; they tend to view social service agencies as negative and oriented toward removing children from their parents. Instead, prisoners may choose to maintain contact with people through telephone calls, letters, and visits. However, even when motivated to keep in contact, frequent telephone calls and visits are expensive, particularly when prisoners live several hundred miles from their home community.

Recently, innovative mechanisms have been tested to enhance the ability of prisoners to maintain contact with their social networks. For example, prisoners can visit with approved individuals by way of video. The video calls eliminate the travel costs and time for friends or family members, but concerns remain. For example, although video programs such as Skype are free for use, the video visits are costly for prisoners (about $20). This cost may be due to the contracts used to obtain video visit equipment by prisons, thus making this a privatized service. Further, family members or friends must travel to the location where the video system is set up for operation.

While prison managers may view visits and contact with family and friends as a luxury, the psychological literature suggests that more interaction with individuals in a person's social network tends to improve the odds of building trust (Cook 2005). Findings also suggest that the trust built from frequent interactions with informal social networks can foster the development of generalized trust (Cook, Hardin, and Levi 2007; Glanville and Andersson 2013). Therefore, frequent interactions between prisoners and their social networks have the potential to build trust not only with friends and family but also in formal relationships (e.g., with prison and parole staff). A point to consider for prison managers is that prisoners who engage in frequent interactions with their loved ones may be more likely to establish trust with others.

F. GED Education Programs

Around 40 percent of prisoners do not have a high school diploma or the equivalent GED; this figure is about 2.3 times greater than the general population (Harlow 2003). It is a common assumption that prisoners get involved in criminal activities in part due to their lack of education and (corresponding) reduced employment opportunities (Piehl 1994; Wilson, Gallagher, and MacKenzie 2000; Andrews and Bonta 2010). It follows that prisoners who participate in vocational and educational programming while incarcerated will show improved prospects for obtaining employment when released, and that education is viewed as a gateway to prosocial behavior. This approach to rehabilitation argues that prisoners are "reformed" through education. Two major assumptions follow this line of thought: (a) education works as a "one size fits all" approach, and (b) prisoners choose to further their education and believe that the education is beneficial. In general, obtaining a GED is viewed as a needed asset that will increase earnings and employment, but there is little recognition in the general GED literature about the null impact of obtaining a GED. Various studies question the value of obtaining a GED since it does not overcome the differences with those who receive a high school diploma in terms of employment and earning capacity (Heckman 2000), and it is suggested that a GED does not address the noncognitive skills needed in the workplace (e.g., interpersonal skills, tenacity, maturation) (Heckman and Rubinstein 2001). Coupling a GED with specialized vocational skills appears to be the preferred method of advancing individuals who did not complete high school.

While education programs are lauded as a mechanism of reform for prisoners, it is not clear that all prisoners benefit equally from the programs or that all prisoners see the programs as valuable. Further, any potentially positive effects of educational programs could be muted by the problems associated with obtaining employment with a criminal record. In one of the few meta-analyses of education and vocational studies conducted, Wilson, Gallagher, and MacKenzie (2000) examined 33 comparison group evaluations. They found that education program participants were slightly less likely to return to prison and more likely to obtain employment compared to nonparticipants. However, they note that 89 percent of the studies had poor methodology, including possible selection bias in who participates in education and employment programs and the lack of good comparison groups.

Perhaps the mixed findings with regard to the relationship between education and vocational programming in prison and criminal justice outcomes should affect the ways in which these programs are recommended at initial classification. For example, is it beneficial for states to require offenders to obtain a GED during incarceration as a means of bolstering their chances to obtain employment after release? While this policy has potential, a strengths-based component to this policy would likely be more effective at improving outcomes. This would involve a session between a staff member and the prisoner where a discussion would take place, using motivational interviewing techniques, about what is useful and important from the prisoner's perspective. This discussion would give more ownership to the prisoner with regard to his or her education and vocational planning rather than mandating GED programming outright. This approach would also give prison staff the opportunity to assess the prisoner's pathway to crime to determine whether it was facilitated by education and employment deficits. In other words, are deficits in this domain a primary criminogenic need for the prisoner? If education and vocational needs are present but not a primary contributor to the prisoner's offending pathway, providing education and vocational programming while incarcerated will be less likely to achieve the desired goal of reducing recidivism and improving the prisoner's prospects upon release. Prison staff should be tasked with providing educational and vocational recommendations that are tied to individualized risk assessments.

III. The Missing Component: Legitimacy

The legitimacy of justice organizations, or the belief by the general public that justice organizations are entitled to make decisions about and should be deferred to in justice matters, has emerged as a major theme in criminal justice research in recent years (Tyler 2005, 2006a). While a handful of studies have been conducted in the courts, a majority of the empirical work investigating the role of legitimacy in the criminal justice system has been conducted with police agencies. In short, this body of literature suggests that individuals are more likely to accept the decisions made by police when they perceive that police are interacting with them in a fair manner (Tyler 2006a), when police allow them to communicate and provide their own side of the situation (Dai et al. 2011), and when police treat them with dignity and respect (Kane 2005; Mastrofski et al. 2015).

As noted by Levi, Sacks, and Tyler, legitimacy is "a concept meant to capture the beliefs that bolster willing obedience" (2009, p. 354). Therefore, it is not surprising that a majority of legitimacy studies have been conducted with police and have explored the extent that people are willing to obey the law (Tyler 2006b). It is also not surprising that existing studies examining legitimacy in prisons have examined the relationship between legitimacy and the extent that prisoners engage in misconduct. Following findings from the police literature, it is assumed that prisoners who perceive staff as legitimate will be more willing to defer to them as authority figures. Thus far, this has held true in a handful of studies. For example, Reisig and Mesko (2009) found that when prisoners reported that corrections officers were just in their actions, they were less likely to have accrued official misconducts and less likely to have self-reported misconducts. Some recent research in the Netherlands has also shown a connection between perceived legitimacy of prison staff and subsequent adjustment to prison, with individuals less likely to experience mental health problems when they perceived staff as legitimate during the first three months of incarceration (Beijersbergen et al. 2013).

Another study comparing the social environment of a prison boot camp with a "regular" prison found that attitudes toward legitimacy of the justice system can change based on the environment. Franke et al. (2010) found that the reinforcing nature of the boot camp and integrity in programming improved the prisoner's perception of the legitimacy of authority figures. This did not occur in the "regular" prison, where attitudes toward authority declined. Tyler sums up the potential value of better understanding legitimacy in prison settings:

> Two questions that both are relevant to corrections policy can be distinguished. The first is whether any negative imprisonment costs can be mitigated by procedural fairness during the experience. If prisons are breeding grounds for de-legitimation and crime, then evidence that this effect can be mitigated is important. The findings of this study [Franke, Bierie, and MacKenzie, 2010] suggest that such mitigation can occur. It would be more valuable to demonstrate that fair treatment in prison can build legitimacy. One core argument of Tyler and Fagan (2008) is that the police can increase their legitimacy even while delivering negative outcomes if they deliver those outcomes through fair procedures—an argument untested in correctional settings. In either case, however, the implication is the same; emphasize fair procedures in correctional settings the same as in policing and in the courts. Doing so should minimize the negative implications of incarceration and maximize the likelihood of positive gains. (Tyler 2010, p. 129)

The prison regime, including the culture of the prison, the social context for providing programming and services, and the behavior of the administrators and staff toward prisoners, affects the prison experience. Further, the prison experience may have important and deliberative impacts on the behavior of prisoners after release. A negative prison experience would be one where the rules and procedures are not fairly applied, where antisocial behaviors and attitudes are common among prisoners and staff, and where humane treatment is scarce. The prison environment also has a widespread impact on the safety and security of the prison, its integrity, and the type of interactions that foster positive behavior. In essence, the culture of a prison alone can be influential over prison policies and programs. Efforts that emphasize not only positive criminal justice outcomes but also the well-being of the prisoners, support for change, and provisions of quality programming are likely to generate more legitimate views from prisoners.

The goal of prison settings should not be limited to achieving social order. After all, most staff-to-inmate ratios suggest that prisoners could easily take over the prison, but they do not. And even though they maintain order and follow the orders of staff, it is unlikely that all prisoners consider the prison environment to be legitimate. Perhaps they follow rules for secondary gains, such as earning valued early release or obtaining extra favors from staff. But following rules is not the same as legitimacy; legitimacy in prison encompasses additional, complex dynamics. Jackson et al. (2010, p. 3) argue that the additional neces- sary dynamic is "a degree of regularity and a sense of trust." Liebling (2004) argues that acceptability is the key—order and stability cannot be achieved without acceptance. In both definitions, a positive element is present beyond simply order and stability. From a prison legitimacy lens, the goal of safety and security may be intertwined with positive elements in a manner that achieves positive criminal justice outcomes.

IV. Conclusion

The RNR framework, reentry, and good-time credit are important reinventions and advancements in prison policy that, if adopted, have the potential to improve prison per- formance and prisoner outcomes. Most of the benefits will be found in improved legitimacy of the prisons and prison regimes, and through attention to a culture that supports the three goals of prisons—safety and security, offender change and well-being, and reduced recidi- vism. The beginning of this chapter reviewed how these policy shifts can be implemented, and we highlighted the need for more research to better understand the extent to which these policy approaches can affect criminal justice outcomes, improve the well-being of prisoners, and improve safety and security in prisons.

Contemporary programming options also have some benefits that can be realized if they are aligned with different policies that focus on these three goals instead of focusing solely on prison security and safety. Many of the innovative programs have the potential to emphasize building on the strengths of individuals to improve their cognitive decision- making skills, interpersonal skills, and ability to develop prosocial attachments. A myriad of programing has this potential, but these programs are infrequently offered (see Taxman, Perdoni, and Harrison 2007). In fact, a major challenge is to increase the percentage of prisoners who have access to programming, to implement high-quality programming, and to create programs consistent with prisoner needs.

The future of prison policies and programs lies in a better understanding of the legiti- macy of the policies and programs from the perceptions of prisoners. If prisoners perceive rules, procedures, and practices as fair, appropriate, and equally applied, and when they trust authority, then perhaps they will feel as though they can enter society with meaningful skills and opportunities for positive outcomes. Themes of legitimacy also bring attention to the practices that may undermine good-quality programs in prisons. Examining the issues related to legitimacy in prison environments and how they affect policies and programming should drive the next generation of research.

REFERENCES

Andrews, Don A., and James Bonta. 2010. *The Psychology of Criminal Conduct*, 5th ed. New Providence, NJ: Matthew Bender and Company.

Andrews, Don A., James Bonta, and J. Stephen Wormith. 2006. "The Recent Past and Near Future of Risk and/or Need Assessment." *Crime and Delinquency* 52:7–27.

Beijersbergen, Karen A., Anja J. Dirkzwager, Veroni I. Eichelsheim, Peter H. Laan, and Paul Nieuwbeerta. 2013. "Procedural Justice and Prisoners' Mental Health Problems: A Longitudinal Study." *Criminal Behaviour and Mental Health*, doi: 10.1002/cbm.1881.

Benda, Brent, Nancy J. Toombs, and Mark Peacock. 2003. "Discriminators of Types of Recidivism Among Boot Camp Graduates in a Five-Year Follow-Up Study." *Journal of Criminal Justice* 31:539–551.

Braithwaite, John. 1989. *Crime, Shame and Reintegration*. Cambridge: Cambridge University Press.

Braithwaite, John. 2000. "Shame and Criminal Justice." *Canadian Journal of Criminology* 42:281–298.

Braithwaite, John. 2002. "Setting Standards for Restorative Justice." *British Journal of Criminology* 42:563–577.

Cohen, Stanley. 1985. *Visions of Social Control: Crime, Punishment and Classification*. Cambridge: Polity Press.

Cook, Karen Schweers. 2005. "Networks, Norms, and Trust: The Social Psychology of Social Capital, 2004 Cooley Mead Award Address." *Social Psychology Quarterly* 68:4–14.

Cook, Karen Schweers, Russell Hardin, and Margaret Levi. 2007. *Cooperation Without Trust?* New York: Russell Sage Foundation.

Cullen, Francis T., and Paul Gendreau. 2000. "Assessing Correctional Rehabilitation: Policy, Practice, Prospects." In *National Institute of Justice Criminal Justice 2000: Changes in Decision Making and Discretion in the Criminal Justice System*, edited by Julie Horney. Washington, DC: Department of Justice, National Institute of Justice.

Dai, Mengyan, James Frank, and Ivan Sun. 2011. "Procedural Justice During Police–citizen Encounters: The Effects of Process-based Policing on Citizen Compliance and Demeanor." *Journal of Criminal Justice* 39: 159–168.

DiIulio, John. 1990. *Governing Prisons*. New York: Free Press.

Duwe, Grant, and Michelle King. 2013. "Can Faith-Based Correctional Programs Work? An Outcome Evaluation of the Inner-Change Freedom Initiative in Minnesota." *International Journal of Offender Therapy and Comparative Criminology* 57:813–841.

Ellsworth, Phoebe C., and Samuel R. Gross. 1994. "Hardening of the Attitudes: Americans Views on the Death Penalty." *Journal of Social Issues* 50:19–52.

Franke, Derrick, David Bierie, and Doris Layton Mackenzie. 2010. "Legitimacy in Corrections: A Randomized Experiment Comparing a Boot Camp with a Prison." *Criminology and Public Policy* 9:89–117.

French, Sheila A., and Paul Gendreau. 2006. "Reducing Prison Misconducts: What Works!" *Criminal Justice and Behavior* 33:185–218.

Garland, David. 2001. *The Culture of Control: Crime and Social Order in Contemporary Society.* Oxford: Oxford University Press.

Glanville, Jennifer L., and Matthew A. Andersson. 2013. "Do Social Connections Create Trust? An Examination Using New Longitudinal Data." *Social Forces* 92:545–562.

Guterman, Jeffrey T. 2006. *Mastering the Art of Solution-Focused Counseling.* Alexandria, VA: American Counseling Association.

Hanson, R. Karl, and Kelly Morton-Bourgon. 2004. *Predictors of Sexual Recidivism: An Updated Meta-Analysis.* Ottawa, Ontario, Canada: Public Works and Government Services.

Harkrader, Todd, Todd W. Burke, and Stephen S. Owen. 2004. "Pound Puppies: The Rehabilitative Uses of Dogs in Correctional Facilities." *Corrections Today* 66:74–79.

Harlow, Caroline Wolf. 2003. *Education and Correctional Populations.* Washington, DC: Bureau of Justice Statistics, NCJ 195670.

Heckman, James J. 2000. "Policies to Foster Human Capital." *Research in Economics* 54:3–56.

Heckman, James J., and Yona Rubinstein. 2001. "The Importance of Noncognitive Skills: Lessons from the GED Testing Program." *American Economic Review* 91:145–149.

Jackson, Jonathan, Tom R. Tyler, Ben Bradford, Dominic Taylor, and Mike Shiner. 2010. "Legitimacy and Procedural Justice in Prisons." *Prison Service Journal* 191:4–10.

Johnson, Byron R. 2004. "Religious Programs and Recidivism Among Former Inmates in Prison Fellowship Programs: A Long-term Follow-up Study." *Justice Quarterly* 21:329–354.

Johnson, Byron R., and David B. Larson. 2003. *The Inner-Change Freedom Initiative: A Preliminary Evaluation of a Faith-Based Prison Program.* Philadelphia: Center for Research on Religion and Urban Civil Society.

Johnson, Byron R., David B. Larson, and Timothy C. Pitts. 1997. "Religious Programs, Institutional Adjustment, and Recidivism Among Former Inmates in Prison Fellowship Programs." *Justice Quarterly* 14:145–166.

Kane, Robert. 2005. "Linking Compromised Police Legitimacy to Violent Crime in Structurally Disadvantaged Communities." *Criminology* 43:469–498.

Kirsch, Laura G., and Judith V. Becker. 2006. "Sexual Offending: Theory of Problem, Theory of Change, and Implications for Treatment Effectiveness." *Aggression and Violent Behavior* 11:208–224.

Landenberger, Nana A., and Mark W. Lipsey. 2005. "The Positive Effects of Cognitive Behavioral Programs for Offenders: A Meta-Analysis of Factors Associated with Effective Treatment." *Journal of Experimental Criminology* 1:451–476.

Latessa, Edward J., Richard Lemke, Matthew Makarios, and Paula Smith. 2010. "Creation and Validation of the Ohio Risk Assessment System (ORAS)." *Federal Probation* 74:16–22.

Levi, Margaret, Audrey Sacks, and Tom Tyler. 2009. "Conceptualizing Legitimacy, Measuring Legitimating Beliefs." *American Behavioral Scientist* 53:354–375.

Liebling, Alison, and Helen Arnold. 2004. *Prisons and Their Moral Performance: A Study of Values, Quality, and Prison Life.* Oxford: Oxford University Press.

Lindsay, William R., Tony Ward, Tom Morgan, and Iris Wilson. 2007. "Self-Regulation of Sex Offending, Future Pathways and the Good Lives Model: Applications and Problems." *Journal of Sexual Aggression* 13:37–50.

Marques, Janice, David M. Day, Craig Nelson, and Michael H. Miner. 1989. "The Sex Offender Treatment and Evaluation Program: California's Relapse Prevention Program." In *Relapse Prevention with Sex Offenders*, edited by D. Richard Laws. New York: Guilford.

Mastrofski, Stephen, Tal Jonathan-Zamir, Shomron Moyal, and James J. Willis. 2015. "Predicting Procedural Justice in Police-Citizen Encounters." *Criminal Justice and Behavior* 43:119–139.

Miller, William R., and Stephen Rollnick. 2013. *Motivational Interviewing: Preparing People for Change*, 2nd ed. New York: Guilford Press.

Monahan, Lynn Hunt, James J. Monahan, Mario T. Gaboury, and Patricia A. Niesyn. 2004. "Victims' Voices in the Correctional Setting: Cognitive Gains in an Offender Education Program." *Journal of Offender Rehabilitation* 39:21–33.

National Institute of Corrections. 2002. *Transition from Prison to the Community Initiative*. Washington, DC: National Institute of Corrections.

National Institute of Corrections. 2004. *Corrections-Based Services for Victims of Crime*. Washington, DC: U.S. Department of Justice, Office for Victims of Crime.

National Institute of Corrections. 2009. *Listen and Learn Facilitator Manual and Participant Workbook*. Washington, D.C.: US Department of Justice, Office for Victims of Crime.

Pattavina, April, and Faye Taxman. 2013. "Using Discrete-Event Simulation Modeling to Estimate the Impact of RNR Program Implementation on Recidivism Level." In *Simulation Strategies to Reduce Recidivism*, edited by Faye Taxman and April Pattavina. New York: Springer.

Phelps, Michelle S. 2012. "The Place of Punishment: Variation in the Provision of Inmate Services Staff Across the Punitive Turn." *Journal of Criminal Justice* 40:348–357.

Piehl, Anne Morrison. 1994. *Learning While Doing Time*. Unpublished report. Cambridge, MA: John F. Kennedy School of Government.

Purvis, Mayumi, Tony Ward and Simone Shaw. 2013. *Applying the Good Lives Model to the Case Management of Sexual Offenders: A Practical Guide for Probation Officers, Parole Officers, and Case Workers*. Brandon, VT: Safer Society Press.

Reisig, Michael D., and Gorazd Mesko. 2009. "Procedural Justice, Legitimacy, and Prisoner Misconduct." *Psychology, Crime and Law* 15:41–59.

Smith, Elsie J. 2006. "The Strength-Based Counseling Model." *Counseling Psychologist* 34:13–69.

Strimple, Earl O. 2003. "A History of Prison Inmate-Animal Interaction Programs." *American Behavioral Scientist* 47:70–78.

Taxman, Faye S., Michael S. Caudy, and April Pattavina. 2013. "Risk-Need-Responsivity (RNR): Leading Towards Another Generation of the Model." In *Simulation Strategies to Reduce Recidivism*, edited by Faye Taxman and April Pattavina. New York: Springer.

Taxman, Faye S., Matthew L. Perdoni, and Michael S. Caudy. 2013. "The Plight of Providing Appropriate Substance Abuse Treatment Services to Offenders: Modeling the Gaps in Service Delivery." *Victims and Offenders* 8:70–93.

Taxman, Faye, Matthew Perdoni, and Lana Harrison. 2007. "Treatment for Adult Offenders: A Review of the State of the State." *Journal of Substance Abuse Treatment* 32:239–254.

Taxman, Faye S., Douglas Young, and James M. Byrne. 2003. "Transforming Offender Reentry into Public Safety: Lessons from OJP's Reentry Partnership Initiative." *Justice Research and Policy* 5:101–128.

Tyler, Tom R. 2005. "Policing in Black and White: Ethnic Group Differences in Trust and Confidence in the Police." *Police Quarterly* 8:322–342.

Tyler, Tom R. 2006a. *Why People Obey the Law*. Princeton, NJ: Princeton University Press.

Tyler, Tom R. 2006b. "Psychological Perspectives on Legitimacy and Legitimation." *Annual Review of Psychology* 57:375–400.

Tyler, Tom R. 2010. "Legitimacy in Corrections: Policy Implications." *Criminology and Public Policy* 9:127–134.

Tyler, Tom, and Jeffrey Fagan. 2008. "Legitimacy and Cooperation: Why Do People Help the Police Fight Crime in Their Communities?" *Ohio State Journal of Criminal Law* 6:231–275.

Walsh, Anthony. 2001. *Correctional Assessment, Casework, and Counseling.* Alexandria, VA: American Correctional Association.

Ward, Tony, and Mark Brown. 2004. "The Good Lives Model and Conceptual Issues in Offender Rehabilitation." *Psychology, Crime, and Law* 10:243–257.

Ward, Tony, and Theresa A. Gannon. 2006. "Rehabilitation, Etiology and Self-Regulation: The Comprehensive Good Lives Model of Treatment for Sexual Offenders." *Aggression and Violent Behavior* 11:77–94.

Ward, Tony, and William L. Marshall. 2004. "Good Lives, Etiology and the Rehabilitation of Sex Offenders: A Bridging Theory." *Journal of Sexual Aggression* 10:153–169.

Ward, Tony, and Claire A. Stewart. 2003. "The Treatment of Sex Offenders: Risk Management and Good Lives." *Professional Psychology: Research and Practice* 34:353–360.

Weinrath, Michael, and Ron Coles. 2003. "Third Generation Prison Classification: The Manitoba Case." *Criminal Justice Studies* 16:305–316.

Whitehead, Paul R., Tony Ward, and Rachael M. Collie. 2007. "Time for a Change: Applying the Good Lives Model of Rehabilitation to a High-Risk Violent Offender." *International Journal of Offender Therapy and Comparative Criminology* 51:578–598.

Willis, Gwenda, and Tony Ward. 2013. "The Good Lives Model: Evidence that It Works." In *What Works in Offender Rehabilitation: An Evidence Based Approach to Assessment and Treatment*, edited by Leam Craig, Theresa A. Gannon, and Louise Dixon. West Sussex, UK: John Wiley and Sons.

Willis, Gwenda, Tony Ward, and Jill S. Levenson. 2013. "The Good Lives Model (GLM): An Evaluation of GLM Operationalization in North American Treatment Programs." *Sexual Abuse: A Journal of Research and Treatment* 26:58–81.

Wilson, David B., Catherine A. Gallagher, and Doris L. MacKenzie. 2000. "A Meta-Analysis of Corrections-Based Education, Vocation, and Work Programs for Adult Offenders." *Journal of Research in Crime and Delinquency* 37:347–368.

Yates, Pamela M., and David Francesca Prescott. 2011. *Building a Better Life: A Good Lives and Self-Regulation Workbook.* Brandon, VT: Safer Society Press.

Yates, Pamela M., David Prescott, and Tony Ward. 2010. *Applying the Good Lives and Self-Regulation Models to Sex Offender Treatment: A Practical Guide for Clinicians.* Brandon, VT: Safer Society Press.

Young, Mark C., John Gartner, Thomas O'Connor, David Larson, and Kevin N. Wright. 1995. "Long-term Recidivism Among Federal Inmates Trained as Volunteer Prison Ministers." *Journal of Offender Rehabilitation* 22:97–118.

....

CHAPTER 30

USEFUL VERSUS HARMFUL
PRISON POLICIES

....

JOHN WOOLDREDGE

EACH contribution to this volume touches on a critical issue related to the incarceration of offenders with discussions of policies that have either given rise to a specific problem or are a response to the problem. An integration of ideas conveyed across some of these essays reveals that the evolution of "useful" corrections policy has primarily reflected an increasingly humanitarian view of offenders (chapters 3, 8, 10, 14, 18, 19, 22–25), a growing awareness of both short- and long-term adverse effects of incarceration on offenders and the general population (chapters 1, 2, 4–9, 11–17, 22, 24–28), and greater reliance on empirically based strategies, where applicable, such as in the areas of treatment and reintegration (chapters 18–23, 27–29). Several contributors have also suggested that more effective solutions to various problems involve collaborations across multiple agencies in order to ensure long-term solutions while minimizing unanticipated ill effects of new strategies that might become problems for other state agencies (see, for example, Susan Turner's discussion of strategies for effectively reintegrating prisoners back into their communities upon release and Faye Taxman and Brandy Blasko's overview of effective treatment programs for prisoners). Interagency collaboration and ongoing communication are necessary for new policies to succeed, reflecting the need to deal with problems related to incarceration within a context larger than the prison to permit more realistic considerations of the necessary resources for and potential limitations of new strategies.

In contrast, other essays in this collection suggest that policies generating new or additional problems linked to incarceration have resulted from the decisions of individuals who are more punishment-oriented, who are further removed from the prison experience, and who possess the influence and power to shape prison resources as well as the composition of inmate populations (politicians and judges as well as police and prosecutors) (see, for example, Dan Mears' and Josh Cochran's discussion of sentencing practices that send disproportionate numbers of economically disadvantaged offenders to prison and Ben Steiner's description of a link between the political movement to "get tougher" with offenders and prison violence in the United States). While there is no question that punishment-oriented prison administrators do exist, they seem generally savvier about the potential ill effects of draconian prison policies because they are embedded in the system and have first-hand experience with their unanticipated consequences for maintaining good order. In other words, a key attribute of those who have promoted harmful policies is the dissonance between what they believe prisons *should* do versus what a prison environment can tolerate before producing additional problems. Considering that the most powerful in the aforementioned group are elected officials (politicians and court actors), one cannot ignore the roles of changing public attitudes and of the media for influencing harmful policy.

The avoidance of "harmful" corrections policies, or strategies that have harmed the welfare of prisoners and prison personnel, is a difficult task considering all possible ill effects that must be anticipated prior to policy implementation. This chapter provides more specific insight into the parameters of this task with an integration of ideas touched on by contributors to this volume. In particular, identifying the common sources to harmful policies suggest ways to shape more effective policies in the future. Section I provides a discussion of what I consider to be some of the most harmful corrections strategies implemented in industrialized countries (particularly in the United States) during the twentieth and twenty-first centuries, the actual harms inflicted on prisoners and prison staff, and the common denominators of these strategies. Section II considers the relevance of broader political ideologies as opposed to placing too much emphasis on the role of sentencing laws per se for generating some of these harms. Section III identifies some of the biggest obstacles that must be overcome to avoid the evolution of potentially useful policy into harmful policy. Finally, Section IV provides an overview of the common themes identified throughout the chapter, highlights the importance of cumulative knowledge and ongoing empirical research on best practices, and then turns to a discussion of the current relevance of retribution as a guiding philosophy of punishment. The main highlights of this chapter are as follows:

- Common denominators of policies with harmful effects on prisoners and prison staff include heavier emphases on punishment (as opposed to treatment) advocated by politicians and court actors who are further removed from the prison experience.
- Common denominators of policies that have generally improved the welfare of prisoners and/or staff include grounding in an increasingly humanitarian view of offenders, a growing awareness of both short- and long-term adverse effects of incarceration on offenders and the general population, greater reliance on empirically based strategies, and interagency collaborations to ensure long-term solutions while minimizing unanticipated ill effects.
- Some of the biggest harms to prisoners and staff reflect a heavier focus on punishment/ incapacitation and the movement toward more formal rationality in decision making and management, overreliance on risk assessment, sentencing practices that have changed the composition of inmate populations, and a greater use of coercive (administrative) controls for inmate management.
- The consequences of harmful policies have included a proliferation of street gangs and drug trades inside prisons; increased rates of inmate crime, victimization, and suicide; greater use of punitive segregation and solitary confinement that, when combined with longer stays, can result in psychological problems for certain types of inmates; growing numbers of women who must endure the emotional stress of separation from their children; more widespread hardships on the families of both women and men in prison; rising numbers of inmates with special needs; and higher postrelease failure

rates (recidivism or parole violations) due to greater demands on community corrections and inadequate social supports.

- A handful of substantive barriers to successfully translating potentially useful policy into practice exist, including an inability to anticipate the long-term consequences of specific policies and strategies for the welfare of prisoners and prison staff, inadequate resources for translating policies into practice, unwillingness among some politicians and prison officials to lessen the ill effects of particular deprivations of incarceration, the dangers to inmate and staff safety posed by the composition of particular inmate populations, and managing large offender populations.

Despite my previous comments regarding more punishment-oriented public officials, the discussion of the ill effects of corrections policies is not intended to be an indictment of a retributive philosophy per se given that most prison sentences are guided to some extent by a society's belief that offenders should be deprived of certain liberties to "balance" their damage to the commonwealth. My focus here is on the common roots of strategies with unintended consequences that ultimately hinder the achievement of particular goals, regardless of whether those goals reflected a punitive orientation. It is important to recognize a distinction between a retributive (punitive) orientation per se and a *more* punitive orientation, however, since the latter can undermine the former by generating hardships not equally distributed across prisoners.

I. Harmful Polices and Their Effects on Prisons and Prisoners

Some of the problems faced by prisoners and prison personnel described in this volume stem from the massive increase in inmate populations that began in the late twentieth century across some industrialized nations. Recent trends in declining inmate populations across the United States and some other countries might therefore lead to speculation that problems emerging from the prison "boom" will subside as these populations become smaller. It is important to address this issue before proceeding to provide proper context for my subsequent discussion as well as to underscore the relevance of the contributions to this volume related directly to the era of mass incarceration.

A. Placing Trends in Decreasing Inmate Populations in Perspective

Most of the contributions to this volume were completed during 2014–2015, when both state and federal prison populations in the United States were declining. By year-end 2014, the latest available data at the time of this composition, state prison populations had been declining since 2010 (from 1.40 million to 1.35 million, except for an increase from 1.35 million to 1.36 million between 2012 and 2013), and the federal prison population had been dropping since 2012 (from 218,000 to 211,000) (Carson 2015). At year-end 2014, there were

1.56 million persons held in state and federal prisons (Carson 2015), which is comparable to the combined populations in 2006. All of the authors with essays pertaining directly to prison populations (Part I) acknowledged at the time of their writing that US prison populations had recently begun to decline but that it was too soon to determine whether the trend would continue based on the available data. Perhaps we can be more confident now that this is, in fact, a trend of decreasing populations, at least at the state level. However, there are several reasons why we cannot assume that these declines mark an immediate remedy to some of the critical issues highlighted by the contributors to Part I and why the issues reviewed by these scholars will remain relevant for years to come.

Arguably the most important reason why prison populations in the United States will remain a concern in the foreseeable future is because the U.S. prison population in 2014 was still over five times larger than the population at the beginning of the prison "boom" (see Figure 1.1 in Lynch and Verma, this volume). Returning to the population levels of the 1970s (hovering in the 200,000s) will take patience at the rate of the current decline, if ever achieved. A second reason, as discussed by Mazzerole, Rynne, and McPhedran (this volume), is that the annual incarceration rate of the United States remains the highest of any other country in the world even when adjusting for population size. As they noted, roughly half of all persons incarcerated in the world are in the United States, China, and Russia. Whereas the United States incarcerated over 700 persons per 100,000 population in 2013 (this estimate includes both prisons and jails), other countries incarcerated fewer than 100 persons per 100,000 population (Walmsley 2013).

A third reason why the size of U.S. prison populations will remain a critical issue in years to come is because many states continue to confine more prisoners than the sum of design capacities across all facilities in each of those states (over half of all states in 2014, derived from tables provided by Carson 2015), which poses safety risks to both staff and inmates considering that design capacities reflect, in part, the maximum population size that can be managed most effectively without incurring additional safety risks (not to mention additional operating costs exceeding economies of scale). Finally, even if the U.S. prison population manages to drop to 1970 levels within a few years (an unlikely scenario), discussions of the causes and consequences of large prison populations are critical for informing policies to prevent repeating these mistakes.

Returning to the discussion immediately prior to this section, it could be argued that many of the critical issues facing U.S. prisons and prisoners today were fed, at least in part, by the prison population boom of the late twentieth century. A careful review of the essays in Part I provides a compelling argument that the era of mass incarceration was fed, in turn, by more punitive sentencing philosophies upheld by public officials combined with the resources available for implementing those philosophies. Growing support for more punitive sentencing of criminals in conjunction with increased resources for prison construction contributed to mass incarceration in the United States beginning in the 1970s (see Lynch and Verma; Mears and Cochran, this volume). Other countries also experienced a "get tough" movement around this time (see King, this volume), resulting in a similar manifestation of rising prison populations although not nearly of the same magnitude as in the United States. Here is a noteworthy example of noncorrections agencies influencing harmful policy, where more than 30 years of mass incarceration contributed to a proliferation of street gangs and drug trades inside prisons (see Decker and Pyrooz; Wheatley, Weekes, Moser, and Thibault, this volume); increased rates of inmate crime, victimization, and suicide (Canning and Dvoskin; Steiner; Wolff); greater use of punitive segregation and solitary confinement (Gendreau and Labreque; Marquart and Trulson); growing numbers of women who must endure the emotional stress of separation from their children (Wright and Cain); more widespread hardships on the families of both women and men in prison (Rodriguez and Turanovic); rising numbers of inmates with special needs (Lane and Lanza-Kaduce; Manchak and Morgan); and higher postrelease failure rates (recidivism or parole violations) due to greater demands on community corrections and inadequate social supports (Taxman and Blasko; Turner).

B. Sentencing Manifestations of "Getting Tougher" with Offenders and Formal Rationality in Prison Management

The "get tough" movement beginning in the late 1970s culminated in determinate sentencing schemes across most of the United States, some with sentencing guidelines, three-strikes laws, mandatory minimum sentences or sentence enhancements for both certain types of offenses and offenders, and truth-in-sentencing. Despite some (limited) evidence that prison populations in particular states were reduced in the short run by the implementation of some of these laws (see, for example, Marvell's [1995] discussion of sentencing guidelines in nine states), no empirical evidence has emerged to date indicating that the aggregation of these laws contributed to decreasing prison populations in either the short or long term. The exact nature of whether and how both state-specific and federal sentencing laws influenced mass incarceration across the entire United States during the late twentieth century has yet to be rigorously examined. Nonetheless, there seems to be little debate over the idea that these laws were manifestations of much larger social and political forces that ultimately drove mass incarceration (as discussed in this volume by Clear and Frost, and Lynch and Verma). Efforts to quantify the specific contributions of sentencing policies to mass incarceration, such as mandatory minimums and truth-in-sentencing, can be useful if the greater relevance of broader movements are kept in perspective. All such policies reflect the shifting orientations of criminal justice officials who wield the greatest control over the flow of individuals in and out of the system, including city administrators and police chiefs interested in beefing up drug enforcement and "hot spots" policing (Braga, Papachristos, and Hureau 2014), prosecutors wishing to convey a stronger emphasis on "community justice" (Rose and Clear, 1998), and judges who are concerned with public perceptions of their abilities to reduce public harm (Steffensmeier, Ulmer, and Kramer 1998). Framing crime issues as matters of "public health" may be feeding these pursuits as opposed to changing them, as even greater responsibility is laid on these officials to reduce crime.

It would be unfair to claim that *all* problems faced by prisoners today are the result of the shift to a more punitive ideology and, in turn, the dramatic increase in prison populations, given that elements of these problems have always existed due to the nature of incarceration itself. Victimization rates in prison have always been higher than in the general population, for example, a likely consequence of placing so many motivated offenders in close physical proximity to vulnerable victims (Wooldredge and Steiner 2014). However, a more punitive ideology may increase the magnitude of some of these problems, such as larger populations creating greater opportunities for motivated offenders to be successful in their criminal pursuits inside prison. Due in part to the rapid growth in prison populations in the United States during the 1980s and increased threats to safety, Feeley and Simon (1992) argued that the primary goal of imprisonment in the United States evolved during the 1980s into the management of large criminal populations with a heavier focus on risk assessment and custodial classification. This move to more "actuarial thinking" (Feeley and Simon 1992: 452) has occurred across most segments of the U.S. criminal justice system and has shifted emphases away from individual considerations (e.g., rehabilitating prisoners) toward decision-making based on formal rationality (e.g., greater uniformity in treatment) (Ulmer and Kramer 1996).

DiIulio (1987) espoused the growing relevance of formal administrative controls for reducing inmate deviance during the era of mass incarceration in the United States, arguing that inmate deviance had become more heavily linked to poor facility management resulting from rising populations (see also Useem and Kimball 1989). His "administrative control theory" was introduced during a period when the dramatic rise in U.S. prison populations served to change the social order of prisons and led to a greater reliance on formal controls by prison management to maintain institutional safety (Simon 2000). "Formal controls" include both coercive controls (e.g., loss of good time, punitive segregation, and loss of privileges) and remunerative controls (e.g., paid jobs and recreation). However, a greater focus on inmate compliance with rules might not necessarily facilitate inmate management if it comes at the expense of treatment and addressing the sources of offenders' criminality. Failure to address the sources of criminality allows these forces to persist and to generate rule "resistance" during confinement.

C. Greater Emphasis on Risk Assessment

In fairness to those who advocate management over treatment, the shift away from more humanitarian goals and toward custodial risk assessment and management during the era of mass incarceration could be construed as recognition of the inevitable nature of inmate deviance. The heavier focus on risk assessment, however, appears to have only redistributed misconduct across prisons as well as across units in the same facility. The California Department of Corrections, for example, built large warehouse prisons for lowerrisk inmates and supermax prisons for "high-risk" inmates. Irwin (2005) observed that levels of violence are considerably lower in the warehouse facilities relative to the supermax prisons even though the latter are much more "secure." This idea suggests that inmate population composition is more relevant than coercive controls for shaping levels of inmate crime and victimization, given that crime rates are higher in more secure prisons. At best, the heavier emphasis on risk assessment and management may only be changing the spatial patterns of offending in prison rather than reducing levels of crime and victimization. At worst, placing the most dangerous offenders together in the same space could be escalating the problem (Wooldredge and Steiner 2014). Although officially recorded assault rates in U.S. prisons appear to have declined since the 1980s (e.g., Useem and Piehl 2006; Association of State Corrections Administrators 2010), there is no concrete evidence that this has resulted from more effective prison policies. The higher prison admission rates of lower risk offenders, for example, might have created the illusion of less crime by increasing the population base used in the calculation of these rates. Self-report data on crimes and victimization experiences are needed to fully assess the linkages between greater use of formal controls and trends in inmate crime and victimization.

D. The Changing Composition of Inmate Populations

The process of mass incarceration also did not operate uniformly across race and ethnic groups in the United States, resulting in an even greater over-representation of African Americans and Latinos in prisons relative to their representations in the general population (for discussions in this volume, see Mears and Cochran; Rodriguez and Turanovic). Nationwide support for more punitive punishments *in general* in conjunction with various "War on Drugs" movements and a focus by court actors on controlling offenders they deem to be the highest risks to community safety have resulted in the mass warehousing of the most socially and economically disadvantaged minorities who are among the most cynical toward legal authority and who shape the inmate cultures of medium and maximum security facilities/units across the United States (Steiner and Wooldredge 2008). The development and sustenance of inmate cultures promoting legal cynicism and the illegitimacy of prison officers and administrators have potential implications for levels of misconduct inside prison as well as postrelease recidivism rates (see Crewe and Laws, this volume).

Crime prevention strategies involving enforcement-based approaches to policing "hot spot" areas in disadvantaged urban neighborhoods might feed this process (Weisburd and Braga 2013), especially if these are areas where some of the most disadvantaged minorities reside in U.S. cities. There is an irony to the recent foci of policing scholars on (a) reducing crime by focusing on select geographic areas (Braga and Weisburd 2010), and (b) improving citizens' perceptions of the police in more disadvantaged communities (Tyler 2004). These two processes necessarily work against each other, and the prevailing emphasis on hot spot policing provides sustenance to the high levels of legal cynicism among minority prisoners by funneling disproportionate numbers of residents less inclined to recognize the legitimacy of power holders into prisons, with the highest concentrations of these individuals placed into the harshest prison environments that further attenuate mainstream values and marginalize these prisoners from conventional society. Similar to how these processes work to feed crime in the most disadvantaged urban neighborhoods (Sampson and Wilson 1995; Krivo and Peterson 1996; Wacquant 2001; Warner 2003; Sampson and Bean 2006), the impact of these processes may be even stronger in higher security prisons and units with greater densities of persons with substantial deficits in social and human capital.

Even with further reductions in the numbers of people sent to prison, the expansion of particular crime prevention strategies such as hot spots policing in conjunction with greater emphases on prison management and risk assessment may only exacerbate the barriers to achieving good order in prisons by perpetuating a migratory loop for the highest risk offenders between the most economically disadvantaged urban neighborhoods, where these individuals most often reside, and maximum security units/prisons, where many of these same individuals are sent upon conviction. Short of restructuring sentencing practices to send proportionately fewer minorities to prison (such as lessening the severity of drug offenses for which minorities are more often incarcerated relative to whites), as well as different strategies for the placement and management of "high-risk" offenders (see King this volume), U.S. prison populations will remain primarily black and Latino in the foreseeable future with even higher concentrations of minorities in the most dangerous environments.

More attention should be paid to evaluating risk assessment strategies for their impact on violence levels in higher security prisons. Toward the end of reducing violence in the higher risk prison environments, which, in turn, might reduce the intensity of the migratory loop between more crime-ridden prisons and neighborhoods, efforts should be made to avoid reaching a critical mass of serious offenders with the least regard for legal authority. Except for supermax prisons, redistributing some of the higher risk inmates across state facilities might be more feasible if prison populations continue to generally decline and a larger number of lower risk offenders are supervised in the community. As opposed to shutting facilities down completely as a state's prison population declines overall (see Camp this volume), which seems to be a trend in states like Indiana, Kentucky, and Ohio, it might be more useful in the long run to keep those facilities operational at lower capacities. Researchers familiar with data on prison transfers in a state can attest to the frequency of inmate mobility between prisons, particularly during the first few months of incarceration when initial classifications are tweaked due to margins of error in risk scores. Allowing prison administrators the flexibility to redistribute offenders initially classified as "higher risk" throughout a system might further help to compensate for errors made in initial screening due to opportunities to observe how these prisoners behave in less secure settings.

To be realistic, such a strategy would not involve shifting very high-risk prisoners into lower security prisons and units but instead might involve moving certain groups of higher risk offenders such as some first-time violent offenders, older violent offenders, or younger property offenders. Other factors would also have to be considered (e.g., recency of gang involvement inside or outside prison). Coupled with lowering the density of prison populations over time, striving for greater "balance" among offender groups could reduce some of the anxieties of first-time violent offenders who otherwise might have been placed with higher concentrations of high-risk offenders.

E. Greater Use of Administrative Controls over Prisoners

DiIulio's (1987) administrative control perspective on inmate management underscores the relevance of both remunerative controls (paid jobs, recreation, etc.) and coercive controls (loss of good time, punitive segregation, loss of privileges, etc.) for maintaining institutional safety, and both types increased in use across U.S. prisons during the era of mass incarceration. However, I am not aware of convincing empirical evidence suggesting that increasing the use of coercive controls corresponds with decreasing rates of inmate crime. Moreover, increasing the use of coercive controls necessarily increases corrections budgets due to greater use of restrictive housing, more proactive enforcement of rules and corresponding infraction hearings, and longer sentences due to loss of good time (where it still exists). Yet, these expanding investments have not made prisons generally safer for inmates and staff, and there is some evidence to even suggest that greater use of coercive tactics by correctional officers undermines their legitimacy in the eyes of inmates (Wooldredge and Steiner 2016; King this volume).

Government officials' inability or unwillingness to keep prison populations at or below design capacities in some states also poses a problem when coupled with tougher sentencing laws designed to lengthen time served by higher risk offenders who pose the biggest management problems for custodial staff. California is a good example, where the state was operating at 137 percent of capacity in 2014 while the state courts were adding 10 years to convicted violent offenders' prison sentences if they were known gang affiliates. These types of gang enhancement laws also exist in other states and reflect the "warehousing" ideology described by Feeley and Simon (1992). When these types of laws are enacted, the blanket administration of these laws is necessary to avoid disparities in prison terms that would otherwise result from sporadic applications. Nonetheless, such formal rationality in the administration of more punitive sentencing could actually weaken the safety of prison environments for both inmates and staff by generating higher densities of more dangerous offenders for long periods of time. These types of policies might be reconsidered in strategies to improve the safety of these environments.

Similar to a greater use of coercive controls, there has also been an increase in the use of remunerative controls (e.g., program participation and paid jobs) across U.S. prisons. These types of controls stand in contrast to coercive controls because they promote conformity to the rules without the threat of punishment and are, therefore, less likely to feed inmates' cynicism toward staff and to undermine the legitimacy of prison authorities (Colvin 2007). Remunerative controls are also "administrative" controls in DiIulio's (1987) framework, and, in contrast to coercive controls, there is some evidence to suggest that these have been useful for reducing inmate rule violations (Useem and Reisig 1999; Camp et al. 2003; Huebner 2003; Steiner 2009). Therefore, even though U.S. prison systems now function to "arrange" inmates in ways that make inevitable certain levels of misconduct in certain types of facilities, those that rely more heavily on remunerative (versus coercive) controls may experience lower crime rates, perhaps due to a more humane orientation of facility staff.

There are limits in terms of the effectiveness of remunerative controls, however, in that they are in short supply relative to inmate demands (due to limited budgets) and because they cannot effectively remove many of the opportunities for criminal activity in a prison environment. The first limitation is a by-product of housing large numbers of motivated offenders in close physical proximity to each other, and prisoners vary in their vulnerability to both violent and property victimizations (Wooldredge and Steiner 2014). Even if criminal opportunities were reduced for prisoners engaged in paid jobs or education programs, there is a "replacement effect" in prison due to ample numbers of inmates not engaged in these types of activities at any single point in time.

Regarding the second limitation of remunerative controls for creating safer environments, prisons can generate stressful living conditions based on the unpredictability of how other inmates and particular staff will behave. The more constructive activities provided by remunerative controls can easily be countered in prison due to stressful living conditions and the large numbers of prisoners with a fair amount of idle time on any given day, potentially obscuring any substantive *aggregate* level improvements in prison safety provided by remunerative controls.

Another barrier to the potential effectiveness of remunerative controls are the generally high levels of suspicion and cynicism toward legal authority in prison populations, potentially undermining the ability of prison staff, particularly correctional officers, to establish themselves as legitimate authority in the eyes of inmates (Bottoms 1999). Most prisoners understand the need for rules of behavior, but their inability to trust staff to effectively assist them on a day-to-day basis and to help resolve problems as they arise can lead some prisoners to take matters into their own hands to cope with their frustrations when basic needs are not met and/or to handle conflicts with other inmates. Their perceived inability to count on staff in times of need can lead to rule violations as coping mechanisms (e.g., Black 1983; Toch and Grant 1989; Anderson 1999; Kirk and Papachristos 2011; Liebling this volume). Higher levels of cynicism toward authority, such as in higher risk populations with proportionately more violent offenders, might lead to greater reluctance to participate in programs offered by the administration and a greater willingness to rely on deviant means to need satisfaction. Differences in perceived legitimacy of prison staff and programs even among inmates in the same facility might lead to differences in how amenable inmates are to participating in work and programs as means to facilitate their adaptation to incarceration. Aside from breaking rules for self-gratification, the most cynical inmates will sometimes embrace nonconformity to rules as a symbol of their resistance to prison authority and the status quo (Milovanovic and Thomas 1989). In short, the availability of remunerative controls may not be enough to effectively reduce crime rates in certain types of inmate populations given how these populations have been shaped over the past several decades. More research on the viability and effectiveness of remunerative controls for reducing inmate crime rates is needed before placing too much hope in this strategy for improving the management of inmate populations.

It might be more realistic to expect remunerative controls to have a prison-wide impact on safety when inmate populations are smaller and these services reach a large portion of the population, in conjunction with environments that convey the support of these programs by both noncustodial and custodial staff (Colvin 1992). A climate that nurtures respect for inmates and the importance of facilitating need satisfaction is a precursor for establishing inmates' perceptions of these services as legitimate and useful (Liebling this volume). An adequate supply of these services and a climate of support must coexist before we can expect these services to have a prison-level impact on crime and other rule infractions. Prison administrators who seek to develop more "moral" prison environments with these means, as described by Liebling (2004), may go a long way to reducing misconduct rates and overall levels of cynicism toward prison authority.

As mentioned previously, the greater emphasis on prison management and risk assessment in the United States has created a migratory loop for the highest risk offenders between the most economically disadvantaged urban neighborhoods and maximum security units/prisons. Ironically, it is the offenders housed in the most secure facilities that pose the highest risk of recidivism due to the most restricted access to programs existing within these prisons, and yet many (if not most) of these individuals are released to urban neighborhoods with the most criminal opportunities in conjunction with limited services for aftercare and successful reentry (Petersilia 2005; Turner this volume) and with the largest proportions of residents with severe deficits in social and human capital. It is naïve to expect that these individuals will not recidivate without priorities placed on more effective reentry approved prison programs for high-risk offenders simultaneously with considerably more aftercare services available to them in their neighborhoods of origin.

II. THE HARMFUL EFFECTS OF SENTENCING LAWS VERSUS BROADER POLITICAL IDEOLOGIES

As mentioned earlier, the exact nature of whether and how both state-specific and federal sentencing laws influenced mass incarceration across the entire United States during the late twentieth century has yet to be rigorously examined. Even so, and counter to the opinions of casual observers, court scholars are skeptical about a causal relationship between sentencing policies and imprisonment levels due to the ability of judges to depart from recommended sentences even under the most structured schemes (Kramer and Ulmer 1996; Ulmer and Kramer 1996; Shermer and Johnson 2010; Frost and Clear this volume; Lynch and Verma this volume). At the aggregate level, this might create the appearance of a disjuncture between policies designed to increase punitiveness and/or the structure of sentencing decisions versus actual incarceration rates and numbers of inmates held in prisons. A careful review of the more rigorous (but still relatively few) studies of sentencing policies and prison populations conducted to date also does not provide greater clarity on linkages between the two in that longitudinal and cross-sectional studies have revealed both positive effects of more contemporary sentencing policies (including elements of more structured sentencing and/or "tougher" sentencing) on prison populations (Langan 1991; Joyce 1992; D'Alessio and Stolzenberg 1995; Turner et al. 1999; Nicholson-Crotty 2004), as well as negative effects (Marvell 1995; Marvell and Moody 1997; Sorensen and Stemen 2002; Nicholson-Crotty 2004; Steiner and Wooldredge 2008). Marvell (1995) and Turner et al. (1999) also found that similar policies had different effects in different states. Nicholson-Crotty (2004) provided an example of this, where the implementation of mandatory sentencing guidelines coincided with a drop in incarceration rates only in states where these guidelines were linked to correctional resources. By contrast, states adopting mandatory guidelines *not* linked to correctional resources experienced a rise in incarceration rates.

A. Only "Modest" Effects of Sentencing Laws on Prison Populations?

In conjunction with these mixed findings, no one has ever uncovered anything more than "modest" effects of sentencing policies on prison admissions. For example, Sorensen and Stemen's (2002) cross-sectional analysis of prison admission rates revealed that, although sentencing guidelines coincided with significantly lower admission rates, stronger predictors included index crime rates and citizen political ideology (see also a cross-sectional analysis of prison crowding by Steiner and Wooldredge 2008). On the other hand, Blumstein and Beck (1999) observed that fluctuations in prison populations *over time* did not correspond very well with fluctuations in crime rates, which underscores a possible difference between cross-sectional and longitudinal effects.

A possible reason for these anomalous findings could relate to analyses of different sentencing policies, some of which were designed for multiple reasons (such as sentencing guidelines designed to reduce judicial discretion while also being more consistent with a retributive versus treatment philosophy) versus others implemented for the purposes of deterrence and/or incapacitation (e.g., three-strikes laws; see Tahamont and Chalfin this volume). Whereas more punitive practices might lead to *increases* in incarceration rates and prison populations, more structured sentencing schemes might generate *lower* rates and populations. Granted, there is some overlap in the ideas of increasing the structure of sentencing decisions and getting tougher with offenders, but this overlap does not necessarily translate into policies that should always *increase* prison populations. The implementation of more structured sentencing schemes, such as the sentencing guideline grids enacted in Minnesota and by the federal government in the 1980s, could be interpreted as a response to "getting tougher" with offenders but in the sense of increasing uniformity and certainty in set punishments for specific offenses as opposed to increasing the severity of punishments for these crimes. Many such schemes were derived from the average sentences for particular offenses distributed under indeterminate sentencing (Miethe 1987; Lynch and Verma this volume), so they should not be considered uniformly more punitive for the same offenses. Also, some of these reforms were accompanied by revisions to felony statutes that actually downgraded the seriousness of certain offenses (Wooldredge et al. 2005).

Whereas sentencing policies designed specifically to increase the structure of legal decision-making could either deflate or inflate the numbers of inmates held in state prisons (relative to the size of the general population), policies designed to "get tougher" with offenders would be expected to uniformly increase a state's use of imprisonment. Policies intended to increase the odds and/or the length of imprisonment for certain types of offenses and offenders include mandatory prison time for use of firearms, mandatory prison time for habitual offenders, life without parole for certain offenses, higher percentages of time served under truth-in-sentencing, and three-strikes laws. Some of these policies might also serve to reduce discretion, such as mandatory minimum prison terms, but these are all "get tough" policies that *should* be linked to higher rather than lower levels of imprisonment. However, some judges have expressed dissatisfaction with policies designed to reduce their discretion because they consider themselves to be the experts on sentencing (Griffin and Wooldredge 2001), and the prevailing wisdom seems to be that judges operating under guidelines generally disfavor restrictions on their discretion (Tonry 1987; Knapp 1993). Prior to the *Mistretta* decision in which the Supreme Court upheld the constitutionality of the Federal Sentencing Reform Act of 1987, 200 federal district court judges ruled the federal sentencing guidelines to be unconstitutional (Knapp and Hauptley 1989; Stith and Cabranes 1998). Scholars have speculated that judges are capable of maneuvering around limits placed on their sentencing discretion (Rathke 1982; Miethe 1987) and that prosecutors might begin to exercise more discretion as judges exercise less (Alschuler 1978, 1988; Lagoy, Hussey, and Kramer 1979; Tonry and Coffee 1987). Aside from plea bargaining, prosecutors may seek to preserve individualized justice under more structured sentencing through their control of or influence on decisions such as the severity of formal charges. The means available to court actors to maneuver around the sentences dictated by more structured schemes suggests that sentencing policies by themselves will be limited in their impact on incarceration rates and prison populations.

B. Policy Liberalism and the Use of Imprisonment

Revising existing sentencing schemes or adopting new policies does not necessarily ensure that changes to sentencing laws will have the desired effects, especially among judges who do not agree with the specific changes and underlying goals. Judges' political beliefs and philosophical orientations may not jibe with revised sentencing goals, perhaps leading some judges to maneuver around some of these policies through sentence enhancements and/or the types of plea bargains they are likely to accept from attorneys. Sentencing policies rarely reflect input from the majority of a judiciary, not to mention that these policies are often implemented to address state legislators' perceptions of problems *with* the judiciary such as disparate sentencing. Judges are also elected officials, so the political environment of a state or county may have more to do with shaping imprisonment levels relative to sentencing reforms if the punishment philosophies of judges are linked to the political culture of their jurisdiction. Efforts to control prison populations through sentencing policy alone is insufficient without considering the punishment philosophies of elected officials in conjunction with the loopholes in the sentencing process via plea bargaining and the provision of upward/downward departures in states with sentencing guidelines.

Scholars have uncovered significant empirical relationships between citizens' political ideologies and incarceration rates (Greenberg and West 2001; Jacobs and Carmichael 2001; Percival 2010), and relevant discussions have focused on differences between conservatives and liberals in levels of tolerance toward offenders and the different priorities of these groups regarding incapacitation versus crime prevention (Scheingold 1984; Tonry 1996; Beckett and Western 2001). Political environments might be conceptualized as reflecting dominant political ideologies, although some of the more meaningful distinctions between "Democrat" and "Republican" or between "liberal" and "conservative" have become blurred over time. A more meaningful index might reflect a cross-section of social and economic policies implemented in a state, such as the state-level index of support for liberal policy choices developed by Gray (2006). This scale is typical of indices often examined by political scientists for identifying differences between political districts in social and economic policies over which liberals and conservatives often disagree (e.g., strictness of gun control policies, facilitating welfare eligibility, degree of taxing the rich, more facilitative abortion laws, and unionization laws to facilitate collective bargaining). Using U.S. prison incarceration rates per 100,000 state residents in 2009, reported by the Bureau of Justice Statistics, I found a fairly strong correlation between Gray's (2006) index of "state policy liberalism" and annual incarceration rates (Pearson's $r = -.52$) (Wooldredge 2012). This general relationship could reflect a more liberal stance by state officials on issues related to prison conditions (including considerations of the size of inmate populations). The concept of "policy liberalism" is more nuanced than other political indicators such as dominant political party or the proportion of an electorate voting Democrat or Republican.

Although not a perfect relationship, there is also a noticeable correspondence at the state level between the annual expenditures per inmate in state prisons and policy liberalism (i.e., states with higher per diem expenditures tend to adopt more liberal social policies) (Wooldredge 2012). To some extent these higher costs of incarceration could reflect greater interest among government officials in the welfare of prisoners in their state. Judges in these states might be more attentive to the possible ill effects of prison crowding on inmate well-being and effective management and may consider whether facilities are crowded in their sentencing decisions. Judges in more conservative states, on the other hand, may not consider prison crowding in their decisions if they adopt a less benevolent perspective of prisoners. There is evidence that state court judges are divided on the issue of whether they should consider prison population size when sentencing offenders, with roughly half of them considering this to be a legislative responsibility only (Wooldredge and Gordon 1997). For these judges, the burden of having to consider whether state prisons are crowded necessarily interferes with the administration of justice and the distribution of proportionate sentences. Judges who consider the size of prison populations to be their responsibility, on the other hand, might be less concerned with legally rational decision making (neutral applications of the law) and more interested in deriving sentences based on substantively rational decision making (Savelsberg 1992), considering not only the unique circumstances of offenders but also the implications of their decisions for other aspects of the criminal justice system (such as system efficiency) (Steffensmeier, Ulmer, and Kramer 1998). More structured sentencing schemes reflect efforts to impose formal rationality on judges, and yet substantively rational decision making may be most relevant to controlling prison population flow. Direct tests of whether political environments are more relevant than sentencing policies for shaping prison incarceration rates are needed to place in perspective whether changes in sentencing laws are enough to effectively control the size of prison populations.

The previous discussion suggests that political climates might be more relevant than sentencing policies for shaping prison populations. Although scholars have attributed causal effects of public opinion on criminal justice policy (Roberts 1992), it is also possible that public opinion simply reflects gradations of "liberalism" in a state, and it is the culture that ultimately shapes policies per se as opposed to public outcries related to specific public events. Obvious exceptions can be found in some sentencing laws that are enacted hastily in response to moral panic over sensational cases (e.g., sex offender registration laws and AMBER Alerts). More commonly, however, public "pressures" may have less influence on state policies compared to the philosophies of state legislatures, which are only modestly influenced by the public via the electorate process and rarely involve reactions to very specific public outcries. Public disillusionment with the U.S. criminal justice system in the 1980s might have been fed to a large extent by media portrayals of the system as being too lenient with offenders (Roberts 1992; see also Frost and Clear, this volume, for a nuanced discussion). Even so, the causal link between *public* opinion and the enactment of tougher laws and stiffer penalties on individuals convicted of crimes has never been empirically established.

III. Challenges to Implementing Useful Prison Policies

The greatest challenge to deriving and implementing useful prison policies might lie in trying to anticipate possible negative impacts of a policy on all relevant components of the criminal justice system (e.g., how particular sentencing reforms designed to reduce disparities in prison sentences might impact incarceration rates and the size of prison populations). Also, policy implementation is not always uniform across jurisdictions, even aside from ideological differences that may lead practitioners to maneuver around certain policies. In particular, the get-tough movement was "uneven" across the United States. The country experienced a 500 percent increase in the prison population overall after the late 1970s, yet not every state experienced the same increase. Moreover, states continued to vary considerably in annual incarceration rates and new prison construction. In short, variation in practices can exist even with similar policies.

A. Inadequate Resources and an Unwillingness to Lessen the "Deprivations" of Incarceration

Between-state differences in policy implementation are, in part, likely manifestations of differences in available resources. For example, governments often focus on cutting corrections budgets in times of economic hardship, such as during the Great Recession of the twenty-first century, and the intensity of these hardships usually vary to some extent across states. In particular, prison facilities and operations are often impacted but to varying degrees. For example, it is possible that the cuts to corrections budgets during the Great Recession precipitated the relatively recent decline in prison populations discussed earlier, but state-level contributions to the overall decline are very uneven and follow some of the state-level differences in prison crowding mentioned previously. It is ironic that legislators who were previously supportive of tougher sentencing laws also supported cutting prison expenditures in the late 2000s, possibly reflecting casual attention to and careless attitudes about the use of incarceration. Government reactions to the recession varied across states, such as in Colorado and Kansas where the priority was to close existing facilities versus New Jersey's and Ohio's focus on using more alternatives to incarceration (Steinhauer 2009). Uneven *declines* in incarceration rates, when they occur, may be more a product of budget woes rather than changing punishment ideologies.

Aside from the need for adequate resources to implement more useful corrections policies, many of the more recent and useful policies described in this volume reflect changing attitudes of both practitioners and academics regarding the "need" for certain deprivations that have historically been imposed on prisoners. That is, the effectiveness of certain policies may depend, in part, on a willingness to lessen or even abandon some of these pains of imprisonment. Much of this evolution reflects recognition of the unanticipated consequences of such deprivations on an individual's psychological well-being and subsequent behaviors (for examples, see Bonta and Wormith, this volume). Even so, this has not uniformly translated into more enlightened thinking among politicians and correctional administrators and, as such, has resulted in an uneven evolution of inmate civil rights and privileges across jurisdictions. Jacobs (1980) once argued that the mere occurrence of the "inmate rights movement" (a civil rights movement within prisons) during the 1960s and early 1970s did not guarantee these rights in practice (see also Carroll, Calci, and Wilson this volume). Depriving inmates of personal freedoms was once a key element of their punishment (Sykes 1958), but these deprivations can undermine the effectiveness of treatment and reentry programs (as discussed in this volume by Manchak and Roberts, and Turner).

The Eighth Amendment prohibits the imposition of cruel and unusual punishment and is applicable to state prisons through the due process clause of the Fourteenth Amendment.

The U.S. Supreme Court has held that correctional practices are "cruel and unusual" when they are disproportionately severe for the offense, they are of such character as to "shock the conscience," they go beyond that which is necessary to achieve their aim, and the method of imposition is arbitrary (Barak 2007). Aside from greater uniformity across states regarding the abandonment of these more extreme forms of abuse (Marquart and Trulson this volume), however, differences in treatment remain across jurisdictions and also across prisons within the same jurisdiction (the latter resulting from differences in inmate populations, as described earlier).

B. Inmate Population Composition and Size

Even if treatment by prison staff were uniform across jurisdictions, different inmate populations create different odds of inmate-on-inmate victimization between facilities and units based on how the composition of these populations have changed over time due to heavier emphases on risk management. An important problem that has received considerable attention in the twenty-first century is the sexual victimization of inmates by other inmates and staff. The Prison Rape Elimination Act was enacted in 2003 to address this problem, beginning with an assessment of the magnitude of prison rape across the United States. Despite federal government investments in this program, however, there appears to be no decline in the sexual victimization rates of state prisoners in recent years (see related Bureau of Justice Statistics reports available at www.bjs.gov/). Latest reports indicate that allegations of sexual victimizations actually rose by 40 percent between 2005 and 2011 although the rate of substantiated incidents did not significantly change during the same period (Rantala, Rexroat, and Beck 2014).

Roughly 0.45 percent of adults held in state and federal prisons in 2011 alleged that they were sexually victimized by either inmates or staff (Rantala, Rexroat, and Beck 2014), with the highest rates reported in Washington state (2.6 percent), Nebraska (2.5 percent), Kansas (1.9 percent), Iowa (1.6 percent), and Florida (1.0 percent) (derived from Rantala, Rexroat, and Beck 2014).

It may be the case that potentially useful prison policies do not stand a chance for success in states with very large inmate populations. The fivefold increase in the U.S. prison population between the late 1970s and the mid-2000s generated several new concerns for prison administrators including prison crowding and its impact on order and safety, insufficient medical care (particularly for the much larger numbers of inmates over 50), more limited access to active forms of recreation, and longer wait lists for paid jobs, vocational training, academic education classes, and psychological counseling (Camp et al. 2003). The safety of both staff and inmates is the top priority of prison wardens because unsafe facilities open opportunities for collective violence (Useem this volume), individual victimizations and corresponding civil suits, and staff problems including low morale, high absenteeism, and fast turnover. Yet, larger inmate populations may increase the risks of both individual and collective violence, attempted escapes, staff assaults, and violations of inmates' rights by officers. Aside from bringing motivated offenders physically closer to one another and inhibiting effective supervision by officers, inmates are more likely to manifest the ill effects of depression and anxiety in more crowded facilities and units (Wooldredge 1997).

New prison construction and adding on to existing facilities has been a popular means adopted by most states to address these problems, although it is also the most expensive tactic considering the additional costs of maintaining and staffing these facilities and units. However, this strategy has become less popular over time considering budget crises faced by the federal government and all state governments. Building more prisons has also never been an effective solution to crowding because it simply allows judges to send more offenders to prison, particularly drug offenders (Blumstein and Beck 1999). In some ways, rising prison populations in certain states may have been facilitated by new prison construction and renovations given that some states doubled or tripled their design capacities (e.g., Indiana and Ohio). Not all states adopted this strategy to the same degree, however, which also contributed to between-state differences in prison population growth rates over time.

Following from this discussion, a handful of factors pose the biggest barriers to effectively implementing useful prison policies. These factors include an inability or unwillingness to anticipate the long-term consequences of specific policies and strategies for the welfare of prisoners and prison staff, inadequate resources for translating policies into practice, unwillingness among some politicians and prison officials to lessen the ill effects of particular deprivations of incarceration, the dangers to inmate and staff safety posed by the composition of particular inmate populations, and managing large offender populations. These factors also vary in levels and intensity across states, thus inhibiting the ability to implement useful policies *uniformly* across jurisdictions.

IV. CONCLUSION

Despite the uneven strides that have been made in the development of useful prison policies, the historical and empirical reviews of prisons and imprisonment provided by the contributors to this volume offer a wealth of insight into the common denominators of harmful versus useful policies, not to mention the specific consequences of harmful policies, which can have unanticipated effects in both the short and long term. While this cumulative knowledge offers a roadmap for the development of useful policies and the avoidance of harmful policies, ongoing research is needed in all areas covered in this volume to ensure that past mistakes are not repeated and that new policies have the best chance for success. Evidence-based practices are necessary in all aspects of institutional corrections and are not just limited to effective programming.

A theme that has emerged over time is that harmful policies often have had their roots in heavier emphases on punishment as opposed to treatment advocated by politicians and court actors who are further removed from the prison experience. On the other hand, historical themes regarding the development of useful policies are that these policies have reflected an increasingly humanitarian view of offenders, a growing awareness of both short- and long-term adverse effects of incarceration on offenders and the general population, greater reliance on empirically based strategies, and interagency collaborations to ensure long-term solutions while minimizing unanticipated ill effects. Also important to consider, however, is that the identification of these themes is not enough to simply avoid "bad" practices given the existence of a handful of substantive barriers to successfully translating potentially useful policy into practice. Aside from the obvious need for adequate resources, we must anticipate the unwillingness of some politicians and prison officials to lessen the ill effects of certain deprivations of incarceration, and to consider the dangers to inmate and staff safety posed by the composition of some inmate populations, and the difficulties with managing large offender populations.

Earlier I mentioned that it is the *heavier* focus on retribution as opposed to retribution per se that may underlie some of the problems with corrections policies. An inherent difficulty with retaining retribution as an incarceration philosophy beyond its use as a guiding sentencing philosophy, however, is that it is purely symbolic and difficult to defend from a utilitarian standpoint of crime control in mass society. The feasibility of achieving retribution with imprisonment is questionable at best, given the sheer number of factors that interfere with a government's ability to distribute punishments that are both commensurate with the crimes and consistent across similarly situated offenders (due to the existence of plea bargaining, extra-legal disparities in imprisonment, inefficient clearance rates, and the questionable assumption that different terms of confinement equate to differences in the harms inflicted on society by the crimes committed). In conjunction with the idea that restoring moral balance serves no utilitarian function and is therefore an unconvincing defense of such an expensive use of confinement, even retribution per se is becoming outmoded as a punishment philosophy.

There can be little debate over the clarity of retribution in theory, and there is a certain poetry to the idea that harm inflicted on an offender in proportion to the crime committed will restore moral balance and strengthen the social order, where two "wrongs" can make a "right." On the other hand, this philosophy can only work in smaller populations with a relatively small number of crimes that can be rank ordered in seriousness in conjunction with a relatively high certainty of detection. As soon as industrialized nations reached the point of having to settle for grading punishments according to broad categories of offense groups (felony 1's, felony 2's, etc.) in conjunction with population sizes that prohibited relatively high odds of detection, the ideas of restoring moral balance and pursuing justice based on equity were abandoned in practice. Yet, this is not necessarily a bad thing given that the prison experience itself could *never* have been proportionate to the offense given the many unique individual experiences of prisoners that differentiate one fixed prison sentence from any other of equal length (as demonstrated throughout the chapters of this volume). Although the tide has yet to turn substantially, the growing number of enlightened practitioners and academics who rally around the importance of not inflicting undue harms on prisoners have managed to uncover some very useful corrections strategies and policies that will allow us to move away from incapacitation as a popular "solution" to crime control.

REFERENCES

Alschuler, Albert. 1978. "Sentencing Reform and Prosecutorial Power: A Critique of Recent Proposals for Fixed and Presumptive Sentencing." *University of Pennsylvania Law Review* 126:550–577.

Alschuler, Albert. 1988. "Departures and Plea Agreements under the Sentencing Guidelines." *Federal Rules Decisions* 117:459–476.

Anderson, Elijah. 1999. *Code of the Street: Decency, Violence, and the Moral Life of the Inner City*. New York: W. W. Norton.

Association of State Corrections Administrators. 2010. *Violence and Safety in American Corrections: What the Research Shows*. Washington, DC: Congressional Research Service.

Barak, Greg. 2007. *Battleground Criminal Justice*. Westport, CT: Greenwood.

Beckett, Katherine, and Bruce Western. 2001. "Governing Social Marginality: Welfare, Incarceration, and the Transformation of State Policy." *Punishment and Society* 3:43–59.

Black, Donald. 1983. "Crime as Social Control." *American Sociological Review* 48:34–45.

Blumstein, Alfred, and Allen Beck. 1999. "Population Growth in U.S. Prisons, 1980–1996." In *Crime and Justice: An Annual Review of Research*, Vol. 26, edited by Michael Tonry and Joan Petersilia. Chicago: University of Chicago Press.

Bottoms, Anthony. 1999. "Interpersonal Violence and Social Order in Prison." In *Crime and Justice: An Annual Review of Research*, Vol. 26, edited by Michael Tonry and Joan Petersilia. Chicago: University of Chicago Press.

Braga, Anthony A., Andrew V. Papachristos, and David M. Hureau. 2014. "The Effects of Hot Spots Policing on Crime: An Updated Systematic Review and Meta-analysis." *Justice Quarterly* 31:633–663.

Braga, Anthony A., and David L. Weisburd. 2010. *Policing Problem Places: Crime Hot Spots and Effective Prevention*. New York: Oxford University Press.

Camp, Scott, Gerald Gaes, Neal Langan, and William Saylor. 2003. "The Influence of Prisons on Inmate Misconduct: A Multilevel Investigation." *Justice Quarterly* 20:501–533.

Carson, Elizabeth Ann. 2015. *Prisoners in 2014*. Washington, DC: U.S. Department of Justice, Bureau of Justice Statistics.

Colvin, Mark. 1992. *The Penitentiary in Crisis: From Accommodation to Riot in New Mexico*. Albany: SUNY Press.

Colvin, Mark. 2007. "Applying Differential Coercion and Social Support Theory to Prison Organizations: The Case of the Penitentiary of New Mexico." *The Prison Journal* 87:367–387.

D'Alessio, Stuart, and Lisa Stolzenberg. 1995. "The Impact of Sentencing Guidelines on Jail Incarceration in Minnesota." *Criminology* 33:283–302.

DiIulio, John. 1987. *Governing Prisons: A Comparative Study of Correctional Management*. New York: Free Press.

Feeley, Malcolm, and Jonathan Simon. 1992. "The New Penology: Notes on the Emerging Strategy of Corrections and its Implications." *Criminology* 30:449–474.

Gray, Virginia. 2006. "The Socioeconomic and Political Contexts of States." In *Politics in the American States*, 8th ed., edited by Virginia Gray and Russell Hanson. Washington, DC: CQ Press.

Greenberg, David, and Valerie West. 2001. "State Prison Populations and Their Growth, 1971–1991." *Criminology* 39:615–654.

Griffin, Timothy, and John Wooldredge. 2001. "Judicial Reactions to Sentencing Reform in Ohio." *Crime and Delinquency* 47:491–512.

Huebner, Beth. 2003. "Administrative Determinants of Inmate Violence: A Multilevel Analysis." *Journal of Criminal Justice* 31:107–117.

Irwin, John. 2005. *The Warehouse Prison: Disposal of the New Dangerous Class*. Los Angeles: Roxbury Press.

Jacobs, David, and Jason Carmichael. 2001. "The Politics of Punishment across Time and Space: A Pooled Time-Series Analysis of Imprisonment Rates." *Social Forces* 80:61–91.

Jacobs, James. 1980. "The Prisoners' Rights Movement and its Impact, 1960–1980." In *Crime and Justice: A Review of Research*, Vol. 2, edited by Norval Morris and Michael Tonry. Chicago: University of Chicago Press.

Joyce, Nola. 1992. "A View of the Future: The Effect of Policy on Prison Population Growth." *Crime & Delinquency* 38:357–368.

Kirk, David, and Andrew Papachristos. 2011. "Cultural Mechanisms and the Persistence of Neighborhood Violence." *The American Journal of Sociology* 116:1190–1233.

Knapp, Kay. 1993. "Allocation of Discretion and Accountability within Sentencing Structures." *University of Colorado Law Review* 64:679–705.

Knapp, Kay, and Denis Hauptley. 1989. "U.S. Sentencing Guidelines in Perspective: A Theoretical Background and Overview." In *The U.S. Sentencing Guidelines: Implications for Criminal Justice*, edited by Dean Champion. New York: Praeger.

Kramer, John, and Jeffrey Ulmer. 1996. "Sentencing Disparity and Departure from Guidelines." *Justice Quarterly* 13:81–105.

Krivo, Lauren, and Ruth Peterson. 1996. "Extremely Disadvantaged Neighborhoods and Urban Crime." *Social Forces* 75:619–648.

Lagoy, Stephen, Frederick Hussey, and John Kramer 1979. "The Prosecutorial Function and Its Relation to Determinate Sentencing Structures." In *The Prosecutor*, Vol. 2, edited by William McDonald. Beverly Hills, CA: SAGE.

Langan, Patrick. 1991. "America's Soaring Prison Population." *Science* 251:1568–1573.

Liebling Alison. 2004. *Prisons and Their Moral Performance: A Study of Values, Quality, and Prison Life*. New York: Oxford University Press.

Marvell, Thomas. 1995. "Sentencing Guidelines and Prison Population Growth." *Journal of Criminal Law and Criminology* 85:696–707.

Marvell, Thomas, and Carlisle Moody. 1997. "Age-Structure Trends and Prison Populations." *The Journal of Criminal Justice* 25:115–124.

Miethe, Terance. 1987. "Charging and Plea Bargaining Practices under Determinate Sentencing: An Investigation of the Hydraulic Displacement of Discretion." *Journal of Criminal Law and Criminology* 78:155–176.

Milovanovic, Dragan, and Jim Thomas. 1989. "Overcoming the Absurd: Prisoner Litigation as Primitive Rebellion." *Social Problems* 36:48–60.

Nicholson-Crotty, Sean. 2004. "The Impact of Sentencing Guidelines on State-Level Sanctions: An Analysis over Time." *Crime & Delinquency* 50:395–411.

Percival, Garrick. 2010. "Ideology, Diversity, and Imprisonment: Considering the Influence of Local Politics on Racial and Ethnic Minority Incarceration Rates." *Social Science Quarterly* 91:1063–1082.

Petersilia, Joan. 2005. "From Cell to Society: Who Is Returning Home?" In *Prisoner Reentry and Crime in America*, edited by Jeremy Travis and Christy Visher. New York: Cambridge University Press.

Rantala, Ramona, Jessica Rexroat, and Allen J. Beck. 2014. *Survey of Sexual Violence in Adult Correctional Facilities, 2009–11—Statistical Tables*. Washington, DC: U.S. Department of Justice, Bureau of Justice Statistics. http://www.bjs.gov/content/pub/pdf/ssvacf0911st.pdf

Rathke, Stephen. 1982. "Plea Negotiating Under the Sentencing Guidelines." *Hamline Law Review* 5:271–291.

Roberts, Julian. 1992. "Public Opinion, Crime, and Criminal Justice." In *Crime and Justice: A Review of Research*, Vol. 16, edited by Norval Morris and Michael Tonry. Chicago: University of Chicago Press.

Rose, Dina, and Todd Clear. 1998. "Incarceration, Social Capital, and Crime: Implications for Social Disorganization Theory." *Criminology* 36:441–479.

Sampson, Robert, and Lydia Bean. 2006. "Cultural Mechanisms and Killing Fields: A Revised Theory of Community-level Racial Inequality." In *The Many Colors of Crime: Inequalities of Race, Ethnicity, and Crime in America*, edited by Ruth Peterson, Lauren Krivo, and John Hagan. New York: New York University Press.

Sampson, Robert, and William Wilson. 1995. "Toward a Theory of Race, Crime, and Urban Inequality." In *Crime and Inequality*, edited by John Hagan and Ruth Peterson. Stanford, CA: Stanford University Press.

Savelsberg, Joachim. 1992. "Law That Does Not Fit Society: Sentencing Guidelines as a Neoclassical Reaction to the Dilemmas of Substantivized Law." *American Journal of Sociology* 97:1346–1381.

Scheingold, Stuart. 1984. *The Politics of Law and Order: Street Crime and Public Policy*. New York: Longman.

Shermer, Lauren O'Neill, and Brian Johnson. 2010. "Criminal Prosecutions: Examining Prosecutorial Discretion and Charge Reductions in U.S. Federal District Courts." *Justice Quarterly* 27:394–430.

Simon, Jonathan. 2000. "From the Big House to the Warehouse: Rethinking Prisons and State Government in the 20th Century." *Punishment and Society* 2:213–234.

Sorensen, Jon, and Don Stemen. 2002. "The Effect of State Sentencing Policies on Incarceration Rates." *Crime & Delinquency* 48:456–475.

Steffensmeier, Darrell, Jeffrey Ulmer, and John Kramer. 1998. "The Interaction of Race, Gender, and Age in Criminal Sentencing: The Punishment Cost of Being Young, Black, and Male." *Criminology* 36:763–797.

Steiner, Benjamin. 2009. "Assessing the Static and Dynamic Influences on Inmate Violence Levels." *Crime & Delinquency* 55:134–161.

Steiner, Benjamin, and John Wooldredge. 2008. "Comparing State versus Facility Level Effects on Crowding in U.S. Correctional Facilities." *Crime & Delinquency* 54:259–290.

Steinhauer, Jennifer. 2009. "To Cut Costs, States Relax Prison Policies." *The New York Times*, March 24.

Stith, Kate, and Jose Cabranes. 1998. *Fear of Judging: Sentencing Guidelines in the Federal Courts*. Chicago: University of Chicago Press.

Sykes, Gresham. 1958. *The Society of Captives*. Princeton, NJ: Princeton University Press.

Toch, Hans, and J. Douglas Grant. 1989. "Noncoping and Maladaptation in Confinement" In *The American Prison*, edited by Lynne Goodstein and Doris MacKenzie. New York: Plenum.

Tonry, Michael. 1987. *Sentencing Reform Impacts*. Washington, DC: U.S. Department of Justice, National Institute of Justice.

Tonry, Michael. 1996. *Sentencing Matters*. New York: Oxford University Press.

Tonry, Michael, and John Coffee. 1987. "Enforcing Sentencing Guidelines: Plea Bargaining and Review Mechanisms." In *The Sentencing Commission and its Guidelines*, edited by Andrew Von Hirsch, Michael Tonry, and Kay Knapp. Boston: Northeastern University Press.

Turner, Susan, Peter Greenwood, Elsa Chen, and Terry Fain. 1999. "The Impact of Truth-in-Sentencing and Three Strikes Legislation: Prison Populations, State Budgets, and Crime Rates." *Stanford Law and Policy Review* 11:75–91.

Tyler, Tom. 2004. "Enhancing Police Legitimacy." *Annals of the American Academy of Political and Social Science* 593:84–99.

Ulmer, Jeffrey, and John Kramer. 1996. "Court Communities under Sentencing Guidelines: Dilemmas of Formal Rationality and Sentencing Disparity." *Criminology* 34:383–407.

Useem, Bert, and Peter Kimball. 1989. *States of Siege: U.S. Prison Riots, 1971–1986*. New York: Oxford University Press.

Useem, Bert, and Anne Piehl. 2006. "Prison Buildup and Disorder." *Punishment and Society* 8:81–115.

Useem, Bert, and Michael Reisig. 1999. "Collective Action in Prisons: Protests, Disturbances, and Riots." *Criminology* 37:735–759.

Wacquant, Loic. 2001. "Deadly Symbiosis: When Ghetto and Prison Meet and Mesh." *Punishment and Society* 3:95–134.

Walmsley, Roy. 2013. *World Prison Population List*, 10th ed. London: International Centre for Prison Studies.

Warner, Barbara. 2003. "The Role of Attenuated Culture in Social Disorganization Theory." *Criminology* 41:73–97.

Weisburd, David L., and Anthony A. Braga. 2013. "The Importance of Legitimacy in Hot Spots Policing." *Community Policing Dispatch* 6(9). https://cops.usdoj.gov/html/dispatch/09-2013/the_importance_of_legitimacy_in_hot_spots_policing.asp

Wooldredge, John. 1997. "Explaining Variation in Perceptions of Inmate Crowding." *Prison Journal* 77:27–40.

Wooldredge, John. 2012. "State Corrections Policy." In *Politics in the American States*, Vol. 10. edited by Russell Hanson and Virginia Gray. Washington, DC: CQ Press.

Wooldredge, John, and Jill Gordon. 1997. "Predicting the Estimated Use of Alternatives to Incarceration." *Journal of Quantitative Criminology* 13:121–142.

Wooldredge, John, Timothy Griffin, and Fritz Rauschenberg. 2005. "Sentencing Reform and Reductions in the Disparate Treatment of Felony Defendants." *Law and Society Review* 39:835–874.

Wooldredge, John, and Benjamin Steiner. 2014. "A Bi-Level Framework for Understanding Prisoner Victimization." *Journal of Quantitative Criminology* 30:141–162.

Wooldredge, John, and Benjamin Steiner. 2016. "The Exercise of Power in Prison Organizations and Implications for Legitimacy." *Journal of Criminmal Law and Criminology* 106:125–166.

Index

Page references for figures are indicated by *f* and for tables by *t*.